HALSBURY'S
Laws of England

FOURTH EDITION
1996 REISSUE

Volume 7(2)

HALSBURY'S

Laws of England

FOURTH EDITION
1996 REISSUE

LORD HAILSHAM OF ST. MARYLEBONE

Lord High Chancellor of Great Britain
1970–74 and 1979–87

Volume 7(2)

BUTTERWORTHS

LONDON   1996

UNITED KINGDOM	Butterworths, a Division of Reed Elsevier (UK) Ltd Halsbury House, 35 Chancery Lane, **London** WC2A 1EL and 4 Hill Street, **Edinburgh** EH2 3JZ
AUSTRALIA	Butterworths, **Sydney, Melbourne, Brisbane, Adelaide, Perth, Canberra** and **Hobart**
CANADA	Butterworths Canada Ltd, **Toronto** and **Vancouver**
HONG KONG	Butterworths Asia, **Hong Kong**
IRELAND	Butterworth (Ireland) Ltd, **Dublin**
MALAYSIA	Malayan Law Journal Sdn Bhd, **Kuala Lumpur**
NEW ZEALAND	Butterworths of New Zealand Ltd, **Wellington** and **Auckland**
SINGAPORE	Butterworths Asia, **Singapore**
SOUTH AFRICA	Butterworth Publishers (Pty) Ltd, **Durban**
USA	Michie, **Charlottesville**, Virginia

FIRST EDITION

Published in 31 volumes between 1907 and 1917 under the Editorship of the Rt. Hon. the Earl of Halsbury, Lord High Chancellor of Great Britain, 1885–86, 1886–92 and 1895–1905

SECOND EDITION

Published in 37 volumes between 1931 and 1942 under the Editorship of the Rt. Hon. the Viscount Hailsham, Lord High Chancellor of Great Britain, 1928–29 and 1935–38

THIRD EDITION

Published in 43 volumes between 1952 and 1964 under the Editorship of the Rt. Hon. the Viscount Simonds, Lord High Chancellor of Great Britain, 1951–54

FOURTH EDITION

Published in 56 volumes between 1973 and 1987 under the Editorship of the Rt. Hon. Lord Hailsham of St. Marylebone, Lord High Chancellor of Great Britain, 1970–74 and 1979–87

ISBN   (complete set, standard binding) 0 406 03400 1
(this volume, standard binding) 0 406 04576 3

Typeset by Thomson Litho Ltd, East Kilbride, Scotland
Printed and bound in Great Britain by
Clays Ltd, St Ives plc

Editor in Chief

THE RIGHT HONOURABLE

LORD HAILSHAM OF ST. MARYLEBONE

LORD HIGH CHANCELLOR OF GREAT BRITAIN

1970–74 and 1979–87

The Title Companies in Volume 7(2) has been contributed by:

T. PETER E. CURRY

of The Middle Temple and Lincoln's Inn,
one of Her Majesty's Counsel; a Bencher of The Middle Temple

BRENDA M. HANNIGAN, M.A., LL.M.,

a Solicitor of the Supreme Court of Ireland,
Senior Lecturer in Law, University of Southampton

LLOYD TAMLYN, LL.B.,

of Gray's Inn, Barrister

The law stated in this volume is in general that in force on 1 April 1996, although subsequent changes have been included wherever possible.

TABLE OF CONTENTS

REFERENCES AND ABBREVIATIONS

ACT	Australian Capital Territory
A-G	Attorney General
Adv-Gen	Advocate General
affd	affirmed
affg	affirming
Alta	Alberta
App	Appendix
art	article
Aust	Australia
B	Baron
BC	British Columbia
C	Command Paper (of a series published before 1900)
c	chapter number of an Act
CA	Court of Appeal
CAC	Central Arbitration Committee
CA in Ch	Court of Appeal in Chancery
CB	Chief Baron
CCA	Court of Criminal Appeal
CC Fees Order 1982	County Court Fees Order 1982 (SI 1982/1706) as subsequently amended (see the current County Court Practice)
CCR	County Court Rules 1981 (SI 1981/1687) as subsequently amended (see the current County Court Practice)
CCR	Court for Crown Cases Reserved
C-MAC	Courts-Martial Appeal Court
CO	Crown Office
COD	Crown Office Digest
Can	Canada
Cd	Command Paper (of the series published 1900–18)
Cf	compare
ch	chapter
cl	clause
Cm	Command Paper (of the series published 1986 to date)
Cmd	Command Paper (of the series published 1919–56)
Cmnd	Command Paper (of the series published 1956–86)
Comr	Commissioner
Corpn	Corporation
Court Forms (2nd Edn)	Atkin's Encyclopaedia of Court Forms in Civil Proceedings, 2nd Edn. See note 2, p 13 post

Court Funds Rules 1987	Court Funds Rules 1987 (SI 1987/821) as subsequently amended (see the current Supreme Court Practice and County Court Practice)
DC..	Divisional Court
DPP...	Director of Public Prosecutions
EAT	Employment Appeal Tribunal
EC...	European Community
ECJ..	Court of Justice of the European Community
ECSC	European Coal and Steel Community
EEC...	European Economic Community
Edn..	Edition
EFTA.......................................	European Free Trade Association
Euratom	European Atomic Energy Community
Ex Ch	Court of Exchequer Chamber
ex p	ex parte
Fed..	Federal
Forms & Precedents (5th Edn)......	Encyclopaedia of Forms and Precedents other than Court Forms, 5th Edn. See note 2, p *13* post
GLC	Greater London Council
HC..	High Court
HL	House of Lords
H of C	House of Commons
IRC...	Inland Revenue Commissioners
Ir..	Ireland
J...	Justice
JA...	Judge of Appeal
JC...	Justiciary Cases
Kan...	Kansas
LA..	Lord Advocate
LC...	Lord Chancellor
LCC	London County Council
LCJ...	Lord Chief Justice
LJ	Lord Justice of Appeal
LoN...	League of Nations
MR	Master of the Rolls
Man..	Manitoba
n	note
NB	New Brunswick
NI	Northern Ireland
NS...	Nova Scotia
NSW	New South Wales
NZ..	New Zealand
Nfld..	Newfoundland
OJ	The Official Journal of the European Community published by the Office for Official Publications of the European Community
Ont	Ontario

P	President
PC	Judicial Committee of the Privy Council
PEI	Prince Edward Island
QBD	Queen's Bench Division of the High Court
Qld	Queensland
Que	Quebec
r	rule
RDC	Rural District Council
RPC	Restrictive Practices Court
RSC	Rules of the Supreme Court 1965 (SI 1965/1776) as subsequently amended (see the current Supreme Court Practice)
reg	regulation
Res	Resolution
revsd	reversed
Rly	Railway
s	section
SA	South Africa
S Aust	South Australia
SC	Supreme Court
SC Fees Order 1980	Supreme Court Fees Order 1980 (SI 1980/821) as subsequently amended (see the current Supreme Court Practice)
SI	Statutory Instruments published by authority
SR & O	Statutory Rules and Orders published by authority
SR & O Rev 1904	Revised Edition comprising all Public and General Statutory Rules and Orders in force on 31 December 1903
SR & O Rev 1948	Revised Edition comprising all Public and General Statutory Rules and Orders and Statutory Instruments in force on 31 December 1948
SRNI	Statutory Rules of Northern Ireland
Sask	Saskatchewan
Sch	Schedule
Sess	Session
TS	Treaty Series
Tas	Tasmania
UDC	Urban District Council
UN	United Nations
V-C	Vice-Chancellor
Vict	Victoria
W Aust	Western Australia

NOTE 1. A general list of the abbreviations of law reports and other sources used in this work can be found in vol 54 (Reissue) Consolidated Table of Cases at p *v* et seq.

NOTE 2. Where references are made to other publications, the volume number precedes and the page number follows the name of the publication; eg the reference '12 Forms & Precedents (5th Edn) 44' refers to volume 12 of the Encyclopaedia of Forms and Precedents, page 44.

NOTE 3. An English statute is cited by short title or, where there is no short title, by regnal year and chapter number together with the name by which it is commonly known or a description of its subject matter and date. In the case of a foreign statute, the mode of citation generally follows the style of citation in use in the country concerned with the addition, where necessary, of the name of the country in parentheses.

NOTE 4. A statutory instrument is cited by short title, if any, followed by the year and number, or, if unnumbered, the date.

TABLE OF STATUTES

This Table relates only to statutes cited in Volume 7(1) and Volume 7(2). A consolidated Table for Volumes 7(1), 7(2) and 7(3) appears in Volume 7(3).

TABLE OF
STATUTORY INSTRUMENTS

This Table relates only to statutory instruments cited in Volume 7(1) and Volume 7(2). A consolidated Table for Volumes 7(1), 7(2) and 7(3) appears in Volume 7(3).

TABLE OF
EUROPEAN COMMUNITY
LEGISLATION

This Table relates only to legislation cited in Volume 7(1) and Volume 7(2). A consolidated Table for Volumes 7(1), 7(2) and 7(3) appears in Volume 7(3).

TABLE OF CASES

This Table relates only to cases cited in Volumes 7(1) and 7(2). A consolidated
Table for Volumes 7(1), 7(2) and 7(3) appears in Volume 7(3).

PARA

PARA

PARA

C

PARA

D

PARA

H

PARA

Table of Cases

PARA

Q

PARA

R

PARA

PARA

Decisions of the European Court of Justice are listed below numerically. These decisions are also included in the preceding alphabetical list.

COMPANIES

Volume 7(3)

6. CORPORATE INSOLVENCY

(16) ACCOUNTS

(i) Accounting Records

801. Duty to keep accounting records. Every company must keep accounting records which are sufficient to show and explain the company's transactions, and are such as to:

(1) disclose with reasonable accuracy, at any time, the financial position of the company at that time; and

(2) enable the directors to ensure that any balance sheet[1] and profit and loss account[2] duly prepared[3] comply with the requirements of the Companies Act 1985[4].

The accounting records must in particular contain entries from day to day of all sums of money received and expended by the company, and the matters in respect of which the receipt and expenditure takes place, and a record of the assets and liabilities of the company[5].

If the company's business involves dealing in goods, the accounting records must contain:

(a) statements of stock held by the company at the end of each financial year[6] of the company;

(b) all statements of stocktakings from which any such statement of stock as is mentioned in head (a) above has been or is to be prepared; and

(c) except in the case of goods sold by way of ordinary retail trade, statements of all goods sold and purchased showing the goods and the buyers and sellers in sufficient detail to enable all these to be identified[7].

A parent company[8] which has a subsidiary undertaking[9] in relation to which the above requirements do not apply must take reasonable steps to secure that the undertaking keeps such accounting records as to enable the directors of the parent company to ensure that any balance sheet and profit and loss account duly prepared[10] comply with the requirements of the Companies Act 1985[11].

If a company fails to comply with any of the above provisions, every officer[12] of the company who is in default is guilty of an offence unless he shows that he acted honestly and that in the circumstances in which the company's business was carried on the default was excusable[13]. Otherwise he is liable on conviction on indictment to imprisonment for a term not exceeding two years or a fine, or to both, or on summary conviction to imprisonment for a term not exceeding six months or a fine not exceeding the statutory maximum, or to both[13].

---

1 For the meaning of 'balance sheet' see para 826 post.

2 For the meaning of 'profit and loss account' see para 826 post.

3 Ie under the Companies Act 1985 Pt VII (ss 221-262A) (as amended): see infra and para 802 et seq post.

4 Ibid s 221(1) (substituted by the Companies Act 1989 s 2). An accountant may not exercise a lien for unpaid fees over the accounting records of a company which are required by statute to be kept in specific places for certain periods available for inspection: *DTC (CNC) Ltd v Gary Sargent & Co* (1996) Times, 25 January.

5 Companies Act 1985 s 221(2) (substituted by the Companies Act 1989 s 2).

6 For the meaning of 'financial year' see para 806 post.

7 Companies Act 1985 s 221(3) (substituted by the Companies Act 1989 s 2).

8 For the meaning of 'parent company' see para 828 post.

9 For the meaning of 'subsidiary undertaking' see para 828 post.

10 See note 3 supra.

11 Companies Act 1985 s 221(4) (substituted by the Companies Act 1989 s 2).

12 For the meaning of 'officer' see para 641 ante.

13 Companies Act 1985 s 221(5), (6) (substituted by the Companies Act 1989 s 2); Companies Act 1985 s 730, Sch 24 (amended by the Companies Act 1989 s 23, Sch 10 para 24(1), (2)). For the meaning of 'officer who is in default' and 'the statutory maximum' see para 1161 post.

802. Where and for how long records to be kept. A company's accounting records must be kept at its registered office or such other place as the directors think fit, and must at all times be open to inspection by the company's officers[1].

If accounting records are kept at a place outside Great Britain, accounts and returns with respect to the business dealt with in the accounting records so kept must be sent to, and kept at, a place in Great Britain, and must at all times be open to such inspection[2]. The accounts and returns to be sent to Great Britain must be such as to disclose with reasonable accuracy the financial position of the business in question at intervals of not more than six months, and enable the directors to ensure that the company's balance sheet[3] and profit and loss account[4] comply with the requirements of the Companies Act 1985[5].

If a company fails to comply with any of the above provisions[6], every officer of the company who is in default is guilty of an offence unless he shows that he acted honestly and that in the circumstances in which the company's business was carried on the default was excusable[7]. Otherwise he is liable on conviction on indictment to imprisonment for a term not exceeding two years or a fine, or to both, or on summary conviction to imprisonment for a term not exceeding six months or a fine not exceeding the statutory maximum, or to both[7].

Accounting records which a company is required so to keep must be preserved by it:

(1) in the case of a private company[8], for three years from the date on which they are made; and

(2) in the case of a public company[9], for six years from the date on which they are made[10].

An officer of a company is guilty of an offence if he fails to take all reasonable steps for securing compliance by the company with its duties as to the preservation of its accounting records, or if he has intentionally caused any default by the company in relation thereto; and he is liable on conviction on indictment to imprisonment for a term not exceeding two years or a fine, or to both, or on summary conviction to imprisonment for a term not exceeding six months or a fine not exceeding the statutory maximum, or to both[11].

1 Companies Act 1985 s 222(1) (substituted by the Companies Act 1989 s 2). For the meaning of 'officer' see para 641 ante. As to the provisions applicable where the entries are not recorded in legible form see para 656 ante.
2 Companies Act 1985 s 222(2) (substituted by the Companies Act 1989 s 2).
3 For the meaning of 'balance sheet' see para 826 post.
4 For the meaning of 'profit and loss account' see para 826 post.
5 Companies Act 1985 s 222(3) (substituted by the Companies Act 1989 s 2).
6 Ie any provision of the Companies Act 1985 s 222(1)-(3) (as substituted): see supra.
7 Ibid s 222(4) (substituted by the Companies Act 1989 s 2); Companies Act 1985 s 730, Sch 24 (amended by the Companies Act 1989 s 23, Sch 10 para 24(1), (2)). For the meaning of 'officer who is in default' and 'the statutory maximum' see para 1161 post.
8 For the meaning of 'private company' see para 82 ante.
9 For the meaning of 'public company' see para 82 ante.
10 Companies Act 1985 s 222(5) (substituted by the Companies Act 1989 s 2). This is subject to any provision contained in rules made under the Insolvency Act 1986 s 411 (see para 2800 post): Companies Act 1985 s 222(5) (as so substituted).
11 Ibid s 222(6) (substituted by the Companies Act 1989 s 2); Companies Act 1985 s 730, Sch 24 (amended by the Companies Act 1989 Sch 10 para 24(1), (2)).

803. Accounting standards. 'Accounting standards' means statements of standard accounting practice issued by such body or bodies as may be prescribed by regulations[1]; and references to accounting standards applicable to a company's annual accounts[2] are to such standards as are, in accordance with their terms, relevant to the company's circumstances and to the accounts[3].

The Secretary of State may make grants to or for the purposes of bodies concerned with:

(1) issuing accounting standards;
(2) overseeing and directing the issuing of such standards; or
(3) investigating departures from such standards or from the accounting require-
    ments of the Companies Act 1985 and taking steps to secure compliance with
    them[4].

1   Companies Act 1985 s 256(1) (substituted by the Companies Act 1989 s 19). Such regulations may
    contain such transitional and other supplementary and incidental provisions as appear to the Secretary
    of State to be appropriate: Companies Act 1985 s 256(4) (substituted by the Companies Act 1989 s 19).
    In exercise of the power so conferred the Secretary of State made the Accounting Standards (Prescribed
    Body) Regulations 1990, SI 1990/1667, prescribing The Accounting Standards Board Limited for the
    purposes of the Companies Act 1985 s 256(1) (as so substituted): see the Accounting Standards
    (Prescribed Body) Regulations 1990 reg 2.
2   For the meaning of 'annual accounts' see para 817 note 2 post.
3   Companies Act 1985 s 256(2) (substituted by the Companies Act 1989 s 19).
4   Companies Act 1985 s 256(3) (substituted by the Companies Act 1989 s 19).

804. Articles dealing with accounts. In view of the statutory duties imposed on directors in relation to accounts[1], they clearly have an implied right of inspection[2]. As a rule shareholders have no right to inspect the company's books of account unless the articles so provide[3]. Beneficiaries of shares held by directors as trustees cannot require the trustee directors to disclose information obtained by them in the exercise of their powers of inspection as directors[4].

Absent members of a company are affected by the information furnished by the directors at a general meeting and bound by the proceedings as to matters within its competence[5].

1   See paras 801–803 ante and para 806 et seq post. The statutory right of inspection conferred by the
    Companies Act 1948 s 147(3) was repealed by the Companies Act 1976 s 42(2), Sch 3 and not replaced.
    This statutory right carried the right to be assisted by an accountant: *Healey v Healey Homes Ltd* [1973]
    IR 309. An article directing directors to cause accounts to be laid before the company, prepared in
    accordance with the statutory provisions, does not confer on an individual shareholder the right to
    compel compliance therewith: *Devlin v Slough Estates Ltd* (1982) 126 Sol Jo 623.
2   Directors have a common law right to inspect all the company's documents: *Burn v London and South
    Wales Coal Co* [1890] WN 209; *Conway v Petronius Clothing Co Ltd* [1978] 1 All ER 185, [1978] 1 WLR
    72 (motion for inspection adjourned pending outcome of meeting to consider director's removal from
    office). It is submitted that articles of association may restrict the common law right but not so as to
    impede a director in carrying out his statutory duties.
3   See the Companies (Tables A to F) Regulations 1985, SI 1985/805, Schedule, Table A art 109 which
    provides that no member (as such) is to have any right of inspecting any accounting records or other
    book or document of the company, except as conferred by statute or authorised by the directors or by
    ordinary resolution of the company. As to Table A generally see para 529 et seq ante; and as to the right
    of inspection after the commencement of a winding up see para 2845 post.
4   *Butt v Kelson* [1952] Ch 197, sub nom *Re Butt, Butt v Kelson* [1952] 1 All ER 167, CA; cf *Re Whichelow,
    Bradshaw v Orpen* [1953] 2 All ER 1558, [1954] 1 WLR 5.
5   *Re Norwich Yarn Co, ex p Bignold* (1856) 22 Beav 143 at 165; *Evans v Smallcombe* (1868) LR 3 HL 249.

805. Power of Secretary of State to alter accounting requirements. The Secretary of State may by regulations made by statutory instrument modify the statutory provisions[1] relating to accounts[2].

Regulations which:

(1) add to the classes of documents required to be prepared, laid before the company in general meeting or delivered to the registrar;

(2) restrict the classes of company which have the benefit of any exemption, exception or special provision;

(3) require additional matter to be included in a document of any class; or

(4) otherwise render the requirements of the statutory provisions relating to accounts more onerous,

may not be made unless a draft of the instrument containing the regulations has been laid before Parliament and approved by a resolution of each House[3]. Otherwise a statutory instrument containing regulations under these provisions is subject to annulment in pursuance of a resolution of either House of Parliament[4].

Such regulations may:

(a) make different provision for different cases or classes of case;

(b) repeal and re-enact provisions with modifications of form or arrangement, whether or not they are modified in substance;

(c) make consequential amendments or repeals in other provisions of the Companies Act 1985 or in other enactments; and

(d) contain such transitional and other incidental and supplementary provisions as the Secretary of State thinks fit[5].

1 Ie the Companies Act 1985 Pt VII (ss 221-262A) (as amended): see paras 801-803 ante and para 806 et seq post.

2 Ibid s 257(1) (substituted by the Companies Act 1989 s 20). In exercise of the power so conferred the Secretary of State made the Companies Act 1985 (Miscellaneous Accounting Amendments) Regulations 1996, SI 1996/189.

3 Companies Act 1985 s 257(2) (substituted by the Companies Act 1989 s 20).

4 Companies Act 1985 s 257(3) (substituted by the Companies Act 1989 s 20).

5 Companies Act 1985 s 257(4) (substituted by the Companies Act 1989 s 20). Any modification by regulations so made of the Companies Act 1985 s 258 (as substituted) or Sch 10A (as added) (parent and subsidiary undertakings: see paras 828, 829 post) does not apply for the purposes of the enactments outside the Companies Acts unless the regulations so provide: Companies Act 1985 s 257(5) (substituted by the Companies Act 1989 s 20). For the meaning of 'the Companies Acts' see para 60 note 1 ante.

(ii) Financial Year and Accounting Reference Periods

806. Company's financial year. A company's 'financial year' is determined as follows[1].

Its first financial year begins with the first day of its first accounting reference period[2] and ends with the last day of that period or such other date, not more than seven days before or after the end of that period, as the directors may determine[3].

Subsequent financial years begin with the day immediately following the end of the company's previous financial year and end with the last day of its next accounting reference period or such other date, not more than seven days before or after the end of that period, as the directors may determine[4].

In relation to an undertaking[5] which is not a company, references in the Companies Act 1985 to its financial year are to any period in respect of which a profit and loss account[6] of the undertaking is required to be made up, by its constitution or by the law under which it is established, whether that period is a year or not[7].

The directors of a parent company[8] must secure that, except where in their opinion there are good reasons against it, the financial year of each of its subsidiary undertakings[9] coincides with the company's own financial year[10].

1 Companies Act 1985 s 223(1) (substituted by the Companies Act 1989 s 3); Companies Act 1985 s 742(1) (substituted by the Companies Act 1989 s 23, Sch 10 para 15).
2 For the meaning of 'accounting reference period' see para 807 post.
3 Companies Act 1985 s 223(2) (substituted by the Companies Act 1989 s 3).
4 Companies Act 1985 s 223(3) (substituted by the Companies Act 1989 s 3).
5 For these purposes, 'undertaking' means a body corporate or partnership or an unincorporated association carrying on a trade or business, with or without a view to profit: Companies Act 1985 s 259(1) (substituted by the Companies Act 1989 s 22).
6 For the meaning of 'profit and loss account' see para 826 post.
7 Companies Act 1985 s 223(4) (substituted by the Companies Act 1989 s 3).
8 For the meaning of 'parent company' see para 828 post.
9 For the meaning of 'subsidiary undertaking' see para 828 post.
10 Companies Act 1985 s 223(5) (substituted by the Companies Act 1989 s 3).

807. Accounting reference periods and accounting reference date. A company's accounting reference periods are determined according to its accounting reference date[1].

A company incorporated before 1 April 1996 may, at any time before the end of the period of nine months beginning with the date of its incorporation, by notice in the prescribed form[2] given to the registrar of companies specify its accounting reference date, that is the date on which its accounting reference period ends in each calendar year[3]. Failing such notice, the accounting reference date of such a company is:

(1) in the case of a company incorporated before 1 April 1990, 31 March;
(2) in the case of a company incorporated after 1 April 1990, the last day of the month in which the anniversary of its incorporation falls[4].

The accounting reference date of a company incorporated on or after 1 April 1996 is the last day of the month in which the anniversary of its incorporation falls[5].

A company's first accounting reference period is the period of more than six months but not more than 18 months, beginning with the date of its incorporation and ending with its accounting reference date[6]. Its subsequent accounting reference periods are successive periods of 12 months beginning immediately after the end of the previous accounting reference period and ending with its accounting reference date[7].

In certain circumstances a company may nevertheless alter its accounting reference date[8].

1 Companies Act 1985 s 224(1) (substituted by the Companies Act 1989 s 3); Companies Act 1985 s 742(1) (substituted by the Companies Act 1989 s 23, Sch 10 para 15).
2 For the prescribed form of notice see the Companies (Forms) (Amendment) Regulations 1990, SI 1990/572, reg 4(1), Sch 2, Form 224.
3 Companies Act 1985 s 224(2) (substituted by the Companies Act 1989 s 3; amended by the Companies Act 1985 (Miscellaneous Accounting Amendments) Regulations 1996, SI 1996/189, reg 2(1), (2)); Companies Act 1985 s 742(1) (substituted by the Companies Act 1989 Sch 10 para 15).
4 Companies Act 1985 s 224(3) (substituted by the Companies Act 1989 s 3; amended by the Companies Act 1989 (Commencement No 4 and Transitional and Savings Provisions) Order 1990, SI 1990/355, art 15; the Companies Act 1985 (Miscellaneous Accounting Amendments) Regulations 1996 reg 2(1), (3)).
5 Companies Act 1985 s 224(3A) (added by the Companies Act 1985 (Miscellaneous Accounting Amendments) Regulations 1996 reg 2(1), (4)).
6 Companies Act 1985 s 224(4) (substituted by the Companies Act 1989 s 3).

7 Companies Act 1985 s 224(5) (substituted by the Companies Act 1989 s 3).
8 Companies Act 1985 s 224(6) (substituted by the Companies Act 1989 s 3). As to such alteration see para 808 post.

808. Alteration of accounting reference date. A company may by notice in the prescribed form[1] given to the registrar of companies specify a new accounting reference date[2] having effect in relation to the company's current accounting reference period[3] and subsequent periods or the company's previous accounting reference period[4] and subsequent periods[5].

The notice must state whether the current or previous accounting reference period:

(1) is to be shortened, so as to come to an end on the first occasion on which the new accounting reference date falls or fell after the beginning of the period; or

(2) is to be extended, so as to come to an end on the second occasion on which that date falls or fell after the beginning of the period[6].

A notice[7] stating that the current or previous accounting reference period is to be extended is ineffective, except as mentioned below, if given less than five years after the end of an earlier accounting reference period of the company which was so extended[8]; but this provision does not apply:

(a) to a notice given by a company which is a subsidiary undertaking[9] or parent undertaking[10] of another EEA undertaking[11] if the new accounting reference date coincides with that of the other EEA undertaking or, where that undertaking is not a company, with the last day of its financial year[12]; or

(b) where an administration order is in force[13],

or where the Secretary of State directs that it should not apply, which he may do with respect to a notice which has been given or which may be given[14].

An accounting reference date may not in any case, unless an administration order is in force[15], be extended so as to exceed 18 months; and a notice is ineffective if the current or previous accounting reference period as extended in accordance with the notice would exceed that limit[16].

1 For the prescribed form of notice see the Companies (Forms) (Amendment) Regulations 1996, SI 1996/594, reg 2, Schedule, Form 225. For the prescribed version of the form in Welsh see the Companies (Welsh Language Forms and Documents) Regulations 1996, SI 1996/595, reg 2, Schedule, Form 225CYM.
2 For the meaning of 'accounting reference date' see para 807 ante.
3 For the meaning of 'accounting reference period' see para 807 ante.
4 For these purposes, a company's 'previous accounting reference period' means that immediately preceding its current accounting reference period: Companies Act 1985 s 225(1) (substituted by the Companies Act 1989 s 3; amended by the Companies Act 1985 (Miscellaneous Accounting Amendments) Regulations 1996, SI 1996/189, reg 3(1), (2)).
5 Companies Act 1985 s 225(1) (as substituted and amended: see note 4 supra). A notice under s 225(1) (as so substituted and amended) may not be given in respect of a previous accounting reference period if the period allowed for laying and delivering accounts and reports in relation to that period has already expired: s 225(5) (substituted by the Companies Act 1989 s 3; amended by the Companies Act 1985 (Miscellaneous Accounting Amendments) Regulations 1996 reg 3(1), (5)).
6 Companies Act 1985 s 225(3) (substituted by the Companies Act 1989 s 3).
7 Ie a notice under the Companies Act 1985 s 225(1) (as substituted and amended): see supra.
8 Ie by virtue of ibid s 225 (as substituted and amended).
9 For the meaning of 'subsidiary undertaking' see para 828 ante.
10 For the meaning of 'parent undertaking' see para 828 ante.
11 For these purposes, 'EEA undertaking' means an undertaking established under the law of any part of the United Kingdom or the law of any other EEA State: Companies Act 1985 s 225(7) (added by the Companies Act 1985 (Miscellaneous Accounting Amendments) Regulations 1996 reg 3(1), (6)). 'EEA State' means a State which is a Contracting Party to the Agreement on the European Economic Area signed at Oporto on 2 May 1992, as adjusted by the Protocol signed at Brussels on 17 March 1993 and by

EC Council Decision 1/95 of 10 March 1995: Companies Act 1985 s 262(1) (substituted by the Companies Act 1989 s 22; amended by the Companies Act 1985 (Miscellaneous Accounting Amendments) Regulations 1996 reg 12(1)). As to the European Economic Area see para 299 note 2 ante.

12 For the meaning of 'financial year' see para 806 ante.

13 Ie under the Insolvency Act 1986 Pt II (ss 8-27) (as amended): see para 2080 et seq post.

14 Companies Act 1985 s 225(4) (substituted by the Companies Act 1989 s 3; amended by the Companies Act 1985 (Miscellaneous Accounting Amendments) Regulations 1996 reg 3(1), (4)).

15 See note 13 supra.

16 Companies Act 1985 s 225(6) (substituted by the Companies Act 1989 s 3).

(iii) Accounting Principles

A. GENERAL PRINCIPLES

809. General principles. The amounts to be included in respect of all items shown in a company's accounts must be determined in accordance with the principles below[1]. If, however, it appears to the directors of a company that there are special reasons for departing from any of those principles in preparing the company's accounts in respect of any financial year[2], they may do so, but particulars of the departure, the reasons for it and its effect must be given in a note to the accounts[3].

The principles determining the amounts to be so included are:

(1) the company is to be presumed to be carrying on business as a going concern[4];

(2) accounting policies must be applied consistently within the same accounts and from one financial year to the next[5];

(3) the amount of any item must be determined on a prudent basis, and in particular:

    (a) only profits realised[6] at the balance sheet date[7] are to be included in the profit and loss account[8]; and

    (b) all liabilities and losses which have arisen or are likely to arise in respect of the financial year to which the accounts relate or a previous financial year are to be taken into account, including those which only became apparent between the balance sheet date and the date on which it is signed on behalf of the board of directors in pursuance of the statutory obligation[9] in that behalf[10];

(4) all income and charges relating to the financial year to which the accounts relate are to be taken into account, without regard to the date of receipt or payment[11];

(5) in determining the aggregate amount of any item, the amount of each individual asset or liability that falls to be taken into account must be determined separately[12].

1 Companies Act 1985 s 226(3), Sch 4 Pt II Section A para 9. In the case of an unregistered company (see para 1765 et seq post), Sch 4 (as amended) has effect as if (1) item K.II in balance sheet Format 1 (as amended) (see para 832 post) and liability item A.II in balance sheet Format 2 (as amended) (see para 833 post); (2) Sch 4 para 51(2) (as amended) (see para 847 post); and (3) Sch 4 Pt V (paras 71-73) (see para 936 post), were omitted: Companies (Unregistered Companies) Regulations 1985, SI 1985/680, reg 6(h) (amended by SI 1990/438).

2 For the meaning of 'financial year' see para 806 ante.

3 Companies Act 1985 Sch 4 para 15. As to notes to the accounts see paras 838 et seq, 887 et seq post.

4 Ibid Sch 4 para 10.

5 Ibid Sch 4 para 11 (substituted by the Companies Act 1989 s 4(2), Sch 1 paras 1, 5).

6 For these purposes, references to 'realised profits' and 'realised losses', in relation to a company's accounts, are to such profits of the company as fall to be treated as realised in accordance with principles generally accepted, at the time when the accounts are prepared, with respect to the determination for accounting purposes of realised profits or losses; but this is without prejudice to (1) the construction of

any other expression, where appropriate, by reference to accepted accounting principles or practice; or (2) any specific provision for the treatment of profits or losses of any description as realised: Companies Act 1985 s 262(3) (substituted by the Companies Act 1989 s 22); Companies Act 1985 s 742(2) (substituted by the Companies Act 1989 s 23, Sch 10 para 15).

7 For these purposes, 'balance sheet date' means the date as at which the balance sheet was made up: Companies Act 1985 s 262(1) (substituted by the Companies Act 1989 s 22); Companies Act 1985 s 742(1) (substituted by the Companies Act 1989 Sch 10 para 15).

8 For the meaning of 'profit and loss account' see para 826 post.

9 Ie the Companies Act 1985 s 233 (as substituted): see para 937 post.

10 Ibid Sch 4 para 12 (amended by the Companies Act 1989 Sch 10 para 20).

11 Companies Act 1985 Sch 4 para 13.

12 Ibid Sch 4 para 14.

B. HISTORICAL COST ACCOUNTING RULES

810. Historical cost accounting rules; preliminary. Subject to the adoption of alternative accounting rules[1], the amounts to be included in respect of all items shown in a company's accounts must be determined in accordance with the rules below[2], known as 'the historical cost accounting rules'[3].

Subject to any provision for depreciation or diminution in value[4] made in accordance with the following provisions[5], the amount to be included in respect of any fixed asset[6] must be its purchase price[7] or production cost[8]. In the case of any fixed asset which has a limited useful economic life, the amount of its purchase price or production cost, or, where it is estimated that any such asset will have a residual value at the end of the period of its useful economic life, its purchase price or production cost less that estimated residual value, must be reduced by provisions for depreciation calculated to write off that amount systematically over the period of the asset's useful economic life[9].

Where a fixed asset investment of a description falling to be included under either of the balance sheet formats[10] has diminished in value, provisions for diminution in value may be made in respect of it and the amount to be included in respect of it may be reduced accordingly; and any such provisions which are not shown in the profit and loss account[11] must be disclosed, either separately or in aggregate, in a note to the accounts[12]. Provisions for diminution in value must be made in respect of any fixed asset which has diminished in value if the reduction in its value is expected to be permanent, whether its useful economic life is limited or not, and the amount to be included in respect of it must be reduced accordingly; and any such provisions which are not shown in the profit and loss account must be disclosed, either separately or in aggregate, in a note to the accounts[13]. Where the reasons for which any provision was so made[14] have ceased to apply to any extent, that provision must be written back to the extent that it is no longer necessary; and any amounts so written back which are not shown in the profit and loss account must be disclosed, either separately or in aggregate, in a note to the accounts[15].

1 See para 813 et seq post.

2 Companies Act 1985 s 226(3), Sch 4 Pt II Section B para 16.

3 See ibid Sch 4 Pt II Section B heading; Pt II Section C para 29(1); Pt VII paras 76, 82.

4 References to provisions for depreciation or diminution in value of assets are to any amount written off by way of providing for depreciation or diminution in value of assets: ibid Sch 4 paras 76, 88(1). Any reference in the statutory profit and loss account formats (see paras 834-837 post) to the depreciation of, or amounts written off, assets of any description is to any provision for depreciation or diminution in value of assets of that description: Sch 4 paras 76, 88(2).

5 Ie made in accordance with ibid Sch 4 para 18 or 19: see infra.

6 For these purposes, 'fixed assets' means assets of a company which are intended for use on a continuing basis in the company's activities; and 'current assets' means assets not intended for such use: ibid s 262(1) (substituted by the Companies Act 1989 s 22); Companies Act 1985 s 742(1) (substituted by the Companies Act 1989 s 23, Sch 10 para 15). See *Tudor Heights Ltd (in liquidation) v United Dominions Corpn Finance* [1977] 1 NZLR 532 ('fixed assets' are those assets which are 'permanently' with the company for the purpose of carrying out its business undertakings and are not confined to those assets which are fixed by physical attachment to the premises).

7 For these purposes, 'purchase price', in relation to an asset of a company or of any raw materials or consumables used in the production of any such asset includes any consideration, whether in cash or otherwise, given by the company in respect of that asset or in respect of those materials or consumables, as the case may be: Companies Act 1985 s 262(1) (as substituted: see note 6 supra).

8 Ibid Sch 4 para 17.
9 Ibid Sch 4 para 18.
10 Ie under item B.III: see paras 832, 833 post.
11 For the meaning of 'profit and loss account' see para 826 post.
12 Companies Act 1985 Sch 4 para 19(1). As to notes to the accounts see para 838 et seq post.
13 Ibid Sch 4 para 19(2).
14 Ie in accordance with ibid Sch 4 para 19(1) or (2): see supra.
15 Ibid Sch 4 para 19(3).

811. Rules for determining particular fixed asset items and current assets.
Notwithstanding that an item in respect of 'development costs' is included under 'fixed assets'[1] in the statutory balance sheet formats[2], an amount may only be included in a company's balance sheet[3] in respect of development costs in special circumstances[4]. If any amount is included in a company's balance sheet in respect of development costs, the following information must be given in a note to the accounts[5]:

(1) the period over which the amount of those costs originally capitalised[6] is being or is to be written off; and

(2) the reasons for capitalising the development costs in question[7].

The application of the rules as to fixed assets[8] in relation to goodwill, in any case where goodwill is treated as an asset, is subject to the following provisions[9]. The amount of the consideration for any goodwill acquired by a company must be reduced by provisions for depreciation[10] calculated to write off that amount systematically over a period chosen by the directors of the company[11]; the period chosen must not exceed the useful economic life of the goodwill in question[12]. In any case where any goodwill acquired by a company is shown or included as an asset in the company's balance sheet, the period chosen for writing off the consideration for that goodwill and the reasons for choosing that period must be disclosed in a note to the accounts[13].

The amount to be included in respect of any current asset[14] is its purchase price[15] or production cost[16]. If, however, the net realisable value of any current asset is lower than its purchase price or production cost, the amount to be included in respect of that asset is the net realisable value[17].

1 For the meaning of 'fixed assets' see para 810 note 6 ante.
2 See paras 832, 833 post.
3 For the meaning of 'balance sheet' see para 826 post.
4 Companies Act 1985 s 226(3), Sch 4 Pt II Section B para 20(1).
5 As to notes to the accounts see para 838 et seq post.
6 For these purposes, 'capitalisation', in relation to work or costs, means treating that work or those costs as a fixed asset: Companies Act 1985 s 262(1) (substituted by the Companies Act 1989 s 22).
7 Companies Act 1985 Sch 4 para 20(2).
8 Ie those contained in ibid Sch 4 paras 17-19: see para 810 ante.
9 Ibid Sch 4 para 21(1).
10 For the meaning of references to provisions for depreciation see para 810 note 4 ante.
11 Companies Act 1985 Sch 4 para 21(2).

12 Ibid Sch 4 para 21(3).
13 Ibid Sch 4 para 21(4).
14 For the meaning of 'current assets' see para 810 note 6 ante.
15 For the meaning of 'purchase price' see para 810 note 7 ante.
16 Companies Act 1985 Sch 4 para 22.
17 Ibid Sch 4 para 23(1). Where the reasons for which any provision for diminution in value was made in accordance with Sch 4 para 23(1) have ceased to apply to any extent, that provision must be written back to the extent that it is no longer necessary: Sch 4 para 23(2).

812. Miscellaneous and supplementary provisions. Where the amount repayable on any debt owed by a company is greater than the value of the consideration received in the transaction giving rise to the debt, the amount of the difference may be treated as an asset[1]. Where any such amount is so treated, it must be written off by reasonable amounts each year and must be completely written off before repayment of the debt; and, if the current amount is not shown as a separate item in the company's balance sheet[2], it must be disclosed in a note to the accounts[3].

Assets which fall to be included amongst the fixed assets[4] of a company under the item 'tangible assets'[5], or amongst the current assets[6] of a company under the item 'raw materials and consumables'[7], may be included at a fixed quantity and value, if they are of a kind which are constantly being replaced, where their overall value is not material to assessing the company's state of affairs and their quantity, value and composition are not subject to material variation[8].

The purchase price[9] of an asset must be determined by adding to the actual price paid any expenses incidental to its acquisition[10]. The production cost of an asset must be determined by adding to the purchase price of the raw materials and consumables used the amount of the costs incurred by the company which are directly attributable to the production of that asset[11]. In addition there may be included in the production cost of an asset:

(1) a reasonable proportion of the costs incurred by the company which are only indirectly attributable to the production of that asset, but only to the extent that they relate to the period of production; and

(2) interest on capital borrowed to finance the production of that asset, to the extent that it accrues in respect of the period of production;

provided, however, in a case within head (2) above that the inclusion of the interest in determining the cost of that asset and the amount of the interest so included is disclosed in a note to the accounts[12].

In the case of current assets, distribution costs may not be included in production costs[13]. Where there is no record of the purchase price or production cost of any asset of a company or of any price, expenses or costs relevant for determining its purchase price or production cost in accordance with the above provisions, or any such record cannot be obtained without unreasonable expense or delay, its purchase price or production cost must be taken for the purposes of any of the above provisions[14] to be the value ascribed to it in the earliest available record of its value made on or after its acquisition or production by the company[15].

Subject to the qualification mentioned below, the purchase price or production cost of any assets which fall to be included under any item shown in a company's balance sheet under the general item 'stocks'[16], and any assets which are fungible assets[17] (including investments), may be determined by the application of any of the following methods in relation to any such assets of the same class; and the method chosen must be one which appears to the directors to be appropriate in the circumstances of the company[18]. Those methods are the method known as 'first in, first out' (FIFO); the method know as 'last in, first out' (LIFO); a weighted average price; and any other method similar to any of the methods mentioned above[19].

Where in the case of any company:

(a) the purchase price or production cost of assets falling to be included under any item shown in the company's balance sheet has been determined by the application of any method so permitted; and

(b) the amount shown in respect of that item differs materially from the relevant alternative amount given below,

the amount of that difference must be disclosed in a note to the accounts[20].

For the purposes of head (b) above, the relevant alternative amount, in relation to any item shown in a company's balance sheet, is the amount which would have been shown in respect of that item if assets of any class included under that item at an amount determined by any permitted method had instead been included at their replacement cost as at the balance sheet date[21]. The relevant alternative amount may, however, be determined by reference to the most recent actual purchase price or production cost before the balance sheet date of assets of any class included under the item in question instead of by reference to their replacement cost as at that date, but only if the former appears to the directors of the company to constitute the more appropriate standard of comparison in the case of assets of that class[22].

1 Companies Act 1985 s 226(3), Sch 4 Pt II Section B para 24(1).
2 For the meaning of 'balance sheet' see para 826 post.
3 Companies Act 1985 Sch 4 para 24(2). As to notes to the accounts see paras 838 et seq, 887 et seq post.
4 For the meaning of 'fixed assets' see para 810 note 6 ante.
5 Ie under item B.II in the statutory balance sheet formats: see paras 832, 833 post.
6 For the meaning of 'current assets' see para 810 note 6 ante.
7 Ie under item C.I(1) in the statutory balance sheet formats: see paras 832, 833 post.
8 Companies Act 1985 Sch 4 para 25.
9 For the meaning of 'purchase price' see para 810 note 7 ante.
10 Companies Act 1985 Sch 4 para 26(1).
11 Ibid Sch 4 para 26(2).
12 Ibid Sch 4 para 26(3).
13 Ibid Sch 4 para 26(4).
14 Ie ibid Sch 4 paras 17-23: see paras 810, 811 ante.
15 Ibid Sch 4 para 28.
16 Ie under item C.I in the statutory balance sheet formats: see paras 832, 833 post.
17 For these purposes, assets of any description are to be regarded as 'fungible' if assets of that description are substantially indistinguishable one from another: Companies Act 1985 Sch 4 para 27(6).
18 Ibid Sch 4 para 27(1).
19 Ibid Sch 4 para 27(2).
20 Ibid Sch 4 para 27(3).
21 Ibid Sch 4 para 27(4). For the meaning of 'balance sheet date' see para 809 note 7 ante.
22 Ibid Sch 4 para 27(5).

C. ALTERNATIVE ACCOUNTING RULES

813. Alternative accounting rules. The historical cost accounting rules[1], with certain omissions[2], are referred to below as the depreciation rules; and subsequent references to the historical cost accounting rules do not include the depreciation rules as they apply by virtue of the relevant provisions[3] below[4]. Subject to certain qualifications[5], the amounts to be included in respect of assets[6] of any description next mentioned[7] may be determined on any basis so mentioned[8].

The alternative accounting rules provide that intangible fixed assets, other than goodwill, may be included at their current cost[9]. Tangible fixed assets may be included at a market value determined as at the date of their last valuation or at their current cost[10]. Fixed asset investments of any description falling to be included under either of the statutory balance sheet formats[11] may be included either at a market value determined as at the date of their last valuation, or at a value determined on any basis which appears to the directors to be appropriate in the circumstances of the company; but in the latter case particulars of the method of valuation adopted and of the reasons for adopting it must be disclosed in a note to the accounts[12]. Current asset investments of any description falling to be included under either of the statutory balance sheet formats[13] may be included at their current cost[14]. Stocks may be included at their current cost[15].

1 As to the historical cost accounting rules see para 810 et seq ante.
2 Ie with the omission of the Companies Act 1985 s 226(3), Sch 4 paras 16, 21, 25-28: see paras 810-812 ante.
3 Ie ibid Sch 4 Pt II Section C para 32: see para 814 post.
4 Ibid Sch 4 para 29.
5 Ie those contained in ibid Sch 4 paras 32-34 (as amended): see paras 814, 815 post.
6 For the meaning of 'fixed assets' and 'current assets' see para 810 note 6 ante.
7 Ie mentioned in the Companies Act 1985 Sch 4 para 31: see infra.
8 Ibid Sch 4 para 30.
9 Ibid Sch 4 para 31(1).
10 Ibid Sch 4 para 31(2).
11 Ie under item B.III: see paras 832, 833 post.
12 Companies Act 1985 Sch 4 para 31(3). As to notes to the accounts see paras 838 et seq, 887 et seq post.
13 Ie under item C.III: see paras 832, 833 post.
14 Companies Act 1985 Sch 4 para 31(4).
15 Ibid Sch 4 para 31(5).

814. Application of the depreciation rules. Where the value of any asset of a company is determined on any basis mentioned in the alternative accounting rules[1], that value will be, or (as the case may require) be the starting point for determining, the amount to be included in respect of that asset in the company's accounts, instead of its purchase price[2] or production cost or any value previously so determined for that asset; and the depreciation rules[3] will apply accordingly in relation to any such asset with the substitution for any reference to its purchase price or production cost of a reference to the value most recently determined for that asset on any basis mentioned in the alternative accounting rules[4].

The amount of any provision for depreciation[5] required in the case of any fixed asset[6] by the depreciation rules as so applied[7] is referred to below as the adjusted amount, and the amount of any provision which would be so required in the case of that asset according to the historical cost accounting rules[8] is referred to as the historical cost amount[9]. Where the above provision applies in the case of any fixed asset, the amount of any provision for depreciation in respect of that asset:

(1) included in any item shown in the profit and loss account in respect of amounts written off assets of the description in question; or
(2) taken into account in stating any item so shown which is required by the notes on the statutory profit and loss account formats[10] to be stated after taking into account any necessary provisions for depreciation or diminution in value of assets included under it,

may be the historical cost amount instead of the adjusted amount, provided that the amount of any difference between the two is shown separately in the profit and loss account[11] or in a note to the accounts[12].

1 Ie the rules set out in the Companies Act 1985 s 226(3), Sch 4 Pt II Section C para 31: see para 813 ante.
2 For the meaning of 'purchase price' see para 810 note 7 ante.
3 For the meaning of 'the depreciation rules' see para 813 ante.
4 Companies Act 1985 Sch 4 para 32(1).
5 For the meaning of references to provisions for depreciation see para 810 note 4 ante.
6 For the meaning of 'fixed asset' see para 810 note 6 ante.
7 Ie by the Companies Act 1985 Sch 4 paras 18 or 19 (see para 810 ante) as applied by Sch 4 para 32(1) (see supra).
8 As to the historical cost accounting rules see para 810 et seq ante.
9 Companies Act 1985 Sch 4 para 32(2).
10 Ie by note (14): see paras 834–837 post.
11 For the meaning of 'profit and loss account' see para 826 post.
12 Companies Act 1985 Sch 4 para 32(3). As to notes to the accounts see paras 838 et seq, 887 et seq post.

815. Additional information to be provided in case of departure from historical cost accounting rules. Where the amounts to be included in respect of assets covered by any items shown in a company's accounts have been determined on any basis mentioned in the alternative accounting rules[1], the items affected and the basis of valuation adopted in determining the amounts of the assets in question in the case of each such item must be disclosed in a note to the accounts[2]. In the case of each balance sheet[3] item affected (except stocks) either the comparable amounts[4] determined according to the historical cost accounting rules[5], or the differences between those amounts and the corresponding amounts actually shown in the balance sheet in respect of that item, must be shown separately in the balance sheet or in a note to the accounts[6].

With respect to any determination of the value of an asset of a company on any basis mentioned in the alternative accounting rules, the amount of any profit or loss arising from that determination (after allowing, where appropriate, for any provisions for depreciation or diminution in value made otherwise than by reference to the value so determined and any adjustments of any such provisions made in the light of that determination) must be credited or, as the case may be, debited to a separate reserve ('the revaluation reserve')[7]. The amount of the revaluation reserve must be shown in the company's balance sheet under a separate sub-heading in the position given for the item 'revaluation reserve' in the statutory balance sheet formats[8] but need not be shown under that name[9]. An amount may be transferred:

(1) from the revaluation reserve to the profit and loss account[10], if the amount was previously charged to that account or represents realised profit[11] or on capitalisation[12];

(2) to or from the revaluation reserve in respect of the taxation relating to any profit or loss credited or debited to the reserve;

and the revaluation reserve must be reduced to the extent that the amounts transferred to it are no longer necessary for the purposes of the valuation method used[13]. The revaluation reserve must not otherwise[14] be reduced[15]. The treatment for taxation purposes of amounts credited or debited to the revaluation reserve must be disclosed in a note to the accounts[16].

1 As to the alternative accounting rules see infra and paras 813, 814 ante.
2 Companies Act 1985 s 226(3), Sch 4 Pt II Section C para 33(1), (2). As to notes to the accounts see paras 838 et seq, 887 et seq post.
3 For the meaning of 'balance sheet' see para 826 post.
4 For these purposes, references in relation to any item to the comparable amounts determined as there mentioned are references to (1) the aggregate amount which would be required to be shown in respect of that item if the amounts to be included in respect of all the assets covered by that item were determined according to the historical cost accounting rules; and (2) the aggregate amount of the

cumulative provisions for depreciation or diminution in value (see para 810 note 4 ante) which would be permitted or required in determining those amounts according to those rules: Companies Act 1985 Sch 4 para 33(4).

5 As to the historical cost accounting rules see para 810 et seq ante.

6 Companies Act 1985 Sch 4 para 33(3).

7 Ibid Sch 4 para 34(1).

8 Ie ibid Sch 4 Pt I Section B Formats 1 or 2: see paras 832, 833 respectively post.

9 Ibid Sch 4 para 34(2).

10 For the meaning of 'profit and loss account' see para 826 post.

11 For the meaning of references to 'realised profit' see para 809 note 6 ante.

12 For these purposes, 'capitalisation', in relation to an amount standing to the credit of the revaluation reserve, means applying it in wholly or partly paying up unissued shares in the company to be allotted to members of the company as fully or partly paid shares: Companies Act 1985 Sch 4 para 34(3A) (substituted by the Companies Act 1989 s 4(2), Sch 1 paras 1, 6; amended by the Companies Act 1985 (Miscellaneous Accounting Amendments) Regulations 1996, SI 1996/189, reg 14(1), Sch 1 paras 1, 4(1), (3)).

13 Companies Act 1985 Sch 4 para 34(3) (substituted by the Companies Act 1989 Sch 1 paras 1, 6; amended by the Companies Act 1985 (Miscellaneous Accounting Amendments) Regulations 1996 Sch 1 paras 1, 4(1), (2)). The amendments made by the Companies Act 1989 Sch 1 para 6 to the Companies Act 1985 Sch 4 para 34 are not to be construed as requiring the reinstatement of any amount to the revaluation reserve with respect to any reduction of that reserve which took place in a financial year of a company prior to the first financial year for which the company is required to prepare accounts under the new Pt VII (ss 221–262A) (as amended): Companies Act 1989 (Commencement No 4 and Transitional and Saving Provisions) Order 1990, SI 1990/355, art 7, Sch 2 para 6.

14 Ie except as mentioned in the Companies Act 1985 Sch 4 para 34 (as amended).

15 Ibid Sch 4 para 34(3B) (substituted by the Companies Act 1989 Sch 1 paras 1, 6).

16 Companies Act 1985 Sch 4 para 34(4).

(iv) Annual Accounts

816. Duty to prepare individual company accounts. The directors of every company must prepare for each financial year[1] of the company a balance sheet[2] as at the last day of the year and a profit and loss account[3], those accounts being called the company's 'individual accounts'[4].

The balance sheet must give a true and fair view[5] of the state of affairs of the company as at the end of the financial year; and the profit and loss account must give a true and fair view of the profit or loss of the company for the financial year[6].

A company's individual accounts must comply with the statutory provisions[7] as to the form and content of the balance sheet and profit and loss account and additional information to be provided by way of notes to the accounts[8].

Where compliance with those statutory provisions, and the other provisions of the Companies Act 1985 as to the matters to be included in a company's individual accounts, or in notes to those accounts, would not be sufficient to give a true and fair view, the necessary additional information must be given in the accounts or in a note to them[9].

If in special circumstances compliance with any of those provisions is inconsistent with the requirement to give a true and fair view, the directors must depart from that provision to the extent necessary to give a true and fair view[10]. Particulars of any such departure, the reasons for it and its effect must be given in a note to the accounts[10].

1 For the meaning of 'financial year' see para 806 ante.

2 For the meaning of 'balance sheet' see para 826 post. As to its form and content see paras 832, 833 post.

3 For the meaning of 'profit and loss account' see para 826 post. As to its form and content see paras 834–837 post.

4 Companies Act 1985 s 226(1) (substituted by the Companies Act 1989 s 4(1)).

5   For these purposes, 'true and fair view' refers (1) in the case of individual accounts, to the requirement of the Companies Act 1985 s 226(2) (as substituted); and (2) in the case of group accounts, to the requirement of s 227(3) (as substituted) (see para 875 post): s 262(1) (substituted by the Companies Act 1989 s 22). See also *Lloyd Cheyham & Co Ltd v Littlejohn & Co* [1987] BCLC 303 (while the Statements of Standard Practice are not rigid rules, they are very strong evidence of what is the proper standard to be adopted).

6   Companies Act 1985 s 226(2) (substituted by the Companies Act 1989 s 4(1)).

7   Ie the Companies Act 1985 s 226(3), Sch 4 (as amended): see para 809 et seq ante and para 831 et seq post.

8   Ibid s 226(3) (substituted by the Companies Act 1989 s 4(1)). As to notes to the accounts see paras 838 et seq, 887 et seq post.

9   Companies Act 1985 s 226(4) (substituted by the Companies Act 1989 s 4(1)).

10   Companies Act 1985 s 226(5) (substituted by the Companies Act 1989 s 4(1)).

817. Accounts and reports to be laid before company in general meeting. The directors of a company must in respect of each financial year[1] lay before the company in general meeting copies of the company's annual accounts[2], the directors' report[3] and the auditors' report[4] on those accounts[5].

If the above requirements are not complied with before the end of the period allowed for laying and delivering accounts and reports[6], every person who immediately before the end of that period was a director[7] of the company is guilty of an offence and liable on summary conviction to a fine not exceeding the statutory maximum or, on conviction after continued contravention, to a daily default fine not exceeding one-tenth of the statutory maximum[8].

It is a defence for a person charged with such an offence to prove that he took all reasonable steps for securing that those requirements would be complied with before the end of that period[9]. It is not, however, a defence to prove that the documents in question were not in fact prepared as required[10] by the statutory provisions[11].

1   For the meaning of 'financial year' see para 806 ante.

2   For these purposes, 'annual accounts' means (1) the individual accounts required by the Companies Act 1985 s 226 (as substituted) (see para 816 ante); and (2) any group accounts required by s 227 (as substituted) (see para 875 post); but see also s 230 (as substituted) (treatment of individual profit and loss account where group accounts are prepared: see para 878 post): s 262(1) (substituted by the Companies Act 1989 s 22); Companies Act 1985 s 742(1) (substituted by the Companies Act 1989 s 23, Sch 10 para 15).

3   As to the directors' report see para 1066 et seq post.

4   As to the auditors' report see paras 1059-1061 post.

5   Companies Act 1985 s 241(1) (substituted by the Companies Act 1989 s 11).

6   As to the period allowed for laying and delivering accounts see para 822 post.

7   For the meaning of 'director' see para 543 note 1 ante.

8   Companies Act 1985 s 241(2) (substituted by the Companies Act 1989 s 11); Companies Act 1985 s 730, Sch 24 (amended by the Companies Act 1989 s 23, Sch 10 para 24(1), (2)). For the meaning of 'the statutory maximum' and 'daily default fine' see para 1161 post.

9   Companies Act 1985 s 241(3) (substituted by the Companies Act 1989 s 11).

10   Ie as required by the Companies Act 1985 Pt VII (ss 221-262A) (as amended): see para 801 et seq ante and para 818 et seq post.

11   Ibid s 241(4) (substituted by the Companies Act 1989 s 11).

818. Accounts and reports to be delivered to the registrar. The directors of a company must in respect of each financial year[1] deliver to the registrar of companies a copy of the company's annual accounts[2] together with a copy of the directors' report[3] for that year and a copy of the auditors' report[4] on those accounts[5]. If any document comprised in those accounts or reports is in a language other than English, the directors must[6] annex to the copy of that document delivered a translation of it into English, certified in the prescribed manner[7] to be a correct translation[8].

If the above requirements are not complied with before the end of the period allowed for laying and delivering accounts and reports[9], every person who immediately before the end of that period was a director of the company is guilty of an offence and liable on summary conviction to a fine not exceeding the statutory maximum or, on conviction after continued contravention, to a daily default fine not exceeding one-tenth of the statutory maximum[10].

Further, if the directors of the company fail to make good the default within 14 days after the service of a notice on them requiring compliance, the court may, on the application of any member or creditor of the company or of the registrar, make an order directing the directors, or any of them, to make good the default within such time as may be specified in the order[11]. The court's order may provide that all costs of and incidental to the application shall be borne by the directors[11].

It is a defence for a person charged with an offence under the above provisions to prove that he took all reasonable steps for securing that the above requirements would be complied with before the end of the period allowed for laying and delivering accounts and reports[12]. It is not, however, a defence in any proceedings under the above provisions to prove that the documents in question were not in fact prepared as required[13] by the statutory provisions[14].

1 For the meaning of 'financial year' see para 806 ante.
2 For the meaning of 'annual accounts' see para 817 note 2 ante.
3 As to the directors' report see para 1066 et seq post.
4 As to the auditors' report see paras 1059-1061 post.
5 Companies Act 1985 s 242(1) (substituted by the Companies Act 1989 s 11).
6 Ie subject to the Companies Act 1985 s 710B(6) (as added) (delivery of certain Welsh documents without a translation): see para 90 ante.
7 For these purposes, a translation of a document into English is certified to be a correct translation:
  (1) if the translation was made in the United Kingdom, by:
    (a) a notary public in any part of the United Kingdom;
    (b) a solicitor (if the translation was made in Scotland), a solicitor of the Supreme Court of Judicature of England and Wales (if it was made in England or Wales), or a solicitor of the Supreme Court of Judicature of Northern Ireland (if it was made in Northern Ireland);
    (c) a person certified by a person mentioned in heads (1)(a) and (1)(b) supra to be known to him to be competent to translate the document into English; or
  (2) if the translation was made outside the United Kingdom, by:
    (a) a notary public;
    (b) a person authorised in the place where the translation was made to administer an oath;
    (c) any of the British officials mentioned in the Commissioners for Oaths Act 1889 s 6 (as amended); or
    (d) a person certified by a person mentioned in heads (2)(a), (2)(b) or (2)(c) supra, to be known to him to be competent to translate the document into English:
Companies (Forms) (Amendment) Regulations 1990, SI 1990/572, reg 5(1), (2). The British officials mentioned in the Commissioners for Oaths Act 1889 s 6 (as amended) are: every British ambassador, envoy, minister, chargé d' affaires, and secretary of embassy or legation exercising his functions in any foreign country, and every British consul-general, consul, vice-consul, acting consul, pro-consul, and consular agent, acting consul-general, acting vice-consul and acting consular agent exercising his functions in any foreign place: s 6(1) (amended by the Commissioners for Oaths Act 1891 s 2).
    The Companies (Forms) (Amendment) Regulations 1990 reg 5(1) applies also for the purposes of the Companies Act 1985 s 228(2)(f) (as substituted and amended) (see para 876 post), s 243(4) (as substituted and amended) (see para 821 post) and s 702(1) (as substituted) (see para 1825 post): Companies (Forms) (Amendment) Regulations 1990 reg 5(2).

8 Companies Act 1985 s 242(1) (substituted by the Companies Act 1989 s 11; amended by the Welsh Language Act 1993 s 30(1), (4)).
9 As to the period allowed for laying and delivering accounts see para 822 post.
10 Companies Act 1985 s 242(2) (substituted by the Companies Act 1989 s 11); Companies Act 1985 s 730, Sch 24 (amended by the Companies Act 1989 s 23, Sch 10 para 24(1), (2)). For the meaning of 'the statutory maximum' and 'daily default fine' see para 1161 post.
11 Companies Act 1985 s 242(3) (substituted by the Companies Act 1989 s 11).
12 Companies Act 1985 s 242(4) (substituted by the Companies Act 1989 s 11).
13 Ie prepared as required by the Companies Act 1985 Pt VII (ss 221-262A) (as amended): see para 801 et seq ante and para 819 et seq post.
14 Ibid s 242(5) (substituted by the Companies Act 1989 s 11).

819. Civil penalty for failure to deliver accounts. Where the statutory requirements relating to the delivery to the registrar of companies of accounts and reports[1] are not complied with before the end of the period allowed for laying and delivering accounts and reports[2], the company is liable to a civil penalty[3]. This is in addition to any liability of the directors[4] under those statutory provisions[5].

The amount of the penalty is determined by reference to the length of the period between the end of the period allowed for laying and delivering accounts and reports and the day on which the requirements are complied with, and whether the company is a public[6] or private[7] company, as follows[8]:

LENGTH OF PERIOD	PUBLIC COMPANY	PRIVATE COMPANY
Not more than three months	£500	£100
More than three months but not more than six months	£1,000	£250
More than six months but not more than 12 months	£2,000	£500
More than 12 months	£5,000	£1,000

The penalty may be recovered by the registrar and must be paid by him into the Consolidated Fund[9].

It is not a defence in proceedings under the above provisions to prove that the documents in question were not in fact prepared as required by the statutory provisions[10].

1 Ie the Companies Act 1985 s 242(1) (as substituted): see para 818 ante.
2 As to the period for laying and delivering accounts and reports see para 822 post.
3 Companies Act 1985 s 242A(1) (added by the Companies Act 1989 s 11).
4 Ie under the Companies Act 1985 s 242 (as substituted and amended): see para 818 ante.
5 Ibid s 242A(1) (as added: see note 3 supra).
6 For the meaning of 'private company' see para 82 ante.
7 For the meaning of 'public company' see para 82 ante.
8 Companies Act 1985 s 242A(2) (added by the Companies Act 1989 s 11).
9 Companies Act 1985 s 242A(3) (added by the Companies Act 1989 s 11).
10 Companies Act 1985 s 242A(4) (added by the Companies Act 1989 s 11).

820. Delivery and publication of accounts in ECUs. The amounts set out in the annual accounts[1] of a company may also be shown in the same accounts translated into ECUs[2].

When complying with their statutory duty to deliver to the registrar of companies accounts and reports[3], the directors of a company may deliver to the registrar an additional copy of the company's annual accounts in which the relevant amounts have been translated into ECUs[4].

In both cases the amounts must have been translated at the relevant exchange rate[5] prevailing on the balance sheet date[6] and that rate must be disclosed in the notes to the accounts[7].

1 For the meaning of 'annual accounts' see para 817 note 2 ante.
2 Companies Act 1985 s 242B(1) (added by the Companies Act 1985 (Accounts of Small and Medium-sized Enterprises and Publication of Accounts in ECUs) Regulations 1992, SI 1992/2452, reg 3). For these purposes, 'ECU' means a unit with a value equal to the value of the unit of account known as the ecu used in the European Monetary System: Companies Act 1985 s 242B(5) (added by the Companies Act 1985 (Accounts of Small and Medium-sized Enterprises and Publication of Accounts in ECUs) Regulations 1992 reg 3).
3 Ie under the Companies Act 1985 s 242 (as substituted): see para 818 ante.
4 Ibid s 242B(2) (added by the Companies Act 1985 (Accounts of Small and Medium-sized Enterprises and Publication of Accounts in ECUs) Regulations 1992 reg 3). For the purposes of the Companies Act 1985 s 240 (as substituted and amended) (see para 938 post), any additional copy of the company's annual accounts delivered to the registrar under s 242B(2) (as so added) is treated as statutory accounts of the company and, in the case of such a copy, references in s 240 (as substituted and amended) to the auditors' report under s 235 (as substituted) (see para 1059 post) are to be read as references to the auditors' report on the annual accounts of which it is a copy: s 242B(4) (added by the Companies Act 1985 (Accounts of Small and Medium-sized Enterprises and Publication of Accounts in ECUs) Regulations 1992 reg 3).
5 For these purposes, 'relevant exchange rate' means the rate of exchange used for translating the value of the ecu for the purposes of the European Monetary System: Companies Act 1985 s 242B(5) (as added: see note 2 supra).
6 For the meaning of 'balance sheet date' see para 809 note 7 ante.
7 Companies Act 1985 s 242B(3) (added by the Companies Act 1985 (Accounts of Small and Medium-sized Enterprises and Publication of Accounts in ECUs) Regulations 1992 reg 3).

821. Accounts of subsidiary undertakings to be appended in certain cases. The following provisions apply where at the end of the financial year[1] a parent company[2] has as a subsidiary undertaking[3]:

(1) a body corporate[4] incorporated outside Great Britain which does not have an established place of business[5] in Great Britain; or

(2) an unincorporated undertaking,

which is excluded[6] from consolidation on the basis that it is an undertaking with activities different from the undertakings included in the consolidation[7].

There must be appended to the copy of the company's annual accounts[8] delivered to the registrar of companies[9] a copy of the undertaking's latest individual accounts[10] and, if it is a parent undertaking[11], its latest group accounts[12]. If the accounts appended are required by law to be audited, a copy of the auditors' report[13] must also be appended[14].

The accounts must be for a period ending not more than 12 months before the end of the financial year for which the parent company's accounts are made up[15].

If any document required to be appended is in a language other than English, the directors must[16] annex to the copy of that document delivered a translation of it into English, certified in the prescribed manner[17] to be a correct translation[18].

The above requirements are subject to the following qualifications:

(a) an undertaking is not required to prepare for these purposes accounts which would not otherwise be prepared, and, if no accounts satisfying the above requirements are prepared, none need be appended;

(b) a document need not be appended if it would not otherwise be required to be published, or made available for public inspection, anywhere in the world, but in that case the reason for not appending it must be stated in a note to the company's accounts[19];

(c) where an undertaking and all its subsidiary undertakings are excluded from consolidation[20], the accounts of such of the subsidiary undertakings of that undertaking as are included in its consolidated group accounts need not be appended[21].

The penalties and statutory defences which apply in the case of default in delivering accounts and reports to the registrar of companies[22] apply[23] also in relation to the requirements of the above provisions[24].

1 For the meaning of 'financial year' see para 806 ante.
2 For the meaning of 'parent company' see para 828 post.
3 For the meaning of 'subsidiary undertaking' see para 828 post.
4 For the meaning of 'body corporate' see para 89 note 8 ante.
5 For the meaning of 'place of business' see para 63 note 1 ante.
6 Ie in accordance with the Companies Act 1985 s 229(4) (as substituted): see para 877 post.
7 Ibid s 243(1) (substituted by the Companies Act 1989 s 11).
8 For the meaning of 'annual accounts' see para 817 note 2 ante.
9 Ie in accordance with the Companies Act 1985 s 242 (as substituted): see para 818 ante.
10 For the meaning of 'individual accounts' see para 816 ante.
11 For the meaning of 'parent undertaking' see para 828 post.
12 Companies Act 1985 s 243(2) (substituted by the Companies Act 1989 s 11).
13 As to the auditors' report see paras 1059-1061 post.
14 Companies Act 1985 s 243(2) (as substituted: see note 12 supra).
15 Ibid s 243(3) (substituted by the Companies Act 1989 s 11).
16 Ie subject to the Companies Act 1985 s 710B(6) (delivery of certain Welsh documents without a translation): see para 90 ante.
17 For the prescribed manner of certification see para 818 note 7 ante.
18 Companies Act 1985 s 243(4) (substituted by the Companies Act 1989 s 11; amended by the Welsh Language Act 1993 s 30(1), (4)).
19 As to notes to the accounts see paras 838 et seq, 887 et seq post.
20 Ie in accordance with the Companies Act 1985 s 229(4) (as substituted): see para 877 post.
21 Ibid s 243(5) (substituted by the Companies Act 1989 s 11).
22 Ie the Companies Act 1985 s 242(2)-(4) (as substituted): see para 818 ante.
23 Ie as they apply in relation to the requirements of ibid s 242(1) (as substituted): see para 818 ante.
24 Ibid s 243(6) (substituted by the Companies Act 1989 s 11).

822. Period allowed for laying and delivering accounts and reports. The period allowed for laying and delivering accounts and reports is:
(1) for a private company[1], ten months after the end of the relevant accounting reference period[2]; and
(2) for a public company[3], seven months after the end of that period[4].

If, however, the relevant accounting reference period is the company's first and is a period of more than 12 months, the period allowed is:
(a) ten months or seven months, as the case may be, from the first anniversary of the incorporation of the company; or
(b) three months from the end of the accounting reference period,
whichever last expires[5].

Where a company carries on business, or has interests, outside the United Kingdom, the Channel Islands and the Isle of Man, the directors may, in respect of any financial year, give to the registrar of companies before the end of the period allowed under the above provisions a notice in the prescribed form[6] stating that the company so carries on business or has such interests and claiming a three-month extension of the period allowed for laying and delivering accounts and reports; and, upon such a notice being given, the period is extended accordingly[7].

If the relevant accounting period is treated as shortened[8], the period allowed for laying and delivering accounts is that applicable in accordance with the above provisions or three months from the date of the notice altering the accounting reference date, whichever last expires[9].

If for any special reason the Secretary of State thinks fit, he may, on an application made before the expiry of the period otherwise allowed, by notice in writing to a company extend that period by such further period as may be specified in the notice[10].

1 For the meaning of 'private company' see para 82 ante.
2 For the meaning of 'public company' see para 82 ante.
3 For these purposes, 'the relevant accounting reference period' means the accounting reference period by reference to which the financial year for the accounts in question was determined: Companies Act 1985 s 244(6) (substituted by the Companies Act 1989 s 11). For the meaning of 'financial year' see para 806 ante; and for the meaning of 'accounting reference period' see para 807 ante.
4 Companies Act 1985 s 244(1) (substituted by the Companies Act 1989 s 11). The Companies Act 1985 s 244(1) (as so substituted) is subject to s 244(2)-(6) (as substituted): s 244(1) (as so substituted).
5 Ibid s 244(2) (substituted by the Companies Act 1989 s 11).
6 For the prescribed form of notice see the Companies (Forms) (Amendment) Regulations 1990, SI 1990/572, reg 3, Sch 2, Form 244.
7 Companies Act 1985 s 244(3) (substituted by the Companies Act 1989 s 11).
8 Ie by virtue of a notice under the Companies Act 1985 s 225 (as substituted and amended): see para 808 ante.
9 Ibid s 244(4) (substituted by the Companies Act 1989 s 11).
10 Companies Act 1985 s 244(5) (substituted by the Companies Act 1989 s 11). The functions conferred on the Secretary of State by the Companies Act 1985 s 244(5) (as so substituted) may be exercised by, or by employees of, such person (if any) as may be authorised in that behalf by the Secretary of State: Contracting Out (Functions in relation to the Registration of Companies) Order 1995, SI 1995/1013, art 5, Sch 3 para 1(b). As to the contracting out of functions of the Secretary of State generally see paras 1508, 1509 post.

823. Persons entitled to receive copies of accounts and reports. A copy of the company's annual accounts[1], together with a copy of the directors' report[2] for the financial year[3] and of the auditors' report[4] on those accounts must be sent to every member of the company, every holder of the company's debentures and every person who is entitled to receive notice of general meetings, not less than 21 days before the date of the meeting at which copies of those documents are[5] to be laid[6].

Copies need not be sent:
(1) to a person who is not entitled to receive notices of general meetings and of whose address the company is unaware; or
(2) to more than one of the joint holders of shares or debentures none of whom is entitled to receive such notices; or
(3) in the case of joint holders of shares or debentures some of whom are, and some not, entitled to receive such notices, to those who are not so entitled[7].

In the case of a company not having a share capital, copies need not be sent to anyone who is not entitled to receive notices of general meetings of the company[8].

If copies are sent less than 21 days before the date of the meeting, they are deemed, notwithstanding that fact, to have been duly sent if it is so agreed by all the members entitled to attend and vote at the meeting[9].

If default is made in complying with the above provisions, the company, and every officer of it who is in default, is guilty of an offence and liable on conviction on indictment to a fine, or on summary conviction to a fine not exceeding the statutory maximum[10].

Where copies are sent out under the above provisions over a period of days, references elsewhere in the Companies Act 1985 to the day on which copies are sent out are to be construed as references to the last day of that period[11].

1 For the meaning of 'annual accounts' see para 817 note 2 ante.
2 As to the directors' report see para 1066 et seq post.
3 For the meaning of 'financial year' see para 806 ante.
4 As to the auditors' report see paras 1059-1061 post.
5 Ie in accordance with the Companies Act 1985 s 241 (as substituted): see para 817 ante.
6 Ibid s 238(1) (substituted by the Companies Act 1989 s 10).
7 Companies Act 1985 s 238(2) (substituted by the Companies Act 1989 s 10).
8 Companies Act 1985 s 238(3) (substituted by the Companies Act 1989 s 10).
9 Companies Act 1985 s 238(4) (substituted by the Companies Act 1989 s 10).
10 Companies Act 1985 s 238(5) (substituted by the Companies Act 1989 s 10); Companies Act 1985 s 730,
    Sch 24 (amended by the Companies Act 1989 s 23, Sch 10 para 24(1), (2)). For the meaning of 'the
    statutory maximum', 'officer who is in default' and 'daily default fine' see para 1161 post.
11 Companies Act 1985 s 238(6) (substituted by the Companies Act 1989 s 10).

824. Right to demand copies of accounts and reports. Any member of a
company and any holder of a company's debentures is entitled to be furnished, on
demand and without charge, with a copy of the company's last annual accounts[1] and
directors' report[2] and a copy of the auditors' report[3] on those accounts[4]. This entitlement is to a single copy of those documents, but that is in addition to any copy to which
a person may otherwise[5] be entitled[6].

If a demand under the above provisions is not complied with within seven days, the
company, and every officer of it who is in default, is guilty of an offence and liable on
summary conviction to a fine not exceeding one-fifth of the statutory maximum and,
on conviction after continued contravention, to a daily default fine not exceeding
one-fiftieth of the statutory maximum[7].

If in proceedings for such an offence the issue arises whether a person had already
been so furnished with a copy of the relevant document, it is for the defendant to prove
that he had[8].

1 For the meaning of 'annual accounts' see para 817 note 2 ante.
2 As to the directors' report see para 1066 et seq post.
3 As to the auditors' report see paras 1059, 1061 post.
4 Companies Act 1985 s 239(1) (substituted by the Companies Act 1989 s 10).
5 Ie under the Companies Act 1985 s 238 (as substituted): see para 823 ante.
6 Ibid s 239(2) (substituted by the Companies Act 1989 s 10).
7 Companies Act 1985 s 239(3) (substituted by the Companies Act 1989 s 10); Companies Act 1985 s 730,
    Sch 24 (amended by the Companies Act 1989 s 23, Sch 10 para 24(1), (2)). For the meaning of 'officer
    who is in default', 'the statutory maximum', and 'daily default fine' see para 1161 post.
8 Companies Act 1985 s 239(4) (substituted by the Companies Act 1989 s 10).

(v) Form and Content of Company Individual Accounts other than of Banking and Insurance Companies

A. GENERAL RULES

825. Form and content of accounts generally. A company's individual accounts[1]
must comply with the statutory provisions[2] as to the form and content of the balance
sheet[3] and profit and loss account[4] and additional information to be provided by way of
notes to the accounts[5].

1 For the meaning of 'individual accounts' see para 816 ante.
2 Ie the Companies Act 1985 s 226(3), Sch 4 (as amended): see para 809 et seq ante and para 831 et seq
    post.

3 The balance sheet must give a true and fair view of the state of affairs of the company as at the end of the financial year: see ibid s 226(2) and para 816 ante.

4 The profit and loss account must give a true and fair view of the profit or loss of the company for the financial year: see ibid s 226(2) and para 816 ante.

5 Ibid s 226(3) (substituted by the Companies Act 1989 s 4(1)). As to notes to accounts see para 838 et seq post.

826. Meaning of 'annual accounts', 'balance sheet' and 'profit and loss account'. References to a company's annual accounts, or to a balance sheet or profit and loss account, include notes to the accounts giving information which is required by any provision of the Companies Act 1985, and required or allowed by any such provision to be given in a note to company accounts[1]. In the case of an undertaking[2] not trading for profit, any reference to a profit and loss account is to an income and expenditure account; and references to profit and loss and, in relation to group accounts[3], to a consolidated profit and loss account are to be construed accordingly[4].

1 Companies Act 1985 s 261(2) (substituted by the Companies Act 1989 s 22); Companies Act 1985 s 742(1) (substituted by the Companies Act 1989 s 23, Sch 10 para 15).

2 For the meaning of 'undertaking' see para 806 note 5 ante.

3 As to group accounts see para 875 et seq post.

4 Companies Act 1985 s 262(2) (substituted by the Companies Act 1989 s 22).

827. Meaning of 'subsidiary', 'holding company' and 'wholly-owned subsidiary'. A company[1] is a 'subsidiary' of another company, its 'holding company', if that other company:

(1) holds a majority of the voting rights[2] in it; or

(2) is a member of it and has the right to appoint or remove a majority of its board of directors[3]; or

(3) is a member of it and controls alone, pursuant to an agreement with other shareholders or members, a majority of the voting rights in it,

or if it is a subsidiary of a company which is itself a subsidiary of that other company[4].

A company is a 'wholly-owned subsidiary' of another company if it has no members except that other and that other's wholly-owned subsidiaries or persons acting on behalf of that other or its wholly-owned subsidiaries[5].

Rights which are exercisable only in certain circumstances are taken into account only when the circumstances have arisen, and for so long as they continue to obtain, or when the circumstances are within the control of the person having the rights; and rights which are normally exercisable but are temporarily incapable of exercise must continue to be taken into account[6].

Rights held by a person[7] in a fiduciary capacity are treated as not held by him[8].

Rights held by a person as nominee for another are treated as held by the other; and rights are regarded as held as nominee for another if they are exercisable only on his instructions or with his consent or concurrence[9].

Rights attached to shares held by way of security are treated as held by the person providing the security:

(a) where apart from the right to exercise them for the purpose of preserving the value of the security, or of realising it, the rights are exercisable only in accordance with his instructions;

(b) where the shares are held in connection with the granting of loans as part of normal business activities and apart from the right to exercise them for the purpose of preserving the value of the security, or of realising it, the rights are exercisable only in his interests[10].

Rights are treated as held by a company if they are held by any of its subsidiaries; and nothing in the above provisions[11] is to be construed as requiring rights held by a company to be treated as held by any of its subsidiaries[12].

The voting rights in a company are to be reduced by any rights held by the company itself[13].

The Secretary of State may by regulations amend the above provisions so as to alter the meaning of the expressions 'holding company', 'subsidiary' or 'wholly-owned subsidiary'[14].

Furthermore, for the purposes of the EC Treaty[15], the conduct of a subsidiary can be imputed to its parent company whether or not it has its own separate legal personality, and whether or not it is a wholly-owned subsidiary[16].

1 For these purposes, and for the purposes of the Companies Act 1985 s 736A (as substituted) (see infra), 'company' includes any body corporate: ss 736(3), 736A(12) (substituted by the Companies Act 1989 s 144(1)). For the meaning of 'body corporate' see para 89 note 8 ante.

2 For these purposes, and for the purposes of the Companies Act 1985 s 736(1)(c) (as substituted) (see text head (3) infra), the references to the voting rights in a company are to the rights conferred on shareholders in respect of their shares or, in the case of a company not having a share capital, on members, to vote at general meetings of the company on all, or substantially all, matters: s 736A(1), (2) (substituted by the Companies Act 1989 s 144(1)).

3 For these purposes, the reference to the right to appoint or remove a majority of the board of directors is to the right to appoint or remove directors holding a majority of the voting rights at meetings of the board on all, or substantially all, matters; and, for those purposes (1) a company is treated as having the right to appoint to a directorship if a person's appointment to it follows necessarily from his appointment as director of the company or the directorship is held by the company itself; and (2) a right to appoint or remove which is exercisable only with the consent or concurrence of another person must be left out of account unless no other person has a right to appoint or, as the case may be, remove in relation to that directorship: Companies Act 1985 s 736A(1), (3) (substituted by the Companies Act 1989 s 144(1)).

4 Companies Act 1985 s 736(1) (substituted by the Companies Act 1989 s 144(1)). Any reference in any enactment, including any enactment contained in subordinate legislation within the meaning of the Interpretation Act 1978, to a 'subsidiary' or 'holding company' within the meaning of the Companies Act 1985 s 736 is to be read, subject to any express amendment or saving made by or under the Companies Act 1989, as referring to a subsidiary or holding company as defined in the Companies Act 1985 s 736 as substituted by the Companies Act 1989 s 144: s 144(2).

5 Companies Act 1985 s 736(2) (substituted by the Companies Act 1989 s 144(1)).

6 Companies Act 1985 s 736A(4) (substituted by the Companies Act 1989 s 144(1)).

7 For these purposes, references in any provision of the Companies Act 1985 s 736A(5)-(10) (as substituted) (see infra) to rights held by a person include rights falling to be treated as held by him by virtue of any other provision of s 736A(5)-(10) (as substituted) but not rights which by virtue of any such provision are to be treated as not held by him: s 736A(11) (substituted by the Companies Act 1989 s 144(1)).

8 Companies Act 1985 s 736A(5) (substituted by the Companies Act 1989 s 144(1)).

9 Companies Act 1985 s 736A(6) (substituted by the Companies Act 1989 s 144(1)).

10 Companies Act 1985 s 736A(7) (substituted by the Companies Act 1989 s 144(1)). For these purposes, rights are treated as being exercisable in accordance with the instructions or in the interests of a company if they are exercisable in accordance with the instructions of or, as the case may be, the interests of any subsidiary or holding company of that company or any subsidiary of a holding company of that company: Companies Act 1985 s 736A(9) (substituted by the Companies Act 1989 s 144(1)).

11 Ie the Companies Act 1985 s 736A(6) or (7) (as substituted): see supra.

12 Ibid s 736A(8) (substituted by the Companies Act 1989 s 144(1)).

13 Companies Act 1985 s 736A(10) (substituted by the Companies Act 1989 s 144(1)).

14 Companies Act 1985 s 736B(1) (substituted by the Companies Act 1989 s 144(3)). The regulations may make different provision for different cases or classes of case and may contain such incidental and supplementary provisions as the Secretary of State thinks fit: Companies Act 1985 s 736B(2) (substituted by the Companies Act 1989 s 144(3)). Any such regulations must be made by statutory instrument which is subject to annulment in pursuance of a resolution of either House of Parliament: Companies Act 1985 s 736B(3) (substituted by the Companies Act 1989 s 144(3)). Any amendment so made by regulations does not apply for the purposes of enactments outside the Companies Acts unless the

regulations so provide: Companies Act 1985 s 736B(4) (substituted by the Companies Act 1989 s 144(3)). So much of the Interpretation Act 1978 s 23(3) as applies s 17(2)(a) (effect of repeal and re-enactment: see STATUTES vol 44(1) (Reissue) para 1303) to deeds, instruments and documents other than enactments does not apply in relation to any repeal and re-enactment effected by any such regulations: Companies Act 1985 s 736B(5) (substituted by the Companies Act 1989 s 144(3)). For the meaning of 'the Companies Acts' see para 60 note 1 ante.

15 Ie the EC Treaty (Treaty establishing the European Economic Community (Rome, 25 March 1957; TS 1 (1973); Cmnd 5179); Treaty on European Union (Maastricht, 7 February 1992; Cm 1934) Title II art G para (1). See further EUROPEAN COMMUNITIES.

16 *Re Continental Can Co Inc* [1972] CMLR D11, overruled on other grounds by Case 6/72 *Europemballage Corpn and Continental Can Co Inc v EC Commission* [1973] ECR 215, [1973] CMLR 199, ECJ. The question of control of the conduct of the subsidiary was regarded more a question of fact than of actual definition of what constituted a subsidiary for this purpose.

828. Parent and subsidiary undertakings; in general. The expressions 'parent undertaking' and 'subsidiary undertaking' are to be construed as follows; and a 'parent company' means a parent undertaking which is a company[1].

An undertaking is a parent undertaking in relation to another undertaking, a subsidiary undertaking, if:

(1) it holds a majority of the voting rights[2] in the undertaking; or

(2) it is a member of the undertaking and has the right to appoint or remove a majority of its board of directors[3]; or

(3) it has the right to exercise a dominant influence over the undertaking[4] by virtue of provisions contained in the undertaking's memorandum or articles or by virtue of a control contract[5]; or

(4) it is a member of the undertaking and controls alone, pursuant to an agreement with other shareholders or members, a majority of the voting rights[6] in the undertaking[7].

For these purposes, an undertaking is treated as a member of another undertaking if any of its subsidiary undertakings is a member of that undertaking or if any shares[8] in that other undertaking are held by a person acting on behalf of the undertaking or any of its subsidiary undertakings[9].

An undertaking is also a parent undertaking in relation to another undertaking, a subsidiary undertaking, if it has a participating interest[10] in the undertaking and it actually exercises a dominant influence[11] over it or it and the subsidiary undertaking are managed on a unified basis[12].

A parent undertaking is treated as the parent undertaking of undertakings in relation to which any of its subsidiary undertakings are, or are to be treated as, parent undertakings; and references to its subsidiary undertakings are to be construed accordingly[13].

1 Companies Act 1985 s 258(1) (substituted by the Companies Act 1989 s 21(1)); Companies Act 1985 s 742(1) (substituted by the Companies Act 1989 s 23, Sch 10 para 15). For the meaning of 'undertaking' see para 806 note 5 ante. See also para 829 post.

2 For these purposes, and for the purposes of the Companies Act 1985 s 258(2)(d) (see text head (4) infra), the references to the voting rights in an undertaking are to the rights conferred on shareholders in respect of their shares or, in the case of an undertaking not having a share capital, on members, to vote at general meetings of the undertaking on all, or substantially all, matters: s 258(6), Sch 10A paras 1, 2(1) (added by the Companies Act 1989 s 21(2), Sch 9). In relation to an undertaking which does not have general meetings at which matters are decided by the exercise of voting rights, the references to the holding of a majority of the voting rights in the undertaking are to be construed as references to having the right under the constitution of the undertaking to direct the overall policy of the undertaking or to alter the terms of its constitution: Companies Act 1985 Sch 10A paras 1, 2(2) (added by the Companies Act 1989 Sch 9).

3 For these purposes, the reference to the right to appoint or remove a majority of the board of directors is to the right to appoint or remove directors holding a majority of the voting rights at meetings of the board on all, or substantially all, matters: Companies Act 1985 Sch 10A paras 1, 3(1) (added by the Companies Act 1989 Sch 9). An undertaking is treated as having the right to appoint to a directorship if (1) a person's appointment to it follows necessarily from his appointment as director of the undertaking; or (2) the directorship is held by the undertaking itself: Companies Act 1985 Sch 10A paras 1, 3(2) (added by the Companies Act 1989 Sch 9). A right to appoint or remove which is exercisable only with the consent or concurrence of another person must be left out of account unless no other person has a right to appoint or, as the case may be, remove in relation to that directorship: Companies Act 1985 Sch 10A paras 1, 3(3) (added by the Companies Act 1989 Sch 9).

4 For these purposes, an undertaking is not regarded as having the right to exercise a dominant influence over another undertaking unless it has a right to give directions with respect to the operating and financial policies of that other undertaking which its directors are obliged to comply with whether or not they are for the benefit of that other undertaking: Companies Act 1985 Sch 10A paras 1, 4(1) (added by the Companies Act 1989 Sch 9). The Companies Act 1985 Sch 10A para 4 (as added) is not to be read as affecting the construction of the expression 'actually exercises a dominant influence' in s 258(4)(a) (as substituted) (see infra): Sch 10A paras 1, 4(3) (added by the Companies Act 1989 Sch 9).

5 For these purposes, a 'control contract' means a contract in writing conferring such a right which (1) is of a kind authorised by the memorandum or articles of the undertaking in relation to which the right is exercisable; and (2) is permitted by the law under which that undertaking is established: Companies Act 1985 Sch 10A paras 1, 4(2) (added by the Companies Act 1989 Sch 9). See also note 4 supra.

6 See note 2 supra.

7 Companies Act 1985 s 258(2) (substituted by the Companies Act 1989 s 21(1)).

8 For these purposes, references to shares (1) in relation to an undertaking with a share capital, are to allotted shares; (2) in relation to an undertaking with capital but no share capital, are to rights to share in the capital of the undertaking; and (3) in relation to an undertaking without capital, are to interests conferring any right to share in the profits or liability to contribute to the losses of the undertaking or giving rise to an obligation to contribute to the debts or expenses of the undertaking in the event of a winding up: Companies Act 1985 s 259(2) (substituted by the Companies Act 1989 s 22).

9 Companies Act 1985 s 258(3) (substituted by the Companies Act 1989 s 21(1)).

10 For the meaning of 'participating interest' see para 830 post.

11 See note 4 supra.

12 Companies Act 1985 s 258(4) (substituted by the Companies Act 1989 s 21(1)).

13 Companies Act 1985 s 258(5) (substituted by the Companies Act 1989 s 21(1)).

829. Parent and subsidiary undertakings; exercise of rights. Rights which are exercisable only in certain circumstances are to be taken into account only when the circumstances have arisen, and for so long as they obtain or when the circumstances are within the control of the person having the rights[1]. Rights which are normally exercisable but are temporarily incapable of exercise must continue to be taken into account[2].

Rights held by a person[3] in a fiduciary capacity are to be treated as not held by him[4]. Rights held by a person as nominee for another are to be treated as held by the other[5]; and rights are to be regarded as held by a nominee for another if they are exercisable only on his instructions or with his consent or concurrence[6].

Rights attached to shares[7] held by way of security are to be treated as held by the person providing the security:

(1) where apart from the right to exercise them for the purpose of preserving the value of the security, or of realising it, the rights are exercisable only in accordance with his instructions; and

(2) where the shares are held in connection with the granting of loans as part of normal business activities and apart from the right to exercise them for the purpose of preserving the value of the security, or of realising it, the rights are exercisable only in his interests[8].

Rights are to be treated as held by a parent undertaking if they are held by any of its subsidiary undertakings[9].

The voting rights in an undertaking must be reduced by any rights held by the undertaking itself[10].

1 Companies Act 1985 s 258(6), Sch 10A paras 1, 5(1) (added by the Companies Act 1989 s 21(2), Sch 9).
2 Companies Act 1985 Sch 10A paras 1, 5(2) (added by the Companies Act 1989 Sch 9).
3 For these purposes, references in any provision of the Companies Act 1985 Sch 10A paras 6-10 (as added) (see infra) to rights held by a person include rights falling to be treated as held by him by virtue of any other provision of Sch 10A paras 6-10 (as added) but not rights which by virtue of any such provision are to be treated as not held by him: Sch 10A paras 1, 11 (added by the Companies Act 1989 Sch 9).
4 Companies Act 1985 Sch 10A paras 1, 6 (added by the Companies Act 1989 Sch 9).
5 Companies Act 1985 Sch 10A paras 1, 7(1) (added by the Companies Act 1989 Sch 9).
6 Companies Act 1985 Sch 10A paras 1, 7(2) (added by the Companies Act 1989 Sch 9).
7 For the meaning of 'shares' see para 828 note 8 ante.
8 Companies Act 1985 Sch 10A paras 1, 8 (added by the Companies Act 1989 Sch 9).
9 Companies Act 1985 Sch 10A paras 1, 9(1) (added by the Companies Act 1989 Sch 9). Nothing in the Companies Act 1985 Sch 10A paras 7 or 8 (as added) (see supra) is to be construed as requiring rights held by a parent undertaking to be treated as held by any of its subsidiary undertakings: Sch 10A paras 1, 9(2) (added by the Companies Act 1989 Sch 9). For the purposes of the Companies Act 1985 Sch 10A para 8 (as added), rights are to be treated as being exercisable in accordance with the instructions or in the interests of an undertaking if they are exercisable in accordance with the instructions of or, as the case may be, in the interests of any group undertaking: Sch 10A paras 1, 9(3) (added by the Companies Act 1989 Sch 9). For these purposes, 'group undertaking', in relation to an undertaking, means an undertaking which is a parent undertaking or subsidiary undertaking of that undertaking or a subsidiary undertaking of any parent undertaking of that undertaking: Companies Act 1985 s 259(5) (substituted by the Companies Act 1989 s 22). For the meaning of 'parent undertaking' and 'subsidiary undertaking' see para 828 ante.
10 Companies Act 1985 Sch 10A paras 1, 10 (added by the Companies Act 1989 Sch 9).

830. Participating interests. 'Participating interest' means an interest held by an undertaking[1] in the shares[2] of another undertaking which it holds on a long-term basis for the purpose of securing a contribution to its activities by the exercise of control or influence arising from or related to that interest[3]. A holding of 20% or more of the shares of an undertaking is presumed to be a participating interest unless the contrary is shown[4].

For these purposes, an interest held on behalf of an undertaking is treated as held by it[5].

For the purposes of these provisions as they apply in relation to the expression 'participating interest' in the definition of subsidiary undertaking[6]:

(1) there must be attributed to an undertaking any interests held by any of its subsidiary undertakings; and

(2) the reference[7] to the purpose and activities of an undertaking include the purposes and activities of any of its subsidiary undertakings and of the group[8] as a whole[9].

In the statutory balance sheet and profit and loss formats[10] 'participating interest' does not include an interest in a group undertaking[11].

For the purpose of these provisions as they apply in relation to the expression 'participating interest' in those formats as they apply to group accounts and in the provisions relating to undertakings to be accounted for as associated undertakings in group accounts[12], the references in the above provisions[13] to the interest held by, and the purposes and activities of, the undertaking concerned are to be construed as references to the interest held by, and the purposes and activities of, the group[14].

1 For the meaning of 'undertaking' see para 806 note 5 ante.
2 For these purposes, the reference to an interest in shares includes (1) an interest which is convertible into an interest in shares; and (2) an option to acquire shares or any such interest; and an interest or option falls within heads (1) or (2) supra notwithstanding that the shares to which it relates are, until the conversion or the exercise of the option, unissued: Companies Act 1985 s 260(3) (substituted by the Companies Act 1989 s 22). For the meaning of 'shares' see para 828 note 8 ante.
3 Companies Act 1985 s 260(1) (substituted by the Companies Act 1989 s 22).
4 Companies Act 1985 s 260(2) (substituted by the Companies Act 1989 s 22).
5 Companies Act 1985 s 260(4) (substituted by the Companies Act 1989 s 22).
6 Ie in the Companies Act 1985 s 258(4) (as substituted): see para 828 ante.
7 Ie the reference in ibid s 260(1) (as substituted): see supra.
8 For these purposes, 'group' means a parent undertaking and its subsidiary undertakings: ibid s 262(1) (substituted by the Companies Act 1989 s 22). For the meaning of 'parent undertaking' and 'subsidiary undertaking' see para 828 ante.
9 Companies Act 1985 s 260(5) (substituted by the Companies Act 1989 s 22).
10 Ie the formats set out in the Companies Act 1985 s 226(3), Sch 4 Pt I (paras 1–8 (as amended): see para 832 et seq post) and s 260(6), Sch 9A Pt I Ch I (paras 1–12 (as added): insurance companies).
11 Ibid s 260(6) (substituted by the Companies Act 1989 s 22; amended by the Companies Act 1985 (Insurance Companies Accounts) Regulations 1993, SI 1993/3246, reg 5(1), Sch 2 para 4). For the meaning of 'group undertaking' see para 829 note 9 ante.
12 Ie the Companies Act 1985 s 227(4), Sch 4A para 20 (as added): see para 886 post.
13 Ie the references in ibid s 260(1)–(4) (as substituted): see supra.
14 Ibid s 260(7) (substituted by the Companies Act 1989 s 22). For these purposes, 'group' means a group within the meaning of the Companies Act 1985 Sch 4A para 1 (as added) (see para 879 post): s 260(7) (as so substituted).

831. General rules. Subject to the following provisions[1], every balance sheet[2] of a company must show the items listed in either of the balance sheet formats[3]; and every profit and loss account[4] of a company must show the items listed in any one of the profit and loss account formats[5]; in either case in the order and under the headings and sub-headings given in the format adopted[6].

Where, in accordance with the above provisions, a company's balance sheet or profit and loss account for any financial year[7] has been prepared by reference to one of such formats, the directors of the company must adopt the same format in preparing the accounts for subsequent financial years of the company unless in their opinion there are special reasons for a change[8]. Particulars of any change in the format so adopted in preparing a company's balance sheet or profit and loss account must be disclosed, and the reasons for the change must be explained, in a note to the accounts in which the new format is first adopted[9].

Any item so required[10] to be shown in a company's balance sheet or profit and loss account may be shown in greater detail than required by the format adopted[11]. A company's balance sheet or profit and loss account may include an item representing or covering the amount of any asset or liability, income or expenditure not otherwise covered by any of the items listed in the format adopted, but the following must not be treated as assets in any company's balance sheet: preliminary expenses; expenses of, and commission on, any issue of shares or debentures; and costs of research[12].

In preparing a company's balance sheet or profit and loss account the directors of the company must adapt the arrangement and headings and sub-headings otherwise so required in respect of items to which an Arabic number is assigned in the format adopted, in any case where the special nature of the company's business requires such adaptation[13]. Items to which Arabic numbers are assigned in any of such formats may be combined in a company's accounts for any financial year if either:

(1) their individual amounts are not material to assessing the state of affairs or profit or loss of the company for that year; or

(2) the combination facilitates that assessment;
but in a case within head (2) above the individual amounts of any items so combined must be disclosed in a note to the accounts[14].

A heading or sub-heading corresponding to an item listed in the format adopted in preparing a company's balance sheet or profit and loss account must not be included if there is no amount to be shown for that item in respect of the financial year to which the balance sheet or profit and loss account relates[15]. Every profit and loss account of a company must show:

(a) the amount of the company's profit or loss on ordinary activities before taxation[16]; and

(b) separately as additional items any amount set aside or proposed to be set aside to, or withdrawn or proposed to be withdrawn from, reserves, the aggregate amount of any dividends paid and proposed and, if it is not shown in the notes to the accounts, the aggregate amount of any dividends proposed[17].

In respect of every item shown in a company's balance sheet or profit and loss account the corresponding amount for the financial year immediately preceding that to which the balance sheet or profit and loss account relates must also be shown[18]. Where that corresponding amount is not comparable with the amount to be shown for the item in question in respect of the financial year to which the balance sheet or profit and loss account relates, the former amount must be adjusted and particulars of the adjustment and the reasons for it must be disclosed in a note to the accounts[19]. Amounts in respect of items representing assets or income may not be set off against amounts in respect of items representing liabilities or expenditure (as the case may be), or vice versa[20].

1　See para 832 et seq post.
2　For the meaning of 'balance sheet' see para 826 ante.
3　See paras 832, 833 post. A statement of the amount of debentures outstanding made in a balance sheet is a sufficient acknowledgment of the debt due under the debentures within the meaning of the Limitation Act 1980 s 30(2): *Re Atlantic and Pacific Fibre Importing and Manufacturing Co Ltd* [1928] Ch 836; and see *Jones v Bellegrove Properties Ltd* [1949] 1 All ER 498; affd [1949] 2 KB 700, [1949] 2 All ER 198, CA (where parol evidence was admitted to dissect a debit entry 'sundry creditors' so as to constitute that entry a sufficient acknowledgment to a member-creditor). See also *Re Gee & Co (Woolwich) Ltd* [1975] Ch 52, [1974] 1 All ER 1149 (where the accounts were adopted at a general meeting attended by or by the representatives of every member of the company, so that there was no breach of fiduciary duty by the creditor directors who signed the same). No such acknowledgment is, however, made unless the debt appears in the balance sheet as a debt existing at the time it was signed: *Consolidated Agencies Ltd v Bertram Ltd* [1965] AC 470, [1964] 3 All ER 282, PC. A statement made in a balance sheet signed by the directors relating to arrears of their own remuneration is not a sufficient acknowledgment to prevent the operation of the Limitation Act 1980: *Re Coliseum (Barrow) Ltd* [1930] 2 Ch 44; and cf *John Shaw and Sons (Salford) Ltd v Shaw* [1935] 2 KB 113, CA (debt owing by directors); *Re Transplanters (Holding Co) Ltd* [1958] 2 All ER 711, [1958] 1 WLR 822; *McMenigall v Central Refrigeration Services Ltd* [1963] SLT (Notes) 8. See further LIMITATION OF ACTIONS vol 28 paras 878, 880 et seq.
4　For the meaning of 'profit and loss account' see para 826 ante.
5　See paras 834-837 post.
6　Companies Act 1985 s 226(3), Sch 4 para 1(1). Schedule 4 para 1(1) is not to be read as requiring the heading or sub-heading for any item to be distinguished by any letter or number assigned to that item in the format adopted: Sch 4 para 1(2).
7　For the meaning of 'financial year' see para 806 ante.
8　Companies Act 1985 Sch 4 para 2(1).
9　Ibid Sch 4 para 2(2). As to notes to the accounts see para 838 et seq post.
10　Ie by ibid Sch 4 para 1: see supra.
11　Ibid Sch 4 para 3(1).
12　Ibid Sch 4 para 3(2).
13　Ibid Sch 4 para 3(3).

14 Ibid Sch 4 para 3(4).
15 Ibid Sch 4 para 3(5). Schedule 4 para 3(5) does not apply in any case where an amount can be shown for the item in question in respect of the financial year immediately preceding that to which the balance sheet or profit and loss account relates, and that amount must be shown under the heading or sub-heading required by Sch 4 para 1 for that item: Sch 4 para 4(3).
16 Ibid Sch 4 para 3(6).
17 Ibid Sch 4 para 3(7) (amended by the Companies Act 1985 (Miscellaneous Accounting Amendments) Regulations 1996, SI 1996/189, reg 14(1), Sch 1 paras 1, 2).
18 Companies Act 1985 Sch 4 para 4(1).
19 Ibid Sch 4 para 4(2).
20 Ibid Sch 4 para 5.

B. FORMATS FOR BALANCE SHEET

832. Balance sheet formats; Format 1. The items to be listed in a balance sheet prepared in accordance with Format 1[1] are as follows[2]:

A Called up share capital not paid[3]

B Fixed assets[4]

   I Intangible assets
     1 Development costs
     2 Concessions, patents, licences, trade marks and similar rights and assets[5]
     3 Goodwill[6]
     4 Payments on account

   II Tangible assets
     1 Land and buildings
     2 Plant and machinery
     3 Fixtures, fittings, tools and equipment
     4 Payments on account and assets in course of construction

   III Investments
     1 Shares in group undertakings[7]
     2 Loans to group undertakings
     3 Participating interests[8]
     4 Loans to undertakings in which the company has a participating interest
     5 Other investments other than loans
     6 Other loans
     7 Own shares[9]

C Current assets

   I Stocks
     1 Raw materials and consumables
     2 Work in progress
     3 Finished goods and goods for resale
     4 Payments on account

   II Debtors[10]
     1 Trade debtors
     2 Amounts owed by group undertakings
     3 Amounts owed by undertakings in which the company has a participating interest

4 Other debtors
5 Called up share capital not paid[11]
6 Prepayments and accrued income[12]

III Investments
1 Shares in group undertakings
2 Own shares[13]
3 Other investments

IV Cash at bank and in hand

D Prepayments and accrued income[14]

E Creditors: amounts falling due within one year

1 Debenture loans[15]
2 Bank loans and overdrafts
3 Payments received on account[16]
4 Trade creditors
5 Bills of exchange payable
6 Amounts owed to group undertakings
7 Amounts owed to undertakings in which the company has a participating interest
8 Other creditors including taxation and social security[17]
9 Accruals and deferred income[18]

F Net current assets (liabilities)[19]

G Total assets less current liabilities

H Creditors: amounts falling due after more than one year

1 Debenture loans[20]
2 Bank loans and overdrafts
3 Payments received on account[21]
4 Trade creditors
5 Bills of exchange payable
6 Amounts owed to group undertakings
7 Amounts owed to undertakings in which the company has a participating interest
8 Other creditors including taxation and social security[22]
9 Accruals and deferred income[23]

I Provisions for liabilities and charges[24]

1 Pensions and similar obligations
2 Taxation, including deferred taxation
3 Other provisions

J Accruals and deferred income[25]

K Capital and reserves

I Called up share capital[26]
II Share premium account
III Revaluation reserve
IV Other reserves

1 Capital redemption reserve
2 Reserve for own shares
3 Reserves provided for by the articles of association
4 Other reserves

V Profit and loss account

1 As to the statutory formats see para 831 ante.
2 Companies Act 1985 s 226(3), Sch 4 Pt I Section B (amended by the Companies Act 1989 s 4(2), Sch 1 paras 1-4). References to the items listed in any of the formats are to those items read together with any of the notes following the formats which apply to any of those items, and the requirement imposed by the Companies Act 1985 Sch 4 para 1 to show the items listed in any such format in the order adopted in the format is subject to any provisions in those notes for alternative positions for any particular items: Sch 4 para 6. A number in brackets following any item in any of the statutory formats is a reference to the note of that number in the notes following the formats: Sch 4 para 7. In the notes following the formats (1) the heading of each note gives the required heading or sub-heading for the item to which it applies and a reference to any letters and numbers assigned to that item in the statutory formats (taking a reference in the case of Format 2 of the balance sheet formats to the item listed under 'Assets' or under 'Liabilities' as the case may require); and (2) references to a numbered format are to the balance sheet format or, as the case may require, to the profit and loss account format of that number: Sch 4 para 8.
3 For the meaning of 'called-up share capital' see para 174 ante. This item may be shown in either of the two positions given in Formats 1 and 2: ibid Sch 4 Balance Sheet Formats note (1).
4 For the meaning of 'fixed assets' see para 810 note 6 ante.
5 Amounts in respect of assets must only be included in a company's balance sheet under this item if either (1) the assets were acquired for valuable consideration and are not required to be shown under goodwill; or (2) the assets in question were created by the company itself: Companies Act 1985 Sch 4 Balance Sheet Formats note (2).
6 Amounts representing goodwill must only be included to the extent that the goodwill was acquired for valuable consideration: ibid Sch 4 Balance Sheet Formats note (3).
7 For the meaning of 'group undertaking' see para 829 note 9 ante.
8 For the meaning of 'participating interest' see para 830 ante.
9 The nominal value of the shares held must be shown separately: Companies Act 1985 Sch 4 Balance Sheet Formats note (4).
10 The amount falling due after more than one year must be shown separately for each item included under debtors: ibid Sch 4 Balance Sheet Formats note (5).
11 See note 3 supra.
12 This item may be shown in either of the two positions given in Formats 1 and 2 (as amended): Companies Act 1985 Sch 4 Balance Sheet Formats note (6).
13 See note 9 supra.
14 See note 12 supra.
15 The amount of any convertible loans must be shown separately: Companies Act 1985 Sch 4 Balance Sheet Formats note (7). A loan is treated as falling due for repayment, and an instalment of a loan is treated as falling due for payment, on the earliest date on which the lender could require repayment or (as the case may be) payment, if he exercised all options and rights available to him: Sch 4 paras 76, 85.
16 Payments received on account of orders must be shown for each of items E.3 and H.3 in Format 1 and item C.3 in Format 2 in so far as they are not shown as deductions from stocks: ibid Sch 4 Balance Sheet Formats note (8).
17 The amount for creditors in respect of taxation and social security must be shown separately from the amount for other creditors: ibid Sch 4 Balance Sheet Formats note (9).
18 The two positions given for this item in Format 1 at E.9 and H.9 are an alternative to the position at J, but, if the item is not shown in a position corresponding to that at J, it may be shown in either or both of the other two positions (as the case may require). The two positions given for this item in Format 2 (see para 816 post) are alternatives: ibid Sch 4 Balance Sheet Formats note (10).
19 In determining the amount to be shown for this item any amounts shown under 'prepayments and accrued income' must be taken into account wherever shown: ibid Sch 4 Balance Sheet Formats note (11).
20 See note 15 supra.
21 See note 16 supra.
22 See note 17 supra.
23 See note 18 supra.

24 References to provisions for liabilities or charges are to any amount retained as reasonably necessary for the purpose of providing for any liability or loss which is either likely to be incurred, or certain to be incurred, but uncertain as to amount or as to the date on which it will arise: Companies Act 1985 Sch 4 paras 76, 89.

25 See note 18 supra.

26 The amount of allotted share capital and the amount of called-up share capital which has been paid up must be shown separately: Companies Act 1985 Sch 4 Balance Sheet Formats note (12).

833. Balance sheet formats; Format 2. The items to be listed in a balance sheet prepared in accordance with Format 2[1] are as follows[2]:

ASSETS

A Called up share capital not paid[3]

B Fixed assets[4]

  I Intangible assets
    1 Development costs
    2 Concessions, patents, licences, trade marks and similar rights and assets[5]
    3 Goodwill[6]
    4 Payments on account

  II Tangible assets
    1 Land and buildings
    2 Plant and machinery
    3 Fixtures, fittings, tools and equipment
    4 Payments on account and assets in course of construction

  III Investments
    1 Shares in group undertakings[7]
    2 Loans to group undertakings
    3 Participating interests[8]
    4 Loans to undertakings in which the company has a participating interest
    5 Other investments other than loans
    6 Other loans
    7 Own shares[9]

C Current assets

  I Stocks
    1 Raw materials and consumables
    2 Work in progress
    3 Finished goods and goods for resale
    4 Payments on account

  II Debtors[10]
    1 Trade debtors
    2 Amounts owed by group undertakings
    3 Amounts owed by undertakings in which the company has a participating interest
    4 Other debtors
    5 Called up share capital not paid[11]
    6 Prepayments and accrued income[12]

III Investments
    1 Shares in group undertakings
    2 Own shares[13]
    3 Other investments

IV Cash at bank and in hand

D Prepayments and accrued income[14]

LIABILITIES

A Capital and reserves

  I Called up share capital[15]

  II Share premium account

  III Revaluation reserve

  IV Other reserves
    1 Capital redemption reserve
    2 Reserve for own shares
    3 Reserves provided for by the articles of association
    4 Other reserves

  V Profit and loss account

B Provisions for liabilities and charges[16]

    1 Pensions and similar obligations
    2 Taxation including deferred taxation
    3 Other provisions

C Creditors[17]

    1 Debenture loans[18]
    2 Bank loans and overdrafts
    3 Payments received on account[19]
    4 Trade creditors
    5 Bills of exchange payable
    6 Amounts owed to group undertakings
    7 Amounts owed to undertakings in which the company has a participating interest
    8 Other creditors including taxation and social security[20]
    9 Accruals and deferred income[21]

D Accruals and deferred income[21]

1 As to the statutory formats see para 831 ante.
2 Companies Act 1985 s 226(3), Sch 4 Pt I Section B (amended by the Companies Act 1989 s 4(2), Sch 1 paras 1–4). See also para 832 note 2 ante.
3 See para 832 note 3 ante.
4 For the meaning of 'fixed assets' see para 810 note 6 ante.
5 See para 832 note 5 ante.
6 See para 832 note 6 ante.
7 For the meaning of 'group undertaking' see para 829 note 9 ante.
8 For the meaning of 'participating interest' see para 830 ante.
9 See para 832 note 9 ante.
10 See para 832 note 10 ante.
11 See note 3 supra.
12 See para 832 note 12 ante.

13 See note 9 supra.
14 See note 12 supra.
15 See para 832 note 26 ante.
16 See para 832 note 24 ante.
17 Amounts falling due within one year and after one year must be shown separately for each of these items and for the aggregate of all these items: Companies Act 1985 Sch 4 Balance Sheet Formats note (13) (amended by the Companies Act 1985 (Miscellaneous Accounting Amendments) Regulations 1996, SI 1996/189, reg 14(1), Sch 1 paras 1, 3).
18 See para 832 note 15 ante.
19 See para 832 note 16 ante.
20 See para 832 note 17 ante.
21 See para 832 note 18 ante.

C. FORMATS FOR PROFIT AND LOSS ACCOUNT

834. Profit and loss account formats; Format 1. The items to be included in a profit and loss account prepared in accordance with Format 1[1] are as follows[2]:

1 Turnover[3]
2 Cost of sales[4]
3 Gross profit or loss
4 Distribution costs[4]
5 Administrative expenses[4]
6 Other operating income
7 Income from shares in group undertakings[5]
8 Income from participating interests[6]
9 Income from other fixed asset investments[7]
10 Other interest receivable and similar income[7]
11 Amounts written off investments
12 Interest payable and similar charges[8]
13 Tax on profit or loss on ordinary activities
14 Profit or loss on ordinary activities after taxation
15 Extraordinary income
16 Extraordinary charges
17 Extraordinary profit or loss
18 Tax on extraordinary profit or loss
19 Other taxes not shown under the above items
20 Profit or loss for the financial year[9]

1 As to the statutory formats see para 831 ante.
2 Companies Act 1985 s 226(3), Sch 4 Pt I Section B (amended by the Companies Act 1989 s 4(2), Sch 1 paras 1–4). See also para 832 note 2 ante.
3 For these purposes, 'turnover', in relation to a company, means the amounts derived from the provision of goods and services falling within the company's ordinary activities, after deduction of trade discounts, VAT and any other taxes based on the amounts so derived: Companies Act 1985 s 262(1) (substituted by the Companies Act 1989 s 22).
4 These items must be stated after taking into account any necessary provisions for depreciation or diminution in value of assets: Companies Act 1985 Sch 4 Profit and Loss Account Formats note (14). The amount of any provisions for depreciation or diminution in value of tangible and intangible fixed assets falling to be shown under items 7(a) and A.4(a) respectively in Formats 2 and 4 (see paras 835, 837 post) must be disclosed in a note to the accounts in any case where the profit and loss account is prepared by reference to Format 1 or Format 3: Sch 4 Profit and Loss Account Formats note (17). As to such provisions see para 810 note 4 ante; and as to notes to the accounts see para 838 et seq post.

5 For the meaning of 'group undertaking' see para 829 note 9 ante.
6 For the meaning of 'participating interest' see para 830 ante.
7 Income and interest derived from group undertakings must be shown separately from income and interest derived from other sources: Companies Act 1985 Sch 4 Profit and Loss Account Formats note (15) (amended by the Companies Act 1989 s 4(2), Sch 1 paras 1-4).
8 The amount payable to group undertakings must be shown separately: Companies Act 1985 Sch 4 Profit and Loss Account Formats note (16) (amended by the Companies Act 1989 Sch 1 paras 1-4).
9 For the meaning of 'financial year' see para 806 ante.

835. Profit and loss account formats; Format 2. The items to be included in a profit and loss account prepared in accordance with Format 2[1] are as follows[2]:

1 Turnover[3]
2 Change in stocks of finished goods and in work in progress
3 Own work capitalised[4]
4 Other operating income
5 (a) Raw materials and consumables
   (b) Other external charges
6 Staff costs[5]:
   (a) Wages and salaries
   (b) Social security costs
   (c) Other pension costs
7 (a) Depreciation[6] and other amounts written off tangible and intangible fixed assets
   (b) Exceptional amounts written off current assets
8 Other operating charges
9 Income from shares in group undertakings[7]
10 Income from participating interests[8]
11 Income from other fixed asset investments[9]
12 Other interest receivable and similar income[9]
13 Amounts written off investments
14 Interest payable and similar charges[10]
15 Tax on profit or loss on ordinary activities
16 Profit or loss on ordinary activities after taxation
17 Extraordinary income
18 Extraordinary charges
19 Extraordinary profit or loss
20 Tax on extraordinary profit or loss
21 Other taxes not shown under the above items
22 Profit or loss for the financial year

1 As to the statutory formats see para 831 ante.
2 Companies Act 1985 s 226(3), Sch 4 Pt I Section B (amended by the Companies Act 1989 s 4(2), Sch 1 paras 1-4). See also para 832 note 2 ante.
3 For the meaning of 'turnover' see para 834 note 3 ante.
4 For the meaning of 'capitalisation' see para 811 note 6 ante.
5 For these purposes, 'social security costs' means any contributions by the company to any state social security or pension scheme, fund or arrangement: Companies Act 1985 Sch 4 paras 76, 94(1). 'Pension costs' includes any costs incurred by the company in respect of any pension scheme established for the purpose of providing pensions for persons currently or formerly employed by the company, any sums set aside for the future payment of pensions directly by the company to current or former employees and any pensions paid directly to such persons without having first been set aside: Sch 4 paras 76, 94(2) (substituted by the Companies Act 1985 (Miscellaneous Accounting Amendments) Regulations 1996,

SI 1996/189, reg 14(1), Sch 1 paras 1, 16(1), (2)). Any amount stated in respect of the item 'social security costs' or in respect of the item 'wages and salaries' in the company's profit and loss account is to be determined by reference to payments made or costs incurred in respect of all persons employed by the company during the financial year who are taken into account in determining the relevant annual number for the purposes of information supplementing the profit and loss account: Companies Act 1985 Sch 4 paras 76, 94(3) (amended by the Companies Act 1985 (Miscellaneous Accounting Amendments) Regulations 1996 Sch 1 paras 1, 16(1), (3)). As to such supplementary information see para 851 post. For the meaning of 'financial year' see para 806 ante.

6 As to provisions for depreciation see para 810 note 5 ante. For the meaning of 'fixed assets' and 'current assets' see para 810 note 6 ante.

7 For the meaning of 'group undertaking' see para 829 note 9 ante.

8 For the meaning of 'participating interest' see para 830 ante.

9 See para 834 note 7 ante.

10 See para 834 note 8 ante.

836. Profit and loss account formats; Format 3. The items to be included in a profit and loss account prepared in accordance with Format 3[1] are as follows[2]:

A Charges

    1 Cost of sales[3]

    2 Distribution costs[3]

    3 Administrative expenses[3]

    4 Amounts written off investments

    5 Interest payable and similar charges[4]

    6 Tax on profit or loss on ordinary activities

    7 Profit or loss on ordinary activities after taxation

    8 Extraordinary charges

    9 Tax on extraordinary profit or loss

   10 Other taxes not shown under the above items

   11 Profit or loss for the financial year[5]

B Income

    1 Turnover[6]

    2 Other operating income

    3 Income from shares in group undertakings[7]

    4 Income from participating interests[8]

    5 Income from other fixed asset investments[9]

    6 Other interest receivable and similar income[9]

    7 Profit or loss on ordinary activities after taxation

    8 Extraordinary income

    9 Profit or loss for the financial year

1 As to the statutory formats see para 831 ante.

2 Companies Act 1985 s 226(3), Sch 4 Pt I Section B (amended by the Companies Act 1989 s 4(2), Sch 1 paras 1-4). See also para 832 note 2 ante.

3 See para 834 note 4 ante.

4 See para 834 note 8 ante.

5 For the meaning of 'financial year' see para 806 ante.

6 For the meaning of 'turnover' see para 834 note 3 ante.

7 For the meaning of 'group undertaking' see para 829 note 9 ante.

8 For the meaning of 'participating interest' see para 830 ante.

9 See para 834 note 7 ante.

837. Profit and loss account formats; Format 4. The items to be included in a profit and loss account prepared in accordance with Format 4[1] are as follows[2]:

A Charges
    1 Reduction in stocks of finished goods and in work in progress
    2 (a) Raw materials and consumables
       (b) Other external charges
    3 Staff costs[3]:
       (a) Wages and salaries
       (b) Social security costs
       (c) Other pension costs
    4 (a) Depreciation[4] and other amounts written off tangible and intangible fixed assets
       (b) Exceptional amounts written off current assets
    5 Other operating charges
    6 Amounts written off investments
    7 Interest payable and similar charges[5]
    8 Tax on profit or loss on ordinary activities
    9 Profit or loss on ordinary activities after taxation
    10 Extraordinary charges
    11 Tax on extraordinary profit or loss
    12 Other taxes not shown under the above items
    13 Profit or loss for the financial year[6]

B Income
    1 Turnover[7]
    2 Increase in stocks of finished goods and in work in progress
    3 Own work capitalised[8]
    4 Other operating income
    5 Income from shares in group undertakings[9]
    6 Income from participating interests[10]
    7 Income from other fixed asset investments[11]
    8 Other interest receivable and similar income[11]
    9 Profit or loss on ordinary activities after taxation
    10 Extraordinary income
    11 Profit or loss for the financial year

1 As to the statutory formats see para 831 ante.
2 Companies Act 1985 s 226(3), Sch 4 Pt I Section B (amended by the Companies Act 1989 s 4(2), Sch 1 paras 1-4). See also para 832 note 2 ante.
3 As to staff costs see para 835 note 5 ante.
4 As to provisions for depreciation see para 810 note 4 ante. For the meaning of 'fixed assets' and 'current assets' see para 810 note 6 ante.
5 See para 834 note 8 ante.
6 For the meaning of 'financial year' see para 806 ante.
7 For the meaning of 'turnover' see para 834 note 3 ante.
8 For the meaning of 'capitalisation' see para 811 note 6 ante.
9 For the meaning of 'group undertaking' see para 829 note 9 ante.
10 For the meaning of 'participating interest' see para 830 ante.
11 See para 834 note 7 ante.

D. NOTES TO THE ACCOUNTS

(A) *In general*

838. Notes to the accounts. Any information required[1] in the case of any company must, if not given in the company's accounts, be given by way of a note to those accounts[2]. Information required[3] to be given in notes to a company's annual accounts[4] may be contained in the accounts or in a separate document annexed to the accounts[5].

The information which may be given in either the accounts or notes to the accounts relates to:

(1) the disclosure of accounting policies[6];

(2) information supplementing the balance sheet[7];

(3) information supplementing the profit and loss account[8].

Special provisions apply where a company is a parent company or subsidiary undertaking[9] and where a company is an investment company[10].

The information which must be disclosed in notes to the accounts comprises:

(a) particulars of related undertakings[11];

(b) chairman's and directors' emoluments, pensions and compensation for loss of office[12];

(c) loans, quasi-loans and other dealings in favour of directors[13]; and

(d) other transactions, arrangements and agreements[14].

1 Ie by the Companies Act 1985 s 226(3), Sch 4 paras 36-58 (as amended): see para 839 et seq post.
2 Ibid Sch 4 para 35.
3 Ie by ibid Pt VII (ss 221-262A) (as amended): see para 801 et seq ante and para 839 et seq post.
4 For the meaning of 'annual accounts' see para 817 note 2 ante.
5 Companies Act 1985 s 261(1) (substituted by the Companies Act 1989 s 22).
6 See the Companies Act 1985 Sch 4 paras 36, 36A (as added) and para 839 post.
7 See ibid Sch 4 paras 37-51 (as amended) and paras 841-847 post.
8 See ibid Sch 4 paras 52-58 (as amended) and paras 848-852 post.
9 See ibid Sch 4 Pt IV (para 59A) (as substituted) and para 887 post. For the meaning of 'parent company' and 'subsidiary undertaking' see para 828 ante.
10 See ibid Sch 4 Pt V (paras 71-73) and para 936 post.
11 See ibid s 231(1), Sch 5 (as substituted and amended) and para 853 et seq post.
12 See ibid s 232(1), (2), Sch 6 Pt I (paras 1-14) (as substituted) and para 865 et seq post.
13 See ibid Sch 6 Pt II (paras 15-27) (as renumbered and amended): see para 871 et seq post.
14 See ibid Sch 6 Pt III (paras 28-30) (as renumbered and amended): see para 874 post.

839. Information supplementary to the accounts; in general. Any information required in the case of any company by the following statutory provisions[1] must, if not given in the company's accounts, be given by way of a note to those accounts[2]. Such information either (as the case may be) supplements the information given with respect to any particular items shown in the balance sheet[3] or is otherwise relevant to assessing the company's state of affairs in the light of the information so given[4]; or supplements the information given with respect to any particular items shown in the profit and loss account[5], or otherwise provides particulars of income or expenditure of the company or of circumstances affecting the items shown in the profit and loss account[6].

The accounting policies[7] adopted by the company in determining the amounts to be included in respect of items shown in the balance sheet and in determining the profit or loss of the company must be stated (including such policies with respect to the depreciation and diminution in value of assets)[8].

It must be stated whether the accounts have been prepared in accordance with applicable accounting standards[9] and particulars of any material departure from those standards and the reason for it must be given[10].

1 Ie those contained in the Companies Act 1985 s 226(3), Sch 4 Pt III (paras 35–58) (as amended): see infra and para 840 et seq post.
2 Ibid s 226(3), Sch 4 para 35.
3 For the meaning of 'balance sheet' see para 826 ante.
4 Companies Act 1985 Sch 4 para 37.
5 For the meaning of 'profit and loss account' see para 826 ante.
6 Companies Act 1985 Sch 4 para 52.
7 As to possible accounting policies see ibid Sch 4 Pt II Section A: Accounting Principles (as amended) (see paras 809–815 ante); Section B: Historical Cost Accounting Rules (see para 810 ante) and Section C: Alternative Accounting Rules (as amended) (see para 813 ante).
8 Ibid Sch 4 para 36.
9 For the meaning of 'accounting standards' see para 803 ante.
10 Companies Act 1985 Sch 4 para 36A (added by the Companies Act 1989 s 4(2), Sch 1 paras 1, 7).

(B) *Information supplementing both Balance Sheet and Profit and Loss Account*

840. In general. Where sums originally denominated in foreign currencies have been brought into account under any items shown in the balance sheet[1] or profit and loss account[2], the basis on which those sums have been translated into sterling must be stated[3].

Subject to certain exceptions[4], in respect of every item stated in a note to the accounts[5], the corresponding amount for the financial year[6] immediately preceding that to which the accounts relate must also be stated, and, where the corresponding amount is not comparable, it must be adjusted and particulars of the adjustment and the reasons for it must be given[7].

1 For the meaning of 'balance sheet' see para 826 ante.
2 For the meaning of 'profit and loss account' see para 826 ante.
3 Companies Act 1985 s 226(3), Sch 4 para 58(1).
4 The exceptions are any amounts stated by virtue of any of the following provisions of the Companies Act 1985: (1) s 227(4), Sch 4A para 13 (as added and amended) (see para 882 post);(2) s 231, Sch 5 paras 2, 8(3), 16, 21(1)(d), 22(4), (5), 24(3), (4), 27(3), (4) (as substituted) (see paras 855, 860, 890, 893, 894, 895 post); (3) s 232, Sch 6 Pt II (paras 15–27 (as renumbered and amended): see para 871 et seq post), Sch 6 Pt III (paras 28–30 (as renumbered and amended): see para 874 post); and (4) s 226(3), Sch 4 paras 42, 46 (see paras 842, 844 post): Sch 4 para 58(3) (amended by the Companies Act 1989 s 4(2), Sch 1 paras 1, 10).
5 See para 838 ante.
6 For the meaning of 'financial year' see para 806 ante.
7 Companies Act 1985 Sch 4 para 58(2).

(C) *Information supplementing the Balance Sheet*

841. Share capital and debentures. With respect to the company's share capital, particulars of the authorised share capital, and, where shares of more than one class have been allotted, the number and aggregate nominal value of shares of each class allotted must be given[1]. In the case of any part of the allotted share capital that consists of redeemable shares[2], particulars of the earliest and latest dates on which the company has power to redeem those shares, whether those shares must be redeemed in any event or are liable to be redeemed at the option of the company or of the shareholder and whether any (and, if so, what) premium is payable on redemption, must be given[3].

If the company has allotted any shares during the financial year[4], particulars of the classes of shares allotted and, as respects each class of shares, the number allotted, their aggregate nominal value and the consideration received by the company for the allotment must be given[5].

With respect to any contingent right to the allotment of shares[6] in the company, particulars of the number, description and amount of the shares in relation to which the right is exercisable, the period during which it is exercisable and the price to be paid for the shares allotted must be given[7].

If the company has issued any debentures during the financial year to which the accounts relate, particulars of the classes of debentures issued and, as respects each class of debentures, the amount issued and the consideration received by the company for the issue must be given[8]. Where any of the company's debentures are held by a nominee of or trustee for the company, the nominal amount of the debentures and the amount at which they are stated in the accounting records kept by the company[9] must be stated[10].

1 Companies Act 1985 s 226(3), Sch 4 para 38(1).
2 As to redeemable shares see para 219 et seq ante.
3 Companies Act 1985 Sch 4 para 38(2).
4 For the meaning of 'financial year' see para 806 ante.
5 Companies Act 1985 Sch 4 para 39 (amended by the Companies Act 1985 (Miscellaneous Accounting Amendments) Regulations 1996, SI 1996/189, reg 14(1), Sch 1 paras 1, 5).
6 For these purposes, 'contingent right to the allotment of shares' means any option to subscribe for shares and any other right to require the allotment of shares to any person whether arising on the conversion into shares of securities of any other description or otherwise: Companies Act 1985 Sch 4 para 40(2).
7 Ibid Sch 4 para 40(1).
8 Ibid Sch 4 para 41(1) (amended by the Companies Act 1985 (Miscellaneous Accounting Amendments) Regulations 1996 Sch 1 paras 1, 6).
9 Ie in pursuance of the Companies Act 1985 s 221 (as substituted): see para 801 ante.
10 Ibid Sch 4 para 41(3).

842. Fixed assets. In respect of each item which is, or would but for its inclusion combined with other assets[1] be, shown under the general item 'fixed assets'[2] in the company's balance sheet[3] the following information must be given:

(1) the appropriate amounts[4] in respect of that item as at the date of the beginning of the financial year[5] and as at the balance sheet date[6] respectively;

(2) the effect on any amount shown in the balance sheet in respect of that item of any revision of the amount in respect of any assets included under that item made during that year on any basis mentioned in the alternative accounting rules[7], acquisitions during that year of any assets, disposals during that year of any assets and any transfers of assets of the company to and from that item during that year[8].

In respect of each such item the cumulative amount of provisions for depreciation or diminution[9] in value of assets included under that item as at the date of the beginning of the financial year and as at the balance sheet date, the amount of any such provisions made in respect of the financial year, the amount of any adjustments made in respect of any such provisions during that year in consequence of the disposal of any assets and the amount of any other adjustments made in respect of any such provisions during that year must also be stated[10].

Where any fixed assets of the company, other than listed investments[11], are included under any item shown in the company's balance sheet at an amount determined on any basis mentioned in the alternative accounting rules, the following information must be given:

(a) the years, so far as they are known to the directors, in which the assets were severally valued and the several values; and

(b) in the case of assets that have been valued during the financial year, the names of the persons who valued them or particulars of their qualifications for doing so and, whichever is stated, the bases of valuation used by them[12].

In relation to any amount which is or would but for its inclusion combined with other assets be shown in respect of the item 'land and buildings' in the company's balance sheet, there must be stated how much of that amount is ascribable to land of freehold tenure and how much to land of leasehold tenure; and how much of the amount ascribable to land of leasehold tenure is ascribable to land held on long lease[13] and how much to land held on short lease[14].

1   As to the possibility of such combination see the Companies Act 1985 s 226(3), Sch 4 Pt I Section A para 3(4)(b) and para 831 ante.

2   For the meaning of 'fixed assets' see para 810 note 6 ante.

3   For the meaning of 'balance sheet' see para 826 ante.

4   For these purposes, the reference to the appropriate amounts in respect of any item as at any date there mentioned is a reference to amounts representing the aggregate amounts determined, as at that date, in respect of assets falling to be included under that item on either of the following bases, that is to say (1) on the basis of purchase price or production cost, determined in accordance with the Companies Act 1985 Sch 4 paras 26, 27 (see para 812 ante) or on any basis mentioned in Sch 4 Pt II Section C para 31 (see para 813 ante), leaving out of account in either case any provisions for depreciation or diminution in value: Sch 4 para 42(2). For the meaning of 'purchase price' see para 810 note 7 ante.

5   For the meaning of 'financial year' see para 806 ante.

6   For the meaning of 'balance sheet date' see para 809 note 7 ante.

7   Ie the Companies Act 1985 Sch 4 Pt II Section C para 31: see para 813 ante.

8   Ibid Sch 4 para 42(1).

9   For the meaning of references to provisions for depreciation or diminution see para 810 note 4 ante.

10 Companies Act 1985 Sch 4 para 42(3).

11 For these purposes, 'listed investment' means an investment as respects which there has been granted a listing on a recognised investment exchange other than an overseas investment exchange within the meaning of the Financial Services Act 1986, or on any stock exchange of repute outside Great Britain: Companies Act 1985 Sch 4 paras 76, 84 (amended by the Financial Services Act 1986 s 212(2), Sch 16 para 23(b)). For the meaning of 'recognised investment exchange' see para 223 note 1 ante; and for the meaning of 'overseas investment exchange' see para 223 note 1 ante.

12 Companies Act 1985 Sch 4 para 43.

13 For these purposes, 'long lease' means a lease in the case of which the portion of the term for which it was granted remaining unexpired at the end of the financial year is not less than 50 years: ibid Sch 4 paras 76, 83(1). 'Short lease' means a lease which is not a long lease: Sch 4 paras 76, 83(2). 'Lease' includes an agreement for a lease: Sch 4 paras 76, 83(3).

14 Ibid Sch 4 para 44.

843. Investments. In respect of the amount of each item which is, or would but for its inclusion combined with other assets[1] be, shown in the company's balance sheet[2] under the general item 'investments', whether as fixed assets[3] or as current assets[3], there must be stated how much of that amount is ascribable to listed investments[4].

Where the amount of any listed investments is so stated for any item, the following amounts must also be stated:

(1) the aggregate market value of those investments where it differs from the amount so stated; and

(2) both the market value and the stock exchange value of any investments of which the former value is, for the purposes of the accounts, taken as being higher than the latter[5].

1 As to the possibility of such combination see the Companies Act 1985 s 226(3), Sch 4 Pt I Section A para
   3(4)(b) and para 831 ante.
2 For the meaning of 'balance sheet' see para 826 ante.
3 For the meaning of 'fixed assets' and 'current assets' see para 810 note 6 ante.
4 Companies Act 1985 Sch 4 para 45(1) (amended by the Financial Services Act 1986 s 212(2), Sch 16 para
   23(a); the Companies Act 1985 (Miscellaneous Accounting Amendments) Regulations 1996, SI
   1996/189, reg 14(1), Sch 1 paras 1, 7)). For the meaning of 'listed investment' see para 842 note 11 ante.
5 Companies Act 1985 Sch 4 para 45(2).

844. Reserves and provisions. Where any amount is transferred to or from any
reserves, or to any provisions[1] for liabilities and charges, or from any provision for
liabilities and charges otherwise than for the purpose for which the provision was
established, and the reserves or provisions are, or would but for their inclusion
combined with other items[2] be, shown as separate items in the company's balance
sheet[3], the following information must be given in respect of the aggregate of reserves
or provisions included in the same item[4].

That information is:

(1) the amount of the reserves or provisions as at the date of the beginning of the
     financial year[5] and as at the balance sheet date[6] respectively;

(2) any amounts transferred to or from the reserves or provisions during that year;
     and

(3) the source and application respectively of any amounts so transferred[7].

Particulars must be given of each provision included in the item 'other provisions' in
the company's balance sheet in any case where the amount of that provision is
material[8].

The amount of any provision for deferred taxation must be stated separately from
the amount of any provision for other taxation[9].

1 For the meaning of 'provisions' see para 832 note 24 ante.
2 As to the possibility of such combination see the Companies Act 1985 s 226(3), Sch 4 Pt I Section A para
   3(4)(b) and para 831 ante.
3 For the meaning of 'balance sheet' see para 826 ante.
4 Companies Act 1985 Sch 4 para 46(1).
5 For the meaning of 'financial year' see para 806 ante.
6 For the meaning of 'balance sheet date' see para 809 note 7 ante.
7 Companies Act 1985 Sch 4 para 46(2).
8 Ibid Sch 4 para 46(3). Amounts which in the particular context of any provision of Sch 4 (as amended)
   are not material may be disregarded for the purposes of that provision: Sch 4 paras 76, 86.
9 Ibid Sch 4 para 47 (substituted by the Companies Act 1989 s 4(2), Sch 1 paras 1, 8).

845. Details of indebtedness. In respect of each item shown under 'creditors'[1] in
the company's balance sheet[2] there must be stated the aggregate of the following
amounts, that is to say:

(1) the amount of any debts included under that item which are payable or
     repayable otherwise than by instalments and fall due for payment or repayment
     after the end of the period of five years beginning with the day next following
     the end of the financial year[3]; and

(2) the amount of any debts so included which are payable or repayable by
     instalments any of which fall due for payment after the end of that period[4].

In relation to each debt falling so to be taken into account, the terms of payment or
repayment and the rate of any interest payable on the debt must be stated[5]; but, if the
number of debts is such that, in the opinion of the directors, compliance with this

requirement would result in a statement of excessive length, it is sufficient to give a general indication of the terms of payment or repayment and the rates of any interest payable on the debts[6].

In respect of each item shown under 'creditors' in the company's balance sheet there must be stated the aggregate amount of any debts included under that item in respect of which any security has been given by the company and an indication of the nature of the securities so given[7].

If any fixed cumulative dividends on the company's shares are in arrear, there must be stated the amount of the arrears and the period for which the dividends, or, if there is more than one class, each class of them, are in arrear[8].

1   For these purposes, items which would but for their having been combined with other items pursuant to the Companies Act 1985 s 226(3), Sch 4 Pt I Section A para 3(4)(b) (see para 831 ante) have been shown under this heading are included: Sch 4 para 48(5).
2   For the meaning of 'balance sheet' see para 826 ante.
3   For the meaning of 'financial year' see para 806 ante.
4   Companies Act 1985 Sch 4 para 48(1) (substituted by the Companies Act 1985 (Miscellaneous Accounting Amendments) Regulations 1996, SI 1996/189, reg 14(1), Sch 1 paras 1, 8). Where amounts falling due to creditors within one year and after more than one year are distinguished in the balance sheet, the reference in the Companies Act 1985 Sch 4 para 48(1) (as so substituted) is to the latter of those categories: Sch 4 para 48(5)(a).
5   Ibid Sch 4 para 48(2).
6   Ibid Sch 4 para 48(3).
7   Ibid Sch 4 para 48(4). Where amounts falling due to creditors within one year and after more than one year are distinguished in the balance sheet, the reference in Sch 4 para 48(4) is to both categories: Sch 4 para 48(5)(b).
8   Ibid Sch 4 para 49.

846. Guarantees and other financial commitments.   Particulars must be given of any charge on the assets of the company to secure the liabilities of any other person, including, where practicable, the amount secured[1]. The following information must be given with respect to any other contingent liability not provided for:

(1)   the amount or estimated amount of that liability;
(2)   its legal nature; and
(3)   whether any valuable security has been provided by the company in connection with that liability and, if so, what[2].

There must be stated, where practicable, the aggregate amount or estimated amount of contracts for capital expenditure, so far as not provided for[3].

Particulars must be given of any pension commitments included under any provision shown in the company's balance sheet and any such commitments for which no provision has been made; and, where any such commitment relates wholly or partly to pensions payable to past directors of the company, separate particulars must be given of that commitment so far as it relates to such pensions[4].

Particulars must also be given of any other financial commitments which have not been provided for and are relevant to assessing the company's state of affairs[5].

1   Companies Act 1985 s 226(3), Sch 4 para 50(1).
2   Ibid Sch 4 para 50(2).
3   Ibid Sch 4 para 50(3) (amended by the Companies Act 1985 (Miscellaneous Accounting Amendments) Regulations 1996, SI 1996/189, reg 14(1), Sch 1 paras 1, 9).
4   Companies Act 1985 Sch 4 para 50(4).
5   Ibid Sch 4 para 50(5).

847. Miscellaneous matters. Particulars must be given of any case where the purchase price or production cost of any asset is for the first time determined[1] in a case where the price or cost is unknown[2].

Where any outstanding loans made under certain statutory provisions[3] authorising the giving of financial assistance by a company for the purchase of its own shares are included under any item shown in the company's balance sheet, the aggregate amount of those loans must be disclosed for each item in question[4].

1 Ie under the Companies Act 1985 s 226(3), Sch 4 para 28: see para 812 ante.
2 Ibid Sch 4 para 51(1).
3 Ie under ibid s 153(4)(b), (bb) or (c) (as amended) (see para 274 ante) or s 155 (see para 276 ante).
4 Ibid Sch 4 para 51(2) (amended by the Companies Act 1989 s 4(2), Sch 1 paras 1, 9).

(D) *Information supplementing the Profit and Loss Account*

848. Separate statement of certain items of income and expenditure. The amount of the interest on or any similar charges in respect of bank loans and overdrafts and loans of any other kind made to the company must be stated[1].

1 Companies Act 1985 s 226(3), Sch 4 para 53(1), (2) (amended by the Companies Act 1985 (Miscellaneous Accounting Amendments) Regulations 1996, SI 1996/189, reg 14(1), Sch 1 paras 1, 11(1), (2)). The Companies Act 1985 Sch 4 para 53(2) (as so amended) does not apply to interest or charges on loans to the company from group undertakings, but, with that exception, it applies to interest or charges on all loans, whether made on the security of debentures or not: Sch 4 para 53(2) proviso (amended by the Companies Act 1989 s 4(2), Sch 1 paras 1, 2(1)). For the meaning of 'group undertaking' see para 829 note 9 ante.

849. Particulars of tax. Particulars must be given of any special circumstances which affect liability in respect of taxation of profits, income or capital gains for the financial year[1] or liability in respect of taxation of profits, income or capital gains for succeeding financial years[2]. The following amounts must be stated:

(1) the amount of the charge for United Kingdom corporation tax;
(2) if that amount would have been greater but for relief from double taxation, the amount which it would have been but for such relief;
(3) the amount of the charge for United Kingdom income tax; and
(4) the amount of the charge for taxation imposed outside the United Kingdom of profits, income and, so far as charged to revenue, capital gains[3].

These amounts must be stated separately in respect of each of the amounts which is, or would but for their inclusion combined with other items[4] be, shown under the following items in the profit and loss account, that is to say 'tax on profit or loss on ordinary activities' and 'tax on extraordinary profit or loss'[5].

1 For the meaning of 'financial year' see para 806 ante.
2 Companies Act 1985 s 226(3), Sch 4 para 54(2).
3 Ibid Sch 4 para 54(3).
4 As to the possibility of such combination see ibid Sch 4 Pt I Section A para 3(4)(b) and para 831 ante.
5 Ibid Sch 4 para 54(3).

850. Particulars of turnover. If in the course of the financial year[1] the company has carried on business of two or more classes that, in the opinion of the directors, differ substantially from each other, there must be stated in respect of each class (describing it) the amount of the turnover[2] attributable to that class[3]. If in the course of the financial year the company has supplied markets[4] that, in the opinion of the directors, differ substantially from each other, the amount of the turnover attributable to each such market must also be stated[5]. In analysing for the purposes of these provisions the source, in terms of business or in terms of market, of turnover, the directors of the company must have regard to the manner in which the company's activities are organised[6].

For the above purposes, classes of business which, in the opinion of the directors, do not differ substantially from each other must be treated as one class; and markets which, in the opinion of the directors, do not differ substantially from each other must be treated as one market; and any amounts properly attributable to one class of business or, as the case may be, to one market which are not material may be included in the amount stated in respect of another[7].

Where in the opinion of the directors the disclosure of any information so required would be seriously prejudicial to the interests of the company, that information need not be disclosed, but the fact that any such information has not been disclosed must be stated[8].

1 For the meaning of 'financial year' see para 806 ante.
2 For the meaning of 'turnover' see para 834 note 3 ante.
3 Companies Act 1985 s 226(3), Sch 4 para 55(1) (amended by the Companies Act 1985 (Miscellaneous Accounting Amendments) Regulations 1996, SI 1996/189, reg 14(1), Sch 1 paras 1, 13(1), (2)).
4 For these purposes, 'market' means a market delimited by geographical bounds: Companies Act 1985 Sch 4 para 55(2).
5 Ibid Sch 4 para 55(2).
6 Ibid Sch 4 para 55(3) (amended by the Companies Act 1985 (Miscellaneous Accounting Amendments) Regulations 1996 Sch 1 paras 1, 13(1), (3)).
7 Companies Act 1985 Sch 4 para 55(4).
8 Ibid Sch 4 para 55(5).

851. Particulars of staff. The following information must be given with respect to the employees of the company:

(1) the average number of persons employed by the company in the financial year[1]; and

(2) the average number of persons so employed within each category of persons employed by the company[2].

The average number so required is to be determined by dividing the relevant annual number by the number of months in the financial year[3]. The relevant annual number is to be determined by ascertaining for each month in the financial year, for the purposes of head (1) above, the number of persons employed under contracts of service by the company in that month, whether throughout the month or not; for the purposes of head (2) above, the number of persons in the category in question of persons so employed; and, in either case, adding together all the monthly numbers[4].

In respect of all persons employed by the company during the financial year who are taken into account in determining the relevant annual number for the purposes of head (1) above, there must also be stated the aggregate amounts respectively of wages and salaries paid or payable in respect of that year to those persons, social security costs[5] incurred by the company on their behalf and other pension costs[5] so incurred, save in so far as those amounts or any of them are stated in the profit and loss account[6]. The categories of persons employed by the company by reference to which the number required to be disclosed by head (2) above is to be determined may be such as the directors may select, having regard to the manner in which the company's activities are organised[7].

1 For the meaning of 'financial year' see para 806 ante.
2 Companies Act 1985 s 226(3), Sch 4 para 56(1).
3 Ibid Sch 4 para 56(2) (amended by the Companies Act 1985 (Miscellaneous Accounting Amendments) Regulations 1996, SI 1996/189, reg 14(1), Sch 1 paras 1, 14(1), (2)).
4 Companies Act 1985 Sch 4 para 56(3) (amended by the Companies Act 1985 (Miscellaneous Accounting Amendments) Regulations 1996 Sch 1 paras 1, 14(1), (3)).
5 For the meaning of 'social security costs' and 'pension costs' see para 835 note 5 ante.
6 Companies Act 1985 Sch 4 para 56(4). For the meaning of 'profit and loss account' see para 826 ante.
7 Ibid para 56(5).

852. Miscellaneous matters. Where any amount relating to any preceding financial year[1] is included in any item in the profit and loss account[2], the effect must be stated[3]. Particulars must be given of any extraordinary income or charges arising in the financial year[4]. The effect of any transactions that are exceptional by virtue of size or incidence, though they fall within the ordinary activities of the company, must also be stated[5].

1 For the meaning of 'financial year' see para 806 ante.
2 For the meaning of 'profit and loss account' see para 826 ante.
3 Companies Act 1985 s 226(3), Sch 4 para 57(1).
4 Ibid Sch 4 para 57(2).
5 Ibid Sch 4 para 57(3).

(E) *Related Undertakings*

853. Disclosure required in notes to accounts. The prescribed information[1] must be given in notes to a company's annual accounts[2]. The information so required need not be disclosed with respect to an undertaking[3] which is established under the law of a country outside the United Kingdom or carries on business outside the United Kingdom, if, in the opinion of the directors of the company, the disclosure would be seriously prejudicial to the business of that undertaking, or to the business of the company or any of its subsidiary undertakings[4], and the Secretary of State agrees that the information need not be disclosed[5]. Where advantage is taken of that provision, that fact must be stated in a note to the company's annual accounts[6].

If the directors of the company are of the opinion that the number of undertakings in respect of which the company is required to disclose information under any of the statutory provisions[7] is such that compliance with that provision would result in information of excessive length being given, the information need only be given in respect of:

(1) the undertakings whose results or financial position, in the opinion of the directors, principally affected the figures shown in the company's annual accounts; and

(2) undertakings excluded[8] from consolidation[9].

If advantage is taken of that provision:

(a) there must be included in the notes to the company's annual accounts a statement that the information is given only with respect to such undertakings[10]; and

(b) the full information, both that which is disclosed in the notes to the accounts and that which is not, must be annexed to the company's next annual return[11].

If a company fails to comply with head (b) above, the company, and every officer of it who is in default, is liable on summary conviction to a fine not exceeding one-fifth of the statutory maximum and, on conviction after continued contravention, to a daily default fine not exceeding one-fiftieth of the statutory maximum[12].

1 Ie the information specified in the Companies Act 1985 s 231(1), Sch 5 (as substituted and amended): see para 854 et seq post. In the case of an unregistered company (see para 1765 et seq post), Sch 5 (as substituted) has effect as if Sch 5 paras 10, 29 (sic) were omitted: Companies (Unregistered Companies) Regulations 1985, SI 1985/680, reg 6(hh) (added by SI 1990/438). The Companies Act 1985 Sch 5 paras 10, 19 (as substituted) are, however, repealed by the Companies Act 1985 (Miscellaneous Accounting Amendments) Regulations 1996, SI 1996/189, reg 14(3), Sch 3 paras 1, 10, 23.
2 Companies Act 1985 s 231(1) (substituted by the Companies Act 1989 s 6(1)). For the meaning of 'annual accounts' see para 817 note 2 ante. Where the company is not required to prepare group accounts, the information specified in the Companies Act 1985 Sch 5 Pt I (paras 1-13 (as substituted and amended): see para 854 et seq post) must be given: s 231(2) (substituted by the Companies Act 1989 s 6(1)). As to companies required to prepare group accounts see para 888 et seq post.
3 For the meaning of 'undertaking' see para 806 note 5 ante.
4 For the meaning of 'subsidiary undertaking' see para 828 ante.
5 Companies Act 1985 s 231(3) (substituted by the Companies Act 1989 s 6(1)). The Companies Act 1985 s 231(3) (as so substituted) does not apply in relation to the information required under Sch 5 paras 6 or 9A (as respectively substituted and added) (see paras 858, 861 post): s 231(3) (as so substituted; amended by the Partnerships and Unlimited Companies (Accounts) Regulations 1993, SI 1993/1820, reg 11(1); the Companies Act 1985 (Miscellaneous Accounting Amendments) Regulations 1996 reg 15(1)).
6 Companies Act 1985 s 231(4) (substituted by the Companies Act 1989 s 6(1)).
7 Ie any provision of the Companies Act 1985 Sch 5 (as substituted and amended).
8 Ie excluded under ibid s 229(3) or (4) (as substituted): see para 877 post.
9 Ibid s 231(5) (substituted by the Companies Act 1989 s 6(1); amended by the Companies Act 1985 (Miscellaneous Accounting Amendments) Regulations 1996 reg 15(1)).
10 Ie such undertakings as are mentioned in the Companies Act 1985 s 231(5) (as substituted): see supra.
11 Ibid s 231(6) (substituted by the Companies Act 1989 s 6(1)). For these purposes, the 'next annual return' means that delivered to the registrar of companies after the accounts in question have been approved under the Companies Act 1985 s 233 (as substituted) (see para 937 post): s 231(6) (as so substituted).
12 Ibid s 231(7) (substituted by the Companies Act 1989 s 6(1)); Companies Act 1985 s 730, Sch 24 (amended by the Companies Act 1989 s 23, Sch 10 para 24(1), (2)). For the meaning of 'officer who is in default', 'the statutory maximum' and 'daily default fine' see para 1161 post.

854. Subsidiary undertakings. The following information must be given where at the end of the financial year[1] the company has subsidiary undertakings[2].

The name of each subsidiary undertaking must be stated[3].

There must be stated with respect to each subsidiary undertaking:

(1) if it is incorporated outside Great Britain, the country in which it is incorporated;

(2) if it is unincorporated, the address of its principal place of business[4].

The reason why the company is not required to prepare group accounts[5] must be stated[6]. If the reason is that all the subsidiary undertakings of the company fall within the exclusions provided for[7], it must be stated with respect to each subsidiary undertaking which of those exclusions applies[8].

1 For the meaning of 'financial year' see para 806 ante.
2 Companies Act 1985 s 231(1), (2), Sch 5 para 1(1) (substituted by the Companies Act 1989 s 6(2), Sch 3). For the meaning of 'subsidiary undertaking' see para 828 ante.
3 Companies Act 1985 Sch 5 para 1(2) (substituted by the Companies Act 1989 s 6(2), Sch 3).
4 Companies Act 1985 Sch 5 para 1(3) (substituted by the Companies Act 1989 Sch 3; amended by the Companies Act 1985 (Miscellaneous Accounting Amendments) Regulations 1996, SI 1996/189, reg 14(3), Sch 3 paras 1, 2). For the meaning of 'place of business' see para 63 note 1 ante.
5 As to group accounts see para 875 et seq post.
6 Companies Act 1985 Sch 5 para 1(4) (substituted by the Companies Act 1989 Sch 3).
7 Ie in the Companies Act 1985 s 229 (as substituted): see para 877 post.
8 Ibid Sch 5 para 1(5) (substituted by the Companies Act 1989 Sch 3).

855. Holdings in subsidiary undertakings. There must be stated in relation to shares of each class held by the company in a subsidiary undertaking[1] the identity of the class and the proportion of the nominal value of the shares of that class represented by those shares[2].

The shares held by or on behalf of the company itself must be distinguished from those attributed to the company which are held by or on behalf of a subsidiary undertaking[3].

1 For the meaning of 'subsidiary undertaking' see para 828 ante.
2 Companies Act 1985 s 231(1), (2), Sch 5 para 2(1) (substituted by the Companies Act 1989 s 6(2), Sch 3).
3 Companies Act 1985 Sch 5 para 2(2) (substituted by the Companies Act 1989 Sch 3).

856. Financial information about subsidiary undertakings. There must be disclosed with respect to each subsidiary undertaking[1]:

(1) the aggregate amount of its capital and reserves as at the end of its relevant financial year[2]; and

(2) its profit and loss for that year[3].

That information need not be given if the company is exempt[4] from the requirement to prepare group accounts[5] or if the company's investment in the subsidiary undertaking is included in the company's accounts by way of the equity method of valuation[6]. Nor need that information be given if:

(a) the subsidiary undertaking is not required by any provision of the Companies Act 1985 to deliver a copy of its balance sheet for its relevant financial year and does not otherwise publish that balance sheet in Great Britain or elsewhere; and

(b) the company's holding is less than 50% of the nominal value of the shares in the undertaking[7].

Information otherwise required by these provisions need not be given if it is not material[8].

1 For the meaning of 'subsidiary undertaking' see para 828 ante.
2 For these purposes, the 'relevant financial year' of a subsidiary undertaking is (1) if its financial year ends with that of the company, that year; and (2) if not, its financial year ending last before the end of the company's financial year: Companies Act 1985 s 231(1), (2), Sch 5 para 3(5) (substituted by the Companies Act 1989 s 6(2), Sch 3). For the meaning of 'financial year' see para 806 ante.
3 Companies Act 1985 Sch 5 para 3(1) (substituted by the Companies Act 1989 Sch 3).
4 Ie by virtue of the Companies Act 1985 s 228 (as substituted and amended) (parent company included in accounts of larger group): see para 876 post.
5 Ibid Sch 5 para 3(2) (substituted by the Companies Act 1989 Sch 3).
6 Companies Act 1985 Sch 5 para 3(2A) (added by the Companies Act 1985 (Miscellaneous Accounting Amendments) Regulations 1996, SI 1996/189, reg 14(3), Sch 3 paras 1, 3). Under the equity method of valuation an investment is included in the company's accounts at cost, or at a valuation relating to the investment at the date of acquisition, increased (or decreased) by the investing company's interest in the increase (or decrease) in the post-acquisition profits and reserves of the body corporate whose shares comprise the investment.
7 Companies Act 1985 Sch 5 para 3(3) (substituted by the Companies Act 1989 Sch 3).
8 Companies Act 1985 Sch 5 para 3(4) (substituted by the Companies Act 1989 Sch 3).

857. Financial years of subsidiary undertakings. Where disclosure is made[1] with respect to a subsidiary undertaking[2] and that undertaking's financial year[3] does not end with that of the company, there must be stated in relation to that undertaking the date on which its last financial year ended (last before the end of the company's financial year)[4].

1 Ie under the Companies Act 1985 s 231(1), (2), Sch 5 para 3(1): see para 856 ante.
2 For the meaning of 'subsidiary undertaking' see para 828 ante.
3 For the meaning of 'financial year' see para 806 ante.
4 Companies Act 1985 Sch 5 para 4(1) (substituted by the Companies Act 1985 (Miscellaneous Accounting Amendments) Regulations 1996, SI 1996/189, reg 14(3), Sch 3 paras 1, 4)).

858. Shares and debentures of company held by subsidiary undertakings.
The number, description and amount of the shares in the company held by or on behalf of its subsidiary undertakings[1] must be disclosed[2]; but this provision does not apply in relation to shares in the case of which the subsidiary undertaking is concerned as personal representative or, subject as follows, as trustee[3]. The exception for shares in relation to which the subsidiary undertaking is concerned as trustee does not apply if the company, or any subsidiary undertaking of the company, is beneficially interested under the trust, otherwise than by way of security only for the purposes of a transaction entered into by it in the ordinary course of a business which includes the lending of money[4].

1 For the meaning of 'subsidiary undertaking' see para 828 ante.
2 Companies Act 1985 s 231(1), (2), Sch 5 para 6(1) (substituted by the Companies Act 1989 s 6(2), Sch 3; amended by the Companies Act 1985 (Miscellaneous Accounting Amendments) Regulations 1996, SI 1996/189, reg 14(3), Sch 3 paras 1, 6(1), (2)).
3 Companies Act 1985 Sch 5 para 6(2) (substituted by the Companies Act 1989 Sch 3; amended by the Companies Act 1985 (Miscellaneous Accounting Amendments) Regulations 1996 Sch 3 paras 1, 6(1), (3)).
4 Companies Act 1985 Sch 5 para 6(3) (substituted by the Companies Act 1989 Sch 3; amended by the Companies Act 1985 (Miscellaneous Accounting Amendments) Regulations 1996 Sch 3 paras 1, 6(1), (3)). The Companies Act 1985 Sch 2 (as amended) (see para 859 post) has effect for the interpretation of the reference in Sch 5 para 6(3) (as so substituted and amended) to a beneficial interest under a trust: Sch 5 para 6(4) (substituted by the Companies Act 1989 Sch 3).

859. Meaning of 'beneficial interest'. Where shares[1] in an undertaking[2] are held on trust for the purposes of a pension scheme[3] or an employees' share scheme[4], there must be disregarded any residual interest[5] which has not vested in possession[6], being an interest of the undertaking or any of its subsidiary undertakings[7].
Where shares in an undertaking are held on trust, there must be disregarded:
(1) if the trust is for the purposes of a pension scheme, any such rights as are mentioned in heads (a) and (b) below;
(2) if the trust is for the purposes of an employees' share scheme, any such rights as are mentioned in head (a) below[8].
The rights referred to are:
(a) any charge or lien on, or set-off against, any benefit or other right or interest under the scheme for the purpose of enabling the employer[9] or former employer of a member of the scheme to obtain the discharge of a monetary obligation due to him from the member; and
(b) any right to receive from the trustee of the scheme, or as trustee of the scheme to retain, an amount that can be recovered or retained in respect of the deduction of premiums from a refund of pension contributions[10] or otherwise as reimbursement or partial reimbursement for any contributions equivalent premium paid[11] in connection with the scheme[12].

Where an undertaking is a trustee, there must be disregarded any rights which the undertaking has in its capacity as trustee, including, in particular, any right to recover its expenses or to be remunerated out of the trust property and any right to be indemnified out of that property for any liability incurred by reason of any act or omission of the undertaking in the performance of its duties as trustee[13].

1 For these purposes, 'shares', in relation to an undertaking, has the same meaning as in the Companies Act 1985 Pt VII (ss 221-262A (as amended): see para 828 note 8 ante): Sch 2 para 9(1), (2) (added by the Companies Act 1989 s 23, Sch 10 para 18(1), (7)).

2 For these purposes, 'undertaking' has the same meaning as in the Companies Act 1985 Pt VII (ss 221-262A (as amended): see para 806 note 5 ante): Sch 2 para 9(1), (2) (as added: see note 1 supra).

3 For these purposes, 'pension scheme' means any scheme for the provision of benefits consisting of or including relevant benefits for or in respect of employees or former employees; and 'relevant benefits' means any pension, lump sum, gratuity or other like benefit given or to be given on retirement or on death or in anticipation of retirement or, in connection with past service, after retirement or death: ibid Sch 2 para 9(1), (4) (added by the Companies Act 1989 Sch 10 para 18(1), (7)). For these purposes, and for the purposes of the Companies Act 1985 Sch 2 para 7(2) (see infra), 'employee' and 'employer' are to be read as if a director of an undertaking were employed by it: Sch 2 para 9(1), (5) (added by the Companies Act 1989 Sch 10 para 18(1), (7)).

4 For the meaning of 'employee share scheme' see para 120 note 8 ante.

5 For these purposes, 'residual interest' means a right of the undertaking in question (the 'residual beneficiary') to receive any of the trust property in the event of (1) all the liabilities arising under the scheme having been satisfied or provided for; or (2) the residual beneficiary ceasing to participate in the scheme; or (3) the trust property at any time exceeding what is necessary for satisfying the liabilities arising or expected to arise under the scheme: Companies Act 1985 Sch 2 para 6(2) (added by the Companies Act 1989 Sch 10 para 18(1), (7)). References to a right include a right dependent on the exercise of a discretion vested by the scheme in the trustee or any other person; and references to liabilities arising under a scheme include liabilities that have resulted or may result from the exercise of any such discretion: Companies Act 1985 Sch 2 para 6(3) (added by the Companies Act 1989 Sch 10 para 18(1), (7)).

6 For these purposes, a residual interest vests in possession (1) in a case within the Companies Act 1985 Sch 2 para 6(2)(a) (as added) (see note 5 head (1) supra), on the occurrence of the event there mentioned, whether or not the amount of the property receivable pursuant to the right there mentioned is then ascertained; (2) in a case within Sch 2 para 6(2)(b) or (c) (as added) (see note 5 heads (2), (3) supra), when the residual beneficiary becomes entitled to require the trustee to transfer to that beneficiary any of the property receivable pursuant to that right: Sch 2 para 6(4) (added by the Companies Act 1989 Sch 10 para 18(1), (7)).

7 Companies Act 1985 Sch 2 para 6(1) (added by the Companies Act 1989 Sch 10 para 18(1), (7)).

8 Companies Act 1985 Sch 2 para 7(1) (added by the Companies Act 1989 Sch 10 para 18(1), (7)).

9 See note 3 supra.

10 Ie under the Pension Schemes Act 1993 s 61: see SOCIAL SECURITY AND PENSIONS.

11 Ie under ibid Pt III Ch III (ss 50-68): see SOCIAL SECURITY AND PENSIONS.

12 Companies Act 1985 Sch 2 para 7(2) (added by the Companies Act 1989 Sch 10 para 18(1), (7); amended by the Pension Schemes Act 1993 s 190, Sch 8 para 16(b); the Pensions Act 1995 s 151, Sch 5 para 11).

13 Companies Act 1985 Sch 2 para 8 (added by the Companies Act 1989 Sch 10 para 18(1), (7)).

860. Significant holdings in undertakings other than subsidiary undertakings. The following information must be given where at the end of the financial year[1] the company has a significant holding[2] in an undertaking which is not a subsidiary undertaking[3] of the company[4].

The name of the undertaking must be stated[5].

There must be stated:

(1) if the undertaking is incorporated outside Great Britain, the country in which it is incorporated;

(2) if it is unincorporated, the address of its principal place of business[6].

There must also be stated:
(a) the identity of each class of shares in the undertaking held by the company; and
(b) the proportion of the nominal value of the shares of that class represented by those shares[7].

There must also be stated the aggregate amount of the capital and reserves of the undertaking as at the end of its relevant financial year[8] and its profit or loss for that year[9]. That information need not, however, be given if:
(i) the company is exempt[10] from the requirement to prepare group accounts; and
(ii) the investment of the company in all undertakings in which it has such a holding[11] is shown, in aggregate, in the notes to the accounts by way of the equity method of valuation[12].

That information need not be given in respect of an undertaking if:
(A) the undertaking is not required by any provision of the Companies Act 1985 to deliver a copy of its balance sheet for its relevant financial year and does not otherwise publish that balance sheet in Great Britain or elsewhere; and
(B) the company's holding is less than 50% of the nominal value of the shares in the undertaking[13].

Information otherwise required by the above provisions need not be given if it is not material[14].

1 For the meaning of 'financial year' see para 806 ante.
2 For these purposes, a holding is significant if (1) it amounts to 20% or more of the nominal value of any class of shares in the undertaking; or (2) the amount of the holding (as stated or included in the company's accounts) exceeds one-fifth of the amount (as so stated) of the company's assets: Companies Act 1985 s 231(1), (2), Sch 5 para 7(2) (substituted by the Companies Act 1989 s 6(2), Sch 3; amended by the Companies Act 1985 (Miscellaneous Accounting Amendments) Regulations 1996, SI 1996/189, reg 14(3), Sch 3 paras 1, 7). For the meaning of 'undertaking' see para 806 note 5 ante.
3 For the meaning of 'subsidiary undertaking' see para 828 ante.
4 Companies Act 1985 Sch 5 para 7(1) (substituted by the Companies Act 1989 Sch 3).
5 Companies Act 1985 Sch 5 para 8(1) (substituted by the Companies Act 1989 Sch 3).
6 Companies Act 1985 Sch 5 para 8(2) (substituted by the Companies Act 1989 Sch 3; amended by the Companies Act 1985 (Miscellaneous Accounting Amendments) Regulations 1996 Sch 3 paras 1, 8). For the meaning of 'place of business' see para 63 note 1 ante.
7 Companies Act 1985 Sch 5 para 8(3) (substituted by the Companies Act 1989 Sch 3).
8 For these purposes, the 'relevant financial year' of an undertaking is (1) if its financial year ends with that of the company, that year; and (2) if not, its financial year ending last before the end of the company's financial year: Companies Act 1985 Sch 5 para 9(5) (substituted by the Companies Act 1989 Sch 3).
9 Companies Act 1985 Sch 5 para 9(1) (substituted by the Companies Act 1989 Sch 3; amended by the Companies Act 1985 (Miscellaneous Accounting Amendments) Regulations 1996 Sch 3 paras 1, 9).
10 Ie by virtue of the Companies Act 1985 s 228 (as substituted and amended): see para 876 post.
11 Ie such a holding as is mentioned in ibid Sch 5 para 9(1) (as substituted): see supra.
12 Ibid Sch 5 para 9(2) (substituted by the Companies Act 1989 Sch 3). As to the equity method of valuation see para 856 note 6 ante.
13 Companies Act 1985 Sch 5 para 9(3) (substituted by the Companies Act 1989 Sch 3).
14 Companies Act 1985 Sch 5 para 9(4) (substituted by the Companies Act 1989 Sch 3).

861. Membership of certain undertakings. The information required by the following provisions must be given where at the end of the financial year[1] the company is a member[2] of a qualifying undertaking[3].
There must be stated:
(1) the name and legal form of the undertaking; and
(2) the address of the undertaking's registered office (whether in or outside Great Britain) or, if it does not have such an office, its head office (whether in or outside Great Britain)[4].

Information otherwise required by the above provisions[5] need not be given if it is not material[6].

Where the undertaking is a qualifying partnership, there must also be stated either:

(a) that a copy of the latest accounts of the undertaking has been or is to be appended to the copy of the company's accounts sent to the registrar of companies[7]; or

(b) the name of at least one body corporate (which may be the company) in whose group accounts the undertaking has been or is to be dealt with on a consolidated basis[8].

Information otherwise required by head (b) above need not be given if the notes to the company's accounts disclose that advantage has been taken[9] of the statutory exemption[10].

1 For the meaning of 'financial year' see para 806 ante.
2 Any reference to the members of a qualifying partnership is to be construed, in relation to a limited partnership, as a reference to its general partner or partners: Partnerships and Unlimited Companies (Accounts) Regulations 1993, SI 1993/1820, reg 2(2) (applied by the Companies Act 1985 s 231(1), Sch 5 para 9A(6) (added by the Partnerships and Unlimited Companies (Accounts) Regulations 1993 reg 11(2))).
3 Companies Act 1985 Sch 5 para 9A(1) (added by the Partnerships and Unlimited Companies (Accounts) Regulations 1993 reg 11(2)). For these purposes, 'qualifying undertaking' means a qualifying partnership or a qualifying company: Companies Act 1985 Sch 5 para 9A(6) (as added: see note 2 supra). For the meaning of 'qualifying partnership' see para 931 post; and for the meaning of 'qualifying company' see para 117 note 12 ante.
4 Ibid Sch 5 para 9A(2) (added by the Partnerships and Unlimited Companies (Accounts) Regulations 1993 reg 11(2)).
5 Ie by the Companies Act 1985 Sch 5 para 9A(2) (as added): see supra.
6 Ibid Sch 5 para 9A(4) (added by the Partnerships and Unlimited Companies (Accounts) Regulations 1993 reg 11(2)).
7 Ie under the Companies Act 1985 s 242 (as substituted): see para 818 ante.
8 Ibid Sch 5 para 9A(3) (added by the Partnerships and Unlimited Companies (Accounts) Regulations 1993 reg 11(2)). For these purposes, 'dealt with on a consolidated basis' means dealt with by the method of full consolidation, the method of proportional consolidation or the equity method of accounting: Partnerships and Unlimited Companies (Accounts) Regulations 1993 reg 2(2) (applied by the Companies Act 1985 Sch 5 para 9A(6) (as added: see note 2 supra).
9 Ie of the exemption conferred by the Partnerships and Unlimited Companies (Accounts) Regulations 1993 reg 7: see para 934 post.
10 Companies Act 1985 Sch 5 para 9A(5) (added by the Partnerships and Unlimited Companies (Accounts) Regulations 1993 reg 11(2)).

862. Parent undertaking drawing up accounts for larger group. Where the company is a subsidiary undertaking[1], the following information must be given with respect to the parent undertaking[2] of the largest group of undertakings for which group accounts are drawn up and of which the company is a member and the smallest such group of undertakings[3].

The name of the parent undertaking must be stated[4].

There must be stated:

(1) if the undertaking is incorporated outside Great Britain, the country in which it is incorporated;

(2) if it is unincorporated, the address of its principal place of business[5].

If copies of the group accounts are available to the public, there must also be stated the addresses from which copies of the accounts can be obtained[6].

1 For the meaning of 'subsidiary undertaking' see para 828 ante.
2 For the meaning of 'parent undertaking' see para 828 ante.

3 Companies Act 1985 s 231(1), (2), Sch 5 para 11(1) (substituted by the Companies Act 1989 s 6(2), Sch 3).
4 Companies Act 1985 Sch 5 para 11(2) (substituted by the Companies Act 1989 Sch 3).
5 Companies Act 1985 Sch 5 para 11(3) (substituted by the Companies Act 1989 Sch 3; amended by the Companies Act 1985 (Miscellaneous Accounting Amendments) Regulations 1996, SI 1996/189, reg 14(3), Sch 3 paras 1, 11). For the meaning of 'place of business' see para 63 note 1 ante.
6 Companies Act 1985 Sch 5 para 11(4) (substituted by the Companies Act 1989 Sch 3).

863. Identification of ultimate parent company. Where the company[1] is a subsidiary undertaking[2], the following information must be given with respect to the company, if any, regarded by the directors as being the company's ultimate parent company[3].

The name of that company must be stated[4].

If known to the directors, there must be stated, if that company is incorporated outside Great Britain, the country in which it is incorporated[5].

1 For these purposes, 'company' includes any body corporate: Companies Act 1985 s 231(1), (2), Sch 5 para 12(4) (substituted by the Companies Act 1989 s 6(2), Sch 3). For the meaning of 'body corporate' see para 89 note 8 ante.
2 For the meaning of 'subsidiary undertaking' see para 828 ante.
3 Companies Act 1985 Sch 5 para 12(1) (substituted by the Companies Act 1989 Sch 3). For the meaning of 'parent company' see para 828 ante.
4 Companies Act 1985 Sch 5 para 12(2) (substituted by the Companies Act 1989 Sch 3).
5 Companies Act 1985 Sch 5 para 12(3) (substituted by the Companies Act 1989 Sch 3; amended by the Companies Act 1985 (Miscellaneous Accounting Amendments) Regulations 1996, SI 1996/189, reg 14(3), Sch 3 paras 1, 12).

864. References to shares held by company. References to shares held by a company are to be construed as follows[1].

For the purposes of the statutory provisions relating to information about subsidiary undertakings[2]:

(1) there must be attributed to the company any shares held by a subsidiary undertaking[3], or by a person acting on behalf of the company or a subsidiary undertaking; but

(2) there must be treated as not held by the company any shares held on behalf of a person other than the company or a subsidiary undertaking[4].

For the purpose of the statutory provisions relating to information about undertakings other than subsidiary undertakings[5]:

(a) there must be attributed to the company shares held on its behalf by any person; but

(b) there must be treated as not held by a company shares held on behalf of a person other than the company[6].

For the purposes of any of those provisions, shares held by way of security are to be treated as held by the person providing the security:

(i) where apart from the right to exercise them for the purpose of preserving the value of the security, or of realising it, the rights attached to the shares are exercisable only in accordance with his instructions; and

(ii) where the shares are held in connection with the granting of loans as part of normal business activities and apart from the right to exercise them for the purpose of preserving the value of the security, or of realising it, the rights attached to the shares are exercisable only in his interests[7].

1 Companies Act 1985 s 231(1), (2), Sch 5 para 13(1) (substituted by the Companies Act 1989 s 6(2), Sch 3).

2 Ie the Companies Act 1985 Sch 5 paras 2-4 (as substituted): see paras 855-857 ante.
3 For the meaning of 'subsidiary undertaking' see para 828 ante.
4 Companies Act 1985 Sch 5 para 13(2) (substituted by the Companies Act 1989 Sch 3; amended by the Companies Act 1985 (Miscellaneous Accounting Amendments) Regulations 1996, SI 1996/189, reg 14(3), Sch 3 paras 1, 13).
5 Ie the Companies Act 1985 Sch 5 paras 7-9 (as substituted): see paras 858-860 ante.
6 Ibid Sch 5 para 13(3) (substituted by the Companies Act 1989 Sch 3).
7 Companies Act 1985 Sch 5 para 13(4) (substituted by the Companies Act 1989 Sch 3).

(F) *Emoluments and other Benefits of Directors and Others*

865. In general. The information relating to the emoluments and other benefits of directors and others[1] must be given in notes to a company's annual accounts[2]; but this information is required to be given only so far as it is contained in the company's books and papers[3] or the company has the right to obtain it from the person concerned[4].

It is the duty of any director of a company, and any person who is or has at any time in the preceding five years been an officer of the company, to give notice to the company of such matters relating to himself as may be necessary[5].

A person who makes default in complying with the above provisions is guilty of an offence and liable on summary conviction to a fine not exceeding one-fifth of the statutory maximum[6].

1 Ie the Companies Act 1985 s 232, Sch 6 (as amended): see para 866 et seq post. Schedule 6 Pt I (paras 1-14) (as substituted) relates to the emoluments of directors (including emoluments waived), pensions of directors and past directors, compensation for loss of office to directors and past directors and sums paid to third parties in respect of directors' services; Sch 6 Pt II (paras 15-27) (as amended and renumbered) relates to loans, quasi-loans and other dealings in favour of directors and connected persons; and Pt III (paras 28-30) (as renumbered) relates to transactions, arrangements and agreements made by the company or a subsidiary undertaking for officers of the company other than directors: s 232(2) (substituted by the Companies Act 1989 s 6(3)).
2 Companies Act 1985 s 232(1) (substituted by the Companies Act 1989 s 6(3)). For the meaning of 'annual accounts' see para 817 note 2 ante.
3 For these purposes, 'books and papers' and 'books or papers' include accounts, deeds, writings and documents: Companies Act 1985 s 744.
4 Ibid Sch 6 para 14 (substituted by the Companies Act 1989 s 6(4), Sch 4 paras 1-3).
5 Companies Act 1985 s 232(3) (substituted by the Companies Act 1989 s 6(3)).
6 Companies Act 1985 s 232(4) (substituted by the Companies Act 1989 s 6(3)); Companies Act 1985 s 730, Sch 24 (amended by the Companies Act 1989 s 23, Sch 10 para 24(1), (2)). For the meaning of 'the statutory maximum' see para 1161 post.

866. Aggregate amount of directors' emoluments. The aggregate amount[1] of directors' emoluments[2] must be shown[3]. This means the emoluments paid to or receivable by any person in respect of:
  (1) his services as a director of the company; or
  (2) his services while director of the company:
    (a) as director of any of its subsidiary undertakings[4]; or
    (b) otherwise in connection with the management of the affairs of the company or any of its subsidiary undertakings[5].
There must also be shown, separately, the aggregate amount within heads (1) and (2)(a) above and the aggregate amount within head (2)(b) above[6].

1 The following provisions apply with respect to the amounts to be shown under the Companies Act 1985 s 232, Sch 6 para 1 (as substituted) (see infra), Sch 6 para 7 (as substituted) (see para 868 post), Sch 6 para 8 (as substituted) (see para 869 post) and Sch 6 para 9 (as substituted) (see para 870 post): Sch 6 para

10(1) (substituted by the Companies Act 1989 s 6(4), Sch 4 paras 1-3). The amount in each case includes all relevant sums paid by or receivable from (1) the company; and (2) the company's subsidiary undertakings; and (3) any other person, except sums to be accounted for to the company or any of its subsidiary undertakings or, by virtue of the Companies Act 1985 ss 314, 315 (see para 609 ante), to past or present members of the company or any of its subsidiaries or any class of those members: Sch 6 para 10(2) (substituted by the Companies Act 1989 Sch 4 paras 1-3). References to amounts paid to or receivable by a person include amounts paid to or receivable by a person connected with him or a body corporate controlled by him, but not so as to require an amount to be counted twice: Companies Act 1985 Sch 6 para 10(4) (substituted by the Companies Act 1989 Sch 4 paras 1-3). For these purposes, references to a person being 'connected' with a director and to a director 'controlling' a body corporate are to be construed in accordance with the Companies Act 1985 s 346 (see para 607 ante): Sch 6 para 13(1), (4) (substituted by the Companies Act 1989 Sch 4 paras 1-3). For the meaning of 'subsidiary undertaking' see note 4 infra.

The amounts to be shown for any financial year under the Companies Act 1985 Sch 6 paras 1, 7, 8 and 9 (as substituted) are the sums receivable in respect of that year, whenever paid, or, in the case of sums not receivable in respect of a period, the sums paid during that year: Sch 6 para 11(1) (substituted by the Companies Act 1989 Sch 4 paras 1-3). Where, however (a) any sums are not shown in a note to the accounts for the relevant financial year on the ground that the person receiving them is liable to account for them as mentioned in the Companies Act 1985 Sch 6 para 10(2) (as substituted) (see supra), but the liability is thereafter wholly or partly released or is not enforced within a period of two years; or (b) any sums paid by way of expenses allowance are charged to United Kingdom income tax after the end of the relevant financial year, those sums are to be shown, to the extent to which the liability is released or not enforced or they are charged as mentioned supra, as the case may be, in a note to the first accounts in which it is practicable to show them and must be distinguished from the amounts to be shown apart from this provision: Sch 6 para 11(2) (substituted by the Companies Act 1989 Sch 4 paras 1-3).

Where it is necessary to do so for the purpose of making any distinction required by the Companies Act 1985 Sch 6 paras 1-11 (as substituted) in an amount to be shown in compliance with Sch 6 Pt I (paras 1-14) (as substituted), the directors may apportion any payments between the matters in respect of which these have been paid or are receivable in such manner as they think appropriate: Sch 6 para 12 (substituted by the Companies Act 1989 Sch 4 paras 1-3).

2   For these purposes, the 'emoluments' of a person include (1) fees and percentages; (2) sums paid by way of expenses allowance, so far as those sums are chargeable to United Kingdom income tax; (3) contributions paid in respect of him under any pension scheme; and (4) the estimated money value of any other benefits received by him otherwise than in cash; and emoluments in respect of a person's accepting office as director are treated as emoluments in respect of his services as director: Companies Act 1985 Sch 6 para 1(4) (substituted by the Companies Act 1989 Sch 4 paras 1-3). For the meaning of 'pension scheme' see para 868 note 3 post.

3   Companies Act 1985 Sch 6 para 1(1) (substituted by the Companies Act 1989 Sch 4 paras 1-3). See also para 865 ante.

4   For these purposes, a reference to a subsidiary undertaking of the company (1) in relation to a person who is or was, while a director of the company, a director also, by virtue of the company's nomination, direct or indirect, of any other undertaking, includes, subject to head (2) infra, that undertaking, whether or not it is or was in fact a subsidiary undertaking of the company; and (2) for the purposes of the Companies Act 1985 Sch 6 paras 1-7 (as substituted), including any provision of Sch 6 Pt I (paras 1-14) (as substituted) referring to Sch 6 para 1 (as substituted), is to an undertaking which is a subsidiary undertaking at the time the services were rendered, and for the purposes of Sch 6 para 8 (as substituted) to a subsidiary undertaking immediately before the loss of office as director: Sch 6 para 13(1), (2) (substituted by the Companies Act 1989 Sch 4 paras 1-3). For the usual meaning of 'subsidiary undertaking' see para 828 ante.

5   Companies Act 1985 Sch 6 para 1(2) (substituted by the Companies Act 1989 Sch 4 paras 1-3).

6   Companies Act 1985 Sch 6 para 1(3) (substituted by the Companies Act 1989 Sch 4 paras 1-3).

867. Details of chairman's and directors' emoluments. Where the company is a parent company[1] or a subsidiary undertaking[2], or where the aggregate amount of directors' emoluments[3] is £60,000 or more, the information required by the following provisions must be given with respect to the emoluments of the chairman and directors, and emoluments waived[4].

The emoluments[5] of the chairman[6] must be shown[7]. Where there has been more than one chairman during the year, the emoluments of each must be stated so far as attributable to the period during which he was chairman[8]. The emoluments of a person need not be shown if his duties as chairman were wholly or mainly discharged outside the United Kingdom[9].

The following information must be given with respect to the emoluments of directors[10]. There must be shown the number of directors whose emoluments fell within each of the following bands: not more than £5,000; more than £5,000 but not more than £10,000; more than £10,000 but not more than £15,000; and so on[11].

If the emoluments of any of the directors exceeded that of the chairman, there must be shown the greatest amount of emoluments of any director[12].

There must be shown the number of directors who have waived rights to receive emoluments which, but for the waiver, would have fallen to be included in the amount shown[13] and the aggregate amount of those emoluments[14].

1 For the meaning of 'parent company' see para 828 ante.
2 For the meaning of 'subsidiary undertaking' see para 866 note 4 ante.
3 Ie the amount shown in compliance with the Companies Act 1985 s 232, Sch 6 para 1(1) (as substituted): see para 866 ante.
4 Ibid Sch 6 para 2 (substituted by the Companies Act 1989 s 6(4), Sch 4 paras 1–3). See also para 865 ante.
5 For these purposes, and for the purposes of the Companies Act 1985 Sch 6 para 4 (as substituted) (see infra), 'emoluments' has the same meaning as in Sch 6 para 1 (as substituted) (see para 866 note 1 ante), except that it does not include contributions paid in respect of a person under a pension scheme: Sch 6 para 5 (substituted by the Companies Act 1989 Sch 4 paras 1–3). For the meaning of 'pension scheme' see para 868 note 3 post.
6 For these purposes, the 'chairman' means the person elected by the directors to be chairman of their meetings, and includes a person who, though not so elected, holds an office, however designated, which in accordance with the company's constitution carries with it functions substantially similar to those discharged by a person so elected: Companies Act 1985 Sch 6 para 3(2) (substituted by the Companies Act 1989 Sch 4 paras 1–3).
7 Companies Act 1985 Sch 6 para 3(1) (substituted by the Companies Act 1989 Sch 4 paras 1–3).
8 Companies Act 1985 Sch 6 para 3(3) (substituted by the Companies Act 1989 Sch 4 paras 1–3).
9 Companies Act 1985 Sch 6 para 3(4) (substituted by the Companies Act 1989 Sch 4 paras 1–3).
10 Companies Act 1985 Sch 6 para 4(1) (substituted by the Companies Act 1989 Sch 4 paras 1–3).
11 Companies Act 1985 Sch 6 para 4(2) (substituted by the Companies Act 1989 Sch 4 paras 1–3). The information required by the Companies Act 1985 Sch 6 para 4(2) (as so substituted) need not be given in respect of a director who discharged his duties as such wholly or mainly outside the United Kingdom; and any such director must be left out of account for the purposes of Sch 6 para 4(3) (as substituted) (see infra): Sch 6 para 4(5) (substituted by the Companies Act 1989 Sch 4 paras 1–3).
12 Companies Act 1985 Sch 6 para 4(3) (substituted by the Companies Act 1989 Sch 4 paras 1–3). Where more than one person has been chairman during the year, the reference to the emoluments of the chairman is to the aggregate of the emoluments of each person who has been chairman, so far as attributable to the period during which he was chairman: Companies Act 1985 Sch 6 para 4(4) (substituted by the Companies Act 1989 Sch 4 paras 1–3). See also note 11 supra.
13 Ie under the Companies Act 1985 Sch 6 para 1(1) (as substituted): see para 866 ante.
14 Ibid Sch 6 para 6(1) (substituted by the Companies Act 1989 Sch 4 paras 1–3). For these purposes, it is to be assumed that a sum not receivable in respect of a period would have been paid at the time at which it was due; and, if such a sum was payable only on demand, it is deemed to have been due at the time of the waiver: Companies Act 1985 Sch 6 para 6(2) (substituted by the Companies Act 1989 Sch 4 paras 1–3).

868. Pensions of directors and past directors. There must be shown the aggregate amount[1] of directors' or past directors' pensions[2]. This amount does not, however, include any pension paid or receivable under a pension scheme[3] if the scheme is such that the contributions under it are substantially adequate for the maintenance of the scheme; but, subject to this, it includes any pension paid or receivable in respect of any services of a director or past director[4], whether to or by him or, on his nomination or by virtue of dependence on or other connection with him, to or by any other person[5].

The amount shown must distinguish between pensions in respect of services as director, whether of the company or any of its subsidiary undertakings[6], and other pensions[7].

1 As to the amounts to be so included see para 866 note 1 ante.
2 Companies Act 1985 s 232, Sch 6 para 7(1) (substituted by the Companies Act 1989 s 6(4), Sch 4 paras 1-3). For these purposes, references to pensions include benefits otherwise than in cash and, in relation to so much of a pension as consists of such a benefit, references to its amount are to the estimated money value of the benefit: Companies Act 1985 Sch 6 para 7(4) (substituted by the Companies Act 1989 Sch 4 paras 1-3). The amount of any such benefit must also be disclosed: Sch 6 para 7(4) (as so substituted). 'Pension' includes any superannuation allowance, superannuation gratuity or similar payment: Companies Act 1985 Sch 6 para 13(1), (3)(a) (substituted by the Companies Act 1989 Sch 4 paras 1-3). See also para 865 ante.
3 For these purposes, 'pension scheme' means a scheme for the provision of pensions in respect of services as a director or otherwise which is maintained in whole or in part by means of contributions: Companies Act 1985 Sch 6 para 13(1), (7)(b) (substituted by the Companies Act 1989 Sch 4 paras 1-3). 'Contribution', in relation to a pension scheme, means any payment, including an insurance premium, paid for the purposes of the scheme by or in respect of persons rendering services in respect of which pensions will or may become payable under the scheme except that it does not include any payment in respect of two or more persons if the amount paid in respect of each of them is not ascertainable: Companies Act 1985 Sch 6 para 13(1), (7)(c) (substituted by the Companies Act 1989 Sch 4 paras 1-3).
4 Ie any such services as are mentioned in the Companies Act 1985 Sch 6 para 1(2) (as substituted): see para 866 ante.
5 Ibid Sch 6 para 7(2) (substituted by the Companies Act 1989 Sch 4 paras 1-3).
6 For the meaning of 'subsidiary undertaking' see para 866 note 4 ante.
7 Companies Act 1985 Sch 6 para 7(3) (substituted by the Companies Act 1989 Sch 4 paras 1-3).

869. Compensation to directors for loss of office. There must be shown the aggregate amount[1] of any compensation[2] to directors or past directors in respect of loss of office[3]. This amount includes compensation received or receivable by a director or past director for:

(1) loss of office as director of the company; or
(2) loss, while director of the company or on or in connection with his ceasing to be a director of it, of any other office in connection with the management of the company's affairs or any office as director or otherwise in connection with the management of the affairs of any subsidiary undertaking of the company;

and must distinguish between compensation in respect of the office of director, whether of the company or any of its subsidiary undertakings, and compensation in respect of other offices[4].

1 As to the amounts to be so included see para 866 note 1 ante.
2 For these purposes, references to compensation include benefits otherwise than in cash and, in relation to such compensation, references to its amount are to the estimated money value of the benefit: Companies Act 1985 s 232, Sch 6 para 8(3) (substituted by the Companies Act 1989 s 6(4), Sch 4 paras 1-3). The nature of any such compensation must be disclosed: Companies Act 1985 Sch 6 para 8(3) (as so substituted). References to compensation for loss of office include compensation in consideration for, or in connection with, a person's retirement from office: Sch 6 para 8(4) (substituted by the Companies Act 1989 Sch 4 paras 1-3).
3 Companies Act 1985 Sch 6 para 8(1) (substituted by the Companies Act 1989 Sch 4 paras 1-3). For these purposes, the amount to be so shown must distinguish between the sums respectively paid by or receivable from the company, the company's subsidiary undertakings and persons other than the company and its subsidiary undertakings: Companies Act 1985 Sch 6 para 10(3) (substituted by the Companies Act 1989 Sch 4 paras 1-3). For the meaning of 'subsidiary undertaking' see para 866 note 4 ante.
4 Companies Act 1985 Sch 6 para 8(2) (substituted by the Companies Act 1989 Sch 4 paras 1-3).

870. Sums paid to third parties in respect of directors' services. There must be shown the aggregate amount[1] of any consideration[2] paid to or receivable by third parties[3] for making available the services of any person:

(1) as director of the company; or

(2) while director of the company, as director of any of its subsidiary undertakings or otherwise in connection with the management of the affairs of the company or any of its subsidiary undertakings[4].

1 As to the amounts to be so included see para 866 note 1 ante.

2 For these purposes, the reference to consideration includes benefits otherwise than in cash and, in relation to such consideration, the reference to its amount is to the estimated money value of the benefit: Companies Act 1985 s 232, Sch 6 para 9(2) (substituted by the Companies Act 1989 s 6(4), Sch 4 paras 1-3).

3 For these purposes, the reference to third parties is to persons other than the director himself or a person connected with him or body corporate controlled by him or the company or any of its subsidiary undertakings: Companies Act 1985 Sch 6 para 9(3) (substituted by the Companies Act 1989 Sch 4 paras 1-3). For the meaning of references to a person being 'connected' with a director and to a director 'controlling' a body corporate see para 868 note 1 ante; and for the meaning of 'subsidiary undertaking' see para 866 note 4 ante.

4 Companies Act 1985 Sch 6 para 9(1) (substituted by the Companies Act 1989 Sch 4 paras 1-3).

(G) *Loans, Quasi-loans and other Dealings in favour of Directors*

871. Particulars of disclosure in relation to loans etc to company directors. The group accounts of a holding company[1], or, if it is not required to prepare group accounts its individual accounts[2], must contain the required particulars of:

(1) any transaction or arrangement of a financial kind generally restricted[3] entered into by the company or a subsidiary[4] of the company for[5] a person who at any time during the financial year[6] was a director[7] of the company or its holding company or was connected with[8] such a director;

(2) an agreement by the company or by a subsidiary of the company to enter into any such transaction or arrangement for a person who was at any time during the financial year a director of the company or its holding company or was connected with such a director; and

(3) any other transaction or arrangement with the company or a subsidiary of it in which a person who at any time during the financial year was a director of the company or of its holding company had, directly or indirectly, a material interest[9].

The accounts prepared by a company other than a holding company must contain the required particulars of:

(a) any transaction or arrangement of a financial kind generally restricted[10] entered into by the company for a person who at any time during the financial year was a director of it or its holding company or was connected with such a director;

(b) an agreement by the company to enter into any such transaction or arrangement for a person who was at any time during the financial year a director of the company or its holding company or was connected with such a director; and

(c) any other transaction or arrangement with the company in which a person who at any time during the financial year was a director of the company or of its holding company had, directly or indirectly, a material interest[11].

The above obligations do not apply in relation to a transaction, arrangement or agreement between one company and another in which a director of the former or of its subsidiary or holding company is interested only by virtue of his being a director of the latter; a contract of service between a company and one of its directors or a director of its holding company, or between a director of a company and any of that company's subsidiaries; a transaction, arrangement or agreement which was not entered into during the financial year and which did not subsist at any time during that year[12].

The above obligations apply, however, whether or not:

(i) the transaction or arrangement was prohibited by the provisions[13] of the Companies Act 1985;

(ii) the person for whom it was made was a director of the company or was connected with a director of it at the time it was made;

(iii) in the case of a transaction or arrangement made by a company which at any time during a financial year is a subsidiary of another company, it was a subsidiary of that other company at the time the transaction or arrangement was made[14].

Neither head (3) nor head (c) above applies in relation to any transaction or arrangement if each party to the transaction or arrangement which is a member of the same group of companies (meaning a holding company and its subsidiaries) as the company entered into the transaction or arrangement in the ordinary course of business, and the terms of the transaction or arrangement are not less favourable to any such party than it would be reasonable to expect if the interest mentioned in head (3) or, as the case may be, head (c) above had not been an interest of a person who was a director of the company or of its holding company[15].

Neither head (3) nor head (c) above applies in relation to any transaction or arrangement if:

(A) the company is a member of a group of companies (meaning a holding company and its subsidiaries); and

(B) either the company is a wholly-owned subsidiary[16] or no body corporate (other than the company or a subsidiary of the company) which is a member of the group of companies which includes the company's ultimate holding company was a party to the transaction or arrangement; and

(C) the director in question was at some time during the relevant period associated with the company; and

(D) the material interest of the director in question in the transaction or arrangement would not have arisen if he had not been associated with the company at any time during the relevant period[17].

1 For the meaning of 'holding company' see para 827 ante.

2 For the meaning of 'individual accounts' see para 816 ante.

3 Ie by the Companies Act 1985 s 330: see para 598 ante.

4 For the meaning of 'subsidiary' see para 827 ante.

5 For these purposes, the Companies Act 1985 s 331(9) (see para 598 notes 9, 12 ante) applies as to the interpretation of references to a transaction or arrangement being made 'for' a person: Sch 6 para 27(1)(b) (renumbered by the Companies Act 1989 s 6(4), Sch 4 para 4(1), (2)).

6 For the meaning of 'financial year' see para 806 ante.

7 For these purposes, 'director' includes a shadow director: Companies Act 1985 Sch 6 para 27(2) (renumbered and amended by the Companies Act 1989 Sch 4 paras 4(1), (2), 5). For the meaning of 'director' and 'shadow director' see para 543 note 1 ante.

8 For these purposes, the Companies Act 1985 s 346 (see para 607 ante) applies as to the interpretation of references to a person being 'connected with' a director of a company: Sch 6 para 27(1)(d) (renumbered by the Companies Act 1989 Sch 4 para 4(1), (2)).

9 Companies Act 1985 s 232(1), (2), Sch 6 para 15 (renumbered and amended by the Companies Act 1989 Sch 4 para 4(1),(2),(4)). For the purposes of the Companies Act 1985 Sch 6 para 15(c) (as so renumbered and amended) (see text head (3) supra), and for the purposes of Sch 6 para 16(c) (as renumbered) (see text head (c) infra), a transaction or arrangement between a company and a director of it or its holding company, or a person connected with such a director, is to be treated (if it would not otherwise be so) as

a transaction, arrangement or agreement in which that director is interested: Sch 6 para 17(1) (renumbered by the Companies Act 1989 Sch 4 para 4(1), (2)). An interest in such a transaction or arrangement is not 'material' if in the board's opinion it is not so; but this is without prejudice to the question whether or not such an interest is material in a case where the board has not considered the matter: Companies Act 1985 Sch 6 para 17(2) (renumbered by the Companies Act 1989 Sch 4 para 4(1), (2)). 'The board' means the directors of the company preparing the accounts, or a majority of those directors, but excluding in either case the director whose interest it is: Companies Act 1985 Sch 6 para 17(2) (as so renumbered).

10 See note 3 supra.
11 Companies Act 1985 Sch 6 para 16 (renumbered by the Companies Act 1989 Sch 4 para 4(1), (2)). See also note 9 supra.
12 Companies Act 1985 Sch 6 para 18 (renumbered by the Companies Act 1989 Sch 4 para 4(1), (2)).
13 Ie by the Companies Act 1985 s 330: see para 598 ante.
14 Ibid Sch 6 para 19 (renumbered by the Companies Act 1989 Sch 4 para 4(1), (2)).
15 Companies Act 1985 Sch 6 para 20 (renumbered by the Companies Act 1989 Sch 4 para 4(1), (2)).
16 For the meaning of 'wholly-owned subsidiary' see para 827 ante.
17 Companies Act 1985 Sch 6 para 21 (renumbered by the Companies Act 1989 Sch 4 para 4(1), (2)).

872. The required particulars. The particulars required are those of the principal terms of the transaction, arrangement or agreement[1].

Without prejudice to the generality of the above provisions, the following particulars are required:

(1) a statement of the fact either that the transaction, arrangement or agreement was made or subsisted (as the case may be) during the financial year[2];

(2) the name of the person for[3] whom it was made and, where that person is or was connected with[4] a director[5] of the company or of its holding company[6], the name of that director;

(3) in the case of any other transaction or arrangement with the company in which a person who at any time during the financial year was a director of the company or of its holding company had, directly or indirectly, a material interest[7], the name of the director with the material interest and the nature of that interest;

(4) in the case of a loan or an agreement for a loan or an arrangement where the transaction is initially made by a third party[8] relating to a loan:

    (a) the amount of the liability of the person to whom the loan was or was agreed to be made, in respect of principal and interest, at the beginning and at the end of the financial year;

    (b) the maximum amount of that liability during that year;

    (c) the amount of any interest which, having fallen due, has not been paid; and

    (d) the amount of any provision[9] made in respect of any failure or anticipated failure by the borrower to repay the whole or part of the loan or to pay the whole or part of any interest on it;

(5) in the case of a guarantee[10] or security or an arrangement whereby the company assumes liability[11] relating to a guarantee or security:

    (a) the amount for which the company (or its subsidiary[12]) was liable under the guarantee or in respect of the security both at the beginning and at the end of the financial year;

    (b) the maximum amount for which the company may become so liable; and

    (c) any amount paid and any liability incurred by the company (or its subsidiary) for the purpose of fulfilling the guarantee or discharging the security, including any loss incurred by reason of the enforcement of the guarantee or security; and

(6) in the case of any transaction, arrangement or agreement other than those mentioned in heads (4) and (5) above, the value[13] of the transaction or arrangement or (as the case may be) the value of the transaction or arrangement to which the agreement relates[14].

Heads (3) to (6) above do not apply in the case of a loan or quasi-loan made or agreed to be made by a company to or for a body corporate which is either a body corporate of which that company is a wholly-owned subsidiary[15], or a wholly-owned subsidiary of a body corporate of which that company is a wholly-owned subsidiary or a wholly-owned subsidiary of that company, if particulars of that loan, quasi-loan or agreement for it would not have been required to be included in that company's annual accounts if the first-mentioned body corporate had not been associated with a director of that company at any time during the relevant period[16].

1 Companies Act 1985 s 232(1), (2), Sch 6 para 22(1) (renumbered by the Companies Act 1989 s 6(4), Sch 4 para 4(1), (2)).
2 For the meaning of 'financial year' see para 806 ante.
3 As to the circumstances in which such a transaction or arrangement is made 'for' a person see para 871 note 5 ante.
4 For the meaning of 'connected with' see para 871 note 8 ante.
5 For the meaning of 'director' see para 871 note 6 ante.
6 For the meaning of 'holding company' see para 827 ante.
7 Ie in a case where the Companies Act 1985 Sch 6 paras 15(c) (as renumbered) or Sch 6 para 16(c) (as renumbered) applies: see para 871 heads (3), (c) respectively ante.
8 Ie an agreement within ibid s 330(6) or (7): see para 598 ante.
9 For the meaning of 'provision' see para 832 note 24 ante.
10 For these purposes, the Companies Act 1985 s 331(2) (see para 598 note 2 ante) applies as regards the meaning of 'guarantee': Sch 6 para 27(1)(a) (renumbered by the Companies Act 1989 Sch 4 para 4(1), (2)).
11 Ie an arrangement within the the Companies Act 1985 s 330(6): see para 598 ante.
12 For the meaning of 'subsidiary' see para 827 ante.
13 For these purposes, the Companies Act 1985 s 340 (as amended) (see para 603 ante) applies in assigning values to transactions and arrangements: Sch 6 para 27(1)(c) (renumbered by the Companies Act 1989 Sch 4 para 4(1), (2)).
14 Companies Act 1985 Sch 6 para 22(2) (renumbered by the Companies Act 1989 Sch 4 para 4(1), (2)).
15 For the meaning of 'wholly-owned subsidiary' see para 827 ante.
16 Companies Act 1985 Sch 6 para 23 (renumbered by the Companies Act 1989 Sch 4 para 4(1), (2)).

873. Excluded transactions. In relation to a company's accounts for a financial year[1], disclosure[2] is not required in the case of transactions of a kind mentioned below which are made by the company or a subsidiary[3] of it for[4] a person who at any time during that financial year was a director[5] of the company or of its holding company[6] or was connected with[7] such a director, if the aggregate of the values[8] of each transaction, arrangement or agreement so made for that director or any person connected with him, less the amount (if any) by which the liabilities of the person for whom the transaction or arrangement was made has been reduced, did not at any time during the financial year exceed £5,000[9]. The transactions in question are credit transactions[10], guarantees[11] provided or securities entered into in connection with credit transactions, arrangements within the statutory prohibitions[12] relating to credit transactions and agreements to enter into credit transactions[13].

In relation to a company's accounts for a financial year, disclosure is not required[14] in the case of any transaction or arrangement with a company in which a director of the company or any of its subsidiaries in which a director of the company or its holding company had, directly or indirectly, a material interest if:

(1) the value of each such transaction or arrangement in which that director had (directly or indirectly) a material interest and which was made after the commencement of the financial year with the company or any of its subsidiaries; and

(2) the value of each such transaction or arrangement which was made before the commencement of the financial year less the amount (if any) by which the liabilities of the person for whom the transaction or arrangement was made have been reduced,

did not at any time during the financial year exceed in the aggregate £1,000[15] or, if more, did not exceed £5,000[15] or 1% of the value of the net assets[16] of the company preparing the accounts in question as at the end of the financial year, whichever is the less[17].

1   For the meaning of 'financial year' see para 806 ante.
2   Ie in accordance with the Companies Act 1985 s 232(1), Sch 6 Pt II (paras 15-27) (as renumbered and amended): see para 871 ante.
3   For the meaning of 'subsidiary' see para 827 ante.
4   As to the circumstances in which a transaction or arrangement is made 'for' a person see para 871 note 5 ante.
5   For the meaning of 'director' see para 871 note 6 ante.
6   For the meaning of 'holding company' see para 827 ante.
7   For the meaning of 'connected with' see para 871 note 8 ante.
8   As to assigning values to transactions and arrangements see para 872 note 13 ante.
9   Companies Act 1985 Sch 6 para 24(1) (renumbered by the Companies Act 1989 s 6(4), Sch 4 paras 1, 6(1), (2)). The Companies Act 1985 s 345 (power of the Secretary of State to alter sums by statutory instrument: see para 599 note 5 ante) applies as if the money sum specified in Sch 6 para 24 (as renumbered) or Sch 6 para 25 (as renumbered) (see infra) were specified in Pt X (ss 311-347 (as amended): see para 562 et seq ante): Sch 6 para 26 (renumbered by the Companies Act 1989 Sch 4 paras 1, 6(1), (2)).
10 For these purposes, the Companies Act 1985 s 331(7) (see para 598 note 11 ante) applies as regards the meaning of 'credit transaction': Sch 6 para 27(1)(a) (renumbered by the Companies Act 1989 Sch 4 paras 1, 4(1), (2)).
11 For the meaning of 'guarantee' see para 872 note 10 ante.
12 Ie those contained in the Companies Act 1985 s 330(6) or (7): see para 598 ante.
13 Ibid Sch 6 para 24(2) (renumbered by the Companies Act 1989 Sch 4 paras 1, 6(1), (2)).
14 Ie by virtue of the Companies Act 1985 Sch 6 paras 15(c) or 16(c) (as renumbered and amended): see para 871 heads (3), (c) respectively ante.
15 See note 9 supra.
16 For these purposes, a company's net assets are the aggregate of its assets, less the aggregate of its liabilities, 'liabilities' to include any provision for liabilities or charges within the Companies Act 1985 Sch 4 para 89 (see para 832 note 24 ante): Sch 6 para 25 (renumbered by the Companies Act 1989 Sch 4 paras 1, 6(1), (2)).
17 Companies Act 1985 Sch 6 para 25 (as renumbered: see note 16 supra).

874. Particulars of disclosure in relation to loans etc to company's officers.
The following provisions apply in relation to the following classes of transactions, arrangements and agreements:

(1) loans, guarantees[1] and securities relating to loans and arrangements of a kind generally restricted by statute[2];

(2) quasi-loans[3], guarantees and securities relating to quasi-loans and arrangements of a kind generally restricted by statute[4];

(3) credit transactions[5], guarantees and securities relating to credit transactions and arrangements of a kind generally restricted by statute[6].

The accounts must contain a statement, in relation to such transactions, arrangements and agreements made by the company or a subsidiary[7] of it for[8] persons who at any time during the financial year[9] were officers of the company but not directors or shadow directors[10], of the aggregate amounts outstanding[11] at the end of the financial year under transactions, arrangements and agreements within heads (1), (2) and (3) above; and the numbers of officers for whom the transactions, arrangements and agreements falling within each of heads (1), (2) and (3) above were made[12].

These provisions do not apply to transactions, arrangements and agreements made by the company for an officer of the company if the aggregate amount outstanding at the end of the financial year under the transactions, arrangements and agreements so made for that officer does not exceed £2,500[13].

1 For these purposes, the Companies Act 1985 s 331(2) (see para 598 note 2 ante) applies as regards the meaning of 'guarantee': Sch 6 para 30(a) (renumbered by the Companies Act 1989 s 6(4), Sch 4 para 4(1), (2)).
2 Ie of a kind described in the Companies Act 1985 s 330(6), (7): see para 598 ante.
3 For these purposes, ibid s 331(3) (see para 598 note 7 ante) applies as regards the meaning of 'quasi-loan': Sch 6 para 30(a) (as renumbered: see note 1 supra).
4 See note 2 supra.
5 For these purposes, the Companies Act 1985 s 331(7) (see para 598 note 11 ante) applies as regards the meaning of 'credit transaction': Sch 6 para 30(a) (as renumbered: see note 1 supra).
6 Ibid Sch 6 para 28 (renumbered by the Companies Act 1989 Sch 4 para 4(1), (2)). As to the statutory restrictions see note 2 supra.
7 For the meaning of 'subsidiary' see para 827 ante.
8 For these purposes, the Companies Act 1985 s 331(9) (see para 598 notes 9, 12 ante) applies as to the interpretation of references to a transaction or arrangement being made 'for' a person: Sch 6 para 30(b) (renumbered by the Companies Act 1989 Sch 4 para 4(1), (2)).
9 For the meaning of 'financial year' see para 806 ante.
10 For the meaning of 'shadow director' see para 543 note 1 ante.
11 For these purposes, 'amount outstanding' means the amount of the outstanding liabilities of the person for whom the transaction, arrangement or agreement was made, or, in the case of a guarantee or security, the amount guaranteed or secured: Companies Act 1985 Sch 6 para 30 (renumbered by the Companies Act 1989 Sch 4 para 4(1), (2)).
12 Companies Act 1985 Sch 6 para 29(1) (renumbered by the Companies Act 1989 Sch 4 para 4(1), (2)).
13 Companies Act 1985 Sch 6 para 29(2) (renumbered by the Companies Act 1989 Sch 4 para 4(1), (2)). The Companies Act 1985 s 345 (power of the Secretary of State to alter sums by statutory instrument: see para 599 note 5 ante) applies as if the money sum specified in Sch 6 para 29 (as renumbered) were specified in Pt X (ss 311-347 (as amended): see para 562 et seq ante): Sch 6 para 29(3) (renumbered by the Companies Act 1989 Sch 4 paras 1, 6(1), (2)).

(vi) Group Accounts

A. IN GENERAL

875. Duty to prepare group accounts. If at the end of a financial year[1] a company is a parent company[2], the directors must, as well as preparing individual accounts[3] for the year, prepare group accounts[4]. Group accounts must be consolidated accounts comprising:

(1) a consolidated balance sheet[5] dealing with the state of affairs of the parent company and its subsidiary undertakings[6]; and

(2) a consolidated profit and loss account[7] dealing with the profit or loss of the parent company and its subsidiary undertakings[8].

The accounts must give a true and fair view[9] of the state of affairs as at the end of the financial year, and the profit or loss for the financial year, of the undertakings included in the consolidation[10] as a whole, so far as concerns members of the company[11].

A company's group accounts must comply with the statutory provisions[12] as to the form and content of the consolidated balance sheet and consolidated profit and loss account and additional information to be provided by way of notes to the accounts[13].

Where compliance with those statutory provisions, and the other provisions of the Companies Act 1985 as to the matters to be included in a company's group accounts or in notes to those accounts, would not be sufficient to give a true and fair view, the necessary additional information must be given in the accounts or in a note to them[14].

If in special circumstances compliance with any of those provisions is inconsistent with the requirement to give a true and fair view, the directors must depart from that provision to the extent necessary to give a true and fair view[15]. Particulars of any such departure, the reasons for it and its effect must be given in a note to the accounts[15].

1 For the meaning of 'financial year' see para 806 ante.
2 For the meaning of 'parent company' see para 827 ante.
3 For the meaning of 'individual accounts' see para 816 ante.
4 Companies Act 1985 s 227(1) (substituted by the Companies Act 1989 s 5(1)).
5 For the meaning of 'balance sheet' see para 826 ante. As to its form and content see paras 832, 833 ante.
6 For the meaning of 'subsidiary undertaking' see para 828 post.
7 For the meaning of 'profit and loss account' see para 826 ante. As to its form and content see paras 834-837 ante.
8 Companies Act 1985 s 227(2) (substituted by the Companies Act 1989 s 5(1)).
9 For the meaning of 'true and fair view' see para 816 note 5 ante.
10 For these purposes, 'included in the consolidation', in relation to group accounts, or 'included in consolidated group accounts', means that the undertaking is included in the accounts by the method of full, and not professional, consolidation; and references to an undertaking excluded from consolidation are to be construed accordingly: Companies Act 1985 s 262(1) (substituted by the Companies Act 1989 s 22).
11 Companies Act 1985 s 227(3) (substituted by the Companies Act 1989 s 5(1)).
12 Ie the Companies Act 1985 s 227(4), Sch 4A (as added and amended): see para 879 et seq post.
13 Ibid s 227(4) (substituted by the Companies Act 1989 s 5(1)). As to notes to group accounts see para 887 et seq post.
14 Companies Act 1985 s 227(5) (substituted by the Companies Act 1989 s 5(1)).
15 Companies Act 1985 s 227(6) (substituted by the Companies Act 1989 s 5(1)).

876. Exemption for parent companies included in accounts of larger group. A company is exempt from the requirement to prepare group accounts[1] if it is itself a subsidiary undertaking[2] and its immediate parent undertaking[3] is established under the law of a member State of the European Community in the following cases:

(1) where the company is a wholly-owned subsidiary[4] of that parent undertaking;

(2) where the parent undertaking holds more than 50% of the shares[5] in the company and notice requesting the preparation of group accounts has not been served on the company by shareholders holding in aggregate more than half of the remaining shares in the company or 5% of the total shares in the company[6].

Such notice must be served not later than six months after the end of the financial year[7] before that to which it relates[8].

Exemption is conditional upon compliance with all of the following conditions:

(a) that the company is included in consolidated accounts for a larger group drawn up to the same date, or to an earlier date in the same financial year, by a parent undertaking established under the law of a member State of the European Community;

(b) that those accounts are drawn up and audited, and that parent undertaking's annual report[9] is drawn up, in accordance with the provisions of the Seventh Directive[10];

(c) that the company discloses in its individual accounts[11] that it is exempt from the obligation to prepare and deliver group accounts;

(d) that the company states in its individual accounts the name of the parent undertaking which draws up the group accounts referred to above and:
   (i) if it is incorporated outside Great Britain, the country in which it is registered;
   (ii) if it is unincorporated, the address of its principal place of business;

(e) that the company delivers to the registrar of companies, within the period allowed for delivering its individual accounts, copies of those group accounts and of the parent undertaking's annual report, together with the auditors' report on them; and

(f) subject to the statutory right to deliver certain Welsh documents without a translation[12], that, if any document comprised in accounts and reports delivered in accordance with head (e) above is in a language other than English, there is annexed to the copy of that document delivered a translation of it into English, certified in the prescribed manner[13] to be a correct translation[14].

The exemption does not apply to a company any of whose securities[15] are listed on a stock exchange in any member State of the European Community[16].

1 As to the requirement to prepare group accounts see para 875 ante.

2 For the meaning of 'subsidiary undertaking' see para 828 ante.

3 For the meaning of 'parent undertaking' see para 828 ante.

4 For these purposes, shares held by directors of a company for the purpose of complying with any share qualification requirement are to be disregarded in determining whether the company is a wholly-owned subsidiary: Companies Act 1985 s 228(4) (substituted by the Companies Act 1989 s 5(3)). For the meaning of 'wholly-owned subsidiary' see para 827 ante.

5 For these purposes, shares held by a wholly-owned subsidiary of the parent undertaking, or held on behalf of the parent undertaking or a wholly-owned subsidiary, are to be attributed to the parent undertaking: Companies Act 1985 s 228(5) (substituted by the Companies Act 1989 s 5(3)).

6 Companies Act 1985 s 228(1) (substituted by the Companies Act 1989 s 5(3)).

7 For the meaning of 'financial year' see para 806 ante.

8 Companies Act 1985 s 228(1) (as substituted: see note 6 supra).

9 For these purposes, 'annual report', in relation to a company, means the directors' report required by ibid s 234 (as substituted and amended) (see para 1066 post): s 262(1) (substituted by the Companies Act 1989 s 22).

10 Ie the European Council Seventh Company Law Directive on consolidated accounts of 13 June 1983 (OJ L193, 18.7.1983, p 1), where applicable as modified by the provisions of EC Council Directive 86/635 (OJ L372, 31.12.1986, p 1) or EC Council Directive 91/674 (OJ L374, 31.12.91, p 7).

11 For the meaning of 'individual accounts' see para 816 ante.

12 Ie the Companies Act 1985 s 710B(6) (as added): see para 90 ante.

13 For the prescribed manner of certification see para 818 note 7 ante.

14 Companies Act 1985 s 228(2) (substituted by the Companies Act 1989 s 5(3); amended by the Companies Act 1985 (Disclosure of Branches and Bank Accounts) Regulations 1992, SI 1992/3178, reg 4; the Companies Act 1985 (Insurance Companies Accounts) Regulations 1993, SI 1993/3246, reg 5(1), Sch 2 para 1; the Welsh Language Act 1993 s 30(1), (3); the Companies Act 1985 (Miscellaneous Accounting Amendments) Regulations 1996, SI 1996/189, reg 4).

15 For these purposes, 'securities' includes (1) shares and stock; (2) debentures, including debenture stock, loan stock, bonds, certificates of deposit and other instruments creating or acknowledging indebtedness; (3) warrants or other instruments entitling the holder to subscribe for securities falling within heads (1) or (2) supra; and (4) certificates or other instruments which confer (a) property rights in respect of a security falling within heads (1), (2) or (3) supra; (b) any right to acquire, dispose of, underwrite or convert a security, being a right to which the holder would be entitled if he held any such security to which the certificate or other instrument relates; or (c) a contractual right, other than an option, to acquire any such security otherwise than by subscription: Companies Act 1985 s 228(6) (substituted by the Companies Act 1989 s 5(3)).

16 Companies Act 1985 s 228(3) (substituted by the Companies Act 1989 s 5(3)).

877. Subsidiary undertakings included in the consolidation. Subject to the exceptions authorised or required by the following provisions, all the subsidiary undertakings[1] of the parent company[2] must be included in the consolidation[3].

A subsidiary undertaking may be excluded from consolidation if its inclusion is not material for the purpose of giving a true and fair view[4]; but two or more undertakings may be excluded only if they are not material taken together[5].

In addition, a subsidiary undertaking may be excluded from consolidation where:

(1) severe long-term restrictions substantially hinder the exercise of the rights of the parent company[6] over the assets or management of that undertaking; or

(2) the information necessary for the preparation of group accounts cannot be obtained without disproportionate expense or undue delay; or

(3) the interest of the parent company[7] is held exclusively with a view to subsequent resale and the undertaking has not previously been included in consolidated group accounts prepared by the parent company[8].

Where the activities of one or more subsidiary undertakings are so different from those of other undertakings to be included in the consolidation that their inclusion would be incompatible with the obligation to give a true and fair view, those undertakings must be excluded from consolidation; but this provision does not apply merely because some of the undertakings are industrial, some commercial and some provide services, or because they carry on industrial or commercial activities involving different products or provide different services[9].

Where all the subsidiary undertakings of a parent company fall within the above exclusions, no group accounts are required[10].

1 For the meaning of 'subsidiary undertaking' see para 828 ante.
2 For the meaning of 'parent company' see para 828 ante.
3 Companies Act 1985 s 229(1) (substituted by the Companies Act 1989 s 5(3)).
4 For the meaning of 'true and fair view' see para 816 note 5 ante.
5 Companies Act 1985 s 229(2) (substituted by the Companies Act 1989 s 5(3)).
6 For these purposes, the reference to the rights of the parent company is to rights held by or attributed to the company for the purposes of the Companies Act 1985 s 258 (as substituted) (meaning of 'parent company': see para 828 ante) in the absence of which it would not be the parent company: s 229(3) (substituted by the Companies Act 1989 s 5(3)).
7 For these purposes, the reference to the interest of the parent company is to interests held by or attributed to the company for the purposes of the Companies Act 1985 s 258 (as substituted) in the absence of which it would not be the parent company: s 229(3) (as substituted: see note 6 supra).
8 Ibid s 229(3) (as substituted: see note 6 supra).
9 Ibid s 229(4) (substituted by the Companies Act 1989 s 5(3)).
10 Companies Act 1985 s 229(5) (substituted by the Companies Act 1989 s 5(3)).

878. Treatment of individual profit and loss account where group accounts prepared. The following provisions apply with respect to the individual profit and loss account[1] of a parent company[2] where:

(1) the company is required to prepare and does prepare group accounts in accordance with the Companies Act 1985; and

(2) the notes to the company's individual balance sheet show the company's profit and loss for the financial year[3] determined in accordance with that Act[4].

The profit and loss account need not contain the statutory information otherwise required[5] supplementing the profit and loss account[6].

The profit and loss account must be approved[7] by the board of directors but may be omitted[8] from the company's annual accounts[9].

The exemption conferred by the above provisions is conditional upon its being disclosed in the company's annual accounts that the exemption applies[10].

1 For the meaning of 'profit and loss account' see para 826 ante.
2 For the meaning of 'parent company' see para 828 ante.
3 For the meaning of 'financial year' see para 806 ante.
4 Companies Act 1985 s 230(1) (substituted by the Companies Act 1989 s 5(4)).
5 Ie the information specified in the Companies Act 1985 s 226(3), Sch 4 paras 52–57: see paras 839, 840, 848–852 ante.
6 Ibid s 230(2) (substituted by the Companies Act 1989 s 5(4)).
7 Ie in accordance with the Companies Act 1985 s 233(1) (as substituted): see para 937 post.
8 Ie for the purposes of ibid ss 231–245C (as substituted and amended).
9 Ibid s 230(3) (substituted by the Companies Act 1989 s 5(4)).
10 Companies Act 1985 s 230(4) (substituted by the Companies Act 1989 s 5(4)).

B. FORM AND CONTENT OF GROUP ACCOUNTS

879. General rules. Group accounts must comply, so far as practicable, with the statutory provisions relating to the amount of the auditors' remuneration[1] and the form and content of company accounts[2] as if the undertakings[3] included in the consolidation ('the group') were a single company[4].

In particular, for the purposes of the provisions[5] relating to dealings with or interests in group undertakings, as they apply to group accounts:

(1) any subsidiary undertakings[6] of the parent company[7] not included in the consolidation must be treated as subsidiary undertakings of the group; and

(2) if the parent company is itself a subsidiary undertaking, the group must be treated as a subsidiary undertaking of any parent undertaking of that company, and the reference to fellow subsidiary undertakings[8] must be construed accordingly[9].

Where the parent company is treated as an investment company[10], the group must be similarly treated[11].

1 Ie the Companies Act 1985 s 390A(3) (as added): see para 1042 post.
2 Ie ibid s 226(3), Sch 4 (as amended): see para 801 et seq ante.
3 For the meaning of 'undertaking' see para 806 note 5 ante.
4 Companies Act 1985 s 227(4), Sch 4A para 1(1) (added by the Companies Act 1989 s 5(2), Sch 2; amended by the Companies Act 1985 (Miscellaneous Accounting Amendments) Regulations 1996, SI 1996/189, reg 14(2), Sch 2 paras 1, 2).
5 Ie the Companies Act 1985 Sch 4 para 59 (sic). Schedule 4 para 59 is, however, repealed by the Companies Act 1985 (Miscellaneous Accounting Amendments) Regulations 1996 reg 14(1), Sch 1 paras 1, 15.
6 For the meaning of 'subsidiary undertaking' see para 828 ante.
7 For the meaning of 'parent company' see para 828 ante.
8 For these purposes, references to 'fellow subsidiary undertakings' are to undertakings which are subsidiary undertakings of the same parent undertaking but are not parent undertakings or subsidiary undertakings of each other: Companies Act 1985 s 259(4) (substituted by the Companies Act 1989 s 22).
9 Companies Act 1985 Sch 4A para 1(2) (added by the Companies Act 1989 Sch 2).
10 Ie for the purposes of the Companies Act 1985 Sch 4 Pt V (paras 71–73): see para 936 post.
11 Ibid Sch 4A para 1(2) (added by the Companies Act 1989 Sch 2).

880. Consolidated accounts of holding company and subsidiaries. The consolidated balance sheet[1] and profit and loss account[2] must incorporate in full the information contained in the individual accounts[3] of the undertakings[4] included in the consolidation, subject to the adjustments authorised or required by the following provisions[5] and to such other adjustments, if any, as may be appropriate in accordance with generally accepted accounting principles or practice[6].

If the financial year[7] of a subsidiary undertaking[8] included in the consolidation does not end with that of the parent company[9], the group accounts must be made up:

(1) from the accounts of the subsidiary undertaking for its financial year last ending before the end of the parent company's financial year, provided that year ended no more than three months before that of the parent company; or

(2) from interim accounts prepared by the subsidiary undertaking as at the end of the parent company's financial year[10].

Where assets and liabilities to be included in the group accounts have been valued or otherwise determined by undertakings according to accounting rules differing from those used for the group accounts, the values or amounts must be adjusted so as to accord with the rules used for the group accounts[11]. If it appears to the directors of the parent company that there are special reasons for departing from the above provisions[12], they may do so, but particulars of any such departure, the reasons for it and its effect must be given in a note to the accounts[13]. Such adjustments need not, however, be made if they are not material for the purpose of giving a true and fair view[14].

Any differences of accounting rules as between a parent company's individual accounts for a financial year and its group accounts must be disclosed in a note to the latter accounts and the reasons for the difference given[15].

Amounts which in the particular context of any statutory provision[16] are not material may be disregarded for the purposes of that provision[17].

1 For the meaning of 'balance sheet' see para 826 ante.
2 For the meaning of 'profit and loss account' see para 826 ante.
3 For the meaning of 'individual accounts' see para 816 ante.
4 For the meaning of 'undertaking' see para 806 note 5 ante.
5 Ie the provisions of the Companies Act 1985 s 227(4), Sch 4A paras 2(2), 3-22 (as added and amended): see infra and para 881 et seq post.
6 Ibid Sch 4A para 2(1) (added by the Companies Act 1989 s 5(2), Sch 2).
7 For the meaning of 'financial year' see para 806 ante.
8 For the meaning of 'subsidiary undertaking' see para 828 ante.
9 For the meaning of 'parent company' see para 828 ante.
10 Companies Act 1985 Sch 4A para 2(2) (added by the Companies Act 1989 Sch 2; amended by the Companies Act 1985 (Miscellaneous Accounting Amendments) Regulations 1996, SI 1996/189, reg 14(2), Sch 2 paras 1, 3).
11 Companies Act 1985 Sch 4A para 3(1) (added by the Companies Act 1989 Sch 2).
12 Ie the Companies Act 1985 Sch 4A para 3(1) (as added): see supra.
13 Ibid Sch 4A para 3(2) (added by the Companies Act 1989 Sch 2). As to notes to group accounts see para 887 et seq post.
14 Companies Act 1985 Sch 4A para 3(3) (added by the Companies Act 1989 Sch 2). For the meaning of 'true and fair view' see para 816 note 5 ante.
15 Companies Act 1985 Sch 4A para 4 (added by the Companies Act 1989 Sch 2).
16 Ie any provision of the Companies Act 1985 Sch 4A (as added).
17 Ibid Sch 4A para 5 (added by the Companies Act 1989 Sch 2).

881. Elimination of group transactions. Debts and claims between undertakings[1] included in the consolidation, and income and expenditure relating to transactions between such undertakings, must be eliminated in preparing the group accounts[2].

Where profits and losses resulting from transactions between undertakings included in the consolidation are included in the book value of assets, they must be eliminated in preparing group accounts[3]. The elimination so required may be effected in proportion to the group's interest in the shares of the undertakings[4].

The above provisions[5] need not be complied with if the amounts concerned are not material for the purpose of giving a true and fair view[6].

1 For the meaning of 'undertaking' see para 806 note 5 ante.
2 Companies Act 1985 s 227(4), Sch 4A para 6(1) (added by the Companies Act 1989 s 5(2), Sch 2).

3 Companies Act 1985 Sch 4A para 6(2) (added by the Companies Act 1989 Sch 2).
4 Companies Act 1985 Sch 4A para 6(3) (added by the Companies Act 1989 Sch 2).
5 Ie the Companies Act 1985 Sch 4A para 6(1), (2) (as added): see supra.
6 Ibid Sch 4A para 6(4) (added by the Companies Act 1989 Sch 2). For the meaning of 'true and fair view' see para 816 note 5 ante.

882. Acquisition and merger accounting. The following provisions apply where an undertaking[1] becomes a subsidiary undertaking[2] of the parent company[3]. That event is referred to in those provisions as an 'acquisition'; and references to the 'undertaking acquired' are to be construed accordingly[4].

An acquisition must be accounted for by the acquisition method of accounting unless the conditions for accounting for it as a merger are met and the merger method of accounting is adopted[5].

The acquisition method of accounting is as follows[6]. The identifiable[7] assets and liabilities of the undertaking acquired must be included in the consolidated balance sheet at their fair values as at the date of acquisition[8]. The income and expenditure of the undertaking acquired must be brought into the group accounts only as from the date of the acquisition[9]. There must be set off against the acquisition cost[10] of the interest in the shares of the undertaking held by the parent company and its subsidiary undertakings the interest of the parent company and its subsidiary undertakings in the adjusted capital and reserves[11] of the undertaking acquired[12]. The resulting amount, if positive, is to be treated as goodwill and, if negative, as a negative consolidation difference[13].

The conditions for accounting for an acquisition as a merger are:

(1) that at least 90% of the nominal value of the relevant shares[14] in the undertaking acquired is held by or on behalf of the parent company and its subsidiary undertakings;

(2) that the proportion referred to in head (1) above was attained pursuant to an arrangement providing for the issue of equity shares by the parent company or one or more of its subsidiary undertakings;

(3) that the fair value of any consideration other than the issue of equity shares given pursuant to the arrangement by the parent company and its subsidiary undertakings did not exceed 10% of the nominal value of the equity shares issued; and

(4) that adoption of the merger method of accounting accords with generally accepted accounting principles or practice[15].

The merger method of accounting is as follows[16]. The assets and liabilities of the undertaking acquired must be brought into the group accounts at the figures at which they stand in the undertaking's accounts, subject to any adjustment[17] authorised or required[18]. The income and expenditure of the undertaking acquired must be included in the group accounts for the entire financial year[19], including the period before the acquisition[20]. The group accounts must show corresponding amounts relating to the previous financial year as if the undertaking acquired had been included in the consolidation throughout that year[21].

There must be set off against the aggregate of:

(a) the appropriate amount in respect of qualifying shares[22] issued by the parent company or its subsidiary undertakings in consideration for the acquisition of shares in the undertaking acquired; and

(b) the fair value of any other consideration for the acquisition of shares in the undertaking acquired, determined as at the date when those shares were acquired, the nominal value of the issued share capital of the undertaking acquired held by the parent company and its subsidiary undertakings[23]. The resulting amount must be shown as an adjustment to the consolidated reserves[24].

Where a group is acquired, the above provisions[25] apply with the following adaptations[26]. References to shares of the undertaking acquired are to be construed as references to shares of the parent undertaking of the group[27]. Other references to the undertaking acquired are to be construed as references to the group; and references to the assets and liabilities, income and expenditure and capital and reserves of the undertaking acquired are to be construed as references to the assets and liabilities, income and expenditure and capital and reserves of the group after making the set-offs and other adjustments required[28] in the case of group accounts[29].

The following information with respect to acquisitions taking place in the financial year must be given in a note to the accounts[30].

There must be stated:

(i) the name of the undertaking acquired or, where a group was acquired, the name of the parent undertaking of that group; and

(ii) whether the acquisition has been accounted for by the acquisition or the merger method of accounting;

and, in relation to an acquisition which significantly affects the figures shown in the group accounts, the following further information must be given[31].

The composition and fair value of the consideration for the acquisition given by the parent company and its subsidiary undertakings must be stated[32].

Where the acquisition method of accounting has been adopted, the book values immediately prior to the acquisition, and the fair values at the date of acquisition, of each class of assets and liabilities of the undertaking or group acquired must be stated in tabular form, including a statement of the amount of any goodwill or negative consolidation difference arising on the acquisition, together with an explanation of any significant adjustments made[33].

Where the merger method of accounting has been adopted, an explanation must be given of any significant adjustments made in relation to the amounts of the assets and liabilities of the undertaking or group acquired, together with a statement of any resulting adjustment to the consolidated reserves, including the restatement of opening and consolidated reserves[34].

There must also be stated in a note to the accounts the cumulative amount of goodwill resulting from acquisition in that and earlier financial years which has been written off otherwise than in the consolidated profit and loss account for that or any earlier financial year[35]. That figure must be shown net of any goodwill attributable to subsidiary undertakings or businesses disposed of prior to the balance sheet date[36].

Where during the financial year there has been a disposal of an undertaking or group which significantly affects the figures shown in the group accounts, there must be stated in a note to the accounts the name of that undertaking or, as the case may be, of the parent undertaking of that group and the extent to which the profit or loss shown in the group accounts is attributable to profit or loss of that undertaking or group[37].

The information required by the above provisions[38] need not be disclosed with respect to an undertaking which is established under the law of a country outside the United Kingdom or carries on business outside the United Kingdom, if in the opinion of the directors of the parent company the disclosure would be seriously prejudicial to the business of that undertaking or to the business of the parent company or any of its subsidiary undertakings and the Secretary of State agrees that the information should not be disclosed[39].

1 For the meaning of 'undertaking' see para 806 note 5 ante.
2 For the meaning of 'subsidiary undertaking' see para 828 ante.
3 Companies Act 1985 s 227(4), Sch 4A para 7(1) (added by the Companies Act 1989 s 5(2), Sch 2). For the meaning of 'parent company' see para 828 ante.
4 Companies Act 1985 Sch 4A para 7(2) (added by the Companies Act 1989 Sch 2).
5 Companies Act 1985 Sch 4A para 8 (added by the Companies Act 1989 Sch 2).
6 Companies Act 1985 Sch 4A para 9(1) (added by the Companies Act 1989 Sch 2).
7 For these purposes, the 'identifiable' assets or liabilities of the undertaking acquired means the assets or liabilities which are capable of being disposed of or discharged separately, without disposing of a business of the undertaking: Companies Act 1985 Sch 4A para 9(2) (added by the Companies Act 1989 Sch 2).
8 Companies Act 1985 Sch 4A para 9(2) (as added: see note 7 supra).
9 Ibid Sch 4A para 6(3) (added by the Companies Act 1989 Sch 2).
10 For these purposes, 'the acquisition cost' means the amount of any cash consideration and the fair value of any other consideration, together with such amount, if any, in respect of fees and other expenses of the acquisition as the company may determine: Companies Act 1985 Sch 4A para 9(4) (added by the Companies Act 1989 Sch 2).
11 For these purposes, 'the adjusted capital and reserves' of the undertaking acquired means its capital and reserves at the date of the acquisition after adjusting the identifiable assets and liabilities of the undertaking to fair values as at that date: Companies Act 1985 Sch 4A para 9(4) (as added: see note 10 supra).
12 Ibid Sch 4A para 9(4) (as added: see note 10 supra).
13 Ibid Sch 4A para 9(5) (added by the Companies Act 1989 Sch 2).
14 For these purposes, the reference to the 'relevant shares' in an undertaking acquired is to those carrying unrestricted rights to participate both in distributions and in the assets of the undertaking upon liquidation: Companies Act 1985 Sch 4A para 10(2) (added by the Companies Act 1989 Sch 2).
15 Companies Act 1985 Sch 4A para 10(1) (added by the Companies Act 1989 Sch 2).
16 Companies Act 1985 Sch 4A para 11(1) (added by the Companies Act 1989 Sch 2).
17 Ie any adjustment authorised or required by the Companies Act 1985 Sch 4A (as added and amended).
18 Ibid Sch 4A para 11(2) (added by the Companies Act 1989 Sch 2).
19 For the meaning of 'financial year' see para 806 ante.
20 Companies Act 1985 Sch 4A para 11(3) (added by the Companies Act 1989 Sch 2).
21 Companies Act 1985 Sch 4A para 11(4) (added by the Companies Act 1989 Sch 2).
22 For these purposes, 'qualifying shares' means (1) shares in relation to which the Companies Act 1985 s 131 (as amended) (see para 189 ante) applies, in respect of which the appropriate amount is the nominal value; or (2) shares in relation to which s 132 (see para 190 ante) applies, in respect of which the appropriate amount is the nominal value together with any minimum premium value within the meaning of s 132 (see para 190 ante): Sch 4A para 11(7) (added by the Companies Act 1989 Sch 2).
23 Companies Act 1985 Sch 4A para 11(5) (added by the Companies Act 1989 Sch 2).
24 Companies Act 1985 Sch 4A para 11(6) (added by the Companies Act 1989 Sch 2).
25 Ie the Companies Act 1985 Sch 4A paras 9-11 (as added): see supra.
26 Ibid Sch 4A para 12(1) (added by the Companies Act 1989 Sch 2).
27 Companies Act 1985 Sch 4A para 12(2) (added by the Companies Act 1989 Sch 2).
28 Ie required by the Companies Act 1985 Sch 4A (as added and amended).
29 Ibid Sch 4A para 12(3) (added by the Companies Act 1989 Sch 2).
30 Companies Act 1985 Sch 4A para 13(1) (added by the Companies Act 1989 Sch 2). As to notes to group accounts see para 887 et seq post.
31 Companies Act 1985 Sch 4A para 13(2) (added by the Companies Act 1989 Sch 2).
32 Companies Act 1985 Sch 4A para 13(3) (added by the Companies Act 1989 Sch 2).
33 Companies Act 1985 Sch 4A para 13(5) (added by the Companies Act 1989 Sch 2). In ascertaining for the purposes of the Companies Act 1985 Sch 4A para 13(5) (as so added) or Sch 4A para 13(6) (as added) (see infra) the profit or loss of a group, the book values and fair values of assets and liabilities of a group or the amount of the assets and liabilities of a group, the set-offs and other adjustments required by Sch 4A (as added and amended) in the case of group accounts must be made: Sch 4A para 13(7) (added by the Companies Act 1989 Sch 2; amended by the Companies Act 1985 (Miscellaneous Accounting Amendments) Regulations 1996, SI 1996/189, reg 14(2), Sch 2 paras 1, 4(1), (3)).
34 Companies Act 1985 Sch 4A para 13(6) (added by the Companies Act 1989 Sch 2). See also note 33 supra.
35 Companies Act 1985 Sch 4A para 14(1) (added by the Companies Act 1989 Sch 2; amended by the Companies Act 1985 (Miscellaneous Accounting Amendments) Regulations 1996 Sch 2 paras 1, 5).

36 Companies Act 1985 Sch 4A para 14(2) (added by the Companies Act 1989 Sch 2). For the meaning of 'balance sheet date' see para 809 note 7 ante.
37 Companies Act 1985 Sch 4A para 15 (added by the Companies Act 1989 Sch 2).
38 Ie the Companies Act 1985 Sch 4A paras 13, 14 or 15 (as added and amended): see supra.
39 Ibid Sch 4A para 16 (added by the Companies Act 1989 Sch 2).

883. Minority interests. The statutory formats[1] have effect in relation to group accounts with the following additions[2].

In the Balance Sheet Formats a further item headed 'Minority interests' must be added:

(1) in Format 1, either after item J or at the end (after item K); and

(2) in Format 2, under the general heading 'LIABILITIES', between items A and B;

and under that item must be shown the amount of capital and reserves attributable to shares in subsidiary undertakings[3] included in the consolidation held by or on behalf of persons other than the parent company[4] and its subsidiary undertakings[5].

In the Profit and Loss Account Formats a further item headed 'Minority interests' must be added:

(a) in Format 1, between items 14 and 15;

(b) in Format 2, between items 16 and 17;

(c) in Format 3, between items 7 and 8 in both sections A and B; and

(d) in Format 4, between items 9 and 10 in both sections A and B;

and under that item must be shown the amount of any profit or loss on ordinary activities attributable to shares in subsidiary undertakings included in the consolidation held by or on behalf of persons other than the parent company and its subsidiary undertakings[6].

In the Profit and Loss Formats a further item headed 'Minority interests' must be added:

(i) in Format 1, between items 18 and 19;

(ii) in Format 2, between items 20 and 21;

(iii) in Format 3, between items 9 and 10 in section A and between items 8 and 9 in section B; and

(iv) in Format 4, between items 11 and 12 in section A and between items 10 and 11 in section B;

and under that item must be shown the amount of any profit or loss on extraordinary activities attributable to shares in subsidiary undertakings included in the consolidation held by or on behalf of persons other than the parent company and its subsidiary undertakings[7].

1 Ie the formats in the Companies Act 1985 s 226(3), Sch 4 (as amended): see para 832 et seq ante.
2 Ibid s 227(4), Sch 4A para 17(1) (added by the Companies Act 1989 s 5(2), Sch 2).
3 For the meaning of 'subsidiary undertaking' see para 828 ante.
4 For the meaning of 'parent company' see para 828 ante.
5 Companies Act 1985 Sch 4A para 17(2) (added by the Companies Act 1989 Sch 2). For the purposes of the Companies Act 1985 Sch 4 para 3(3), (4) (see para 831 ante), the additional item required by Sch 4A para 17(2) (as so added) is to be treated as one to which a letter is assigned: Sch 4A para 17(5)(a) (added by the Companies Act 1989 Sch 2).
6 Companies Act 1985 Sch 4A para 17(3) (added by the Companies Act 1989 Sch 2). For the purposes of the Companies Act 1985 Sch 4 para 3(3), (4) (see para 831 ante), the additional item required by Sch 4A para 17(3) (as so added) and Sch 4A para 17(4) (as added) (see infra) is to be treated as one to which an Arabic number is assigned: Sch 4A para 17(5)(b) (added by the Companies Act 1989 Sch 2).
7 Companies Act 1985 Sch 4A para 17(4) (added by the Companies Act 1989 Sch 2). See also note 6 supra.

884. Interests in subsidiary undertakings excluded from consolidation. The interest of the group in subsidiary undertakings[1] excluded from consolidation[2] and the amount of profit or loss attributable to such an interest must be shown in the consolidated balance sheet or, as the case may be, in the consolidated profit and loss account by the equity method of accounting, including dealing with any goodwill[3] arising[4].

1 For the meaning of 'subsidiary undertaking' see para 828 ante.
2 Ie under the Companies Act 1985 s 229(4) (as substituted): see para 877 ante.
3 Ie any goodwill arising in accordance with ibid s 226(3), Sch 4 paras 17-19, 21: see paras 810, 811 ante.
4 Ibid s 227(4), Sch 4A para 18 (added by the Companies Act 1989 s 5(2), Sch 2).

885. Joint ventures. Where an undertaking[1] included in the consolidation manages another undertaking jointly with one or more undertakings not included in the consolidation, that other undertaking ('the joint venture') may, if it is not a body corporate or a subsidiary undertaking[2] of the parent company[3], be dealt with in the group accounts by the method of proportional consolidation[4].

The statutory provisions relating to the preparation of consolidated accounts[5] apply, with any necessary modifications, to proportional consolidation under these provisions[6].

1 For the meaning of 'undertaking' see para 806 note 5 ante.
2 For the meaning of 'subsidiary undertaking' see para 828 ante.
3 For the meaning of 'parent company' see para 828 ante.
4 Companies Act 1985 s 227(4), Sch 4A para 19(1) (added by the Companies Act 1989 s 5(2), Sch 2).
5 Ie the provisions of the Companies Act 1985 Pt VII (ss 221-262A) (as amended).
6 Ibid Sch 4A para 19(2) (added by the Companies Act 1989 Sch 2).

886. Associated undertakings. An 'associated undertaking' means an undertaking[1] in which an undertaking included in the consolidation has a participating interest and over whose operating and financial policy it exercises a significant influence, and which is not a subsidiary undertaking[2] of the parent company[3] or a joint venture[4]. Where an undertaking holds 20% or more of the voting rights[5] in another undertaking, it is presumed to exercise such an influence over it unless the contrary is shown[6].

The statutory formats[7] have effect in relation to group accounts with the following modifications[8].

In the Balance Sheet Formats the items headed 'Participating interests', that is:
    (1) in Format 1, item B.III.3; and
    (2) in Format 2, item B.III.3 under the heading 'ASSETS',
must be replaced by two items, 'Interests in associated undertakings' and 'Other participating interests'[9].

In the Profit and Loss Account Formats the items headed 'Income from participating interests', that is:
    (a) in Format 1, item 8;
    (b) in Format 2, item 10;
    (c) in Format 3, item B.4; and
    (d) in Format 4, item B.6,
must be replaced by two items, 'Income from interests in associated undertakings' and 'Income from other participating interests'[10].

The interest of an undertaking in an associated undertaking, and the amount of profit or loss attributable to such an interest, must be shown by the equity method of accounting, including dealing with any goodwill[11] arising[12].

Where the associated undertaking is itself a parent undertaking[13], the net assets and profits or losses to be taken into account are those of the parent and its subsidiary undertakings, after making any consolidation adjustments[14].

The equity method of accounting need not be applied if the amounts in question are not material for the purpose of giving a true and fair view[15].

1 For the meaning of 'undertaking' see para 806 note 5 ante.
2 For the meaning of 'subsidiary undertaking' see para 828 ante.
3 For the meaning of 'parent company' see para 828 ante.
4 Companies Act 1985 s 227(4), Sch 4A para 20(1) (added by the Companies Act 1989 s 5(2), Sch 2). For these purposes, 'joint venture' means a joint venture dealt with in accordance with the Companies Act 1985 Sch 4A para 19 (as added) (see para 885 ante): Sch 4A para 20(1) (as so added).
5 The provisions of ibid Sch 10A paras 5-11 (as added) (see para 829 ante) apply in determining for these purposes whether an undertaking holds 20% or more of the voting rights in another undertaking: Sch 4A para 20(4) (added by the Companies Act 1989 Sch 2). The voting rights in an undertaking means the rights conferred on shareholders in respect of their shares or, in the case of an undertaking not having a share capital, on members, to vote at general meetings of the undertaking on all, or substantially all, matters: Companies Act 1985 Sch 4A para 20(3) (added by the Companies Act 1989 Sch 2).
6 Companies Act 1985 Sch 4A para 20(2) (added by the Companies Act 1989 Sch 2).
7 Ie the formats set out in the Companies Act 1985 s 226(3), Sch 4 (as amended): see para 832 et seq ante.
8 Ibid Sch 4A para 21(1) (added by the Companies Act 1989 Sch 2).
9 Companies Act 1985 Sch 4A para 21(2) (added by the Companies Act 1989 Sch 2).
10 Companies Act 1985 Sch 4A para 21(3) (added by the Companies Act 1989 Sch 2).
11 Ie any goodwill arising in accordance with the Companies Act 1985 Sch 4 paras 17-19, 21: see paras 810, 811 ante.
12 Ibid Sch 4A para 22(1) (added by the Companies Act 1989 Sch 2).
13 For the meaning of 'parent undertaking' see para 828 ante.
14 Companies Act 1985 Sch 4A para 22(2) (added by the Companies Act 1989 Sch 2).
15 Companies Act 1985 Sch 4A para 22(3) (added by the Companies Act 1989 Sch 2). For the meaning of 'true and fair view' see para 816 note 5 ante.

C. NOTES TO THE ACCOUNTS

(A) *Information supplementing the Balance Sheet*

887. Guarantees and other financial commitments in favour of group undertakings. Commitments falling within the provisions relating to guarantees and other financial commitments[1] which are undertaken on behalf of or for the benefit of:

(1) any parent undertaking[2] or fellow subsidiary undertaking[3]; or

(2) any subsidiary undertaking[4] of the company,

must be stated separately from the other commitments; and commitments within head (1) above must be stated separately from those within head (2) above[5].

1 Ie commitments within the Companies Act 1985 s 226(3), Sch 4 para 50(1)-(5) (as amended): see para 846 ante.
2 For the meaning of 'parent undertaking' see para 828 ante.
3 For the meaning of 'fellow subsidiary undertaking' see para 879 note 8 ante.
4 For the meaning of 'subsidiary undertaking' see para 828 ante.
5 Companies Act 1985 Sch 4 para 59A (added by the Companies Act 1989 s 4(2), Sch 1 paras 1, 11(1), (2)).

(B) *Related Undertakings*

888. Disclosure required in notes to accounts. The prescribed information[1] must be given in notes to a company's annual accounts[2]. The information so required need not be disclosed with respect to an undertaking[3] which is established under the law of a country outside the United Kingdom or carries on business outside the United Kingdom, if, in the opinion of the directors of the company, the disclosure would be seriously prejudicial to the business of that undertaking, or to the business of the company or any of its subsidiary undertakings[4], and the Secretary of State agrees that the information need not be disclosed[5]. Where advantage is taken of that provision, that fact must be stated in a note to the company's annual accounts[6].

If the directors of the company are of the opinion that the number of undertakings in respect of which the company is required to disclose information under any of the statutory provisions[7] is such that compliance with that provision would result in information of excessive length being given, the information need only be given in respect of:

(1) the undertakings whose results or financial position, in the opinion of the directors, principally affected the figures shown in the company's annual accounts; and

(2) undertakings excluded[8] from consolidation[9].

If advantage is taken of that provision:

(a) there must be included in the notes to the company's annual accounts a statement that the information is given only with respect to such undertakings[10]; and

(b) the full information, both that which is disclosed in the notes to the accounts and that which is not, must be annexed to the company's next annual return[11].

If a company fails to comply with head (b) above, the company, and every officer of it who is in default, is liable on summary conviction to a fine not exceeding one-fifth of the statutory maximum and, on conviction after continued contravention, to a daily default fine not exceeding one-fiftieth of the statutory maximum[12].

1 Ie the information specified in the Companies Act 1985 s 231(1), Sch 5 (as substituted and amended): see para 889 et seq post. As to the application of Sch 5 (as substituted and amended) to unregistered companies see para 853 note 1 ante.

2 Ibid s 231(1) (substituted by the Companies Act 1989 s 6(1)). For the meaning of 'annual accounts' see para 817 note 2 ante. Where the company is required to prepare group accounts, the information specified in the Companies Act 1985 Sch 5 Pt II (paras 14-32 (as substituted and amended): see para 889 et seq post) must be given: s 231(2) (substituted by the Companies Act 1989 s 6(1)). As to companies not required to prepare group accounts see para 853 et seq ante.

3 For the meaning of 'undertaking' see para 806 note 5 ante.

4 For the meaning of 'subsidiary undertaking' see para 828 ante.

5 Companies Act 1985 s 231(3) (substituted by the Companies Act 1989 s 6(1)). The Companies Act 1985 s 231(3) (as so substituted) does not apply in relation to the information required under Sch 5 paras 20 or 28A (as respectively substituted and added) (see paras 892, 896 post): s 231(3) (as so substituted; amended by the Partnerships and Unlimited Companies (Accounts) Regulations 1993, SI 1993/1820, reg 11(1); the Companies Act 1985 (Miscellaneous Accounting Amendments) Regulations 1996, SI 1996/189, reg 15(1)).

6 Companies Act 1985 s 231(4) (substituted by the Companies Act 1989 s 6(1)).

7 Ie any provision of the Companies Act 1985 Sch 5 (as substituted and amended).

8 Ie excluded under ibid s 229(3) or (4) (as substituted): see para 877 ante.

9 Ibid s 231(5) (substituted by the Companies Act 1989 s 6(1); amended by the Companies Act 1985 (Miscellaneous Accounting Amendments) Regulations 1996 reg 15(1)).

10 Ie such undertakings as are mentioned in the Companies Act 1985 s 231(5) (as substituted): see supra.

11 Ibid s 231(6) (substituted by the Companies Act 1989 s 6(1)). For these purposes, the 'next annual return' means that delivered to the registrar of companies after the accounts in question have been approved under the Companies Act 1985 s 233 (as substituted) (see para 937 post): s 231(6) (as so substituted).

12 Ibid s 231(7) (substituted by the Companies Act 1989 s 6(1)); Companies Act 1985 s 730, Sch 24 (amended by the Companies Act 1989 s 23, Sch 10 para 24(1), (2)). For the meaning of 'officer who is in default', 'the statutory maximum' and 'daily default fine' see para 1161 post.

889. Subsidiary undertakings. The following information must be given with respect to the undertakings[1] which are subsidiary undertakings[2] of the parent company[3] at the end of the financial year[4].

The name of each undertaking must be stated[5].

There must be stated:

(1) if the undertaking is incorporated outside Great Britain, the country in which it is incorporated;

(2) if it is unincorporated, the address of its principal place of business[6].

It must also be stated whether the subsidiary undertaking is included in the consolidation and, if it is not, the reasons for excluding it from consolidation must be given[7].

It must also be stated with respect to each subsidiary undertaking by virtue of which of the statutory conditions[8] it is a subsidiary of its immediate parent undertaking[9]. That information need not, however, be given if the relevant condition is that relating to the holding of a majority of the voting rights[10] and the immediate parent undertaking holds the same proportion of the shares in the undertaking as it holds voting rights[11].

1 For the meaning of 'undertaking' see para 806 note 5 ante.
2 For the meaning of 'subsidiary undertaking' see para 828 ante.
3 For the meaning of 'parent company' see para 828 ante.
4 Companies Act 1985 s 231(1), (2), Sch 5 para 15(1) (substituted by the Companies Act 1989 s 6(2), Sch 3).
5 Companies Act 1985 Sch 5 para 15(2) (substituted by the Companies Act 1989 Sch 3).
6 Companies Act 1985 Sch 5 para 15(3) (substituted by the Companies Act 1989 Sch 3; amended by the Companies Act 1985 (Miscellaneous Accounting Amendments) Regulations 1996, SI 1996/189, reg 14(3), Sch 3 paras 1, 14). For the meaning of 'place of business' see para 63 note 1 ante.
7 Companies Act 1985 Sch 5 para 15(4) (substituted by the Companies Act 1989 Sch 3).
8 Ie which of the conditions specified in the Companies Act 1985 s 258(2) or (4) (as substituted): see para 828 ante.
9 Ibid Sch 5 para 15(5) (substituted by the Companies Act 1989 Sch 3). For the meaning of 'parent undertaking' see para 828 ante.
10 The relevant condition is that specified in the Companies Act 1985 s 258(2)(a): see para 828 ante.
11 Ibid Sch 5 para 15(5) (as substituted: see note 9 supra).

890. Holdings in subsidiary undertakings. The following information must be given with respect to shares of a subsidiary undertaking[1] held:

(1) by the parent company[2]; and

(2) by the group[3];

and the information under heads (1) and (2) above must, if different, be shown separately[4].

There must be stated:

(a) the identity of each class of shares held; and

(b) the proportion of the nominal value of the shares of that class represented by those shares[5].

1 For the meaning of 'subsidiary undertaking' see para 828 ante.
2 For the meaning of 'parent company' see para 828 ante.
3 For these purposes, 'the group' means the group consisting of the parent company and its subsidiary undertakings: Companies Act 1985 s 231(1), (2), Sch 5 para 14 (substituted by the Companies Act 1989 s 6(2), Sch 3).
4 Companies Act 1985 Sch 5 para 16(1) (substituted by the Companies Act 1989 Sch 3).
5 Companies Act 1985 Sch 5 para 16(2) (substituted by the Companies Act 1989 Sch 3).

891. Financial information about subsidiary undertakings not included in the consolidation. There must be shown with respect to each subsidiary undertaking[1] not included in the consolidation the aggregate amount of its capital and reserves as at the end of its relevant financial year[2] and its profit or loss for that year[3].

That information need not be given if the group's[4] investment in the undertaking is included in the accounts by way of the equity method of valuation[5] or if:

(1) the undertaking is not required by any provision of the Companies Act 1985 to deliver a copy of its balance sheet for its relevant financial year and does not otherwise publish that balance sheet in Great Britain or elsewhere; and

(2) the holding of the group is less than 50% of the nominal value of the shares in the undertaking[6].

Information otherwise required by these provisions need not be given if it is not material[7].

1 For the meaning of 'subsidiary undertaking' see para 828 ante.
2 For these purposes, the 'relevant financial year' of a subsidiary undertaking is (1) if its financial year ends with that of the company, that year; and (2) if not, its financial year ending last before the end of the company's financial year: Companies Act 1985 s 231(1), (2), Sch 5 para 17(4) (substituted by the Companies Act 1989 s 6(2), Sch 3).
3 Companies Act 1985 Sch 5 para 17(1) (substituted by the Companies Act 1989 Sch 3).
4 For the meaning of 'group' see para 890 note 3 ante.
5 As to the equity method of valuation see para 856 note 6 ante.
6 Companies Act 1985 Sch 5 para 17(2) (substituted by the Companies Act 1989 Sch 3).
7 Companies Act 1985 Sch 5 para 17(3) (substituted by the Companies Act 1989 Sch 3).

892. Shares and debentures of company held by subsidiary undertakings. The number, description and amount of the shares in the company held by or on behalf of its subsidiary undertakings[1] must be disclosed[2]; but this provision does not apply in relation to shares in the case of which the subsidiary undertaking is concerned as personal representative or, subject as follows, as trustee[3]. The exception for shares in relation to which the subsidiary undertaking is concerned as trustee does not apply if the company or any of its subsidiary undertakings is beneficially interested under the trust[4], otherwise than by way of security only for the purpose of a transaction entered into by it in the ordinary course of a business which includes the lending of money[5].

1 For the meaning of 'subsidiary undertaking' see para 828 ante.
2 Companies Act 1985 s 231(1), (2), Sch 5 para 20(1) (substituted by the Companies Act 1989 s 6(2), Sch 3; amended by the Companies Act 1985 (Miscellaneous Accounting Amendments) Regulations 1996, SI 1996/189, reg 14(3), Sch 3 paras 1, 17(1), (2)).
3 Companies Act 1985 Sch 5 para 20(2) (substituted by the Companies Act 1989 Sch 3; amended by the Companies Act 1985 (Miscellaneous Accounting Amendments) Regulations 1996 Sch 3 paras 1, 17(1), (3)).
4 The Companies Act 1985 Sch 2 (as amended) (see para 859 ante) has effect for the interpretation of the reference to a beneficial interest under a trust: Sch 5 para 20(4) (substituted by the Companies Act 1989 Sch 3).
5 Companies Act 1985 Sch 5 para 20(3) (substituted by the Companies Act 1989 Sch 3; amended by the Companies Act 1985 (Miscellaneous Accounting Amendments) Regulations 1996 Sch 3 paras 1, 17(1), (3)).

893. Joint ventures. The following information must be given where an undertaking[1] is dealt with in the consolidated accounts by the method of proportional consolidation:

(1) the name of the undertaking;

(2) the address of the principal place of business[2] of the undertaking;

(3) the factors on which joint management of the undertaking is based; and

(4) the proportion of the capital of the undertaking held by undertakings included in the consolidation[3].

Where the financial year[4] of the undertaking did not end with that of the company, there must be stated the date on which a financial year of the undertaking last ended before that date[5].

1 For the meaning of 'undertaking' see para 806 note 5 ante.
2 For the meaning of 'place of business' see para 63 note 1 ante.
3 Companies Act 1985 s 231(1), (2), Sch 5 para 21(1) (substituted by the Companies Act 1989 s 6(2), Sch 3).
4 For the meaning of 'financial year' see para 806 ante.
5 Companies Act 1985 Sch 5 para 21(2) (substituted by the Companies Act 1989 Sch 3).

894. Associated undertakings. The following information must be given where an undertaking[1] included in the consolidation has an interest in an associated undertaking[2].

The name of the associated undertaking must be stated[3].

There must be stated:

(1) if the undertaking is incorporated outside Great Britain, the country in which it is incorporated;

(2) if it is unincorporated, the address of its principal place of business[4].

The following information must be given with respect to the shares of the undertaking held by the parent company and by the group[5]; and the information under heads (1) and (2) below must be shown separately[6].

There must be stated:

(a) the identity of each class of shares held; and

(b) the proportion of the nominal value of the shares of that class represented by those shares[7].

1 For the meaning of 'undertaking' see para 806 note 5 ante.
2 Companies Act 1985 s 231(1), (2), Sch 5 para 22(1) (substituted by the Companies Act 1989 s 6(2), Sch 3). For these purposes, 'associated undertaking' has the meaning given by the Companies Act 1985 s 227(4), Sch 4A para 20 (as added) (see para 886 ante); and the additional information required by Sch 5 para 22 (as added) must be given notwithstanding that Sch 4A para 22(3) (as added) (see para 886 ante) applies in relation to the accounts themselves: Sch 5 para 22(6) (substituted by the Companies Act 1989 Sch 3).
3 Companies Act 1985 Sch 5 para 22(2) (substituted by the Companies Act 1989 Sch 3).
4 Companies Act 1985 Sch 5 para 22(3) (substituted by the Companies Act 1989 Sch 3; amended by the Companies Act 1985 (Miscellaneous Accounting Amendments) Regulations 1996, SI 1996/189, reg 14(3), Sch 3 paras 1, 18). For the meaning of 'place of business' see para 63 note 1 ante.
5 For the meaning of 'the group' see para 890 note 3 ante.
6 Companies Act 1985 Sch 5 para 22(4) (substituted by the Companies Act 1989 Sch 3).
7 Companies Act 1985 Sch 5 para 22(5) (substituted by the Companies Act 1989 Sch 3).

895. Other significant holdings of parent company or group. The following information[1] must be given where at the end of the financial year[2] the parent company[3] has a significant holding[4] in an undertaking which is not one of its subsidiary undertakings[5] and does not fall within the statutory provisions[6] relating to joint ventures or associated undertakings[7].

The name of the undertaking must be stated[8].

There must be stated:

(1) if the undertaking is incorporated outside Great Britain, the country in which it is incorporated;

(2) if it is unincorporated, the address of its principal place of business[9].

The following information must be given with respect to the shares of the undertaking held by the parent company[10]. There must be stated the identity of each class of shares held and the proportion of the nominal value of the shares of that class represented by those shares[11].

There must also be stated the aggregate amount of the capital and reserves of the undertaking as at the end of its relevant financial year[12] and its profit or loss for that year[13]. That information need not be given in respect of an undertaking if the undertaking is not required by any provision of the Companies Act 1985 to deliver a copy of its balance sheet for its relevant financial year and does not otherwise publish that balance sheet in Great Britain or elsewhere and the company's holding is less than 50% of the nominal value of the shares in the undertaking[14].

Information otherwise required by the above provisions need not be given if it is not material[15].

The information required by the following provisions[16] must be given where at the end of the financial year the group[17] has a significant holding[18] in an undertaking which is not a subsidiary undertaking of the parent company and does not fall within the statutory provisions relating to joint ventures or associated undertakings[19].

The name of the undertaking must be stated[20].

There must be stated:

(a) if the undertaking is incorporated outside Great Britain, the country in which it is incorporated;

(b) if it is unincorporated, the address of its principal place of business[21].

The following information must be given with respect to the shares of the undertaking held by the group[22]. There must be stated the identity of each class of shares held and the proportion of the nominal value of the shares of that class represented by those shares[23].

There must also be stated the aggregate amount of the capital and reserves of the undertaking as at the end of its relevant financial year[24] and its profit or loss for that year[25]. That information need not be given in respect of an undertaking if the undertaking is not required by any provision of the Companies Act 1985 to deliver a copy of its balance sheet for its relevant financial year and does not otherwise publish that balance sheet in Great Britain or elsewhere and the holding of the group is less than 50% of the nominal value of the shares in the undertaking[26].

Information otherwise required by the above provisions need not be given if it is not material[27].

1   Ie the information required by the Companies Act 1985 s 231(1), (2), Sch 5 paras 24, 25 (as substituted): see infra.

2   For the meaning of 'financial year' see para 806 ante.

3   For the meaning of 'parent company' see para 828 ante.

4   For these purposes, a holding is significant if (1) it amounts to 20% or more of the nominal value of any class of shares in the undertaking; or (2) the amount of the holding (as stated or included in the company's individual accounts) exceeds one-fifth of the amount of its assets (as so stated): Companies Act 1985 Sch 5 para 23(2) (substituted by the Companies Act 1989 s 6(2), Sch 3; amended by the Companies Act 1985 (Miscellaneous Accounting Amendments) Regulations 1996, SI 1996/189, reg 14(3), Sch 3 paras 1, 19). For the meaning of 'undertaking see para 806 note 5 ante.

5   For the meaning of 'subsidiary undertaking' see para 828 ante.

6   Ie does not fall within the Companies Act 1985 Sch 5 para 21 (as substituted) (see para 893 ante) or Sch 5 para 22 (as substituted) (see para 894 ante), as the case may be.

7   Ibid Sch 5 para 23(1) (substituted by the Companies Act 1989 Sch 3).

8　Companies Act 1985 Sch 5 para 24(1) (substituted by the Companies Act 1989 Sch 3).
9　Companies Act 1985 Sch 5 para 24(2) (substituted by the Companies Act 1989 Sch 3; amended by the Companies Act 1985 (Miscellaneous Accounting Amendments) Regulations 1996 Sch 3 paras 1, 20). For the meaning of 'place of business' see para 63 note 1 ante.
10　Companies Act 1985 Sch 5 para 24(3) (substituted by the Companies Act 1989 Sch 3).
11　Companies Act 1985 Sch 5 para 24(4) (substituted by the Companies Act 1989 Sch 3).
12　For these purposes, the 'relevant financial year' of an undertaking is (1) if its financial year ends with that of the company, that year; (2) if not, its financial year ending last before the end of the company's financial year: Companies Act 1985 Sch 5 para 25(4) (substituted by the Companies Act 1989 Sch 3).
13　Companies Act 1985 Sch 5 para 25(1) (substituted by the Companies Act 1989 Sch 3; amended by the Companies Act 1985 (Miscellaneous Accounting Amendments) Regulations 1996 Sch 3 paras 1, 21).
14　Companies Act 1985 Sch 5 para 25(2) (substituted by the Companies Act 1989 Sch 3).
15　Companies Act 1985 Sch 5 para 25(3) (substituted by the Companies Act 1989 Sch 3).
16　Ie the information required by the Companies Act 1985 Sch 5 paras 27, 28 (as substituted): see infra.
17　For the meaning of 'the group' see para 890 note 3 ante.
18　For these purposes, a holding is significant if (1) it amounts to 20% or more of the nominal value of any class of shares in the undertaking; or (2) the amount of the holding (as stated or included in the group accounts) exceeds one-fifth of the amount of its assets (as so stated): Companies Act 1985 Sch 5 para 26(2) (substituted by the Companies Act 1989 Sch 3; amended by the Companies Act 1985 (Miscellaneous Accounting Amendments) Regulations 1996 Sch 3 paras 1, 19).
19　Companies Act 1985 Sch 5 para 26(1) (substituted by the Companies Act 1989 Sch 3).
20　Companies Act 1985 Sch 5 para 27(1) (substituted by the Companies Act 1989 Sch 3).
21　Companies Act 1985 Sch 5 para 27(2) (substituted by the Companies Act 1989 Sch 3; amended by the Companies Act 1985 (Miscellaneous Accounting Amendments) Regulations 1996 Sch 3 paras 1, 22).
22　Companies Act 1985 Sch 5 para 27(3) (substituted by the Companies Act 1989 Sch 3).
23　Companies Act 1985 Sch 5 para 27(4) (substituted by the Companies Act 1989 Sch 3).
24　For these purposes, the 'relevant financial year' of an outside undertaking is (1) if its financial year ends with that of the parent company, that year; (2) if not, its financial year ending last before the end of the parent company's financial year: Companies Act 1985 Sch 5 para 28(4) (substituted by the Companies Act 1989 Sch 3).
25　Companies Act 1985 Sch 5 para 28(1) (substituted by the Companies Act 1989 Sch 3; amended by the Companies Act 1985 (Miscellaneous Accounting Amendments) Regulations 1996 Sch 3 paras 1, 21).
26　Companies Act 1985 Sch 5 para 28(2) (substituted by the Companies Act 1989 Sch 3).
27　Companies Act 1985 Sch 5 para 28(3) (substituted by the Companies Act 1989 Sch 3).

896. Parent company's or group's membership of certain undertakings. The information required by the following provisions must be given where at the end of the financial year[1] the company is a member[2] of a qualifying undertaking[3].

There must be stated:
(1)　the name and legal form of the undertaking; and
(2)　the address of the undertaking's registered office (whether in or outside Great Britain) or, if it does not have such an office, its head office (whether in or outside Great Britain)[4].

Information otherwise required by the above provisions[5] need not be given if it is not material[6].

Where the undertaking is a qualifying partnership, there must also be stated either:
(a)　that a copy of the latest accounts of the undertaking has been or is to be appended to the copy of the company's accounts sent to the registrar of companies[7]; or
(b)　the name of at least one body corporate (which may be the company) in whose group accounts the undertaking has been or is to be dealt with on a consolidated basis[8].

Information otherwise required by head (b) above need not be given if the notes to the company's accounts disclose that advantage has been taken[9] of the statutory exemption[10].

1 For the meaning of 'financial year' see para 806 ante.
2 Any reference to the members of a qualifying partnership is to be construed, in relation to a limited partnership, as a reference to its general partner or partners: Partnerships and Unlimited Companies (Accounts) Regulations 1993, SI 1993/1820, reg 2(2) (applied by the Companies Act 1985 s 231(1), Sch 5 para 28A(6) (added by the Partnerships and Unlimited Companies (Accounts) Regulations 1993 reg 11(3))).
3 Companies Act 1985 Sch 5 para 28A(1) (added by the Partnerships and Unlimited Companies (Accounts) Regulations 1993 reg 11(3)). For these purposes, 'qualifying undertaking' means a qualifying partnership or a qualifying company: Companies Act 1985 Sch 5 para 28A(6) (as added: see note 2 supra). For the meaning of 'qualifying partnership' see para 931 post; and for the meaning of 'qualifying company' see para 117 note 13 ante.
4 Companies Act 1985 Sch 5 para 28A(2) (added by the Partnerships and Unlimited Companies (Accounts) Regulations 1993 reg 11(3)).
5 Ie by the Companies Act 1985 Sch 5 para 28A(2) (as added): see supra.
6 Ibid Sch 5 para 28A(4) (added by the Partnerships and Unlimited Companies (Accounts) Regulations 1993 reg 11(3)).
7 Ie under the Companies Act 1985 s 242 (as substituted and amended): see para 818 ante.
8 Ibid Sch 5 para 28A(3) (added by the Partnerships and Unlimited Companies (Accounts) Regulations 1993 reg 11(3)). For these purposes, 'dealt with on a consolidated basis' means dealt with by the method of full consolidation, the method of proportional consolidation or the equity method of accounting: Partnerships and Unlimited Companies (Accounts) Regulations 1993 reg 2(2) (applied by the Companies Act 1985 Sch 5 para 28A(6) (as added: see note 2 supra).
9 Ie the exemption conferred by the Partnerships and Unlimited Companies (Accounts) Regulations 1993 reg 7: see para 934 post.
10 Companies Act 1985 Sch 5 para 28A(5) (added by the Partnerships and Unlimited Companies (Accounts) Regulations 1993 reg 11(3)).

897. Parent undertaking drawing up accounts for larger group. Where the parent company[1] is itself a subsidiary undertaking[2], the following information must be given with respect to that parent undertaking[3] of the company which heads the largest group of undertakings for which group accounts are drawn up and of which that company is a member and the smallest such group of undertakings[4].

The name of the parent undertaking must be stated[5].

There must be stated:

(1) if the undertaking is incorporated outside Great Britain, the country in which it is incorporated;

(2) if it is unincorporated, the address of its principal place of business[6].

If copies of the group accounts are available to the public, there must also be stated the addresses from which copies of the accounts can be obtained[7].

1 For the meaning of 'parent company' see para 828 ante.
2 For the meaning of 'subsidiary undertaking' see para 828 ante.
3 For the meaning of 'parent undertaking' see para 828 ante.
4 Companies Act 1985 s 231(1), (2), Sch 5 para 30(1) (substituted by the Companies Act 1989 s 6(2), Sch 3).
5 Companies Act 1985 Sch 5 para 30(2) (substituted by the Companies Act 1989 Sch 3).
6 Companies Act 1985 Sch 5 para 30(3) (substituted by the Companies Act 1989 Sch 3; amended by the Companies Act 1985 (Miscellaneous Accounting Amendments) Regulations 1996, SI 1996/189, reg 14(3), Sch 3 paras 1, 24). For the meaning of 'place of business' see para 63 note 1 ante.
7 Companies Act 1985 Sch 5 para 30(4) (substituted by the Companies Act 1989 Sch 3).

898. Identification of ultimate parent company. Where the parent company[1] is itself a subsidiary undertaking[2], the following information must be given with respect to the company, if any, regarded by the directors as being that company's ultimate parent company[3].

The name of that company must be stated[4].

If known to the directors, there must be stated, if that company is incorporated outside Great Britain, the country in which it is incorporated[5].

1 For the meaning of 'parent company' see para 828 ante. For these purposes, 'company' includes any body corporate: Companies Act 1985 s 231(1), (2), Sch 5 para 31(4) (substituted by the Companies Act 1989 s 6(2), Sch 3). For the meaning of 'body corporate' see para 89 note 8 ante.
2 For the meaning of 'subsidiary undertaking' see para 828 ante.
3 Companies Act 1985 Sch 5 para 31(1) (substituted by the Companies Act 1989 Sch 3).
4 Companies Act 1985 Sch 5 para 31(2) (substituted by the Companies Act 1989 Sch 3).
5 Companies Act 1985 Sch 5 para 31(3) (substituted by the Companies Act 1989 Sch 3; amended by the Companies Act 1985 (Miscellaneous Accounting Amendments) Regulations 1996, SI 1996/189, reg 14(3), Sch 3 paras 1, 25).

899. References to shares held by parent company or group. References[1] to shares held by the parent company[2] or the group[3] are to be construed as follows[4].

For the purposes of the statutory provisions relating to information about holdings in subsidiary and other undertakings[5]:

(1) there must be attributed to the parent company any shares held on its behalf by any person; but

(2) there must be treated as not held by the parent company shares held on behalf of a person other than the company[6].

References to shares held by the group are to any shares held by or on behalf of the parent company or any of its subsidiary undertakings[7]; but there must be treated as not held by the group any shares held on behalf of a person other than the parent company or any of its subsidiary undertakings[8].

Shares held by way of security are to be treated as held by the person providing the security:

(a) where apart from the right to exercise them for the purpose of preserving the value of the security, or of realising it, the rights attached to the shares are exercisable only in accordance with his instructions; and

(b) where the shares are held in connection with the granting of loans as part of normal business activities and apart from the right to exercise them for the purpose of preserving the value of the security, or of realising it, the rights attached to the shares are exercisable only in his interests[9].

1 Ie references in the Companies Act 1985 s 231(1), (2), Sch 5 Pt II (paras 14-32) (as substituted and amended): see para 889 et seq ante.
2 For the meaning of 'parent company' see para 828 ante.
3 For the meaning of 'the group' see para 890 note 3 ante.
4 Companies Act 1985 Sch 5 para 32(1) (substituted by the Companies Act 1989 s 6(2), Sch 3).
5 Ie for the purposes of the Companies Act 1985 Sch 5 para 16 (as substituted) (see para 890 ante), Sch 5 para 22(4), (5) (as substituted) (see para 894 ante), Sch 5 paras 23-25 (as substituted) (see para 895 ante).
6 Ibid Sch 5 para 32(2) (substituted by the Companies Act 1989 Sch 3).
7 For the meaning of 'subsidiary undertaking' see para 828 ante.
8 Companies Act 1985 Sch 5 para 32(3) (substituted by the Companies Act 1989 Sch 3).
9 Companies Act 1985 Sch 5 para 32(4) (substituted by the Companies Act 1989 Sch 3).

(vii) Special Cases

A. SMALL AND MEDIUM-SIZED COMPANIES AND GROUPS

(A) *In general*

900. Exemptions for small and medium-sized companies. A company which qualifies as a small or medium-sized company[1] in relation to a financial year[2] is exempt from disclosure with respect to compliance with accounting standards[3] and is entitled to the exemptions[4] with respect to the delivery to the registrar of companies[5] of individual accounts[6] and other documents for that financial year[7].

A company which qualifies as a small company in relation to a financial year is entitled to the statutory exemptions[8] with respect to the preparation of annual accounts for that year if its balance sheet contains, above the signature on behalf of the board[9]:

(1) a statement to the effect that advantage has been taken, in the preparation of the accounts, of special exemptions applicable to small companies; and

(2) a statement of the grounds on which, in the directors' opinion, the company is entitled to those exemptions[10].

A company is not entitled to the above exemptions if it is, or was at any time within the financial year to which the accounts relate a public company[11], a banking[12] or insurance[13] company, or an authorised person under the Financial Services Act 1986[14], or it is or was at any time during that year a member of an ineligible group[15]. A group is ineligible if any of its members is:

(a) a public company or a body corporate[16] which, not being a company, has power under its constitution to offer its shares or debentures to the public and may lawfully exercise that power;

(b) an authorised institution under the Banking Act 1987[17];

(c) an insurance company to which Part II of the Insurance Companies Act 1982[18] applies; or

(d) an authorised person under the Financial Services Act 1986[19].

A parent company[20] is not treated as qualifying as a small company in relation to a financial year unless the group[21] headed by it qualifies as a small group[22], and is not treated as qualifying as a medium-sized company in relation to a financial year unless that group qualifies as a medium-sized group[23].

1 As to qualification of a company as small or medium-sized see para 901 post.

2 For the meaning of 'financial year' see para 806 ante.

3 Ie the requirements of the Companies Act 1985 s 226(3), Sch 4 para 36A (as added): see para 839 ante.

4 Ie the exemptions provided by ibid s 246(1)(b), Sch 8 Pt III (paras 16-26) (as substituted and amended): see paras 911-913 post.

5 Ie under ibid s 242 (as substituted): see para 818 ante.

6 For the meaning of 'individual accounts' see para 816 ante.

7 Companies Act 1985 s 246(1) (substituted by the Companies Act 1989 s 13(1); amended by the Companies Act 1985 (Accounts of Small and Medium-sized Enterprises and Publication of Accounts in ECUs) Regulations 1992, SI 1992/2452, reg 4(2)(a)).

8 Ie the exemptions provided by the Companies Act 1985 Sch 8 Pt I (paras 1-14) (as substituted and amended): see paras 904-910 post.

9 Ie the signature required by ibid s 233 (as substituted): see para 937 post.

10 Ibid s 246(1A) (added by the Companies Act 1985 (Accounts of Small and Medium-sized Enterprises and Publication of Accounts in ECUs) Regulations 1992 reg 4(1); amended by the Companies Act 1985 (Miscellaneous Accounting Amendments) Regulations 1996, SI 1996/189, reg 7(1), (2)(a), (b)). As to the statutory exemption for a company which qualifies as a small company with respect to the preparation of a directors' report see para 1067 post.

11 For the meaning of 'public company' see para 82 ante.

12 For the meaning of 'banking company' see para 117 note 8 ante.

13 For the meaning of 'insurance company' see para 117 note 9 ante.

14 For the meaning of 'authorised person' see para 294 note 7 ante.

15 Companies Act 1985 s 246(3) (substituted by the Companies Act 1989 s 13(1); amended by the Companies Act 1985 (Accounts of Small and Medium-sized Enterprises and Publication of Accounts in ECUs) Regulations 1992 reg 4(2)(c)).

16 For the meaning of 'body corporate' see para 89 note 8 ante.

17 For the meaning of 'authorised institution' see BANKING vol 3(1) (Reissue) para 17.

18 Ie the Insurance Companies Act 1982 Pt II (ss 15-71) (as amended): see INSURANCE vol 25 (Reissue) para 803. The Companies Act 1985 s 246(4) (as substituted: see note 19 infra) has effect as if the reference to an insurance company to which the Insurance Companies Act 1982 Pt II (ss 15-71) (as amended) applies included a reference to an insurance company lawfully carrying on insurance business in the United Kingdom: see the Insurance Companies (Third Insurance Directives) Regulations 1994, SI 1994/1696, reg 68(1), Sch 8 Pt I para 9(1)(a) and INSURANCE.

19 Companies Act 1985 s 246(4) (substituted by the Companies Act 1989 s 13(1)).

20 For the meaning of 'parent company' see para 828 ante.

21 For the meaning of 'group' see para 830 note 8 ante.

22 As to qualification as a small group see para 903 post.

23 Companies Act 1985 s 246(5) (substituted by the Companies Act 1989 s 13(1)). As to qualification as a medium-sized group see para 903 post.

901. Qualification of company as small or medium-sized. A company qualifies as small or medium-sized in relation to a financial year[1] if the qualifying conditions are met:

(1) in the case of the company's first financial year, in that year; and

(2) in the case of any subsequent financial year, in that year and the preceding year[2].

A company is treated as qualifying as small or medium-sized in relation to a financial year:

(a) if it so qualified[3] in relation to the previous financial year or was treated as so qualifying under head (b) below; or

(b) if it was treated as so qualifying in relation to the previous year and the qualifying conditions are met in the year in question[4].

The qualifying conditions are met by a company in a year in which it satisfies two or more of the following requirements[5]:

SMALL COMPANY

1. Turnover[6]	Not more than £2.8 million
2. Balance sheet total[7]	Not more than £1.4 million
3. Number of employees[8]	Not more than 50

MEDIUM-SIZED COMPANY

1. Turnover	Not more than £11.2 million
2. Balance sheet total	Not more than £5.6 million
3. Number of employees	Not more than 250.

For a period which is a company's financial year but not in fact a year the maximum figures for turnover must be proportionately adjusted[9].

1 For the meaning of 'financial year' see para 806 ante.

2 Companies Act 1985 s 247(1) (substituted by the Companies Act 1989 s 13(1)).

3 Ie under the Companies Act 1985 s 247(1) (as substituted): see supra.

4 Ibid s 247(2) (substituted by the Companies Act 1989 s 13(1); amended by the Companies Act 1985 (Accounts of Small and Medium-sized Enterprises and Publication of Accounts in ECUs) Regulations 1992, SI 1992/2452, reg 5(1), (2)).

5 Companies Act 1985 s 247(3) (substituted by the Companies Act 1989 s 13(1); amended by the Companies Act 1985 (Accounts of Small and Medium-sized Enterprises and Publication of Accounts in ECUs) Regulations 1992 reg 5(1), (3), (4)).

6 For the meaning of 'turnover' see para 816 note 5 ante.

7 For these purposes, 'the balance sheet total' means, in relation to a company's financial year: (1) where in the company's accounts Format 1 (as amended) of the balance sheet formats (see para 832 ante) is adopted, the aggregate of the amounts shown in the balance sheet under the headings corresponding to items A to D in that Format; and (2) where Format 2 (as amended) is adopted (see para 833 ante), the aggregate of the amounts shown under the general heading 'Assets': Companies Act 1985 s 247(5) (substituted by the Companies Act 1989 s 13(1)).

8 For these purposes, 'the number of employees' means the average number of persons employed by the company in the year, determined on a monthly basis: Companies Act 1985 s 247(6) (substituted by the Companies Act 1989 s 13(1); amended by the Companies Act 1985 (Miscellaneous Accounting Amendments) Regulations 1996, SI 1996/189, reg 8). That number is to be determined by applying the method of calculation prescribed by the Companies Act 1985 s 226(3), Sch 4 para 56(2), (3) (as amended) (see para 851 ante) for determining the corresponding number required to be stated in a note to the company's accounts: s 247(6) (as so substituted and amended).

9 Ibid s 247(4) (substituted by the Companies Act 1989 s 13(1)).

902. Exemptions for small and medium-sized groups. A parent company[1] need not prepare group accounts[2] for a financial year[3] in relation to which the group[4] headed by that company qualifies as a small or medium-sized group[5] and is not an ineligible group[6].

A group is ineligible if any of its members is:

(1) a public company[7] or body corporate[8] which, not being a company, has power under its constitution to offer its shares or debentures to the public and may lawfully exercise that power;

(2) an authorised institution under the Banking Act 1987[9];

(3) an insurance company to which Part II of the Insurance Companies Act 1982[10] applies; or

(4) an authorised person[11] under the Financial Services Act 1986[12].

1 For the meaning of 'parent company' see para 828 ante.
2 As to group accounts see para 875 et seq ante.
3 For the meaning of 'financial year' see para 806 ante.
4 For the meaning of 'group' see para 830 note 8 ante.
5 As to qualification of a group as small or medium-sized see para 903 post.
6 Companies Act 1985 s 248(1) (substituted by the Companies Act 1989 s 13(3)).
7 For the meaning of 'public company' see para 82 ante.
8 For the meaning of 'body corporate' see para 89 note 8 ante.
9 For the meaning of 'authorised institution' see BANKING vol 3(1) (Reissue) para 17.
10 Ie the Insurance Companies Act 1982 Pt II (ss 15–71) (as amended): see INSURANCE vol 25 (Reissue) para 803. The Companies Act 1985 s 248(2) (as substituted: see note 12 infra) has effect as if the reference to an insurance company to which the Insurance Companies Act 1982 Pt II (ss 15–71) (as amended) applies included a reference to an insurance company lawfully carrying on insurance business in the United Kingdom: see the Insurance Companies (Third Insurance Directives) Regulations 1994, SI 1994/1696, reg 68(1), Sch 8 Pt I para 9(1)(b) and INSURANCE.
11 For the meaning of 'authorised person' see para 294 note 7 ante.
12 Companies Act 1985 s 248(2) (substituted by the Companies Act 1989 s 13(3)).

903. Qualification of group as small or medium-sized. A group[1] qualifies as small or medium-sized in relation to a financial year[2] if the qualifying conditions are met:

(1) in the case of the parent company's[3] first financial year, in that year; and

(2) in the case of any subsequent financial year, in that year and the preceding year[4].

A group is treated as qualifying as small or medium-sized in relation to a financial year:

(a) if it so qualified[5] in relation to the previous financial year or was treated as so qualifying under head (b) below; or

(b) if it was treated as so qualifying in relation to the previous year by virtue of head (a) above and the qualifying conditions are met in the year in question[6].

The qualifying conditions are met by a group in a year in which it satisfies two or more of the following requirements[7]:

SMALL GROUP

1. Aggregate turnover[8]	Not more than £2.8 million net (or £3.36 million gross)
2. Aggregate balance sheet total	Not more than £1.4 million net (or £1.68 million gross)
3. Aggregate number of employees	Not more than 50

MEDIUM-SIZED GROUP

1. Aggregate turnover	Not more than £11.2 million net (or £13.44 million gross)
2. Aggregate balance sheet total	Not more than £5.6 million net (or £6.72 million gross)
3. Aggregate number of employees	Not more than 250.

The aggregate figures must be ascertained by aggregating the relevant figures determined in the prescribed manner[9] for each member of the group[10].

The figures for each subsidiary undertaking[11] must be those included in its accounts for the relevant financial year, that is:

(i) if its financial year ends with that of the parent company, that financial year; and

(ii) if not, its financial year ending last before the end of the financial year of the parent company[12].

If those figures cannot be obtained without disproportionate expense or undue delay, the latest available figures must be taken[13].

1 For the meaning of 'group' see para 830 note 8 ante.
2 For the meaning of 'financial year' see para 806 ante.
3 For the meaning of 'parent company' see para 828 ante.
4 Companies Act 1985 s 249(1) (substituted by the Companies Act 1989 s 13(3)).
5 Ie under the Companies Act 1985 s 249(1) (as substituted): see supra.
6 Ibid s 249(2) (substituted by the Companies Act 1989 s 13(1); amended by the Companies Act 1985 (Accounts of Small and Medium-sized Enterprises and Publication of Accounts in ECUs) Regulations 1992, SI 1992/2452, reg 6(1), (2)).
7 Companies Act 1985 s 249(3) (substituted by the Companies Act 1989 s 13(1); amended by the Companies Act 1985 (Accounts of Small and Medium-sized Enterprises and Publication of Accounts in ECUs) Regulations 1992 reg 6(1), (3), (4)).
8 For the meaning of 'turnover' see para 816 note 5 ante.
9 Ie in accordance with the Companies Act 1985 s 247 (as substituted and amended): see para 901 ante.
10 Ibid s 249(4) (substituted by the Companies Act 1989 s 13(3)). In relation to the aggregate figures for turnover and balance sheet total, 'net' means with the set-offs and other adjustments required by the Companies Act 1985 s 227(4), Sch 4A (as added) (see para 879 et seq ante) in the case of group accounts and 'gross' means without those set-offs and other adjustments; and a company may satisfy the relevant requirements on the basis of either the net or the gross figure: s 249(4) (as so substituted).
11 For the meaning of 'subsidiary undertaking' see para 828 ante.
12 Companies Act 1985 s 249(5) (substituted by the Companies Act 1989 s 13(1)).
13 Companies Act 1985 s 249(6) (substituted by the Companies Act 1989 s 13(1)).

(B) *Preparation of Annual Accounts*

904. Balance sheet; in general. In the case of its individual accounts[1], a small company[2] may, in preparing its balance sheet[3] according to the statutory balance sheet formats[4], apply all or any of the permitted[5] modifications[6]. Where any such modifications are so applied, the statutory provisions relating to the form and contents of a company's accounts[7] must be read as if the balance sheet formats were the formats as modified; and references to the formats and the items in them are to be construed accordingly[8].

The notes on the balance sheet formats continue to apply to items which have been renumbered or combined[9] into other items[10]. For the purpose of the statutory power to adapt or combine items[11], any new item which may be included in a balance sheet[12] is treated as one to which an Arabic number is assigned[13].

1 For the meaning of 'individual accounts' see para 816 ante.
2 As to qualification of a company as small see para 901 ante.
3 For the meaning of 'balance sheet' see para 826 ante.
4 Ie the balance sheet formats set out in the Companies Act 1985 s 226(3), Sch 4 Pt I Section B (as amended): see paras 832, 833 ante.
5 Ie the modifications permitted by ibid s 246, Sch 8 Pt I paras 3, 4 (as added): see paras 905, 906 post.
6 Ibid Sch 8 Pt I Section A paras 1, 2(1) (added by the Companies Act 1985 (Accounts of Small and Medium-sized Enterprises and Publication of Accounts in ECUs) Regulations 1992, SI 1992/2452, reg 4(3), Schedule paras 1(3), 2).
7 Ie the Companies Act 1985 Sch 4 (as amended).
8 Ibid Sch 8 Pt I Section A paras 1, 2(2) (added by the Companies Act 1985 (Accounts of Small and Medium-sized Enterprises and Publication of Accounts in ECUs) Regulations 1992 Schedule paras 1(3), 2).
9 Ie under the Companies Act 1985 Sch 8 Pt I paras 3 or 4 (as added).
10 Ibid Sch 8 Pt I Section A paras 1, 2(3) (added by the Companies Act 1985 (Accounts of Small and Medium-sized Enterprises and Publication of Accounts in ECUs) Regulations 1992 Schedule paras 1(3), 2).
11 Ie the Companies Act 1985 Sch 4 paras 3(3), (4): see para 831 ante.
12 Ie by virtue of ibid Sch 8 Pt I paras 3, 4 (as added).
13 Ibid Sch 8 Pt I Section A paras 1, 2(4) (added by the Companies Act 1985 (Accounts of Small and Medium-sized Enterprises and Publication of Accounts in ECUs) Regulations 1992 Schedule paras 1(3), 2).

905. Balance sheet; Format 1. In the case of the individual accounts[1] of a small company[2], Format 1[3] may be modified as follows[4].

Of the items (development costs etc) required to be shown as sub-items of item B.I (intangible assets) there need only be shown the item 'goodwill' and the other items may be combined in a new item 'other intangible assets', to be shown after 'goodwill'[5].

Of the items (land and other buildings etc) required to be shown as sub-items of item B.II (tangible assets) there need only be shown the item 'land and buildings' and the other items may be combined in a new item 'plant and machinery etc', to be shown after 'land and buildings'[6].

The following items (required to be shown as sub-items of item B.III (investments)) may be combined as follows:

(1) item B.III.1 (shares in group undertakings) may be combined with item B.III.3 (participating interests) in a new item under the heading 'shares in group undertakings and participating interests', to be shown as the first item under the heading 'investments';

(2) item B.III.2 (loans to group undertakings) may be combined with item B.III.4 (loans to undertakings in which the company has a participating interest) in a

new item under the heading 'loans to group undertakings and undertakings in which the company has a participating interest', to be shown after the new item mentioned in head (1) above;

(3) item B.III.6 (other loans) may be combined with item B.III.7 (own shares) in a new item under the heading 'others', to be shown after item B.III.5 (other investments other than loans)[7].

Of the items (raw materials and consumables etc) required to be shown as sub-items of item C.I (stocks) there need only be shown the item 'payments on account' and the other items may be combined in a new item 'stocks', to be shown before 'payments on account'[8].

The following items (required to be shown as sub-items of item C.II (debtors)) may be combined as follows:

(a) item C.II.2 (amounts owed by group undertakings) may be combined with item C.II.3 (amounts owed by undertakings in which the company has a participating interest) in a new item under the heading 'amounts owed by group undertakings and undertakings in which the company has a participating interest', to be shown after item C.II.1 (trade debtors);

(b) item C.II.4 (other debtors) may be combined together with item C.II.5 (called-up share capital not paid) and item C.II.6 (prepayments and accrued income) in a new item under the heading 'others', to be shown after the new item mentioned in head (a) above[9].

Of the items (shares in group undertakings etc) required to be shown as sub-items of item C.III (investments) there need only be shown the item 'shares in group undertakings' and the other items may be combined in a new item 'other investments', to be shown after 'shares in group undertakings'[10].

The following items (required to be shown as sub-items of item E (creditors: amounts falling due within one year)) may be combined as follows:

(i) item E.6 (amounts owed to group undertakings) may be combined with item E.7 (amounts owed to undertakings in which the company has a participating interest) in a new item under the heading 'amounts owed to group undertakings and undertakings in which the company has a participating interest', to be shown after item E.2 (bank loans and overdrafts) and item E.4 (trade creditors); and

(ii) item E.1 (debenture loans), item E.3 (payments received on account), item E.5 (bills of exchange payable), item E.8 (other creditors including taxation and social security) and item E.9 (accruals and deferred income) may be combined in a new item under the heading 'other creditors', to be shown after the new item mentioned in head (i) above[11].

The following items (required to be shown as sub-items of item H (creditors: amounts falling due after more than one year)) may be combined as follows:

(A) item H.6 (amounts owed to group undertakings) may be combined with item H.7 (amounts owed to undertakings in which the company has a participating interest) in a new item under the heading 'amounts owed to group undertakings and undertakings in which the company has a participating interest', to be shown after item H.2 (bank loans and overdrafts) and item H.4 (trade creditors); and

(B) item H.1 (debenture loans), item H.3 (payments received on account), item H.5 (bills of exchange payable), item H.8 (other creditors including taxation and social security) and item H.9 (accruals and deferred income) may be combined in a new item under the heading 'other creditors', to be shown after the new item mentioned in head (A) above[12].

The items (pensions and similar obligations etc) required to be shown as sub-items of item I (provisions for liabilities and charges) and the items (capital redemption reserve etc) required to be shown as sub-items of item K.IV (other reserves) need not be shown[13].

1 For the meaning of 'individual accounts' see para 816 ante.
2 As to qualification of a company as small see para 901 ante.
3 Ie the format set out in the Companies Act 1985 s 226(3), Sch 4 Pt I Section B (as amended): see para 832 ante.
4 Ibid s 246, Sch 8 Pt I Section A paras 1, 3(1) (added by the Companies Act 1985 (Accounts of Small and Medium-sized Enterprises and Publication of Accounts in ECUs) Regulations 1992, SI 1992/2452, reg 4(3), Schedule paras 1(3), 2).
5 Companies Act 1985 Sch 8 Pt I Section A paras 1, 3(2) (added by the Companies Act 1985 (Accounts of Small and Medium-sized Enterprises and Publication of Accounts in ECUs) Regulations 1992 Schedule paras 1(3), 2).
6 Companies Act 1985 Sch 8 Pt I Section A paras 1, 3(3) (added by the Companies Act 1985 (Accounts of Small and Medium-sized Enterprises and Publication of Accounts in ECUs) Regulations 1992 Schedule paras 1(3), 2).
7 Companies Act 1985 Sch 8 Pt I Section A paras 1, 3(4) (added by the Companies Act 1985 (Accounts of Small and Medium-sized Enterprises and Publication of Accounts in ECUs) Regulations 1992 Schedule paras 1(3), 2).
8 Companies Act 1985 Sch 8 Pt I Section A paras 1, 3(5) (added by the Companies Act 1985 (Accounts of Small and Medium-sized Enterprises and Publication of Accounts in ECUs) Regulations 1992 Schedule paras 1(3), 2).
9 Companies Act 1985 Sch 8 Pt I Section A paras 1, 3(6) (added by the Companies Act 1985 (Accounts of Small and Medium-sized Enterprises and Publication of Accounts in ECUs) Regulations 1992 Schedule paras 1(3), 2).
10 Companies Act 1985 Sch 8 Pt I Section A paras 1, 3(7) (added by the Companies Act 1985 (Accounts of Small and Medium-sized Enterprises and Publication of Accounts in ECUs) Regulations 1992 Schedule paras 1(3), 2).
11 Companies Act 1985 Sch 8 Pt I Section A paras 1, 3(8) (added by the Companies Act 1985 (Accounts of Small and Medium-sized Enterprises and Publication of Accounts in ECUs) Regulations 1992 Schedule paras 1(3), 2).
12 Companies Act 1985 Sch 8 Pt I Section A paras 1, 3(9) (added by the Companies Act 1985 (Accounts of Small and Medium-sized Enterprises and Publication of Accounts in ECUs) Regulations 1992 Schedule paras 1(3), 2).
13 Companies Act 1985 Sch 8 Pt I Section A paras 1, 3(10) (added by the Companies Act 1985 (Accounts of Small and Medium-sized Enterprises and Publication of Accounts in ECUs) Regulations 1992 Schedule paras 1(3), 2).

906. Balance sheet; Format 2. In the case of the individual accounts[1] of a small company[2], Format 2[3] may be modified as follows[4].

Of the items (development costs etc) required to be shown as sub-items of item B.I (intangible assets) under the general heading 'ASSETS' there need only be shown the item 'goodwill' and the other items may be combined in a new item 'other intangible assets', to be shown after 'goodwill'[5].

Of the items (land and buildings etc) required to be shown as sub-items of item B.II (tangible assets) under the general heading 'ASSETS' there need only be shown the item 'land and buildings' and the other items may be combined in a new item 'plant and machinery etc', to be shown after 'land and buildings'[6].

The following items (required to be shown as sub-items of item B.III (investments) under the general heading 'ASSETS') may be combined as follows:

(1) item B.III.1 (shares in group undertakings) may be combined with item B.III.3 (participating interests) in a new item under the heading 'shares in group

undertakings and participating interests', to be shown as the first item under the heading 'investments';

(2) item B.III.2 (loans to group undertakings) may be combined with item B.III.4 (loans to undertakings in which the company has a participating interest) in a new item under the heading 'loans to group undertakings and undertakings in which the company has a participating interest', to be shown after the new item mentioned in head (1) above; and

(3) item B.III.6 (other loans) may be combined with item B.III.7 (own shares) in a new item under the heading 'others', to be shown after item B.III.5 (other investments other than loans)[7].

Of the items (raw materials and consumables etc) required to be shown as sub-items of item C.I (stocks) under the general heading 'ASSETS' there need only be shown the item 'payments on account' and the other items may be combined in a new item 'stocks', to be shown before 'payments on account'[8].

The following items (required to be shown as sub-items of item C.II (debtors) under the general heading 'ASSETS') may be combined as follows:

(a) item C.II.2 (amounts owed by group undertakings) may be combined with item C.II.3 (amounts owed by undertakings in which the company has a participating interest) in a new item under the heading 'amounts owed by group undertakings and undertakings in which the company has a participating interest', to be shown after item C.II.1 (trade debtors);

(b) item C.II.4 (other debtors) may be combined together with item C.II.5 (called-up share capital not paid) and item C.II.6 (prepayments and accrued income) in a new item under the heading 'others', to be shown after the new item mentioned in head (a) above[9].

Of the items (shares in group undertakings etc) required to be shown as sub-items of item C.III (investments) under the general heading 'ASSETS' there need only be shown the item 'shares in group undertakings' and the other items may be combined in a new item 'other investments', to be shown after 'shares in group undertakings'[10].

The following items (required to be shown as sub-items of item C (creditors) under the general heading 'LIABILITIES') may be combined as follows:

(i) item C.6 (amounts owed to group undertakings) may be combined with item C.7 (amounts owed to undertakings in which the company has a participating interest) in a new item under the heading 'amounts owed to group undertakings and undertakings in which the company has a participating interest', to be shown after the items for 'bank loans and overdrafts' and 'trade creditors'; and

(ii) item C.1 (debenture loans), item C.3 (payments received on account), item C.5 (bills of exchange payable), item C.8 (other creditors including taxation and social security) and item C.9 (accruals and deferred income) may be combined in a new item under the heading 'other creditors', to be shown after the new item mentioned in head (i) above[11].

The items (pensions and similar obligations etc) required to be shown as sub-items of item B (provisions for liabilities and charges) under the general heading 'LIABIL-ITIES' and the items (capital redemption reserve etc) required to be shown as sub-items of item A.IV (other reserves) under the general heading 'LIABILITIES' need not be shown[12].

1 For the meaning of 'individual accounts' see para 816 ante.
2 As to qualification of a company as small see para 901 ante.
3 Ie the format set out in the Companies Act 1985 s 226(3), Sch 4 Pt I Section B (as amended) para 833 ante.

4 Ibid s 246, Sch 8 Pt I Section A paras 1, 4(1) (added by the Companies Act 1985 (Accounts of Small and Medium–sized Enterprises and Publication of Accounts in ECUs) Regulations 1992, SI 1992/2452, reg 4(3), Schedule paras 1(3), 2).
5 Companies Act 1985 Sch 8 Pt I Section A paras 1, 4(2) (added by the Companies Act 1985 (Accounts of Small and Medium–sized Enterprises and Publication of Accounts in ECUs) Regulations 1992 Schedule paras 1(3), 2).
6 Companies Act 1985 Sch 8 Pt I Section A paras 1, 4(3) (added by the Companies Act 1985 (Accounts of Small and Medium–sized Enterprises and Publication of Accounts in ECUs) Regulations 1992 Schedule paras 1(3), 2).
7 Companies Act 1985 Sch 8 Pt I Section A paras 1, 4(4) (added by the Companies Act 1985 (Accounts of Small and Medium–sized Enterprises and Publication of Accounts in ECUs) Regulations 1992 Schedule paras 1(3), 2).
8 Companies Act 1985 Sch 8 Pt I Section A paras 1, 4(5) (added by the Companies Act 1985 (Accounts of Small and Medium–sized Enterprises and Publication of Accounts in ECUs) Regulations 1992 Schedule paras 1(3), 2).
9 Companies Act 1985 Sch 8 Pt I Section A paras 1, 4(6) (added by the Companies Act 1985 (Accounts of Small and Medium–sized Enterprises and Publication of Accounts in ECUs) Regulations 1992 Schedule paras 1(3), 2).
10 Companies Act 1985 Sch 8 Pt I Section A paras 1, 4(7) (added by the Companies Act 1985 (Accounts of Small and Medium–sized Enterprises and Publication of Accounts in ECUs) Regulations 1992 Schedule paras 1(3), 2).
11 Companies Act 1985 Sch 8 Pt I Section A paras 1, 4(8) (added by the Companies Act 1985 (Accounts of Small and Medium–sized Enterprises and Publication of Accounts in ECUs) Regulations 1992 Schedule paras 1(3), 2).
12 Companies Act 1985 Sch 8 Pt I Section A paras 1, 4(9) (added by the Companies Act 1985 (Accounts of Small and Medium–sized Enterprises and Publication of Accounts in ECUs) Regulations 1992 Schedule paras 1(3), 2).

907. Notes on balance sheet formats. In the case of the individual accounts[1] of a small company[2] with regard to the notes on the balance sheet formats[3], a small company:

(1) in the case both of Format 1 and of Format 2, need not comply with the requirements of note (5)[4] if it discloses in the notes to its accounts the aggregate amount included under 'debtors' (item C.II in Format 1 and item C.II under the general heading 'ASSETS' in Format 2) falling due after more than one year; and

(2) in the case of Format 2, need not comply with the requirements of note (13)[5] if it discloses in the notes to its accounts the aggregate amount included under 'creditors' (item C under the general heading 'LIABILITIES') falling due within one year and the aggregate amount falling due after one year[6].

1 For the meaning of 'individual accounts' see para 816 ante.
2 As to qualification of a company as small see para 901 ante.
3 Ie the formats set out in the Companies Act 1985 s 226(3), Sch 4 Pt I Section B (as amended): see paras 832, 833 ante.
4 See para 832 note 10 ante.
5 See para 833 note 17 ante.
6 Companies Act 1985 s 246, Sch 8 Pt I Section A paras 1, 5 (added by the Companies Act 1985 (Accounts of Small and Medium–sized Enterprises and Publication of Accounts in ECUs) Regulations 1992, SI 1992/2452, reg 4(3), Schedule paras 1(3), 2).

908. Notes to the accounts. In the case of its individual accounts[1], a small company[2] need not set out in the notes thereto any information required by the following items:

(1) contingent rights to allotment of shares[3];
(2) debentures[4];

(3) land and buildings[5];
(4) provision for taxation[6];
(5) particulars of debts[7];
(6) the nature of security given for debts[8];
(7) loans provided by way of financial assistance for the purchase of its own shares[9];
(8) dividend[10];
(9) a separate statement of certain items of income and expenditure[11];
(10) particulars of tax[12];
(11) particulars of staff[13].

Where any assets are included in the accounts of a small company at a value determined by the application of a permitted method[14], the notes to the accounts need not disclose certain information[15].

A small company may comply with the provisions relating to the disclosure of debts repayable in more than five years[16] as if those provisions stated that the information required by them was to be given in aggregate for all items shown under 'creditors' in the company's balance sheet rather than in respect of each such item[17].

A small company need not give particulars[18] of turnover[19]. If, however, the company has supplied geographical markets outside the United Kingdom during the financial year in question, the notes to the accounts must state the percentage of its turnover that, in the opinion of the company's directors, is attributable to those markets[20].

A small company need not comply with the provisions[21] relating to dealings with or interests in group undertakings[22]; nor need it give information relating to the following matters[23]:

(a) the financial years of subsidiary undertakings[24];
(b) the valuation of investment in subsidiary undertakings by the equity method[25];
(c) the breakdown of the aggregate amount of directors' emoluments[26];
(d) details of the chairman's and directors' emoluments[27];
(e) pensions of directors and past directors[28].

1 For the meaning of 'individual accounts' see para 816 ante.
2 As to qualification of a company as small see para 901 ante.
3 Ie the Companies Act 1985 s 226(3), Sch 4 para 40: see para 841 ante.
4 Ie ibid Sch 4 para 41 (as amended): see para 841 ante.
5 Ie ibid Sch 4 para 44: see para 842 ante.
6 Ie ibid Sch 4 para 47 (as substituted): see para 844 ante.
7 Ie ibid Sch 4 para 48(2): see para 845 ante.
8 Ie ibid Sch 4 para 48(4)(b): see para 845 ante.
9 Ie ibid Sch 4 para 51(2): see para 847 ante.
10 Ie ibid Sch 4 para 51(3) (sic). Schedule 4 para 51(3) is, however, repealed by the Companies Act 1985 (Miscellaneous Accounting Amendments) Regulations 1996, SI 1996/189, reg 14(1), Sch 1 paras 1, 10.
11 Ie the Companies Act 1985 Sch 4 para 53 (as amended): see para 848 ante.
12 Ie ibid Sch 4 para 54 (as amended): see para 849 ante.
13 Ibid s 246, Sch 8 Pt I Section A paras 1, 6 (added by the Companies Act 1985 (Accounts of Small and Medium-sized Enterprises and Publication of Accounts in ECUs) Regulations 1992, SI 1992/2452, reg 4(3), Schedule paras 1(3), 2). The particulars of staff are otherwise required by the Companies Act 1985 Sch 4 para 56 (as amended) (see para 851 ante): Sch 8 Pt I Section A paras 1, 6 (as so added).
14 Ie a method permitted by ibid Sch 4 para 27: see para 812 ante.
15 Ibid Sch 8 Pt I Section A paras 1, 7 (added by the Companies Act 1985 (Accounts of Small and Medium-sized Enterprises and Publication of Accounts in ECUs) Regulations 1992 Schedule paras 1(3), 2). The information which need not be disclosed is any information required by the Companies Act 1985 Sch 4 para 27(3) (see para 812 ante): Sch 8 Pt I Section A paras 1, 7 (as so added).
16 Ie ibid Sch 4 para 48(1) (as substituted): see para 845 ante.

17 Ibid Sch 8 Pt I Section A paras 1, 8 (added by the Companies Act 1985 (Accounts of Small and Medium-sized Enterprises and Publication of Accounts in ECUs) Regulations 1992 Schedule paras 1(3), 2).

18 Ie the information required by the Companies Act 1985 Sch 4 para 55 (as amended): see para 850 ante.

19 Ibid Sch 8 Pt I Section A paras 1, 9(1) (added by the Companies Act 1985 (Accounts of Small and Medium-sized Enterprises and Publication of Accounts in ECUs) Regulations 1992 Schedule paras 1(3), 2). For the meaning of 'turnover' see para 816 note 5 ante.

20 Companies Act 1985 Sch 8 Pt I Section A paras 1, 9(2) (added by the Companies Act 1985 (Accounts of Small and Medium-sized Enterprises and Publication of Accounts in ECUs) Regulations 1992 Schedule paras 1(3), 2). For these purposes, the Companies Act 1985 Sch 4 para 55(3) (as amended) (see para 850 ante) applies: Sch 8 Pt I Section A paras 1, 9(3) (added by the Companies Act 1985 (Accounts of Small and Medium-sized Enterprises and Publication of Accounts in ECUs) Regulations 1992 Schedule paras 1(3), 2).

21 Ie the Companies Act 1985 Sch 4 para 59 (sic). Schedule 4 para 59 is, however, repealed by the Companies Act 1985 (Miscellaneous Accounting Amendments) Regulations 1996 Sch 1 paras 1, 15.

22 Companies Act 1985 Sch 8 Pt I Section A paras 1, 10 (added by the Companies Act 1985 (Accounts of Small and Medium-sized Enterprises and Publication of Accounts in ECUs) Regulations 1992 Schedule paras 1(3), 2).

23 Companies Act 1985 Sch 8 Pt I Section A paras 1, 11, 12 (added by the Companies Act 1985 (Accounts of Small and Medium-sized Enterprises and Publication of Accounts in ECUs) Regulations 1992 Schedule paras 1(3), 2).

24 Ie the Companies Act 1985 s 231, Sch 5 para 4 (as substituted): see para 857 ante.

25 Ie ibid Sch 5 para 5(2) (sic). Schedule 5 para 5(2) is, however, repealed by the Companies Act 1985 (Miscellaneous Accounting Amendments) Regulations 1996 reg 14(3), Sch 3 paras 1, 5.

26 Ie the Companies Act 1985 s 232, Sch 6 para 1(3) (as added): see para 866 ante.

27 Ie ibid Sch 6 paras 2-5 (as added): see para 867 ante.

28 Ie ibid Sch 6 para 7 (as added): see para 868 ante.

909. Group accounts. Where a small company[1] has prepared individual accounts[2] for a financial year[3] with any of the statutory exemptions[4] and is preparing group accounts[5] in respect of the same year, it may prepare those group accounts in accordance with those statutory exemptions[6].

In preparing the consolidated balance sheet the company:

(1) when using either balance sheet format[7], must not combine item B.III.1 (shares in group undertakings) with item B.III.3 (participating interests); and

(2) when applying specified exemptions[8], must read the reference to the new item[9] as a reference to the two items which will in each case replace[10] item B.III.3[11].

The general rule relating to the form and content of group accounts[12] has effect subject to the exemptions in question[13].

1 As to qualification of a company as small see para 901 ante.

2 For the meaning of 'individual accounts' see para 816 ante.

3 For the meaning of 'financial year' see para 806 ante.

4 Ie any exemptions set out in the Companies Act 1985 s 246, Sch 8 Section A (paras 1-12) (as added): see paras 904-908 ante.

5 As to group accounts see para 875 et seq ante.

6 Companies Act 1985 Sch 8 Pt I Section B para 13(1) (added by the Companies Act 1985 (Accounts of Small and Medium-sized Enterprises and Publication of Accounts in ECUs) Regulations 1992, SI 1992/2452, reg 4(3), Schedule paras 1(3), 2).

7 Ie either balance sheet format set out in the Companies Act 1985 s 226(3), Sch 4 Pt I Section B (as amended): see paras 832, 833 ante.

8 Ie the exemptions set out in ibid Sch 8 Pt I Section A para 3(4)(b) (as added) (see para 905 ante) or para 4(4)(b) (as added) (see para 906 ante).

9 Ie the new item mentioned in ibid Sch 8 Pt I Section A para 3(4)(a) (as added) (see para 905 ante) or para 4(4)(a) (as added) (see para 906 ante).

10 Ie by virtue of ibid s 227(4), Sch 4A para 21 (as added): see para 886 ante.

11 Ibid Sch 8 Pt I Section B para 13(2) (added by the Companies Act 1985 (Accounts of Small and Medium-sized Enterprises and Publication of Accounts in ECUs) Regulations 1992 Schedule paras 1(3), 2).

12 Ie the Companies Act 1985 Sch 4A para 1(1) (as added): see para 879 ante.

13 Ibid Sch 8 Pt I Section B para 13(3) (added by the Companies Act 1985 (Accounts of Small and Medium-sized Enterprises and Publication of Accounts in ECUs) Regulations 1992 Schedule paras 1(3), 2).

910. Supplementary provisions. The following provisions apply where a small company[1] has prepared annual accounts[2] in accordance with any of the statutory exemptions[3].

The annual accounts of the company are not deemed, by reason only of the fact that advantage has been taken of any of those statutory exemptions, not to give a true and fair view[4] as required by the Companies Act 1985[5].

Where a company is entitled to, and has taken advantage of, any of those statutory exemptions, the auditors are only required[6] to state whether in their opinion the annual accounts have been properly prepared in accordance with the provisions of the Companies Act 1985 relating to small companies[7].

1 As to qualification of a company as small see para 901 ante.

2 For the meaning of 'annual accounts' see para 816 ante.

3 Companies Act 1985 s 246, Sch 8 Pt I Section C para 14(1) (added by the Companies Act 1985 (Accounts of Small and Medium-sized Enterprises and Publication of Accounts in ECUs) Regulations 1992, SI 1992/2452, reg 4(3), Schedule paras 1(3), 2).

4 For the meaning of 'true and fair view' see para 816 note 5 ante.

5 Companies Act 1985 Sch 8 Pt I Section C para 14(2) (added by the Companies Act 1985 (Accounts of Small and Medium-sized Enterprises and Publication of Accounts in ECUs) Regulations 1992 Schedule paras 1(3), 2).

6 Ie by the Companies Act 1985 s 235(2) (as substituted): see para 1059 post.

7 Ibid Sch 8 Pt I Section C para 14(3) (added by the Companies Act 1985 (Accounts of Small and Medium-sized Enterprises and Publication of Accounts in ECUs) Regulations 1992 Schedule paras 1(3), 2).

(C) *Delivery of Accounts*

911. Small companies. A small company[1] may deliver a copy of an abbreviated version of the full balance sheet, showing only those items to which a letter or Roman number is assigned in the statutory balance sheet format adopted[2] but in other respects corresponding to the full balance sheet[3]. If a copy of the abbreviated balance sheet is delivered, there must be disclosed in it or in a note to the company's accounts delivered:

(1) the aggregate of the amounts required by note (5)[4] of the notes to the balance sheet formats to be shown separately for each item included under debtors (amounts falling due after one year); and

(2) the aggregate of the amounts required by note (13)[5] to be shown separately for each item included under creditors in Format 2 (amounts falling due within one year or after more than one year)[6].

The statutory provisions[7] relating to the signing of the copy of the balance sheet delivered to the registrar of companies apply to the copy of an abbreviated balance sheet delivered in accordance with the above provisions[8].

A copy of the company's profit and loss account need not be delivered[9], nor a copy of the directors' report[10].

Of the information required[11] to be given in notes to accounts if not given in the accounts themselves only the information relating to the following matters need be given[12]:

(a) accounting policies[13];
(b) share capital[14];
(c) particulars of allotments[15];
(d) fixed assets[16];
(e) particulars of debts[17];
(f) basis of conversion of foreign currency amounts into sterling[18];
(g) corresponding amounts for the previous financial year[19].

Of the information required[20] to be given in notes to the accounts, the information relating to the following matters need not be given[21]:

(i) financial years of subsidiary undertakings[22];
(ii) additional information about subsidiary undertakings[23];
(iii) shares and debentures of a company held by its subsidiary undertakings[24];
(iv) arrangements attracting merger relief[25].

Of the information required[26] to be given in notes to the accounts the information relating to directors' and the chairman's emoluments, pensions and compensation[27] need not be given[28]. Nor need the amount of the auditors' remuneration[29] be given[30].

  1 As to qualification of a company as small see para 901 ante.
  2 Ie under the Companies Act 1985 s 226(3), Sch 4 Pt I (as amended): see paras 832, 833 ante.
  3 Ibid s 246, Sch 8 Pt III Section A para 17(1) (substituted by the Companies Act 1989 s 13(2), Sch 9; renumbered by the Companies Act 1985 (Accounts of Small and Medium-sized Enterprises and Publication of Accounts in ECUs) Regulations 1992, SI 1992/2452, reg 4(3), Schedule para 1(2)).
  4 See para 832 note 10 ante.
  5 See para 833 note 17 ante.
  6 Companies Act 1985 Sch 8 Pt III Section A para 17(2) (substituted by the Companies Act 1989 Sch 9; renumbered by the Companies Act 1985 (Accounts of Small and Medium-sized Enterprises and Publication of Accounts in ECUs) Regulations 1992 Schedule para 1(2)).
  7 Ie the Companies Act 1985 s 233 (as substituted): see para 937 post.
  8 Ibid Sch 8 Pt III Section A para 17(3) (substituted by the Companies Act 1989 Sch 9; renumbered by the Companies Act 1985 (Accounts of Small and Medium-sized Enterprises and Publication of Accounts in ECUs) Regulations 1992 Schedule para 1(2)).
  9 Companies Act 1985 Sch 8 Pt III Section A para 18 (substituted by the Companies Act 1989 Sch 9; renumbered by the Companies Act 1985 (Accounts of Small and Medium-sized Enterprises and Publication of Accounts in ECUs) Regulations 1992 Schedule para 1(2)).
 10 Companies Act 1985 Sch 8 Pt III Section A para 20 (substituted by the Companies Act 1989 Sch 9; renumbered by the Companies Act 1985 (Accounts of Small and Medium-sized Enterprises and Publication of Accounts in ECUs) Regulations 1992 Schedule para 1(2)).
 11 Ie by the Companies Act 1985 Sch 4 Pt III (as amended): see para 838 et seq ante.
 12 Ibid Sch 8 Pt III Section A para 19(1) (substituted by the Companies Act 1989 Sch 9; renumbered and amended by the Companies Act 1985 (Accounts of Small and Medium-sized Enterprises and Publication of Accounts in ECUs) Regulations 1992 Schedule paras 1(2), 4(1), (2)).
 13 Ie the Companies Act 1985 Sch 4 para 36: see para 839 ante.
 14 Ie ibid Sch 4 para 38: see para 841 ante.
 15 Ie ibid Sch 4 para 39 (as amended): see para 841 ante.
 16 Ie ibid Sch 4 para 42, so far as it relates to those items to which a letter or Roman number is assigned in the balance sheet format adopted.
 17 Ie ibid Sch 4 para 48(1) (as substituted), Sch 4 para 48(4)(a): see para 845 ante.
 18 Ie ibid Sch 4 para 58(1): see para 840 ante.
 19 Ie ibid Sch 4 para 58(2), so far as it relates to amounts stated in a notice to the company's accounts by virtue of a requirement of Sch 4 (as amended) or under any other provision of the Companies Act 1985: see para 840 ante.
 20 Ie by ibid s 231, Sch 5 (as substituted and amended): see para 854 et seq ante.

21 Ibid Sch 8 Pt III Section A para 19(2) (substituted by the Companies Act 1989 Sch 9; renumbered by the Companies Act 1985 (Accounts of Small and Medium-sized Enterprises and Publication of Accounts in ECUs) Regulations 1992 Schedule para 1(2)).
22 Ie the Companies Act 1985 Sch 5 para 4 (as substituted): see para 857 ante.
23 Ie ibid Sch 5 para 5 (sic). Schedule 5 para 5 is, however, repealed by the Companies Act 1985 (Miscellaneous Accounting Amendments) Regulations 1996, SI 1996/189, reg 14(3), Sch 3 paras 1, 5.
24 Ie the Companies Act 1985 Sch 5 para 6 (as substituted): see para 858 ante.
25 Ie ibid Sch 5 para 10 (sic). Schedule 5 para 10 is, however, repealed by the Companies Act 1985 (Miscellaneous Accounting Amendments) Regulations 1996 Sch 3 paras 1, 10.
26 Ie by the Companies Act 1985 s 232, Sch 6 (as amended): see para 866 et seq ante.
27 Ie ibid Sch 6 Pt I (paras 1-14) (as added): see para 865 et seq ante.
28 Ibid Sch 8 Pt III Section A para 19(3) (substituted by the Companies Act 1989 Sch 9; renumbered by the Companies Act 1985 (Accounts of Small and Medium-sized Enterprises and Publication of Accounts in ECUs) Regulations 1992 Schedule para 1(2)).
29 Ie the information required by the Companies Act 1985 s 390A(3) (as substituted): see para 1042 post.
30 Ibid Sch 8 Pt III Section A para 19(4) (added by the Companies Act 1985 (Accounts of Small and Medium-sized Enterprises and Publication of Accounts in ECUs) Regulations 1992 Schedule paras 1(2), 4(1), (3)).

912. Medium-sized companies. A medium-sized company[1] may deliver a profit and loss account in which specified items listed in the profit and loss account formats[2] are combined as one item under the heading 'gross profit and loss'[3].

Particulars of turnover[4] need not be given[5].

1 As to qualification of a company as medium-sized see para 901 ante.
2 Ie the formats set out in the Companies Act 1985 s 262(3), Sch 4 Pt I (as amended): see paras 834-837 ante. These items are:
   (1) items 1, 2, 3 and 6 in Format 1 (see para 834 ante);
   (2) items 1-5 in Format 2 (see para 835 ante);
   (3) items A.1, B.1, B.2 in Format 3 (see para 836 ante); and
   (4) items A.1, A.2 and B.1-B.4 in Format 4 (see para 837 ante).
3 Ibid s 246, Sch 8 Pt III Section B para 21 (substituted by the Companies Act 1989 s 13(2), Sch 9; renumbered by the Companies Act 1985 (Accounts of Small and Medium-sized Enterprises and Publication of Accounts in ECUs) Regulations 1992, SI 1992/2452, reg 4(3), Schedule para 1(2)).
4 Ie the information required by the Companies Act 1985 Sch 4 para 55 (as amended): see para 850 ante.
5 Ibid Sch 8 Pt III Section B para 22 (substituted by the Companies Act 1989 Sch 9; renumbered by the Companies Act 1985 (Accounts of Small and Medium-sized Enterprises and Publication of Accounts in ECUs) Regulations 1992 Schedule para 1(2)).

913. Supplementary provisions. Where the directors of a small[1] or medium-sized[2] company take advantage of the relevant statutory exemptions[3], the company's balance sheet must contain:

(1) a statement that advantage is taken of the relevant statutory exemptions; and
(2) a statement of the grounds on which, in the directors' opinion, the company is entitled to those exemptions[4].

The statements must appear in the balance sheet immediately above the required[5] signature[6].

If the directors of a company propose to take advantage of the relevant statutory exemptions, it is the auditors' duty to provide them with a report stating whether in their opinion the company is entitled to those exemptions and whether the documents to be proposed to be delivered are properly prepared[7]. The accounts delivered must be accompanied by a special report of the auditors stating that in their opinion the company is entitled to the exemptions claimed in the directors' statement and the accounts to be delivered are properly prepared[8]. In such a case a copy of the auditors' report[9] need not be delivered separately, but the full text of it must be reproduced in the special report; and, if the report is qualified[10], there must be included in the special report any further material necessary to understand the qualification[11]. The statutory provisions relating to signature of the auditors' report[12] apply[13] to such a special report[14].

Where advantage is taken of the relevant statutory exemptions, the statutory requirements in connection with the publication of accounts[15] have effect with the following adaptations[16]. Accounts duly delivered[17] and accounts in the form in which they would otherwise be required to be delivered[18] are[19] both 'statutory accounts'[20]; and references to the auditors' report[21] are to be read, in relation to accounts duly delivered[22] as references to the special report[23].

1   As to qualification of a company as small see para 901 ante.
2   As to qualification of a company as medium-sized see para 901 ante.
3   Ie the exemptions conferred by the Companies Act 1985 s 246, Sch 8 Pt III Section A or Section B (as substituted and renumbered): see paras 911, 912 respectively ante.
4   Ibid Sch 8 Pt III Section C para 23(1) (substituted by the Companies Act 1989 s 13(2), Sch 9; renumbered and amended by the Companies Act 1985 (Accounts of Small and Medium-sized Enterprises and Publication of Accounts in ECUs) Regulations 1992, SI 1992/2452, reg 4(3), Schedule paras 1(2), 4(1), (4), (5)). The Companies Act 1985 Sch 8 paras 23, 24 (as substituted and renumbered) do not apply where the company is exempt by virtue of s 250 (as substituted and amended) (dormant companies: see para 1058 post) from the obligation to appoint auditors: Sch 8 Pt III Section C para 25 (substituted by the Companies Act 1989 Sch 9; renumbered and amended by the Companies Act 1985 (Accounts of Small and Medium-sized Enterprises and Publication of Accounts in ECUs) Regulations 1992 Schedule paras 1(2), 4(7)). Nor does the Companies Act 1985 Sch 8 para 24 (as substituted) apply where the company is exempt by virtue of s 249A (as added) (certain categories of small companies: see para 1054 post) from the obligation to appoint auditors: Sch 8 para 25A (added by the Companies Act 1985 (Audit Exemption) Regulations 1994, SI 1994/1935, reg 4, Sch 1 para 5).
5   Ie the signature required by the Companies Act 1985 s 233 (as substituted): see para 937 post.
6   Ibid Sch 8 Pt III Section C para 23(2) (substituted by the Companies Act 1989 Sch 9; renumbered and amended by the Companies Act 1985 (Accounts of Small and Medium-sized Enterprises and Publication of Accounts in ECUs) Regulations 1992 Schedule paras 1(2), 4(6); amended by the Companies Act 1985 (Miscellaneous Accounting Amendments) Regulations 1996, SI 1996/189, reg 15(4)(b)).
7   Companies Act 1985 Sch 8 Pt III Section C para 24(1) (substituted by the Companies Act 1989 Sch 9; renumbered and amended by the Companies Act 1985 (Accounts of Small and Medium-sized Enterprises and Publication of Accounts in ECUs) Regulations 1992 Schedule paras 1(2), 4(4)). See also note 4 supra.
8   Companies Act 1985 Sch 8 Pt III Section C para 24(2) (substituted by the Companies Act 1989 Sch 9; renumbered by the Companies Act 1985 (Accounts of Small and Medium-sized Enterprises and Publication of Accounts in ECUs) Regulations 1992 Schedule paras 1(2), 4(4)).
9   Ie under the Companies Act 1985 s 235 (as substituted): see para 1059 post.
10 For these purposes, 'qualified', in relation to an auditors' report, means that the report does not state the auditors' unqualified opinion that the accounts have been properly prepared in accordance with the Companies Act 1985 or, in the case of an undertaking not required to prepare accounts in accordance with that Act, under any corresponding legislation under which it is required to prepare accounts: s 262(1) (substituted by the Companies Act 1989 s 22).
11 Companies Act 1985 Sch 8 Pt III Section C para 24(3) (substituted by the Companies Act 1989 Sch 9; renumbered by the Companies Act 1985 (Accounts of Small and Medium-sized Enterprises and Publication of Accounts in ECUs) Regulations 1992 Schedule paras 1(2), 4(4)).
12 Ie the Companies Act 1985 s 236 (as substituted): see para 1060 post.
13 Ie as it applies to a report under ibid s 235 (as substituted).
14 Ibid Sch 8 Pt III Section C para 24(4) (substituted by the Companies Act 1989 Sch 9; renumbered by the Companies Act 1985 (Accounts of Small and Medium-sized Enterprises and Publication of Accounts in ECUs) Regulations 1992 Schedule paras 1(2), 4(4)).
15 Ie the Companies Act 1985 s 240 (as substituted and amended): see para 938 post.
16 Ibid Sch 8 Pt III Section C para 26(1) (substituted by the Companies Act 1989 Sch 9; renumbered and amended by the Companies Act 1985 (Accounts of Small and Medium-sized Enterprises and Publication of Accounts in ECUs) Regulations 1992 Schedule paras 1(2), 4(4)).
17 Ie in accordance with the Companies Act 1985 Sch 8 Pt III (paras 16-26) (as substituted and amended): see paras 911, 912 ante.

18 Ie apart from ibid Sch 8 Pt III (paras 16–26) (as substituted and amended).

19 Ie for the purposes of ibid s 240 (as substituted).

20 Ibid Sch 8 Pt III Section C para 26(2) (substituted by the Companies Act 1989 Sch 9; renumbered and amended by the Companies Act 1985 (Accounts of Small and Medium-sized Enterprises and Publication of Accounts in ECUs) Regulations 1992 Schedule paras 1(2), 4(8)).

21 Ie in the Companies Act 1985 s 235 (as substituted).

22 See note 17 supra.

23 Companies Act 1985 Sch 8 Pt III Section C para 26(3) (substituted by the Companies Act 1989 Sch 9; renumbered and amended by the Companies Act 1985 (Accounts of Small and Medium-sized Enterprises and Publication of Accounts in ECUs) Regulations 1992 Schedule paras 1(2), 4(8); amended by the Companies Act 1985 (Miscellaneous Accounting Amendments) Regulations 1996 reg 15(4)(c)). For these purposes, 'the special report' means the special report under the Companies Act 1985 Sch 8 para 24 (as substituted and renumbered) (see supra): Sch 8 para 26(3) (as so substituted, renumbered and amended).

B. LISTED PUBLIC COMPANIES

(A) *Summary Financial Statements*

914. Provision of summary financial statement to shareholders. A public company[1] whose shares or debentures, or any class of whose shares or debentures, are listed[2] need not, in such cases as may be specified in regulations made by the Secretary of State, and provided that any conditions so specified are complied with, send copies of the specified documents[3] to entitled persons[4], but may instead send them a summary financial statement[5]. Copies of those documents must, however, be sent to any entitled person who wishes to receive them; and the Secretary of State may by regulations make provision as to the manner in which it is to be ascertained, whether before or after he becomes an entitled person, whether an entitled person wishes to receive them[6].

The summary financial statement must be derived from the company's annual accounts[7] and the directors' report[8] and must be in such form and contain such information as may be specified by regulations made by the Secretary of State[9].

Every summary financial statement must:

(1) state that it is only a summary of information in the company's annual accounts and the directors' report;

(2) contain a statement by the company's auditors of their opinion as to whether the summary financial statement is consistent with those accounts and that report and complies with the requirements of these provisions and the regulations made thereunder;

(3) state whether the auditors' report[10] on the annual accounts was unqualified or qualified[11] and, if it was qualified, set out the report in full together with any further material needed to understand the qualification;

(4) state whether the auditors' report on the annual accounts contained a statement that the accounting records or returns are inadequate or that the accounts do not agree with the records and returns[12] or that the auditors failed to obtain the necessary information and explanations[13] and, if so, set out the statement in full[14].

If default is made in complying with the above provisions or regulations made thereunder, the company, and every officer of it who is in default, is guilty of an offence and liable on summary conviction to a fine not exceeding one-fifth of the statutory maximum[15].

The statutory requirements in connection with the publication of accounts[16] do not apply in relation to the provision to entitled persons of a summary financial statement in accordance with the above provisions[17].

1 For the meaning of 'public company' see para 82 ante.
2 For these purposes, 'listed' means admitted to the Official List of The International Stock Exchange of the United Kingdom and the Republic of Ireland Limited (see para 281 ante): Companies Act 1985 s 251(1) (substituted by the Companies Act 1989 s 15; amended by the Companies Act 1985 (Amendment of Sections 250 and 251) Regulations 1992, SI 1992/3003, reg 3(1), (3)). As to the change of name of The International Stock Exchange of the United Kingdom and the Republic of Ireland Limited following the separation of the Irish Stock Exchange from the London Stock Exchange see para 21 note 8 ante.
3 Ie the documents referred to in the Companies Act 1985 s 238(1) (as substituted): see para 823 ante.
4 For these purposes, 'entitled persons', in relation to a company, means such of the persons specified in ibid s 238(1)(a)–(c) (as substituted) as are or would apart from s 251 (as substituted and amended) be entitled to be sent copies of those documents relating to the company which are referred to in s 238(1) (as substituted): s 251(1) (as substituted and amended: see note 2 supra).
5 Ibid s 251(1) (as substituted and amended: see note 2 supra). Regulations under s 251 (as substituted and amended) must be made by statutory instrument which is subject to annulment in pursuance of a resolution of either House of Parliament: s 251(5) (substituted by the Companies Act 1989 s 15). In exercise of the power so conferred the Secretary of State made the Companies (Summary Financial Statement) Regulations 1995, SI 1995/2092 (see para 915 et seq post) which came into force on 1 September 1995: reg 1.
6 Companies Act 1985 s 251(2) (substituted by the Companies Act 1989 s 15; amended by the Companies Act 1985 (Amendment of Sections 250 and 251) Regulations 1992 reg 3(1), (4)).
7 For the meaning of 'annual accounts' see para 817 note 2 ante.
8 As to the directors' report see para 1066 et seq post.
9 Companies Act 1985 s 251(3) (substituted by the Companies Act 1989 s 15).
10 As to the auditors' report see paras 1059–1061 post.
11 For the meaning of 'qualified' see para 913 note 10 ante.
12 Ie a statement under the Companies Act 1985 s 237(2) (as substituted): see para 1061 post.
13 Ie a statement under ibid s 237(3) (as substituted): see para 1061 post.
14 Ibid s 251(4) (substituted by the Companies Act 1989 s 15).
15 Companies Act 1985 s 251(6) (substituted by the Companies Act 1989 s 15); Companies Act 1985 s 730, Sch 24 (amended by the Companies Act 1989 s 23, Sch 10 para 24(1), (3)). For the meaning of 'officer who is in default' and 'the statutory maximum' see para 1161 post.
16 Ie the Companies Act 1985 s 240 (as substituted): see para 938 post.
17 Ibid s 251(7) (substituted by the Companies Act 1989 s 15; amended by the Companies Act 1985 (Amendment of Sections 250 and 251) Regulations 1992 reg 3(1), (5)).

915. Cases in which sending of summary financial statement prohibited. A listed public company[1] may not send a summary financial statement to an entitled person[2] instead of copies of its full accounts and reports[3], in any case where it is prohibited from doing so by any relevant provision[4] in its memorandum or articles of association or, where the entitled person is a holder of the company's debentures, in any instrument constituting or otherwise governing any of the company's debentures of which that person is a holder[5].

1 For these purposes, 'listed public company' means a public company whose shares or debentures, or any class of whose shares or debentures, are listed within the meaning of the Companies Act 1985 s 251(1) (as substituted) (see para 914 note 2 ante): Companies (Summary Financial Statement) Regulations 1995, SI 1995/2092, reg 2.
2 For these purposes, 'entitled persons' means the same as in the Companies Act 1985 s 251 (as substituted) (see para 914 note 4 ante): Companies (Summary Financial Statement) Regulations 1995 reg 2.
3 For these purposes, 'full accounts and reports' means a company's annual accounts, the directors' report and the auditors' report on those accounts required to be sent to entitled persons under the Companies Act 1985 s 238(1) (as substituted) (see para 823 ante); and 'full', in relation to any balance sheet, profit

and loss account, group accounts or directors' report means any such document comprised in the full accounts and reports: Companies (Summary Financial Statement) Regulations 1995 reg 2.

4 For these purposes, any provision (however expressed) which requires copies of the full accounts and reports to be sent to entitled persons, or which forbids the sending of summary financial statements under the Companies Act 1985 s 251 (as substituted) (see para 914 ante) is a relevant provision: Companies (Summary Financial Statement) Regulations 1995 regs 2, 3(2).

5 Ibid reg 3(1).

916. Ascertainment of entitled persons' wishes. A listed public company[1] may not send a summary financial statement to an entitled person[2] in place of copies of its full accounts and reports[3], unless the company has ascertained that the entitled person does not wish to receive copies of those documents[4].

Whether or not an entitled person wishes to receive copies of the full accounts and report for a financial year is to be ascertained:

(1) from any relevant notification[5] in writing he has given to the company (either as an entitled person or as a person who is entitled, whether conditionally or unconditionally, to become an entitled person in relation to the company, but who has not yet become such an entitled person) as to whether he wishes to receive copies of the full accounts and reports or as to whether he wishes, instead of copies of those documents, to receive summary financial statements; or

(2) failing any such express notification, from any failure to respond to an opportunity given to the entitled person (including for this purpose a person[6] who is entitled, whether conditionally or unconditionally, to become an entitled person in relation to the company, but who has not yet become such an entitled person) to elect to receive copies of the full accounts and reports either in response to a notice sent by the company[7] or as part of a relevant consultation of his wishes[8] by the company[9].

A company may not send a summary financial statement to an entitled person in relation to any financial year in place of copies of the full accounts and reports unless the period for laying and delivering full accounts and reports[10] for that year has not expired and the summary financial statement has been approved by the board of directors and the original statement signed on behalf of the board by a director of the company[11].

1 For the meaning of 'listed public company' see para 915 note 1 ante.
2 For the meaning of 'entitled persons' see para 915 note 2 ante.
3 For the meaning of 'full accounts and reports' see para 915 note 3 ante.
4 Companies (Summary Financial Statement) Regulations 1995, SI 1995/2092, reg 4(1).
5 For these purposes, a notification is a relevant notification with respect to a financial year if it relates to that year (whether or not it has been given at the invitation of the company) and if it is received by the company not later than 28 days before the first date on which copies of the full accounts and reports are sent out to the entitled persons in compliance with the Companies Act 1985 s 238(1) (as substituted) (see para 823 ante) with respect to the financial year: Companies (Summary Financial Statement) Regulations 1995 regs 2, 4(3).
6 Ie a person to whom ibid reg 4(5) applies.
7 Ie under ibid reg 5: see para 917 post.
8 Ie under ibid reg 6: see para 918 post.
9 Ibid regs 2, 4(2), (5).
10 Ie under the Companies Act 1985 s 244 (as substituted): see para 822 ante.
11 Companies (Summary Financial Statement) Regulations 1995 regs 2, 4(4).

917. Consultation by notice. A listed public company[1] may give a notice to an entitled person[2] (including for this purpose a person[3] who is entitled, whether conditionally or unconditionally, to become an entitled person in relation to the company, but who has not yet become such an entitled person), by sending it by post or giving it in any other manner authorised by the company's articles, which must:

(1) state that for the future, so long as he is an entitled person, he will be sent a summary financial statement for each financial year instead of a copy of the company's full accounts and reports[4], unless he notifies the company that he wishes to receive full accounts and reports;

(2) state that the summary financial statement for a financial year will contain a summary of the company's or group's profit and loss account, balance sheet and directors' report for that year;

(3) state that the printed card or form accompanying the notice[5] must be returned by a date specified in the notice, being a date at least 21 days after service of the notice and not less than 28 days before the first date on which copies of the full accounts and reports for the next financial year for which the entitled person is entitled to receive them are sent out to entitled persons[6];

(4) include a statement in a prominent position to the effect that a summary financial statement will not contain sufficient information to allow as full an understanding of the results and state of affairs of the company or group as would be provided by the full annual accounts and reports and that members and debenture holders requiring more detailed information have the right to obtain, free of charge, a copy of the company's last full accounts and reports; and

(5) state that the summary financial statement will contain a statement by the company's auditors as to whether the summary financial statement is consistent with the full accounts and reports for the year in question, whether it complies with the statutory requirements[7] and whether the report on the accounts was qualified[8].

The notice must be accompanied by a printed card or form, in respect of which any postage necessary for its return to the company has been, or will be, paid by the company, which is so worded as to enable an entitled person (including for this purpose a person[9] who is entitled, whether conditionally or unconditionally, to become an entitled person in relation to the company, but who has not yet become such an entitled person), by marking a box and returning the card or form, to notify the company that he wishes to receive full accounts and reports for the next financial year for which he is entitled to receive them as an entitled person and for all future financial years thereafter[10]. The company need not, however, pay the postage in respect of the return of the printed card or form in the following circumstances:

(a) if the address of a member to which notices are sent in accordance with the company's articles is not within an EEA State[11];

(b) if the address of a debenture holder to which notices are sent in accordance with the terms of any instrument constituting or otherwise governing the debentures of which he is a holder is not within an EEA State; or

(c) if the address of a person[12] who is entitled, whether conditionally or uncon-ditionally, to become an entitled person in relation to the company, but who has not yet become such an entitled person to which notices are sent, in accordance with the contractual provisions whereunder he has a right, conditionally or unconditionally, to become an entitled person, is not within an EEA State[13].

1 For the meaning of 'listed public company' see para 915 note 1 ante.
2 For the meaning of 'entitled persons' see para 915 note 2 ante.
3 Ie a person to whom the Companies (Summary Financial Statement) Regulations 1995, SI 1995/2092, reg 4(5) applies.
4 For the meaning of 'full accounts and reports' see para 915 note 3 ante.

5 Ie in accordance with the Companies (Summary Financial Statement) Regulations 1995 reg 5(2): see infra.
6 Ie in compliance with the Companies Act 1985 s 238(1) (as substituted): see para 823 ante.
7 Ie the requirements of ibid s 251 (as substituted) (see para 914 ante) and the Companies (Summary Financial Statement) Regulations 1995.
8 Ibid reg 5(1). For the meaning of 'qualified' see para 913 note 10 ante.
9 See note 3 supra.
10 Companies (Summary Financial Statement) Regulations 1995 reg 5(2).
11 For these purposes, 'EEA State' means a State which is a Contracting Party to the Agreement on the European Economic Area signed at Oporto on 2 May 1992, as adjusted by the Protocol signed at Brussels on 17 March 1993 and by EC Council Decision 1/95 of 10 March 1995: Companies (Summary Financial Statement) Regulations 1995 reg 2. As to the European Economic Area see para 299 note 2 ante.
12 See note 3 supra.
13 Companies (Summary Financial Statement) Regulations 1995 reg 5(3).

918. Relevant consultation. A listed public company[1] may conduct a relevant consultation to ascertain the wishes of an entitled person[2]. For these purposes, a relevant consultation of the wishes of an entitled person is a notice given to the entitled person (including for this purpose a person[3] who is entitled, whether conditionally or unconditionally, to become an entitled person in relation to the company, but who has not yet become such an entitled person), by sending it by post or giving it in any other manner authorised by the company's articles, which:

(1) states that for the future, so long as he is an entitled person, he will be sent a summary financial statement instead of the full accounts and reports[4] of the company, unless he notifies the company in writing that he wishes to continue to receive full accounts and reports;

(2) accompanies a copy of the full accounts and reports;

(3) accompanies a copy of a summary financial statement, prepared in accordance with the relevant statutory provisions[5], with respect to the financial year covered by those full accounts and reports and which is identified in the notice as an example of the document which the entitled person will receive for the future, so long as he is an entitled person, unless he notifies the company to the contrary; and

(4) is accompanied by a printed card or form, in respect of which any postage necessary for its return to the company has been, or will be, paid by the company, which is so worded as to enable an entitled person (including for this purpose a person[6] who is entitled, whether conditionally or unconditionally, to become an entitled person in relation to the company, but who has not yet become such an entitled person), by marking a box and returning the card or form, to notify the company that he wishes to receive full accounts and reports for the next financial year for which he is entitled to receive them as an entitled person and for all future financial years thereafter[7].

1 For the meaning of 'listed public company' see para 915 note 1 ante.
2 Companies (Summary Financial Statement) Regulations 1995, SI 1995/2092, reg 6(1). For the meaning of 'entitled persons' see para 915 note 2 ante.
3 Ie a person to whom ibid reg 4(5) applies.
4 For the meaning of 'full accounts and reports' see para 915 note 3 ante.
5 Ie the Companies Act 1985 s 251 (as substituted) (see para 914 ante) and the Companies (Summary Financial Statement) Regulations 1995.
6 See note 3 supra.
7 Companies (Summary Financial Statement) Regulations 1995 reg 6(2). Regulation 5(3) (see para 917 ante) applies in respect of the payment of postage for the return of the printed card or form referred to in reg 6(2)(d) (see text head (4) supra): reg 6(3).

(B) *Form and Content of Summary Financial Statements*

919. Provisions applying to all companies and groups. Every summary financial statement issued by a listed public company[1] in place of full accounts and reports[2] must comply with these provisions[3].

The summary financial statement must state the name of the person who signed it on behalf of the board[4].

The summary financial statement of a company which is not required to prepare group accounts[5] must include a statement in a prominent position to the effect that the summary financial statement does not contain sufficient information to allow as full an understanding of the results and state of affairs of the company as would be provided by the full annual accounts and reports, and that members and debenture holders requiring more detailed information have the right to obtain, free of charge, a copy of the company's last full accounts and reports[6].

The summary financial statement of a company which is required to prepare group accounts[7] must include a statement in a prominent position to the effect that the summary financial statement does not contain sufficient information to allow as full an understanding of the results of the group and state of affairs of the company or of the group as would be provided by the full annual accounts and reports, and that members and debenture holders requiring more detailed information have the right to obtain, free of charge, a copy of the company's last full accounts and reports[8].

The summary financial statement must contain a clear, conspicuous statement:

(1) of how members and debenture holders can obtain, free of charge, a copy of the company's last full accounts and reports; and

(2) of how members and debenture holders may elect in writing to receive full accounts and reports in place of summary financial statements for all future financial years[9].

1 For the meaning of 'listed public company' see para 915 note 1 ante.
2 For the meaning of 'full accounts and reports' see para 915 note 3 ante.
3 Companies (Summary Financial Statement) Regulations 1995, SI 1995/2092, reg 7(1).
4 Ibid reg 7(2).
5 Ie under the Companies Act 1985 Pt VII (ss 221–262A) (as amended): see para 801 et seq ante.
6 Companies (Summary Financial Statement) Regulations 1995 reg 7(3).
7 See note 5 supra.
8 Companies (Summary Financial Statement) Regulations 1995 reg 7(4).
9 Ibid reg 7(5).

920. Companies and groups other than banking and insurance companies and groups. The summary financial statement of a listed public company[1], other than a banking[2] or insurance[3] company, the directors of which are not required to prepare group accounts[4] must be in the prescribed form, and contain the prescribed information[5], so far as applicable to such a company[6].

The summary financial statement of a listed public company, other than the parent company of a banking or insurance group, the directors of which are required to prepare group accounts[7] must be in the prescribed form, and contain the prescribed information[8], so far as applicable to such a company[9].

1 For the meaning of 'listed public company' see para 915 note 1 ante.
2 For these purposes, 'banking company' means a company the directors of which prepare accounts for a financial year in accordance with the special provisions of the Companies Act 1985 Pt VII (ss 221–262A) (as amended) relating to banking companies (see paras 926–928 post): Companies (Summary Financial Statement) Regulations 1995, SI 1995/2092, reg 2.

3 For these purposes, 'insurance company' means a company the directors of which prepare accounts for a financial year in accordance with the special provisions of the Companies Act 1985 Pt VII (ss 221-262A) (as amended) relating to insurance companies (see paras 926, 927 post): Companies (Summary Financial Statement) Regulations 1995 reg 2.

4 Ie under the Companies Act 1985 Pt VII (ss 221-262A) (as amended): see para 801 et seq ante.

5 Ie must be in the form, and contain the information, required by the Companies (Summary Financial Statement) Regulations 1995 reg 8(1), Sch 1. The requirements are: form of summary financial statement (Sch 1 para 1); summary directors' report (Sch 1 para 2); summary profit and loss account: companies not required to prepare group accounts (Sch 1 para 3); summary profit and loss account: companies required to prepare group accounts (Sch 1 para 4); summary balance sheet: companies not required to prepare group accounts (Sch 1 para 5); summary balance sheet: companies required to prepare group accounts (Sch 1 para 6); corresponding amounts (Sch 1 para 7).

6 Ibid reg 8(1).

7 See note 4 supra.

8 Ie must be in the form, and contain the information, required by the Companies (Summary Financial Statement) Regulations 1995 Sch 1: see note 5 supra.

9 Ibid reg 8(2).

921. Banking companies and groups. The summary financial statement of a listed public company[1] which is in relation to the financial year in question a banking company[2] the directors of which are not required to prepare group accounts[3] must be in the prescribed form, and contain the prescribed information[4], so far as applicable to such a company[5].

The summary financial statement of a listed public company which is the parent company of a banking group must be in the prescribed form, and contain the prescribed information[6], so far as applicable to such a company[7].

1 For the meaning of 'listed public company' see para 915 note 1 ante.

2 For the meaning of 'banking company' see para 920 note 2 ante.

3 Ie under the Companies Act 1985 Pt VII (ss 221-262A) (as amended): see para 801 et seq ante.

4 Ie must be in the form, and contain the information, required by the Companies (Summary Financial Statement) Regulations 1995, SI 1995/2092, reg 9(1), Sch 2. The requirements are: form of summary financial statement (Sch 2 para 1); summary directors' report (Sch 2 para 2); summary profit and loss account: companies not required to prepare group accounts (Sch 2 para 3); summary profit and loss account: companies required to prepare group accounts (Sch 2 para 4); summary balance sheet: companies not required to prepare group accounts (Sch 2 para 5); summary balance sheet: companies required to prepare group accounts (Sch 2 para 6); corresponding amounts (Sch 2 para 7).

5 Ibid reg 9(1).

6 Ie must be in the form, and contain the information, required by ibid Sch 2: see note 4 supra.

7 Ibid reg 9(2).

922. Insurance companies and groups. The summary financial statement of a listed public company[1] which is in relation to the financial year in question an insurance company[2] the directors of which are not required to prepare group accounts[3] must be in the prescribed form, and contain the prescribed information[4], so far as applicable to such a company[5].

The summary financial statement of a listed public company which is the parent company of an insurance group must be in the prescribed form, and contain the prescribed information[6], so far as applicable to such a company[7].

1 For the meaning of 'listed public company' see para 915 note 1 ante.

2 For the meaning of 'insurance company' see para 920 note 3 ante.

3 Ie under the Companies Act 1985 Pt VII (ss 221-262A) (as amended): see para 801 et seq ante.

4 Ie must be in the form, and contain the information, required by the Companies (Summary Financial Statement) Regulations 1995, SI 1995/2092, reg 10(1), Sch 3. The requirements are: application of

provisions (Sch 3 para 1); form of summary financial statement (Sch 3 para 2); summary directors' report (Sch 3 para 3); summary profit and loss account: companies not required to prepare group accounts (Sch 3 para 4); summary profit and loss account: companies required to prepare group accounts (Sch 3 para 5); summary balance sheet: companies not required to prepare group accounts (Sch 3 para 6); summary balance sheet: companies required to prepare group accounts (Sch 3 para 7); corresponding amounts (Sch 3 para 8); transitional arrangements: definition (Sch 3 para 9); summary profit and loss account under transitional arrangements (Sch 3 para 10); summary balance sheet under transitional arrangements (Sch 3 para 11); companies preparing alternative form group accounts (Sch 3 para 12).

5 Ibid reg 10(1).
6 Ie must be in the form, and contain the information, required by ibid Sch 3: see note 4 supra.
7 Ibid reg 10(2).

C. PRIVATE COMPANIES

923. Election to dispense with laying of accounts and reports before general meeting. A private company[1] may elect by elective resolution[2] to dispense with the laying of accounts and reports before the company in general meeting[3]. An election has effect in relation to the accounts and reports in respect of the financial year[4] in which the election is made and subsequent financial years[5].

Whilst an election is in force, the references to the laying of accounts before the company in general meeting in the statutory provisions relating to the accounts on which the auditors are to report[6], the accounts by reference to which distributions are justified[7] and the accounts relevant for determining a company's net assets for the purposes of ascertaining whether approval is required for certain transactions[8] are to be read as references to the sending of copies of the accounts to members and others[9]; and the statutory requirement[10] that the auditors' statement be laid before the company in general meeting is to be read as a requirement that it be sent to members and others along with the copies of the accounts sent[11] to them[12].

If an election ceases to have effect, the statutory provisions relating to the accounts and reports to be laid before the company in general meeting[13] apply in relation to the accounts and reports in respect of the financial year in which the election ceases to have effect and subsequent financial years[14].

1 For the meaning of 'private company' see para 82 ante.
2 Ie by elective resolution in accordance with the Companies Act 1985 s 379A (as added): see para 686 ante.
3 Ibid s 252(1) (substituted by the Companies Act 1989 s 16).
4 For the meaning of 'financial year' see para 806 ante.
5 Companies Act 1985 s 252(2) (substituted by the Companies Act 1989 s 16).
6 Ie the Companies Act 1985 s 235(1) (as substituted): see para 1059 post.
7 Ie ibid s 270(3), (4): see para 707 ante.
8 Ie ibid s 320(2) (as amended): see para 611 ante.
9 Ie under ibid s 238(1) (as substituted): see para 823 ante.
10 Ie the requirement in ibid s 271(4): see para 708 ante.
11 See note 9 supra.
12 Companies Act 1985 s 252(3) (substituted by the Companies Act 1989 s 16).
13 Ie the Companies Act 1985 s 241 (as substituted): see para 817 ante.
14 Ibid s 252(4) (substituted by the Companies Act 1989 s 16).

924. Right of shareholder to require laying of accounts and reports. Where an election by a private company to dispense with the laying of accounts and reports before the company in general meeting[1] is in force, the copies of the accounts and reports sent out[2] must not be sent out less than 28 days before the end of the period allowed for laying and delivering accounts and reports[3] and must be accompanied, in the case of a member of the company, by a notice informing him of his right to require the laying of the accounts and reports before a general meeting[4].

Before the end of the period of 28 days beginning with the day on which the accounts and reports are so sent out, any member or auditor of the company may by notice in writing deposited at the registered office of the company require that a general meeting be held for the purpose of laying the accounts and reports before the company[5]. If the directors do not, within 21 days from the date of the deposit of such a notice, proceed duly to convene a meeting, the person who deposited the notice may do so himself[6]. A meeting so convened must not be held more than three months from that date and must be convened in the same manner, as nearly as possible, as that in which meetings are to be convened by directors[7]. Where the directors do not duly convene a meeting, any reasonable expenses incurred by reason of that failure by the person who deposited the notice must be made good to him by the company, and must be recouped by the company out of any fees, or other remuneration in respect of their services, due or to become due to such of the directors as were in default[8]. The directors are deemed not to have duly convened a meeting if they convene a meeting for a date more than 28 days after the date of the notice convening it[9].

1 Ie an election under the Companies Act 1985 s 252 (as substituted): see para 923 ante. For the meaning of 'private company' see para 82 ante.
2 Ie in accordance with ibid s 238(1) (as substituted): see para 823 ante.
3 As to the period for laying and delivering accounts see para 822 ante.
4 Companies Act 1985 s 253(1) (substituted by the Companies Act 1989 s 16). The Companies Act 1985 s 238(5) (as substituted) (penalty for default: see para 823 ante) applies in relation to the requirements of s 253(1) (as so substituted) as to the requirements contained in s 238 (as substituted): s 253(1) (as so substituted).
5 Ibid s 253(2) (substituted by the Companies Act 1989 s 16).
6 Companies Act 1985 s 253(3) (substituted by the Companies Act 1989 s 16).
7 Companies Act 1985 s 253(4) (substituted by the Companies Act 1989 s 16).
8 Companies Act 1985 s 253(5) (substituted by the Companies Act 1989 s 16).
9 Companies Act 1985 s 253(6) (substituted by the Companies Act 1989 s 16).

D. UNLIMITED COMPANIES

925. Exemption from requirement to deliver accounts and reports. The directors of an unlimited company are not required[1] to deliver to the registrar of companies accounts and reports in respect of a financial year[2] if the following conditions are met[3]. The conditions are that at no time during the relevant accounting reference period[4]:

(1) has the company been, to its knowledge, a subsidiary undertaking[5] of an undertaking which was then limited;

(2) have there been, to its knowledge, exercisable, by or on behalf of two or more undertakings which were then limited, rights which, if exercisable by one of them, would have made the company a subsidiary undertaking of it; and

(3) has the company been a parent company[6] of an undertaking which was then limited[7].

The references to an undertaking being limited at a particular time are to an undertaking, under whatever law established, the liability of whose members is at that time limited[7].

The exemption conferred by the above provisions does not apply if the company is a banking[8] or insurance[9] company or the parent company of a banking[10] or insurance[11] group, or the company is a qualifying company[12] or at any time during the relevant accounting period the company carried on business as the promoter of a trading stamp scheme within the Trading Stamps Act 1964[13].

1 Ie by the Companies Act 1985 s 242 (as substituted and amended): see para 818 ante.
2 For the meaning of 'financial year' see para 806 ante.
3 Companies Act 1985 s 254(1) (substituted by the Companies Act 1989 s 17). Where a company is so exempt from the obligation to deliver accounts, the Companies Act 1985 s 240 (as substituted) (see para 938 post) has effect with the following modifications: (1) in s 240(3)(b) for the words from 'whether statutory accounts' to 'have been delivered to the registrar' the words 'that the company is exempt from the requirement to deliver statutory accounts' must be substituted; and (2) in s 240(5) for the words 'as required to be delivered to the registrar under section 242' the words 'as prepared in accordance with this Part and approved by the board of directors' must be substituted: s 254(4) (substituted by the Companies Act 1989 s 17).
4 For the meaning of 'accounting reference period' see para 807 ante.
5 For the meaning of 'subsidiary undertaking' see para 828 ante; and for the meaning of 'undertaking' see para 806 ante.
6 For the meaning of 'parent company' see para 828 post.
7 Companies Act 1985 s 254(2) (substituted by the Companies Act 1989 s 17).
8 For the meaning of 'banking company' see para 117 note 8 ante.
9 For the meaning of 'insurance company' see para 117 note 9 ante.
10 For the meaning of 'banking group' see para 927 note 2 post.
11 For the meaning of 'insurance group' see para 927 note 5 ante.
12 For the meaning of 'qualifying company' see para 117 note 12 ante.
13 Companies Act 1985 s 254(3) (substituted by the Companies Act 1989 s 17; amended by the Partnerships and Unlimited Companies (Accounts) Regulations 1993, SI 1993/1820, reg 10; the Companies Act 1985 (Insurance Companies Accounts) Regulations 1993, SI 1993/3246, regs 5(1), 7, Sch 2 para 2). As to trading stamp schemes see SALE OF GOODS vol 41 para 899.

E. BANKING AND INSURANCE COMPANIES AND GROUPS

926. Special provisions for banking and insurance companies. A banking company[1] must prepare its individual accounts[2] in accordance with special statutory provisions[3]; and an insurance company[4] must prepare its individual accounts in accordance with special statutory provisions[5]. Accounts so prepared must contain a statement that they are prepared in accordance with the special provisions relating to banking companies or to insurance companies, as the case may be[6].

1 For the meaning of 'banking company' see para 117 note 8 ante.
2 For the meaning of 'individual accounts' see para 816 ante.
3 Companies Act 1985 s 255(1) (substituted by the Companies Act 1985 (Bank Accounts) Regulations 1991, SI 1991/2705, regs 3, 9). The special statutory provisions are the Companies Act 1985 s 255(1), Sch 9 Pt I (paras 1–87) (substituted by the Companies Act 1985 (Bank Accounts) Regulations 1991, SI 1991/2705, reg 5, Sch 1; amended by the Companies Act 1985 (Bank Accounts) Regulations 1994, SI 1994/233, reg 4(1); the Companies Act 1985 (Miscellaneous Accounting Amendments) Regulations 1996, SI 1996/189, reg 14(6), Sch 4): Companies Act 1985 s 255(1) (as so substituted). In relation to the preparation of individual accounts in accordance with Pt VII (ss 221–262A) (as amended), the references to s 226(3), Sch 4 (as amended) in s 226(4), (5) (relationship between specific requirements and duty to give a true and fair view: see para 816 ante) are to be read as references to the provisions of Sch 9 Pt I (paras 1–87) (as so substituted and amended), in the case of the accounts of banking companies, or to the provisions of s 255(2), Sch 9A Pt I (paras 1–86) (substituted by the Companies Act 1985 (Insurance Companies Accounts) Regulations 1993, SI 1993/3246, reg 4, Sch 1; the Insurance Companies (Reserves) Act 1995 s 3(1)-(3); the Companies Act 1985 (Miscellaneous Accounting Amendments) Regulations 1996 reg 14(7), Sch 5), in the case of the accounts of insurance companies: Companies Act 1985 s 255(4) (substituted by the Companies Act 1985 (Bank Accounts) Regulations 1991 regs 3, 9).
4 For the meaning of 'insurance company' see para 117 note 9 ante.
5 Companies Act 1985 s 255(2) (substituted by the Companies Act 1985 (Bank Accounts) Regulations 1991 regs 3, 9; amended by the Companies Act 1985 (Insurance Companies Accounts) Regulations

1993 reg 2(1)). The special statutory provisions are the Companies Act 1985 Sch 9A Pt I (paras 1–86) (as substituted and amended: see note 3 supra): s 255(1) (as so substituted). See also note 3 supra.

6 Ibid s 255(3) (substituted by the Companies Act 1985 (Bank Accounts) Regulations 1991 regs 3, 9).

927. Special provisions for banking and insurance groups. The parent company[1] of a banking group[2] must prepare group accounts[3] in accordance with special statutory provisions[4]; and the parent company of an insurance group[5] must prepare group accounts in accordance with special statutory provisions[6].

Accounts so prepared must contain a statement that they are prepared in accordance with the special statutory provisions relating to banking groups or to insurance groups, as the case may be[7].

1 For the meaning of 'parent company' see para 828 ante.

2 For these purposes, references to a banking group are to a group where the parent company is a banking company or where (1) the parent company's principal subsidiary undertakings are wholly or mainly credit institutions; and (2) the parent company does not itself carry on any material business apart from the acquisition, management and disposal of interests in subsidiary undertakings: Companies Act 1985 s 255A(4) (added by the Companies Act 1989 s 18(1); substituted by the Companies Act 1985 (Insurance Companies Accounts) Regulations 1993, SI 1993/3246, reg 3(2)). For the meaning of 'banking company' see para 117 note 8 ante; and for the meaning of 'subsidiary undertaking' see para 828 ante. 'Credit institution' means a credit institution as defined in EC Council Directive 77/780 (OJ L322, 17.12.77, p 30) art 1 (see BANKING), that is to say an undertaking whose business is to receive deposits or other repayable funds from the public and to grant credits for its own account: Companies Act 1985 s 262(1) (substituted by the Companies Act 1989 s 22; amended by the Companies Act 1985 (Disclosure of Branches and Bank Accounts) Regulations 1992, SI 1992/3178, regs 7, 8(b)).

For the purposes of the Companies Act 1985 s 255A(4) (as so added and substituted) and s 255A(5) (as added and substituted) (see infra): (a) a parent company's principal subsidiary undertakings are the subsidiary undertakings of the company whose results or financial position would principally affect the figures shown in the group accounts; and (b) the management of interests in subsidiary undertakings includes the provision of services to such undertakings: s 255A(5A) (added by the Companies Act 1985 (Insurance Companies Accounts) Regulations 1993 reg 3(2)).

In relation to the preparation of group accounts in accordance with the special statutory provisions: (i) the references to the provisions of the Companies Act 1985 s 227(4), Sch 4A (as added) in s 227(5), (6) (as substituted) (relationship between specific requirements and duty to give a true and fair view: see para 875 ante) are to be read as references to those provisions as modified by s 255A(1), Sch 9 Pt II (paras 1–7) (substituted by the Companies Act 1985 (Bank Accounts) Regulations 1991, SI 1991/2705, reg 5, Sch 1; amended by the Welsh Language Act 1993 ss 30(1), (4), 35(1), Sch 2), in the case of the group accounts of a banking group, or s 255A(2), Sch 9A Pt II (paras 1, 2) (substituted by the Companies Act 1985 (Insurance Companies Accounts) Regulations 1993 reg 4, Sch 1), in the case of the group accounts of an insurance group; and (ii) the reference to the Companies Act 1985 Sch 4 paras 52–57 (as amended) (see paras 839, 848–852 ante) in s 230(2) (as substituted) (relief from obligation to comply therewith where group accounts are prepared: see para 878 ante) are to be read as a reference to Sch 9 Pt I paras 75–77, 80, 81 (substituted by the Companies Act 1985 (Bank Accounts) Regulations 1991 Sch 1), in the case of the group accounts of a banking group, and as a reference to the Companies Act 1985 Sch 9A Pt I paras 73, 74, 79, 80 (substituted by the Companies Act 1985 (Insurance Companies Accounts) Regulations 1993 Sch 1), in the case of the group accounts of an insurance group: Companies Act 1985 s 255A(6) (added by the Companies Act 1989 s 18(1); substituted by the Companies Act 1985 (Bank Accounts) Regulations 1991 regs 3, 9; amended by the Companies Act 1985 (Insurance Companies Accounts) Regulations 1993 reg 3(3); the Companies Act 1985 (Miscellaneous Accounting Amendments) Regulations 1996, SI 1996/189, reg 15(2)).

3 As to group accounts see para 875 et seq ante.

4 Companies Act 1985 s 255A(1) (added by the Companies Act 1989 s 18(1); substituted by the Companies Act 1985 (Bank Accounts) Regulations 1991 regs 3, 9). The special statutory provisions are the Companies Act 1985 Sch 9 Pt II (paras 1–7) (as substituted and amended: see note 2 supra): s 255A(1) (as so added and substituted).

5 For these purposes, references to an insurance group are to a group where the parent company is an insurance company or where (1) the parent company's principal subsidiary undertakings are wholly or mainly insurance companies; and (2) the parent company does not itself carry on any material business apart from the acquisition, management and disposal of interests in subsidiary undertakings: ibid

s 255A(5) (added by the Companies Act 1989 s 18(1); substituted by the Companies Act 1985 (Insurance Companies Accounts) Regulations 1993 reg 3(2)). For the meaning of 'insurance company' see para 117 note 9 ante.
6 Companies Act 1985 s 255A(2) (added by the Companies Act 1989 s 18(1); substituted by the Companies Act 1985 (Bank Accounts) Regulations 1991 regs 3, 9; amended by the Companies Act 1985 (Insurance Companies Accounts) Regulations 1993 reg 3(1)). The special statutory provisions are the Companies Act 1985 Sch 9A Pt II (paras 1, 2) (as substituted and amended: see note 2 supra): s 255A(2) (as so added, substituted and amended). See also note 2 supra.
7 Ibid s 255A(3) (added by the Companies Act 1989 s 18(1); substituted by the Companies Act 1985 (Bank Accounts) Regulations 1991 regs 3, 9).

928. Modification of disclosure requirements in relation to banking company or group. In relation to a banking company[1], or the parent company[2] of a banking group[3], the statutory provisions relating to the disclosure of information in respect of related undertakings[4] have effect subject to special additional disclosure requirements[5]; and, in relation to a banking company, or the holding company[6] of a credit institution[7], the statutory provisions relating to the disclosure of information in respect of emoluments and other benefits of directors and others[8] have effect subject to additional disclosure requirements[9].

1 For the meaning of 'banking company' see para 117 note 8 ante.
2 For the meaning of 'parent company' see para 828 ante.
3 For the meaning of 'banking group' see para 927 note 2 ante.
4 Ie the Companies Act 1985 s 231, Sch 5 (as substituted and amended): see paras 853 et seq, 888 et seq ante.
5 Ibid s 255B(1) (added by the Companies Act 1989 s 18(1); substituted by the Companies Act 1985 (Bank Accounts) Regulations 1991, SI 1991/2705, regs 3, 9; amended by the Companies Act 1985 (Disclosure of Branches and Bank Accounts) Regulations 1992, SI 1992/3178, regs 6, 8(b)). The additional disclosure requirements are those contained in the Companies Act 1985 s 255B(1), Sch 9 Pt III (para 1) (substituted by the Companies Act 1985 (Bank Accounts) Regulations 1991 reg 5, Sch 1): Companies Act 1985 s 255B(1) (as so added, substituted and amended).
6 For the meaning of 'holding company' see para 827 ante.
7 For the meaning of 'credit institution' see para 927 note 2 ante.
8 Ie the Companies Act 1985 s 232, Sch 6 (as amended): see para 865 et seq ante.
9 Ibid s 255B(2) (added by the Companies Act 1989 s 18(1); substituted by the Companies Act 1985 (Bank Accounts) Regulations 1991 regs 3, 9; amended by the Companies Act 1985 (Bank Accounts) Regulations 1994, SI 1994/233, reg 3). The additional disclosure requirements are those contained in the Companies Act 1985 s 255B(2), Sch 9 Pt IV (paras 1-3) (substituted by the Companies Act 1989 s 18(3), (4), Sch 7 Pt IV; amended by the Companies Act 1985 (Bank Accounts) Regulations 1994 reg 5(1)-(5)): Companies Act 1985 s 255B(2) (as so added, substituted and amended).

F. BANKING PARTNERSHIPS

929. In general. The Secretary of State may by regulations apply to banking partnerships[1], subject to such exceptions, adaptations and modifications as he considers appropriate, the statutory provisions[2] relating to accounts applying to banking companies[3]. Such regulations must be made by statutory instrument[4]; and no such regulations may be made unless a draft of the instrument containing the regulations has been laid before Parliament and approved by a resolution of each House[5].

1 For these purposes, 'banking partnership' means a partnership which is an authorised institution under the Banking Act 1987 (see BANKING vol 3(1) (Reissue) para 17): Companies Act 1985 s 255D(2) (added by the Companies Act 1989 s 18(2)).
2 Ie the provisions of the Companies Act 1985 Pt VII (ss 221-262A) (as amended): see para 801 et seq ante.
3 Ibid s 255D(1) (added by the Companies Act 1989 s 18(2)). At the date at which this volume states the law no such regulations had been made.

4 Companies Act 1985 s 255D(3) (added by the Companies Act 1989 s 18(2)).
5 Companies Act 1985 s 255D(4) (added by the Companies Act 1989 s 18(2)).

G. PARTNERSHIPS AND UNLIMITED COMPANIES

930. Preparation of accounts of qualifying partnerships. The persons who are members of a qualifying partnership[1] at the end of any financial year[2] of the partnership must, in respect of that year:

(1) prepare the like annual accounts and annual report; and

(2) cause to be prepared such an auditors' report,

as would be required under the Companies Act 1985[3] if the partnership were a company formed and registered under that Act[4].

The accounts so required must be prepared within a period of ten months beginning immediately after the end of the financial year and must state that they are prepared under these provisions[5].

1 For the meaning of 'qualifying partnership' see para 931 post.
2 For these purposes, 'financial year', in relation to a qualifying partnership, means any period of not more than 18 months in respect of which a profit and loss account of the partnership is required to be made up by or in accordance with its constitution or, failing any such requirement, each period of 12 months beginning with 1 April: Partnerships and Unlimited Companies (Accounts) Regulations 1993, SI 1993/1820, reg 2(1).
3 Ie under the Companies Act 1985 Pt VII (ss 221-262A) (as amended): see para 801 et seq ante.
4 Partnerships and Unlimited Companies (Accounts) Regulations 1993 regs 2(1), 4(1). Regulation 4 is subject to reg 7 (see para 934 post): reg 4(1). As to the penalties for non-compliance see para 935 post.
    Accounts prepared under reg 4 must comply with the requirements of the Companies Act 1985 Pt VII (ss 221-262A) (as amended) as to the content of accounts subject to the following, namely (1) the provisions of s 259(2), (3) (meaning of references to shares and other expressions); (2) the omission of the provisions mentioned in the Partnerships and Unlimited Companies (Accounts) Regulations 1993 reg 4(3), Schedule para 2(1) (see infra); and (3) any necessary modifications to take account of the fact that partnerships are unincorporated: Schedule para 1(1). For the purposes of the provisions of the Companies Act 1985 Pt VII (ss 221-262A) (as amended) as applied to accounts so prepared, the Partnerships and Unlimited Companies (Accounts) Regulations 1993 are to be regarded as part of the requirements of the Companies Act 1985: Partnerships and Unlimited Companies (Accounts) Regulations 1993 Schedule para 1(2).
    The provisions referred to in Schedule para 1(1)(b) (see head (2) supra) are:
    (a) the Companies Act 1985 s 226(3), Sch 4 para 3(6) (see para 831 ante);
    (b) in Sch 4 para 3(2), the words from 'adopted' to the end (see para 831 ante);
    (c) Sch 4 para 20 (see para 811 ante);
    (d) Sch 4 paras 36A (as added), 41, 43, 44, 45, 50(3)(b), 51(2), 53 (as amended), 54 (see paras 839, 841-843, 846-849 ante);
    (e) s 227(4), Sch 4A paras 13(3)-(5) (as amended), 14, 15 (as added) (see para 882 ante);
    (f) s 231, Sch 5 paras 4, 5 (sic), 10 (sic), 12, 18 (sic), 19 (sic), 29 (sic) (see paras 857, 863 ante);
    (g) s 232, Sch 6 paras 2-6, 8, 9 (as substituted) (see paras 867, 869, 870 ante); and
    (h) s 234, Sch 7 (as amended) (see para 1070 et seq post) except Sch 7 para 6 (as amended) (see para 1073 post):
    Partnerships and Unlimited Companies (Accounts) Regulations 1993 Schedule para 2(1). Schedule para 2(1) is not, however, to be construed as affecting the requirement to give a true and fair view under the Companies Act 1985 s 226 (as substituted) (see para 816 ante) and s 227 (as substituted) (see para 875 ante): Partnerships and Unlimited Companies (Accounts) Regulations 1993 Schedule para 2(2). The Companies Act 1985 Sch 5 paras 5, 10, 18, 19, 29 (as substituted) are, however, repealed by the Companies Act 1985 (Miscellaneous Accounting Amendments) Regulations 1996, SI 1996/189, reg 14(3), Sch 3 paras 1, 5, 10, 15, 16, 23.
    The Companies Act 1989 Pt II (ss 24-54) (eligibility for appointment as auditors: see para 955 et seq post) applies to auditors appointed for the purposes of the Partnerships and Unlimited Companies (Accounts) Regulations 1993 reg 4 as if qualifying partnerships were companies formed and registered under the Companies Act 1985, subject to any necessary modifications to take account of the fact that

partnerships are unincorporated: Partnerships and Unlimited Companies (Accounts) Regulations 1993 Schedule para 3.
5 Ibid reg 4(2).

931. Meaning of 'qualifying partnership'. A partnership which is governed by the laws of any part of Great Britain is a qualifying partnership if each of its members[1] is:

(1) a limited company[2]; or

(2) an unlimited company, or a Scottish firm, each of whose members is a limited company[3].

Where the members of a qualifying partnership include:

(a) an unlimited company, or a Scottish firm, each of whose members is a limited company; or

(b) a member of another partnership each of whose members is a limited company or an unlimited company, or a Scottish firm, each of whose members is a limited company,

any reference to the members of the qualifying partnership includes a reference to the members of that company, firm or other partnership[4].

The statutory requirements[5] apply without regard to any change in the members of a qualifying partnership which does not result in its ceasing to be such a partnership[6].

1 For these purposes, any reference to the members of a qualifying partnership is to be construed, in relation to a limited partnership, as a reference to its general partner or partners: Partnerships and Unlimited Companies (Accounts) Regulations 1993, SI 1993/1820, reg 2(1). 'Limited partnership' means a partnership formed in accordance with the Limited Partnerships Act 1907 (see PARTNERSHIP vol 35 (Reissue) para 205 et seq); and 'general partner' has the same meaning as in the Limited Partnerships Act 1907 (see PARTNERSHIP vol 35 (Reissue) para 207): Partnerships and Unlimited Companies (Accounts) Regulations 1993 reg 2(1).
2 For these purposes, 'limited company' means a company limited by shares or limited by guarantee: ibid reg 2(1).
3 Ibid regs 2(1), 3(1). Any reference in reg 3(1) or reg 3(2) (see infra) to a limited company, an unlimited company, a Scottish firm or another partnership includes a reference to any comparable undertaking incorporated in or formed under the law of any country or territory outside Great Britain: regs 2(1), 3(4).
4 Ibid regs 2(1), 3(2). See also note 3 supra.
5 Ie ibid regs 4–8: see para 932 et seq post.
6 Ibid regs 2(1), 3(3).

932. Delivery of accounts of qualifying partnership to registrar and others. Each limited company[1] which is a member of a qualifying partnership[2] at the end of any financial year[3] of the partnership must append to the copy of its annual accounts which is next delivered to the registrar of companies[4] a copy of the accounts[5] of the partnership prepared for that year[6].

A limited company which is a member of a qualifying partnership must supply to any person upon request:

(1) the name of each member which is to deliver, or has delivered, a copy of the latest accounts of the partnership to the registrar[7]; and

(2) the name of each member incorporated in a member State other than the United Kingdom which is[8] to publish, or has published, the latest accounts of the partnership[9].

1 For the meaning of 'limited company' see para 931 note 2 ante.
2 For the meaning of 'qualifying partnership' see para 931 ante.
3 For the meaning of 'financial year' see para 930 note 2 ante.

4 Ie in accordance with the Companies Act 1985 s 242 (as substituted and amended): see para 818 ante.
5 For these purposes, 'the accounts', in relation to a qualifying partnership, means the annual accounts, the annual report and the auditors' report required by the Partnerships and Unlimited Companies (Accounts) Regulations 1993, SI 1993/1820, reg 4 (see para 930 ante): reg 2(1).
6 Ibid regs 2(1), 5(1). Regulation 5(1) is subject to reg 7 (see para 934 post): reg 5(1). As to the penalties for non-compliance see para 935 post.
7 Ie under ibid reg 5(1): see supra.
8 Ie in accordance with the provisions of EC Council Directive 78/660 (OJ L222, 14.8.78, p 11) or EC Council Directive 83/349 (OJ L193, 18.7.83, p 1).
9 Partnerships and Unlimited Companies (Accounts) Regulations 1993 reg 5(2).

933. Publication of accounts of qualifying partnership at head office. The following provisions apply where a qualifying partnership's[1] head office is in Great Britain and each of its members is:

(1) an undertaking comparable to a limited company[2] which is incorporated in a country or territory outside the United Kingdom; or

(2) an undertaking comparable to an unlimited company or partnership which is incorporated in or formed under the law of such a country or territory and each of whose members is such an undertaking as is mentioned in head (1) above[3].

The above provisions do not, however, apply where any member of a qualifying partnership is:

(a) an undertaking comparable to a limited company which is incorporated in a member State other than the United Kingdom; or

(b) an undertaking comparable to an unlimited company or partnership which is incorporated in or formed under the law of such a State and each of whose members is such an undertaking as is mentioned in head (a) above,

and (in either case) the latest accounts of the qualifying partnership have been or are to be appended to the accounts of any member of the partnership and published[4] under the law of that State[5].

The members of the qualifying partnership:

(i) must make the latest accounts of the partnership available for inspection by any person, without charge and during business hours, at the head office of the partnership; and

(ii) if any document comprised in those accounts is in a language other than English, must annex to that document a translation of it into English, certified[6] to be a correct translation[7].

A member of the qualifying partnership must supply to any person upon request:

(A) a copy of the accounts required by head (i) above to be made available for inspection; and

(B) a copy of any translation required by head (ii) above to be annexed to any document comprised in those accounts,

at a price not exceeding the administrative cost of making the copy[8].

1 For the meaning of 'qualifying partnership' see para 931 ante.
2 For the meaning of 'limited company' see para 931 note 2 ante.
3 Partnerships and Unlimited Companies (Accounts) Regulations 1993, SI 1993/1820, reg 6(1). Regulation 6(1) is subject to reg 6(2) (see infra) and reg 7 (see para 934 post): reg 6(1). As to the penalties for non-compliance see para 935 post.
4 Ie and in accordance with the provisions of EC Council Directive 78/660 (OJ L222, 14.8.78, p 11) or EC Council Directive 83/349 (OJ L193, 18.7.83, p 1).
5 Partnerships and Unlimited Companies (Accounts) Regulations 1993 reg 6(2).
6 Ie in accordance with the Companies (Forms) (Amendment) Regulations 1990, SI 1990/572, reg 5: see para 867 note 7 ante.

7 Partnerships and Unlimited Companies (Accounts) Regulations 1993 reg 6(3).
8 Ibid reg 6(4).

934. Exemption where accounts consolidated. The members of a qualifying partnership[1] are exempt from the requirements to prepare[2], deliver to the registrar[3] and publish[4] accounts if the partnership is dealt with on a consolidated basis[5] in group accounts prepared by:

(1) a member of the partnership which is established under the law of a member State; or

(2) a parent undertaking of such a member which is so established,

and (in either case) the following conditions are complied with[6]:

(a) that the group accounts are prepared and audited under the law of the member State concerned[7]; and

(b) the notes to those accounts disclose that advantage has been taken of the exemption conferred by these provisions[8].

Where advantage is taken of the exemption conferred by these provisions, any member of the qualifying partnership which is a limited company[9] must disclose on request the name of at least one member or parent undertaking in whose group accounts the partnership has been or is to be dealt with on a consolidated basis[10].

1 For the meaning of 'qualifying partnership' see para 931 ante.
2 Ie the Partnerships and Unlimited Companies (Accounts) Regulations 1993, SI 1993/1820, reg 4: see para 930 ante.
3 Ie ibid reg 5: see para 932 ante.
4 Ie ibid reg 6: see para 933 ante.
5 For these purposes, 'dealt with on a consolidated basis' means dealt with by the method of full consolidation, the method of proportional consolidation or the equity method of accounting: ibid reg 2(1).
6 Ie in accordance with EC Council Directive 83/349 (OJ L193, 18.7.83, p 1) (as amended): see para 5 ante.
7 Partnerships and Unlimited Companies (Accounts) Regulations 1993 reg 7(1).
8 Ibid reg 7(2).
9 For the meaning of 'limited company' see para 931 note 2 ante.
10 Partnerships and Unlimited Companies (Accounts) Regulations 1993 reg 7(3). As to the penalties for non-compliance see para 935 post.

935. Penalties for non-compliance. If, in respect of a financial year[1] of a qualifying partnership[2], the requirement to prepare accounts[3] is not complied with within the period specified[4], every person who was a member of the partnership or a director of such a member at the end of that year is guilty of an offence and liable on summary conviction to a fine not exceeding level 5 on the standard scale[5].

If the accounts of a qualifying partnership:

(1) a copy of which is delivered to the registrar of companies[6]; or

(2) which are made available for inspection[7],

do not comply with the requirement to prepare accounts[8], every person who, at the time when the copy was so delivered or, as the case may be, the accounts were first made available for inspection, was a member of the partnership or a director of such a member is guilty of an offence and liable on summary conviction to a fine not exceeding level 5 on the standard scale[9].

If a member of a qualifying partnership fails to comply with the provisions relating to the delivery of accounts to the registrar[10], the publication of accounts at head office[11] or the disclosure on request of the name of at least one member or parent undertaking in whose group accounts the partnership has been or is to be dealt with on a consolidated basis[12], that member and any director of that member is guilty of an offence and liable on summary conviction to a fine not exceeding level 5 on the standard scale[13].

It is a defence for a person charged with an offence under the above provisions to show that he took all reasonable steps for securing that the requirements in question would be complied with[14].

The statutory provisions relating to summary proceedings[15], offences by bodies corporate[16] and criminal proceedings against unincorporated bodies[17] apply to an offence under the above provisions[18].

1 For the meaning of 'financial year' see para 930 note 2 ante.
2 For the meaning of 'qualifying partnership' see para 931 ante.
3 Ie the Partnerships and Unlimited Companies (Accounts) Regulations 1993, SI 1993/1820, reg 4(1): see para 930 ante.
4 Ie the period referred to in ibid reg 4(2): see para 930 ante.
5 Ibid reg 8(1). For the meaning of 'the standard scale' see CRIMINAL LAW vol 11(2) (Reissue) para 808.
6 Ie under ibid reg 5: see para 932 ante.
7 Ie under ibid reg 6: see para 933 ante.
8 See note 3 supra.
9 Partnerships and Unlimited Companies (Accounts) Regulations 1993 reg 8(2).
10 Ie ibid reg 5.
11 Ie ibid reg 6.
12 Ie ibid reg 7(3): see para 934 ante.
13 Ibid reg 8(3).
14 Ibid reg 8(4).
15 Ie the Companies Act 1985 s 731: see para 1164 post.
16 Ie ibid s 733 (as amended): see para 1162 post.
17 Ie ibid s 734 (as amended): see para 1163 post.
18 Partnerships and Unlimited Companies (Accounts) Regulations 1993 regs 2(1), 8(5).

H. INVESTMENT COMPANIES

936. Special provisions where the company is an investment company. The general provisions applicable to a revaluation reserve[1] do not apply to the amount of any profit or loss arising from a determination of the value of any investments of an investment company[2] on any basis applicable to investments falling to be included in either of the statutory balance sheet formats[3] under the alternative accounting rules[4].

Any provisions made[5] in the case of an investment company in respect of the diminution in value of any fixed asset investments[6] need not be charged to the company's profit and loss account provided they are either:

(1) charged against any reserve account to which any amount so excluded from the general provisions applicable to a revaluation reserve has been credited; or

(2) shown as a separate item in the company's balance sheet under the sub-heading 'other reserves'[7].

Any distribution made by an investment company which reduces the amount of its net assets[8] to less than the aggregate of its called-up share[9] capital and undistributable reserves[10] must be disclosed in a note to the company's accounts[11].

1 Ie the Companies Act 1985 s 226(3), Sch 4 para 34 (as amended): see para 815 ante.
2 For these purposes, a company is to be treated as an investment company in relation to any financial year of the company if (1) during the whole of that year it was an investment company as defined in ibid s 266 (as amended) (see para 703 ante); and (2) it was not at any time during that year prohibited under s 265(4) (as amended) (see para 703 ante) from making a distribution by virtue of s 265 (as amended): Sch 4 para 73. For the meaning of 'financial year' see para 806 ante.

3 Ie under item B.III: see paras 832, 833 ante.
4 Companies Act 1985 Sch 4 para 71(1). As to the alternative accounting rules see para 813 ante.
5 Ie by virtue of ibid Sch 4 para 19(1) or (2): see para 810 ante.
6 For these purposes, 'fixed asset investment' means any asset falling to be included under any item shown in the company's balance sheet under the sub-division 'investments' under the general item 'fixed assets': ibid Sch 4 para 71(3). For the meaning of 'balance sheet' see para 826 ante.
7 Ibid Sch 4 para 71(2).
8 For these purposes, a company's net assets are the aggregate of its assets less the aggregate of its liabilities: ibid Sch 4 para 72(2). 'Liabilities' includes any provision for liabilities or charges within Sch 4 para 89 (see para 832 note 24 ante): Sch 4 para 72(2).
9 For the meaning of 'called-up share capital' see para 174 ante.
10 For these purposes, 'undistributable reserves' has the meaning given by the Companies Act 1985 s 264(3) (see para 702 note 5 ante): Sch 4 para 72(2).
11 Ibid Sch 4 para 72(1).

(viii) Signature and Publication of Accounts

937. Approval and signing of accounts. A company's annual accounts[1] must be approved by the board of directors and signed on behalf of the board by a director of the company[2]. The signature must be on the company's balance sheet[3].

Every copy of the balance sheet which is laid before the company in general meeting or which is otherwise circulated, published or issued, must state the name of the person who signed the balance sheet on behalf of the board[4].

The copy of the company's balance sheet which is delivered to the registrar of companies must be signed on behalf of the board by a director of the company[5].

If annual accounts are approved which do not comply with the requirements of the Companies Act 1985, every director of the company who is a party to their approval and who knows that they do not comply or is reckless as to whether they comply is guilty of an offence and liable on conviction on indictment to a fine or on summary conviction to a fine not exceeding the statutory maximum[6]. For this purpose, every director of the company at the time the accounts are approved is to be taken to be a party to their approval unless he shows that he took all reasonable steps to prevent their being approved[7].

If a copy of the balance sheet:

(1) is laid before the company, or otherwise circulated, published or issued, without the balance sheet having been signed as required by the above provisions or without the required statement of the signatory's name being included; or

(2) is delivered to the registrar without being signed as required by the above provisions,

the company, and every officer of it who is in default, is guilty of an offence and liable on summary conviction to a fine not exceeding one-fifth of the statutory maximum[8].

1 For the meaning of 'annual accounts' see para 817 note 2 ante.
2 Companies Act 1985 s 233(1) (substituted by the Companies Act 1989 s 7).
3 Companies Act 1985 s 233(2) (substituted by the Companies Act 1989 s 7). For the meaning of 'balance sheet' see para 826 ante.
4 Companies Act 1985 s 233(3) (substituted by the Companies Act 1989 s 7).
5 Companies Act 1985 s 233(4) (substituted by the Companies Act 1989 s 7).
6 Companies Act 1985 s 233(5) (substituted by the Companies Act 1989 s 7); Companies Act 1985 s 730, Sch 24 (amended by the Companies Act 1989 s 23, Sch 10 para 24(1), (3)). For the meaning of 'the statutory maximum' see para 1161 post.
7 Companies Act 1985 s 233(5) (as substituted: see note 6 supra).
8 Ibid s 233(6) (substituted by the Companies Act 1989 s 7); Companies Act 1985 s 730, Sch 24 (amended by the Companies Act 1989 Sch 10 para 24(1), (2)). For the meaning of 'officer who is in default' see para 1161 post.

938. Requirements in connection with publication of accounts. If a company publishes[1] any of its statutory accounts[2], they must be accompanied by the relevant auditors' report[3].

A company which is required to prepare group accounts for a financial year must not publish its statutory individual accounts for that year without also publishing with them its statutory group accounts[4].

If a company publishes non-statutory accounts[5], it must publish with them a statement indicating:

(1) that they are not the company's statutory accounts;

(2) whether the statutory accounts dealing with any financial year with which the non-statutory accounts purport to deal have been delivered to the registrar of companies;

(3) whether the company's auditors have made a report[6] on the statutory accounts for any such financial year and, if no such report has been made, whether the company's reporting accountant[7] has made a report in respect of certain categories of small company[8] on the statutory accounts for any such financial year; and

(4) whether any auditors' report so made was qualified[9] or contained a statement[10] that the accounting records or returns were inadequate, that the accounts did not agree with the records and returns or that the auditors failed to obtain necessary information and explanations or whether any report made in respect of certain categories of small company[11] was qualified;

and it must not publish with the non-statutory accounts any auditors' report or any report made in respect of certain categories of small company[12].

A company which contravenes the above provisions, and any officer of it who is in default, is guilty of an offence and liable on summary conviction to a fine not exceeding one-fifth of the statutory maximum[13].

1 For these purposes, a company is regarded as publishing a document if it publishes, issues or circulates it or otherwise makes it available for public inspection in a manner calculated to invite members of the public generally, or any class of members of the public, to read it: Companies Act 1985 s 240(4) (substituted by the Companies Act 1989 s 10).

2 For these purposes, references to a company's statutory accounts are to its individual or group accounts for a financial year as required to be delivered to the registrar of companies under the Companies Act 1985 s 242 (as substituted and amended) (see para 818 ante): s 240(5) (substituted by the Companies Act 1989 s 10). For the meaning of 'individual accounts' see para 816 ante; and for the meaning of 'financial year' see para 806 ante. As to the duty to prepare group accounts see para 875 ante.

3 Companies Act 1985 s 240(1) (substituted by the Companies Act 1989 s 10; amended by the Companies Act 1985 (Audit Exemption) Regulations 1994, SI 1994/1935, reg 4, Sch 1 para 1(1), (2)). For these purposes, 'the relevant auditors' report' means the report under the Companies Act 1985 s 235 (as substituted) (see para 1059 post) or, as the case may be, the relevant report made for the purposes of s 249A(2) (as added) (see para 1054 post): s 240(1) (as so substituted and amended).

4 Ibid s 240(2) (substituted by the Companies Act 1989 s 10).

5 For these purposes, references to the publication by a company of 'non-statutory accounts' are to the publication of (1) any balance sheet or profit and loss account relating to, or purporting to deal with, a financial year of the company; or (2) an account in any form purporting to be a balance sheet or profit and loss account for the group consisting of the company and its subsidiary undertakings relating to, or purporting to deal with, a financial year of the company, otherwise than as part of the company's statutory accounts: Companies Act 1985 s 240(5) (as substituted: see note 2 supra). For the meaning of 'balance sheet' and 'profit and loss account' see para 826 ante; for the meaning of 'group' see para 830 note 8 ante; and for the meaning of 'subsidiary undertaking' see para 828 ante.

6 Ie under ibid s 235 (as substituted).

7 For the meaning of 'the reporting accountant' see para 1056 post.

8 Ie a report for the purposes of the Companies Act 1985 s 249A(2) (as added): see para 1054 post.

9 For the meaning of 'qualified' see para 913 note 10 ante.

10 Ie under the Companies Act 1985 s 237(2) or (3) (as substituted): see para 1061 post.
11 See note 8 supra.
12 Companies Act 1985 s 240(3) (substituted by the Companies Act 1989 s 10; amended by the Companies Act 1985 (Audit Exemption) Regulations 1994 Sch 1 para 1(1), (3)). For these purposes, 'auditors' report' means a report under the Companies Act 1985 s 235 (as substituted): s 240(3) (as so substituted).
13 Ibid s 240(6) (substituted by the Companies Act 1989 s 10); Companies Act 1985 s 730, Sch 24 (amended by the Companies Act 1989 s 23, Sch 10 para 24(1), (2)). For the meaning of 'the statutory maximum' and 'officer in default' see para 1161 post.

939. Certain companies to publish periodical statements. Every company, being an insurance company[1] or a deposit, provident or benefit[2] society, must, before it commences business, and also on the first Monday in February and the first Tuesday in August in every year during which it carries on business, make a statement in the statutory form[3], or as near to it as circumstances admit[4]. A copy of the statement must be put up in a conspicuous place in the company's registered office[5], and in every branch office or place where the business of the company is carried on[6].

If default is made in complying with this obligation, the company, and every officer of it who is in default, is liable on summary conviction to a fine not exceeding one-fifth of the statutory maximum and, on conviction after continued contravention, to a daily default fine not exceeding one-fiftieth of the statutory maximum[7].

1   For the purposes of the Companies Act 1985, a company which carries on the business of insurance in common with any other business or businesses is deemed an insurance company (s 720(5)); but s 720 does not apply in the case of an insurance company to which the Insurance Companies Act 1982 Pt II (ss 15–71 (as amended): see INSURANCE vol 25 (Reissue) para 803 et seq) applies if the company complies with the provisions of that Act as to the accounts and balance sheet to be prepared annually and deposited by such a company (Companies Act 1985 s 720(6)).
2   Such activities are more normally carried on under the legislation applying to industrial and provident societies: see INDUSTRIAL AND PROVIDENT SOCIETIES vol 24 (Reissue) para 1 et seq.
3   The prescribed form set out in the Companies Act 1985 Sch 23 reads:

FORM OF STATEMENT TO BE PUBLISHED BY CERTAIN COMPANIES UNDER SECTION 720
*The share capital of the company is   , divided into shares of   each.
The number of shares issued is
Calls to the amount of   pounds per share have been made, under which the sum of pounds has been received.
The liabilities of the company on the first day of January (*or* July) were-
    Debts owing to sundry persons by the company.
        On judgment (in Scotland, in respect of which decree has been granted), £
        On speciality, £
        On notes or bills, £
        On simple contracts, £
        On estimated liabilities, £
The assets of the company on that day were-
    Government securities [*stating them*]
    Bills of exchange and promissory notes, £
    Cash at the bankers, £
    Other securities, £
*If the company has no share capital the portion of the statement relating to capital and shares must be omitted.
    The Secretary of State may, by regulations in a statutory instrument, subject to annulment in pursuance of a resolution of either House of Parliament, alter the form in Sch 23: s 720(7). At the date at which this volume states the law no such regulations had been made.
4   Ibid s 720(1). In the case of an EC company, s 720 does not apply if the company complies with provisions of law of its home State as to the accounts and balance sheet to be prepared annually and deposited with the supervisory authority in that State by such a company: see the Insurance Companies (Third Insurance Directives) Regulations 1994, SI 1994/1696, reg 68(1), Sch 8 Pt I para 9(6) and INSURANCE.

5 As to the registered office see para 150 ante.

6 Companies Act 1985 s 720(2). Every member and every creditor of the company is entitled to a copy of the statement on payment of a sum not exceeding two pence: s 720(3). The figure has been rounded down in consequence of the withdrawal of the halfpenny from 31 December 1984.

7 Ibid ss 720(4), 730, Sch 24. For the meaning of 'officer who is in default', 'the statutory maximum' and 'daily default fine' see para 1161 post.

(ix) Revision of Defective Accounts

A. VOLUNTARY REVISION BY DIRECTORS

940. Voluntary revision of annual accounts. If it appears to the directors of a company that any annual accounts[1] of the company did not comply with the requirements of the Companies Act 1985, they may prepare revised accounts[2]. Where copies of the previous accounts have been laid before the company in general meeting or delivered to the registrar of companies, the revisions must be confined to:

(1) the correction of those respects in which the previous accounts did not comply with the requirements of that Act; and

(2) the making of any necessary consequential alterations[3].

The Secretary of State may make provision by regulations as to the application of the provisions of the 1985 Act in relation to revised annual accounts[4]. The regulations may in particular:

(a) make different provision according to whether the previous accounts are replaced or are supplemented by a document indicating the corrections to be made;

(b) make provision with respect to the functions of the company's auditors or reporting accountant[5] in relation to the revised accounts;

(c) require the directors to take such steps as may be specified in the regulations where the previous accounts have been sent out to members and others[6], laid before the company in general meeting or delivered to the registrar of companies, or where a summary financial statement based on the previous accounts or report has been sent to members[7];

(d) apply the provisions of the Companies Act 1985, including those creating criminal offences, subject to such additions, exceptions and modifications as are specified in the regulations[8].

Any such regulations must be made by statutory instrument which is subject to annulment in pursuance of a resolution of either House of Parliament[9].

1 For the meaning of 'annual accounts' see para 817 note 2 ante.

2 Companies Act 1985 s 245(1) (substituted by the Companies Act 1989 s 12). As to the revision of defective directors' reports see para 1078 et seq post.

3 Companies Act 1985 s 245(2) (substituted by the Companies Act 1989 s 12).

4 Companies Act 1985 s 245(3) (substituted by the Companies Act 1989 s 12). In exercise of the power so conferred the Secretary of State made the Companies (Revision of Defective Accounts and Report) Regulations 1990, SI 1990/2570 (amended by SI 1992/3075; SI 1994/1935; SI 1995/2092; SI 1996/315): see para 941 et seq post.

5 For the meaning of 'the reporting accountant' see para 1056 post.

6 Ie under the Companies Act 1985 s 238(1) (as substituted): see para 823 ante.

7 Ie under ibid s 251 (as substituted and amended): see para 914 et seq ante.

8 Ibid s 245(4) (substituted by the Companies Act 1989 s 12; amended by the Companies Act 1985 (Audit Exemption) Regulations 1994, SI 1994/1935, reg 4, Sch 1 Pt I para 2).

9 Companies Act 1985 s 245(5) (substituted by the Companies Act 1989 s 12).

941. Content of revised accounts. The provisions of the Companies Act 1985 as to the matters to be included in the annual accounts of a company[1] apply to the revised accounts[2] as if the revised accounts were prepared and approved by the directors as at the date of the original[3] annual accounts[4].

1 As to the matters to be included see para 801 et seq ante. In particular, the Companies Act 1985 s 226(2) (as substituted) (see para 816 ante) and s 227(3) (as substituted) (see para 875 ante) apply so as to require a true and fair view to be shown in the revised accounts of the matters therein referred to, viewed as at the date of the original annual accounts: Companies (Revision of Defective Accounts and Report) Regulations 1990, SI 1990/2570, regs 2, 3(2). The Companies Act 1985 s 226(3), Sch 4 para 12(b) (as amended) (see para 809 head (3)(b) ante) applies to revised accounts as if the reference therein to the date on which the accounts were signed was to the date of the original annual accounts: Companies (Revision of Defective Accounts and Report) Regulations 1990 regs 2, 3(3).

2 For these purposes, 'revised accounts' means revised annual accounts of a company prepared by the directors under the Companies Act 1985 s 245 (as substituted and amended) (see para 940 ante), either through revision by replacement or revision by supplementary note; in the latter case the revised accounts comprise the original annual accounts together with the supplementary note: Companies (Revision of Defective Accounts and Report) Regulations 1990 reg 2. For the meaning of 'original' see note 3 infra.

3 For these purposes, 'original', in relation to annual accounts, means the annual accounts which are the subject of revision by revised accounts and, in relation to abbreviated accounts, within the meaning of ibid reg 13(1) (see para 948 post) or a summary financial statement, means abbreviated accounts or a summary financial statement based on the original annual accounts: reg 2. 'Revision by replacement' means revision by the preparation of a replacement set of accounts in substitution for the original annual accounts (reg 2); and 'revision by supplementary note' means revision by the preparation of a note indicating corrections to be made to the original annual accounts (reg 2).

4 Ibid regs 2, 3(1). For these purposes, 'date of the original annual accounts' means the date on which the original annual accounts were approved by the board of directors under the Companies Act 1985 s 233 (as substituted) (see para 937 ante): Companies (Revision of Defective Accounts and Report) Regulations 1990 reg 2. As to the content of revised directors' reports see para 1079 post.

  Regulation 3(1) is subject to reg 16(1): reg 3(1). Where the provisions of the Companies Act 1985 as to the matters to be included in the annual accounts of a company or, as the case may be, in a directors' report have been amended after the date of the original annual accounts or, as the case may be, directors' report but prior to the date of revision, references in the Companies (Revision of Defective Accounts and Report) Regulations 1990 reg 3 (see supra and para 1079 post) and reg 6(3) (see para 943 post) to the provisions of the Companies Act 1985 are to be construed as references to the provisions of the 1985 Act as in force at the date of the original annual accounts or, as the case may be, directors' report: Companies (Revision of Defective Accounts and Report) Regulations 1990 regs 2, 16(1). For these purposes, 'date of revision' means the date on which revised accounts are approved by the board of directors under reg 4 (see para 942 post): reg 2.

942. Approval and signature of revised accounts. The statutory provisions relating to the approval and signing of accounts[1] apply to revised accounts[2], save that, in the case of revision by supplementary note[3], they apply as if they required a signature on the supplementary note instead of on the company's balance sheet[4].

Where copies of the original[5] annual accounts have been sent out to members[6], laid before the company in general meeting[7] or delivered to the registrar of companies[8], the directors must, before approving the revised accounts[9], cause statements as to the following matters to be made in a prominent position in the revised accounts (in the case of a revision by supplementary note, in that note):

(1) in the case of revision by replacement[10]:

    (a) that the revised accounts replace the original annual accounts for the financial year, specifying it;

    (b) that they are now the statutory accounts of the company for that financial year;

    (c) that they have been prepared as at the date of the original annual accounts[11] and not as at the date of revision[12] and accordingly do not deal with events between those dates;

    (d) the respects in which the original annual accounts did not comply with the requirements of the Companies Act 1985; and

    (e) any significant amendments made consequential upon the remedying of those defects;

  (2) in the case of revision by a supplementary note:

    (a) that the note revises in certain respects the original annual accounts of the company and is to be treated as forming part of those accounts; and

    (b) that the annual accounts have been revised as at the date of the original annual accounts and not as at the date of revision and accordingly do not deal with events between those dates,

and must, when approving the revised accounts, cause the date on which the approval is given to be stated in them (in the case of revision by supplementary note, in that note)[13].

1 Ie the Companies Act 1985 s 233 (as substituted): see para 937 ante.
2 For the meaning of 'revised accounts' see para 941 note 2 ante.
3 For the meaning of 'revision by supplementary note' see para 941 note 3 ante.
4 Companies (Revision of Defective Accounts and Report) Regulations 1990, SI 1990/2570, regs 2, 4(1). As to the approval and signature of revised directors' reports see para 1080 post.
5 For the meaning of 'original' see para 941 note 3 ante.
6 Ie under the Companies Act 1985 s 238(1) (as substituted): see para 823 ante.
7 Ie under ibid s 241(1) (as substituted): see para 817 ante.
8 Ie under ibid s 242(1) (as substituted): see para 818 ante.
9 Ie under ibid s 233 (as substituted).
10 For the meaning of 'revision by replacement' see para 941 note 3 ante.
11 For the meaning of 'date of the original annual accounts' see para 941 note 4 ante.
12 For the meaning of 'date of revision' see para 941 note 4 ante.
13 Companies (Revision of Defective Accounts and Report) Regulations 1990 regs 2, 4(2). The Companies Act 1985 s 233(5) (as substituted) (see para 937 ante) applies with respect to a failure to comply with the Companies (Revision of Defective Accounts and Report) Regulations 1990 reg 4(2) as if the requirements of reg 4(2) were requirements of the Companies Act 1985: Companies (Revision of Defective Accounts and Report) Regulations 1990 reg 4(2).

943. Auditors' report on revised accounts and revised report. A company's current auditors must make a report or, as the case may be, a further report[1] to the company's members under these provisions on any revised accounts[2] prepared[3].

Where, however, the auditors' report on the original[4] annual accounts was not made by the company's current auditors, the directors of the company may resolve that the report so required[5] is to be made by the person or persons who made that report, provided that that person or those persons agree to do so and he or they would be qualified for appointment as auditor of the company[6].

An auditors' report under these provisions must state whether in the auditors' opinion the revised accounts have been properly prepared in accordance with the provisions of the Companies Act 1985[7], and in particular whether a true and fair view, seen as at the date the original annual accounts were approved, is given by the revised accounts with respect to the specified[8] matters[9]. The report must state whether in the auditors' opinion the original annual accounts failed to comply with the 1985 Act in the respects identified by the directors (in the case of revision by replacement[10]) in the required statement[11] or (in the case of revision by supplementary note[12]) in the supplementary note[13].

The auditors must also consider whether the information contained in the directors' report for the financial year for which the annual accounts are prepared[14] is consistent with those accounts; and, if they are of the opinion that it is not, they must state that fact in their report under these provisions[15].

An auditors' report under these provisions, upon being signed[16], is, as from the date of signature, the auditors' report on the annual accounts of the company in place of the report on the original annual accounts[17].

Where a company's reporting accountant[18] has, prior to the preparation of the revised accounts, made a report[19] on the original annual accounts, he must make a further report to the company's members under these provisions on any revised accounts prepared[20] by him[21]. The directors may, however, resolve that the further report is to be made by a person who was not the original reporting accountant, but is qualified to act as the reporting accountant of the company[22]. Such a report, upon being signed by the reporting accountant, is, as from the date of the signature, the report on the annual accounts of the company[23] in place of the report on the original annual accounts[24].

Where, as a result of the revisions to the accounts, a company which, in respect of the original accounts, was exempt from audit because it met the total exemption conditions[25], becomes a company which is eligible for exemption only because it meets the report conditions[26], it must cause a report to be prepared[27] in accordance with the revised accounts[28]. Where, as a result of the revisions to the accounts, the company is no longer entitled to exemption from audit[29], the company must cause an auditors' report on the revised accounts to be prepared[30]. The report so made[31] or auditors' report must be delivered to the registrar within 28 days after the date of revision[32] of the revised accounts[33].

1 Ie under the Companies Act 1985 s 235 (as substituted): see para 1059 post.
2 For the meaning of 'revised accounts' see para 941 note 2 ante.
3 Companies (Revision of Defective Accounts and Report) Regulations 1990, SI 1990/2570, regs 2, 6(1) (amended by SI 1996/315). The Companies Act 1985 s 237 (as substituted and amended) (see para 1061 post) applies mutatis mutandis; and s 235(1) (as substituted) does not apply with respect to the revised accounts: Companies (Revision of Defective Accounts and Report) Regulations 1990 regs 2, 6(1). As to the auditors' report on a revised report alone see para 1081 post.
4 For the meaning of 'original' see para 941 note 3 ante.
5 Ie by the Companies (Revision of Defective Accounts and Report) Regulations 1990 reg 6(1): see supra.
6 Ibid reg 6(2). As to qualification for appointment as auditor of a company see para 955 et seq post.
7 Ie as the provisions of the Companies Act 1985 have effect under the Companies (Revision of Defective Accounts and Report) Regulations 1990.
8 Ie the matters specified in the Companies Act 1985 s 235(2)(a)-(c) (as substituted): see para 1059 heads (1)-(3) post.
9 Companies (Revision of Defective Accounts and Report) Regulations 1990 reg 6(3). Regulation 6(3) is subject to reg 16(1) (see para 941 note 4 ante): reg 6(3).
10 For the meaning of 'revision by replacement' see para 941 note 3 ante.
11 Ie the statement required by the Companies (Revision of Defective Accounts and Report) Regulations 1990 reg 4(2)(a)(iv): see para 942 head (1)(d) ante.
12 For the meaning of 'revision by supplementary note' see para 941 note 3 ante.
13 Companies (Revision of Defective Accounts and Report) Regulations 1990 reg 6(3). See also note 9 supra.
14 Ie which is, if the report has been revised under the Companies (Revision of Defective Accounts and Report) Regulations 1990 (see para 1078 et seq post), that revised report.
15 Ibid reg 6(4).

16 Ie under the Companies Act 1985 s 236 (as substituted): see para 1060 post. Section 236 (as substituted) applies to an auditors' report under the Companies (Revision of Defective Accounts and Report) Regulations 1990 reg 6 as it applies to an auditors' report under the Companies Act 1985 s 235(1) (as substituted) mutatis mutandis: Companies (Revision of Defective Accounts and Report) Regulations 1990 reg 6(5).

17 Ibid reg 6(6).

18 For the meaning of 'the reporting accountant' see para 1056 post.

19 Ie for the purposes of the Companies Act 1985 s 249A(2) (as added): see para 1054 post.

20 Ie prepared under ibid s 245 (as substituted and amended): see para 940 ante.

21 Companies (Revision of Defective Accounts and Report) Regulations 1990 reg 6A(1) (added by SI 1994/1935). The Companies Act 1985 s 249C (as added) (see para 1056 post) applies mutatis mutandis: Companies (Revision of Defective Accounts and Report) Regulations 1990 reg 6A(1) (as so added).

22 Ibid reg 6A(2) (added by SI 1994/1935).

23 See note 19 supra.

24 Companies (Revision of Defective Accounts and Report) Regulations 1990 reg 6A(4) (added by SI 1994/1935). The Companies Act 1985 s 236(2)-(4) (as added) (see para 1060 post) applies to a report under the Companies (Revision of Defective Accounts and Report) Regulations 1990 reg 6A (as added) as it applies, by virtue of the Companies Act 1985 s 249A(2)(a) (as added) (see para 1054 post), to a report made for the purposes of s 249A(2) (as added): Companies (Revision of Defective Accounts and Report) Regulations 1990 reg 6A(3) (added by SI 1994/1935).

25 Ie by virtue of the Companies Act 1985 s 249A(1) (as added): see para 1054 post.

26 Ie by virtue of ibid s 249A(2) (as added): see para 1054 post.

27 Ie in accordance with ibid s 249C (as added): see para 1056 post.

28 Companies (Revision of Defective Accounts and Report) Regulations 1990 reg 6B(1) (added by SI 1994/1935). The Companies Act 1985 s 242(2)-(5) (as substituted) (see para 818 ante) applies with respect to a failure to comply with the requirements of the Companies (Revision of Defective Accounts and Reports) Regulations 1990 reg 6B (as added) as it applies with respect to a failure to comply with the requirements of the Companies Act 1985 s 242(1) (as substituted and amended) (see para 818 ante) but as if (1) the references in s 242(2), (4) (as substituted) to 'the period allowed for laying and delivering accounts and reports' were references to the period of 28 days referred to in the Companies (Revision of Defective Accounts and Report) Regulations 1990 reg 6B(3) (as added) (see infra); and (2) the references in the Companies Act 1985 s 242(5) (as substituted) to 'the documents in question' and 'this Part' were respectively a reference to the documents referred to in the Companies (Revision of Defective Accounts and Report) Regulations 1990 reg 6B(3) (as added) and to the provisions of the Companies Act 1985 Pt VII (ss 221-262A (as amended): see para 801 et seq ante) as applied by the Companies (Revision of Defective Accounts and Report) Regulations 1990: reg 6B(4) (added by SI 1994/1935).

29 Ie under the Companies Act 1985 s 249A(1) or (2) (as added).

30 Companies (Revision of Defective Accounts and Report) Regulations 1990 reg 6B(2) (added by SI 1994/1935). See also note 28 supra.

31 See note 27 supra.

32 For the meaning of 'date of revision' see para 941 note 4 ante.

33 Companies (Revision of Defective Accounts and Report) Regulations 1990 reg 6B(3) (added by SI 1994/1935). See also note 28 supra.

944. Effect of revision. Upon the directors approving revised accounts[1], the provisions of the Companies Act 1985 have effect as if the revised accounts were, as from the date of their approval, the annual accounts of the company in place of the original[2] annual accounts[3]. In particular, the revised accounts are thereupon the company's annual accounts for the relevant financial year for the purposes of the statutory provisions relating to the right to demand copies of accounts and reports[4], the requirements in connection with the publication of accounts[5], the entitlement of persons to receive copies of accounts and reports[6], the duty to lay accounts and reports before the company in general meeting[7] and the delivery of accounts and reports to the registrar of companies[8], if the requirements of those provisions have not been complied with prior to the date of revision[9].

1 Ie under the Companies (Revision of Defective Accounts and Report) Regulations 1990, SI 1990/2570, reg 4: see para 942 ante. For the meaning of 'revised accounts' see para 941 note 2 ante.
2 For the meaning of 'original' see para 941 note 3 ante.
3 Companies (Revision of Defective Accounts and Report) Regulations 1990 regs 2, 8(1). As to the effect of revision of directors' reports see para 1082 post.
4 Ie the Companies Act 1985 s 239 (as substituted): see para 824 ante.
5 Ie ibid s 240(5) (as substituted): see para 938 ante.
6 Ie ibid s 238 (as substituted): see para 823 ante.
7 Ie ibid s 241 (as substituted): see para 817 ante.
8 Ie ibid s 242 (as substituted): see para 818 ante.
9 Companies (Revision of Defective Accounts and Report) Regulations 1990 regs 2, 8(2). For the meaning of 'date of revision' see para 941 note 4 ante.

945. Publication of revised accounts. The following provisions have effect where the directors have prepared revised accounts[1] and copies of the original[2] accounts have been sent[3] to any person entitled to receive a copy[4].

The directors must send to any such person:

(1) in the case of a revision by replacement[5], a copy of the revised accounts, together with a copy of the auditors' report on those accounts; or

(2) in the case of revision by supplementary note[6], a copy of that note together with a copy of the auditors' report on the revised accounts,

not more than 28 days after the date of revision[7].

The directors must also, not more than 28 days after the revision, send a copy of the revised accounts, together with a copy of the auditors' report on those accounts to any person who is not a person entitled to receive a copy under the above provisions but who is, as at the date of revision:

(a) a member of the company;

(b) a holder of the company's debentures; or

(c) a person who is entitled to receive notice of general meetings,

unless the company would be entitled[8] at that date to send to that person a summary financial statement[9].

1 Ie under the Companies Act 1985 s 245 (as substituted and amended): see para 940 ante. For the meaning of 'revised accounts' see para 941 note 2 ante.
2 For the meaning of 'original' see para 941 note 3 ante.
3 Ie under the Companies Act 1985 s 238 (as substituted): see para 823 ante.
4 Companies (Revision of Defective Accounts and Report) Regulations 1990, SI 1990/2570, regs 2, 10(1). The Companies Act 1985 s 238(5) (as substituted) (see para 823 ante) applies to a default in complying with the Companies (Revision of Defective Accounts and Report) Regulations 1990 reg 10 (as amended) as if the provisions of reg 10 (as amended) were provisions of the Companies Act 1985 s 238 (as substituted) and as if the reference therein to 'the company and every officer of it who is in default' were a reference to each of the directors who approved the revised accounts under the Companies (Revision of Defective Accounts and Report) Regulations 1990 reg 4 (see para 942 ante): reg 10(4). As to publication of revised directors' reports see para 1083 post.
5 For the meaning of 'revision by replacement' see para 941 note 3 ante.
6 For the meaning of 'revision by supplementary note' see para 941 note 3 ante.
7 Companies (Revision of Defective Accounts and Report) Regulations 1990 reg 10(2). For the meaning of 'date of revision' see para 941 note 4 ante.
8 Ie under the Companies Act 1985 s 251 (as substituted and amended): see para 914 et seq ante.
9 Companies (Revision of Defective Accounts and Report) Regulations 1990 reg 10(3) (amended by SI 1992/3075; SI 1996/315). The Companies Act 1985 s 238(2), (3) (as substituted) (see para 823 ante) applies to the Companies (Revision of Defective Accounts and Report) Regulations 1990 reg 10(3) as it has effect with respect to the Companies Act 1985 s 238(1) (as substituted): Companies (Revision of Defective Accounts and Report) Regulations 1990 regs 2, 10(3).

Where, prior to the date of revision of the original annual accounts, the company had completed sending out copies of those accounts under the Companies Act 1985 s 238 (as substituted) (see para 823 ante), references in that Act to the day on which accounts are sent out under s 238 (as substituted) are to be construed as referring to the day on which the original accounts were sent out (applying s 238(6) (as substituted) as necessary), notwithstanding that those accounts have been revised; where the company had not completed, prior to the date of revision, the sending out of copies of those accounts under s 238 (as substituted), such references are to the day, or the last day, on which the revised accounts are sent out: Companies (Revision of Defective Accounts and Report) Regulations 1990 reg 10(5).

946. Laying of revised accounts. Where the directors have prepared revised accounts[1] and copies of the original[2] annual accounts have been laid[3] before a general meeting, a copy of the revised accounts, together with a copy of the auditors' report on those accounts must be laid before the next general meeting of the company held after the date of revision[4] at which any annual accounts for a financial year are laid, unless the revised accounts have already been laid before an earlier general meeting[5].

1 Ie under the Companies Act 1985 s 245 (as substituted and amended): see para 940 ante. For the meaning of 'revised accounts' see para 941 note 2 ante.
2 For the meaning of 'original' see para 941 note 3 ante.
3 Ie under the Companies Act 1985 s 241 (as substituted): see para 817 ante.
4 For the meaning of 'date of revision' see para 941 note 4 ante.
5 Companies (Revision of Defective Accounts and Report) Regulations 1990, SI 1990/2570, regs 2, 11(1), (2). The Companies Act 1985 s 241(2)-(4) (as substituted) (see para 817 ante) applies with respect to a failure to comply with the requirements of the Companies (Revision of Defective Accounts and Report) Regulations 1990 reg 11 as it has effect with respect to a failure to comply with the requirements of the Companies Act 1985 s 241(1) (as substituted) (see para 817 ante) but as if (1) the reference in s 241(2) (as substituted) to 'the period allowed for laying and delivering accounts and reports' were a reference to the period between the date of revision of the revised accounts or, as the case may be, the revised report and the date of the next general meeting of the company held after the date of revision at which any annual accounts for a financial year are laid; and references in s 241(2), (3) (as substituted) to 'that period' are to be construed accordingly; and (2) the references in s 241(4) (as substituted) to 'the documents in question' and 'this Part' were respectively a reference to the documents referred to in the Companies (Revision of Defective Accounts and Report) Regulations 1990 reg 11(3)(a) (see head (1) supra) and the provisions of the Companies Act 1985 Pt VII (ss 221-262A (as amended): see para 801 et seq ante) as applied by the Companies (Revision of Defective Accounts and Report) Regulations 1990: reg 11(3). For the meaning of 'revised report' see para 1079 note 2 post. As to the laying of revised directors' reports see para 1084 post.

947. Delivery to the registrar of revised accounts. Where the directors have prepared revised accounts[1] and a copy of the original[2] annual accounts have been delivered to the registrar of companies[3], the directors of the company must, within 28 days of the date of revision[4], deliver to the registrar:

(1) in the case of a revision by replacement[5], a copy of the revised accounts, together with a copy of the auditors' report on those accounts; or

(2) in the case of a revision by supplementary note[6], a copy of that note, together with a copy of the auditors' report on the revised accounts[7].

1 Ie under the Companies Act 1985 s 245 (as substituted and amended): see para 940 ante. For the meaning of 'revised accounts' see para 941 note 2 ante.
2 For the meaning of 'original' see para 941 note 3 ante.
3 Ie under the Companies Act 1985 s 242 (as substituted and amended): see para 818 ante.
4 For the meaning of 'date of revision' see para 941 note 4 ante.
5 For the meaning of 'revision by replacement' see para 941 note 3 ante.
6 For the meaning of 'revision by supplementary note' see para 941 note 3 ante.
7 Companies (Revision of Defective Accounts and Report) Regulations 1990, SI 1990/2570, regs 2, 12(1), (2). The Companies Act 1985 s 242(2)-(5) (as substituted) (see para 818 ante) applies with respect to a failure to comply with the requirements of the Companies (Revision of Defective Accounts and Report) Regulations 1990 reg 12 as it applies with respect to a failure to comply with the requirements

of the Companies Act 1985 s 242(1) (as substituted and amended) (see para 818 ante) but as if (1) the references in s 242(2), (4) (as substituted) to 'the period allowed for laying and delivering accounts and reports' were a reference to the period of 28 days referred to in the Companies (Revision of Defective Accounts and Report) Regulations 1990 reg 12(2) (see supra); and the reference in the Companies Act 1985 s 242(2) (as substituted) to 'that period' is to be construed accordingly; (2) the references in s 242(5) (as substituted) to 'the documents in question' and 'this Part' were respectively a reference to the documents referred to in the Companies (Revision of Defective Accounts and Report) Regulations 1990 reg 12(3)(a) (see head (1) supra) and the provisions of the Companies Act 1985 Pt VII (ss 221-262A (as amended): see para 801 et seq ante) as applied by the Companies (Revision of Defective Accounts and Report) Regulations 1990: reg 12(3). As to delivery of revised directors' reports see para 1085 post.

948. Small and medium-sized companies. Where the directors have prepared revised accounts[1] and the company has, prior to the date of revision[2], delivered to the registrar of companies accounts which take advantage of the exemptions for a small or medium-sized company ('abbreviated accounts')[3], the following provisions apply[4].

Where the abbreviated accounts so delivered to the registrar would, if they had been prepared by reference to the revised accounts, not comply with the provisions of the Companies Act 1985, whether because the company would not have qualified as a small or, as the case may be, medium-sized company in the light of the revised accounts or because the accounts have been revised in a manner which affects the content of the abbreviated accounts, the directors of the company must cause the company either:

(1) to deliver to the registrar a copy of the revised accounts, together with a copy of the directors' report[5] and the auditors' report[6] on the revised accounts; or

(2) if on the basis of the revised accounts they would be entitled under the 1985 Act to do so, to prepare further accounts[7] and deliver them to the registrar together with a statement as to the effect of the revisions made[8].

Where the abbreviated accounts would, if they had been prepared by reference to the revised accounts, comply with the requirements of the 1985 Act, the directors of the company must cause the company to deliver to the registrar:

(a) a note stating that the annual accounts of the company for the relevant financial year, specifying it, have been revised in a respect which has no bearing on the abbreviated accounts delivered for that year; together with

(b) a copy of the auditors' report on the revised accounts[9].

Revised abbreviated accounts or a note under these provisions must be delivered to the registrar within 28 days after the date of revision of the revised accounts[10].

Where the directors have delivered to the registrar abbreviated accounts which do not comply with the provisions of the 1985 Act for reasons other than those specified above[11], the directors of the company must cause the company:

(i) to prepare further abbreviated accounts[12]; and

(ii) to deliver those accounts to the registrar within 28 days after the date of revision together with a statement as to the effect of the revisions made[13].

1 Ie under the Companies Act 1985 s 245 (as substituted and amended): see para 940 ante. For the meaning of 'revised accounts' see para 941 note 2 ante.
2 For the meaning of 'date of revision' see para 941 note 4 ante.
3 Ie the Companies Act 1985 s 246 (as substituted and amended): see para 900 ante.
4 Companies (Revision of Defective Accounts and Report) Regulations 1990, SI 1990/2570, regs 2, 13(1). The Companies Act 1985 s 242(2)-(5) (as substituted) (see para 818 ante) applies with respect to a failure to comply with the requirements of the Companies (Revision of Defective Accounts and Reports) Regulations 1990 reg 13 as it applies with respect to a failure to comply with the requirements of the Companies Act 1985 s 242(1) (as substituted and amended) (see para 818 ante) but as if (1) the references in s 242(2), (4) (as substituted) to 'the period allowed for laying and delivering accounts and reports' were a reference to the period of 28 days referred to in the Companies (Revision of Defective Accounts and Report) Regulations 1990 reg 13(4) (see infra); and the reference in the Companies Act

1985 s 242(2) (as substituted) to 'that period' is to be construed accordingly; (2) the references in s 242(5) (as substituted) to 'the documents in question' and 'this Part' were respectively a reference to the documents referred to in the Companies (Revision of Defective Accounts and Report) Regulations 1990 reg 13(2)(a) or (b) (see text heads (1), (2) infra) or, as the case may be, reg 13(3)(a), (b) (see text heads (a), (b) infra) and to the provisions of the Companies Act 1985 Pt VII (ss 221-262A (as amended): see para 801 et seq ante) as applied by the Companies (Revision of Defective Accounts and Report) Regulations 1990: reg 13(5).

Regulation 13 has effect subject to reg 16(2): reg 13(1). Where the provisions of the Companies Act 1985 s 246 (as substituted and amended) and Sch 8 (as substituted and amended) as to the matters to be included in abbreviated accounts, within the meaning of the Companies (Revision of Defective Accounts and Report) Regulations 1990 reg 13(1), have been amended after the date of delivery of the original abbreviated accounts but prior to the date of revision of the revised accounts or report, references in reg 13 or reg 13A (as added) (see infra) to the provisions of the Companies Act 1985 or to any particular provision thereof are to be construed as references to the provisions of the Companies Act 1985, or to the particular provision, as in force at the date of delivery of the original abbreviated accounts: Companies (Revision of Defective Accounts and Report) Regulations 1990 reg 16(2) (amended by SI 1996/315).

5 As to the directors' report see para 1066 et seq post.
6 As to the auditors' report on the revised accounts see para 943 ante.
7 Ie under the Companies Act 1985 s 246 (as substituted and amended), in accordance with the provisions of s 246 (as substituted and amended) and s 246, Sch 8 (as substituted and amended) (see para 904 et seq ante).
8 Companies (Revision of Defective Accounts and Report) Regulations 1990 regs 2, 13(2). See also note 4 supra.
9 Ibid reg 13(3). See also note 4 supra.
10 Ibid reg 13(4). See also note 4 supra.
11 Ie specified in ibid reg 13(2): see supra.
12 See note 7 supra.
13 Companies (Revision of Defective Accounts and Report) Regulations 1990 regs 2, 13A(1), (2) (added by SI 1996/315). Regulation 13A (as added) has effect subject to reg 16(2) (see note 4 supra): reg 13A(1) (as so added). The Companies Act 1985 s 242(2)-(5) (as substituted) (see para 818 ante) applies with respect to a failure to comply with the requirements of the Companies (Revision of Defective Accounts and Report) Regulations 1990 reg 13A (as added) as it applies with respect to a failure to comply with the requirements of the Companies Act 1985 s 242(1) (as substituted and amended) (see para 818 ante) but as if (1) the references in s 242(2), (4) (as substituted) to 'the period allowed for laying and delivering accounts and reports' were a reference to the period of 28 days referred to in the Companies (Revision of Defective Accounts and Report) Regulations 1990 reg 13A(2) (as so added); and the reference in the Companies Act 1985 s 242(2) (as substituted) to 'that period' is to be construed accordingly; (2) the references in s 242(5) (as substituted) to 'the documents in question' were a reference to the documents referred to in the Companies (Revision of Defective Accounts and Report) Regulations 1990 reg 13A(2)(a) (see text head (i) supra) and to the provisions of the Companies Act 1985 Pt VII (ss 221-262A (as amended): see para 801 et seq ante) as applied by the Companies (Revision of Defective Accounts and Report) Regulations 1990: reg 13A(3) (added by SI 1996/315).

949. Summary financial statements. Where the directors have prepared[1] revised accounts[2] or a revised report[3] and a summary financial statement based upon the original[4] annual accounts or report has been sent to any person[5], the following provisions apply[6].

Where the summary financial statement would, if it had been prepared by reference to the revised accounts or revised report, not comply with the statutory requirements[7], the directors of the company must cause the company to prepare a further summary financial statement[8] and to send that statement to:

(1) any person who received a copy of the original summary financial statement; and

(2) any person to whom the company would be entitled, as at the date the revised summary financial statement is prepared, to send a summary financial statement for the current financial year[9].

A summary financial statement so prepared must contain a short statement of the revisions made and their effect[10].

Where the summary financial statement would, if it had been prepared by reference to the revised accounts or revised report, comply with the statutory requirements[11], the directors must cause the company to send to the persons referred to in heads (1) and (2) above a note stating that the annual accounts of the company for the relevant financial year, specifying it, or, as the case may be, the directors' report have or has been revised in a respect which has no bearing on the summary financial statement for that year[12]. If the auditors' report[13] on the revised accounts or revised report is qualified, a copy of that report must be attached to the note sent out under these provisions[14].

A summary financial statement revised, or a note prepared, under these provisions, must be sent to the persons referred to in heads (1) and (2) above within 28 days after the date of revision[15] of the revised account or revised report[16].

1 Ie under the Companies Act 1985 s 245 (as substituted and amended): see para 940 ante and para 1078 post.
2 For the meaning of 'revised accounts' see para 941 note 2 ante.
3 For the meaning of 'revised report' see para 1079 note 2 post.
4 For the meaning of 'original' see para 941 note 3 ante.
5 Ie under the Companies Act 1985 251 (as substituted and amended): see para 914 ante.
6 Companies (Revision of Defective Accounts and Report) Regulations 1990, SI 1990/2570, regs 2, 14(1) (amended by SI 1992/3075). The Companies Act 1985 s 251(6) (as substituted) applies with respect to a failure to comply with the Companies (Revision of Defective Accounts and Report) Regulations 1990 reg 14 (as amended) as if the provisions of reg 14 were provisions of the Companies Act 1985 s 251 (as substituted and amended) and as if the reference therein to 'the company and every officer of it who is in default' were a reference to each of the directors of the company who approved the revised accounts under the Companies (Revision of Defective Accounts and Report) Regulations 1990 reg 4 (see para 942 ante) or the revised report under reg 5 (see para 1080 post): reg 14(6).
   Regulation 14 (as amended) has effect subject to reg 16(3) (as amended): reg 14(1) (as so amended). Where the provisions of the Companies Act 1985 s 251 (as substituted and amended) or of the Companies (Summary Financial Statement) Regulations 1995, SI 1995/2092 (see para 915 et seq ante) as to the matters to be included in a summary financial statement have been amended after the date of the sending out of the original summary financial statement but prior to the date of revision of the revised accounts or report, references in the Companies (Revision of Defective Accounts and Report) Regulations 1990 reg 14 (as amended) to the Companies Act 1985 s 251 (as substituted and amended) or to the Companies (Summary Financial Statement) Regulations 1995 are to be construed as references to the Companies Act 1985 s 251 (as substituted and amended) or to the Companies (Summary Financial Statement) Regulations 1995 as in force at the date of the sending out of the original summary financial statements: Companies (Revision of Defective Accounts and Report) Regulations 1990 reg 16(3) (amended by SI 1995/2092).
7 Ie the requirements of the Companies Act 1985 s 251 (as substituted and amended) or the Companies (Summary Financial Statement) Regulations 1995 made thereunder.
8 See note 5 supra.
9 Companies (Revision of Defective Accounts and Report) Regulations 1990 regs 2, 14(2) (amended by SI 1995/2092). The Companies Act 1985 s 251(1)-(4), (7) (as substituted and amended) applies mutatis mutandis to a summary financial statement under the Companies (Revision of Defective Accounts and Report) Regulations 1990 reg 14(2) (as so amended): reg 14(2) (as so amended).
10 Ibid reg 14(3).
11 See note 7 supra.
12 Companies (Revision of Defective Accounts and Report) Regulations 1990 regs 2, 14(4) (amended by SI 1995/2092).
13 Ie under ibid reg 6 (as amended) (see para 943 ante) or reg 7 (as amended) (see para 1081 post).
14 Ibid reg 14(4) (as amended: see note 12 supra).
15 For the meaning of 'date of revision' see para 941 note 4 ante.
16 Companies (Revision of Defective Accounts and Report) Regulations 1990 reg 14(5).

950. Certain categories of small companies exempt from audit. Where a company which meets the total exemption condition[1] is exempt from the provisions of the Companies Act 1985[2] relating to the audit of accounts, the Companies (Revision of Defective Accounts and Report) Regulations 1990[3] have effect as if any reference to an auditors' report, or to the making of such a report, were omitted[4].

Where a company which meets the report conditions[5] is exempt from the provisions of the Companies Act 1985[6] relating to the audit of accounts, specified provisions[7] of the Companies (Revision of Defective Accounts and Report) Regulations 1990 have effect as if:

(1) references to the auditors' report on any accounts were references to the report made[8] in respect of those accounts; and

(2) references to the auditors' report on a revised directors' report were omitted[9].

1 Ie where a company is exempt by virtue of the Companies Act 1985 s 249A(1) (as added): see para 1054 post.
2 Ie the provisions of ibid Pt VII (ss 221-262A) (as amended): see para 1054 et seq post.
3 Ie the Companies (Revision of Defective Accounts and Report) Regulations 1990, SI 1990/2570 (amended by SI 1992/3075; SI 1994/1935; SI 1995/2092; SI 1996/315): see para 941 et seq ante.
4 Ibid reg 14A(1) (added by SI 1994/1935).
5 Ie where a company is exempt by virtue of the Companies Act 1985 s 249A(2) (as added): see para 1054 post.
6 See note 2 supra.
7 Ie the Companies (Revision of Defective Accounts and Report) Regulations 1990 regs 10-13: see paras 945-948 ante.
8 Ie for the purposes of the Companies Act 1985 s 249A(2) (as added).
9 Companies (Revision of Defective Accounts and Report) Regulations 1990 reg 14A(2) (added by SI 1994/1935).

951. Dormant companies. Where a company has passed a resolution[1] exempting itself from the requirements of the Companies Act 1985[2] relating to the audit of accounts, the Companies (Revision of Defective Accounts and Report) Regulations 1990[3] apply as if they omitted any reference to an auditors' report, or to the making of such a report[4].

1 Ie under the Companies Act 1985 s 250 (as substituted and amended): see para 1058 post.
2 Ie the provisions of ibid Pt VII (ss 221-262A) (as amended): see para 1054 et seq post.
3 Ie the Companies (Revision of Defective Accounts and Report) Regulations 1990, SI 1990/2570 (amended by SI 1992/3075; SI 1994/1935; SI 1995/2092; SI 1996/315): see para 941 et seq ante.
4 Ibid reg 15.

B. REVISION FOLLOWING SECRETARY OF STATE'S NOTICE

952. Secretary of State's notice in respect of annual accounts. Where copies of a company's annual accounts[1] have been sent out[2] or a copy of a company's annual accounts has been laid before the company in general meeting or delivered to the registrar of companies, and it appears to the Secretary of State that there is, or may be, a question whether the accounts comply with the requirements of the Companies Act 1985, he may give notice to the directors of the company indicating the respects in which it appears to him that such a question arises, or may arise[2]. The notice must specify a period of not less than one month for the directors to give him an explanation of the accounts or prepare revised accounts[3].

If at the end of the specified period, or such longer period as he may allow, it appears to the Secretary of State that no satisfactory explanation of the accounts has been given and that the accounts have not been revised so as to comply with the requirements of the 1985 Act, he may, if he thinks fit, apply to the court[4].

The above provisions apply equally to revised annual accounts, in which case the references to revised accounts are to be read as references to further revised accounts[5].

1 For the meaning of 'annual accounts' see para 817 note 2 ante.
2 Companies Act 1985 s 245A(1) (substituted by the Companies Act 1989 s 12).
3 Companies Act 1985 s 245A(2) (substituted by the Companies Act 1989 s 12).
4 Companies Act 1985 s 245A(3) (substituted by the Companies Act 1989 s 12).
5 Companies Act 1985 s 245A(4) (substituted by the Companies Act 1989 s 12).

C. APPLICATION TO THE COURT

953. Application to the court in respect of defective accounts. An application may be made to the court:

(1) by the Secretary of State after having duly served notice[1]; or

(2) by a person authorised by the Secretary of State for these purposes[2],

for a declaration that the annual accounts of a company do not comply with the requirements of the Companies Act 1985 and for an order requiring the directors of the company to prepare revised accounts[3]. Notice of the application, together with a general statement of the matters at issue in the proceedings, must be given by the applicant to the registrar of companies for registration[4].

If the court orders the preparation of revised accounts, it may give directions with respect to the auditing of accounts, the revision of any directors' report or summary financial statement and the taking of steps by the directors to bring the making of the order to the notice of persons likely to rely on the previous accounts, and such other matters as the court thinks fit[5].

If the court finds that the accounts did not comply with the requirements of the 1985 Act, it may order that all or part of the costs of and incidental to the application and any reasonable expenses incurred by the company in connection with or in consequence of the preparation of revised accounts shall be borne by such of the directors as were party to the approval of the defective accounts; and, for these purposes, every director of the company at the time the accounts were approved is taken to have been a party to their approval unless he shows that he took all reasonable steps to prevent their being approved[6]. Where the court makes such an order, it must have regard to whether the directors party to the approval of the defective accounts knew or ought to have known that the accounts did not comply with the requirements of the 1985 Act; and it may exclude one or more directors from the order or order the payment of different amounts by different directors[7].

On the conclusion of proceedings on an application under the above provisions, the applicant must give to the registrar for registration an office copy of the court order or, as the case may be, notice that the application has failed or been withdrawn[8].

The above provisions apply equally to revised annual accounts, in which case the references to revised accounts are to be read as references to further revised accounts[9].

1 Ie under the Companies Act 1985 s 245A (as substituted): see para 952 ante.
2 As to the persons so authorised see para 954 post.
3 Companies Act 1985 s 245B(1) (substituted by the Companies Act 1989 s 12). An application under the Companies Act 1985 s 245B(1) (as so substituted) must be made by originating motion: RSC Ord 102 r 3(1).
4 Companies Act 1985 s 245B(2) (substituted by the Companies Act 1989 s 12).
5 Companies Act 1985 s 245B(3) (substituted by the Companies Act 1989 s 12).
6 Companies Act 1985 s 245B(4) (substituted by the Companies Act 1989 s 12).
7 Companies Act 1985 s 245B(5) (substituted by the Companies Act 1989 s 12).

8 Companies Act 1985 s 245B(6) (substituted by the Companies Act 1989 s 12).
9 Companies Act 1985 s 245B(7) (substituted by the Companies Act 1989 s 12).

954. Other persons authorised to apply to the court. The Secretary of State may authorise for the purposes of making an application to the court in respect of defective accounts[1] any person appearing to him:

(1) to have an interest in, and to have satisfactory procedures directed to securing, compliance by companies with the accounting requirements of the Companies Act 1985;

(2) to have satisfactory procedures for receiving and investigating complaints about the annual accounts of companies; and

(3) otherwise to be a fit and proper person to be authorised[2].

A person may be authorised generally or in respect of particular classes of case; and different persons may be authorised in respect of different classes of case[3].

The Secretary of State may refuse to authorise a person if he considers that his authorisation is unnecessary having regard to the fact that there are one or more other persons who have been or are likely to be authorised[4].

Authorisation must be by order made by statutory instrument which is subject to annulment in pursuance of a resolution of either House of Parliament[5].

Where authorisation is revoked, the revoking order may make such provision as the Secretary of State thinks fit with respect to pending proceedings[6].

Neither a person so authorised, nor any officer, servant or member of the governing body of such a person, is liable in damages for anything done or purporting to be done for the purpose of or in connection with:

(a) the taking of steps to discover whether there are grounds for an application to the court;

(b) the determination whether or not to make such an application; or

(c) the publication of its reasons for any such decision,

unless the act or omission is shown to have been in bad faith[7].

1 Ie for the purposes of the Companies Act 1985 s 245B (as substituted): see para 953 ante.
2 Ibid s 245C(1) (substituted by the Companies Act 1989 s 12).
3 Companies Act 1985 s 245C(2) (substituted by the Companies Act 1989 s 12).
4 Companies Act 1985 s 245C(3) (substituted by the Companies Act 1989 s 12).
5 Companies Act 1985 s 245C(4) (substituted by the Companies Act 1989 s 12). In exercise of the power so conferred the Secretary of State made the Companies (Defective Accounts) (Authorised Person) Order 1991, SI 1991/13, authorising The Financial Reporting Review Panel Limited for the purposes of the Companies Act 1985 s 245B (as substituted): see the Companies (Defective Accounts) (Authorised Person) Order 1991 preamble, art 3.
6 Companies Act 1985 s 245C(5) (substituted by the Companies Act 1989 s 12).
7 Companies Act 1985 s 245C(6) (substituted by the Companies Act 1989 s 12).

(17) AUDITORS AND AUDIT

(i) Auditors

A. ELIGIBILITY FOR APPOINTMENT

(A) *In general*

955. Purposes of the statutory provisions. The main purposes of the statutory provisions relating to eligibility for appointment as a company auditor[1] are to secure that only persons who are properly supervised and appropriately qualified are appointed company auditors, and that audits by persons so appointed are carried out properly and with integrity and with a proper degree of independence[2].

1 Ie the Companies Act 1989 Pt II (ss 24-54): see para 956 et seq post.
2 Ibid s 24(1).

956. Eligibility for appointment. A person is eligible for appointment as a company auditor[1] only if he is a member of a recognised supervisory body[2] and is eligible for the appointment under the rules[3] of that body[4]. An individual or a firm[5] may be appointed a company auditor[6]. Where, however, a person only retains an authorisation granted under the Companies Act 1967[7], that person's eligibility for appointment is[8] restricted[9].

1 For these purposes, a 'company auditor' means a person appointed as auditor under the Companies Act 1985 Pt XI Ch V (ss 384-394A (as amended): see para 1027 et seq post); and the expressions 'company audit' and 'company audit work' are to be construed accordingly: Companies Act 1989 s 24(2). 'Company' means any company or other body to which the Companies Act 1985 s 384 (as substituted) (see para 1027 post) applies: Companies Act 1989 s 53(1).
2 For the meaning of 'supervisory body' see para 962 post. As to the recognition of supervisory bodies see para 962 et seq post.
3 For the meaning of references to the rules of a supervisory body see para 962 head (b) post.
4 Companies Act 1989 s 25(1).
5 For these purposes, 'firm' means a body corporate or a partnership: ibid s 53(1).
6 Ibid s 25(2).
7 Ie in the cases to which ibid s 34 applies: see para 990 post.
8 Ie is restricted by ibid s 34.
9 Ibid s 25(3).

957. Effect of appointment of partnership. The following provisions apply to the appointment as company auditor[1] of a partnership constituted under the law of England and Wales or Northern Ireland or under the law of any other country or territory in which a partnership is not a legal person[2].

The appointment is, unless a contrary intention appears, an appointment of the partnership as such and not of the partners[3]. Where the partnership ceases, the appointment is treated as extending to:

(1) any partnership which succeeds to the practice of that partnership and is eligible for the appointment; and

(2) any person who succeeds to that practice having previously carried it on in partnership and is eligible for the appointment[4].

For this purpose, a partnership is regarded as succeeding to the practice of another partnership only if the members of the successor partnership are substantially the same as those of the former partnership; and a partnership or other person is regarded as succeeding to the practice of a partnership only if it or he succeeds to the whole or substantially the whole of the business of the former partnership[5]. Where the partnership ceases and no person succeeds to the appointment[6], the appointment may with the consent of the company be treated as extending to a partnership or other person eligible for the appointment who succeeds to the business of the former partnership or to such part of it as is agreed by the company shall be treated as comprising the appointment[7].

1 For the meaning of 'company auditor' and 'company' see para 956 note 1 ante.
2 Companies Act 1989 s 26(1).
3 Ibid s 26(2).

4 Ibid s 26(3).
5 Ibid s 26(4).
6 Ie under ibid s 26(3): see supra.
7 Ibid s 26(5).

958. Ineligibility on ground of lack of independence. A person is ineligible for appointment as company auditor[1] of a company if he is:

(1) an officer or employee of the company; or

(2) a partner or employee of such a person, or a partnership of which such a person is a partner,

or if he is ineligible by virtue of heads (1) or (2) above for appointment as company auditor of any associated undertaking[2] of the company; but, for this purpose, an auditor is not regarded as an officer or employee of the company[3].

A person is also ineligible for appointment as company auditor of a company if there exists between him or any associate[4] of his and the company or any associated undertaking a connection of any such description as may be specified by regulations made by the Secretary of State[5].

1 For the meaning of 'company auditor' and 'company' see para 956 note 1 ante.
2 For these purposes, 'associated undertaking', in relation to a company, means a parent undertaking or subsidiary undertaking of the company or a subsidiary undertaking of any parent undertaking of the company: Companies Act 1989 s 27(3). 'Parent undertaking' and 'subsidiary undertaking' have the same meaning as in the Companies Act 1985 Pt VII (ss 221-262A (as amended): see para 828 ante): Companies Act 1989 s 53(1).
3 Ibid s 27(1). As to the effect of ineligibility see para 960 post; and as to a second audit where an audit has beeen carried out by an ineligible person see para 961 post.
4 For the meaning of 'associate' see para 959 post.
5 Companies Act 1989 s 27(2). Regulations must be made by statutory instrument which is subject to annulment in pursuance of a resolution of either House of Parliament (s 27(4)); and they may make different provisions for different cases (s 27(2)). At the date at which this volume states the law no such regulations had been made.

959. Meaning of 'associate'. 'Associate', in relation to a person, is to be construed[1] as follows[2].

In relation to an individual, 'associate' means:

(1) that individual's spouse or minor child or stepchild;

(2) any body corporate of which that individual is a director[3]; and

(3) any employee or partner of that individual[4].

In relation to a body corporate, 'associate' means:

(a) any body corporate of which that body is a director;

(b) any body corporate in the same group[5] as that body; and

(c) any employee or partner of that body or of any body corporate in the same group[6].

In relation to a Scottish firm, or a partnership constituted under the law of any other country or territory in which a partnership is a legal person, 'associate' means:

(i) any body corporate of which the firm[7] is a director;

(ii) any employee of or a partner in the firm; and

(iii) any person who is an associate of a partner in the firm[8].

In relation to a partnership constituted under the law of England and Wales or Northern Ireland, or the law of any other country or territory in which a partnership is not a legal person, 'associate' means any person who is an associate of any of the partners[9].

1   Ie in the Companies Act 1989 Pt II (ss 24–54): see paras 955–958 ante and para 960 et seq post.
2   Ibid s 52(1).
3   For these purposes, 'director', in relation to a body corporate, includes any person occupying in relation
    to it the position of a director, by whatever name called, and any person in accordance with whose
    directions or instructions, not being advice given in a professional capacity, the directors of the body are
    accustomed to act: ibid s 53(1).
4   Ibid s 52(2).
5   For these purposes, 'group', in relation to a body corporate, means the body corporate, any other body
    corporate which is its holding company or subsidiary and any other body corporate which is a subsidiary
    of that holding company: ibid s 53(1). 'Holding company' and 'subsidiary' have the same meaning as in
    the Companies Act 1985 s 736 (as substituted) (see para 827 ante): Companies Act 1989 s 53(1).
6   Ibid s 52(3).
7   For the meaning of 'firm' see para 956 note 5 ante.
8   Companies Act 1989 s 52(4).
9   Ibid s 52(5).

960. Effect of ineligibility. No person may act as a company auditor[1] if he is
ineligible for appointment to the office[2]. If, during his term of office, a company
auditor becomes ineligible for appointment to the office, he must thereupon vacate
office and must forthwith give notice in writing to the company concerned that he has
vacated it by reason of ineligibility[3]. A person who acts as company auditor in
contravention of the above provisions[4], or fails to give notice of vacating his office as so
required[5], is guilty of an offence and liable on conviction on indictment to a fine, or on
summary conviction to a fine not exceeding the statutory maximum[6].

In the case of a continued contravention he is liable on a second or subsequent
summary conviction, instead of the fine mentioned above, to a fine not exceeding
one-tenth of the statutory maximum in respect of each day on which the contravention is continued[7].

In proceedings against a person for any offence under the above provisions it is a
defence for him to show that he did not know and had no reason to believe that he was,
or had become, ineligible for appointment[8].

1   For the meaning of 'company auditor' and 'company' see para 956 note 1 ante.
2   Companies Act 1989 s 28(1).
3   Ibid s 28(2). As to the service of notices see para 1024 post.
4   Ie in contravention of ibid s 28(1): see supra.
5   Ie as required by ibid s 28(2): see supra.
6   Ibid s 28(3). For the meaning of 'the statutory maximum' see para 1161 post. As to offences by bodies
    corporate, partnerships and unincorporated associations see para 1001 post; as to the time limit for the
    prosecution of offences see para 1003 post; and as to jurisdiction and procedure in respect of offences see
    para 1004 post.
7   Ibid s 28(4).
8   Ibid s 28(5).

961. Secretary of State's power to require second audit. Where a person
appointed company auditor[1] was, for any part of the period during which the audit was
conducted, ineligible for appointment[2] to that office, the Secretary of State may direct
the company concerned to retain a person eligible for appointment as auditor[3] of the
company:

(1) to audit the relevant accounts again; or
(2) to review the first audit and to report (giving his reasons) whether a second audit
    is needed;

and the company must comply with such a direction within 21 days of its being given[4].
If a second audit is recommended, the company must forthwith take such steps as are

necessary to comply with the recommendation[5]. A direction so given is, on the application of the Secretary of State, enforceable by injunction[6].

Where a direction is so given, the Secretary of State must send a copy of the direction to the registrar of companies; and the company must, within 21 days of receiving any report under head (2) above, send a copy of it to the registrar of companies[7].

Any statutory or other provisions applying in relation to the first audit apply, so far as practicable, in relation to a second audit[8].

If a company fails to comply with the above requirements, it is guilty of an offence and liable on summary conviction to a fine not exceeding the statutory maximum; and, in the case of continued contravention, it is liable on a second or subsequent summary conviction, instead of the fine mentioned above, to a fine not exceeding one-tenth of the statutory maximum in respect of each day on which the contravention is continued[9].

If a person accepts an appointment, or continues to act, as company auditor at a time when he knows he is ineligible, the company concerned may recover from him any costs incurred by it in complying with the above requirements[10].

1 For the meaning of 'company auditor' and 'company' see para 956 note 1 ante.
2 As to the effect of ineligibility see para 960 ante.
3 As to eligibility for appointment see para 955 et seq ante and para 962 et seq post.
4 Companies Act 1989 s 29(1). As to the service of directions see para 1024 post.
5 Ibid s 29(2).
6 Ibid s 29(6).
7 Ibid s 29(3). The provisions of the Companies Act 1985 relating to the delivery of documents to the registrar apply for the purposes of the Companies Act 1989 s 29(3): s 29(3).
8 Ibid s 29(4).
9 Ibid s 29(5). For the meaning of 'the statutory maximum' see para 1161 post. As to offences by bodies corporate, partnerships and unincorporated associations see para 1001 post; as to the time limit for the prosecution of offences see para 1003 post; and as to jurisdiction and procedure in respect of offences see para 1004 post.
10 Ibid s 29(7).

(B) *Recognition of Supervisory Bodies*

962. Supervisory bodies. A 'supervisory body' means a body established in the United Kingdom[1], whether a body corporate or an unincorporated association, which maintains and enforces rules as to:

(1) the eligibility of persons to seek appointment as company auditors[2]; and

(2) the conduct of company audit work[3],

which are binding on persons seeking appointment or acting as company auditors either because they are members of that body or because they are otherwise subject to its control[4].

References to:

(a) the members of a supervisory body are to the persons who, whether or not members of the body, are subject to its rules in seeking appointment or acting as company auditors[5];

(b) the rules of a supervisory body are to the rules, whether or not laid down by the body itself, which the body has power to enforce and which are[6] relevant[7];

(c) guidance issued by a supervisory body are to guidance issued or any recommendation made by it to all or any class of its members or persons seeking to become members which would, if it were a rule, fall within head (b) above[8].

1 For these purposes, a body is regarded as 'established in the United Kingdom' if and only if (1) it is incorporated or formed under the law of the United Kingdom or a part of the United Kingdom; or (2) its central management and control is exercised in the United Kingdom; and any reference to a qualification 'obtained in the United Kingdom' is to a qualification obtained from such a body: Companies Act 1989 s 53(2).
2 As to eligibility for appointment see para 955 et seq ante and para 963 et seq post. For the meaning of 'company auditor' and 'company' see para 956 note 1 ante.
3 For the meaning of 'company audit work' see para 956 note 1 ante.
4 Companies Act 1989 s 30(1). The provisions of s 30(5), Sch 11 Pts I, II (paras 1-16) (see para 963 et seq post) have effect with respect to the recognition of supervisory bodies for the purposes of Pt II (ss 24-54) (see para 955 et seq ante and para 963 et seq post): s 30(5).
5 Ibid s 30(2).
6 Ie are relevant for the purposes of ibid Pt II (ss 24-54).
7 Ibid s 30(3). This includes rules relating to the admission and expulsion of members of the body, so far as relevant for the purposes of Pt II (ss 24-54): s 30(3).
8 Ibid s 30(4).

963. Application for recognition of supervisory body. A supervisory body[1] may apply to the Secretary of State for an order declaring it to be a recognised supervisory body[2]. Any such application must be made in such manner as the Secretary of State may direct and must be accompanied by such information as the Secretary of State may reasonably require for the purpose of determining the application[3]. At any time after receiving an application and before determining it the Secretary of State may require the applicant to furnish additional information[4]. The directions and requirements so given or imposed may differ as between different applications[5]. Any information to be so furnished to the Secretary of State must, if he so requires, be in such form or verified in such manner as he may specify[6]. Every application must be accompanied by a copy of the applicant's rules[7] and of any guidance[8] issued by the applicant which is intended to have continuing effect and is issued in writing or other legible form[9].

1 For the meaning of 'supervisory body' see para 962 ante.
2 Companies Act 1989 s 30(5), Sch 11 para 1(1).
3 Ibid Sch 11 para 1(2). As to the service of directions see para 1024 post.
4 Ibid Sch 11 para 1(3).
5 Ibid Sch 11 para 1(4).
6 Ibid Sch 11 para 1(5).
7 For the meaning of references to the rules of a supervisory body see para 962 head (b) ante.
8 For the meaning of references to guidance issued by a supervisory body see para 962 head (c) ante.
9 Companies Act 1989 Sch 11 para 1(6).

964. Holding of appropriate qualification. The supervisory body[1] must have rules[2] to the effect that a person is not eligible for appointment as a company auditor[3] unless:
(1) in the case of an individual, he holds an appropriate qualification[4];
(2) in the case of a firm[5], the individuals responsible for company audit work[6] on behalf of the firm hold an appropriate qualification and the firm is controlled by qualified persons[7].
This does not, however, prevent the body from imposing more stringent requirements[8]. A firm which has ceased to comply with the conditions in head (2) above may be permitted to remain eligible for appointment as a company auditor for a period of not more than three months[9].
The following provisions explain what is meant by a firm being 'controlled by qualified persons'[10]. For this purpose, references to a person being qualified are, in

relation to an individual, to his holding an appropriate qualification, and, in relation to a firm, to its being eligible for appointment as a company auditor[11]. A firm is to be treated as controlled by qualified persons if, and only if:

(a) a majority of the members of the firm are qualified persons; and

(b) where the firm's affairs are managed by a board of directors, committee or other management body, a majority of the members of that body are qualified persons or, if the body consists of two persons only, that at least one of them is a qualified person[12].

A majority of the members of a firm means:

(i) where under the firm's constitution matters are decided upon by the exercise of voting rights, members holding a majority of the rights to vote on all, or substantially all, matters;

(ii) in any other case, members having such rights under the constitution of the firm as enable them to direct its overall policy or alter its constitution[13].

A majority of the members of the management body of a firm means:

(A) where matters are decided at meetings of the management body by the exercise of voting rights, members holding a majority of the rights to vote on all, or substantially all, matters at such meetings;

(B) in any other case, members having such rights under the constitution of the firm as enable them to direct its overall policy or alter its constitution[14].

1 For the meaning of 'supervisory body' see para 962 ante.
2 For the meaning of references to the rules of a supervisory body see para 962 head (b) ante.
3 As to eligibility for appointment see para 955 et seq ante and para 965 et seq post. For the meaning of 'company auditor' and 'company' see para 956 note 1 ante.
4 For the meaning of 'appropriate qualification' see para 978 post.
5 For the meaning of 'firm' see para 956 note 5 ante.
6 For the meaning of 'company audit work' see para 956 note 1 ante.
7 Companies Act 1989 s 30(5), Sch 11 para 4(1).
8 Ibid Sch 11 para 4(2).
9 Ibid Sch 11 para 4(3).
10 Ibid Sch 11 para 5(1). The provisions of the Companies Act 1985 s 258(6), Sch 10A paras 5–11 (as added) (rights to be taken into account and attribution of rights: see para 829 ante) apply for the purposes of the Companies Act 1989 Sch 11 para 5: Sch 11 para 5(6).
11 Ibid Sch 11 para 5(2). See also note 10 supra.
12 Ibid Sch 11 para 5(3). See also note 10 supra.
13 Ibid Sch 11 para 5(4). See also note 10 supra.
14 Ibid Sch 11 para 5(5). See also note 10 supra.

965. Auditors to be fit and proper persons. The supervisory body[1] must have adequate rules[2] and practices designed to ensure that the persons eligible under its rules for appointment as a company auditor[3] are fit and proper persons to be so appointed[4]. The matters which the body may take into account for this purpose in relation to a person must include:

(1) any matter relating to any person who is or will be employed by or associated with him for the purposes of or in connection with company audit work[5]; and

(2) in the case of a body corporate, any matter relating to any director[6] or controller[7] of the body, to any other body corporate in the same group[8] or to any director or controller of any such other body; and

(3) in the case of a partnership, any matter relating to any of the partners, any director or controller[9] of any of the partners, any body corporate in the same group as any of the partners and any director or controller of any such other body[10].

1   For the meaning of 'supervisory body' see para 962 ante.
2   For the meaning of references to the rules of a supervisory body see para 962 head (b) ante.
3   As to eligibility for appointment see para 955 et seq ante and para 966 et seq post. For the meaning of 'company auditor' and 'company' see para 956 note 1 ante.
4   Companies Act 1989 s 30(5), Sch 11 para 6(1).
5   For the meaning of 'company audit work' see para 956 note 1 ante.
6   For the meaning of 'director' see para 959 note 3 ante.
7   For these purposes, 'controller', in relation to a body corporate, means a person who either alone or with any associate or associates is entitled to exercise or control the exercise of 15% or more of the rights to vote on all, or substantially all, matters at general meetings of the body or another body corporate of which it is a subsidiary: Companies Act 1989 Sch 11 para 6(3). For the meaning of 'associate' see para 959 ante; and for the meaning of 'subsidiary' see para 959 note 5 ante.
8   For the meaning of 'group' see para 959 note 5 ante.
9   See note 7 supra.
10 Companies Act 1989 Sch 11 para 6(2).

966. Professional integrity and independence. The supervisory body[1] must have adequate rules[2] and practices designed to ensure:

(1) that company audit work[3] is conducted properly and with integrity; and

(2) that persons are not appointed company auditor[4] in circumstances in which they have any interest likely to conflict with the proper conduct of the audit[5].

The body must also have adequate rules and practices designed to ensure that no firm[6] is eligible under its rules for appointment as a company auditor unless the firm has arrangements to prevent individuals who do not hold an appropriate qualification[7] and persons who are not members of the firm from being able to exert any influence over the way in which an audit is conducted in circumstances in which that influence would be likely to affect the independence or integrity of the audit[8].

1   For the meaning of 'supervisory body' see para 962 ante.
2   For the meaning of references to the rules of a supervisory body see para 962 head (b) ante.
3   For the meaning of 'company audit work' and 'company' see para 956 note 1 ante.
4   For the meaning of 'company auditor' see para 956 note 1 ante.
5   Companies Act 1989 s 30(5), Sch 11 para 7(1).
6   For the meaning of 'firm' see para 956 note 5 ante.
7   For the meaning of 'appropriate qualification' see para 978 post.
8   Companies Act 1989 Sch 11 para 7(2).

967. Technical standards. The supervisory body[1] must have rules[2] and practices as to the technical standards to be applied in company audit work[3] and as to the manner in which those standards are to be applied in practice[4].

1   For the meaning of 'supervisory body' see para 962 ante.
2   For the meaning of references to the rules of a supervisory body see para 962 head (b) ante.
3   For the meaning of 'company audit work' and 'company' see para 956 note 1 ante.
4   Companies Act 1989 s 30(5), Sch 11 para 8.

968. Procedures for maintaining competence. The supervisory body[1] must have rules[2] and practices designed to ensure that persons eligible under its rules for appointment as a company auditor[3] continue to maintain an appropriate level of competence in the conduct of company audits[4].

1   For the meaning of 'supervisory body' see para 962 ante.
2   For the meaning of references to the rules of a supervisory body see para 962 head (b) ante.
3   As to eligibility for appointment see para 955 et seq ante and para 969 et seq post. For the meaning of 'company auditor' and 'company' see para 956 note 1 ante.
4   Companies Act 1989 s 30(5), Sch 11 para 9.

969. Monitoring and enforcement. The supervisory body[1] must have adequate arrangements and resources for the effective monitoring and enforcement of compliance with its rules[2]. The arrangements for monitoring may make provision for that function to be performed on behalf of the body (and without affecting its responsibility) by any other body or person who is able and willing to perform it[3].

1 For the meaning of 'supervisory body' see para 962 ante.
2 Companies Act 1989 s 30(5), Sch 11 para 10(1). For the meaning of references to the rules of a supervisory body see para 962 head (b) ante.
3 Ibid Sch 11 para 10(2).

970. Membership, eligibility and discipline. The rules[1] and practices of the supervisory body[2] relating to:
 (1) the admission and expulsion of members;
 (2) the grant and withdrawal of eligibility for appointment as a company auditor[3]; and
 (3) the discipline it exercises over its members,
must be fair and reasonable and include adequate provision for appeals[4].

1 For the meaning of references to the rules of a supervisory body see para 962 head (b) ante.
2 For the meaning of 'supervisory body' see para 962 ante.
3 As to eligibility for appointment see para 955 et seq ante and para 971 et seq post. For the meaning of 'company auditor' and 'company' see para 956 note 1 ante.
4 Companies Act 1989 s 30(5), Sch 11 para 11.

971. Investigation of complaints. The supervisory body[1] must have effective arrangements for the investigation of complaints:
 (1) against persons who are eligible under its rules to be appointed company auditor[2]; or
 (2) against the body in respect of matters arising out of its functions as a supervisory body[3].
The arrangements may make provision for the whole or part of that function to be performed by and to be the responsibility of a body or person independent of the body itself[4].

1 For the meaning of 'supervisory body' see para 962 ante.
2 As to eligibility for appointment see para 955 et seq ante and para 972 et seq post. For the meaning of 'company auditor' and 'company' see para 956 note 1 ante.
3 Companies Act 1989 s 30(5), Sch 11 para 12(1).
4 Ibid Sch 11 para 12(2).

972. Meeting of claims arising out of audit work. The supervisory body[1] must have adequate rules[2] or arrangements designed to ensure that persons eligible under its rules for appointment as a company auditor[3] take such steps as may reasonably be expected of them to secure that they are able to meet claims against them arising out of company audit work[4]. This may be achieved by professional indemnity insurance or other appropriate arrangements[5].

1 For the meaning of 'supervisory body' see para 962 ante.
2 For the meaning of references to the rules of a supervisory body see para 962 head (b) ante.
3 As to eligibility for appointment see para 955 et seq ante and para 973 et seq post. For the meaning of 'company auditor' and 'company' see para 956 note 1 ante.

4 Companies Act 1989 s 30(5), Sch 11 para 13(1). For the meaning of 'company audit work' see para 956
   note 1 ante.
5 Ibid Sch 11 para 13(2).

973. Rules for compliance by members of supervisory body. The supervisory
body[1] must have rules[2] requiring persons eligible under its rules for appointment as a
company auditor[3] to comply with any obligations imposed on them by regulations
made[4] by the Secretary of State[5].

1 For the meaning of 'supervisory body' see para 962 ante.
2 For the meaning of references to the rules of a supervisory body see para 962 head (b) ante.
3 As to eligibility for appointment see para 955 et seq ante and para 974 et seq post. For the meaning of
   'company auditor' and 'company' see para 956 note 1 ante.
4 Ie under the Companies Act 1989 s 35 (see para 991 post) or s 36 (see para 995 post).
5 Ibid s 30(5), Sch 11 para 14.

974. Taking account of costs of compliance. The supervisory body[1] must have
satisfactory arrangements for taking account, in framing its rules[2], of the cost to those to
whom the rules would apply of complying with those rules and any other controls to
which they are subject[3].

1 For the meaning of 'supervisory body' see para 962 ante.
2 For the meaning of references to the rules of a supervisory body see para 962 head (b) ante.
3 Companies Act 1989 s 30(5), Sch 11 para 15.

975. Promotion and maintenance of standards. The supervisory body[1] must be
able and willing to promote and maintain high standards of integrity in the conduct of
company audit work[2] and to co-operate, by the sharing of information and otherwise,
with the Secretary of State and any other authority, body or person having responsibility in the United Kingdom for the qualification, supervision or regulation of
auditors[3].

1 For the meaning of 'supervisory body' see para 962 ante.
2 For the meaning of 'company audit work' and 'company' see para 956 note 1 ante.
3 Companies Act 1989 s 30(5), Sch 11 para 16.

976. Grant and refusal of recognition. The Secretary of State may, on an application duly made[1] and after being furnished with all such information as he may
require[2], make or refuse to make an order (a 'recognition order') declaring the
applicant to be a recognised supervisory body[3]. The Secretary of State must not,
however, make a recognition order unless it appears to him, from the information
furnished by the body and having regard to any other information in his possession,
that the statutory requirements for recognition[4] are satisfied as respects that body[5]. The
Secretary of State may refuse to make a recognition order in respect of a body if he
considers that its recognition is unnecessary having regard to the existence of one or
more other bodies which maintain and enforce rules as to the appointment and
conduct of company auditors[6] and which have been or are likely to be recognised[7].
Where the Secretary of State refuses an application for a recognition order, he must

give the applicant written notice to that effect specifying which requirements in the opinion of the Secretary of State are not satisfied or stating that the application is refused on the ground[8] that he considers that its recognition is unnecessary[9]. A recognition order must state the date on which it takes effect[10].

1 Ie duly made in accordance with the Companies Act 1989 s 30(5), Sch 11 para 1: see para 963 ante.
2 Ie under ibid Sch 11 para 1.
3 Ibid Sch 11 para 2(1). For the meaning of 'supervisory body' see para 962 ante.
4 Ie the requirements of ibid Sch 11 Pt II (paras 4-16): see para 964 et seq ante.
5 Ibid Sch 11 para 2(2).
6 For the meaning of 'company auditor' and 'company' see para 956 note 1 ante.
7 Companies Act 1989 Sch 11 para 2(3).
8 Ie the ground mentioned in ibid Sch 11 para 2(3): see supra.
9 Ibid Sch 11 para 2(4). As to the service of notices see para 1024 post.
10 Ibid Sch 11 para 2(5).

977. Revocation of recognition. A recognition order[1] may be revoked by a further order made by the Secretary of State if at any time it appears to him:

(1) that any statutory requirement for recognition[2] is not satisfied in the case of the body to which the recognition order relates ('the recognised body');

(2) that the recognised body has failed to comply with any obligation to which it is subject[3]; or

(3) that the continued recognition of the body is undesirable having regard to the existence of one or more other bodies which have been or are to be recognised[4].

An order revoking a recognition order must state the date on which it takes effect and that date must not be earlier than three months after the day on which the revocation order is made[5]. The order may contain such transitional provisions as the Secretary of State thinks necessary or expedient[6].

Before revoking a recognition order, the Secretary of State must give written notice of his intention to do so to the recognised body, take such steps as he considers reasonably practicable for bringing the notice to the attention of members of the body and publish it in such manner as he thinks appropriate for bringing it to the attention of any other persons who are in his opinion likely to be affected[7]. A body on which a notice is so served, any member of the body and any other person who appears to the Secretary of State to be affected may within three months after the date of service or publication, or within such longer time as the Secretary of State may allow, make written representations to the Secretary of State and, if desired, oral representations to a person appointed for that purpose by the Secretary of State; and the Secretary of State must have regard to any representations so made in determining whether to revoke the recognition order[8].

If in any case the Secretary of State considers it essential to do so in the public interest, he may revoke a recognition order without regard to the restriction imposed by the above provisions[9] and notwithstanding that no notice has been given or published[10] or that the time for making representations in pursuance of such a notice has not expired[11].

A recognition order may be revoked at the request or with the consent of the recognised body[12].

On making an order revoking a recognition order, the Secretary of State must give the body written notice of the making of the order, take such steps as he considers reasonably practicable for bringing the making of the order to the attention of members of the body, and publish a notice of the making of the order in such manner as he thinks appropriate for bringing it to the attention of any other persons who are in his opinion likely to be affected[13].

1 For the meaning of 'recognition order' see para 976 ante.
2 Ie any requirement of the Companies Act 1989 s 30(5), Sch 11 Pt II (paras 4–16): see para 964 et seq ante.
3 Ie by virtue of ibid Pt II (ss 24–54): see para 955 et seq ante and para 978 et seq post.
4 Ibid Sch 11 para 3(1).
5 Ibid Sch 11 para 3(2).
6 Ibid Sch 11 para 3(7).
7 Ibid Sch 11 para 3(3). A notice under Sch 11 para 3(3) must state the reasons for which the Secretary of State proposes to act and give particulars of the rights conferred by Sch 11 para 3(5) (see infra): Sch 11 para 3(4). As to the service of notices see para 1024 post.
8 Ibid Sch 11 para 3(5).
9 Ie the restriction imposed by ibid Sch 11 para 3(2): see supra.
10 Ie under ibid Sch 11 para 3(3): see supra.
11 Ibid Sch 11 para 3(6).
12 Ibid Sch 11 para 3(8). Any such revocation is not subject to the restrictions imposed by Sch 11 para 3(1),(2) (see supra) or the requirements of Sch 11 para 3(3)–(5) (see supra): Sch 11 para 3(8).
13 Ibid Sch 11 para 3(9).

(C) *Recognition of Professional Qualification*

978. Meaning of 'appropriate qualification'. A person holds an appropriate qualification[1] if:

(1) he was qualified[2] for appointment as auditor of a company[3] immediately before 1 January 1990 and immediately before 1 October 1991;

(2) he holds a recognised professional qualification[4] obtained in the United Kingdom[5]; or

(3) he holds an approved overseas qualification[6] and satisfies any additional educational requirements which are[7] applicable[8].

A person who immediately before 1 January 1990 and immediately before 1 October 1991 was qualified for appointment as auditor of a company[9] otherwise than by virtue of membership of a recognised body[10]:

(a) is treated as holding an appropriate qualification for 12 months from 1 October 1991; and

(b) continues to be so treated if within that period he notifies the Secretary of State that he wishes to retain the benefit of his qualification[11].

The notice must be in writing and must contain such information as the Secretary of State may require[11].

If a person fails to give such notice within the time allowed, he may apply to the Secretary of State, giving such information as would have been required in connection with a notice; and the Secretary of State may, if he is satisfied that there was good reason why the applicant did not give notice in time and that the applicant genuinely intends to practise as an auditor in Great Britain, direct that he shall be treated as holding[12] an appropriate qualification[13].

A person who:

(i) began before 1 January 1990 a course of study or practical training leading to a professional qualification in accountancy offered by a body established in the United Kingdom[14]; and

(ii) obtained that qualification on or after that date and before 1 January 1996,

is treated as holding an appropriate qualification if the qualification is approved by the Secretary of State[15].

Approval must not be given unless the Secretary of State is satisfied that the body concerned has or, as the case may be, had at the relevant time adequate arrangements to ensure that the qualification is or was awarded only to persons educated and trained to a standard equivalent to that required in the case of a recognised professional qualification[16].

A person is not to be regarded as holding an appropriate qualification[17] except in the above cases[18].

 1 Ie for the purposes of the Companies Act 1989 Pt II (ss 24–54): see para 955 et seq ante and para 979 et seq post.
 2 Ie by virtue of membership of a body recognised for the purposes of the Companies Act 1985 s 389(1)(a) (repealed).
 3 For the meaning of 'company' see para 956 note 1 ante.
 4 As to recognised professional qualifications see para 979 et seq post.
 5 For the meaning of 'obtained in the United Kingdom' see para 962 note 1 ante.
 6 As to approval of overseas qualifications see para 989 post.
 7 Ie in accordance with the Companies Act 1989 s 33(4): see para 989 post.
 8 Ibid s 31(1).
 9 Ie under the Companies Act 1985 s 389 (repealed).
10 Ie a body recognised for the purposes of ibid s 389(1)(a) (repealed).
11 Companies Act 1989 s 31(2).
12 Ie as holding an appropriate qualification for the purposes of ibid Pt II (ss 24–54).
13 Ibid s 31(3).
14 For the meaning of 'established in the United Kingdom' see para 962 note 1 ante.
15 Companies Act 1989 s 31(4).
16 Ibid s 31(5).
17 See note 1 supra.
18 Companies Act 1989 s 31(6).

979. Qualifying bodies and recognised professional qualifications. A 'qualifying body' means a body established in the United Kingdom[1], whether a body corporate or an unincorporated association, which offers a professional qualification in accountancy[2].

References to the rules of a qualifying body are to the rules, whether or not laid down by the body itself, which the body has power to enforce and which are[3] relevant[4]. This includes rules relating to:

(1) admission to or expulsion from a course of study leading to a qualification;
(2) the award or deprivation of a qualification; or
(3) the approval of a person for the purposes of giving practical training or the withdrawal of such approval,

so far as relevant[5].

References to guidance issued by any such body are to any guidance which the body issues, or any recommendation it makes to all or any class of persons holding or seeking to hold a qualification, or approved or seeking to be approved by the body for the purpose of giving practical training which would, if it were a rule, fall within[6] the above provisions[7].

 1 For the meaning of 'established in the United Kingdom' see para 962 note 1 ante.
 2 Companies Act 1989 s 32(1). As to the recognition of a professional qualification offered by a qualifying body see para 980 et seq post.
 3 Ie for the purposes of ibid Pt II (ss 24–54): see para 955 et seq ante and para 980 et seq post.
 4 Ibid s 32(2).
 5 Ibid s 32(3).
 6 Ie would fall within ibid s 32(2): see supra.
 7 Ibid s 32(4).

980. Application for recognition of professional qualification. A qualifying body[1] may apply to the Secretary of State for an order declaring a qualification offered by it to be[2] a recognised professional qualification[3]. Any such application:

(1) must be made in such manner as the Secretary of State may direct; and
(2) must be accompanied by such information as the Secretary of State may reasonably require for the purpose of determining the application[4].

At any time after receiving an application and before determining it the Secretary of State may require the applicant to furnish additional information[5]. The directions and requirements so given or imposed may differ as between different applications[6]. Any information to be so furnished to the Secretary of State must, if he so requires, be in such form or verified in such manner as he may specify[7]. In the case of examination standards, the verification required may include independent moderation of the examinations over such period as the Secretary of State considers necessary[7]. Every application must be accompanied by a copy of the applicant's rules[8] and of any guidance[9] issued by it which is intended to have continuing effect and is issued in writing or other legible form[10].

1 For the meaning of 'qualifying body' see para 979 ante.
2 Ie for the purposes of the Companies Act 1989 Pt II (ss 24–54): see para 955 et seq ante and para 981 et seq post.
3 Ibid s 32(4), Sch 12 para 1(1).
4 Ibid Sch 12 para 1(2). As to the punishment of persons who furnish false information for the purposes of such an application see para 1001 post; and as to the payment of fees by applicants see para 1022 post.
5 Ibid Sch 12 para 1(3).
6 Ibid Sch 12 para 1(4).
7 Ibid Sch 12 para 1(5).
8 For the meaning of references to the rules of qualifying body see para 979 ante.
9 For the meaning of references to guidance issued by a qualifying body see para 979 ante.
10 Companies Act 1989 Sch 12 para 1(6).

981. Entry requirements. The qualification must only be open to persons who have attained university entrance level or have a sufficient period of professional experience[1].

In relation to a person who has not been admitted to a university or other similar establishment in the United Kingdom, attaining university entrance level means:

(1) being educated to such a standard as would entitle him to be considered for such admission on the basis of academic or professional qualifications obtained in the United Kingdom[2] and recognised by the Secretary of State to be of an appropriate standard, or academic or professional qualifications obtained outside the United Kingdom which the Secretary of State considers to be of an equivalent standard; or
(2) being assessed on the basis of written tests of a kind appearing to the Secretary of State to be adequate for the purpose, with or without oral examination, as of such a standard of ability as would entitle him to be considered for such admission[3].

The assessment, tests or oral examination referred to in head (2) above may be conducted by the qualifying body[4] or by some other body approved by the Secretary of State[5].

1 Companies Act 1989 s 32(4), Sch 12 para 4(1). For the meaning of references to a sufficient period of professional experience see para 983 post.
2 For the meaning of 'obtained in the United Kingdom' see para 962 note 1 ante.

3 Companies Act 1989 Sch 12 para 4(2).
4 For the meaning of 'qualifying body' see para 979 ante.
5 Companies Act 1989 Sch 12 para 4(3).

982. Course of theoretical instruction. The qualification must be restricted to persons who have completed a course of theoretical instruction in the prescribed subjects[1] or have a sufficient period of professional experience[2].

  1 Ie the subjects prescribed for the purposes of the Companies Act 1989 s 32(4), Sch 12 para 7: see para 984 post.
  2 Ibid Sch 12 para 5. For the meaning of references to a sufficient period of professional experience see para 983 post.

983. Sufficient period of professional experience. The references[1] to a sufficient period of professional experience are to not less than seven years' experience in a professional capacity in the fields of finance, law and accountancy[2].

Periods of theoretical instruction in the fields of finance, law and accountancy may be deducted from the required period of professional experience, provided the instruction lasted at least one year and is attested by an examination recognised by the Secretary of State for these purposes, but the period of professional experience may not be so reduced by more than four years[3].

The period of professional experience together with the practical training required in the case of persons satisfying the statutory requirement[4] by virtue of having a sufficient period of professional experience must not be shorter than the course of theoretical instruction[5] and the practical training required in the case of persons satisfying that statutory requirement by virtue of having completed such a course[6].

  1 Ie in the Companies Act 1989 s 32(4), Sch 12 para 4 (see para 981 ante) or Sch 12 para 5 (see para 982 ante).
  2 Ibid Sch 12 para 6(1).
  3 Ibid Sch 12 para 6(2).
  4 Ie ibid Sch 12 para 5.
  5 Ie referred to in ibid Sch 12 para 5.
  6 Ibid Sch 12 para 6(3).

984. Examination. The qualification must be restricted to persons who have passed an examination, at least part of which is in writing, testing theoretical knowledge of the subjects prescribed for these purposes by regulations made by the Secretary of State and ability to apply that knowledge in practice, and requiring a standard of attainment at least equivalent to that required to obtain a degree from a university or similar establishment in the United Kingdom[1].

The qualification may be awarded to a person without his theoretical knowledge of a subject being tested by examination if he has passed a university or other examination of equivalent standard in that subject or holds a university degree or equivalent qualification in it[2].

The qualification may be awarded to a person without his ability to apply his theoretical knowledge of a subject in practice being tested by examination if he has received practical training in that subject which is attested by an examination or diploma recognised by the Secretary of State for these purposes[3].

Regulations under the above provisions must be made by statutory instrument which is subject to annulment in pursuance of a resolution of either House of Parliament[4].

1 Companies Act 1989 s 32(4), Sch 12 para 7(1). The subjects prescribed for these purposes are (1) auditing; (2) analysis and critical assessment of annual accounts; (3) general accounting; (4) cost and management accounting; (5) consolidated accounts; (6) internal control; (7) standards relating to the preparation of annual and consolidated accounts and to methods of valuing balance sheet items and of computing profits and losses; (8) legal and professional standards and professional guidance relating to the statutory auditing of accounting documents and to those carrying out such audits; (9) those aspects of the following which are relevant to auditing: (a) company law; (b) the law of insolvency and similar procedures; (c) tax law; (d) civil and commercial law; (e) social security law and law of employment; (f) information and computer systems; (g) business, general and financial economics; (h) mathematics and statistics; and (i) basic principles of financial management of undertakings: Company Auditors (Examinations) Regulations 1990, SI 1990/1146, reg 2, Schedule.
2 Companies Act 1989 Sch 12 para 7(2).
3 Ibid Sch 12 para 7(3).
4 Ibid Sch 12 para 7(4).

985. Practical training. The qualification must be restricted to persons who have completed at least three years' practical training of which part was spent being trained in company audit work[1] and a substantial part was spent being trained in company audit work or other audit work of a description approved by the Secretary of State as being similar to company audit work[2].

The training must be given by persons approved by the body offering the qualification as persons as to whom the body is satisfied, in the light of undertakings given by them and the supervision to which they are subject (whether by the body itself or some other body or organisation), that they will provide adequate training[3].

At least two-thirds of the training must be given by a fully-qualified auditor, that is, a person eligible[4] to be appointed as a company auditor or satisfying the corresponding requirements of the law of Northern Ireland or another member State of the European Community[5].

1 For these purposes, 'company audit work' includes the work of a person appointed as auditor under the Companies (Northern Ireland) Order 1986, SI 1986/1032, or under the law of a country or territory outside the United Kingdom where it appears to the Secretary of State that the law and practice with respect to the audit of company accounts is similar to that in the United Kingdom: Companies Act 1989 s 32(4), Sch 12 para 8(1). For the meaning of 'company audit work' and 'company' generally see para 956 note 1 ante.
2 Ibid Sch 12 para 8(1).
3 Ibid Sch 12 para 8(2).
4 Ie in accordance with ibid Pt II (ss 24-54): see para 955 et seq ante and para 986 et seq post.
5 Ibid Sch 12 para 8(3).

986. The body offering the qualification. The body offering the qualification must have rules and arrangements adequate to ensure compliance with the statutory requirements[1] and adequate arrangements for the effective monitoring of its continued compliance with those requirements[2].

The arrangements must include arrangements for monitoring the standard of its examinations and the adequacy of the practical training to be given by the persons approved by it for that purpose[3].

1 Ie the Companies Act 1989 s 32(4), Sch 12 paras 4-8: see paras 981-985 ante.
2 Ibid Sch 12 para 9(1).
3 Ibid Sch 12 para 9(2).

987. Grant and refusal of recognition. On an application duly made[1] and after being furnished with all such information as he may require[2], the Secretary of State may make or refuse to make an order (a 'recognition order') declaring the qualification in respect of which the application was made to be[3] a recognised professional qualification[4].

The Secretary of State must not make a recognition order unless it appears to him, from the information furnished by the applicant and having regard to any other information in his possession, that the statutory requirements[5] are satisfied as respects the qualification[6].

Where the Secretary of State refuses an application for a recognition order, he must give the applicant a written notice to that effect specifying which requirements, in his opinion, are not satisfied[7].

A recognition order must state the date on which it takes effect[8].

1   Ie in accordance with the Companies Act 1989 s 32(4), Sch 12 para 1: see para 980 ante.
2   Ie under ibid Sch 12 para 1.
3   Ie for the purposes of ibid Pt II (ss 24-54): see para 955 et seq ante and para 988 et seq post.
4   Ibid Sch 12 para 2(1). As to refusal of recognition on grounds related to competition see para 1015 post.
    For the punishment of bodies which falsely describe themselves as recognised qualifying bodies see para 1001 post; and as to the payment of periodical fees by such bodies see para 1022 post.
5   Ie the requirements of ibid Sch 12 Pt II (paras 4-9): see paras 981-986 ante.
6   Ibid Sch 12 para 2(2).
7   Ibid Sch 12 para 2(3). As to the service of notices see para 1024 post.
8   Ibid Sch 12 para 2(4).

988. Revocation of recognition. A recognition order[1] may be revoked by a further order made by the Secretary of State if at any time it appears to him that any of the statutory requirements[2] is not satisfied in relation to the qualification to which the recognition order relates or that the qualifying body[3] has failed to comply with any obligation to which it is[4] subject[5].

An order revoking a recognition order must state the date on which it takes effect and that date must not be earlier than three months after the day on which the revocation order is made[6].

Before revoking a recognition order the Secretary of State must give written notice of his intention to do so to the qualifying body, take such steps as he considers reasonably practicable for bringing the notice to the attention of persons holding the qualification or in the course of studying for it and publish it in such manner as he thinks appropriate for bringing it to the attention of any other persons who are in his opinion likely to be affected[7]. Such a notice must state the reasons for which the Secretary of State proposes to act and give particulars of the following statutory rights[8]. A body on which a notice is so served, any person holding the qualification or in the course of studying for it and any other person who appears to the Secretary of State to be affected may within three months after the date of service or publication, or within such longer time as the Secretary of State may allow, make written representations to the Secretary of State and, if desired, oral representations to a person appointed for that purpose by the Secretary of State; and the Secretary of State must have regard to any representations so made in determining whether to revoke the recognition order[9].

If in any case the Secretary of State considers it essential to do so in the public interest, he may revoke a recognition order without regard to the above restriction[10] and notwithstanding that no notice has been given or published[11] or that the time for making representations in pursuance of such a notice has not expired[12].

An order revoking a recognition order may contain such transitional provisions as the Secretary of State thinks necessary or expedient[13].

A recognition order may be revoked at the request or with the consent of the qualifying body and any such revocation is not subject to the above restrictions[14] or the requirements[15] mentioned above[16].

On making an order revoking a recognition order the Secretary of State must give the qualifying body written notice of the making of the order, take such steps as he considers reasonably practicable for bringing the making of the order to the attention of persons holding the qualification or in the course of studying for it and publish a notice of the making of the order in such manner as he thinks appropriate for bringing it to the attention of any other persons who are in his opinion likely to be affected[17].

1 For the meaning of 'recognition order' see para 987 ante.
2 Ie any requirement of the Companies Act 1989 s 32(4), Sch 12 Pt II (paras 4–9): see paras 981–986 ante.
3 For the meaning of 'qualifying body' see para 979 ante.
4 Ie by virtue of the Companies Act 1989 Pt II (ss 24–54): see para 955 et seq ante and para 989 et seq post.
5 Ibid Sch 12 para 3(1). As to the making of a compliance order by the court instead of the revocation of a recognition order see para 999 post.
6 Ibid Sch 12 para 3(2).
7 Ibid Sch 12 para 3(3). As to the service of notices see para 1024 post.
8 Ibid Sch 12 para 3(4).
9 Ibid Sch 12 para 3(5).
10 Ie the restriction imposed by ibid Sch 12 para 3(2): see supra.
11 Ie under ibid Sch 12 para 3(3): see supra.
12 Ibid Sch 12 para 3(6).
13 Ibid Sch 12 para 3(7).
14 Ie the restrictions imposed by ibid Sch 12 para 3(1),(2): see supra.
15 Ie the requirements of ibid Sch 12 para 3(3)–(5): see supra.
16 Ibid Sch 12 para 3(8).
17 Ibid Sch 12 para 3(9).

989. Approval of overseas qualifications. The Secretary of State may declare that persons who:

(1) are qualified to audit accounts under the law of a specified country or territory outside the United Kingdom; or

(2) hold a specified professional qualification in accountancy recognised under the law of a country or territory outside the United Kingdom,

shall be regarded[1] as holding an approved overseas qualification[2].

A qualification must not be so approved by the Secretary of State unless he is satisfied that it affords an assurance of professional competence equivalent to that afforded by a recognised professional qualification[3].

In exercising the power so conferred the Secretary of State may have regard to the extent to which persons eligible[4] for appointment as a company auditor or holding a professional qualification duly recognised[4] are recognised by the law of the country or territory in question as qualified to audit accounts there[5].

The Secretary of State may direct that a person holding an approved overseas qualification shall not be treated as holding an appropriate qualification[6] unless he holds such additional educational qualifications as the Secretary of State may specify for the purpose of ensuring that such persons have an adequate knowledge of the law and practice in the United Kingdom relevant to the audit of accounts[7].

Different directions may be given in relation to different qualifications[8].

The Secretary of State may, if he thinks fit, having regard to the above considerations[9], withdraw his approval of an overseas qualification in relation to persons becoming qualified as mentioned in head (1) above, or obtaining such a qualification as is mentioned in head (2) above, after such date as he may specify[10].

1 Ie for the purposes of the Companies Act 1989 Pt II (ss 24–54): see para 955 et seq ante and para 990 et seq post.
2 Ibid s 33(1).
3 Ibid s 33(2).
4 Ie under ibid Pt II (ss 24–54).
5 Ibid s 33(3).
6 See note 1 supra.
7 Companies Act 1989 s 33(4). As to the service of directions see para 1024 post.
8 Ibid s 33(5).
9 Ie the considerations mentioned in ibid s 33(2),(3): see supra.
10 Ibid s 33(6).

990. Eligibility of individuals retaining only authorisation under the Companies Act 1967. A person whose only appropriate qualification is that he retains an authorisation granted by the Board of Trade or the Secretary of State under the Companies Act 1967[1] is eligible only for appointment as auditor of an unquoted company[2]. These provisions do not authorise the appointment of such a person as auditor of a company that carries on business as the promoter of a trading stamp scheme[3].

1 Ie under the Companies Act 1967 s 13(1) (repealed).
2 Companies Act 1989 s 34(1). For these purposes, a company is 'unquoted' if, at the time of the person's appointment, no shares or debentures of the company, or of a parent undertaking of which it is a subsidiary undertaking, have been quoted on a stock exchange (in Great Britain or elsewhere) or offered (whether in Great Britain or elsewhere) to the public for subscription or purchase: s 34(2). For the meaning of 'company' see para 956 note 1 ante; and for the meaning of 'parent undertaking' and 'subsidiary undertaking' see para 958 note 2 ante.
   References to a person eligible for appointment as company auditor under s 25 (see para 956 ante) in enactments relating to eligibility for appointment as auditor of a body other than a company do not include a person to whom s 34 applies: s 34(4). For these purposes, 'enactment' includes an enactment contained in subordinate legislation within the meaning of the Interpretation Act 1978 (see STATUTES vol 44(1) (Reissue) para 1232 note 2): Companies Act 1989 s 53(1).
3 Ibid s 34(3). For these purposes, 'trading stamp scheme' means a trading stamp scheme within the meaning of the Trading Stamps Act 1964 (see SALE OF GOODS vol 41 para 899 note 4): Companies Act 1989 s 34(3).

(D) *Duties of Recognised Bodies*

991. Register of auditors. The Secretary of State must make regulations requiring the keeping of a register of:

(1) the individuals and firms[1] eligible for appointment as company auditor[2]; and

(2) the individuals holding an appropriate qualification[3] who are responsible for company audit work[4] on behalf of such firms[5].

The regulations must provide that each person's entry in the register shall give his name and address[6] and, in the case of a person eligible as mentioned in head (1) above, the name of the relevant supervisory body[7], together with such other information as may be specified by the regulations[8].

The regulations may impose such obligations as the Secretary of State thinks fit:

(a) on recognised supervisory bodies;

(b) on persons eligible for appointment as company auditor; and

(c) on any person with whom arrangements are made by one or more recognised supervisory bodies with respect to the keeping of the register[9].

The regulations may include provision:

(i) requiring the register to be open to inspection at such times and places as may be specified in the regulations or determined in accordance with them;

(ii) enabling a person to require a certified copy of an entry in the register; and

(iii) authorising the charging of fees for inspection, or the provision of copies, of such reasonable amount as may be specified in the regulations or determined in accordance with them;

and may contain such other supplementary and incidental provisions as the Secretary of State thinks fit[10].

Such regulations must be made by statutory instrument which is subject to annulment in pursuance of a resolution of either House of Parliament[11].

The obligations imposed by regulations under the above provisions on such persons as are mentioned in heads (a) and (c) above are enforceable on the application of the Secretary of State by injunction[12].

1 For the meaning of 'firm' see para 956 note 5 ante.

2 As to eligibility for appointment see para 955 et seq ante and para 992 et seq post. For the meaning of 'company auditor' and 'company' see para 956 note 1 ante.

3 For the meaning of 'appropriate qualification' see para 978 ante.

4 For the meaning of 'company audit work' see para 956 note 1 ante.

5 Companies Act 1989 s 35(1). In exercise of the power so conferred the Secretary of State made the Companies Act 1989 (Register of Auditors and Information about Audit Firms) Regulations 1991, SI 1991/1566 (see paras 992-994 post) which came into force on 1 October 1991: reg 1. As to the punishment of persons falsely describing themselves as registered auditors see para 1001 post.

6 For these purposes, 'address' means (1) in relation to an individual, his usual residential or business address; and (2) in relation to a firm, its registered or principal office in Great Britain: Companies Act 1989 s 53(1).

7 For the meaning of 'supervisory body' see para 962 ante.

8 Companies Act 1989 s 35(2).

9 Ibid s 35(3).

10 Ibid s 35(4).

11 Ibid s 35(5).

12 Ibid s 35(6).

992. Keeping and maintenance of register of auditors. The recognised supervisory bodies[1], or, if there is only one recognised supervisory body, that recognised supervisory body, must keep a register of:

(1) the individuals and firms eligible for appointment as company auditor[2]; and

(2) the individuals holding an appropriate qualification[3] who are responsible for company audit work on behalf of such firms[4].

Each person's entry in the register must give:

(a) his name and address; and

(b) in the case of a person eligible as mentioned in head (1) above, the name of the relevant supervisory body[5].

The responsibilities of each supervisory body, or, if there is only one supervisory body, of that supervisory body, in connection with the above obligation is to be determined as follows[6].

Where there is more than one recognised supervisory body, each recognised supervisory body must co-operate with each other recognised supervisory body for the purpose of ensuring that each enters information on the register[7].

Each recognised supervisory body, or, if there is only one recognised supervisory body, that supervisory body, must take reasonable care to ensure that, at all times:

(i) the register accurately states the individuals and firms eligible for appointment as company auditor under its rules and the individuals holding an appropriate qualification who are responsible for company audit work on behalf of such firms;

(ii) the names and addresses shown on the register relating to persons falling within head (i) above are correct; and

(iii) its name appears on the register by virtue of head (b) above only if the person in question is eligible for appointment as company auditor under its rules[8].

1 As to eligibility for appointment see para 955 et seq ante and para 993 et seq post.
2 As to the recognition of supervisory bodies see para 962 et seq ante.
3 As to holding an appropriate qualification see para 964 ante.
4 Companies Act 1989 (Register of Auditors and Information about Audit Firms) Regulations 1991, SI 1991/1566, reg 2(1).
5 Ibid reg 2(2).
6 Ibid reg 2(3).
7 Ibid reg 3(1).
8 Ibid reg 3(2). To the extent that reg 3(2) imposes a duty on a recognised supervisory body to take reasonable care to ensure that the register is amended to reflect changes in the information specified therein, the recognised supervisory body in question is to be regarded as having discharged that duty if it ensures that the register is appropriately amended within the period of ten business days beginning with the day on which it becomes aware of the relevant change: reg 3(3). For these purposes, 'business day' means any day which is not Saturday, Sunday, Christmas Day, Good Friday or a bank holiday within the meaning of the Banking and Financial Dealings Act 1971 (see TIME vol 45 para 1119 et seq): Companies Act 1989 (Register of Auditors and Information about Audit Firms) Regulations 1991 reg 2.

993. Place of keeping and inspection of register. The register[1] must be kept at the principal office in the United Kingdom of one of the recognised supervisory bodies[2] or, if there is only one recognised supervisory body, at the principal office in the United Kingdom of that body[3].

The recognised supervisory body, at whose principal office the register is kept must ensure that it is open to inspection by any person during a period of at least two hours between the hours of 9 am and 5 pm in any business day[4].

The recognised supervisory bodies, or, if there is only one recognised supervisory body, that recognised supervisory body, must ensure that the register may be inspected in each of the following ways, that is to say, alphabetically and by reference to recognised supervisory bodies[5].

The recognised supervisory bodies, or, if there is only one recognised supervisory body, that recognised supervisory body, may charge a fee for inspection of the register or any part of it not exceeding £2.50 for each hour, or part of an hour, that is spent in conducting an inspection[6].

1 For these purposes, 'the register' means the register to be kept under the Companies Act 1989 (Register of Auditors and Information about Audit Firms) Regulations 1991, SI 1991/1566, reg 2 (see para 992 ante): reg 2.
2 As to the recognition of supervisory bodies see para 962 et seq ante.
3 Companies Act 1989 (Register of Auditors and Information about Audit Firms) Regulations 1991 reg 5(1).
4 Ibid reg 5(2). For the meaning of 'business day' see para 992 note 8 ante.
5 Ibid reg 5(3).
6 Ibid reg 5(4).

994. Copies of entries on register. The recognised supervisory bodies[1], or, if there is only one recognised supervisory body, that recognised supervisory body, must ensure that any person may obtain a copy of any entry in the register[2], being a copy which is certified to be a true copy of the relevant entry by or on behalf of a recognised supervisory body[3].

The recognised supervisory bodies, or, if there is only one recognised supervisory body, that recognised supervisory body, may charge a person a fee not exceeding five pence for a copy of an entry in the register[4].

The recognised supervisory bodies, or, if there is only one recognised supervisory body, that recognised supervisory body, must ensure that it is possible for a person to require copies of entries both alphabetically and by reference to recognised supervisory bodies[5].

1 As to the recognition of supervisory bodies see para 962 et seq ante.
2 For the meaning of 'the register' see para 993 note 1 ante.
3 Companies Act 1989 (Register of Auditors and Information about Audit Firms) Regulations 1991, SI 1991/1566, reg 7(1).
4 Ibid reg 7(2).
5 Ibid reg 7(3).

995. Information about firms to be available to public. The Secretary of State must make regulations requiring recognised supervisory bodies[1] to keep and make available to the public the following information with respect to the firms[2] eligible under their rules[3] for appointment as company auditor:

(1) in relation to a body corporate, the name and address[4] of each person who is a director[5] of the body corporate or holds any shares in it;

(2) in relation to a partnership, the name and address of each partner,
and such other information as may be specified in the regulations[6].

The regulations may impose such obligations as the Secretary of State thinks fit:
(a) on recognised supervisory bodies;
(b) on persons eligible for appointment as company auditor;
(c) on any person with whom arrangements are made by one or more recognised supervisory bodies with respect to the keeping of the information[7].

The regulations may include provision:
(i) requiring that the information be open to inspection at such times and places as may be specified in the regulations or determined in accordance with them;
(ii) enabling a person to require a certified copy of the information or any part of it; and
(iii) authorising the charging of fees for inspection, or the provision of copies, of such reasonable amount as may be specified in the regulations or determined in accordance with them;
and may contain such other supplementary and incidental provisions as the Secretary of State thinks fit[8].

The regulations may make different provision in relation to different descriptions of information and may contain such other supplementary and incidental provisions as the Secretary of State thinks fit[9].

Such regulations must be made by statutory instrument which is subject to annulment in pursuance of a resolution of either House of Parliament[10].

The obligations imposed by regulations under the above provisions on such persons as are mentioned in heads (a) or (c) above are enforceable on the application of the Secretary of State by injunction[11].

1 For the meaning of 'supervisory body' see para 962 ante. As to the recognition of supervisory bodies see para 962 et seq ante.

2 For the meaning of 'firm' see para 956 note 5 ante.
3 For the meaning of references to the rules of a supervisory body see para 962 head (b) ante.
4 For the meaning of 'address' see para 991 note 6 ante.
5 For the meaning of 'director' see para 959 note 1 ante.
6 Companies Act 1989 s 36(1). In exercise of the power so conferred the Secretary of State made the Companies Act 1989 (Register of Auditors and Information about Audit Firms) Regulations 1991, SI 1991/1566 (see para 996 post) which came into force on 1 October 1991: reg 1.
7 Companies Act 1989 s 36(2).
8 Ibid s 36(3).
9 Ibid s 36(4).
10 Ibid s 36(5).
11 Ibid s 36(6).

996. Information about firms to be available to the public; inspection and copies of information. A recognised supervisory body[1] must keep and make available to the public the following information in relation to each firm eligible under its rules for appointment as company auditor:

(1) where the firm is a body corporate, the name and address of each person who is a director of the body or holds any shares in it; and

(2) where the firm is a partnership, the name and address of each partner,

indicating which of the persons mentioned in heads (1) and (2) above is responsible for company audit work on behalf of the firm[2].

A recognised supervisory body must ensure that the information it is required so to keep and make available to the public[3] is open to inspection by any person during a period of at least two hours between the hours of 9 am and 5 pm in every business day[4] at its principal office in the United Kingdom[5].

A recognised supervisory body must ensure that the information may be inspected in each of the following ways, that is to say, alphabetically and by reference to firm[6].

A recognised supervisory body may charge a fee for inspection of the information or any part of it not exceeding £2.50 for each hour, or part of an hour, spent by a person in conducting an inspection[7].

A recognised supervisory body must ensure that any person may obtain a copy of the whole or any part of the information which it is required so to keep certified by the body to be a true copy of the relevant information[8].

A recognised supervisory body may charge a person a fee not exceeding five pence for a copy of the information it keeps relating to any director of or shareholder in a firm which is a body corporate or any partner in a firm which is a partnership[9].

A recognised supervisory body must ensure that it is possible for a person to require copies of information both alphabetically and by reference to firm[10].

1 As to the recognition of supervisory bodies see para 962 et seq ante.
2 Companies Act 1989 (Register of Auditors and Information about Audit Firms) Regulations 1991, SI 1991/1566, reg 4.
3 Ie by virtue of ibid reg 4: see supra.
4 For the meaning of 'business day' see para 992 note 8 ante.
5 Companies Act 1989 (Register of Auditors and Information about Audit Firms) Regulations 1991 reg 6(1).
6 Ibid reg 6(2).
7 Ibid reg 6(3).
8 Ibid reg 8(1).
9 Ibid reg 8(2).
10 Ibid reg 8(3).

997. Matters to be notified to the Secretary of State. The Secretary of State may require a recognised supervisory[1] or qualifying[2] body:

(1) to notify him forthwith of the occurrence of such events as he may specify in writing and to give him such information in respect of those events as is so specified;

(2) to give him, at such times or in respect of such periods as he may specify in writing, such information as is so specified[3].

The notices and information required to be given are such as the Secretary of State may reasonably require for the exercise[4] of his functions[5].

The Secretary of State may require information so given to be given in a specified form or verified in a specified manner[6].

Any notice or information required to be so given must be given in writing unless the Secretary of State specifies or approves some other manner[7].

1 For the meaning of 'supervisory body' see para 962 ante. As to the recognition of supervisory bodies see para 962 et seq ante.
2 For the meaning of 'qualifying body' see para 979 ante. As to the recognition of qualifying bodies see para 979 et seq ante.
3 Companies Act 1989 s 37(1).
4 Ie the exercise of his functions under ibid Pt II (ss 24–54): see para 955 et seq ante and para 998 et seq post.
5 Ibid s 37(2).
6 Ibid s 37(3).
7 Ibid s 37(4).

998. Power to call for information. The Secretary of State may by notice in writing require a recognised supervisory[1] or qualifying[2] body to give him such information as he may reasonably require for the exercise[3] of his functions[4].

The Secretary of State may require that any information which he so requires shall be given within such reasonable time and verified in such manner as he may specify[5].

1 For the meaning of 'supervisory body' see para 962 ante. As to the recognition of supervisory bodies see para 962 et seq ante.
2 For the meaning of 'qualifying body' see para 979 ante. As to the recognition of qualifying bodies see para 979 et seq ante.
3 Ie the exercise of his functions under the Companies Act 1989 Pt II (ss 24–54): see para 955 et seq ante and para 999 et seq post.
4 Ibid s 38(1). As to the service of notices see para 1024 post.
5 Ibid s 38(2).

999. Compliance orders. If at any time it appears to the Secretary of State:

(1) in the case of a recognised supervisory body[1], that any requirement relating to the recognition of such a body[2] is not satisfied;

(2) in the case of a recognised professional qualification[3], that any requirement relating to the recognition of such a qualification[4] is not satisfied; or

(3) that a recognised supervisory or qualifying body has failed to comply with an obligation to which it is subject[5],

he may, instead of revoking the relevant recognition order, make an application to the court[6].

If, on such an application, the court decides that the statutory provision or requirement in question is not satisfied or, as the case may be, that the body has failed to comply with the obligation in question, it may order the supervisory or qualifying body in question to take such steps as the court directs for securing that the statutory provision or requirement is satisfied or that the obligation is complied with[7].

The jurisdiction conferred by the above provisions is exercisable by the High Court[8].

1 For the meaning of 'supervisory body' see para 962 ante. As to the recognition of supervisory bodies see para 962 et seq ante.
2 Ie any requirement of the Companies Act 1989 s 30(5), Sch 11: see para 963 et seq ante.
3 As to the recognition of professional qualifications see para 979 et seq ante.
4 Ie any requirement of the Companies Act 1989 s 32(4), Sch 12: see para 980 et seq ante.
5 Ie by virtue of ibid Pt II (ss 24-54): see para 955 et seq ante and para 1000 et seq post.
6 Ibid s 39(1).
7 Ibid s 39(2).
8 Ibid s 39(3).

1000. Directions to comply with international obligations. If it appears to the Secretary of State:

(1) that any action proposed to be taken by a recognised supervisory[1] or qualifying[2] body, or a body established by order of the Secretary of State[3], would be incompatible with Community obligations or any other international obligations of the United Kingdom; or

(2) that any action which that body has power to take is required for the purpose of implementing any such obligations,

he may direct the body not to take or, as the case may be, to take the action in question[4].

A direction may include such supplementary or incidental requirements as the Secretary of State thinks necessary or expedient[5].

A direction under the above provisions is enforceable on the application of the Secretary of State by injunction[6].

1 For the meaning of 'supervisory body' see para 962 ante. As to the recognition of supervisory bodies see para 962 et seq ante.
2 For the meaning of 'qualifying body' see para 979 ante. As to the recognition of qualifying bodies see para 979 et seq ante.
3 Ie under the Companies Act 1989 s 46: see para 1005 post.
4 Ibid s 40(1). As to the service of directions see para 1024 post.
5 Ibid s 40(2).
6 Ibid s 40(3).

(E) *Offences*

1001. False and misleading statements. A person commits an offence if for the purposes of or in connection with any application[1] or in purported compliance with any requirement imposed on him[2] he furnishes information which he knows to be false or misleading in a material particular or recklessly furnishes information which is false or misleading in a material particular[3]. A person guilty of such an offence is liable on conviction on indictment to imprisonment for a term not exceeding two years or a fine, or to both, or on summary conviction to imprisonment for a term not exceeding six months or a fine not exceeding the statutory maximum, or to both[4].

It is an offence for a person whose name does not appear on the register of auditors[5] to describe himself as a registered auditor or so to hold himself out as to indicate, or be reasonably understood to indicate, that he is a registered auditor[6]. It is also an offence for a body which is not a recognised supervisory[7] or qualifying[8] body to describe itself as so recognised or so to describe itself or hold itself out as to indicate, or be reasonably understood to indicate, that it is so recognised[9]. A person guilty of such an offence[10] is liable on summary conviction to imprisonment for a term not exceeding six months or a fine not exceeding level 5 on the standard scale, or to both[11]. Where contravention of the above provisions[12] involves a public display of the offending description, the maximum fine that may be imposed is, in place of that mentioned above, an amount equal to level 5 on the standard scale multiplied by the number of days for which the display has continued[13]. It is, however, a defence for a person charged with such an offence[14] to show that he took all reasonable precautions and exercised all due diligence to avoid the commission of the offence[15].

1 Ie under the Companies Act 1989 Pt II (ss 24–54): see para 955 et seq ante and para 1002 et seq post.
2 Ie by or under ibid Pt II (ss 24–54).
3 Ibid s 41(1).
4 Ibid s 41(4). For the meaning of 'the statutory maximum' see para 1161 post. As to offences by bodies corporate, partnerships and unincorporated associations see para 1002 post; as to time limits for the prosecution of offences see para 1003 post; and as to jurisdiction and procedure in respect of offences see para 1004 post.
5 Ie the register kept under regulations under ibid s 35: see paras 991–994 ante.
6 Ibid s 41(2).
7 For the meaning of 'supervisory body' see para 962 ante. As to the recognition of supervisory bodies see para 962 et seq ante.
8 For the meaning of 'qualifying body' see para 979 ante. As to the recognition of qualifying bodies see para 979 et seq ante.
9 Companies Act 1989 s 41(3).
10 Ie an offence under ibid s 41(2) or (3): see supra.
11 Ibid s 41(5). For the meaning of 'the standard scale' see CRIMINAL LAW vol 11(2) (Reissue) para 808.
12 Ie ibid s 41(2) or (3).
13 Ibid s 41(5).
14 See note 10 supra.
15 Companies Act 1989 s 41(6).

1002. Offences by bodies corporate, partnerships and unincorporated associations. Where an offence[1] committed by a body corporate is proved to have been committed with the consent or connivance of, or to be attributable to any neglect on the part of, a director[2], manager, secretary or other similar officer of the body, or a person purporting to act in any such capacity, he, as well as the body corporate, is guilty of the offence and liable to be proceeded against and punished accordingly[3]. Where the affairs of a body corporate are managed by its members, the above provisions apply in relation to the acts and defaults of a member in connection with his functions of management as to a director of a body corporate[4].

Where an offence[5] committed by a partnership is proved to have been committed with the consent or connivance of, or to be attributable to any neglect on the part of, a partner, he, as well as the partnership, is guilty of the offence and liable to be proceeded against and punished accordingly[6].

Where an offence[7] committed by an unincorporated association (other than a partnership) is proved to have been committed with the consent or connivance of, or to be attributable to any neglect on the part of, any officer of the association or any member of its governing body, he, as well as the association, is guilty of the offence and liable to be proceeded against and punished accordingly[8].

1 Ie an offence under the Companies Act 1989 Pt II (ss 24–54): see para 955 et seq ante and para 1003 et seq post.

2 For the meaning of 'director' see para 959 note 3 ante.
3 Companies Act 1989 s 42(1). As to jurisdiction and procedure in respect of offences see para 1004 post.
4 Ibid s 42(2).
5 See note 1 supra.
6 Companies Act 1989 s 42(3).
7 See note 1 supra.
8 Companies Act 1989 s 42(4).

1003. Time limit for prosecution of offences. An information relating to an offence[1] which is triable by a magistrates' court in England and Wales may be so tried on an information laid at any time within 12 months after the date on which evidence sufficient in the opinion of the Director of Public Prosecutions or the Secretary of State to justify the proceedings comes to his knowledge[2]. These provisions do not, however, authorise the trial of an information laid more than three years after the commission of the offence[3].

For the above purposes, a certificate of the Director of Public Prosecutions or the Secretary of State as to the date on which such evidence as is referred to above came to his knowledge is conclusive evidence[4].

1 Ie an offence under the Companies Act 1989 Pt II (ss 24–54): see para 955 et seq ante and para 1004 et seq post.
2 Ibid s 43(1). Nothing in s 43 affects proceedings within the time limits prescribed by the Magistrates' Courts Act 1980 s 127(1) (see MAGISTRATES): Companies Act 1989 s 43(5).
3 Ibid s 43(2).
4 Ibid s 43(4).

1004. Jurisdiction and procedure in respect of offences. Summary proceedings for an offence[1] may, without prejudice to any jurisdiction exercisable apart from these provisions, be taken against a body corporate or unincorporated association at any place at which it has a place of business and against an individual at any place where he is for the time being[2].

Proceedings for an offence alleged to have been committed[3] by an unincorporated association must be brought in the name of the association (and not in that of any of its members); and, for the purposes of any such proceedings, any rules of court relating to the service of documents apply as in relation to a body corporate[4].

A fine imposed on an unincorporated association on its conviction of such an offence must be paid out of the funds of the association[5].

1 Ie an offence under the Companies Act 1989 Pt II (ss 24–54): see para 955 et seq ante and para 1005 et seq post.
2 Ibid s 44(1). The Criminal Justice Act 1925 s 33 (as amended) and the Magistrates' Courts Act 1980 s 46, Sch 3 (as amended) (procedure on charge of offence against a corporation: see MAGISTRATES) apply in a case in which an unincorporated association is charged in England and Wales with an offence under the Companies Act 1989 Pt II (ss 24–54) as they apply in the case of a corporation: s 44(3).
3 Ie under ibid Pt II (ss 24–54).
4 Ibid s 44(2).
5 Ibid s 44(5).

(F) *Delegation Orders*

1005. Delegation of functions of the Secretary of State. The Secretary of State may by order (a 'delegation order') establish a body corporate to exercise his functions[1].

A delegation order has the effect of transferring to the body established by it, subject to such exceptions and reservations as may be specified in the order, all the functions of the Secretary of State except such functions relating to the prevention of restrictive practices[2] as are excepted by regulations[3] and his functions in relation to the body itself; and the order may also confer on the body such other functions supplementary or incidental to those transferred as appear to the Secretary of State to be appropriate[4].

Any transfer of the functions under the provisions relating to the power to call for information[5] and directions to comply with international obligations[6] must be subject to the reservation that they remain exercisable concurrently by the Secretary of State; and any transfer of the functions of refusing to approve an overseas qualification, or withdrawing such approval, on the grounds of lack of reciprocity[7] must be subject to the reservation that the function is exercisable only with the consent of the Secretary of State[8].

A delegation order may be amended or, if it appears to the Secretary of State that it is no longer in the public interest that the order should remain in force, revoked by a further order under these provisions[9].

Where functions are transferred or resumed, the Secretary of State may by order confer or, as the case may be, take away such other functions supplementary or incidental to those transferred or resumed as appear to him to be appropriate[10].

An order under these provisions must be made by statutory instrument[11]. An order which has the effect of transferring or resuming any functions must not be made unless a draft of it has been laid before and approved by resolution of each House of Parliament; and any other description of order is subject to annulment in pursuance of a resolution of either House of Parliament[12].

1 Companies Act 1989 s 46(1). For these purposes, 'functions' means functions under Pt II (ss 24–54) (see para 955 et seq ante and para 1006 et seq post): s 46(1). Section 46 comes into force on such day as the Secretary of State may appoint by order made by statutory instrument: s 215(2). At the date at which this volume states the law no such order had been made.
2 Ie functions under ibid s 47(1), Sch 14 Pt I (paras 1–7): see para 1014 et seq post.
3 Ie regulations under ibid s 47: see para 1014 post.
4 Ibid s 46(2). See also note 1 supra.
5 Ie under ibid s 38: see para 998 ante.
6 Ie under ibid s 40: see para 1000 ante.
7 Ie on the grounds referred to in ibid s 33(3): see para 989 ante.
8 Ibid s 46(3). See also note 1 supra.
9 Ibid s 46(4). See also note 1 supra.
10 Ibid s 46(5). See also note 1 supra.
11 Ibid s 46(7). See also note 1 supra.
12 Ibid s 46(8). See also note 1 supra.

1006. Status. The body established by a delegation order[1] is not to be regarded as acting on behalf of the Crown; and its members, officers and employees are not to be regarded as Crown servants[2].

1 Ie under the Companies Act 1989 s 46: see para 1005 ante.
2 Ibid s 46(6), Sch 13 paras 1, 2. The provisions of Sch 13 (see para 1007 et seq post) have effect in relation to a body established by a delegation order under s 46; and any power to make provisions by order is to make provision by order under s 46: Sch 13 para 1. Schedule 13 comes into force on such day as the Secretary of State may appoint by order made by statutory instrument: s 215(2). At the date at which this volume states the law no such order had been made.

1007. Name, members and chairman. The body established by a delegation order[1] is to be known by such name as may be specified in the delegation order[2].

The body must consist of such persons, not being less than eight, as the Secretary of State may appoint after such consultation as he thinks appropriate; and the chairman of the body must be such person as the Secretary of State may appoint from amongst its members[3].

The Secretary of State may make provision by order as to the terms on which the members of the body are to hold and vacate office and as to the terms on which a person appointed chairman is to hold and vacate the office of chairman[4].

1 Ie under the Companies Act 1989 s 46: see para 1005 ante.
2 Ibid s 46(6), Sch 13 para 3(1). As to the application of the provisions of Sch 13 see para 1006 note 2 ante.
3 Ibid Sch 13 para 3(2).
4 Ibid Sch 13 para 3(3).

1008. Financial provisions. The body established by a delegation order[1] must pay to its chairman and members such remuneration, and such allowances in respect of expenses properly incurred by them in the performance of their duties, as the Secretary of State may determine[2].

As regards any chairman or member in whose case the Secretary of State so determines, the body must pay or make provision for the payment of:
(1) such pension, allowance or gratuity to or in respect of that person on his retirement or death; or
(2) such contributions or other payment towards the provision of such a pension, allowance or gratuity,
as the Secretary of State may determine[3].

Where a person ceases to be a member of the body otherwise than on the expiry of his term of office and it appears to the Secretary of State that there are special circumstances which might make it right for him to receive compensation, the body must make a payment to him by way of compensation of such amount as the Secretary of State may determine[4].

1 Ie under the Companies Act 1989 s 46: see para 1005 ante.
2 Ibid s 46(6), Sch 13 para 4(1). As to the application of the provisions of Sch 13 see para 1006 note 2 ante.
3 Ibid Sch 13 para 4(2).
4 Ibid Sch 13 para 4(3).

1009. Proceedings. The delegation order[1] may contain such provision as the Secretary of State considers appropriate with respect to the proceedings of the body established by the order[2].

The order may, in particular:
(1) authorise the body to discharge any functions by means of committees consisting wholly or partly of members of the body;
(2) provide that the validity of proceedings of the body, or of any such committee, is not affected by any vacancy among the members or any defect in the appointment of any member[3].

1 For the meaning of 'delegation order' see para 1005 ante.
2 Companies Act 1989 s 46(6), Sch 13 para 5(1). As to the application of the provisions of Sch 13 see para 1006 note 2 ante.
3 Ibid Sch 13 para 5(2).

1010. Fees. The body established by the delegation order[1] may retain fees payable to it[2].

The fees must be applied for meeting the expenses of the body in discharging its functions and for any purposes incidental to those functions[3]. Those expenses include any expenses incurred by the body on such staff, accommodation, services and other facilities as appear to it to be necessary or expedient for the proper performance of its functions[4].

In prescribing the amount of fees in the exercise of the functions transferred to it, the body must prescribe such fees as appear to it sufficient to defray those expenses, taking one year with another[5].

Any exercise by the body of the power to prescribe fees requires the approval of the Secretary of State; and the Secretary of State may, after consultation with the body, by order vary or revoke any regulations made by it prescribing fees[6].

1 Ie under the Companies Act 1989 s 46: see para 1005 ante.
2 Ibid s 46(6), Sch 13 para 6(1). As to the application of the provisions of Sch 13 see para 1006 note 2 ante.
3 Ibid Sch 13 para 6(2).
4 Ibid Sch 13 para 6(3).
5 Ibid Sch 13 para 6(4).
6 Ibid Sch 13 para 6(5).

1011. Legislative functions. Regulations made by the body established by a delegation order[1] in the exercise of the functions transferred to it must be made by instrument in writing, but not by statutory instrument[2]. The instrument must specify the provision[3] under which it is made[4].

The Secretary of State may by order impose such requirements as he thinks necessary or expedient as to the circumstances and manner in which the body must consult on any regulations it proposes to make[5].

Immediately after an instrument is made, it must be printed and made available to the public with or without payment[6]. A person is not to be taken to have contravened any regulation if he shows that at the time of the alleged contravention the instrument containing the regulation had not been so made available[7].

The production of a printed copy of an instrument purporting to be made by the body on which is indorsed a certificate signed by an officer of the body authorised by it for the purpose and stating:

(1) that the instrument was made by the body;
(2) that the copy is a true copy of the instrument; and
(3) that on a specified date the instrument was made available to the public[8],

is prima facie evidence of the facts stated in the certificate[9]. A certificate purporting to be so signed is deemed to have been duly signed unless the contrary is shown[10]. Any person wishing in any legal proceedings to cite an instrument made by the body may require the body to cause a copy of it to be indorsed with such a certificate[11].

1 Ie under the Companies Act 1989 s 46: see para 1005 ante.
2 Ibid s 46(6), Sch 13 para 7(1). As to the application of the provisions of Sch 13 see para 1006 note 2 ante.
3 Ie the provision of ibid Pt II (ss 24–54): see para 955 et seq ante and para 1012 et seq post.
4 Ibid Sch 13 para 7(2).
5 Ibid Sch 13 para 7(3).
6 Ibid Sch 13 para 8(1).
7 Ibid Sch 13 para 8(2).
8 Ie as required by ibid Sch 13 para 8: see supra.
9 Ibid Sch 13 para 9(1).
10 Ibid Sch 13 para 9(2).
11 Ibid Sch 13 para 9(3).

1012. Report and accounts. The body established by a delegation order[1] must at least once in each year for which the delegation order is in force make a report to the Secretary of State on the discharge of the functions transferred to it and on such other matters as the Secretary of State may by order require[2]. The Secretary of State must lay before Parliament copies of each report so received by him[3].

The Secretary of State may, with the consent of the Treasury, give directions to the body with respect to its accounts and the audit of its accounts; and it is the duty of the body to comply with the directions[4].

A person must not be appointed auditor of the body unless he is eligible for appointment[5] as a company auditor[6].

1 Ie under the Companies Act 1989 s 46: see para 1005 ante.
2 Ibid s 46(6), Sch 13 para 10(1). As to the application of the provisions of Sch 13 see para 1006 note 2 ante.
3 Ibid Sch 13 para 10(2).
4 Ibid Sch 13 para 10(3). As to the service of directions see para 1024 post.
5 Ie under ibid s 25: see para 956 ante.
6 Ibid Sch 13 para 10(4).

1013. Other supplementary provisions. The transfer of a function to a body established by a delegation order[1] does not affect anything previously done in the exercise of the function transferred; and the resumption of a function so transferred does not affect anything previously done in exercise of the function resumed[2]. The Secretary of State may by order make such transitional and other supplementary provision as he thinks necessary or expedient in relation to the transfer or resumption of a function[3].

The provision that may be made in connection with the transfer of a function includes, in particular, provision:

(1) for modifying or excluding any statutory provision[4] in its application to the function transferred;

(2) for applying to the body established by the delegation order, in connection with the function transferred, any provision applying to the Secretary of State which is contained in or made under any other enactment[5];

(3) for the transfer of any property, rights or liabilities from the Secretary of State to that body;

(4) for the carrying on and completion by that body of anything in process of being done by the Secretary of State when the order takes effect;

(5) for the substitution of that body for the Secretary of State in any instrument, contract or legal proceedings[6].

The provision that may be made in connection with the resumption of a function includes, in particular, provision:

(a) for the transfer of any property, rights or liabilities from that body to the Secretary of State;

(b) for the carrying on and completion by the Secretary of State of anything in process of being done by that body when the order takes effect;

(c) for the substitution of the Secretary of State for that body in any instrument, contract or legal proceedings[7].

Where a delegation order is revoked, the Secretary of State may by order make provision for the payment of compensation to persons ceasing to be employed by the body established by the delegation order and as to the winding up and dissolution of the body[8].

1 Ie under the Companies Act 1989 s 46: see para 1005 ante.
2 Ibid s 46(6), Sch 13 para 11(1). As to the application of the provisions of Sch 13 see para 1006 note 2 ante.
3 Ibid Sch 13 para 11(2).
4 Ie any provision of ibid Pt II (ss 24–54): see para 955 et seq ante and para 1014 et seq post.
5 For the meaning of 'enactment' see para 990 note 2 ante.
6 Companies Act 1989 Sch 13 para 11(3).
7 Ibid Sch 13 para 11(4).
8 Ibid Sch 13 para 12.

(G) *Restrictive Practices and Competition Law*

1014. In general. The following provisions[1] have effect with respect to certain matters relating to restrictive practices and competition law[2].

The Secretary of State may make provision by regulations as to the discharge of certain functions[3] when a delegation order[4] is in force[5]. The regulations may:

(1) except any function from the effect of the delegation order;

(2) modify any of specified provisions[6]; and

(3) impose such duties on the body established by the delegation order, the Secretary of State and Director General of Fair Trading[7] as appear to the Secretary of State to be appropriate[8].

The regulations must contain such provision as appears to the Secretary of State to be necessary or expedient for reserving to him the decision to refuse recognition[9] or to exercise certain[10] statutory powers[11]. For that purpose, the regulations may prohibit the body from granting a recognition order[12] without the leave of the Secretary of State and empower the Secretary of State to direct the body to exercise its powers in such manner as may be specified in the directions[13].

Regulations under the above provisions must be made by statutory instrument which is subject to annulment in pursuance of a resolution of either House of Parliament[14].

1 Ie the provisions of the Companies Act 1989 s 47(1), Sch 14: see para 1015 et seq post.
2 Ibid s 47(1).
3 Ie the functions under ibid Sch 14 paras 1–7: see para 1015 et seq post.
4 For the meaning of 'delegation order' see para 1005 ante.
5 Companies Act 1989 s 47(2). Section 47(2) and s 47(6) (see infra) come into force on such day as the Secretary of State may appoint by order made by statutory instrument: s 215(2). At the date at which this volume states the law no such order had been made.
6 Ie any of the provisions of ibid Sch 14 paras 1–7.
7 As to the Director General of Fair Trading see TRADE AND INDUSTRY vol 47 (Reissue) para 504 et seq.
8 Companies Act 1989 s 47(3).
9 Ie on the ground mentioned in ibid Sch 14 para 1(3): see para 1015 post.
10 Ie the powers conferred by ibid Sch 14 para 6: see para 1020 post.
11 Ibid s 47(4).
12 For the meaning of 'recognition order' see para 976 ante (supervisory bodies) and para 987 ante (qualifying bodies).
13 Companies Act 1989 s 47(5). As to the service of directions see para 1024 post.
14 Ibid s 47(6). See also note 5 supra.

1015. Refusal of recognition on grounds related to competition. Before deciding whether to make a recognition order in respect of a supervisory body[1] or professional qualification[2], the Secretary of State must send to the Director General of Fair Trading ('the Director')[3] a copy of the rules[4] and of any guidance[5] which the Secretary of State is required to consider in making that decision together with such other information as the Secretary of State considers will assist the Director[6].

The Director must consider whether the rules or guidance have, or are intended or likely to have, to any significant extent the effect[7] of restricting, distorting or preventing competition, and must report to the Secretary of State; and the Secretary of State must have regard to his report in deciding whether to make a recognition order[8].

The Secretary of State must not make a recognition order if it appears to him that the rules and any guidance of which copies are furnished with the application have, or are intended or likely to have, to any significant extent the effect of restricting, distorting or preventing competition, unless it appears to him that the effect is reasonably justifiable having regard[9] to the statutory purposes[10].

1 See para 962 et seq ante.
2 See para 978 et seq ante.
3 As to the Director General of Fair Trading see TRADE AND INDUSTRY vol 47 (Reissue) para 504 et seq.
4 For the meaning of references to rules see para 962 head (b) ante (supervisory bodies) and para 979 ante (qualifying bodies).
5 For the meaning of references to guidance see para 962 head (c) ante (supervisory bodies) and para 979 ante (qualifying bodies).
6 Companies Act 1989 s 47(1), Sch 14 para 1(1).
7 In determining whether any guidance has, or is likely to have, any particular effect, the Secretary of State and the Director General of Fair Trading may assume that the persons to whom it is addressed will act in conformity with it: ibid Sch 14 para 7(3).
8 Ibid Sch 14 para 1(2).
9 Ie having regard to the purposes of ibid Pt II (ss 24–54): see para 955 et seq ante and para 1016 et seq post.
10 Ibid Sch 14 para 1(3).

1016. Notification of changes to rules or guidance. Where a recognised supervisory[1] or qualifying[2] body amends, revokes or adds to its rules[3] or guidance[4] in a manner which may reasonably be regarded as likely to restrict, distort or prevent competition to any significant extent or otherwise to affect the question whether the recognition order[5] granted to the body should continue in force, it must within seven days give the Secretary of State written notice of the amendment, revocation or addition[6].

Notice need not be so given of the revocation of guidance not intended to have continuing effect or issued otherwise than in writing or other legible form, or of any amendment or addition to guidance which does not result in or consist of guidance which is intended to have continuing effect and is issued in writing or other legible form[7].

1 For the meaning of 'supervisory body' see para 962 ante. As to the recognition of supervisory bodies see para 962 et seq ante.
2 For the meaning of 'qualifying body' see para 979 ante. As to the recognition of qualifying bodies see para 979 et seq ante.
3 For the meaning of references to rules see para 962 head (b) ante (supervisory bodies) and para 979 ante (qualifying bodies).
4 For the meaning of references to guidance see para 962 head (c) ante (supervisory bodies) and para 979 ante (qualifying bodies).

5 For the meaning of 'recognition order' see para 976 ante (supervisory bodies) and para 987 ante (qualifying bodies).
6 Companies Act 1989 s 47(1), Sch 14 para 2(1).
7 Ibid Sch 14 para 2(2).

1017. Continuing scrutiny by the Director General of Fair Trading. The Director General of Fair Trading[1] must keep under review the rules[2] made or guidance[3] issued by a recognised supervisory[4] or qualifying[5] body and, if he is of the opinion that any rules or guidance of such a body have, or are intended or likely to have, to any significant extent the effect[6] of restricting, distorting or preventing competition, he must report his opinion to the Secretary of State, stating what in his opinion the effect is or is likely to be[7].

The Secretary of State must send to the Director copies of any notice received by him[8], together with such other information as he considers will assist the Director[9]. The Director may report to the Secretary of State his opinion that any matter mentioned in such a notice does not have, and is not intended or likely to have, to any significant extent the effect of restricting, distorting or preventing competition[10].

The Director may from time to time consider whether:

(1) any practices of a recognised supervisory or qualifying body in its capacity as such; or

(2) any relevant practices[11] required or contemplated by the rules or guidance of such a body or otherwise attributable to its conduct in its capacity as such,

have, or are intended or likely to have, to any significant extent the effect of restricting, distorting or preventing competition and, if so, what that effect is or is likely to be; and, if he is of that opinion, he must make a report to the Secretary of State stating his opinion and what the effect is or is likely to be[12].

1 As to the Director General of Fair Trading see TRADE AND INDUSTRY vol 47 (Reissue) para 504 et seq.
2 For the meaning of references to rules see para 962 head (b) ante (supervisory bodies) and para 979 ante (qualifying bodies).
3 For the meaning of references to guidance see para 962 head (c) ante (supervisory bodies) and para 979 ante (qualifying bodies).
4 For the meaning of 'supervisory body' see para 962 ante. As to the recognition of supervisory bodies see para 979 et seq ante.
5 For the meaning of 'qualifying body' see para 979 ante. As to the recognition of qualifying bodies see para 979 et seq ante.
6 As to the criterion for determining whether any guidance has, or is likely to have, any particular effect see para 1015 note 7 ante.
7 Companies Act 1989 s 47(1), Sch 14 para 3(1).
8 Ie under ibid Sch 14 para 2: see para 1016 ante.
9 Ibid Sch 14 para 3(2).
10 Ibid Sch 14 para 3(3).
11 The practices relevant for these purposes in the case of a recognised supervisory body are practices engaged in for the purposes of, or in connection with, appointment as a company auditor or the conduct of company audit work by persons who are eligible under its rules for appointment as a company auditor or hold an appropriate qualification and are directors or other officers of bodies corporate which are so eligible or partners in, or employees of, partnerships which are so eligible: ibid Sch 14 para 3(5). The practices relevant for these purposes in the case of a recognised qualifying body are (1) practices engaged in by persons in the course of seeking to obtain a recognised professional qualification from that body; and (2) practices engaged in by persons approved by the body for the purposes of giving practical training to persons seeking such a qualification and which relate to such training: Sch 14 para 3(6). For the meaning of 'company audit work' see para 956 note 1 ante; and for the meaning of 'appropriate qualification' see para 978 ante. As to the recognition of professional qualifications see para 979 et seq ante.
12 Ibid Sch 14 para 3(4).

1018. Investigatory powers of the Director General of Fair Trading. The following powers are exercisable by the Director General of Fair Trading[1] for the purpose of investigating any matter in connection with his statutory[2] functions[3].

The Director may by a notice in writing require any person to produce, at a time and place specified in the notice, to the Director or to any person appointed by him for the purpose, any documents which are specified or described in the notice and which are documents in his custody or under his control and relating to any matter relevant to the investigation[4].

The Director may by a notice in writing require any person to furnish to the Director such information as may be specified or described in the notice, and specify the time within which and the manner and form in which any such information is to be furnished[5].

A person may not be required under the above provisions to produce any document or disclose any information which he would be entitled to refuse to produce or disclose on grounds of legal professional privilege in proceedings in the High Court[6].

1 As to the Director General of Fair Trading see TRADE AND INDUSTRY vol 47 (Reissue) para 504 et seq.
2 Ie his functions under the Companies Act 1989 s 47(1), Sch 14 para 1 (see para 1015 ante) or Sch 14 para 3 (see para 1017 ante).
3 Ibid Sch 14 para 4(1). The Fair Trading Act 1973 s 85(6)-(8) (as amended) (see TRADE AND INDUSTRY vol 47 (Reissue) para 141 note 6) applies in relation to a notice under the Companies Act 1989 Sch 14 para 4 as it applies in relation to a notice under the Fair Trading Act 1973 s 85(1) but as if in s 85(7) (as substituted) for the words from 'any one' to 'the Commission' there were substituted 'the Director': Companies Act 1989 Sch 14 para 4(5).
4 Ibid Sch 14 para 4(2). As to the service of notices see para 1024 post.
5 Ibid Sch 14 para 4(3).
6 Ibid Sch 14 para 4(4). As to legal professional privilege see CRIMINAL LAW vol 11(2) (Reissue) para 1163; EVIDENCE vol 17 para 237.

1019. Publication of the Director General's reports. If he thinks fit, the Director General of Fair Trading[1] may publish any report made[2] by him[3].

He must exclude from a published report, so far as practicable, any matter which relates to the affairs of a particular person (other than the supervisory[4] or qualifying[5] body concerned) the publication of which would or might in his opinion seriously and prejudicially affect the interests of that person[6].

1 As to the Director General of Fair Trading see TRADE AND INDUSTRY vol 47 (Reissue) para 504 et seq.
2 Ie under the Companies Act 1989 s 47(1), Sch 14 para 1 (see para 1015 ante) or Sch 14 para 3 (see para 1017 ante).
3 Ibid Sch 14 para 5(1).
4 For the meaning of 'supervisory body' see para 962 ante. As to the recognition of supervisory bodies see para 962 et seq ante.
5 For the meaning of 'qualifying body' see para 979 ante. As to the recognition of qualifying bodies see para 979 et seq ante.
6 Companies Act 1989 Sch 14 para 5(2).

1020. Powers exercisable by the Secretary of State in consequence of report. The powers:

(1) to revoke the recognition order[1] granted to the body concerned;

(2) to direct it to take specified steps for the purpose of securing that the rules[2], guidance[3] or practices in question do not have the effect mentioned below; and

(3) to make alterations in the rules of the body for that purpose,

are exercisable by the Secretary of State if, having received and considered a report[4] from the Director General of Fair Trading[5], it appears to him that any rules made or guidance issued by a recognised supervisory[6] or qualifying[7] body or any specified practices[8] have, or are intended or likely to have, to any significant extent the effect[9] of restricting, distorting or preventing competition and that that effect is greater than is reasonably justifiable having regard to the relevant statutory[10] purposes[11].

Before the Secretary of State exercises the power conferred by heads (2) or (3) above, he must:

(a) give written notice of his intention to do so to the body concerned and take such steps (whether by publication or otherwise) as he thinks appropriate for bringing the notice to the attention of any other person who in his opinion is likely to be affected by the exercise of the power; and

(b) have regard to any representations made within such time as he considers reasonable by the body or any such other person[12].

Such a notice must give particulars of the manner in which the Secretary of State proposes to exercise the power in question and state the reasons for which he proposes to act; and the statement of reasons may include matters contained in any report received[13] by him[14].

A direction by the Secretary of State under the above provisions is, on his application, enforceable by injunction[15].

The fact that any rules made by a recognised supervisory or qualifying body have been altered by the Secretary of State, or pursuant to a direction of the Secretary of State, under the above provisions does not preclude their subsequent alteration or revocation by that body[16].

1   For the meaning of 'recognition order' see para 976 ante (supervisory bodies) and para 987 ante (qualifying bodies). The provisions of the Companies Act 1989 s 30(5), Sch 11 para 3(2)-(5),(7),(9) (see para 977 ante) or, as the case may be, s 32(4), Sch 12 (see para 978 et seq ante) have effect in relation to the revocation of a recognition order under s 47(1), Sch 14 para 6(2)(a) as they have effect in relation to the revocation of such an order under Sch 11 or, as the case may be, Sch 12: s 47(1), Sch 14 para 6(3).
2   For the meaning of references to rules see para 962 head (b) ante (supervisory bodies) and para 979 ante (qualifying bodies).
3   For the meaning of references to guidance see para 962 head (c) ante (supervisory bodies) and para 979 ante (qualifying bodies).
4   Ie under the Companies Act 1989 Sch 14 para 3(1) or (4): see para 1017 ante.
5   As to the Director General of Fair Trading see TRADE AND INDUSTRY vol 47 (Reissue) para 504 et seq.
6   For the meaning of 'supervisory body' see para 962 ante. As to the recognition of supervisory bodies see para 962 et seq ante.
7   For the meaning of 'qualifying body' see para 979 ante. As to the recognition of qualifying bodies see para 979 et seq ante.
8   Ie any such practices as are mentioned in the Companies Act 1989 Sch 14 para 3(4).
9   As to the criterion for determining whether any guidance has, or is likely to have, any particular effect see para 1015 note 7 ante.
10 Ie the purposes of the Companies Act 1989 Pt II (ss 24-54): see para 955 et seq ante and para 1021 et seq post.
11 Ibid Sch 14 para 6(1),(2).
12 Ibid Sch 14 para 6(4). As to the service of notices see para 1024 post.
13 Ie under ibid Sch 14 para 4: see para 1018 ante.
14 Ibid Sch 14 para 6(5).
15 Ibid Sch 14 para 7(1).
16 Ibid Sch 14 para 7(2).

1021. Consequential exemptions from competition law. For the purposes of determining whether a monopoly situation[1] exists by reason of the supply of services by or for a group of two or more persons[2], no account is to be taken of the rules[3] of or guidance[4] issued by a recognised supervisory[5] or qualifying[6] body or conduct constituting a specified[7] practice[8].

Where a recognition order[9] is revoked, there must be disregarded for the above purposes any such conduct as is there mentioned[10] which occurred while the order was in force[11].

Where on a monopoly reference[12] not limited to the facts[13] the Monopolies and Mergers Commission[14] finds that a monopoly situation[15] exists and:

(1) that the person (or, if more than one, any of the persons) in whose favour it exists is a recognised supervisory or qualifying body or a person of a specified description[16]; or

(2) that any such person's conduct in doing anything to which the rules of such a body relate is subject to guidance issued by the body,

the Commission, in making its report on that reference, must exclude from its consideration the question whether the rules or guidance of the body concerned, or the acts or omissions of that body in its capacity as such, operate or may be expected to operate against the public interest[17].

The Restrictive Trade Practices Act 1976 does not apply to an agreement for the constitution of a recognised supervisory or qualifying body in so far as it relates to rules or guidance issued by the body, and incidental matters connected therewith, including any term deemed[18] to be contained in it[19]. Nor does the 1976 Act apply to an agreement the parties to which consist of or include a recognised supervisory or qualifying body or any specified person[20], by reason that it includes any terms the inclusion of which is required or contemplated by the rules or guidance of that body[21].

Where an agreement so ceases to be subject to registration:

(a) the Director General of Fair Trading[22] must remove from the register maintained by him any particulars which are entered or filed in that register in respect of the agreement; and

(b) any proceedings in respect of the agreement which are pending before the Restrictive Practices Court must be discontinued[23].

Where a recognition order is revoked, the above provisions[24] continue to apply for a period of six months beginning with the day on which the revocation takes effect, as if the order were still in force[25].

Where an agreement which has been exempt from registration ceases to be exempt in consequence of the revocation of a recognition order, the time within which particulars of the agreement are to be furnished[26] is the period of one month beginning with the day on which the agreement ceased to be exempt from registration[27].

Where in the case of an agreement registered under the 1976 Act a term ceases to fall within the above provisions[28] in consequence of the revocation of a recognition order and particulars of that term have not previously been furnished to the Director under that Act, those particulars must be furnished to him within the period of one month beginning with the day on which the term ceased so to fall[29].

No course of conduct constituting any specified practice[30] constitutes an anti-competitive practice for the purposes of the Competition Act 1980[31]. Where a recognition order is revoked, there is not to be treated as an anti-competitive practice any such course of conduct[32] which occurred while the order was in force[33].

1 Ie within the meaning of the Fair Trading Act 1973: see TRADE AND INDUSTRY vol 47 (Reissue) para 114.

2 Ie exists by reason of the circumstances mentioned in ibid s 7(1)(c): see TRADE AND INDUSTRY vol 47 (Reissue) para 114.

3 For the meaning of references to rules see para 962 head (b) ante (supervisory bodies) and para 979 ante (qualifying bodies).

4 For the meaning of references to guidance see para 962 head (c) ante (supervisory bodies) and para 979 ante (qualifying bodies).

5 For the meaning of 'supervisory body' see para 962 ante. As to the recognition of supervisory bodies see para 962 et seq ante.

6 For the meaning of 'qualifying body' see para 979 ante. As to the recognition of qualifying bodies see para 979 et seq ante.

7 Ie such a practice as is mentioned in the Companies Act 1989 s 47(1), Sch 14 para 3(4): see para 1017 ante.

8 Ibid Sch 14 para 8(1).

9 For the meaning of 'recognition order' see para 976 ante (supervisory bodies) and para 987 ante (qualifying bodies). As to revocation of recognition see para 977 ante (supervisory bodies) and para 988 ante (qualifying bodies).

10 Ie in the Companies Act 1989 Sch 14 para 8(1): see supra.

11 Ibid Sch 14 para 8(2).

12 Ie under the Fair Trading Act 1973 s 50 (as amended) (see TRADE AND INDUSTRY vol 47 (Reissue) para 120) or s 51 (as amended) (see TRADE AND INDUSTRY vol 47 (Reissue) para 122).

13 Ie a reference falling within ibid s 49: see TRADE AND INDUSTRY vol 47 (Reissue) para 118.

14 As to the Monopolies and Mergers Commission see TRADE AND INDUSTRY vol 47 (Reissue) para 111 et seq.

15 See note 1 supra.

16 Ie a person of a description mentioned in the Companies Act 1989 Sch 14 para 3(5) or (6): see para 1017 ante.

17 Ibid Sch 14 para 8(3).

18 Ie by virtue of the Restrictive Trade Practices Act 1976 s 8(2) (see TRADE AND INDUSTRY vol 47 (Reissue) para 219) or s 16(3) (see TRADE AND INDUSTRY vol 47 (Reissue) para 228).

19 Companies Act 1989 Sch 14 para 9(1).

20 See note 16 supra.

21 Companies Act 1989 Sch 14 para 9(2).

22 As to the Director General of Fair Trading see TRADE AND INDUSTRY vol 47 (Reissue) para 504 et seq.

23 Companies Act 1989 Sch 14 para 9(3).

24 Ie ibid Sch 14 para 9(1),(2): see supra.

25 Ibid Sch 14 para 9(4).

26 Ie in accordance with the Restrictive Trade Practices Act 1976 s 24, Sch 2: see TRADE AND INDUSTRY vol 47 (Reissue) paras 245, 246.

27 Companies Act 1989 Sch 14 para 9(5).

28 Ie ibid Sch 14 para 9(2): see supra.

29 Ibid Sch 14 para 9(6) (amended by the Deregulation and Contracting Out Act 1994 ss 39, 81(1), Sch 11 para 9, Sch 17).

30 Ie any such practice as is mentioned in the Companies Act 1989 Sch 14 para 3(4): see supra.

31 Ibid Sch 14 para 10(1).

32 Ie any such course of conduct as is mentioned in ibid Sch 14 para 10(1): see supra.

33 Ibid Sch 14 para 10(2).

(H) *Supplementary Provisions*

1022. Fees. An applicant for a recognition order[1] must pay such fee in respect of his application as may be prescribed[2]; and no application is to be regarded as duly made unless this provision is complied with[3].

Every recognised supervisory[4] or qualifying[5] body must pay such periodical fees to the Secretary of State as may be prescribed[6].

Fees received by the Secretary of State[7] must be paid into the Consolidated Fund[8].

1 Ie under the Companies Act 1989 Pt II (ss 24–54): see para 955 et seq ante.

2 For these purposes, 'prescribed' means prescribed by regulations made by the Secretary of State, which may make different provision for different cases or classes of case: ibid s 45(3).

3 Ibid s 45(1). In exercise of the power so conferred the Secretary of State made the Company Auditors (Recognition Orders) (Application Fees) Regulations 1990, SI 1990/1206, which came into force on 2 July 1990: reg 1.

4 For the meaning of 'supervisory body' see para 962 ante. As to the recognition of supervisory bodies see para 962 et seq ante.

5 For the meaning of 'qualifying body' see para 979 ante. As to the recognition of qualifying bodies see para 979 et seq ante.
6 Companies Act 1989 s 45(2). In exercise of the power so conferred the Secretary of State made the Companies Act 1989 (Recognised Supervisory Bodies) (Periodical Fees) Regulations 1993, SI 1993/1881, which came into force on 16 August 1993: reg 1.
7 Ie by virtue of the Companies Act 1989 Pt II (ss 24–54).
8 Ibid s 45(3).

1023. Exemption from liability for damages. Neither a recognised supervisory body[1], nor any of its officers or employees or members of its governing body, is liable in damages for anything done or omitted in the discharge or purported discharge of functions to which these provisions apply, unless the act or omission is shown to have been in bad faith[2].

These provisions apply to the functions of the body so far as relating to, or to matters arising out of:

(1) such rules[3], practices, powers and arrangements of the body to which the statutory provisions[4] apply; or
(2) the obligations with which the body is required[5] to comply;
(3) any guidance[6] issued by the body; or
(4) the obligations to which the body is[7] subject[8].

Neither a body established by a delegation order, nor any of its members, officers or employees, is liable in damages for anything done or omitted in the discharge or purported discharge of the functions exercisable by virtue of a delegation order[9], unless the act or omission is shown to have been in bad faith[10].

1 For the meaning of 'supervisory body' see para 962 ante. As to the recognition of supervisory bodies see para 962 et seq ante.
2 Companies Act 1989 s 48(1).
3 For the meaning of references to rules see para 962 head (b) ante.
4 Ie the Companies Act 1989 s 30(5), Sch 11 Pt II (paras 4–16): see para 964 et seq ante.
5 For the meaning of references to guidance see para 962 head (c) ante.
6 Ie by the Companies Act 1989 Sch 11 para 16: see para 975 ante.
7 Ie by virtue of ibid Pt II (ss 24–54): see para 955 et seq ante.
8 Ibid s 48(2).
9 Ie an order under ibid s 46: see para 1005 ante.
10 Ibid s 48(3). Section 48(3) (see infra) comes into force on such day as the Secretary of State may appoint by order made by statutory instrument: s 215(2). At the date at which this volume states the law no such order had been made.

1024. Service of notices etc. The following provisions have effect in relation to any notice, direction or other document required or authorised[1] to be given to or served on any person other than the Secretary of State[2].

Any such document may be given to or served on the person in question by delivering it to him, by leaving it at his proper address[3] or by sending it by post to him at that address[4].

Any such document may:

(1) in the case of a body corporate, be given to or served on the secretary or clerk of that body;
(2) in the case of a partnership, be given to or served on any partner;
(3) in the case of an unincorporated association other than a partnership, be given to or served on any member of the governing body of the association[5].

For these purposes, and for the purposes of the statutory provisions relating to service of documents by post[6], the proper address of any person is his last known address, whether of his residence or of a place where he carries on business or is employed, and also:

   (a) in the case of a person who is eligible under the rules of a recognised supervisory body[7] for appointment as company auditor and who does not have a place of business in the United Kingdom, the address of that body;

   (b) in the case of a body corporate, its secretary or its clerk, the address of its registered or principal office in the United Kingdom;

   (c) in the case of an unincorporated association, other than a partnership, or a member of its governing body, its principal office in the United Kingdom[8].

1 Ie under the Companies Act 1989 Pt II (ss 24-54): see para 955 et seq ante.
2 Ibid s 49(1).
3 For the meaning of 'address' see para 991 note 6 ante.
4 Companies Act 1989 s 49(2).
5 Ibid s 49(3).
6 Ie the Interpretation Act 1978 s 7 (see STATUTES vol 44(1) (Reissue) para 1388) in its application to the Companies Act 1989 s 49.
7 For the meaning of 'supervisory body' see para 962 ante. As to the recognition of supervisory bodies see para 962 et seq ante.
8 Companies Act 1989 s 49(4).

1025. Power to make consequential amendments. The Secretary of State may by regulations make such amendments of enactments[1] as appear to him to be necessary or expedient in consequence of the statutory provisions relating to eligibility for appointment as company auditor[2] having effect in place of the former provisions[3] of the Companies Act 1985[4]. That power extends to making such amendments as appear to the Secretary of State necessary or expedient of enactments referring by name to the bodies of accountants duly recognised[5] and enactments making with respect to other statutory auditors[6] provision as to the matters dealt with in relation to company auditors[7] under the Companies Act 1985[8].

The provision which may be made with respect to other statutory auditors includes provision as to:

   (1) eligibility for the appointment;

   (2) the effect of appointing a partnership which is not a legal person and the manner of exercise of the auditor's rights in such a case; and

   (3) ineligibility on the ground of lack of independence or any other ground[9].

The regulations may contain such supplementary, incidental and transitional provision as appears to the Secretary of State to be necessary or expedient[10].

The Secretary of State must not make regulations under the above provisions with respect to any statutory auditors without the consent of:

   (a) the Minister responsible for their appointment or responsible for the body or person by, or in relation to whom, they are appointed; or

   (b) if there is no such Minister, the person by whom they are appointed[11].

Regulations under the above provisions must be made by statutory instrument which is subject to annulment in pursuance of a resolution of either House of Parliament[12].

1 For the meaning of 'enactment' see para 990 note 3 ante.
2 Ie by or under the Companies Act 1989 Pt II (ss 24-54): see para 955 et seq ante.
3 Ie the Companies Act 1985 s 389 (repealed).
4 Companies Act 1989 s 50(1). In exercise of the power so conferred the Secretary of State made the Companies Act 1989 (Eligibility for Appointment as Company Auditor) (Consequential Amendments) Regulations 1991, SI 1991/1997 (amended by SI 1995/1163); the Companies Act 1989 Part II

(Consequential Amendments) Regulations 1995, SI 1995/1163; and the Companies Act 1989 Part II (Consequential Amendment) (No 2) Regulations 1995, SI 1995/2723.

5 Ie recognised for the purposes of the Companies Act 1985 s 389(1)(a) (repealed).
6 For these purposes, a 'statutory auditor' means a person appointed auditor in pursuance of any enactment authorising or requiring the appointment of an auditor or auditors: Companies Act 1989 s 50(6).
7 Ie by the Companies Act 1985 s 389 (repealed).
8 Companies Act 1989 s 50(2).
9 Ibid s 50(3).
10 Ibid s 50(4).
11 Ibid s 50(5).
12 Ibid s 50(7).

1026. Power to make provision in consequence of changes affecting accountancy bodies. The Secretary of State may by regulations make such amendments of enactments[1] as appear to him to be necessary or expedient in consequence of any change of name, merger or transfer of engagements affecting a recognised supervisory or qualifying body[2] or a body of accountants referred to in, or approved, authorised or otherwise recognised for the purposes of, any other enactment[3].

Such regulations must be made by statutory instrument which is subject to annulment in pursuance of a resolution of either House of Parliament[4].

1 For the meaning of 'enactment' see para 990 note 2 ante.
2 Ie under the Companies Act 1989 Pt II (ss 24–54): see para 955 et seq ante.
3 Ibid s 51(1). At the date at which this volume states the law no such regulations had been made.
4 Ibid s 51(2).

B. APPOINTMENT

1027. Duty to appoint auditors. Every company must appoint an auditor or auditors[1], subject to the exemption[2] in the case of certain companies[3].

Auditors must be appointed at a general meeting at which accounts are laid[4], except in the case of a private company[5] which has elected[6] to dispense with the laying of accounts, in which case the appointment must be made[7] in accordance with the alternative statutory provisions[8].

1 Ie in accordance with the Companies Act 1985 Pt XI Ch V (ss 384–394A) (as amended): see infra and para 1028 et seq post.
2 Ie the exemption conferred by ibid s 388A (as added): see para 1033 post.
3 Ibid s 384(1) (substituted by the Companies Act 1989 s 119(1); amended by the Companies Act 1985 (Audit Exemption) Regulations 1994, SI 1994/1935, reg 4, Sch 1 para 4). References in the Companies Act 1985 Pt XI Ch V (ss 383–394A) (as amended) to the end of the time for appointing auditors are to the end of the time within which an appointment must be made under s 385(2) (as substituted) (see para 1028 post) or s 385A(2) (as added) (see para 1029 post), according to whichever of those provisions applies: s 384(3) (substituted by the Companies Act 1989 s 119(1)).
4 Ie appointed in accordance with the Companies Act 1985 s 385 (as substituted): see para 1028 post.
5 For the meaning of 'private company' see para 82 ante.
6 Ie in accordance with the Companies Act 1985 s 252 (as substituted): see para 923 ante.
7 Ie in accordance with ibid s 385A (as added): see para 1029 post.
8 Ibid s 384(2) (added by the Companies Act 1989 s 119(1)).

1028. Appointment at general meeting at which accounts are laid. The following provisions apply to every public company[1] and to a private company[2] which has not elected[3] to dispense with the laying of accounts[4].

The company must, at each general meeting at which accounts are laid, appoint an auditor or auditors to hold office from the conclusion of that meeting until the conclusion of the next general meeting at which accounts are laid[5].

The first auditors of the company may be appointed by the directors at any time before the first general meeting of the company at which accounts are laid; and auditors so appointed hold office until the conclusion of that meeting[6]. If the directors fail so to exercise their powers, the power may be exercised by the company in general meeting[7].

1 For the meaning of 'public company' see para 82 ante.
2 For the meaning of 'private company' see para 82 ante.
3 Ie in accordance with the Companies Act 1985 s 252 (as substituted): see para 923 ante.
4 Ibid s 385(1) (substituted by the Companies Act 1989 s 119(1)). The Companies Act 1985 s 385 (as substituted) has effect subject to s 386 (as substituted) (see para 1030 post) under which a private company may elect to dispense with the obligation to appoint auditors annually: s 384(4) (substituted by the Companies Act 1989 s 119(1)).
5 Companies Act 1985 s 385(2) (substituted by the Companies Act 1989 s 119(1)).
6 Companies Act 1985 s 385(3) (substituted by the Companies Act 1989 s 119(1)).
7 Companies Act 1985 s 385(4) (substituted by the Companies Act 1989 s 119(1)).

1029. Appointment by private company which is not obliged to lay accounts. The following provisions apply to a private company[1] which has elected[2] to dispense with the laying of accounts before the company in general meeting[3].

Auditors must be appointed by the company in general meeting before the end of the period of 28 days beginning with the day on which copies of the company's annual accounts[4] for the previous financial year[5] are sent to members[6] or, if notice is given[7] requiring the laying of accounts before the company in general meeting, the conclusion of that meeting[8]. Auditors so appointed hold office from the end of that period or, as the case may be, the conclusion of that meeting until the end of the time for appointing auditors for the next financial year[9].

The first auditors of the company may be appointed by the directors at any time before:

(1) the end of the period of 28 days beginning with the day on which copies of the company's first annual accounts are sent to members; or

(2) if notice is given[10] requiring the laying of the accounts before the company in general meeting, the beginning of that meeting;

and auditors so appointed hold office until the end of that period or, as the case may be, the conclusion of that meeting[11]. If the directors fail so to exercise their powers, the powers may be exercised by the company in general meeting[12].

Auditors holding office when the election is made continue, unless the company in general meeting determines otherwise, to hold office until the end of the time for appointing auditors for the next financial year; and auditors holding office when an election ceases to have effect continue to hold office until the conclusion of the next general meeting of the company at which accounts are laid[13].

1 For the meaning of 'private company' see para 82 ante.
2 Ie in accordance with the Companies Act 1985 s 252 (as substituted): see para 923 ante.
3 Ibid s 385A(1) (added by the Companies Act 1989 s 119(1)). The Companies Act 1985 s 385A (as added) has effect subject to s 386 (as substituted) (see para 1030 post) under which a private company may elect to dispense with the obligation to appoint auditors annually: s 384(4) (substituted by the Companies Act 1989 s 119(1)).
4 For the meaning of 'annual accounts' see para 817 note 2 ante.
5 For the meaning of 'financial year' see para 806 ante.

6 Ie under the Companies Act 1985 s 238 (as substituted): see para 823 ante.
7 Ie under ibid s 253(2) (as substituted): see para 924 ante.
8 Ibid s 385A(2) (added by the Companies Act 1989 s 119(1)).
9 See note 6 supra.
10 See note 7 supra.
11 Companies Act 1985 s 385A(3) (substituted by the Companies Act 1989 s 119(1)).
12 Companies Act 1985 s 385A(4) (substituted by the Companies Act 1989 s 119(1)).
13 Companies Act 1985 s 385A(5) (substituted by the Companies Act 1989 s 119(1)).

1030. Election by private company to dispense with annual appointment. A private company[1] may elect by elective resolution[2] to dispense with the obligation to appoint auditors annually[3].

When such an election is in force, the company's auditors are deemed to be reappointed for each succeeding financial year[4] on the expiry of the time for appointing auditors for that year, unless:

(1) a resolution has been passed[5] by virtue of which the company is exempt from the obligation to appoint auditors; or

(2) a resolution has been passed[6] to the effect that their appointment should be brought to an end[7].

If the election ceases to be in force, the auditors then holding office continue to hold office:

(a) where the statutory provisions relating to the appointment of auditors at a general meeting at which accounts are laid[8] then apply, until the conclusion of the next general meeting of the company at which accounts are laid;

(b) where the statutory provisions relating to the appointment of auditors by a private company which is not obliged to lay accounts[9] then apply, until the end of the time for appointing auditors[10] for the next financial year[11].

No account is to be taken of any loss of the opportunity of further deemed reappointment under the above provisions in ascertaining the amount of any compensation or damages payable to an auditor on his ceasing to hold office for any reason[12].

1 For the meaning of 'private company' see para 82 ante.
2 Ie in accordance with the Companies Act 1985 s 379A (as added): see para 686 ante.
3 Ibid s 386(1) (substituted by the Companies Act 1989 s 119(1)).
4 For the meaning of 'financial year' see para 806 ante.
5 Ie under the Companies Act 1985 s 250 (as amended): see para 1058 post.
6 Ie under ibid s 393 (as substituted): see para 1051 post.
7 Ibid s 386(2) (substituted by the Companies Act 1989 s 119(1)).
8 Ie the Companies Act 1985 s 385 (as substituted): see para 1028 ante.
9 Ie ibid s 385A (as added): see para 1029 ante.
10 Ie under ibid s 385A (as added).
11 Ibid s 386(3) (substituted by the Companies Act 1989 s 119(1)).
12 Companies Act 1985 s 386(4) (substituted by the Companies Act 1989 s 119(1)).

1031. Appointment by the Secretary of State in default of appointment by company. If in any case no auditors are appointed, reappointed or deemed to be reappointed before the end of the time for appointing auditors[1], the Secretary of State may appoint a person to fill the vacancy[2].

In such a case the company must within one week of the end of the time for appointing auditors give notice to the Secretary of State of his power having become exercisable[3].

If a company fails to give the required notice, the company, and every officer of it who is in default, is guilty of an offence and liable on summary conviction to a fine not exceeeding one-fifth of the statutory maximum and, on conviction after continued contravention, to a daily default fine not exceeding one-fiftieth of the statutory maximum[4].

1 For the meaning of references to the end of the time for appointing auditors see para 1027 note 3 ante.
2 Companies Act 1985 s 387(1) (substituted by the Companies Act 1989 s 119(1)).
3 Companies Act 1985 s 387(2) (substituted by the Companies Act 1989 s 119(1)).
4 Companies Act 1985 s 387(2) (as substituted: see note 3 supra), s 730, Sch 24 (amended by the Companies Act 1989 s 119(2)). For the meaning of 'officer who is in default', 'the statutory maximum' and 'daily default fine' see para 1161 post.

1032. Casual vacancies. The directors, or the company in general meeting, may fill a casual vacancy in the office of auditor[1].

While such a vacancy continues, any surviving or continuing auditor or auditors may continue to act[2].

Special notice[3] is required for a resolution at a general meeting of a company filling a casual vacancy in the office of auditor or reappointing as auditor a retiring auditor who was appointed by the directors to fill a casual vacancy[4].

On receipt of notice of such an intended resolution the company must forthwith send a copy of it to the person proposed to be appointed and, if the casual vacancy was caused by the resignation of an auditor, to the auditor who resigned[5].

1 Companies Act 1985 s 388(1) (substituted by the Companies Act 1989 s 119(1)).
2 Companies Act 1985 s 388(2) (substituted by the Companies Act 1989 s 119(1)).
3 As to special notice see para 687 ante.
4 Companies Act 1985 s 388(3) (substituted by the Companies Act 1989 s 119(1)).
5 Companies Act 1985 s 388(4) (substituted by the Companies Act 1989 s 119(1)).

1033. Companies exempt from obligation to appoint auditors. A company which, being a small company or dormant, is exempt[1] from the statutory provisions[2] relating to the audit of accounts is also exempt from the obligation to appoint auditors[3].

The following provisions apply if a company which has been exempt from those provisions ceases to be so exempt[4].

Where the statutory provisions relating to the appointment of auditors at a general meeting at which accounts are laid apply[5], the directors may appoint auditors at any time before the next meeting of the company at which accounts are to be laid; and auditors so appointed hold office until the conclusion of that meeting[6].

Where the statutory provisions relating to the appointment of auditors by a private company not obliged to lay accounts[7] apply, the directors may appoint auditors at any time before:

(1) the end of the period of 28 days beginning with the day on which copies of the company's annual accounts[8] are next sent[9] to members; or

(2) if notice is given[10] requiring the laying of the accounts before the company in general meeting, the beginning of that meeting;

and auditors so appointed hold office until the end of that period or, as the case may be, the conclusion of that meeting[11].

If the directors fail to exercise their powers under the above provisions[12], the powers may be exercised by the company in general meeting[13].

1 Ie by virtue of the Companies Act 1985 s 249A (as added) (certain categories of small companies: see para 1054 post) or s 250 (as substituted and amended) (dormant companies: see para 1058 post).
2 Ie the provisions of ibid Pt VII (ss 221-262A) (as amended): see para 1054 et seq post.

3 Ibid s 388A(1) (added by the Companies Act 1989 s 119(1); substituted by the Companies Act 1985 (Audit Exemption) Regulations 1994, SI 1994/1935, reg 3(1)).

4 Companies Act 1985 s 388A(2) (added by the Companies Act 1989 s 119(1); substituted by the Companies Act 1985 (Audit Exemption) Regulations 1994 reg 3(1)).

5 Ie the Companies Act 1985 s 385 (as substituted): see para 957 ante.

6 Ibid s 388A(3) (added by the Companies Act 1989 s 119(1); substituted by the Companies Act 1985 (Audit Exemption) Regulations 1994 reg 3(1)).

7 Ie the Companies Act 1985 s 385A (as added): see para 1029 ante.

8 For the meaning of 'annual accounts' see para 817 note 2 ante.

9 Ie under the Companies Act 1985 s 238 (as substituted): see para 823 ante.

10 Ie under ibid s 253(2) (as substituted): see para 924 ante.

11 Ibid s 388A(4) (added by the Companies Act 1989 s 119(1); substituted by the Companies Act 1985 (Audit Exemption) Regulations 1994 reg 3(1)).

12 Ie the Companies Act 1985 s 388A(3) or (4) (as added and substituted): see supra.

13 Ibid s 388A(5) (added by the Companies Act 1989 s 119(1); substituted by the Companies Act 1985 (Audit Exemption) Regulations 1994 reg 3(1)).

C. RIGHTS AND DUTIES

1034. Rights to information. The auditors of a company have a right of access at all times to the company's books, accounts and vouchers, and are entitled to require from the company's officers such information and explanations as they think necessary for the performance of their duties as auditors[1]. The court will not, however, enforce this right by mandatory injunction where it is doubtful until after a general meeting has been held whether the company wishes the auditors to continue as such[2].

A company cannot by its articles preclude its auditors from obtaining or availing themselves of the information to which they are entitled by statute as material for their reports[3].

An officer of a company commits an offence if he knowingly or recklessly makes to the company's auditors a statement, whether written or oral, which:

(1) conveys or purports to convey any information or explanations which the auditors require, or are entitled to require, as auditors of the company; and

(2) is misleading, false or deceptive in a material particular[4].

A person guilty of such an offence is liable on conviction on indictment to imprisonment for a term not exceeding two years or a fine, or to both, or on summary conviction to imprisonment for a term not exceeding six months or a fine not exceeding the statutory maximum, or to both[5].

A subsidiary undertaking[6] which is a body corporate incorporated in Great Britain, and the auditors of such an undertaking, must give to the auditors of any parent company[7] of the undertaking such information and explanations as they may reasonably require for the purposes of their duties as auditors of that company[8]. If a subsidiary undertaking fails to comply with that obligation, the undertaking, and every officer of it who is in default, is guilty of an offence and liable on summary conviction to a fine not exceeding one-fifth of the statutory maximum; and, if an auditor fails without reasonable excuse to comply with that obligation, he is guilty of an offence and liable on summary conviction to a fine not exceeding one-fifth of the statutory maximum[9].

A parent company having a subsidiary undertaking which is not a body corporate incorporated in Great Britain must, if required by its auditors to do so, take all such steps as are reasonably open to it to obtain from the subsidiary undertaking such information and explanations as they may reasonably require for the purposes of their duties as auditors of that company[10]. If a parent company fails to comply with that obligation, the company, and every officer of it who is in default, is guilty of an offence and liable on summary conviction to a fine not exceeding one-fifth of the statutory maximum[11].

1 Companies Act 1985 s 389A(1) (added by the Companies Act 1989 s 120(1)).
2 *Cuff v London and County Land and Building Co Ltd* [1912] 1 Ch 440, CA.
3 *Newton v Birmingham Small Arms Co Ltd* [1906] 2 Ch 378. As to the report see para 1059 post.
4 Companies Act 1985 s 389A(2) (added by the Companies Act 1989 s 120(1)).
5 Companies Act 1985 s 389A(2) (as added: see note 4 supra), s 730, Sch 24 (amended by the Companies Act 1989 s 120(3)). For the meaning of 'the statutory maximum' see para 1161 post.
6 For the meaning of 'subsidiary undertaking' see para 828 ante.
7 For the meaning of 'parent company' see para 828 ante.
8 Companies Act 1985 s 389A(3) (added by the Companies Act 1989 s 120(1)).
9 Companies Act 1985 s 389A(3) (as added: see note 8 supra), s 730, Sch 24 (amended by the Companies Act 1989 s 120(3)). For the meaning of 'officer who is in default' see para 1161 post. The Companies Act 1985 s 734 (as amended) (criminal proceedings against unincorporated bodies: see para 1163 post) applies to an offence under s 389A(3) (as so added): s 389A(5) (added by the Companies Act 1989 s 120(3)).
10 Companies Act 1985 s 389A(4) (added by the Companies Act 1989 s 120(1)).
11 Companies Act 1985 s 389A(4) (as added: see note 10 supra), s 730, Sch 24 (amended by the Companies Act 1989 s 120(3)).

1035. Right to attend company meetings etc. A company's auditors are entitled:

(1) to receive all notices of, and other communications relating to, any general meeting which a member of the company is entitled to receive;

(2) to attend any general meeting of the company; and

(3) to be heard at any general meeting which they attend on any part of the business of the meeting which concerns them as auditors[1].

In relation to a written resolution proposed to be agreed to by a private company[2], the company's auditors are entitled:

(a) to receive all such communications relating to the resolution as are required[3] to be supplied to a member of the company;

(b) to give notice[4] of their opinion that the resolution concerns them as auditors and should be considered by the company in general meeting or, as the case may be, by a meeting of the relevant class of members of the company;

(c) to attend any such meeting; and

(d) to be heard at any such meeting which they attend on any part of the business of the meeting which concerns them as auditors[5].

The right to attend or be heard at a meeting is exercisable in the case of a body corporate or partnership by an individual authorised by it in writing to act as its representative at the meeting[6].

1 Companies Act 1985 s 390(1) (substituted by the Companies Act 1989 s 120(1)). As to the rights of auditors who have been removed see para 1047 post; and as to the rights of auditors who have resigned see para 1050 post.
2 Ie in accordance with the Companies Act 1985 s 381A (as added): see para 697 ante. For the meaning of 'private company' see para 82 ante.
3 Ie by virtue of ibid s 381A(7), Sch 15A (as added): see para 697 ante.
4 Ie in accordance with ibid s 381B (as added): see para 698 ante.
5 Ibid s 390(2) (substituted by the Companies Act 1989 s 120(1)).
6 Companies Act 1985 s 390(3) (substituted by the Companies Act 1989 s 120(1)).

1036. Provisions in articles. The articles of association of a company sometimes make provision for audit and the duties of auditors[1]. As regards indemnity clauses in articles or in contracts, auditors are in the same position as directors[2].

1 This was the position under the Companies Act 1948 Sch 1, Table A art 130 (as amended) but the Companies (Tables A to F) Regulations 1985, SI 1985/805, Schedule, Table A (amended by SI 1985/1052) makes no such provision. As to Table A generally see para 529 et seq ante; and as to the articles impliedly forming part of the contract between the company and its auditors see *Re City Equitable Fire Insurance Co Ltd* [1925] Ch 407 at 520, 521, CA and paras 142, 144 ante.

2 See the Companies Act 1985 s 310 (as amended) and para 623 ante.

1037. Auditors' duties; in general. It is the duty of an auditor to verify not merely the arithmetical accuracy of the balance sheet, but its substantial accuracy[1], and to see that it includes the particulars required by the articles and by statute, and contains a correct representation of the state of the company's affairs. While, therefore, it is not his duty to consider whether the business is prudently conducted, he is bound to consider and report to the shareholders whether the balance sheet shows the company's true financial position. To do this he must examine the books and take reasonable care to see that their contents are substantially accurate[2]. Except in special cases he should place before the shareholders the necessary information as to the company's true financial position, and not merely indicate the means of acquiring it[3].

Apart from his statutory duty, which cannot be removed by the articles or an agreement, the exact duties of an auditor are regulated by the contract under which he is employed[4]. The statutory duty is not absolute but depends upon the explanations furnished and information given; but an auditor must ask for information on matters which call for further explanation[4]. An auditor must take steps to learn his statutory duties and, if there are any, his duties under the articles[5].

It is his duty to consider whether payments made by the company before the audit were authorised by the articles[5], and he will be liable for improper payments made by the directors and naturally resulting from his breach of duty[6]. So an auditor who reports confidentially to the directors the insufficiency of the securities on which the capital is invested and the difficulty of realisation, but who only reports to the shareholders that the value depends on realisation, with the result that the shareholders ignorantly approve an improper dividend, is liable to make good the amount paid[7]. An auditor should not be content with a certificate that securities are in the possession of any person or body of persons, however trustworthy, unless the certificate is given by a bank or other person who in the ordinary course of business would usually be entrusted with securities[8].

1 See *Fomento (Sterling Area) Ltd v Selsdon Fountain Pen Co Ltd* [1958] 1 All ER 11 at 23, [1958] 1 WLR 45 at 61, HL per Lord Denning.

2 *Re London and General Bank (No 2)* [1895] 2 Ch 673, CA; *Re City Equitable Fire Insurance Co Ltd* [1925] Ch 407 at 501, CA (where the duties of auditors are elaborately discussed and the previous decisions on the subject are collected). See also *Lloyd Cheyham & Co Ltd v Littlejohn & Co* [1987] BCLC 303.

3 *Re London and General Bank (No 2)* [1895] 2 Ch 673, CA.

4 *Re City Equitable Fire Insurance Co Ltd* [1925] Ch 407 at 501, CA. As to possible liability for negligent statements apart from contract see *Hedley Byrne & Co Ltd v Heller & Partners Ltd* [1964] AC 465, [1963] 2 All ER 575, HL and TORT. Cf *Scott Group Ltd v McFarlane* [1978] 1 NZLR 553 (duties owed only to company and its officers and third parties to whom the auditors either themselves show accounts or know the accounts are to be shown so as to induce them to act thereon). As to the duties of auditors employed to check the amount of royalties payable under a special agreement see *Fomento (Sterling Area) Ltd v Selsdon Fountain Pen Co Ltd* [1958] 1 All ER 11, [1958] 1 WLR 45, HL and *Haig v Bamford* (1976) 72 DLR (3d) 68 (Can SC).

5 *Re Republic of Bolivia Exploration Syndicate Ltd* [1914] 1 Ch 139 (auditors held entitled to rely on the special circumstances of the case); and see *Thomas v Devonport Corpn* [1900] 1 QB 16, CA.

6 *Spackman v Evans* (1868) LR 3 HL 171 at 235, 236.

7 *Re London and General Bank (No 2)* [1895] 2 Ch 673, CA.

8 *Re City Equitable Fire Insurance Co Ltd* [1925] Ch 407 at 501, CA.

1038. Auditors' duty towards third parties. The duty of care owed by auditors to members of a company arises by reason of their statutory position and obligations[1]. That duty is towards shareholders in their capacity as shareholders[2]. The auditors of a public company owe no duty of care to a member of the public at large who relies on the company's accounts to buy shares in the company because the court will not deduce a relationship of proximity between the auditors and a member of the public when to do so would give rise to unlimited liability on the part of the auditors[3]. Nor do auditors owe a duty of care to an individual shareholder in the company who wishes to buy more shares in the company, since an individual shareholder is in no better a position than a member of the public at large and the auditors' statutory duty to prepare accounts is owed to the body of shareholders as a whole, the purpose for which accounts are prepared and audited being to enable the shareholders as a body to exercise informed control of the company and not to enable individual shareholders to buy shares with a view to profit[3].

Auditors owe a duty of care to third parties only where a special duty has been assumed by the third party and there is an intention on the part of the auditors that the third party should rely on the audit[4]; but the position may be different where auditors are carrying out a special duty for a specific purpose[5]. Where, however, the auditors, on the evidence, have no reason to know that the company intends to supply the auditors' reports to potential investors, there is no relationship between the auditors and potential or existing investors who are not company shareholders, even though the auditors' reports may foreseeably come into their hands and be relied upon[6].

1   As to the auditors' position generally see para 955 et seq ante and para 1039 et seq post.
2   *Caparo Industries plc v Dickman* [1990] 2 AC 605, [1990] 1 All ER 568, HL. The three criteria for the imposition of a duty of care are foreseeability of damage, proximity of relationship and the reasonableness or otherwise of imposing a duty: *Caparo Industries plc v Dickman* supra.
    The decision in *Caparo Industries plc v Dickman* supra largely reflects the dissenting judgment of Denning LJ in *Candler v Crane Christmas & Co* [1951] 2 KB 164 at 179-184, [1951] 1 All ER 426 at 433-436, CA, described as a 'masterly analysis [which required] little, if any, amplification or modification in the light of later authority' by Lord Bridge of Harwich in *Caparo Industries plc v Dickman* supra at 623 and at 577.
3   *Caparo Industries plc v Dickman* [1990] 2 AC 605, [1990] 1 All ER 568, HL.
4   *Anthony v Wright* [1995] 1 BCLC 236 (claim against auditors by persons who were beneficiaries of assets administered in trust by the company in which the beneficiaries were also shareholders; trust assets misappropriated; beneficiaries claimed that, in failing to discover the misappropriation, the auditors were in breach of their duty of care to the beneficiaries; claim failed). See also *Berg Sons & Co Ltd v Mervyn Hampton Adams* [1993] BCLC 1045 (no duty of care on the part of the auditors towards creditors and lenders); *Deloitte Haskins & Sells v National Mutual Life Nominees Ltd* [1993] AC 774, [1993] 2 All ER 1015, PC (no duty of care on the part of the auditors of a deposit-taking business towards the trustees for the depositors).
5   *Morgan Crucible Co plc v Hill Samuel & Co Ltd* [1991] Ch 259; sub nom *Morgan Crucible Co Ltd v Hill Samuel Bank Ltd* [1991] 1 All ER 148, CA (if during the course of a contested take-over bid the directors and financial advisers of the target company made express representations after an identified bidder had emerged intending that the bidder would rely on those representations, they owed the bidder a duty of care not to be negligent in making representations which might mislead him).
6   *Al Saudi Banque v Clark Pixley (a firm)* [1990] Ch 313, [1989] 3 All ER 361.

1039. Auditors' position. Auditors are not agents of the company so as to affect the members with knowledge which they have acquired while auditing the accounts, as, for example, of directors' unauthorised acts[1]. Nevertheless they are officers of the company, and may be proceeded against for misfeasance[2]. The court has the same power of granting relief to auditors in respect of negligence, default, breach of duty or breach of trust as it has of granting relief to directors[3].

1   *Leeds Estate Building and Investment Co v Shepherd* (1887) 36 ChD 787; *Re London and General Bank (No 2)* [1895] 2 Ch 673 at 683, CA per Lindley LJ. The auditor must show reasonable skill, care and caution in the performance of his duties, but he is not bound to be a detective, and is 'a watch-dog, not a bloodhound': *Re Kingston Cotton Mill Co (No 2)* [1896] 2 Ch 279 at 288, CA. He must come to his task with an inquiring mind, suspecting that someone may have made a mistake somewhere: *Fomento (Sterling Area) Ltd v Selsdon Fountain Pen Co Ltd* [1958] 1 All ER 11 at 23, [1958] 1 WLR 45 at 61, HL per Lord Denning. See also that case at 15 and at 51 per Viscount Simonds; and see *Squire, Cash Chemist v Ball, Baker & Co* (1911) 106 LT 197, CA; *Fox & Son v Morrish, Grant & Co* (1918) 35 TLR 126. Standards of auditing are now more stringent, and the older cases may have to be read with this in mind: *Re Thomas Gerrard & Son Ltd* [1968] Ch 455, [1967] 2 All ER 525. See also para 1037 ante.

2   *Re London and General Bank (No 2)* [1895] 2 Ch 673, CA; *Re Kingston Cotton Mill Co* [1896] 1 Ch 6, CA; and see para 2448 et seq post; *Re Western Counties Steam Bakeries and Milling Co* [1897] 1 Ch 617, CA. As to criminal liability see *R v Shacter* [1960] 2 QB 252, [1960] 1 All ER 61, CCA.

3   See the Companies Act 1985 s 727 and para 624 ante.

1040. Auditors of trade unions. A trade union must in respect of each accounting period appoint an auditor or auditors to audit the accounts contained in its annual return[1]. A person is not qualified to be the auditor or one of the auditors of a trade union unless he is eligible for appointment as a company auditor[2].

The auditor or auditors of a trade union must make a report to it on the accounts audited by him or them and contained in its annual return[3].

Every auditor of a trade union has a right of access to accounting records and other documents, a right to require information and explanations for the performance of his duty as auditor and the right to attend general meetings of members, or delegates of members, of the trade union, to receive notices of any such general meeting and to be heard at any such meeting on any part of the meeting which concerns him as auditor[4].

1   See the Trade Union and Labour Relations (Consolidation) Act 1992 s 33(1) and TRADE AND INDUSTRY vol 47 (Reissue) para 1042. As to the appointment and removal of auditors see TRADE AND INDUSTRY vol 47 (Reissue) para 1043.

2   See ibid s 34(1) and TRADE AND INDUSTRY vol 47 (Reissue) para 1042.

3   See ibid s 36 and TRADE AND INDUSTRY vol 47 (Reissue) para 1044.

4   See ibid s 37 and TRADE AND INDUSTRY vol 47 (Reissue) para 1045.

1041. Rights as to working papers. The working papers prepared by a firm of accountants in the course of producing a balance sheet for a company for audit purposes are the property of the accountants and not of the company, and may be ordered to be produced on discovery in litigation between the firm and one of their employees engaged in the audit. Correspondence in which the firm was acting as agent for the company is, however, the property of the company and is not to be produced[1].

1   *Chantrey Martin & Co v Martin* [1952] 2 QB 286, [1953] 2 All ER 691, CA (where the production of working papers was ordered subject to an undertaking by the person seeking the discovery not to disclose their contents otherwise than for the purposes of the litigation; the court considered that a plea that the discovery should not be ordered by reason of the embodiment of information which was the subject of professional confidence between the firm and its clients was not a ground for refusing the order). As to the production of documents generally see DISCOVERY.

D.   REMUNERATION

1042. In general. The remuneration[1] of auditors appointed by the company in general meeting must be fixed by the company in general meeting or in such manner as the company in general meeting may determine[2].

The remuneration of auditors appointed by the directors or the Secretary of State must be fixed by the directors or the Secretary of State, as the case may be[3].

There must be stated in a note[4] to the company's annual accounts[5] the amount of the remuneration of the company's auditors in their capacity as such[6].

The above provisions apply in relation to benefits in kind as to payments in cash; and in relation to any such benefit references to its amount are to its estimated money value[7]. The nature of any such benefit must also be disclosed[7].

1 For these purposes, 'remuneration' includes sums paid in respect of expenses: Companies Act 1985 s 390A(4) (substituted by the Companies Act 1989 s 121).
2 Companies Act 1985 s 390A(1) (substituted by the Companies Act 1989 s 121).
3 Companies Act 1985 s 390A(2) (substituted by the Companies Act 1989 s 121).
4 As to notes to the accounts see paras 838 et seq, 887 et seq ante.
5 For the meaning of 'annual accounts' see para 817 note 2 ante.
6 Companies Act 1985 s 390A(3) (substituted by the Companies Act 1989 s 121).
7 Companies Act 1985 s 390A(5) (substituted by the Companies Act 1989 s 121).

1043. Remuneration for non-audit work. The Secretary of State may make provision by regulations for securing the disclosure of the amount of any remuneration received or receivable by a company's auditors or their associates in respect of services other than those of auditors in their capacity as such[1].

The regulations may:

(1) provide that 'remuneration' includes sums paid in respect of expenses;
(2) apply in relation to benefits in kind as to payments in cash, and in relation to any such benefit require disclosure of its nature and its estimated money value;
(3) define 'associate' in relation to an auditor;
(4) require the disclosure of remuneration in respect of services rendered to associated undertakings of the company; and
(5) define 'associated undertaking' for that purpose[2].

The regulations may require the auditors to disclose the relevant information in their report or require the relevant information to be disclosed in a note[3] to the company's accounts and require the auditors to supply the directors of the company with such information as is necessary to enable that disclosure to be made[4].

The regulations may make different provision for different cases[5].

Regulations under the above provisions must be made by statutory instrument which is subject to annulment in pursuance of a resolution of either House of Parliament[6].

1 Companies Act 1985 s 390B(1) (substituted by the Companies Act 1989 s 121). In exercise of the power so conferred the Secretary of State made the Companies Act 1985 (Disclosure of Remuneration for Non-Audit Work) Regulations 1991, SI 1991/2128 (amended by SI 1995/1520) (see paras 1044-1046 post) which came into force on 14 October 1991: reg 1.
2 Companies Act 1985 s 390B(2) (substituted by the Companies Act 1989 s 121).
3 As to notes to the accounts see paras 838 et seq, 887 et seq ante.
4 Companies Act 1985 s 390B(3) (substituted by the Companies Act 1989 s 121).
5 Companies Act 1985 s 390B(4) (substituted by the Companies Act 1989 s 121).
6 Companies Act 1985 s 390B(5) (substituted by the Companies Act 1989 s 121).

1044. Persons who are to be regarded as associates of a company's auditors. The following provisions apply in order to determine whether a person is to be regarded as an associate of a company's auditors in any financial year of a company in relation to which disclosure must be made in the annual accounts[1] of that company relating to that year[2].

Where a company's auditors are a body corporate, each of the following is to be regarded as an associate of theirs in a relevant financial year:

(1) any partnership in which the auditors were, at any time in the financial year, a partner;

(2) any partnership in which a director[3] of the auditors was, at any time in the financial year, a partner;

(3) any body corporate which was, at any time in the financial year, in the same group[4] as the auditors;

(4) any body corporate which was an associated undertaking[5] of the auditors or of a body corporate in the same group as the auditors at any time in the financial year;

(5) any body corporate in which any director of the auditor either alone or with any associate of the auditors was, at any time in the financial year, entitled to exercise, or control the exercise of, 20% or more of the voting rights at any general meeting and any body corporate which was, at any time in the financial year, in the same group as any such body corporate; and

(6) any director of the auditors[6].

Where a company's auditors are a partnership, each of the following is to be regarded as an associate of theirs in a relevant financial year:

(a) any other partnership which had, at any time in the financial year, a partner in common with the auditors;

(b) any body corporate which was, at any time in the financial year, a partner in the auditors;

(c) any body corporate in which, whether alone or with any associate of the auditors, the auditors or any partner in the auditors was, at any time in the financial year, entitled to exercise, or control the exercise of, 20% or more of the voting rights at any general meeting;

(d) any body corporate which was, at any time in the financial year, in the same group as any such body corporate as is mentioned in heads (b) or (c) above; and

(e) any partner in the auditors[7].

Where a company's auditor is an individual, each of the following is to be regarded as an associate of his in a relevant financial year:

(i) any partnership in which the auditor was, at any time in the financial year, a partner; and

(ii) any body corporate in which the auditor or any associate of his was, at any time in the financial year, entitled to exercise, or control the exercise of, 20% or more of the voting rights at any general meeting and any body corporate which was, at any time in that year, in the same group as any such body corporate[8].

Each of the following is to be regarded as an associate of a company's auditors in a relevant financial year whether the auditors are a body corporate, a partnership or an individual, that is to say, any person who was, at any time in that financial year, entitled to receive 20% or more of the auditors' profits and any person of whose profits the auditors were, in that financial year, entitled to receive 20% or more[9].

1 Ie by virtue of the Companies Act 1985 (Disclosure of Remuneration for Non-Audit Work) Regulations 1991, SI 1991/2128, reg 5: see para 1046 post.

2 Ibid regs 2, 3(1). Regulation 3 is subject to reg 7 (as added) (see para 1045 post): reg 3(1) (amended by SI 1995/1520).

3 For these purposes, 'director' has the same meaning as in the Companies Act 1989 s 53(1) (see para 959 note 3 ante): Companies Act 1985 (Disclosure of Remuneration for Non-Audit Work) Regulations 1991 reg 2.

4 For these purposes, 'group' has the same meaning as in the Companies Act 1989 s 53(1) (see para 959 note 5 ante): Companies Act 1985 (Disclosure of Remuneration for Non-Audit Work) Regulations 1991 reg 2.

5 For these purposes, 'associated undertaking', in relation to a company, means any undertaking which, in accordance with the Companies Act 1985 s 258 (as substituted) (see para 828 ante), is a subsidiary undertaking of the company other than a subsidiary undertaking formed under the law of a country or territory outside the United Kingdom: Companies Act 1985 (Disclosure of Remuneration for Non-Audit Work) Regulations 1991 reg 2.

6 Ibid regs 2, 3(2).

7 Ibid regs 2, 3(3).

8 Ibid regs 2, 3(4).

9 Ibid regs 2, 3(5).

1045. Persons who are not to be regarded as associates of a company's auditors. A body corporate is not to be regarded as an associate of a company's auditors in a relevant financial year:

(1) if[1] the relevant director[2] of the auditors was entitled to exercise, or control the exercise of, 20% or more of the voting rights at any general meeting of such body corporate solely by virtue of acting as an insolvency practitioner[3] in relation to any person, or in his capacity as a receiver, or a receiver and manager, of the property of a company[4], or a judicial factor on the estate of any person;

(2) if[5] the auditors or the relevant partner in the auditors were or was entitled to exercise, or control the exercise of, 20% or more of the voting rights at any general meeting of such body corporate solely by virtue of acting as an insolvency practitioner in relation to any person, or in his capacity as a receiver, or a receiver and manager, of the property of a company, or a judicial factor on the estate of any person;

(3) if[6] neither the auditor nor any associate of his was entitled to exercise, or control the exercise of, 20% or more of the voting rights at any general meeting of such body corporate otherwise than by virtue of acting as an insolvency practitioner in relation to any person, or in his capacity as a receiver, or a receiver and manager, of the property of a company, or a judicial factor on the estate of any person[7].

1 Ie by virtue of the Companies Act 1985 (Disclosure of Remuneration for Non-Audit Work) Regulations 1991, SI 1991/2128, reg 3(2)(e): see para 1044 head (5) ante.

2 For the meaning of 'director' see para 1044 note 3 ante.

3 For these purposes, 'act as an insolvency practitioner' is to be construed in accordance with the Insolvency Act 1986 s 388 (see para 2007 post): Companies Act 1985 (Disclosure of Remuneration for Non-Audit Work) (Amendment) Regulations 1995, SI 1995/1520, reg 2.

4 For these purposes, any reference to 'a receiver, or a receiver or manager, of the property of a company' includes a receiver, or, as the case may be, a receiver or manager, of part only of that property: ibid reg 2.

5 Ie by virtue of the Companies Act 1985 (Disclosure of Remuneration for Non-Audit Work) Regulations 1991 reg 3(3)(c): see para 1044 head (c) ante.

6 Ie by virtue of ibid reg 3(4)(b): see para 1044 head (ii) ante.

7 Ibid reg 7 (added by SI 1995/1520).

1046. Disclosure of remuneration for non-audit work. There must be disclosed in notes[1] to the annual accounts[2] of a company relating to each financial year beginning on or after 1 October 1991[3]:

(1) the aggregate of the remuneration[4], if any, in respect of work carried out in that year of the company's auditors during that year and of any person who is treated[5] as having been an associate of the company's auditors in that year; and

(2) the aggregate of the remuneration, if any, in respect of work carried out during the previous financial year of the company's auditors and of any person who is treated[5] as having been an associate of the company's auditors in that previous financial year,

for services other than those of the auditors in their capacity as such supplied to the company and to an associated undertaking[6] of the company in any case in which the company's auditors or any associates of the company's auditors are auditor of the relevant associated undertaking[7].

The above provisions apply to benefits in kind as to payments in cash and, in relation to any such benefit, its nature and its estimated value must also be disclosed in the note[8].

The auditors of a company must supply the directors of the company with such information as is necessary to enable the relevant associates to be identified for the above purposes[9].

In relation to a company which qualifies as small or medium-sized[10], the information specified above is not required to be disclosed in notes to the annual accounts of the company relating to the financial year in respect of which the company is entitled[11] to the statutory exemptions[12].

1 As to notes to the accounts see paras 838 et seq, 887 et seq ante.
2 For the meaning of 'annual accounts' see para 817 note 2 ante.
3 Disclosure of remuneration is not, however, required for a financial year beginning before 1 October 1991: Companies Act 1985 (Disclosure of Remuneration for Non-Audit Work) Regulations 1991, SI 1991/2128, reg 5(3). For the meaning of 'remuneration' see note 4 infra.
4 For these purposes, 'remuneration' includes sums paid in respect of expenses: ibid reg 2.
5 Ie by virtue of ibid reg 3: see para 1044 ante.
6 For the meaning of 'associated undertaking' see para 1044 note 5 ante.
7 Companies Act 1985 (Disclosure of Remuneration for Non-Audit Work) Regulations 1991 reg 5(1). Where more than one person has been appointed as a company's auditor in a single financial year, reg 5(1) has effect to require separate disclosure in respect of remuneration of each such person and their associates: reg 5(4).
8 Ibid reg 5(2).
9 Ibid reg 6.
10 Ie by virtue of the Companies Act 1985 s 247 (as substituted and amended): see para 901 ante.
11 Ie entitled to the exemptions mentioned in ibid s 246 (as substituted and amended): see para 900 ante.
12 Companies Act 1985 (Disclosure of Remuneration for Non-Audit Work) Regulations 1991 reg 4.

E. REMOVAL, RESIGNATION ETC

1047. Removal of auditors. A company may by ordinary resolution[1] at any time remove an auditor from office, notwithstanding anything in any agreement between it and him[2].

Where a resolution removing an auditor is passed at a general meeting of a company, the company must within 14 days give notice of that fact in the prescribed form[3] to the registrar of companies[4]. If, however, a company fails to give the notice so required, the company, and every officer of it who is in default, is guilty of an offence and liable on summary conviction to a fine not exceeding one-fifth of the statutory maximum and, on conviction after continued contravention, to a daily default fine not exceeding one-fiftieth of the statutory maximum[5].

Nothing in these provisions is to be taken as depriving a person removed thereunder of compensation or damages payable to him in respect of the termination of his appointment as auditor or of any appointment terminating with that as auditor[6].

An auditor of a company who has been removed has, notwithstanding his removal, the statutory rights[7] in relation to any general meeting of the company at which his term of office would otherwise have expired or at which it is proposed to fill the vacancy caused by his removal[8]. In such a case the references to matters concerning the auditors as auditors are to be construed as references to matters concerning him as a former auditor[8].

1 As to ordinary resolutions see para 681 ante.
2 Companies Act 1985 s 391(1) (substituted by the Companies Act 1989 s 122(1)). The Companies Act 1985 s 381A (as added) (written resolutions of private companies: see para 697 post) does not apply to a resolution under s 391 (as substituted) removing an auditor before the expiration of his term of office: s 381A(7), Sch 15A para 1(b) (added by the Companies Act 1989 s 114(1)).
3 For the prescribed form of notice see the Companies (Forms) (Amendment) Regulations 1995, SI 1995/736, reg 3, Sch 2, Form 391.
4 Companies Act 1985 s 391(2) (substituted by the Companies Act 1989 s 122(1)).
5 Companies Act 1985 s 391(2) (as substituted: see note 4 supra), s 730, Sch 24 (amended by the Companies Act 1989 s 122(2)). For the meaning of 'the statutory maximum', 'officer who is in default' and 'daily default fine' see para 1161 post.
6 Companies Act 1985 s 391(3) (substituted by the Companies Act 1989 s 122(1)).
7 Ie the rights conferred by the Companies Act 1985 s 390 (as substituted): see para 1035 ante.
8 Ibid s 391(4) (substituted by the Companies Act 1989 s 122(1)).

1048. Rights of auditors who are removed or not reappointed. Special notice[1] is required for a resolution at a general meeting of a company removing an auditor before the expiration of his term of office or appointing as auditor a person other than a retiring auditor[2].

On receipt of notice of such an intended resolution the company must forthwith send a copy of it to the person proposed to be removed or, as the case may be, to the person proposed to be appointed and to the retiring auditor[3].

The auditor proposed to be removed or, as the case may be, the retiring auditor may make with respect to the intended resolution representations in writing to the company, not exceeding a reasonable length, and request their notification to members of the company[4].

The company must, unless the representations are received by it too late for it to do so:

(1) in any notice of the resolution given to members of the company, state the fact of the representations having been made; and

(2) send a copy of the representations to every member of the company to whom notice of the meeting is or has been sent[5].

If a copy of any such representations is not sent out as required because received too late or because of the company's default, the auditor may, without prejudice to his right to be heard orally, require that the representations be read out at the meeting[6].

Copies of the representations need not be sent out and the representations need not be read at the meeting if, on the application either of the company or of any other person claiming to be aggrieved, the court is satisfied that the rights conferred by the above provisions are being abused to secure needless publicity for defamatory matter; and the court may order the company's costs on the application to be paid in whole or in part by the auditor, notwithstanding that he is not a party to the application[7].

1 As to special notice see para 687 ante.
2 Companies Act 1985 s 391A(1) (substituted by the Companies Act 1989 s 122(1)).
3 Companies Act 1985 s 391A(2) (substituted by the Companies Act 1989 s 122(1)).
4 Companies Act 1985 s 391A(3) (substituted by the Companies Act 1989 s 122(1)).

5 Companies Act 1985 s 391A(4) (substituted by the Companies Act 1989 s 122(1)).
6 Companies Act 1985 s 391A(5) (substituted by the Companies Act 1989 s 122(1)).
7 Companies Act 1985 s 391A(6) (substituted by the Companies Act 1989 s 122(1)). The application is by originating summons: RSC Ord 102 r 2.

1049. Resignation of auditors. An auditor of a company may resign his office by depositing a notice in writing to that effect at the company's registered office[1]. The notice is not, however, effective unless it is accompanied by the requisite statement[2] by him[3].

An effective notice of resignation operates to bring the auditor's term of office to an end as of the date on which the notice is deposited or on such later date as may be specified in it[4].

The company must within 14 days of the deposit of a notice of resignation send a copy of the notice to the registrar of companies[5]. If default is made in complying with that requirement, the company, and every officer of it who is in default, is guilty of an offence and liable on indictment to a fine or on summary conviction to a fine not exceeding the statutory maximum and, on conviction after continued contravention, to a daily default fine not exceeding one-tenth of the statutory maximum[6].

1 Companies Act 1985 s 392(1) (substituted by the Companies Act 1989 s 122(1)). As to the company's registered office see para 150 ante.
2 Ie the statement required by the Companies Act 1985 s 394 (as substituted): see para 1052 post.
3 Ibid s 392(1) (as substituted: see note 1 supra).
4 Ibid s 392(2) (substituted by the Companies Act 1989 s 122(1)).
5 Companies Act 1985 s 392(3) (substituted by the Companies Act 1989 s 122(1)).
6 Companies Act 1985 s 392(3) (as substituted: see note 5 supra), s 730, Sch 24 (amended by the Companies Act 1989 s 122(2)). For the meaning of 'the statutory maximum', 'officer who is in default' and 'daily default fine' see para 1161 post.

1050. Rights of resigning auditors. The following provisions apply where an auditor's notice of resignation is accompanied by a statement of circumstances which he considers should be brought to the attention of members or creditors of the company[1].

He may deposit with the notice a signed requisition calling on the directors of the company forthwith duly to convene an extraordinary general meeting of the company for the purpose of receiving and considering such explanation of the circumstances connected with his resignation as he may wish to place before the meeting[2].

He may request the company to circulate to its members:

(1) before the meeting convened on his requisition; or

(2) before any general meeting at which his term of office would otherwise have expired or at which it is proposed to fill the vacancy caused by his resignation,

a statement in writing, not exceeding a reasonable length, of the circumstances connected with his resignation[3].

The company must, unless the statement is received too late for it to comply:

(a) in any notice of the meeting given to members of the company, state the fact of the statement having been made; and

(b) send a copy of the statement to every member of the company to whom notice of the meeting is or has been sent[4].

If the directors do not within 21 days from the date of the deposit of a requisition proceed duly to convene a meeting for a day not more than 28 days after the date on which the notice convening the meeting is given, every director who failed to take all reasonable steps to secure that a meeting was convened as mentioned above is guilty of an offence and liable on indictment to a fine or on summary conviction to a fine not exceeding the statutory maximum[5].

If a copy of the statement mentioned above is not sent out as required because received too late or because of the company's default, the auditor may, without prejudice to his right to be heard orally, require that the statement be read out at the meeting[6].

Copies of a statement need not be sent out and the statement need not be read out at the meeting if, on the application either of the company or of any other person who claims to be aggrieved, the court is satisfied that the rights conferred by the above provisions are being abused to secure needless publicity for defamatory matter; and the court may order the company's costs on such an application to be paid in whole or in part by the auditor, notwithstanding that he is not a party to the application[7].

An auditor who has resigned has, notwithstanding his resignation, the statutory rights[8] in relation to any such general meeting of the company as is mentioned in heads (1) or (2) above[9].

1 Companies Act 1985 s 392A(1) (substituted by the Companies Act 1989 s 122(1)).
2 Companies Act 1985 s 392A(2) (substituted by the Companies Act 1989 s 122(1)).
3 Companies Act 1985 s 392A(3) (substituted by the Companies Act 1989 s 122(1)).
4 Companies Act 1985 s 392A(4) (substituted by the Companies Act 1989 s 122(1)).
5 Companies Act 1985 s 392A(5) (substituted by the Companies Act 1989 s 122(1)); Companies Act 1985 s 730, Sch 24 (amended by the Companies Act 1989 s 122(2)). For the meaning of 'the statutory maximum' see para 1161 post.
6 Companies Act 1985 s 392A(6) (substituted by the Companies Act 1989 s 122(1)).
7 Companies Act 1985 s 392A(7) (substituted by the Companies Act 1989 s 122(1)). The application is by originating summons: RSC Ord 102 r 2.
8 Ie the rights conferred by the Companies Act 1985 s 390 (as substituted): see para 1035 ante.
9 Ibid s 392A(8) (substituted by the Companies Act 1989 s 122(1)). In such a case the references in the Companies Act 1985 s 390 (as substituted) to matters concerning the auditors as auditors are to be construed as references to matters concerning him as a former auditor: s 392A(8) (as so substituted).

1051. Termination of appointment of auditors not appointed annually. When an election by a private company to dispense with an annual appointment of auditors is in force[1], any member of the company may deposit notice in writing at the company's registered office[2] proposing that the appointment be brought to an end[3]. No member may, however, deposit more than one such notice in any financial year[4] of the company[5].

If such a notice is deposited, it is the duty of the directors:

(1) to convene a general meeting of the company for a date not more than 28 days after the date on which the notice was given; and

(2) to propose at the meeting a resolution in a form enabling the company to decide whether the appointment of the company's auditors should be brought to an end[6].

If the decision of the company at the meeting is that the appointment of the auditors should be brought to an end, the auditors are not deemed to be reappointed when next they would be and, if the notice was deposited within the period immediately following the distribution of accounts[7], any deemed reappointment for the financial year following that to which those accounts relate which has already occurred ceases to have effect[8].

If the directors do not within 14 days from the date of the deposit of the notice proceed duly to convene a meeting, the member who deposited the notice (or, if there was more than one, any of them) may himself convene the meeting, but any meeting so convened must not be held after the expiration of three months from that date[9].

A meeting convened under these provisions by a member must be convened in the same manner, as nearly as possible, as that in which meetings are to be convened by directors[10].

Any reasonable expenses incurred by a member by reason of the failure of the directors duly to convene a meeting must be made good to him by the company; and any such sums must be recouped by the company from such of the directors as were in default out of any sums payable, or to become payable, by the company by way of fees or other remuneration in respect of their services[11].

The above provisions have effect notwithstanding anything in any agreement between the company and its auditors; and no compensation or damages are payable by reason of the auditors' appointment being terminated under the above provisions[12].

1 Ie an election under the Companies Act 1985 s 386 (as substituted): see para 1030 ante.
2 As to the company's registered office see para 150 ante.
3 Companies Act 1985 s 393(1) (substituted by the Companies Act 1989 s 122(1)).
4 For the meaning of 'financial year' see para 806 ante.
5 Companies Act 1985 s 393(1) (as substituted: see note 3 supra).
6 Ibid s 393(2) (substituted by the Companies Act 1989 s 122(1)).
7 For these purposes, the period immediately following the distribution of accounts means the period beginning with the day on which copies of the company's annual accounts are sent to members of the company under the Companies Act 1985 s 238 (as substituted) (see para 823 ante) and ending 14 days after that day: s 393(3) (substituted by the Companies Act 1989 s 122(1)). For the meaning of 'annual accounts' see para 817 note 2 ante.
8 Companies Act 1985 s 393(3) (as substituted: see note 7 supra).
9 Ibid s 393(4) (substituted by the Companies Act 1989 s 122(1)).
10 Companies Act 1985 s 393(5) (substituted by the Companies Act 1989 s 122(1)).
11 Companies Act 1985 s 393(6) (substituted by the Companies Act 1989 s 122(1)).
12 Companies Act 1985 s 393(7) (substituted by the Companies Act 1989 s 122(1)).

1052. Statement by person ceasing to hold office as auditor. Where an auditor ceases for any reason to hold office, he must deposit at the company's registered office[1] a statement of any circumstances connected with his ceasing to hold office which he considers should be brought to the attention of the members or creditors of the company or, if he considers that there are no such circumstances, a statement that there are none[2].

In the case of resignation, the statement must be deposited along with the notice of resignation; in the case of failure to seek reappointment, the statement must be deposited not less than 14 days before the end of the time allowed for next appointing auditors[3]; in any other case, the statement must be deposited not later than the end of the period of 14 days beginning with the date on which he ceases to hold office[4].

If the statement is of circumstances which the auditor considers should be brought to the attention of the members or creditors of the company, the company must within 14 days of the deposit of the statement either:

(1) send a copy of it to every person who is entitled[5] to be sent copies of the accounts; or
(2) apply to the court[6].

The company must, if it applies to the court, notify the auditor of the application[7].

Unless the auditor receives notice of such an application before the end of the period of 21 days beginning with the day on which he deposited the statement, he must within a further seven days send a copy of the statement to the registrar of companies[8].

If the court is satisfied that the auditor is using the statement to secure needless publicity for defamatory matter:

(a) it must direct that copies of the statement need not be sent out; and

(b) it may further order the company's costs on the application to be paid in whole or in part by the auditor, notwithstanding that he is not a party to the application;

and the company must within 14 days of the court's decision send to the persons mentioned in head (1) above a statement setting out the effect of the order[9].

If the court is not so satisfied, the company must within 14 days of the court's decision send copies of the statement to the persons mentioned in head (1) above and notify the auditor of the court's decision; and the auditor must within seven days of receiving such notice send a copy of the statement to the registrar[10].

1 As to the company's registered office see para 150 ante.
2 Companies Act 1985 s 394(1) (substituted by the Companies Act 1989 s 123(1)). As to offences see para 1053 post.
3 For the meaning of references to the end of the time for appointing auditors see para 1027 note 3 ante.
4 Companies Act 1985 s 394(2) (substituted by the Companies Act 1989 s 123(1)).
5 Ie under the Companies Act 1985 s 238 (as substituted): see para 823 ante.
6 Ibid s 394(3) (substituted by the Companies Act 1989 s 123(1)). The application is by originating summons: RSC Ord 102 r 2.
7 Companies Act 1985 s 394(4) (substituted by the Companies Act 1989 s 123(1)).
8 Companies Act 1985 s 394(5) (substituted by the Companies Act 1989 s 123(1)).
9 Companies Act 1985 s 394(6) (substituted by the Companies Act 1989 s 123(1)).
10 Companies Act 1985 s 394(7) (substituted by the Companies Act 1989 s 123(1)).

1053. Offences. If a person ceasing to hold office as auditor fails to comply with his duty to deposit the required statement as to the circumstances of his ceasing to hold office[1], he is guilty of an offence and liable on indictment to a fine or on summary conviction to a fine not exceeding the statutory maximum[2]. In proceedings for such an offence it is a defence for the person charged to show that he took all reasonable steps and exercised all due diligence to avoid the commission of the offence[3].

If a company makes default in complying with the requirements as to the statement of a person ceasing to hold office as auditor[4], the company, and every officer of it who is in default, is guilty of an offence and liable on conviction on indictment to a fine or on summary conviction to a fine not exceeding the statutory maximum and, on conviction after continued contravention, to a daily default fine not exceeding one-tenth of the statutory maximum[5].

1 Ie fails to comply with the Companies Act 1985 s 394 (as substituted): see para 1052 ante.
2 Ibid s 394A(1) (substituted by the Companies Act 1989 s 123(1)); Companies Act 1985 s 730, Sch 24 (amended by the Companies Act 1989 s 123(2)). For the meaning of 'the statutory maximum' see para 1161 post. The Companies Act 1985 s 733 (as amended) (liability of individuals for corporate default: see para 1162 post) and s 734 (as amended) (criminal proceedings against unincorporated bodies: see para 1163 post) apply to an offence under s 394A(1) (as so substituted): s 394A(3) (substituted by the Companies Act 1989 s 123(1)).
3 Companies Act 1985 s 394A(2) (substituted by the Companies Act 1989 s 123(1)).
4 Ie makes default in complying with the Companies Act 1985 s 394 (as substituted).
5 Ibid s 394A(4) (substituted by the Companies Act 1989 s 123(1)); Companies Act 1985 s 730, Sch 24 (amended by the Companies Act 1989 s 123(2)). For the meaning of 'officer who is in default' and 'daily default fine' see para 1161 post.

(ii) Exemptions from Audit

A. CERTAIN CATEGORIES OF SMALL COMPANY

1054. In general. A company which meets the total exemption conditions in respect of a financial year[1] is exempt[2] from the statutory provisions relating to the audit of accounts[3] in respect of that year[4].

A company which meets the report conditions in respect of a financial year is exempt[5] from the statutory provisions relating to the audit of accounts in respect of that year if the directors cause a report in respect of the company's individual accounts[6] for that year to be duly prepared[7] and made to the company's members[8].

The total exemption conditions are met by a company in respect of a financial year if:

(1) it qualifies as a small company in relation to that year[9];
(2) its turnover in that year is not more than £90,000; and
(3) its balance sheet total[10] for that year is not more than £1.4 million[11].

The report conditions are met by a company in respect of a financial year if:

(a) it qualifies as a small company in relation to that year[12];
(b) its turnover in that year is more than £90,000 but not more than £350,000; and
(c) its balance sheet total for that year is not more than £1.4 million[13].

For a period which is a company's financial year but not in fact a year the maximum figures for turnover or gross income must be proportionately adjusted[14].

1 For the meaning of 'financial year' see para 806 ante.
2 Ie subject to the Companies Act 1985 s 249B (as added): see para 1055 post.
3 Ie the provisions of ibid Pt VII (ss 221–262A) (as amended): see para 1059–1061 post.
4 Ibid s 249A(1) (added by the Companies Act 1985 (Audit Exemption) Regulations 1994, SI 1994/1935, reg 2). Where the directors of a company have taken advantage of the exemption so conferred (1) the Companies Act 1985 s 238 (as substituted) (see para 823 ante) and s 239 (as substituted) (see para 824 ante) have effect with the omission of references to the auditors' report; (2) no copy of an auditors' report need be delivered to the registrar of companies or laid before the company in general meeting; (3) s 271(3)-(5) (as substituted) (see para 708 ante) does not apply: s 249E(1) (added by the Companies Act 1985 (Audit Exemption) Regulations 1994 reg 2).
5 See note 2 supra.
6 For the meaning of 'individual accounts' see para 816 ante.
7 Ie in accordance with the Companies Act 1985 s 249C (as added): see para 1056 post.
8 Ibid s 249A(2) (added by the Companies Act 1985 (Audit Exemption) Regulations 1994 reg 2). Where the directors of a company have taken advantage of the exemption so conferred (1) the Companies Act 1985 s 236(2)-(4) (as substituted) (see para 1060 post) has effect with the substitution for references to the auditors and the auditors' report of references to the reporting accountant and the report made for the purposes of s 249A(2) (as so added) respectively; (2) s 238 (as substituted) and s 239 (as substituted), s 241 (as substituted) (see para 817 ante) and s 242 (as substituted and amended) (see para 818 ante) have effect with the substitution for references to the auditors' report of references to the report made for the purposes of s 249A(2) (as so added); (3) s 271(3)-(5) (as substituted) does not apply; (4) s 389A(1),(2) (as added) (see para 1034 ante) has effect with the substitution for references to the auditors of references to the reporting accountant: s 249E(2) (added by the Companies Act 1985 (Audit Exemption) Regulations 1994 reg 2).
9 Ie for the purposes of the Companies Act 1985 s 246 (as substituted and amended): see para 900 ante.
10 For these purposes, 'balance sheet total' has the meaning given by ibid s 247(5) (as substituted) (see para 901 note 7 ante): s 249A(7) (added by the Companies Act 1985 (Audit Exemption) Regulations 1994 reg 2).
11 Companies Act 1985 s 249A(3) (added by the Companies Act 1985 (Audit Exemption) Regulations 1994 reg 2). In relation to any company which is a charity, the Companies Act 1985 s 249A(3)(b) (see text head (2) supra) has effect with the substitution for the reference to turnover of a reference to gross income: s 249A(5)(a) (added by the Companies Act 1985 (Audit Exemption) Regulations 1994 reg 2). For these purposes, 'gross income' means the company's income from all sources, as shown in the

company's income and expenditure account: Companies Act 1985 s 249A(7) (as added: see note 10 supra).

12 See note 9 supra.

13 Companies Act 1985 s 249A(4) (added by the Companies Act 1985 (Audit Exemption) Regulations 1994 reg 2). In relation to any company which is a charity, the Companies Act 1985 s 249A(4)(b) (see text head (b) supra) has effect with the substitution for the reference to turnover of a reference to gross income and for the reference to £350,000 of a reference to £250,000: s 249A(5)(b) (added by the Companies Act 1985 (Audit Exemption) Regulations 1994 reg 2).

14 Companies Act 1985 s 249A(6) (added by the Companies Act 1985 (Audit Exemption) Regulations 1994 reg 2).

1055. Cases where exemptions are not available. A company is not entitled to the statutory exemption from audit[1] in respect of a financial year[2] if at any time within that year:

(1) it was a public company[3];
(2) it was a banking[4] or insurance[5] company;
(3) it was enrolled in the list maintained by the Insurance Brokers Registration Council[6];
(4) it was an authorised person or an appointed representative[7];
(5) it was a special register body[8] or an employers' association[9];
(6) it was a parent company[10] or a subsidiary undertaking[11].

A company which would otherwise fall within head (6) above by virtue of its being a subsidiary undertaking for any period within a financial year is not to be treated as so falling if it is dormant[12] throughout that period[13].

Any member or members holding not less in the aggregate than 10% in nominal value of the company's issued share capital or any class of it or, if the company does not have a share capital, not less than 10% in number of the members of the company, may, by notice in writing deposited at the registered office[14] of the company during a financial year, but not later than one month before the end of that year, require the company to obtain an audit of its accounts for that year[15]. Where a notice has been so deposited, the company is not entitled to the statutory exemption from audit[16] in respect of the financial year to which the notice relates[17].

A company is not entitled to the statutory exemption from audit[18] unless its balance sheet[19] contains a statement[20] by the directors to the effect:

(a) that for the year in question the company was entitled to the statutory exemption from audit[21];
(b) that no notice has been deposited[22] in relation to its accounts for the financial year; and
(c) that the directors acknowledge their responsibilities for ensuring that the company keeps accounting records which comply with the statutory requirements[23] and preparing accounts which give a true and fair view[24] of the state of affairs of the company as at the end of the financial year and of its profit[25] or loss[25] for the financial year[26] and which otherwise comply with the provisions of the Companies Act 1985 relating to accounts, so far as applicable to the company[27].

1 Ie the exemption conferred by the Companies Act 1985 s 249A(1) or (2) (as added): see para 1054 ante.
2 For the meaning of 'financial year' see para 806 ante.
3 For the meaning of 'public company' see para 82 ante.
4 For the meaning of 'banking company' see para 117 note 8 ante.
5 For the meaning of 'insurance company' see para 117 note 9 ante.
6 Ie the list maintained under the Insurance Brokers (Registration) Act 1977 s 4: see INSURANCE vol 25 (Reissue) para 876.
7 Ie under the Financial Services Act 1986: see MONEY.

8 Ie as defined in the Trade Union and Labour Relations (Consolidation) Act 1992 s 117(1): see TRADE AND INDUSTRY vol 47 (Reissue) para 1007.

9 Ie as defined in ibid s 122: see TRADE AND INDUSTRY vol 47 (Reissue) para 1201.

10 For the meaning of 'parent company' see para 828 ante.

11 Companies Act 1985 s 249B(1) (added by the Companies Act 1985 (Audit Exemption) Regulations 1994, SI 1994/1935, reg 2; amended by the Companies Act 1985 (Miscellaneous Accounting Amendments) Regulations 1996, SI 1996/189, reg 10(1),(2)). For the meaning of 'subsidiary undertaking' see para 828 ante.

12 Ie within the meaning of the Companies Act 1985 s 250 (as added and amended): see para 1058 post.

13 Ibid s 249B(1A) (added by the Companies Act 1985 (Miscellaneous Accounting Amendments) Regulations 1996 reg 10(1),(3)).

14 As to the company's registered office see para 150 ante.

15 Companies Act 1985 s 249B(2) (added by the Companies Act 1985 (Audit Exemption) Regulations 1994 reg 2).

16 See note 1 supra.

17 Companies Act 1985 s 249B(3) (added by the Companies Act 1985 (Audit Exemption) Regulations 1994 reg 2).

18 See note 1 supra.

19 For the meaning of 'balance sheet' see para 826 ante.

20 The statement so required must appear in the balance sheet above the signature required by the Companies Act 1985 s 233 (as substituted) (see para 937 ante): s 249B(5) (added by the Companies Act 1985 (Audit Exemption) Regulations 1994 reg 2; amended by the Companies Act 1985 (Miscellaneous Accounting Amendments) Regulations 1996 reg 10(1),(5)).

21 Ie exemption under the Companies Act 1985 s 249A(1) or (2) (as added), as the case may be.

22 Ie under ibid s 249B(2) (as added): see supra.

23 Ie ibid s 221 (as substituted): see para 801 ante.

24 For the meaning of 'true and fair view' see para 816 note 5 ante.

25 For the meaning of references to profit or loss see para 809 note 6 ante.

26 Ie in accordance with the Companies Act 1985 s 226 (as substituted): see para 816 ante.

27 Ibid s 249B(4) (added by the Companies Act 1985 (Audit Exemption) Regulations 1994 reg 2; amended by the Companies Act 1985 (Miscellaneous Accounting Amendments) Regulations 1996 reg 10(1),(4)).

1056. The required report. The required report[1] must be prepared by a person ('the reporting accountant') who is eligible[2] for appointment[3]. It must state whether in the opinion of the reporting accountant making it:

(1) the accounts of the company for the financial year[4] in question are in agreement with the accounting records kept by the company[5];

(2) having regard only to, and on the basis of, the information contained in those accounting records, those accounts have been drawn up in a manner consistent with specified statutory provisions[6], so far as applicable to the company[7].

The report must also state that in the opinion of the reporting accountant, having regard only to, and on the basis of, the information contained in the accounting records kept by the company[8], the company satisfied the report conditions[9] for the financial year in question and did not fall within any of the cases where that exemption is not available[10] at any time within that financial year[11].

The report must state the name of the reporting accountant and be signed by him[12].

Where the reporting accountant is a body corporate or partnership, any reference to the signing of the report, or any copy of the report, by the reporting accountant is a reference to signature in the name of the body corporate or partnership by a person authorised to sign on its behalf[13].

1 Ie the report required for the purposes of the Companies Act 1985 s 249A(2) (as added): see para 1054 ante.

2 Ie eligible under ibid s 249D (as added): see para 1057 post.

3 Companies Act 1985 s 249C(1) (added by the Companies Act 1985 (Audit Exemption) Regulations 1994, SI 1994/1935, reg 2).

4 For the meaning of 'financial year' see para 806 ante.
5 Ie under the Companies Act 1985 s 221 (as substituted): see para 801 ante.
6 The statutory provisions so specified are (1) ibid s 226(3) (as substituted) (see para 816 ante) and Sch 4 (as amended) (see para 816 et seq ante); (2) s 231 (as substituted and amended) (see paras 853, 888 ante) and Sch 5 paras 7-9A, 13(1),(3),(4) (as substituted) (see paras 860, 861, 864 ante); and (3) s 232 (as substituted) (see para 865 ante) and Sch 6 (as amended) (see para 866 et seq ante), where appropriate as modified by s 246(1)(a),(1A) (as substituted and amended) (see para 900 ante) and Sch 8 Pt I Section A (as substituted) (see paras 904-908 ante): s 249C(6) (added by the Companies Act 1985 (Audit Exemption) Regulations 1994 reg 2).
7 Companies Act 1985 s 249C(2) (added by the Companies Act 1985 (Audit Exemption) Regulations 1994 reg 2).
8 See note 5 supra.
9 Ie the requirements of the Companies Act 1985 s 249A(4) (as added) (see para 1054 ante) or, where the company is a charity, the requirements of s 249A(4) (as added) as modified by s 294A(5) (as added) (see para 1054 notes 11, 13 ante).
10 Ie did not fall within ibid s 249B(1)(a)-(f) (as added): see para 1055 heads (1)-(6) ante.
11 Ibid s 249C(3) (added by the Companies Act 1985 (Audit Exemption) Regulations 1994 reg 2).
12 Companies Act 1985 s 249C(4) (added by the Companies Act 1985 (Audit Exemption) Regulations 1994 reg 2).
13 Companies Act 1985 s 249C(5) (added by the Companies Act 1985 (Audit Exemption) Regulations 1994 reg 2).

1057. The reporting accountant. The reporting accountant[1] must be either:

(1) any member of a specified body[2] who, under the rules of the body[3], is entitled to engage in public practice and is not ineligible for appointment[4] as a reporting accountant; or

(2) any person, whether or not a member of any such body, who is subject to the rules of any such body in seeking appointment or acting as auditor[5] and, under those rules, is eligible for appointment[5] as auditor[6].

An individual, a body corporate or a partnership may be appointed as a reporting accountant[7].

1 For the meaning of 'the reporting accountant' see para 1056 ante.
2 The bodies so specified are: the Institute of Chartered Accountants in England and Wales; the Institute of Chartered Accountants of Scotland; the Institute of Chartered Accountants in Ireland; the Chartered Association of Certified Accountants; and the Association of Authorised Public Accountants: Companies Act 1985 s 249D(3) (added by the Companies Act 1985 (Audit Exemption) Regulations 1994, SI 1994/1935, reg 2; amended by the Companies Act 1985 (Audit Exemption) (Amendment) Regulations 1995, SI 1995/589, reg 2(1),(3)).
3 For these purposes, references to the rules of a specified body are to the rules, whether or not laid down by the body itself, which the body has power to enforce and which are relevant for the purposes of the Companies Act 1989 Pt II (ss 24-54) (see para 955 et seq ante) or the Companies Act 1985 s 249D (as added); and this includes rules relating to the admission and expulsion of members of the body, so far as relevant for the purposes of the Companies Act 1989 Pt II (ss 24-54) or the Companies Act 1985 s 249D (as added): s 249D(1A) (added by the Companies Act 1985 (Audit Exemption) (Amendment) Regulations 1995 reg 2(1),(2)).
4 For these purposes, a person is ineligible for appointment by a company as reporting accountant if he would be ineligible for appointment as an auditor of that company under the Companies Act 1989 s 27 (ineligibility on ground of lack of independence: see para 958 ante): Companies Act 1985 s 249D(4) (added by the Companies Act 1985 (Audit Exemption) Regulations 1994 reg 2).
5 Ie under the Companies Act 1985 Pt XI Ch V (ss 384-394A) (as amended): see para 1027 et seq ante.
6 Ibid s 249D(1) (added by the Companies Act 1985 (Audit Exemption) Regulations 1994 reg 2; substituted by the Companies Act 1985 (Audit Exemption) (Amendment) Regulations 1995 reg 2(1),(2)).
7 Companies Act 1985 s 249D(2) (added by the Companies Act 1985 (Audit Exemption) Regulations 1994 reg 2). The Companies Act 1989 s 26 (effect of appointment of a partnership: see para 957 ante) applies to the appointment as reporting accountant of a partnership constituted under the law of England and Wales or Northern Ireland, or under the law of any other country or territory in which a partnership is not a legal person: Companies Act 1985 s 249D(2) (as so added).

B. DORMANT COMPANIES

1058. Dormant companies. A company may by special resolution[1] make itself exempt from the statutory provisions relating to the audit of accounts[2] in the following cases:

(1) if the company has been dormant[3] from the time of its formation;

(2) if the company has been dormant since the end of the previous financial year[4] and:

(a) is entitled in respect of its individual accounts[5] for that year to the statutory exemptions conferred[6] on a small company[7], or would be so entitled but for being a member of an ineligible group[8]; and

(b) is not required to prepare group accounts[9] for that year,

by a special resolution passed at a general meeting of the company at any time after copies of the annual accounts and reports for that year have been duly[10] sent out[11].

A company may not, however, pass such a resolution if it is a banking[12] or insurance[13] company or an authorised person[14] under the Financial Services Act 1986[15].

Where a company is, at the end of a financial year, so exempt from the statutory provisions relating to the audit of accounts:

(i) the provisions relating to the right to receive or demand copies of accounts and reports[16] have effect with the omission of references to the auditors' report;

(ii) no copies of an auditors' report need be laid before the company in general meeting;

(iii) no copy of an auditors' report need be delivered to the registrar of companies and, if none is delivered, the copy of the balance sheet so delivered must contain a statement by the directors, in a position above the signature on behalf of the board[17], to the effect that the company was dormant throughout the financial year; and

(iv) the company is treated as entitled in respect of its individual accounts for that year to the statutory exemptions conferred on a small company notwithstanding that it is a member of an ineligible group[18].

Where a company which is so exempt from the statutory provisions relating to the audit of accounts ceases to be dormant or would no longer qualify (for any other reason) to make itself exempt by passing a resolution under the above provisions, it thereupon ceases to be so exempt[19].

1 As to special resolutions see para 683 ante.

2 As to the audit of accounts see paras 1059-1061 post.

3 For these purposes, a company is 'dormant' during a period in which no significant accounting transaction occurs, ie no transaction which is required by the Companies Act 1985 s 221 (as substituted) (see para 801 ante) to be entered in the company's accounting records; and a company ceases to be dormant on the occurrence of such a transaction; and for this purpose there must be disregarded any transaction arising from the taking of shares in the company by a subscriber to the memorandum in pursuance of an undertaking of his in the memorandum: s 250(3) (substituted by the Companies Act 1989 s 14).

4 For the meaning of 'financial year' see para 806 ante.

5 For the meaning of 'individual accounts' see para 816 ante.

6 Ie the exemptions conferred by the Companies Act 1985 s 246 (as substituted and amended): see para 900 ante.

7 As to the qualification of a company as small see para 901 ante.

8 For the meaning of 'ineligible group' see paras 900, 902 ante.

9 As to group accounts see para 875 et seq ante.

10 Ie in accordance with the Companies Act 1985 s 238(1) (as substituted): see para 823 ante.

11 Ibid s 250(1) (substituted by the Companies Act 1989 s 14; amended by the Companies Act 1985 (Amendment of Sections 250 and 251) Regulations 1992, SI 1992/3003, reg 2(1)-(3)).
12 For the meaning of 'banking company' see para 117 note 8 ante.
13 For the meaning of 'insurance company' see para 117 note 9 ante.
14 For the meaning of 'authorised person' see para 294 note 7 ante.
15 Companies Act 1985 s 250(2) (substituted by the Companies Act 1989 s 14; amended by the Companies Act 1985 (Miscellaneous Accounting Amendments) Regulations 1996, SI 1996/189, reg 11(1),(2)).
16 Ie the Companies Act 1985 ss 238, 239 (as substituted): see paras 823, 824 ante.
17 Ie the signature required by ibid s 233(4) (as substituted): see para 937 ante.
18 Ibid s 250(4) (substituted by the Companies Act 1989 s 14; amended by the Companies Act 1985 (Miscellaneous Accounting Amendments) Regulations 1996 reg 11(1),(3)(a),(b)).
19 Companies Act 1985 s 250(5) (substituted by the Companies Act 1989 s 14).

(iii) Auditors' Report

1059. Auditors' duty to report. A company's auditors must make a report to the company's members on all annual accounts[1] of the company of which copies are to be laid before the company in general meeting during their tenure of office[2].

The auditors' report must state whether in the auditors' opinion the annual accounts have been properly prepared in accordance with the Companies Act 1985, and in particular whether a true and fair view[3] is given:

(1) in the case of an individual balance sheet[4], of the state of affairs of the company as at the end of the financial year[5];

(2) in the case of an individual profit and loss account[6], of the profit[7] or loss[7] of the company for the financial year;

(3) in the case of group accounts[8], of the state of affairs as at the end of the financial year, and the profit or loss for the financial year, of the undertakings[9] included in the consolidation as a whole, so far as concerns members of the company[10].

The auditors must consider whether the information given in the directors' report[11] for the financial year for which the annual accounts are prepared is consistent with those accounts; and, if they are of opinion that it is not, they must state that fact in their report[12].

1 For the meaning of 'annual accounts' see para 817 note 2 ante.
2 Companies Act 1985 s 235(1) (substituted by the Companies Act 1989 s 9).
3 For the meaning of 'true and fair view' see para 816 note 5 ante.
4 For the meaning of 'balance sheet' see para 826 ante.
5 For the meaning of 'financial year' see para 806 ante.
6 For the meaning of 'profit and loss account' see para 826 ante.
7 For the meaning of 'profit' and 'loss' see para 809 note 6 ante.
8 As to group accounts see para 875 et seq ante.
9 For the meaning of 'undertaking' see para 806 note 5 ante.
10 Companies Act 1985 s 235(2) (substituted by the Companies Act 1989 s 9).
11 As to the directors' report see para 1066 et seq post.
12 Companies Act 1985 s 235(3) (substituted by the Companies Act 1989 s 9).

1060. Signature of auditors' report. The auditors' report must state the names of the auditors and be signed[1] by them[2].

Every copy of the auditors' report which is laid before the company in general meeting, or which is otherwise circulated, published or issued, must state the names of the auditors[3].

The copy of the auditors' report which is delivered to the registrar of companies must state the names of the auditors and be signed by them[4].

If a copy of the auditors' report:

(1) is laid before the company, or otherwise circulated, published or issued, without the required statement of the auditors' names; or

(2) is delivered to the registrar without the required statement of the auditors' names or without being signed as required by these provisions,

the company, and every officer of it who is in default, is guilty of an offence and liable on summary conviction to a fine not exceeding one-fifth of the statutory maximum[5].

1 For these purposes, references to signature by the auditors are, where the office of auditor is held by a body corporate or partnership, to signature in the name of the body corporate or partnership by a person authorised to sign on its behalf: Companies Act 1985 s 236(5) (substituted by the Companies Act 1989 s 9).

2 Companies Act 1985 s 236(1) (substituted by the Companies Act 1989 s 9).

3 Companies Act 1985 s 236(2) (substituted by the Companies Act 1989 s 9).

4 Companies Act 1985 s 236(3) (substituted by the Companies Act 1989 s 9).

5 Companies Act 1985 s 236(4) (substituted by the Companies Act 1989 s 9); Companies Act 1985 s 730, Sch 24 (amended by the Companies Act 1989 s 23, Sch 10 para 24(1),(3)). For the meaning of 'officer who is in default' and 'the statutory maximum' see para 1161 post.

1061. Duties of auditors. A company's auditors must, in preparing their report, carry out such investigations as will enable them to form an opinion as to:

(1) whether proper accounting records have been kept by the company and proper returns adequate for their audit have been received from branches not visited by them; and

(2) whether the company's individual accounts[1] are in agreement with the accounting records and returns[2].

If the auditors are of opinion that proper accounting records have not been kept, or that proper returns for their audit have not been received from branches not visited by them, or, if the company's individual accounts are not in agreement with the accounting records and returns, the auditors must state that fact in their report[3].

If the auditors fail to obtain all the information and explanations which, to the best of their knowledge and belief, are necessary for the purposes of their audit, they must state that fact in their report[4].

If the statutory requirements relating to the disclosure of information as to the emoluments and other benefits of directors and others[5] are not complied with in the annual accounts[6], the auditors must include in their report, so far as they are reasonably able to do so, a statement giving the required particulars[7].

If the directors of the company have taken advantage of the exemption for small and medium-sized groups from the need to prepare group accounts[8] and in the auditors' opinion they were not entitled to do so, the auditors must state that fact in their report[9].

1 For the meaning of 'individual accounts' see para 816 ante.

2 Companies Act 1985 s 237(1) (substituted by the Companies Act 1989 s 9).

3 Companies Act 1985 s 237(2) (substituted by the Companies Act 1989 s 9).

4 Companies Act 1985 s 237(3) (substituted by the Companies Act 1989 s 9).

5 Ie the requirements of the Companies Act 1985 s 232, Sch 6 (as amended): see para 866 et seq ante.

6 For the meaning of 'annual accounts' see para 817 note 2 ante.

7 Companies Act 1985 s 237(4) (substituted by the Companies Act 1989 s 9).

8 Ie the exemption conferred by the Companies Act 1985 s 248 (as substituted): see para 902 ante.

9 Ibid s 237(4A) (added by the Companies Act 1985 (Miscellaneous Accounting Amendments) Regulations 1996, SI 1996/189, reg 6).

(18) ANNUAL RETURNS

(i) In general

1062. Duty to deliver annual returns. Every company must deliver to the registrar of companies successive annual returns each of which is made up to a date not later than the date which is from time to time the company's 'return date', that is:

(1) the anniversary of the company's incorporation; or

(2) if the company's last return delivered[1] was made up to a different date, the anniversary of that date[2].

Each return must be in the prescribed form[3], must contain the required information[4] and must be signed by a director[5] or the secretary of the company; and it must be delivered to the registrar within 28 days after the date to which it is made up[6].

If a company fails so to deliver an annual return before the end of the period of 28 days after a return date, the company is guilty of an offence and liable on summary conviction to a fine not exceeding the statutory maximum and, on conviction after continued contravention, to a daily default fine not exceeding one-tenth of the statutory maximum[7]. The contravention continues until such time as an annual return made up to that return date and complying with the above provisions[8], except as to date of delivery, is delivered by the company to the registrar[9]. Where a company is guilty of such an offence, every director[10] or secretary of the company is similarly liable unless he shows that he took all reasonable steps to avoid the commission or continuation of the offence[11].

1 Ie in accordance with the Companies Act 1985 Pt XI Ch III (ss 363-365) (as substituted): see infra and paras 1063-1065 post. For these purposes, the references to a return being delivered 'in accordance with Pt XI Ch III (ss 363-365) (as amended)' are (1) in relation to a return made on or after 1 October 1990, to a return with respect to which all the requirements of s 363(2) (as substituted) (see infra) are complied with; (2) in relation to a return made before 1 October 1990, to a return with respect to which the formal and substantive requirements of Pt XI Ch III (ss 363-365) as it then had effect were complied with, whether or not the return was delivered in time: s 363(5) (substituted by the Companies Act 1989 s 139(1); amended by the Companies Act 1989 (Commencement No 7 and Transitional and Saving Provisions) Order 1990, SI 1990/1707, art 7).

2 Companies Act 1985 s 363(1) (substituted by the Companies Act 1989 s 139(1)). Where a company was, immediately before 1 October 1990, in default with respect to the delivery of one or more annual returns, the Companies Act 1989 s 139 does not affect its obligation to make such a return, in accordance with the Companies Act 1985 Pt XI Ch III (ss 363-365) as it then had effect, or any liability arising from failure to do so: Companies Act 1989 s 139(2).

3 For the prescribed form of annual return see the Companies (Forms) (Amendment) Regulations 1995, SI 1995/736, reg 3, Sch 2, Form 363a. For the prescribed version of that form in Welsh see the Companies (Welsh Language Forms and Documents) (Amendment) Regulations 1995, SI 1995/734, reg 4, Schedule, Form 363CWM.

4 Ie the information required by or under the Companies Act 1985 ss 364-365 (as substituted): see paras 1063-1065 post.

5 For these purposes, a shadow director is not deemed to be a director: ibid s 365(3) (substituted by the Companies Act 1989 s 139(1)). For the meaning of 'director' and 'shadow director' see para 543 note 1 ante.

6 Companies Act 1985 s 363(2) (substituted by the Companies Act 1989 s 139(1)). The fee payable for registration of an annual return is £18: Companies (Fees) Regulations 1991, SI 1991/1206, reg 4, Schedule, Fee 2 (substituted by SI 1994/2217).

7 Companies Act 1985 s 363(3) (substituted by the Companies Act 1989 s 139(1)); Companies Act 1985 s 730, Sch 24 (amended by the Companies Act 1989 s 139(3)). For the meaning of 'the statutory maximum' and 'daily default fine' see para 1161 post.

8 Ie the Companies Act 1985 s 363(2) (as substituted): see supra.

9 Ibid s 363(3) (as substituted: see note 7 supra).

10 For these purposes, a shadow director is deemed to be a director: ibid s 365(3) (as substituted: see note 5 supra).
11 Ibid s 365(4) (substituted by the Companies Act 1989 s 139(1)).

(ii) Contents

1063. In general. Every annual return[1] must state the date to which it is made up and must contain the following information:
(1) the address of the company's registered office[2];
(2) the type[3] of company it is and its principal business activities[4];
(3) the name and address[5] of the company secretary;
(4) the name and address[5] of every director[6] of the company;
(5) in the case of an individual director:
  (a) his nationality, date of birth and business occupation; and
  (b) such particulars of other directorships and former names as are required to be contained in the company's register of directors[7];
(6) in the case of any corporate director, such particulars of other directorships as would be required to be contained in that register in the case of an individual;
(7) if the register of members[8] is not kept at the company's registered office, the address of the place where it is kept;
(8) if any register of debenture holders[9], or duplicate of any such register or a part of it, is not kept at the company's registered office, the address of the place where it is kept;
(9) if the company has elected:
  (a) to dispense[10] with the laying of accounts and reports before the company in general meeting; or
  (b) to dispense[11] with the holding of annual general meetings,
  a statement to that effect[12].

1 As to the duty to deliver annual returns see para 1062 ante.
2 As to the registered office see para 150 ante.
3 The information as to the company's type must be given by reference to the classification scheme prescribed for these purposes: Companies Act 1985 s 364(2) (substituted by the Companies Act 1989 s 139(1)). With effect from 1 October 1990, the classification scheme so prescribed is (1) T1: public limited company; (2) T2: private company limited by shares; (3) T3: private company limited by guarantee without share capital; (4) T4: private company limited by shares exempt under the Companies Act 1985 s 30 (see para 112 ante); (5) T5: private company limited by guarantee exempt under s 30; (6) T6: private unlimited company with share capital; and (7) T7: private unlimited company without share capital: Companies (Forms Amendment No 2 and Company's Type and Principal Business Activities) Regulations 1990, SI 1990/1766, reg 5(1), Sch 3 Pt I. A company required to deliver an annual return under the Companies Act 1985 s 699 (as amended) (Channel Islands and Isle of Man companies: see para 1784 post) or s 718 (unregistered companies: see para 1765 et seq post) must give the type of company it is by reference to the category which is, in the opinion of its directors, the most appropriate to its circumstances: Companies (Forms Amendment No 2 and Company's Type and Principal Business Activities) Regulations 1990 Sch 3 Pt I.
4 The information as to the company's principal business activities may be given by reference to one or more categories of any prescribed system of classifying business activities: Companies Act 1985 s 364(3) (substituted by the Companies Act 1989 s 139(1)). With effect from 6 May 1996, the Standard Industrial Classification of Economic Activities 1992, with the addition of the code set out in the Companies (Forms Amendment No 2 and Company's Type and Principal Business Activities) Regulations 1990 reg 5(2), Sch 3 Pt II (substituted by SI 1996/1105), is so prescribed: reg 5(2) (substituted by SI 1996/1105). The code so added is '9600 residents property management company': Sch 3 Pt II (as so substituted). 'The Standard Industrial Classification of Economic Activities 1992' means the edition published by Her Majesty's Stationery Office in August 1993 of the publication of that name prepared

by the Central Statistical Office: Companies (Forms Amendment No 2 and Company's Type and Principal Business Activities) Regulations 1990 reg 2 (amended by SI 1996/1105). Notwithstanding the provisions of the Companies (Principal Business Activities) (Amendment) Regulations 1996, SI 1996/1105, reg 2, the system of classifying business activities which was prescribed for the purpose of the Companies Act 1985 s 364(3) (as so substituted) by the Companies (Forms Amendment No 2 and Company's Type and Principal Business Activities) Regulations 1990 reg 5(2) (as originally made) may continue to be used in relation to an annual return delivered to the registrar of companies on or before 5 May 1997 instead of the system prescribed for that purpose by the Companies (Principal Business Activities) (Amendment) Regulations 1996: reg 3.

5 For these purposes, a person's 'name' and 'address' mean, respectively: (1) in the case of an individual, his Christian name (or other forename) and surname and his usual residential address; (2) in the case of a corporation or Scottish firm, its corporate or firm name and its registered or principal office: Companies Act 1985 s 364(4) (substituted by the Companies Act 1989 s 139(1)). In the case of a peer, or an individual usually known by a title, the title may be stated instead of his Christian name (or other forename) and surname or in addition to either or both of them: Companies Act 1985 s 364(5) (substituted by the Companies Act 1989 s 139(1)). Where all the partners in a firm are joint secretaries, the name and principal office of the firm may be stated instead of the names and addresses of the partners: Companies Act 1985 s 363(6) (substituted by the Companies Act 1989 s 139(1)).

6 For these purposes, a shadow director is deemed to be a director: Companies Act 1985 s 365(3) (substituted by the Companies Act 1989 s 139(1)). For the meaning of 'director' and 'shadow director' see para 543 note 1 ante.

7 As to the register of directors see para 560 ante.

8 As to the register of members see para 378 et seq ante.

9 As to the register of debenture holders see para 1293 post.

10 Ie under the Companies Act 1985 s 252 (as substituted): see para 923 ante.

11 Ie under ibid s 366A (as added): see para 659 ante.

12 Ibid s 364(1) (substituted by the Companies Act 1989 s 139(1)).

1064. Particulars of share capital and shareholders. The annual return[1] of a company having a share capital must contain the following information with respect to its share capital and members[2].

The return must state the total number of issued shares of the company at the date to which the return is made up and the aggregate nominal value of those shares[3].

The return must state with respect to each class of shares in the company:

(1) the nature of the class; and

(2) the total number and aggregate nominal value of issued shares of that class at the date to which the return is made up[4].

The return must contain a list of the names and addresses of every person who:

(a) is a member of the company on the date to which the return is made up; or

(b) has ceased to be a member of the company since the date to which the last return was made up, or, in the case of the first return, since the incorporation of the company;

and, if the names are not arranged in alphabetical order, the return must have annexed to it an index sufficient to enable the name of any person in the list to be easily found[5].

The return must also state:

(i) the number of shares of each class held by each member of the company at the date to which the return is made up; and

(ii) the number of shares of each class transferred since the date to which the last return was made up, or, in the case of the first return, since the incorporation of the company, by each member or person who has ceased to be a member, and the dates of registration of the transfers[6].

The return may, if either of the two immediately preceding returns has given the full particulars required[7], give only such particulars as relate to persons ceasing to be or becoming members since the date of the last return and to shares transferred since that date[8].

The above provisions[9] do not, however, require the inclusion of particulars entered in an overseas branch register[10] if copies of those entries have not been received at the company's registered office by the date to which the return is made up; but those particulars must be included in the company's next annual return after they are received[11].

Where the company has converted any of its shares into stock, the return must give the corresponding information in relation to that stock, stating the amount of stock instead of the number or nominal value of shares[12].

 1 As to the duty to deliver annual returns see para 1062 ante.
 2 Companies Act 1985 s 364A(1) (substituted by the Companies Act 1989 s 139(1)).
 3 Companies Act 1985 s 364A(2) (substituted by the Companies Act 1989 s 139(1)).
 4 Companies Act 1985 s 364A(3) (substituted by the Companies Act 1989 s 139(1)).
 5 Companies Act 1985 s 364A(4) (substituted by the Companies Act 1989 s 139(1)).
 6 Companies Act 1985 s 364A(5) (substituted by the Companies Act 1989 s 139(1)).
 7 Ie by the Companies Act 1985 s 364A(4),(5) (as substituted): see supra.
 8 Ibid s 364A(6) (substituted by the Companies Act 1989 s 139(1)).
 9 Ie the Companies Act 1985 s 364A(4),(5) (as substituted).
 10 As to the overseas branch register see paras 398-400 ante.
 11 Companies Act 1985 s 364A(7) (substituted by the Companies Act 1989 s 139(1)).
 12 Companies Act 1985 s 364A(8) (substituted by the Companies Act 1989 s 139(1)).

1065. Supplementary provisions. The Secretary of State may by regulations make further provision as to the information to be given in a company's annual return, which may amend or repeal the statutory provisions[1] relating to the contents of the return[2]. Such regulations must be made by statutory instrument which is subject to annulment in pursuance of a resolution of either House of Parliament[3].

 1 Ie the Companies Act 1985 s 364 (as substituted) (see para 1063 ante) and s 364A (as substituted) (see para 1064 ante).
 2 Ibid s 365(1) (substituted by the Companies Act 1989 s 139(1)).
 3 Companies Act 1985 s 365(2) (substituted by the Companies Act 1989 s 139(1)). At the date at which this volume states the law no such regulations had been made.

(19) DIRECTORS' REPORTS

(i) In general

1066. Duty to prepare report. The directors of a company must for each financial year[1] prepare a report:

(1) containing a fair review of the development of the business of the company and its subsidiary undertakings[2] during the financial year and of their position at the end of it[3]; and

(2) stating the amount, if any, which the directors recommend should be paid as dividend[4].

The report must also state the names of the persons who, at any time during the financial year, were directors of the company, and the principal activities of the company and its subsidiary undertakings in the course of the year, and any significant change in those activities in the year[5]. The report must also comply with the statutory provisions[6] as regards the disclosure of the specified matters[7].

In the case of any failure to comply with the statutory provisions as to the preparation of a directors' report and the contents of the report[8], every person who was a director of the company immediately before the end of the period for laying and delivering accounts and reports for the financial year in question is guilty of an offence and liable on conviction on indictment to a fine, or on summary conviction to a fine not exceeding the statutory maximum[9]. In proceedings against a person for such an offence it is a defence for him to prove that he took all reasonable steps for securing compliance with the requirements in question[10].

1   For the meaning of 'financial year' see para 806 ante.
2   For the meaning of 'subsidiary undertaking' see para 828 ante.
3   Companies Act 1985 s 234(1)(a) (substituted by the Companies Act 1989 s 8(1)).
4   Companies Act 1985 s 234(1)(b) (substituted by the Companies Act 1989 s 8(1); amended by the Companies Act 1985 (Miscellaneous Accounting Amendments) Regulations 1996, SI 1996/189, reg 5(1),(2)).
5   Companies Act 1985 s 235(2) (substituted by the Companies Act 1989 s 8(1)).
6   Ie the Companies Act 1985 s 234(3), Sch 7 (as amended). Schedule 7 Pt I (paras 1-6 (as amended): see para 1070 et seq post) relates to matters of a general nature, including changes in asset values, directors' shareholdings and other interests and contributions for political and charitable purposes; Pt II (paras 7, 8) (see para 1074 post) relates to the acquisition by a company of its own shares or a charge on them; Pt III (para 9) (see para 1075 post) relates to the employment, training and advancement of disabled persons; Pt V (para 11) (see para 1076 post) relates to the involvement of employees in the affairs, policy and performance of the company; and Pt VI (para 12) (see para 1077 post) relates to the company's policy on the payment of creditors: s 234(4) (substituted by the Companies Act 1989 s 8(1); amended by the Companies Act 1985 (Miscellaneous Accounting Amendments) Regulations 1996 reg 5(1),(3)(a), (b)).
7   Companies Act 1985 s 234(3) (substituted by the Companies Act 1989 s 8(1)).
8   Ie the Companies Act 1985 ss 234, 234A, Sch 7 (as amended): see supra and para 1070 et seq post.
9   Ibid s 234(5) (substituted by the Companies Act 1989 s 8(1)); Companies Act 1985 s 730, Sch 24 (amended by the Companies Act 1989 s 23, Sch 10 para 24(1),(2)). For the meaning of 'the statutory maximum' see para 1161 post.
10 Companies Act 1985 s 234(6) (substituted by the Companies Act 1989 s 8(1)).

1067. Small companies. A company which qualifies as a small company[1] in relation to a financial year[2] is entitled to the statutory exemptions[3] with respect to the preparation of a directors' report for that year if the report contains, above the signature on behalf of the board[4]:

(1) a statement to the effect that advantage has been taken, in the preparation of the report, of special exemptions applicable to small companies; and

(2) where the company's balance sheet for that year does not contain a statement of the grounds on which, in the directors' opinion, the company is entitled to the exemptions[5], a statement of the grounds on which, in the directors' opinion, the company is entitled to those exemptions[6].

A company is not entitled to the above exemption if it is, or was at any time within the financial year to which the accounts relate, a public company[7], a banking[8] or insurance[9] company, or an authorised person under the Financial Services Act 1986[10], or it is or was at any time during that year a member of an ineligible group[11].

The directors' report of a small company need not then give any of the information in respect of the following[12]:

(a) a fair review of business, the amount to be paid as dividend and the amount to be carried to reserves[13];

(b) a statement of the market value of fixed assets where it is substantially different from the balance sheet[14];

(c) miscellaneous disclosures[15];

(d) employee involvement[16].

A parent company[17] is not treated as qualifying as a small company in relation to a financial year unless the group[18] headed by it qualifies as a small group[19], and is not treated as qualifying as a medium-sized company in relation to a financial year unless that group qualifies as a medium-sized group[20].

1 As to qualification of a company as small or medium-sized see para 901 ante.
2 For the meaning of 'financial year' see para 806 ante.
3 Ie the exemptions provided by the Companies Act 1985 s 246, Sch 8 Pt II (para 15) (as added): see infra.
4 Ie the signature required by ibid s 234A (as added): see para 1068 post.
5 Ie a statement under ibid s 246(1A)(b) (as added): see para 900 ante.
6 Ibid s 246(1B) (added by the Companies Act 1985 (Accounts of Small and Medium-sized Enterprises and Publication of Accounts in ECUs) Regulations 1992, SI 1992/2452, reg 4(1); amended by the Companies Act 1985 (Miscellaneous Accounting Amendments) Regulations 1996, SI 1996/189, reg 7(1),(2)).
7 For the meaning of 'public company' see para 82 ante.
8 For the meaning of 'banking company' see para 117 note 8 ante.
9 For the meaning of 'insurance company' see para 117 note 9 ante.
10 For the meaning of 'authorised person' see para 294 note 7 ante.
11 Companies Act 1985 s 246(3) (substituted by the Companies Act 1989 s 13(1); amended by the Companies Act 1985 (Accounts of Small and Medium-sized Enterprises and Publication of Accounts in ECUs) Regulations 1992 reg 4(2)(c)). For the meaning of 'ineligible group' see para 900 ante.
12 Companies Act 1985 Sch 8 Pt II para 15 (added by the Companies Act 1985 (Accounts of Small and Medium-sized Enterprises and Publication of Accounts in ECUs) Regulations 1992 Schedule paras 1(3), 3; amended by the Companies Act 1985 (Miscellaneous Accounting Amendments) Regulations 1996 reg 15(4)(a)).
13 Ie the Companies Act 1985 s 234(1)(a),(b) (as substituted and amended): see para 1066 heads (1), (2) ante.
14 Ie ibid Sch 7 para 1(2): see para 1070 post.
15 Ie ibid Sch 7 para 6: see para 1073 post.
16 Ie ibid Sch 7 para 11: see para 1076 post.
17 For the meaning of 'parent company' see para 828 ante.
18 For the meaning of 'group' see para 830 note 8 ante.
19 As to qualification as a small group see para 903 ante.
20 Companies Act 1985 s 246(5) (substituted by the Companies Act 1989 s 13(1)). As to qualification as a medium-sized group see para 903 post.

1068. Approval and signing of directors' report. The directors' report[1] must be approved by the board of directors and signed on behalf of the board by a director or the secretary of the company[2].

Every copy of the directors' report which is laid before the company in general meeting[3], or which is otherwise circulated, published or issued, must state the name of the person who signed it on behalf of the board[4].

The copy of the directors' report which is delivered[5] to the registrar of companies must be signed on behalf of the board by a director or the secretary of the company[6].

If a copy of the report:

(1) is laid before the company, or otherwise circulated, published or issued, without the report having been signed as required by these provisions or without the required statement of the signatory's name being included; or

(2) is delivered to the registrar without being signed as required by these provisions,

the company, and every officer of it who is in default, is guilty of an offence and liable on summary conviction to a fine not exceeding one-fifth of the statutory maximum[7].

1 As to the duty to prepare the directors' report see para 1066 ante; and as to the contents of the directors' report see para 1070 et seq post.
2 Companies Act 1985 s 234A(1) (substituted by the Companies Act 1989 s 8(1)).

3 Ie pursuant to the Companies Act 1985 s 241 (as substituted): see para 817 ante.
4 Ibid s 234A(2) (substituted by the Companies Act 1989 s 8(1)).
5 Ie pursuant to the Companies Act 1985 s 242 (as substituted and amended): see para 818 ante.
6 Ibid s 234A(3) (substituted by the Companies Act 1989 s 8(1)).
7 Companies Act 1985 s 234A(4) (substituted by the Companies Act 1989 s 8(1)); Companies Act 1985 s 730, Sch 24 (amended by the Companies Act 1989 s 23, Sch 10 para 24(1),(3)). For the meaning of 'officer who is in default' and 'the statutory maximum' see para 1161 post.

1069. False statements by directors. Where an officer of a body corporate[1] (or person purporting to act as such), with intent to deceive members or creditors[2] of the body corporate about its affairs, publishes or concurs in publishing a written statement or account which to his knowledge is or may be misleading, false or deceptive in a material particular, he is liable on conviction on indictment to imprisonment for a term not exceeding seven years, or on summary conviction to imprisonment for a term not exceeding six months or a fine not exceeding the prescribed sum, or to both[3].

Where the affairs of the body corporate are managed by its members, these provisions apply to any statement which a member publishes or concurs in publishing in connection with his functions of management as if he were an officer of the body corporate[4].

1 The provisions of the Theft Act 1968 s 19 apply to an unincorporated association as they apply to a body corporate: see s 19(1)–(3).
2 For these purposes, a person who has entered into a security for the benefit of a body corporate is to be treated as a creditor of it: ibid s 19(2).
3 Ibid s 19(1); Magistrates' Courts Act 1980 ss 17, 32(1), Sch 1 para 28. For the meaning of 'the prescribed sum' see CRIMINAL LAW vol 11(2) (Reissue) para 807. As to the imposition of a fine in lieu of or in addition to the sentence see the Powers of Criminal Courts Act 1973 s 30(1) (as amended) and CRIMINAL LAW vol 11(2) (Reissue) para 1232.
4 Theft Act 1968 s 19(3).

(ii) Contents

1070. Asset values. If, in the case of such of the fixed assets of the company or of any of its subsidiary undertakings[1] as consist in interests in land, their market value, as at the end of the financial year[2], differs substantially from the amount at which they are included in the balance sheet[3], and the difference, in the directors' opinion, is of such significance as to require that the attention of members of the company or of holders of its debentures should be drawn to it, the report must indicate the difference with such degree of precision as is practicable[4].

1 For the meaning of 'subsidiary undertaking' see para 828 ante.
2 For the meaning of 'financial year' see para 806 ante.
3 For the meaning of 'balance sheet' see para 826 ante.
4 Companies Act 1985 s 234(3), Sch 7 para 1(2) (amended by the Companies Act 1985 (Miscellaneous Accounting Amendments) Regulations 1996, SI 1996/189, reg 15(3)).

1071. Directors' interests. The information required by the following provisions[1] must be given in the directors' report, or by way of notes to the company's annual accounts, with respect to each person who at the end of the financial year[2] was a director of the company[3].

It must be stated with respect to each director whether, according to the register[4], he was at the end of the financial year interested in shares in or debentures[5] of the company or any other body corporate in the same group[6]. If he was so interested, there must be stated the number of shares in and amount of debentures of each body (specifying it) in which, according to the register, he was then interested[7]. If a director was interested at the end of the financial year in shares in or debentures of the company or any other body corporate in the same group:

(1) it must also be stated whether, according to the register, he was at the beginning of the financial year, or, if he was not then a director, when he became one[8], interested in shares in or debentures of the company or any other body corporate in the same group; and

(2) if he was so interested, there must be stated the number of shares in and amount of debentures of each body (specifying it) in which, according to the register, he was then interested[9].

It must be stated with respect to each director whether, according to the register, any right to subscribe for shares in or debentures of the company or another body corporate in the same group was during the financial year granted to, or exercised by, the director or a member of his immediate family[10]. If any such right was granted to, or exercised by, any such person during the financial year, there must be stated the number of shares in and amount of debentures of each body (specifying it) in respect of which, according to the register, the right was granted or exercised[11].

1 Ie the Companies Act 1985 s 234(3), Sch 7 para 2A (as substituted) and Sch 7 para 2B (as substituted): see infra.
2 For the meaning of 'financial year' see para 806 ante.
3 Companies Act 1985 Sch 7 para 2(1) (substituted by the Companies Act 1989 s 8(2), Sch 5 paras 1, 3).
4 For these purposes, 'the register' means the register of directors' interests kept by the company under the Companies Act 1985 s 325 (see para 571 ante): Sch 7 para 2(2)(a) (substituted by the Companies Act 1989 Sch 5 paras 1, 3).
5 For these purposes, references to an interest in shares or debentures have the same meaning as in the Companies Act 1985 s 324 (see para 564 ante); and references to the interest of a director include any interest falling to be treated as his for the purposes of s 324: Sch 7 para 2A(4) (substituted by the Companies Act 1989 Sch 5 paras 1, 3).
6 Companies Act 1985 Sch 7 para 2A(1) (substituted by the Companies Act 1989 Sch 5 paras 1, 3). For these purposes, references to a body corporate being in the same group as the company are to its being a subsidiary or holding company, or another subsidiary of a holding company, of the company: Companies Act 1985 Sch 7 para 2(2)(b) (substituted by the Companies Act 1989 Sch 5 paras 1, 3). For the meaning of 'body corporate' see para 89 note 8 ante; for the meaning of 'group' see para 830 note 8 ante; for the meaning of 'subsidiary' see para 827 ante; and for the meaning of 'parent company' see para 828 ante.
7 Companies Act 1985 Sch 7 para 2A(2) (substituted by the Companies Act 1989 Sch 5 paras 1, 3).
8 For these purposes, the reference to the time when a person became a director is, in the case of a person who became a director on more than one occasion, to the time when he first became a director: Companies Act 1985 Sch 7 para 2A(5) (substituted by the Companies Act 1989 Sch 5 paras 1, 3).
9 Companies Act 1985 Sch 7 para 2A(3) (substituted by the Companies Act 1989 Sch 5 paras 1, 3).
10 Companies Act 1985 Sch 7 para 2B(1) (substituted by the Companies Act 1989 Sch 5 paras 1, 3). For these purposes, a director's 'immediate family' means his or her spouse and minor children; and 'children' includes stepchildren: Companies Act 1985 Sch 7 para 2B(3) (substituted by the Companies Act 1989 Sch 5 paras 1, 3). The reference to a member of the director's immediate family does not, however, include a person who is himself or herself a director of the company: Companies Act 1985 Sch 7 para 2B(4) (substituted by the Companies Act 1989 Sch 5 paras 1, 3). As to the attainment of majority at the age of 18 see the Family Law Reform Act 1969 s 1 and CHILDREN vol 5(2) (Reissue) para 601.
11 Companies Act 1985 Sch 7 para 2B(2) (substituted by the Companies Act 1989 Sch 5 paras 1, 3).

1072. Political and charitable gifts. The following provisions apply if the company, not being the wholly-owned subsidiary[1] of a company incorporated in Great

Britain, has in the financial year[2] given money for political purposes[3] or charitable purposes[4], or both[5].

If the money given exceeded £200 in amount, there must be contained in the directors' report for the year:

(1) in the case of each of the purposes for which money has been given, a statement of the amount of money given for that purpose[6];

(2) in the case of political purposes for which money has been given, the following particulars (so far as applicable):

    (a) the name of each person to whom money has been given for those purposes exceeding £200 in amount and the amount of money given; and

    (b) if money exceeding £200 in amount has been given by way of donation or subscription to a political party, the identity of the party and the amount of money given[7].

The above provisions do not apply to a company which, at the end of the financial year, has subsidiaries which have, in that year, given money as mentioned above but which is not itself the wholly-owned subsidiary of a company incorporated in Great Britain[8]. In such a case, however, if the amount of money so given in that year by the company and the subsidiaries between them exceeds £200, there must be contained in the directors' report for the year:

    (i) in the case of each of the purposes for which money has been given by the company and the subsidiaries between them, a statement of the amount of money given for that purpose[9]; and

    (ii) in the case of political purposes for which money has been given, the like particulars, so far as applicable, as are required[10] by the above provisions[11].

1 For the meaning of 'wholly-owned subsidiary' see para 827 ante.
2 For the meaning of 'financial year' see para 806 ante.
3 For these purposes, a company is to be treated as giving money for political purposes if, directly or indirectly: (1) it gives a donation or subscription to a political party of the United Kingdom or any part of it; or (2) it gives a donation or subscription to a person who, to the company's knowledge, is carrying on, or proposing to carry on, any activities which can, at the time at which the donation or subscription was given, reasonably be regarded as likely to affect public support for such a political party as is mentioned supra: Companies Act 1985 s 234(3), Sch 7 para 5(1),(2).
4 For these purposes, 'charitable purposes' mean purposes which are exclusively charitable: ibid Sch 7 para 5(1),(4). Money given for charitable purposes to a person who, when it was given, was ordinarily resident outside the United Kingdom is to be left out of account: Sch 7 para 5(1),(3).
5 Ibid Sch 7 para 3(1).
6 Ibid Sch 7 para 3(2)(a).
7 Ibid Sch 7 para 3(2)(b).
8 Ibid Sch 7 para 4(1).
9 Ibid Sch 7 para 4(2)(a).
10 Ie required by ibid Sch 7 para 3: see supra.
11 Ibid Sch 7 para 4(2)(b).

1073. Miscellaneous items. The directors' report must contain:

(1) particulars of any important events affecting the company or any of its subsidiary undertakings[1] which have occurred since the end of the financial year[2];

(2) an indication of likely future developments in the business of the company and of its subsidiary undertakings;

(3) an indication of the activities, if any, of the company and its subsidiary undertakings in the field of research and development; and

(4) unless the company is an unlimited company, an indication of the existence of branches[3] of the company outside the United Kingdom[4].

1　For the meaning of 'subsidiary undertaking' see para 828 ante.
2　For the meaning of 'financial year' see para 806 ante.
3　Ie as defined by the Companies Act 1985 s 698(2) (as added): see para 1791 note 2 post.
4　Ibid s 234(3), Sch 7 para 6 (amended by the Companies Act 1989 s 8(2), Sch 5 paras 1, 2(2); the Companies Act 1985 (Disclosure of Branches and Bank Accounts) Regulations 1992, SI 1992/3178, regs 3, 8(a)).

1074. Disclosure required by company acquiring its own shares or a charge on them. Disclosure is required in the directors' report where shares in a company:

  (1) are purchased by that company or are acquired by it by forfeiture[1] or surrender in lieu of forfeiture[2], or in pursuance of the statutory power[3] to purchase its own shares[4]; or

  (2) are acquired by another person in circumstances where he is a nominee for the company[5] or where he acquires the shares with financial assistance given by the company[6] and the company has a beneficial interest therein[7]; or

  (3) are made subject to a lien or other charge taken, whether expressly or otherwise, by the company and permitted by one of the exceptions[8] from the general rule against a company having a lien or charge on its own shares[9].

The directors' report with respect to a financial year[10] must then state:

  (a) the number and nominal value of the shares so purchased, the aggregate amount of the consideration paid by the company for such shares and the reasons for their purchase;

  (b) the number and nominal value of the shares so acquired by the company, acquired by another person in such circumstances and so charged respectively during the financial year;

  (c) the maximum number and nominal value of shares which, having been so acquired by the company, acquired by another person in such circumstances or so charged, whether or not during that year, are held at any time by the company or that other person during that year;

  (d) the number and nominal value of the shares so acquired by the company, acquired by another person in such circumstances or so charged, whether or not during that year, which are disposed of by the company or that other person or cancelled by the company during that year;

  (e) where the number and nominal value of the shares of any particular description are stated in pursuance of any of heads (a) to (d) above, the percentage of the called-up share capital[11] which shares of that description represent;

  (f) where any of the shares have been so charged, the amount of the charge in each case; and

  (g) where any of the shares have been disposed of by the company or the person who acquired them in such circumstances for money or money's worth, the amount or value of the consideration in each case[12].

1　See para 443 ante.
2　See para 441 ante.
3　Ie in pursuance of the Companies Act 1985 s 143(3): see para 362 ante.
4　Ibid s 234(3), Sch 7 para 7(a).
5　Ie pursuant to ibid s 146(1)(c): see para 366 ante.
6　Ie pursuant to ibid s 146(1)(d): see para 366 ante.
7　Ibid Sch 7 para 7(b).
8　Ie ibid s 150(2) or (4) (see para 214 ante) or the Companies Consolidation (Consequential Provisions) Act 1985 s 6(3) (see para 214 ante).
9　Companies Act 1985 Sch 7 para 7(c).

10 For the meaning of 'financial year' see para 806 ante.
11 For the meaning of 'paid-up share capital' see para 445 ante.
12 Companies Act 1985 Sch 7 para 8.

1075. Disclosure concerning employment etc of disabled persons. The following provisions apply to the directors' report where the average number of persons employed[1] by the company in each week during the financial year[2] exceeded 250[3]. That average number is the quotient derived by dividing, by the number of weeks in the financial year, the number derived by ascertaining, in relation to each of those weeks, the number of persons who, under contracts of service, were employed in the week, whether throughout it or not, by the company, and adding up the numbers ascertained[4].

In that case the directors' report must contain a statement describing such policy as the company has applied during the financial year:

(1) for giving full and fair consideration to applications for employment by the company made by disabled persons[5], having regard to their particular aptitudes and abilities;

(2) for continuing the employment of, and for arranging appropriate training for, employees of the company who have become disabled persons during the period when they were employed by the company; and

(3) otherwise for the training, career development and promotion of disabled persons employed by the company[6].

1 For these purposes, 'employment' means employment other than employment to work wholly or mainly outside the United Kingdom; and 'employed' and 'employee' are to be construed accordingly: Companies Act 1985 s 234(3), Sch 7 para 9(4)(a).
2 For the meaning of 'financial year' see para 806 ante.
3 Companies Act 1985 Sch 7 para 9(1).
4 Ibid Sch 7 para 9(2).
5 For these purposes, 'disabled person' means the same as in the Disabled Persons (Employment) Act 1944 (see EMPLOYMENT vol 16 (Reissue) para 218 note 2): Companies Act 1985 Sch 7 para 9(4)(b).
6 Ibid Sch 7 para 9(3).

1076. Employee involvement. The following provisions apply where the average number of persons employed by the company in each week during the financial year[1] exceeded 250[2]. That average number is the quotient derived by dividing by the number of weeks in the financial year the number derived by ascertaining, in relation to each of those weeks, the number of persons who, under contracts of service, were employed in the week, whether throughout it or not, by the company, and adding up the numbers ascertained[3].

In that case the directors' report must contain a statement describing the action that has been taken during the financial year to introduce, maintain or develop arrangements aimed at:

(1) providing employees[4] systematically with information on matters of concern to them as employees;

(2) consulting employees or their representatives on a regular basis, so that the views of employees can be taken into account in making decisions which are likely to affect their interests;

(3) encouraging the involvement of employees in the company's performance through an employees' share scheme[5] or by some other means;

(4) achieving a common awareness on the part of all employees of the financial and economic factors affecting the performance of the company[6].

1 For the meaning of 'financial year' see para 806 ante.
2 Companies Act 1985 s 234(3), Sch 7 para 11(1).
3 Ibid Sch 7 para 11(2). For these purposes, no regard is to be had to a person employed to work wholly or mainly outside the United Kingdom: Sch 7 para 11(4).
4 For these purposes, 'employee' does not include a person employed to work wholly or mainly outside the United Kingdom: ibid Sch 7 para 11(4).
5 For the meaning of 'employees' share scheme' see para 120 note 8 ante.
6 Companies Act 1985 Sch 7 para 11(1),(3).

1077. Policy on the payment of creditors. The following provisions apply to a report by the directors of a company for a financial year[1] if:

(1) the company was at any time within the financial year a public company[2]; or
(2) the company did not qualify[3] as small or medium-sized in relation to the financial year and was at any time within the year a member of a group[4] of which the parent company[5] was a public company[6].

The report must, with respect to the financial year immediately following that covered by the report, state:

(a) whether in respect of some or all of its suppliers[7] it is the company's policy to follow the code or standard on payment practice and, if so, the name of the code or standard and the place where the information about, and copies of, the code or standard can be obtained;
(b) whether in respect of some or all of its suppliers it is the company's policy to settle the terms of payment with those suppliers when agreeing the terms of each transaction, to ensure that those suppliers are made aware of the terms of payment, and to abide by the terms of payment;
(c) where the company's policy is not as mentioned in heads (a) or (b) above in respect of some or all of its suppliers, what its policy is with respect to the payment of those suppliers[8].

If the company's policy is different for different suppliers or classes of suppliers, the report must identify the suppliers or classes of suppliers to which the different policies apply[9].

1 For the meaning of 'financial year' see para 806 ante.
2 For the meaning of 'public company' see para 82 ante.
3 Ie by virtue of the Companies Act 1985 s 247 (as substituted and amended): see para 901 ante.
4 For the meaning of 'group' see para 830 note 8 ante.
5 For the meaning of 'parent company' see para 828 ante.
6 Companies Act 1985 s 234(3), Sch 7 para 12(1) (added by the Companies Act 1985 (Miscellaneous Accounting Amendments) Regulations 1996, SI 1996/189, reg 14(5)).
7 For these purposes, a supplier is any person whose claim on the reporting company in respect of goods or services supplied would be included under 'trade creditors' within 'Creditors; amounts falling due within one year' in a balance sheet drawn up in accordance with balance sheet Format 1 (as amended) (see para 832 ante): Companies Act 1985 Sch 7 para 12(4) (added by the Companies Act 1985 (Miscellaneous Accounting Amendments) Regulations 1996 reg 14(5)).
8 Companies Act 1985 Sch 7 para 12(2) (added by the Companies Act 1985 (Miscellaneous Accounting Amendments) Regulations 1996 reg 14(5)).
9 Companies Act 1985 Sch 7 para 12(3) (added by the Companies Act 1985 (Miscellaneous Accounting Amendments) Regulations 1996 reg 14(5)).

(iii) Revision of Defective Reports

1078. Voluntary revision of directors' report. If it appears to the directors of a company that any directors' report did not comply with the requirements of the Companies Act 1985, they may prepare a revised report[1]. Where copies of the report have been laid before the company in general meeting or delivered to the registrar of companies, the revisions must be confined to:

(1) the correction of those respects in which the previous report did not comply with the requirements of that Act; and

(2) the making of any necessary consequential alterations[2].

The Secretary of State may make provision by regulations as to the application of the provisions of the 1985 Act in relation to a revised directors' report[3]. The regulations may in particular:

(a) make different provision according to whether the previous report is replaced or is supplemented by a document indicating the corrections to be made;

(b) make provision with respect to the functions of the company's auditors or reporting accountant[4] in relation to the revised report;

(c) require the directors to take such steps as may be specified in the regulations where the previous report has been sent out to members and others[5], laid before the company in general meeting or delivered to the registrar of companies, or where a summary financial statement based on the previous report has been sent to members[6];

(d) apply the provisions of the Companies Act 1985, including those creating criminal offences, subject to such additions, exceptions and modifications as are specified in the regulations[7].

Any such regulations must be made by statutory instrument which is subject to annulment in pursuance of a resolution of either House of Parliament[8].

1 Companies Act 1985 s 245(1) (substituted by the Companies Act 1989 s 12). As to the revision of defective accounts see para 940 et seq ante.
2 Companies Act 1985 s 245(2) (substituted by the Companies Act 1989 s 12).
3 Companies Act 1985 s 245(3) (substituted by the Companies Act 1989 s 12). In exercise of the power so conferred the Secretary of State made the Companies (Revision of Defective Accounts and Report) Regulations 1990, SI 1990/2570 (amended by SI 1992/3075; SI 1994/1935; SI 1995/2092; SI 1996/315): see para 1079 et seq post.
4 For the meaning of 'the reporting accountant' see para 1056 ante.
5 Ie under the Companies Act 1985 s 238(1) (as substituted): see para 823 ante.
6 Ie under ibid s 251 (as substituted and amended): see para 914 et seq ante.
7 Ibid s 245(4) (substituted by the Companies Act 1989 s 12; amended by the Companies Act 1985 (Audit Exemption) Regulations 1994, SI 1994/1935, reg 4, Sch 1 Pt I para 2).
8 Companies Act 1985 s 245(5) (substituted by the Companies Act 1989 s 12).

1079. Content of revised report. The provisions of the Companies Act 1985 as to the matters to be included in a directors' report[1] apply to a revised report[2] as if the revised report was prepared and approved by the directors of the company as at the date of the original[3] directors' report[4].

1 As to the matters to be included see para 1070 et seq ante.
2 For these purposes, 'revised report' means a revised directors' report prepared by the directors under the Companies Act 1985 s 245 (as substituted and amended) (see para 1078 ante), either through revision by replacement or revision by supplementary note; in the latter case the revised report comprises the original directors' report together with the supplementary note: Companies (Revision of Defective Accounts and Report) Regulations 1990, SI 1990/2570, reg 2. 'Revision by replacement' means revision by the preparation of a replacement directors' report in substitution for the original directors' report (reg 2); and 'revision by supplementary note' means revision by the preparation of a note indicating corrections to be made to the original directors' report (reg 2). For the meaning of 'original' see note 3 infra.

3 For these purposes, 'original', in relation to a directors' report, means the directors' report which is the subject of revision by a revised report: ibid reg 2.
4 Ibid regs 2, 3(4). For these purposes, 'date of the original directors' report' means the date on which the original directors' report was approved by the board of directors under the Companies Act 1985 s 234A (as substituted) (see para 1068 ante): Companies (Revision of Defective Accounts and Report) Regulations 1990 reg 2. For the meaning of references in reg 3 to the provisions of the Companies Act 1985 see para 941 note 4 ante. As to the content of revised annual accounts see para 941 ante.

1080. Approval and signature of revised report. The statutory provisions relating to the approval and signing of the directors' report[1] apply to a revised report[2], save that in the case of revision by supplementary note[3], they apply as if they required the signature to be on the supplementary note[4].

Where the original[5] directors' report has been sent out to members[6], laid before the company in general meeting[7] or delivered to the registrar of companies[8], the directors must, before approving the revised report[9], cause statements as to the following matters to be made in a prominent position in the revised report (in the case of a revision by supplementary note, in that note):

(1) in the case of revision by replacement[10]:
  (a) that the revised report replaces the original report for the financial year, specifying it;
  (b) that it has been prepared as at the date of the original directors' report[11] and not as at the date of revision[12] and accordingly does not deal with any events between those dates;
  (c) the respects in which the original directors' report did not comply with the requirements of the Companies Act 1985; and
  (d) any significant amendments made consequential upon the remedying of those defects;

(2) in the case of revision by a supplementary note:
  (a) that the note revises in certain respects the original directors' report of the company and is to be treated as forming part of that report; and
  (b) that the directors' report has been revised as at the date of the original directors' report and not as at the date of the revision and accordingly does not deal with events between those dates;

and must, when approving the revised report, cause the date on which the approval is given to be stated in them (in the case of a revision by supplementary note, in that note)[13].

1 Ie the Companies Act 1985 s 234A (as substituted): see para 1068 ante.
2 For the meaning of 'revised report' see para 1079 note 2 ante.
3 For the meaning of 'revision by supplementary note' see para 1079 note 2 ante.
4 Companies (Revision of Defective Accounts and Report) Regulations 1990, SI 1990/2570, regs 2, 5(1). As to approval and signature of revised annual accounts see para 942 ante.
5 For the meaning of 'original' see para 1079 note 3 ante.
6 Ie under the Companies Act 1985 s 238(1) (as substituted): see para 823 ante.
7 Ie under ibid s 241(1) (as substituted): see para 817 ante.
8 Ie under ibid s 242(1) (as substituted): see para 818 ante.
9 Ie under ibid s 234A (as substituted).
10 For the meaning of 'revision by replacement' see para 1079 note 2 ante.
11 For the meaning of 'date of the original directors' report' see para 1079 note 4 ante.
12 For these purposes, 'date of revision' means the date on which a revised report is approved by the board of directors under the Companies (Revision of Defective Accounts and Report) Regulations 1990 reg 5: reg 2.

13 Ibid regs 2, 5(2). The Companies Act 1985 s 234(5) (as substituted) (see para 1066 ante) applies with
    respect to a failure to comply with the Companies (Revision of Defective Accounts and Report)
    Regulations 1990 reg 5(2) as if the requirements of reg 5(2) were requirements of the Companies Act
    1985 Pt VII (ss 221-262A (as amended): see para 801 et seq ante): Companies (Revision of Defective
    Accounts and Report) Regulations 1990 regs 2, 5(2).

1081. Auditors' report on revised report alone. A company's current auditors
must make a report or, as the case may be, a further report[1] to the company's members
under these provisions on any revised report[2] prepared if the relevant annual accounts
have not been revised at the same time[3].

Where, however, the auditors' report on the annual accounts for the financial year
covered by the revised report was not made by the company's current auditors, the
directors of the company may resolve that the report so required[4] is to be made by the
person or persons who made that report, provided that that person or those persons
agree to do so and he or they would be qualified for appointment as auditors of the
company[5].

The report must state that the auditors have considered whether the information
given in the revised report is consistent with the annual accounts for the relevant year,
specifying it, and:

(1) if they are of the opinion that it is; or
(2) if they are of the opinion that it is not,

they must state that fact in their report[6].

1 Ie under the Companies Act 1985 s 235 (as substituted): see para 1059 ante.
2 For the meaning of 'revised report' see para 1079 note 2 ante.
3 Companies (Revision of Defective Accounts and Report) Regulations 1990, SI 1990/2570, reg 7(1)
   (amended by SI 1996/315). The Companies Act 1985 s 236 (as substituted) (signature of auditors'
   report: see para 1060 ante) applies to an auditors' report under the Companies (Revision of Defective
   Accounts and Report) Regulations 1990 reg 7 as it applies to an auditors' report under the Companies
   Act 1985 s 235(1) (as substituted) (see para 1059 ante) mutatis mutandis: Companies (Revision of
   Defective Accounts and Report) Regulations 1990 reg 7(4). As to the auditors' report on revised
   accounts and a revised report see para 943 ante.
4 Ie by ibid reg 7(1): see supra.
5 Ibid reg 7(2).
6 Ibid reg 7(3).

1082. Effect of revision. Upon the directors' approving a revised report[1], the
provisions of the Companies Act 1985 have effect as if the revised report was, as from
the date of its approval, the directors' report in place of the original[2] directors' report[3].
In particular, the revised report is thereupon the directors' report for the relevant
financial year for the purposes of the statutory provisions relating to the right to
demand copies of reports[4], the entitlement of persons to receive copies of reports[5], the
duty to lay reports before the company in general meeting[6] and the delivery of reports
to the registrar of companies[7], if the requirements of those provisions have not been
complied with prior to the date of revision[8].

1 Ie under the Companies (Revision of Defective Accounts and Report) Regulations 1990, SI 1990/
   2570, reg 5: see para 1080 ante. For the meaning of 'revised report' see para 1079 note 2 ante.
2 For the meaning of 'original' see para 1079 note 3 ante.
3 Companies (Revision of Defective Accounts and Report) Regulations 1990 regs 2, 9(1) (amended by
   SI 1996/315). As to the effect of revision of annual accounts see para 944 ante.
4 Ie the Companies Act 1985 s 239 (as substituted): see para 824 ante.

5 Ie ibid s 238 (as substituted): see para 823 ante.
6 Ie ibid s 241 (as substituted): see para 817 ante.
7 Ie ibid s 242 (as substituted and amended): see para 818 ante.
8 Companies (Revision of Defective Accounts and Report) Regulations 1990 regs 2, 9(2). For the meaning of 'date of revision' see para 1080 note 12 ante.

1083. Publication of revised report. The following provisions have effect where the directors have prepared a revised report[1] and copies of the original[2] report have been sent[3] to any person entitled to receive a copy[4].

The directors must send to any such person:

(1) in the case of a revision by replacement[5], a copy of the revised report, together with a copy of the auditors' report on that report; or

(2) in the case of revision by supplementary note[6], a copy of that note together with a copy of the auditors' report on the revised report,

not more than 28 days after the date of revision[7].

The directors must also, not more than 28 days after the revision, send a copy of the revised report, together with a copy of the auditors' report on that report to any person who is not a person entitled to receive a copy under the above provisions but who is, as at the date of revision:

(a) a member of the company;

(b) a holder of the company's debentures; or

(c) a person who is entitled to receive notice of general meetings,

unless the company would be entitled[8] at that date to send to that person a summary financial statement[9].

1 Ie under the Companies Act 1985 s 245 (as substituted and amended): see para 1078 ante. For the meaning of 'revised report' see para 1079 note 2 ante.
2 For the meaning of 'original' see para 1079 note 3 ante.
3 Ie under the Companies Act 1985 s 238 (as substituted): see para 823 ante.
4 Companies (Revision of Defective Accounts and Report) Regulations 1990, SI 1990/2570, regs 2, 10(1). The Companies Act 1985 s 238(5) (as substituted) (see para 823 ante) applies to a default in complying with the Companies (Revision of Defective Accounts and Report) Regulations 1990 reg 10 (as amended) as if the provisions of reg 10 (as amended) were provisions of the Companies Act 1985 s 238 (as substituted) and as if the reference therein to 'the company and every officer of it who is in default' were a reference to each of the directors who approved the revised report under the Companies (Revision of Defective Accounts and Report) Regulations 1990 reg 5 (see para 1080 ante): reg 10(4). As to publication of revised annual accounts see para 945 ante.
5 For the meaning of 'revision by replacement' see para 1079 note 2 ante.
6 For the meaning of 'revision by supplementary note' see para 1079 note 2 ante.
7 Companies (Revision of Defective Accounts and Report) Regulations 1990 reg 10(2). For the meaning of 'date of revision' see para 1080 note 12 ante.
8 Ie under the Companies Act 1985 s 251 (as substituted and amended): see para 914 et seq ante.
9 Companies (Revision of Defective Accounts and Report) Regulations 1990 reg 10(3) (amended by SI 1992/3075; SI 1996/315). The Companies Act 1985 s 238(2),(3) (as substituted) (see para 823 ante) applies to the Companies (Revision of Defective Accounts and Report) Regulations 1990 reg 10(3) as it has effect with respect to the Companies Act 1985 s 238(1) (as substituted): Companies (Revision of Defective Accounts and Report) Regulations 1990 regs 2, 10(3).

1084. Laying of revised report. Where the directors have prepared a revised report[1] and copies of the original[2] report have been laid[3] before a general meeting, a copy of the revised report, together with a copy of the auditors' report on that report must be laid before the next general meeting of the company held after the date of revision⁴ at which any annual accounts for a financial year are laid, unless the revised report has already been laid before an earlier general meeting⁵.

1   Ie under the Companies Act 1985 s 245 (as substituted and amended): see para 1078 ante. For the meaning of 'revised report' see para 1079 note 2 ante.
2   For the meaning of 'original' see para 1079 note 3 ante.
3   Ie under the Companies Act 1985 s 241 (as substituted): see para 817 ante.
4   For the meaning of 'date of revision' see para 1080 note 12 ante.
5   Companies (Revision of Defective Accounts and Report) Regulations 1990, SI 1990/2570, regs 2, 11(1),(2). The Companies Act 1985 s 241(2)-(4) (as substituted) (see para 817 ante) applies with respect to a failure to comply with the requirements of the Companies (Revision of Defective Accounts and Report) Regulations 1990 reg 11 as it has effect with respect to a failure to comply with the requirements of the Companies Act 1985 s 241(1) (as substituted) (see para 817 ante) but as if (1) the reference in s 241(2) (as substituted) to 'the period allowed for laying and delivering accounts and reports' were a reference to the period between the date of revision of the revised accounts or, as the case may be, the revised report and the date of the next general meeting of the company held after the date of revision at which any annual accounts for a financial year are laid; and references in s 241(2),(3) (as substituted) to 'that period' are to be construed accordingly; and (2) the references in s 241(4) (as substituted) to 'the documents in question' and 'this Part' were respectively a reference to the documents referred to in the Companies (Revision of Defective Accounts and Report) Regulations 1990 reg 11(3)(a) (see head (1) supra) and the provisions of the Companies Act 1985 Pt VII (ss 221-262A (as amended): see para 801 et seq ante) as applied by the Companies (Revision of Defective Accounts and Report) Regulations 1990: reg 11(3). For the meaning of 'revised accounts' see para 941 note 2 ante. As to the laying of revised accounts see para 946 ante.

1085. Delivery to the registrar of revised report. Where the directors have prepared a revised report¹ and a copy of the original² report has been delivered to the registrar of companies³, the directors of the company must, within 28 days of the date of revision⁴, deliver to the registrar:

(1)   in the case of a revision by replacement⁵, a copy of the revised report, together with a copy of the auditors' report on that report; or

(2)   in the case of a revision by supplementary note⁶, a copy of that note, together with a copy of the auditors' report on the revised report⁷.

1   Ie under the Companies Act 1985 s 245 (as substituted and amended): see para 1078 ante. For the meaning of 'revised report' see para 1079 note 2 ante.
2   For the meaning of 'original' see para 1079 note 3 ante.
3   Ie under the Companies Act 1985 s 242 (as substituted and amended): see para 818 ante.
4   For the meaning of 'date of revision' see para 1080 note 12 ante.
5   For the meaning of 'revision by replacement' see para 1079 note 2 ante.
6   For the meaning of 'revision by supplementary note' see para 1079 note 2 ante.
7   Companies (Revision of Defective Accounts and Report) Regulations 1990, SI 1990/2570, regs 2, 12(1),(2). The Companies Act 1985 s 242(2)-(5) (as substituted) (see para 818 ante) applies with respect to a failure to comply with the requirements of the Companies (Revision of Defective Accounts and Reports) Regulations 1990 reg 12 as it applies with respect to a failure to comply with the requirements of the Companies Act 1985 s 242(1) (as substituted and amended) (see para 818 ante) but as if (1) the reference in s 242(2),(4) (as substituted) to 'the period allowed for laying and delivering accounts and reports' were a reference to the period of 28 days referred to in the Companies (Revision of Defective Accounts and Report) Regulations 1990 reg 12(2) (see supra); and the reference in the Companies Act 1985 s 242(2) (as substituted) to 'that period' is to be construed accordingly; (2) the references in s 242(5) (as substituted) to 'the documents in question' and 'this Part' were respectively a reference to the documents referred to in the Companies (Revision of Defective Accounts and Report) Regulations 1990 reg 12(2) and the provisions of the Companies Act 1985 Pt VII (ss 221-262A (as amended): see para 801 et seq ante) as applied by the Companies (Revision of Defective Accounts and Report) Regulations 1990: reg 12(3).

(20) POWERS AND LIABILITIES OF COMPANIES

(i) In general

1086. Powers of registered companies. Although a company registered under the Companies Act 1985 is a body corporate[1], it does not have all the powers of a corporation at common law[2]. Its powers are limited to:

(1) those expressly given by the Companies Act 1985;

(2) those which are incidental to its being a statutory corporation;

(3) those expressly given by its memorandum of association; and

(4) those incidental to the powers so given.

Moreover, a company is subject to the common law and to statutory provisions which affect the conduct of its affairs or business, like any other person[3], and may come within the scope of special statutory restrictions as, for example, those enabling restriction or winding-up orders to be made if the business is carried on by or on behalf of enemies or enemy subjects[4] or those restricting the transfer of businesses abroad[5].

If a petition for an administration order has been presented[6], the court may, by interim order, restrict the exercise of any powers of the company, whether by reference to the consent of the court, or of a person qualified to act as an insolvency practitioner[7] in relation to the company, or otherwise[8].

1 See the Companies Act 1985 s 13(3) and para 92 ante.

2 See para 97 ante and CORPORATIONS vol 9 para 1326.

3 'Person' includes a corporation: see the Interpretation Act 1978 ss 5, 22(1), 23(1), Sch 1, Sch 2 para 4(1)(a) and STATUTES vol 44(1) (Reissue) para 1382. A limited company may be a 'respectable and responsible person' within the meaning of a proviso against assigning a lease without the landlord's consent: *Willmott v London Road Car Co Ltd* [1910] 2 Ch 525, CA; *Re Greater London Properties Ltd's Lease, Taylor Bros (Grocers) Ltd v Covent Garden Properties Co Ltd* [1959] 1 All ER 728, [1959] 1 WLR 503.

4 See the Trading with the Enemy Act 1939 s 3A (as added) and WAR vol 49 para 154.

5 See para 95 ante.

6 See para 2082 et seq post.

7 As to insolvency practitioners and their qualification see para 2007 et seq post.

8 See the Insolvency Act 1986 s 9(4),(5) and para 2088 post. The court may make any other order it thinks fit: see s 9(4) and para 2088 post.

1087. Limit on exercise of companies' powers. Unless it is a private company, a company under the Companies Act 1985 does not acquire the right to exercise all its powers immediately on incorporation, for it must comply with certain statutory requirements before it may either properly commence business or exercise its borrowing powers or enter into binding contracts[1].

1 See para 652 ante.

1088. Statutory duties of companies. A company has certain statutory duties, attaching to it from the time of its incorporation, for example[1]:

(1) to have a registered office and give notice of any change in its situation to the registrar of companies[2];

(2) to keep its name on each of its offices or places of business[3];

(3) to keep and allow inspection of such registers of directors and secretaries[4], directors' share interests[5], members[6], substantial individual interests in share capital of a public company[7], and mortgages and charges[8] as are required by the Companies Act 1985;

(4) to make the returns of allotments[9] and annual returns[10] required;
(5) to deliver for registration contracts in respect of shares issued for a consideration other than cash[11];
(6) to issue share certificates and debentures within the statutory period[12];
(7) to hold annual general meetings required by the Companies Act 1985[13];
(8) to register transfers of shares on request by the transferor in the same manner and subject to the same conditions as if the request were made by the transferee[14];
(9) to issue copies of the memorandum in accordance with the alterations made in it[15];
(10) if it has a common seal, to have its name engraved in legible characters on the seal[16];
(11) to have its name mentioned in all its business letters and in all notices and other official publications, and in all bills of exchange, promissory notes, indorsements, cheques and orders for money or goods purporting to be signed by or on behalf of the company, and in all its bills of parcels, invoices, receipts and letters of credit[17]; and
(12) to keep proper accounting records[18] and lay before the members in general meeting copies of the company's annual accounts, the directors' report and the auditors' report on those accounts[19].

1 The list given here is not exhaustive.
2 See the Companies Act 1985 s 287 (as substituted) and para 150 ante.
3 See ibid s 348 and para 152 ante.
4 See ibid s 288 (as amended) and para 560 ante.
5 See ibid s 325 and para 571 ante.
6 See ibid s 352 and para 378 et seq ante.
7 See ibid Pt VI (ss 198-220) (as amended) and para 735 et seq ante.
8 See ibid s 401 and para 1310 post.
9 See ibid s 88(2)(a) and para 478 ante.
10 See ibid ss 363-365 (as substituted) and para 1062 et seq ante.
11 See ibid s 88(2)(b) and para 478 ante.
12 See ibid s 185 (as amended); paras 482, 483 ante; and para 1282 post.
13 See ibid s 366 and para 658 ante.
14 See ibid s 183(4) and para 510 ante.
15 See ibid s 20 and para 101 ante.
16 See ibid s 350 (as substituted) and para 98 ante.
17 See ibid s 349 and para 1134 post.
18 See ibid s 221 (as substituted) and para 801 ante.
19 See ibid s 241 (as substituted) and para 817 ante.

1089. Exercise of general statutory powers. Some statutory powers may be exercised, subject to conditions, by an incorporated company even though they are not conferred either by its memorandum of association or by its articles, such as its powers to change its name[1], or to close the register of members for a limited period[2].

1 See the Companies Act 1985 s 28(1) and para 160 ante.
2 See ibid s 358 and para 390 ante. Notwithstanding s 358 or any other enactment, a participating issuer may not close a register of securities relating to a participating security without the consent of the Operator: see the Uncertificated Securities Regulations 1995, SI 1995/3272, reg 22 and para 390 ante.

1090. Statutory powers exercisable only if given by articles. Many of the powers conferred by the Companies Act 1985 may be exercised by a company only if authorised to exercise them by its articles[1]. These include the power:

(1) if it has a common seal, to have an official seal for use abroad[2];
(2) to pay underwriting commissions in respect of share capital[3];
(3) to make provision for different amounts to be paid on its shares, with pro-portionate dividends[4];
(4) to alter the conditions of its memorandum relating to share capital by increasing, consolidating or sub-dividing its shares, or by converting paid-up shares into stock, or reconverting stock or cancelling unissued shares and reducing its capital accordingly[5];
(5) to reduce its share capital[6];
(6) to issue redeemable shares[7];
(7) to purchase its own shares[8];
(8) to issue share warrants to bearer[9];
(9) to alter its memorandum by special resolution so as to render the liability of its directors unlimited[10];
(10) by a resolution of its directors to provide for employees on cessation or transfer of the business of the company or any of its subsidiaries[11].

1 For the meaning of 'articles' see para 140 note 2 ante. This list is not exhaustive.
2 See the Companies Act 1985 s 39(1) (as amended) and para 1117 post.
3 See ibid s 97(2) (as amended) and para 194 ante.
4 See ibid s 119 and paras 271, 417, 719 ante.
5 See ibid s 121(1) and paras 174, 201, 205, 207, 209, 218 ante.
6 See ibid s 135(1) and para 241 ante.
7 See ibid s 159(1) and para 219 ante.
8 See ibid s 162(1) and para 222 ante.
9 See ibid s 188(1) (as substituted) and para 493 ante.
10 See ibid s 307 and para 627 ante.
11 See ibid s 719(3)(b) and para 1101 post. This power may alternatively be taken in the memorandum: s 719(3)(b).

1091. Powers exercisable only by special resolution. A special resolution[1] is required by the Companies Act 1985 for the exercise of certain powers[2]. These include the power:
(1) to change the company's name[3];
(2) to alter the company's objects as stated in its memorandum of association[4];
(3) to alter its articles of association[5];
(4) to reduce the company's capital[6];
(5) to turn an existing liability on shares into a reserve liability[7];
(6) to alter the memorandum of association so as to make the liability of directors or managers unlimited[8]; and
(7) as a rule, to wind up voluntarily[9].

1 As to special resolutions see para 683 ante.
2 This list is not exhaustive.
3 See the Companies Act 1985 s 28(1) and para 160 ante.
4 See ibid s 4 (as substituted) and para 1184 post.
5 See ibid s 9(1) and para 538 ante.
6 See ibid s 135(1) and para 241 ante.
7 See ibid s 120 and para 177 ante.
8 See ibid s 307(1) and para 627 ante.
9 See the Insolvency Act 1986 s 84(1)(b) and para 2698 post. The company may also, by special resolution, resolve that it be wound up by the court: see s 122(1)(a) and para 2202 et seq post.

1092. Stock Exchange requirements. If a company is to obtain admission to the Official List of The Stock Exchange[1], it must undertake to observe certain obligations once its securities have been admitted to listing[2].

1 As to the Official List of The Stock Exchange see para 281 ante and STOCK EXCHANGE vol 45 para 5.
2 See para 282 ante.

(ii) Company's Powers; Limitation of Powers

A. IN GENERAL

1093. In general. Under the Companies Act 1948 a company could be incorporated for carrying out any lawful purpose only[1].

The Companies Act 1985[2] provided, however, that, in favour of a person dealing with a company in good faith, any transaction decided on by the directors was deemed to be one which it was within the capacity of the company to enter into, and the power of the directors to bind the company was deemed to be free of any limitation under the memorandum or articles[3]. That Act further provided that a party to a transaction so decided on was not bound to inquire as to the capacity of the company to enter into it or as to any such limitation on the powers of the directors, and was presumed to have acted in good faith unless the contrary was proved[4].

The statutory provisions relating to a company's capacity contained in the Companies Act 1985 have been further expanded in respect of:

(1) a company's capacity not being limited by its memorandum[5];
(2) the directors' power to bind the company[6]; and
(3) there being no duty to inquire as to the capacity of a company or the authority of its directors[7].

The new provisions largely abolish the effect of the old ultra vires doctrine on relations between a company and third parties and confer protection on such parties, unless they have acted in bad faith, in respect of acts beyond the authority of the board of directors. Thus, the ultra vires doctrine[8], although otherwise substantially modified, remains in relation to the accountability of directors, subject to the new statutory provisions, and in relation to transactions by a company with a person who is not acting in good faith. Nor do the new statutory provisions affect the operation of a constructive trust, if the facts give rise to one[9].

1 See the Companies Act 1948 s 1 (repealed). Thus, under the rule in *Royal British Bank v Turquand* (1856) 6 E & B 327, a person was presumed to have ensured that the transaction was consistent with such of the company's public documents eg its memorandum and articles, special and extraordinary resolutions, as were open to public inspection. The company was, therefore, held not to be bound in such cases as *Irvine v Union Bank of Australia* (1877) 2 App Cas 366, PC (where no special resolution had been filed to authorise the transaction in question as was required by the articles) and *Howard v Patent Ivory Manufacturing Co* (1888) 38 ChD 156 (where articles permitted borrowing over a certain limit by the directors only with special authorisation which had not been given). As to the harshness of the ultra vires doctrine see further *Re Jon Beauforte (London) Ltd* [1953] Ch 131, [1953] 1 All ER 634; *Re Introductions Ltd, Introductions Ltd v National Provincial Bank Ltd* [1970] Ch 199, [1968] 1 All ER 887, CA.
2 Ie the Companies Act 1985 s 35 (re-enacting the European Communities Act 1972 s 9(1)).
3 See the Companies Act 1985 s 35(1) (repealed).
4 See ibid s 35(2) (repealed).
5 See ibid s 35 (as substituted) and para 1107 post.
6 See ibid s 35A (as substituted) and para 1108 post.
7 See ibid s 35B (as substituted) and para 1109 post.
8 See the cases cited in note 1 supra.

9 See *International Sales and Agencies Ltd v Marcus* [1982] 3 All ER 551, [1982] 2 CMLR 46; *Rolled Steel Products (Holdings) Ltd v British Steel Corpn* [1986] Ch 246, [1985] 3 All ER 52, CA; and TRUSTS vol 48 (Reissue) para 585 et seq.

B. POWERS UNDER THE COMPANY'S CONSTITUTION; STATUTORY POWERS

1094. Company's objects. The memorandum of association of a company is its charter, defining the objects of its existence and operations[1].

The memorandum must state the objects of the company[2]. This means that it must delimit and identify the objects in such a manner that the reader may identify the field of industry within which the corporate activities are to be confined[3]. The registrar of companies may refuse to register a memorandum which does not comply with the provisions of the Companies Act 1985[3].

The memorandum usually sets out as objects of the company many of the powers which the company would be entitled to exercise in carrying out its objects[4]. There is no objection to objects being framed by reference to the directors' opinion as to whether they may be advantageously carried on by the company in connection with or as ancillary to its general business[5].

Notwithstanding the above provisions, the validity of an act done by a company may not be called into question on the ground of lack of capacity by reason of anything in the company's memorandum[6]; and, in favour of a person dealing with a company in good faith, the power of the board of directors to bind the company is deemed to be free of any limitation under the company's constitution[7].

1 As to alteration of the memorandum see para 99 ante and para 1184 post.
2 See the Companies Act 1985 s 2(1)(c) and para 84 ante.
3 *Cotman v Brougham* [1918] AC 514 at 522, HL.
4 *Cotman v Brougham* [1918] AC 514 at 522, 523, HL (where the practice of inserting powers in the objects clause is criticised). The registrar of companies does not refuse to register a memorandum on the ground that its objects are stated with too great particularity, but he would probably do so if they were stated vaguely or too generally. The registration, if made, is conclusive: *Cotman v Brougham* supra at 522; and see para 86 note 1 ante.
5 *Bell Houses Ltd v City Wall Properties Ltd* [1966] 2 QB 656, [1966] 2 All ER 674, CA; *H A Stephenson & Son Ltd v Gillanders, Arbuthnot & Co* (1931) 45 CLR 476 (Aust HC); *H & A Logging Co Ltd v Random Services Corpn Ltd* (1967) 63 DLR (2d) 6 (BC CA); *American Home Assurance Co v Tjmond Properties Ltd* [1984] NZLR 452.
6 See the Companies Act 1985 s 35(1) (as substituted) and para 1107 post.
7 See ibid s 35A(1) (as substituted), para 1093 ante and para 1108 post.

1095. Construction of objects clause of memorandum. The ordinary rules applicable to construing documents apply to the construction of the objects clause of a memorandum of association. The first question is, what is the fair construction of the memorandum as a whole? General words following a particular specification may be construed ejusdem generis, but there is no special rule of interpretation by reference to what are supposed to be the main or principal objects of a company where the question is whether something done or proposed to be done is ultra vires[1]; though this consideration may be of importance where the question is whether the company ought to be wound up on the ground that its substratum is gone[2]. Although the subjective intent with which a transaction is carried out by the directors may result in a charge of misfeasance against them, and, if participated in by the other contracting party, may entitle the company to rescind the contract, such intent is irrelevant to the question whether the transaction is intra vires the company[3].

Where the memorandum provides that the objects set out in each sub-clause of the objects clause of the memorandum are to be construed as separate objects and not limited by reference to any other clause or the name of the company, such a provision operates to make each of those objects intra vires[4], but it does not operate to turn what is properly a power into an object in itself[5].

Where the company's memorandum states that the object of the company is to carry on business as a general commercial company:

(1) the object of the company is to carry on any trade or business whatsoever; and

(2) the company has power to do all such things as are incidental or conducive to the carrying on of any trade or business by it[6].

1 *Cotman v Brougham* [1918] AC 514, HL; *Pedlar v Road Block Gold Mines of India Ltd* [1905] 2 Ch 427; cf *Stephens v Mysore Reefs (Kangundy) Mining Co Ltd* [1902] 1 Ch 745; *Re German Date Coffee Co* (1882) 20 ChD 169 at 188, CA; *Re New Finance and Mortgage Co Ltd* [1975] Ch 420, [1975] 1 All ER 684 ('and merchants generally' covers all purely commercial occupations). The name of the company may be important in construing wide objects: see *Re Crown Bank* (1890) 44 ChD 634; *Re Coolgardie Consolidated Gold Mines Ltd* (1897) 76 LT 269, CA; and see *Re London and Edinburgh Shipping Co Ltd* 1909 SC 1; *Butler v Northern Territories Mines of Australia Ltd* (1906) 96 LT 41.

   For some purposes (see eg the Rating and Valuation (Miscellaneous Provisions) Act 1955 s 8(1) (repealed)), it is necessary to discover what is the main object of a company. This inquiry involves not merely the construction of the memorandum but also evidence on the further question of which activities have in fact been so far the main objects: *North of England Zoological Society v Chester RDC* [1959] 3 All ER 116, [1959] 1 WLR 773, CA. As to the construction of a memorandum of association on an originating summons see para 1177 post.

   As to the abolition of the doctrine of ultra vires in favour of a third party dealing with the company in good faith see para 1093 ante and paras 1107-1109 post.

2 See para 2209 post.

3 *Charterbridge Corpn Ltd v Lloyds Bank Ltd* [1970] Ch 62, [1969] 2 All ER 1185.

4 *Cotman v Brougham* [1918] AC 514, HL, overruling on this point *Stephens v Mysore Reefs (Kangundy) Mining Co Ltd* [1902] 1 Ch 745; *Anglo-Overseas Agencies Ltd v Green* [1961] 1 QB 1, [1960] 3 All ER 244.

5 *Re Introductions Ltd, Introductions Ltd v National Provincial Bank Ltd* [1970] Ch 199, [1969] 1 All ER 887, CA (where a clause conferring a power to borrow was held incapable of being a wholly independent object). As to mitigation of the harshness of the ultra vires rule as exemplified in this case in respect of a third party dealing with the company in good faith see para 1093 ante and paras 1107-1109 post. Cf *Re Horsley & Weight Ltd* [1982] Ch 442, [1982] 3 All ER 1045, CA (where a provision of the memorandum relating to the granting of pensions was construed as an independent object of the company). See also *Rolled Steel Products (Holdings) Ltd v British Steel Corpn* [1986] Ch 246, [1985] 3 All ER 52, CA (but as to this case see para 1102 text and note 5 post).

6 See the Companies Act 1985 s 3A (as added) and para 86 ante.

1096. Construction of contemporaneous memorandum and articles. The articles of association are subordinate to the memorandum[1]. However, where, as is usually the case, the memorandum and articles are contemporaneous documents, the ordinary rule of construction applies, according to which an ambiguity in one document may be explained by the other or an inconsistency may be explained by taking the two together[2]. As regards matters which the Companies Act 1985 requires to be in the memorandum, that instrument is dominant, and the articles cannot be read to modify its provisions[3]. As regards matters which are, but need not have been, stated in the memorandum, such as the rights of different classes of shareholders, the memorandum cannot be overridden by the articles[4], although the articles may be referred to for the purpose of explaining or supplementing its provisions as to such matters[5].

1 See para 146 ante.
2 *Anderson's Case* (1877) 7 ChD 75 at 99, CA; *Harrison v Mexican Rly Co* (1875) LR 19 Eq 358; *London Financial Association v Kelk* (1884) 26 ChD 107 at 135; *Re South Durham Brewery Co* (1885) 31 ChD 261, CA. Cf *Angostura Bitters (Dr J G B Siegert & Sons) Ltd v Kerr* [1933] AC 550, PC; and *Re Duncan Gilmour & Co Ltd, Duncan Gilmour & Co Ltd v Inman* [1952] 2 All ER 871 (where there was no ambiguity in the memorandum, which accordingly prevailed).
3 *Guinness v Land Corpn of Ireland Ltd* (1882) 22 ChD 349 at 381, CA; *Re Phoenix Bessemer Steel Co* (1875) 44 LJ Ch 683; and see *Ashbury Railway Carriage and Iron Co v Riche* (1875) LR 7 HL 653.
4 *Andrews v Gas Meter Co* [1897] 1 Ch 361 at 369, CA; *Re Southern Brazilian Rio Grande do Sul Rly Co Ltd* [1905] 2 Ch 78; and see *Ashbury v Watson* (1885) 30 ChD 376, CA (subsequent alteration of articles).
5 *Re Southern Brazilian Rio Grande do Sul Rly Co Ltd* [1905] 2 Ch 78 at 84; and see the cases cited in note 2 supra.

1097. Meaning of 'ultra vires'. The term 'ultra vires' in its proper sense denotes some act or transaction on the part of a corporation which, although not unlawful or contrary to public policy if done by an individual, is yet beyond the corporation's legitimate powers as defined by the statute under which it is formed, or the statutes which are applicable to it, or by its memorandum of association; although in favour of a third party dealing with the company in good faith the doctrine no longer applies[1]. The term is not appropriate in relation to any act or transaction which is beyond the lawful powers of any person. Thus, the term is used in two senses: beyond the powers of the company; and beyond the powers of the directors under the authority conferred on them by the company or its constitution[2]. Acts of directors which should not be undertaken by them without the sanction of the members of the company are, however, often described as acts ultra vires the directors[3].

Exercises by the directors of powers for purposes other than the promotion of the objects of the company are also often denominated as being ultra vires[4].

1 See para 1093 ante and paras 1107–1109 post.
2 The term was also used in two different ways in relation exclusively to the powers of a company in *Rolled Steel Products (Holdings) Ltd v British Steel Corpn* [1982] Ch 478, [1982] 3 All ER 1057 per Vinelott J. On appeal, however, the Court of Appeal considered that such use of the term could lead to confusion and that the term should be confined rigidly to 'describing acts which are beyond the corporate capacity of a company': see [1986] Ch 246 at 297, [1985] 3 All ER 52 at 87, CA per Slade LJ and at 303 and at 91 per Browne-Wilkinson LJ.
3 As to the director's liability to the company for causing it to commit ultra vires acts see para 615 ante; and as to his liability in tort see para 621 ante.
4 See para 1102 post. As to the proposition that no exercise of a power can be ultra vires if the exercise is in literal compliance with the wording of the power, irrespective of its object, see para 1102 text and note 5 post.

1098. Acts ultra vires the company. Subject always to the exception in favour of a person dealing with the company in good faith[1], the company's objects as stated in its memorandum cannot be departed from[2] unless and until altered under the Companies Act 1985[3]. An attempted departure is as invalid as if the memorandum were a statute of incorporation; it is ultra vires the company and cannot be validated by the assent of a general meeting of the members or of every individual member[4], or by taking judgment against the company by consent[5], or by estoppel[6].

A transaction will not be ultra vires the company if it falls within the proper construction of its memorandum, even if the directors cause the transaction to be entered into for an improper reason. This may have consequences, such as claims by the company against the directors for misfeasance or against the other contracting party for rescission, but cannot render the contract ultra vires[7]. A transaction which is beyond the powers conferred on the directors but within the powers of the company may, however, be ratified by an ordinary resolution of the members in general meeting, although to authorise such acts in the future an alteration of the articles by special resolution is required[8].

Some of the statutory forms of memorandum include among the objects of a company 'the doing of all such other things as are incidental or conducive to the attainment of the above object'[9]. Even without these words the same powers would be implied[10].

A corporation in a matter intra vires cannot be heard to deny a transaction to which all the shareholders have given their assent, even when such assent has been given in an informal manner, or by conduct, as distinct from a formal resolution at a duly convened meeting[11]. If shareholders require directors to make certain decisions, or approve the decisions which the directors have already taken, then such decisions become the acts of the company, and binding on it, so that thereafter it cannot sue its directors in negligence[12]. It is otherwise if the shareholders or directors are acting fraudulently[13].

1 See para 1093 ante and paras 1107-1109 post.
2 As to the alteration of objects set out in the memorandum see para 1184 et seq post. See also CORPORATIONS.
3 See para 99 ante.
4 *Ashbury Railway Carriage and Iron Co v Riche* (1875) LR 7 HL 653; *East Anglian Rlys Co v Eastern Counties Rly Co* (1851) 11 CB 775; *Towers v African Tug Co* [1904] 1 Ch 558 at 566, CA.
5 *Great North-West Central Rly Co v Charlebois* [1899] AC 114 at 124, PC; *Re Jon Beauforte (London) Ltd* [1953] Ch 131, [1953] 1 All ER 634 (cited in para 1093 note 1 ante).
6 *Bishop v Balkis Consolidated Co Ltd* (1890) 25 QBD 77 at 84 (affd 25 QBD 512, CA); *Re Home and Foreign Investment and Agency Co Ltd* [1912] 1 Ch 72 at 81; and see *British Mutual Banking Co Ltd v Charnwood Forest Rly Co* (1887) 18 QBD 714 at 718, CA; *Balkis Consolidated Co v Tomkinson* [1893] AC 396 at 407, 415, HL; *South London Greyhound Racecourses Ltd v Wake* [1931] 1 Ch 496 at 506.
7 *Charterbridge Corpn Ltd v Lloyds Bank Ltd* [1970] Ch 62, [1969] 2 All ER 1185. As to the exercise of the company's powers cf para 1102 note 5 post.
8 *Grant v United Kingdom Switchback Rlys Co* (1888) 40 ChD 135, CA; and see *Hogg v Cramphorn* [1967] Ch 254, [1966] 3 All ER 420; *Bamford v Bamford* [1970] Ch 212, [1968] 2 All ER 655; para 1125 post.
9 See the Companies (Tables A to F) Regulations 1985, SI 1985/805, reg 2, Schedule, Tables B, C, D, E. Cf *Bell Houses Ltd v City Wall Properties Ltd* [1966] 2 QB 656, [1966] 2 All ER 674, CA (power to carry on any business which directors considered could be carried on advantageously with its general business).
10 *A-G v Great Eastern Rly Co* (1880) 5 App Cas 473 at 481, HL; *Dundee Harbour Trustees v Nicol* [1915] AC 550 at 556, 557, HL; *Deuchar v Gas Light and Coke Co* [1925] AC 691, HL; and see *City of Winnipeg v Canadian Pacific Rly Co* [1953] AC 618 at 630, [1953] 2 All ER 988 at 993, PC.
11 *Walton v Bank of Nova Scotia* (1965) 52 DLR (2d) 506; *CPHC Holding Co Ltd v Western Pacific Trust Co* (1973) 36 DLR (3d) 431 (BC SC); *Re Horsley & Weight Ltd* [1982] Ch 442, [1982] 3 All ER 1045, CA; *Multinational Gas and Petrochemical Co v Multinational Gas and Petrochemical Services Ltd* [1983] Ch 258, [1983] 2 All ER 563, CA.
12 *A-G for Canada v Standard Trust Co of New York* [1911] AC 498, PC; *Re Express Engineering Works Ltd* [1920] 1 Ch 466, CA; *Re Horsley & Weight Ltd* [1982] Ch 442, [1982] 3 All ER 1045, CA (where Cuming Bruce and Templeman LJJ reserved their views on the situation where what had been done by the directors amounted to misfeasance: see at 455, 1055 per Cuming Bruce LJ and at 456, 1056 per Templeman LJ).
13 *A-G Reference (No 2 of 1982)* [1984] QB 624, [1984] 2 All ER 216, CA.

1099. Examples of ultra vires acts. Subject always to the exception in favour of a person dealing with the company in good faith[1], it is not sufficient for the proposed transaction to be convenient if it is not incidental[2]. In the absence of a special power in the memorandum, it is ultra vires for any company to take shares in another carrying on a different class of business[3]; for one company to amalgamate with another company[4]; for a company which has power to invest on second mortgages, and which is a second mortgagee, to guarantee payment of the prior mortgage debt for good consideration[5]; for a company with power to lend to guarantee the debts of a company promoted by it[6]; unless first sanctioned[7], for a company to treat its former employees not merely generously but beyond all entitlement[8]; for a company authorised by its memorandum to make and deal in railway carriages to purchase a concession for a foreign railway[9]; for a bill-broking company to take shares in a banking company for the purpose of increasing its own business[10]; and for a body dedicated to preventing cruelty to animals to pay money over to a political party whose aims include such an aim, but with no obligation to expend the money in any particular manner[11].

1 See paras 1093 ante and paras 1107-1109 post.
2 *LCC v A-G* [1902] AC 165, HL; *A-G v Mersey Rly Co* [1907] AC 415, HL.
3 *Re Lands Allotment Co* [1894] 1 Ch 616, CA; cf *Re Barned's Banking Co, ex p Contract Corpn* (1867) 3 Ch App 105 (where there was power in the memorandum). In the case of a banking company no express power is required, as it is an inherent part of its business that it should advance money on securities such as shares: see *Royal Bank of India's Case* (1869) 4 Ch App 252; *Re Financial Corpn, Goodson's Claim* (1880) 28 WR 760. In *Re William Thomas & Co* [1915] 1 Ch 325, a company with a power of amalgamating was held to have a power to sell part of its undertaking for shares, although apart from the power of amalgamation there was no other authority for it to hold shares in another company. As to accepting shares by way of compromise and not for investment see *Re Lands Allotment Co* supra.
4 *Re European Society Arbitration Acts, ex p British Nation Life Assurance Association (Liquidators)* (1878) 8 ChD 679, CA. A power to amalgamate does not include a power to force partly-paid shares on a member: *Re European Society Arbitration Acts, ex p British Nation Life Assurance Association (Liquidators)* supra. As to amalgamation generally see para 1460 et seq post.
5 *Small v Smith* (1884) 10 App Cas 119, HL.
6 *Re Queen Anne and Garden Mansions Co* (1894) 1 Mans 460.
7 See para 1102 post.
8 *Parke v Daily News Ltd* [1962] Ch 927, [1962] 2 All ER 929.
9 *British and Foreign Railway Plant Co Ltd v Ashbury Carriage and Iron Co Ltd, Smith v Ashbury etc Co* (1869) 20 LT 360; *Ashbury Railway Carriage and Iron Co v Riche* (1875) LR 7 HL 653; and see *Guinness v Land Corpn of Ireland Ltd* (1882) 22 ChD 349, CA.
10 *Joint Stock Discount Co v Brown* (1866) LR 3 Eq 139 (subsequent proceedings (1869) LR 8 Eq 381); cf *Re West of England Bank, ex p Booker* (1880) 14 ChD 317.
11 *Simmonds v Heffer* [1983] BCLC 298.

1100. Examples of acts not ultra vires. It is not ultra vires for a trading company[1], without any special powers to do so, to pay a pension to the family of a deceased officer[2]; or to give gratuities to its employees[3]; or to pay a loss not within the terms of a policy[4]; or to pay a reasonable brokerage for placing its shares[5]; or to let off a large part of a hotel for government offices[6]; or to take a larger house than necessary and underlet a portion[7]. A company established to buy a special brewery, but with general powers, may buy a different one, even though it will not have enough money left to buy the first[8]. A trading company may borrow, with or without security[9]; or accept bills of exchange[10]; or deposit its title deeds to secure an overdraft[11]; or issue debenture stock as collateral security[12].

A company formed to work a patent may purchase it[13]. A company whose powers include that of promoting may promote another company, subscribe shares, and pay the expenses of the promotion[14]. A chemical company may distribute money to scientific institutions in the United Kingdom for the furtherance of scientific education and research[15]. A company formed for the development of salt concessions and the manufacture of salt may export salt[16].

In these and similar cases it is a question dependent on the true construction of the memorandum of association and all the circumstances of the case whether the proceeding in question will facilitate or is otherwise incidental to the business which the company was formed to carry on[17]. In conducting its business a company may do what any other person conducting the same kind of business may do[18]. No act of the company can be ultra vires if on the true construction of its memorandum it is intra vires[19].

An act of a company is not ultra vires merely because it is in breach of a statutory provision which renders the act voidable[20].

1   Where a company is registered without the word 'limited' or words 'plc' but with limited liability, the power to give pensions depends on its memorandum: *Cyclists' Touring Club v Hopkinson* [1910] 1 Ch 179.

2   *Henderson v Bank of Australasia* (1888) 40 ChD 170; cf *Re Lee, Behrens & Co Ltd* [1932] 2 Ch 46, applied in *Re W & M Roith Ltd* [1967] 1 All ER 427, [1967] 1 WLR 432, but criticised in *Charterbridge Corpn Ltd v Lloyds Bank Ltd* [1970] Ch 62, [1969] 2 All ER 118 and purportedly overruled in *Rolled Steel Products (Holdings) Ltd v British Steel Corpn* [1986] Ch 246, [1985] 3 All ER 52, CA; but see para 1102 note 5 post. As to income tax exemption in respect of the income of approved retirement benefit schemes see SOCIAL SECURITY AND PENSIONS. Company pension schemes are sometimes set up by arrangement with insurance companies and sometimes by establishing a trust complying with the requirements of the Social Security Act 1973 s 69 (as amended) and regulations thereunder, thus gaining exemption from the rule against perpetuities: see ibid s 69(1) and PERPETUITIES vol 35 (Reissue) para 1044.

3   *Hampson v Price's Patent Candle Co* (1876) 45 LJ Ch 437; cf *Warren v Lambeth Waterworks* (1905) 21 TLR 685; and see *Re Birkbeck Permanent Benefit Building Society* [1913] 1 Ch 400.

4   *Taunton v Royal Insurance Co* (1864) 2 Hem & M 135; and see para 1102 post.

5   *Metropolitan Coal Consumers' Association v Scrimgeour* [1895] 2 QB 604, CA. As to brokerage see para 200 ante.

6   *Simpson v Westminster Palace Hotel Co* (1860) 8 HL Cas 712.

7   *Re London and Colonial Co, Horsey's Claim* (1868) LR 5 Eq 561.

8   *Syers v Brighton Co Ltd, Wright v Brighton Brewery Co Ltd* (1864) 11 LT 560; cf *Re Langham Skating Rink Co* (1877) 5 ChD 669 at 685, CA.

9   See para 1234 post.

10 *Peruvian Rlys Co v Thames and Mersey Marine Insurance Co, Re Peruvian Rlys Co* (1867) 2 Ch App 617, distinguishing *Bateman v Mid-Wales Rly Co* (1866) LR 1 CP 499.

11 *Re Patent File Co, ex p Birmingham Banking Co* (1870) 6 Ch App 83.

12 *Whitehaven Joint Stock Banking Co v Reed* (1886) 54 LT 360, CA.

13 *Leifchild's Case* (1865) LR 1 Eq 231.

14 *Butler v Northern Territories Mines of Australia* (1906) 96 LT 41; *Re Financial Corpn, Goodson's Claim* (1880) 28 WR 760.

15 *Evans v Brunner, Mond & Co Ltd* [1921] 1 Ch 359.

16 *Egyptian Salt and Soda Co Ltd v Port Said Association Ltd* [1931] AC 677, PC.

17 A company may purchase land on a joint account (*London Financial Association v Kelk* (1884) 26 ChD 107); an insurance company may compromise claims (*Bath's Case* (1878) 8 ChD 334, CA); a banking company may be empowered to guarantee payment of interest on debentures in another company (*Re West of England Bank, ex p Booker* (1880) 14 ChD 317); a company may be empowered to guarantee the debenture stock of another company (*Re Friary Holyroyd and Healy's Breweries Ltd* (1922) 67 Sol Jo 97, 126); a newspaper company may pay the cost of defending the editor in a libel action (*Breay v Royal British Nurses' Association* [1897] 2 Ch 272, CA); a colliery company may purchase a colliery (*Re Baglan Hall Colliery Co* (1870) 5 Ch App 346; *Johns v Balfour* (1889) 5 TLR 389), or sell land to a builder for the erection of cottages (*Re Kingsbury Collieries Ltd and Moore's Contract* [1907] 2 Ch 259).

18 *Breay v Royal British Nurses' Association* [1897] 2 Ch 272 at 277, CA. Cf *Investment Trust Corpn Ltd v Singapore Traction Co Ltd* [1935] Ch 615 (where it was held to be intra vires for one company to get rid of the management by another company whose remuneration was a charge on annual profits by payment of a capital sum raised by the issue of debenture stock).

19 *Bell Houses Ltd v City Wall Properties Ltd*]1966] 2 QB 656, [1966] 2 All ER 674, CA; *Charterbridge Corpn Ltd v Lloyds Bank Ltd* [1970] Ch 62, [1969] 2 All ER 1185. As to the true construction of powers see para 1102 note 5 post.
20 *Finance and Issue Ltd v Canadian Produce Corpn Ltd* [1905] 1 Ch 37 at 45.

1101. Power of company to provide for employees on cessation or transfer of business. The powers of a company include, if they would not otherwise do so apart from these provisions, power to make the following provision for the benefit of persons employed or formerly employed by the company or any of its subsidiaries[1], that is to say, provision in connection with the cessation or the transfer to any person of the whole or part of the undertaking of the company or that subsidiary[2].

The power so conferred is exercisable notwithstanding that its exercise is not in the best interests of the company[3]. The power which a company may exercise by virtue only of the above provisions may be exercised by the company only if sanctioned:

(1) in a case not falling within heads (2) or (3) below, by an ordinary resolution of the company; or

(2) if so authorised by the memorandum or articles, a resolution of the directors; or

(3) if the memorandum or articles require the exercise of the power to be sanctioned by a resolution of the company of some other description for which more than a simple majority of the members voting is necessary, with the sanction of a resolution of that description;

and, in any case, after compliance with any other requirements of the memorandum or articles applicable to its exercise[4].

Any payment which may be made by a company under the above provisions may, if made before the commencement of any winding up of the company, be made out of profits of the company which are available for dividend[5].

1 For the meaning of 'subsidiary' see para 827 ante.
2 Companies Act 1985 s 719(1). This provision negatives the effect of the decisions in *Hutton v West Cork Rly Co* (1883) 23 ChD 654, CA; *Stroud v Royal Aquarium and Summer and Winter Garden Society Ltd* (1903) 89 LT 243; *Warren v Lambeth Waterworks* (1905) 21 TLR 685; *Parke v Daily News Ltd* [1962] Ch 927, [1962] 2 All ER 929.
    For the purposes of the Companies Act 1985 s 719, a company which immediately before the commencement of the Companies Act 1989 s 144(1) (ie 1 November 1990) was a subsidiary of another company is not to be treated as ceasing to be such a subsidiary by reason of s 144(1) (substituted meaning of 'subsidiary', 'holding company' and 'wholly-owned subsidiary': see para 827 ante) coming into force: s 144(4), Sch 18 para 36.
3 Companies Act 1985 s 719(2).
4 Ibid s 719(3).
5 Ibid s 719(4).

1102. Ultra vires exercise of powers. Although contained in the memorandum of association, any provision which is in its essential nature a power[1] and not an object[2] will be treated as being such; inclusion in the memorandum does not turn what is properly a power into an object[3]. Any such provision is subject, in the same manner as an implied power[4], to the limitation that it is only an exercise of that power for the purposes of furthering the objects of the company which is intra vires[5]. Any transaction not so effected is prima facie void[6].

Since this involves an inquiry into the objective of the directors in carrying out the transaction which the other party concerned, typically but not exclusively a lender[7], is not bound to carry out[8] (as distinct, for example, from ensuring that any conditions actually surrounding the power as set out in the memorandum have been fulfilled) the law has stopped short of depriving an unsuspecting third party of a remedy[9]. So far as he is concerned, it is sufficient if he has no knowledge that the transaction, which could be a perfectly proper one, is not such[10]. Accordingly, even apart from the abolition of the doctrine of ultra vires in favour of a person dealing with the company in good faith[11], if such a person is not on notice as to the intentions of the directors regarding the use to which the benefit of what is capable of being a perfectly proper contract is put, the company will not be allowed to plead the defence of ultra vires against him[12].

In those cases where there has been an ultra vires exercise of a power, the remedy of tracing is available to the other party to the contract[13].

1   See *Re Introductions Ltd, Introductions Ltd v National Provincial Bank Ltd* [1970] Ch 199, [1969] 1 All ER 887, CA.

2   See *Re Horsley & Weight Ltd* [1982] Ch 442, [1982] 3 All ER 1045, CA (where a provision of the memorandum relating to the granting of pensions was construed as an independent object of the company). Cf *Re W and M Roith Ltd* [1967] 1 All ER 427, [1967] 1 WLR 432.

3   See *Re Introductions Ltd, Introductions Ltd v National Provincial Bank Ltd* [1970] Ch 199, [1969] 1 All ER 887, CA. 'You cannot convert a power into an object merely by saying so': *Re Introductions Ltd, Introductions Ltd v National Provincial Bank Ltd* supra at 210 and at 889 per Harman LJ.

4   If the terms of the power did, on its true construction or import, authorise its exercise for any purpose other than the fulfilment of the company's objects, such power would itself be ultra vires: see *Re Birkbeck Permanent Benefit Building Society* [1912] 2 Ch 183 at 230, CA per Buckley LJ.

5   *Sinclair v Brougham* [1914] AC 398, HL; *Colman v Eastern Counties Rly Co* (1846) 10 Beav 1; *Re Lee, Behrens & Co Ltd* [1932] 2 Ch 46; *Re Jon Beauforte (London) Ltd* [1953] Ch 131, [1953] 1 All ER 634; *Re Introductions Ltd, Introductions Ltd v National Provincial Bank Ltd* [1970] Ch 199, [1969] 1 All ER 887, CA; *International Sales and Agencies Ltd v Marcus* [1982] 3 All ER 551, [1982] 2 CMLR 46; cf *Charterbridge Corpn Ltd v Lloyds Bank Ltd* [1970] Ch 62, [1969] 2 All ER 1185 and *Rolled Steel Products (Holdings) Ltd v British Steel Corpn* [1986] Ch 246, [1985] 3 All ER 52, CA, in neither of which cases was any reference made to *Sinclair v Brougham* supra. *Rolled Steel Products (Holdings) Ltd v British Steel Corpn* supra sought to explain *Re Introductions Ltd, Introductions Ltd v National Provincial Bank Ltd* supra as involving not the doctrine of ultra vires but the rule in *Royal British Bank v Turquand* (1856) 6 E & B 327 (see para 1137 post).

    The difference between the two views, having regard to the Companies Act 1985 ss 35-35B (as substituted) (see para 1093 ante and paras 1107-1109 post), will now be material only in cases where ss 35-35B (as substituted) do not apply because there is no 'dealing' ie typically in the case of the making of a gratuitous payment as in *Re Lee, Behrens & Co Ltd* supra which was (consistently with this view) disapproved in *Charterbridge Corpn Ltd v Lloyds Bank Ltd* supra, and purported to be overruled by *Rolled Steel Products (Holdings) Ltd v British Steel Corpn* supra. Cf *Ashbury Rly Carriage and Iron Co v Riche* (1875) LR 7 HL 653 (words 'general contractors' construed in light of other clauses of memorandum).

6   *Sinclair v Brougham* [1914] AC 398, HL. For an example of a case where the intentions of the directors might have made an action otherwise ultra vires intra vires see *Re Lands Allotment Co* [1894] 1 Ch 616, CA.

7   See *Sinclair v Brougham* [1914] AC 398, HL (lender); *Re Jon Beauforte (London) Ltd* [1953] Ch 131, [1953] 1 All ER 634 (suppliers of veneer and coke).

8   *Re David Payne & Co Ltd* [1904] 2 Ch 608, CA; *Cotman v Brougham* [1918] AC 514 at 521, HL per Lord Parker; *Re Introductions Ltd, Introductions Ltd v National Provincial Bank Ltd* [1970] Ch 199 at 210, [1969] 1 All ER 887 at 890, CA per Harman LJ.

9   *Re David Payne Ltd* [1904] 2 Ch 608, CA.

10   For cases where the other party to the transaction was on notice see *Sinclair v Brougham* [1914] AC 398, HL (loans); *Re Jon Beauforte (London) Ltd* [1953] Ch 131, [1953] 1 All ER 634 (supply of veneers and coke).

11   Ie by the Companies Act 1985 ss 35-35B (as substituted): see para 1093 ante and paras 1107-1109 post.

12   *Re David Payne Ltd* [1904] 2 Ch 608, CA.

13   Ie as in *Sinclair v Brougham* [1914] AC 398, HL and *Re Jon Beauforte (London) Ltd* [1953] Ch 131, [1953] 1 All ER 634 (where the order dismissing appeals from the liquidator's rejection of proofs expressly reserved all questions of tracing).

1103. Company exceeding statutory powers.
Even if apparently authorised to do so by its articles or by its memorandum of association[1], a company cannot lawfully

do anything beyond the powers given by the Companies Act 1985[2]. Thus, it cannot purchase its own shares[3] save in compliance with the statutory requirements[4]; or, except in certain cases, lend money for the purchase of its shares[5]; or issue unauthorised capital[6] or reduce or repay capital without complying with the statutory requirements[7]; or distribute bonus shares gratuitously[8]; or allot shares at a discount[9]; or pay dividends on shares out of capital[10]; or make presents to directors out of capital[11]; or make payments for the benefit of a section only of the shareholders, such as paying the costs of a prosecution for libel[12] or the costs of prosecuting an action not instituted by itself, even though it is for the company's benefit[13].

1 *Trevor v Whitworth* (1887) 12 App Cas 409 at 430, HL; *Re Castle Crag SS Co, Raine's Case* (1888) 4 TLR 302; *Re Mersina and Adana Construction Co* (1889) 5 TLR 680; *General Property Investment Co v Matheson's Trustees* (1888) 16 R 282.

2 This position is not affected by the Companies Act 1985 ss 35-35B (as substituted) (see para 1093 ante and paras 1107-1109 post), but in respect of any lawful transaction entered into by a person dealing with the company in good faith, the power of the directors to bind the company or to authorise others to do so is deemed to be free of any limitation under the company's constitution: see *Re Crossmore Electrical and Civil Engineering Ltd* [1989] BCLC 137; *Re a Company (No 004502 of 1988), ex p Johnson* [1992] BCLC 701.

3 *Trevor v Whitworth* (1887) 12 App Cas 409, HL (overruling *Re Dronfield Silkstone Coal Co* (1880) 17 ChD 76); *Re Balgooley Distillery Co* (1886) 17 LR Ir 239, CA; *Taylor v Pilsen, Joel and General Electric Light Co* (1884) 27 ChD 268; *Phosphate of Lime Co Ltd v Green* (1871) LR 7 CP 43; *Cree v Somervail* (1879) 4 App Cas 648, HL.

4 See paras 222, 232 ante.

5 See para 273 et seq ante.

6 *Bank of Hindustan, China and Japan Ltd v Alison* (1871) LR 6 CP 222 (where an applicant for new shares was held not estopped from denying that he was a shareholder).

7 See para 215 et seq ante.

8 *Re Eddystone Marine Insurance Co* [1893] 3 Ch 9, CA; *Welton v Saffery* [1897] AC 299, HL.

9 See paras 187, 465 ante.

10 See para 701 et seq ante.

11 *Re George Newman & Co* [1895] 1 Ch 674, CA; and see para 272 ante.

12 *Pickering v Stephenson* (1872) LR 14 Eq 322 at 340; *Studdert v Grosvenor* (1886) 33 ChD 528. These two decisions were adversely commented on by Lindley LJ in *Cullerne v London and Suburban General Permanent Building Society* (1890) 25 QBD 485 at 490, CA, on the question of the directors' liability to repay funds improperly paid ultra vires the company.

13 *Kernaghan v Williams* (1868) LR 6 Eq 228; *Re Liverpool Household Stores Association* (1890) 59 LJ Ch 616.

1104. Prevention of ultra vires acts. Any shareholder has the right to resist any attempt by a company to act ultra vires, and the court will interpose on his behalf by way of injunction[1]. If an agreement is entered into by two companies, an injunction will not be granted to restrain one of them from acting under the agreement at the suit of a shareholder of the other company, on the ground that, so far as regards the former company, the agreement is ultra vires[2].

Proceedings by representative shareholders to protect the rights of members generally are discussed subsequently[3].

1 *Simpson v Westminster Palace Hotel Co* (1860) 8 HL Cas 712 at 717; and see *Mosely v Koffyfontein Mines Ltd* [1911] 1 Ch 73, CA; affd sub nom *Koffyfontein Mines Ltd v Mosely* [1911] AC 409, HL. It is thought that this position is unaffected by the Companies Act 1985 ss 35-35B (as substituted) (see para 1093 ante and paras 1107-1109 post); but, if the contract has already been entered into in good faith on the part of the other contracting party, clearly no injunction could be obtained to prevent the contract being fulfilled. An injunction will not be granted to restrain a company from doing something within its objects on the ground that it will thereby be incapacitated from doing something else within its objects: *Syers v Brighton Brewery Co Ltd, Wright v Brighton Brewery Co Ltd* (1864) 11 LT 560.

2 *Maunsell v Midland Great Western (Ireland) Rly Co* (1863) 1 Hem & M 130. See also para 1093 ante and paras 1107-1109 post.

3 See para 1171 post; cf para 1111 post.

1105. Guarantee of ultra vires act. A guarantee by an individual of the performance by a company of an ultra vires contract is enforceable if it is made in good faith and the contract is not illegal or contrary to public policy[1].

1   *Garrard v James* [1925] Ch 616; *Chambers v Manchester and Milford Rly Co* (1864) 5 B & S 588; *Yorkshire Railway Wagon Co v Maclure* (1881) 19 ChD 478 (affd on other grounds (1882) 21 ChD 309, CA).

1106. Recovery of money paid under ultra vires contract. A claim for money had and received is not maintainable for money paid to a company under an ultra vires contract of borrowing[1], although premiums paid in respect of an ultra vires policy may be recoverable[2].

1   *Sinclair v Brougham* [1914] AC 398, HL. As to tracing see para 1237 post.
2   *Re Phoenix Life Assurance Co* (1862) 2 John & H 441; *Flood v Irish Provident Assurance Co Ltd and Hibernian Bank Ltd* [1912] 2 Ch 597n, 46 ILT 214, CA; and see INSURANCE vol 25 (Reissue) para 447.

C. MODIFICATIONS OF THE ULTRA VIRES DOCTRINE

1107. Company's capacity not limited by its memorandum. The validity of an act done by a company may not be called into question on the ground of lack of capacity by reason of anything in the company's memorandum[1].

A member of the company may bring proceedings to restrain the doing of an act which would otherwise be beyond the company's capacity; but no such proceedings lie in respect of an act to be done in fulfilment of a legal obligation arising from a previous act of the company[2].

It remains the duty of the directors to observe any limitations on their powers flowing from the company's memorandum; and action by the directors which would otherwise[3] be beyond the company's capacity may only be ratified by the company by special resolution[4]. A resolution ratifying such action does not affect any liability incurred by the directors or any other person; and relief from any such liability must be agreed to separately by special resolution[4].

1   Companies Act 1985 s 35(1) (substituted by the Companies Act 1989 s 108(1)). The operation of the Companies Act 1985 s 35 (as substituted) is restricted by the Charities Act 1993 s 65(1) (see CHARITIES vol 5(2) (Reissue) para 226) and the Companies Act 1989 s 112(3) in relation to companies which are charities; and the Companies Act 1985 s 322A (as added) (see para 613 ante) has effect notwithstanding s 35 (as substituted): s 35(4) (substituted by the Companies Act 1989 s 108(1); amended by the Charities Act 1993 s 98(1), Sch 6 para 20(1),(2)).
    In the case of an unregistered company (see para 1765 et seq post) (1) for references to the memorandum or articles of association of a company there must be substituted references to any instrument constituting or regulating the company; (2) the Companies Act 1985 s 35 (as substituted) has effect as though it were expressed to be without prejudice to any rule of law which gives to a person dealing with a company incorporated by letters patent or by royal charter any greater protection in relation to the capacity of such a company than that afforded by s 35 (as substituted): Companies (Unregistered Companies) Regulations 1985, SI 1985/680, reg 6(a),(c) (amended by SI 1990/2571).
2   Companies Act 1985 s 35(2) (substituted by the Companies Act 1989 s 108(1)).
3   Ie but for the Companies Act 1985 s 35(1) (as substituted): see supra.
4   Ibid s 35(3) (substituted by the Companies Act 1989 s 108(1)).

1108. Powers of directors to bind the company. In favour of a person dealing with a company in good faith, the power of the board of directors to bind the company, or authorise others to do so, is deemed to be free of any limitation under the company's constitution[1].

For these purposes:

(1) a person 'deals with' a company if he is a party to any transaction or other act to which the company is a party;

(2) a person is not regarded as acting in bad faith by reason only of his knowing that an act is beyond the powers of the directors under the company's constitution; and

(3) a person is presumed to have acted in good faith unless the contrary is proved[2].

The above provisions do not, however, affect any right of a member of the company to bring proceedings to restrain the doing of an act which is beyond the powers of the directors; but no such proceedings lie in respect of an act to be done in fulfilment of a legal obligation arising from a previous act of the company[3]. Nor do the above provisions affect any liability incurred by the directors, or any other person, by reason of the directors' exceeding their powers[4].

1 Companies Act 1985 s 35A(1) (substituted by the Companies Act 1989 s 108(1)). For these purposes, the references to limitations on the directors' powers under the company's constitution include limitations deriving (1) from a resolution of the company in general meeting or a meeting of any class of shareholders; or (2) from any agreement between the members of the company or of any class of shareholders: Companies Act 1985 s 35A(3) (substituted by the Companies Act 1989 s 108(1)).

    The operation of the Companies Act 1985 s 35A (as substituted) is restricted by the Charities Act 1993 s 65(1) (see CHARITIES vol 5(2) (Reissue) para 226) and the Companies Act 1989 s 112(3) in relation to companies which are charities; and the Companies Act 1985 s 322A (as added) (see para 613 ante) has effect notwithstanding s 35A (as substituted): Companies Act 1985 s 35A(6) (substituted by the Companies Act 1989 s 108(1); amended by the Charities Act 1993 s 98(1), Sch 6 para 20(1),(2)).

2 Companies Act 1985 s 35A(2) (substituted by the Companies Act 1989 s 108(1)). See also *TCB Ltd v Gray* [1986] Ch 621, [1986] 1 All ER 587 (manner in which the company's seal is to be affixed; lack of good faith could not be presumed merely from failure to inquire); *Thompson v J Barke & Co (Caterers) Ltd* 1975 SLT 67 (cheque drawn on company account by director for the purpose of paying off his private account; regularity of transaction suspect; other party put on inquiry); and the cases cited in para 1093 note 1 ante.

3 Companies Act 1985 s 35A(4) (substituted by the Companies Act 1989 s 108(1)).

4 Companies Act 1985 s 35A(5) (substituted by the Companies Act 1989 s 108(1)).

1109. No duty to inquire as to capacity of company or authority of directors. A party to a transaction with a company is not bound to inquire as to whether it is permitted by the company's memorandum or as to any limitations on the powers of the board of directors to bind the company or authorise others to do so[1].

1 Companies Act 1985 s 35B (substituted by the Companies Act 1989 s 108(1)). In the case of an unregistered company (see para 1765 et seq post) (1) for references to the memorandum or articles of association of a company there must be substituted references to any instrument constituting or regulating the company; (2) the Companies Act 1985 s 35B (as so substituted) has effect as though it were expressed to be without prejudice to any rule of law which gives to a person dealing with a company incorporated by letters patent or by royal charter any greater protection in relation to the capacity of such a company than that afforded by s 35B (as so substituted): Companies (Unregistered Companies) Regulations 1985, SI 1985/680, reg 6(a),(c) (amended by SI 1990/2571).

(iii) Exercise of Company's Powers

1110. When court will not interfere. The court has no jurisdiction to interfere with the internal management of a company acting within its powers. To redress a wrong done to the company or to recover money or damages due to it the action must prima facie be brought by the company itself[1], if the matter constituting the cause of action is a cause of action properly belonging to the company or the general body of members[2]. Where, however, the persons against whom relief is sought hold and control the majority of the shares, and will not permit an action to be brought in the company's name, shareholders complaining may bring an action in their own names and on behalf of the others.

In such an action the plaintiffs have no larger right to relief than the company would have if plaintiff; they cannot complain of acts which are valid if done with the approval of the majority of shareholders, or are capable of being confirmed by the majority, and may maintain their action only when the acts complained of are of a fraudulent character or where, without fraud, the directors and majority shareholders are guilty of a breach of duty which not only harms the company but benefits those shareholders[3], or where the acts complained of are ultra vires the company, or where the majority propose to effect by an ordinary resolution that which may effectively be done only by an extraordinary or special resolution[4], mere irregularity or informality which may be remedied by the majority being insufficient[5]. Thus, directors will not be restrained from making or enforcing calls in good faith[6]; or from applying the proceeds in a particular manner[7]; or from applying the proceeds of the issue of new shares to purposes other than those for which the issue was made[8]; or from cancelling unissued shares[9]; or from otherwise applying the funds of the company within its powers[10]; and they will not be interfered with as regards the manner in which profits are ascertained[11]; or as to distributing profits while debts are unpaid[12]; or as regards selecting the place where a general meeting of the company is to be held[13]; or as regards drawing up the accounts in accordance with their business judgment exercised in good faith[14].

---

1   *Burland v Earle* [1902] AC 83 at 93, PC; and see *Foss v Harbottle* (1843) 2 Hare 461 (where the allegation was that no board was in existence); *Mozley v Alston* (1847) 1 Ph 790 (where the election of directors was said to be invalid); *Morris v Morris* [1877] WN 6; *Harben v Phillips* (1883) 23 ChD 14, CA (where elected directors claimed to act against the wish of the majority of the members); and see *Bainbridge v Smith* (1889) 41 ChD 462, CA; *Marshall's Valve Gear Co Ltd v Manning, Wardle & Co Ltd* [1909] 1 Ch 267; *Quin & Axtens Ltd v Salmon* [1909] AC 442, HL; *MacDougall v Gardiner* (1875) 1 ChD 13, CA (where the court was asked for a declaration and injunction on the ground of alleged illegality by the chairman declaring a meeting adjourned); *Burland v Earle* supra (dividing profits, carrying forward or forming a reserve fund, and making investments); *Campbell v Australian Mutual Provident Society* (1908) 77 LJPC 117, PC (extending a company's business to other countries where there is a general power to do so); *Foster v Foster* [1916] 1 Ch 532 (where it was unsuccessfully contended that, by ratifying the appointment of one of their members as managing director, the majority were appropriating some of the company's assets to themselves); *Last v Buller & Co Ltd* (1919) 36 TLR 35 (where an injunction to restrain a modification of rights and cancellations of arrears of dividend was refused); *Harris v A Harris Ltd* 1936 SC 183; *Birch v Sullivan* [1958] 1 All ER 56, [1957] 1 WLR 1247 (statement of claim by individual shareholder, not alleging that it was impossible for company to sue, defective). See also *Prudential Assurance Co Ltd v Newman Industries Ltd (No 2)* [1982] Ch 204, [1982] 1 All ER 354, CA.

2   *Edwards v Halliwell* [1950] 2 All ER 1064, CA.

3   *Daniels v Daniels* [1978] Ch 406, [1978] 2 All ER 89.

4   *Baillie v Oriental Telephone and Electric Co Ltd* [1915] 1 Ch 503, CA.

5   *Burland v Earle* [1902] AC 83, PC; *Menier v Hooper's Telegraph Works* (1874) 9 Ch App 350; *MacDougall v Gardiner* (1875) 1 ChD 13 at 25, CA; *Normandy v Ind, Coope & Co Ltd* [1908] 1 Ch 84; *Hoole v Great Western Rly Co* (1867) 3 Ch App 262; *Cockburn v Newbridge Sanitary Steam Laundry Co Ltd and Llewellyn* [1915] 1 IR 237 at 249, CA (where the transaction in respect of which the minority sued was ultra vires and tainted with criminality); *Alexander v Automatic Telephone Co* [1900] 2 Ch 56, CA (where it was held that the action may be brought against the company and the alleged wrongdoers); and see *Clinch v Financial Corpn* (1868) 4 Ch App 117 (action to restrain irregular amalgamation); *Atwool v Merryweather* (1867) LR 5 Eq 464n; *Hope v International Financial Society* (1876) 4 ChD 327, CA; *Mason v Harris* (1879) 11 ChD 97, CA; *Pavlides v Jensen* [1956] Ch 565, [1956] 2 All ER 518 (no such action will lie where negligence alone on the part of the directors is alleged); *Heyting v Dupont* [1964] 2 All ER 273, [1954] 1 WLR 843, CA (damage to the company must be shown); *Smith v Croft (No 2)* [1988] Ch 114, [1987] 3

All ER 909 (majority of independent shareholders opposed to litigation). An interlocutory injunction until trial has been granted where the majority were insufficient in numbers to demand a poll: see *Cory v Reindeer SS Ltd* (1915) 31 TLR 530. If the shareholder names the company as co-plaintiff, in a proper case the court may grant an interim injunction and direct a meeting to be held: see para 1170 post.

6 *Bailey v Birkenhead, Lancashire and Cheshire Junction Rly Co* (1850) 12 Beav 433; *Anglo-Universal Bank v Baragnon* (1881) 45 LT 362, CA.

7 *Cooper v Shropshire Union Rly and Canal Co* (1849) 6 Ry & Can Cas 136.

8 *Yetts v Norfolk Rly Co* (1849) 3 De G & Sm 293.

9 *Re Swindon Town Football Co Ltd* [1990] BCLC 467 (a company would only be prevented from cancelling shares under the Companies Act 1985 s 121(2)(e) (see para 218 ante) where a person had entered into a contract to take the shares in question; where a person had unilaterally consented to take shares, the shares had not been 'agreed to be taken' within s 121(2)(e)).

10 *Taunton v Royal Insurance Co* (1864) 2 Hem & M 135; *Bank of Turkey v Ottoman Co* (1866) LR 2 Eq 366.

11 *Stevens v South Devon Rly Co* (1851) 9 Hare 313; *Browne v Monmouthshire Rly and Canal Co* (1851) 13 Beav 32; *Lambert v Neuchatel Asphalte Co Ltd* (1882) 51 LJ Ch 882.

12 *Re Mercantile Trading Co, Stringer's Case* (1869) 4 Ch App 475; and see *Lord v Governor & Co of Copper Miners* (1848) 2 Ph 740 at 742, 751 and the cases cited in note 10 supra. As to the interference by the court as to dividends see further para 721 ante.

13 *Martin v Walker* (1918) 145 LT Jo 377.

14 *Devlin v Slough Estates Ltd* [1983] BCLC 497.

1111. When court will interfere. The court will interfere to prevent a fraudulent sale by a promoter to the company[1]; or to prevent fraud on a minority[2], as where an arrangement is being carried out beneficial only to the majority of shareholders[3]; or where resolutions have been passed for altering the articles in the interest of a majority to enable them to expropriate a minority[4]; or where a resolution has been passed for the transfer of a controlling interest in a company which may involve a complete transformation of the company[5]; or where directors are withholding payment of calls on their own shares while making calls on those of other persons[6]; or where the directors have sold the company's land at an undervalue to one of their number[7]; or where the company is existing only for the purpose of being wound up and gratuities are voted to its employees and directors[8]; or where a resolution has been passed by the votes of the holder of the majority of the shares which has the effect of appropriating to his own use a contract which belongs in equity to the company[9]; or stifling an action by the company against him[10]; or where resolutions have been passed on winding up purporting to divide the assets in fraud of a class of shareholders[11]; or where the chairman of a meeting has improperly rejected votes[12]; or where a proper notice of the purpose of a meeting involving payments to directors has not been given[13]; or where shares are being issued to secure a majority of votes[14]; or where the majority of directors exclude the minority from meetings of the board or a committee of it[15]; or where the company is conducting its business in an illegal way[16]. Such actions will, however, lie only where those who have been guilty of the fraud are in control of the company[17].

For the purpose of deciding whether the action should be allowed to proceed, the question whether the plaintiff has a reasonable cause of action should be decided as a preliminary issue on the balance of probabilities, not on the mere allegations in the statement of claim[18]. In such cases, the shareholder has no independent right of action based on an allegation of damage to the sale price of his shares occasioned by the damage to the company[19].

1 *Atwool v Merryweather* (1867) LR 5 Eq 464n; *Duckett v Gover* (1877) 6 ChD 82; *Mason v Harris* (1879) 11 ChD 97, CA.

2 *Gray v Lewis* (1873) 8 Ch App 1035; *Spokes v Grosvenor Hotel Co* [1897] 2 QB 124, CA; *Daniels v Daniels* [1978] Ch 406, [1978] 2 All ER 89. As to the court's statutory powers where the company's affairs are being conducted in a manner oppressive to minorities see the Companies Act 1985 s 459 (as amended) and para 1405 et seq post.

3 *Menier v Hooper's Telegraph Works* (1874) 9 Ch App 350. Cf *Castello v London General Omnibus Co Ltd* (1912) 107 LT 575, CA; *North-West Transportation Co Ltd and Beatty v Beatty* (1887) 12 App Cas 589, PC; *Dominion Cotton Mills Ltd v Amyot* [1912] AC 546, PC; *Greenhalgh v Arderne Cinemas Ltd* [1951] Ch 286, [1950] 2 All ER 1120, CA; *Clemens v Clemens Bros Ltd* [1976] 2 All ER 268. Cf *Rights and Issues Investment Trust Ltd v Stylo Shoes Ltd* [1965] Ch 250, [1964] 3 All ER 628 (alteration of voting rights held in good faith for benefit of company as a whole).

4 *Brown v British Abrasive Wheel Co* [1919] 1 Ch 290; and see para 540 ante.

5 *Clark v Workman* [1920] 1 IR 107.

6 *Alexander v Automatic Telephone Co* [1900] 2 Ch 56, CA.

7 *Daniels v Daniels* [1978] Ch 406, [1978] 2 All ER 89.

8 *Hutton v West Cork Rly Co* (1883) 23 ChD 654, CA; *Stroud v Royal Aquarium and Summer and Winter Garden Society Ltd* (1903) 89 LT 243; *Parke v Daily News Ltd* [1962] Ch 927, [1962] 2 All ER 929; but, as to the power of the company in this regard if the proper steps are taken, see now the Companies Act 1985 s 719 and para 1101 ante.

9 *Cook v Deeks* [1916] 1 AC 554, PC.

10 *Estmanco (Kilner House) Ltd v Greater London Council* [1982] 1 All ER 437, [1982] 1 WLR 2 (additionally the actions of the GLC were designed to prevent the other shareholders from ever acquiring voting rights and stultifying the purpose for which the company was formed).

11 *Griffith v Paget* (1877) 5 ChD 894.

12 *Pender v Lushington* (1877) 6 ChD 70; *Marks v Financial News Ltd* (1919) 35 TLR 681.

13 *Kaye v Croydon Tramways Co* [1898] 1 Ch 358, CA; *Clarkson v Davies* [1923] AC 100, PC; and see para 596 ante.

14 *Fraser v Whalley* (1864) 2 Hem & M 10; *Punt v Symons & Co Ltd* [1903] 2 Ch 506; *Piercy v Mills & Co* [1920] 1 Ch 77. Cf *Hogg v Cramphorn Ltd* [1967] Ch 254, [1966] 3 All ER 420 (majority given opportunity to sanction shares purported to have been issued improperly by directors); *Bamford v Bamford* [1970] Ch 212, [1969] 1 All ER 969, CA (same point).

15 See para 587 ante.

16 See *Powell v Kempton Park Racecourse Co Ltd* [1897] 2 QB 242, CA.

17 *Prudential Assurance Co Ltd v Newman Industries Ltd (No 2)* [1982] Ch 204, [1982] 1 All ER 354, CA.

18 *Prudential Assurance Co Ltd v Newman Industries Ltd (No 2)* [1982] Ch 204 at 221, 222, [1982] 1 All ER 354 at 366, CA.

19 *Prudential Assurance Co Ltd v Newman Industries Ltd (No 2)* [1982] Ch 204 at 222, 223, [1982] 1 All 354 at 366, 367, CA.

1112. Effect of liquidation. Once the company has gone into liquidation, it is no longer possible for a minority shareholders', or derivative, action to be brought[1]. The reason such an action is allowed in the first place depends upon the impossibility of the plaintiffs' obtaining relief in any other manner. Once the company has gone into liquidation, the right to bring an action in the name of the company passes to the liquidator, and, if he is unwilling to bring any action which the minority shareholders consider ought to be brought, they may apply to the court for assistance[2]. This may take the form of an order that the liquidator does himself bring the action in the name of the company, or that the minority shareholders themselves be given leave to bring the action in the name of the company. In all cases, leave will normally be given only on terms that the liquidator, and the assets of the company, are completely indemnified against the consequences of an unfavourable outcome of the litigation[3].

Alternatively, in so far as any of the proposed defendants are persons who have taken part in the formation or promotion of the company, or any past or present director or officer of the company, any contributory may obtain relief directly against him under the misfeasance provisions of the Insolvency Act 1986[4].

1 *Ferguson v Wallbridge* [1935] 3 DLR 66, PC; *Fargro Ltd v Godfroy* [1986] 3 All ER 279, [1986] 1 WLR 1134.

2 Ie in a voluntary winding up under the Insolvency Act 1986 s 112 (see para 2771 post) and in a compulsory liquidation under s 167(3) (see para 2340 post). See also *Ferguson v Wallbridge* [1935] 3 DLR 66 at 83, PC per Lord Blanesburgh.

3 See *Cape Breton Co v Fenn* (1881) 17 ChD 198, CA at 200 per Malins VC and at 208 per Cotton LJ.
4 Ie the Insolvency Act 1986 s 212: see para 2448 et seq post. See also *Ferguson v Wallbridge* [1935] 3 DLR 66 at 83, 84, PC per Lord Blanesburgh.

(iv) Agency

1113. How a company may act. A company, not being a physical person, may only act either by the resolution of its members in general meeting, or by its agents[1]. It is not the agent of its members[2], and a member as such is not the agent[3] of the company[4], the company being a separate entity or legal person apart from its members, who are not, even collectively, the company[5]. The legal position of a company, as so stated, must be regarded in relation to its contracts[6], to torts committed by it[7], and to its liabilities as regards acts which, if committed by individuals, would bring them within the criminal law[8].

A company exists because there is a rule, usually in a statute, which says that a persona ficta is deemed to exist and to have certain powers, rights and duties of a natural person; and the company exercises these through natural persons as its agents, those acts being attributable to the company[9]. It also makes itself subject to the general rules by which liability for the acts of others can be attributed to natural persons, such as estoppel and ostensible authority in contract and vicarious liability in tort[9].

1 *Ferguson v Wilson* (1866) 2 Ch App 77 at 89. For a consideration of the position of the directors see para 1115 post.
2 *Ferguson v Wilson* (1866) 2 Ch App 77 at 89; *Salomon v A Salomon & Co Ltd* [1897] AC 22 at 31, 51, 57, HL.
3 Unless the contrary intention appears, 'agent' in the Companies Act 1985 does not include a person's counsel acting as such: s 744.
4 Machen's Modern Law of Corporation s 1301; *Oakes v Turquand and Harding* (1867) LR 2 HL 325 at 358.
5 *Flitcroft's Case* (1882) 21 ChD 519 at 536, CA; *John Foster & Sons v IRC* [1894] 1 QB 516 at 528, CA; *Society of Practical Knowledge v Abbott* (1840) 2 Beav 559 at 567; *Re Sheffield and South Yorkshire Permanent Building Society* (1889) 22 QBD 470 at 476; *Farrar v Farrars Ltd* (1888) 40 ChD 395 at 410, CA; and see para 92 text and note 4 ante.
6 See paras 1126–1145 post.
7 See paras 1152–1156 post.
8 See para 1157 et seq post.
9 *Meridian Global Funds Management Asia Ltd v Securities Commission* [1995] 2 AC 500 at 506, [1995] 3 All ER 918 at 922, 923, PC per Lord Hoffmann.

1114. Appointment of agents. The appointment of an agent[1] by a company need not be made under its corporate seal; it may employ an agent or employee to do ordinary services without a deed[2].

1 For the meaning of 'agent' see para 1113 note 3 ante.
2 See AGENCY vol 1(2) (Reissue) para 26; CORPORATIONS vol 9 para 1371. As to the form of a company's contracts generally see para 1129 et seq post.

1115. Directors' position as company's agents. The directors are agents of the company[1]. Wherever an agent is liable, they are liable; and, where the liability would attach to the principal, and the principal only, the liability is the company's liability[2]. It does not follow that they are the only agents of the company; and they, or the company in general meeting where its powers in this respect are not exclusively vested in the directors, may appoint other agents of the company, by whose acts it will be bound[3]. For example, the secretary is able to bind the company in all administrative matters[4], and clerks in a company's registered office, in the absence of evidence to the contrary, are deemed to have authority during business hours in the absence of the secretary to receive notices on the company's behalf[5].

In practice, it is clear that in many companies most of the transactions are carried out by employees of the company, not by the directors; and such employees will in most cases have actual authority to bind the company in the matters with which their employment is concerned.

1 See para 582 ante.
2 *Ferguson v Wilson* (1866) 2 Ch App 77 at 89, 90.
3 *Smith v Hull Glass Co* (1852) 11 CB 897. As to the authority of a secretary see para 647 ante.
4 See para 647 ante.
5 *Truman's Case* [1894] 3 Ch 272. See further para 1147 post.

1116. Attorney to execute deeds abroad. By writing under its common seal[1] a company may empower any person, either generally or in respect of any specified matters, as its attorney, to execute deeds on its behalf in any place elsewhere than in the United Kingdom[2]. A deed executed by such an attorney on behalf of the company has the same effect as if it were executed under the company's common seal[3].

1 A company need no longer have a common seal: see para 1130 post.
2 Companies Act 1985 s 38(1) (amended by the Companies Act 1989 s 130(7), Sch 17 para 1(1),(2); the Law Reform (Miscellaneous Provisions) (Scotland) Act 1990 s 74(1),(2), Sch 8 para 33(2), Sch 9).
3 Companies Act 1985 s 38(2) (substituted by the Companies Act 1989 Sch 17 para 1(1),(3)).

1117. Company's seal for use abroad. If authorised by its articles, a company which has a common seal[1] whose objects require or comprise the transaction of business in foreign countries may have for use in any territory, district or place elsewhere than in the United Kingdom an official seal, which must be a facsimile of its common seal, with the addition on its face of the name of every territory, district or place where it is to be used[2].

A company having an official seal for use in any such territory, district or place may, by writing under its common seal, authorise any person appointed for the purpose in that territory, district or place to affix the official seal to any deed or other document to which the company is party in that territory, district or place[3].

The authority of any such agent continues, as between the company and a person dealing with such an agent, during the period, if any, mentioned in the instrument conferring the authority, or, if no period is there mentioned, then until notice of the revocation or determination of the agent's authority has been given to the person dealing with him[4].

The person affixing the official seal must certify in writing on the deed or other instrument to which the seal is affixed the date on which and the place at which it is affixed[5].

When duly affixed to a document, the official seal has the same effect as the company's common seal[6].

1 A company need no longer have a common seal: see para 1130 post.
2 Companies Act 1985 s 39(1) (amended by the Companies Act 1989 s 130(7), Sch 17 para 2(1),(2)).
3 Companies Act 1985 s 39(3) (amended by the Companies Act 1989 Sch 17 para 2(1),(4); the Law Reform (Miscellaneous Provisions) (Scotland) Act 1990 s 74(1),(2), Sch 8 para 33(3), Sch 9).

4 Companies Act 1985 s 39(4).
5 Ibid s 39(5).
6 Ibid s 39(2) (substituted by the Companies Act 1989 Sch 17 para 2(1),(3)).

1118. Official seal for security documents. A company which has a common seal[1] may have, for use for sealing securities issued by the company and for sealing documents creating or evidencing securities so issued, an official seal which is a facsimile of its common seal with the addition on its face of the word 'Securities'[2]. When duly affixed to a document, the official seal has the same effect as the company's common seal[2].

A company which was incorporated before 12 February 1979[3] and which has such an official seal may use the seal for sealing such securities and documents notwithstanding anything in any instrument constituting or regulating the company or in any instrument made before that date which relates to any securities issued by the company[4]. Any provision of such an instrument which requires any such securities or documents to be signed does not apply to the securities or documents if they are sealed with that seal[5].

1 A company need no longer have a common seal: see para 1130 post.
2 Companies Act 1985 s 40 (amended by the Companies Act 1989 s 130(7), Sch 17 para 3(1)-(3)). In the case of an unregistered company (see para 1765 et seq post) in the Companies Act 1985 s 40 (as so amended) for the reference to the common seal of the company there must be substituted a reference to the common or other authorised seal of the company: Companies (Unregistered Companies) Regulations 1985, SI 1985/680, reg 6(d) (amended by SI 1990/1394).
3 Ie the date on which the Stock Exchange (Completion of Bargains) Act 1976 was brought into force.
4 Companies Consolidation (Consequential Provisions) Act 1985 s 11(1).
5 Ibid s 11(2).

1119. Company's liability in contract for agent's acts. A company is liable in respect of contracts made by its agents when acting within the scope of their authority, provided that the contract is within the company's powers[1], but not for acts or representations not within that scope[2]. The question whether the act or representation was committed or made by the agent for his own benefit or for the benefit of the company is irrelevant[3]. Similarly, the company may be bound by the knowledge of, or notice given to, a subordinate official[4].

1 See AGENCY vol 1(2) (Reissue) para 133 et seq; CORPORATIONS vol 9 para 1334. For the limitations on a principal's liability in respect of contracts made by an agent see *Re International Contract Co, Pickering's Claim* (1871) 6 Ch App 525 and AGENCY vol 1(2) (Reissue) para 139 et seq; and for an analysis of this subject see *Meridian Global Funds Management Asia Ltd v Securities Commission* [1995] 2 AC 500 at 506, [1995] 3 All ER 918 at 922, 923, PC.
2 *Kleinwort, Sons & Co v Associated Automatic Machine Corpn Ltd* (1934) 151 LT 1, HL; *George Whitechurch Ltd v Cavanagh* [1902] AC 117, HL (secretary falsely certifying transfers of shares); *Ruben v Great Fingall Consolidated* [1906] AC 439, HL (secretary issuing fraudulent certificates); *Shaw v Port Philip Gold Mining Co Ltd* (1884) 13 QBD 103. The effect of the first two cases in so far as they relate to certification of transfers was negatived by the Companies Act 1948 s 79 (repealed: see now the Companies Act 1985 s 184 and para 512 ante).
  It is not within the scope of a manager's duties to make an unusual contract (*Re Cunningham & Co Ltd, Simpson's Claim* (1887) 36 ChD 532; *Houghton & Co v Nothard, Lowe and Wills* [1927] 1 KB 246, CA (affd on other grounds [1928] AC 1, HL); cf *Cartmell's Case* (1874) 9 Ch App 691); nor is it within the ostensible authority of a provincial manager of a bank to draw or indorse cheques (*Kreditbank Cassel GmbH v Schenkers* [1927] 1 KB 826, CA); nor is the resident agent of a mining company authorised to borrow money to pay wages, although warrants of distress have been issued (*Hawtayne v Bourne* (1841) 7 M & W 595); nor may a local agent grant a policy (*Linford v Provincial Horse and Cattle Insurance Co* (1864)

34 Beav 291); nor is it within the scope of a secretary's duties to make representations as to the financial arrangements of a company with its contractors (*Barnett v South London Tramways Co* (1887) 18 QBD 815, CA), or to make false statements to induce an investor to take shares (*Newlands v National Employers' Accident Association Ltd* (1885) 54 LJQB 428, CA). See further AGENCY vol 1(2) (Reissue) para 136.

3 *Lloyd v Grace, Smith & Co* [1912] AC 716, HL, which overruled many dicta to the effect that the act or representation had to be committed for the benefit of the principal.

4 *Evans v Employers Mutual Insurance Association Ltd* [1936] 1 KB 505. As to notice of assignments see CHOSES IN ACTION vol 6 (Reissue) para 20.

1120. Company's liability in tort for agent's acts. A company is liable to be sued for a tort committed by its agent if an action in tort would lie against an individual and the agent is acting in the course of his employment or within the actual or ostensible scope of his authority, and the act complained of is one which the company might possibly be authorised by its constitution to commit[1]. In general, the cause of action arises whenever the relevant person or body, not necessarily the directors, made the relevant decision[2].

A company may also be liable for the torts and contracts of its agents under the doctrine of estoppel[3], when they are either acting within their apparent authority[4] or apparently acting within their actual authority[5].

An action based on fraudulent misrepresentation as to the credit, trade or dealings of third persons made for the purpose of obtaining credit, money or goods cannot be maintained unless the misrepresentation is in writing signed by the party to be charged[6]. A company may only make such a representation by deed[7], and therefore signature by an agent, such as a manager, is not sufficient to charge the company[8], but the agent may himself be liable[9].

1 See AGENCY vol 1(2) (Reissue) para 162 et seq; CORPORATIONS vol 9 para 1375; *New Brunswick and Canada Rly and Land Co v Conybeare* (1862) 9 HL Cas 711 at 738 (shares taken on directors' fraudulent representations); *Ranger v Great Western Rly Co* (1854) 5 HL Cas 72; *Western Bank of Scotland v Addie* (1867) LR 1 Sc & Div 145, HL (or of managers); *Houldsworth v City of Glasgow Bank* (1880) 5 App Cas 317, HL; *Refuge Assurance Co Ltd v Kettlewell* [1909] AC 243, HL; *Barwick v English Joint Stock Bank* (1867) LR 2 Exch 259 (fraud of agents); *Re United Service Co, Johnston's Claim* (1870) 6 Ch App 212; *Mackay v Commercial Bank of New Brunswick* (1874) LR 5 PC 394; *Swire v Francis* (1877) 3 App Cas 106, PC (deceit); *Mersey Docks and Harbour Board Trustees v Gibbs* (1866) LR 1 HL 93 (negligence); *Edwards v Midland Rly Co* (1880) 6 QBD 287; *Kemp v Courage & Co* (1890) 7 TLR 50 (malicious prosecution; trover); *Goff v Great Northern Rly Co* (1861) 3 E & E 672; *Cornford v Carlton Bank* [1899] 1 QB 392; *Lambert v Great Eastern Rly Co* [1909] 2 KB 776, CA (false imprisonment); *Yarborough v Bank of England* (1812) 16 East 6; *Butler v Manchester, Sheffield and Lincolnshire Rly Co* (1888) 21 QBD 207, CA (assault); *Pratt v British Medical Association* [1919] 1 KB 244 (boycotting medical practitioner); *Citizens' Life Assurance Co v Brown* [1904] AC 423, PC (malicious libel); *Whitfield v South Eastern Rly Co* (1858) EB & E 115; *E Hulton & Co v Jones* [1910] AC 20, HL (libel); *Finburgh v Moss Empires Ltd* 1908 SC 928 (slander); *M'Adam v City and Suburban Dairies Ltd* 1911 SC 430 (slander); *Aiken v Caledonian Rly Co* 1913 SC 66 (slander); *Mandelston v North British Rly Co* 1917 SC 442 (slander); *Maund v Monmouthshire Canal Co* (1842) 4 Man & G 452; *Eastern Counties Rly Co v Broom* (1851) 6 Exch 314, Ex Ch (trespass); *Green v London General Omnibus Co* (1859) 7 CBNS 290 (obstruction in business); *United Telephone Co v London and Globe Telephone and Maintenance Co* (1884) 26 ChD 766 (infringement of patent). No sensible distinction may be drawn between the case of fraud and the case of any other wrong: *Barwick v English Joint Stock Bank* (1867) LR 2 Exch 259, Ex Ch; *London County Freehold and Leasehold Properties Ltd v Berkeley Property and Investment Co Ltd* [1936] 2 All ER 1039 (fraudulent misrepresentation). See also *Briess v Woolley* [1954] AC 333, [1954] 1 All ER 909, HL (fraudulent misrepresentation in negotiation of sale of shares by director authorised to act as shareholders' agent); and see para 1152 post.

2 *Multinational Gas and Petrochemical Co v Multinational Gas and Petrochemical Services Ltd* [1983] Ch 258, [1983] 2 All ER 563, CA; *Meridian Global Funds Management Asia Ltd v Securities Commission* [1995] 2 AC 500, [1995] 3 All ER 918, PC.

3 *Smith v Hull Glass Co* (1852) 11 CB 897 at 928; *Re Henry Bentley & Co and Yorkshire Breweries, ex p Harrison* (1893) 69 LT 204, CA. Thus, as a principal is estopped from denying the full authority of his agent where the limitation of it is not disclosed, an application for shares which is conditional in the

hands of the applicant's agent may be absolute in the hands of the company: *Re Henry Bentley & Co and Yorkshire Breweries, ex p Harrison* supra; and see AGENCY vol 1(2) (Reissue) para 29. A concealed limitation of the directors' powers does not bind third persons without notice: *Commercial Mutual Marine Insurance Co v Union Mutual Insurance Co* (1856) 19 Howard 318; and see the Companies Act 1985 ss 35-35B (as substituted) and paras 1093, 1107-1109 ante. Where those provisions do not apply, there can be no estoppel as regards acts ultra vires the company.

4   *Sutton v Tatham* (1839) 10 Ad & El 27 at 30; *Trott v National Discount Co* (1900) 17 TLR 37.
5   *Bryant, Powis and Bryant v La Banque du Peuple* [1893] AC 170, PC; *Hambro v Burnand* [1904] 2 KB 10, CA; *Cuthbert v Robarts, Lubbock & Co* [1909] 2 Ch 226 at 235, CA; *Re Land Credit Co of Ireland, ex p Overend, Gurney & Co* (1869) 4 Ch App 460, distinguished in *Premier Industrial Bank Ltd v Carlton Manufacturing Co Ltd and Crabtree Ltd* [1909] 1 KB 106. The last-named case was expressly dissented from in *Dey v Pullinger Engineering Co* [1921] 1 KB 77 (where the principle laid down in *Royal British Bank v Turquand* (1856) 6 E & B 327, was applied). As to the principle in *Royal British Bank v Turquand* supra see para 1137 post; and as to agency by estoppel see AGENCY vol 1(2) (Reissue) para 29.
6   See the Statute of Frauds Amendment Act 1828 s 6 and MISREPRESENTATION vol 31 para 1106.
7   *Bishop v Balkis Consolidated Co* (1890) 25 QBD 77; affd, without touching this point, 25 QBD 512, CA.
8   *Bishop v Balkis Consolidated Co* (1890) 25 QBD 77 (affd 25 QBD 512, CA); *Swift v Jewsbury and Goddard* (1874) LR 9 QB 301, Ex Ch; *Hirst v West Riding Union Banking Co Ltd* [1901] 2 KB 560, CA. Cf *Barwick v English Joint Stock Bank* (1867) LR 2 Exch 259 (where the statutory defence (see note 6 supra) was not raised).
9   *Swift v Jewsbury and Goddard* (1874) LR 9 QB 301.

1121. Company's liability for agents' criminal acts. In general, a corporation is in the same position in relation to criminal liability as a natural person and may be convicted of common law and statutory offences, including those requiring mens rea. There are, however, crimes which a corporation is incapable of committing or of which a corporation cannot be found guilty as a principal[1].

1   See para 1158 post and CRIMINAL LAW vol 11(1) (Reissue) para 35.

1122. Position of company's agents. The agent of a company cannot normally obtain an injunction to prevent his discharge, since the court will not usually specifically enforce a contract of personal service; but he will be left to his action for damages[1]. Agents of a company are in the position of agents of an individual, except that their principal is a corporate body and must act in accordance with its memorandum and articles[2]. An agent of a company has a right to be repaid the expenses incurred by him in the performance of his agency[3].

1   *Mair v Himalaya Tea Co* (1865) LR 1 Eq 411; *Johnson v Shrewsbury and Birmingham Rly Co* (1853) 3 De GM & G 914. See, however, *Hill v C A Parsons & Co Ltd* [1972] Ch 305, [1971] 3 All ER 1345, CA; and *C H Giles & Co Ltd v Morris* [1972] 1 All ER 960, [1972] 1 WLR 307 (specific performance of execution of service agreement). As to a director see para 639 et seq ante.
2   *Imperial Hydropathic Hotel Co, Blackpool v Hampson* (1882) 23 ChD 1 at 13, CA.
3   *Re Famatina Development Corpn Ltd* [1914] 2 Ch 271, CA. As to the expenses of defending criminal proceedings see *Tomlinson v Scottish Amalgamated Silks Ltd (Liquidators)* 1935 SC (HL) 1; and see AGENCY vol 1(2) (Reissue) para 123 et seq.

1123. Agent's liability for contracts. An agent may become liable on a contract made by him on behalf of a company if it is made in his own name and it does not appear from the document that he did not intend to contract as principal; and, where there is an ambiguity in this respect on the face of the document, parol evidence is admissible to explain it[1]. When an agent expressly contracts on behalf of his company or makes a contract in its name, he is not personally liable to the other contracting party in the absence of fraud or misrepresentation[2] unless he expressly or impliedly warrants an authority which he does not have or a state of facts which does not exist[3], in which case the contracting party has a remedy against him[3]. Thus, borrowing by the directors is a warranty that they as directors, or the company, as the case may be, have power to borrow[4]. A director or other agent may, however, act in such a way as to expose himself to liability for breach of trust[5].

1   *McCollin v Gilpin* (1881) 6 QBD 516, CA; *Re International Contract Co, Pickering's Claim* (1871) 6 Ch App 525; and see AGENCY vol 1(2) (Reissue) paras 169, 171.
2   *Godwin v Francis* (1870) LR 5 CP 295 (misrepresentation of authority); *Chapman v Smethurst* [1909] 1 KB 927, CA (promissory note); *Premier Industrial Bank Ltd v Carlton Manufacturing Co Ltd and Crabtree Ltd* [1909] 1 KB 106; *Landes v Marcus and Davids* (1909) 25 TLR 478; *H B Etlin Co v Asselstyne* (1962) 34 DLR (2d) 91 (Ont CA); *Elkington & Co v Hürter* [1892] 2 Ch 452; *Ferguson v Wilson* (1866) 2 Ch App 77; *Gadd v Houghton* (1876) 1 ExD 357, CA; *Bondina Ltd v Rollaway Shower Blinds Ltd* [1986] 1 All ER 564, [1986] 1 WLR 517, CA; and see AGENCY vol 1(2) (Reissue) para 170.
3   *Collen v Wright* (1857) 8 E & B 647, Ex Ch; and see AGENCY vol 1(2) (Reissue) para 172. Directors are liable on bills accepted by them for the company without authority: *West London Commercial Bank Ltd v Kitson* (1884) 13 QBD 360, CA; and see para 1145 post.
4   *Chapleo v Brunswick Permanent Building Society* (1881) 6 QBD 696, CA; *Richardson v Williamson and Lawson* (1871) LR 6 QB 276; *Looker v Wrigley* (1882) 9 QBD 397; *Whitehaven Joint Stock Banking Co v Reed* (1886) 54 LT 360, CA.
5   *Wilson v Lord Bury* (1880) 5 QBD 518, CA.

1124. Agent's liability for torts. An agent who commits a tort in the course of his employment is himself liable in damages to the full amount[1], and, if more than one agent, each agent is so liable[2]. This applies to a company's agent in the same way as to any person's agent; but one of two or more agents is not liable for the acts of the other unless he has expressly or impliedly authorised such acts[3].

Directors are not responsible to third persons for torts committed by sub-agents of the company properly appointed, unless they themselves committed or knowingly procured the commission of the tortious acts[4].

1   As to the liability of an agent for torts see AGENCY vol 1(2) (Reissue) para 176.
2   An officer of the company may be a joint tortfeasor with the company itself: *The Radiant* [1958] 2 Lloyd's Rep 596 (managing director aware of defects in equipment which contributed to accident); *C Evans & Sons Ltd v Spritebrand Ltd* [1985] 2 All ER 415, [1985] 1 WLR 317, CA. As to proceedings against and contributions between joint and several tortfeasors see the Civil Liability (Contribution) Act 1978 and TORT vol 45 para 1234 et seq.
3   *Cargill v Bower* (1878) 10 ChD 502; and see AGENCY vol 1(2) (Reissue) para 31. As to the liability of directors for the torts of a company see para 615 note 1 ante.
4   *Weir v Bell* (1878) 3 ExD 238, CA; *Betts v De Vitre* (1868) 3 Ch App 429 at 441, CA; *Cargill v Bower* (1878) 10 ChD 502; *The Radiant* [1958] 2 Lloyd's Rep 596. See further AGENCY vol 1(2) (Reissue) paras 69-71, 112.

1125. Ratification of agents' acts. In all cases where the doctrine of ultra vires has been abolished[1], no question of ratification can arise, save where statute confers such a power[2]. The following propositions apply where that doctrine still governs.

A company cannot confirm or ratify anything which is beyond the powers[3] expressed or implied in the memorandum of association or conferred by statute[4].

A transaction by the directors which is beyond their own powers but within the company's powers may be ratified by a resolution of the company in general meeting or even by acquiescence, provided the shareholders have knowledge of the facts relating to the transaction to be ratified or the means of knowledge are available to them[5].

By resolution at a subsequent meeting a company may ratify any business which it has purported to transact at a meeting informally called[6]. Such a ratification will not be implied merely from the fact that the shareholders have seen and passed without comment the balance sheet or formal documents[7], but it may be implied from acquiescence[8]. A contract entered into by directors at a meeting irregularly constituted may be ratified at a subsequent duly constituted meeting, and is sufficiently ratified by an action being brought by the company to enforce it[9]. A company may ratify the institution and conduct of litigation commenced in its name without proper authority, but, until ratified, the proceedings may be stayed[10].

1 See paras 1093, 1107-1109 ante.
2 See the Companies Act 1985 s 35(3) (as substituted) and para 1107 ante.
3 *Oakbank Oil Co v Crum* (1882) 8 App Cas 65 at 71, HL; *Ashbury Railway Carriage and Iron Co v Riche* (1875) LR 7 HL 653 at 668; *Preston v Liverpool, Manchester and Newcastle-upon-Tyne Junction Rly Co (Proprietors)* (1856) 5 HL Cas 605; *Athy Guardians v Murphy* [1896] 1 IR 65; *James v Eve* (1873) LR 6 HL 335; *Re Empress Engineering Co* (1880) 16 ChD 125, CA; *Re Exchange Banking Co, Flitcroft's Case* (1882) 21 ChD 519, CA; *Re Dale and Plant Ltd* (1889) 43 ChD 255; *Mann and Beattie v Edinburgh Northern Tramways Co* [1893] AC 69, HL.
4 See para 1086 et seq ante.
5 *Grant v United Kingdom Switchback Rlys Co* (1888) 40 ChD 135, CA; *Irvine v Union Bank of Australia* (1877) 2 App Cas 366, PC; and see *Srimati Premila Devi v Peoples Bank of Northern India Ltd* [1938] 4 All ER 337, PC; *Bamford v Bamford* [1970] Ch 212, [1969] 1 All ER 969, CA (issue of shares voidable on assumption of improper motives in directors ratified by company in general meeting after full and frank disclosure); *Baillie v Oriental Telephone and Electric Co Ltd* [1915] 1 Ch 503, CA (insufficient notice of effect of resolution to ratify irregular payment of remuneration); *Re Bank of Hindustan, China and Japan, Campbell's Case* (1873) 9 Ch App 1 (irregular amalgamation); *Sewell's Case* (1868) 3 Ch App 131; *Re London and New York Investment Corpn* [1895] 2 Ch 860 (increase of capital, made without the previous sanction of a resolution required by the articles, validated by a subsequent resolution); *Phosphate of Lime Co v Green* (1871) LR 7 CP 43 (what is a sufficient intimation to shareholders); *Spackman v Evans* (1868) LR 3 HL 171; *Houldsworth v Evans* (1868) LR 3 HL 263; *Re Republic of Bolivia Exploration Syndicate Ltd* [1914] 1 Ch 139 at 176 (approving of balance sheet); cf *Re Railway and General Light Improvement Co, Marzetti's Case* (1880) 42 LT 206, CA; and see *Imperial Mercantile Credit Association (Liquidators) v Coleman* (1873) LR 6 HL 189; *London Financial Association v Kelk* (1884) 26 ChD 107 at 152; and see para 584 ante. As to ratification after repudiation by the other party see AGENCY vol 1(2) (Reissue) para 73. A contract entered into by an agent in his own name and without authority cannot be ratified: *Keighley, Maxsted & Co v Durant* [1901] AC 240, HL. As to ratification generally see AGENCY vol 1(2) (Reissue) para 72 et seq.
6 *Briton Medical, General and Life Association v Jones (2)* (1889) 61 LT 384. Possibly ratification may be effected by the individual consents of all the shareholders without a meeting: see para 696 ante.
7 *Blackburn and District Benefit Building Society v Cunliffe, Brooks & Co* (1885) 29 ChD 902, CA.
8 *London Financial Association v Kelk* (1884) 26 ChD 107; *Evans v Smallcombe* (1868) LR 3 HL 249. See also *Maclae v Sutherland* (1854) 3 E & B 1; *Re Magdalena Steam Navigation Co* (1860) John 690; *Phosphate of Lime Co v Green* (1871) LR 7 CP 43; *Reuter v Electric Telegraph Co* (1856) 6 E & B 341.
9 *Re Portuguese Consolidated Copper Mines Ltd, ex p Badman, ex p Bosanquet* (1890) 45 ChD 16 at 26, 27, CA. See also *Re Land and Credit Co of Ireland, ex p Overend, Gurney & Co* (1869) 4 Ch App 460 at 473 (where it was said that formal ratification is not necessary); *Re State of Wyoming Syndicate* [1901] 2 Ch 431.
10 *Danish Mercantile Co Ltd v Beaumont* [1951] Ch 680, [1951] 1 All ER 925, CA (proceedings a nullity until ratified); approved in *Alexander Ward & Co Ltd v Samyang Navigation Co Ltd* [1975] 2 All ER 424, [1975] 1 WLR 673, HL (company with no directors; two individuals brought action on company's behalf to recover debt without authority; action ratified by liquidator). See also *Airways Ltd v Bowen* [1985] BCLC 355, CA. As to a solicitor's liability for costs where he institutes proceedings without authority see SOLICITORS vol 44(1) (Reissue) para 173.

(v) Contracts

A. CONTRACTS BEFORE INCORPORATION OR COMMENCEMENT OF BUSINESS

1126. Extent of company's liability. A company is not bound by contracts purporting to be entered into on its behalf by its promoters or other persons before its incorporation[1]. After incorporation it cannot ratify or adopt any such contract because in such cases there is no agency and the contract is that of the parties making it[2]. The adoption and confirmation by a directors' resolution of a contract made before the incorporation of the company by persons purporting to act on its behalf does not create any contractual relation between it and the other party to the contract, or impose any obligation on it towards him[3].

The principle that there is no agency before the company is incorporated does not apply where a company, awaiting a certificate of incorporation on change of name, purports to contract in the new name; in such a case no personal liability attaches to a director for contracts authorised by him or made by him on behalf of the company in the new name[4].

  1 See para 51 ante; *F J Neale (Glasgow) Ltd v Vickery* 1973 SLT (Sh Ct) 88 (new company formed with same name as old company and taking over assets and goodwill not liable on old company's contracts). The person purporting to enter into such a contract is personally liable upon it: *Kelner v Baxter* (1866) LR 2 CP 174; *Wilson & Co v Baker, Lees & Co* (1901) 17 TLR 473. A contract which purports to be made by or on behalf of a company at a time when the company has not been formed has effect, subject to any agreement to the contrary, as one made with the person purporting to act for the company or as agent for it; and he is personally liable on the contract accordingly: see the Companies Act 1985 s 36C (as substituted) and para 54 ante. See also *Phonogram Ltd v Lane* [1982] QB 938, [1981] 3 All ER 182, CA. A contract cannot purport to be made on behalf of a company not yet formed if no one had thought of the new company at the time of contracting: *Cotronic (UK) Ltd v Dezonie* [1991] BCLC 721, CA (parties contracted with first company which in fact had been struck off the register and dissolved and, when this was discovered years later, a second company was incorporated; it was impossible to say that the contract purported to be made by or on behalf of the second company). The person actually issuing an invoice showing chargeable VAT is liable for that amount if he issues such invoices in the name of a company before its incorporation: *Customs and Excise Comrs v Wells* [1982] 1 All ER 920. A solicitor who prepares the memorandum and articles cannot recover his costs for doing so from the company when it is incorporated (*Re English and Colonial Produce Co Ltd* [1906] 2 Ch 435, CA), or even the fees required to be paid on the registration of the company (*Re National Motor Mail-Coach Co Ltd, Clinton's Claim* [1908] 2 Ch 515, CA, overruling the decision of Buckley J in *Re English and Colonial Produce Co Ltd* supra at 439, which was not appealed against on this point); and see *Smith v Brown* [1896] AC 614, PC.

  2 *Kelner v Baxter* (1866) LR 2 CP 174; *Scott v Lord Ebury* (1867) LR 2 CP 255; *Re Northumberland Avenue Hotel Co* (1886) 33 ChD 16, CA; *Re Dale and Plant Ltd* (1889) 61 LT 206; *Falcke v Scottish Imperial Insurance Co* (1886) 34 ChD 234 at 249, CA; *Natal Land and Colonisation Co v Pauline Colliery Syndicate* [1904] AC 120, PC; *Bagot Pneumatic Tyre Co v Clipper Pneumatic Tyre Co* [1901] 1 Ch 196 (affd [1902] 1 Ch 146, CA); *North Sydney Investment and Tramway Co v Higgins* [1899] AC 263 at 721, PC; *Bridgetown Co-operative Society v Whelan* [1917] 2 IR 39. See also AGENCY vol 1(2) (Reissue) para 76.

  3 *North Sydney Investment and Tramway Co v Higgins* [1899] AC 263, PC; *Re Johannesburg Hotel Co, ex p Zoutpansberg Prospecting Co* [1891] 1 Ch 119 at 128, CA.

  4 *Oshkosh B'Gosh Inc v Dan Marbel Inc Ltd* [1989] BCLC 507, CA.

1127. Adoption of pre-incorporation contracts. In order that the company may be bound by agreements entered into before its incorporation, there must be a new contract to the effect of the previous agreement[1]; although this new contract may be inferred from the company's acts when incorporated[2], except where such acts are done in the mistaken belief that the agreement is binding[3].

If the company has notice of a contract made before its incorporation between the persons under whom it claims property of which it takes possession and a former owner of the property, whereby a charge or incumbrance was imposed on the property, the company takes subject to the charge or incumbrance, although it is not liable to be sued for breach of the contract[4].

It is the duty of directors of a company which is formed to adopt and enter into a contract to make careful and full inquiries before finally committing the company to it and to act as prudent men of affairs would in their own business[5].

1 *Melhado v Porto Alegre Rly Co* (1874) LR 9 CP 503; *Re Hereford and South Wales Waggon and Engineering Co* (1876) 2 ChD 621, CA; *Re Empress Engineering Co* (1880) 16 ChD 125 at 128, CA (and see at 130, where *Spiller v Paris Skating Rink Co* (1878) 7 ChD 368 is criticised); *Re Rotherham Alum and Chemical Co* (1883) 25 ChD 103, CA; *Tinnevelly Sugar Refining Co Ltd v Mirrlees, Watson and Varyan Co Ltd* 1894 31 SLR 823; cf *Hutchison v Surrey Consumers Gaslight and Coke Association* (1851) 11 CB 689; *Payne v New South Wales Coal and Intercolonial Steam Navigation Co* (1854) 10 Exch 283.

2 *Re Empress Engineering Co* (1880) 16 ChD 125 at 128, CA; *Re Rotherham Alum and Chemical Co* (1883) 25 ChD 103, CA; *Howard v Patent Ivory Manufacturing Co, Re Patent Ivory Manufacturing Co* (1888) 38 ChD 156; and see *Browning v Great Central Mining Co* (1860) 5 H & N 856; *Touche v Metropolitan Rly Warehousing Co* (1871) 6 Ch App 671. As to the last-mentioned case see *Gandy v Gandy* (1885) 30 ChD 57 at 67, CA.

3 *Re Northumberland Avenue Hotel Co* (1886) 33 ChD 16, CA; *Bagot Pneumatic Tyre Co v Clipper Pneumatic Tyre Co* [1901] 1 Ch 196 at 203 (affd [1902] 1 Ch 146, CA).

4 *Werderman v Société Générale d'Electricité* (1881) 19 ChD 246, CA, as explained in *Bagot Pneumatic Tyre Co v Clipper Pneumatic Tyre Co* [1902] 1 Ch 146 at 157, CA. It may be, however, that the original assignor might succeed by suing in the name of the intermediate assignee: *Werderman v Société Générale d'Electricité* supra at 161, 162. As to lien see *Gifford v Mashonaland Development Co (Willoughby's) Ltd* (1902) 18 TLR 274, HL.

5 See *Overend, Gurney & Co v Gibb and Gibb* (1872) LR 5 HL 480; *Twycross v Grant* (1877) 2 CPD 469 at 494, CA. As to the disclosures to be made to the company as regards profit and other matters see para 48 ante.

1128. Contracts made before company entitled to commence business.
Any contract, including a contract of borrowing, made by a company to be registered as a public company before the issue of the registrar's certificate to the effect that it is entitled to do business and exercise borrowing powers[1] is, nevertheless, not invalid on that account[2]. If, however, the company fails to comply with its obligations under any such contract within 21 days from being called upon to do so, the directors of the company are jointly and severally liable to indemnify the other party to the transaction in respect of any loss or damage suffered by him by reason of the company's failure to comply with those obligations[2].

1 Ie under the Companies Act 1985 s 117(2): see paras 82, 104, 652 ante.
2 See ibid s 117(8) and paras 616, 653 ante.

B. FORM OF CONTRACT; AUTHENTICATION OF DOCUMENTS

1129. Company contracts.
Under the law of England and Wales a contract may be made:

(1) by a company by writing under its common seal[1]; or
(2) on behalf of a company, by any person acting under its authority, express or implied;

and any formalities required by law in the case of a contract made by an individual also apply, unless a contrary intention appears, to a contract made by or on behalf of a company[2].

1 A company need no longer have a common seal: see para 1130 post.
2 Companies Act 1985 s 36 (substituted by the Companies Act 1989 s 130(1)). See also para 54 note 2 ante. As to the name of the company being engraved on its seal see para 1134 post; as to appointing a person to execute deeds abroad see para 1116 ante; as to the company's power to have an official seal for use abroad see para 1118 ante; and as to execution of deeds by corporations generally see CORPORATIONS vol 9 para 1217 et seq. See also DEEDS vol 12 paras 1335, 1336.

In the case of an unregistered company (see para 1765 et seq post) in the Companies Act 1985 s 36 (as so substituted) for the reference to the common seal of the company there must be substituted a reference to the common or other authorised seal of the company: Companies (Unregistered Companies) Regulations 1985, SI 1985/680, reg 6(d) (amended by SI 1990/1394).

The Companies Act 1985 s 36 (as so substituted) applies to companies incorporated outside Great Britain with the specified adaptations and modifications; and references in s 36 (as so substituted) to a company are to be construed as references to a company incorporated outside Great Britain: Foreign Companies (Execution of Documents) Regulations 1994, SI 1994/950, regs 2, 3 (amended by SI 1995/1729). The Companies Act 1985 s 36 (as so substituted) so applies as if (1) after the word 'common seal' in s 36(a) (as so substituted) (see text head (1) supra) there were inserted 'or in any manner permitted by the laws of the territory in which the company is incorporated for the execution of documents by such a company'; and (2) for s 36(b) (as so substituted) (see text head (2) supra) there were substituted:

'(b) on behalf of a company, by any person who, in accordance with the laws of the territory in which the company is incorporated, is acting under the authority, express or implied, of that company':

Foreign Companies (Execution of Documents) Regulations 1994 reg 4(1).

1130. Execution of documents. Under the law of England and Wales, the following provisions have effect with respect to the execution of documents by a company[1].

A document is executed by a company by the affixing of its common seal[2]. A company need not have a common seal, however, and the following provisions apply whether it does or not[3].

A document signed by a director and the secretary of a company, or by two directors of a company, and expressed, in whatever form of words, to be executed by the company has the same effect as if executed under the common seal of the company[4].

A document executed by a company which makes it clear on its face that it is intended by the person or persons making it to be a deed has effect, upon delivery, as a deed; and it is presumed, unless a contrary intention is proved, to be delivered upon its being so executed[5].

In favour of a purchaser[6] a document is deemed to have been duly executed by a company if it purports to be signed by a director and the secretary of the company, or by two directors of the company; and, where it makes it clear on its face that it is intended by the person or persons making it to be a deed, to have been delivered upon its being executed[7].

1 Companies Act 1985 s 36A(1) (substituted by the Companies Act 1989 s 130(2)). See also para 54 note 2 ante. In the case of an unregistered company (see para 1765 et seq post) in the Companies Act 1985 s 36A (as substituted) for the reference to the common or other authorised seal of the company there must be substituted a reference to the common or other authorised seal of the company: Companies (Unregistered Companies) Regulations 1985, SI 1985/680, reg 6(d) (amended by SI 1990/1394).

The Companies Act 1985 s 36A (as substituted) applies to companies incorporated outside Great Britain with the specified adaptations and modifications; and references in s 36A (as substituted) to a company are to be construed as references to a company incorporated outside Great Britain: Foreign Companies (Execution of Documents) Regulations 1994, SI 1994/950, regs 2, 3 (amended by SI 1995/1729). The Companies Act 1985 s 36A (as substituted) so applies as if:

(1) at the end of s 36A(2) (as substituted) (see infra) there were inserted ', or if it is executed in any manner permitted by the laws of the territory in which the company is incorporated for the execution of documents by such a company'; and

(2) for s 36A(4) (as substituted) (see infra) there were substituted:
    '(4) A document which:

(a) is signed by a person or persons who, in accordance with the laws of the territory in which the company is incorporated, is or are acting under the authority (express or implied) of that company; and

(b) is expressed (in whatever form of words) to be executed by the company,

has the same effect in relation to that company as it would have in relation to a company incorporated in England and Wales if executed under the common seal of a company so incorporated.'; and

(3) in s 36A(6) (as substituted) (see infra) for the words from 'a director' to 'directors of the company' there were substituted 'a person or persons who, in accordance with the laws of the territory in which the company is incorporated, is or are acting under the authority (express or implied) of that company':

Foreign Companies (Execution of Documents) Regulations 1994 reg 5.

2 Companies Act 1985 s 36A(2) (substituted by the Companies Act 1989 s 130(2)). See also note 1 supra.

3 Companies Act 1985 s 36A(3) (substituted by the Companies Act 1989 s 130(2)).

4 Companies Act 1985 s 36A(4) (substituted by the Companies Act 1989 s 130(2)). See also note 1 supra.

5 Companies Act 1985 s 36A(5) (substituted by the Companies Act 1989 s 130(2)).

6 For these purposes, 'purchaser' means a purchaser in good faith for valuable consideration and includes a lessee, mortgagee or other person who for valuable consideration acquires an interest in property: Companies Act 1985 s 36A(6) (substituted by the Companies Act 1989 s 130(2)).

7 Companies Act 1985 s 36A(6) (as substituted: see note 6 supra).

1131. Contracts under seal. A document is executed by a company by the affixing of its common seal[1]; but a company need no longer have a common seal[2]. If the company does have a common seal, the articles will almost invariably contain provisions as to its affixation[3]. If these provisions are apparently complied with, the company will be bound as against a person dealing with it in good faith[4]. If no particular formalities are prescribed, whoever, as a matter of practice, manages the affairs of a company may use the seal for those acts which he is authorised to perform[5]. Contracts required in the case of individuals to be under seal are those which are made without valuable consideration. Conveyances of land, leases, assignments and surrenders of leases, assignments of ships and shares in ships, and transfers of shares in companies must also in most cases be under seal[6].

In favour of a purchaser a document is deemed to have been duly executed by a company if it purports to be signed by a director and the secretary of the company, or by two directors of the company; and, where it makes it clear on its face that it is intended by the person or persons making it to be a deed, to have been delivered upon its being executed[7]. If, however, the document is a forgery, it does not bind the company[8].

1 See the Companies Act 1985 s 36A(2) (as added) and para 1130 ante. As to the name of the company being engraved on its common seal see para 1134 post; and as to appointing a person to seal contracts abroad see para 1117 ante.

2 See ibid s 36A(3) (as added) and para 1130 ante.

3 See eg the Companies (Tables A to F) Regulations 1985, SI 1985/805, Schedule, Table A art 101 which provides that the seal is only to be used by the authority of the directors or of a committee of the directors; and that the directors may determine who shall sign any instrument to which the seal is affixed and, unless otherwise so determined, it must be signed by a director and by the secretary or by a second director. Such an article, at any rate when read with other articles, may be directory only: *Re Hansard Publishing Union Ltd* (1892) 8 TLR 280, CA; *Landowners West of England and South Wales Land Drainage and Inclosure Co v Ashford* (1880) 16 ChD 411.

4 *Re County Life Assurance Co* (1870) 5 Ch App 288 at 293. See also *Re Athenaeum Life Assurance Society, ex p Eagle Insurance Co* (1858) 4 K & J 549; *Re Barned's Banking Co, ex p Contract Corpn* (1867) 3 Ch App 105; *County of Gloucester Bank v Rudry Merthyr Steam and House Coal Colliery Co* [1895] 1 Ch 629, CA; *Ruben v Great Fingall Consolidated* [1906] AC 439, HL; *Re Fireproof Doors Ltd, Umney v Fireproof Doors Ltd* [1916] 2 Ch 142; cf *Mayor Constables and Co Merchants of the Staple of England v Governors and Co of the Bank of England* (1887) 21 QBD 160, CA; *Davies v R Bolton & Co* [1894] 3 Ch 678. Directors who

subscribe a deed in accordance with articles of association are not signing as witnesses attesting its execution: see *Shears v Jacob* (1866) LR 1 CP 513; *Deffell v White* (1866) LR 2 CP 144 (bills of sale).

5 *Re Barned's Banking Co, ex p Contract Corpn* (1867) 3 Ch App 105 at 116.

6 See DEEDS vol 12 para 1307 et seq.

7 See the Companies Act 1985 s 36A(6) and para 1130 ante. A document signed by a director and the secretary of a company, or by two directors of a company, and expressed, in whatever form of words, to be executed by the company has the same effect as if executed under the common seal of the company: see s 36A(4) and para 1130 ante.

8 *Ruben v Great Fingall Consolidated* [1906] AC 439, HL.

1132. Written contracts.

A contract which, if made between private persons, would be required by law to be in writing, signed by the parties to be charged therewith, may be made on behalf of the company in writing signed[1] by any person acting under its authority, express or implied[2]. A contract so made is effectual in law and binds the company and its successors and all other parties to it; it may be varied or discharged in the same manner in which it is authorised so to be made.

Contracts may be validly made between companies on a Sunday[3]. Accuracy in naming the company is not essential if it can be uniquely identified from all the surrounding circumstances[4].

Many contracts when made by individuals are required by statute to be in writing and duly signed[5]; and such a contract, if made by a company, must comply with the like formalities[6]. A director's signature to a resolution referring to a draft agreement may be sufficient for this purpose[7].

1 The signature may consist of the company's stamp: *McDonald v John Twiname Ltd* [1953] 2 QB 304, [1953] 2 All ER 589, CA (apprenticeship agreement). An instrument which fails as a deed because of lack of delivery may yet take effect as an instrument in writing: *Windsor Refrigerator Co Ltd v Branch Nominees Ltd* [1961] Ch 375, [1961] 1 All ER 277, CA.

2 See the Companies Act 1985 s 36(b) (as substituted) and para 1129 ante. See also *Beer v London and Paris Hotel Co* (1875) LR 20 Eq 412. As to bills and notes see paras 1142-1145 post. The Corporate Bodies' Contracts Act 1960 does not apply to companies: see s 2 (as amended) and CORPORATIONS vol 9 para 1370.

3 *Rolloswin Investments Ltd v Chromolit Portugal Cutelarias e Produtos Metálicos SARL* [1970] 2 All ER 673, [1970] 1 WLR 912; and see TIME vol 45 para 1122.

4 *F Goldsmith (Sicklesmere) Ltd v Baxter* [1970] Ch 85, [1969] 3 All ER 733 (company named as 'Goldsmith Coaches (Sicklesmere) Ltd').

5 See CONTRACT vol 9 para 217 et seq; DEEDS vol 12 para 1441 et seq.

6 See the Companies Act 1985 s 36 (as substituted) and para 1129 ante.

7 *Jones v Victoria Graving Dock Co* (1877) 2 QBD 314, CA; *Howard v Patent Ivory Manufacturing Co, Re Patent Ivory Manufacturing Co* (1888) 38 ChD 156; *Wilson v West Hartlepool Rly Co* (1865) 2 De GJ & Sm 475.

1133. Parol contracts.

A contract which, if made between private persons, would by law be valid, although made by parol only, and not reduced into writing, may be made by parol on behalf of the company by any person acting under its authority, express or implied[1]. A contract so made is effectual in law and binds the company and its successors; it may be varied or discharged in the same manner in which it is authorised so to be made[2].

A company is liable, equally with an individual, to be estopped by the acts of its agents, for example by a parol consent to an act even though no resolution on the subject has been passed[3].

1 See the Companies Act 1985 s 36(b) (as substituted) and para 1129 ante.

2 This proposition contains the provisions of ibid s 36(2) (as originally enacted). Those provisions are not, however, re-enacted in s 36 (as substituted) but the proposition nevertheless remains correct.

3 See *Bourke v Alexandra Hotel Co Ltd* (1877) 25 WR 393; on appeal 25 WR 782, CA.

1134. Requirements as to use of company's name. A company which has a common seal[1] must have its name[2] engraved in legible characters on its seal[3].

Every company must have its name mentioned[4] in legible characters:

(1) in all business letters of the company;

(2) in all notices and other official publications[5];

(3) in all bills of exchange, promissory notes, indorsements, cheques and orders for money or goods purporting to be signed by or on behalf of the company; and

(4) in all its bills of parcels, invoices, receipts and letters of credit[6].

If a company fails to comply with any of the above provisions[7], it is liable on summary conviction to a fine not exceeding one-fifth of the statutory maximum[8].

If an officer of a company or a person on its behalf uses or authorises the use of any seal purporting to be a seal of the company on which its name is not so engraved, he is liable on summary conviction to a fine not exceeding one-fifth of the statutory maximum[9].

If an officer of a company or a person on its behalf:

(a) issues or authorises the issue of any business letter of the company, or any notice or other official publication of the company in which the company's name is not so mentioned[10]; or

(b) issues or authorises the issue of any bill of parcels, invoice, receipt or letter of credit of the company in which its name is not so mentioned,

he is liable on summary conviction to a fine not exceeding one-fifth of the statutory maximum[11].

If an officer of a company or a person on its behalf signs or authorises to be signed on behalf of the company any bill of exchange, promissory note, indorsement, cheque or order for money or goods in which the company's name is not so mentioned[12], he is liable on summary conviction to a fine not exceeding one-fifth of the statutory maximum[13]; and he is further personally liable to the holder of the bill of exchange, promissory note, cheque or order for money or goods for the amount of it, unless it is duly paid by the company[14].

Although documents omitting the company's name cannot therefore be relied on as against the company, moneys paid under them to persons known to represent the company are not on that account payable over again[15].

1 A company need no longer have a common seal: see para 1130 ante.

2 As to permitted contractions in relation to the words 'limited', 'public limited company' and their Welsh equivalents, which may be included as part of the ordinary name of the company, see the Companies Act 1985 s 27(4) and para 155 ante. Apart therefrom, 'company' may apparently be abbreviated for present purposes to 'Coy', 'limited' to 'ltd' and 'and' to '&': see *F Stacey & Co Ltd v Wallis* (1912) 106 LT 544; *Banque de l'Indochine et de Suez SA v Euroseas Group Finance Co Ltd* [1981] 3 All ER 198.

3 See the Companies Act 1985 s 350(1) (as substituted) and para 98 ante.

4 As to compliance with the requirement that the company's name must be mentioned see *F Stacey & Co Ltd v Wallis* (1912) 106 LT 544.

5 As to whether an advertisement is included in 'other official publications' see *General Radio Co v General Radio Co (Westminster) Ltd* [1957] RPC 471 at 484, 485 per Roxburgh J.

6 Companies Act 1985 s 349(1). Breach of these provisions will not deprive the company of the right to protect a trade name used separately from its corporate name: *Pearks Gunston and Tee Ltd v Thompson Talmey & Co* (1901) 18 RPC 185, CA; *H E Randall Ltd v British and American Shoe Co* [1902] 2 Ch 354; approved in *Employers' Liability Insurance Corpn v Sedgwick, Collins & Co* [1927] AC 95 at 120, HL. As to the contents of business letters and order forms see further para 1135 post. As to bills and notes see paras 1142-1145 post.

7 Ie the Companies Act 1985 s 349(1) or s 350(1) (as substituted): see supra.

 8 Ibid ss 349(2), 350(1) (substituted by the Companies Act 1989 s 130(7), Sch 17 para 7); Companies Act 1985 s 730, Sch 24. For the meaning of 'the statutory maximum' see para 1161 post.
 9 Ibid ss 350(2), 730, Sch 24.
10 Ie as required by ibid s 349(1): see supra.
11 Ibid ss 349(3), 730, Sch 24.
12 See note 10 supra.
13 Companies Act 1985 ss 349(4), 730, Sch 24.
14 Ibid s 349(4); *Scottish and Newcastle Breweries Ltd v Blair* 1967 SLT 72 (failure to comply with what is now the Companies Act 1985 s 349(1) rendered those purporting to sign on behalf of the company personally liable). See also *Durham Fancy Goods Ltd v Michael Jackson (Fancy Goods) Ltd* [1968] 2 QB 839, [1968] 2 All ER 987 (same situation, but holders estopped from enforcing personal liability as they had initiated the misdescription of the company); *Hendon v Adelman* (1973) 117 Sol Jo 631 (cheque printed by bank for 'L & R Agencies Ltd' gave as the company's name 'L R Agencies Ltd': signatories to cheque personally liable); *British Airways Board v Parish* [1979] 2 Lloyd's Rep 361, CA ('limited' omitted). The director who signed is liable not as surety but for breach of statutory duty: *Maxform SpA v B Mariani and Goodville Ltd* [1981] 2 Lloyd's Rep 54, CA (signature in trading name not sufficient to avoid personal liability); *Banque de l'Indochine et de Suez SA v Euroseas Group Finance Co Ltd* [1981] 3 All ER 198 (abbreviation of 'company' to 'co' no breach); *John Wilkes (Footwear) Ltd v Lee International (Footwear) Ltd* [1985] BCLC 444, CA (officer of the company authorised the placing of an order for goods on the company's behalf by a company servant in a written form omitting the company's name). In the case of orders for goods, 'holder' means the person to whom the order was given: *Civil Service Co-operative Society Ltd v Chapman* (1914) 30 TLR 679.
15 *Mahony v East Holyford Mining Co* (1875) LR 7 HL 869 at 893; *Beer v London and Paris Hotel Co* (1875) LR 20 Eq 412.

1135. Requirements as to contents of business letters and order forms. Every company must have the following particulars mentioned in legible characters in all its business letters and order forms of the company:

(1) the place of its registration and the number with which it is registered[1];
(2) the address of its registered office[2];
(3) in the case of an investment company[3], the fact that it is such a company[4]; and
(4) in the case of a limited company exempt from the obligation to use the word 'limited' as part of its name, the fact that it is a limited company[5].

If, in the case of a company having a share capital, there is any reference to the amount of share capital on the stationery used for any such letters or on the company's order forms, the reference must be to paid-up share capital[6].

If a company fails to comply with any of the above provisions, it is liable on summary conviction to a fine not exceeding one-fifth of the statutory maximum; and, if an officer of a company or a person on its behalf issues or authorises the issue of any business letter or order form which does not so comply, he is liable on summary conviction to a fine not exceeding one-fifth of the statutory maximum[7].

 1 Companies Act 1985 s 351(1)(a). As to the registration of the company see para 88 ante. In the case of an unregistered company (see para 1765 et seq post) in s 351(1) for s 351(1)(a)-(d) the following is to be substituted:
     '(a) whether the company has its principal office in England, Wales or Scotland, as the case may be, and the number which has been allocated to the company by the registrar of companies;
      (b) the address of its principal office; and
      (c) the manner in which it was incorporated and, if it is a limited company, that fact':
     Companies (Unregistered Companies) Regulations 1985, SI 1985/680, reg 6(f).
 2 Companies Act 1985 s 351(1)(b). As to the registered office see para 150 ante.
 3 Ie as defined in ibid s 266 (as amended): see para 703 ante.
 4 Ibid s 351(1)(c).
 5 Ibid s 351(1)(d). As to registration without the word 'limited' see paras 112-114 ante.
 6 Ibid s 351(2). As to paid-up capital see para 175 ante.
 7 Ibid ss 351(5)(a),(b), 730, Sch 24. For the meaning of 'the statutory maximum' see para 1161 post.

1136. Authentication of documents. A document or proceeding requiring authentication by a company is sufficiently authenticated for the purposes of the law of England and Wales by the signature of a director, secretary or other authorised officer of the company[1].

1 Companies Act 1985 s 41 (amended by the Companies Act 1989 s 130(7), Sch 17 para 4).

C. COMPANIES' CONTRACTS IN GENERAL

1137. Notice of constitution of company. In all cases where the doctrine of ultra vires has been abolished[1], the contracting party will not need to know anything about the constitution of the company. This will be the usual position, but in all other cases persons contracting with a company, whether or not they are shareholders, are bound to know, or are precluded from denying that they know, the constitution of the company and its powers as given by statute and the memorandum and articles[2]. They cannot complain that a contract which is ultra vires is void[3] and cannot be enforced[4], or that the company may be restrained from carrying it out[5]. This doctrine of constructive notice of a company's registered documents is a purely negative one which does not operate against a company, but only in its favour[6].

Persons contracting with a company and dealing in good faith[7] have always been entitled to assume that acts within its constitution and powers have been properly and duly performed, and were never bound to inquire whether acts of internal management have been regular[8]. This rule does not, however, apply to a director, or de facto director, who contracts with the company, as he should know the true position[9]. In any case persons contracting with the company must take the articles in force to be those registered, and they are not entitled to assume that a special resolution has been passed pursuant to the articles, for that would have to be registered[10], and where the act is within the company's power only on the fulfilment of a statutory condition, persons dealing with it are bound to ascertain whether the condition has been fulfilled[11]. An irregularity may be cured by a special article validating certain acts of the officers notwithstanding any irregularity[12]; but the particular act to be protected must on the face of it comply with the articles[13].

1 See paras 1093, 1107–1109 ante.
2 See *Peel's Case* (1867) 2 Ch App 674; *Sewell's Case* (1868) 3 Ch App 131 at 140; *Re Bank of Hindustan, China and Japan, Campbell's Case* (1873) 9 Ch App 1; *Griffith v Paget* (1877) 6 ChD 511 at 517; and *Oakbank Oil Co v Crum* (1882) 8 App Cas 65 at 70, HL (as to shareholders); *Ernest v Nicholls* (1857) 6 HL Cas 401 at 419; and *Mahony v East Holyford Mining Co* (1875) LR 7 HL 869 at 893 (as to outsiders). See also para 145 ante.
3 *Ashbury Railway Carriage and Iron Co v Riche* (1875) LR 7 HL 653 at 668; *Great North-West Central Rly Co v Charlebois* [1899] AC 114, PC; *James v Eve* (1873) LR 6 HL 335; *Re Jon Beauforte (London) Ltd* [1953] Ch 131, [1953] 1 All ER 634. Provisions which are severable may be valid: *Wall v London and Northern Assets Corpn* [1898] 2 Ch 469, CA.
4 *Ellis v Colman, Bates and Husler* (1858) 25 Beav 662.
5 *Charlton v Newcastle and Carlisle Rly Co and North-Eastern Rly Co* (1859) 34 LTOS 22; *Hattersley v Earl Shelburne* (1862) 31 LJ Ch 873; *Maunsell v Midland Great Western (Ireland) Rly Co* (1863) 1 Hem & M 130. A contract to take shares, good on the face of it, may be enforced, even though a collateral contract is illegal (*Odessa Tramways Co v Mendel* (1878) 8 ChD 235, CA), if the two are sufficiently severable.
6 *Houghton & Co v Nothard, Lowe and Wills Ltd* [1927] 1 KB 246, CA (affd [1928] AC 1, HL); *Rama Corpn Ltd v Proved Tin and General Investments Ltd* [1952] 2 QB 147, [1952] 1 All ER 554.
7 Cf *Rolled Steel Products (Holdings) Ltd v British Steel Corpn* [1986] Ch 246, [1985] 3 All ER 52, CA (where the dealing was not in good faith).
8 *Royal British Bank v Turquand* (1856) 6 E & B 327 (where a power to borrow could only be exercised with the sanction of a general meeting which had not been held). This statement in the text of the

so-called 'rule in Turquand's Case' was cited with approval by Lord Simonds in *Morris v Kanssen* [1946] AC 459 at 474, [1946] 1 All ER 586 at 592, HL. See now the Companies Act 1985 ss 35-35B (as substituted) and paras 1093, 1107-1109 ante.

See also *Landowners West of England and South Wales Land Drainage and Inclosure Co v Ashford* (1880) 16 ChD 411 (where the order of a statutory meeting was held to be directory only); *Heiton v Waverley Hydropathic Co* (1877) 4 R 830 (where the meeting had been irregularly summoned); *Agar v Athenaeum Life Assurance Society* (1858) 3 CBNS 725; *Re Athenaeum Life Assurance Society, ex p Eagle Insurance Co* (1858) 4 K & J 549 (issue of debentures not duly authorised); *Prince of Wales Assurance Co v Harding* (1858) EB & E 183 (policies); *Re British Provident Life and Fire Assurance Society, Grady's Case* (1863) 1 De GJ & Sm 488 (no consent by a general meeting); *Reuter v Electric Telegraph Co* (1856) 6 E & B 341 (where an oral contract was upheld, the constitution requiring special formalities); *Bargate v Shortridge* (1855) 5 HL Cas 297 (irregular registration of transfer by directors); *County of Gloucester Bank v Rudry Merthyr Steam and House Coal Colliery Co* [1895] 1 Ch 629, CA (mortgage executed at a board meeting of less than a quorum); *Cox v Dublin City Distillery (No 2)* [1915] 1 IR 345, CA; *Re Fireproof Doors Ltd, Umney v Fireproof Doors Ltd* [1916] 2 Ch 142 (debentures issued at a board meeting where there was an insufficient quorum); *Mahony v East Holyford Mining Co* (1875) LR 7 HL 869 at 893 (bankers honouring cheques signed by a self-appointed board); *Re County Life Assurance Co* (1870) 5 Ch App 288 at 293 (policy issued by de facto directors); *Montreal and St Lawrence Light and Power Co v Robert* [1906] AC 196, PC (contract made on a resolution of directors less than a quorum); *Owen and Ashworth's Claim, Whitworth's Claim* [1901] 1 Ch 115, CA (security given for debts in similar circumstances, following *Re Scottish Petroleum Co* (1883) 23 ChD 413, CA (allotment of shares)); *Duck v Tower Galvanizing Co* [1901] 2 KB 314 (debenture issued, although no directors had been appointed and no resolution of the company had been passed); *Gillies v Craigton Garage Co* 1935 SC 423 (borrowing without sanction of a general meeting); *Freeman and Lockyer (a firm) v Buckhurst Park Properties (Mangal) Ltd* [1964] 2 QB 480, [1964] 1 All ER 630, CA (company bound by acts of person held out as managing director); *Hely-Hutchinson v Brayhead Ltd* [1968] 1 QB 549 at 573, [1967] 3 All ER 98, CA (similar point); *Albert Gardens (Manly) Pty Ltd v Mercantile Credits Ltd* (1973) 9 ALR 653 (Aust HC) (security given by invalidly appointed directors); *IRC v Ufitec Group Ltd* [1977] 3 All ER 924 (company permitting chairman to continue negotiations estopped from denying his authority to contract). See also *Re David Payne & Co Ltd, Young v David Payne & Co Ltd* [1904] 2 Ch 608, CA; *Re Marseilles Extension Rly Co, ex p Credit Foncier and Mobilier of England* (1871) 7 Ch App 161 (purposes of borrowing); *Totterdell v Fareham Blue Brick and Tile Co Ltd* (1866) LR 1 CP 674. As to bills of exchange see paras 1142-1145 post.

9 *Morris v Kanssen* [1946] AC 459, [1946] 1 All ER 586, HL (invalid allotment of shares to a de facto director). Cf *Hely-Hutchinson v Brayhead Ltd* [1968] 1 QB 549 at 573, [1967] 3 All ER 98, CA (director entitled to rely on managing director's ostensible authority).

10 *Irvine v Union Bank of Australia* (1877) 2 App Cas 366, PC.

11 *Pacific Coast Coal Mines Ltd v Arbuthnot* [1917] AC 607, PC.

12 As to the effect of defects in the appointment of directors or managers see para 545 ante. For an article validating acts notwithstanding such irregularity see para 545 note 7 ante.

13 *Davies v R Bolton & Co* [1894] 3 Ch 678 at 688.

1138. Exercise of delegated powers.

Where there is a power of delegation to a committee of directors or a managing director, a person contracting with the company may assume that that power has been duly exercised[1]. Where there is a power of delegation to agents, a person is entitled to assume only that such powers as are within the ostensible authority of such an agent have been so delegated[2]; but, where an agreement entered into by a director is unusual, a person contracting with the company through that director is put upon inquiry as to whether the necessary power has been delegated to that director[3]. A person who has only ostensible authority to do an act or make a representation cannot make a representation which may be relied upon as giving a further agent an ostensible authority which he would not otherwise have had[4].

Where a power of delegation has been exercised, the subsequent act of the agent within the scope of his authority is binding on the company as against the person with whom the company is contracting; but, if the power of delegation has not been exercised, a person is not entitled to rely on the supposed exercise of the power unless he actually knew of its existence, because there is no estoppel in such circumstances[5].

A company which has appointed a manager of its business is bound by contracts made by him in the usual course of the business, even though sufficient powers have not in fact been delegated to him; and, where goods are supplied to the order of unauthorised persons, the company is liable if the goods are received and used for the purposes of its trade[6].

1   *Biggerstaff v Rowatt's Wharf Ltd* [1896] 2 Ch 93, CA; *Re Fireproof Doors Ltd, Umney v Fireproof Doors Ltd* [1916] 2 Ch 142; *Clay Hill Brick and Tile Co Ltd v Rawlings* [1938] 4 All ER 100 (payment by valid cheque to managing director equivalent to payment in cash to company); *Hely-Hutchinson v Brayhead Ltd* [1968] 1 QB 549 at 573, [1967] 3 All ER 98, CA (act within managing director's ostensible authority). As to the importance, when entering into a contract on behalf of a company, of so stating in unmistakable terms, see *The Swan* [1968] 1 Lloyd's Rep 5 and AGENCY vol 1(2) (Reissue) para 169; as to delegation see generally AGENCY vol 1(2) (Reissue) para 63 et seq; and as to the position of a person contracting with the company in good faith see paras 1092, 1107-1109 ante.

2   *Kreditbank Cassel GmbH v Schenkers Ltd* [1927] 1 KB 826, CA; *British Thomson-Houston Co Ltd v Federated European Bank Ltd* [1932] 2 KB 176, CA; *Freeman and Lockyer (a firm) v Buckhurst Park Properties (Mangal) Ltd* [1964] 2 QB 480, [1964] 1 All ER 630, CA; *Hely-Hutchinson v Brayhead Ltd* [1968] 1 QB 549 at 573, [1967] 3 All ER 98, CA; *Armagas Ltd v Mundogas SA, The Ocean Forest* [1986] AC 717, [1986] 2 All ER 385, HL (no ostensible authority to make contract; no actual or ostensible authority to inform other party of alleged approval by board of company).

3   *Houghton & Co v Nothard, Lowe and Wills Ltd* [1927] 1 KB 246, CA (affd [1928] AC 1, HL, this point not being discussed); *Kreditbank Cassel GmbH v Schenkers Ltd* [1927] 1 KB 826, CA; *Rama Corpn Ltd v Proved Tin and General Investments Ltd* [1952] 2 QB 147, [1952] 1 All ER 554 (a correct decision on its facts, but the suggestion of Slade J at 161 and at 563 that the earlier cases were conflicting is not justified: see *Freeman and Lockyer (a firm) v Buckhurst Park Properties (Mangal) Ltd* [1964] 2 QB 480, [1964] 1 All ER 630, CA at 493, 494, and at 638 per Willmer LJ, at 508, 509 and at 647 per Diplock LJ).

4   *Crabtree-Vickers Pty Ltd v Australian Direct Mail Advertising & Addressing Co Pty Ltd* (1975) 7 ALR 527 (Aust HC); *British Bank of the Middle East v Sun Life Assurance Co of Canada (UK) Ltd* [1983] 2 Lloyd's Rep 9, HL.

5   *Kreditbank Cassel GmbH v Schenkers Ltd* [1927] 1 KB 826, CA; *Houghton & Co v Nothard, Lowe and Wills Ltd* [1927] 1 KB 246 at 266, CA per Sargant LJ. For reservations see *Houghton & Co v Nothard, Lowe and Wills Ltd* supra at 266 per Sargant LJ; and *Rama Corpn Ltd v Proved Tin and General Investments Ltd* [1952] 2 QB 147, [1952] 1 All ER 554.

6   *Smith v Hull Glass Co* (1852) 11 CB 897.

1139. Notice of irregularity. Actual or constructive notice of an irregularity prevents a person contracting with the company obtaining the protection of the rule that the regularity of internal management may be relied on[1], except where he is claiming for value through another who had no notice[2]. A person does not obtain the protection of the rule where he was put on inquiry by the circumstances out of which the transaction with the company arose[3].

Further, the rule does not operate to protect a person who has accepted a document which is a forgery[4].

1   *Irvine v Union Bank of Australia* (1877) 2 App Cas 366, PC; *Wandsworth and Putney Gas-Light and Coke Co v Wright* (1870) 22 LT 404. Circumstances in which there is actual or constructive notice arise where a director is himself claiming (*Howard v Patent Ivory Manufacturing Co* (1888) 38 ChD 156 at 170; *Re Greymouth-Point Elizabeth Rly and Coal Co Ltd, Yuill v Greymouth-Point Elizabeth Rly and Coal Co Ltd* [1904] 1 Ch 32), although he is only a de facto director (*Morris v Kanssen* [1946] AC 459, [1946] 1 All ER 586, HL); where a copy of the articles was supplied to the creditor (*Davies v R Bolton & Co* [1894] 3 Ch 678); where the company's solicitor was claiming (*Re General Provident Assurance Co Ltd* (1869) 38 LJ Ch 320). Cf *Hely-Hutchinson v Brayhead Ltd* [1968] 1 QB 549 at 573, [1967] 3 All ER 98, CA (director acting as an individual not in his capacity as a director; no notice). The employment by a woman of her husband as agent to apply for debentures has been held not to affect the woman with all the husband knew as a director: *Re Fireproof Doors Ltd, Umney v Fireproof Doors Ltd* [1916] 2 Ch 142.

Quaere whether the fact that a person has actual notice of an irregularity may prevent him from contracting with the company in good faith, so as to take advantage of the abolition of the ultra vires

rule by the Companies Act 1985 ss 35-35B (as substituted): see paras 1093, 1107-1109 ante. Constructive notice would not appear to produce this result.
2 *Owen and Ashworth's Claim, Whitworth's Claim* [1901] 1 Ch 115, CA.
3 *A L Underwood Ltd v Bank of Liverpool and Martins* [1924] 1 KB 775; *Houghton & Co v Nothard, Lowe and
Wills Ltd* [1927] 1 KB 246, CA (affd [1928] AC 1, HL, this point not being discussed); *B Liggett
(Liverpool) Ltd v Barclays Bank Ltd* [1928] 1 KB 48.
4 *Kreditbank Cassel GmbH v Schenkers Ltd* [1927] 1 KB 826, CA, applying *Ruben v Great Fingall
Consolidated* [1906] AC 439, HL; *South London Greyhound Racecourses Ltd v Wake* [1931] 1 Ch 496.

1140. Statements in offer documents as to contracts. In relation to offers of
listed securities[1], the listing particulars must contain a summary of the principal
contents of each material contract, not being a contract entered into in the ordinary
course of business, entered into by any member of the group within the two years
immediately preceding the publication of the listing particulars, including particulars
of dates, parties, terms and conditions, any consideration passing to or from the issuer
or any member of the group, unless such contracts have been available for inspection in
the last two years, in which case it will be sufficient to refer to them collectively as being
available for inspection[2].

The question whether representations in offer documents on the faith of which a
contract is made may be read as part of the contract with the company is one of
construction of the contract and the offer documents read together[3].

1 As to offers of listed securities see para 281 et seq ante.
2 See the *Listing Rules* r 6.C.20. As to the *Listing Rules* generally see para 282 ante.
3 *British Equitable Assurance Co Ltd v Baily* [1906] AC 35, HL (policy of assurance); *Jacobs v Batavia and
General Plantations Trust Ltd* [1924] 2 Ch 329, CA.

1141. Assignment of contracts. The question how far the benefit of a commercial
contract is assignable by or to a company is decided on the same principles as in the case
of an individual, and depends on the circumstances of each case[1].

1 *Tolhurst v Associated Portland Cement Manufacturers (1900) Ltd* [1903] AC 414, HL; *Kemp v Baerselman*
[1906] 2 KB 604, CA; and see CHOSES IN ACTION vol 6 (Reissue) paras 16, 90; CONTRACT vol 9 para
338.

D. BILLS AND NOTES

1142. Power to deal with bills and notes. A non-trading company has no general
power to incur liability on bills of exchange or promissory notes and, although it may
transfer the property in a bill or note, it cannot incur liability on it unless its instrument
of incorporation expressly or by clear implication confers the power[1]. The Companies
Act 1985[2] does not give to every company incorporated under it, as an incident of its
incorporation, the power of accepting bills or issuing negotiable instruments, but
leaves such power to be determined on the construction of its memorandum and
articles[3]. If they are silent on the subject, the power may be inferred where the nature of
the company's business involves such a power[4].

A proviso in a bill of exchange by an unlimited company professing to limit the
liability under the bill is void[5].

1 *Peruvian Rlys Co v Thames and Mersey Marine Insurance Co, Re Peruvian Rlys Co* (1867) 2 Ch App 617 at
623. As to inferring the power from the course of dealing see *Bramah v Roberts* (1837) 5 Scott 172. The

following companies have been held not to be trading companies which have as such the implied power: a waterworks company (*Broughton v Manchester and Salford Waterworks Co* (1819) 3 B & Ald 1); a cemetery company (*Steele v Harmer* (1845) 14 M & W 831); a gas company (*Bramah v Roberts* (1837) 5 Scott 172); a salt company (*Bult v Morrell* (1840) 12 Ad & El 745); a salvage company (*Thompson v Universal Salvage Co* (1848) 1 Exch 694); a mining company (*Hawtayne v Bourne* (1841) 7 M & W 595; *Dickinson v Valpy* (1829) 10 B & C 128 at 137); a railway company incorporated by statute (*Bateman v Mid-Wales Rly Co* (1866) LR 1 CP 499). 'Trade' has a more restricted significance than 'business': see para 22 ante.

2 As to the necessity of mentioning the company's name in all instruments see para 1134 ante; and as to the personal liability of directors accepting a bill for the company, but omitting the word 'limited', see para 1145 post.

3 *Peruvian Rlys Co v Thames and Mersey Marine Insurance Co, Re Peruvian Rlys Co* (1867) 2 Ch App 617.

4 *Re General Estates Co, ex p City Bank* (1868) 3 Ch App 758 (where a land and building company was held to have the power); and see *East London Waterworks Co v Bailey* (1827) 4 Bing 283 at 288; *Slark v Highgate Archway Co* (1814) 5 Taunt 792; *Murray v East India Co* (1821) 5 B & Ald 204; *Dickinson v Valpy* (1829) 10 B & C 128; *Steele v Harmer* (1845) 14 M & W 831. As to the power of a liquidator see para 2337 et seq post.

5 *Re State Fire Insurance Co, ex p Meredith's and Conver's Claim* (1863) 1 New Rep 510.

1143. Signature on bill or note. Where in the case of an individual a bill or note is required to be signed, it is sufficient, in the case of a company, if it is signed on behalf of the company by any person acting on its authority or if it is sealed with the corporate seal, but a company's bill or note is not required to be under seal[1].

A bill of exchange or promissory note is deemed to have been made, accepted or indorsed on behalf of a company if made, accepted or indorsed in the name of, or by or on behalf or on account of, the company by a person acting under its authority[2]. It is not necessary that a formal resolution of the directors should be passed that bills should be accepted[3]; and, where a director without authority accepts bills on behalf of a company whose articles give power to delegate the duty of accepting bills to one director, the company is liable to a holder in due course, even though the delegation has not in fact taken place[4].

1 Bills of Exchange Act 1882 s 91; and see *Re General Estates Co, ex p City Bank* (1868) 3 Ch App 758 at 762, 763 and para 1132 ante.

2 Companies Act 1985 s 37; and see *Re Barber & Co, ex p Agra Bank* (1870) LR 9 Eq 725; cf *Herald v Connah* (1876) 34 LT 885.

3 *Re Land Credit Co of Ireland, ex p Overend, Gurney & Co* (1869) 4 Ch App 460 at 473.

4 *Dey v Pullinger Engineering Co* [1921] 1 KB 77, dissenting from *Premier Industrial Bank Ltd v Carlton Manufacturing Co Ltd and Crabtree Ltd* [1909] 1 KB 106; but cf *Kreditbank Cassel GmbH v Schenkers Ltd* [1927] 1 KB 826, CA (branch manager of bank); *A L Underwood Ltd v Bank of Liverpool and Martins* [1924] 1 KB 775, CA; *B Liggett (Liverpool) Ltd v Barclays Bank Ltd* [1928] 1 KB 48 (as to being put on inquiry); and see para 981 ante. A signature 'for and on behalf of a company, X, director' is not a signature by procuration within the Bills of Exchange Act 1882 s 25, and does not put the person taking the bill on inquiry as to the actual authority of the director to sign: *Alexander Stewart & Son of Dundee Ltd v Westminster Bank Ltd* [1926] WN 126; revsd on other grounds [1926] WN 271, CA. As to signature by procuration see BILLS OF EXCHANGE vol 4(1) (Reissue) para 375.

1144. Holders' duties to inquire. A holder in due course[1] is not concerned to see that the agent's authority has been strictly followed[2]. Where no express authority has been given to the agent, the company is not liable if the bill is given to meet an unusual occurrence or emergency not in the ordinary course of business[3]. Where a holder has notice that the agent had only a limited authority, he is in the same position as if he had inquired into the extent of that authority[4].

1 As to holders in due course see BILLS OF EXCHANGE vol 4(1) (Reissue) para 308.

2 *Re Land Credit Co of Ireland, ex p Overend, Gurney & Co* (1869) 4 Ch App 460 (where bills were authorised on condition that security was deposited); *Hambro v Burnard* [1904] 2 KB 10, CA (where the agent acted for his own purposes); *Thompson v Wesleyan Newspaper Association* (1849) 8 CB 849 (where the authorised amount was exceeded); *Re State Fire Insurance Co, ex p Meredith's and Conver's Claim* (1863) 1 New Rep 510.

3 *Re Cunningham & Co Ltd, Simpson's Claim* (1887) 36 ChD 532; *Hawtayne v Bourne* (1841) 7 M & W 595; *Re Moseley Green Coal and Coke Co, ex p Official Liquidator* (1864) 10 LT 819.

4 *Reckitt v Barnett, Pembroke and Slater Ltd* [1929] AC 176, HL: *John v Dodwell & Co* [1918] AC 563, PC; *Bryant, Powis and Bryant v La Banque du Peuple* [1893] AC 170, PC; *Gompertz v Cook* (1903) 20 TLR 106; *Reid v Rigby & Co* [1894] 2 QB 40; *Stagg v Elliott* (1862) 12 CBNS 373; *National Bank of Scotland Ltd v Dewhurst, The Gonchar and the Izgar* (1896) 1 Com Cas 318; *Jacobs v Morris* [1902] 1 Ch 816, CA. See further AGENCY vol 1(2) (Reissue) para 135.

1145. Liability of company's officers. If the company is liable on the bill, its authorised agents are not personally liable, even though they used words apparently sufficient to render them so liable, such as 'I promise' or 'We promise'[1], provided the signatures are expressed to be on behalf of the company as principal or in a representative capacity[2]. Thus, if a bill is directed to a company and accepted by its directors describing themselves as directors of the (named) company, the company alone is liable[3]; but words describing them as being officers of the company do not of themselves exempt them[4].

Where a company has no power to accept, an acceptance by directors and secretary 'for and on behalf of the company' makes them personally liable on a warranty of authority[5], but there is no implied warranty that the company has funds at its bank to meet a cheque or acceptance[6]. If a loan is made to a director who has become liable on a bill accepted for the company's purposes, it is a question of evidence whether the loan is made to him personally or to the company[7].

Under the Companies Act 1985 officers of a company are personally liable on a bill of exchange or similar document if the name of the company is not mentioned in the document in legible characters and the company fails to pay on it[8]. The company's name is not properly mentioned if the word 'limited' or 'public limited company' (or their Welsh equivalents) is or are omitted from it[9], or if additions are made to it[10]; but, if the company's name appears on the face of the bill, it is a sufficient mention and the name need not appear again in the acceptance[11].

1 *Chapman v Smethurst* [1909] 1 KB 927, CA; *H B Etlin Co Ltd v Asselstyne* (1962) 34 DLR (2d) 191 (Ont CA); *Bondina Ltd v Rollaway Shower Blinds Ltd* [1986] 1 All ER 564, [1986] 1 WLR 517, CA; *Lindus v Melrose* (1858) 3 H & N 177, Ex Ch; *Halford v Cameron's Coalbrook Steam Coal and Swansea and Loughor Rly Co* (1851) 16 QB 442; *Forbes v Marshall* (1855) 11 Exch 166; *Aggs v Nicholson* (1856) 1 H & N 165.

2 *Alexander v Sizer* (1869) LR 4 Exch 102; *Dutton v Marsh* (1871) LR 6 QB 361 at 364; *Landes v Marcus and Davids* (1909) 25 TLR 478; *Leadbitter v Farrow* (1816) 5 M & S 345; *Mare v Charles* (1856) 5 E & B 978; *Liverpool Borough Bank v Walker* (1859) 4 De G & J 24; *W and T Avery Ltd v Charlesworth* (1914) 31 TLR 52, CA. Even so, evidence is admissible to show the defendant signed in his personal capacity: *Rolfe Lubell & Co v Keith* [1979] 1 All ER 860.

Alternatively, the form of the document may indicate that the signatories are intended to be liable jointly with the company: *Glatt v Ritt* (1973) 34 DLR (3d) 295 (Ont HC). See further AGENCY vol 1(2) (Reissue) para 171.

3 *Okell v Charles* (1876) 34 LT 822, CA.

4 *Courtauld v Saunders* (or *Sanders*) (1867) 16 LT 562; *Dutton v Marsh* (1871) LR 6 QB 361 (notwithstanding that the company's seal was also affixed to the note); *Penkivil v Connell* (1850) 5 Exch 381; *Jones v Jackson* (1870) 22 LT 828; *Kettle v Dunster and Wakefield* (1927) 138 LT 158 (signed by the receiver of a company); *F Stacey & Co Ltd v Wallis* (1912) 106 LT 544; *Brebner v Henderson* 1925 SC 643. See also *Elliott v Bax-Ironside* [1925] 2 KB 301, CA (where bills were accepted by two directors on behalf of a company and indorsed by the company and the two directors, and it was held that the signatures were intended to create a personal liability on the directors); explained in *Britannia Electric Lamp Works Ltd v*

Mandler & Co Ltd and Mandler [1939] 2 KB 129 at 135, [1939] 2 All ER 469 at 472 per Branson J; and see BILLS OF EXCHANGE vol 4(1) (Reissue) paras 376, 377, 396. See also AGENCY vol 1(2) (Reissue) para 140.

5 *West London Commercial Bank v Kitson* (1884) 13 QBD 360, CA; cf *Liverpool Borough Bank v Walker* (1859) 4 De G & J 24.

6 *Beattie v Lord Ebury* (1874) LR 7 HL 102.

7 *Colley v Smith* (1838) 2 Mood & R 96; cf *McCollin v Gilpin* (1881) 6 QBD 516, CA.

8 See the Companies Act 1985 s 349(1)(c),(4) and para 1134 ante; *Scottish and Newcastle Breweries Ltd v Blair* 1967 SLT 72. Cf *Durham Fancy Goods Ltd v Michael Jackson (Fancy Goods) Ltd* [1968] 2 QB 839, [1968] 2 All ER 987 (holders estopped from enforcing personal liability as they had initiated the misdescription of the company); a trading name is not sufficient: *Maxform SpA v B Mariani and Goodville Ltd* [1981] 2 Lloyd's Rep 54, CA. As to the obligation to put the company's name on bills of exchange etc and the penalty for non-compliance see para 1134 ante.

9 *Penrose v Martyr* (1858) EB & F 499; *Atkins (or Atkin) & Co v Wardle* (1889) 58 LJQB 377. The abbreviation 'Ltd' has always been sufficient for this purpose: *F Stacey & Co Ltd v Wallis* (1912) 106 LT 544. As to permitted contractions in relation to the words 'limited', 'public limited company' and their Welsh equivalents, which may be included as part of the ordinary name of the company, see the Companies Act 1985 s 27(4) and para 155 ante. Apart therefrom, 'company' may apparently be abbreviated for present purposes to 'Coy' and 'and' to '&': see *F Stacey & Co Ltd v Wallis* supra; *Banque de l'Indochine et de Suez SA v Euroseas Group Finance Co Ltd* [1981] 3 All ER 198.

10 *Nassau Steam Press v Tyler* (1894) 70 LT 376.

11 *F Stacey & Co Ltd v Wallis* (1912) 106 LT 544; *Dermatine Co Ltd v Ashworth* (1905) 21 TLR 510 (where the word 'limited' was omitted by accident, the words of acceptance being on a rubber stamp which overlapped the edge of the bill).

(vi) Notice

1146. Notice to company. A document[1] may be served on a company by leaving it at, or sending it by post to, the company's registered office[2]. If service is effected by post, it is deemed to be effected by properly addressing, prepaying[3], and posting a letter containing the notice[4] by ordinary or registered post[5] or by the recorded delivery service[6]. Unless the contrary is proved, it is deemed to have been effected at the time at which the letter would have been delivered in the ordinary course of post[7]. It is sufficient that the letter is addressed with substantial accuracy[8], but giving the letter to a postman who is not authorised to receive letters for the post is not 'posting'[9].

1 For these purposes, 'document' includes summons, notice, order and other legal process, and registers: Companies Act 1985 s 744.

2 Ibid s 725(1). Under the Fire Precautions Act 1971 service of notices by virtue of that Act includes service at any person's proper address; in the case of the secretary or clerk of a body corporate, the proper address is the address of its registered or principal office: s 38(3). The company cannot rely upon any change of its registered office unless the change has been officially notified: see para 71 ante.

3 See *Walthamstow UDC v Henwood* [1897] 1 Ch 41.

4 It follows from this that a default judgment obtained because the writ never in fact reached the company cannot be set aside as of right; the company must file an affidavit of merits: *Saga of Bond Street Ltd v Avalon Promotions Ltd* [1972] 2 QB 325, [1972] 2 All ER 545, CA; *A/S Cathrineholm v Norequipment Trading Ltd* [1972] 2 QB 314, [1972] 2 All ER 538, CA, which expressly followed the decision in *Saga of Bond Street Ltd v Avalon Promotions Ltd* supra, and rejected the contrary view expressed in *Thomas Bishop Ltd v Helmville Ltd* [1972] 1 QB 464, [1972] 1 All ER 365, CA; sed quaere.

5 *TO Supplies (London) Ltd v Jerry Creighton Ltd* [1952] 1 KB 42, [1951] 2 All ER 992.

6 Recorded Delivery Service Act 1962 s 1(1).

7 See the Interpretation Act 1978 s 7, Sch 2 para 3 and STATUTES vol 44(1) (Reissue) para 1388. For similar provisions in articles of association see the Companies (Tables A to F) Regulations 1985, SI 1985/805, Schedule, Table A art 115 (amended by SI 1985/1052) (cited in para 1149 note 1 post).

8 *Liverpool Marine Insurance Co v Haughton* (1874) 23 WR 93.

9 *Re London and Northern Bank, ex p Jones* [1900] 1 Ch 220.

1147. Notice to officers. In order that notice to a company may be effectual it should either be given to the company through its proper officers[1] or received by it in the course of its business[2]. Notice to a director or other officer of the company in that character is sufficient[3], but not a notice received by him in the course of a transaction in which he is not concerned as such director or officer[4] or as a director of another company[5], or if it relates to a matter which he is not bound to[6], and does not[7], disclose, or in which he is acting fraudulently[8] or irregularly[9]. Oral notice to a sitting board will suffice[10].

An oral notice given to a clerk of the company at its registered office, in office hours, and during the absence of the secretary, is good notice to the company itself[11], as is an oral notice given to a managing director or the secretary in the course of his duties as such[12].

The notice which a company receives through its officers or other agents is not properly called constructive notice, but is actual notice[13]. Notice or knowledge of facts possessed by an agent of a company does not of necessity preclude the recovery by the company of money paid under a mistake of fact, where the agent had no idea that the matter to which his knowledge was relevant was being acted upon[14].

1 *Re Eyles, ex p Stright* (1832) Mont 502; *Alletson v Chichester* (1875) LR 10 CP 319. As to notice of a trust see para 385 ante.
2 As to notice of assignments given to officers of companies see CHOSES IN ACTION vol 6 (Reissue) para 57.
3 *Re Carew's Estate Act (No 2)* (1862) 31 Beav 39 at 46; *Gale v Lewis* (1846) 9 QB 730; *Bank of Ireland v Cogry Spinning Co* [1900] 1 IR 219; *Re European Bank, ex p Oriental Commercial Bank* (1870) 5 Ch App 358.
4 *Société Générale de Paris v Tramways Union Co* (1884) 14 QBD 424, CA; affd sub nom *Société Générale de Paris v Walker* (1885) 11 App Cas 20, HL (where it was suggested that a director might be personally liable in disregarding a notice); *Peruvian Rlys Co v Thames and Mersey Marine Insurance Co, Re Peruvian Rlys Co* (1867) 2 Ch App 617; *North British Insurance Co v Hallett* (1861) 7 Jur NS 1263; *Powles v Page* (1846) 3 CB 16.
5 *Re Marseilles Extension Rly Co, ex p Crédit Foncier and Mobilier of England* (1871) 7 Ch App 161.
6 *Re David Payne & Co Ltd, Young v David Payne & Co Ltd* [1904] 2 Ch 608, CA (where the same person was director of both contracting companies); *Deep Sea Fishery Co's (Ltd) Claim* [1902] 1 Ch 507; *Re Hampshire Land Co* [1896] 2 Ch 743.
7 *Lagunas Nitrate Co v Lagunas Syndicate* [1899] 2 Ch 392 at 431, 432, CA.
8 *Re European Bank, ex p Oriental Commercial Bank* (1870) 5 Ch App 358; *Re Hirth, ex p Trustee* [1899] 1 QB 612 at 625, CA; cf *Cave v Cave* (1880) 15 ChD 639; *Ruben v Great Fingall Consolidated* [1906] AC 439, HL; *Gluckstein v Barnes* [1900] AC 240 at 247, HL: *Re Hampshire Land Co* [1896] 2 Ch 743; applied in *Kwei Tek Chao (Trading as Zung fu Co) v British Traders and Shippers Ltd* [1954] 2 QB 459, [1954] 1 All ER 779; *Houghton & Co v Nothard, Lowe and Wills Ltd* [1928] AC 1, HL; *Belmont Finance Corpn Ltd v Williams Furniture Ltd* [1979] Ch 250, [1979] 1 All ER 118, CA. See *G L Baker Ltd v Medway Building and Supplies Ltd* [1958] 2 All ER 532; new trial ordered on other grounds [1958] 3 All ER 540, [1958] 1 WLR 1216, CA.
9 *Re Hampshire Land Co* [1896] 2 Ch 743.
10 *Re Worcester, ex p Agra Bank* (1868) 3 Ch App 555.
11 *Truman's Case* [1894] 3 Ch 272; and see *Re Natal Investment Co Ltd, Wilson's Case* (1869) 20 LT 962.
12 *Jaeger's Sanitary Woollen System Co Ltd v Walker & Sons* (1897) 77 LT 180, CA; *Alletson v Chichester* (1875) LR 10 CP 319.
13 *Espin v Pemberton* (1859) 3 De G & J 547. As to constructive notice see para 1148 post.
14 *Anglo-Scottish Beet Sugar Corpn Ltd v Spalding UDC* [1937] 2 KB 607, [1937] 3 All ER 335; *Turvey v Dentons (1923) Ltd* [1953] 1 QB 218, [1952] 1 All ER 1025. As to when notice to an agent is regarded also as notice to his principal see AGENCY vol 1(2) (Reissue) para 149.

1148. Constructive notice. A company is subject to the rule that, where the conduct of a party charged with notice shows that he had suspicions of a state of facts the knowledge of which would affect his legal rights, but that he deliberately refrained from making inquiries, he will be treated as having had notice[1], though he is not entitled to claim for his own advantage to be treated as having knowledge of the facts which inquiry would have disclosed[2]. Nevertheless, generally speaking the equitable doctrines of constructive notice are not applicable to purely commercial transactions[3].

1 *Jones v Smith* (1841) 1 Hare 43.
2 *Houghton & Co v Nothard, Lowe and Wills Ltd* [1927] 1 KB 246, CA; affd [1928] AC 1, HL.
3 *Manchester Trust v Furness* [1895] 2 QB 539, CA; *Greer v Downs Supply Co* [1927] 2 KB 28, CA.

1149. Notice by company in general. Articles of association generally provide how notices should be given by the company to its members[1]. Provisions in articles as to service of notices on members generally apply only to notices relating to the ordinary business of the company, and service in the manner set out by them is not in itself sufficient to fix a shareholder with knowledge of the falsity of a misrepresentation which would entitle him to repudiate his shares[2]. Similarly, such a provision that service of a notice at the registered address was to be good did not necessarily apply to give validity to substituted service of a debtor's summons at the address on the company register[3].

1 See eg the Companies (Tables A to F) Regulations 1985, SI 1985/805, Schedule, Table A arts 111-116 (amended by SI 1985/1052). Under art 111 any notice to be given to or by any person pursuant to the articles must be in writing. Under art 112 any notice may be given by the company to a member either personally or by sending it by post in a prepaid envelope addressed to the member at his registered address or by leaving it at that address. A member whose registered address is not within the United Kingdom and who gives to the company an address within the United Kingdom at which notices may be given to him is entitled to have notices given to him at that address, but otherwise no such member is entitled to receive any notice from the company. In the case of joint holders of a share, all notices are to be given to the one whose name stands first in the register of members in respect of the joint holding, and notice so given is sufficient notice to all the joint holders. Under art 113 a member present either in person or by proxy at any meeting whether of the company or of the holders of any class of shares in the company is deemed to have received notice of the meeting and, where requisite, of the purposes for which it was called. Under art 114 every person who becomes entitled to a share is bound by any notice given in respect of that share which, before his name is entered in the register of members, has been duly given to a person from whom he derives his title. Under art 115 (amended by SI 1985/1052) proof that an envelope containing a notice was properly addressed, prepaid and posted is conclusive evidence that notice was given; and it will be deemed to be given at the expiration of 48 hours after the envelope containing it was posted. Under art 116 a notice may be given to the persons entitled to a share in consequence of the death or bankruptcy of a member by sending or delivering it in any manner authorised by the articles for the giving of notice to a member, addressed to them by name, or by the title of representatives of the deceased, or trustee of the bankrupt or by any like description at the address, if any, within the United Kingdom supplied for that purpose by the persons claiming to be so entitled. Until such an address has been supplied, notice may be given in any manner in which it might have been given if the death or bankruptcy had not occurred. The requirement of the Companies Act 1985 s 378 that notice has been 'duly given' means given in accordance with s 370 or with the articles if they provide otherwise: *Re Anglo-International Bank Ltd* [1943] Ch 233 at 237. As to the computation of days of the period required for the giving of notices see the cases cited in para 660 note 4 ante.
2 *Re London and Staffordshire Fire Insurance Co* (1883) 24 ChD 149; and see *Peak v Gurney* (1873) LR 6 HL 377.
3 *Re Studer, ex p Chatteris* (1875) 10 Ch App 227.

1150. Notice by company in special cases. Even if the articles do not so provide[1], it is unnecessary to give notice of meetings to shareholders who reside abroad[2].

When a member has died[3], a notice addressed to him at his registered address is good, if the company has no notice of his death[4]; but not if the directors are aware of the death[5], in which case, unless the articles themselves otherwise provide[6], a notice required by the articles to be served on members need not be sent at all, even to the personal representatives, unless they have been registered as members[7].

A notice sent to all the members on the register at the date of sending out is good, even though the register is subsequently rectified with effect retrospective to a day prior to that date[8].

1 As regards notices of general meetings the Companies (Tables A to F) Regulations 1985, SI 1985/805, Schedule, Table A arts 111, 112, 116 require that notice be given to (1) every member except those members who (having no registered address within the United Kingdom) have not supplied to the company an address within the United Kingdom for the giving of notices to them; and (2) every person upon whom the ownership of a share devolves by reason of his being a legal personal representative or trustee in bankruptcy of a member.

2 *Re Union Hill Silver Co Ltd* (1870) 22 LT 400, followed in *Re Newcastle United Football Co Ltd* [1932] WN 109, and *Re Warden and Hotchkiss Ltd* [1945] Ch 270, [1945] 1 All ER 507, CA; and see *Halifax Sugar Refining Co v Francklyn* (1890) 59 LJ Ch 591.

3 As to the cases in which the Companies (Tables A to F) Regulations 1985 Schedule, Table A (as amended) applies see art 116 (cited in para 1149 note 1 ante).

4 *New Zealand Gold Extraction Co (Newbery-Vautin Process) v Peacock* [1894] 1 QB 622, CA (notice of a call).

5 *James v Buena Ventura Nitrate Grounds Syndicate Ltd* [1896] 1 Ch 456 at 465, CA (offer of new shares); followed in *Ward v Dublin North City Milling Co Ltd* [1919] 1 IR 5 (forfeiture of unclaimed dividends).

6 See the Companies (Tables A to F) Regulations 1985 Schedule, Table A art 116 (cited in para 1149 note 1 ante).

7 *Allen v Gold Reefs of West Africa Ltd* [1900] 1 Ch 656, CA (meeting to alter articles to prejudice of deceased).

8 *Re Sussex Brick Co* [1904] 1 Ch 598, CA.

1151. Notice by company to debenture holders. For the purpose of calling a meeting of the holders of bearer debentures, in the absence of special provision, notice by advertisement is sufficient[1]. Such a notice will be deemed to have been given on the date of the publication of the advertisement[2].

1 *Mercantile Investment and General Trust Co v International Co of Mexico* (1891) cited in [1893] 1 Ch 484n at 488n, CA.

2 *Mercantile Investment and General Trust Co v International Co of Mexico* (1891) cited in [1893] 1 Ch 484n at 489n, CA.

(vii) Torts

1152. Company's liability for agents' torts. In a sense, every tort is ultra vires, for no corporation is formed for the purpose of committing wrongs, but a company is not thereby exempted from tortious liability[1]. It is liable for torts such as, for example, malicious prosecution[2], libel[3] or fraudulent misrepresentation[4] committed by its agents in the course of their employment, even though no express command or privity of the company is proved[5].

1 Machen's Law of Modern Corporations s 1072; and see *Yarborough v Bank of England* (1812) 16 East 6; and CORPORATIONS vol 9 para 1374 et seq. As to vicarious liability for agents' torts see para 1120 ante; and see AGENCY vol 1(2) (Reissue) para 162 et seq.

2 *Cornford v Carlton Bank Ltd* [1900] 1 QB 22, CA; cf *Bank of New South Wales v Owston* (1879) 4 App Cas 270, PC; *Bank of New South Wales v Piper* [1897] AC 383, PC.

3 *Nevill v Fine Art and General Insurance Co* [1897] AC 68, HL; *Citizens' Life Assurance Co v Brown* [1904] AC 423, PC.

4 *Lloyd v Grace, Smith & Co* [1912] AC 716, HL, overruling a dictum in *Barwick v English Joint Stock Bank* (1867) LR 2 Exch 259 at 266, which had been approved in subsequent cases. Cf *Briess v Woolley* [1954] AC 333, [1954] 1 All ER 909, HL (where the negotiations for the sale of shares by the managing director in which the false representations were made were held to have been authorised by the shareholders and

the shareholders were in consequence liable). As to the rescission of contracts to take shares on the ground of misrepresentation see MISREPRESENTATION vol 31 para 1082 et seq. Liability for fraud will not be established against a company in the absence of specific allegations against officials: see *Smith and Houston Ltd v Metal Industries (Salvage) Ltd* (1953) 103 L Jo 734, Ct of Sess.

5　It is possible that a company may sometimes be liable for the tortious acts of its liquidator: see *Metropolitan Bank Ltd v Pooley* (1885) 10 App Cas 210 at 218, HL per Lord Selborne LC. See also para 1120 ante.

1153. Misrepresentation. Persons who have been induced to enter into transactions with a company for the purchase of chattels or goods by misrepresentation may, instead of claiming rescission with a return of money paid, elect to retain the goods or chattels and recover any damages which have been sustained[1].

The statutory liability[2] as to misstatements in listing particulars or a prospectus does not affect any liability which any person may incur under the general law apart from that liability[3]. In respect of the liability so incurred, the remedies for misrepresentation open to an allottee of shares, but not necessarily to a transferee of his shares[4], or to a person in whose favour an allotment of shares is renounced[5], are:

(1) rectification of the register of members and consequent relief;
(2) rescission of the contract[6];
(3) damages in an action of deceit[7] or negligent misrepresentation[8] or negligent misstatement[9];
(4) compensation or damages under the statutory provisions[10]; and
(5) criminal proceedings[11].

1　See the Misrepresentation Act 1967 s 2(2) and MISREPRESENTATION vol 31 para 1136.
2　Ie the liability under the Financial Services Act 1986 s 150 (as amended) and s 154A (as added) (listed securities) and the Public Offers of Securities Regulations 1995, SI 1995/1537, reg 14 (unlisted securities): see para 339 et seq ante.
3　Financial Services Act 1986 s 150(4); Public Offers of Securities Regulations 1995 reg 14(4). As to the exemptions from liability for non-compliance see paras 348, 351 ante.
4　*Hyslop v Morel* (1891) 7 TLR 263; *Andrews v Mockford* [1896] 1 QB 372, CA. As to sub-underwriters see para 199 ante.
5　*Collins v Associated Greyhound Racecourses Ltd* [1930] 1 Ch 1 at 14, CA.
6　See para 324 ante.
7　See para 332 ante.
8　See the Misrepresentation Act 1967 s 2 and para 338 ante.
9　See para 338 ante.
10　See para 347 ante (listed securities) and para 350 ante (unlisted securities).
11　See para 354 ante.

1154. Defamation at company meetings etc. An action will not lie for slanders uttered at a meeting of a company, provided the allegations are germane to its affairs and there is no malice, for to that extent the occasion is privileged; moreover complaints made to the directors or managers touching the conduct of its affairs are similarly privileged[1]. Even away from meetings of the company a shareholder has a qualified privilege in making communications to another shareholder as such[2].

Neither a company nor its directors are liable in an action for libel if, without malice, they circulate among the shareholders an auditor's report reflecting on one of the agents[3].

1　*Harris v Thompson* (1853) 13 CB 333. See further LIBEL.
2　*Quartz Hill Consolidated Gold Mining Co v Beall* (1882) 20 ChD 501, CA.

3   *Lawless v Anglo-Egyptian Cotton and Oil Co* (1869) LR 4 QB 262; cf *Nevill v Fine Art and General Insurance Co* [1897] AC 68, HL; *Philadelphia, Wilmington and Baltimore Railroad Co v Quigley* 62 US (21 How) 202 (1858). As to statements in official reports in a winding up by official receivers and other officials see para 2287 et seq post.

1155. Defamation in newspaper reports. The publication in a newspaper[1] of a fair and accurate report or summary of the proceedings at a general meeting of any company or association constituted, registered or certified by or under any Act or incorporated by royal charter, not being a private company[2], is privileged unless the publication is proved to be made with malice[3]. This privilege will not afford a defence to a libel action if it is proved that the defendant has been requested by the plaintiff to publish in the newspaper in which the original publication was made a reasonable letter or statement by way of explanation or contradiction and has refused or neglected to do so, or has done so in a manner not adequate or not reasonable having regard to all the circumstances[4]. Nor will the privilege protect the publication of any matter the publication of which is prohibited by law, or of any matter which is not of public concern and the publication of which is not for the public benefit[5].

1   For these purposes, 'newspaper' means any paper containing public news or observations on it, or consisting wholly or mainly of advertisements, which is printed for sale and is published in the United Kingdom either periodically or in parts or numbers at intervals not exceeding 36 days: Defamation Act 1952 s 7(5).
2   For the meaning of 'private company' see para 82 ante.
3   Defamation Act 1952 s 7(1), Schedule para 11.
4   Ibid s 7(2).
5   Ibid s 7(3). Nothing in these provisions is to be construed as limiting or abridging any privilege subsisting immediately prior to 30 November 1952 otherwise than by virtue of the Law of Libel Amendment Act 1888 s 4 (which gave qualified privilege to certain newspaper reports), now repealed by the Defamation Act 1952 s 18(3): see ss 7(4), 18(1). On a summary criminal charge, where evidence of a publication in a newspaper having been for the public benefit was admissible by statute, it was held that a report of charges made against officers of the company was not privileged as being of matters of public concern or for the public benefit in publication: *Ponsford v Financial Times Ltd and Hart* (1900) 16 TLR 248. See further LIBEL vol 28 paras 128, 287.

1156. Torts committed against companies. A company may sue for any damage done to it in its corporate capacity by a tort not of a purely personal nature, such as a libel affecting its property, or a libel reflecting on the management of its trade or business, or attacking its financial position[1]. It is unnecessary to prove special damage[2].

An action will lie by a trading company in respect of the malicious and unreasonable presentation of a winding-up petition against it[3].

Where the company is a victim of a conspiracy to which its directors acting on its behalf are parties, the company will not be considered a co-conspirator, and may recover damages from the directors if it suffers loss as a result of the conspiracy[4].

1   *Metropolitan Saloon Omnibus Co v Hawkins* (1859) 4 H & N 87; *Thorley's Cattle Food Co v Massam* (1880) 14 ChD 763, CA; *Slazengers Ltd v C Gibbs & Co* (1916) 33 TLR 35; and see *Rubber Improvement Ltd v Daily Telegraph Ltd* [1964] AC 234, [1963] 2 All ER 151, HL (subsequent proceedings sub nom *Lewis v Daily Telegraph Ltd (No 2)* [1964] 2 QB 601, [1964] 1 All ER 705, CA); and see CORPORATIONS vol 9 para 1378.
2   *South Hetton Coal Co v North-Eastern News Association* [1894] 1 QB 133, CA; *Linotype Co Ltd v British Empire Type-setting Machine Co Ltd* (1899) 81 LT 331, HL.
3   *Quartz Hill Gold Mining Co v Eyre* (1883) 11 QBD 674, CA; and see para 2210 post.
4   *Belmont Finance Corpn Ltd v Williams Furniture Ltd* [1979] Ch 250, [1979] 1 All ER 118, CA (conspiracy to cause company to breach what is now the Companies Act 1985 s 151: see para 273 ante).

(viii) Crimes and Offences

1157. Directing mind of company. Since a company cannot act of itself, but only through an individual, and even then not necessarily through one and the same individual, the question arises whether, on the one hand, a person so acting is acting as a living embodiment of the company, or whether, on the other hand, he is merely acting as the company's employee or agent[1].

For most civil purposes it is not necessary to decide the matter, since, usually as a result of the doctrine of ostensible authority, the company will be bound by the acts of the person acting on its behalf[2]. The question is, however, often a live one so far as the criminal law is concerned, since for the acts of a person who may properly be classified as 'the directing mind of the company'[3] the company will undoubtedly be liable criminally if those acts are in breach of any of the provisions of the criminal law[4]; but, if the person who has acted is merely an employee or agent, the company may well be able to refute any charge or take advantage of any exempting provision based on actual fault in the actor[5].

The directors may delegate part of their functions of management in such a way as to make their delegate an embodiment of the company within the sphere of the delegation; but they do not do this merely because, of necessity, ministerial functions have to be delegated[6]. Once the facts relating to the precise position of the person alleged to form the directing mind of the company have been ascertained, it is a question of law whether that person, in doing a particular act, is or is not to be regarded as the company[7]. The main considerations are the relative position in the company which he holds and the extent to which, as a matter of fact, he is in actual control of its operations or a section of them without effective superior control[8].

---

1 See *Tesco Supermarkets Ltd v Nattrass* [1972] AC 153 at 170, [1971] 2 All ER 127 at 131, 132, HL per Lord Reid. Where a company's rights and obligations cannot be determined either by the primary rules of attribution, expressed in its constitution or implied by law, for determining what acts are to be attributed to the company, or by the application of the general principles of agency or vicarious liability, the question of attribution for a particular substantive rule is a matter of interpretation or construction of that rule. If the court decides that the substantive rule is intended to apply to a company, it then has to decide how the rule is intended to apply and whose act or knowledge or state of mind is for that purpose intended to count as the act, knowledge or state of mind of the company. Although in some cases that can be determined by applying the test of whose was the 'directing mind and will' of the company so that his fault or knowledge becomes the company's fault or knowledge, that test is not appropriate in all cases: *Meridian Global Funds Management Asia Ltd v Securities Commission* [1995] 2 AC 500, [1995] 3 All ER 918, PC, applying *Tesco Supermarkets Ltd v Nattrass* supra. See also *R v Coroner for East Kent, ex p Spooner* (1987) 88 Crim App Rep 10, DC (corporate manslaughter).

2 See para 1137 et seq ante. For cases under the Landlord and Tenant Act 1954 s 30(1)(f), involving a consideration of the landlord's intention, see LANDLORD AND TENANT vol 27(1) (Reissue) para 590 et seq.

3 See *Lennard's Carrying Co Ltd v Asiatic Petroleum Co Ltd* [1915] AC 705 at 731, 714, HL per Viscount Haldane LC; and *HL Bolton (Engineering) Co Ltd v T J Graham & Sons Ltd* [1957] 1 QB 159 at 172, [1956] 3 All ER 624 at 630, CA per Denning LJ. If there is just one such person, he cannot conspire with the company, since conspiracy requires two minds: *R v McDonnell* [1966] 1 QB 233, [1966] 1 All ER 193.

4 This will not be so, however, where the directors or other directing minds are acting for their own benefit at the expense of the company, or in order to deprive the company of part of its assets: see eg *Belmont Finance Corpn Ltd v Williams Furniture Ltd* [1979] Ch 250, [1979] 1 All ER 118, CA.

5 *Tesco Supermarkets Ltd v Nattrass* [1972] AC 153, [1971] 2 All ER 127, HL; *Dumfries and Maxwelltown Co-operative Society v Williamson* 1950 JC 76; *John Henshall (Quarries) Ltd v Harvey* [1965] 2 QB 233, [1965] 1 All ER 725, DC (lorry of excessive weight allowed on road); *Magna Plant Ltd v Mitchell* (1966) 110 Sol Jo 349, DC (unmaintained vehicle allowed on road).

6 *Tesco Supermarkets Ltd v Nattrass* [1972] AC 153, [1971] 2 All ER 127, HL (delegation to branch managers).

7　*Tesco Supermarkets Ltd v Nattrass* [1972] AC 153 at 170, 173, [1971] 2 All ER 127 at 131, 134, HL per Lord Reid; *Essendon Engineering Co Ltd v Maile* [1982] RTR 260, DC (no evidence as to responsibilities of guilty employee, so company not liable).
8　*DPP v Kent and Sussex Contractors Ltd* [1944] KB 146, [1944] 1 All ER 119, DC; *R v ICR Haulage Ltd* [1944] KB 551, [1944] 1 All ER 691, CCA. Cf *R v Andrews Weatherfoil Ltd* [1972] 1 All ER 65, [1972] 1 WLR 118, CA (not every 'high executive' binds the company).

1158. Criminal liability of company. A company can commit crimes only by its agent, who must himself be responsible for the crime[1]. A company cannot be guilty of any criminal offences which, by their very nature, may be committed only by natural persons (such as bigamy) nor of those which cannot be committed vicariously (such as perjury)[2]. A company cannot be indicted for a crime where the only punishment is imprisonment[3].

Apart from such exceptions, a company may be guilty both of statutory[4] and common law[5] offences, even though the latter involve mens rea[6], this element being identified in the directing mind of the company[7]. This could be the board of directors, the managing director, the manager or any other person to whom the board has delegated the governing executive authority of the company[7].

1　See *R v Grubb* [1915] 2 KB 683, CCA.
2　Per curiam in *R v ICR Haulage Ltd* [1944] KB 551 at 554, [1944] 1 All ER 691 at 693, CCA; and see the earlier cases discussed in *DPP v Kent and Sussex Contractors Ltd* [1944] KB 146, [1944] 1 All ER 119.
3　*R v ICR Haulage Ltd* [1944] KB 551 at 554, 557, [1944] 1 All ER 691 at 693, 694, CCA.
4　See eg *Brentnall and Cleland Ltd v LCC* [1945] 1 KB 115, [1944] 2 All ER 552 (offences against weights and measures legislation). In all enactments (including those relating to offences) 'person' includes a body corporate unless a contrary intention appears: Interpretation Act 1978 s 5, Sch 1, Sch 2 para 4(5). As to penalties under the Companies Act 1985 see para 1161 post and eg *R v Tyler and International Commercial Co* [1891] 2 QB 588, CA (default in complying with the Companies Act 1862 s 26 (annual list of members) (repealed)).
5　*R v ICR Haulage Ltd* [1944] KB 551, [1944] 1 All ER 691, CCA.
6　*R v ICR Haulage Ltd* [1944] KB 551, [1944] 1 All ER 691, CCA, doubting *R v Cory Bros & Co* [1927] 1 KB 810.
7　*Canadian Dredge & Dock Co Ltd v R* (1985) 19 CCC (3d) 1 (Can SC). As to the directing mind of the company, and as to the rules of attribution relating to acts of natural persons attributed to a company, see para 1157 ante.

1159. Criminal liability of officers. In all cases of fraud where two or more persons such as directors co-operate, an indictment for conspiracy will normally lie[1]; but, where only one person is the directing mind of the company[2], a charge of conspiracy with the company will not lie, as there are not the necessary two minds concerned[3]. Where the conspiracy is to commit a fraud on the company or to deprive it of part of its assets, the natural persons to the conspiracy being the company's directors, a charge of conspiracy will not lie against the company, even though the company, through the agency of the conspiring directors, carries out part of the conspired acts[4].

Directors and other officers of companies are by statute indictable for many criminal acts[5]. Directors, officers and members may be liable for the theft of the company's property[6] or for false accounting[7]. Directors and officers may be liable for the making of false statements[8]. Further, if the company itself has obtained property[9] or a pecuniary advantage[10] by deception, or has falsely accounted[11], and the offence is proved to have been committed with the consent or connivance of any director, manager, secretary or other similar officer[12] of the company, he, as well as the company, is guilty of the offence, and is liable to be proceeded against and punished accordingly[13].

An officer or member of a company cannot refuse to give evidence in civil proceedings about such matters, or to comply with any order made in any such proceedings, for example an order to answer interrogatories; but no statement or admission made by him in answering a question put or in complying with such an order will be admissible in evidence against that person or, unless the marriage took place after the making of the statement or admission, against his spouse in proceedings for any of the above offences[14].

The Companies Act 1985, the Insolvency Act 1986 and the Company Directors Disqualification Act 1986 include many provisions rendering directors and others liable to imprisonment[15]. In some cases the offender is punishable as if he had been guilty of contempt of court[16]. Many of the offences punishable are those committed in connection with a company which is being wound up[17].

1 *Twycross v Grant* (1877) 2 CPD 469 at 493, CA (directors receiving presents etc from promoters); *Re Gold Co* (1879) 11 ChD 701 at 723, CA (watering the capital); *Burnes v Pennell* (1849) 2 HL Cas 497 at 524 (publishing false statements); *R v De Berenger* (1814) 3 M & S 67 (inducing purchase of shares); *Scott v Brown, Doering, McNab & Co* [1892] 2 QB 724 at 730, CA; *R v Aspinall* (1876) 2 QBD 48, CA (inducing the Committee of the Stock Exchange to grant a quotation of shares); *R v Barber* (1887) 3 TLR 491 (paying a concealed profit to a broker). An agreement between two or more persons to purchase shares in a company in order to induce persons thereafter purchasing shares in it to believe, contrary to the fact, that there is a bona fide market in the shares, and that there is a real premium, being an offence indictable as a conspiracy, no action may be maintained in respect of such an agreement or purchase of shares: *Scott v Brown, Doering, McNab & Co* supra. See also *Taylor v Chester* (1869) LR 4 QB 309; *Begbie v Phosphate Sewage Co* (1876) 1 QBD 679.

2 See para 1157 ante.

3 *R v McDonnell* [1966] 1 QB 233, [1966] 1 All ER 193.

4 *Belmont Finance Corpn Ltd v Williams Furniture Ltd* [1979] Ch 250, [1979] 1 All ER 118, CA.

5 Modern statutes sometimes provide that, where an offence created by the particular statute which has been committed by a body corporate is proved to have been committed with the consent or connivance of, or to be attributable to any neglect on the part of, a director, manager, secretary or other similar officer of the body corporate, or any person who was purporting to act in any such capacity, he, as well as the body corporate, is guilty of that offence: see eg the Clean Air Act 1993 s 52 and PUBLIC HEALTH. As to statutory offences of which directors or other officers may be guilty see the titles in this work relevant to the particular subject; and see eg the Official Secrets Act 1920 and CRIMINAL LAW.

6 See the Theft Act 1968 s 1 and CRIMINAL LAW vol 11(1) (Reissue) para 541.

7 See ibid s 17 and CRIMINAL LAW vol 11(1) (Reissue) para 572.

8 See ibid s 19 and paras 354, 1069 ante.

9 See ibid s 15 and CRIMINAL LAW vol 11(1) (Reissue) para 567.

10 See ibid s 16 (as amended) and CRIMINAL LAW vol 11(1) (Reissue) para 568.

11 See ibid s 17 and CRIMINAL LAW vol 11(1) (Reissue) para 572.

12 This extends also to a person purporting to act as such: ibid s 18(1).

13 Ibid s 18(1). Where the affairs of a company are managed by its members, these provisions apply in relation to the member's acts and defaults in connection with his management functions as if he were a director: s 18(2). Section 18 applies also in relation to offences by bodies corporate which are not registered under the Companies Act 1985: Theft Act 1968 s 18.

14 Ibid s 31(1). When an act done by a person is first disclosed by him without making any objection during cross-examination in a civil action, it is not disclosed by him 'in consequence of any compulsory process of any court of law' (the phrase used in the Larceny Act 1861 s 85 (repealed), which is now replaced by the Theft Act 1968 s 31(1)): *R v Noel* [1914] 3 KB 848, CCA. See also *R v Gunnell* (1886) 55 LT 786, CCR; *R v Strahan, Paul and Bates* (1855) 7 Cox CC 85; *R v Oliver* (1909) 3 Cr App Rep 246, CCA; and CRIMINAL LAW vol 11(2) (Reissue) para 1161.

15 See the Companies Act 1985 s 95 (authorising the inclusion in a statement setting out the reasons for a resolution disapplying pre-emption rights of misleading false or deceptive matter: see para 462 ante); s 110 (making misleading, false or deceptive statement to valuer of non-cash asset: see para 473 ante); s 143 (company acquiring its own shares otherwise than in accordance with statutory provisions: see para 362 ante); s 151 (company giving financial assistance towards acquisition of own shares: see para 273 ante); s 156 (making statutory declaration in connection with financial assistance given by private company for purchase of its own shares without having reasonable grounds for opinion expressed: see

para 276 ante); s 173 (similar offence in connection with statutory declaration relating to a payment out of capital by a private company for redemption or purchase of its own shares: see para 234 ante); s 221 (as substituted) (officer of company failing to keep accounting records: see para 802 ante); s 323 (dealing in options to buy or sell company's listed shares or debentures: see para 614 ante); s 324 (failing to notify interest in company's shares; making false statement in purported notification: see para 564 ante); s 328 (failing to notify company that members of his family have, or have exercised, options to buy shares or debentures; making false statements in purported notification: see para 566 ante); s 342(1) (authorising or permitting company to enter into transaction or arrangement knowing or suspecting that it contravened the provisions on loans to directors: see para 605 ante); s 342(2) (company entering into transaction or arrangement for a director in contravention of those provisions: see para 605 ante); s 342(3) (procuring a company to enter into transaction or arrangement known to be contrary to those provisions: see para 605 ante); s 450 (as amended) (destroying or mutilating company documents; falsifying such documents or making false entries; parting with such documents or altering them or making omissions: see para 1388 post); s 458 (being a party to carrying on company's business with intent to defraud creditors, or for any fraudulent purpose: see para 1160 post); the Insolvency Act 1986 s 89 (making statutory declaration of company's solvency without reasonable grounds for opinion: see para 2700 post); s 206 (as amended) (fraud in anticipation of winding up: see para 2664 post); s 207 (entering into transactions in fraud of company's creditors: see para 2667 post); s 208 (misconducting himself in course of winding up: see para 2665 post); s 209 (destroying, falsifying etc the company's books: see para 2666 post); s 210 (making material omission from statement relating to company's affairs: see para 2668 post); s 211 (making false representation or fraud for purpose of obtaining creditors' consent to an agreement in connection with winding up: see para 2669 post); the Company Directors Disqualification Act 1986 s 11 (undischarged bankrupt acting as director: see para 1423 post); s 13 (acting in contravention of a disqualification order: see para 1443 post).

This list is not exhaustive. The offence of impersonation under the Companies Act 1948 s 84 (repealed) was one for which imprisonment could be ordered: see now the Theft Act 1968 s 15 and CRIMINAL LAW vol 11(1) (Reissue) para 567.

16 See eg the Companies Act 1985 s 436 (as amended) (failing to attend before, produce documents to or answer questions put by inspectors) and para 1379 post.

17 See para 2664 et seq post.

1160. Punishment for fraudulent trading. If any business of a company is carried on[1] with intent to defraud[2] creditors of the company or creditors of any other person, or for any fraudulent purpose[3], every person who was knowingly a party to the carrying on[4] of the business in that manner is liable on conviction on indictment to imprisonment for a term not exceeding seven years or a fine, or to both, or on summary conviction to imprisonment for a term not exceeding six months or a fine not exceeding the statutory maximum, or to both[5]. The allegation of intent to defraud contains an ingredient of dishonesty without which finding no jury would be entitled to convict[6].

It must be dishonesty on the part of those who are carrying on the business of the company; if such persons are themselves acting honestly, but have been induced to carry on the business by the fraudulent representations of others, no such action will lie against those who have so induced the carrying on of the business[7].

Where a person carries on the business of two companies with the fraudulent intent of defrauding the companies' customers, he commits the offence of fraudulent trading[8].

1 One transaction may be sufficient: *Re Gerald Cooper Chemicals Ltd* [1978] Ch 262, [1978] 2 All ER 49. Where the only allegation is the bare fact of preferring one creditor over another, such preference will not per se be sufficient to constitute fraud: *Re Sarflax Ltd* [1979] Ch 592, [1979] 1 All ER 529.

2 The persons who actually carry on the business must be guilty of fraud, and a holding company cannot be liable otherwise than as a knowing party to such conduct: *Re Augustus Barnett & Son Ltd* [1986] BCLC 170.

3 Prior to the coming into force of the Companies Act 1981 s 96 on 22 December 1981 such an allegation could only have been made in the course of the winding up of the company. However, s 96 (repealed:

see now the Companies Act 1985 s 458) does not apply to acts which took place prior to its coming into effect: *R v Sutcliffe-Williams and Gaskell* [1983] Crim LR 255.

4 A person who, although not a director, manages the business in consultation with a director is within this description: *Re Peake and Hall* [1985] PCC 87, Isle of Man HC. A creditor who knowingly receives money procured by carrying on a business with intent to defraud may be liable (see *Re Gerald Cooper Chemicals Ltd* [1978] Ch 262, [1978] 2 All ER 49); but not a secretary who merely performs the duties appropriate to that office (*Re Maidstone Buildings Provisions Ltd* [1971] 3 All ER 363, [1971] 1 WLR 1085). Similarly a financial adviser who fails to give advice is not by reason of that fact alone so liable (*Re Maidstone Buildings Provisions Ltd* supra); nor a director who did not concern himself with the company's financial affairs (*Re Peake and Hall* supra). Where there is an issue as to whether the accused falls within the Companies Act 1985 s 458, that issue must be put to the jury with clear guidance as to the meaning of 'a party to the carrying on of the business of the company': *R v Miles* [1992] Crim LR 657, CA.

5 Companies Act 1985 ss 458, 730, Sch 24. Section 458 applies whether or not the company has been, or is in the course of being, wound up: s 458. For the meaning of 'the statutory maximum' see para 1161 post. As to the possible unlimited liability of such persons in a winding up see further para 2670 post.

6 See *Re Patrick and Lyon Ltd* [1933] Ch 786; *DPP v Schildkamp* [1971] AC 1, [1969] 3 All ER 1640, HL; *R v Rollafson* [1969] 2 All ER 833, [1969] 1 WLR 815, CA. 'Intent to defraud creditors' may in general be properly inferred if the company continues to carry on business and incurs debts when to the knowledge of the persons responsible there is no reasonable prospect of those debts being paid: *Re William C Leitch Bros Ltd* [1932] 2 Ch 71.

7 *Re Augustus Barnett & Son Ltd* [1986] BCLC 170 (directors of parent company induced directors of subsidiary to carry on business by fraudulently promising financial support; liability might have rested in deceit, but not under these statutory provisions).

8 *R v Kemp* [1988] QB 645, [1988] 2 WLR 975, CA. See also *R v Seillon* [1982] Crim LR 676, CA.

1161. Punishment of offences. In many cases the Companies Act 1985 and the Insolvency Act 1986 impose either imprisonment or a fine, or both, upon companies and their officers who fail to comply with the statutory requirements. Schedule 24 to the Companies Act 1985 and Schedule 10 to the Insolvency Act 1986 have effect with respect to the way in which such offences under those Acts are punishable on conviction[1].

In relation to an offence under a provision of either Act specified in the first column of the appropriate Schedule (the general nature of the offence being described in the second column), the third column shows whether the offence is punishable on conviction on indictment, or on summary conviction, or either in the one way or the other[2].

The fourth column of the appropriate Schedule shows, in relation to an offence, the maximum punishment by way of fine or imprisonment under the appropriate Act which may be imposed on a person convicted of the offence in the way specified in relation to it in the third column (that is to say, on indictment or summarily), a reference to a period of years or months being to a term of imprisonment of that duration[3].

The fifth column shows (in relation to an offence for which there is an entry in that column) that a person convicted of the offence after continued contravention is liable to a daily default fine, that is to say, he is liable on a second or subsequent summary conviction of the offence to the fine specified in that column for each day on which the contravention is continued (instead of the penalty specified for the offence in the fourth column of the appropriate Schedule)[4].

For the purpose of any enactment in the Companies Acts[5] which provides that an officer of a company or other body who is in default is liable to a fine or penalty, the expression 'officer who is in default' means any officer of the company or other body who knowingly and wilfully authorises or permits the default, refusal or contravention mentioned in that enactment[6]; and for the purpose of any enactment in the Insolvency Act 1986 which provides that an officer of a company who is in default is liable to a fine or penalty, the expression 'officer who is in default' means any officer of the company who knowingly and wilfully authorises or permits the default, refusal or contravention mentioned in that enactment[7].

With reference to a fine or penalty on summary conviction for an offence, 'the statutory maximum' means the prescribed sum[8] within the meaning of the Magistrates' Courts Act 1980[9].

1   Companies Act 1985 s 730(1); Insolvency Act 1986 s 430(1).
2   Companies Act 1985 s 730(2); Insolvency Act 1986 s 430(2).
3   Companies Act 1985 s 730(3); Insolvency Act 1986 s 430(3).
4   Companies Act 1985 s 730(4); Insolvency Act 1986 s 430(4).
5   For the meaning of 'the Companies Acts' see para 60 note 1 ante.
6   Companies Act 1985 s 730(5) (amended by the Companies Act 1989 s 145, Sch 19 para 17).
7   Insolvency Act 1986 s 430(5).
8   Ie within the meaning of the Magistrates' Courts Act 1980 s 32 (as amended): see MAGISTRATES vol 29 para 397. The present maximum is £5,000: see s 32(9) (amended by the Criminal Justice Act 1991 s 17(2)(c)).
9   Interpretation Act 1978 s 5, Sch 1 (amended by the Criminal Justice Act 1988 s 170(1), Sch 15 para 58(b)).

1162. Offences by bodies corporate. Where a body corporate[1] is guilty of a specified offence[2] and it is proved that the offence occurred with the consent or connivance of, or was attributable to any neglect on the part of any director[3], manager, secretary or other similar officer of the body, or any person who was purporting to act in any such capacity, he as well as the body corporate is guilty of that offence and is liable to be proceeded against and punished accordingly[4].

Where the affairs of a body corporate are managed by its members, the above provisions apply in relation to the acts and defaults of a member in connection with his functions of management as if he were a director of the body corporate[5].

1   For the meaning of 'body corporate' see para 89 note 8 ante.
2   Ie an offence under any of the Companies Act 1985 s 210 (see para 745 ante), s 216(3) (see para 752 ante), s 394A(1) (as added) (see para 1053 ante), s 447 (as amended) (see para 1386 post), s 448 (as substituted) (see para 1393 post), s 449 (as amended) (see para 1387 post), s 450 (as amended) (see para 1388 post) and s 451 (as amended) (see para 1386 post).
3   For these purposes, 'director', in relation to an offence under any of ibid ss 447–451 (as amended), includes a shadow director: s 733(4). For the meaning of 'director' and 'shadow director' see para 543 note 1 ante.
4   Ibid s 733(1) (amended by the Insolvency Act 1985 s 109, Sch 6 para 7(2); the Insolvency Act 1986 s 439(1), Sch 13 Pt I; the Companies Act 1989 s 123(3)).
5   Companies Act 1985 s 733(3) (amended by the Companies Act 1989 s 212, Sch 24).

1163. Criminal proceedings against unincorporated bodies. Proceedings for an offence alleged to have been committed under specified provisions of the Companies Act 1985[1] by an unincorporated body must be brought in the name of that body (and not in that of any of its members); and, for the purposes of any such proceedings, any rules of court relating to the service of documents apply as if that body were a corporation[2].

A fine imposed on an unincorporated body on its conviction of such an offence must be paid out the funds of that body[3].

Where such an offence committed by a partnership is proved to have been committed with the consent or connivance of, or to be attributable to any neglect on the part of, a partner, he as well as the partnership is guilty of the offence and liable to be proceeded against and punished accordingly[4].

Where such an offence committed by an unincorporated body (other than a partnership) is proved to have been committed with the consent or connivance of, or to be attributable to any neglect on the part of, any officer of the body or any member of its governing body, he as well as the body is guilty of the offence and liable to be proceeded against and punished accordingly[5].

1 Ie under the Companies Act 1985 s 389A(3) (as added) (see para 1034 ante), s 394A(1) (as added) (see para 1053 ante), s 447 (as amended) (see para 1386 post), s 448 (as substituted) (see para 1393 post), s 449 (as amended) (see para 1387 post), s 450 (as amended) (see para 1388 post) or s 451 (as amended) (see para 1386 post).
2 Ibid s 734(1) (amended by the Companies Act 1989 ss 120(2), 123(4)). In a case in which an unincorporated body is charged in England and Wales with such an offence, the Criminal Justice Act 1925 s 33 (as amended) and the Magistrates' Courts Act 1980 s 46, Sch 3 (as amended) (procedure on charge of an offence against a corporation: see MAGISTRATES) have effect in like manner as in the case of a corporation so charged: Companies Act 1985 s 734(3).
3 Ibid s 734(2).
4 Ibid s 734(5) (added by the Companies Act 1989 s 145, Sch 19 para 18).
5 Companies Act 1985 s 734(6) (added by the Companies Act 1989 Sch 19 para 18).

1164. Prosecution of offences. Summary proceedings for any offence under the Companies Acts[1] or the Insolvency Act 1986[2] may, without prejudice to any jurisdiction exercisable apart from these provisions, be taken against a body corporate at any place at which it has a place of business[3], and against any other person at any place at which he is for the time being[4].

An information relating to such an offence which is triable by a magistrates' court in England and Wales may be so tried if it is laid at any time within three years after the commission of the offence and within 12 months after the date on which evidence sufficient in the opinion of the Director of Public Prosecutions or the Secretary of State, as the case may be, to justify the proceedings comes to his knowledge[5]. For these purposes, a certificate of the Director of Public Prosecutions or the Secretary of State, as the case may be, as to the date on which such evidence came to his knowledge is conclusive evidence of it[6].

On a summons for default in making annual returns a magistrates' court is not bound to accept the register as conclusive, but should accept it as correct unless it is clearly proved that the entries and the returns based on them are so false and misleading as not to be in compliance with the Companies Act 1985[7].

1 For the meaning of 'the Companies Acts' see para 60 note 1 ante.
2 Ie the Insolvency Act 1986 Pts I–VII (ss 1–251) (as amended).
3 For the meaning of 'place of business' see para 63 note 1 ante.
4 Companies Act 1985 s 731(1); Insolvency Act 1986 s 431(1). As to summary proceedings see MAGISTRATES vol 29 para 301 et seq; as to appeals to the Crown Court see CRIMINAL LAW vol 11(2) (Reissue) para 677 et seq; and as to appeals on a case stated to the High Court see also MAGISTRATES vol 29 para 472. An appeal against a refusal of mandamus to compel a magistrate to issue process to lead to the recovery of a penalty under the Companies Act 1985 is an appeal from a judgment of the High Court in a criminal cause or matter and hence no appeal lies under the Supreme Court Act 1981 s 18(1)(a): *R v Tyler and International Commercial Co* [1891] 2 QB 588, CA. However, an appeal lies to the House of Lords from any decision of the Divisional Court or the criminal division of the Court of Appeal in a criminal cause or matter provided that court certifies that a point of law of general public importance is involved, and the court below, or the House of Lords itself, gives leave: see the Administration of Justice Act 1960 s 1(1)(a),(2); the Criminal Appeal Act 1968 s 33 and CRIMINAL LAW vol 11(2) (Reissue) paras 1437, 1491.
5 Companies Act 1985 s 731(2); Insolvency Act 1986 s 431(2). This is notwithstanding anything in the Magistrates' Courts Act 1980 s 127(1) (see MAGISTRATES): Companies Act 1985 s 731(2); Insolvency Act 1986 s 431(4).

6   Companies Act 1985 s 731(4); Insolvency Act 1986 s 431(4).
7   See *Re Briton, Medical and General Life Association* (1888) 39 ChD 61, following *Grosvenor Bank Co v Boaler* (1885) 49 JP 774. The High Court has the right to issue a writ of prohibition to the court of summary jurisdiction if it considers that that court is exceeding its jurisdiction: *Re Briton, Medical and General Life Association* supra at 64.

1165. Prosecution by public authorities. In respect of some offences[1], proceedings may not be instituted in England and Wales except by or with the consent of the Secretary of State or the Director of Public Prosecutions[2]. In respect of other offences[3], such proceedings may be instituted only by or with the consent of either the Secretary of State or the Director of Public Prosecutions or the Industrial Assurance Commissioner[4]. In the case of one offence[5] only, proceedings may be instituted only by or with the consent of the Secretary of State[6].

1   Ie under any of the Companies Act 1985 s 210 (see para 745 ante), s 324 (see para 564 ante) or s 329 (as amended) (see para 567 ante).
2   Ibid s 732(1),(2)(a). As to the saving for privileged communications see para 1168 post.
3   Ie under ibid ss 447-451 (as amended): see para 1386 et seq post.
4   Ibid s 732(1),(2)(b).
5   Ie under ibid s 455: see para 1396 post.
6   Ibid s 732(1),(2)(c).

1166. Production of books where offence suspected. If, on an application[1] made to a judge of the High Court by the Director of Public Prosecutions, the Secretary of State or a chief officer of police[2], there is shown to be reasonable cause to believe that any person has, while an officer of a company, committed an offence in connection with the management of the company's affairs, and that evidence of the commission of the offence is to be found in any books or papers[3] of or under the control of the company, an order may be made:

(1)   authorising any person named in it to inspect such books or papers or any of them for the purpose of investigating and obtaining evidence of the offence; or

(2)   requiring the secretary of the company or such other officer of it as may be named in the order to produce the books or papers or any of them to a person named in the order at a place so named[4].

The above provisions also apply in relation to any books or papers of a person carrying on the business of banking so far as they relate to the company's affairs, as they apply to any books or papers of or under the company's control, except that no order may be made in relation to them under head (2) above[5].

1   The application is by ex parte originating summons: RSC Ord 102 r 2(3).
2   'Chief officer of police' means, in relation to the City of London, the Commissioner of the City of London Police; in relation to the metropolitan police district, the Commissioner of Police of the Metropolis; in relation to a county, or a combined area, the chief constable: Police Act 1964 s 62(b), Sch 8 (applied by the Interpretation Act 1978 s 5, Sch 1).
3   For these purposes, 'books and papers' or 'books or papers' includes accounts, deeds, writings and documents: Companies Act 1985 s 744.
4   Ibid s 721(1),(2). The judge's decision is not appealable: s 721(4); *Re Racal Communications Ltd* [1981] AC 374, [1980] 2 All ER 634, HL.
5   Companies Act 1985 s 721(3).

1167. Admissibility of evidence. In any proceedings, whether or not under the Insolvency Act 1986, a statement of affairs prepared for the purposes of any provision of that Act which was derived from the Insolvency Act 1985[1], and any other statement made in pursuance of a requirement imposed by or under any such provision or by or under rules made[2] under the Insolvency Act 1986 may be used in evidence against any person making or concurring in making the statement[3].

1   See para 2805 note 1 post.
2   Ie made under the Insolvency Act 1986 s 411: see para 2800 post.
3   Ibid s 433.

1168. Saving for privileged communications. Where proceedings are instituted under the Companies Acts[1] against any person by the Director of Public Prosecutions or by or on behalf of the Secretary of State, nothing in those Acts is to be taken to require any person to disclose information which he is entitled to refuse to disclose on grounds of legal professional privilege[2].

1   For the meaning of 'the Companies Acts' see para 60 note 1 ante. In the Companies Act 1985 s 732(3) references to the Companies Acts include certain provisions of the Insolvency Act 1986, and also the Company Directors Disqualification Act 1986: see para 20 text to note 12 and note 12 ante.
2   Companies Act 1985 s 732(3).

(ix) Actions and Proceedings

1169. Company's name in litigation. A company registered under the Companies Act 1985 or the Acts which it replaces is a body corporate[1] and may only sue or be sued in its corporate name[2]. Proceedings by a company under the Insolvency Act 1986 against an insolvent individual are considered elsewhere[3].

The change of a company's name does not render defective any legal proceedings by or against it; and any legal proceedings that might have been continued or commenced against it by its former name may be continued or commenced against it by its new name[4]. Where the name of a limited company is changed after a cause or matter by or against it has been instituted, the new name must be substituted in all future proceedings in the cause or matter, and the former name mentioned in brackets[5].

1   See the Companies Act 1985 s 13(3) and para 92 ante.
2   *Re Hodges* (1873) 8 Ch App 204; *Pilbrow v Pilbrow's Atmospheric Rly Co* (1846) 3 CB 730. In *Springate v Questier* [1952] 2 All ER 21 notice of an intended prosecution under the Road Traffic Act 1972 s 179(2)(c) (repealed: see now the Road Traffic Offenders Act 1988 s 1(1)(c),(2)) was held to have been validly served on a limited company, though the word 'limited' was omitted; and see CORPORATIONS vol 9 para 1215. As to the amendment of misnomers in writs see *Etablissement Baudelot v R Graham & Co Ltd* [1953] 2 QB 271, [1953] 1 All ER 149, CA (French trading firm wrongly described as incorporated company) and PRACTICE AND PROCEDURE vol 37 para 224.
3   See BANKRUPTCY.
4   See the Companies Act 1985 s 28(7) and para 160 ante.
5   *Practice Direction* [1965] 1 All ER 43, [1965] 1 WLR 120.

1170. Control of company's litigation. As regards litigation by an incorporated company, as a rule the directors are the persons who have authority to act for the company[1]; but, in the absence of any contract to the contrary in the articles of association, the majority of the members are entitled to decide, even to the extent of overruling the directors, whether an action in the company's name should be begun or allowed to proceed[2]. The secretary of a company cannot institute proceedings in its name in the absence of express authority to do so[3]; but proceedings begun without proper authority may subsequently be ratified[4].

Any objection that an action in the name of the company is not properly authorised should be raised at the outset by an application to have the name of the company struck out; if not so raised, it may be raised when it comes to the attention of the court or the defendant that this is the case[5]. Where appropriate, the action may be adjourned so that the issue as to the initial authorisation, or subsequent ratification, of the proceedings may be tried[5].

1 See para 582 ante; *Harben v Phillips* (1883) 23 ChD 14 at 29, CA.
2 See *Marshall's Valve Gear Co Ltd v Manning, Wardle & Co Ltd* [1909] 1 Ch 267 at 272; *Pender v Lushington* (1877) 6 ChD 70; *Duckett v Gover* (1877) 6 ChD 82; *Harben v Phillips* (1883) 23 ChD 14, CA; cf *Automatic Self-Cleansing Filter Syndicate Co Ltd v Cuninghame* [1906] 2 Ch 34, CA; *Gramophone and Typewriter Ltd v Stanley* [1908] 2 KB 89 at 98, 105, CA; *Quin & Axtens Ltd v Salmon* [1909] AC 442, HL; *Re Olderfleet Shipbuilding and Engineering Co Ltd* [1922] 1 IR 26. As to joining the company as plaintiff see *Harben v Phillips* supra.
3 *Daimler Co Ltd v Continental Tyre and Rubber Co (Great Britain) Ltd* [1916] 2 AC 307, HL. As to the court procedure where there is want of authority to sue see *Russian Commercial and Industrial Bank v Comptoir d'Escompte de Mulhouse* [1925] AC 112, HL; *John Shaw & Sons (Salford) Ltd v Shaw* [1935] 2 KB 113, CA; and PRACTICE AND PROCEDURE vol 37 para 442.
4 *Danish Mercantile Co Ltd v Beaumont* [1951] Ch 680, [1951] 1 All ER 925, CA, approved in *Alexander Ward & Co Ltd v Samyang Navigation Co Ltd* [1975] 2 All ER 424, [1975] 1 WLR 673, HL (company without directors; two individuals brought action on company's behalf to recover debt without authority; acts of individuals subsequently ratified by liquidator).
5 *Airways Ltd v Bowen* [1985] BCLC 355, CA.

1171. Actions in respect of corporate wrongs. In an action to redress a wrong done to a company or to recover money or damages alleged to be due to it, the company is the only proper plaintiff[1], but its name should be used as plaintiff only by direction of the company or its directors[2]. Where the members complaining represent the majority of the company, the action may be brought in the company's name, even though the directors object[3]. The court may allow the matter to stand so that a company meeting may be held to decide whether the action should proceed in the company's name[4]. At such a meeting the votes of the persons complained of cannot be excluded[5]. Nevertheless, proceedings may be brought by any member or members in his or their own name or names where such authority cannot be obtained and the act complained of is of a fraudulent character or oppressive or is ultra vires the company[6], or is criminal[7]; or where the wrongdoers control the majority of votes[8]; or where the result would otherwise be that the company was carrying out by an ordinary resolution something which could be properly carried out only by a special resolution[9], or by any other resolution requiring a prescribed majority[10]. The question whether the action will lie at all should, if possible, be decided as a preliminary issue, and not left for determination at the trial[11].

In such a case the plaintiff should distinctly allege the true nature of the act complained of and the impossibility of getting the company to impeach its validity[12]. Persons who were themselves parties to the wrongful act cannot raise the question by action[13]; and a shareholder who has knowingly received and retained the proceeds of an act ultra vires the company is not a proper person to sue[14], unless he is proposing to restrain future ultra vires acts[15]. Similarly, if for any other reason it would be inequitable to allow the plaintiff to bring such an action, the defendant may raise the plaintiff's conduct as a defence thereto[16].

In all such cases the company must be made a defendant[17]. If the directors are themselves the wrongdoers, it is proper to add them as defendants[18]; and, where the subject matter of the action is an agreement between the company and a stranger, it is proper to make him a defendant[19]. Except as expressly mentioned, the court has no jurisdiction to interfere with the internal management of companies acting within their powers[20]. Where those seeking to bring a minority shareholders' action in fact control the company, so that they are in a position to cause the company to bring the action, such an action is wholly misconceived[21].

If the company is in liquidation, a minority shareholders' action will not lie[22]; the correct course for an aggrieved shareholder to take is to persuade the liquidator, against a suitable indemnity, to bring the action or, if he is unwilling to do so, to apply to the court for leave to bring the action in the name of the liquidator[23].

1 *Foss v Harbottle* (1843) 2 Hare 461; and see the statement of the rule in *Edwards v Halliwell* [1950] 2 All ER 1064 at 1066, CA per Jenkins LJ; and see further para 1113 et seq ante. In *Duckett v Gover* (1877) 6 ChD 82, the company was made defendant in the first instance and leave was given to amend by making it plaintiff; cf *Mason v Harris* (1879) 11 ChD 97, CA. Damage to the company must be shown: *Heyting v Dupont* [1964] 2 All ER 273, [1964] 1 WLR 843, CA. The rule will not be applied if it would frustrate the will of the majority: *Hodgson v National and Local Government Officers Association* [1972] 1 All ER 15, [1972] 1 WLR 130.

2 *Compagnie de Mayville v Whitley* [1896] 1 Ch 788 at 803, CA.

3 *MacDougall v Gardiner* (1875) 1 ChD 13 at 22, CA; *Pender v Lushington* (1877) 6 ChD 70; *Imperial Hydropathic Hotel Co, Blackpool v Hampson* (1882) 23 ChD 1, CA; *Harben v Phillips* (1883) 23 ChD 14, CA.

4 See *Danish Mercantile Co Ltd v Beaumont* [1951] Ch 680 at 687, [1951] 1 All ER 925 at 930, CA; and *SBA Properties Ltd v Cradock* [1967] 2 All ER 610, [1967] 1 WLR 716 (application adjourned pending hearing of winding-up petition). See also the cases cited in para 1170 note 3 ante.

5 *Mason v Harris* (1879) 11 ChD 97 to 107, CA.

6 *Burland v Earle* [1902] AC 83 at 93, PC; *Edwards v Halliwell* [1950] 2 All ER 1064 at 1067, CA per Jenkins LJ; and see generally para 1113 et seq ante; *Pavlides v Jensen* [1956] Ch 565, [1956] 2 All ER 518 (gross negligence not sufficient).

7 *Cockburn v Newbridge Sanitary Steam Laundry Co Ltd and Llewellyn* [1915] 1 IR 237 at 249, CA.

8 *Russell v Wakefield Waterworks Co* (1875) LR 20 Eq 474 at 482; *Prudential Assurance Co Ltd v Newman Industries Ltd (No 2)* [1982] Ch 204, [1982] 1 All ER 354, CA. As to the procedure for striking out such an action see *Smith v Croft (No 2)* [1987] 3 All ER 909, [1987] 3 WLR 405.

9 *Baillie v Oriental Telephone and Electric Co Ltd* [1915] 1 Ch 503, CA.

10 See *Edwards v Halliwell* [1950] 2 All ER 1064, CA.

11 *Prudential Assurance Co Ltd v Newman Industries Ltd (No 2)* [1982] Ch 204, [1982] 1 All ER 354, CA; *Estmanco (Kilner House) Ltd v Greater London Council* [1982] 1 All ER 437, [1982] 1 WLR 2. As to the plaintiff's right to obtain an indemnity in respect of his costs from the company see *Wallersteiner v Moir (No 2)* [1975] QB 373, [1975] 1 All ER 849, CA; *Smith v Croft* [1986] 2 All ER 551, [1986] 1 WLR 580 (for subsequent proceedings see [1987] BCLC 355); *Jaybird Group Ltd v Greenwood* [1986] BCLC 319. Such an order will not be made unless the action is for the benefit of shareholders: *Watts v Midland Bank plc* [1986] BCLC 15 (company hopelessly insolvent).

12 *Cannon v Trask* (1875) LR 20 Eq 669 at 676; and see *Gray v Lewis* (1873) 8 Ch App 1035 at 1050; *Anderson v Midland Rly Co* [1902] 1 Ch 369 at 375; *Solomons v Laing* (1850) 12 Beav 377; *Mason v Harris* (1879) 11 ChD 97, CA; *Mills v Northern Rly of Buenos Ayres Co* (1870) 5 Ch App 621; *Birch v Sullivan* [1958] 1 All ER 56, [1957] 1 WLR 1247.

13 *Whitwam v Watkin* (1898) 78 LT 188 (where the plaintiffs became shareholders for the purpose of bringing the action).

14 *Towers v African Tug Co* [1904] 1 Ch 558, CA.

15 *Mosely v Koffyfontein Mines Ltd* [1911] 1 Ch 73, CA (distinguishing *Towers v African Tug Co* [1904] 1 Ch 558, CA); affd on another point sub nom *Koffyfontein Mines Ltd v Mosely* [1911] AC 409, HL.

16 *Nurcombe v Nurcombe* [1985] 1 All ER 65, [1985] 1 WLR 370, CA (plaintiff had proceeded in matrimonial proceedings against her husband on the basis that a profit he had made as a director of the company belonged to him and not the company).

17 *Silber Light Co v Silber* (1879) 12 ChD 717; *Spokes v Grosvenor Hotel Co* [1897] 2 QB 124, CA; *Towers v African Tug Co* [1904] 1 Ch 558 at 571, CA.

18 *Ferguson v Wilson* (1866) 2 Ch App 77 at 90.

19 *Russell v Wakefield Waterworks Co* (1875) LR 20 Eq 474 at 481.

20 *MacDougall v Gardiner* (1875) 1 ChD 13, CA; *Wall v London and Northern Assets Corpn* [1898] 2 Ch 469 at 483, CA; *Burland v Earle* [1902] AC 83, PC.

21 *Watts v Midland Bank plc* [1986] BCLC 15 (action against receiver for alleged improper discharge of his duties; no obstacle to company bringing the action itself).

22 *Ferguson v Wallbridge* [1935] 3 DLR 66, PC; *Fargro Ltd v Godfroy* [1986] 3 All ER 279, [1986] 1 WLR 1134.

23 As to such procedure (approved in the cases cited in note 20 supra) see *Cape Breton Co v Fenn* (1881) 17 ChD 198, CA; and para 2341 post.

1172. Unauthorised use of company's name. If the name of the company has been wrongly used as plaintiff, it will be struck out as plaintiff[1], but may be added as defendant[2]. The solicitor[3] or the person who instructed him and who was also plaintiff[4] may be ordered to pay the costs of a company improperly made plaintiff and of the defendant[5]. However, where, in bringing the action in the company's name, the plaintiffs substantially represent the wishes of the majority of the shareholders, the plaintiffs' costs may be directed to be paid by the company[6]. Where the action is properly brought in the company's name, the solicitors for those who unsuccessfully apply in its name for a stay may be ordered to pay the costs personally[7].

1 *Atwool v Merryweather* (1867) LR 5 Eq 464n at 468n; *Pender v Lushington* (1877) 6 ChD 70; *Oystermouth Rly or Tramroad Co v Morris* [1876] WN 129, 192; *West End Hotels Syndicate Ltd v Bayer* (1912) 29 TLR 92.

2 *Silber Light Co v Silber* (1879) 12 ChD 717.

3 *Newbiggin-by-the-Sea Gas Co v Armstrong* (1879) 13 ChD 310, CA; *John Morley Building Co v Barras* [1891] 2 Ch 386; *Gold Reefs of Western Australia Ltd v Dawson* [1897] 1 Ch 115; *West End Hotels Syndicate Ltd v Bayer* (1912) 29 TLR 92.

4 *Compagnie de Mayville v Whitley* [1896] 1 Ch 788 at 810, CA; and see *Wandsworth and Putney Gas-Light and Coke Co v Wright* (1870) 22 LT 404.

5 See *Silber Light Co v Silber* (1879) 12 ChD 717. Where a solicitor had originally authority to defend an action for a company which was afterwards dissolved, he was ordered to pay the costs of the plaintiff as from the date on which he might with due diligence have known of the dissolution: *Salton v New Beeston Cycle Co* [1900] 1 Ch 43. The proper order would now date from the dissolution itself: see *Yonge v Toynbee* [1910] 1 KB 215, CA. As to the effect of solicitors acting without authority see SOLICITORS vol 44(1) (Reissue) para 132.

6 *Re Imperial Hydropathic Hotel Co, Blackpool v Hampson* (1882) 23 ChD 1, CA.

7 *Marshall's Valve Gear Co Ltd v Manning, Wardle & Co Ltd* [1909] 1 Ch 267 at 275.

1173. Action by company member for individual wrong. Proceedings may be maintained by a member of a company when the matter is one which affects his individual rights[1]; and in a proper case he may obtain an injunction against the company in aid of his right[2].

A shareholder seeking to enforce an individual right against the company is not entitled to an advance order for an indemnity as to costs[3].

1 *Pender v Lushington* (1877) 6 ChD 70 at 80; *Edwards v Halliwell* [1950] 2 All ER 1064, CA.

2 See *Pulbrook v Richmond Consolidated Mining Co* (1878) 9 ChD 610; *Munster v Cammell Co* (1882) 21 ChD 183; *Kyshe v Alturas Gold Co* (1888) 36 WR 496; *Turnbull v West Riding Athletic Club Leeds Ltd* (1894) 70 LT 92; *Catesby v Burnett* [1916] 2 Ch 325 (where an injunction was granted restraining two former directors from continuing to act, and restraining the company from refusing to allow two duly elected directors to act as such); *Norman v Mitchell* (1854) 5 De GM & G 648; *Johnson v Lyttle's Iron Agency* (1877) 5 ChD 687, CA; *Goulton v London Architectural Brick and Tile Co* [1877] WN 141 (where an injunction was granted to restrain an illegal forfeiture of shares); *Jones v Pacaya Rubber and Produce Co Ltd* [1911] 1 KB 455, CA (forfeiture restrained pending trial of action for rescission of contract to take shares); *British Murac Syndicate Ltd v Alperton Rubber Co Ltd* [1915] 2 Ch 186 (where a company was restrained from altering its articles of association in breach of agreement with a member); *Lawson v Financial News Ltd* (1917) 34 TLR 52, CA (issue of debenture stock to directors and employees restrained); *Nelson v Anglo-American Land Mortgage Agency Co* [1897] 1 Ch 130 (where an injunction was

granted to restrain interference by a company with shareholders and debenture holders, in the exercise of their statutory rights to inspect, at all reasonable times, the register of mortgages of the company); *Cory v Reindeer SS Ltd* (1915) 31 TLR 530 (where an interlocutory injunction was granted to restrain the company from acting upon resolutions which had been passed against the wishes of the majority of the shareholders); *Last v Buller & Co Ltd* (1919) 36 TLR 35; *Tatham v Palace Restaurants Ltd* (1909) 53 Sol Jo 743; *Hayes v Bristol Plant Hire Ltd* [1957] 1 All ER 685, [1957] 1 WLR 499 (action for wrongful exclusion of a director from the boardroom).

3 *Re a Company (Case No 005136 of 1986)* [1987] BCLC 82. The principle in *Wallersteiner v Moir (No 2)* [1975] QB 373, [1975] 1 All ER 849, CA is confined to minority shareholders' actions: see paras 1110-1112 ante.

1174. Representative action. Where an action is brought by a member of a company to enforce or protect the rights of members generally, the plaintiff usually sues on behalf of himself and the other members. This form of action is encouraged by the court as it avoids conflict as to the persons who are entitled to put forward the company as plaintiff[1]. The court has a discretion to order that the company shall indemnify the plaintiff against the costs incurred in the action[2]; and even in a proper case to order that the company shall pay a proportion of those costs as the action proceeds, without waiting until its conclusion[3]. The test is whether an independent board, exercising the standard of care which a prudent business man would exercise in his own affairs, would have decided to bring the action[4].

1 *Alexander v Automatic Telephone Co* [1900] 2 Ch 56, CA. As to ultra vires acts cf para 1110 ante. As to actions by one or more persons on behalf of all persons having the same interest see RSC Ord 15 r 12; CCR Ord 5 r 5; *Duke of Bedford v Ellis* [1901] AC 1, HL; *Wood v McCarthy* [1893] 1 QB 775; and COUNTY COURTS vol 10 para 129; PRACTICE AND PROCEDURE vol 37 para 232 et seq. See further paras 1175, 1176 post.

2 *Wallersteiner v Moir (No 2)* [1975] QB 373, [1975] 1 All ER 849, CA. The plaintiff should accordingly, if he considers it appropriate, after the issue of the writ apply ex parte to the master for directions whether there is a reasonable case for the shareholder to bring the action at the expense of the company down to some particular stage, when the matter can be reviewed: *Wallersteiner v Moir (No 2)* supra. In the absence of special circumstances, the master should, however, require the matter to be dealt with inter partes, and should ensure that the intending plaintiff's evidence should, save as to matters of privilege and such matters, if any, as would defeat the success of the action, be disclosed to the company so as to enable it to answer it if it can. The views of genuinely independent shareholders should also be taken into account in considering whether the action should be allowed to proceed at the expense of the company: *Smith v Croft* [1986] 2 All ER 551, [1986] 1 WLR 580. Such relief is in any event available only in a minority shareholders' action; it is not available to a shareholder whose individual rights have been infringed: *Re a Company (Case No 005136 of 1986)* [1987] BCLC 82.

3 *Smith v Croft* [1986] 2 All ER 551, [1986] 1 WLR 580.

4 *Wallersteiner v Moir (No 2)* [1975] QB 373 at 404, [1975] 1 All ER 849 at 869, CA per Buckley LJ; *Smith v Croft* [1986] 2 All ER 551, [1986] 1 WLR 580; *Jaybird Group Ltd v Greenwood* [1986] BCLC 319.

1175. Representative parties. Where numerous persons have the same interest in any proceedings[1], as where a member of a company sues to enforce or protect the rights of members generally, the plaintiff may sue, unless the court otherwise orders, as representing all, or all except one or some of the members[2]. No consent is required from those on whose behalf the plaintiff purports to sue[3]. A plaintiff suing on behalf of a class must specify the class as accurately as possible[4]; but the fact that the interest of some members of the class is different from that of the plaintiff so suing does not make the action defective[5]. The fact that the plaintiff is suing on behalf of himself and others should be stated in the title of the pleading, and not merely in the indorsement on the writ or in the statement of claim[6].

Whatever is a defence against the plaintiff suing in a representative capacity is a defence to the action, even though other persons on whose behalf he is suing might maintain the action[7]. A plaintiff suing in a representative capacity will not be ordered to add as co-plaintiffs those on whose behalf he sues[8], or to disclose their names and addresses[9]. If anyone objects to the plaintiff suing on his behalf, he should apply by summons to have himself added as a defendant[10]; but the application must be made promptly[11].

The court will not allow a person to represent himself and others as defendants unless it is satisfied that he is authorised to represent the others[12].

The judgment in a representative action binds all the members of the class of defendants represented[13].

If the plaintiff is suing as a creditor and a trustee is appointed in his bankruptcy whilst the action is pending, the right of action vests in his trustee, and, unless the trustee intervenes, the action will be dismissed[14].

1 Ie other than proceedings under RSC Ord 15 r 13, as to which a representation order is appropriate: see RSC Ord 15 rr 12(1), 13 and PRACTICE AND PROCEDURE vol 37 paras 232, 233.
2 RSC Ord 15 r 12(1).
3 *White v Carmarthen etc Rly Co* (1863) 1 Hem & M 786; *Bloxam v Metropolitan Rly Co* (1868) 3 Ch App 337. As to the plaintiff's right to discontinue the action see *Handford v Storie* (1825) 2 Sim & St 196; *Re Alpha Co Ltd, Ward v Alpha Co* [1903] 1 Ch 203.
4 *Marshall v South Staffordshire Tramways Co* [1895] 2 Ch 36, CA.
5 *Hallows v Fernie* (1868) 3 Ch App 467; *Watson v Cave* (1881) 17 ChD 19, CA.
6 *Re Tottenham, Tottenham v Tottenham* [1896] 1 Ch 628, explaining *Eyre v Cox* (1876) 24 WR 317; *Worraker v Pryer* (1876) 2 ChD 109; *Dover Picture Palace Ltd and Pessers v Dover Corpn and Crundall, Wraith, Gurr and Knight* (1913) 11 LGR 971, CA.
7 *Burt v British Nation Life Assurance Association* (1859) 4 De G & J 158; *Scarth v Chadwick* (1850) 14 Jur 300.
8 *De Hart v Stevenson* (1876) 1 QBD 313; *Janson v Property Insurance Co Ltd* (1913) 30 TLR 49.
9 *Leathley v McAndrew & Co* [1875] WN 259.
10 *Wilson v Church* (1878) 9 ChD 552; *Watson v Cave* (1881) 17 ChD 19, CA; *Fraser v Cooper, Hall & Co* (1882) 21 ChD 718; *May v Newton* (1887) 34 ChD 347.
11 *Conybeare v Lewis* (1883) 48 LT 527.
12 *Morgan's Brewery Co v Crosskill* [1902] 1 Ch 898. As to appointing parties to represent absent persons see RSC Ord 15 rr 13, 15 and PRACTICE AND PROCEDURE vol 37 paras 235, 236.
13 *City of London Sewers Comrs v Gellatly* (1876) 3 ChD 610 at 615; and see *Friends Provident and Century Life Office v Investment Trust Corpn Ltd* [1951] 2 All ER 632 at 634, HL; and as to a judgment against trustees for debenture holders binding the debenture holders see *Cox v Dublin City Distillery Co Ltd (No 3)* [1917] 1 IR 203, CA.
14 *Wolff v Van Boolen* (1906) 94 LT 502. As to actions by trustees in bankruptcy see BANKRUPTCY.

1176. When representative action may be brought. A representative action is properly brought[1] by a shareholder to prevent the improper declaration or payment of dividends[2], or the misapplication of the company's funds[3], or purchase by the company of its own shares[4], or an improper reduction of capital[5], or improper forfeiture of shares[6], or to stop directors from making calls unfairly[7], or to make them account for money received by them[8], or to make them pay damages to the company[9], or to prevent loans to them[10], or to impeach the validity of resolutions as to the issue of shares or otherwise[11].

An action may be brought by an applicant for shares on behalf of himself and other depositors when the company is abortive and no shares have been issued[12]. Where another class of shareholders has a conflicting interest, they should be made defendants[13].

In an action against directors for misrepresentation, several persons may join as plaintiffs[14].

1 As to representative actions by debenture holders see para 1368 post.

2 *Hoole v Great Western Rly Co* (1867) 3 Ch App 262; *Bloxam v Metropolitan Rly Co* (1868) 3 Ch App 337; *Wood v Odessa Waterworks Co* (1889) 42 ChD 636; cf *Carlisle v South Eastern Rly Co* (1850) 1 Mac & G 689 (payment of dividends actually declared; not restrained); *Salisbury v Metropolitan Rly Co* (1870) 18 WR 484 at 486; *Will v United Lankat Plantations Co Ltd* [1912] 2 Ch 571, CA; affd [1914] AC 11, HL; cf *Fawcett v Laurie* (1860) 1 Drew & Sm 192 at 202, 203. As to actions by creditors or debenture holders to restrain the payment of improper dividends see para 743 ante.

3 *Guinness v Land Corpn of Ireland Ltd* (1882) 22 ChD 349, CA; *Smith v Duke of Manchester* (1883) 24 ChD 611 (costs of dismissed winding-up petition by directors); *Studdert v Grosvenor* (1886) 33 ChD 528 (as to the points decided in this case see *Peel v London and North Western Rly Co* [1907] 1 Ch 5, CA); *Tomkinson v South-Eastern Rly Co* (1887) 35 ChD 675; *Lyde v Eastern Bengal Rly Co* (1866) 36 Beav 10; *Vance v East Lancashire Rly Co* (1856) 3 K & J 50 (application to Parliament); *Warburton v Huddersfield Industrial Society* [1892] 1 QB 817, CA; *Evans v Brunner, Mond & Co Ltd* [1921] 1 Ch 359.

4 *Hope v International Financial Society* (1876) 4 ChD 327, CA; *Rowell v John Rowell & Sons Ltd* [1912] 2 Ch 609.

5 *Bannatyne v Direct Spanish Telegraph Co* (1886) 34 ChD 287, CA.

6 *Sweny v Smith* (1869) LR 7 Eq 324.

7 *Alexander v Automatic Telephone Co* [1900] 2 Ch 56, CA.

8 *Shaw v Holland* [1900] 2 Ch 305, CA; *Bryson v Warwick and Birmingham Canal Co* (1853) 4 De GM & G 711.

9 *Spokes v Grosvenor Hotel Co* [1897] 2 QB 124, CA.

10 *Bluck v Mallalue* (1859) 27 Beav 398.

11 *Andrews v Gas Meter Co* [1897] 1 Ch 361, CA; *Preston v Grand Collier Dock Co* (1840) 11 Sim 327; *McEllistrim v Ballymacelligott Co-operative Agricultural and Dairy Society Ltd* [1919] AC 548, HL.

12 *Moseley v Cressey's Co* (1865) LR 1 Eq 405.

13 *Hoole v Great Western Rly Co* (1867) 3 Ch App 262 at 277, 278 per Rolt LJ.

14 *Drincqbier v Wood* [1899] 1 Ch 393.

1177. Mode of application to court. The Companies Act 1985 provides for many applications to be made to the court with reference to the companies which are subject to its provisions, and the mode of making applications under the Act is dealt with by the rules[1].

Questions as to the true meaning of the memorandum or articles of a company may be decided by the court in proceedings begun by originating summons. The court may decide the question as between the company and the shareholder who is the other party to the summons[2], but will not usually appoint a defendant shareholder to represent a class, or decide the question so as to bind the class unless a meeting of the members of the class is first called and nominates a person to represent the class[3].

1 See RSC Ord 102 and the Insolvency Rules 1986, SI 1986/1925 (amended by SI 1987/1919; SI 1989/397; SI 1991/495; SI 1993/602; SI 1995/586) (see para 2800 et seq post). The mode in which the applications are to be made in the High Court under RSC Ord 102 (ie by originating summons, by originating motion or by petition: see RSC Ord 102 rr 2–4) is dealt with elsewhere in this title in each case in connection with the section of the Companies Act 1985 which provides for the application. Applications are made in the county court by petition if a like application to the High Court would be so made: CCR Ord 49 r 3. Other applications are made by originating application: CCR Ord 3 r 4(1).

As to the practice in the companies court relating to applications which are to be made to a judge in open court, applications which are to be made to the registrar and applications which may be dealt with by the chief clerk see *Practice Direction* [1987] 1 All ER 107, [1987] 1 WLR 53.

2 *Mason v Schuppisser* (1899) 81 LT 147; *Re William Thomas & Co Ltd* [1915] 1 Ch 325.

3 *Morgan's Brewery Co v Crosskill* [1902] 1 Ch 898.

1178. Admissions by agents. In cases of express authorisation, an admission by an agent of the company is an admission by the company itself, where the statement or act is made or done in the ordinary course of employment[1]. A statement made by a director to the shareholders at a general meeting is not an admission which may be used by a shareholder against the company, being a statement by the agent of the company and of the shareholders to his joint principals[2].

In any civil proceedings between the company and a third person, a statement contained in a document is admissible as evidence of any fact stated in it of which direct oral evidence would be admitted, if the document is or forms part of a record compiled by a person acting under a duty from information which was supplied by a person, whether acting under a duty or not, who had, or may reasonably be supposed to have had, personal knowledge of the matters dealt with in that information and which, if not supplied by that person to the compiler of the record directly, was supplied by him to the compiler indirectly through one or more intermediaries each acting under a duty[3].

1 See AGENCY vol 1(2) (Reissue) para 148; *Lampson & Co v London and India Dock Joint Co* (1901) 17 TLR 663; *Simmons v London Joint Stock Bank* (1890) 62 LT 427; *Re Royal Bank of Australia, Meux's Executors' Case* (1852) 2 De GM & G 522 at 533; *Bruff v Great Northern Rly Co* (1858) 1 F & F 344; and see EVIDENCE vol 17 para 72. As to representations by agents see para 1119 ante.
2 *Re Devala Provident Gold Mining Co* (1883) 22 ChD 593; and see AGENCY vol 1(2) (Reissue) para 148.
3 See the Civil Evidence Act 1968 s 4(1) and EVIDENCE vol 17 para 58; cf *Shrewsbury v Blount* (1841) 2 Man & G 475. Cf the Civil Evidence Act 1968 s 1 (hearsay evidence admissible in certain cases), s 2 (out of court statements admissible in certain cases), s 3 (witnesses' previous statements), s 5 (statements produced by computers); and see EVIDENCE vol 17 paras 55, 56, 59, 288. Conversations among principals and between them and their agent are admissible to prove good faith: *Shrewsbury v Blount* supra. As to the discovery of documents and interrogatories see para 1180 post and DISCOVERY.

1179. Presumption that acts properly performed. It is presumed in favour of third persons or members of the company that acts which are proved to have been performed have been properly performed, so that the burden of proving the contrary is thrown upon the company[1].

1 See EVIDENCE vol 17 paras 118, 119; *Knight's Case* (1867) 2 Ch App 321 (forfeiture of shares held to be valid although there was no proof of a directors' resolution to that effect); *Clarke v Imperial Gas Light and Coke Co* (1832) 4 B & Ad 315; and see *Re Fireproof Doors Ltd, Umney v Fireproof Doors Ltd* [1916] 2 Ch 142.

1180. Discovery and interrogatories. An officer of a company need not be made a party to an action, in order to obtain discovery of documents[1]. An order for discovery against a company will require the affidavit verifying the list of documents to be made by a responsible or proper officer or member; normally the company secretary should make the affidavit, but the order may name any officer or member who has personal knowledge as to the documents in the company's possession[2].

If a company is a party to an action, the opposite party may apply to the court for an order allowing him to serve interrogatories on such officer or member of the company as may be specified in the order[3].

These subjects are considered fully elsewhere[4].

1 *Cooke v Oceanic Steam Co* [1875] WN 220; *Dyke v Stephens* (1885) 30 ChD 189 at 191; cf *Wilson v Church* (1878) 9 ChD 552 (interrogatories). As to orders for discovery see RSC Ord 24 r 3 and DISCOVERY vol 13 para 9 et seq.
2 See *A-G v North Metropolitan Tramways Co* [1892] 3 Ch 70 at 74.
3 See RSC Ord 26 r 2 and DISCOVERY vol 13 para 129.
4 See DISCOVERY vol 13 para 100 et seq.

1181. Enforcement of judgments and orders against company. Judgment against a company[1] may be enforced by writ of fieri facias, as in the case of a natural person[2]. Any judgment or order against the company requiring it to do an act within a specified time or requiring it to abstain from doing an act may, by leave of the court, be enforced by sequestration against its property, or by committal against any of its directors or other officers, or by writ of sequestration against their property[3]. For this purpose an undertaking given to the court and embodied in a court order has the same effect as a judgment or order[4]. A company cannot be attached for contempt of court[5], but the court may inflict an appropriate fine[6]; and sequestration will be ordered if the company contumaciously refuses to obey, though not in the case of casual or accidental and unintentional disobedience[7].

1 Unless the contrary appears, a company is included in the word 'person' in the Rules of the Supreme Court: Interpretation Act 1978 ss 5, 22(1), 23(1), Sch 1, Sch 2 para 4(1)(a); RSC Ord 1 r 3.

2 *Worral Waterworks Co v Lloyd* (1866) LR 1 CP 719; *Spokes v Banbury Board of Health* (1865) LR 1 Eq 42; and see EXECUTION vol 17 para 462 et seq. If a winding-up petition is presented founded on a judgment debt, the petition was not a mode of enforcing the judgment so as to be covered by a civil aid certificate given in the original action (*Re Parker Davies and Hughes Ltd* [1953] 2 All ER 1158, [1953] 1 WLR 1349); but following a change in the wording of the relevant rules this decision becomes obsolete: *Re Peretz Co Ltd* [1965] Ch 200, [1964] 3 All ER 633.

3 RSC Ord 45 r 5(1). The remedies against the company, and against its directors for committal, are alternative: *Iberian Trust Ltd v Founders Trust and Investment Co Ltd* [1932] 2 KB 87; and see *Benabo v William Jay & Partners Ltd* [1941] Ch 52, [1940] 4 All ER 196. It was formerly not necessary that the judgment or order which had been disobeyed should have been served personally on the company, as service on the company's solicitors was sufficient (*Aberdonia Cars Ltd v Brown, Hughes and Strachen Ltd* (1915) 59 Sol Jo 598 (sequestration)), at all events where the order was merely prohibitive (see *Ronson Products Ltd v Ronson Furniture Ltd* [1966] Ch 603, [1966] 2 All ER 381). Personal service on the director affected is now essential: RSC Ord 45 r 7(3). Execution may be issued against shareholders or public officers of joint stock companies which were registered under 7 & 8 Vict c 110 (Joint Stock Companies) (1844), or the Country Bankers Act 1826, and have not been re-registered under the Joint Stock Companies Acts (see para 11 note 2 ante); but such a proceeding is now so rare as to be practically obsolete: see Lindley's Law of Companies (6th Edn) 400 et seq and cf para 1645 post. As to personal service on directors, the statement in an order of the time within which it is to be obeyed under RSC Ord 42 r 2 and committal generally see CONTEMPT vol 9 para 98.

4 *Biba Ltd v Stratford Investments Ltd* [1973] Ch 281, [1972] 3 All ER 1041.

5 *R v Windham* (1776) 1 Cowp 377; *Re Hooley, ex p Hooley* (1899) 79 LT 706.

6 *R v J G Hammond & Co Ltd* [1914] 2 KB 866; *R v Hutchison, ex p McMahon* [1936] 2 All ER 1514.

7 *Fairclough v Manchester Ship Canal Co* [1897] WN 7, CA. On the true construction of RSC Ord 45 r 5, under which a director or other officer of a company may be committed or have his property sequestrated where the company disobeys an injunction, such a person is not rendered liable in contempt merely by virtue of his office and his knowledge that the order sought to be enforced was made, but will be liable only if he can otherwise be shown to be in contempt under the general law of contempt; in the absence of mens rea or an actus reus, such a director or other officer of a company will not be liable in contempt: *Director General of Fair Trading v Buckland* [1990] 1 All ER 545, [1990] 1 WLR 920. Where, however, a company is ordered by the court not to do certain acts or to give an undertaking to the like effect and a director of the company is aware of that order or undertaking, the director is under a duty to take reasonable steps to ensure that the order or undertaking is obeyed; and, if he wilfully fails to take those steps and the order or undertaking is breached, he may be punished for contempt unless he reasonably believes that some other director or officer of the company is taking them: *A-G for Tuvalu v Philatelic Distribution Corpn Ltd* [1990] 2 All ER 216, [1990] 1 WLR 926, CA.

1182. Practice in general. A company must employ a solicitor to initiate legal proceedings[1], except in the county court[2]. No special formalities are required for the appointment[3], and in the absence of evidence to the contrary, the solicitor on the record is presumed to have been validly appointed[4]. Normally a company may appear in open court only by counsel[5], or, where he has a right of audience, by a solicitor, except that in the county court it may by leave of the judge appear by an agent[6]. However, the court can, pursuant to its inherent power to regulate its own proceedings, permit a director of a company to appear as an advocate on its behalf; but it will do so only in exceptional circumstances, such as where the company's assets are frozen by a Mareva injunction so that it cannot instruct solicitors[7]. Where a director is a party to litigation to which his company is also a party, the court may allow the director to appear in person for purposes which are also those of the company[7].

A statement of claim against a company, if it states the corporate title, need not allege that the company is a corporation or state how it was incorporated[8]. In a debenture holders' action the writ of summons must be entitled in the matter of the company[9].

Where a transaction by a company is within its powers but is about to be carried out without the necessary sanction of a general meeting, an injunction may be granted until the meeting has been held to sanction the transaction[10].

Where a company is seeking an interlocutory injunction, the court may accept its undertaking as to damages, unless its solvency is questioned. However, the practice requiring an undertaking by a director or other responsible person is still, as a rule, followed[11].

If a petition for the winding up of a company is presented, an action pending against it may be stayed or restrained[12]; and a winding-up order or the appointment of a provisional liquidator prevents any action or proceeding being proceeded with or commenced against the company or its property without the court's leave[13]. Where a company goes into voluntary liquidation, any action against it may be brought or continued unless it is stayed or restrained[14].

1 As to service of proceedings see para 151 ante; and as to the retaining of a solicitor by a company see SOLICITORS vol 44(1) (Reissue) para 108. As to the position where proceedings are instituted in the name of a company without authority and later ratified see para 1125 ante.
2 *Charles P Kinnell & Co Ltd v Harding, Wace & Co* [1918] 1 KB 405, CA.
3 See the Companies Act 1985 s 36 (as substituted) and para 1129 ante and s 36A (as added) and para 1130 ante.
4 *Thames Haven Dock and Rly Co v Hall* (1843) 5 Man & G 274; *Faviell v Eastern Counties Rly Co* (1848) 2 Exch 344.
5 See Bro Abr, Corporations, 28; *Scriven v Jescott (Leeds) Ltd* (1908) 53 Sol Jo 101; *Tritonia Ltd v Equity and Law Life Assurance Society* [1943] AC 584, [1943] 2 All ER 401, HL (arguing appeal before House of Lords); *Frinton and Walton UDC v Walton and District Sand and Mineral Co Ltd* [1938] 1 All ER 649 (company cannot be represented by managing director); cf *Re G J Mannix Ltd* [1984] 1 NZLR 309 (NZ CA) (residual discretion in courts of New Zealand).
6 *Charles P Kinnell & Co v Harding, Wace & Co* [1918] 1 KB 405, CA.
7 *Arbuthnot Leasing International Ltd v Havelet Leasing Ltd* [1991] 1 All ER 591; sub nom *ALI Finance Ltd v Havelet Leasing Ltd* [1992] 1 WLR 455. Where a company director acts for the company in court, with the company's authority, the company is the litigant and it is not entitled to recover its costs as a litigant in person: *Jonathan Alexander Ltd v Proctor* [1996] 2 All ER 334, [1996] 1 WLR 518, CA.
8 *Woolf v City Steam Boat Co* (1849) 7 CB 103.
9 See para 1366 post.
10 *Kaye v Croydon Tramways Co* [1898] 1 Ch 358, CA; *Towers v African Tug Co* [1904] 1 Ch 558, CA; *Lawson v Financial News Ltd* (1917) 34 TLR 52, CA.
11 *Manchester and Liverpool Banking Co v Parkinson* (1888) 60 LT 47; *East Molesey Local Board v Lambeth Waterworks Co* [1892] 3 Ch 289, CA; 1 Seton's Judgments and Orders (7th Edn) 510.
12 See the Insolvency Act 1986 s 126(1) and para 2646 et seq post.
13 See ibid s 130 and para 2251 post.
14 See para 2773 post.

1183. Security for costs by company. Where a limited company is plaintiff[1] in any action or other legal proceeding[2], the court having jurisdiction in the matter may[3], if it appears by credible testimony that there is reason to believe that the company will be unable to pay the costs of the defendant if successful in his defence, require sufficient security to be given for those costs, and may stay all proceedings until the security is given[4]. This provision does not apply to an unlimited company, even if it is in winding up[5], or enable security to be ordered to be given by the liquidator of a company, even where he has no means, either when he is applying by misfeasance summons or is coming to the court in exercise of any other statutory duty[6]; nor does it apply to a company incorporated in Scotland or Northern Ireland, although in such cases security may be ordered in the usual way under the provisions of the Rules of the Supreme Court[7]. The fact of a company being in liquidation is prima facie evidence that it will, if unsuccessful, be unable to pay the defendant's costs, even if the liquidation occurs while the action is pending[8]. The mere fact that a company has issued a debenture charging all its assets to secure the repayment of money then or at any time owing to a particular person is not itself a sufficient reason for ordering security[9]. A defendant company is not obliged to give security[10]; nor need it do so if it is plaintiff in an action against a person who is suing it in another action in regard to the same subject matter[11].

If, however, there is a counterclaim or separate action to impeach the transaction in respect of which the original action is brought, security may be ordered[12], but the amount of the security should be determined by the claim alone, and not by the cross claim[13]. In interpleader proceedings if both parties are in substance claimants, and are in a similar financial position, an order for security may only be made by one upon giving the like security as the other is ordered to give[14]. The amount of security required should equal the probable amount of costs payable[15], but the court has an absolute discretion as to the amount of the security, and as to when, in what manner and on what terms it is to be given[16].

Where a company appeals from a winding-up order against it, security for costs may be required[17].

Where security for costs is sought against a plaintiff company, it is not necessary for the company, in order to have the application dismissed, to adduce evidence that it will or may be unable to pursue the proceedings if the order is granted[18].

1 Where a company successfully brought an action as plaintiff and the decision was appealed against, the company was not, as respondent to the appeal, ordered to give security: *Star Fire and Burglary Insurance Co v Davidson & Sons* (1902) 4 F 997.

2 For these purposes, 'other legal proceeding' refers to any matter in which the jurisdiction of the court is invoked by an originating process other than a writ, the word 'plaintiff' indicating not a person who would be conventionally described as a plaintiff but covering a person who has invoked the jurisdiction of the court by whatever originating process he has selected. Thus the Companies Act 1985 s 726 covers proceedings commenced by petition: *Re Unisoft Group Ltd* [1993] BCLC 528.

3 *Sir Lindsay Parkinson & Co Ltd v Triplan Ltd* [1973] QB 609, [1973] 2 All ER 273, CA (discretion exercisable according to all the circumstances of the particular case). In exercising its discretion to order security for costs where the plaintiff is ordinarily resident out of the jurisdiction, the court will take into account, as an important but not a decisive factor, the substantial and improved rights of enforcement available to a defendant under the Civil Jurisdiction and Judgments Act 1982: *Porzelack KG v Porzelack (UK) Ltd* [1987] 1 All ER 1074, [1987] 1 WLR 420. Whether the court will make such an order depends on what is just having regard to all the circumstances of the case: *Porzelack KG v Porzelack (UK) Ltd* supra. The court will only have jurisdiction to award security if it appears by credible testimony that there is reason to believe that the company will, and not merely may, be unable to pay the defendant's costs if successful in its defence: *Europa Holdings Ltd v Circle Industries (UK) plc* [1993] BCLC 320, CA. As to whether security for costs is available in respect of a counterclaim by the defendant see *Hutchison Telephone (UK) Ltd v Ultimate Response Ltd* [1993] BCLC 307, CA.

4 Companies Act 1985 s 726(1). Remission of the case to the county court does not deprive the judge in the county court of his power under s 726 to order security: *Plascyoed Collieries Co Ltd v Partridge, Jones & Co Ltd* (1911) 104 LT 807, DC. Security may be ordered up to a certain stage of the proceedings, with liberty to apply: *Western of Canada Oil, Lands and Works Co v Walker* (1875) 10 Ch App 628. The fact that there was another plaintiff, whose claim only slightly overlapped the plaintiff company's claim, was held not to be a ground for excusing the company from giving security in *John Bishop (Caterers) Ltd v National Union Bank Ltd* [1973] 1 All ER 707. Where it appeared that no assets had been collected in the

winding up of a plaintiff company, and that all the shareholders who did not dispute the allotment of shares had paid in full, the court ordered security: *Southampton, Isle of Wight and Portsmouth Improved Steam Boat Co Ltd v Pinnock* (1863) 11 WR 978. In *Bilcon Ltd v Fegmay Investments Ltd* [1966] 2 QB 221, [1966] 2 All ER 513, security was ordered in a reference to arbitration. See also *Pearson v Naydler* [1977] 3 All ER 531, [1977] 1 WLR 899 (security ordered where there was a natural person as co-plaintiff with the company).

5 *United Ports Insurance Co v Hill* (1870) LR 5 QB 395.
6 *Re Strand Wood Co Ltd* [1904] 2 Ch 1, CA. In such a case the liquidator may be ordered to pay the costs personally: see para 2354 post. As to security for costs by a foreign company as petitioning creditor see para 2235 post.
7 *DSQ Property Co Ltd v Lotus Cars Ltd* [1987] 1 WLR 127, not following *Wilson Vehicle Distributions Ltd v Colt Car Co Ltd* [1984] BCLC 93, and distinguishing *Raeburn v Andrews* (1874) LR 9 QB 118. Security is ordered under RSC Ord 23 r 1(1)(a).
8 *Northampton Coal, Iron and Waggon Co v Midland Waggon Co* (1878) 7 ChD 500, CA; *Pure Spirit Co v Fowler* (1890) 25 QBD 235; *Re Diamond Fuel Co* (1879) 13 ChD 400, CA; *Re Photographic Artists' Co-operative Supply Association* (1883) 23 ChD 370, CA; *Lydney and Wigpool Iron Ore Co v Bird* (1883) 23 ChD 358 at 359; *City of Moscow Gas Co v International Financial Society Ltd* (1872) 7 Ch App 225 at 229.
9 *Universal Aircraft Ltd v Hickey* (4 May 1943, unreported) (cited in the Supreme Court Practice 1995 para 23/1-3/14); *Tudor Furnishers Ltd v Montague & Co and Finer Production Co Ltd* [1950] Ch 113 at 115, [1950] 1 All ER 65 at 66.
10 *Accidental and Marine Insurance Co v Mercati* (1866) LR 3 Eq 200; *Maatschappij Voor Fondsenbezit v Shell Transport and Trading Co* [1923] 2 KB 166, CA; *Naamlooze Vennootschap Beleggings Compagnie 'Uranus' v Bank of England* [1948] 1 All ER 465, CA.
11 *Accidental and Marine Insurance Co v Mercati* (1866) LR 3 Eq 200.
12 *Strong v Carlyle Press* (1893) 37 Sol Jo 357; *City of Moscow Gas Co v International Financial Society* (1872) 7 Ch App 225; *Washoe Mining Co v Ferguson* (1866) LR 2 Eq 371; and see *Sinclair v Glasgow and London Contract Corpn* (1904) 6 F 818; *Freehold Land and Brickmaking Co v Spargo* [1868] WN 94. As to security when the plaintiff is out of the jurisdiction see *Naamlooze Venootschap Beleggings Compagnie 'Uranus' v Bank of England* [1948] 1 All ER 465, CA.
13 *T Sloyan & Sons (Builders) Ltd v Brothers of Christian Instruction* [1974] 3 All ER 715 (arbitration).
14 *Tudor Furnishers Ltd v Montague & Co and Finer Production Co Ltd* [1950] Ch 113, [1950] 1 All ER 65.
15 *Imperial Bank of China, India, and Japan v Bank of Hindustan, China and Japan* (1866) 1 Ch App 437; *Dominion Brewery Ltd v Foster* (1897) 77 LT 507, CA.
16 RSC Ord 23 rr 1(1), 2. As to security for costs generally see PRACTICE AND PROCEDURE vol 37 para 298 et seq.
17 See para 2791 post.
18 *Trident International Freight Services Ltd v Manchester Ship Canal Co* [1990] BCLC 263, CA. An application for security may be dismissed if the plaintiff company shows, whether expressly or impliedly, that there is a probability that it will be unable to pursue the action if the order is granted. On an application for security for costs it is not appropriate to go into the merits of the case unless it can be clearly demonstrated one way or the other that there is a high probability of success or failure: *Trident International Freight Services Ltd v Manchester Ship Canal Co* supra.

(x) Alteration of Objects

1184. Company's power to alter objects. A company[1] may by special resolution[2] alter its memorandum with respect to the statement of the company's objects[3]. If an application is made for an order for the alteration to be cancelled[4], an alteration does not have effect except in so far as it is confirmed by the court[5].

A company is not entitled to rely against other persons on any alteration of its memorandum if the alteration had not been officially notified at the material time and is not shown by the company to have been known at that time to the person concerned, or if the material time fell on or before the fifteenth day after the date of official notification or, where the fifteenth day was a non-business day, on or before the next day that was not, and it is shown that the person concerned was unavoidably prevented from knowing of the event at that time[6].

Where a charity is a company or other body corporate having power to alter the instruments establishing or regulating it as a body corporate, no exercise of that power which has the effect of the body ceasing to be a charity is valid so as to affect the application of any property acquired under any disposition or agreement previously made otherwise than for full consideration in money or money's worth, or any property representing property so acquired[7].

1   For the meaning of 'company' see para 11 note 1 ante. Under the Companies (Memorandum of Association) Act 1890 (repealed), there was some doubt as to which companies could alter their objects without registering under the Companies Act 1862 (repealed): see *Re General Credit Co* [1891] WN 153; *Re Nitrophosphate and Odams Chemical Manure Co Ltd* [1893] WN 141; *Re Hong Kong and China Gas Co Ltd* (1898) 43 Sol Jo 77; *Re Copiapo Mining Co Ltd* (1899) 43 Sol Jo 368; *Re Euphrates and Tigris Steam Navigation Co Ltd* [1904] 1 Ch 360.

2   As to special resolutions see para 683 ante. A company which has no members cannot pass a special resolution, and accordingly no alteration may be sanctioned: *Re Blackburn Philanthropic Assurance Co Ltd* [1914] 2 Ch 430.

3   Companies Act 1985 s 4(1) (substituted by the Companies Act 1989 s 110(2)). The alteration must be an alteration of the objects of the company (*Re Society for Promoting Employment of Women* (1927) 71 Sol Jo 583), but need not be an alteration of the objects clause, as all the objects are not necessarily contained in that clause (*Incorporated Glasgow Dental Hospital v Lord Advocate* 1927 SC 400). See further *Re Scientific Poultry Breeders' Association Ltd* [1933] Ch 227, CA. For a consideration of the Companies Act 1985 s 4 (as originally enacted) see 66 LQR 493.

    If the court's order requires the company not to make any, or any specified, alteration in its memorandum (see para 1185 post), the company does not then have power without the leave of the court to make any such alteration in breach of that requirement: s 5(6).

4   Ie under ibid s 5: see para 1185 post.

5   Ibid s 4(2) (substituted by the Companies Act 1989 s 110(2)).

6   See the Companies Act 1985 s 42 and para 71 ante.

7   See the Charities Act 1993 s 64(1)(a) and CHARITIES vol 5(2) (Reissue) para 225.

1185. Cancelling alteration of objects. Where a company's memorandum has been altered by special resolution[1], application may be made to the court for the alteration to be cancelled[2]. Such an application may be made:

(1)   by the holders of not less in the aggregate than 15% in nominal value of the company's issued share capital or any class of it or, if the company is not limited by shares, not less than 15% of the company's members; or

(2)   by the holders of not less than 15% of the company's debentures entitling the holders to object to alterations of its objects[3];

but an application may not be made by any person who has consented to, or voted in favour of, the alteration[4].

The application[5] must be made within 21 days after the date on which the resolution altering the company's objects was passed, and may be made on behalf of the persons entitled to make the application by such one or more of their number as they may appoint in writing for the purpose[6].

On such an application the court may make an order confirming the alteration either wholly or in part and on such terms and conditions as it thinks fit and may, if it thinks fit, adjourn the proceedings in order that an arrangement may be made to its satisfaction for the purchase of the interests of dissentient members, and may give such directions and make such orders as it thinks expedient for facilitating or carrying into effect any such arrangement[7].

If the court thinks fit, its order may provide for the purchase by the company of the shares of any members of the company and for the reduction accordingly of its capital, and may make such alterations in the company's memorandum and articles as may be required in consequence of that provision[8].

If the court's order requires the company not to make any, or any specified, alteration in its memorandum or articles, the company does not then have power without the leave of the court to make any such alteration in breach of that requirement[9].

An alteration in the memorandum or articles of a company made by virtue of an order under these provisions, other than one made by resolution of the company, is of the same effect as if duly made by resolution[10]; and the Companies Act 1985 applies accordingly to the memorandum or articles as so altered[11].

1   Ie under the Companies Act 1985 s 4 (as substituted): see para 1184 ante.
2   Ibid s 5(1).
3   The debentures entitling the holders to object to alterations of a company's objects are any debentures secured by a floating charge which were issued or first issued before 1 December 1947, or form part of the same series as any debentures so issued; and a special resolution altering a company's objects requires the same notice to the holders of any such debentures as to members of the company: ibid s 5(8). In the absence of provisions regulating the giving of notice to any such debenture holders, the provisions of the company's articles regulating the giving of notice to members apply: s 5(8). See *Re Hampstead Garden Suburb Trust Ltd* [1962] Ch 806, [1962] 2 All ER 879.
4   Companies Act 1985 s 5(2). See *Re Hampstead Garden Suburb Trust Ltd* [1962] Ch 806, [1962] 2 All ER 879.
5   The application is by petition under RSC Ord 102 r 4(1)(a). As to the disclosure of the applicant's title to make the petition and the communication to him of authority to petition on behalf of other objectors see the cases cited in para 184 note 1 ante.
6   Companies Act 1985 s 5(3).
7   Ibid s 5(4).
8   Ibid s 5(5).
9   Ibid s 5(6).
10 As to such effect see para 538 ante and para 1187 post.
11 Companies Act 1985 s 5(7).

1186. Notices to registrar. Where a company passes a resolution altering its objects, then, if with respect to the resolution no application is made to the court[1], the company must within 15 days from the end of the period for making such an application deliver to the registrar of companies a printed copy of its memorandum as altered[2]. If, however, an application is made to the court, the company must forthwith give notice in the prescribed form[3] of that fact to the registrar and within 15 days from the date of any order cancelling or confirming the alteration deliver to the registrar an office copy of the order and, in the case of an order confirming the alteration, a printed copy of the memorandum as altered[4]. Where there has been an application to the court, the court may by order at any time extend the time for the delivery of documents to the registrar for such period as the court may think proper[5].

If a company makes default in giving notice or delivering any document to the registrar of companies as required by these provisions, the company, and every officer of it who is in default, is liable on summary conviction to a fine not exceeding one-fifth of the statutory maximum and, on conviction after continued contravention, to a daily default fine not exceeding one-fiftieth of the statutory maximum[6].

1   Ie under the Companies Act 1985 s 5: see para 1185 ante.
2   Ibid s 6(1)(a). As to official notification see para 1184 ante.
3   For the prescribed form of notice see the Companies (Forms) (Amendment) Regulations 1995, SI 1995/736, reg 3, Sch 2, Form 6.
4   Companies Act 1985 s 6(1)(b).
5   Ibid s 6(2).
6   Ibid ss 6(3), 730, Sch 24. For the meaning of 'officer who is in default', 'the statutory maximum' and 'daily default fine' see para 1161 ante.

1187. Validity of alteration. The validity of an alteration of a company's memorandum with respect to the objects of the company may not be questioned on the ground that it was not authorised[1] except in proceedings taken for the purpose (whether under these provisions[2] or otherwise) before the expiration of 21 days after the date of the resolution in that behalf[3]. Where such proceedings are taken other than under these provisions, the provisions as to notices to be given[4] apply to such proceedings and, if the proceedings are dismissed, the order has effect as if it were an order confirming the alteration, and, if in the proceedings the alteration is declared invalid, as if it were an order cancelling the alteration[5].

1 Ie authorised by the Companies Act 1985 s 4 (as substituted): see para 1184 ante.
2 Ie under ibid s 5: see para 1185 ante.
3 Ibid s 6(4).
4 Ie ibid s 6(1)–(3): see para 1186 ante.
5 Ibid s 6(5).

(21) OWNERSHIP AND DISPOSITION OF PROPERTY

1188. Company's power to hold land. Any company incorporated under the Companies Act 1985 or the former Companies Acts[1], or registered, though not formed, under that Act or the former Companies Acts, has always had power to hold land in the United Kingdom[2].

The fact that a company holds land does not make its shares an interest in land within the Law of Property (Miscellaneous Provisions) Act 1989[3], or, where it is established for charitable purposes, render it necessary to obtain any consent of the Charity Commissioners to the sale of its land which would not be required if it was not incorporated[4].

The power of holding land imposes no restriction on the mode in which the company may acquire land, which may therefore be taken on lease, if required for the purposes of the company as stated in the memorandum of association[5]. The company may let the land acquired so far as the company's objects expressly or impliedly authorise the letting of its property[6].

1 For the meaning of 'the former Companies Acts' see para 11 note 2 ante.
2 As to companies admitted to the Official List of the Stock Exchange see para 1189 note 1 post. Formerly a company formed for the purpose of promoting art, science, religion, charity or any other like object, not involving the acquisition of gain by the company or by its individual members, could not without the licence of the Board of Trade hold more than two acres of land, although the Board might license any such company to hold land in such quantity and subject to such conditions as the Board thought fit: see the Companies Act 1948 s 14(1) proviso (repealed).
3 Ie the Law of Property (Miscellaneous Provisions) Act 1989 s 2: see SALE OF LAND. See also the Companies Act 1985 s 182(1)(a) (under which the shares or other interest of any member are personal estate, transferable as provided by the articles, and are not of the nature of real estate: see para 437 ante) and *Bligh v Brent* (1837) 2 Y & C Ex 268; *Humble v Mitchell* (1839) 11 Ad & El 205. See further STOCK EXCHANGE.
4 *Re Church Army* (1906) 75 LJ Ch 467, CA; and see *Re Society for Training Teachers of the Deaf and Whittle's Contract* [1907] 2 Ch 486. See also CHARITIES vol 5(2) (Reissue) para 222.
5 If the company takes premises which are the best for its purposes, it is no objection to the validity of the lease that the premises are too large and that part will have to be sublet: *Re London and Colonial Co, Horsey's Claim* (1868) LR 5 Eq 561 at 562 n (1). Directors entering into an agreement for a lease in their own names are personally liable: *Kay v Johnson* (1864) 2 Hem & M 118. As to the effect of the dissolution of the company on leases see paras 2692-2694 post.
6 A lease of the company's undertaking may be sanctioned as a term in a scheme of arrangement made under the Companies Act 1985 s 425 (as amended) (see para 1447 post): see *Re Dynevor, Dyffryn and Neath Abbey Collieries Co* (1879) 11 ChD 605, CA. As to schemes of arrangement see para 1447 et seq post.

1189. Personalty. An incorporated company may hold personal property to any extent without licence from any government department[1]. Its powers in this respect may, however, be limited by its memorandum of association, and, whatever the memorandum says, it cannot (save in the manner provided by the Companies Act 1985[2]) purchase its own shares[3]; but it may buy up its debentures for the purpose of redeeming or reissuing them[4], or redeem redeemable shares[5].

Where a person transfers property to a company for the purpose of defeating his creditors[6], its title to the property may in certain cases be displaced in favour of his trustee in bankruptcy[6]. A bill of sale to a company must state its address and description[7].

1 See CORPORATIONS. As to the classification etc of transactions, principally acquisitions and disposals, by a company admitted to the Official List of the Stock Exchange, and as to the additional requirements for take-overs and mergers (see para 1193 et seq post), see the *Listing Rules* Ch 10 (rr 10.1–10.50). As to the *Listing Rules* see para 282 ante.
2 See para 219 et seq ante.
3 *Trevor v Whitworth* (1887) 12 App Cas 409, HL.
4 See the Companies Act 1985 s 194 and para 1272 post.
5 See para 219 et seq ante.
6 See BANKRUPTCY.
7 *Altree v Altree* [1898] 2 QB 267; and see BILLS OF SALE vol 4(1) (Reissue) para 696.

1190. Joint ownership. Being a body corporate, a company is capable of acquiring and holding any real or personal property in joint tenancy in the same manner as if it were an individual[1]. Where it and an individual or another or several other bodies corporate become entitled to any such property in circumstances or by virtue of any instrument which would, if the company had been an individual, have created a joint tenancy, they are entitled to the property as joint tenants[2]. Such acquisition and holding are, however, subject to the like conditions and restrictions which attach to the acquisition and holding of property by a body corporate in severalty[3].

1 Bodies Corporate (Joint Tenancy) Act 1899 s 1(1).
2 Ibid s 1(1). On the dissolution of a body corporate which is a joint tenant the property devolves on the other joint tenant: s 1(2).
3 Ibid s 1(1) proviso.

1191. Directors' duties as to property. The directors of a company have generally under the articles duties as to maintaining and keeping in repair the company's property[1].

1 *Re Floating Dock Co of St Thomas Ltd* [1895] 1 Ch 691.

1192. Company's power to sell property. A company has extensive powers of selling its personal property as incidental to the management of its business[1]. A power to sell its business for shares in another company will not be implied[2], but the whole business and undertaking[3] or a part of the undertaking may be sold if the sale is authorised by the memorandum of association[4] and may with the same express authority be sold for shares in another company[5].

Even if its memorandum purports to give it power to do so, a company which is proposed to be wound up cannot sell all its assets and undertaking and provide for the distribution of the proceeds in the winding up otherwise than in accordance with the statutory provisions[6].

An agreement for sale is not necessarily bad on the ground that one of its terms is the payment of a bonus to the directors of the selling company, unless the bonus is in fact a bribe to them[7]; but it is not lawful to make any such payment to a director unless particulars of it, including the actual amount, are disclosed to the members of the company and approved by them[8].

1 *Wilson v Miers* (1861) 10 CBNS 348 at 366. For special tax provisions on sales between associated companies see the Income and Corporation Taxes Act 1988 ss 770, 772-775 (as amended) and INCOME TAXATION vol 23 (Reissue) para 1581 et seq; the Capital Allowances Act 1990 s 157 and INCOME TAXATION vol 23 (Reissue) para 338; the Value Added Tax Act 1994 ss 43 (as amended), 46(1) and VALUE ADDED TAX.

2 *Re European Society Arbitration Acts, ex p British National Life Assurance Association (Liquidators)* (1878) 8 ChD 679, CA; and see *Bisgood v Henderson's Transvaal Estates Ltd* [1908] 1 Ch 743, CA.

3 *Re Borax Co, Foster v Borax Co* [1901] 1 Ch 326, CA, disapproving *Re Borax Co, Foster v Borax Co* [1899] 2 Ch 130; and see *Mason v Motor Traction Co Ltd* [1905] 1 Ch 419; *Loeffler v Donna Thereza Christina Rly Co Ltd* (1901) 18 TLR 149; *Booth v New Afrikander Gold Mining Co Ltd* [1903] 1 Ch 295 at 313, CA. As to the principles governing the assessment of a company to corporation tax on profits arising on such a sale see INCOME TAXATION vol 23 (Reissue) paras 866, 867.

4 *Grant v United Kingdom Switchback Rly Co* (1888) 40 ChD 135, CA; *Re H H Vivian & Co Ltd, Metropolitan Bank of England and Wales Ltd v H H Vivian & Co Ltd* [1900] 2 Ch 654; *Wall v London and Northern Assets Corpn* [1898] 2 Ch 479, CA. As to exemptions from capital and transfer stamp duty in cases of reconstruction or amalgamation of companies see para 1491 et seq post.

5 *Re William Thomas & Co Ltd* [1915] 1 Ch 325; *Re Barned's Banking Co* (1867) 3 Ch App 105.

6 *Bisgood v Henderson's Transvaal Estates Ltd* [1908] 1 Ch 743, CA. As to reconstructions and amalgamations see para 1460 post; and as to distributions in a winding up see para 2571 et seq post.

7 *Southall v British Mutual Life Assurance Society* (1871) 6 Ch App 614.

8 See the Companies Act 1985 s 313 and para 609 ante.

(22) THE TAKE-OVER CODE

1193. The necessity for the Code. It has been long established under company law that a director occupies a fiduciary position towards the company of which he is a director, but it is equally well established that he owes no fiduciary duty towards any individual shareholder in the company[1]. Accordingly, the general law is virtually silent as to the duties of a board of directors when faced by a take-over bid for the company beyond the duty to be honest and not to mislead[2], or as to the duties of the intending acquirer, beyond the duty not to misuse confidential information[3]. Where the company proposed to be acquired is a shell company, whose assets consist largely of cash, there is always a real possibility of a breach of the statutory provisions prohibiting the provision of financial assistance for the purchase of the company's own shares[4] or of some other criminal act, such as a conspiracy to cheat and defraud minority shareholders, taking place[5].

There are, however, many steps which a company threatened by a take-over bid may take in order to hamper one bidder or prefer another, such as the issue of unissued shares[6], the alteration of voting rights attached to a particular class of shares[7], or the reduction of the company's capital[8]. Some of these steps, particularly the issue of shares, might be taken by the board alone[9]; and, although such an issue might successfully be challenged as being beyond the powers of the directors, in many cases the issue could only be set aside, if at all, after considerable litigation, which would deter the making of the offer.

Clearly, as a matter of business and fairness, the directors ought always to act in the best interests of their shareholders, unmotivated by their own personal consider-ations[10]; and since the general law did not provide a suitable code, it was left to the City institutions to provide one, and delimit the sanctions for any breach[11].

1   See para 591 ante.
2   *Gething v Kilner* [1972] 1 All ER 1166, [1972] 1 WLR 337; *Coleman v Myers* [1977] 2 NZLR 225, NZ CA. This latter case suggests that, in certain circumstances, the directors may owe a duty to disclose matters as to which they know, or have reason to believe, their shareholders are inadequately informed.
    The problem which was recognised from the beginning, but was not addressed, is that the interests of the company as an entity (as distinct from its shareholders) might be different from the interests of its shareholders. The fiduciary duty is owed to the company, not to the individual shareholders, whether treated as individuals or as a body; moreover, interests of individual shareholders differ among themselves. A further complication is the duty statutorily imposed on directors to have regard to the interests of employees: see para 582 ante. On a take-over bid there can be at least three competing interests: those of the company itself; those of its employees; and those of its shareholders.
3   *Dunford & Elliot v Johnson & Firth Brown* [1977] 1 Lloyd's Rep 505, CA (information given to acquirer in confidence: use would normally have been restrained but unreasonable in circumstances to do so).
4   See the Companies Act 1985 ss 151-154 (as amended) and paras 273-275 ante.
5   See eg *R v Sinclair* [1968] 3 All ER 241, [1968] 1 WLR 1246, CA (conspiracy to cheat and defraud by using company's assets in a manner known to be not in the company's best interests and prejudicial to minority shareholders); *Selangor United Rubber Estates Ltd v Cradock (No 3)* [1968] 2 All ER 1073, [1968] 1 WLR 1555 (breach of the Companies Act 1948 s 54 (repealed)).
6   See eg *Hogg v Cramphorn Ltd* [1967] Ch 254, [1966] 3 All ER 420 (issue by directors of shares with inflated voting rights to trustees for employees; allottees entitled to retain without such inflated rights; company given opportunity to ratify acts of directors); *Bamford v Bamford* [1970] Ch 212 at 228, [1969] 1 All ER 969, CA (voidable issue of shares by directors ratified by company).
7   See eg *Rights and Issues Investment Trust Ltd v Stylo Shoes Ltd* [1965] Ch 250, [1964] 3 All ER 628.
8   See eg *IRC v Brebner* [1967] 2 AC 18, [1967] 1 All ER 779, HL.
9   See the text to note 5 supra.
10 As to the necessity for disclosure, and ratification by the company in general meeting, of any sums proposed to be paid to the directors by way of compensation for loss of office see paras 608-610 ante.
11 As to the Secretary of State's power to prohibit or restrict take-overs see the Fair Trading Act 1973 s 73, Sch 8 (as amended) and TRADE AND INDUSTRY vol 47 (Reissue) paras 127, 143 et seq.

1194. The City Code on Take-overs and Mergers. It was in the circumstances described above[1] that in 1959 the Governor of the Bank of England set up the City Working Party, consisting of representatives of the Accepting Houses Committee, the Association of Investment Trust Companies, the Association of Unit Trust Managers, the British Insurance Association, the Committee of London Clearing Bankers, the Confederation of British Industry, the Issuing Houses Association, the National Association of Pension Funds, and the Stock Exchange, London, for the purpose of considering good business practice in the conduct of take-overs and mergers.

This body produced the City Code on Take-overs and Mergers, which of necessity represented a code of business ethics, not a code of law[2]. The current version of this Code is issued on the authority of the Panel on Take-overs and Mergers[3]. The Panel works on a day-to-day basis through its executive, headed by the Director General; and the executive is responsible for the general administration of the Code[4]. This includes, either on its own initiative or at the instigation of third parties, the conduct of investigations, and the monitoring of relevant dealings, in connection with the Code[4].

The executive is available both for consultation and to give rulings on points of interpretation before or during take-over or merger transactions⁴. The Listing Rules impose additional requirements⁵.

1 See para 1193 ante.
2 As to judicial recognition of the Code see *Crabtree v Hinchcliffe* [1972] AC 707 at 730, [1971] 3 All ER 967 at 976, HL per Lord Reid and at 740 and at 984 per Viscount Dilhorne.
3 Copies of the current Code, now published in loose-leaf format, may be obtained from the secretary of the Panel on Take-overs and Mergers, PO Box No 226, The Stock Exchange Building, London EC2P 2JX. The Code comprises:
    (1) Section A: Introduction;
    (2) Section B: General Principles;
    (3) Section C: Definitions;
    (4) Section D (rr 1-3): the Approach, Announcements and Independent Advice;
    (5) Section E (rr 4-8): Dealings and Restrictions on the Acquisition of Shares and Rights over Shares;
    (6) Section F (r 9): the Mandatory Offer and its Terms;
    (7) Section G (rr 10-13): the Voluntary Offer and its Terms;
    (8) Section H (rr 14-18): Provisions applicable to all Offers;
    (9) Section I (rr 19-22): Conduct during the Offer;
    (10) Section J (rr 23-27): Documents from the Offeror and the Offeree Board;
    (11) Section K (r 28): Profit Forecasts;
    (12) Section L (r 29): Asset Valuations;
    (13) Section M (rr 30-34): Timing and Revision;
    (14) Section N (r 35): Restrictions following Offers and Possible Offers;
    (15) Section O (r 36): Partial Offers;
    (16) Section P (r 37): Redemption or Purchase by a Company of its own Securities;
    (17) Section Q (r 38): Dealings by Connected Exempt Market-makers;
    (18) Appendix 1: Whitewash Guidance Note;
    (19) Appendix 2: Formula Offers Guidance Note;
    (20) Appendix 3: Directors' Responsibilities and Conflicts of Interest;
    (21) Appendix 4: Receiving Agents' Code of Practice.
4 *The City Code on Take-overs and Mergers* Introduction para 2(b).
5 As to the *Listing Rules* see para 282 ante.

1195. Scope of the Code. In determining whether or not The City Code on Take-overs and Mergers applies, it is the nature of the company which is the offeree or potential offeree company, or in which control may change or be consolidated, that is relevant¹. The Code applies to offers for all listed and unlisted public companies (and, where appropriate, statutory and chartered companies) considered by the Panel on Take-overs and Mergers to be resident in the United Kingdom, the Channel Islands or the Isle of Man¹. The Code also applies to offers for certain private companies considered to be so resident¹.

1 See *The City Code on Take-overs and Mergers* Introduction para 4(a).

1196. Transactions to which the Code applies. The City Code on Take-overs and Mergers is concerned with take-over and merger transactions, however effected, of all relevant companies¹; these include partial offers, offers by a parent company for shares in its subsidiary and certain other transactions where control² of a company is to be obtained or consolidated³. References in the Code to 'take-overs' and 'offers' include, where appropriate, all such transactions³. The Code does not in general⁴ apply to offers for non-voting, non-equity capital⁵.

1   As to the companies within the scope of the Code see para 1195 ante.
2   'Control' means a holding or aggregate holdings of shares carrying 30% or more of the voting rights of a company, irrespective of whether the holding or holdings gives or give de facto control; and 'voting rights' means all the voting rights attributable to the share capital of a company which are currently exercisable at a general meeting: *The City Code on Take-overs and Mergers* Definitions.
3   See *The City Code on Take-overs and Mergers* Introduction para 4(b).
4   Ie unless the offers are ones required by *The City Code on Take-overs and Mergers* r 15.
5   See *The City Code on Take-overs and Mergers* Introduction para 4(b).

1197. General principles of the Code. It is intended that the spirit, as well as the precise wording, of the following general principles should be observed[1]:

(1)   all shareholders of the same class of an offeree company must be treated similarly by an offeror;

(2)   during the course of an offer, or when an offer is in contemplation, neither an offeror, nor the offeree company, nor any of their respective advisers may furnish information to some shareholders which is not made available to all shareholders; this principle does not apply to the furnishing of information in confidence by the offeree company to a bona fide potential offeror or vice versa;

(3)   an offeror should only announce an offer after the most careful and responsible consideration; such an announcement should be made only when the offeror has every reason to believe that it can and will continue to be able to implement the offer; responsibility in this connection also rests on the financial adviser to the offeror;

(4)   shareholders must be given sufficient information and advice to enable them to reach a properly informed decision and must have sufficient time to do so; no relevant information should be withheld from them;

(5)   any document or advertisement addressed to shareholders containing information or advice from an offeror or the board of the offeree company or their respective advisers must, as is the case with a prospectus, be prepared with the highest standards of care and accuracy;

(6)   all parties to an offer must use every endeavour to prevent the creation of a false market in the securities of an offeror or offeree company; parties involved in offers must take care that statements are not made which may mislead shareholders or the market;

(7)   at no time after a bona fide offer has been communicated to the board of an offeree company, or after the board of an offeree company has reason to believe that a bona fide offer might be imminent, may any action be taken by the board of the offeree company in relation to the affairs of the company, without the approval of the shareholders in general meeting, which could effectively result in any bona fide offer being frustrated or in the shareholders being denied an opportunity to decide on its merits;

(8)   rights of control must be exercised in good faith and the oppression of a minority is wholly unacceptable;

(9)   directors of an offeror and the offeree company must always, in advising their shareholders, act only in their capacity as directors and not have regard to their personal or family shareholdings or to their personal relationships with the companies; it is the shareholders' interests taken as a whole, together with those of employees and creditors, which should be considered when the directors are giving advice to shareholders; directors of the offeree company should give careful consideration before they enter into any commitment with an offeror (or anyone else) which would restrict their freedom to advise their

shareholders in the future; such commitments may give rise to conflicts of interest or result in a breach of the directors' fiduciary duties;

(10) where control of a company is acquired by a person, or persons acting in concert, a general offer to all other shareholders is normally required; a similar obligation may arise if control is consolidated; where an acquisition is contemplated as a result of which a person may incur such an obligation, he must, before making the acquisition, ensure that he can and will continue to be able to implement such an offer.

1 *The City Code on Take-overs and Mergers* General Principles 1-10.

1198. Breaches of the Code. The City Code on Take-overs and Mergers has not, and does not seek to have, the force of law[1]. The executive of the Panel on Take-overs and Mergers may, however, institute disciplinary proceedings when it considers that there has been a breach of the Code. In such a case, the executive invites the person concerned to appear before the Panel. He is informed in writing of the alleged breach and of the matters which the executive will present. If subsequently any additional matter of a material nature becomes relevant, he may request an adjournment. If the Panel finds that there has been a breach, it may have recourse to private reprimand, to public censure, to reporting the offender's conduct to another regulatory body, for example the Department of Trade and Industry, the Stock Exchange, the Securities and Investments Board or the relevant self-regulating organisation, and/or to requiring further action to be taken, as it thinks fit. The executive may itself deal with a disciplinary matter where the party which is to be subject to disciplinary action agrees the facts and the action proposed by the executive[2]. At hearings before the Panel the case is presented in person by the parties or their advisers; but it is not normal practice to allow presentation of a case by a legal representative. It is the Panel's policy in the case of important decisions to publish its conclusions and the reasons for them so that its activities may be explained to the public. The Panel will normally announce its decision to the parties immediately, essentially as informal guidance. The decision will be constituted, where appropriate, by a written statement issued as promptly as possible after the hearing[3].

There is a right of appeal where the Panel finds a breach of the Code and proposes to take disciplinary action, where it is alleged that the Panel has acted outside its jurisdiction or in respect of any refusal by the Panel to recognise, or any decision of the Panel to cease to recognise, a market-maker or fund manager as an exempt market-maker or exempt fund manager, as the case may be. An appeal may in other cases be made to the Appeal Committee with leave of the Panel but no application for leave to appeal may be made to the Appeal Committee itself. In all cases notice of appeal must be given within two business days of the decision in question. The Panel will normally suspend publication in full of its findings during this time, although an appropriate interim announcement may have to be made. If there is no appeal, any publication by the Panel will follow immediately. If there is an appeal, publication is further suspended until after the decision of the Appeal Committee. If an appeal is upheld, the appellant is consulted on the form of statement, if any, which is to be published. If an appeal is dismissed, normally the findings of the Panel are published and any steps decided upon by way of action implemented[4].

1 See *The City Code on Take-overs and Mergers* Introduction para 1(c).
2 See *The City Code on Take-overs and Mergers* Introduction para 1(d).
3 See *The City Code on Take-overs and Mergers* Introduction para 1(e).
4 See *The City Code on Take-overs and Mergers* Introduction para 1(f).

1199. Sanctions for breach of the Code. The City Code on Take-overs and Mergers and the Panel on Take-overs and Mergers not having the force of law, the sanctions available are different from those which are available in a court of law. Private reprimand and public censure are the two main sanctions; and in this connection it must be borne in mind that reputation in the City of London is, or used to be, highly prized. In a more flagrant case the Panel may take action designed to deprive the offender temporarily or, if necessary, permanently of his ability to enjoy the facilities of the securities market[1].

Having regard to the fact that the Panel performs a public duty its decisions are subject to judicial review[2]. The internal right of appeal must first be exercised before the court will consider intervening. The Panel is the body charged with the duty of evaluating the evidence and finding the facts, and the court will not normally substitute itself as the fact finding tribunal. However, it will interfere if the Panel has misdirected itself in law, if its decision is so outrageous in its defiance of logic or accepted moral standards that no sensible person who had applied his mind to the question could have arrived at it, or if there has been a departure from the procedural rules governing its conduct[2]. Pending any review by the court, those affected by the Panel's decision, and the Panel itself, must treat its decisions as valid and binding[2].

1 See *The City Code on Take-overs and Mergers* Introduction paras 2, 6. As to the securities market see STOCK EXCHANGE.
2 *R v Panel on Take-overs and Mergers, ex p Datafin plc* [1987] QB 815, [1987] 1 All ER 564, CA. The test of whether particular acts or decisions of a body, such as the Panel on Take-overs and Mergers, whose constitution, functions and powers are sui generis should be subject to judicial review is whether, considering the matter in the round, something has gone wrong with that body's procedure such as to cause real injustice and require the intervention of the court: *R v Panel on Take-overs and Mergers, ex p Guinness plc* [1990] 1 QB 146, [1989] 1 All ER 509, CA (decision whether to adjourn a hearing essentially a matter for the exercise of judicial discretion by the court or tribunal seised of the matter; and, where a right of appeal from the decision-making body existed but was not exercised, the court would grant relief by way of judicial review only in exceptional circumstances).

1200. Provisions for facilitating take-over bids. Statutory provision enables a bidder who obtains not less than 90% of the outstanding shares of any particular class not already owned by him to acquire compulsorily the remaining shares of that class[1]. There is also provision for relief from stamp duty in certain circumstances[2].

1 See the Companies Act 1985 ss 428-430F (as substituted) and para 1202 et seq post.
2 See para 1491 et seq post.

1201. References of take-overs to the Monopolies and Mergers Commission. When it appears to the Secretary of State that it is or may be the fact that two or more enterprises have at a specified time or in specified circumstances, ceased to be distinct enterprises, and that either:

    (1) as a result a specified market share condition prevails, or does so to a greater extent, with respect to the supply of goods or services of any description; or
    (2) the value of the assets taken over exceeds £70 million,

and, further, that the merger does not constitute a concentration having a Community dimension for the purposes of the EC Merger Regulation, he may refer the matter to the Monopolies and Mergers Commission[1].

If the report of the Commission is adverse, he may exercise powers to remedy or prevent the adverse effects specified in the report[2].

He may also make such a reference to the Commission in anticipation of a merger[3].

A transfer of a newspaper or of newspaper assets to a newspaper proprietor whose newspapers have an average circulation per day of publication amounting, together with that of the newspaper concerned in the transfer, to 500,000 or more copies, is unlawful and void unless the transfer is made with the written consent given, either conditionally or unconditionally, by the Secretary of State[4]. Normally he requires a report from the Monopolies and Mergers Commission[5].

1 See the Fair Trading Act 1973 s 64(1) (as amended) and TRADE AND INDUSTRY vol 47 (Reissue) para 127. As to the exercise of the Secretary of State's discretion to decide which mergers to refer to the Monopolies and Mergers Commission see *Lonrho plc v Secretary of State for Trade and Industry* [1989] 2 All ER 609, sub nom *R v Secretary of State for Trade and Industry, ex p Lonrho plc* [1989] 1 WLR 525, HL; as to the restrictions on the Secretary of State's powers of referral to the Commission where prior notice of a merger has been given see the Fair Trading Act 1973 ss 75A–75F (as added) and TRADE AND INDUSTRY vol 47 (Reissue) para 131; and as to the Secretary of State's power to accept appropriate statutory undertakings instead of making a reference to the Commission see ss 75G–75K (as added and amended) and TRADE AND INDUSTRY vol 47 (Reissue) para 132. As to the merger of water enterprises see TRADE AND INDUSTRY vol 47 (Reissue) para 133.
2 See ibid s 73(2), Sch 8 (as amended) and TRADE AND INDUSTRY vol 47 (Reissue) paras 127, 143 et seq.
3 See ibid s 75 (as amended) and TRADE AND INDUSTRY vol 47 (Reissue) para 129. As to restrictions on share dealings where a merger reference is made under s 75 (as amended) see TRADE AND INDUSTRY vol 47 (Reissue) para 130.
4 See ibid s 58(1) and TRADE AND INDUSTRY vol 47 (Reissue) para 126.
5 See ibid s 58(2) and TRADE AND INDUSTRY vol 47 (Reissue) para 126.

(23) TAKE-OVER OFFERS

1202. Take-over offers. In these provisions[1] 'a take-over offer' means an offer to acquire all the shares, or all the shares of any class or classes, in a company (other than shares which at the date of the offer are already held by the offeror), being an offer on terms which are the same in relation to all the shares to which the offer relates or, where those shares include shares of different classes, in relation to all the shares of each class[2]. For this purpose, 'shares' means shares which have been allotted on the date of the offer but a take-over offer may include among the shares to which it relates all or any shares that are subsequently allotted before a date specified in or determined in accordance with the terms of the offer[3]. Similarly, for the purpose of these provisions, 'the offeror' means, subject to the provisions relating to joint offers[4], the person making a take-over offer and 'the company' means the company whose shares are the subject of the offer[5].

The terms offered in relation to any shares are, for the purposes of these provisions, to be treated as being the same in relation to all the shares or, as the case may be, all the shares of a class to which the offer relates notwithstanding any permitted variation[6]. A variation is so permitted where:

(1) the law of a country or territory outside the United Kingdom precludes an offer of consideration in the form or any of the forms specified in the terms in question or precludes it except after compliance by the offeror with conditions with which he is unable to comply or which he regards as unduly onerous; and

(2) the variation is such that the persons to whom an offer of consideration in that form is precluded are able to receive consideration otherwise than in that form but of substantially equivalent value[7].

The above reference[8] to shares already held by the offeror includes a reference to shares which he has contracted to acquire but is not to be construed as including shares which are the subject of a contract binding the holder to accept the offer when it is made, being a contract entered into by the holder either for no consideration and under seal or for no consideration other than a promise by the offeror to make the offer[9]. Where the terms of an offer make provision for their revision and for acceptances on the previous terms to be treated as acceptances on the revised terms, the revision is not to be regarded for the purposes of these provisions as the making of a fresh offer and references to the date of the offer are accordingly to be construed as references to the date on which the original offer was made[10].

1   Ie the Companies Act 1985 Pt XIIIA (ss 428-430F) (substituted by the Financial Services Act 1986 s 172(1), Sch 12): see infra and paras 1203-1210 post. These provisions came into force on 30 April 1987 (see the Financial Services Act 1986 (Commencement No 3) Order 1986, SI 1986/2246) and do not affect any case in which the offer in respect of the scheme or contract mentioned in these provisions was made before that date: Financial Services Act 1986 s 172(2). Nothing in the Companies Act 1989 s 144(1) (substituted meaning of 'subsidiary', 'holding company' and 'wholly-owned subsidiary': see para 827 ante) affects the operation of the Companies Act 1985 Pt XIIIA (ss 428-430F) (as so substituted) in relation to a take-over offer made before the commencement of the Companies Act 1989 s 144(1) (ie 1 November 1990): s 144(4), Sch 18 para 35.
2   Companies Act 1985 s 428(1) (as substituted: see note 1 supra).
3   Ibid s 428(2) (as substituted: see note 1 supra). See *Re Simo Securities Trust Ltd* [1971] 3 All ER 999, [1971] 1 WLR 1455.
4   Ie the Companies Act 1985 s 430D (as substituted): see para 1208 post.
5   Ibid s 428(8) (as substituted: see note 1 supra). In s 428 (as substituted: see note 1 supra) references to the offeror are to be construed as references to the joint offerors or any of them: s 430D(4) (as substituted: see note 1 supra).
6   Ibid s 428(3) (as substituted: see note 1 supra).
7   Ibid s 428(4) (as substituted: see note 1 supra).
8   Ie in ibid s 428(1) (as substituted): see supra.
9   Ibid s 428(5) (as substituted: see note 1 supra).
10 Ibid s 428(7) (as substituted: see note 1 supra).

1203.   Right of offeror to buy out minority shareholders.   If, in a case in which a take-over offer[1] does not relate to shares of different classes, the offeror[2] has by virtue of acceptances of the offer acquired or contracted to acquire not less than nine-tenths in value of the shares[3] to which the offer relates, he may give notice to the holder of any shares to which the offer relates which the offeror has not acquired or contracted to acquire that he desires to acquire those shares[4].

If, in a case in which a take-over offer relates to shares of different classes, the offeror has by virtue of acceptances of the offer acquired or contracted to acquire not less than nine-tenths in value of the shares of any class to which the offer relates, he may give notice to the holder of any shares of that class which the offeror has not acquired or contracted to acquire that he desires to acquire those shares[5].

No notice may be so given unless the offeror has acquired or contracted to acquire the shares necessary to satisfy the specified minimum[6] before the end of the period of four months[7] beginning with the date of the offer; and no such notice may be given after the end of the period of two months beginning with the date on which he has acquired or contracted to acquire shares which satisfy that minimum[8].

Any notice under these provisions must be given in the prescribed manner[9]; and, when the offeror gives the first notice in relation to an offer, he must send a copy of it to the company together with a statutory declaration by him in the prescribed form[10] stating that the conditions for the giving of the notice are satisfied[11]. Any person who fails to send a copy of the required notice or statutory declaration or makes such a declaration knowing it to be false or without having reasonable grounds for believing it to be true is liable on conviction on indictment to imprisonment for a term not exceeding two years or a fine, or to both, or on summary conviction to imprisonment for a term not exceeding six months or a fine not exceeding the statutory maximum, or to both, and, on conviction after continued contravention, to a daily default fine not exceeding one-fiftieth of the statutory maximum[12]. If any person is so charged with an offence for failing to send a copy of a notice[13], it is a defence for him to prove that he took reasonable steps for securing compliance with that requirement[14].

Where during the period within which a take-over offer can be accepted the offeror acquires or contracts to acquire any of the shares to which the offer relates but otherwise than by virtue of acceptances of the offer, then, if:

(1) the value of the consideration for which they are acquired or contracted to be acquired ('the acquisition consideration') does not at that time exceed the value of the consideration specified in the terms of the offer; or

(2) those terms are subsequently revised so that, when the revision is announced, the value of the acquisition consideration, at the time mentioned in head (1) above, no longer exceeds the value of the consideration specified in those terms,

the offeror is to be treated for the purposes of these provisions as having acquired or contracted to acquire those shares by virtue of acceptances of the offer; but in any other case those shares are to be treated as excluded from those to which the offer relates[15].

1 For the meaning of 'take-over offer' see para 1202 ante.
2 For the meaning of 'the offeror' see para 1202 ante.
3 For the meaning of 'shares' see para 1202 ante.
4 Companies Act 1985 s 429(1) (substituted by the Financial Services Act 1986 s 172(1), Sch 12).
5 Companies Act 1985 s 429(2) (substituted by the Financial Services Act 1986 Sch 12).
6 Ie the minimum specified in the Companies Act 1985 s 429(1) or (2) (as substituted): see supra.
7 It is competent for the transferee company to fix a shorter period within the four months during which the offer must be accepted: see *Re Western Manufacturing (Reading) Ltd, Miles v Adamant Engineering Co (London) Ltd* [1956] Ch 436, [1955] 3 All ER 733 (period of under four months unobjectionable).
8 Companies Act 1985 s 429(3) (substituted by the Financial Services Act 1986 Sch 12).
9 For the purposes of the Companies Act 1985 s 429(4) (as substituted) (see infra) and s 430A(3) (as substituted) (see para 1205 post), a notice to a holder of shares in the company must be given to him in the prescribed form either personally or by sending it to him by post: Companies (Forms) (Amendment) Regulations 1987, SI 1987/752, reg 4(1). For the prescribed form of notice see reg 5(2), Sch 2 Pt II, Form 429(4). Where such a notice cannot be given personally or by post because the holder of the shares is the holder of a share warrant to bearer, the notice must be given (1) in a case where the articles of association or the regulations of the company provide that notice to such holders of shares may be given by advertisement, by advertisement in the manner so provided; and (2) in any other case, by advertisement in the Gazette: reg 4(2). Where a notice is so sent to a holder of shares by post, it must be sent to him (a) at his address in the United Kingdom registered in the books of the company; (b) if no such address is registered, to the address, if any, in the United Kingdom given by him to the company for the giving of notices to him; or (c) if no address in the United Kingdom is registered or has been so notified, to his address outside the United Kingdom registered in the books of the company: reg 4(3). Where a notice is so sent to a holder of shares by post (i) if it is sent to an address in the United Kingdom, it must be sent by recorded delivery; and (ii) if it is sent to an address outside the United Kingdom, it must be sent by airmail, if that form of post is available: reg 4(4). For the meaning of 'the Gazette' see para 70 note 1 ante.
10 For the prescribed form of statutory declaration see ibid Sch 2 Pt II, Form 429 dec.
11 Companies Act 1985 s 429(4) (substituted by the Financial Services Act 1986 Sch 12). Where the offeror is a company, whether or not a company within the meaning of the Companies Act 1985 (see para 11 note 1 ante), the statutory declaration must be signed by a director: s 429(5) (substituted by the Financial Services Act 1986 Sch 12).
12 Companies Act 1985 s 429(6) (substituted by the Financial Services Act 1986 Sch 12); Companies Act 1985 s 730, Sch 24 (amended by the Financial Services Act 1986 s 212(2), Sch 16 para 27). For the meaning of 'the statutory maximum' and 'daily default fine' see para 1161 ante.
13 Ie as required by the Companies Act 1985 s 429(4) (as substituted): see supra.

14 Ibid s 429(7) (substituted by the Financial Services Act 1986 Sch 12).
15 Companies Act 1985 s 429(8) (substituted by the Financial Services Act 1986 Sch 12).

1204. Effect of notice to buy out minority shareholder. Subject to the powers of the court[1], the following provisions have effect where a notice is given[2] to buy out a minority shareholder[3]. The offeror[4] is entitled and bound to acquire those shares on the terms of the offer[5].

Where the terms of an offer are such as to give the holder of any shares[6] a choice of consideration, the notice must give particulars of the choice and state:

(1) that the holder of the shares may within six weeks from the date of the notice indicate his choice by a written communication sent to the offeror at an address specified in the notice; and

(2) which consideration specified in the offer is to be taken as applying in default of his so indicating a choice;

and the terms of the offer mentioned above[7] are to be determined accordingly[8]. This provision applies whether or not any time limit or other conditions applicable to the choice under the terms of the offer can still be complied with; and, if the consideration chosen by the holder of the shares:

(a) is not cash and the offeror[9] is no longer able to provide it; or

(b) was to have been provided by a third party who is no longer bound or able to provide it,

the consideration is to be taken to consist of an amount of cash payable by the offeror which at the date of the notice is equivalent to the chosen consideration[10].

At the end of six weeks from the date of the notice the offeror must forthwith:

(i) send a copy of the notice to the company; and

(ii) pay or transfer to the company the consideration for the shares to which the notice relates[11].

If the shares to which the notice relates are registered, the copy of the notice sent to the company under head (i) above must be accompanied by an instrument of transfer executed on behalf of the shareholder by a person appointed by the offeror[12]; and on receipt of that instrument the company must register the offeror as the holder of those shares[13]. If the shares to which the notice relates are transferable by the delivery of warrants or other instruments, the copy of the notice sent to the company under head (i) above must be accompanied by a statement to that effect; and the company must on receipt of the statement issue the offeror[14] with warrants or other instruments in respect of the shares and those already in issue in respect of the shares become void[15]. Where the consideration referred to in head (ii) above consists of shares or securities to be allotted by the offeror[16], the reference in head (ii) above to the transfer of the consideration is to be construed as a reference to the allotment of the shares or securities to the company[17].

Any sum and any other consideration received by a company under head (ii) above must be held by the company on trust for the person entitled to the shares in respect of which the sum or other consideration was received[18]. Any sum and any dividend or other sum accruing from any other consideration received by a company under head (ii) above must be paid into a separate bank account, being an account the balance on which bears interest at an appropriate rate and can be withdrawn by such notice, if any, as is appropriate[19]. Where, after reasonable inquiry[20] made at such intervals as are reasonable, the person entitled to any consideration so held on trust cannot be found and 12 years have elapsed since the consideration was received or the company is wound up, the consideration (together with any interest, dividend or other benefit that has accrued from it) must be paid into court[21].

These provisions cannot be used to enable the majority simply to expropriate a small minority by arranging an ostensible take-over[22]. A dissenting minority may properly complain if they are being subjected to a compulsory purchase as a result of a breach on the part of the board of the company of the duty to be honest and not to mislead shareholders[23].

1 Ie under the Companies Act 1985 s 430C (as substituted): see para 1207 post.
2 Ie under ibid s 429 (as substituted): see para 1203 ante.
3 Ibid s 430(1) (substituted by the Financial Services Act 1986 s 172(1), Sch 12).
4 For the meaning of 'the offeror' see para 1202 ante. However, in the Companies Act 1985 s 430(4)(a) (as substituted) (see head (a) infra) references to the offeror being no longer able to provide the relevant consideration are to be construed as references to none of the joint offerors being able to do so: s 430D(6) (substituted by the Financial Services Act 1986 Sch 12). In the Companies Act 1985 s 430(6),(7) (as substituted) (see infra) references to the offeror are to be construed as references to the joint offerors or such of them as they may determine: s 430D(5) (substituted by the Financial Services Act 1986 Sch 12). In the Companies Act 1985 s 430(8) (as substituted) (see infra) references to the offeror are to be construed as references to the joint offerors or any of them: s 430D(4) (substituted by the Financial Services Act 1986 Sch 12). As to joint offers see para 1208 post.
5 Companies Act 1985 s 430(2) (substituted by the Financial Services Act 1986 Sch 12). A compulsory transfer under this provision is subject to ad valorem stamp duty as a conveyance or transfer on sale: *Ridge Nominees Ltd v IRC* [1962] Ch 376 at 391, [1961] 3 All ER 1108, CA. As to such duty see para 513 note 1 ante.
6 For the meaning of 'shares' see para 1202 ante.
7 Ie in the Companies Act 1985 s 430(2) (as substituted): see supra.
8 Ibid s 430(3) (substituted by the Financial Services Act 1986 Sch 12).
9 See note 4 supra.
10 Companies Act 1985 s 430(4) (substituted by the Financial Services Act 1986 Sch 12). This gives statutory effect to the decision in *Re Carlton Holdings Ltd, Worster v Priam Instruments Ltd* [1971] 2 All ER 1082, [1971] 1 WLR 918 (where the scheme included a cash alternative or 'put option' exercisable against a third party and it was held that the company was bound to acquire on those terms even though the date for exercising the option had passed).
11 Companies Act 1985 s 430(5) (substituted by the Financial Services Act 1986 Sch 12).
12 See note 4 supra.
13 Companies Act 1985 s 430(6) (substituted by the Financial Services Act 1986 Sch 12).
14 See note 4 supra.
15 Companies Act 1985 s 430(7) (substituted by the Financial Services Act 1986 Sch 12).
16 See note 4 supra.
17 Companies Act 1985 s 430(8) (substituted by the Financial Services Act 1986 Sch 12).
18 Companies Act 1985 s 430(9) (substituted by the Financial Services Act 1986 Sch 12).
19 Companies Act 1985 s 430(10) (substituted by the Financial Services Act 1986 Sch 12).
20 The expense of any such inquiry may be defrayed out of the money or other property held on trust for the person or persons to whom the inquiry relates: Companies Act 1985 s 430(15) (substituted by the Financial Services Act 1986 Sch 12).
21 Companies Act 1985 s 430(11) (substituted by the Financial Services Act 1986 Sch 12).
22 *Re Bugle Press Ltd, Re Houses and Estates Ltd* [1961] Ch 270 at 279, [1960] 3 All ER 791, CA (transferee company a mere alias for majority shareholder).
23 See *Gething v Kilner* [1972] 1 All ER 1166, [1972] 1 WLR 337 (where, in the absence of bad faith on the part of the boards of the two companies, the court refused to grant interlocutory injunctions restraining the board of the transferor company from recommending acceptance of the offer and the transferee company from declaring the offer unconditional); cf *Coleman v Myers* [1977] 2 NZLR 225, NZ CA (in certain circumstances the directors may owe a duty to disclose matters of which they are aware, or have reason to believe, that their shareholders are inadequately informed).

1205. Right of minority shareholder to be bought out by offeror. If a take-over offer[1] relates to all the shares[2] in a company and at any time before the end of the period within which the offer can be accepted:

(1) the offeror[3] has by virtue of acceptances of the offer acquired or contracted to acquire some (but not all) of the shares to which the offer relates; and

(2) those shares, with or without any other shares in the company which he has acquired or contracted to acquire, amount to not less than nine-tenths in value of all the shares in the company,

the holder of any shares to which the offer relates who has not accepted the offer may by a written communication addressed to the offeror require him to acquire those shares[4].

If a take-over offer relates to shares of any class or classes and at any time before the end of the period within which the offer can be accepted:

(a) the offeror has by virtue of acceptances of the offer acquired or contracted to acquire some (but not all) of the shares of any class to which the offer relates; and

(b) those shares, with or without any other shares of that class which he has acquired or contracted to acquire, amount to not less than nine-tenths in value of all the shares of that class,

the holder of any shares of that class who has not accepted the offer may by a written communication addressed to the offeror require him to acquire those shares[5].

Within one month of the time specified in either of the above provisions[6], as the case may be, the offeror must give any shareholder who has not accepted the offer notice in the prescribed manner[7] of the rights that are exercisable by him under the appropriate provision; and, if the notice is given before the end of the period within which the offer can be accepted, it must state that the offer is still open for acceptance[8]. Such a notice may specify a period for the exercise of the rights conferred by these provisions and in that event the rights are not exercisable after the end of that period; but no such period may end less than three months after the end of the period within which the offer can be accepted[9].

If the offeror fails to comply with this obligation[10], he and, if the offeror is a company, every officer of the company who is in default or to whose neglect the failure is attributable, is liable on conviction on indictment to a fine, or on summary conviction to a fine not exceeding the statutory maximum and, on conviction after continued contravention, to a daily default fine not exceeding one-fiftieth of the statutory maximum[11]. If an offeror, other than a company, is so charged, it is a defence for him to prove that he took all reasonable steps for securing compliance with this obligation[12].

1 For the meaning of 'take-over offer' see para 1202 ante.

2 For the meaning of 'shares' see para 1202 ante. For the purposes of the Companies Act 1985 s 430A(1)(b),(2)(b) (as substituted) (see infra), the reference to shares which the offeror has acquired or contracted to acquire includes a reference to shares which any associate of his has acquired or contracted to acquire: s 430E(3) (substituted by the Financial Services Act 1986 s 172(1), Sch 12). For the meaning of 'associate' see para 1209 post. As to joint offers see para 1208 post.

3 For the meaning of 'the offeror' see para 1202 ante.

4 Companies Act 1985 s 430A(1) (substituted by the Financial Services Act 1986 Sch 12).

5 Companies Act 1985 s 430A(2) (substituted by the Financial Services Act 1986 Sch 12).

6 Ie in the Companies Act 1985 s 430A(1) or (2) (as substituted): see supra.

7 For the prescribed form of notice see the Companies (Forms) (Amendment) Regulations 1987, SI 1987/752, reg 5(2), Sch 2 Pt II, Form 430A. As to the procedure for sending such notice see para 1203 note 9 ante.

8 Companies Act 1985 s 430A(3) (substituted by the Financial Services Act 1986 Sch 12). No such notice need be given if the offeror has given the shareholder a notice in respect of the shares in question under the Companies Act 1985 s 429 (as substituted) (see para 1203 ante): s 430A(5) (substituted by the Financial Services Act 1986 Sch 12).

9 Companies Act 1985 s 430A(4) (substituted by the Financial Services Act 1986 Sch 12).

10 Ie the obligation in the Companies Act 1985 s 430A(3) (as substituted): see supra.

11 Ibid s 430A(6) (substituted by the Financial Services Act 1986 Sch 12); Companies Act 1985 s 730, Sch 24 (amended by the Financial Services Act 1986 s 212(2), Sch 16 para 27). For the meaning of 'officer who is in default', 'the statutory maximum' and 'daily default fine' see para 1161 ante.

12 Companies Act 1985 s 430A(7) (substituted by the Financial Services Act 1986 Sch 12).

1206. Effect of requirement by minority shareholder to be bought out. Subject to the powers of the court[1], the following provisions have effect where a shareholder exercises his rights to be bought out[2] under the above provisions in respect of any shares[3]. The offeror[4] is entitled and bound to acquire those shares on the terms of the offer or on such other terms as may be agreed[5]. Where the terms of an offer are such as to give the holder of shares a choice of consideration, the holder of the shares may indicate his choice when requiring the offeror to acquire them and the notice given[6] to the holder:

(1) must give particulars of the choice and of the rights conferred by this provision; and

(2) may state which consideration in the offer is to be taken as applying in default of his indicating a choice;

and the terms of the offer on which the shares are to be acquired are to be determined accordingly[7].

The above provisions[8] apply whether or not any time limit or other conditions applicable to the choice under the terms of the offer can still be complied with; and, if the consideration chosen by the holder of the shares:

(a) is not cash and the offeror[9] is no longer able to provide it; or

(b) was to have been provided by a third party who is no longer bound or able to provide it,

the consideration is to be taken to consist of an amount of cash payable by the offeror which at the date when the holder of the shares requires the offeror to acquire them is equivalent to the chosen consideration[10].

1 Ie the Companies Act 1985 s 430C (as substituted): see para 1207 post.

2 Ie under ibid s 430A (as substituted): see para 1205 ante.

3 Ibid s 430B(1) (substituted by the Financial Services Act 1986 s 172(1), Sch 12).

4 For the meaning of 'the offeror' see para 1202 ante. However, in the Companies Act 1985 s 430B(4)(a) (as substituted) (see text head (a) infra) references to the offeror being no longer able to provide the relevant consideration are to be construed as references to none of the joint offerors being able to do so: s 430D(6) (substituted by the Financial Services Act 1986 Sch 12). As to joint offers see para 1208 post.

5 Companies Act 1985 s 430B(2) (substituted by the Financial Services Act 1986 Sch 12).

6 Ie under the Companies Act 1985 s 430A(3) (as substituted): see para 1205 ante.

7 Ibid s 430B(3) (substituted by the Financial Services Act 1986 Sch 12).

8 Ie the Companies Act 1985 s 430B(3) (as substituted): see supra.

9 See note 4 supra.

10 Companies Act 1985 s 430B(4) (substituted by the Financial Services Act 1986 Sch 12).

1207. Applications to the court. Where a notice is given by an offeror[1] to the holder of any shares to buy him out[2], the court[3] may, on application[4] made by the holder within six weeks from the date on which the notice was given, order that the offeror shall not be entitled and bound to acquire the shares, or specify terms of acquisition different from those of the offer[5]. If such an application is pending at the end of six weeks from the date of the notice, the obligation[6] on the offeror to send notice to the company and pay or transfer the consideration to the company does not have effect until the application has been disposed of[7]. Where the holder of any shares exercises his rights to require the offeror[8] to buy his shares[9], the court may, on an application made by him or the offeror, order that the terms on which the offeror is entitled and bound to acquire the shares shall be such as the court thinks fit[10].

No order for costs may be made against a shareholder making any such application unless the court considers that the application was unnecessary, improper or vexatious, or that there has been unreasonable delay in making the application or unreasonable conduct on his part in conducting the proceedings on the application[11].

Where a take-over offer[12] has not been accepted to the extent necessary for entitling the offeror[13] to give notices entitling him to buy out minority shareholders[14], the court may, on the application of the offeror, make an order authorising him to give such notices[14] if satisfied:

(1) that the offeror[15] has after reasonable inquiry been unable to trace one or more of the persons holding shares to which the offer relates;

(2) that the shares which the offeror has acquired or contracted to acquire by virtue of acceptances of the offer, together with the shares held by the person or persons mentioned in head (1) above, amount to not less than the required minimum[16]; and

(3) that the consideration offered is fair and reasonable;

but the court must not make such an order unless it considers that it is just and equitable to do so having regard, in particular, to the number of shareholders who have been traced but who have not accepted the offer[17].

1 For the meaning of 'the offeror' see para 1202 ante. However, in the Companies Act 1985 s 430C (as substituted) references to the offeror are to be construed as references to the joint offerors except that any application under s 430C(3) or (5) (as substituted) (see infra) may be made by any of them and the reference in s 430C(5)(a) (as substituted) (see text head (1) infra) to the offeror having been unable to trace one or more of the persons holding shares is to be construed as a reference to none of the offerors having been able to do so: s 430D(7) (substituted by the Financial Services Act 1986 s 172(1), Sch 12). As to joint offers see para 1208 post.

2 Ie under the Companies Act 1985 s 429 (as substituted): see para 1203 ante.

3 For the meaning of 'the court' see para 161 note 4 ante.

4 The application is by originating summons in the expedited form: RSC Ord 102 r 2(1),(2). Formerly discovery would not have been ordered *(Re Press Caps Ltd* [1948] 2 All ER 638; and see *Re Press Caps Ltd* [1949] Ch 434 at 446, [1949] 1 All ER 1013 at 1018, CA per Evershed LJ) but see now RSC Ord 24 r 3.

5 Companies Act 1985 s 430C(1) (substituted by the Financial Services Act 1986 Sch 12). The court will make no such order unless the dissentient shareholder establishes that notwithstanding the views of the majority the scheme is unfair: *Re Hoare & Co Ltd* (1933) 150 LT 374; *Re Evertite Locknuts Ltd* [1945] Ch 220, [1945] 1 All ER 401; *Re Press Caps Ltd* [1949] Ch 434, [1949] 1 All ER 1013, CA; *Re Sussex Brick Co Ltd* [1961] Ch 289n, [1960] 1 All ER 772n; *Nidditch v Calico Printers' Association Ltd* 1961 SLT 282; *Re Grierson, Oldham and Adams Ltd* [1968] Ch 17, [1967] 1 All ER 192 (the test of fairness is whether the offer is fair to offerees as a whole, not to the applicant as an individual; the onus of proving that the offer is unfair is a heavy one where the offer price is above the market price). The mere fact that the dissentient shareholder was not provided with all the materials on which he could come to a just conclusion regarding the proposal will not normally be sufficient in itself to establish that the scheme is unfair: *Re Evertite Locknuts Ltd* supra; *Re Press Caps Ltd* supra at 443, 445, 446 and at 1015, 1017, 1018. When the court does make such an order, it may fix any purchase price it thinks fit: see *Re Castner-Kellner Alkali Co Ltd* [1930] 2 Ch 349. The fact that there has been a further amalgamation since the original offer does not affect the position: *Re Castner-Kellner Alkali Co Ltd* supra.

6 Ie in the Companies Act 1985 s 430(5) (as substituted): see para 1204 ante.

7 Ibid s 430C(2) (substituted by the Financial Services Act 1986 Sch 12).

8 See note 1 supra.

9 Ie under the Companies Act 1985 s 430A (as substituted): see para 1205 ante.

10 Ibid s 430C(3) (substituted by the Financial Services Act 1986 Sch 12).

11 Companies Act 1985 s 430C(4) (substituted by the Financial Services Act 1986 Sch 12).

12 For the meaning of 'take-over offer' see para 1202 ante.

13 See note 1 supra.

14 Ie under the Companies Act 1985 s 429(1) or (2) (as substituted): see para 1203 ante.

15 See note 1 supra.
16 Ie the required minimum specified in the Companies Act 1985 s 429(1) or (2) (as substituted): see para 1203 ante.
17 Ibid s 430C(5) (substituted by the Financial Services Act 1986 Sch 12).

1208. Joint offers. A take-over offer[1] may be made by two or more persons jointly, and in that event the above provisions[2] have effect with the following modifications[3]. The conditions for the exercise of the rights thereby conferred[4] on offerors may be satisfied by the joint offerors acquiring or contracting to acquire the necessary shares jointly (as respects acquisitions by virtue of acceptances of the offer) and either jointly or separately (in other cases); and, subject to the following provisions, the rights and obligations of the offeror under the above provisions[5] will be respectively joint rights and joint and several obligations of the joint offerors[6]. It will be a sufficient compliance with any of the above provisions[7] requiring or authorising a notice or other document to be given or sent by or to the joint offerors that it is given or sent by or to any of them; but the statutory declaration in relation to the satisfaction of the conditions for the giving of a notice to buy out minority shareholders[8] must be made by all of them, and, in the case of a joint offeror being a company, must be signed by a director of that company[9].

1 For the meaning of 'take-over offer' see para 1202 ante.
2 Ie the Companies Act 1985 Pt XIIIA (ss 428–430F) (substituted by the Financial Services Act 1986 s 172(1), Sch 12): see paras 1202–1208 ante and paras 1209, 1210 post.
3 Companies Act 1985 s 430D(1) (as substituted: see note 2 supra). This provision reverses the prior law under which these provisions related only to a case where the scheme or contract involved transfer to a single transferee company: *Blue Metal Industries Ltd v Dilley* [1970] AC 827, [1969] 3 All ER 437, PC (decided under a New South Wales enactment in similar terms to the Companies Act 1985 s 428).
   In addition to the modifications noted infra see also paras 1202 note 5, 1204 note 4, 1206 note 4, 1207 note 1 ante and para 1209 note 3 post.
4 Ie conferred by the Companies Act 1985 s 429 (as substituted) (see para 1203 ante) and s 430A (as substituted) (see para 1205 ante).
5 Ie ibid s 429 (as substituted), s 430 (as substituted) (see para 1204 ante), s 430A (as substituted) and s 430B (as substituted) (see para 1206 ante).
6 Ibid s 430D(2) (as substituted: see note 2 supra).
7 See note 2 supra.
8 Ie under the Companies Act 1985 s 429(4) (as substituted): see para 1203 ante.
9 Ibid s 430D(3) (as substituted: see note 2 supra).

1209. Associates. The requirement[1] that a take-over offer[2] must extend to all the shares, or all the shares of any class or classes, in a company is to be regarded as satisfied notwithstanding that the offer does not extend to shares which associates of the offeror[3] hold or have contracted to acquire; but shares which any such associate holds or has contracted to acquire, whether at the time when the offer is made or subsequently, are to be disregarded for the purposes of any reference in these provisions[4] to the shares to which a take-over offer relates[5]. However, where during the period within which a take-over offer can be accepted any associate of the offeror acquires or contracts to acquire any of the shares to which the offer relates, then, if the value of the consideration is within the statutory provision[6] as respects those shares, they are to be treated for those purposes as shares to which the offer relates[7].

For these purposes 'associate', in relation to an offeror, means:
(1) a nominee of the offeror;
(2) a holding company[8], subsidiary[9] or fellow subsidiary[10] of the offeror or a nominee of such a holding company, subsidiary or fellow subsidiary;

(3) a body corporate in which the offeror is substantially interested[11]; or

(4) any person who is, or is a nominee of, a party to an agreement with the offeror for the acquisition of, or of an interest in, the shares which are the subject of the take-over offer, being an agreement which includes[12] certain provisions imposing obligations or restrictions[13].

Where the offeror is an individual, his associates will also include his spouse and any minor[14] child or stepchild of his[15].

1 Ie in the Companies Act 1985 s 428(1) (as substituted): see para 1202 ante.
2 For the meaning of 'take-over offer' see para 1202 ante.
3 For the meaning of 'the offeror' see para 1202 ante. However, in the Companies Act 1985 s 430E (as substituted) references to the offeror are to be construed as references to the joint offerors or any of them: s 430D(4) (substituted by the Financial Services Act 1986 s 172(1), Sch 12). As to joint offers see para 1208 ante.
4 Ie the Companies Act 1985 Pt XIIIA (ss 428-430F) (as substituted): see para 1202 et seq ante and para 1210 post.
5 Ibid s 430E(1) (substituted by the Financial Services Act 1986 Sch 12). Even before this provision a shareholding company which was a wholly-owned subsidiary of the offeror could not have given approval for the purpose of acquiring the shares of dissenting shareholders: *Re Hellenic & General Trust Ltd* [1975] 3 All ER 382, [1976] 1 WLR 123.
6 Ie the Companies Act 1985 s 429(8)(a) or (b) (as substituted): see para 1203 ante.
7 Ibid s 430E(2) (substituted by the Financial Services Act 1986 Sch 12).
8 For the meaning of 'holding company' see para 827 ante.
9 For the meaning of 'subsidiary' see para 827 ante.
10 For these purposes, a company is a fellow subsidiary of another body corporate if both are subsidiaries of the same body corporate but neither is a subsidiary of the other: Companies Act 1985 s 430E(5) (substituted by the Financial Services Act 1986 Sch 12). For the meaning of 'body corporate' see para 89 note 8 ante.
11 For these purposes, an offeror has a substantial interest in a body corporate if (1) that body or its directors are accustomed to act in accordance with his directions or instructions; or (2) he is entitled to exercise or control the exercise of one-third or more of the voting power at general meetings of that body: Companies Act 1985 s 430E(6) (substituted by the Financial Services Act 1986 Sch 12). The Companies Act 1985 s 203(3),(4) (see para 738 ante) applies for the purposes of s 430E(6) (as so substituted) as it applies for the purposes of s 203(2)(b): s 430E(7) (substituted by the Financial Services Act 1986 Sch 12).
12 Ie includes the provisions imposing obligations or restrictions as are mentioned in the Companies Act 1985 s 204(2)(a): see para 739 ante.
13 Ibid s 430E(4) (substituted by the Financial Services Act 1986 Sch 12). The Companies Act 1985 s 204(5),(6) (see para 739 ante) applies to s 430E(4)(d) (as so substituted) (see text head (4) supra) as it applies to s 204: s 430E(7) (as substituted: see note 11 supra).
14 As to the attainment of majority at the age of 18 see the Family Law Reform Act 1969 s 1 and CHILDREN vol 5(2) (Reissue) para 601.
15 Companies Act 1985 s 430E(8) (substituted by the Financial Services Act 1986 Sch 12).

1210. Convertible securities. For the purposes of these provisions[1], securities of a company are to be treated as shares in the company if they are convertible into, or entitle the holder to subscribe for, such shares; and references to the holder of shares or a shareholder are to be construed accordingly[2]. However, this is not to be construed as requiring any securities to be treated:

(1) as shares of the same class as those into which they are convertible or for which the holder is entitled to subscribe; or

(2) as shares of the same class as other securities by reason only that the shares into which they are convertible or for which the holder is entitled to subscribe are of the same class[3].

1 Ie the Companies Act 1985 Pt XIIIA (ss 428-430F) (substituted by the Financial Services Act 1986 s 172(1), Sch 12): see infra and para 1202 et seq ante.
2 Companies Act 1985 s 430F(1) (as substituted: see note 1 supra).
3 Ibid s 430F(2) (as substituted: see note 1 supra).

(24) DEMERGERS

1211. Exempt distributions. The following provisions have effect for facilitating certain transactions whereby trading activities carried on by a single company or group[1] are divided so as to be carried on by two or more companies not belonging to the same group or by two or more independent groups[2].

References in the Corporation Tax Acts[3] to distributions of a company do not apply to any distribution:

(1) consisting of the transfer to all or any of its members[4] by a company ('the distributing company') of shares[5] in one or more companies which are its 75% subsidiaries[6];

(2) consisting of the transfer by a company ('the distributing company') to one or more other companies ('the transferee company or companies') of either a trade[7] or trades or shares in one or more companies which are 75% subsidiaries of the distributing company, and the issue of shares by the transferee company or companies to all or any of the members of the distributing company,

and in respect of which the specified conditions[8] are satisfied[9].

1 For these purposes, except in the Income and Corporation Taxes Act 1988 s 213(11)(c) (see para 1212 head (iii) post), 'group' means a company which has one or more 75% subsidiaries together with that or those subsidiaries: s 218(1). For the meaning of '75% subsidiary' see note 6 infra.

2 Ibid s 213(1). For these purposes, 'exempt distribution' has the meaning given by s 213(2): s 218(1).

3 For these purposes, 'the Corporation Tax Acts' means the enactments relating to the taxation of the income and chargeable gains of companies and company distributions, including provisions relating also to income tax: Income and Corporation Taxes Act 1988 s 831(1)(a).

4 For these purposes, 'member', where the reference is to a member of a company, does not, except in ibid s 214(2)(a) (see para 1214 post), include a person who is a member otherwise than by virtue of holding shares forming part of the company's ordinary share capital: s 218(1). 'Ordinary share capital', in relation to a company, means all the issued share capital (by whatever name called) of the company, other than capital the holders of which have a right to a dividend at a fixed rate but have no other right to share in the profits of the company: s 832(1).

5 For these purposes, 'shares' includes stock: ibid s 218(1).

6 A body corporate is deemed to be a '75% subsidiary' of another body corporate if and so long as not less than 75% of its ordinary share capital is owned directly or indirectly by that other body corporate: ibid s 838(1)(b). In determining for the purposes of s 213(3)-(9) (as amended) (see infra and para 1212 post) whether a company whose shares are transferred by the distributing company is a 75% subsidiary of the distributing company, any share capital of the first-mentioned company which is owned indirectly by the distributing company must be disregarded: s 218(2). In determining for the purposes of ss 213-217 (as amended) (see infra and para 1212 et seq post) whether one company is a 75% subsidiary of another, the other company is to be treated as not being the owner of (1) any share capital which it owns directly in a body corporate if a profit on a sale of the shares would be treated as a trading receipt of its trade; or (2) any share capital which it owns indirectly and which is owned directly by a body corporate for which a profit on the sale of the shares would be a trading receipt: s 218(3). For the meaning of 'trade' see note 7 infra.

7 For these purposes, except in ibid s 218(3) (see note 6 supra), 'trade' does not include dealing in shares, securities, land, trades or commodity futures; and 'trading activities' is to be construed accordingly: s 218(1). The Revenue will, however, regard the requirement that a trade or trades be transferred as satisfied where what is received by the transferee company is a trade. What passes from one company to another will be a parcel of assets comprising what is needed for the carrying on of that trade. The same trade may have been carried on as such by the distributing company; but this is not essential. What is transferred may have been part only of a trade carried on by that company, eg the retail end of a combined manufacturing/retail trade. Or again the assets being transferred may be being brought together for the first time from one or more trades carried on by the distributing company or in the group of which it is a member; assets may even be included which were not previously used in a trade or held by a trading company, eg property may have been held in a property investment company. What matters is that there should be a division of trading activities and that assets transferred should be

transferred to be used in a trade by the transferee company and should be so used. Relief will not be denied solely because some minor asset linked with a trading asset, eg a flat above a shop, is also transferred: Inland Revenue Statement of Practice SP13/80.

8 Ie the conditions specified in the Income and Corporation Taxes Act 1988 s 213(4)–(12) (as amended): see para 1212 post.

9 Ibid s 213(2),(3). Any such distribution is referred to in s 213 (as amended) as an 'exempt distribution': s 213(2).

1212. Conditions to be satisfied. Each relevant company[1] must be resident[2] in the United Kingdom at the time of the distribution[3].

The distributing company[4] must at the time of the distribution be either a trading company[5] or a member of a trading group[6] and each subsidiary whose shares are transferred[7] must at that time be either a trading company or the holding company[8] of a trading group[9].

In a case[10] where the distributing company makes a distribution consisting of the transfer to all or any of its members[11] of shares[12] in one or more companies which are its 75% subsidiaries:

(1) the shares must not be redeemable, must constitute the whole or substantially the whole of the distributing company's holding of the ordinary share capital[13] of the subsidiary and must confer the whole or substantially the whole of the distributing company's voting rights in the subsidiary[14]; and

(2) the distributing company must after the distribution be either a trading company or the holding company of a trading group[15].

In a case[16] where the distributing company is making a distribution consisting of the transfer to one or more other companies of a trade or trades or shares to one or more other companies which are 75% subsidiaries of the distributing company:

(a) if a trade is transferred, the distributing company must either not retain any interest or retain only a minor interest[17] in that trade[18];

(b) if shares in a subsidiary are transferred, those shares must constitute the whole or substantially the whole of the distributing company's holding of the ordinary share capital of the subsidiary and must confer the whole or substantially the whole of the distributing company's voting rights in the subsidiary[19];

(c) the only or main activity of the transferee company or each transferee company after the distribution must be the carrying on of the trade or the holding of the shares transferred to it[20];

(d) the shares issued by the transferee company or each transferee company must not be redeemable, must constitute the whole or substantially the whole of its issued ordinary share capital and must confer the whole or substantially the whole of the voting rights in that company[21]; and

(e) the distributing company must after the distribution be either a trading company or the holding company of a trading group[22].

The distribution must be made wholly or mainly[23] for the purpose of benefiting some or all of the trading activities which before the distribution are carried on by a single company or group and after the distribution will be carried on by two or more companies or groups[24].

The distribution must not form part of a scheme or arrangements the main purpose or one of the main purposes of which is:

(i) the avoidance of tax, including stamp duty[25]; or

(ii) without prejudice to head (i) above, the making of a chargeable payment[26] or what would be such a payment if any of the companies concerned were an unquoted company[27]; or

(iii) the acquisition by any person or persons other than members of the distributing company of control[28] of that company, of any other relevant company or of any company which belongs to the same group[29] as any such company[30]; or

(iv) the cessation of a trade or its sale after[31] the distribution[32].

Where the distributing company is a 75% subsidiary of another company:

(A) the group, or, if more than one, the largest group, to which the distributing company belongs at the time of the distribution must be a trading group[33];

(B) heads (2) and (e) above do not apply[34]; and

(C) the distribution must be followed by one or more other distributions, consisting either of the transfer to all or any of its members of shares in one or more companies which are its 75% subsidiaries or a distribution of such shares to one or more transferee companies followed by the issue of shares by the transferee company or companies to all or any members of the distributing company[35], which satisfy the statutory conditions[36] and result in members of the holding company of the group, or, if more than one, the largest group, to which the distributing company belonged at the time of the distribution becoming members of the transferee company or each transferee company to which a trade was transferred by the distributing company, or the subsidiary or each subsidiary whose shares were transferred by the distributing company, or a company (other than that holding company) of which the company or companies[37] are 75% subsidiaries[38].

1 For these purposes, references to a relevant company are to the distributing company, to each subsidiary whose shares are transferred as mentioned in the Income and Corporation Taxes Act 1988 s 213(3)(a) or (b)(ii) (see para 1211 ante) and to each transferee company mentioned in s 213(3)(b) (see para 1211 ante): ss 213(3), 218(1).

2 As to the residence of companies for tax purposes see INCOME TAXATION vol 23 (Reissue) para 1254.

3 Income and Corporation Taxes Act 1988 s 213(4).

4 For these purposes, 'distributing company' has the meaning given by ibid s 213(2) (see para 1211 ante): s 218(1).

5 For these purposes, 'trading company' means a company whose business consists wholly or mainly of the carrying on of a trade or trades: ibid s 218(1). For the meaning of 'trade' see para 1211 note 7 ante.

6 For these purposes, 'trading group' means a group the business of whose members, taken together, consists wholly or mainly in the carrying on of a trade or trades: ibid s 218(1).

7 Ie as mentioned in ibid s 213(3)(a) or (b)(ii): see para 1211 ante.

8 For these purposes, 'holding company' means a company whose business, disregarding any trade carried on by it, consists wholly or mainly of the holding of shares or securities of one or more companies which are its 75% subsidiaries: ibid s 218(1). For the meaning of '75% subsidiary' see para 1211 note 6 ante.

9 Ibid s 213(5).

10 Ie in a case within ibid s 213(3)(a): see para 1211 head (1) ante.

11 For the meaning of 'member' see para 1211 note 4 ante.

12 For the meaning of 'shares' see para 1211 note 5 ante.

13 For the meaning of 'ordinary share capital' see para 1211 note 4 ante.

14 Income and Corporation Taxes Act 1988 s 213(6)(a). Relief is so given to a distribution to ordinary shareholders only in so far as it is of shares forming part of the ordinary share capital which are transferred or issued. Relief on that distribution will not, however, be denied solely because concurrently there is a transfer or issue, of a kind that does not qualify for relief, of other shares or securities to ordinary shareholders or of shares or securities of any description to preference shareholders, and whether or not that other transfer or issue involves a taxable distribution. Similarly, the words 'substantially the whole' will be regarded as satisfied even where the shareholders give some consideration. However, those other conditions will be taken into account in judging whether all the conditions are satisfied. In the

context of these particular provisions, 'substantially the whole' is taken to mean around 90% or more: Inland Statement of Practice SP18/80.

15 Income and Corporation Taxes Act 1988 s 213(6)(b). Section 213(6)(b) is subject to s 213(7) and s 213(12)(b) (see text head (B) infra): s 213(6)(b). Section 213(6)(b) does not apply if the transfer relates to two or more 75% subsidiaries of the distributing company and that company is dissolved without there having been after the distribution any net assets of the company available for distribution in a winding up or otherwise: s 213(7). By extra-statutory concession, a company will not be regarded as failing to comply with s 213(7) merely because it retains after the distribution sufficient funds to meet the cost of liquidation and to cover what will usually be the negligible amount of share capital remaining; but this concession does not apply where the company retains more than a negligible amount of share capital: Inland Revenue booklet IR1 (1993) C11.

In the Revenue's view, the Income and Corporation Taxes Act 1988 s 213(6)(b),(8)(c),(e) requires that the company should be bona fide trading after the distribution; but in this context the Revenue does not regard 'after' as meaning 'for ever after'. If there were any intention that the conditions would cease to be satisfied at some later time, the application of s 213(10),(11) (see infra) would need to be considered: Inland Revenue Statement of Practice SP13/80.

16 Ie in a case within the Income and Corporation Taxes Act 1988 s 213(3)(b): see para 1211 head (2) ante.

17 There is no statutory definition of 'interest in trade'. In the Revenue's view the expression must be given a wide meaning. A company would clearly retain an interest in trade if it carried it on jointly or otherwise had a right to the profits or assets or to any of them. Other circumstances could, however, exist in which it could be said to have an interest, eg if it was or was entitled to be a main supplier or customer, or possibly as a consequence of the two companies having common management. In these kinds of case the Revenue would not normally argue that the interest was other than a 'minor interest' unless the interest effectively gave control of the trade or of its assets, or a material influence on the profits or their destination. More generally, it will not always be possible to quantify an interest in a trade; but, where this can be done, 'minor' is the opposite of 'substantially the whole' ie around 10% or less: Inland Revenue Statement of Practice SP13/80.

18 Income and Corporation Taxes Act 1988 s 213(8)(a). See also note 14 supra.

19 Ibid s 218(3)(b).

20 Ibid s 218(3)(c). See also note 15 supra.

21 Ibid s 218(3)(d).

22 Ibid s 218(3)(e). See also note 15 supra. Section 218(3)(e) does not apply, however, if there are two or more transferee companies each of which has a trade or shares in a separate 75% subsidiary of the distributing company transferred to it and the distributing company is dissolved without there having been after the distribution any net assets of the company available for distribution in a winding up or otherwise: s 213(9).

23 The word 'mainly' probably means 'more than half' though there is nothing in ibid s 213 to indicate by reference to what this is to be calculated: see *Fawcett Properties Ltd v Buckingham County Council* [1961] AC 636 at 669, [1960] 3 All ER 503 at 512, HL per Lord Morton of Henryton (a town and country planning case). On the meaning of 'wholly or mainly' (or 'exclusively or mainly') see also *Re Hatschek's Patents, ex p Zerenner* [1909] 2 Ch 68 (a patent case); *Miller v Ottilie (Owners)* [1944] 1 KB 188, [1944] 1 All ER 277 (a workers' compensation case); *Franklin v Gramophone Co Ltd* [1948] 1 KB 542 at 555, [1948] 1 All ER 353 at 358, CA per Somervell LJ (a Factory Acts case); *Berthelemy v Neale* [1952] 1 All ER 437, CA (a landlord and tenant case).

24 Income and Corporation Taxes Act 1988 s 213(10).

25 Ibid s 213(11)(a).

26 For these purposes, 'chargeable payment' has the meaning given by ibid s 214(2) (see para 1214 post): s 218(1).

27 Ibid s 213(11)(b). For these purposes, 'unquoted company' means a company which does not satisfy the condition that its shares or some class thereof (disregarding debenture or loan stock, preferred shares or preferred stock) are listed in the Official List of the Stock Exchange and are dealt in on the Stock Exchange regularly or from time to time; but this definition does not apply to a company under the control of, and only of, one or more companies to which this definition does not apply: s 218(1). For the meaning of 'control' see note 28 infra.

28 For these purposes, 'control' is to be construed in accordance with ibid s 416(2)-(6) (see INCOME TAXATION vol 23 (Reissue) para 1295): s 218(1).

29 For these purposes, 'group' means a company which has one or more 51% subsidiaries together with that or those subsidiaries: ibid s 213(11). A body corporate is deemed to be a '51% subsidiary' of another body corporate if and so long as not less than 50% of its ordinary share capital is owned directly or indirectly by that other body corporate: s 838(1)(a). The concurrent sale of another company in the same group as the demerged subsidiary is not necessarily a bar to relief, although it would be so if that

were a main purpose of a scheme or arrangement of which the distribution formed a part: Inland Revenue Statement of Practice SP13/80.

30 Income and Corporation Taxes Act 1988 s 213(11)(c).
31 In the Revenue's view the word 'after' in this context means 'at any time after': Inland Revenue Statement of Practice SP13/80.
32 Income and Corporation Taxes Act 1988 s 213(11)(d).
33 Ibid s 213(12)(a).
34 Ibid s 213(12)(b).
35 Ie distributions falling within ibid s 213(3)(a) or (b)(ii): see para 1211 ante.
36 Ie ibid s 213(4)-(12) (as amended): see supra.
37 Ie the company or companies mentioned in ibid s 213(12)(c)(i) or (ii): see supra.
38 Ibid s 213(12)(c).

1213. Relief from capital gains tax. The following provisions have effect for facilitating certain transactions whereby trading activities carried on by a single company or group[1] are divided so as to be carried on by two or more companies not belonging to the same group or by two or more independent groups[2].

Where a company makes an exempt distribution[3] consisting of the transfer to all or any of its members of shares in one or more companies which are its 75% subsidiaries[4]:

(1) the distribution is not a capital distribution for the purposes of the Taxation of Chargeable Gains Tax Act 1992[5]; and

(2) the statutory provisions relating to reorganisations[6] apply, with the necessary modifications, as if that company and the subsidiary whose shares are transferred were the same company and the distribution were a reorganisation of its share capital[7].

Further, the provisions of the Taxation of Chargeable Gains Tax Act 1992 which apply where a company ceases to be a member of a group[8] do not apply in a case where a company ceases to be a member of a group by reason only of an exempt distribution[9]. This exemption does not, however, apply if, within five years after the making of the exempt distribution, there is a chargeable payment[10]; and the time for so making an assessment[11] by virtue of this provision does not expire before the end of three years after the making of the chargeable payment[12].

1 For these purposes, 'group' means a company which has one or more 75% subsidiaries together with that or those subsidiaries: Taxation of Chargeable Gains Act 1992 s 192(5). For the meaning of '75% subsidiary' see para 1211 note 6 ante. In determining for these purpose whether one company is a 75% subsidiary of another, the other company is to be treated as not being the owner of (1) any share capital which it owns directly in a body corporate if a profit on a sale of the shares would be treated as a trading receipt of its trade; or (2) any share capital which it owns indirectly and which is owned directly by a body corporate for which a profit on the sale of the shares would be a trading receipt: s 192(6).

In the context of demergers and the legislation contained in the Income and Corporation Taxes Act 1988 ss 213-218 (as amended) (see paras 1211, 1212 ante and para 1214 et seq post) a shareholding in a company which is a 75% subsidiary of the distributing company is regarded as constituting an identifiable part of the trade or business of the distributing company. Thus the division of a company involving the transfer of shares in a subsidiary to a newly formed company by way of demerger falling within s 213(3)(b)(ii) (see para 1211 ante) is also regarded as a scheme of reconstruction even though the distributing company and the transferee company may have no common shareholder. The division of a company in this manner involves the reclassification of the shares of the distributing company into separate classes followed by the distribution of the shares in a subsidiary to a newly formed company in consideration of the issue of shares by that company to a particular class of shareholders: Inland Revenue Statement of Practice SP5/85 para 4. This Statement of Practice does not apply to stamp duty or to taxes other than capital gains tax and the charge to corporation tax on capital gains: Inland Revenue Statement of Practice SP5/85 para 5.

2 Taxation of Chargeable Gains Act 1992 s 192(1).

3 For these purposes, 'exempt distribution' means a distribution which is exempt by virtue of the Income and Corporation Taxes Act 1988 s 213(2) (see para 1211 ante): Taxation of Chargeable Gains Act 1992 s 192(5).

4 Ie an exempt distribution which falls within the Income and Corporation Taxes Act 1988 s 213(3)(a): see para 1211 head (1) ante.

5 Ie for the purposes of the Taxation of Chargeable Gains Act 1992 s 122: see CAPITAL GAINS TAXATION vol 5(1) (Reissue) para 243.

6 Ie ibid ss 126–130: see CAPITAL GAINS TAXATION vol 5(1) (Reissue) para 252.

7 Ibid s 192(2).

8 Ie ibid s 178 (as amended) or s 179 (as amended): see CAPITAL GAINS TAXATION vol 5(1) (Reissue) para 162.

9 Ibid s 192(3).

10 For these purposes, 'chargeable payment' has the meaning given in the Income and Corporation Taxes Act 1988 s 214(2) (see para 1211 note 2 ante): Taxation of Chargeable Gains Act 1992 s 192(5).

11 Ie under ibid s 178 (as amended) or s 179 (as amended).

12 Ibid s 192(4).

1214. Chargeable payments connected with exempt distributions. If within five years after the making of an exempt distribution[1] there is a chargeable payment[2]:

(1) the amount or value of the payment is to be treated as income chargeable to tax under Case VI of Schedule D[3];

(2) unless the payment is a transfer of money's worth, the Income and Corporation Taxes Act 1988[4] applies to the payment as if it were an annual sum payable otherwise than out of profits or gains charged to income tax[5];

(3) the payment is regarded as a distribution[6] for certain purposes[7]; and

(4) the payment is not, if it otherwise would be, treated[8] as a repayment of capital[9].

For these purposes, 'a chargeable payment' means any payment made otherwise than for bona fide commercial reasons or forming part of a scheme or arrangement the main purpose or one of the main purposes of which is the avoidance of tax, including stamp duty, being a payment which:

(a) a company concerned in an exempt distribution[10] makes directly or indirectly to a member[11] of that company or of any other company concerned in that distribution[12]; and

(b) is made in connection with, or with any transaction affecting, the shares in that or any such company[13]; and

(c) is not a distribution or exempt distribution or made to another company which belongs to the same group as the company making the payment[14].

1 For the meaning of 'exempt distribution' see para 1211 note 2 ante.

2 For these purposes, references to a payment include references to a transfer of money's worth including the assumption of a liability: Income and Corporation Taxes Act 1988 s 214(6).

3 Ibid s 214(1)(a). As to s 18(2),(3), Schedule D, Case VI (as amended) see INCOME TAXATION vol 23 (Reissue) para 610 et seq.

4 Ie ibid ss 349(1), 350 (as amended): see INCOME TAXATION vol 23 (Reissue) paras 578, 579.

5 Ibid s 214(1)(b).

6 Ie for the purposes of ibid s 337(2) (see INCOME TAXATION vol 23 (Reissue) para 852) and s 338(2)(a) (see INCOME TAXATION vol 23 (Reissue) para 885).

7 Ibid s 214(1)(c) (amended by the Finance Act 1989 s 107, Sch 12 para 10).

8 Ie for the purposes of the Income and Corporation Taxes Act 1988 s 210 (see INCOME TAXATION vol 23 (Reissue) para 884) or s 211 (see INCOME TAXATION vol 23 (Reissue) para 885).

9 Ibid s 214(1)(d).

10 For the meaning of 'member' see para 1211 note 4 ante.

11 For these purposes, references to a company concerned in an exempt distribution are to any relevant company and to any other company which was connected with any such company for the whole or any part of the period beginning with the exempt distribution and ending with the making of the payment which is in question under the Income and Corporation Taxes Act 1988 s 214 (s 214(4)); and a company

is deemed to have been connected in the period so referred to with each company to which a company connected with it was connected in that period (s 214(5)). For these purposes, s 839 (meaning of 'connected persons': see INCOME TAXATION vol 23 (Reissue) para 1250) applies: s 218(4).

12 Ibid s 214(2)(a). Where a company concerned in an exempt distribution is an unquoted company, s 214(2)(a) has effect as if any reference to the making of a payment by, or to a member of, a company concerned in the exempt distribution included a reference to the making of a payment by or to any other person in pursuance of a scheme or arrangements made with the unquoted company or, if the unquoted company is (1) under the control of five or fewer persons; and (2) not under the control of, and only of, a company which is not itself under the control of five or fewer persons, with any of the persons mentioned in head (1) supra: s 214(3). For the meaning of 'unquoted company' see para 1212 note 27 ante; and for the meaning of 'control' see para 1212 note 28 ante.

13 Ibid s 214(2)(b).

14 Ibid s 214(2)(c).

1215. Advance clearance of distributions and payments. A distribution is treated as an exempt distribution[1] in any case in which, before the distribution is made, the Commissioners of Inland Revenue ('the Board') have, on the application of the distributing company, notified that company that the Board is satisfied that it will be such a distribution[2].

A payment[3] is not treated as a chargeable payment[4] in any case in which, before the payment is made, the Board has, on the application of the person intending to make it, notified him that the Board is satisfied that the payment will be made for bona fide commercial reasons and will not form part of any scheme or arrangements the main purpose or one of the main purposes of which is the avoidance of tax, including stamp duty[5]. A company which becomes or ceases to be connected[6] with another company may make such an application as respects any payments that may be made by it at any time after becoming or ceasing to be so connected, whether or not there is any present intention to make any payments; and, where a notification is given by the Board on such an application, no payment to which the notification relates is to be treated as a chargeable payment by reason only of the company being or having been connected with the other company[7].

Any application under these provisions must be in writing and must contain particulars of the relevant transactions and the Board may, within 30 days of the receipt of the application or of any further particulars previously required, by notice in writing require the applicant to furnish further particulars for the purposes of enabling the Board to make its decision; and, if any such notice is not complied with within 30 days or such longer period as the Board may allow, the Board need not proceed further on the application[8].

The Board must notify its decision to the applicant within 30 days of receiving the application or, if the Board gives a notice under the above provisions, within 30 days of the notice being complied with[9].

If the Board notifies the applicant that it is not satisfied as mentioned in the above provisions[10] or does not notify its decision to the applicant within the time specified above, the applicant may within 30 days of the notification or of that time require the Board to transmit the application, together with any notice given and further particulars so furnished, to the Special Commissioners; and in that event any notification by the Special Commissioners has effect for the purposes of obtaining a clearance as if it were a notification by the Board[11].

If any particulars furnished under these provisions do not fully and accurately disclose all facts and circumstances material for the decision of the Board or the Special Commissioners, any resulting notification that the Board or the Commissioners are satisfied as mentioned in the above provisions[12] is void[13].

1 For the meaning of 'exempt distribution' see para 1211 note 2 ante.
2 Income and Corporation Taxes Act 1988 s 215(1). As to application for clearance under s 215(1) see Inland Revenue Statement of Practice SP13/80, Annex.
3 For these purposes, references to a payment are to be construed as in the Income and Corporation Taxes Act 1988 s 214 (as amended) (see para 1214 note 2 ante): s 215(4).
4 For the meaning of 'chargeable payment' see para 1212 note 26 ante.
5 Income and Corporation Taxes Act 1988 s 215(2).
6 For the meaning of 'connected' see para 1214 note 11 ante.
7 Income and Corporation Taxes Act 1988 s 215(3).
8 Ibid s 215(5).
9 Ibid s 215(6).
10 Ie as mentioned in ibid s 215(1) or (2): see supra.
11 Ibid s 215(7).
12 See note 10 supra.
13 Income and Corporation Taxes Act 1988 s 215(8).

1216. Returns. Where a company makes an exempt distribution[1], it must, within 30 days after the distribution, make a return to the inspector of taxes giving particulars of the distribution and of the circumstances by reason of which it is exempt[2].

Where, within five years after the making of an exempt distribution, a person makes a chargeable payment[3] which consists of a transfer of money's worth, he must within 30 days after the transfer make a return to the inspector giving particulars:

(1) of the transaction effecting the transfer;

(2) of the name and address of the recipient or each recipient and the value of what is transferred to him or each of them; and

(3) if the transfer is accompanied by a chargeable payment consisting of a payment of money, of that payment[4].

Where, within five years after the making of an exempt distribution, a person makes a payment or a transfer of money's worth which would be a chargeable payment but for the fact that it is made for bona fide commercial reasons and does not form part of any scheme or arrangements the main purpose or one of the main purposes of which is the avoidance of tax, including stamp duty[5], that person must, within 30 days after the payment or transfer, make a return to the inspector giving particulars:

(a) in the case of a transfer, of the transaction by which it is effected;

(b) of the name and address of the recipient or each recipient and the amount of the payment made, or the value of what is transferred, to him or each of them; and

(c) of the circumstances by reason of which the payment or transfer is not a chargeable payment[6].

1 For the meaning of 'exempt distribution' see para 1211 note 2 ante.
2 Income and Corporation Taxes Act 1988 s 216(1). As to the penalty for failure to comply with this requirement see INCOME TAXATION vol 23 (Reissue) para 1638.
    Section 216(1) requires a company making an exempt distribution to make a return giving particulars (inter alia) 'of the circumstances by reason of which it is exempt'. In many cases a clearance notification will previously have been given by the Board under s 215(1) (see para 1215 ante). Where the distribution is precisely that for which a clearance application was made, all relevant circumstances being as disclosed in that application, it will suffice to refer to the notification and to confirm that it is so: Inland Revenue Statement of Practice SP13/80.
3 For the meaning of 'chargeable payment' see para 1212 note 26 ante.
4 Income and Corporation Taxes Act 1988 s 216(2). As to the penalty for failure to comply with this requirement see INCOME TAXATION vol 23 (Reissue) para 1638.
5 Ie any such scheme or arrangement as is mentioned in ibid s 214(2): see para 1214 ante.
6 Ibid s 216(3). As to the penalty for failure to comply with this requirement see INCOME TAXATION vol 23 (Reissue) para 1638.
    Section 216(3) does not apply where the payment or transfer is one in relation to which a notification under s 215(3) (see para 1215 ante) has effect: s 216(4).

1217. Power to obtain information. Where a distribution[1] has been made and the inspector of taxes has reason to believe that it may form part of certain prohibited schemes or arrangements[2], he may by a notice in writing require any relevant company[3] or any person controlling[4] any such company to furnish him within such time, not being less than 30 days, as may be specified in the notice with:

(1) a declaration in writing stating whether or not, according to information which the company or that person has, or can reasonably obtain, any such scheme or arrangements exist or have existed;

(2) such other information as the inspector may reasonably require[5] and the company or that person has or can reasonably obtain[6].

If the inspector has reason to believe that a person has not delivered an account or made a return which he is required to deliver or make by virtue of the provisions relating to deduction of tax at source from a chargeable payment[7] or the return required if a chargeable payment is made consisting of a transfer of money's worth[8] in respect of any payment or transfer, the inspector may by notice in writing require that person to furnish him within such time, not being less than 30 days, as may be specified in the notice with such information relating to the payment or transfer as he may[9] reasonably require[10].

If the inspector has reason to believe that a payment or transfer has been made within five years after the making of an exempt distribution and that the payment or transfer is a chargeable payment by reason of the existence of a scheme or arrangements made with an unquoted company[11], he may by notice in writing require the person making the payment or transfer or, if that person is a company, any person controlling it to furnish him within such time, not being less than 30 days, as may be specified in the notice with:

(a) a declaration in writing stating whether or not, according to information which that person has, or can reasonably obtain, any such scheme or arrangements exist or have existed;

(b) such other information as the inspector may reasonably require[12] and that person has or can reasonably obtain[13].

Any recipient of a chargeable payment and any person on whose behalf such a payment is received must, if so required by the inspector, state whether the payment received by him or on his behalf is received on behalf of any person other than himself and, if so, the name and address of that person[14].

1 Ie a distribution falling within the Income and Corporation Taxes Act 1988 s 213(3): see para 1211 ante.
2 Ie any such scheme or arrangements as are mentioned in ibid s 213(11): see para 1212 ante.
3 For the meaning of 'relevant company' see para 1212 note 1 ante.
4 For the meaning of 'control' see para 1212 note 28 ante.
5 Ie for the purposes of the Income and Corporation Taxes Act 1988 s 213(11): see para 1212 ante.
6 Ibid s 217(1). As to the penalty for failure to comply with this requirement see INCOME TAXATION vol 23 (Reissue) para 1638.
7 Ie ibid s 214(1)(b): see para 1214 head (2) ante.
8 Ie ibid s 216(2) or (3): see para 1216 ante.
9 Ie for the purposes of ibid s 214: see para 1214 ante.
10 Ibid s 217(2). As to the penalty for failure to comply with this requirement see INCOME TAXATION vol 23 (Reissue) para 1638.
11 Ie ibid s 214(3): see para 1214 ante.
12 See note 9 supra.
13 Income and Corporation Taxes Act 1988 s 217(3). As to the penalty for failure to comply with this requirement see INCOME TAXATION vol 23 (Reissue) para 1638.
14 Ibid s 217(4). As to the penalty for failure to comply with this requirement see INCOME TAXATION vol 23 (Reissue) para 1638.

(25) INSIDER DEALING

(i) In general

1218. The offence of insider dealing. An individual who has information as an insider is guilty of insider dealing if in the specified circumstances[1] he deals in securities[2] that are price-affected securities[3] in relation to the information[4].

An individual who has information as an insider is also guilty of insider dealing if:

(1) he encourages another person to deal in securities that are, whether or not that other knows it, price-affected securities in relation to the information, knowing or having reasonable cause to believe that the dealing would take place in the specified circumstances[5]; or

(2) he discloses the information, otherwise than in the proper performance of the functions of his employment, office or profession, to another person[6].

The circumstances so specified are that the acquisition or disposal in question occurs on a regulated market[7] or that the person dealing relies on a professional intermediary[8] or is himself acting as a professional intermediary[9].

The above provisions do not apply to anything done by an individual acting on behalf of a public sector body[10] in pursuit of monetary policies or policies with respect to exchange rates or the management of public debt or foreign exchange reserves[11]; and no contract is void or unenforceable by reason only of the above provisions[12].

A person has information as an insider if and only if it is, and he knows that it is, inside information[13] and he has it, and knows that he has it, from an inside source[14]. A person has information from an inside source if and only if:

(a) he has it through being a director, employee or shareholder of an issuer[15] of securities or having access to the information by virtue of his employment, office or profession; or

(b) the direct or indirect source of his information is a person within head (a) above[16].

---

1 Ie the circumstances mentioned in the Criminal Justice Act 1993 s 52(3): see infra.

2 For these purposes, a person deals in securities if (1) he acquires or disposes of the securities, whether as principal or agent; or (2) he procures, directly or indirectly, an acquisition or disposal of the securities by any other person: ibid s 55(1). A person procures an acquisition or disposal of a security if the security is acquired or disposed of by a person who is his agent, his nominee or a person who is acting at his direction, in relation to the acquisition or disposal: s 55(4). Section 55(4) is not, however, exhaustive as to the circumstances in which one person may be regarded as procuring an acquisition or disposal of securities by another: s 55(5). 'Acquire', in relation to a security, includes agreeing to acquire the security and entering into a contract which creates the security (s 55(2)); and 'dispose', in relation to a security, includes agreeing to dispose of the security and bringing to an end a contract which created the security (s 55(3)). For the meaning of 'security' see para 1221 post.

3 For these purposes, securities are 'price-affected securities' in relation to inside information, and inside information is 'price-sensitive information' in relation to securities, if and only if the information would, if made public, be likely to have a significant effect on the price of the securities: ibid s 56(2). 'Price' includes value: s 56(3). For the meaning of 'made public' see para 1220 post.

4 Ibid s 52(1). Section 52 is subject to s 53 (see para 1225 post): s 52(4). As to the territorial scope of an offence under s 52(1) see para 1224 post; and as to defences see para 1225 et seq post.

5 See note 1 supra.

6 Criminal Justice Act 1993 s 52(2). See also note 4 supra. As to the territorial scope of an offence under s 52(2) see para 1223 post; and as to defences see para 1225 et seq post.

7 For these purposes, 'regulated market' means any market, however operated, which, by an order made by the Treasury, is identified, whether by name or by reference to criteria prescribed by the order, as a regulated market for the purposes of ibid Pt V (ss 52-64): s 60(1). In exercise of the power so conferred the Treasury made the Insider Dealing (Securities and Regulated Markets) Order 1994, SI 1994/187,

art 9 which came into force on 1 March 1994: art 1. The following are regulated markets for the purposes of the Criminal Justice Act 1993 Pt V (ss 52-64), ie any market which is established under the rules of one of the following investment exchanges: Amsterdam Stock Exchange; Antwerp Stock Exchange; Athens Stock Exchange; Barcelona Stock Exchange; Bavarian Stock Exchange; Berlin Stock Exchange; Bilbao Stock Exchange; Bologna Stock Exchange; Bordeaux Stock Exchange; Bremen Stock Exchange; Brussels Stock Exchange; Copenhagen Stock Exchange; Dusseldorf Stock Exchange; Florence Stock Exchange; Frankfurt Stock Exchange; Genoa Stock Exchange; Ghent Stock Exchange; Hamburg Stock Exchange; Hanover Stock Exchange; Helsinki Stock Exchange; The International Stock Exchange of the United Kingdom and the Republic of Ireland Limited; Liege Stock Exchange; Lille Stock Exchange; Lisbon Stock Exchange; LIFFE Administration & Management; Luxembourg Stock Exchange; Lyon Stock Exchange; Madrid Stock Exchange; Marseille Stock Exchange; Milan Stock Exchange; Nancy Stock Exchange; Nantes Stock Exchange; Naples Stock Exchange; The exchange known as NASDAQ; OMLX, the London Securities and Derivatives Exchange Limited; Oporto Stock Exchange; Oslo Stock Exchange; Palermo Stock Exchange; Paris Stock Exchange; Rome Stock Exchange; Securities Exchange of Iceland; Stockholm Stock Exchange; Stuttgart Stock Exchange; Trieste Stock Exchange; Turin Stock Exchange; Valencia Stock Exchange; Venice Stock Exchange; and Vienna Stock Exchange: Insider Dealing (Securities and Regulated Markets) Order 1994 art 9, Schedule. As to the change of name of The International Stock Exchange of the United Kingdom and the Republic of Ireland Limited following the separation of the Irish Stock Exchange from the London Stock Exchange see para 21 note 8 ante.

Any power under the Criminal Justice Act 1993 Pt V (ss 52-64) to make an order is exercisable by statutory instrument (s 64(1)); but no such order may be made unless a draft of it has been laid before and approved by a resolution of each House of Parliament (s 64(2)). Any such order may make different provision for different cases and may contain such incidental, supplemental and transitional provisions as the Treasury considers expedient: s 64(3).

8 For the meaning of 'professional intermediary' see para 1222 post.

9 Criminal Justice Act 1993 s 52(3).

10 For these purposes, 'public sector body' means (1) the government of the United Kingdom, of Northern Ireland or any country or territory outside the United Kingdom; (2) a local authority in the United Kingdom or elsewhere; (3) any international organisation the members of which include the United Kingdom or another member State; (4) the Bank of England; or (5) the central bank of any sovereign State: ibid s 60(3)(b).

11 Ibid s 63(1).

12 Ibid s 63(2). Cf *Chase Manhattan Equities Ltd v Goodman* [1991] BCLC 897 (which considered the equivalent provision in the Company Securities (Insider Dealing) Act 1985 s 8(3) (repealed) which provided that the transaction was not void or voidable by reason only of the contravention of the statutory provisions; the court found that despite s 8(3) (repealed) the transaction was unenforceable). The wording now contained in the Criminal Justice Act 1993 s 63(2) rules out the approach in *Chase Manhattan Equities Ltd v Goodman* supra.

13 For the meaning of 'inside information' see para 1219 post.

14 Criminal Justice Act 1993 s 57(1).

15 For these purposes, an 'issuer', in relation to any securities, means any company, public sector body or individual by which or by whom the securities have been or are to be issued: ibid s 60(2). 'Company' means any body, whether or not incorporated and wherever incorporated or constituted, which is not a public sector body: s 60(3)(a). Information is to be treated as relating to an issuer of securities which is a company not only where it is about the company but also where it may affect the company's business prospects: s 60(4).

16 Ibid s 57(2).

1219. Meaning of 'inside information'. 'Inside information' means[1] information which:

(1) relates to particular securities[2] or to a particular issuer[3] of securities or to particular issuers of securities and not to securities generally or to issuers of securities generally;

(2) is specific or precise;

(3) has not been made public[4]; and

(4) if it were made public, would be likely to have a significant effect on the price of any securities[5].

1 Ie for the purposes of the Criminal Justice Act 1993 ss 56, 57: see para 1218 ante.
2 For the meaning of 'security' see para 1221 post.
3 For the meaning of 'issuer' see para 1218 note 15 ante.
4 For the meaning of 'made public' see para 1220 post.
5 Criminal Justice Act 1993 s 56(1).

1220. Meaning of 'made public'. 'Made public', in relation to information, is to be construed in accordance with the following provisions[1]; but those provisions are not exhaustive as to the meaning of that expression[2]. Information is made public if:

(1) it is published in accordance with the rules of a regulated market[3] for the purpose of informing investors and their professional advisers;

(2) it is contained in records which, by virtue of any enactment, are open to inspection by the public;

(3) it can be readily acquired by those likely to deal in any securities[4] to which the information relates or of an issuer to which the information relates; or

(4) it is derived from information which has been made public[5].

Information may be treated as made public, even though:

(a) it can be acquired only by persons exercising diligence or expertise;

(b) it is communicated to a section of the public and not to the public at large;

(c) it can be acquired only by observation;

(d) it is communicated only on payment of a fee; or

(e) it is published only outside the United Kingdom[6].

1 Ie in accordance with the Criminal Justice Act 1993 s 58(1),(3): see infra.
2 Ibid s 58(1).
3 For the meaning of 'regulated market' see para 1218 note 7 ante.
4 For the meaning of 'deal in securities' see para 1218 note 2 ante.
5 Criminal Justice Act 1993 s 58(2).
6 Ibid s 58(3).

1221. Meaning of 'security'. 'Security' means a security which falls within any of the following heads:

(1) shares and stock in the share capital of a company[1] ('shares')[2];

(2) any instrument creating or acknowledging indebtedness which is issued by a company or public sector body[3], including, in particular, debentures, debenture stock, loan stock, bonds and certificates of deposit ('debt securities')[4];

(3) any right, whether conferred by warrant or otherwise, to subscribe for shares or debt securities ('warrants')[5];

(4) the rights under any depositary receipt[6];

(5) any option to acquire[7] or dispose[8] of any security falling within any of heads (1) to (4) above or heads (6), (7) below[9];

(6) rights under a contract for the acquisition or disposal of relevant securities[10] under which delivery is to be made at a future date[11] and at a price agreed[11] when the contract is made[12];

(7) rights under a contract which does not provide for the delivery of securities but whose purpose or pretended purpose is to secure a profit or avoid a loss by reference to fluctuations in a share index or other similar factor connected with relevant securities[13], the price of particular relevant securities or the interest rate offered on money placed on deposit[14];

and satisfies any conditions applying to it under an order made by the Treasury for these purposes[15].

The Treasury may by order amend the above provisions[16].

1 For the meaning of 'company' see para 1218 note 15 ante.
2 Criminal Justice Act 1993 s 54(1)(a), Sch 2 para 1.
3 For the meaning of 'public sector body' see para 1218 note 10 ante.
4 Criminal Justice Act 1993 Sch 2 para 2.
5 Ibid Sch 2 para 3.
6 Ibid Sch 2 para 4(1). For these purposes, a 'depositary receipt' means a certificate or other record, whether or not in the form of a document (1) which is issued by or on behalf of a person who holds any relevant securities of a particular issuer; and (2) which acknowledges that another person is entitled to rights in relation to the relevant securities or relevant securities of the same kind: Sch 2 para 4(2). 'Relevant securities' means shares, debt securities and warrants: Sch 2 para 4(3). For the meaning of 'issuer' see para 1218 note 15 ante.
7 For the meaning of 'acquire' see para 1218 note 2 ante.
8 For the meaning of 'dispose' see para 1218 note 2 ante.
9 Criminal Justice Act 1993 Sch 2 para 5.
10 For these purposes, 'relevant securities' means any security falling within any of ibid Sch 2 paras 1-4, 7 (see text heads (1)-(5) supra and head (7) infra): Sch 2 para 6(2)(b).
11 For these purposes, the references to a future date and to a price agreed when the contract is made include references to a date and a price determined in accordance with terms of the contract: ibid Sch 2 para 6(2)(a).
12 Ibid Sch 2 para 6(1).
13 For these purposes, 'relevant securities' means any security falling within any of ibid Sch 2 paras 1-6 (see text heads (1)-(6) supra): Sch 2 para 7(2).
14 Ibid Sch 2 para 7(1).
15 Ibid s 54(1)(a),(b). In the provisions of Pt V (ss 52-64), other than Sch 2 (see supra), any reference to a security is to a security to which Pt V (ss 52-64) applies: s 54(1). In exercise of the power so conferred the Treasury made the Insider Dealing (Securities and Regulated Markets) Order 1994, SI 1994/187, which came into force on 1 March 1994 (art 1) and which specified the following conditions:

    (1) in relation to any security which falls within any of the Criminal Justice Act 1993 Sch 2 paras 1-7 (see text heads (1)-(7) supra), the following condition applies, ie that it is officially listed in a State within the European Economic Area or that it is admitted to dealing on, or has its price quoted on or under the rules of, a regulated market (Insider Dealing (Securities and Regulated Markets) Order 1994 arts 3, 4);

    (2) in relation to a warrant, the following alternative condition applies ie that the right under it is a right to subscribe for any share or debt security of the same class as a share or debt security which satisfies the condition in art 4 (see head (1) supra) (arts 3, 5);

    (3) in relation to a depositary receipt, the following alternative condition applies ie that the rights under it are in respect of any share or debt security which satisfies the condition in art 4 (arts 3, 6);

    (4) in relation to an option or future, the following alternative condition applies ie that the option or rights under the future are in respect of (a) any share or debt security which satisfies the condition in art 4; or (b) any depositary receipt which satisfies the condition in art 4 or art 6 (see head (3) supra) (arts 3, 7);

    (5) in relation to a contract for differences, the following alternative condition applies ie that the purpose or pretended purpose of the contract is to secure a profit or avoid a loss by reference to fluctuations in (a) the price of any shares or debt securities which satisfy the condition in art 4; or (b) an index of the price of such shares or debt securities (arts 3, 8).

For these purposes, a 'State within the European Economic Area' means a State which is a member of the European Communities and the Republics of Austria, Finland and Iceland, the Kingdoms of Norway and Sweden and the Principality of Liechtenstein: art 2. As to the European Economic Area see para 299 note 2 ante.
16 Criminal Justice Act 1993 s 54(2).

1222. Meaning of 'professional intermediary'. A 'professional intermediary' is a person:

    (1) who carries on a business consisting of a specified activity[1] and who holds himself out to the public or any section of the public, including a section of the public constituted by persons such as himself, as willing to engage in any such business; or

(2) who is employed by a person falling within head (1) above to carry out any such activity[2].

The activities so specified are:

(a) acquiring[3] or disposing[4] of securities[5], whether as principal or agent; or

(b) acting as an intermediary between persons taking part in any dealing in securities[6].

A person is not, however, to be treated as carrying on a business consisting of a specified activity[7] if the activity in question is merely incidental to some other activity[8] or merely because he occasionally conducts one of those activities[9].

A person dealing in securities relies on a professional intermediary[10] if and only if a person who is acting as a professional intermediary carries out a specified activity[11] in relation to that dealing[12].

1   Ie an activity mentioned in the Criminal Justice Act 1993 s 59(2): see text heads (1), (2) infra.
2   Ibid s 59(1).
3   For the meaning of 'acquire' see para 1218 note 2 ante.
4   For the meaning of 'dispose' see para 1218 note 2 ante.
5   For the meaning of 'security' see para 1221 ante.
6   Criminal Justice Act 1993 s 59(2). For the meaning of 'deal in securities' see para 1218 note 2 ante.
7   See note 1 supra.
8   Ie some other activity not falling within the Criminal Justice Act 1993 s 59(2).
9   Ibid s 59(3).
10 Ie for the purposes of ibid s 52: see para 1218 ante.
11 See note 1 supra.
12 Criminal Justice Act 1993 s 59(4).

1223. Penalties and prosecution. An individual guilty of insider dealing[1] is liable on conviction on indictment to imprisonment for a term not exceeding seven years or a fine, or to both, or on summary conviction to imprisonment for a term not exceeding six months or a fine not exceeding the statutory maximum, or to both[2].

Proceedings for such an offence may not be instituted in England and Wales except by or with the consent of the Secretary of State or the Director of Public Prosecutions[3].

An individual convicted of insider dealing may also be disqualified from being a company director where the insider dealing offence has some relevant factual connection with the management of a company[4].

1   As to the offence of insider dealing see para 1218 ante.
2   Criminal Justice Act 1993 s 61(1). For the meaning of 'the statutory maximum' see para 1161 ante. As to the territorial scope of insider dealing see para 1224 post; and as to defences see para 1225 et seq post.
3   Ibid s 61(2).
4   *R v Goodman* [1992] BCC 625, CA (company chairman who used knowledge of the company's financial position to carry out insider dealing convicted under the Company Securities (Insider Dealing) Act 1985 (repealed) and also disqualified for ten years under the Company Directors Disqualification Act 1986 s 2 (disqualification where person convicted of indictable offence in connection with (inter alia) the promotion, formation, management or liquidation of a company: see para 1418 post).

1224. Territorial scope of insider dealing. An individual who has information as an insider[1] is not, however, guilty of an offence by dealing in the specified circumstances in securities that are price-affected securities in relation to the information[2] unless:

(1) he was within the United Kingdom at the time when he is alleged to have done any act constituting or forming part of the alleged dealing;

(2) the regulated market[3] on which the dealing is alleged to have occurred is one which, by an order of the Treasury, is identified, whether by name or by reference to criteria prescribed by the order, as being regulated in the United Kingdom[4]; or

(3) the professional intermediary[5] was within the United Kingdom at the time when he is alleged to have done anything by means of which the offence is alleged to have been committed[6].

Nor is an individual who has information as an insider guilty of an offence by encouraging another person to deal in price-affected securities or disclosing the information to another person[7] unless:

(a) he was within the United Kingdom at the time when he is alleged to have disclosed the information or encouraged the dealing; or

(b) the alleged recipient of the information or encouragement was within the United Kingdom at the time when he is alleged to have received the information or encouragement[8].

1 For the meaning of 'information as an insider' see para 1218 ante.
2 Ie an offence under the Criminal Justice Act 1993 s 52(1): see para 1218 ante.
3 For the meaning of 'regulated market' see para 1218 note 7 ante.
4 The regulated markets which are regulated in the United Kingdom for the purpose of the Criminal Justice Act 1993 Pt V (ss 52–64) are any market which is established under the rules of (1) the International Stock Exchange of the United Kingdom and the Republic of Ireland Limited, other than the market which operates in the Republic of Ireland known as the Irish Unit of the International Stock Exchange of the United Kingdom and the Republic of Ireland Limited; (2) LIFFE Administration & Management; and (3) OMLX, the London Securities and Derivatives Exchange Limited: Insider Dealing (Securities and Regulated Markets) Order 1994, SI 1994/187, art 10. As to the change of name of The International Stock Exchange of the United Kingdom and the Republic of Ireland Limited following the separation of the Irish Stock Exchange from the London Stock Exchange see para 21 note 8 ante.
5 For the meaning of 'professional intermediary' see para 1222 ante.
6 Criminal Justice Act 1993 s 62(1).
7 Ie an offence under ibid s 52(2): see para 1218 ante.
8 Ibid s 62(2).

(ii) Defences

1225. General defences. An individual is not guilty of insider dealing[1] by virtue of dealing in securities[2] if he shows:

(1) that he did not at the time expect the dealing to result in a profit[3] attributable to the fact that the information in question was price-sensitive information[4] in relation to the securities; or

(2) that at the time he believed on reasonable grounds that the information had been disclosed widely enough to ensure that none of those taking part in the dealing would be prejudiced by not having the information; or

(3) that he would have done what he did even if he had not had the information[5].

An individual is not guilty of insider dealing by virtue of encouraging another person to deal in securities if he shows:

(a) that he did not at the time expect the dealing to result in a profit attributable to the fact that the information in question was price-sensitive information in relation to the securities; or

(b) that at the time he believed on reasonable grounds that the information had been or would be disclosed widely enough to ensure that none of those taking part in the dealing would be prejudiced by not having the information; or

(c) that he would have done what he did even if he had not had the information[6].

An individual is not guilty of insider dealing by virtue of a disclosure of information if he shows:

   (i) that he did not at the time expect any person, because of the disclosure, to deal in securities in the specified circumstances[7]; or

 (ii) that, although he had such an expectation at the time, he did not expect the dealing to result in a profit attributable to the fact that the information was price-sensitive information in relation to the securities[8].

Special defences[9] apply in the case of market makers, market information and price stabilisation[10].

1 As to the offence of insider dealing see para 1218 ante; as to the penalties see para 1223 ante; and as to the territorial scope of the offence see para 1224 ante.
2 For the meaning of 'deal in securities' see para 1218 note 2 ante; and for the meaning of 'security' see para 1221 ante.
3 For the meaning of 'price-sensitive information' see para 1218 note 3 ante.
4 For these purposes, references to a profit include references to the avoidance of a loss: Criminal Justice Act 1993 s 53(6).
5 Ibid s 53(1). See *R v Cross* [1991] BCLC 125 (burden of proof was on the accused to show that he fell within the equivalent defence under the Company Securities (Insider Dealing) Act 1985).
6 Criminal Justice Act 1993 s 53(2).
7 Ie the circumstances mentioned in ibid s 52(3): see para 1218 ante.
8 Ibid s 53(3).
9 Ie the special defences in ibid s 53(4), Sch 1: see paras 1226–1228 post.
10 Ibid s 53(4). The Treasury may by order amend Sch 1: s 53(5). At the date at which this volume states the law no such order had been made.

1226. Market makers. An individual is not guilty of insider dealing[1] by virtue of dealing in securities[2] or encouraging another person to deal if he shows that he acted in good faith in the course of his business as a market maker or his employment in the business of a market maker[3].

A market maker is a person who:

   (1) holds himself out at all normal times in compliance with the rules of a regulated market[4] or an approved organisation[5] as willing to acquire or dispose of securities; and

   (2) is recognised as doing so under those rules[6].

1 As to the offence of insider dealing see para 1218 ante; as to the penalties see para 1223 ante; and as to the territorial scope of the offence see para 1224 ante.
2 For the meaning of 'deal in securities' see para 1218 note 2 ante; and for the meaning of 'security' see para 1221 ante.
3 Criminal Justice Act 1993 s 53(4), Sch 1 para 1(1).
4 For the meaning of 'regulated market' see para 1218 note 7 ante.
5 For these purposes, 'approved organisation' means an international securities self-regulating organisation approved under the Financial Services Act 1986 ss 1, 2, Sch 1 para 25B (as added) (see MONEY): Criminal Justice Act 1993 Sch 1 para 1(3).
6 Ibid Sch 1 para 1(2).

1227. Market information. An individual is not guilty of insider dealing[1] by virtue of dealing in securities[2] or encouraging another person to deal if he shows that the information which he had as an insider[3] was market information and it was reasonable for an individual in his position to have acted as he did despite having that information as an insider at the time[4]. In determining whether it is reasonable for an individual to do any act despite having market information at the time, there must, in particular, be taken into account the content of the information, the circumstances in which he first had the information and in what capacity and the capacity in which he now acts[5].

An individual is not guilty of insider dealing by virtue of dealing in securities or encouraging another person to deal if he shows:

(1) that he acted in connection with an acquisition[6] or disposal[7] which was under consideration or the subject of negotiation, or in the course of a series of such acquisitions or disposals and with a view to facilitating the accomplishment of the acquisition or disposal or the series of acquisitions or disposals; and

(2) that the information which he had as an insider was market information arising directly out of his involvement in the acquisition or disposal or series of acquisitions or disposals[8].

For these purposes, market information is information consisting of one or more of the following facts:

(a) that securities of a particular kind have been or are to be acquired or disposed of, or that their acquisition or disposal is under consideration or the subject of negotiation;

(b) that securities of a particular kind have not been or are not to be acquired or disposed of;

(c) the number of securities acquired or disposed of or to be acquired or disposed of or whose acquisition or disposal is under consideration or the subject of negotiation;

(d) the price, or range of prices, at which securities have been or are to be acquired or disposed of or the price, or range of prices, at which securities whose acquisition or disposal is under consideration or the subject of negotiation may be acquired or disposed of;

(e) the identity of the persons involved or likely to be involved in any capacity in an acquisition or disposal[9].

1 As to the offence of insider dealing see para 1218 ante; as to the penalties see para 1223 ante; and as to the territorial scope of the offence see para 1224 ante.
2 For the meaning of 'deal in securities' see para 1218 note 2 ante; and for the meaning of 'security' see para 1221 ante.
3 For the meaning of 'information as an insider' see para 1218 ante.
4 Criminal Justice Act 1993 s 53(4), Sch 1 para 2(1).
5 Ibid Sch 1 para 2(2).
6 For the meaning of 'acquire' see para 1218 note 2 ante.
7 For the meaning of 'dispose' see para 1218 note 2 ante.
8 Criminal Justice Act 1993 Sch 1 para 3.
9 Ibid Sch 1 para 4.

1228. Price stabilisation. An individual is not guilty of insider dealing[1] by virtue of dealing in securities[2] or encouraging another person to deal if he shows that he acted in conformity with the price stabilisation rules[3].

1 As to the offence of insider dealing see para 1218 ante; as to the penalties see para 1223 ante; and as to the territorial scope of the offence see para 1223 ante.
2 For the meaning of 'deal in securities' see para 1218 note 2 ante; and for the meaning of 'security' see para 1221 ante.
3 Criminal Justice Act 1993 s 53(4), Sch 1 para 5. For these purposes, 'the price stabilisation rules' means rules which (1) are made under the Financial Services Act 1986 s 48 (as amended) (conduct of business rules: see MONEY); and (2) make provision of a description mentioned in s 48(2)(i) (price stabilisation rules): Criminal Justice Act 1993 Sch 1 para 5(2).

(iii) Disclosure of Information

1229. In general. A company[1] or undertaking[2] which is an issuer of a security[3] admitted to trading[4] on a regulated market[5] (an 'issuer') must inform the public as soon as possible of any major new developments in the issuer's sphere of activity which are not public knowledge and which may, by virtue of their effect on the issuer's assets and liabilities or financial position or on the general course of its business, lead to substantial movements in the price of that security[6].

A recognised investment exchange which regulates and supervises a regulated market on which an issuer's securities are admitted to trading may, however, exempt the issuer from the above obligation[7] if satisfied that the disclosure of the particular information would prejudice the legitimate interests of that issuer[8].

The rules of a recognised investment exchange must, at least, enable the exchange, in the event of a failure by an issuer whose securities are admitted to trading on a regulated market which the exchange regulates and supervises to comply with the above obligation[9], to do any of the following, that is to say:

(1) discontinue the admission of the securities to trading;

(2) suspend trading in the securities;

(3) publish the fact that the issuer has failed to comply with the obligation; and

(4) itself make public any information which the issuer has failed to publish[10].

1 For these purposes, 'company' has the same meaning as in EC Council Directive 89/592 (OJ L334, 18.11.89, p 30) of 13 November 1989 co-ordinating regulations on insider dealing: Traded Securities (Disclosure) Regulations 1994, SI 1994/188, reg 2.

2 For these purposes, 'undertaking' has the same meaning as in EC Council Directive 89/592: Traded Securities (Disclosure) Regulations 1994 reg 2.

3 For the meaning of 'security' see para 1230 post.

4 For these purposes, 'admitted to trading' has the same meaning as in EC Council Directive 89/592: Traded Securities (Disclosure) Regulations 1994 reg 2.

5 For these purposes, 'regulated market' means any market in the United Kingdom on which securities are admitted to trading being a market which is regulated and supervised by a recognised investment exchange and which operates regularly and is accessible directly or indirectly to the public: ibid reg 2. 'Recognised investment exchange' has the meaning given by the Financial Services Act 1986 s 207(1) (see para 223 note 1 ante): Traded Securities (Disclosure) Regulations 1994 reg 2.

6 Ibid reg 3(1).

7 Ie the obligation imposed by ibid reg 3(1): see supra.

8 Ibid reg 3(2).

9 See note 7 supra.

10 Traded Securities (Disclosure) Regulations 1994 reg 3(3). The Financial Services Act 1986 has effect as if the requirement set out in the Traded Securities (Disclosure) Regulations 1994 reg 3(3) was (1) in the case of a recognised investment exchange which is not an overseas investment exchange, among those specified in the Financial Services Act 1986 s 36(2), Sch 4 (requirements for recognition of UK investment exchange: see MONEY); and (2) in the case of an overseas investment exchange, among those mentioned in s 37(7)(a) (revocation of recognition order: see MONEY) and specified in s 40(2) (requirements for recognition of overseas investment exchange etc: see MONEY): Traded Securities (Disclosure) Regulations 1994 reg 4. 'Overseas investment exchange' has the meaning given by the Financial Services Act 1986 s 207(1) (see para 223 note 1 ante): Traded Securities (Disclosure) Regulations 1994 reg 2.

1230. Meaning of 'security'. 'Security' means any security which falls within any of the following heads but does not include an investment which is admitted to the Official List[1]:

(1) shares and stock in the share capital of a company[2] ('shares')[3];

(2) any instrument creating or acknowledging indebtedness which is issued by a company or undertaking[4], including, in particular, debentures, debenture stock, loan stock, bonds and certificates of deposit ('debt securities')[5];

(3) any right, whether conferred by warrant or otherwise, to subscribe for shares or debt securities ('warrants')[6];

(4) the rights under any depositary receipt[7];

(5) any option to acquire or dispose of any security falling within any of heads (1) to (4) above or heads (6), (7) below[8];

(6) rights under a contract for the acquisition or disposal of relevant securities[9] under which delivery is to be made at a future date[10] and at a price agreed[10] when the contract is made[11];

(7) rights under a contract which does not provide for the delivery of securities but whose purpose or pretended purpose is to secure a profit or avoid a loss by reference to fluctuations in a share index or other similar factor connected with relevant securities[12] or the price of particular relevant securities[13].

1 Ie in accordance with the Financial Services Act 1986 Pt IV (ss 142-156B) (as amended): see para 281 et seq ante.
2 For the meaning of 'company' see para 1229 note 1 ante.
3 Traded Securities (Disclosure) Regulations 1994, SI 1994/188, reg 2, Schedule para 1.
4 For the meaning of 'undertaking' see para 1229 note 2 ante.
5 Traded Securities (Disclosure) Regulations 1994 Schedule para 2.
6 Ibid Schedule para 3.
7 Ibid Schedule para 4(1). For these purposes, a 'depositary receipt' means a certificate or other record, whether or not in the form of a document (1) which is issued by or on behalf of a person who holds any relevant securities of a particular issuer; and (2) which acknowledges that another person is entitled to rights in relation to the relevant securities or relevant securities of the same kind: Schedule para 4(2). 'Relevant securities' means shares, debt securities and warrants: Schedule para 4(3).
8 Ibid Schedule para 5.
9 For these purposes, 'relevant securities' means any security falling within any of ibid Schedule paras 1-4, 7 (see text heads (1)-(5) supra and head (7) infra): Schedule para 6(2)(b).
10 For these purposes, the references to a future date and to a price agreed when the contract is made include references to a date and a price determined in accordance with the terms of the contract: ibid Schedule para 6(2)(a).
11 Ibid Schedule para 6(1).
12 For these purposes, 'relevant securities' means any security falling within any of ibid Schedule paras 1-6 (see text heads (1)-(6) supra): Schedule para 7(2).
13 Ibid Schedule para 7(1).

(iv) Investigations

1231. Investigations into insider dealing. If it appears to the Secretary of State that there are circumstances suggesting that an offence under Part V of the Criminal Justice Act 1993[1] may have been committed, he may appoint one or more competent inspectors to carry out such investigations as are requisite to establish whether or not any such offence has been committed and to report the results of their investigations to him[2]. Such appointment may limit the period during which the inspector is to continue his investigation or confine it to particular matters[3]. At any time during the investigation the Secretary of State may vary the appointment by limiting or extending the period during which the inspector is to continue his investigation or by confining the investigation to particular matters[4].

If the inspectors consider that any person is or may be able to give information concerning any such offence, they may require that person:

(1) to produce to them any documents[5] in his possession or under his control which appear to them to be relevant to the investigation;

(2) to attend before them; and

(3) otherwise to give them all assistance in connection with the investigation which he is reasonably able to give;

and it is the duty of that person to comply with that requirement[6].

An inspector may examine on oath any person who he considers is or may be able to give information concerning any such offence, and may administer an oath accordingly[7].

The inspectors must make such interim reports to the Secretary of State as they think fit or he may direct and on the conclusion of the investigation they must make a final report to him[8]. If the Secretary of State thinks fit, he may direct the inspector to take no further steps in the investigation or to take only such further steps as are specified in the direction; and, where an investigation is the subject of such a direction, the inspectors must make a final report to the Secretary of State only where the Secretary of State directs them to do so[9].

A statement made by a person in compliance with a requirement imposed by virtue of these provisions may be used in evidence against him[10]. A person is not required under these provisions to disclose any information or produce any document which he would be entitled to refuse to disclose or produce on grounds of legal professional privilege in proceedings in the High Court[11]. Nor is a person required under these provisions to disclose any information or produce any document in respect of which he owes an obligation of confidence by virtue of carrying on the business of banking unless the person to whom the obligation of confidence is owed consents to the disclosure or production or the making of the requirement was authorised by the Secretary of State[12]. Where a person claims a lien on a document, its production under these provisions is without prejudice to his lien[13].

A person who is convicted on a prosecution instituted as a result of an investigation under these provisions may in the same proceedings be ordered to pay the expenses of the investigation to such extent as may be specified in the order; and there are to be treated as expenses of the investigation, in particular, such reasonable sums as the Secretary of State may determine in respect of general staff costs and overheads[14].

1 Ie the Criminal Justice Act 1993 Pt V (ss 52-64): see para 1218 et seq ante.

2 Financial Services Act 1986 s 177(1) (amended by the Criminal Justice Act 1993 s 79(13), Sch 5 paras 7, 9(1)(a),(b)).

3 Financial Services Act 1986 s 177(2).

4 Ibid s 177(2A) (added by the Companies Act 1989 s 74(1),(2)).

5 For these purposes, 'document' includes information recorded in any form; and, in relation to information recorded otherwise than in legible form, the power to require its production includes power to require the production of a copy of the information in legible form: Financial Services Act 1986 s 177(10) (amended by the Companies Act 1989 s 74(1),(5)).

6 Financial Services Act 1986 s 177(3) (amended by the Criminal Justice Act 1993 Sch 5 paras 7, 9(2)). See *Re an inquiry under the Company Securities (Insider Dealing) Act 1985* [1988] AC 660, [1988] 1 All ER 203, HL.

7 Financial Services Act 1986 s 177(4) (amended by the Criminal Justice Act 1993 Sch 5 paras 7, 9(3)).

8 Financial Services Act 1986 s 177(5).

9 Ibid s 177(5A) (added by the Companies Act 1989 s 74(1),(3)).

10 Financial Services Act 1986 s 177(6).

11 Ibid s 177(7).

12 Ibid s 177(8) (substituted by the Companies Act 1989 s 74(1),(4)).

13 Financial Services Act 1986 s 177(9).

14 Ibid s 177(11) (added by the Companies Act 1989 s 74(1),(6)).

1232. Penalties for failure to co-operate with investigation into insider dealing. If any person refuses to comply with any request for assistance[1] in connection with such an investigation[2] or refuses to answer any question put to him by the inspectors appointed to conduct the investigation with respect to any matter relevant for establishing whether or not any suspected offence has been committed, the inspectors may certify that fact in writing to the court and the court may inquire into the case[3]. If, after hearing any witness who may be produced against or on behalf of the alleged offender and any statement which may be offered in defence, the court is satisfied that he did without reasonable excuse refuse to comply with such a request or answer any such question, the court may:

(1) punish him in like manner as if he had been guilty of contempt of the court[4]; or

(2) direct that the Secretary of State may exercise the powers under these provisions in respect of him;

and the court may give a direction under head (2) above notwithstanding that the offender is not within the jurisdiction of the court if the court is satisfied that he was notified of his right to appear before the court and of the powers available under these provisions[5].

Where the court gives a direction under head (2) above in respect of an authorised person[6], the Secretary of State may serve a notice on him:

(a) cancelling any authorisation of his to carry on investment business after the expiry of a specified period after the service of the notice;

(b) disqualifying him from becoming authorised to carry on investment business after the expiry of a specified period;

(c) restricting any authorisation of his in respect of investment business during a specified period to the performance of contracts entered into before the notice comes into force;

(d) prohibiting him from entering into transactions of a specified kind or entering into them except in specified circumstances or to a specified extent;

(e) prohibiting him from soliciting business from persons of a specified kind or otherwise than from such persons; or

(f) prohibiting him from carrying on business in a specified manner or otherwise than in a specified manner[7].

The period mentioned in heads (a) and (c) above is such period as appears to the Secretary of State reasonable to enable the person on whom the notice is served to complete the performance of any contracts entered into before the notice comes into force and to terminate such of them as are of a continuing nature[8].

Where the court gives a direction under head (2) above in the case of an unauthorised person, the Secretary of State may direct that any authorised person who knowingly transacts investment business of a specified kind, or in specified circumstances or to a specified extent, with or on behalf of that unauthorised person shall be treated as having contravened rules[9] relating to the conduct of investment business or, in the case of a person who is an authorised person by virtue of his membership of a recognised self-regulating organisation[10] or certification by a recognised professional body[11], the rules of that organisation or body[12].

A person is not to be treated for the above purposes[13] as having a reasonable excuse for refusing to comply with a request or answer a question in a case where the offence or suspected offence being investigated relates to dealing by him on the instructions or for the account of another person, by reason that at the time of the refusal he did not know the identity of that other person, or he was subject to the law of a country or territory outside the United Kingdom which prohibited him from disclosing information relating to the dealing without the consent of that other person, if he might have obtained that consent or obtained exemption from that law[14].

A notice so served on a person[15] may be revoked at any time by the Secretary of State by serving a revocation notice on him; and the Secretary of State must revoke such a notice if it appears to him that the person has agreed to comply with the relevant request or answer the relevant question[16]. Such revocation will not have the effect of reviving the authorisation cancelled by the notice except where the person would (apart from the notice) at the time of the revocation be an authorised person by virtue of his membership of a recognised self-regulating organisation or certification by a recognised professional body; but nothing in this provision is to be construed as preventing any person who has been subject to such a notice from again becoming authorised after the revocation of the notice[17].

If it appears to the Secretary of State:

(i)   that a person on whom he serves such a notice is an authorised person by virtue of an authorisation granted by a designated agency[18] or by virtue of membership of a recognised self-regulating organisation or certification by a recognised professional body; or

(ii) that a person on whom he serves a revocation notice was such an authorised person at the time that the notice which is being revoked was served,

he must serve a copy of the notice on that agency, organisation or body[19].

The functions which may be transferred[20] by the Secretary of State to a designated agency include his functions under these provisions but any transfer of those functions must be subject to a reservation that they are to be exercisable by him concurrently with the designated agency and so as to be exercisable by the agency subject to such conditions or restrictions as the Treasury may from time to time impose[21].

1   Ie under the Financial Services Act 1986 s 177(3): see para 1231 ante.
2   Ie an investigation into insider dealing under ibid s 177 (as amended): see para 1231 ante.
3   Ibid s 178(1) (amended by the Criminal Justice Act 1993 s 79(13), Sch 5 paras 7, 10(1)). The Financial Services Act 1986 s 178 (as amended) has effect as if:
    (1)   the reference in s 178(3) (see infra) to an authorised person included a reference to a European investment firm; and
    (2)   the notices which may be served on a European investment firm under s 178(3) included a notice:
        (a)   directing that the Investment Services Regulations 1995, SI 1995/3275, reg 5(1)(a) shall not apply in relation to the firm after the expiry of a specified period after the service of the notice; or
        (b)   directing that during a specified period that provision shall apply in relation to the firm only as respects the performance of contracts entered into before the notice comes into force;
    (3)   the reference in the Financial Services Act 1986 s 178(4) (see infra) to the period mentioned in s 178(3)(a),(c) included a reference to the period mentioned in heads (2)(a), (2)(b) supra;
    (4)   any reference in s 178(5) (see infra) to an unauthorised person did not include a reference to a European investment firm carrying on home-regulated investment business in the United Kingdom; and
    (5)   the reference in s 178(5) to any authorised person included a reference to such a European investment firm:
    Investment Services Regulations 1995 reg 32, Sch 7 para 37(1).
    The Financial Services Act 1986 s 178 (as amended) also has effect as if it included provision that, if it appears to the Secretary of State that a person on whom he serves a notice under s 178(3) is a European investment firm carrying on home-regulated investment business in the United Kingdom or that a person on whom he serves a revocation notice under s 178(7) (see infra) was such a firm at the time when the notice which is being revoked was served, he must serve a copy of the notice on The Securities and Investments Board or, in the case of a firm which is a member of a recognised self-regulating organisation, that organisation: Investment Services Regulations 1995 reg 2(1), Sch 7 para 37(2).
    For these purposes, 'European investment firm' has the meaning given by reg 3 (see MONEY);

'home-regulated investment business', in relation to a European investment firm, means investment business which consists in the provision of one or more listed services which its authorisation as an investment firm authorises it to provide; 'listed service' means a service listed in EC Council Directive 93/22 (OJ L141, 10.5.93, p 27) Annex, Section A or C (see MONEY); and 'recognised self-regulating organisation' has the same meaning as in the Financial Services Act 1986 (see note 10 infra): Investment Services Regulations 1995 reg 2(1).

4 See CONTEMPT OF COURT vol 9 para 101 et seq.

5 Financial Services Act 1986 s 178(2). See *Re an inquiry under the Company Securities (Insider Dealing) Act 1985* [1988] AC 660, [1988] 1 All ER 203, HL.

6 For these purposes, 'authorised person' means a person authorised under the Financial Services Act 1986 Pt I Ch III (ss 7–34) (as amended) to carry on investment business: s 207(1). See STOCK EXCHANGE.

7 Ibid s 178(3). See also note 3 supra.

8 Ibid s 178(4). See also note 3 supra.

9 Ie made pursuant to ibid Pt I Ch V (ss 47–63) (as amended): see STOCK EXCHANGE.

10 For these purposes, 'recognised self-regulating organisation' means a body declared by an order of the Secretary of State for the time being in force to be a recognised self-regulating organisation for the purposes of the Financial Services Act 1986: s 207(1).

11 For these purposes, 'recognised professional body' means a body declared by an order of the Secretary of State for the time being in force to be a recognised professional body for the purposes of the Financial Services Act 1986: s 207(1).

12 Ibid s 178(5). See also note 3 supra.

13 Ie for the purposes of ibid s 178(2): see supra.

14 Ibid s 178(6) (amended by the Criminal Justice Act 1993 Sch 5 paras 7, 10(2)).

15 Ie under the Financial Services Act 1986 s 178(3): see supra.

16 Ibid s 178(7).

17 Ibid s 178(8).

18 For these purposes, 'designated agency' means a body to whom functions exercisable by the Secretary of State have been transferred by means of a delegation order: ibid s 114(1),(3). See STOCK EXCHANGE.

19 Ibid s 178(9).

20 Ie pursuant to ibid s 114 (as amended): see STOCK EXCHANGE.

21 Ibid s 178(10) (amended by the Transfer of Functions (Financial Services) Order 1992, SI 1992/1315, art 10(1), Sch 4 para 3).

(26) BORROWING AND SECURING MONEY

(i) Power to Borrow

1233. Control of borrowing. Treasury consent for the borrowing of money by companies[1] has not been required on and after 11 February 1991[2].

1 Ie under the Borrowing (Control and Guarantees) Act 1946 and the subordinate instruments made thereunder.

2 See the Government Trading Act 1990 s 4(1),(2), Sch 2 Pt I; the Government Trading Act 1990 (Appointed Day) Order 1991, SI 1991/132, art 2.

1234. When power to borrow is implied. A company regulated by the Companies Act 1985 has in general no power to borrow unless authorised by its constitution to do so, either expressly or impliedly; but a trading or commercial company has an implied power to borrow to a reasonable amount for the purposes of its business, and to mortgage or charge all or any part of its property to secure the money so borrowed, even where no express power to borrow or mortgage is given to it, provided that such borrowing or giving of security is not expressly prohibited[1]. No power of borrowing is implied when the company is not a trading or commercial undertaking[2]. In such a case a company may borrow only if authorised to do so by its memorandum of association[3].

Normally, however, no intending lender will be concerned with any such question if he is lending in good faith[4].

1 *Re Badger, Mansell v Viscount Cobham* [1905] 1 Ch 568 at 574; *Re Hamilton's Windsor Ironworks Co, ex p Pitman and Edwards* (1879) 12 ChD 707; and see *Bank of Australasia v Breillat* (1847) 6 Moo PCC 152 (banking company); *Australian Auxiliary Steam Clipper Co v Mounsey* (1858) 4 K & J 733 (shipping company); *Bryon v Metropolitan Saloon Omnibus Co Ltd* (1858) 3 De G & J 123 (omnibus company); *Re Patent File Co, ex p Birmingham Banking Co* (1870) 6 Ch App 83 at 86, 88 (file-making company); *Re International Life Assurance Society, Gibbs and West's Case* (1870) LR 10 Eq 312 (insurance company); *General Auction Estate and Monetary Co v Smith* [1891] 3 Ch 432 (auction company whose objects included discounting approved commercial bills).
2 *Re Badger, Mansell v Viscount Cobham* [1905] 1 Ch 568.
3 In practice the implied power of a trading company to borrow is too indefinite to be relied on, for it is not always easy to decide whether a company is a trading company or not; and, reasonableness being the basis of the power, there is the uncertainty as to what is a reasonable amount and as to whether the borrowing is required for the purposes of the company's business. It is accordingly the almost invariable practice to give an express power to borrow in the memorandum of association.
4 See the Companies Act 1985 s 35A (as substituted) and para 1108 ante.

1235. Examples of loans. An overdraft at a company's bank is a loan[1]. A sale in good faith by a company which has exhausted its borrowing powers, of part of its equipment, accompanied by an agreement on its part to hire the equipment from the purchaser at a rent which will repay the purchase money and interest and enable the company at the end of the term to repurchase the equipment for a nominal consideration, is not a borrowing[2]. A sale of goods in good faith with a proviso that the purchaser may call on the vendor to repurchase them at a profit to the purchaser at the end of four years is not a borrowing; but it is a borrowing where there is not only a sale but also a collateral document providing for the redemption by the vendor of the goods comprised in the sale[3].

1 *Cunliffe, Brooks & Co v Blackburn and District Benefit Building Society* (1884) 9 App Cas 857, HL (affg *Blackburn Building Society v Cunliffe, Brooks & Co* (1882) 22 ChD 61, CA); *Chambers v Manchester and Milford Rly Co* (1864) 5 B & S 588; *Looker v Wrigley* (1882) 9 QBD 397; *Blackburn and District Benefit Building Society v Cunliffe, Brooks & Co* (1885) 29 ChD 902, CA, overruling *Re Cefn Cilcen Mining Co* (1868) LR 7 Eq 88; and *Waterlow v Sharp* (1869) LR 8 Eq 501.
2 *Yorkshire Railway Wagon Co v Maclure* (1882) 21 ChD 309, CA; cf *Manchester, Sheffield, and Lincolnshire Rly Co v North Central Wagon Co* (1888) 13 App Cas 554, HL. As to the distinction between a loan and a sale accompanied by an agreement for rehire cf BILLS OF SALE vol 4(1) (Reissue) para 673 et seq.
3 *Coveney v Persse Ltd* [1910] 1 IR 194, CA.

1236. Limit on borrowing. The Companies Act 1985 does not impose any limit on the amount which may be borrowed; but the memorandum or articles of the company often impose a limit. If the memorandum expressly or impliedly limits the borrowing powers, any borrowing beyond that limit is ultra vires and therefore void and cannot be ratified[1]; but, if the directors merely purport to borrow in excess of their powers, so that the borrowing is beyond the powers of the directors, the company, although not prima facie bound, may ratify that excess[2]. Nevertheless, a lender or other person dealing with the company in good faith is not bound to inquire about the company's capacity to contract with him or about any limitation on the directors' powers[3].

The memorandum may be altered by special resolution so as to extend or remove the limit, unless the memorandum itself expressly prohibits such an alteration[4]. If the limit is imposed only by the articles of association, they may be altered by a special resolution so as extend or remove the limit[5].

Where a company's borrowing powers are limited, any security given for any amount lent to it beyond the limit is void, even if the limit is subsequently increased[6]. Where the security is given in respect of a loan which is to be applied in paying off other loans properly made to the company, the security is good, as the transaction will not result in the limit being exceeded[7].

1 *Ashbury Railway Carriage and Iron Co v Riche* (1875) LR 7 HL 653.
2 See para 1238 post. The Companies (Tables A to F) Regulations 1985, SI 1985/805, Schedule, Table A art 70 provides that the directors may exercise all the powers of the company. As to Table A generally see para 529 et seq ante; and as to Stock Exchange requirements see para 536 ante.
3 See the Companies Act 1985 s 35A (as substituted) and para 1108 ante.
4 See ibid s 17 and para 99 ante.
5 According to *Re Bansha Woollen Mills Co Ltd* (1887) 21 LR Ir 181, where the memorandum imposes no limit on the power to borrow, but the articles limit the power, a general meeting of the company cannot sanction any borrowing in excess of the limit; but probably a company may in such a case ratify a borrowing beyond the limit and in any case may alter the articles: see *Grant v United Kingdom Switchback Railways Co* (1888) 40 ChD 135, CA; cf *Re Olderfleet Shipbuilding and Engineering Co Ltd* [1922] 1 IR 26. See further para 1238 text and note 4 post.
6 *Fountaine v Carmarthen Rly Co* (1868) LR 5 Eq 316; and see *Re Companies Acts, ex p Watson* (1888) 21 QBD 301.
7 *Re Harris Calculating Machine Co, Sumner v Harris Calculating Machine Co* [1914] 1 Ch 920.

1237. Remedies in respect of ultra vires borrowing. If a company borrows money in circumstances which render the borrowing ultra vires, no debt arises either at law or in equity, and the lender cannot recover the money in an action for money had and received or in any other action in personam[1]. A company may, however, repay money so borrowed, and cannot recover any money so repaid[2]. If the loan has been applied in payment of the company's debts or liabilities duly incurred, whether accruing before or after the date of the loan[3], then, even if the lender knew that the borrowing was unauthorised[4], he is entitled to recover the amount so paid[5], and to that extent may hold any securities given to himself[6]; but he is not subrogated to any securities or priorities or rights as to the interest of any creditor paid off with his money[7].

A lender in an ultra vires loan transaction is entitled to a tracing order or, in the case of a mixed fund, a declaration of charge, if the money lent can be traced into any investments or other property held by the company, or held by a volunteer having no better equity[8]. If and so far as the money borrowed cannot be specifically traced, but has increased the company's total assets, the whole available fund will be treated as belonging to the lenders and to the company in proportion to the amounts provided by the lenders and the shareholders respectively; and any losses will be deducted in the same proportions. Thus, where a building society for many years carried on an ultra vires business of banking with money provided partly by shareholders and partly by depositors, the company's assets in a winding up, after providing for the costs of the liquidation, depositors' money which could be specifically traced, and the claims of other creditors, were distributed pari passu among the shareholders and the depositors according to the amounts respectively provided by them[9].

1 *Re National Permanent Benefit Building Society, ex p Williamson* (1869) 5 Ch App 309; *Blackburn Building Society v Cunliffe, Brooks & Co* (1882) 22 ChD 61, CA (affd sub nom *Cunliffe, Brooks & Co v Blackburn and District Benefit Building Society* (1884) 9 App Cas 857, HL); *Baroness Wenlock v River Dee Co* (1885) 10 App Cas 354, HL; *Baroness Wenlock v River Dee Co* (1887) 19 QBD 155, CA; *Sinclair v Brougham* [1914] AC

398, HL. The lender cannot present a winding-up petition: *Re National Permanent Building Society, ex p Williamson* supra.

2   *Sinclair v Brougham* [1914] AC 398 at 426, HL per Lord Haldane, overruling *Blackburn and District Benefit Building Society v Cunliffe, Brooks & Co* (1885) 29 ChD 902, CA; and criticising *Re Companies Acts, ex p Watson* (1888) 21 QBD 301.

3   *Baroness Wenlock v River Dee Co* (1887) 19 QBD 155, CA.

4   *Reversion Fund and Insurance Co Ltd v Maison Cosway Ltd* [1913] 1 KB 364, CA; *Rolled Steel Products (Holdings) Ltd v British Steel Corpn* [1986] Ch 246, [1985] 3 All ER 52, CA. As to the equitable principle applicable see *Re Cleadon Trust Ltd* [1939] Ch 286, [1938] 4 All ER 518, CA.

5   *Sinclair v Brougham* [1914] AC 398, HL; *Re Electric Telegraph Co of Ireland, Troup's Case* (1860) 29 Beav 353; *Re Magdalena Steam Navigation Co* (1860) John 690 at 694; *Re National Permanent Benefit Building Society, ex p Williamson* (1869) 5 Ch App 309; *Cunliffe, Brooks & Co v Blackburn and District Benefit Building Society* (1884) 9 App Cas 857, HL; *Re Bank of Syria, Owen and Ashworth's Claim, Whitworth's Claim* [1901] 1 Ch 115, CA. In *Sinclair v Brougham* supra at 441, Lord Parker refused to express an opinion as to whether this result was arrived at by treating the contract of loan as validated to the extent to which the borrowed money is so applied on the ground that to this extent there is no increase in the company's indebtedness, in which case, if the contract of loan involves a security for the money borrowed, the security would be validated to a like extent, or because the lenders are subrogated to the rights of the legitimate creditors who are paid off. The principle of *Sinclair v Brougham* supra was applied in *Re Airedale Co-operative Worsted Manufacturing Society Ltd* [1933] Ch 639.

6   *Blackburn Building Society v Cunliffe, Brooks & Co* (1882) 22 ChD 61, CA; affd sub nom *Cunliffe, Brooks & Co v Blackburn and District Benefit Building Society* (1884) 9 App Cas 857, HL.

7   *Re Wrexham, Mold and Connah's Quay Rly Co* [1899] 1 Ch 440, CA; *Re Lough Neagh Ship Co, ex p Workman* [1895] 1 IR 533 at 546; *Re Electric Telegraph Co of Ireland, Hoare's Case* (1861) 30 Beav 225; and see the case cited in note 6 supra.

8   *Sinclair v Brougham* [1914] AC 398, HL; *Re Diplock, Diplock v Wintle* [1948] Ch 465 at 532, [1948] 2 All ER 318 at 353 (affd on other grounds sub nom *Ministry of Health v Simpson* [1951] AC 251, [1950] 2 All ER 1137, HL).

9   *Sinclair v Brougham* [1914] AC 398, HL, criticising *Re Guardian Permanent Benefit Building Society* (1882) 23 ChD 440, CA; and see *Re Diplock, Diplock v Wintle* [1948] Ch 465 at 526-532, [1948] 2 All ER 318 at 349-353, CA (affd sub nom *Ministry of Health v Simpson* [1951] AC 251, [1950] 2 All ER 1137, HL). Cf *Re Jon Beauforte (London) Ltd* [1953] Ch 131, [1953] 1 All ER 634 (where none of the contractors had actual knowledge of the company's lack of capacity but it was held that none had a provable claim on the company's liquidation; but as to possible mitigation of the harshness of this decision by the Companies Act 1985 ss 35-35B (as substituted) see paras 1093, 1107-1109 ante).

1238. Borrowing when directors' powers limited. Where the directors' borrowing power is limited to a certain amount, they cannot[1] borrow beyond that amount so as to bind the company[2]. If, however, the borrowing, although in excess of their own powers, is not in excess of the company's powers[3], the borrowing may be ratified by the company in general meeting[4], an ordinary resolution being sufficient for that purpose[5]. Ratification may also be inferred[6].

Where directors may borrow any sum not exceeding two-thirds of the uncalled capital of the company, they may borrow up to two-thirds of the nominal capital not called up, whether issued or unissued[7]. Unless the directors' borrowing powers given by the articles are exclusive, the company may delegate its borrowing powers to an agent by executing a power of attorney[8].

1   Ie save by virtue of the doctrine noted in para 1234 text to note 4 ante.

2   *Re Worcester Corn Exchange Co* (1853) 3 De GM & G 180; *Re Pooley Hall Colliery Co* (1869) 21 LT 690; *Fountaine v Carmarthen Rly Co* (1868) LR 5 Eq 316. As to the directors' liability in such a case see para 1123 ante. If the amount borrowed is not to exceed the amount of preference capital, and there is no such capital, there is no limit on borrowing: *Re Johnston Foreign Patents Co* [1904] 2 Ch 234, CA.

3   Eg if the articles prohibit the directors from borrowing more than a specified amount except with the sanction of the shareholders: cf the Companies (Tables A to F) Regulations 1985, SI 1985/805, Schedule, Table A art 7 and para 1236 note 2 ante. As to Table A generally see para 529 et seq ante.

4   *Irvine v Union Bank of Australia* (1877) 2 App Cas 366, PC (where the company was held not to be bound vis-à-vis a third party on the principle that he could have inspected the public documents to learn that

the special resolution required by the articles to authorise the borrowing had not in fact been filed). This principle of constructive notice appears to be abrogated by the Companies Act 1985 s 35A (as substituted): see para 1108 ante.

5 Cf *Grant v United Kingdom Switchback Rlys Co* (1888) 40 ChD 135, CA.
6 See *Re Magdalena Steam Navigation Co* (1860) John 690.
7 *English Channel SS Co v Rolt* (1881) 17 ChD 715.
8 *Mercantile Bank of India Ltd v Chartered Bank of India, Australia and China and Strauss & Co Ltd* [1937] 1 All ER 231.

1239. Security given by directors. Where directors have power to borrow, then, unless the memorandum or the articles provide otherwise, they may borrow to such an amount and upon such terms and security and for such purposes for the benefit of the company as they think fit. Where directors have power to issue bonds or debentures to secure sums borrowed, they may also borrow on other securities[1].

Directors with power to mortgage may do so for such purposes as to secure a past debt, if the mortgage is not given in such circumstances as to make it a preference[2]; to secure sums owing on a bill of exchange given by directors to secure a debt of the company, even though they have no power to accept such bills[3]; or to indemnify directors against loss on guarantees given by them to the company's creditors[4]. They may issue debentures in satisfaction of the debts of an insolvent business which the company has taken over and against which it has agreed to indemnify the vendor of the business[5], and may give the vendor of a solvent business preference over unsecured creditors in respect of a part of the purchase price[6]. Even if an action to enforce a series of debentures has been begun, they may issue further debentures of the series, provided that a receiver has not been appointed[7].

1 *Commercial Bank of Canada v Great Western Rly Co of Canada* (1865) 3 Moo PCCNS 295, PC. As to perpetual debenture stock see para 1255 post.
2 *Shears v Jacob* (1866) LR 1 CP 513; *Re Inns of Court Hotel Co* (1868) LR 6 Eq 82; *Re Patent File Co, ex p Birmingham Banking Co* (1870) 6 Ch App 83; *Davies v R Bolton & Co Ltd* [1894] 3 Ch 678; and see para 2602 et seq post.
3 *Scott v Colburn* (1858) 26 Beav 276.
4 *Re Pyle Works (No 2)* [1891] 1 Ch 173.
5 *Seligman v Prince & Co* [1895] 2 Ch 617, CA.
6 *Salomon v A Salomon & Co Ltd* [1897] AC 22, HL.
7 *Re Hubbard & Co Ltd, Hubbard v Hubbard & Co Ltd* (1898) 68 LJ Ch 54.

1240. Necessity for good faith. The power to borrow must be exercised in good faith for the benefit of the company, and not for purposes other than those for which it has been conferred[1]. If the power is not exercised for the purposes of the company, the loan cannot be recovered by a person lending with notice of the purpose for which it is to be applied[2]. If he had no notice, he may recover the loan, even though the money was borrowed for an illegal purpose[3]; a lender is not bound to inquire how the money is intended to be applied[4].

If an agent of a company hands to a lender a fully-paid certificate of debenture stock on the security of which he borrows more than he was authorised and appropriates the excess, a lender without notice may prove for the whole sum[5].

Where one company lends money to another, and one person is a director of both companies, the knowledge acquired by him as officer of one company is not imputed to the other company, unless he has some duty to communicate his knowledge to the company sought to be affected by the notice and some duty imposed on him by that company to receive it[6].

1 *Re London and County Assurance Co, Wood's Claim, Brown's Claim* (1861) 30 LJ Ch 373.
2 *Moye v Sparrow* (1870) 18 WR 400 at 402; *Re Durham County Permanent Investment Land and Building Society, Davis's Case* (1871) LR 12 Eq 516, where the directors borrowed money for the purpose of lending it to another society (overruled, so far as it held that the lender was under a duty to inquire for what purposes the borrowing was made, by *Re David Payne & Co Ltd, Young v David Payne & Co Ltd* [1904] 2 Ch 608, CA); *Re Introductions Ltd, Introductions Ltd v National Provincial Bank Ltd* [1970] Ch 199, [1969] 1 All ER 887, CA; and see *Bank of Ireland v Cogry Spinning Co* [1900] 1 IR 219.
3 *Re Marseilles Extension Rly Co, ex p Crédit Foncier and Mobilier of England* (1871) 7 Ch App 161 (money borrowed to buy shares of the company).
4 *Re David Payne & Co Ltd, Young v David Payne & Co Ltd* [1904] 2 Ch 608, CA; *Re Standard Rotary Machine Co Ltd* (1906) 95 LT 829 at 833. It is not the duty of a bank to inquire into the state of accounts between a company and its directors: *Bank of New South Wales v Goulburn Valley Butter Co Pty Ltd* [1902] AC 543, PC.
   As to the necessity for good faith in order that the lender should have the protection of the Companies Act 1985 s 35A (as substituted) see para 1108 ante. Under that enactment, the lender is prima facie no longer affected with constructive notice of the company's powers; but, even before that enactment, there was no duty on the lender to acquaint himself with the company's 'indoor management' as distinguished from its 'external position': see *Royal British Bank v Turquand* (1856) 6 E & B 327, Ex Ch and para 1137 ante.
5 *Robinson v Montgomeryshire Brewery Co* [1896] 2 Ch 841.
6 *Re Hampshire Land Co* [1896] 2 Ch 743; *Re David Payne & Co Ltd, Young v David Payne & Co Ltd* [1904] 2 Ch 608, CA; *J C Houghton & Co v Nothard, Lowe and Wills Ltd* [1928] AC 1, HL; and see *Re Marseilles Extension Rly Co, ex p Crédit Foncier and Mobilier of England* (1871) 7 Ch App 161.

1241. Loan by directors or promoters. Unless prohibited by its memorandum or articles, a director of a company may lend money to the company, provided that, in so doing, he is acting for its benefit, even though the loan is made on the security of a debenture issued at a discount[1].

A trader, when selling his solvent business to a company, even though it consists only of himself and members of his family, may as a general rule lawfully take debentures charged upon all the company's assets in satisfaction of the whole or part of his purchase money[2].

1 *Re Compagnie Générale de Bellegarde, Campbell's Case* (1876) 4 ChD 470.
2 *Salomon v A Salomon & Co Ltd* [1897] AC 22, HL. As to the effect of selling an insolvent business for debentures see *Re Slobodinsky, ex p Moore* [1903] 2 KB 517; and para 1192 ante.

1242. Borrowing by two companies jointly. Where two or more companies join in giving one debenture to secure a joint loan, and thereby purport to charge their several undertakings and assets with payment of the amount advanced, the charge is ultra vires so far as it purports to make one company's assets a security for money lent to the other company or companies; but the charge is good as to each company's assets to the extent of the money actually received by that company[1].

1 *Re Johnston Foreign Patents Co* [1904] 2 Ch 234, CA.

1243. Condition precedent to borrowing. Where directors have power to borrow upon the security of debentures only after a certain proportion of the share capital has been subscribed, any debentures issued before such subscription will be invalid[1].

Although as a general principle any condition precedent to the exercise of a power to borrow or mortgage should be performed, yet, where the condition is a matter pertaining to the internal management of the company, its non-performance does not invalidate a loan by a person acting in good faith without notice, nor any security given in respect of the loan by the company[2]. If the lender is a director, he may be taken to have notice of non-compliance with internal regulations[3]; but a security transferred to him by a person who had no notice will be valid in his hands[4].

1 *West Cornwall Rly Co v Mowatt* (1848) 17 LJ Ch 366. Where the borrowing powers of a company are to arise only upon completion of a portion of its works, the company may before completion, in consideration of a present advance, validly agree to issue debentures to secure the same when it is completed: *Re Bagnalstown and Wexford Rly Co* (1870) IR 4 Eq 505, CA.

2 *Royal British Bank v Turquand* (1856) 6 E & B 327, Ex Ch; *Agar v Athenaeum Life Assurance Society* (1858) 3 CBNS 725; *Fountaine v Carmarthen Rly Co* (1868) LR 5 Eq 316; *Re General Provident Assurance Co, ex p National Bank* (1872) LR 14 Eq 507; *Landowners' West of England and South Wales Land Drainage and Inclosure Co v Ashford* (1880) 16 ChD 411; *Biggerstaff v Rowatt's Wharf Ltd* [1896] 2 Ch 93, CA (powers of managing director relied on); *Re Hampshire Land Co* [1896] 2 Ch 743 (where the power to borrow and issue debentures required the consent of a general meeting of the company, which had not been given); *County of Gloucester Bank v Rudry Merthyr Steam and House Coal Colliery Co* [1895] 1 Ch 629, CA; *Cox v Dublin City Distillery (No 2)* [1915] 1 IR 345, CA; *Re Fireproof Doors Ltd, Umney v Fireproof Doors Ltd* [1916] 2 Ch 142 (debentures issued at a meeting of directors where there was an insufficient quorum); *Davies v R Bolton & Co* [1894] 3 Ch 678 (where the issue of debentures had not been duly authorised by the directors). In *Davies v R Bolton & Co* supra the articles provided that any debentures bearing the company's common seal issued for valuable consideration should be binding on the company, notwithstanding any irregularity touching the directors' authority to issue them. See also *Re Bank of Syria, Owen and Ashworth's Claim, Whitworth's Claim* [1900] 2 Ch 272; on appeal [1901] 1 Ch 115, CA; and see para 1137 et seq ante where the rule in *Royal British Bank v Turquand* supra and subsequent decisions are fully discussed. As to the remedies of a lender who has notice that the borrowing is ultra vires see para 1237 ante. See also *Mercantile Bank of India Ltd v Chartered Bank of India, Australia and China and Strauss & Co Ltd* [1937] 1 All ER 231.

3 *Howard v Patent Ivory Manufacturing Co, Re Patent Ivory Manufacturing Co* (1888) 38 ChD 156 at 170 (cf para 1093 note 1 ante); *Re General Provident Assurance Co Ltd* (1869) 38 LJ Ch 320 at 321 (loan by solicitor of the company). The employment of a director as agent by his wife to apply for debentures on her behalf does not fix her with notice of what he knows or should know as director: *Re Fireproof Doors Ltd, Umney v Fireproof Doors Ltd* [1916] 2 Ch 142.

4 *Re Bank of Syria, Owen and Ashworth's Claim, Whitworth's Claim* [1900] 2 Ch 272.

1244. Assignee's position. Where a security is transferable at law and is legally transferred, an irregularity in the issue cannot be set up against an assignee for value in good faith without notice, even where the original holder had notice of it[1]; but the equitable assignee of a security takes it subject to any equities affecting the person to whom it was originally issued, even though the assignment is taken for value and without notice of the circumstances giving rise to such equities[2], unless the terms of issue otherwise provide[3]. If a debenture defectively created is issued to a person who has no notice of the defect[4], so that the company cannot rely on it, and is then assigned to a person who has notice of the defect, the assignee has a good title to the debenture[5]. The company may be estopped by its conduct from denying the legality of the security as against an assignee for value in good faith who had no notice of any irregularity[6].

1 *Webb v Herne Bay Comrs* (1870) LR 5 QB 642; *Re Romford Canal Co, Carew's Claim* (1883) 24 ChD 85 at 89. A person acting de facto as a director of the company apparently cannot, however, be an assignee for value in good faith without notice of the irregularity, for he should know the true position: see *Morris v Kanssen* [1946] AC 459, [1946] 1 All ER 586, HL.

2 *Athenaeum Life Assurance Society v Pooley* (1858) 3 De G & J 294; *Re Natal Investment Co, Financial Corpn Claim* (1868) 3 Ch App 355; *Christie v Taunton, Delmard & Co, Re Taunton, Delmard, Lane & Co* [1893] 2 Ch 175.

3 *Re Blakely Ordnance Co, ex p New Zealand Banking Corpn* (1867) 3 Ch App 154; *Higgs v Assam Tea Co Ltd* (1869) LR 4 Exch 387; *Re Imperial Land Co of Marseilles, ex p Colborne and Strawbridge* (1870) LR 11 Eq 478.

4 This must include all persons entitled to rely upon the Companies Act 1985 ss 35–35B (as substituted): see paras 1093, 1107–1109 ante.

5 *Re Bank of Syria, Owen and Ashworth's Claim, Whitworth's Claim* [1901] 1 Ch 115, CA.
6 *Re Hercules Insurance Co, Brunton's Claim* (1874) LR 19 Eq 302; *Re Renshaw & Co Ltd* [1908] WN 210; *Re Hansard Publishing Union Ltd* (1892) 8 TLR 280, CA.

1245. Charge on uncalled capital. The property of a company does not include the liability of its members to contribute to its funds[1]; but a mortgage of uncalled capital[2] may be made[3] where either by the memorandum or the articles, whether original or as amended[4], there is express power to mortgage uncalled capital, or where there is a power to mortgage 'the company's properties and rights'[5], or 'property and assets whether existing or future'[6], or 'to receive money on loan. . . upon any security of the company or upon the security of any property of the company'[7], or to borrow money on the security of 'all or any of the real and personal assets. . . of the company'[8], or to borrow 'in such other manner as the company may determine', when the preceding specific powers cover everything it could charge except uncalled capital[9]. A charge on uncalled capital is not authorised by a power to charge the company's 'funds or property'[10], or to charge its 'works, hereditaments, plant, property and effects'[11] or its 'property'[12]; but such a power authorises a charge on calls already made or determined upon[13].

Where a company, with power to charge its uncalled capital, issues debentures charging only its undertaking and its present and after-acquired property, the charge does not include uncalled capital[14]; nor does a charge on 'all the lands, tenements and estates of the company and all their undertaking'[15], or on 'their undertaking and property and receipts and revenues'[16], or on 'their real and personal estate'[17].

If a resolution has been passed under the Companies Act 1985 or the enactments which it replaces prohibiting any portion of the uncalled capital being called up except in the event and for the purpose of the company being wound up[18], directors cannot mortgage that uncalled capital, even if the memorandum of association empowers them to mortgage uncalled capital[19].

Where a temporary loan is made by a bank to a company on the security of its uncalled capital, a charge made by a resolution of the board, that is, by parol, is good, subject to the statutory provisions[20] as to registration[21].

A company limited by guarantee cannot charge the amounts which the members have undertaken to contribute in the event of a winding up[22].

1 *Re Russian Spratts Patent Ltd, Johnson v Russian Spratts Patent Ltd* [1898] 2 Ch 149, CA; *Re Andrew Handyside & Co Ltd* (1911) 131 LT Jo 125.
2 For the meaning of 'uncalled share capital' see para 174 note 14 ante.
3 Such charges require registration: see para 1299 post.
4 *Newton v Anglo-Australian Investment Co's Debenture-holders* [1895] AC 244 at 248, PC; *Jackson v Rainford Coal Co* [1896] 2 Ch 340.
5 *Howard v Patent Ivory Manufacturing Co, Re Patent Ivory Manufacturing Co* (1888) 38 ChD 156.
6 *South Australian Barytes Ltd v Wood* (1976) 12 SASR 527 (Aust SC) (the charge validly included premiums payable on the shares).
7 *Newton v Anglo-Australian Investment Co's Debenture-holders* [1895] AC 244, PC.
8 *Re Pyle Works (No 2)* [1891] 1 Ch 173; and see *Page v International Agency and Industrial Trust Ltd* (1893) 62 LJ Ch 610.
9 *Jackson v Rainford Coal Co* [1896] 2 Ch 340.
10 *Re British Provident Life and Fire Assurance Society, Stanley's Case* (1864) 4 De GJ & Sm 407; *Bower v Foreign and Colonial Gas Co* [1877] WN 222.
11 *Re Sankey Brook Coal Co (No 2)* (1870) LR 10 Eq 381, doubting *Re Colonial and General Gas Co, Lishman's Claim* (1870) 19 WR 344.
12 *Bank of South Australia v Abrahams* (1875) LR 6 PC 265.

13 *Re Sankey Brook Coal Co* (1870) LR 9 Eq 721; *Re International Life Assurance Society, Gibbs and West's Case* (1870) LR 10 Eq 312; *Re Humber Iron Works Co, ex p Warrant Finance Co* (1868) 16 WR 474 (on appeal 16 WR 66).

14 *Re Andrew Handyside & Co Ltd* (1911) 131 LT Jo 125; *Re Russian Spratts Patent Ltd, Johnson v Russian Spratts Patent Ltd* [1898] 2 Ch 149, CA, approving *Re Streatham and General Estates Co* [1897] 1 Ch 15.

15 *King v Marshall* (1864) 33 Beav 565.

16 *Re Marine Mansions Co* (1867) LR 4 Eq 601.

17 *Re Colonial Trusts Corpn, ex p Bradshaw* (1879) 15 ChD 465.

18 As to the creation of reserve capital see the Companies Act 1985 ss 120, 124 and paras 128, 177 respectively ante.

19 *Re Mayfair Property Co, Barlett v Mayfair Property Co* [1898] 2 Ch 28, CA; *Re Pyle Works* (1890) 44 ChD 534 at 587, CA; cf *Newton v Anglo-Australian Investment Co's Debenture-holders* [1895] AC 244, PC.

20 See para 1299 post.

21 *Re Tilbury Portland Cement Co Ltd* (1893) 62 LJ Ch 814.

22 *Re Irish Club Co Ltd* [1906] WN 127; but see *Lloyds Bank Ltd v Morrison & Son Ltd* 1927 SC 571 (where a distinction was drawn between the guarantee by members, which was available only in winding up, and a guarantee, to which both members and non-members might contribute, in respect of liabilities of the company in organising an exhibition, and the benefit of the last-mentioned guarantee was held to be assignable).

1246. Enforcing mortgage of uncalled capital. A mortgage of uncalled capital may be enforced while the company is a going concern by appointing a receiver[1], and either ordering the directors to make calls and pay the proceeds over to the receiver or ordering the receiver to make the calls[2]. Such a charge may also be enforced after the company goes into liquidation[3]; but generally speaking only the liquidator may make and enforce the calls although, on an adequate indemnity being given, a receiver so appointed may obtain leave to use the liquidator's name in proceedings to enforce the calls[4].

The fact that uncalled capital has been charged does not prevent the company from forfeiting shares[5].

1 In *South Australian Barytes Ltd v Wood* (1976) 12 SASR 527 (Aust SC) it was held that the deed of charge validly delegated to a receiver and manager the directors' powers to make calls, the court intimating that such a delegation could in any event easily be implied. However, in that case this power was of only limited use, as it did not extend to instalments of the premium payable on the shares.

2 *Re Phoenix Bessemer Steel Co* (1875) 44 LJ Ch 683; and see *English Channel SS Co v Rolt* (1881) 44 LT 135; *Re Pyle Works* (1890) 44 ChD 534, CA. As to the power of an administrative receiver to call up uncalled capital see para 2154 post.

3 *Re Pyle Works* (1890) 44 ChD 534, CA; *Re Queensland Mercantile and Agency Co Ltd, ex p Australasian Investment Co, ex p Union Bank of Australia* [1891] 1 Ch 536 (affd [1892] 1 Ch 219, CA); *Newton v Anglo-Australian Investment Co's Debenture-holders* [1895] AC 244, PC. A nominee of the debenture holders will not be authorised to collect calls made by the liquidator: *Re Westminster Syndicate Ltd* (1908) 99 LT 924. An assignee of such a charge (invalid as to part) who takes with notice of the winding up, is in no better position than his assignor: *Re Gwelo Matabeleland Exploration and Development Co, Williamson's Claim* [1901] 1 IR 38.

4 *Fowler v Broad's Patent Night Light Co* [1893] 1 Ch 724; *Harrison v St Etienne Brewery Co* (1893) 37 Sol Jo 562.

5 *Re Agency, Land and Finance Co of Australia Ltd* (1903) 20 TLR 41.

1247. After-acquired property. A charge on future or after-acquired property, when sufficiently defined (that is, capable of identification when it is sought to enforce the security) is good[1]; and directors, when so empowered, may effectually charge a company's future or after-acquired property[2].

1 *Tailby v Official Receiver* (1888) 13 App Cas 523 at 530, HL; and see CHOSES IN ACTION vol 6 (Reissue) paras 8, 32.

2 *Bloomer v Union Coal and Iron Co* (1873) LR 16 Eq 383; *Anderson v Butler's Wharf Co Ltd* (1879) 48 LJ Ch
   824; *Re Marine Mansions Co* (1867) LR 4 Eq 601; *Re Panama, New Zealand, and Australian Royal Mail Co*
   (1870) 5 Ch App 318; *Re General South American Co* (1876) 2 ChD 337, CA; *Re Anglo-American Leather
   Cloth Co Ltd* (1880) 43 LT 43, CA (mortgage of business premises and the effects there included
   stock-in-trade for the time being, but not book debts); *Re New Bullas Trading Ltd* [1994] 1 BCLC 485,
   CA (book debts). In *Re Florence Land and Public Works Co, ex p Moor* (1878) 10 ChD 530, CA, a question
   was raised whether the Supreme Court of Judicature Act 1875 s 10 (repealed) affected the powers of
   companies to charge their after-acquired property as against their other creditors, but in *Re Dublin
   Drapery Co, ex p Cox* (1884) 13 LR Ir 174, it was held that the corresponding Supreme Court of
   Judicature (Ireland) Act 1877 s 28(1) did not affect it.

1248. Charge on books, registers etc. As against the liquidator, a company cannot
make a valid charge on any books or documents which it is bound by statute to keep,
such as registers of members and mortgages, minute books and share certificate books,
or books which are required by the liquidator for the performance of his duties, such as
letter books, cash books, bank books and ledgers[1].

1 *Engel v South Metropolitan Brewing and Bottling Co* [1892] 1 Ch 442; *Re Capital Fire Insurance Association*
   (1883) 24 ChD 408, CA; *Re Clyne Tin Plate Co* (1882) 47 LT 439; *Re Anglo-Maltese Hydraulic Dock Co
   Ltd* (1885) 54 LJ Ch 730.

1249. When borrowing power commences. A company registered as a public
company on its original incorporation may not exercise any borrowing powers unless
either the registrar of companies has issued it with a certificate that he is satisfied that the
nominal value of the company's share capital is not less than the authorised minimum[1],
or the company is re-registered as a private company[2]. Such a certificate is conclusive
evidence that the company is entitled to exercise any borrowing powers[3].

Any transaction entered into when no such certificate has been obtained will be
valid; but, if the company fails to comply with its obligations in that connection within
21 days from being called upon to do so, the directors of the company will be jointly
and severally liable to indemnify the lender in respect of any loss or damage suffered by
him in consequence[4]; and the company and any officer of it who is in default will be
liable on conviction on indictment to a fine, or on summary conviction to a fine not
exceeding the statutory maximum[5].

1 For the meaning of 'authorised minimum' see para 652 note 6 ante.
2 See the Companies Act 1985 s 117(1) and para 652 et seq ante.
3 Ibid s 117(6).
4 Ibid s 117(8).
5 Ibid ss 117(7), 730, Sch 24. For the meaning of 'officer who is in default' and 'the statutory maximum'
   see para 1161 ante.

(ii) Debentures and Debenture Stock

A. DESCRIPTION AND CONTENTS OF INSTRUMENTS
OF SECURITY

1250. Meaning of 'debenture'. No precise definition of 'debenture'[1] can be
found[2], but various forms of instruments are called debentures[3]. A debenture is a
document which either creates or acknowledges a debt[4]. The debt secured may be all
moneys due from the company on any account whatsoever, and is then known as an

'all moneys debenture'. Even so, it does not cover moneys due on unsecured loan stock issued to a third party and subsequently acquired by the debenture holder[5]. A document may be a debenture even though, under its terms, the debt is to be repaid out of only a part of the profits[6]. The term 'debenture' is usually associated with a company of some kind, and most debentures are securities given by companies. Nevertheless debentures are often granted by clubs[7] and occasionally by individuals.

The instrument need not describe itself as a debenture even to bring it within the exception from the application of the Bills of Sale Acts 1878 and 1882[8] which exists in favour of debentures of an incorporated company[9], and the use or non-use of the word is not conclusive[10]; but, even though no security other than a promise to pay is given by the instrument, if it is described as a debenture on the face of it, it is a debenture for stamping purposes[11].

1 A certificate or voucher certifying that a sum of money is owing to the person designated in it; a certificate of indebtedness: Oxford English Dictionary (2nd Edn) vol IV p 311.
2 *British India Steam Navigation Co v IRC* (1881) 7 QBD 165 at 168, 169, 172; *Knightsbridge Estates Trust Ltd v Byrne* [1940] AC 613 at 621, 627, [1940] 2 All ER at 405, 406, 410, HL. A document may be a debenture even if it is also accurately describable by another description: see *Pearl Assurance Co Ltd v West Midlands Gas Board* [1950] 2 All ER 844 at 847.
3 *British India Steam Navigation Co v IRC* (1881) 7 QBD 165. Unless the contrary intention appears, 'debenture' in the Companies Act 1985 includes debenture stock, bonds and any other securities of a company whether constituting a charge on the company's assets or not: s 744. This statutory definition applies to s 193: see para 1255 post. Trust deeds securing debentures are themselves debentures within the meaning of the Bills of Sale Act (1878) Amendment Act 1882 s 17 and as such do not require registration as bills of sale: see *Richards v Kidderminster Overseers, Richards v Kidderminster Corpn* [1896] 2 Ch 212 and BILLS OF SALE vol 4(1) (Reissue) para 665. As to the words which will pass debentures in a will see para 1258 note 2 post.
4 *Levy v Abercorris Slate and Slab Co* (1887) 37 ChD 260 at 264n; *Edmonds v Blaina Furnaces Co* (1887) 36 ChD 215; cf *Topham v Greenside Glazed Fire-brick Co* (1887) 37 ChD 281 at 290, 292. See also *R v Findlater* [1939] 1 KB 594, [1939] 1 All ER 82, CCA (where a certificate undertaking to pay insurance for return of capital was held to be a debenture).
5 *Re Quest Cae Ltd* [1985] BCLC 266.
6 *Lemon v Austin Friars Investment Trust Ltd* [1926] Ch 1, CA ('income stock certificates'; characteristics of a debenture discussed).
7 See CLUBS vol 6 (Reissue) para 245.
8 As to the Acts which may be so cited see BILLS OF SALE vol 4(1) (Reissue) para 611.
9 See the Bills of Sale Act (1878) Amendment Act 1882 s 17; *Levy v Abercorris Slate and Slab Co* (1887) 37 ChD 260; and BILLS OF SALE vol 4(1) (Reissue) para 665.
10 *British India Steam Navigation Co v IRC* (1881) 7 QBD 165 at 172; *Speyer Bros v IRC* [1908] AC 92 at 95, HL; *Lemon v Austin Friars Investment Trust Ltd* [1926] Ch 1, CA.
11 *Speyer Bros v IRC* [1908] AC 92, HL; *Re Fireproof Doors Ltd, Umney v Fireproof Doors Ltd* [1916] 2 Ch 142 at 150. As to stamp duty in respect of debentures see para 1292 post.

1251. Form of debenture. Although this is not strictly necessary[1], a debenture is generally issued under the company's seal; but it is doubtful whether the statutory right of a mortgagee to sell where the mortgage is by deed[2] applies to a series of debentures of a company[3]. As a rule, a debenture contains a covenant to pay, generally at some named place, such as the company's office[4], accompanied by some charge or security, in which case the instrument is usually called a 'mortgage debenture'[5]. Debentures sometimes contain a fixed charge, and usually contain a charge by way of floating security[6] on the company's property and undertaking, including, as a rule, its uncalled capital. A debenture is usually one of a series of documents all of which rank pari passu in point of priority, but it may, and often does, consist of one document only[7].

1 *British India Steam Navigation Co v IRC* (1881) 7 QBD 165. A company need no longer have a common seal: see the Companies Act 1985 s 36A(3) (as added) and para 1130 ante.

2 See the Law of Property Act 1925 s 101 and MORTGAGE vol 32 para 712.

3 *Blaker v Herts and Essex Waterworks Co* (1889) 41 ChD 399.

4 *Edmonds v Blaina Furnaces Co* (1887) 36 ChD 215 at 219 per Chitty J. Default in payment at the place named must be proved before any proceedings may be commenced to enforce the security: see *Thorn v City Rice Mills* (1889) 40 ChD 357; *Re Escalera Silver Lead Mining Co Ltd* (1908) 25 TLR 87; but see *Re Harris Calculating Machine Co, Sumner v Harris Calculating Machine Co* [1914] 1 Ch 920 (where the interest, unlike the principal, was not payable at a specified place).

5 *British India Steam Navigation Co v IRC* (1881) 7 QBD 165 at 172. A debenture need not, however, embody a charge: cf *Pearl Assurance Co Ltd v West Midlands Gas Board* [1950] 2 All ER 844 (a decision on the definition of 'securities' in the Gas Act 1948 s 74(1) (repealed)). A covenant binding the company's estate, property and effects to repay a sum mentioned in the bond has been held to constitute a charge: see *Re Florence Land and Public Works Co, ex p Moor* (1878) 10 ChD 530, CA; and see *Re Colonial Trusts Corpn, ex p Bradshaw* (1879) 15 ChD 465. As to the effect on foreign property of a charge given in England as against unsecured creditors abroad see para 1352 post.

6 For the meaning of 'floating charge' and 'floating security' see para 1260 post.

7 See *Robson v Smith* [1895] 2 Ch 118.

1252. Unsecured notes. Sometimes a debenture contains no charge over the company's property whatsoever, in which case it is known as a 'naked debenture'[1], or unsecured note. Where such notes are secured by a trust deed, in the sense that the company covenants to pay the money due under them to trustees, they are sometimes called 'unsecured loan stock'. Notwithstanding the absence of any charge, an unsecured note is properly speaking a debenture[2], and is chargeable with the same stamp duty[3]. Since no charge is created, such notes do not require registration under the Companies Act 1985[4]. Equally the holders of such notes are entitled to no priority over other creditors of the company in the payment of the money due on them and may have their claims expressly postponed by the terms of issue to other classes of creditors such as trade creditors[5].

1 The word 'debenture', which by itself popularly implies the existence of some security (see *Knightsbridge Estates Trust Ltd v Byrne* [1940] AC 613 at 625, [1940] 2 All ER 401 at 407, 408, HL), should not be used alone.

2 See para 1250 note 3 ante.

3 *British India Steam Navigation Co v IRC* (1881) 7 QBD 165.

4 See para 1296 post (registration at the company's office) and para 1299 post (registration with the registrar of companies).

5 Since in a winding up all debts (other than preferential debts) fall to be paid pari passu (see paras 2571, 2768 post), such postponement may normally be effected only by providing for payment to be made to trustees who are to stand possessed of anything received in the first instance upon trust, so far as is required, for the benefit of the creditors intended to be preferred.

1253. Trust deed. Often a trust deed is executed by which property belonging to the company is specifically mortgaged to trustees for the debenture holders further to secure the payment of the money owing on the debentures. Trustees of such a trust deed are in much the same position as any other trustees[1]. Any provision contained in such a trust deed or in any contract with the holders of debentures secured by a trust deed is void in so far as it would have the effect of exempting a trustee of it from, or indemnifying him against, liability for breach of trust where, having regard to the provisions of the trust deed conferring on him any powers, authorities or discretions, he fails to show the degree of care and diligence required of him as trustee[2].

This provision does not invalidate:

(1) a release otherwise validly given in respect of anything done or omitted to be done by a trustee before the giving of the release[3]; or

(2) any provision enabling such a release to be given on the agreement thereto of a majority of not less than three-fourths in value of the debenture holders present

and voting in person or, where proxies are permitted, by proxy at a meeting summoned for the purpose, and either with respect to specific acts or omissions or on the trustee dying or ceasing to act[4].

This provision also does not operate:

(a) to invalidate any provision in force on 1 July 1948 so long as any person then entitled to the benefit of it or afterwards given the benefit of it under the provision set out below remains a trustee of the deed in question[5]; or

(b) to deprive any person of any exemption or right to be indemnified in respect of anything done or omitted to be done by him while any such provision was in force[6].

While any trustee remains entitled to the benefit of such a provision[7], the benefit may be given either to all trustees of the deed, present and future, or to any named trustees or proposed trustees of it, by a resolution passed by a majority of not less than three-fourths in value of the debenture holders present in person or, where proxies are permitted, by proxy at a meeting summoned for the purpose in accordance with the provisions of the deed or, if the deed makes no provision for summoning meetings, a meeting summoned for the purpose in any manner approved by the court[8].

Provisions are usually inserted for the remuneration of trustees, and for this remuneration to be a first charge on the proceeds of sale[9]. Without such a special provision the remuneration is not payable in priority to the debenture holders out of the fund realised by the sale of the assets charged[10]. The question whether the trustees are entitled to remuneration after the appointment of a receiver is one of construction of the trust deed[11].

The solicitor who acts for the trustees has a lien on the trust deed and other documents in his possession as solicitor for the trustees for costs incurred in connection with the trust both before and after the execution of the trust deed[12], unless he has agreed to look for payment of the costs to a third party, for example the company[13].

1 *Re Magadi Soda Co Ltd* (1925) 94 LJ Ch 217 at 219. See generally TRUSTS vol 48 (Reissue) para 501 et seq.
2 Companies Act 1985 s 192(1).
3 Ibid s 192(2)(a).
4 Ibid s 192(2)(b).
5 Ibid s 192(3)(a).
6 Ibid s 192(3)(b).
7 Ie a provision saved by ibid s 192(3): see supra.
8 Ibid s 192(4).
9 *Re Piccadilly Hotel Ltd, Paul v Piccadilly Hotel Ltd* [1911] 2 Ch 534.
10 *Re Accles Ltd, Hodgson v Accles Ltd* (1902) 51 WR 57.
11 *Re Piccadilly Hotel Ltd, Paul v Piccadilly Hotel Ltd* [1911] 2 Ch 534; *Re Anglo-Canadian Lands (1912) Ltd* [1918] 2 Ch 287; *Re British Consolidated Oil Corpn Ltd* [1919] 2 Ch 81 (where the trustees were held to be entitled to remuneration after the appointment of a receiver); *Re Locke and Smith Ltd* [1914] 1 Ch 687, CA (where the trustee was held not so entitled). In the last-named case Eve J proceeded on the basis that the trustee in question had rendered no substantial services, but see the criticism in *Re British Consolidated Oil Corpn Ltd* supra at 90 per Peterson J. It is now usual to provide for the remuneration to be payable notwithstanding the appointment of a receiver.
12 *Re Dee Estates Ltd* [1911] 2 Ch 85.
13 *Re Mason and Taylor* (1878) 10 ChD 729.

1254. Bearer and registered debentures. Debentures may be:

(1) made payable to bearer[1], in which case interest coupons are attached and the principal and interest are payable respectively upon presentation and delivery of the debenture and coupons; or

(2) registered debentures, in which case the principal and interest are payable only to the registered holders, unless they are issued with coupons payable to bearer, in which case the interest is payable on presentation and delivery of the coupons.

A bearer debenture is recognised as a negotiable instrument[2]. Where money is payable on 'presentation' of a debenture or coupon, it must be delivered in order to obtain payment[3].

Where the bearers of some of the debentures cannot be found, it may be necessary for the company or the trustees to apply to the court for directions. The Attorney General should be made a party to the originating summons by which the application is made[4].

1 Formerly bearer debentures were rarely issued, as the ad valorem duty payable on them was larger than the duty upon registered debentures: see *Bechuanaland Exploration Co v London Trading Bank Ltd* [1898] 2 QB 658; but see para 1292 post. Certain debentures to bearer in Scotland are made valid by the Companies Act 1985 s 197. As to special restrictions on the issue of bearer securities and requirements as to deposit of certificates of title see para 493 ante.
2 See para 1275 post.
3 Cf *Bartlett v Holmes* (1853) 13 CB 630.
4 *Re Chillagoe Rly and Mines Ltd, Trust Deed* (1930) 46 TLR 242.

1255. Perpetual debentures. A condition contained in debentures, or in a deed for securing debentures, is not invalid by reason only that the debentures are thereby made irredeemable or redeemable only on the happening of a contingency, however remote, or on the expiration of a period, however long, any rule of equity to the contrary notwithstanding; and this provision applies to debentures whenever issued, and to deeds whenever executed[1].

1 Companies Act 1985 s 193. In view of the statutory definition of 'debenture' (see para 1250 note 3 ante), a mortgage of freehold land may be a 'debenture' within s 193: *Knightsbridge Estates Trust Ltd v Byrne* [1940] AC 613, [1940] 2 All ER 401, HL. As to the modification of rights of redeemable debenture holders by making their debentures irredeemable see para 1286 post. For the meaning of 'redeemable' and 'irredeemable' see *Re Joseph Stocks & Co Ltd* (1909) [1912] 2 Ch 134n at 140n.

1256. Indorsed debenture conditions. It is usual to set out most of the provisions relating to debentures in conditions indorsed on them. Such provisions generally state that the debenture is one of a series of a certain limited number, or for securing a total sum of limited amount, each for a like amount of principal; that all the debentures of the series rank pari passu as a first or other charge and that such charge (except as regards the property, if any, specifically mortgaged) is to be a floating security[1], but so that the company is not to create any charge ranking in priority to, or pari passu with, the debentures of the series.

The conditions also generally provide for registration of the debentures and of transfers of them at the company's office, the non-recognition of equities[2], transfers, payment of interest[3] by warrant, requirements to be observed in the case of joint holders, acceleration of payment of principal in certain specified events[4], the service of notices, and the time and mode of repayment of the principal money secured. A power to appoint a person as receiver or as receiver and manager is usually given, his powers are defined, and provision is made as to the disposal of money which comes into his hands[5]. Power is also usually given to a specified majority of debenture holders of a series to modify the rights of all the holders of the series[6]. In such cases provisions are usually made for the convening and holding of meetings of debenture holders[7].

If there is a trust deed[8], some reference to it in the debentures is advisable, and many of the provisions usually contained in the debenture conditions are then inserted in the trust deed.

1 See para 1260 post.
2 See para 1283 post.
3 Where interest is payable out of net earnings, a company is not entitled to set aside a sum representing profits before ascertaining the amount available for the payment of interest: see *Heslop v Paraguay Central Rly Co Ltd* (1910) 54 Sol Jo 234. Acceptance of a cheque for interest and failure to present it does not release the security: *Re J Defries & Sons Ltd* [1909] 2 Ch 423.
4 Eg on falling into arrear with interest, winding up, seizure in execution or under a distress (*Central Printing Works Ltd v Walker and Nicholson* (1907) 24 TLR 88), or receiving notice of an intention to pay off (*First National Bank of Chicago v Orinoco Shipping and Trading Co Ltd* (1904) 21 TLR 39).
5 See para 1320 post.
6 See para 1286 post.
7 See para 1287 post.
8 See para 1253 ante.

1257. Special clauses in debentures. Debentures and trust deeds often provide for redemption of debentures by drawings[1] and for the formation of a sinking fund, which is to be applicable to the redemption of the debentures either as they are drawn for redemption or pari passu in proportion to the amounts secured by them. Occasionally provisions are made to enable debentures originally payable to bearer to become registered debentures, or vice versa, with rights varied in consequence of the change. Special provisions are required where more than one series of debentures are issued and the company is only in a position to give to the holders of the later series a second or other puisne security on its assets.

1 See para 1289 post.

1258. Charging orders. Debentures may be made the subject of a charging order[1], as they are now included in the statutory definition of 'stock'[2].

1 Ie under RSC Ord 50 rr 1–7, implementing the provisions of the Charging Orders Act 1979: see EXECUTION.
2 For these purposes, 'stock' includes shares, debentures and any securities of the body concerned, whether or not constituting a charge on the assets of that body: Charging Orders Act 1979 s 6(1). The assets which may be charged under that Act now include stock of any body, other than a building society, incorporated within England and Wales, and stock of any body incorporated outside England and Wales or of any state or territory outside the United Kingdom, being stock registered in a register kept at any place within England and Wales: s 2(2)(b)(ii),(iii). Formerly the power to make a charging order was restricted to 'stocks and shares' where 'stock' bore its usual meaning of consolidated shares: *Sellar v Charles Bright & Co Ltd* [1904] 2 KB 446, CA. Debentures may, however, pass in a gift by will of 'all my stocks and shares': see *Re Purnchard's Will Trusts, Public Trustee v Pelly* [1948] Ch 312, [1948] 1 All ER 790; and WILLS vol 50 para 480.

1259. Debenture stock. Debenture stock is generally constituted and secured by a trust deed containing a charge upon the property of the company. A stock certificate is issued to each allottee or transferee of stock stating (inter alia) in the case of registered stock, that the person named in it is the registered proprietor or, in the case of bearer stock, that the bearer is the proprietor of the amount of stock mentioned in it, and having printed on it the conditions on which the stock is issued and held[1].

Where a debenture stock deed does not contain any direct covenant with the stockholder to pay him interest, a stockholder whose interest is in arrear is not entitled to present a winding-up petition against the company as a creditor[2].

1 See *Re Melbourne Brewery and Distillery* [1901] 1 Ch 453 (where it was held that slight breaches of the covenants in the trust deed would not entitle the stockholder to present a petition).
2 *Re Dunderland Iron Ore Co Ltd* [1909] 1 Ch 446.

B. FLOATING CHARGE OR SECURITY

1260. Meaning of 'floating charge' and 'floating security'. The terms 'floating charge' and 'floating security' mean a charge or security which is not to be put into immediate operation, but is to float so that the company is to be allowed to carry on its business. It contemplates, for example, that book debts may be extinguished by payment, and other book debts may come in and take the place of those which have disappeared. While a specific charge is one which without more fastens on ascertained and definite property or property capable of being ascertained and defined, a floating charge moves with the property which it is intended to affect until some event occurs or some act is done which causes it to settle and fasten on the subject of the charge within its reach and grasp[1]. The language used in the debenture is not conclusive; what is described as a 'fixed charge' may nevertheless create a floating charge if on construction it is a charge on present and future assets which, in the ordinary course of business, would be changing from time to time[2]. It is of the essence of a floating charge that it remains dormant until the undertaking charged ceases to be a going concern, or until the person in whose favour the charge is created intervenes. His right to intervene may be suspended by agreement, but, if there is no such agreement, he may exercise his right whenever he pleases after default[3].

Mortgage debentures usually contain a charge upon the undertaking of the company and all its property[4], real or personal, whether present or future, and may or may not give a charge upon uncalled capital[5]. The conditions usually provide that the charge so given shall be a floating charge or security. Where a series of debentures or debenture stock is secured by a trust deed[6], then, in addition to specific property of the company being assigned by it to the trustees to secure the debentures or stock, a floating charge is generally given upon all the other property of the company, present or future, and its undertaking, and in some cases its uncalled capital.

A general charge may be construed as a floating security even though the instrument does not expressly so describe it. Thus, a charge on the undertaking of a company constitutes a floating charge on all its property[7], and debentures given to bind a company and all its estate, property and effects[8], or its real and personal estate[9], constitute a floating security.

A floating charge may extend to part only of the company's assets[10], such as all the present and future book debts together with the securities for them[11], the profits of certain schemes for developing land[12], or the furniture and effects 'which now are or which may from time to time be placed upon or used in or about' certain specified premises[13]. It may also arise from a contract of sale of goods on credit terms reserving the equitable ownership in the goods to the vendor[14] or from a contractual lien on sub-freights[15].

1 *Illingworth v Houldsworth* [1904] AC 355 at 358, HL. A floating charge was formerly unknown to the law of Scotland, and such a charge given by a company registered in Scotland over assets in England was void: see *Carse v Coppen* 1951 SC 233. The law of Scotland was changed to enable companies to give security by way of floating charge in 1961: see now the Companies Act 1985 Pt XVIII (ss 462-487) (as amended).
2 *Re Brightlife Ltd* [1987] Ch 200, [1986] 3 All ER 673; *Re Armagh Shoes Ltd* [1984] BCLC 405; cf *Siebe Gorman & Co Ltd v Barclays Bank Ltd* [1979] 2 Lloyd's Rep 142; *Re Keenan Bros Ltd* [1986] BCLC 242, Ir

SC (it is possible in principle to create a fixed charge over present or future book debts; provisions of charges indicated this was the intention). See also *Re CCG International Enterprises Ltd* [1993] BCLC 1428 (debenture created fixed charge over the proceeds of insurance policies).

3 *Governments Stock and other Securities Investment Co v Manila Rly Co* [1897] AC 81 at 86, HL; and see *Evans v Rival Granite Quarries Ltd* [1910] 2 KB 979, CA. The parties to a charge may make provision for the floating charge to become fixed or to 'crystallise' on the happening of a defined event: *Re Brightlife Ltd* [1987] Ch 200, [1986] 3 All ER 673; following *Re Manurewa Transport Ltd* [1971] NZLR 909. A floating charge over land contained in a debenture constitutes an interest in land: *Driver v Broad* [1893] 1 QB 744, CA; *Re Dawson Pattisson v Bathurst* [1915] 1 Ch 626, CA.

4 'Property' or 'assets' includes goodwill: *Re Leas Hotel Co* [1902] 1 Ch 332.

5 As to charges on uncalled capital see para 1245 ante.

6 As to trust deeds see para 1253 ante.

7 *Re Panama, New Zealand and Australian Royal Mail Co* (1870) 5 Ch App 318; *Marshall v Rogers & Co* (1898) 14 TLR 217; cf *Re New Clydach Sheet and Bar Iron Co* (1868) LR 6 Eq 514; and see *National Provincial and Union Bank of England Ltd v Charnley* [1924] 1 KB 431, CA.

8 *Re Florence Land and Public Works Co, ex p Moor* (1878) 10 ChD 530, CA.

9 *Re Colonial Trusts Corpn, ex p Bradshaw* (1879) 15 ChD 465.

10 *Re Yorkshire Woolcombers' Association Ltd* [1903] 2 Ch 284, CA; affd sub nom *Illingworth v Houldsworth* [1904] AC 355, HL.

11 *Re Yorkshire Woolcombers' Association Ltd* [1903] 2 Ch 284, CA; affd sub nom *Illingworth v Houldsworth* [1904] AC 355, HL. Cf *Siebe Gorman & Co Ltd v Barclays Bank Ltd* [1979] 2 Lloyd's Rep 142; *Re Keenan Bros Ltd* [1986] BCLC 242, Ir SC (cited in note 2 supra).

12 *Hoare v British Columbia Development Association* (1912) 107 LT 602.

13 *National Provincial Bank of England Ltd v United Electric Theatres Ltd* [1916] 1 Ch 132.

14 *Re Bond Worth Ltd* [1980] Ch 228, [1979] 3 All ER 919. Cf *Borden (UK) Ltd v Scottish Timber Products Ltd* [1981] Ch 25, [1979] 3 All ER 961, CA (where the product is used in a manufacturing process in accordance with the intentions of the parties and becomes part of a new product, it ceases to exist, and the retention of title clause no longer operates. If the cost is intended to be charged on the new product, or its proceeds of sale, this is a charge created by the company requiring registration under the Companies Act 1985 s 395 (as amended) (see para 1299 post)); *Re Peachdart Ltd* [1984] Ch 131, [1983] 3 All ER 204. As to retention of title clauses see further para 1301 post.

15 *Annangel Glory Cia Naviera SA v M Golodetz Ltd* [1988] 1 Lloyd's Rep 45.

1261. Effect of floating charge. A floating security being only a charge on the assets for the time being, the company may in the ordinary course of its business[1], unless it is otherwise agreed and until the security becomes fixed, sell[2], let, mortgage[3], or otherwise deal with[4] any of its assets, just as if the floating charge had not been created[5]. It follows that, if the company enters into a specifically enforceable agreement to sell, the subsequent crystallisation of the charge will not afford a defence to an action by the purchaser for specific performance[6]. Where a company has created a floating charge on its undertaking and assets and has reserved power to mortgage its property, it cannot in general create another general floating charge over all the assets to rank in priority to, or pari passu with, the first floating charge[7]; but, where the company has reserved power to charge specified assets, it may create a floating charge on those assets in priority to the general floating charge[8].

Even before a floating security becomes fixed or 'crystallised', the debenture holders are entitled to an injunction to restrain the company from parting with its assets otherwise than in the ordinary course of its business, as, for example, when, with a view to its ceasing to be going concern, it agrees to sell all its property[9].

Moreover, each asset within the scope of the floating charge must be regarded as equitably assigned to the debenture holder by way of charge as soon as it comes into the ownership of the company, so that, if such asset is a debt, no right of set-off of any subsequently acquired debt could defeat the debenture holder's interest[10]. In some provisions of the Insolvency Act 1986, however, the word 'assets' includes assets subject to a floating charge, so as to render them available for the costs and expenses of a winding up in priority to the claims of the debenture holders[11].

The administrator of a company[12] may dispose of, or otherwise exercise his powers in relation to, any property of the company which is subject to a security which, as created, was a floating charge[13].

1 As to what acts or payments are considered to come within the ordinary course of business see *Willmott v London Celluloid Co* (1886) 34 ChD 147, CA; *Re Hubbard & Co Ltd, Hubbard v Hubbard & Co Ltd* (1898) 68 LJ Ch 54; *Re H H Vivian & Co Ltd, Metropolitan Bank of England and Wales Ltd v H H Vivian & Co Ltd* [1900] 2 Ch 654; *Cox Moore v Peruvian Corpn Ltd* [1908] 1 Ch 604; *Hamer v London, City and Midland Bank Ltd* (1918) 87 LJKB 973; cf *Re Borax Co, Foster v Borax Co* [1901] 1 Ch 326, CA; *Re Old Bushmills Distillery Co, ex p Brett* [1897] 1 IR 488, CA; *Wallace v Evershed* [1899] 1 Ch 891; *Cox v Dublin Distillery Co* [1906] 1 IR 446. There may be a right of set-off while the charge floats: *Edward Nelson & Co Ltd v Faber & Co* [1903] 2 KB 367. The rights of a contractor under a hire purchase agreement entered into prior to the creation of a floating charge take priority over the charge: *Re Samuel Allen & Sons Ltd* [1907] 1 Ch 575; *Re Morrison, Jones and Taylor Ltd* [1914] 1 Ch 50, CA; and see HIRE PURCHASE vol 22 para 132. A purchaser to whom the property has passed under the Sale of Goods Act 1979 is entitled to goods purchased as against a receiver subsequently appointed, even though the purchaser has not taken the goods from the company's premises: see *Hamer v London, City and Midland Bank Ltd* supra.

2 *Re H H Vivian & Co Ltd, Metropolitan Bank of England and Wales Ltd v H H Vivian & Co Ltd* [1900] 2 Ch 654. A purchaser from a company of land subject to a charge expressed to be a floating security until default in payment is entitled to evidence that there has been no default: *Re Horne and Hellard* (1885) 29 ChD 736.

3 *Re Florence Land and Public Works Co, ex p Moor* (1878) 10 ChD 530, CA; *Re Hamilton's Windsor Ironworks Co* (1879) 12 ChD 707; *Ward v Royal Exchange Shipping Co, ex p Harrison* (1887) 58 LT 174; *Re Hubbard & Co Ltd, Hubbard v Hubbard & Co Ltd* (1898) 68 LJ Ch 54. The priority of a specific mortgage of a chose in action over a floating charge on it is not displaced by notice by the receiver for the debenture holders of his appointment: *Re Ind, Coope & Co Ltd* [1911] 2 Ch 223.

4 See *George Barker (Transport) Ltd v Eynon* [1974] 1 All ER 900, [1974] 1 WLR 462, CA (creation of inchoate contractual right which crystallised after security became fixed).

5 *Robson v Smith* [1895] 2 Ch 118 at 124; *Biggerstaff v Rowatt's Wharf Ltd* [1896] 2 Ch 93 at 103, CA. This is so even if the charge is described as a first charge: *Wheatley v Silkstone and Haigh Moor Coal Co* (1885) 29 ChD 715; *Cox Moore v Peruvian Corpn Ltd* [1908] 1 Ch 604. An express power to carry on business until default does not give creditors who have supplied goods any priority: *Re Anglo-American Leather Cloth Co Ltd* (1880) 43 LT 43, CA.

6 *Freevale Ltd v Metrostore (Holdings) Ltd* [1984] Ch 199, [1984] 1 All ER 495 (specific performance against company after appointment of receiver of contract made in ordinary course of business before appointment).

7 *Smith v English and Scottish Mercantile Investment Trust Ltd* (1896) 40 Sol Jo 717; *Re Benjamin Cope & Sons Ltd* [1914] 1 Ch 800, explained and approved in *Re Automatic Bottle Makers* [1926] Ch 412, CA.

8 *Re Automatic Bottle Makers* [1926] Ch 412, CA.

9 *Hubbuck v Helms* (1887) 56 LJ Ch 536; but see *Re H H Vivian & Co Ltd, Metropolitan Bank of England and Wales Ltd v H H Vivian & Co Ltd* [1900] 2 Ch 654 (sale of a branch business); and *Re Borax Co, Foster v Borax Co* [1901] 1 Ch 326, CA (where nearly the whole assets were sold, but the company continued business as the holders of shares).

10 *N W Robbie & Co Ltd v Witney Warehouse Co Ltd* [1963] 3 All ER 613, [1963] 1 WLR 1324, CA (debt sought to be set off assigned to party fixed with knowledge of appointment of receiver); *Lynch v Ardmore Studios (Ireland) Ltd* [1966] IR 133 (similar principle). Cf *Rother Iron Works Ltd v Canterbury Precision Engineers Ltd* [1974] 1 QB 1, [1973] 1 All ER 394, CA (debt owed by company before appointment of receiver set off against subsequent debt). Similarly, the debenture holder is entitled to the moneys due in respect of the debt, even if actually received by the company after crystallisation without regard to the Insolvency Act 1986 s 127 (avoidance of dispositions of property after commencement of winding up: see para 2460 post): *Re Margart Pty Ltd, Hamilton v Westpac Banking Corpn* [1985] BCLC 314 (NSW SC).

11 *Re Barleycorn Enterprises Ltd, Mathias and Davies (a firm) v Down* [1970] Ch 465, [1970] 2 All ER 155, CA; distinguished in *Re M C Bacon Ltd* [1991] Ch 127, [1990] 3 WLR 646; and see para 2569 post.

12 As to administrators see para 2092 et seq post.

13 See the Insolvency Act 1986 s 15(1),(3) and para 2098 post. The holder of the security nevertheless has the same priority in respect of any property of the company directly or indirectly representing the property disposed of as he would have had in respect of the property subject to the security: s 15(4).

1262. Restrictions on operation of floating charge. It is usual to qualify the operation of a floating security by providing that the company shall not create a mortgage or charge on all or any of the assets, ranking in priority to or pari passu with the charge given by the debentures[1]. The mere existence of such a restriction in a debenture containing a specific charge on certain assets does not enable a floating charge on the remaining assets to be implied[2].

Such a restriction does not prevent a solicitor from acquiring a lien having priority over the floating charge[3], or a mortgagee of an insurance policy, without notice of such provision, from acquiring priority by giving notice to the insurance company[4]; or a person without notice from acquiring a charge on specific property in priority to the debentures[5]. This restriction does not prevent a vendor who leaves the purchase price of property acquired from him by the company on mortgage from obtaining priority for that mortgage[6], or a lender who provides the purchase price of property acquired by the company in consideration of a first mortgage from obtaining priority for that mortgage[7].

Similarly, where a specific mortgagee, being a bank, knows that debentures have been issued, and even holds some of the same series as security for an account of another company, the bank is not affected with notice of the restriction[8] and the registration of particulars of debentures pursuant to the Companies Act 1985, or earlier Acts[9], although it amounts to constructive notice of the debentures, does not amount to constructive notice of the restriction, at any rate where particulars of the restriction are not also registered[10].

Where such a restriction exists, and a company transfers goods to creditors at a fair price to find money to carry on the company's business, then, even though the creditors are not dealers in such goods, the transaction will be held to be a sale and not an infringement of the restriction, provided that the transfer is an out and out sale[11].

1 See para 1261 text and notes 7, 8 ante.
2 *Grigson v Taplin & Co* (1915) 85 LJ Ch 75.
3 *Brunton v Electrical Engineering Corpn* [1892] 1 Ch 434.
4 *English and Scottish Mercantile Investment Co v Brunton* [1892] 2 QB 700, CA.
5 *Re Castell and Brown Ltd, Roper v Castell and Brown Ltd* [1898] 1 Ch 315. Cf *Re Woodroffes (Musical Instruments) Ltd* [1986] Ch 366, [1985] 2 All ER 908 (express postponement of second charge).
6 *Wilson v Kelland* [1910] 2 Ch 306.
7 *Re Connolly Bros Ltd (No 2), Wood v Connolly Bros Ltd* [1912] 2 Ch 25, CA. See also *Security Trust Co v Royal Bank of Canada* [1976] AC 503, [1976] 1 All ER 381, PC.
8 *Re Valletort Sanitary Steam Laundry Co Ltd, Ward v Valletort Sanitary Steam Laundry Co Ltd* [1903] 2 Ch 654.
9 As to registration see para 1299 post.
10 *Re Standard Rotary Machine Co Ltd* (1906) 95 LT 829 at 834; *Wilson v Kelland* [1910] 2 Ch 306; *G and T Earle Ltd v Hemsworth RDC* (1928) 44 TLR 605 (affd 44 TLR 758, CA). In the case of a land charge for securing money created by a company before 1 January 1970 or so created at any time as a floating charge, registration under the Companies (Consolidation) Act 1908 s 93 (repealed), the Companies Act 1929 s 79 (repealed), the Companies Act 1948 s 95 (repealed) or the Companies Act 1985 ss 395–398 (as amended) was or is sufficient in place of registration under the Land Charges Act 1972, and had or has effect as if the land charge had been registered under the 1972 Act: s 3(7),(8) (amended by the Companies Consolidation (Consequential Provisions) Act 1985 s 30, Sch 2); *Property Discount Corpn v Lyon Group Ltd* [1981] 1 All ER 379, [1981] 1 WLR 300, CA. The registration of any instrument or matter in any register kept under the Land Charges Act 1972 or any local land charges register is deemed to constitute actual notice of such instrument or matter, and of the fact of such registration, to all persons and for all purposes connected with the land affected: see the Law of Property Act 1925 s 198(1) (as amended); EQUITY vol 16 (Reissue) para 768; and LAND CHARGES vol 26 para 716. It appears that these provisions do not alter the effect of the cases above cited.
11 *Re Old Bushmills Distillery Co, ex p Brett* [1897] 1 IR 488, CA.

1263. When floating charge becomes fixed. If the company ceases its business[1] (but not if it ceases to be a going concern, in so far as there is any difference)[2] or if it is wound up, or if a receiver is appointed or some event happens upon which the charge is to become a fixed charge[3], the security ceases to be a floating security and becomes a fixed charge, and the company cannot thereafter deal with any part of the property so charged except subject to the charge[4]. It does not, however, automatically crystallise on the crystallisation of a subsequent floating charge[5].

Where the security merely provides that the company is at liberty to deal with the property charged until the happening of a specified event, the security continues to be a floating one after the happening of that event until a receiver is appointed or until the company goes into liquidation[6]. The mere issue of a writ asking for a receiver is not sufficient to affect the company's power of disposition[7].

1 *Governments Stock and other Securities Investment Co v Manila Rly Co* [1897] AC 81 at 86, HL per Lord MacNaghten; *Hubbuck v Helms* (1887) 56 LJ Ch 536; *Robson v Smith* [1895] 2 Ch 118; *Re Victoria Steamboats Ltd, Smith v Wilkinson* [1897] 1 Ch 158; *Davey & Co v Williamson & Sons Ltd* [1898] 2 QB 194; *Re Yorkshire Woolcombers' Association Ltd* [1903] 2 Ch 284, CA (affd on another point sub nom *Illingworth v Holdsworth* [1904] AC 355, HL); *Edward Nelson & Co v Faber & Co* [1903] 2 KB 367; *Evans v Rival Granite Quarries Ltd* [1910] 2 KB 979, CA; *Re Crompton & Co Ltd* [1914] 1 Ch 954; *Re Woodroffes (Musical Instruments) Ltd* [1986] Ch 366, [1985] 2 All ER 908.

2 *Re Woodroffes (Musical Instruments) Ltd* [1986] Ch 366, [1985] 2 All ER 908.

3 Eg such as notice being given to this effect pursuant to the terms of the charge: *Re Brightlife Ltd* [1987] Ch 200, [1986] 3 All ER 673, following *Re Manurewa Transport Ltd* [1971] NZLR 909.

4 *Governments Stock and other Securities Investment Co v Manila Rly Co* [1897] AC 81, HL; *Re Panama, New Zealand and Australian Royal Mail Co* (1870) 5 Ch App 318; *Hodson v Tea Co* (1880) 14 ChD 859; *Wallace v Universal Automatic Machines Co* [1894] 2 Ch 547, CA; *Re Horne and Hellard* (1885) 29 ChD 736 (where the charge was to be a floating charge until default). As to the appointment of a receiver by the court where the security is in jeopardy see para 1348 post. Notice of the appointment should be given to the persons carrying on the company's business: see *Re Arauco Co Ltd* (1898) 79 LT 336.

5 *Re Woodroffes (Musical Instruments) Ltd* [1986] Ch 366, [1985] 2 All ER 908 (decided under the Companies Act 1948 (repealed)). The result of this was that the holder of the first floating charge ranked first to the extent of the moneys due to the holder of the second floating charge (but crystallised at the date of appointment of the receivers); the preferential creditors ranked second; the holder of the first floating charge to the extent of the balance of its charge ranked third; and the holder of the crystallised second floating charge ranked last. Under the present law the preferential creditors would have ranked first because priority is now given to preferential creditors over the holders of charges which 'as created' were floating charges: see para 1334 post.

6 *Governments Stock and other Securities Investment Co v Manila Rly Co* [1897] AC 81, HL; *Biggerstaff v Rowatt's Wharf Ltd* [1896] 2 Ch 93, CA; *Edward Nelson & Co v Faber & Co* [1903] 2 KB 367; *Evans v Rival Granite Quarries Ltd* [1910] 2 KB 979, CA. Cf text to note 3 supra.

7 *Re Hubbard & Co Ltd, Hubbard v Hubbard & Co Ltd* (1898) 68 LJ Ch 54.

1264. Effect of attachment of debts. Where, after a judgment creditor has obtained and served on a company a garnishee order absolute attaching debts due from the company to the judgment debtor[1], the company borrows money on the security of a debenture comprising all its assets, and execution is then levied to enforce the attachment on its goods, the title of a receiver subsequently appointed under the debenture prevails over that of the garnishor[2]. Where judgment is obtained against a company and the judgment creditor serves a garnishee order nisi on a person owing the company a debt which is at the time subject to a floating charge in a debenture, the title of the debenture holder prevails over that of the creditor, even though his receiver is appointed after the service of the order[3], and the receiver's title prevails even if the garnishee order is made absolute before he is appointed[4], unless the money has been actually paid over under the order[5]; and, even if debentures are irregularly issued, the rights of the holder, if he had no notice of the irregularity, prevail over those of an execution creditor[6]. The court will not, however, restrain an execution from proceeding or refuse to make a garnishee order absolute unless the debenture holder takes some step to turn his security from a floating into a fixed charge[7].

1   As to attachment of debts see RSC Ord 49 and EXECUTION vol 17 para 525.
2   *Geisse v Taylor* [1905] 2 KB 658.
3   *Norton v Yates* [1906] 1 KB 112; *Re Combined Weighing and Advertising Machine Co* (1889) 43 ChD 99, CA; cf *Robson v Smith* [1895] 2 Ch 118; *Re Watt, ex p Joselyne* (1878) 8 ChD 327 at 330, CA.
4   *Cairney v Back* [1906] 2 KB 746 (where the money claimed was paid into court).
5   *Robson v Smith* [1895] 2 Ch 118, as explained in *Norton v Yates* [1906] 1 KB 112 at 123.
6   *Duck v Tower Galvanizing Co* [1901] 2 KB 314.
7   *Evans v Rival Granite Quarries Ltd* [1910] 2 KB 979, CA (explaining *Re Standard Manufacturing Co* [1891] 1 Ch 627, CA; *Re Opera Ltd* [1891] 3 Ch 260, CA; *Davey & Co v Williamson & Sons* [1898] 2 QB 194; *Re London Pressed Hinge Co Ltd* [1905] 1 Ch 576 (on the grounds that in all those cases either the charge had crystallised or steps had been taken with that object); overruling dicta in *Cairney v Back* [1906] 2 KB 746); and see *Simultaneous Colour Printing Syndicate v Foweraker* [1901] 1 KB 771, cited in argument but not explained; and see *Taunton v Sheriff of Warwickshire* [1895] 2 Ch 319, CA. A receiver seeking to oust the execution creditor must prove the validity of his appointment: *Kasofsky v Kreegers* [1937] 4 All ER 374. See generally EXECUTION vol 17 para 401 et seq.

1265. Effect of execution or distress. Where, after giving a floating charge on all its property, a company has its goods seized under a writ of fieri facias[1] and, either with or without an arrangement with the execution creditor, pays to the sheriff daily a sum out of its daily takings to avoid a sale and to enable the business to go on, a receiver subsequently appointed on behalf of debenture holders is not entitled to the moneys so received even where they remain in the sheriff's hands[2].

A distress levied though not completed by sale before a floating charge becomes fixed[3], or a distress for rates even after a receiver has been appointed[4], has priority over the debenture holders.

1   As to writs of fieri facias see RSC Ord 47 r 1 and EXECUTION vol 17 para 462 et seq.
2   *Robinson v Burnell's Vienna Bakery Co* [1904] 2 KB 624; *Heaton and Dugard Ltd v Cutting Bros Ltd* [1925] 1 KB 655.
3   *Re Roundwood Colliery Co, Lee v Roundwood Colliery Co* [1897] 1 Ch 373, CA; *Biggerstaff v Rowatt's Wharf Ltd* [1896] 2 Ch 93, CA. As to cases where the company is an undertenant see the Law of Distress Amendment Act 1908 and DISTRESS vol 13 para 250 et seq.
4   *Re Marriage, Neave & Co, North of England Trustee, Debenture and Assets Corpn v Marriage, Neave & Co* [1896] 2 Ch 663, CA; *Re Adolphe Crosbie Ltd* (1909) 74 JP 25; cf *Richards v Kidderminster Overseers* [1896] 2 Ch 212; *Husey v London Electric Supply Corpn* [1902] 1 Ch 411, CA; *Re British Fullers Earth Co, Gibbs v British Fullers Earth Co* (1901) 17 TLR 232. As to distress for rates see DISTRESS vol 13 para 397 et seq.

1266. Effect of floating charge becoming fixed. When a floating security upon all the property or assets of the company becomes fixed, it constitutes a charge upon all the property or assets then belonging to the company. It has priority over any subsequent equitable charges[1] and over unsecured creditors[2], and over money advanced to the liquidator to carry on the business of the company, even though the advances were made with the sanction of the court in the winding up, and over the costs of the liquidators other than costs of realisation[3]; but it is subject to all then existing charges and to the payment of debts which by statute are made payable out of property subject to a floating security or which, when created, was a floating security, in priority to the money thereby secured[4] and to all rights in course of being acquired under the Limitation Act 1980, if the full period of time ultimately runs[5]. A floating charge on all the undertaking and property of a company including uncalled capital constitutes a charge on money recovered by a liquidator in misfeasance proceedings[6] as well as on calls got in by him[7].

1 See para 1263 text and note 1 ante.
2 *Re Marine Mansions Co* (1867) LR 4 Eq 601; *Panama, New Zealand and Australian Royal Mail Co* (1870) 5 Ch App 318; *Re Anglo-American Leather Cloth Co Ltd* (1880) 43 LT 43, CA; *Re General South American Co* (1876) 2 ChD 337, CA.
3 *Re Regent's Canal Ironworks Co, ex p Grissell* (1875) 3 ChD 411, CA.
4 See the Insolvency Act 1986 ss 40, 175 and paras 1334, 2523 respectively post.
5 *Halpin v Cremin* [1954] IR 19.
6 As to such proceedings see para 2448 et seq post.
7 *Re Anglo-Austrian Printing and Publishing Union, Brabourne v Anglo-Austrian Printing and Publishing Union* [1895] 2 Ch 891; *Re Regent's Canal Ironworks Co, ex p Grissell* (1875) 3 ChD 411, CA. Contrast *Re Yagerphone Ltd* [1935] Ch 392 (preference; sum recovered from creditor by liquidator).

C. ISSUE AND REISSUE OF DEBENTURES

1267. Enforcement of agreement to issue debentures. A contract with a company to take up and pay for debentures or debenture stock of the company may be enforced by an order for specific performance[1]; but, where debentures have been issued payable by instalments and have been forfeited, the company cannot enforce payment[2]. No action may be brought on an agreement to purchase debentures or debenture stock containing a charge on land, unless the agreement is in writing, incorporating all the expressly agreed terms of the agreement in one document or, where agreements are exchanged, in each signed by or on behalf of each party to the agreement[3].

1 Companies Act 1985 s 195. The remedy of specific performance first conferred by the Companies Act 1907 (repealed) was not available in the case of a contract entered into prior to that Act: *Re Smelting Corpn Ltd* [1915] 1 Ch 472.
2 *Kuala Pahi Rubber Estates Ltd v Mowbray* (1914) 111 LT 1072, CA.
3 *Driver v Broad* [1893] 1 QB 744, CA (decided under that part of the Statute of Frauds (1677) s 4 which was replaced by the Law of Property Act 1925 s 40 (repealed), itself replaced by the Law of Property (Miscellaneous Provisions) Act 1989 s 2).

1268. Lender's position. Where a company borrows money and agrees to give a debenture to secure the amount when called upon, the agreement is valid as an equitable security[1], subject to any statutory requirements as to registration[2] and to the law as to preference[3]. A floating charge contained in a debenture may in certain circumstances be invalid[4].

Under an agreement to issue debentures of a certain series to a creditor, he will be entitled to rank pari passu with the holders of the series even though no debentures are issued to him[5].

Where directors of a company deposit incomplete mortgage bonds by way of security in pursuance of written agreements, a valid charge is created, independently of the bonds, upon the property which the bonds purport to charge[6], and an agreement to issue a debenture may be implied from an irregularly issued debenture[7].

1 *Re Queensland Land and Coal Co, Davis v Martin* [1894] 3 Ch 181; *Pegge v Neath and District Tramways Co Ltd* [1898] 1 Ch 183; *Simultaneous Colour Printing Syndicate v Foweraker* [1901] 1 KB 771; *Ross v Army and Navy Hotel Co* (1886) 34 ChD 43, CA. An agreement by a company to assign a debenture in another company by way of security to a bank in place of a security released under the agreement does not itself constitute the company a trustee of the debenture if obtained after the first-named company goes into liquidation: see *Bank of Scotland v Macleod* [1914] AC 311, HL. In *Dublin City Distillery Ltd v Doherty* [1914] AC 823, HL, it was held that holders of debentures issued after the Companies Act 1900 (repealed), and therefore requiring registration, but secured by a trust deed executed before that Act and therefore not requiring registration, were entitled as beneficiaries under the trust deed to a lien on the debentures for the amount of their advances to the extent of the property comprised in the deed.

2 See para 1299 et seq post.
3 See para 2602 et seq post.
4 See para 2620 et seq post.
5 *Re Queensland Land and Coal Co, Davis v Martin* [1894] 3 Ch 181; *Pegge v Neath and District Tramways Co Ltd* [1898] 1 Ch 183. Where a person subscribed for debentures on the terms of a prospectus which stated that the debentures were first mortgage debentures and were to be secured upon the entire property of the company, it was held that he was entitled to a charge on it pari passu with the other debenture holders, even though no debentures were issued and the company had gone into liquidation: *Re New Durham Salt Co, Stevenson's Case* (1890) 2 Meg 360. Nevertheless, if the statement as to charge had been omitted from the prospectus, he would have had no charge: *Re New Durham Salt Co, Quin's Case* (1890) 2 Meg 360. As to the effect of scheduling creditors to a company's purchase agreement under which creditors are to have debentures see *Re Harden Star etc Co Ltd, Morris v Harden Star etc Co Ltd* (1903) 47 Sol Jo 368.
6 *Re Strand Music Hall Co* (1865) 3 De GJ & Sm 147.
7 *Re Fireproof Doors Ltd, Umney v Fireproof Doors Ltd* [1916] 2 Ch 142.

1269. Issue of debentures. An issue of debentures or debenture stock will not be valid until all conditions precedent to the exercise of the power to issue them have been performed[1], unless any such condition relates to acts of internal management, when its non-observance does not necessarily invalidate the issue[2]. Where a company has power to issue debentures or debenture stock, the issue may be made on such terms and for such amount and for such purposes as the company thinks fit, subject to any restrictions or prohibitions contained in its memorandum or articles of association. Sealing debentures without delivery is not sufficient to constitute issuing them[3]; but sealing and delivering undated debentures is an issue, even though the names of the holders are omitted[4].

The issue of a writ in a debenture holders' action does not of itself prevent the company from issuing unissued debentures of the series in respect of some of which the proceedings are taken[5].

1 See para 1243 ante.
2 As to inquiry into acts of internal management see para 1137 ante; and as to the issue of debenture certificates see para 1282 post.
3 *Mowatt v Castle Steel and Iron Works Co* (1886) 34 ChD 58, CA.
4 *Re Perth Electric Tramways Ltd, Lyons v Tramways Syndicate Ltd and Perth Electric Tramways Ltd* [1906] 2 Ch 216; cf *A-G v Liverpool Corpn* [1902] 1 KB 411. An allotment of debentures and entry in the register of debentures without the issue of certificates is a sufficient issue to constitute the allottee a debenture holder so as to enable him to vote under the modification of rights clause: *Dey v Rubber and Mercantile Corpn Ltd* [1923] 2 Ch 528.
5 *Re Hubbard & Co Ltd* (1898) 68 LJ Ch 54.

1270. Offers of debentures for subscription or sale. Offers of debentures for subscription or sale are governed by the same statutory provisions as apply to company securities generally[1].

Prima facie the terms of offer documents inviting subscriptions for debentures cannot be considered for the purpose of adding to or explaining the terms or conditions contained in the debenture itself[2], and a transferee cannot rely on the offer documents for this purpose, even where the agreement for allotment expressly refers to the terms of the offer documents[3]. Nevertheless, in the case of an original allottee, the agreement for allotment may incorporate the terms of the offer documents as an additional or collateral contract[4].

Debenture offer documents generally state that application for debentures must be accompanied by a remittance, and that, if any instalment payable in respect of the debentures is not punctually paid, the payments already made may be forfeited. Where debentures or debenture stock are allotted upon the terms that they be paid for by instalments, it is usual to issue provisional bearer scrip certificates to the subscribers, to be exchanged for definitive debentures or for stock certificates when all the instalments are paid, and to indorse upon the scrip certificates the payments of the several instalments. When the instalments are paid, the bearer of the certificate is entitled to have the debentures or stock certificate issued to him[5]. If the instalments are not fully paid before the company goes into liquidation, a holder may safely refuse to pay any further instalments without prejudicing his position as a secured creditor for previous instalments, even if the certificate provides that failure to pay any instalment when due will empower the company to forfeit previous instalments[6]; but it appears that, in the event of the security being enforced, such a holder would not be entitled to share in the distribution of the fund realised until after he has paid up in full the instalments still owing[7].

1 See para 281 et seq ante (listed securities) and para 300 et seq ante (unlisted securities).
2 *Re Chicago and North West Granaries Co Ltd* [1898] 1 Ch 263.
3 *Re Tewkesbury Gas Co, Tysoe v Tewkesbury Gas Co* [1911] 2 Ch 279; affd [1912] 1 Ch 1, CA; and see *British Equitable Assurance Co v Baily* [1906] AC 35, HL.
4 *Jacobs v Batavia and General Plantations Trust Ltd* [1924] 1 Ch 287; affd [1924] 2 Ch 329, CA, distinguishing and explaining the cases referred to in note 3 supra.
5 As to the issue of certificates see further para 1282 post.
6 *Re Consolidated Land Co, Ellerby's Claim* (1872) 20 WR 855.
7 In *Re Smelting Corpn* [1915] 1 Ch 472, holders of partly paid debentures were held to be entitled to share in proportion to the amounts which they had paid up. This decision was based on the ground that the debentures had been issued prior to the Companies Act 1907 s 16 (repealed: see now the Companies Act 1985 s 195 and para 1267 ante), before which specific performance of a contract to take debentures could not be enforced, so that the unpaid instalments did not constitute a debt due to the company. It appears from the reasoning in that case that in the case of a debenture issued since the 1907 Act a contrary principle would apply: cf *Re Rhodesia Goldfields Ltd* [1910] 1 Ch 239 (where a debenture holder was indebted to the company in respect of profits received as a director and the rule in *Cherry v Boultbee* (1839) 4 My & Cr 442 (see BANKRUPTCY vol 3(2) (Reissue) para 547) was held to apply).

1271. Issue of debentures at a discount. A company which has power to borrow on debentures may issue them at a discount[1]. Thus, where a director takes some of the debentures at the rate of discount allowed to other persons, he is not liable to account for the discount[2]. A company cannot, however, issue debentures at a discount upon the terms that they shall be exchangeable, at the holder's option, for paid-up shares in the company of the same amount as the face value of the debentures, where such an issue is a means of allotting shares at a discount[3].

1 *Re Compagnie Générale de Bellegarde, Campbell's Case* (1876) 4 ChD 470; *Re Anglo-Danubian Steam Navigation and Colliery Co* (1875) LR 20 Eq 339; cf *Re Regent's Canal Ironworks Co* (1876) 3 ChD 43, CA.
2 *Campbell's Case* (1876) 4 ChD 470. As to the disclosure of interests in debentures held by a director see the Companies Act 1985 s 324(1) and para 564 ante.
3 *Mosely v Koffyfontein Mines Ltd* [1904] 2 Ch 108, CA. See further *Famatina Development Corpn Ltd v Bury* [1910] AC 439, HL; and as to the statutory prohibition on the allotment of shares at a discount see paras 187, 465 ante. As to registration of debentures see para 1299 post.

1272. Reissue of debentures. Where, at any time, a company has redeemed debentures previously issued, then, unless provision to the contrary, whether express or implied, is contained in the articles or in any contract entered into by the company, or unless, by passing a resolution to that effect or by some other act, the company has manifested its intention that the debentures are to be cancelled, the company has, and is deemed always to have had, power to reissue the debentures, either by reissuing the same debentures or by issuing other debentures in their place[1]. On a reissue of redeemed debentures, the person entitled to the debentures has, and is deemed always to have had, the same priorities as if the debentures had never been redeemed[2]. Where a company has power to reissue debentures which have been redeemed, particulars with respect to the debentures which may be so reissued must be included as a note to the company's accounts[3].

Where a company has, at any time, deposited any of its debentures to secure advances from time to time on current account or otherwise, the debentures are not deemed to have been redeemed by reason only of the company's account having ceased to be in debit whilst the debentures remained so deposited[4].

The reissue of a debenture or the issue of another debenture in its place under the power which by these provisions is given to or deemed to be possessed by a company is to be treated as the issue of a new debenture for the purpose of stamp duty[5]; but it is not to be so treated for the purpose of any provision limiting the amount or number of debentures to be issued[6]. This applies whenever the issue or reissue was made[6]. A person lending money on the security of a debenture so reissued which appears to be duly stamped may give the debenture in evidence in any proceedings for enforcing his security without payment of the stamp duty or any penalty in respect of it, unless he had notice or, but for his negligence, might have discovered, that the debenture was not duly stamped; but in that case the company is liable to pay the proper stamp duty and penalty[7].

Where any debentures which were redeemed before 1 November 1929[8] have been reissued after that date and before 1 July 1948[9] or are or have been reissued after that date, the reissue does not prejudice, and is deemed never to have prejudiced, any right or priority which any person would have had under or by virtue of any mortgage or charge created before that date if the corresponding provisions in the Companies (Consolidation) Act 1908[10], as originally enacted, had been enacted[11] in the Companies Act 1948 and the Companies Act 1985, instead of the corresponding provisions in those Acts respectively[12].

Under the usual modification power in a debenture trust deed the deed may be altered so as to give a right to reissue debentures[13].

1 Companies Act 1985 s 194(1). The new debentures must contain the same terms as the originals with the same date for redemption: *Re Antofagasta (Chile) and Bolivia Rly Co Ltd's Trust Deed, Antofagasta (Chile) and Bolivia Rly Co Ltd's Trust Deed v Schroeder* [1939] Ch 732, [1939] 2 All ER 461.

2 Companies Act 1985 s 194(2).

3 See ibid s 228(1), Sch 4 para 41(2) and para 841 ante.

4 Ibid s 194(3).

5 As to stamp duty see para 1292 post.

6 Companies Act 1985 s 194(4).

7 Ibid s 194(5).

8 Ie the commencement date of the Companies Act 1928 (repealed).

9 Ie the commencement date of the Companies Act 1948 (repealed).

10 Ie the Companies (Consolidation) Act 1908 s 104 (repealed), which provided that, upon the reissue of redeemed debentures, the person entitled to the debentures would have the same rights and priorities as if the debentures had not previously been issued.

11 Ibid s 104 (repealed) was amended by the Companies Act 1928 s 45 (repealed), with a saving in relation to debentures redeemed before 1 November 1929 and reissued thereafter.

12 Companies Consolidation (Consequential Provisions) Act 1985 s 13. The corresponding provisions are the Companies Act 1948 s 90 (repealed) and the Companies Act 1985 s 194.

13 *Re Kent Collieries Ltd, Day v Kent Collieries Ltd* (1907) 23 TLR 559, CA. As to the power of modification see para 1286 post; and as to the registration of reissued debentures see para 1306 text and notes 4, 5 post.

1273. Priority. Subject to the necessity of registration[1], the ordinary rules regulating the priority of mortgages[2] apply to debentures, including the ordinary equitable rules relating to marshalling and subrogation[3].

If two successive securities are created by a company, both of which purport to give a first floating charge, the security which is prior in date will take priority over that which is later in date, whether or not the holders of the later security have notice of the earlier one[4]. If a series of first debentures is not secured by legal mortgage and a series of second debentures is secured by a legal mortgage of specific property, the first series giving only a floating charge, then, as to the specific property, the second debentures rank in priority to the first debentures, unless the specific charge is made subject to the prior floating charge[5].

1 See para 1299 post.
2 See MORTGAGE vol 32 para 551 et seq.
3 *P X Nuclear Cameron v A M F International* (1982) 16 NIJB.
4 *Smith v English and Scottish Mercantile Investment Trust Ltd* (1896) 40 Sol Jo 717; *Re Benjamin Cope & Sons Ltd* [1914] 1 Ch 800; but distinguish *Re Automatic Bottle Makers* [1926] Ch 412, CA (where the trust deed creating the first floating charge reserved to the company power to mortgage certain specific assets and it was held that the power might be exercised by the creation of a floating charge over those assets with priority over the first charge). A second debenture does not acquire priority over a first debenture which is not registered within the time limit where the time is subsequently extended and the first debenture is registered within the time as so extended: *Watson v Duff Morgan and Vermont (Holdings) Ltd* [1974] 1 All ER 794, [1974] 1 WLR 450, following *Ram Narain v Radha Kishen Moti Lal Chamaria Firm* (1929) LR 57 Ind App 76, PC, in preference to *Re Monolithic Building Co, Tacon v Monolithic Building Co* [1915] 1 Ch 643, CA. See also para 1299 note 21 post.
5 *Re Robert Stephenson & Co Ltd* [1913] 2 Ch 201, CA; *Re Camden Brewery Ltd* (1911) 106 LT 598n, CA; and as to the power of a company to charge specifically property subject to a floating charge, the restrictions which may be imposed on that power and the effect of those restrictions see para 1260 et seq ante.

1274. Priorities of debenture holders. Where debentures contain a charge upon property, but nothing is stated as to their being a series or ranking pari passu in point of charge, they rank in priority in order of time of issue[1], even when all are issued on the same day[2]. As a general rule, however, debentures provide that all the debentures constituting the series are to rank pari passu as a charge upon the property charged. If so, on a division of the proceeds of realisation between the various debenture holders, some of whom have been paid interest up to the date of the crystallisation of the charge, those who have not been paid interest are not entitled to be paid arrears of interest before the proceeds are distributed; but the amount due to each holder for capital and interest must be ascertained and the proceeds divided pari passu according to the amounts so due to each[3].

When part of a series of first debentures remains unissued, and then there is another series of debentures expressed to be subject to the previous series, any of the first debentures issued after the second series ranks in priority to the second series[4]. A holder of second debentures ranking after an issue of first debentures may not set off the debt due on his second debentures against a debt due from him to the company[5].

1 *James v Boythorpe Colliery Co* (1890) 2 Meg 55.
2 *Gartside v Silkstone and Dodworth Coal and Iron Co* (1882) 21 ChD 762; *Howard v Patent Ivory Manufacturing Co, Re Patent Ivory Manufacturing Co* (1888) 38 ChD 156 at 171.
3 *Re Midland Express Ltd, Pearson v Midland Express Ltd* [1914] 1 Ch 41, CA.
4 *Lister v Henry Lister & Son Ltd* (1893) 62 LJ Ch 568.
5 *H Wilkins & Elkington Ltd v Milton* (1916) 32 TLR 618.

D. TRANSFER OF DEBENTURES

1275. Transfer of debentures by delivery. Being a negotiable instrument[1], a bearer debenture is transferable by delivery so as to pass the property in it to a holder for value in good faith, and entitle him, upon delivery of it to the company, to obtain payment of the principal secured when due, and to sue in his own name upon the debenture[2].

1 *Bechuanaland Exploration Co v London Trading Bank* [1898] 2 QB 658; *Edelstein v Schuler & Co* [1902] 2 KB 144. Cf *Goodwin v Robarts* (1876) 1 App Cas 476, HL, apparently overruling *Crouch v Crédit Foncier of England* (1873) LR 8 QB 374 (where it was held that the company might lawfully refuse to pay the bona fide transferee for value of a stolen debenture payable to bearer, even though he had no notice of the theft: see *Bechuanaland Exploration Co v London Trading Bank* supra at 669 et seq per Kennedy J).

2 In certain cases decided before the negotiability of bearer debentures had been fully established (see note 1 supra), the holder for value in good faith of a bearer debenture was held entitled to prove on the debentures without being subject to equities between the company and the persons to whom the debentures were originally issued: see *Re Blakely Ordnance Co, ex p New Zealand Corpn* (1867) 3 Ch App 154; *Re General Estates Co, ex p City Bank* (1868) 3 Ch App 758 (where the question arose whether the instrument was not in fact a promissory note); *Re Imperial Land Co of Marseilles, ex p Colborne and Strawbridge* (1870) LR 11 Eq 478 at 490, 491, 494 (where the question also arose whether the instrument was a promissory note). Contrast *Re Natal Investment Co, Financial Corpn Claim* (1868) 3 Ch App 355; but see comments on the last-mentioned case in *Re General Estates Co, ex p City Bank* supra at 762; *Re Imperial Land Co of Marseilles, ex p Colborne and Strawbridge* supra at 493; *Higgs v Assam Tea Co* (1869) LR 4 Exch 387 at 395; *Crouch v Crédit Foncier of England* (1873) LR 8 QB 374 at 385; *Re Romford Canal Co, Pocock's Claim, Trickett's Claim, Carew's Claim* (1883) 24 ChD 85 at 91, 92.

1276. Transfer of debentures by instrument. According to the ordinary form, a registered debenture is legally transferable only by an instrument of transfer duly executed or signed and by registration in the company's books. The conditions of registered debentures usually provide that the company must keep a register of the debentures at its registered office, containing the names, addresses and descriptions of the registered holders and particulars of the debentures held by them respectively; that every transfer must be in writing under the hand of the registered holder or his legal personal representatives; that, upon delivery of the transfer at the registered office with the prescribed fee and such evidence of identity or title as the company may reasonably require, the transfer is to be registered, and a note of the registration is to be indorsed on the debenture; and that the company will be entitled to retain the transfer[1]. The simplified form of transfer introduced by the Stock Transfer Act 1963 applies to debentures[2].

When the principal and interest secured by the debenture are to be paid to the registered holder for the time being without regard to any equities subsisting between the company and the original or any intermediate holder, and the conditions as to transfer are similar to those mentioned above, a liquidator is bound to register the transfer, even if made after the liquidation commenced, and after judgment in a debenture holders' action, but before any notice of a claim by the company against the transferor[3].

1 Under such provisions a person entitled by transmission is not bound to produce a transfer before registration: *Edwards v Ransomes and Rapier Ltd* (1930) 143 LT 594.

2 See the Stock Transfer Act 1963 ss 1, 4(1) (as amended) and para 506 ante.

3 *Re Goy & Co Ltd, Farmer v Goy & Co Ltd* [1900] 2 Ch 149; cf *Re Palmer's Decoration and Furnishing Co* [1904] 2 Ch 743; *Re Brown and Gregory Ltd, Shepheard v Brown and Gregory Ltd, Andrews v Brown and Gregory Ltd* [1904] 1 Ch 627; *Re Richard Smith & Co* [1901] 1 IR 73; *Re Rhodesia Goldfields Ltd* [1910] 1 Ch 239.

1277. Necessity for proper instrument of transfer. Notwithstanding anything in the articles of a company, it is not lawful for a company to register a transfer of its debentures unless a proper instrument of transfer[1] has been delivered to the company or the transfer is an exempt transfer within the Stock Transfer Act 1982[2] or is in accordance with regulations made[3] under the Companies Act 1989[4]; but this does not prejudice any power of the company to register as a debenture holder any person to whom the right to any debentures of the company has been transmitted by operation of law[5].

1 As to instruments of transfer see para 505 note 3 ante.
2 As to exempt transfers within the Stock Transfer Act 1982, which in its relation to companies affects only debentures issued by the Agricultural Mortgage Corporation PLC, the Commonwealth Development Finance Company Ltd, Finance for Industry Public Limited Company and the Scottish Agricultural Securities Corporation Ltd, see s 2, Sch 1 para 6(1) and STOCK EXCHANGE vol 45 para 125. See also *Re Greene, Greene v Greene* [1949] Ch 333, [1949] 1 All ER 167.
3 Ie under the Companies Act 1989 s 207: see para 496 note 4 ante.
4 Companies Act 1985 s 183(1) (amended by the Uncertificated Securities Regulations 1995, SI 1995/3272, reg 40(2)(a)).
5 Companies Act 1985 s 183(2). As to transmission by operation of law see para 518 ante.

1278. Notice of refusal to register transfer. If a company refuses to register a transfer of debentures, it must, within two months after the date on which the transfer was lodged with it, send to the transferee notice of the refusal[1]. If default is made in complying with this provision, the company, and every officer of it who is in default, is liable on summary conviction to a fine not exceeding one-fifth of the statutory maximum and, on conviction after continued contravention, to a daily default fine not exceeding one-fiftieth of the statutory maximum[2].

1 Companies Act 1985 s 183(5).
2 Ibid ss 183(6), 730, Sch 24. For the meaning of 'officer who in default', 'the statutory maximum' and 'daily default fine' see para 1161 ante.

1279. Forged transfers. If the company registers a forged transfer of debentures, the true owner may obtain a cancellation of the registration and the delivery of the debentures[1]; or, if the debentures are redeemed by the company and the sums secured are paid to the transferee under a forged transfer, the company is primarily liable to the true owner for the sums so paid, without prejudice to any rights it may have against the transferee[2].

The provisions of the Forged Transfers Acts 1891 and 1892 apply to the debentures and debenture stock of a company, as well as to shares[3].

1 *Cottam v Eastern Counties Rly Co* (1860) 1 John & H 243 (where one of three trustees forged the signatures of his co-trustees).
2 See para 515 ante and the cases there cited relating to transfers of shares and stock.
3 See para 516 ante.

1280. Transfer of debenture by way of mortgage. The principles applicable to mortgages of shares apply to mortgages of debentures which are transferable by registration of an instrument of transfer in the company's books[1].

1 See para 519 ante.

1281. Certification of transfers. The certification by a company of any instrument of transfer of its debentures is to be taken as a representation by it to any person acting on the faith of the certification that there have been produced to the company such documents as on their face show a prima facie title to the debentures in the transferor named in the instrument of transfer (which includes a brokers transfer[1]), but is not to be taken as a representation that the transferor has any title to the debentures[2]. Where, however, a person acts on the faith of a false certification by a company made negligently, the company is under the same liability to him as if the certification had been made fraudulently[3].

For the purposes of the above provisions:

(1) an instrument of transfer is deemed to be certificated if it bears the words 'certificate lodged', or words to the like effect[4];

(2) the certification of an instrument of transfer is deemed made by a company if the person issuing the instrument is a person authorised to issue certificated instruments of transfer on the company's behalf and the certification is signed by a person authorised to certificate transfers on the company's behalf or by an officer or servant either of the company or of a body corporate so authorised[5];

(3) a certification is deemed to be signed by a person if it purports to be authenticated by his signature or initials, whether handwritten or not, and it is not shown that the signature or initials was or were placed there neither by himself nor by a person authorised to use the signature or initials for the purpose of certificating transfers on the company's behalf[6].

1 See the Stock Transfer Act 1963 s 2(2) and para 506 ante.
2 Companies Act 1985 s 184(1); and see *Bishop v Balkis Consolidated Co Ltd* (1890) 25 QBD 512 at 519, 520, CA.
3 Companies Act 1985 s 184(2).
4 Ibid s 184(3)(a).
5 Ibid s 184(3)(b).
6 Ibid s 184(3)(c).

1282. Issue of debentures and certificates. Unless the conditions of issue of the debentures or debenture stock otherwise provide, every company must, within two months after the allotment of any of its debentures or debenture stock, and within two months after the date on which a transfer[1] of any such debentures or debenture stock is lodged with it, complete and have ready for delivery the debentures and the certificates of all debenture stock allotted or transferred[2].

This provision does not apply in the case of a transfer to any person where, by virtue of regulations under the Stock Transfer Act 1982[3], he is not entitled to a certificate or other document of, or evidencing title in respect of, the debentures or debenture stock transferred; but, if in such a case the transferee subsequently becomes entitled to such a certificate or other document by virtue of any provision of those regulations and gives notice in writing of that fact to the company, the above provision has effect as if the reference to the date of the lodging of the transfer were a reference to the date of the notice[4].

A company of which debentures are or debenture stock is allotted to a recognised clearing house[5] or a nominee[6] of a recognised clearing house or of a recognised investment exchange[7], or with which a transfer is lodged for transferring any debentures or debenture stock of the company to such a clearing house or nominee, is not required, in consequence of the allotment or the lodging of the transfer, to comply with the above provisions[8].

If default is made in complying with the above provisions, the company, and every officer of it who is in default, is liable on summary conviction to a fine not exceeding one-fifth of the statutory maximum and, on conviction after continued contravention, to a daily default fine not exceeding one-fiftieth of the statutory maximum[9].

If a company on which a notice has been served requiring it to make good any default in complying with this provision, fails to make good the default within ten days after the service of the notice, the court may, on the application[10] of the person entitled to have the certificates or the debentures delivered to him, make an order directing the company and any officer of it to make good the default within such time as may be specified in the order; and any such order may provide that all costs of and incidental to the application are to be borne by the company or any officer of it responsible for the default[11].

1 For these purposes, the expression 'transfer' means a transfer duly stamped and otherwise valid or an exempt transfer within the Stock Transfer Act 1982 (see STOCK EXCHANGE) and does not include such a transfer as for any reason the company is entitled to refuse to register and does not register: Companies Act 1985 s 185(2).
2 Ibid s 185(1). See also para 482 text and note 3 ante.
3 Ie the Stock Transfer Act 1982 s 3: see para 1277 ante. This relates to a computer-based system of transfer established by the Bank of England and the Stock Exchange for the transfer of 'specified securities' as defined in s 2. At present only the securities listed in ibid Sch 1 (as amended) (securities traded in the gilt-edged market), the Stock Transfer (Specified Securities) Order 1988, SI 1988/231, art 2, Schedule and the Stock Transfer (Specified Securities) Order 1991, SI 1991/340, art 2, Schedule are so specified: see STOCK EXCHANGE.
4 Companies Act 1985 s 185(3).
5 For the meaning of 'recognised clearing house' see para 482 note 6 ante.
6 No person is a nominee for this purpose unless he is a person designated for this purpose in the rules of the recognised investment exchange in question: Companies Act 1985 s 185(4) (amended by the Financial Services Act 1986 s 194(5)(c)). See STOCK EXCHANGE.
7 For the meaning of 'recognised investment exchange' see para 223 note 1 ante.
8 Companies Act 1985 s 185(4) (amended by the Financial Services Act 1986 s 194(5)(d)). In the case of an unregistered company (see para 1765 et seq post) the Companies Act 1985 s 185(4) (as so amended) has effect as if for the words 'subsection (1)' there were substituted 'any provision of any instrument constituting or regulating the company': Companies (Unregistered Companies) Regulations 1985, SI 1985/680, reg 6(e).
9 Companies Act 1985 ss 185(5), 730, Sch 24. For the meaning of 'officer who is in default', 'the statutory maximum' and 'daily default fine' see para 1161 ante.
10 The application is by originating summons in the expedited form: RSC Ord 102 r 2(1),(2).
11 Companies Act 1985 s 185(6),(7). As to the procedure see para 484 ante.

E. EQUITIES AFFECTING DEBENTURES

1283. Freedom from equities. Debenture conditions are usually so framed as to give the registered holder for the time being the absolute right to receive the money secured by the debentures, and similar conditions are used in the case of debenture stock[1]. The usual conditions in the case of debentures make the principal money and interest payable to the registered holder without regard to any equities subsisting between the company and the original or any intermediate holder. Such a provision is binding upon the company[2]. The conditions also usually provide that the registered holder's receipt shall be a good discharge for the money secured, and that the company shall not be bound to inquire into his title or to take notice of any trust affecting that money, or be affected by notice, express or implied, of the right or claim of any other person to that money or instrument[3].

In the absence of any special conditions, the assignee of a debenture takes it subject to any equities subsisting between the company and the original holder, even though the assignment was for value and the assignee had no notice of the circumstances giving rise to such equities[4]. The company may, however, be estopped from setting up such equities against the assignee either by the form of the debenture itself[5], or by registering the transferee as the holder[6], by accepting notice of assignment, even though it does not register the transfer[7], by informing the transferee that registration is unnecessary[8], by previous contract[9], or by a judgment previously recovered against the company for interest on the debentures[10].

1 As to bearer debentures being negotiable see para 1275 ante.
2 *Re Goy & Co Ltd, Farmer v Goy & Co Ltd* [1900] 2 Ch 149; *Robinson v Montgomeryshire Brewery Co* [1896] 2 Ch 841; *Hilger Analytical Ltd v Rank Precision Industries Ltd* [1984] BCLC 301; and see the cases cited in para 1276 note 3 ante.
3 *Re Blakely Ordnance Co, ex p New Zealand Banking Corpn* (1867) 3 Ch App 154.
4 *Athenaeum Life Assurance Society v Pooley* (1858) 3 De G & J 294; *Re China SS Co, ex p Mackenzie* (1869) LR 7 Eq 240; *Re Natal Investment Co, Financial Corpn Claim* (1868) 3 Ch App 355; *Christie v Taunton, Delmard, Lane & Co, Re Taunton, Delmard, Lane & Co* [1893] 2 Ch 175. It is otherwise if a document, which is called a debenture, is a negotiable instrument: *Re General Estates Co, ex p City Bank* (1868) 3 Ch App 758; *Re Imperial Land Co of Marseilles, ex p Colborne and Strawbridge* (1870) LR 11 Eq 478; and see para 1275 note 2 ante.
5 *Higgs v Assam Tea Co* (1869) LR 4 Exch 387; *Re General Estates Co, ex p City Bank* (1868) 3 Ch App 758; *Re Agra and Masterman's Bank, ex p Asiatic Banking Corpn* (1867) 2 Ch App 391; *Hilger Analytical Ltd v Rank Precision Industries Ltd* [1984] BCLC 301.
6 *Higgs v Assam Tea Co* (1869) LR 4 Exch 387; *Re Northern Assam Tea Co, ex p Universal Life Assurance Co* (1870) LR 10 Eq 458; and see *Re South Essex Estuary Co, Carey's Claim* [1873] WN 17.
7 *Re Hercules Insurance Co, Brunton's Claim* (1874) LR 19 Eq 302; *Christie v Taunton, Delmard, Lane & Co, Re Taunton, Delmard, Lane & Co* [1893] 2 Ch 175.
8 *Re Colonial and General Gas Co, Lishman's Claim* (1870) 23 LT 40.
9 *Higgs v Assam Tea Co* (1869) LR 4 Exch 387; *Dickson v Swansea Vale Rly Co* (1868) LR 4 QB 44.
10 *Re South Essex Gas-Light and Coke Co, Hulett's Case* (1862) 2 John & H 306; *Re South Essex Estuary Co, ex p Chorley* (1870) LR 11 Eq 157. As to irregularities in issue see para 1244 ante.

1284. Clogging the equity of redemption. Debentures and other mortgages or charges issued by a company are not excepted from the rule against clogging the equity of redemption[1]. Thus, in the case of a loan to a company on the security of a mortgage of debenture stock, an option given to the lender to purchase the stock within a certain period at a discount is a clog on the equity of redemption and void[2]. A term in a debenture providing for payment of a bonus out of the net profit of the company for an unlimited period until the amount specified has been discharged constitutes a clog on the equity[3]; but a term in a debenture giving the holder a right in a winding up to share in surplus assets is not a clog on the equity[4]. A debenture may be made irredeemable[5].

1 *Jarrah Timber and Wood Paving Corpn Ltd v Samuel* [1903] 2 Ch 1 at 11, CA (affd sub nom *Samuel v Jarrah Timber and Wood Paving Corpn Ltd* [1904] AC 323, HL); and see *Noakes & Co Ltd v Rice* [1902] AC 24, HL; *Browne v Ryan* [1901] 2 IR 653, CA; *Bradley v Carritt* [1903] AC 253, HL; *Knightsbridge Estates Trust Ltd v Byrne* [1940] AC 613, [1940] 2 All ER 401, HL. Cf *De Beers Consolidated Mines Ltd v British South Africa Co* [1912] AC 52, HL; *Kreglinger v New Patagonia Meat and Cold Storage Co Ltd* [1914] AC 25, HL, in both of which cases it was held that the stipulation claimed to be a clog on the equity formed part of a collateral contract, in the first-named case independent of the mortgage, in the second-named case as a condition of the company obtaining the loan. See further MORTGAGE vol 32 para 585 et seq.
2 *Jarrah Timber and Wood Paving Corpn Ltd v Samuel* [1903] 2 Ch 1, CA; affd sub nom *Samuel v Jarrah Timber and Wood Paving Corpn Ltd* [1904] AC 323, HL.

3 *Re Rainbow Syndicate Ltd, Owen v Rainbow Syndicate Ltd* [1916] WN 178.
4 *Re Cuban Land Co Ltd* [1921] 2 Ch 147.
5 See para 1255 ante.

1285. Set-off. A debenture holder cannot set off a debt due from him to the company against the amount due from the company to him on his debentures. Before winding up[1] a company may set off a call made on a member against money owing to him on registered debentures, even though prior to the date of the call he has equitably mortgaged his debentures, provided that no notice of the mortgage has been given to the company before the calls were made[2].

1 *Re Brown and Gregory Ltd* [1904] 1 Ch 627.
2 *Christie v Taunton, Delmard, Lane & Co, Re Taunton, Delmard, Lane & Co* [1893] 2 Ch 175.

F. MODIFICATION OF RIGHTS; MEETINGS

1286. Modification clause. It is common to insert in debenture trust deeds, and in the conditions indorsed on debentures, provisions for calling meetings of the debenture holders and enabling a specified majority to bind the whole body of holders to a modification, compromise or release of their rights against the company or the security.

Under a power to sanction any modification or compromise of the debenture holders' rights a mortgage may be given priority over the debentures[1], or the date of payment may be postponed[2], or redeemable debentures may be converted into irredeemable debentures[3], or the company may be permitted to redeem debentures below par at a price which is in excess of the stock exchange quotation[4]. In such cases the court will not imply a condition that the power should be exercised only in the event of some serious occasion arising[5]. The power does not, however, allow the majority of the debenture holders to authorise a sale of the company's assets and the appropriation of the proceeds of sale in redeeming debentures by the purchase at the lowest price tendered after an invitation to the debenture holders[6]; nor does it authorise the debenture holders to delegate to a committee the power of further modifying the scheme for modification to which they have agreed[7]. The extinction of rights against the company, as by accepting shares in a new company in exchange for the debentures, is neither a 'modification' nor a 'compromise' of rights[8] unless there is some dispute or difficulty in enforcing those rights[9].

Under a power to sanction any compromise or arrangement which the court would have jurisdiction to sanction[10], guarantors of debentures may be released from their guarantee, interest may be increased, new trustees of the debenture trust deed may be appointed, and payments to a sinking fund established by the debenture trust deed may be discontinued[11], or debenture holders may be bound to accept preference shares in a new company, to which the assets charged by the debentures are sold, in lieu of their debentures[12]. Where, however, there is no express power to compromise, a mere power given to the majority to bind all the debenture holders as if they had consented does not enable the majority to bind the whole body to an arrangement whereby the rights declared by the trust deed are altered[13].

1 *Follit v Eddystone Granite Quarries* [1892] 3 Ch 75; cf *Re Dominion of Canada Freehold Estate and Timber Co Ltd* (1886) 55 LT 347.
2 *Finlay v Mexican Investment Corpn* [1897] 1 QB 517; and see *Walker v Elmore's German and Austro-Hungarian Metal Co Ltd* (1901) 85 LT 767, CA.

3 *Northern Assurance Co Ltd v Farnham United Breweries Ltd* [1912] 2 Ch 125; *Re Joseph Stocks & Co Ltd* (1909) [1912] 2 Ch 134n.
4 *Meade-King v Usher's Wiltshire Brewery Ltd* (1928) 44 TLR 298.
5 *Northern Assurance Co Ltd v Farnham United Breweries Ltd* [1912] 2 Ch 125.
6 *Re New York Taxicab Co Ltd, Sequin v New York Taxicab Co Ltd* [1913] 1 Ch 1.
7 *British America Nickel Corpn v M J O'Brien Ltd* [1927] AC 369, PC.
8 *Mercantile Investment and General Trust Co v International Co of Mexico* (1891) cited at [1893] 1 Ch 484n, CA; cf *Re Labuan and Borneo Ltd* (1901) 18 TLR 216. Such a transaction may be effected under a power to sanction a scheme for reconstruction or amalgamation: see *Re W H Hutchinson & Sons Ltd* (1915) 31 TLR 324.
9 *Sneath v Valley Gold Ltd* [1893] 1 Ch 477, CA; *Mercantile Investment and General Trust Co v River Plate Trust, Loan and Agency Co* [1894] 1 Ch 578; and see *Wright v Revelstoke* (1914) Times, 7 February.
10 See para 1447 et seq post.
11 *Shaw v Royce Ltd* [1911] 1 Ch 138.
12 *Re Labuan and Borneo Ltd* (1901) 18 TLR 216.
13 *Hay v Swedish and Norwegian Rly Co* (1889) 5 TLR 460, CA.

1287. Meetings. In connection with the modification of rights clause[1], it is usual to provide in the case of debentures, where the issue is small, that the power may be exercised by writing under the hand of the holders of a specified nominal amount of the debentures; but, where the power is contained in a debenture trust deed, provisions are usually inserted for the power to be exercised by a resolution passed at a meeting of the debenture holders[2]. These provisions are also usually inserted in debentures where the issue is large and is not secured by a trust deed. For purposes of voting at such meetings, persons entitled to an immediate issue of debentures, but to whom certificates have not been issued, are entitled to vote[3]. A debenture holder may vote at a meeting as his interest directs, although, in so voting, he must act in good faith with reference to the interests of the debenture holders as a class; and a majority of debenture holders will not be allowed to oppress a minority[4].

The provisions of the Companies Act 1985 relating to the representation of corporations at meetings of shareholders of another company apply in the same way in the case of meetings of holders of debentures, whether held in pursuance of that Act or any rules made under it, or in pursuance of the provisions contained in any debenture or trust deed[5].

1 See para 1286 ante.
2 The court will compel a company to hold a meeting of debenture holders pursuant to the provisions relating thereto: *Newhouse v Northern Light, Power and Coal Co Ltd* (1915) 139 LT Jo 540.
3 *Dey v Rubber and Mercantile Corpn Ltd* [1923] 2 Ch 528.
4 *Goodfellow v Nelson Line (Liverpool) Ltd* [1912] 2 Ch 324; *British America Nickel Corpn v M J O'Brien Ltd* [1927] AC 369, PC.
5 As to the representation of corporations at meetings see para 678 ante.

1288. Arrangements and compromises. The rights of holders of debentures or debenture stock may be modified by a scheme sanctioned under the statutory provisions relating to arrangements and reconstruction[1]. In an action to administer the trusts of a deed securing debentures or debenture stock, the court may also approve a compromise and bind absent debenture holders, if satisfied that the compromise is for their benefit and that it is expedient to exercise the power; but they are not bound if the order has been obtained by fraud or non-disclosure of material facts[2]. Only non-assenting persons may be so bound; dissentients are not bound and are entitled to payment in full[3]; but they may be compelled to claim within a certain time or be excluded[4].

1 See the Companies Act 1985 s 425 (as amended) and para 1447 et seq post.
2 See RSC Ord 15 r 13(4) and PRACTICE AND PROCEDURE vol 37 para 235.
3 *Collingham v Sloper, Foreign, American and General Investments Trust Co v Sloper* [1894] 3 Ch 716, CA.
4 *Saragossa and Mediterranean Rly Co v Collingham* [1904] AC 159, HL.

G. REDEMPTION OF DEBENTURES

1289. Time for redemption. Debentures of a company become redeemable at the time or on the happening of any of the events specified in the debentures or debenture conditions, or in the trust deed securing the debentures; and the happening of any one or more of such events entitles the company to make immediate repayment and call for a reconveyance of the property charged[1]. Provision is sometimes made for redemption by means of a sinking fund, and for the debentures to be redeemed by drawings[2]. An option is often given to the company at any time after a specified date to redeem at a premium. Unless otherwise agreed, debentures are not redeemable before the date or event specified in them[3]. Where debentures are to be redeemed on or after a specified date, the company may, but is not liable to, redeem them on that date, but it must redeem them on demand after that date[4]. The word 'redeemable', as used in debentures, implies an option and not an obligation to redeem[5].

1 *Re Simmer and Jack East Ltd* (1913) 108 LT 488 (explaining *Re General Motor Cab Co Ltd* (1912) 56 Sol Jo 573 as having decided merely that trustees of a trust deed are not bound to reconvey unless all the debenture holders secured by the trust deed have been satisfied); and see para 1255 ante (perpetual debenture).
2 Periodical drawings of this kind are not within the Lotteries and Amusements Act 1976: see *Wallingford v Mutual Society* (1880) 5 App Cas 685 at 696, 697, 701, 702, HL; cf *Sykes v Beadon* (1879) 11 ChD 170 at 185. As to lotteries see the Lotteries and Amusements Act 1976 Pt I (ss 1-6) (as amended) and BETTING vol 4(1) (Reissue) para 153 et seq. If the debentures to be paid off are to be determined by ballot but provide for their repayment on and after a fixed date, the debentures become repayable after that date, even though no ballot is held: *Re Tewkesbury Gas Co, Tysoe v Tewkesbury Gas Co* [1911] 2 Ch 279; affd [1912] 1 Ch 1, CA.
3 *Hooper v Western Counties and South Wales Telephone Co Ltd* (1892) 68 LT 78.
4 *Re Tewkesbury Gas Co, Tysoe v Tewkesbury Gas Co* [1912] 1 Ch 1, CA.
5 *Re Chicago and North West Granaries Co Ltd, Morrison v Chicago and North West Granaries Co Ltd* [1898] 1 Ch 263; and see *Re Joseph Stocks & Co Ltd* (1909) [1912] 2 Ch 134n; *Edinburgh Corpn v British Linen Bank* [1913] AC 133, HL.

1290. Place of redemption; winding up. If debentures are made payable at a particular place, they must be presented for payment at that place before there can be default in payment[1]. Where no place is fixed, the ordinary rule that a debtor must seek out his creditor applies[2].

The principal money becomes due at the commencement of a winding up, even if the stipulated time for payment has not arrived[3].

Debentures may be issued which are irredeemable or redeemable only on a contingency[4].

1 *Thorn v City Rice Mills* (1889) 40 ChD 357. Cf *Re Harris Calculating Machine Co Ltd* [1914] 1 Ch 920 (where the principal only, and not the interest, was made payable at a fixed place and it was held that default in payment of the principal had taken place because the company had not paid the interest after demand).

2 *Fowler v Midland Electric Corpn for Power Distribution Ltd* [1917] 1 Ch 656, CA.
3 *Hodson v Tea Co* (1880) 14 ChD 859; *Wallace v Universal Automatic Machines Co* [1894] 2 Ch 547, CA.
4 See para 1255 ante. As to clogging the equity see para 1284 ante.

H. STAMP DUTY

1291. Stamp duty on loan capital. No stamp duty is chargeable[1] on any statement of an amount proposed to be served by an issue of loan capital unless the obligation to deliver the statement arose before 1 January 1973[2].

1 Ie under the Finance Act 1899 s 8 (repealed).
2 Finance Act 1973 s 49(2). In any case where duty had been paid in respect of a statement on which, by virtue of s 49(2), duty was not chargeable, the company by whom it was paid might claim repayment of it: s 49(2).

1292. Exemptions for certain categories of loan capital. Stamp duty is not chargeable:
   (1) on the issue of an instrument which relates to loan capital or on the transfer of the loan capital constituted by, or transferable by means of, such an instrument[1];
   (2) on an instrument which transfers loan capital issued or raised by the financial support fund of the Organisation for Economic Co-operation and Development, the Inter-American Development Bank or an organisation which was a designated international organisation at the time of the transfer, whether or not it was such an organisation at the time the loan capital was issued or raised[2];
   (3) on an instrument which transfers any other loan capital except where it is an instrument transferring loan capital which, at the time the instrument is executed, carries a right, exercisable then or later, of conversion into shares or other securities, or to the acquisition of shares or other securities, including loan capital of the same description[3];
   (4) on an instrument transferring loan capital which, at the time the instrument is executed or any earlier time, carries or has carried:
      (a) a right to interest the amount of which exceeds a reasonable commercial return on the nominal amount of the capital;
      (b) a right to interest the amount of which falls or has fallen to be determined to any extent by reference to the results of, or of any part of, a business or to the value of any property; or
      (c) a right on repayment to an amount which exceeds the nominal amount of the capital and is not reasonably comparable with what is generally repayable, in respect of a similar nominal amount of capital, under the terms of issue of loan capital listed in the Official List of the Stock Exchange[4].

1 See the Finance Act 1986 ss 78(3), 79(2) and STAMP DUTIES vol 44(1) (Reissue) para 1101. As to the prospective repeal of s 79(2)–(8) see STAMP DUTIES vol 44(1) (Reissue) para 1101 note 12.
2 See ibid ss 78(4), 79(3) and STAMP DUTIES vol 44(1) (Reissue) para 1101.
3 See ibid s 79(4),(5) and STAMP DUTIES vol 44(1) (Reissue) para 1101.
4 See ibid 79(6) and STAMP DUTIES vol 44(1) (Reissue) para 1101.

I. REGISTER OF DEBENTURES

1293. Where register of debentures may be kept. A company registered in England and Wales may not keep in Scotland and a company registered in Scotland may not keep in England and Wales any register of holders of debentures of the company[1] or any duplicate of any such register or part of any such register which is kept outside Great Britain[2]. Neither a register of holders of debentures of a company nor a duplicate of any such register or part of any such register which is kept outside Great Britain may be kept in England and Wales, in the case of a company registered in England and Wales, or in Scotland, in the case of a company registered in Scotland, elsewhere than:

(1) at the company's registered office; or
(2) at any office of the company at which the work of making it up is done; or
(3) if the company arranges with some other person for the making up of the register or duplicate to be undertaken on its behalf by that other person, at the office of that other person at which the work is done[3].

Where a company keeps, in England and Wales or Scotland, as the case may be, both such a register and such a duplicate, it must keep them at the same place[4].

Every company which keeps any such register or duplicate in England and Wales or Scotland must send to the registrar of companies notice in the prescribed form[5] of the place where the register or duplicate is kept and of any change in that place[6]; but a company is not bound to send such notice where the register or duplicate has, at all times since it came into existence, been kept at the company's registered office[7].

1 There is no statutory provision requiring the keeping of such a register.
2 Companies Act 1985 s 190(1),(2). Cf the provisions as to custody of the register of members: see para 389 ante.
3 Ibid s 190(3).
4 Ibid s 190(4).
5 For the prescribed form of notice see the Companies (Forms) (Amendment) Regulations 1995, SI 1995/736, reg 3, Sch 2, Form 190.
6 Companies Act 1985 s 190(5).
7 Ibid s 190(6).

1294. Inspection of register of debentures. Except when the register of holders of debentures of a company is duly closed[1], every register of holders of debentures of a company must be open to the inspection of the registered holder of any such debentures or any holder of shares in the company without fee, and of any other person on payment of such fee as may be prescribed[2]. The company[3] must make the register available for such inspection for not less than two hours during the period between 9 am and 5 pm on each business day[4]; and it must permit a person inspecting the register to copy any information made available for inspection by means of the taking of notes or the transcription of the information[5]. A company is not, however, obliged to present for inspection a register of debenture holders maintained by it in a manner which groups together entries by reference to whether a debenture holder has given an address in a particular geographical location, is of a particular nationality, has a holding of a certain size, is a natural person or not or is of a particular gender[6]; nor is a company obliged, in providing a copy of a part of a register of debenture holders, to extract entries from the register by reference to whether a debenture holder has given an address in a particular geographical location, is of a particular nationality, has a holding of a certain size, is a natural person or not or is of a particular gender[7].

Any such registered holder of debentures or holder of shares, or any other person, may require a copy of the register of the holders of debentures of the company, or any part of it, on payment of such fee as may be prescribed[8]. A copy of any trust deed for securing an issue of debentures must be forwarded to every holder of any such debentures at his request on payment of such fee as may be prescribed[9].

If inspection is refused, or a copy is refused or not forwarded, the company, and every officer of it who is in default, is liable on summary conviction to a fine not exceeding one-fifth of the statutory maximum and, on conviction after continued contravention, to a daily default fine not exceeding one-fiftieth of the statutory maximum[10]. Where a company is so in default, the court may by order compel an immediate inspection of the register or direct that the copies required be sent to the person requiring them[11].

1 For these purposes, a register is deemed to be duly closed if closed in accordance with provisions contained in the articles or in the debentures, or, in the case of debenture stock, in the stock certificates, or in the trust deed or other document securing the debentures or debenture stock, during such period or periods, not exceeding in the whole 30 days in any year, as may be therein specified: Companies Act 1985 s 191(6). See also *Lemon v Austin Friars Investment Trust Ltd* [1926] Ch 1, CA. The right to inspect does not carry the right to make copies: see *Re Balaghât Gold Mining Co* [1901] 2 KB 665, CA. This right is impliedly excluded because the shareholder may obtain copies on payment. Cf the right to inspect the register of charges where no such provision for obtaining copies on payment is made: see para 1298 text and note 3 post. As to the right to appoint an agent to inspect see the cases cited in para 1298 note 3 post.

Without prejudice to any lesser period of limitation, liability incurred by a company from the making or deletion of an entry in its register of debenture holders, or from a failure to make or delete any such entry, is not enforceable more than 20 years after the date on which the entry was made or deleted or, in the case of any such failure, the failure first occurred: Companies Act 1985 s 191(7).

2 Ibid s 191(1) (amended by the Companies Act 1989 ss 143(4)(a), 212, Sch 24). The fee so prescribed is £2.50 for each hour or part thereof during which the right of inspection is exercised: Companies (Inspection and Copying of Registers, Indices and Documents) Regulations 1991, SI 1991/1998, reg 5, Sch 2 para 1(a). Cf the provisions as to inspection of the register of members: para 390 ante. As to the power to make regulations see para 230 ante.

3 For the meaning of 'company' see para 229 note 14 ante.

4 Companies (Inspection and Copying of Registers, Indices and Documents) Regulations 1991 reg 3(1), (2)(a). For the meaning of 'business day' see para 229 note 15 ante.

5 Ibid reg 3(1),(2)(b). Regulation 3(2)(b) is not, however, to be construed as obliging a company to provide any facilities additional to those provided for the purposes of facilitating inspection: reg 3(3).

6 Ibid reg 4(1),(2).

7 Ibid reg 4(1),(3).

8 Companies Act 1985 s 191(2) (amended by the Companies Act 1989 s 143(4)(b)). The fee so prescribed is, for the first 100 entries or part thereof copied, £2.50; for the next 1,000 entries or part thereof copied, £20.00; and, for every subsequent 1,000 entries or part thereof copied, £15.00: Companies (Inspection and Copying of Registers, Indices and Documents) Regulations 1991 Sch 2 para 2(a).

9 Companies Act 1985 s 191(3) (amended by the Companies Act 1989 s 143(4)(c), Sch 24). The fee so prescribed is ten pence per 100 words, or part thereof, copied: Companies (Inspection and Copying of Registers, Indices and Documents) Regulations 1991 Sch 2 para 3(a).

10 Companies Act 1985 ss 191(4), 730, Sch 24. For the meaning of 'officer who is in default', 'the statutory maximum' and 'daily default fine' see para 1161 ante.

11 Ibid s 191(5). The application is by originating summons in the expedited form: RSC Ord 102 r 2(1),(2). As to the procedure see para 69 ante.

1295. Register of debenture holders kept otherwise than in legible form. Where any register of holders of debentures of a company is kept by a company by recording the matters in question otherwise than in a legible form[1], a company registered in England and Wales may not perform the duty to allow inspection[2] of such a register in Scotland and a company registered in Scotland may not perform such duty in England and Wales[3]. Nor may a company perform the duty so to allow inspection of a register in England and Wales, in the case of a company registered in England and Wales, or in Scotland, in the case of a company registered in Scotland, elsewhere than at:

(1) the registered office of the company;

(2) any other office of the company at which the work of ensuring that the register is duly made up is done; or

(3) if the company arranges with some other person for the carrying out of such work to be undertaken on behalf of the company by that other person, the office of that other person at which the work is done[4].

The normal statutory requirements relating to registers of debenture holders[5] and annual returns[6] do not apply to such a register in so far as they relate to any of the following matters:

(a) the place where the register is permitted to be kept[7];

(b) the giving of notice to the registrar of companies of the place where the register is kept, or of any change in that place[7]; and

(c) the inclusion in the annual return of a statement[8] of the address of the place where the register is kept[9].

Where the place for inspection of such a register is in England and Wales or Scotland, the company must send to the registrar of companies notice in the prescribed form[10] of the place for inspection of that register and of any change in that place[11]. The company is not, however, obliged to give such notice:

(i) where it changes from keeping the register in a legible form to keeping it otherwise than in a legible form and the place for inspection of the register immediately following the change is the same as the place where the register was kept in a legible form immediately prior to the change; or

(ii) where since the register first came into existence it has been kept by recording the matters in question otherwise than in legible form, and the place for inspection has been the registered office of the company[12].

Where the place for inspection of a register is situated in England and Wales, in the case of a company registered in England and Wales, or in Scotland, in the case of a company registered in Scotland, elsewhere than at its registered office, the company must include in its annual return a statement of the address of that place[13]. If a company fails to comply with this provision, the company, and every officer of it who is in default, is liable on summary conviction to a fine not exceeding the statutory maximum and, on conviction after continued contravention, to a daily default fine not exceeding one-tenth of the statutory maximum[14].

Where a register of holders of debentures is kept by recording the matters in question otherwise than in legible form, any reference to such register in any provision of the Companies Act 1985 relating to the place where a duplicate[15] of such register, another register or duplicate of another register is required to be kept, is to be construed as a reference to the place for inspection of the first-mentioned register[16].

1 As to the provisions relating to the register of debenture holders kept in legible form see para 1293 ante.
2 As to the right of inspection of the register see para 1294 ante.
3 Companies (Registers and other Records) Regulations 1985, SI 1985/724, reg 4(1),(2).
4 Ibid reg 4(3).
5 Ie the Companies Act 1985 s 190: see para 1293 ante.
6 Ie ibid ss 363–365 (as substituted): see para 1062 et seq ante.
7 See para 1293 ante.
8 See para 1063 ante.
9 Companies (Registers and other Records) Regulations 1985 reg 4(4).
10 For the prescribed form of notice see the Companies (Registers and other Records) Regulations 1985 reg 5(1), Sch 2, Form 190a.
11 Ibid reg 5(1).
12 Ibid reg 5(2).
13 Ibid reg 5(3).

14 Companies Act 1985 ss 363(7), 730, Sch 24 (applied by the Companies (Registers and other Records) Regulations 1985 reg 5(4)). For the meaning of 'officer who is in default', 'the statutory maximum' and 'daily default fine' see para 1161 ante. For the purposes of the Companies Act 1985 s 363(7), a shadow director is deemed a director and officer: s 363(8). For the meaning of 'shadow director' see para 543 note 1 ante.

15 See eg ibid s 190(1)-(6) and para 1293 ante.

16 Companies (Registers and other Records) Regulations 1985 reg 6(1).

(iii) Registration of Charges

A. REGISTRATION AT THE COMPANY'S OFFICE

1296. Keeping copies of charges. •Every company must cause to be kept at its registered office a copy of every instrument creating any charge requiring registration either at the registered office[1] or at the registrar's office[2]; in the case of a series of uniform debentures, a copy of one debenture of the series is sufficient[3].

1 See para 1297 post.

2 Companies Act 1985 s 406(1). Section 406 is repealed from a day to be appointed by the Companies Act 1989 s 92(a) and replaced from a day to be appointed by the Companies Act 1985 s 411(1),(3) (substituted by the Companies Act 1989 ss 92(a), 101). At the date at which this volume states the law no such days had been appointed. As to the proposed new registration system generally see para 1316 post.

3 Companies Act 1985 s 406(2). See also note 2 supra.

1297. Company's register of charges. Every limited company[1] must keep at its registered office a register of charges[2] and enter in it all charges[3] specifically affecting property of the company, and all floating charges on the company's undertaking or any of its property, giving in each case a short description of the property charged, the amount of the charge and, except in the case of securities to bearer, the names of the persons entitled to it[4]. The property charged, not the instrument, is required to be registered[5].

The omission to enter a charge in the register does not invalidate the charge, even where it is given to a director or other officer of the company[6] or to a shareholder[7]. If an officer of the company knowingly and wilfully authorises or permits the omission of any such entry, he is liable on conviction on indictment to a fine, or on summary conviction to a fine not exceeding the statutory maximum[8]. 'Officer' includes a director, manager or secretary[9]. The company's bankers are not officers[10]; but the solicitor acting in the transaction is an officer[11]. Where directors instruct the secretary to register a charge and he omits to do so, they are not knowingly and wilfully authorising or permitting the omission[12].

1 For the general meaning of 'company' in the Companies Act 1985 Pt XII Ch I (ss 395-409) (as amended) see note 2 infra. For the meaning of 'limited company' see s 1(2) and para 80 ante.

2 The provisions of ibid Pt XII Ch I (ss 395-409 (as amended): registration of charges) extend to charges on property in England and Wales which are created, and to charges on property in England and Wales which is acquired, by a company, whether a company within the meaning of the Companies Act 1985 or not, incorporated outside Great Britain which has an established place of business in England and Wales: s 409(1). For the meaning of 'place of business' see para 63 note 1 ante. In relation to such a company s 406 (see para 1296 ante), and s 407 apply with the substitution, for the reference to the company's registered office, of a reference to its principal place of business in England and Wales: s 409(2). It does not matter that the company ought to have registered under Pt XXIII Ch 1 (ss 691-699 (as amended): see para 1790 et seq post) and did not, nor that it subsequently ceased to have a place of business in England and Wales. Further in s 395 (as amended) (see para 1299 post) as it applies to a

foreign company, the term 'liquidator' means either an English liquidator or the foreign equivalent: *N V Slavenburg's Bank v Intercontinental Natural Resources Ltd* [1980] 1 All ER 955, [1980] 1 WLR 1076. See also *Re Alton Corpn* [1985] BCLC 27. The Companies Act 1985 s 409 is repealed from a day to be appointed by the Companies Act 1989 s 92(b) and replaced from a day to be appointed by the Companies Act 1985 Pt XXIII Ch III (ss 703A–703N) (added by the Companies Act 1989 ss 92(b), 105, Sch 15). At the date at which this volume states the law no such days had been appointed. As to the proposed new registration system in respect of oversea companies generally see para 1827 post.

A company registered in Scotland must register charges over English properties with the registrar of companies in Scotland: Companies Act 1985 s 410(4)(a). Section 410 is repealed from a day to be appointed by the Companies Act 1989 s 92(a). At the date at which this volume states the law no such day had been appointed.

3 In the Companies Act 1985 Pt XII Ch I (ss 395–409) (as amended) 'charge' includes mortgage: s 396(4). Section 396(4) is repealed from a day to be appointed by the Companies Act 1989 s 92(a) and replaced from a day to be appointed by the Companies Act 1985 s 395(2) (substituted by the Companies Act 1989 ss 92(a), 93). At the date at which this volume states the law no such day had been appointed.

4 Companies Act 1985 s 407(1),(2). Section 407 is repealed from a day to be appointed by the Companies Act 1989 s 92(a) and replaced from a day to be appointed by the Companies Act 1985 s 411(2)–(4) (substituted by the Companies Act 1989 ss 92(a), 101). At the date at which this volume states the law no such days had been appointed. As to the proposed new registration system generally see para 1316 post.

As to the provisions applicable where the entries are not recorded in legible form see paras 655, 656 ante (register of charges) and para 1295 ante (register of debenture holders).

5 *Re South Durham Iron Co, Smith's Case* (1879) 11 ChD 579 at 585, CA per Jessel MR (mortgage by deposit). Copies of the instruments creating the charge must be open to inspection: see para 1298 post.

6 *Re Globe New Patent Iron and Steel Co* (1879) 48 LJ Ch 295; *Wright v Horton* (1887) 12 App Cas 371, HL (where Lord Halsbury LC relied to some extent on the fact that only creditors and members of the company could inspect the register; but the register is now open to public inspection: see para 1298 post).

7 *Re General South American Co* (1876) 2 ChD 337, CA.

8 Companies Act 1985 ss 407(3), 730, Sch 24. See also note 4 supra. For the meaning of 'the statutory maximum' see para 1161 ante.

9 Ibid s 744. For the meaning of 'officer' cf also para 1358 post.

10 *Re General Provident Assurance Co, ex p National Bank* (1872) LR 14 Eq 507. This case and those cited in notes 11, 12 infra were decided on the construction of the words of the Companies Act 1862 s 43 (repealed: see now the Companies Act 1985 s 407). Before the decision in *Wright v Horton* (1887) 12 App Cas 371, HL (cited in note 6 supra) it was not clear whether a further penalty was or was not impliedly imposed upon a director, manager or other officer knowingly and wilfully authorising or permitting the omission, so as to make any charge in his favour invalid against the liquidator in a winding up. For a general discussion of the decisions before *Wright v Horton* supra see *Re General Provident Assurance Co, ex p National Bank* supra.

11 *Re Patent Bread Machinery Co, ex p Valpy and Chaplin* (1872) 7 Ch App 289; *Re Hackney Borough Newspaper Co* (1876) 3 ChD 669 at 671; cf *Re International Pulp and Paper Co, Knowles' Mortgage* (1877) 6 ChD 556 at 560; *Re Dublin Drapery Co, ex p Cox* (1884) 13 LR Ir 174.

12 *Re Hackney Borough Newspaper Co* (1876) 3 ChD 669.

1298. Inspection of instruments and register. The copies of instruments creating any charge requiring registration with the registrar of companies[1], and the register of charges kept by the company[2], must be open during business hours (but subject to such reasonable restrictions as the company in general meeting may impose, so that not less than two hours in each day are allowed for inspection) to the inspection of any creditor or member of the company without fee; and the register of charges must also be open to the inspection of any other person on payment of such fee, not exceeding five pence for each inspection, as the company may prescribe[3]. If inspection of the copies or of the register is refused, every officer of the company who is in default is liable on summary conviction to a fine not exceeding one-fifth of the statutory maximum and, on conviction after continued contravention, to a daily default fine not exceeding one-fiftieth of the statutory maximum[4]. If such a refusal occurs in relation to a company registered in England and Wales, the court may by order compel an immediate inspection of the copies or register[5].

1 See para 1299 post.
2 See para 1297 ante.
3 Companies Act 1985 s 408(1),(2). The right to inspect includes a right to take copies (*Nelson v Anglo-American Land Mortgage Agency Co* [1897] 1 Ch 130 at 134), and the right of the shareholder to appoint a solicitor, accountant or other competent person to inspect (*Re Credit Co* (1879) 11 ChD 256; *Bevan v Webb* [1901] 2 Ch 59 at 75, CA; *Norey v Keep* [1909] 1 Ch 561; *Dodd v Amalgamated Marine Workers' Union* [1924] 1 Ch 116, CA; *Re Balaghât Gold Mining Co* [1901] 2 KB 665, CA).
   The Companies Act 1985 s 408 is repealed from a day to be appointed by the Companies Act 1989 s 92(a) and replaced from a day to be appointed by the Companies Act 1985 s 412 (substituted by the Companies Act 1989 ss 92(a), 101). At the date at which this volume states the law no such days had been appointed. As to the proposed new registration system generally see para 1316 post.
4 Companies Act 1985 ss 408(3), 730, Sch 24. See also note 3 supra. For the meaning of 'officer who is in default', 'the statutory maximum' and 'daily default fine' see para 1161 ante.
5 Ibid s 408(4). See also note 3 supra. Application to the court is made by originating summons in the expedited form: RSC Ord 102 r 2(1),(2). As to the procedure see para 69 ante. This power to order inspection ceases when the company goes into liquidation; and in that case the only right of inspection which a creditor or contributory has is in conformity with an order of the winding-up court under the Insolvency Act 1986: see s 155; paras 2329, 2845 post; and *Somerset v Land Securities Co* [1897] WN 29.

B. REGISTRATION AND INSPECTION AT THE REGISTRAR'S OFFICE

1299. Charges required to be registered. Every charge[1] falling under the following heads, created[2] by a company registered in England and Wales[3], requires to be registered with the registrar of companies[4]:

   (1) a charge for the purpose of securing any issue of debentures[5];
   (2) a charge on uncalled share capital of the company[6];
   (3) a charge created or evidenced by an instrument which, if executed by an individual, would require registration as a bill of sale[7];
   (4) a charge on land, wherever situated, or any interest in it, but not including a charge for any rent or other periodical sum issuing out of the land[8];
   (5) a charge on book debts of the company[9], not including the deposit for the purpose of securing an advance to the company of a negotiable instrument to secure payment of any book debts of the company[10];
   (6) a floating charge[11] on the undertaking[12] or property[13] of the company[14];
   (7) a charge on calls made but not paid[15];
   (8) a charge on a ship or aircraft or any share in a ship[16];
   (9) a charge on goodwill or any intellectual property[17].

Subject to the court's power to extend the time for registration[18], so far as any security on the company's property or undertaking is conferred by any such charge[19], the charge is void against the liquidator or administrator[20] and any creditor of the company[21], unless the prescribed particulars[22] of the charge, together with the instrument, if any, by which it is created or evidenced, are delivered to, or received by, the registrar of companies for registration in the manner required[23] within 21 days after the date of the charge's creation[24]. The registrar has otherwise no power to extend this time[25].

It is not actual registration, but delivery of the particulars to the registrar for registration, that preserves the validity of the charge[26]. Nor does the omission to register prejudice any contract or obligation for repayment of the money secured by the charge; and, when a charge becomes void for want of registration, the money secured by it immediately becomes payable[27].

These provisions are not confined to limited companies but extend to all companies registered in England and Wales[28], although the provisions as to registration in a company's register of charges apply only to limited companies[29].

1   For these purposes, 'charge' includes 'mortgage' (see the Companies Act 1985 s 396(4) and para 1297 note 3 ante), but does not include a charging order imposed under the Charging Orders Act 1979 s 1 (*Re Overseas Aviation Engineering (GB) Ltd* [1963] Ch 24, [1962] 3 All ER 12, CA). The provisions relating to registration of charges cannot be evaded by making what is in fact a mortgage or charge in form an absolute assignment: *Re Kent and Sussex Sawmills Ltd* [1947] Ch 177, [1946] 2 All ER 638. Cf *Lloyds and Scottish Finance Ltd v Prentice* (1977) 121 Sol Jo 847, CA; affd sub nom *Lloyds & Scottish Finance Ltd v Cyril Lord Carpets Sales Ltd* (1979) [1992] BCLC 609, HL (assignment construed as absolute). As to charges by foreign companies see para 1297 note 2 ante.

2   A charge such as an unpaid vendor's lien which arises by operation of law is not 'created' within the meaning of these provisions: *London and Cheshire Insurance Co Ltd v Laplagrene Property Co Ltd* [1971] Ch 499, [1971] 1 All ER 766. As to the time of creation see para 1306 post. In the case of the usual arrangement of a conveyance of property where part of the consideration is left outstanding on mortgage, the charge is created after the conveyance and accordingly falls within these provisions: *Capital Finance Co Ltd v Stokes* [1969] 1 Ch 261, [1968] 3 All ER 625, CA.

3   For the meaning of 'company registered in England and Wales' see para 1297 note 1 ante. See also note 25 infra.

4   Companies Act 1985 s 395(1) (amended by the Insolvency Act 1985 s 109, Sch 6 para 10); Companies Act 1985 s 396(1). Section 395 (as amended) and s 396 are repealed from a day to be appointed by the Companies Act 1989 s 92(a) and replaced from a day to be appointed by the Companies Act 1985 ss 395, 396 (substituted by the Companies Act 1989 ss 92(a), 93). At the date at which this volume states the law no such days had been appointed. As to the proposed new registration system generally see para 1316 post.

5   Companies Act 1985 s 396(1)(a). See also note 4 supra. For the meaning of 'debentures' see paras 1250, 1259 ante.

6   Ibid s 396(1)(b). See also note 4 supra. As to what uncalled capital is, and how and to what extent it may be incumbered, see paras 1245, 1246 ante.

7   Ibid s 396(1)(c). See BILLS OF SALE vol 4(1) (Reissue) paras 619, 643-645. It is not sufficient that the instrument, if executed by an individual, would require registration as a bill of sale if it does not also create a charge: *Stoneleigh Finance Ltd v Phillips* [1965] 2 QB 537, [1965] 1 All ER 513, CA (sale of property which did not leave vendor's possession).

8   Companies Act 1985 s 396(1)(d). See also note 4 supra. This does not include an unpaid vendor's lien arising by operation of law: *London and Cheshire Insurance Co Ltd v Laplagrene Property Co Ltd* [1971] Ch 499, [1971] 1 All ER 766; and see *Re Wallis & Simmonds (Builders) Ltd* [1974] 1 All ER 561, [1974] 1 WLR 391 (deposit of title deeds to secure debt owed by third party created equitable charge void against liquidator of depositor company for want of registration). A contract to create, in a particular event, a legal charge is not registrable under the Companies Act 1985 s 395 (as amended) as it does not create a present equitable right to a security, but is merely an agreement than in some future circumstance a security will be created: *Williams v Burlington Investments Ltd* (1977) 121 Sol Jo 424, HL; *Re Gregory Love & Co* [1916] 1 Ch 203. Cf *Re Jackson and Bassford Ltd* [1906] 2 Ch 467 (agreement creating present security interest registrable). The exception of a charge for rent or a periodical sum issuing out of land was introduced by the Companies Act 1948; and by s 458(1) (repealed) the equivalent provisions of earlier Companies Acts were to be deemed never to have applied to such a charge. In the case of a land charge for securing money created by a company before 1 January 1970 or so created at any time as a floating charge, registration under the Companies (Consolidation) Act 1908 s 93 (repealed), the Companies Act 1929 s 79 (repealed), the Companies Act 1948 s 95 (repealed) or the Companies Act 1985 ss 395-398 (as amended) was or is sufficient in place of registration under the Land Charges Act 1972, and had or has effect as if the land charge had been registered under the 1972 Act: s 3(7),(8) (amended by the Companies Consolidation (Consequential Provisions) Act 1985 s 30, Sch 2). All other charges require registration under both Acts. As to compensation for loss due to undisclosed land charges see the Law of Property Act 1969 s 25 (as amended) and LAND CHARGES vol 26 para 717. For a discussion of the relationship between registration of a charge under these provisions and the Land Charges Act 1972 where the registration of an equitable charge was not effected in the name of the owner of the underlying legal estate see *Property Discount Corpn Ltd v Lyon Group Ltd* [1981] 1 All ER

379, [1981] 1 WLR 300, CA. For the purposes of the Companies Act 1985 s 395 (as amended), the holding of debentures entitling the holder to a charge on land is not deemed to be an interest in land: s 396(3).

9 Ibid s 396(1)(e). See also note 4 supra. For the meaning of 'book debts' cf *Shipley v Marshall* (1863) 14 CBNS 566, applied in *Independent Automatic Sales Ltd v Knowles and Foster* [1962] 3 All ER 27, [1962] 1 WLR 974 (where it was held that a deposit of hire purchase agreements with a finance company to secure a loan was registrable as constituting a charge on book debts). A balance at a bank is not normally a book debt: *Re Brightlife Ltd* [1987] Ch 200, [1986] 3 All ER 673; *Northern Bank Ltd v Ross* [1991] BCLC 504 (NI CA). There must be a book debt in existence and included in the contract at the date the charge is created: *Paul & Frank Ltd v Discount Bank (Overseas) Ltd and Board of Trade* [1967] Ch 348, [1966] 2 All ER 922. As to what constitutes a charge on book debts see *Ladenburg & Co v Goodwin, Ferreira & Co Ltd and Garnett* [1912] 3 KB 275; *Saunderson & Co v Clark* (1913) 29 TLR 579; *Re Law, Car and General Insurance Corpn Ltd* (1911) 55 Sol Jo 407 (affd [1911] WN 101, CA); *Re David Allester Ltd* [1922] 2 Ch 211; *Re George Inglefield Ltd* [1933] Ch 1, CA; *Ashby, Warner & Co Ltd v Simmons* [1936] 2 All ER 697, CA; *Re Kent and Sussex Sawmills Ltd* [1947] Ch 177, [1946] 2 All ER 638; *Re Brush Aggregates Ltd* [1983] BCLC 320; *Re Charge Card Services Ltd* [1987] Ch 150, [1986] 3 All ER 289 (affd on other grounds [1989] Ch 497, [1988] 3 All ER 702, CA); *E Pfeiffer Weinkellerei-Weineinkauf GmbH & Co v Arbuthnot Factors Ltd* [1988] 1 WLR 150 (retention of title clause); *Re Welsh Irish Ferries Ltd* [1986] Ch 471, [1985] 3 WLR 610 (contractual lien on sub-freights (see SHIPPING vol 43 para 529) held to constitute a charge on book debts and hence registrable); and see *Annangel Glory Cia Naviera SA v M Golodetz Ltd* [1988] 1 Lloyd's Rep 45 (contract lien on sub-freights held to constitute a floating charge and hence registrable). Where an agreement provided that assignments of debts were to be absolute, the fact that the parties did not operate the transactions in accordance with the terms of the agreement did not make them into charges on book debts: *Lloyds and Scottish Finance Ltd v Cyril Lord Carpets Sales Ltd* (1979) [1992] BCLC 609, HL; *Carreras Rothmans Ltd v Freeman Mathews Treasure Ltd* [1985] Ch 207, [1985] 1 All ER 155. An escrow agreement whereby an account was opened and the moneys paid into it were to be impressed with a trust was held not to be registrable: *Lovell Construction Ltd v Independent Estates plc (in liquidation)* [1994] 1 BCLC 31 (the account created by the escrow agreement was only machinery for effecting payment).

It is not possible to have a charge in favour of a company of its own indebtedness to the chargor: *Re Charge Card Services Ltd* supra. The official view was originally that a company's bank account could properly be regarded as a 'book debt' and that accordingly charges thereover would be accepted for registration. This view changed with effect from March 1985 (see 82 LS Gaz 1535) but was restored with effect from 6 August 1985, after which date such charges were again accepted for registration. Particulars of such charges delivered in the interim period were held pending a decision as to whether they were registrable, and they accordingly thereafter proceeded to registration: see 82 LS Gaz 2868.

10 Companies Act 1985 s 396(2). See also note 4 supra.

11 For the meaning of 'floating charge' or 'floating security' see para 1260 ante.

12 As to what is the 'undertaking' of a company see para 1245 ante.

13 As to what is a company's 'property' see para 1245 ante.

14 Companies Act 1985 s 396(1)(f). See also note 4 supra.

15 Ibid s 396(1)(g). See also note 4 supra.

16 Ibid s 396(1)(h); Mortgaging of Aircraft Order 1972, SI 1972/1268, art 16(2). See also note 4 supra.

17 Companies Act 1985 s 396(1)(j) (amended by the Copyright, Designs and Patents Act 1988 s 303(1), Sch 7 para 31(1)). See also note 4 supra. For these purposes, 'intellectual property' means any patent, trade mark, registered design, copyright or design right and any licence in respect of any such right: Companies Act 1985 s 396(3A) (added by the Copyright, Designs and Patents Act 1988 Sch 7 para 31(2); amended by the Trade Marks Act 1994 s 106(2), Sch 5).

18 See para 1314 post.

19 Where the debentures which had not been registered pursuant to this provision were secured by a charge on some of the property of the company contained in a trust deed which did not require registration, it was held that the debenture holders were entitled to share as beneficiaries to the extent of the charge contained in the trust deed: *Dublin City Distillery v Doherty* [1914] AC 823, HL.

20 As to administrators and administration orders see para 2080 et seq post.

21 See *Re Toomer, ex p Blaiberg* (1883) 23 ChD 254, CA; *Re Monolithic Building Co, Tacon v Monolithic Building Co* [1915] 1 Ch 643, CA (where, in respect of mortgage debentures duly issued to a company director and registered, the director was given priority over a prior mortgage which had not been registered but of the existence of which he had full knowledge); *Re Eric Holmes (Property) Ltd* [1965] Ch 1052, [1965] 2 All ER 333 (where the fact that the date was wrongly stated in the charges and the fact that they were submitted for registration more than 21 days after their creation would not, since they were in fact registered, by themselves have been fatal to their validity as against the liquidator); *Re C L*

Nye Ltd [1971] Ch 442, [1970] 3 All ER 1061, CA (same facts, and result actually the same; as there was no evidence that any other person had given credit to the company between the dates when the charge should have been, and when it was actually, registered, the maxim that nobody could take advantage of his own wrong did not apply); and *Wilde v Australian Trade Equipment Co Pty* (1981) 145 CLR 590 (Aust HC) (order for extension of time made on same day that a petition for winding up presented; registration duly effected; winding-up order and order setting aside order for extension of time made subsequently; held that registration so effected continued valid). See also para 1273 note 4 ante.

22 For the prescribed form of particulars see the Companies (Forms) Regulations 1985, SI 1985/854, reg 4(1), Sch 3, Form 395.

23 See para 1310 post.

24 Companies Act 1985 s 395(1) (as amended: see note 4 supra). See also note 4 supra. The company itself, as distinct from its liquidator, cannot have a cause of action arising out of non-registration: *Independent Automatic Sales Ltd v Knowles and Foster* [1962] 3 All ER 27, [1962] 1 WLR 974. On an equitable charge being avoided as against the liquidator, everything ancillary to it is also made void: *Re Molton Finance Ltd* [1968] Ch 325, [1967] 3 All ER 843, CA.

     As to when a charge is created see para 1306 post; as to charges on foreign property see para 1304 post; as to inconsistency between particulars inserted in the form and the terms of the instrument creating the charge see para 1311 post; as to the penalty for failure to comply with these provisions see para 1308 post, and as to obtaining relief in the event of a failure so to comply see para 1314 post; and as to how far registration is constructive notice see para 1262 text and note 8 ante.

25 It was formerly the practice of the registrar of companies to allow an extension of time for the lodging of a properly completed form if an improperly completed form had been lodged within the 21-day period. This procedure has been held to be without statutory authority and erroneous: *R v Registrar of Companies, ex p Central Bank of India* [1986] QB 1114, [1986] 1 All ER 105, CA, where an order of certiorari had been granted by the court below to quash the registrar's decision to register the charge outside the 21-day period reckoned from the date of its creation. This decision was reversed on appeal, but the criticism of the practice was upheld. As to the present practice adopted by the registrar in the case of incorrectly completed forms see para 1300 post.

26 *N V Slavenburg's Bank v Intercontinental Natural Resources Ltd* [1980] 1 All ER 955, [1980] 1 WLR 1076.

27 Companies Act 1985 s 395(2). See also note 4 supra.

28 Ibid s 395(1). As to charges by foreign companies see para 1297 note 2 ante.

29 See para 1297 ante.

1300. The registrar of companies' current practice. The current practice of the registrar of companies is:

(1) except as provided by the Companies Act 1985[1], copy instruments will not be accepted by the registrar of companies; oversea companies[2] must state in a covering letter where their place of business is within England and Wales or, in appropriate circumstances, state that they have no such place of business;

(2) with the agreement of the presentor, the registrar will amend either within or outside the 21 days[3] errors in the company number and the company name and any other minor clerical or typing error that appears in the words or figures that have been presented on the submitted prescribed form[4] that differ from the accompanying instrument submitted by the presentor;

(3) all other errors or omissions[5] which the registrar highlights within the 21 days will be required to be rectified by the submission of an amended prescribed form within the 21-day period;

(4) if any other error or omission other than those stated in head (2) above is discovered by the registrar after the twenty-first day, or if an amended prescribed form is not returned within the 21 days in relation to head (3) above, then it will be necessary to obtain a court order[6] and there will be no exceptions to that rule[7].

1 Ie by the Companies Act 1985 s 398 (see para 1304 post) or s 400 (see para 1309 post).

2 As to oversea companies see para 1790 et seq post.

3 See para 1299 text to notes 18–25 ante.

4 For the prescribed form of particulars see the Companies (Forms) Regulations 1985, SI 1985/854, reg 4(1), Sch 3, Form 395.
5 Eg omitting reference to 'all other moneys' in the section headed 'Amount secured by the Mortgage or Charge' or referring only to a fixed charge where a floating charge is also created.
6 Ie under the Companies Act 1985 s 404: see para 1314 post.
7 Press Notice dated 28 August 1985 entitled *Registration of Company Charges —Changes in Companies Registration Office Practice Following Court of Appeal Judgment*. The case referred to is *R v Registrar of Companies, ex p Central Bank of India* [1986] QB 1114, [1986] 1 All ER 105, CA.

1301. Retention of title clauses. An ordinary retention of title clause in a contract by a vendor of goods sold to a company and to which the Sale of Goods Act 1979 applies[1], so drawn as to ensure that title in the goods does not pass to the company until payment, or until the goods are sold to a third party, does not require registration under the Companies Act 1985[2]. Just as the company never itself obtains title to the goods, so it cannot create any effective charge over such goods in favour of the vendor[3]. Such a reservation of title will thus be fully effective and enforceable at the appropriate time, for example on the liquidation of the company or against a receiver, in respect of so much of the goods as are then still remaining in the company's hands[4].

In cases where the goods supplied by a vendor to a company are simply resold by the company without alteration, the contract may by appropriate wording provide that the company is also to be regarded as standing in a fiduciary position to the vendor in relation to any goods sold, who may then be entitled to trace his goods into the proceeds of sale[5].

Difficulties arise, however, where the company employs the goods sold to it in the manufacturing process. If the finished product incorporates no other material, there is no reason why the vendor's title should not remain[6]. If the goods are incorporated with others in such a manner that it is possible to separate them out again, then the vendor's title to any such goods still in the hands of the company remains[7]. If, however, the goods sold have for practical purposes lost their identity by being utilised in a non-reversible manufacturing process[8], then, since the vendor never had any title to the whole of the finished product, a retention of title clause by itself will not furnish him with any rights against the manufactured product or its proceeds of sale[9]. Any provision granting any such rights will amount to a charge created by the company and will be accordingly void as against a liquidator or any creditor of the company[10].

Any provisions, other than a simple retention of title clause, may be held to create a charge granted by the company if, on their true construction, that appears to be their intended effect[11].

1 Ie under the Sale of Goods Act 1979 s 19(1): see SALE OF GOODS vol 41 para 731.
2 Ie under the Companies Act 1985 s 396 (as amended): see para 1299 ante.
3 *Clough Mill Ltd v Martin* [1984] 3 All ER 982, [1985] 1 WLR 111, CA.
4 *Aluminium Industrie Vaassen BV v Romalpa Aluminium Ltd* [1976] 2 All ER 552, [1976] 1 WLR 676, CA; *Re Peachdart Ltd* [1984] Ch 131, [1983] 3 All ER 204; *Hendy Lennox (Industrial Engines) Ltd v Grahame Puttick Ltd* [1984] 2 All ER 152, [1984] 1 WLR 485; *Clough Mill Ltd v Martin* [1984] 3 All ER 982, [1985] 1 WLR 111, CA; *John Snow & Co Ltd v DBG Woodcroft & Co Ltd* [1985] BCLC 54.
5 *Aluminium Industrie Vaassen BV v Romalpa Aluminium Ltd* [1976] 2 All ER 552, [1976] 1 WLR 676, CA; cf *Re Andrabell Ltd (in liquidation), Airborne Accessories Ltd v Goodman* [1984] 3 All ER 407 (where the terms of the contract made it impossible to imply a fiduciary relationship); and *E Pfeiffer Weinkellerei-Weineinkauf GmbH & Co v Arbuthnot Factors Ltd* [1988] 1 WLR 150 (clause providing for all claims with respect to the sales by the company to sub-purchasers to be passed on to the vendor pending payment in full of the company's obligations to the vendor constituted a charge on book debts by the company void for want of registration). See also *Compaq Computer Ltd v Abercorn Group Ltd (trading as Osiris)* [1993] BCLC 602.

6 *Clough Mill Ltd v Martin* [1984] 3 All ER 982 at 994, [1985] 1 WLR 111 at 125, CA per Sir John Donaldson MR.
7 *Hendy Lennox (Industrial Engines) Ltd v Grahame Puttick Ltd* [1984] 2 All ER 152, [1984] 1 WLR 485.
8 Eg resin utilised in the production of chip-board as in *Borden (UK) Ltd v Scottish Timber Products Ltd* [1981] Ch 25, [1979] 3 All ER 961, CA.
9 *Clough Mill Ltd v Martin* [1984] 3 All ER 982, [1985] 1 WLR 111, CA. See also *Modelboard Ltd v Outer Box Ltd (in liquidation)* [1993] BCLC 623 (arrangement between the parties created a defeasible interest in the product of the goods and the proceeds from sale; this constituted an interest by way of charge which was voidable for non-registration).
10 *Borden (UK) Ltd v Scottish Timber Products Ltd* [1981] Ch 25, [1979] 3 All ER 961, CA; *Re Bond Worth Ltd* [1980] Ch 228, [1979] 3 All ER 919; *Re Peachdart Ltd* [1984] Ch 131, [1983] 3 All ER 204; *Specialist Plant Services Ltd v Braithwaite Ltd* [1987] BCLC 1, CA. See also *Modelboard Ltd v Outer Box Ltd (in liquidation)* [1993] BCLC 623.
11 *Re Bond Worth Ltd* [1980] Ch 228, [1979] 3 All ER 919 (clause seeking to retain 'equitable and beneficial ownership' of (ie not the legal title to) the raw fibre sold, its proceeds of sale, and the products into which any part of the fibre might become a constituent or into which it might be converted or the proceeds of sale of any such product, held to create a floating equitable charge requiring registration for its effectiveness). See also *Compaq Computer Ltd v Abercorn Group Ltd (trading as Osiris)* [1993] BCLC 602.

1302. Statements as to commission and discount. Where any commission, allowance or discount has been paid or made, either directly or indirectly, by a company to a person in consideration of his subscribing or agreeing to subscribe, whether absolutely or conditionally, for its debentures, or procuring or agreeing to procure subscriptions, whether absolute or conditional, for such debentures, the particulars required to be sent for registration under the above provisions[1] must include particulars as to the amount or rate per cent of the commission, discount or allowance so paid or made; but omission to do this does not affect the validity of the debentures issued[2]. The deposit of debentures as security for a debt of the company is not, however, treated as the issue of the debentures at a discount for the purposes of this provision[3].

1 Ie under the Companies Act 1985 s 395 (as amended): see para 1299 ante.
2 Ibid s 397(2). Section 397(2) and s 397(3) (see infra) are repealed from a day to be appointed by the Companies Act 1989 s 92(a). At the date at which this volume states the law no such day had been appointed. As to the proposed new registration system generally see para 1316 post.
3 Companies Act 1985 s 397(3). See also note 2 supra.

1303. Registration of a series of debentures. Where a series of debentures containing, or giving by reference to another instrument, any charge to the benefit of which the debenture holders of that series are entitled pari passu is created by a company, then it is sufficient[1] if there are delivered to, or received by, the registrar of companies within 21 days after the execution of the deed containing the charge, or, if there is no such deed, after the execution of any debentures of the series, the following particulars in the prescribed form[2]:
(1) the total amount secured by the whole series; and
(2) the dates of the resolutions authorising the issue of the series and the date of the covering deed, if any, by which the security is created or defined; and
(3) a general description of the property charged; and
(4) the names of the trustees, if any, for the debenture holders,
together with the deed containing the charge, or, if there is no such deed, one of the debentures of the series[3].
Where more than one issue is made of debentures in the series, there must be sent to the registrar for entry in the register particulars in the prescribed form[4] of the date and

amount of each issue; but any omission to do this does not affect the validity of any of the debentures issued[5].

1 Ie for the purposes of the Companies Act 1985 s 395 (as amended): see paras 1299, 1302 ante and paras 1304, 1305 post.
2 For the prescribed form of particulars see the Companies (Forms) Regulations 1985, SI 1985/854, reg 4(1), Sch 3, Form 397.
3 Companies Act 1985 s 397(1); and see *Re Spiral Globe Ltd (No 2), Watson v Spiral Globe Ltd* [1902] 2 Ch 209; *Re Harrogate Estates Ltd* [1903] 1 Ch 498; *Cunard SS Co Ltd v Hopwood* [1908] 2 Ch 564. The series of debentures includes all those which, whenever issued, are entitled to the pari passu charge; cf *Re Yolland, Husson and Birkett Ltd, Leicester v Yolland, Husson and Birkett Ltd* [1908] 1 Ch 152, CA. The registration of the particulars mentioned above protects the debentures of the series issued not more than 21 days before registration and all other debentures of the series subsequently issued: *Re Harrogate Estates Ltd* supra. The sealing of debentures is not an issue (*Re N Defries & Co Ltd, Bowen v N Defries & Co Ltd* [1904] 1 Ch 37); but a contract to issue is an issue (*Re Perth Electric Tramways Ltd, Lyons v Tramways Syndicate Ltd and Perth Electric Tramways Ltd* [1906] 2 Ch 216). The delivery of particulars of a series of debentures is a sufficient registration of particulars of an agreement to issue debentures of that series: *Re Fireproof Doors Ltd, Umney v Fireproof Doors Ltd* [1916] 2 Ch 142. As to the penalty for failure to comply with these provisions see para 1308 post; and as to obtaining relief in the event of a failure so to comply see para 1314 post.
   The Companies Act 1985 s 397 is repealed from a day to be appointed by the Companies Act 1989 s 92(a) and replaced from a day to be appointed by the Companies Act 1985 s 408 (substituted by the Companies Act 1989 ss 92(a), 100). At the date at which this volume states the law no such days had been appointed. As to the proposed new registration system generally see para 1316 post.
4 For the prescribed form of particulars see the Companies (Forms) Regulations 1985 Sch 3, Form 397.
5 Companies Act 1985 s 397(1) proviso. See also note 3 supra.

1304. Charge on foreign property. Where a charge is created in the United Kingdom but comprises property outside the United Kingdom, the instrument creating or purporting to create the charge may be sent for registration[1], notwithstanding that further proceedings may be necessary to make the charge valid or effectual according to the law of the country in which the property is situated[2].

In the case of a charge created out of the United Kingdom comprising property situated outside the United Kingdom, the delivery to, and the receipt by, the registrar of companies of a copy, verified in the prescribed manner[3], of the instrument by which the mortgage or charge is created or evidenced, has the same effect for these purposes[4] as the delivery and receipt of the instrument itself[5]. In that case, the particulars and instrument or copy must be delivered to the registrar within 21 days after the date on which the instrument or copy could, in due course of post, and if dispatched with due diligence, have been received in the United Kingdom[6].

1 Ie under the Companies Act 1985 s 395 (as amended): see para 1299 ante.
2 Ibid s 398(3). Section 398 is repealed from a day to be appointed by the Companies Act 1989 s 92(a). At the date at which this volume states the law no such day had been appointed. As to the proposed new registration system generally see para 1316 post.
3 For these purposes, a certificate or verification, as the case may be, that a copy of an instrument by which a charge is created or evidenced is a correct copy must be given by the company which has created the charge, or, where that person is different, by the person who delivered or sent the copy to the registrar; and such a certificate must be signed by or on behalf of the person giving it; where that person is a body corporate, the person signing the certificate on behalf of the body must be an officer of it: Companies (Forms) Regulations 1985, SI 1985/854, reg 7(1),(3). As to the application of this provision in connection with the registration of charges created by companies registered in Scotland see note 5 infra.
4 Ie the Companies Act 1985 ss 395-398 (as amended): see paras 1299-1303 ante.
5 Ibid s 398(1). See also note 2 supra and para 1297 note 2 ante.
   Part XII Ch II (ss 410-424), which enacts provisions akin to those contained in Pt XII Ch I (ss 395-409) (as amended) for the purpose of securing the registration in Scotland of charges created by companies there registered, makes express provision for charges on foreign property corresponding to

s 398: see s 411; the Companies (Forms) Regulations 1985 reg 7(1),(3) (cited in note 3 supra).

As to the position where the charge comprises property situated in Scotland or Northern Ireland see the Companies Act 1985 s 398(4); the Companies (Forms) Regulations 1985 reg 7(1), (3); and para 1305 post.

6 Companies Act 1985 s 398(2). See also note 2 supra.

1305. Charge on property in Scotland or Northern Ireland. Where a charge comprises property situated in Scotland or Northern Ireland, and registration in the country where the property is situated is necessary to make the charge valid or effectual according to the law of that country, the delivery to, and the receipt by, the registrar of companies of a copy, verified in the prescribed manner[1], of the instrument by which the charge is created or evidenced, together with a certificate in the prescribed form[2] stating that the charge was presented for registration in Scotland or Northern Ireland, as the case may be, on the date on which it was so presented, has for the purposes of the above provisions[3], the same effect as the delivery and receipt of the instrument itself[4].

1 For the prescribed manner of verification see para 1304 note 3 ante.
2 For the prescribed form of certificate see the Companies (Forms) Regulations 1985, SI 1985/854, reg 4(1), Sch 3, Form 398.
3 Ie for the purposes of the Companies Act 1985 ss 395–398 (as amended): see paras 1299–1304 ante.
4 Ibid s 398(4). Section 398 is repealed from a day to be appointed by the Companies Act 1989 s 92(a). At the date at which this volume states the law no such day had been appointed. As to the proposed new registration system generally see para 1316 post.

1306. When a charge is created. The charge is created when it is executed[1]. However, where, under an agreement to issue debentures, a company has sealed some debentures, but has not registered them within 21 days, it may cancel them and issue to the lender other debentures, which are valid, if registered within 21 days[2] after they were sealed[3]. Debentures created before the date when registration was required, but validly reissued[4] after that date, are not within the provisions as to registration[5].

1 *Re Spiral Globe Ltd (No 2), Watson v Spiral Globe Ltd* [1902] 2 Ch 209; *Re New London and Suburban Omnibus Co, Appleyard v New London and Suburban Omnibus Co* [1908] 1 Ch 621; *Esberger & Son Ltd v Capital and Counties Bank* [1913] 2 Ch 366; *Re Columbian Fireproofing Co* [1910] 2 Ch 120, CA; *Re Olderfleet Shipbuilding and Engineering Co Ltd* [1922] 1 IR 26; *Transport and General Credit Corpn v Morgan* [1939] Ch 531, [1939] 2 All ER 17.

The Companies Act 1985 s 414 (substituted by the Companies Act 1989 ss 92(a), 103 from a day to be appointed) contains a statutory definition of 'the date of creation of a charge'. At the date at which this volume states the law no such day had been appointed. As to the proposed new registration system generally see para 1316 post.
2 See para 1303 ante.
3 *Re N Defries & Co Ltd, Bowen v N Defries & Co Ltd* [1904] 1 Ch 37.
4 See the Companies Consolidation (Consequential Provisions) Act 1985 s 13 and para 1272 ante.
5 *Re New London and Suburban Omnibus Co, Appleyard v New London and Suburban Omnibus Co* [1908] 1 Ch 621. It seems to follow that, when a debenture is validly reissued, no registration is necessary on the reissue.

1307. Sale of property subject to charge. Where property subject to a mortgage is sold and the proceeds are invested in other property which is conveyed to the company, and then mortgaged by the company to the mortgagee, the latter mortgage requires registration[1]; but the registration of a trust deed securing debenture stock containing specific equitable charges on property is sufficient to cover subsequent legal mortgages of that property to complete the security, and also mortgages of further property substituted under the powers of the deed for property comprised in the original charge[2].

1 *Cornbrook Brewery Co Ltd v Law Debenture Corpn Ltd* [1904] 1 Ch 103, CA; *Capital Finance Co Ltd v Stokes* [1969] 1 Ch 261, [1963] 3 All ER 625, CA. In *Bristol United Breweries Ltd v Abbot* [1908] 1 Ch 279 it was held that, where there was a direct conveyance to the mortgagee, the conveyance need not be registered, because it was not a mortgage or charge created by the company. Such a transaction should now be carried out in such a way as to vest the legal estate in fee simple in the company and a term of years in the mortgagee. Such a conveyance would require to be registered under the Companies Act 1985 s 400 (repealed from a day to be appointed): see para 1309 post.

2 *Cunard SS Co Ltd v Hopwood* [1908] 2 Ch 564 (a case under the Companies Act 1900 s 14(4) (repealed)). The Companies Act 1929 s 79(8) (repealed), the Companies Act 1948 s 95(8) (repealed) and the Companies Act 1985 s 397(1) (see para 1303 ante) are similar in general terms, but the words 'for the purposes of the appropriate section' are added. It is doubtful, however, whether this addition makes s 397(1) inapplicable to mortgages of substituted property which would otherwise require registration under s 400 (see para 1309 post). In any case, failure to comply with s 400 does not affect the validity of the charge.

1308. Company's duty to register charges. It is the duty of a company to send to the registrar of companies for registration the particulars of every charge created by it, and of the issues of debentures of a series requiring registration[1] with the registrar[2]. The registration of any such charge may, however, be effected on the application of any person interested in it[2]. Where the registration is effected on the application of some person other than the company, that person is entitled to recover from the company the amount of any fees properly paid by him to the registrar on the registration[3].

If a company makes default in sending to the registrar for registration the particulars of any charge created by it or of the issues of debentures of a series so requiring registration with the registrar, then, unless the registration has been effected on the application of some other person, the company, and every officer of it who is in default, is liable on conviction on indictment to a fine, or on summary conviction to a fine not exceeding the statutory maximum and, on conviction after continued contravention, to a daily default fine not exceeding one-tenth of the statutory maximum[4].

1 Ie under the Companies Act 1985 ss 395–398 (as amended): see paras 1299–1304 ante.

2 Ibid s 399(1). Section 399 is repealed from a day to be appointed by the Companies Act 1989 s 92(a) and replaced from a day to be appointed by the Companies Act 1985 ss 398–401 (substituted by the Companies Act 1989 ss 92(a), 95, 96). At the date at which this volume states the law no such days had been appointed. As to the proposed new registration system generally see para 1316 post.

3 Companies Act 1985 s 399(2). See also note 2 supra.

4 Ibid ss 399(3), 730, Sch 24. See also note 2 supra. For the meaning of 'officer who is in default', 'the statutory maximum' and 'daily default fine' see para 1161 ante.

1309. Registration of charges existing on property acquired. Where a company registered in England and Wales[1] acquires property which is subject to a charge of any such kind as would, if it had been created by the company after the acquisition of the property, have been required to be registered[2], the company must cause the prescribed particulars[3] of the charge, together with a copy, certified in the prescribed manner[4] to be a correct copy, of the instrument, if any, by which the charge was created or is evidenced, to be delivered to the registrar of companies for registration in the manner required[5] within 21 days after the date on which the acquisition is completed[6]; or, if the property is situated and the charge was created outside Great Britain, within 21 days after the date on which the copy of the instrument could in due course of post, and if dispatched with due diligence, have been received in the United Kingdom[7].

If default is made in complying with this provision, the company, and every officer of it who is in default, is liable on conviction on indictment to a fine, or on summary conviction to a fine not exceeding the statutory maximum and, on conviction after continued contravention, to a daily default fine not exceeding one-tenth of the statutory maximum[8].

1 See paras 1297 note 2, 1299 note 25 ante.
2 See para 1299 ante.
3 For the prescribed form of particulars see the Companies (Forms) Regulations 1985, SI 1985/854, reg 4(1), Sch 3, Form 400 (amended by SI 1987/752).
4 For the prescribed manner of certification see para 1304 note 3 ante.
5 See para 1310 post.
6 Companies Act 1985 s 400(1),(2). Before the Companies Act 1929 (repealed) only charges by a company had to be registered. The Companies Act 1985 s 400 is repealed from a day to be appointed by the Companies Act 1989 s 92(a). At the date at which this volume states the law no such day had been appointed. As to the proposed new registration system generally see para 1316 post.
7 Companies Act 1985 s 400(3). See also note 6 supra.
8 Ibid ss 400(4), 730, Sch 24. See also note 6 supra. For the meaning of 'officer who is in default', 'the statutory maximum' and 'daily default fine' see para 1161 ante.

1310. Register of charges and index. With respect to each company, the registrar of companies must keep a register in the prescribed form[1] of all the charges requiring registration under the Companies Act 1985[2], and must enter in the register with respect to such charges, in the case of a charge to the benefit of which the holders of a series of debentures are entitled, the particulars[3] required to be delivered by the company[4]; and in the case of any other charge:

(1) if it is a charge created by the company, the date of its creation, and if it is a charge which was existing on property acquired by the company, the date of the acquisition of the property; and

(2) the amount secured by the charge; and

(3) short particulars of the property charged; and

(4) the persons entitled to the charge[5].

The register so kept by the registrar must be open to inspection by any person[6].

1 For the prescribed form of register see the Companies (Forms) Regulations 1985, SI 1985/854, reg 4(1), Sch 3, Form 401.
2 Ie under the Companies Act 1985 Pt XII Ch I (ss 395-409) (as amended).
3 Ie the particulars specified in ibid s 397(1): see para 1303 ante.
4 Ibid s 401(1)(a). Section 401(1) and s 401(3) (see infra) are repealed from a day to be appointed by the Companies Act 1989 s 92(a) and replaced from a day to be appointed by the Companies Act 1985 s 397(1),(2) (substituted by the Companies Act 1989 ss 92(a), 94). At the date at which this volume states the law no such days had been appointed. As to the proposed new registration system generally see para 1316 post.
5 Companies Act 1985 s 401(1)(b). See also note 4 supra.
6 Ibid s 401(3). See also note 4 supra. As to the effect of winding up see para 2845 post; and as to notice by registration see para 1262 text and note 8 ante.

1311. Certificate of registration. The registrar of companies must give a certificate either signed by him or authenticated by his official seal[1] of the registration of any charge registered with him, stating the amount secured by it[2]. The certificate is conclusive evidence that the requirements of the Companies Act 1985[3] as to registration have been satisfied[4]; and the court will refuse to go into the question whether the requirements as to registration have been complied with[5].

Thus, it is immaterial, after the certificate has been obtained, that the date of the resolution creating stock is omitted from the particulars filed on registration[6]; and, if the certificate sufficiently identifies the instrument of charge, it is conclusive evidence of the effective registration of the charge in respect of all the property comprised in it, even though the registered particulars of the property charged omit some of such properties[7].

It is equally immaterial that the order for extension of time for registration, if made properly at the time of making, is subsequently set aside. If registration has been effected in the meantime in reliance upon the original order, it remains valid[8].

1   As to the registrar's official seal see para 60 ante.
2   Companies Act 1985 s 401(2)(a). Section 401(2) is repealed from a day to be appointed by the Companies Act 1989 s 92(a) and replaced from a day to be appointed by the Companies Act 1985 s 397(3)-(5) (substituted by the Companies Act 1989 ss 92(a), 94). At the date at which this volume states the law no such days had been appointed. As to the proposed new registration system generally see para 1316 post.
3   Ie the Companies Act 1985 Pt XII Ch I (ss 395-409) (as amended).
4   Ibid s 401(2)(b). See *Re C L Nye Ltd* [1971] Ch 442 at 457, [1970] 3 All ER 1061, CA (date of creation of charge misstated in application which was not made within 21 days; registration nevertheless valid); cf para 1299 note 21 ante.
5   *Re Yolland, Husson and Birkett Ltd, Leicester v Yolland, Husson and Birkett Ltd* [1908] 1 Ch 152, CA; *R v Registrar of Companies, ex p Central Bank of India* [1986] QB 1114, [1986] 1 All ER 105, CA (where it was held that judicial review of the registrar's issue of the certificate was not available, save possibly in cases of fraud or where the application was made by the Attorney General, as the Companies Act 1985 is not expressed to bind the Crown).
6   *Cunard SS Co Ltd v Hopwood* [1908] 2 Ch 564 at 578.
7   *National Provincial and Union Bank of England v Charnley* [1924] 1 KB 431, applied in *Re Mechanisations (Eaglescliffe) Ltd* [1966] Ch 20, [1964] 3 All ER 840; *Re Eric Holmes (Property) Ltd* [1965] Ch 1052, [1965] 2 All ER 333 (cf para 1299 note 21 ante) and *N V Slavenburg's Bank v Intercontinental Natural Resources Ltd* [1980] 1 All ER 955, [1980] 1 WLR 1076.
8   *Wilde v Australian Trade Equipment Co Pty* (1981) 145 CLR 590 (Aust HC).

1312. Indorsement of registration certificate on debentures. The company must cause a copy of every certificate of registration[1] to be indorsed on every debenture or certificate of debenture stock which is issued by the company, and the payment of which is secured by the charge so registered, not being a debenture or certificate of debenture stock issued by it before the charge was created[2].

If a person knowingly and wilfully authorises or permits the delivery of a debenture or certificate of debenture stock requiring indorsement without a copy of the registration certificate being so indorsed upon it, he is, without prejudice to any other liability, liable on summary conviction to a fine not exceeding one-fifth of the statutory maximum[3].

1   Ie given under the Companies Act 1985 s 401: see para 1310 ante.
2   Ibid s 402(1),(2). Section 402 is repealed from a day to be appointed by the Companies Act 1989 s 92(a). At the date at which this volume states the law no such day had been appointed. As to the proposed new registration system generally see para 1316 post.
3   Companies Act 1985 ss 402(3), 730, Sch 24. See also note 2 supra. For the meaning of 'the statutory maximum' see para 1161 ante.

1313. Memorandum of satisfaction or release. On receipt of a statutory declaration in the prescribed form[1] verifying, with respect to a registered charge, that the debt for which the charge was given has been paid or satisfied in whole or in part, or that part of the property or undertaking charged has been released from the charge or has ceased to form part of the company's property or undertaking, the registrar of companies may enter on the register a memorandum of satisfaction in whole or in part, or of the fact that part of the property or undertaking has been released from the charge or has ceased to form part of the company's property or undertaking, as the case may be[2]; and, where he enters a memorandum of satisfaction in whole, he must, if required, furnish the company with a copy of it[3].

1 For the prescribed forms of statutory declaration see the Companies (Forms) Regulations 1985, SI 1985/854, reg 4(1), Sch 3, Form 403a (amended by SI 1987/752) (satisfaction in full or part), Form 403b (amended by SI 1987/752) (release of property from the charge or such property no longer forming part of the company's property or undertaking).

2 Companies Act 1985 s 403(1). As to cancelling and correcting a memorandum of satisfaction see para 1314 post. Section 403 is repealed from a day to be appointed by the Companies Act 1989 s 92(a) and replaced from a day to be appointed by the Companies Act 1985 s 403 (substituted by the Companies Act 1989 ss 92(a), 98). At the date at which this volume states the law no such days had been appointed. As to the proposed new registration system generally see para 1316 post.

3 Companies Act 1985 s 403(2). See also note 2 supra.

C. EXTENSION OF TIME FOR REGISTRATION; RECTIFICATION

1314. When relief may be granted. On being satisfied that the omission to register a charge within the time required[1], or that the omission or misstatement of any particular with respect to any such charge or in a memorandum of satisfaction was accidental[2], or due to inadvertence[3] or to some other sufficient cause[4], or is not of a nature to prejudice the position of the company's creditors or shareholders, or that on other grounds it is just and equitable to grant relief, the court may, on the application[5] of the company or any person interested, and on such terms and conditions as seem to the court just and expedient, order that the time for registration be extended, or, as the case may be, that the omission or misstatement be rectified[6]. There is no jurisdiction to order the deletion of the whole of a registration under these provisions[7]; and there is no power to grant interim relief[8].

It is only in exceptional circumstances that such an extension will be granted after the company has gone into liquidation; but it is such an exceptional case if the only creditor who could be affected thereby does not oppose[9].

1 As to the time allowed for registration see paras 1299, 1303 ante; as to charges on property in Scotland or Northern Ireland or on foreign property see paras 1305, 1304 respectively ante; and as to charges existing on property acquired see para 1309 ante.

2 An accident is a mishap or untoward event not expected or designed: *Fenton v Thorley & Co Ltd* [1903] AC 443, HL; and see *Brintons Ltd v Turvey* [1905] AC 230, HL and other decisions cited in NATIONAL HEALTH vol 33 para 486.

3 'Inadvertence' includes ignorance of the provisions requiring registration (*Re Mendip Press* (1901) 18 TLR 38; *Re Jackson & Co Ltd* [1899] 1 Ch 348; *Re Heathstar Properties Ltd (No 2)* [1966] 1 All ER 1000, [1966] 1 WLR 993 at 999; cf *Re E and F Beattie Ltd* (1901) 45 Sol Jo 671), or a case where the company secretary and the chargee each thinks that the other has registered (*Re Kris Cruisers Ltd* [1949] Ch 138, [1948] 2 All ER 1105).

4 'Some other sufficient cause' covers difficulties arising through the property charged being situated abroad (*Re Tingri Tea Co Ltd* [1901] WN 165; but as to property situated abroad see paras 1304, 1309 ante), and, in the case of debentures, delay at the Stamp Office (*Re Bootle Cold Storage and Ice Co* [1901] WN 54; and see *Re S Abrahams & Sons* [1902] 1 Ch 695).

5 As to the procedure see para 1315 post.

6 Companies Act 1985 s 404(1),(2). The jurisdiction to grant relief conferred by corresponding provisions in earlier Companies Acts in relation to instruments requiring registration under those Acts is preserved by the Interpretation Act 1978 s 16(1), Sch 2 para 3: *Re Lush & Co Ltd* (1913) 108 LT 450. As to the court's power to deal with costs see the Supreme Court Act 1981 s 51 (as substituted) and PRACTICE AND PROCEDURE.

The Companies Act 1985 s 404 is repealed from a day to be appointed by the Companies Act 1989 s 92(a) and replaced from a day to be appointed by the Companies Act 1985 s 402 (substituted by the Companies Act 1989 ss 92(a), 97). At the date at which this volume states the law no such days had been appointed. As to the proposed new registration system generally see para 1316 post.

7 *Re C L Nye Ltd* [1971] Ch 442, [1970] 3 All ER 1061, CA.

8 *Re Heathstar Properties Ltd* [1966] 1 All ER 628, [1966] 1 WLR 993.

9 *Re R M Arnold & Co Ltd* [1984] BCLC 535; cf *Re John Bateson & Co Ltd* [1985] BCLC 259 (where there were no exceptional circumstances).

1315. Procedure. The application must be made by originating summons in the expedited form[1], which should be supported by an affidavit proving the facts relied on as founding the court's jurisdiction to grant relief[2]. It is usually stated in the affidavit that no petition to wind up the company has been presented, no notice convening a meeting for voluntary liquidation has been served, and no judgment against the company has been recovered which is unsatisfied[3]. On an application for extension of time for registration, the court will not as a rule decide the question whether a charge requires registration[4].

There is usually inserted in an order granting an extension of time for registration a proviso that the order is to be without prejudice to any rights acquired prior to actual registration against the persons entitled to the mortgage or charge[5]. The usual form of proviso will not protect ordinary unsecured creditors unless, before actual registration, either they have acquired rights against or affecting the property charged by the debentures[6] or a winding up has commenced[7]; and no express words for their protection will in ordinary cases be inserted[8]. An order extending the time for registration will not usually be made where the liquidation of the company is imminent[9], and a fortiori after the company has gone into liquidation[10]. Where a liquidation is found to be imminent, the decision whether to extend time is a matter of discretion, the overriding question being whether it is just and equitable to grant an extension[11]. Where an administration order does not include as one of its purposes the survival of the company, or survival proves incapable of achievement, the court will nor normally extend time for registration since liquidation is inevitable[12]. In exceptional circumstances, however, an order may be made even after liquidation has commenced[13].

1 RSC Ord 102 r 2(1),(2). As to the procedure on an originating summons under RSC Ord 102 see para 69 ante.

2 *Re Kris Cruisers Ltd* [1949] Ch 138, [1948] 2 All ER 1105. If issues of fact arise, cross-examination on the affidavits may be allowed: *Re Heathstar Properties Ltd* [1966] 1 All ER 628, [1966] 1 WLR 993. For a case where there was a long delay see *Re Telomatic Ltd* [1994] 1 BCLC 90.

3 *Re Bootle Cold Storage and Ice Co* [1901] WN 54; *Re Tingri Tea Co Ltd* [1901] WN 165. These statements in the affidavit are, it appears, unnecessary since the purpose of the discretion given to the court as regards granting registration out of time is to protect secured creditors, not unsecured creditors of the company: see *Re MIG Trust Ltd* [1933] Ch 542 at 571, CA.

4 *Re Cunard SS Co Ltd* [1908] WN 160; *Re Heathstar Properties Ltd (No 2)* [1966] 1 All ER 1000, [1966] 1 WLR 993 at 999.

5 *Re Joplin Brewery Co Ltd* [1902] 1 Ch 79; *Re I C Johnson & Co Ltd* [1902] 2 Ch 101, CA, where the form of proviso settled by the Court of Appeal was as follows: 'Provided always that this order is to be without prejudice to any right which may have been or may be acquired against the holders of the said debentures prior to the time when such debentures shall be actually registered'. The order in that case referred to some only of a series of debentures, the remainder having been registered in due time. See also *Re Kris Cruisers Ltd* [1949] Ch 138, [1948] 2 All ER 1105; *Crew v Cummings* (1888) 21 QBD 420, CA; *Re Parsons, ex p Furber* [1893] 2 QB 122, CA and *Re R M Arnold & Co Ltd* [1984] BCLC 535 (where the addition of this proviso would have rendered the order pointless); cf BILLS OF SALE vol 4(1) (Reissue) para 760. Where liquidation is contemplated, the order should give an opportunity to the

liquidator when appointed to apply for the discharge of the order; for a form see *Re L H Charles & Co Ltd* [1935] WN 15. A liquidator's application for discharge of the order will be by way of a complete rehearing in which the court is not limited to the evidence before the registrar or the grounds on which he based his decision: *Re Braemar Investments Ltd* [1989] Ch 54, [1988] 3 WLR 596.

6   *Re Ehrmann Bros Ltd* [1906] 2 Ch 697, CA; *Re MIG Trust Ltd* [1933] Ch 542, CA.

7   *Re Ehrmann Bros Ltd* [1906] 2 Ch 697, CA; *Re Anglo-Oriental Carpet Manufacturing Co* [1903] 1 Ch 914.

8   *Re Cardiff Workmen's Cottage Co Ltd* [1906] 2 Ch 627; and see *Re MIG Trust Ltd* [1933] Ch 542, CA.

9   *Re Resinoid and Mica Products Ltd* [1983] Ch 132n, [1982] 3 All ER 677n, CA; *Re Ashpurton Estates Ltd* [1983] Ch 110, sub nom *Victoria Housing Estates Ltd v Ashpurton Estates Ltd* [1982] 3 All ER 665, CA.

10 *Re S Abrahams & Sons* [1902] 1 Ch 695 (where the order was refused after the winding up had commenced on the ground that with the protecting proviso it could have no beneficial effect); *Re Resinoid and Mica Products Ltd* [1983] Ch 132n, [1982] 3 All ER 677n, CA; *Re John Bateson & Co Ltd* [1985] BCLC 259; cf *Re Spiral Globe Ltd* [1902] 1 Ch 396 and *Re R M Arnold & Co Ltd* [1984] BCLC 535 (where the proviso was not added for the converse reason); and see *Re Ehrmann Bros Ltd* [1906] 2 Ch 697, CA; *Re L H Charles & Co Ltd* [1935] WN 15 (a case where notices convening a meeting to consider a resolution for voluntary winding up had been sent out, and a provision was added to the order entitling the liquidator, if appointed, to apply to the court to challenge the order).

11 *Re Braemar Investments Ltd* [1989] Ch 54, [1988] 3 WLR 596.

12 *Re Barrow Borough Transport Ltd* [1990] Ch 227, [1989] 3 WLR 858.

13 *Re R M Arnold & Co Ltd* [1984] BCLC 535 (only other person interested in subject matter of charge did not object).

D. PROPOSED NEW REGISTRATION SYSTEM

1316. In general. Part IV of the Companies Act 1989[1] amends the provisions of the Companies Act 1985 relating to the registration of company charges by inserting[2] new provisions with respect to companies registered in Great Britain[3]. The provisions come into force on such day as the Secretary of State may by order made by statutory instrument appoint[4], such day not having yet been appointed.

The proposed new system of registration relates to:

(1) introductory provisions[5];
(2) charges requiring registration[6];
(3) the companies' charges register[7];
(4) a company's duty to deliver particulars of a charge for registration[8];
(5) the effect of failure to deliver particulars for registration[9];
(6) late delivery of particulars[10];
(7) delivery of further particulars[11];
(8) the effect of omissions and errors in registered particulars[12];
(9) a memorandum of a charge ceasing to affect a company's property[13];
(10) the exclusion of voidness as against unregistered charges[14];
(11) restrictions on voidness[15];
(12) the effect of the exercise of a power of sale[16];
(13) the effect of voidness on the obligation secured[17];
(14) particulars of the taking up of the issue of debentures[18];
(15) notice of appointment of a receiver or manager[19];
(16) notice of crystallisation of floating charges etc[20];
(17) the duty to keep copies of instruments and a register of charges[21];
(18) inspection of copies of instruments and the register of charges[22];
(19) the Secretary of State's power to make further provision by regulations[23];
(20) the date of creation of a charge[24];
(21) the prescribed particulars of a charge and related expressions[25];
(22) notice of matters disclosed on the register[26];
(23) the court's power to dispense with signature[27];

(24) the making of regulations[28];

(25) minor definitions[29];

(26) an index of defined expressions[30].

A similar proposed new system is to be introduced with respect to charges created by oversea companies[31].

1 Ie the Companies Act 1989 Pt IV (ss 92–107).
2 Ie in the Companies Act 1985 Pt XXII in place of ss 395–408 (as amended) (registration of charges (England and Wales)) and ss 410–423 (as amended) (registration of charges (Scotland)).
3 Companies Act 1989 s 92(a).
4 See ibid s 215(2).
5 Ie the Companies Act 1985 s 395 (substituted by the Companies Act 1989 ss 92(a), 93).
6 Ie the Companies Act 1985 s 396 (substituted by the Companies Act 1989 ss 92(a), 93).
7 Ie the Companies Act 1985 s 397 (substituted by the Companies Act 1989 ss 92(a), 94).
8 Ie the Companies Act 1985 s 398 (substituted by the Companies Act 1989 ss 92(a), 95).
9 Ie the Companies Act 1985 s 399 (substituted by the Companies Act 1989 ss 92(a), 95).
10 Ie the Companies Act 1985 s 400 (substituted by the Companies Act 1989 ss 92(a), 95).
11 Ie the Companies Act 1985 s 401 (substituted by the Companies Act 1989 ss 92(a), 96).
12 Ie the Companies Act 1985 s 402 (substituted by the Companies Act 1989 ss 92(a), 97).
13 Ie the Companies Act 1985 s 403 (substituted by the Companies Act 1989 ss 92(a), 98).
14 Ie the Companies Act 1985 s 404 (substituted by the Companies Act 1989 ss 92(a), 99).
15 Ie the Companies Act 1985 s 405 (substituted by the Companies Act 1989 ss 92(a), 99).
16 Ie the Companies Act 1985 s 406 (substituted by the Companies Act 1989 ss 92(a), 99).
17 Ie the Companies Act 1985 s 407 (substituted by the Companies Act 1989 ss 92(a), 99).
18 Ie the Companies Act 1985 s 408 (substituted by the Companies Act 1989 ss 92(a), 100).
19 Ie the Companies Act 1985 s 409 (substituted by the Companies Act 1989 ss 92(a), 100).
20 Ie the Companies Act 1985 s 410 (substituted by the Companies Act 1989 ss 92(a), 100).
21 Ie the Companies Act 1985 s 411 (substituted by the Companies Act 1989 ss 92(a), 101).
22 Ie the Companies Act 1985 s 412 (substituted by the Companies Act 1989 ss 92(a), 101).
23 Ie the Companies Act 1985 s 413 (substituted by the Companies Act 1989 ss 92(a), 102).
24 Ie the Companies Act 1985 s 414 (substituted by the Companies Act 1989 ss 92(a), 103).
25 Ie the Companies Act 1985 s 415 (substituted by the Companies Act 1989 ss 92(a), 103).
26 Ie the Companies Act 1985 s 416 (substituted by the Companies Act 1989 ss 92(a), 103).
27 Ie the Companies Act 1985 s 417 (substituted by the Companies Act 1989 ss 92(a), 103).
28 Ie the Companies Act 1985 s 418 (substituted by the Companies Act 1989 ss 92(a), 104).
29 Ie the Companies Act 1985 s 419 (substituted by the Companies Act 1989 ss 92(a), 104).
30 Ie the Companies Act 1985 s 420 (substituted by the Companies Act 1989 ss 92(a), 104).
31 See the Companies Act 1989 ss 92(b), 105, Sch 15 and para 1827 post.

(27) REMEDIES FOR ENFORCING SECURITIES

(i) Remedies under the Security

A. IN GENERAL

1317. Debenture holder's remedies. If the debenture gives no charge on the company's assets, the debenture holder, being an unsecured creditor, has only the rights against the company which any unsecured creditor has against an individual debtor, and also the right to present or support a petition for its winding up. As a general rule, however, the holder of a debenture or debenture stock of a company has a charge or, where the debenture stock is secured by a trust deed, the trustees usually have a legal mortgage on specific assets of the company, and, if so, he or they may enforce the usual remedies of a legal or equitable mortgagee against the company in the same manner as if it were an individual[1]. One of these rights is to have a sale of the property charged, either under the power given by the charge or by statute[2], or with the assistance of the court. If the company goes into liquidation, the rights of a secured creditor under his security are not prejudiced, and the liquidator cannot obtain an injunction to restrain a sale by the secured creditor except on the usual terms of paying the amount due, or, if it is not agreed, paying the amount claimed, into court[3].

The right of the debenture holder to exercise the remedies otherwise open to him is subject to certain statutory restrictions[4].

1 See para 1346 post.
2 See the Law of Property Act 1925 s 101(1)(i) and MORTGAGE vol 32 para 712 et seq; but see also para 1251 text and note 3 ante.
3 See *Re Poole Firebrick and Blue Clay Co* (1873) LR 17 Eq 268; *Walker v Banagher Distillery Co* (1875) 1 QBD 129.
4 As to the position where a petition has been presented for an administration order see para 2083 post; as to the powers of an administrator with regard to a company's property see paras 2097, 2098 post; and as to the powers of an administrative receiver see para 2155 et seq post.

1318. Construction of references to receivers and managers. Except where the context otherwise requires, any reference in the Companies Act 1985 or the Insolvency Act 1986 to a receiver or manager of the property of a company, or to a receiver of it, includes a reference to a receiver or manager, or, as the case may be, to a receiver of part only of that property and to a receiver only of the income arising from that property or from part of it[1]. Any such reference to the appointment of a receiver or manager under powers contained in an instrument includes an appointment made under powers which, by virtue of any enactment, are implied in and have effect as if contained in an instrument[2].

1 Insolvency Act 1986 s 29(1)(a). As to administrative receivers see paras 1344, 2147 et seq post.
2 Ibid s 29(1)(b).

1319. Provisions of the Insolvency Act 1986 in relation to receivers not retrospective. The new law[1] does not apply in relation to any receiver or manager of a company's property who was appointed before 29 December 1986[2] and the relevant provisions of the former law[3] continue to have effect[4]. It follows, therefore, that any person who is appointed an administrative receiver[5] is subject to the new law.

The above provisions are, however, without prejudice to the power conferred by the Insolvency Act 1986 under which company insolvency rules[6] may make transitional provision in connection with the coming into force of those rules; and such provision may apply those rules in relation to the receiver or manager of a company's property notwithstanding that he was appointed before the coming into force of those rules, or of the provision[7] under which they were made[8].

1 For these purposes, 'the new law' means the Insolvency Act 1986 Pt III Ch I (ss 28-49 (as amended): see para 2147 et seq post) and Pt VI (ss 230-246 (as amended): see paras 2149, 2151, 2157, 2158 et seq post, although ss 238-246 (as amended) do not directly affect the position of receivers): s 437, Sch 11 para 2(2).
2 Ie the date on which the Insolvency Act 1986 came into force: see para 2002 post.
3 For these purposes, 'the former law' means the Companies Act 1985 and so much of the Insolvency Act 1986 as replaces the provisions of that Act (without the amendments in the Insolvency Act 1985 Sch 6 paras 15-17: see paras 1330-1334 post), or the associated repeals made by that Act) and any provision of the Insolvency Act 1985 which was in force before 29 December 1986: Insolvency Act 1986 Sch 11 para 2(2).
4 Ibid Sch 11 para 2(1). See paras 1340-1343 post.
5 For the meaning of 'administrative receiver' see para 1344 post. As to administrative receivers generally see para 2147 et seq post.

6 Ie made under the Insolvency Act 1986 s 411: see para 2800 post.
7 Ie ibid s 411: see para 2800 post.
8 Ibid Sch 11 para 2(3).

1320. Appointment of receiver or manager. A debenture or trust deed often gives power to appoint a receiver or manager in specified events[1]. Such a power given in debentures of a series is a fiduciary power; and, if an appointment is made which is not for the benefit of the debenture holders, but with a view to the benefit of the company or third persons, the court will interfere and appoint its own receiver[2]. The appointment of a person as a receiver or manager of a company's property under powers contained in an instrument[3] is, however, of no effect unless it is accepted by that person before the end of the business day[4] next following that on which the instrument of appointment is received by him or on his behalf[5]; and, subject to this, the appointment is deemed to be made at the time at which the instrument of appointment is so received[6]. The date of the document is immaterial[7]. The above provisions apply to the appointment of two or more persons as joint receivers or managers of a company's property under powers contained in an instrument, subject to such modifications as may be prescribed by the rules[8].

The power of a secured creditor to appoint a receiver under his security may be exercised, assuming that all conditions necessary for the appointment have been satisfied, at any time the creditor chooses; and, as regards timing, he owes no duty either to the company or to any guarantors to select any time other than one which suits his own convenience[9]. In making any such appointment, the person making it is under no duty to refrain from so doing because this may cause loss to the company or its unsecured creditors, as, for example, where a liquidator who could do all that the receiver could do has already been appointed[10].

On the making of an administration order[11], any administrative receiver[12] of the company must vacate office[13]; and, where such an order has been made, any receiver of part of the company's property must vacate office on being required to do so by the administrator[14]. During the period for which such an order is in force, no administrative receiver of the company may be appointed[15]; and no other steps may be taken to enforce any security over the company's property, or to repossess goods in the company's possession under any hire-purchase agreement except with the consent of the administrator or the leave of the court[16] and subject, where the court gives leave, to such terms as the court may impose[17].

1 As to the statutory power of a mortgagee by deed to appoint a receiver see the Law of Property Act 1925 s 101(1)(iii) and MORTGAGE vol 32 para 743; but cf para 1251 text and note 3 ante. As to an invalid appointment by deed taking effect as an appointment in writing see *Windsor Refrigerator Co Ltd v Branch Nominees Ltd* [1961] Ch 375, [1961] 1 All ER 277, CA. The power to appoint often arises under the terms of a debenture upon failure by the company to make repayment of all sums due thereunder on demand. Such demand need not specify the actual sum due (*Bank of Baroda v Panessar* [1987] Ch 335, [1986] 3 All ER 751, following *Bunbury Foods Pty Ltd v National Bank of Australasia Ltd* (1984) 54 ALJ 199 (Aust HC); and see *NRG Vision Ltd v Churchfield Leasing Ltd* (1988) 4 BCC 56) but must give the company sufficient time to carry out any necessary mechanics of payment in relation to sums assumed to be already at its disposal (*R A Cripps & Son Ltd v Wickenden* [1973] 2 All ER 606, [1973] 1 WLR 944; *Bank of Baroda v Panessar* supra). If the power to appoint a receiver has become exercisable on the happening of a specified event, the appointment is valid notwithstanding that the reason given for the appointment at the time is not on those grounds but only adduced subsequently; and the power to appoint a receiver is valid even if the charge documents take effect only under hand so that any receiver appointed cannot execute deeds on the company's behalf: *Byblos Bank SAL v Al-Khudhairy* [1987] BCLC 232, CA.

2 *Re Maskelyne British Typewriter Ltd, Stuart v Maskelyne British Typewriter Ltd* [1898] 1 Ch 133, CA; *Re Slogger Automatic Feeder Co Ltd* [1915] 1 Ch 478 (where the order was made on the application of the equitable mortgagees of some of the debentures).

3 For the meaning of 'contained in an instrument' see para 1318 ante.

4 For these purposes, 'business day' means any day other than a Saturday, a Sunday, Christmas Day, Good Friday, or a day which is a bank holiday in any part of Great Britain: Insolvency Act 1986 s 251.

5 Ibid s 33(1)(a). In the case of an appointment made before 29 December 1986 (see para 2002 post) these provisions do not apply and the former law prevails ie assuming that all necessary conditions have been fulfilled, the appointment took effect when the document of appointment was handed to the receiver by a person having the necessary authority: *R A Cripps & Son Ltd v Wickenden* [1973] 2 All ER 606, [1973] 1 WLR 944. For the meaning of 'the former law' see para 1319 note 3 ante.

6 Insolvency Act 1986 s 33(1)(b).

7 *R A Cripps & Son Ltd v Wickenden* [1973] 2 All ER 606, [1973] 1 WLR 944.

8 Insolvency Act 1986 ss 33(2), 251. See also the Insolvency Rules 1986, SI 1986/1925, r 3.1 (as substituted) and para 2152 post.

9 *Shamji v Johnson Matthey Bankers Ltd* [1986] BCLC 278; on appeal [1986] 1 FTLR 329, CA.

10 *Re Potters Oils Ltd (No 2)* [1986] 1 All ER 890, [1986] 1 WLR 201.

11 As to administration orders see para 2080 et seq post.

12 For the meaning of 'administrative receiver' see para 1344 post.

13 Insolvency Act 1986 s 11(1)(b). As to the interrelationship between administration orders and administrative receiverships see para 2148 post.

14 Ibid s 11(2). As to remuneration, expenses and indemnity in this event see para 1338 post.

15 Ibid s 11(3)(b).

16 As to the mode of application and the procedure see para 2814 et seq post.

17 Insolvency Act 1986 s 11(3)(c).

1321. Liability for invalid appointment. Where the appointment of a person as the receiver or manager of a company's property under powers contained in an instrument[1] is discovered to be invalid, whether by virtue of the invalidity of the instrument or otherwise, the court may order the person by whom or on whose behalf the appointment was made to indemnify the person appointed against any liability which arises solely by reason of the invalidity of the appointment[2]. The acts of an individual as administrative receiver[3] of a company are, however, valid notwithstanding any defect in his appointment, nomination or qualifications[4].

1 For the meaning of 'contained in an instrument' see para 1318 ante.

2 Insolvency Act 1986 s 34. In the case of an appointment of a receiver prior to 29 December 1986 (see para 2002 post) the provisions of s 34 will not apply: see para 1319 ante.

3 For the meaning of 'administrative receiver' see para 1344 post. As to administrative receivers generally see para 2147 et seq post.

4 Insolvency Act 1986 s 232.

1322. Effect of appointment of receiver. The appointment of a receiver is one of the events which causes a floating charge to crystallise[1]. As regards all the property comprised in the security over which the receiver is appointed, the directors' powers are of necessity paralysed. The powers exercisable by the receiver depend, however, entirely upon the combination of the precise terms of the debenture and his appointment, as supplemented, in the case of an administrative receiver[2], by certain statutory powers[3] if not inconsistent with the terms of the debenture. The receiver's status, whether as agent for the debenture holders[4] or, as is usual, and is, in the case of an administrative receiver, expressly provided by statute[5], as agent for the company, depends on similar considerations[6].

A person dealing with an administrative receiver of a company in good faith and for value is not, however, concerned to inquire whether the administrative receiver is acting within his powers[7].

The appointment of a receiver normally has no effect upon the company's contracts, except such as cannot well subsist concurrently with the receivership, such as contracts of management. Ordinary contracts of employment, for example, will not be affected[8], save that, if they are adopted by an administrative receiver in the carrying out of his functions, he will become personally liable on them but only to the extent of any qualifying liability[9]. Apart from that, if, as is usual, the receiver has powers of management, the decision whether to cause the company to fulfil existing contracts is solely a matter for his discretion, at any rate where the repudiation of the contract would not adversely affect the realisation of the assets or seriously affect the trading prospects of the company, if it is able to trade in the future[10].

A provision in a debenture empowering the receiver to bring an action in the name of the company whose assets are charged is merely an enabling provision, investing the receiver with the capacity to bring such an action, and does not divest the company's directors of their power to institute proceedings on behalf of the company, provided that the proceedings do not interfere with the receiver's function of getting in the company's assets or prejudicially affect the debenture holder by imperilling the assets[11].

1 See para 1266 ante.
2 For the meaning of 'administrative receiver' see para 1344 post. As to administrative receivers generally see para 2147 et seq post.
3 As to such powers see para 2154 post.
4 See eg *Re Vimbos Ltd* [1900] 1 Ch 470.
5 See the Insolvency Act 1986 s 44(1)(a) (following the Law of Property Act 1925 s 109(2)) and para 2160 post. As in any other case of agency, this agency is determined by the liquidation of the company: see the Insolvency Act 1986 s 44(1)(a) and para 2160 post.
6 See note 4 supra.
7 Insolvency Act 1986 s 42(3).
8 *Re Mack Trucks (Britain) Ltd* [1967] 1 All ER 977, [1967] 1 WLR 780; *Re Foster Clark Ltd's Indenture Trusts, Loveland and Horscroft* [1966] 1 All ER 43 at 49, [1966] 1 WLR 125 at 132 per Plowman J; *Griffiths v Secretary of State for Social Services* [1974] QB 468, [1973] 3 All ER 1184 (employment of managing director under service contract subject to control of board not determined by appointment of receiver); *Re Peek Winch & Tod Ltd* (1980) 130 NLJ 116, [1979] CA Transcript 190, CA.
9 See the Insolvency Act 1986 s 44(1)(b) (as amended) and para 2160 post. For this purpose, he will not be taken to have adopted a contract of employment by reason of anything done or omitted to be done within 14 days after his appointment: see s 44(2) and para 2160 post. In the case of an ordinary receiver (which includes all receivers appointed before 29 December 1986: see para 1319 ante) this provision does not apply, and accordingly employees who continue to work for the company after his appointment will not be regarded as employed by him: see *Nicoll v Cutts* [1985] BCLC 322, CA. See generally RECEIVERS.
10 *Airlines Airspares Ltd v Handley Page Ltd* [1970] Ch 193, [1970] 1 All ER 29n.
11 *Newhart Developments Ltd v Co-operative Commercial Bank Ltd* [1978] QB 814, [1978] 2 All ER 896, CA; distinguished in *Tudor Grange Holdings Ltd v Citibank NA* [1992] Ch 53, [1991] 4 All ER 1.

1323. Rates and taxes. So long as the receiver is the agent of the company, the company remains as rateable occupier of any premises so occupied by it; and the company remains liable to pay any rates[1]. If and when the receiver ceases to be the agent of the company, he or his then principal[2] may become liable to pay the rates, if he takes such possession as constitutes rateable occupation[3].

So far as corporation tax is concerned, if and so long as the receiver is the agent of the company, the tax position of the company remains unchanged, and the company will be the person chargeable to tax. If and when the receiver is not, or ceases to be, the agent of the company, since nevertheless it remains entitled to the benefit of the income produced by the receiver's conduct of its affairs, it would appear that the company would be chargeable thereon[4].

In the case of VAT, since failure to pay the same is a criminal offence[5], although the company continues to be the taxable person so long as the receiver is its agent, the receiver must ensure payment to the Commissioners of Customs and Excise, as he would otherwise be causing the company to commit a criminal act[6]. Once he is not, or ceases to be, the agent of the company, he will himself become a taxable person and so directly responsible therefor[7].

1 *Liverpool Corpn v Hope* [1938] 1 KB 751, [1938] 1 All ER 492, CA (action against receiver for rates dismissed; receiver is under no statutory duty pursuant to the Law of Property Act 1925 s 109(8)(i) (see MORTGAGE vol 32 para 747) owed to the rating authority); *Ratford v Northavon District Council* [1987] QB 357, [1986] 3 All ER 193, DC. The situation would be different if the receiver had dispossessed the company, or taken possession in an independent capacity: *Ratford v Northavon District Council* supra.
2 See para 1336 post.
3 *Richards v Kidderminster Overseers* [1896] 2 Ch 212.
4 See the Income and Corporation Taxes Act 1988 s 8(2) and INCOME TAXATION vol 23 (Reissue) para 840.
5 See the Value Added Tax Act 1994 s 72 and VALUE ADDED TAX.
6 *Re John Willment (Ashford) Ltd* [1979] 2 All ER 615, [1980] 1 WLR 73. The Commissioners of Customs and Excise have no right to demand VAT by virtue of the Law of Property Act 1925 s 109(8)(i): *Re John Willment (Ashford) Ltd* supra.
7 See the Value Added Tax Act 1994 ss 1(2), 4 and VALUE ADDED TAX.

1324. Notification of appointment of receiver. If a person obtains an order for the appointment of a receiver[1] or manager[2] of a company's property or appoints such a receiver or manager under powers contained in an instrument[3], he must, within seven days of the order or of the appointment under those powers, give notice in the prescribed form[4] of the fact to the registrar of companies; and the registrar must enter the fact in the register of charges[5]. Where a person appointed receiver or manager of a company's property under the powers contained in an instrument ceases to act as such receiver or manager, he must on so ceasing give the registrar notice in the prescribed form[6] to that effect; and the registrar must enter the fact in the register of charges[7]. If a person makes default in complying with these requirements, he is liable on summary conviction to a fine not exceeding one-fifth of the statutory maximum and, on conviction after continued contravention, to a daily default fine not exceeding one-fiftieth of the statutory maximum[8].

Where a receiver or manager of the property of a company has been appointed, every invoice, order for goods or business letter issued by or on behalf of the company or its receiver or manager or liquidator, being a document on or in which the company's name appears, must contain a statement that a receiver or manager has been appointed[9]. If default is made in complying with this provision, the company, and any officer or liquidator of the company and any receiver or manager who knowingly and wilfully authorises or permits the default, is liable on summary conviction to a fine not exceeding one-fifth of the statutory maximum[10].

1 For the meaning of 'receiver' see para 1318 ante.
2 For the meaning of 'manager' see para 1318 ante.
3 For the meaning of 'contained in an instrument' see para 1318 ante.
4 For the prescribed form of notice see the Companies (Forms) Regulations 1985, SI 1985/854, reg 4(1), Sch 3, Form 405(1).
5 Companies Act 1985 s 405(1),(3). Section 405 is repealed from a day to be appointed by the Companies Act 1989 s 92(a) and replaced from a day to be appointed by the Companies Act 1985 s 409 (substituted by the Companies Act 1989 ss 92(b), 100). At the date at which this volume states the law no such days had been appointed. As to the proposed new registration system generally see para 1316 ante.
6 For the prescribed form of notice see the Companies (Forms) Regulations 1985 Sch 3, Form 405(2).

7 Companies Act 1985 s 405(2),(3). See also note 5 supra.
8 Ibid ss 405(4), 730, Sch 24. See also note 5 supra. For the meaning of 'the statutory maximum' and 'daily default fine' see para 1161 ante.
9 Insolvency Act 1986 s 39(1).
10 Ibid ss 39(2), 430, Sch 10.

1325. Corporation not to act as receiver. A body corporate[1] is not qualified for appointment as receiver of the property of a company[2]; and an attempt to appoint such a body as receiver is a nullity[3]. Any body corporate which acts as such a receiver is liable on conviction on indictment to a fine, or on summary conviction to a fine not exceeding the statutory maximum[4].

An administrative receiver must be a person who is qualified to act as an insolvency practitioner in relation to the company[5].

1 For these purposes, 'body corporate' does not include a corporation sole, nor a Scottish firm, but includes a company incorporated elsewhere than in Great Britain: Companies Act 1985 s 740 (applied by the Insolvency Act 1986 s 251).
2 Insolvency Act 1986 s 30.
3 *Portman Building Society v Gallwey* [1955] 1 All ER 227, [1955] 1 WLR 96.
4 Insolvency Act 1986 ss 30, 430, Sch 10. For the meaning of 'the statutory maximum' see para 1161 ante.
5 See para 2150 post.

1326. Undischarged bankrupt not to act as receiver or manager. If a person being an undischarged bankrupt acts as receiver or manager of the property of a company on behalf of debenture holders, he is liable on conviction on indictment to imprisonment for a term not exceeding two years or a fine, or to both, or on summary conviction to imprisonment for a term not exceeding six months or a fine not exceeding the statutory maximum, or to both[1]. This provision does not apply, however, to a receiver or a manager acting under an appointment made by the court[2].

1 Insolvency Act 1986 ss 31, 430, Sch 10. For the meaning of 'the statutory maximum' see para 1161 ante.
2 Ibid s 31.

1327. Powers of receiver appointed out of court. The powers of a receiver, other than an administrative receiver[1], appointed out of court depend upon the provisions of the debenture under which he is appointed, together with any appropriate statutory powers[2]. Normally, the debenture will confer upon him power to carry on part of the business of the company, for he will have no such power unless specifically so authorised[3]. If he has such power, he will normally have, as incidental thereto, power to borrow upon the security of the assets in his hands[4]; but he will require express power to borrow on such security in priority to the debenture holders' charge thereon.

1 For the meaning of 'administrative receiver' see para 1344 post. As to the powers of an administrative receiver see para 2154 et seq post.
2 Eg the Law of Property Act 1925 s 109: see MORTGAGE vol 30 para 745.
3 *Bompas v King* (1886) 33 ChD 279.
4 *Robinson Printing Co Ltd v Chic Ltd* [1905] 2 Ch 123.

1328. Getting in uncalled capital. Unless the terms of the instrument under which he was appointed contain provisions to the contrary, an administrative receiver[1] has power to call up any uncalled capital of the company[2]. In all other cases, if uncalled capital is included in the security, the liquidator is the proper person to get it in, and what he receives, less the expenses of making and enforcing the call, is paid to the receiver; but the court may authorise the receiver, on giving a proper indemnity, to get in the calls in the name of the liquidator[3].

1 For the meaning of 'administrative receiver' see para 1344 post. As to administrative receivers generally see para 2147 et seq post.

2 See the Insolvency Act 1986 s 42(1), Sch 1 para 19 and para 2154 post.

3 See the cases cited in para 1355 note 4 post.

1329. Liability of trustees etc for receiver's acts. An administrative receiver[1] of a company is deemed to be the agent of the company unless and until it goes into liquidation[2]. In all other cases the question of his status depends upon the construction of the relevant power of appointment. Where the receiver is appointed under a document which provides that the person appointed receiver is to be the agent of the company, and that the company is alone to be answerable[3] for his acts, contracts and defaults, neither the trustees nor the debenture holders are personally liable in respect of contracts entered into by him, even in respect of contracts entered into after the company has gone into liquidation[4]. In such circumstances he becomes, if the company goes into liquidation, a principal[5], unless by his acts he puts himself in the position of an agent of the debenture holder[6].

When a receiver is declared to be the agent of the company, he has power to sue in its name[7]. Where there is no such provision, he will be the agent primarily of the debenture holders, and they will be liable on his contracts[8], and liable to pay him reasonable remuneration[9].

A receiver who incurs liability in respect of proper contracts is entitled to be indemnified out of the property subject to the security[10].

A receiver may be ordered at the instance of the plaintiff to give discovery of documents belonging to the company but in his possession as receiver in an action against the company and himself as managing director of it[11].

1 For the meaning of 'administrative receiver' see para 1344 post. As to administrative receivers generally see para 2147 et seq post.

2 See the Insolvency Act 1986 s 44(1)(a) and para 2160 post. This is in any event the normal position under the provisions of the instrument of charge.

3 As to the receiver's liability notwithstanding this see, however, para 1330 post.

4 *Gosling v Gaskell* [1897] AC 575, HL, disapproving the dictum of Lord Esher MR in *Owen & Co v Cronk* [1895] 1 QB 265 at 272, CA, that the receiver is the agent of the trustees. Cf the Law of Property Act 1925 s 109(2) which provides that a receiver appointed under the powers conferred by that Act (see para 1320 note 1 ante) 'shall be deemed to be the agent of the mortgagor, and the mortgagor shall be solely responsible for the receiver's acts or defaults unless the mortgage deed otherwise provides'; and see *Deyes v Wood* [1911] 1 KB 806, CA, where the corresponding provision of the Conveyancing Act 1881 s 24(2) (repealed), was, on the construction of the debenture, deemed to be incorporated, but it was held that the mortgage otherwise provided that the receiver was to be the agent of the debenture holder. This case was distinguished in *Cully v Parsons* [1923] 2 Ch 512, where a provision was inserted that a debenture holder should not in making or consenting to the appointment of a receiver incur any liability to him for his remuneration or otherwise. As to a receiver's liability as occupier of a factory see *Meigh v Wickenden* [1942] 2 KB 160, [1942] 2 All ER 68.

5 *Gosling v Gaskell* [1897] AC 575, HL. His status is thus akin to that of a receiver appointed by the court.

6 *American Express International Banking Corpn v Hurley* [1985] 3 All ER 564.

7 *M Wheeler & Co Ltd v Warren* [1928] Ch 840, CA. As to the powers of an administrative receiver see para 2154 et seq post. After a winding-up order has been made, a receiver is entitled to continue an action begun before the order for the grant of a new lease under the Landlord and Tenant Act 1954 Pt II (ss 23-46) (as amended): *Gough's Garages Ltd v Pugsley* [1930] 1 KB 615 (decided under the Landlord and

Tenant Act 1927 (repealed)). As to the renewal of business tenancies generally see LANDLORD AND
TENANT vol 27(1) (Reissue) para 558 et seq.
8 *Robinson Printing Co Ltd v Chic Ltd* [1905] 2 Ch 123; *Re Vimbos Ltd* [1900] 1 Ch 470.
9 *Deyes v Wood* [1911] 1 KB 806, CA.
10 See paras 1330, 1356, 2160 post. Cf *Batten v Wedgwood Coal and Iron Co* (1884) 28 ChD 317; and the
cases cited in para 1356 note 2 post.
11 *Fenton Textile Association Ltd v Lodge* [1928] 1 KB 1, CA. As to the ownership of documents coming into
existence during the receivership see *Gomba Holdings UK Ltd v Minories Finance Ltd* [1989] 1 All ER 261,
[1988] 1 WLR 1231, CA (ownership depends on the capacity in which the receivers acted when they
brought the documents into existence).

1330. Liability of a receiver other than an administrative receiver. A receiver
or manager appointed under powers contained in an instrument[1], other than an
administrative receiver[2], is, to the same extent as if he had been appointed by order of
the court[3]:

(1) personally liable on any contract entered into by him in the performance of his
functions, except in so far as the contract otherwise provides, and on any
contract of employment adopted by him[4] in the performance of those functions[5]; and

(2) entitled in respect of that liability to indemnity out of the assets[6].

The above provisions do not, however, limit any right to indemnity which the
receiver or manager would have apart from it, nor limit his liability on contracts
entered into without authority, nor confer any right to indemnity in respect of that
liability[7].

On the termination of his agency by the liquidation of the company, he will be
personally bound by any contracts made by him, and, if he contracts in the name of the
company, he may be liable for breach of warranty of authority[8]. Otherwise he is
entitled to ratify contracts made by others ostensibly as agents for the company[9].

A receiver for debenture holders who intends to sell the benefit of a contract may be
restrained from doing so if the assignment is one which will not be valid without the
consent of the other party to the contract, and that consent is withheld[10].

Where a receiver has received money from the company and paid it into a
receivership account and the money was obtained by the company wrongfully, the
receiver is not liable personally to repay the money, if, at the time when he paid it in, he
had no knowledge that it had been wrongfully obtained[11]. A receiver is not a debtor to
the company from time to time of the amount which may ultimately prove to be the
balance in his hands after payment of preferential claims and the amount due to
debenture holders[12].

A receiver who is appointed by debenture holders and is acting as their agent is liable
as a trespasser if he deals with assets which are not the property of the company[13].

In realising the property of the company, as in the exercise of all his powers, the
receiver is under a duty not to act negligently[14]. He must obtain the best possible price
he can in all the circumstances of the case. This duty is owed not only to the company
itself, but also to a guarantor of the company's debt[14].

The receiver's conveyance of the company's property even after liquidation is not in
contravention of the provisions of the Insolvency Act 1986 prohibiting dispositions of
the company's property made after the commencement of the winding up without the
leave of the court[15], since the relevant disposition is the charge under which the
receiver was appointed[16].

1 For the meaning of 'contained in an instrument' see para 1318 ante.
2 As to the liability of an administrative receiver see para 2160 post.

3 As to the liability of a receiver appointed by the court see para 1356 post.

4 For these purposes, the receiver or manager is not to be taken to have adopted a contract of employment by reason of anything done or omitted to be done within 14 days after his appointment: Insolvency Act 1986 s 37(2).

5 Ibid s 37(1)(a). See also *Bacal Contracting Ltd v Modern Engineering (Bristol) Ltd* [1980] 2 All ER 655 (receiver joined as defendant ordered pursuant to the Supreme Court of Judicature (Consolidation) Act 1925 s 50(1) (repealed: see now the Supreme Court Act 1981 s 51 (as substituted) and PRACTICE AND PROCEDURE) to pay personally costs of action continued by him after his appointment provided he had recourse to debenture holders). As to the circumstances under which it may be proper to make the receiver a defendant to an action against the company with resultant liability for costs see *Telemetrix plc v Modern Engineers of Bristol (Holdings) plc* [1985] BCLC 213.

In the case of a receiver appointed before 29 December 1986 (see para 2002 post) the former law applies and the receiver is not liable in respect of contracts of employment: see *Griffiths v Secretary of State for Social Services* [1974] QB 468, [1973] 3 All ER 1184; *Nicoll v Cutts* [1985] BCLC 322, CA. For the meaning of 'the former law' see para 1319 note 3 ante.

6 Insolvency Act 1986 s 37(1)(b).

7 Ibid s 37(3).

8 *Gosling v Gaskell* [1987] AC 575, HL; *Thomas v Todd* [1926] 2 KB 511.

9 *Lawson (Inspector of Taxes) v Hosemaster Machine Co Ltd* [1966] 2 All ER 944, [1966] 1 WLR 1300, CA.

10 *Griffiths v Tower Publishing Co Ltd and Moncreiff* [1897] 1 Ch 21.

11 *Owen & Co v Cronk* [1895] 1 QB 265, CA (excessive amount charged for work done by the company; payment obtained by duress); *Bissell v Ariel Motors (1906) Ltd and Walker* (1910) 27 TLR 73 (contract induced by misrepresentation). In *Owen & Co v Cronk* supra at 271, 275 Lord Esher MR and Rigby LJ drew a distinction between the liability of a receiver appointed under an instrument and a receiver appointed by the court; but see text and note 3 supra.

12 *Seabrook Estate Co Ltd v Ford* [1949] 2 All ER 94 (where a judgment creditor of the company sought unsuccessfully to attach money alleged to be owing from the receiver to the company); and see EXECUTION vol 17 para 527.

13 *Re Goldberg (No 2), ex p Page* [1912] 1 KB 606 (where a sale by a bankrupt to a company was set aside as a fraudulent assignment and an act of bankruptcy, and the receiver was held liable as a trespasser to account for the assets of the bankrupt which had come into his hands).

14 *Standard Chartered Bank Ltd v Walker* [1982] 3 All ER 938, [1982] 1 WLR 1410, CA, overruling *Barclays Bank Ltd v Thienel* (1978) 247 Estates Gazette 385 and *Latchford v Beirne* [1981] 3 All ER 705; *American Express International Banking Corpn v Hurley* [1985] 3 All ER 564.

15 Ie the Insolvency Act 1986 s 127: see para 2460 post.

16 *Sowman v David Samuel Trust Ltd* [1978] 1 All ER 616, [1978] 1 WLR 22 (if the debentures under which the receiver is appointed contain a full power of attorney, the receiver and the debenture holders will be able to execute any necessary assurance in the name of the company, since such power continues to subsist, both at common law and under the provisions of the Powers of Attorney Act 1971 s 4, even after the liquidation of the company); *Barrows v Chief Land Registrar* (1977) Times, 20 October.

1331. Application to court for directions. A receiver or manager of the property of a company appointed under powers contained in an instrument[1], or the persons by whom or on whose behalf a receiver or manager has been so appointed[2], may apply to the court for directions in relation to any particular matter arising in connection with the performance of the functions of the receiver or manager[3]. On such an application the court may give such directions, or may make such order declaring the rights of persons before the court or otherwise, as it thinks just[4].

1 For the meaning of 'contained in an instrument' see para 1318 ante.

2 If the appointment was made before 29 December 1986 (see para 2002 post), only the receiver is entitled to make such an application: see para 1319 ante and the Companies Act 1985 s 492(1) (repealed).

3 Insolvency Act 1986 s 35(1). Section 35 is drafted in wide terms and should be given scope wide enough to embrace any dispute concerning a receiver or manager's remuneration. Further, s 35 should be read as a whole; it follows that all those matters which can be the subject of an application under s 35(1) can be the subject of directions or a declaration under s 35(2) and vice versa: *Morris v Lewis* (1996) Times, 29 March.

4 Insolvency Act 1986 s 35(2).

1332. Filing receiver's accounts. Subject to certain exceptions[1], every receiver or manager of a company's property who has been appointed under powers contained in an instrument[2] must deliver to the registrar of companies for registration the requisite accounts of his receipts and payments[3].

The accounts must be delivered within one month, or such longer period as the registrar may allow, after the expiration of 12 months[4] from the date of his appointment and of every subsequent period of six months, and also within one month after he ceases to act as receiver or manager[5]. The requisite accounts must be an abstract in the prescribed form[6] showing:

(1) receipts and payments during the relevant period of 12 or six months[7]; or

(2) where the receiver or manager ceases to act, receipts and payments during the period from the end of the period of 12 or six months to which the last preceding abstract related, or, if no preceding abstract has been so delivered, from the date of his appointment, up to the date of his so ceasing, and the aggregate amount of receipts and payments during all preceding periods since his appointment[8].

A receiver or manager who makes default in complying with the above provisions is liable on summary conviction to a fine not exceeding one-fifth of the statutory maximum and, on conviction after continued contravention, to a daily default fine not exceeding one-fiftieth of the statutory maximum[9].

1 As to the position where the appointment was made before 29 December 1986 see paras 1340, 1341 post; and as to the position where an administrative receiver has been appointed see para 2185 post. For the meaning of 'administrative receiver' see para 1344 post.

2 For the meaning of 'contained in an instrument' see para 1318 ante.

3 Insolvency Act 1986 s 38(1).

4 Before 29 December 1986 when the relevant provisions of the Insolvency Act 1986 were brought into force (see para 2002 post) this period was six months only: see the Companies Act 1985 s 498(2) (repealed).

5 Insolvency Act 1986 s 38(2).

6 For these purposes, 'prescribed' means prescribed by regulations made by statutory instrument by the Secretary of State: ibid s 38(4). For the prescribed form of abstract see the Insolvency Rules 1986, SI 1986/1925, r 12.7, Sch 4, Form 3.6.

7 Before 29 December 1986 this period was uniformly six months: see the Companies Act 1985 s 498(2) (repealed).

8 Insolvency Act 1986 s 38(3).

9 Ibid ss 38(5), 430, Sch 10. For the meaning of 'the statutory maximum' and 'daily default fine' see para 1161 ante.

1333. Default in rendering accounts. A receiver or manager is under a duty, as an accounting party to the company[1], and also, where this is the case, as its agent, to keep and deliver to the company when required full accounts of his dealings with the company's property[2]. This duty, which may be enforced by an action in the ordinary way, is not displaced by the following provisions[2].

If a receiver or manager of a company's property:

(1) having made default in filing, delivering or making any return, account or other document, or in giving any notice, which a receiver or manager is by law required to file, deliver, make or give, fails to make good the default within 14 days after the service on him of a notice requiring him to do so; or

(2) having been appointed under powers contained in an instrument[3], has, after being required at any time by the liquidator of the company to do so, failed to

render proper accounts of his receipts and payments and to vouch them and pay over to the liquidator the amount properly payable to him,

the court may, on an application made for the purpose[4], make an order directing the receiver or manager, as the case may be, to make good the default within such time as may be specified in the order[5].

In the case of default mentioned in head (1) above, application to the court may be made by any member or creditor of the company or by the registrar of companies; and, in the case of the default mentioned in head (2) above, the application must be made by the liquidator[6]. In either case the court's order may provide that all costs of and incidental to the application shall be borne by the receiver or manager, as the case may be[7].

1 See the Law of Property Act 1925 s 109(8) and RECEIVERS.
2 *Smiths Ltd v Middleton* [1979] 3 All ER 842.
3 For the meaning of 'contained in an instrument' see para 1318 ante.
4 As to the mode of application and the procedure see para 2814 et seq post.
5 Insolvency Act 1986 s 41(1). Nothing in s 41 prejudices the operation of any enactment imposing penalties on receivers in respect of any such default as is mentioned in s 41(1): s 41(3). It does not apply, however, in the case of a receiver appointed before 29 December 1986: see para 1319 ante.
6 Ibid s 41(2).
7 Ibid s 41(3).

1334. Payment of preferential debts out of assets subject to floating charge. Where debentures of a company registered in England and Wales are secured by a charge which, as created, was a floating charge, then, if possession is taken, by or on behalf of the holders of any of the debentures, of any property comprised in or subject to the charge, and the company is not, at that time, in course of being wound up[1], the company's preferential debts[2] must be paid out of assets coming to the hands of the person taking possession in priority to any claims for principal or interest in respect of the debentures[3].

Where a receiver is appointed on behalf of the holders of any debentures of a company secured by a charge which, as created, was a floating charge, then, if the company is not at the time in course of being wound up, its preferential debts[4] must be paid out of the assets coming to the hands of the receiver in priority to any claims for principal or interest in respect of the debentures[5].

If a second floating charge crystallises before a prior floating charge, it becomes a fixed charge and takes priority over the uncrystallised floating charge, even if the latter charge subsequently crystallises[6].

Payments so made must be recouped, as far as may be, out of the assets of the company available for payment of general creditors[7].

Where the charge, as created, was partly specific and partly floating, the priority of such preferential payments applies only to the assets secured by the floating charge[8]. They do not obtain priority over all other payments such as the costs of realisation and the receiver's remuneration, but rank immediately before the principal and interest secured by the debentures[9].

A receiver and manager is liable in damages to the preferential creditors if he exhausts the assets in carrying on the company's business on behalf of the debenture holders by paying ordinary debts without first paying the preferential debts[10]; or if, having collected assets, he hands them over to the company with the knowledge that it will transfer them to the debenture holder in satisfaction of his claim without any provision being made for payment of the preferential debts[11]. An action in tort by a preferential creditor for damages for failing to pay his debt out of available assets is not barred by lapse of time if the receiver had sufficient assets to pay the debt at any time within six years[12] before the bringing of the action[13].

1 A company is not in the course of being wound up until a winding-up order has been made: *Re Christonette International Ltd* [1982] 3 All ER 225, [1982] 1 WLR 1245.

2 For these purposes, 'preferential debts' means the categories of debts listed in the Insolvency Act 1986 s 386(1), Sch 6 (as amended) (see para 2523 et seq post); and, for the purposes of Sch 6 (as amended), 'the relevant date' is the date of possession being so taken: Companies Act 1985 s 196(3) (substituted by the Insolvency Act 1986 s 439(1), Sch 13 Pt I).

3 Companies Act 1985 s 196(1),(2) (substituted by the Insolvency Act 1986 Sch 13 Pt I). In the case of a receiver appointed before 29 December 1986 (see para 2002 post), the relevant provisions of the Companies Act 1985 s 196 as originally enacted will apply: see the Insolvency Act 1986 ss 436, 437, 443, Sch 11 para 2 and para 1319 ante. The effect of this is that the property out of which the preferential debts are to be paid is property comprised in a charge which, at the relevant date, was still floating, and the relevant preferential debts are those set out in the Companies Act 1985 Sch 19 (repealed). Nothing in the Companies Consolidation (Consequential Provisions) Act 1985 (which effected the repeal of the Companies Act 1948) affects the priority to which any person may have been entitled under the Companies Act 1948 s 319(1)(a)(ii) (repealed) in respect of a debt of the description specified therein (which included references to profits tax and excess profits tax) or under s 319(1)(f),(g) (repealed) (old workmen's compensation cases): Companies Consolidation (Consequential Provisions) Act 1985 s 21.

4 Ie preferential debts within the meaning given to that expression by the Insolvency Act 1986 s 386 (as amended): see para 2523 et seq post. For the purposes of s 386(1), Sch 6 (as amended), 'the relevant date' is the date of the appointment of the receiver by debenture holders: s 387(1),(4)(a).

5 Ibid s 40(1),(2). This provision applies where the receiver appointed by the debenture holders takes possession even though no appointment has been made by the court: *Re Barnby's Ltd, Fallows v Barnby's Ltd* [1899] WN 103. As to the form of order appointing a receiver so far as it relates to preferential creditors see para 1371 post; and as to the priority given to preferential debts in winding up over the claims of debenture holders under a floating charge see para 2531 post. See also note 3 supra.

6 *Griffiths v Yorkshire Bank plc* [1994] 1 WLR 1427.

7 Companies Act 1985 s 196(4) (substituted by the Insolvency Act 1986 Sch 13 Pt I); Insolvency Act 1986 s 40(3).

8 *Re Lewis Merthyr Consolidated Collieries Ltd* [1929] 1 Ch 498, CA; *Re G L Saunders Ltd* [1986] 1 WLR 215 (where a surplus arising from the sale of assets subject to a fixed charge was ordered to be paid to the company); *Re Griffin Hotel Co Ltd, Joshua Tetley & Son Ltd v Griffin Hotel Co Ltd* [1941] Ch 129, [1940] 4 All ER 324, followed in *Herde v Mahabirsingh* [1992] 1 WLR 869, PC.

9 *Re Glyncorrwg Colliery Co Ltd* [1926] Ch 951, where the assets were held applicable in the following order: (1) costs of realisation; (2) costs including receiver's remuneration; (3) costs, charges and expenses of the debenture trust deed including the trustees' remuneration; (4) plaintiffs' costs of action; (5) preferential creditors; (6) debenture holders. See also paras 1371, 1374 post.

10 *Woods v Winskill* [1913] 2 Ch 303; *Westminster Corpn v Haste* [1950] Ch 442, [1950] 2 All ER 65. If the receiver has disregarded the priority through misrepresentation by the debenture holders' agent, the illegality of which he was unaware is no bar to his enforcement of an indemnity given by the agent: *Westminster City Council v Treby* [1936] 2 All ER 21.

11 *IRC v Goldblatt* [1972] Ch 498, [1972] 2 All ER 202.

12 See the Limitation Act 1980 s 2 and LIMITATION OF ACTIONS.

13 *Westminster Corpn v Haste* [1950] Ch 442, [1950] 2 All ER 65.

1335. Transfer of rights under insurance contracts. On the appointment of a receiver or manager of the company's business or undertaking, or on possession being taken by or on behalf of holders of debentures constituting a floating charge, then, if the company has entered into contracts of insurance against any liability to third parties, its rights against the insurers in respect of that liability are automatically transferred to and vested in the third party; but the third party retains his rights to recover any balance not covered by insurance[1].

1 Third Parties (Rights against Insurers) Act 1930 s 1(1),(4)(b) (amended by the Insolvency Act 1985 s 235(1), Sch 8 para 7(2); the Insolvency Act 1986 s 439(2), Sch 14). See also the Workmen's Compen-

sation Act 1925 s 7(1),(2) (repealed); the Marine and Aviation Insurance (War Risks) Act 1952 s 4 and INSURANCE vol 25 (Reissue) para 795. As to the application of these provisions in winding up see paras 2433, 2515 post.

1336. Change of status on making of order for winding up or administration. Save that on the liquidation of the company the receiver, receiver and manager or administrative receiver[1] ceases to be agent of the company[2] and in general becomes a principal[3], such liquidation has no effect on the status or powers of the receiver. It is, however, possible for the receiver and the debenture holder so to conduct themselves that the receiver becomes the agent of the debenture holder[4].

On the making of an administration order[5], however, any administrative receiver of the company must vacate office[6]. Where an administration order has been made, any receiver of part of the company's property must vacate office on being required to do so by the administrator[7]. Where at any time an administrative receiver of the company has vacated office on the making of an administration order or a receiver of part of the company's property has vacated office on being required to do so by the administrator, his remuneration and any expenses properly incurred by him and any indemnity to which he is entitled out of the assets of the company, are charged on and must be paid out of any property of the company which was in his custody or under his control at that time in priority to any security held by the person by or on whose behalf he was appointed[8]. Neither an administrative receiver who vacates office on the making of an administration order nor a receiver of part of the company's property who has vacated office on being required to do so by the administrator is required on or after so vacating office to take any steps for the purpose of complying with any duty[9] imposed on him to pay the preferential creditors[10].

1 For the meaning of 'administrative receiver' see para 1344 post. As to administrative receivers generally see para 2147 et seq post.
2 As to administrative receivers see the Insolvency Act 1986 s 44(1)(a) and para 2160 post; and as to other receivers see *Gosling v Gaskell* [1897] AC 575.
3 *Thomas v Todd* [1926] 2 KB 511.
4 *American Express International Banking Corpn v Hurley* [1985] 3 All ER 564 (in which case the receiver will be liable to the debenture holder to indemnify him against any loss caused by his negligence).
5 As to administration orders see para 2080 et seq post.
6 See the Insolvency Act 1986 s 11(1)(b) and para 2091 post.
7 See ibid s 11(2) and para 2091 post.
8 See ibid s 11(4) and para 2091 post. Section 11(4) is subject to the general restriction on enforcement of claims while an administration order is in force under s 11(3): see s 11(4) and para 2091 post.
9 Ie pursuant to ibid s 40: see para 1334 ante.
10 Ibid s 11(5).

1337. Court's power to fix remuneration. On an application made by the liquidator of a company, the court may by order fix the amount to be paid by way of remuneration to a person who, under the powers contained in an instrument[1], has been appointed receiver or manager of the property of the company[2]. The power so given is intended to be confined to cases where the remuneration can clearly be seen to be excessive; it is not intended to ensure a routine taxation of the remuneration by the court[3]. Where no such previous order has been made, the court's power extends to fixing the remuneration for any period before the making of the order or the application for it[4], and is exercisable notwithstanding that the receiver or manager has died or ceased to act before the making of the order or the application for it[5]. Where the receiver or manager has been paid or has retained for his remuneration for any period before the making of the order any amount in excess of that so fixed for that period, the court's power extends to requiring him or his personal representatives to account for the excess or such part of it as may be specified[6] in the order; but this power[7] must not be exercised as respects any period before the making of the application for the order, unless in the court's opinion there are special circumstances making it proper for the power to be exercised[8]. On an application made either by the liquidator or by the receiver or manager the court may from time to time vary or amend any such order[9].

The statutory power does not extend to disbursements, the receiver's right to be indemnified in respect thereof depending upon the ordinary law of agency[10].

1 For the meaning of 'contained in an instrument' see para 1318 ante.
2 Insolvency Act 1986 s 36(1).
3 *Re Potters Oils Ltd (No 2)* [1986] 1 All ER 890, [1986] 1 WLR 201.
4 Insolvency Act 1986 s 36(2)(a).
5 Ibid s 36(2)(b).
6 Ibid s 36(2)(c).
7 Ie under ibid s 36(2)(c): see supra.
8 Ibid s 36(2).
9 Ibid s 36(3).
10 *Re Potters Oils Ltd (No 2)* [1986] 1 All ER 890, [1986] 1 WLR 201.

1338. Vacation of office by receiver. A receiver appointed by or on behalf of debenture holders will be displaced by the appointment of a receiver by debenture holders with a higher priority. The instrument under which he was appointed may contain power to remove him, in which case he will vacate office when notice of his removal is received by him[1]. He is in any event liable to be displaced by the appointment of a receiver by the court; and, on the making of an administration order[2], any administrative receiver[3] must vacate office, and any receiver of part of the company's property must vacate office on being required to do so by the administrator[4].

Where at any time the receiver or manager appointed under powers contained in an instrument[5], other than an administrative receiver, vacates office, his remuneration and any expenses properly incurred by him and any indemnity to which he is entitled out of the assets of the company are charged on and must be paid out of any property of the company which is in his custody or under his control at that time in priority to any charge or other security held by that person by or on whose behalf he was appointed[6].

1 *Windsor Refrigerator Co Ltd v Branch Nominees Ltd* [1961] Ch 375.
2 As to administration orders generally see para 2080 et seq post.
3 For the meaning of 'administrative receiver' see para 1344 post. As to administrative receivers generally see para 2147 et seq post.
4 See the Insolvency Act 1986 s 11(1)(b),(2) and para 2091 post.
5 For the meaning of 'contained in an instrument' see para 1318 ante.
6 Insolvency Act 1986 s 37(4).

1339. Cross-border operation of receivership provisions. A receiver[1] appointed under the law of either part of Great Britain in respect of the whole or any part of any property or undertaking of a company and in consequence of the company having created a charge which, as created, was a floating charge, may exercise his powers in the other part of Great Britain so far as their exercise is not inconsistent with the law applicable there[2].

1 For these purposes, 'receiver' includes a manager and a person who is appointed both receiver and manager: Insolvency Act 1986 s 72(2).
2 Ibid s 72(1).

B. TRANSITIONAL PROVISIONS

1340. Obligation to give information when receiver appointed. Where a receiver or manager was appointed under the powers contained in an instrument[1] in relation to the whole or substantially the whole of the property of the company on behalf of the holders of debentures secured by a floating charge, before 29 December 1986[2], certain statutory obligations[3] regarding the giving of notice and of information apply[4]. Where such a receiver is appointed on or after 29 December 1986, he will be an administrative receiver[5] and different provisions[6] apply[7].

1 For the meaning of 'contained in an instrument' see para 1318 ante.
2 Ie the date on which the Insolvency Act 1986 came into force: see para 2002 post.
3 See para 1341 post (where the modifications applicable under the Companies Act 1985 s 495(4) (repealed: see note 7 infra) in the case of an appointment out of court are indicated in the text).
4 Ie ibid ss 495-497 (repealed: see note 7 infra). See para 1341 et seq post.
5 For the meaning of 'administrative receiver' see para 1344 post.
6 See para 2147 et seq post.
7 Ie the Insolvency Act 1986 ss 46-49: see para 2153 et seq post. The provisions of the Companies Act 1985 ss 495-497 are repealed by the Insolvency Act 1986 s 438, Sch 12, but without affecting the position of receivers appointed prior to such repeal: s 437, Sch 11 para 2(1). See para 1319 ante.

1341. Information where receiver or manager appointed. Where, in the case of a company registered in England and Wales, a receiver or manager[1] of the whole, or substantially the whole, of the company's property was appointed on behalf of the holders of any debentures of the company secured by a floating charge before 29 December 1986[2], then, subject to the provisions specified below[3]:

(1) he was required forthwith to send to the company notice of his appointment in the prescribed form[4]; and

(2) within 14 days after receipt of the notice, or such longer period as might have been allowed by the court or the receiver, a statement in the prescribed form[5] as to the affairs of the company had to be made out and submitted to the receiver[6].

Within two months after receipt of the statement, the receiver was required to send:

(a) to the registrar of companies and to the court, a copy of the statement and of any comments he saw fit to make on it and, in the case of the registrar of companies, also a summary of the statement and of his comments, if any, on it; and

(b) to the company, a copy of any such comments or, if he did not see fit to make any comments, a notice to that effect; and

(c) to any trustees for the debenture holders on whose behalf he was appointed, and, so far as he was aware of their addresses, to all such debenture holders, a copy of the summary[7].

If the receiver was appointed under powers contained in an instrument[8], the above provisions[9] had effect with the omission of references to the court; and in any other case references to the court were to the court by which the receiver was appointed[10].

The above provisions did not apply, however, in relation to the appointment of a receiver or manager to act with an existing receiver or manager or in place of a receiver or manager dying or ceasing to act, except that, where it applied to a receiver or manager who died or ceased to act before it had been fully complied with, the references in heads (2), (a), (b) and (c) above to the receiver included his successor and any continuing receiver or manager[11].

If, however, the company was being wound up, the above provisions applied notwithstanding that the receiver or manager and the liquidator were the same person, but with any necessary modifications arising from that fact[12].

If the receiver made default in complying with these provisions, he was liable on summary conviction to a fine not exceeding one-fifth of the statutory maximum and, on conviction after continued contravention, to a daily default fine not exceeding one-fiftieth of the statutory maximum[13].

1 Except where the context otherwise required, any reference in the Companies Act 1985 to a receiver or manager of the property of a company, or to a receiver of it, included a reference to a receiver or manager or, as the case may be, to a receiver of part only of that property and to a receiver only of the income arising from the property or from part of it: s 500(a) (repealed). Cf the Insolvency Act 1986 s 29(1)(a): see para 1318 ante.

2 Ie the date on which the Insolvency Act 1986 came into force: see para 1319 note 2 ante. The Companies Act 1985 s 495 was repealed as from that date by the Insolvency Act 1986 s 438, Sch 12 and replaced by s 46 (see para 2153 post), but leaving receivers appointed before that date still subject to the former law: s 437, Sch 11 Pt I para 2. For the meaning of 'the former law' see para 1319 note 3 ante.

3 Ie subject to the Companies Act 1985 ss 495–497 (repealed): see infra and paras 1342, 1343 post.

4 For the prescribed form of appointment see the Companies (Forms) Regulations 1985, SI 1985/854, reg 4(1), Sch 3, Form 495(2)(a) (revoked by SI 1986/2097). This form still applies in the case of receivers appointed before 29 December 1986 notwithstanding the provisions of the Companies (Forms) (Amendment) Regulations 1986, SI 1986/2097: reg 2(1)(c),(2).

5 For the prescribed form of statement see the Companies (Forms) Regulations 1985 Sch 3, Form 495(3)(a) (receiver appointed under the powers contained in an instrument: see note 8 infra) or Form 495(3)(b) (receiver appointed by the court) (both forms revoked by SI 1986/2097). These forms still apply in the case of receivers appointed before 29 December 1986 notwithstanding the provisions of the Companies (Forms) (Amendment) Regulations 1986: reg 2(1)(c),(2).

6 Companies Act 1985 s 495(1),(2) (repealed: see note 2 supra).

7 Ibid s 495(3) (repealed: see note 2 supra). It was queried by Slade J in *Re Overmark, Smith Warden Ltd* [1982] 3 All ER 513, [1982] 1 WLR 1195 whether statements so prepared or subsequently circulated by the receiver could amount to acknowledgments of indebtedness for the purposes of the Limitation Act 1980. It was sufficient for the decision of that case for Slade J to hold that, even if this were so, the statements related only to the position as at the date of the appointment of the receiver. See also para 2280 post, where the same questions arise in relation to statements submitted on liquidation to the Official Receiver.

8 Except where the context otherwise required, any reference in the Companies Act 1985 to the appointment of a receiver or manager under powers contained in an instrument included a reference to an appointment made under powers which, by virtue of any enactment, were implied in and had effect as if contained in an instrument: s 500(b) (repealed). Cf the Insolvency Act 1986 s 29(1)(b): see para 1318 ante.

9 Ie the Companies Act 1985 s 495(2),(3) (repealed: see note 2 supra).

10 Ibid s 495(4) (repealed: see note 2 supra).

11 Ibid s 495(5) (repealed: see note 2 supra).

12 Ibid s 495(6) (repealed: see note 2 supra).

13 Ibid ss 495(7) (repealed: see note 2 supra), 730, Sch 24. For the meaning of 'the statutory maximum' and 'daily default fine' see para 1161 ante.

1342. Statement of affairs to be submitted to receiver. The company's statement of affairs required[1] to be submitted to the receiver appointed before 29 December 1986[2] or his successor[3] had to show as at the date of the receiver's appointment:

(1) the particulars of the company's assets, debts and liabilities;

(2) the names, residences and occupations of its creditors;

(3) the securities held by them respectively;

(4) the dates when the securities were respectively given; and

(5) such further or other information as might be prescribed[4].

The statement had to be submitted by, and be verified by affidavit of, one or more of the persons who were at the date of the receiver's appointment the directors and by the person who was at that date the secretary of the company, or by such of the following persons as the receiver or his successor, subject to the direction of the court, might require to submit and verify the statement:

(a) those persons who were or had been officers[5] of the company;

(b) those persons who had taken part in the company's formation at any time within one year before the date of the receiver's appointment;

(c) those persons who were in the company's employment, or had been in its employment during that year and were in the receiver's opinion capable of giving the information required;

(d) those persons who were or had been during that year officers of or in the employment of a company which was, or within that year was, an officer of the company to which the statement related[6].

A person making the statement and affidavit had to be allowed, and paid by the receiver or his successor out of his receipts, such costs and expenses incurred in and about the preparation and making of the statement and affidavit as the receiver or his successor might consider reasonable, subject to an appeal to the court[7].

If a person without reasonable excuse made default in complying with these provisions, he was liable on summary conviction to a fine not exceeding one-fifth of the statutory maximum and, on conviction after continued contravention, to a daily default fine not exceeding one-fiftieth of the statutory maximum[8].

1 Ie by the Companies Act 1985 s 495 (repealed): see para 1341 ante.

2 Ie the date on which the Insolvency Act 1986 came into force: see para 1319 note 2 ante. The Companies Act 1985 s 496 has been repealed by the Insolvency Act 1986 s 438, Sch 12 and replaced by s 47: see para 2161 et seq post.

3 References in the Companies Act 1985 s 496 (repealed: see note 2 supra) to the receiver's successor included a continuing receiver or manager: s 496(7) (repealed: see note 2 supra).

4 Ibid s 496(1) (repealed: see note 2 supra). Where the receiver was appointed under powers contained in an instrument (see para 1341 note 8 ante), s 496 (repealed) applied with the substitution for references to the court of references to the Secretary of State, and for references to an affidavit of references to a statutory declaration; and in any other case references to the court were to the court by which the receiver was appointed: s 496(5) (repealed: see note 2 supra). For the prescribed forms see para 1341 note 5 ante. The forms so prescribed embody the particulars and other prescribed information referred to in the text heads (1)–(5) supra: Companies (Forms) Regulations 1985, SI 1985/854, reg 4(2), Sch 4 Pt II (revoked by SI 1986/2097). In relation to any receiver appointed before 29 December 1986 this continues to apply notwithstanding the provisions of the Companies (Forms) (Amendment) Regulations 1986, SI 1986/2097: reg 2(2).

5 For the meaning of 'officer' see para 641 ante.

6 Companies Act 1985 s 496(2),(3) (repealed: see note 2 supra).

7 Ibid s 496(4) (repealed: see note 2 supra).

8 Ibid ss 496(6) (repealed: see note 2 supra), 730, Sch 24. For the meaning of 'the statutory maximum' and 'daily default fine' see para 1161 ante.

1343. Subsequent returns by receiver. Where, in the case of a company registered in England and Wales, the receiver[1] or manager of the whole or substantially the whole of the company's property was appointed before 29 December 1986[2] on behalf of the holders of any debentures of the company secured by a floating charge, he must:

(1) within two months, or such longer period as the court may allow, after the expiration of 12 months from the date of his appointment and of every subsequent period of 12 months; and

(2) within two months, or such longer period as the court may allow after he ceases to act as receiver or manager of the company's property,

send the requisite accounts of his receipts and payments to the registrar of companies, to any trustees for the debenture holders on whose behalf he was appointed, to the company and, so far as he is aware of their addresses, to all such debenture holders[3].

The requisite accounts must be an abstract in the prescribed form[4] showing:

(a) receipts and payments during the relevant period of 12 months; or

(b) where the receiver ceases to act, receipts and payments during the period from the end of the period of 12 months to which the last preceding abstract related, or, if no preceding abstract has been sent under this provision, from the date of his appointment, up to the date of his so ceasing, and the aggregate amount of receipts and payments during all preceding periods since his appointment[5].

This is without prejudice to the receiver's duty to render proper accounts of his receipts and payments to the persons to whom, and at the times at which, he may be required to do so apart from these provisions[6]. In this connection, having regard to his primary duty to the debenture holders, he does not, as agent for the company, owe it any duty to keep it continuously informed as to the state of the receivership; but he may, if not contrary to the interests of the debenture holders, provide information to enable the directors to perform their duties and, assuming they can show a bona fide intention and ability to redeem, he should provide all information necessary for that purpose[7].

These provisions apply, where the company is being wound up, notwithstanding that the receiver or manager and the liquidator are the same person, but with any necessary modifications arising from that fact[8].

If the receiver makes default in complying with these provisions, he is liable on summary conviction to a fine not exceeding one-fifth of the statutory maximum and, on conviction after continued contravention, to a daily default fine not exceeding one-fiftieth of the statutory maximum[9].

1 Nothing in the Companies Act 1985 s 495(5) (repealed) (see para 1341 ante) was to be taken as limiting the meaning of the expression 'the receiver' where used in, or in relation to, s 497(1) or (2) (repealed: see note 2 infra): s 497(3) (repealed: see note 2 infra).

2 Ie the date on which the Insolvency Act 1986 came into force: see para 1319 note 2 ante. The Companies Act 1985 s 497 has been repealed by the Insolvency Act 1986 s 438, Sch 12 and replaced, in relation to administrative receivers, by s 48: see para 2167 post.

3 Companies Act 1985 s 497(1) (repealed: see note 2 supra). Where the receiver was appointed under powers contained in an instrument (see para 1341 note 8 ante), s 497 (repealed) has effect with the substitution of the Secretary of State for the court; and in any other case references to the court are to the court by which the receiver was appointed: s 497(4) (repealed: see note 2 supra).

4 For the prescribed form of abstract see the Companies (Forms) Regulations 1985, SI 1985/854, reg 4(1), Sch 3, Form 497 (revoked by SI 1986/2097). This form still applies notwithstanding the provisions of the Companies (Forms) (Amendment) Regulations 1986, SI 1986/2097: reg 2(1)(c), (2).

5 Companies Act 1985 s 497(2) (repealed: see note 2 supra).

6 Ibid s 497(6) (repealed: see note 2 supra): see para 1333 ante.

7 *Gomba Holdings UK Ltd v Homan* [1986] 3 All ER 94, [1986] 1 WLR 1301.

8 Companies Act 1985 s 497(5) (repealed: see note 2 supra).

9 Ibid ss 497(7) (repealed: see note 2 supra), 730, Sch 24. For the meaning of 'the statutory maximum' and 'daily default fine' see para 1161 ante.

C. ADMINISTRATIVE RECEIVERS

1344. In general. In relation to a company registered in England and Wales, 'administrative receiver' means a receiver or manager[1] of the whole, or substantially the whole, of a company's property[2] appointed after 29 December 1986[3] by or on behalf of the holders of any debentures of the company secured by a charge which, as created, was a floating charge[4], or by such a charge and one or more other securities, or a person who would be such a receiver or manager but for the appointment of some other person as the receiver of part of the company's property[5].

However, since the general purpose and the nature of the statutory scheme relating to the qualifications, functions, powers and duties of administrative receivers are as appropriate to unregistered companies as to registered companies, the scheme of administrative receivership is not confined to appointments of receivers made over the property of registered companies[6].

1 As to the construction of references to receivers and managers see para 1318 ante.
2 For these purposes, 'property' includes money, goods, things in action, land and every description of property wherever situated and also obligations and every description of interest, whether present or future or vested or contingent, arising out of, or incidental to, property: Insolvency Act 1986 s 436.
3 Ie the date on which the Insolvency Act 1986 came into force: see para 2002 post.
4 For these purposes, 'floating charge' means a charge which, as created, was a floating charge and includes a floating charge within the Companies Act 1985 s 462 (Scottish floating charges): Insolvency Act 1986 s 251.
5 Ibid ss 28, 29(2), 443. In Pts I–VII (ss 1–251) (as amended), except in so far as the context otherwise requires, 'insolvency', in relation to a company, includes the appointment of an administrative receiver: s 247(1). As to administrative receivers generally see para 2147 et seq post.
6 *Re International Bulk Commodities Ltd* [1993] Ch 77, [1993] 1 All ER 361.

(ii) Remedies on Application to the Court

A. REMEDIES IN GENERAL

1345. Specific mortgage. A specific legal mortgage or equitable charge given by a company may, subject to the statutory restrictions[1] when an application for an administration order is pending or such an order is in force, be enforced in the same manner as similar securities given by an individual[2].

1 See para 1317 note 4 ante.
2 See MORTGAGE vol 32 para 785 et seq.

1346. Debenture holder's remedies. A debenture holder may obtain the appointment of a receiver or receiver and manager[1]. He may also sue for the recovery of his principal or interest if in arrear; or present a petition for the winding up of the company[2]; or enforce his security by obtaining an order for sale or, in some instances, for foreclosure[3]; or where, as is sometimes the case, the principal money and interest is guaranteed by some other company or person, enforce the guarantee. The passing of a resolution for voluntary winding up does not prevent a debenture holder from commencing proceedings to enforce his security[4], and the court will not restrain the action upon the liquidator's application[5]. Where a compulsory order has been made, a debenture holders' action cannot be begun or proceeded with except with the leave of the winding-up court, but leave is granted as a matter of course unless the same relief is given to the debenture holder in the winding up as he would obtain in the action[6].

During the period beginning with the presentation of a petition for an administration order[7] and ending with the making of such an order or the dismissal of the petition[8]:

(1) no resolution may be passed or order made for the winding up of the company[9];
(2) no steps may be taken to enforce any security over the company's property[10], or to repossess goods in the company's possession under any hire–purchase agree-

ment[11] except with the leave of the court and subject to such terms as the court may impose; and

(3) no other proceedings and no execution or other legal process may be commenced or continued, and no distress may be levied, against the company or its property except with the leave of the court and subject to such terms as the court may impose[12].

During the period for which an administration order is in force:

(a) no resolution may be passed or order made for the winding up of the company;

(b) no administrative receiver[13] of the company may be appointed;

(c) no other steps may be taken to enforce any security over the company's property, or to repossess goods in the company's possession under any hire-purchase agreement, except with the consent of the administrator or the leave of the court and subject, where the court gives leave, to such terms as the court may impose; and

(d) no other proceedings[14] and no execution or other legal process[14] may be commenced or continued, and no distress may be levied, against the company or its property except with the consent of the administrator or the leave of the court and subject, where the court gives leave, to such terms as the court may impose[15].

Provisions may be included in debentures restraining a holder from taking action without the consent of a specified number of the holders of the debentures[16].

1 See paras 1347, 1358 post.
2 See para 2211 post.
3 See para 1364 post.
4 *Re Longdendale Cotton Spinning Co* (1878) 8 ChD 150; *Re Henry Pound, Son and Hutchins* (1889) 42 ChD 402, CA; *Re David Lloyd & Co, Lloyd v David Lloyd & Co* (1877) 6 ChD 339, CA.
5 *Re Longdendale Cotton Spinning Co* (1878) 8 ChD 150.
6 See para 2652 post. As to proof by debenture holders and other secured creditors see para 2556 et seq post.
7 As to administration orders generally see para 2080 et seq post.
8 Where a petition for an administration order is presented at a time when there is an administrative receiver of the company, and the person by or on whose behalf the receiver was appointed has not consented to the making of the order, such period is deemed not to begin unless and until that person so consents: see the Insolvency Act 1986 s 10(3) and para 2083 post.
9 The leave of the court is not required for the presentation of a petition for winding up: see ibid s 10(2)(a) and para 2083 post.
10 The leave of the court is not required for the appointment of an administrative receiver or for his carrying out, whenever appointed, of any of his functions: see ibid s 10(2)(b),(c) and para 2083 post.
11 For these purposes, references to hire-purchase agreements include references to conditional sale agreements, chattel leasing agreements and retention of title agreements: ibid s 10(4). 'Hire purchase agreement' and 'conditional sale agreement' have the same meanings as in the Consumer Credit Act 1974 (see HIRE PURCHASE vol 22 para 37): Insolvency Act 1986 s 436. 'Chattel leasing agreement' means an agreement for the bailment (or, in Scotland, the hiring) of goods which is capable of subsisting for more than three months; and 'retention of title agreement' means an agreement for the sale of goods to a company, being an agreement (1) which does not constitute a charge on goods but (2) under which, if the seller is not paid and the company is wound up, the seller will have priority over all the other creditors of the company as respects the goods or any property representing the goods: s 251. See further para 1301 ante.
12 Ibid s 10(1). See also note 9 supra.
13 For the meaning of 'administrative receiver' see para 1344 ante. As to administrative receivers generally see para 2147 et seq post.
14 For these purposes, the concept of 'proceedings' and 'legal process' embraces all steps in legal proceedings from the issue of the initiating process to their determination in execution or any other forms of enforcement of a judgment: *Re Olympia & York Canary Wharf Ltd* [1993] BCLC 453 (the service of a notice on a company in administration making time of the essence under a contract, or the

acceptance of a repudiatory breach of a contract by a company in administration, whether the company's breach took place before or after the making of the administration order, did not constitute the commencement or continuation of a legal process; accordingly such notice could be served or repudiation accepted without the leave of the court or the consent of the adminsitrator, even though a company was in administration).

15 Insolvency Act 1986 s 11(3). As to the power of the administrator with the authorisation of the court to sell property free from charges etc see para 2098 post.

16 *Pethybridge v Unibifocal Co Ltd* [1918] WN 278.

B. APPOINTMENT OF RECEIVER

1347. Application for appointment of receiver. The appointment of a receiver[1] or a receiver and manager by the court may be obtained upon an originating summons, but it is generally obtained by motion in an action. In addition to claiming the appointment of a receiver and manager, the originating summons or writ usually claims to have the debentures enforced by foreclosure or sale[2], and asks for accounts and inquiries, which will include an account of what is due to the debenture holders upon the security of the debentures, and an inquiry as to what property is comprised in or charged by the debentures[3].

1 As to the position of receivers generally see RECEIVERS.

2 See paras 1364, 1365 post.

3 As to debenture holders' actions generally see para 1366 et seq post; and for orders made for inquiries as to charges see para 1371 post.

1348. When a receiver will be appointed. A receiver or receiver and manager will be appointed by the court where the principal[1] or interest[2] is in arrear; or where the security is in jeopardy, even if no event has happened which either under the debentures or the trust deed makes the security enforceable[3]; or where the company has sold the whole, or substantially the whole, of its undertaking and assets otherwise than in the ordinary course of business, and has ceased to be a going concern[4]; or on an order being made or a resolution being passed for the winding up of the company[5]. In some cases the court will also appoint a receiver in place of a receiver appointed by debenture holders under a power contained in the debentures[6].

1 *Hopkins v Worcester and Birmingham Canal Proprietors* (1868) LR 6 Eq 437.

2 *Bissill v Bradford Tramways Co Ltd* [1891] WN 51; cf *Re New York Taxicab Co Ltd, Sequin v New York Taxicab Co Ltd* [1913] 1 Ch 1 (where the interest was postponed). If the writ in a debenture holders' action is issued before the principal is payable or the interest is in default, the court has jurisdiction to and will appoint a receiver as soon as the money becomes payable: *Re Carshalton Park Estate Ltd, Graham v Carshalton Park Estate Ltd, Turnell v Carshalton Park Estate Ltd* [1908] 2 Ch 62.

3 *Re Tilt Cove Copper Co Ltd* [1913] 2 Ch 588 (where the company was proposing to distribute among its shareholders a reserve fund which constituted practically its only asset); *McMahon v North Kent Ironworks Co* [1891] 2 Ch 148 (where the company was insolvent and its works closed); *Thorn v Nine Reefs Ltd* (1892) 67 LT 93, CA; *Edwards v Standard Rolling Stock Syndicate* [1893] 1 Ch 574; *Re London Pressed Hinge Co Ltd, Campbell v London Pressed Hinge Co Ltd* [1905] 1 Ch 576; *Grigson v Taplin & Co* (1915) 85 LJ Ch 75 (where judgments had been recovered and executions were likely to issue); *Re Victoria Steamboats Ltd, Smith v Wilkinson* [1897] 1 Ch 158 (where a winding-up petition had been presented and creditors were pressing); *Re Braunstein and Marjorlaine Ltd* (1914) 112 LT 25 (where the directors had allowed to pass unchallenged statements by the company's auditors at a general meeting to the effect that, after providing for liabilities, the assets would cover only the principal secured, and one of the directors had stated that the company's credit and funds were exhausted); but cf *Re New York Taxicab Co, Sequin v New York Taxicab Co Ltd* [1913] 1 Ch 1 (where it was held that mere insolvency was not enough, and that there must be threats from creditors or some jeopardy to the assets).

4 *Hubbuck v Helms* (1887) 56 LJ Ch 536; and see *Re Borax Co, Foster v Borax Co* [1901] 1 Ch 326, CA.
5 *Hodson v Tea Co* (1880) 14 ChD 859; *Re Panama, New Zealand and Australian Royal Mail Co* (1870) 5 Ch App 318; cf *Re Crompton & Co Ltd* [1914] 1 Ch 954 (where it was unsuccessfully contended that a provision in the debentures that the security should become enforceable in the event of a winding up otherwise than for reconstruction impliedly prevented the security becoming enforceable on a reconstruction). It would appear, however, that provision may be made in the debenture excluding the operation of this decision: see *Re Crompton & Co Ltd* supra at 965.
6 See para 1320 ante.

1349. Who may be appointed receiver.

The person appointed receiver by the court is usually the person nominated by the plaintiff in an action to enforce the security[1]. The usual practice is to make the appointment upon an affidavit of fitness on the hearing of the motion asking for the appointment, and not on a reference of the matter to chambers. A receiver appointed on a misleading affidavit of fitness will be discharged[2]. Where the notice of motion does not ask for the appointment of any particular person, or an affidavit of fitness is not forthcoming, an order is made for the appointment of a receiver and is referred to chambers to determine who is to be appointed. A body corporate cannot be appointed[3], nor, in the case of the appointment of an administrative receiver[4] (which will be the normal case), may any person other than an insolvency practitioner be appointed[5].

1 See *Budgett v Improved Patent Forced Draught Furnace Syndicate Ltd* [1901] WN 23 (where the plaintiff was appointed). As to the choice of the person to be appointed see further RECEIVERS vol 39 para 845 et seq.
2 *Re Church Press Ltd* (1917) 116 LT 247.
3 See para 1325 ante. As to the position of an undischarged bankrupt see para 1326 ante.
4 For the meaning of 'administrative receiver' see para 1344 ante.
5 See para 2150 post.

1350. Receiver's security.

The receiver's appointment is usually made conditional on his giving security within 21 days, the amount and nature of which is to be settled in chambers; and the usual form of order for the appointment of a receiver provides that the appointment lapses unless the security is given within the time specified or such extended time as may be obtained[1]. If it is important that the receiver should act at once, application is made for liberty for him so to act, and an immediate appointment is made on the plaintiff's undertaking to be personally answerable, pending the completion of the security, for all the liabilities of the receiver which would be covered by the security when completed[2].

Where the applicant is a limited company, an undertaking from the company is not usually accepted, but must be given by some responsible person who signs an undertaking in the court's book. Where such an undertaking is not given, the appointment is conditional, taking effect only upon his giving security in chambers, and any disposition of the mortgaged assets pending completion of the security is not a contempt of court[3].

If the receiver is appointed with power to take possession but the order does not direct security to be given, the appointment takes effect on the making of the order[4]. Where a receiver is appointed until judgment or further order and is continued after judgment, he must give further security[5].

Premiums paid by a receiver to a guarantee society for joining in his security are allowed in his accounts[6].

1 See RSC Ord 30 r 2(2); *Rowley v Desborough* (1916) 60 Sol Jo 429; *Re Sims and Woods Ltd* (1916) 60 Sol Jo 539. As to security of receivers generally see RECEIVERS vol 39 para 858 et seq.

2 *Re Debenture-Holders' Actions* (1900) 16 TLR 256.
3 *Re Watkins, ex p Evans* (1879) 13 ChD 252, CA, explaining *Edwards v Edwards* (1876) 2 ChD 291, CA.
4 *Morrison v Skerne Ironworks Co Ltd* (1889) 60 LT 588.
5 *Brinsley v Lynton and Lynmouth Hotel and Property Co* (1895) 2 Mans 244.
6 *Harris v Sleep* [1897] 2 Ch 80, CA, limited to cases where the receiver was appointed without remuneration, but the modern practice is to allow the receiver to charge such premiums in his accounts even where he is remunerated.

1351. Official receiver or liquidator as receiver. Where application is made to the court to appoint a receiver on behalf of the debenture holders or other creditors of a company which is being wound up by the court, the official receiver may be appointed[1]. Although the debenture holders cannot insist upon their own nominee being appointed or retained in office as against the official receiver or liquidator, the court will not as a rule displace a receiver appointed by the debenture holders or mortgagees under their special powers, and, except under special circumstances, the Court of Appeal will not interfere when the court of first instance has refused to displace a receiver by a liquidator[2].

The court sometimes appoints the liquidator as receiver in respect of some or all of the assets[3]; and he may be appointed in the place of a receiver appointed by the court[4] where the assets are of an unusual character. In such a case the official receiver may be appointed receiver of part of them, leaving the receiver originally appointed to receive the other assets[5]. The liquidator cannot obtain the discharge of the receiver unless with a view to his being appointed receiver in his place[6].

In considering whether the same person shall act as receiver and liquidator, the court usually gives effect to the wishes of the parties most interested in the beneficial realisation of the company's assets[7].

1 Insolvency Act 1986 s 32; and see *British Linen Co v South American and Mexican Co* [1894] 1 Ch 108, CA. As to the official receiver see para 2263 et seq post.
2 *Re Joshua Stubbs Ltd, Barney v Joshua Stubbs Ltd* [1891] 1 Ch 475, CA; *Re Henry Pound, Son and Hutchins* (1889) 42 ChD 402, CA.
3 *Re Joshua Stubbs Ltd, Barney v Joshua Stubbs Ltd* [1891] 1 Ch 475, CA; *Willmott v London Celluloid Co* (1885) 52 LT 642, CA.
4 *Perry v Oriental Hotels Co* (1870) 5 Ch App 420; *Campbell v Compagnie Générale de Bellegarde, Re Compagnie Générale de Bellegarde* (1876) 2 ChD 181; *Tottenham v Swansea Zinc Ore Co Ltd* (1884) 53 LJ Ch 776; *Bartlett v Northumberland Avenue Hotel Co Ltd* (1885) 53 LT 611, CA.
5 *British Linen Co v South American and Mexican Co* [1894] 1 Ch 108, CA.
6 *Strong v Carlyle Press* [1893] 1 Ch 268, CA.
7 *Boyle v Bettws Llantwit Colliery Co* (1876) 2 ChD 726 (where the secured creditor was appointed receiver); *Re Karamelli and Barnett Ltd* [1917] 1 Ch 203 (where a receiver who was also liquidator was removed from the office of liquidator at the request of the unsecured creditors).

1352. Receiver of land abroad. A receiver may be appointed of land out of the jurisdiction[1]. Until what is necessary has been done in accordance with foreign law to put the receiver in possession of that property, no one, whether a British subject or a foreigner, is guilty of contempt of court by taking proceedings in a foreign country with reference to that property[2]; but the company may be ordered to revoke a power of attorney which is being used by the holder to prevent the receiver's agent from obtaining possession of property situated in a foreign country, and to execute a power of attorney in favour of the receiver's agent[3].

1 *Mercantile Investment and General Trust Co v River Plate Trust, Loan and Agency Co* [1892] 2 Ch 303.
2 *Re Maudslay, Sons and Field, Maudslay v Maudslay, Sons and Field* [1900] 1 Ch 602; *Re West Cumberland Iron and Steel Co* [1893] 1 Ch 713; *Re Derwent Rolling Mills Co Ltd* (1905) 21 TLR 701, CA.
3 *Re Huinac Copper Mines Ltd* [1910] WN 218.

1353. Receiver's statutory and other obligations. A receiver or manager appointed by the court is under the same statutory obligations as a receiver appointed under powers contained in an instrument[1]. A receiver, other than an administrative receiver[2], must:

(1) give notification of his appointment[3];
(2) pay the preferential debts[4]; and
(3) deliver receivership accounts to the registrar of companies[5].

An administrative receiver must comply with the statutory obligations in heads (1) and (2) above, and must also:

(a) give certain information as to his appointment[6];
(b) require the submission of a statement of affairs[7];
(c) make a report[8];
(d) furnish information to a creditors' committee[9]; and
(e) furnish VAT certificates[10].

An administrative receiver may be compelled to make good any default in filing, delivering or making any return, account or other document which he is by law required to file, deliver, make or give[11].

An administrative receiver is also under a non-statutory duty to keep and deliver to the company when required full accounts of his dealings with the company's property. This duty is enforced by an action in the ordinary manner[12].

 1 For the meaning of 'contained in an instrument' see para 1318 ante.
 2 For the meaning of 'administrative receiver' see para 1344 ante.
 3 See the Insolvency Act 1986 s 39(1) and para 1324 ante.
 4 See ibid s 40 and para 1334 ante.
 5 See ibid s 38 and para 1332 ante.
 6 See ibid s 46 and para 2153 post.
 7 See ibid s 47 and para 2161 post.
 8 See ibid s 48 and para 2167 post.
 9 See ibid s 49(2) and para 2173 post.
10 See the Insolvency Rules 1986, SI 1986/1925, rr 3.36-3.38 and para 2186 post.
11 See the Insolvency Act 1986 s 41 and para 1333 ante.
12 *Smiths Ltd v Middleton* [1979] 3 All ER 842; and see para 1333 ante.

1354. Default in making returns etc. If a receiver or manager of the property of a company, having made default in filing, delivering or making any return, account[1] or other document or in giving any notice, which a receiver or manager is by law required to file, deliver, make or give, fails to make good the default within 14 days after the service on him of a notice requiring him to do so, the court may, on an application made for the purpose, make an order directing him to make good the default within such time as may be specified in the order[2]. The application, which is by summons in the action in which he was appointed, may be made by any member or creditor of the company or by the registrar of companies and the order may provide that all costs of and incidental to the application shall be borne by the receiver or manager, as the case may be[3].

 1 The accounts are those required by the Insolvency Rules 1986, SI 1986/1925, r 3.32: see para 2185 post. As to the liability of any receiver to deliver accounts beyond those referred to see para 1333 ante.
 2 See the Insolvency Act 1986 s 41(1)(a) and para 1333 ante. Nothing in s 41 prejudices the operation of any enactment imposing penalties on receivers in respect of such default as is mentioned in s 41(1): see s 41(3) and para 1333 ante. See also RSC Ord 30 rr 5, 6 and RECEIVERS vol 39 paras 939, 954.
 3 See the Insolvency Act 1986 s 41(2) and para 1333 ante.

1355. Status of receiver. A receiver appointed by the court is an officer of the court; any interference with him as such receiver is a contempt of court[1]. He is disqualified from purchasing the interests of the debenture holders on whose behalf he has been appointed[2].

The receiver must do his best to collect, get in and realise all the property subject to the security, except uncalled capital[3]. If the company is in liquidation, the liquidator is the proper person to make and enforce the calls, the proceeds of which he pays over to the receiver; but leave may be given to the receiver on giving a proper indemnity to take proceedings in the liquidator's name to enforce the calls[4].

1 See *Ames v Birkenhead Docks (Trustees)* (1855) 20 Beav 332; *Russell v East Anglian Rly Co* (1850) 3 Mac & G 104; and CONTEMPT vol 9 para 34. As to actions against receivers and claims to property in their possession see *Re Maidstone Palace of Varieties Ltd* [1909] 2 Ch 283.
2 *Re Magadi Soda Co Ltd* (1925) 94 LJ Ch 217.
3 Although an administrative receiver (see para 1344 ante) has power to call up any uncalled capital of the company (see the Insolvency Act 1986 s 42, Sch 1 para 19 and para 2154 post), this is effected by deeming the power to be included in the powers conferred by the debenture, unless its terms are inconsistent: see s 42 and para 2154 post. This power is, therefore, not conferred upon such a receiver appointed by the court. The court may order the trustees of a trust deed to deliver possession of the title deeds to the receiver: see *Re Ind, Coope & Co Ltd* (1909) 26 TLR 11, CA. As to a receiver enforcing an order made in his favour for possession of assets of the company see *Savage v Bentley* (1904) 90 LT 641; *Re Derwent Rolling Mills Co Ltd* (1905) 21 TLR 701, CA. A solicitor to a company may retain money in his hands in payment of costs incurred prior to the appointment of the receiver, but must pay over the balance: *Re British Tea Table Co (1897) Ltd* (1909) 101 LT 707. As to the rights of a receiver appointed by the court of retaining rents received by him where a receiver appointed by a prior mortgagee had taken no steps see *Re Metropolitan Amalgamated Estates Ltd* [1912] 2 Ch 497.
4 *Fowler v Broad's Patent Night Light Co* [1893] 1 Ch 724; *Harrison v St Etienne Brewery Co* (1893) 37 Sol Jo 562; *Re Westminster Syndicate Ltd* (1908) 99 LT 924. As to the liquidator's power to make calls see para 2494 post.

1356. Receiver's liability. A receiver appointed by the court is personally liable on the contracts made by him as receiver[1], subject to his right to be indemnified out of the property subject to the debentures[2]. He is not the agent of the company or of the court, or of anyone else[3]. A receiver may, however, by a term in the contract exclude personal liability to a person with whom he contracts[4].

Where a receiver appointed by the court takes possession of leasehold property of the company, whether it is mortgaged by sub-demise to the trustees for debenture holders or is subject to an equitable mortgage, he is not liable for rent to the landlord[5]; and the same rule applies to chattels which have been hired by the company[6]. Even if the receiver has, by court order, sold goods upon which the landlord might have distrained, the court will not order him to pay the landlord out of the proceeds[7], nor, in similar circumstances, will an order be made for payment of rates in default of recovery by distress[8].

1 Cf the Insolvency Act 1986 s 37(1): see para 1330 ante.
2 *Owen & Co v Cronk* [1895] 1 QB 265, CA; *Burt, Boulton and Hayward v Bull* [1895] 1 QB 276, CA; *Re Glasdir Copper Mines Ltd, English Electro-Metallurgical Co Ltd v Glasdir Copper Mines Ltd* [1906] 1 Ch 365 at 368, CA; and see RECEIVERS vol 39 paras 928, 984. As to costs where a receiver is given leave to appeal in proceedings against the company see *Re Griffiths Cycle Corpn Ltd* (1902) 85 LT 776, CA. A receiver signing a bill of exchange as 'R, Receiver X Co Ltd' merely adds words describing him as an agent within the meaning of the Bills of Exchange Act 1882 s 26, and may sue or be sued personally on the bill of exchange: see *Kettle v Dunster and Wakefield* (1927) 138 LT 158 and BILLS OF EXCHANGE vol 4(1) (Reissue) para 377.

3 *Burt, Boulton and Hayward v Bull* [1895] 1 QB 276 at 279, 284, CA; *Re Glasdir Copper Mines Ltd, English Electro-Metallurgical Co Ltd v Glasdir Copper Mines Ltd* [1906] 1 Ch 365, CA; and see *Moss SS Co Ltd v Whinney* [1912] AC 254 at 259, 261, HL.

4 *Re Ernest Hawkins & Co Ltd* (1915) 31 TLR 247.

5 *Hand v Blow* [1901] 2 Ch 721, CA; *Re J W Abbott & Co Ltd, Abbott v J W Abbott & Co Ltd* (1913) 30 TLR 13; *Re Westminster Motor Garage Co, Boyers v Westminster Motor Garage Co* (1914) 84 LJ Ch 753. A receiver is entitled to treat tax paid by him in respect of rent due prior to his appointment as a pro tanto payment of rent: see *Re Sturmey Motors Ltd* [1913] 1 Ch 16; *Re Hayman, Christy and Lilly Ltd (No 2), Christy v Hayman, Christy and Lilly Ltd* [1917] 1 Ch 545; *Consolidated Entertainments Ltd v Taylor* [1937] 4 All ER 432.

6 *Hay v Swedish and Norwegian Rly Co Ltd* (1892) 8 TLR 775.

7 *Hand v Blow* [1901] 2 Ch 721, CA.

8 *Re British Fullers' Earth Co Ltd, Gibbs v British Fullers' Earth Co Ltd* (1901) 17 TLR 232; *Re Mayfair and General Property Trust Ltd, Crang v Mayfair and General Property Trust Ltd* [1945] 2 All ER 523 (where the receiver received 'inclusive rentals').

1357. Applications and proceedings by receiver. A receiver appointed by the court in an action should not apply to the court for directions unless the circumstances are exceptional; as a rule applications should be made by the plaintiff[1].

The question what proceedings a receiver should be allowed to take or continue at the expense of the company's assets is one solely for the discretion of the court, and debenture holders may not prevent a receiver from continuing an action by the company against themselves in another capacity[2].

1 *Parker v Dunn* (1845) 8 Beav 497; *Windschuegl v Irish Polishes Ltd* [1914] 1 IR 33.

2 *Viola v Anglo-American Cold Storage Co* [1912] 2 Ch 305.

C. APPOINTMENT OF MANAGER

1358. When a receiver and manager will be appointed. Where a company on whose assets debentures are charged is a going concern, the court will, at the instance of the debenture holders, appoint not merely a receiver, but a receiver and manager[1], provided that the company is carrying on a business which is included in the charge and which it is advisable to continue in the interests of the debenture holders for the more beneficial realisation of their security. The court will appoint a receiver and manager even where the charge does not in terms include the goodwill if it includes all the company's property or contains other words showing an intention to include the business[2]. If the debenture, as created, was a floating charge comprising the whole, or substantially the whole, of the company's property, so that any receiver appointed under it will be an administrative receiver[3], then, provided that there is nothing inconsistent in any of the provisions of that debenture, such receiver will have power to carry on the business of the company, and will therefore be a manager[4]. Otherwise, to justify the appointment the company's goodwill must be charged, expressly or by implication[5]. In the case, however, of a company incorporated for purposes of a public nature, and having statutory powers and duties, whether incorporated by a special Act or by charter, or under the Companies Act 1985, a holder of debentures or debenture stock cannot obtain the appointment of a manager[6], but an order may be made appointing a receiver of the tolls or other money receivable by the company and charged by the debenture or debenture stock[7].

A special case must be made out for the appointment of a manager by the affidavit supporting the application, and a manager is appointed only for a limited period (usually three months); and any extension of time required must be applied for before the period expires⁸. A receiver and manager will not be allowed the expenses of management incurred after the expiration of the period of his appointment⁹. Where no business is being carried on, or it is not in the interests of the debenture holders to continue it, a receiver only is appointed.

Jeopardy justifies the appointment of a manager of the company's business if there is a probability of a sale¹⁰.

1 *Reid v Explosives Co Ltd* (1887) 19 QBD 264, CA. The provisions of the Companies Act 1985 s 405 (repealed from a day to be appointed) and the Insolvency Act 1986 ss 29(1), 39, 41, 46, 47 apply to receivers and managers appointed by the court: see para 1320 et seq ante.
2 *Peek v Trinsmaran Iron Co* (1876) 2 ChD 115; *Makins v Percy Ibotson & Sons* [1891] 1 Ch 133; *Whitley v Challis* [1892] 1 Ch 64, CA; *Gloucester County Bank v Rudry Merthyr Steam and House Coal Colliery Co* [1895] 1 Ch 629, CA; *Jennings v Jennings* [1898] 1 Ch 378; *Re David and Matthews* [1899] 1 Ch 378; *Edwards v Standard Rolling Stock Syndicate* [1893] 1 Ch 574; and see *Campbell v Lloyd's, Barnett's and Bosanquet's Bank Ltd* [1891] 1 Ch 136n (where a manager was appointed on the application of a mortgagee); *Whitley v Challis* [1892] 1 Ch 64, CA.
3 For the meaning of 'administrative receiver' see para 1344 ante.
4 See the Insolvency Act 1986 s 42(1), Sch 1 para 14 and para 2097 post.
5 *Re Victoria Steamboats Ltd, Smith v Wilkinson* [1897] 1 Ch 158; *Re Leas Hotel Co, Salter v Leas Hotel Co* [1902] 1 Ch 332. As to registration of the manager's appointment see para 1324 ante.
6 *Gardner v London, Chatham and Dover Rly Co, Drawbridge v London, Chatham and Dover Rly Co, Gardner v London, Chatham and Dover Rly Co (No 2), Imperial Mercantile Credit Association v London, Chatham and Dover Rly Co* (1867) 2 Ch App 201; *Blaker v Herts and Essex Waterworks Co* (1889) 41 ChD 399; *Marshall v South Staffordshire Tramways Co* [1895] 2 Ch 36, CA, disapproving *Bartlett v West Metropolitan Tramways Co* [1893] 3 Ch 437, [1894] 2 Ch 286; cf *Re Crystal Palace Co, Fox v Crystal Palace Co* (1911) 104 LT 898, CA (affd sub nom *Saunders v Bevan* (1912) 107 LT 70, HL).
7 *Blaker v Herts and Essex Waterworks Co* (1889) 41 ChD 399; *Re Mitchell's Estate, Mitchell v Moberly* (1877) 6 Ch App 655; *Holdsworth v Davenport* (1876) 3 ChD 185; *Attree v Hawe* (1878) 9 ChD 337, CA. For a form of order see *Re Ticehurst and District Water and Gas Co* (1910) 128 LT Jo 516. See also para 1684 post.
8 *Day v Sykes, Walker & Co Ltd* (1886) 55 LT 763; *Re Victoria Steamboats Ltd, Smith v Wilkinson* [1897] 1 Ch 158. As to appointing a director or receiver and manager see *Budgett v Improved Patent Forced Draught Furnace Syndicate Ltd* [1901] WN 23. For forms of order see *Davies v Vale of Evesham Preserves Ltd* (1895) 73 LT 150.
9 *Re Wood Green and Hornsey Steam Laundry* [1918] 1 Ch 423.
10 *Re Victoria Steamboats Ltd, Smith v Wilkinson* [1897] 1 Ch 158. As to jeopardy see para 1348 ante.

1359. Effect of appointment on current contracts. The appointment by the court of a receiver and manager operates as a dismissal of the company's employees[1]; on his appointment they do not become his employees[2]. An administrative receiver[3] is, however, personally liable on any contract of employment adopted by him in the carrying out of his functions as such administrative receiver, but only to the extent of any qualifying liability[4], although he is not to be taken to have adopted a contract of employment by reason of anything done or omitted to be done within 14 days after his appointment[5].

It is the duty of a receiver and manager to complete contracts entered into by the company prior to his appointment if the completion of the contracts will assist in the preservation of the goodwill[6], but not otherwise[7]. When a receiver and manager has partly performed a continuing contract for the sale of goods between the company and another person and fails to perform the rest of the contract, that other person may set off the damages for breach of the contract against a claim for the purchase money for goods already supplied[8].

1 *Reid v Explosives Co Ltd* (1887) 19 QBD 264, CA; *Midland Counties District Bank Ltd v Attwood* [1905] 1 Ch 357 at 362; and see *Parsons v Sovereign Bank of Canada* [1913] AC 160, PC; *Re Great Cobar Ltd* [1915] 1 Ch 682 at 689. Cf the position where a receiver is appointed out of court: see para 1322 ante.

2 *Re Marriage, Neave & Co, North of England Trustee, Debenture and Assets Corpn v Marriage, Neave & Co* [1896] 2 Ch 663, CA.
3 For the meaning of 'administrative receiver' see para 1344 ante.
4 See the Insolvency Act 1986 s 44(1)(b) (as amended) and para 2160 post.
5 See ibid s 44(2) and para 2160 post. He will be entitled to the usual indemnity out of the assets (see para 1329 ante): see s 44(1)(c) and para 2160 post. Section 44 (as amended) does not limit any right to indemnity which he would have apart from it, nor limit his liability on contracts entered into or adopted without authority, nor confer any right to indemnity in respect of that liability: see s 44(3) and para 2160 post.
6 *Re Newdigate Colliery Ltd* [1912] 1 Ch 468, CA; cf *Re Great Cobar Ltd* [1915] 1 Ch 682.
7 *Re Thames Ironworks, Shipbuilding and Engineering Co Ltd* (1912) 106 LT 674.
8 *Forster v Nixon's Navigation Co Ltd* (1906) 23 TLR 138; *Parsons v Sovereign Bank of Canada* [1913] AC 160, PC.

1360. Prior lien securities. The court sometimes empowers a receiver and manager to borrow money for the purpose of carrying on the company's business or preserving its property, and to secure it by creating a charge having priority to the charge created by the debentures[1]. Unless all the parties interested are before the court, liberty to raise money by a charge having priority over the debentures in order to preserve property in the receiver's possession is granted only where special urgency is shown[2]. It will not be granted to enable a receiver and manager to complete a contract made prior to his appointment unless completion will assist in the preservation of the goodwill[3]. Where a receiver is authorised to borrow generally up to a fixed amount, and he has borrowed a part of the amount and repaid it, his original borrowing power is not diminished[4].

1 *Greenwood v Algesiras (Gibraltar) Rly Co* [1894] 2 Ch 205, CA; and see *Moss SS Co Ltd v Whinney* [1912] AC 254 at 263, HL per Lord Atkinson (where he stated that a receiver had no power to create a prior lien for an existing debt of the company without leave of the court).
2 *Securities and Properties Corpn Ltd v Brighton Alhambra Ltd* (1893) 62 LJ Ch 566.
3 *Re Thames Ironworks, Shipbuilding and Engineering Co Ltd* (1912) 106 LT 674.
4 *Milward v Avill and Smart Ltd* (1897) 4 Mans 403.

1361. Right of indemnity. Where orders are made in order to preserve the company's property and carry on the business, giving the receiver liberty to borrow in priority to the debentures, and he borrows the money from the plaintiff or other parties to the action, and the assets when sold are insufficient to satisfy both the prior lien charges and the receiver's costs and expenses, including remuneration, the costs and expenses have priority over the prior lien charges unless the agreement for loan expressly or impliedly provides otherwise. It is doubtful whether the same rule applies where a stranger makes the advance; and the order ought to state whether the charge to be given by the receiver is to be subject to or free from his right to indemnity[1].

Expenses and liabilities incurred in good faith by a manager in the ordinary course of business are prima facie properly incurred and within the rules as to indemnity; and, where he is authorised to borrow a sum not exceeding a certain limit for the general purposes of the business, the effect is to provide, at the expense of the parties interested, a special fund out of which the manager may indemnify himself. He is not, however, entitled without any further authority to incur expenses and liabilities to an unlimited extent, and to require them to be met out of the assets, since, if he finds that the fund provided by the court is not sufficient, his duty is to cause the matter to be brought before the court, so that it may increase the fund or give him leave to incur further expenses and liabilities. If he incurs expenses and liabilities exceeding the limit without such an application, he is not entitled to be indemnified against them unless he can justify it by showing special circumstances. It is not enough to show that the expenses or liabilities were incurred in good faith and in the ordinary course of business[2].

Where debts are properly incurred by a receiver and manager appointed by the court in carrying on the company's business, the court will see that those debts are satisfied either by the receiver himself or, in the case of his bankruptcy, or if for any other reason it is deemed advisable to do so, by payment direct to the creditors out of the funds in court available for the purpose[3]. Where the receiver and manager has incurred liabilities and is entitled to an indemnity for them out of the estate, but this account is deficient, the creditors may claim only the net amount of the indemnity after deducting the deficiency[4].

1 See *Strapp v Bull, Sons & Co, Shaw v London School Board* [1895] 2 Ch 1, CA; *Re Glasdir Copper Mines Ltd, English Electro-Metallurgical Co Ltd v Glasdir Copper Mines Ltd* [1906] 1 Ch 365, CA; *Re New Zealand Midland Rly Co, Smith v Lubbock* [1901] 2 Ch 357, CA; *Re Boynton Ltd, Hoffman v A Boynton Ltd* [1910] 1 Ch 519.

2 *Re British Power Traction and Lighting Co Ltd, Halifax Joint Banking Co Ltd v British Power Traction and Lighting Co Ltd* [1906] 1 Ch 497; *Re British Power Traction and Lighting Co Ltd, Halifax Joint Stock Banking Co Ltd v British Power Traction and Lighting Co Ltd (No 2)* [1907] 1 Ch 528; *Re Ernest Hawkins & Co Ltd* (1915) 31 TLR 247; cf *Lathom v Greenwich Ferry Co* (1895) 72 LT 790.

3 *Re London United Breweries Ltd, Smith v London United Breweries Ltd* [1907] 2 Ch 511.

4 *Re British Power Traction and Lighting Co Ltd* [1910] 2 Ch 470.

1362. Rates, electricity and gas. Where the court's order appointing the receiver does not direct him to take possession, there is no change of occupation and the company's goods may be distrained for rates[1] in arrear[2]; but there may be a change of occupation where the company is directed to deliver possession to the receiver[3]. Where the order appointing a receiver (other than an administrative receiver[4] where the position is different[5]), does not direct him to take possession, or directs him to take possession only so far as necessary for the purposes of the receivership, the receiver is not entitled to require a supply of electricity[6] or gas[7] and is not protected from liability to pay arrears[8]; and in such a case the supply of electricity[9] or gas[10] may be cut off, unless the receiver pays arrears owing by the company[11].

1 As to rateable occupation generally see RATING vol 39 para 15 et seq; and as to distress for rates see DISTRESS vol 13 para 397 et seq.

2 *Re Marriage, Neave & Co* [1896] 2 Ch 663, CA; *National Provincial Bank of England Ltd v United Electric Theatres Ltd* (1916) as reported in 85 LJ Ch 106. Where the goods of a company are sold under an order made in a debenture holders' action, the rating authority is not entitled to an order for payment of rates due from the company in lieu of its right of distress which can no longer be enforced: see *Re British Fullers' Earth Co Ltd, Gibbs v British Fullers' Earth Co Ltd* (1901) 17 TLR 232; *Gyton v Palmour* [1945] KB 426, [1944] 2 All ER 540. As to the priority of rates due when a receiver is appointed see para 1334 ante.

3 See *Richards v Kidderminster Overseers, Richards v Kidderminster Corpn* [1896] 2 Ch 212; *Madge v Debenture Corpn* (1896) 12 TLR 203 (cases where possession was taken by the receiver appointed under the powers contained in a trust deed securing debentures); *Re Marriage, Neave & Co* [1896] 2 Ch 663 at 671, 672, 674, 676, 678, CA.

4 For the meaning of 'administrative receiver' see para 1344 ante.

5 See para 2157 post.

6 Ie under the Electricity Act 1989 ss 16, 17: see FUEL AND ENERGY vol 19(2) (Reissue) paras 895, 896.

7 Ie under the Gas Act 1986 s 10: see FUEL AND ENERGY vol 19(1) (Reissue) paras 617-619.

8 Ie under the Electricity Act 1989 s 24, Sch 6 para 1(5)(b) (see FUEL AND ENERGY vol 19(2) (Reissue) para 907) or, as the case may be, the Gas Act 1986 s 15, Sch 5 para 7(4)(b) (see FUEL AND ENERGY vol 19(1) (Reissue) para 632).

9 Ie under the Electricity Act 1989 Sch 6 para 1(6)–(8): see FUEL AND ENERGY vol 19(2) (Reissue) para 907. A public electricity supplier may not, however, exercise its power of disconnection as respects any amount which is genuinely in dispute: see Sch 6 para 1(9) and FUEL AND ENERGY vol 19(2) (Reissue) para 907.

10 Ie under the Gas Act 1986 Sch 5 para 7(5)(a): see FUEL AND ENERGY vol 19(1) (Reissue) para 620. A public gas supplier may not, however, exercise its power of disconnection as respects any amount which is genuinely in dispute: see Sch 5 para 7(5A) (as added) and FUEL AND ENERGY vol 19(1) (Reissue) para 620.

11 *Paterson v Gas Light and Coke Co* [1896] 2 Ch 476, CA; *Husey v Gas Light and Coke Co* (1902) 18 TLR 299; contrast *Husey v London Electric Supply Corpn* [1902] 1 Ch 411, CA (where the court, without deciding whether the receiver was a new 'occupier', held him to be in any case disentitled to a supply until he had entered into a contract with the undertakers). These cases were decided partly upon provisions contained in special Acts, but it seems that the same principles will still apply in cases falling under the enactments cited in notes 6-10 supra.

In *Granger v South Wales Electric Power Distribution Co* [1931] 1 Ch 551 a receiver was held entitled to a supply without paying arrears where an undertaker's special Act provided they should give a supply to any person who required a supply.

D. FORECLOSURE OR SALE

1363. Effect of trust deed. Where debentures or debenture stock are secured by a trust deed and the security has become enforceable, the court will, in an action for that purpose, make an order for administration by the court of the trusts of the deed and grant the ordinary relief given in an action for enforcing debentures. In such a case, the right of a debenture holder to begin an action to enforce the debentures, by foreclosure or sale, may be qualified by the trust deed or conditions[1].

Where the objects for which the money was raised by the issue of debentures cannot be carried into effect and part of it remains in the hands of the trustees, the court will, on the application even of a minority of the debenture holders, order the unspent portion to be distributed among the debenture holders after payment of expenses of saving and realising the property charged and costs[2].

1 See *Re Rogers & Co v British and Colonial Colliery Supply Association* (1898) 68 LJQB 14 (where the debenture holder had the right only if the trustees failed to take steps); and see *Cleary v Brazil Rly Co* (1915) 85 LJKB 32.

2 *Collingham v Sloper, Foreign, American and General Investments Trust Co v Sloper* [1893] 2 Ch 96 (on appeal [1894] 3 Ch 716, CA); *National Bolivian Navigation Co v Wilson* (1880) 5 App Cas 176, HL.

1364. Foreclosure. Even under the old procedure, foreclosure could have been obtained in an action or in proceedings begun by originating summons[1]. Where there is a trust deed which does not contain a legal mortgage, the claim should be for a declaration of a charge, execution of the trusts, an account and enforcement of the charge by sale. Where there is no trust deed, foreclosure may be ordered where all the debenture holders are before the court and concur[2]; but foreclosure cannot be ordered in the absence of any one debenture holder[3].

The judgment should give liberty to the defendant company, at any time before foreclosure absolute, to apply to the judge in chambers for payment and transfer to the plaintiff, on account of the money due to him, of any money or securities in court to the credit of the action or in the hands of the receiver[4].

An order for sale may also be obtained in foreclosure proceedings. As a rule it is not made until after judgment has been obtained in the action and notice has been given to all the debenture holders by circular, letter or advertisement; but, where the plaintiff is suing on behalf of himself and other debenture holders and the judge is of the opinion that there must eventually be a sale, he may direct a sale before judgment, or after judgment, before all the persons interested are ascertained, whether served or not[5]. Where the action is not a representative one, the above rule does not apply[6]. Where the order is asked for on motion for judgment on admissions in the pleadings, an affidavit of the facts is required[7]. On such a motion, an immediate sale will be ordered where the property is in jeopardy; but, unless all the subsequent debenture holders are parties, the order will be for sale with the approbation of the judge so that the absent parties may be brought in on the application to approve the conditional contract for sale[8].

1   *Oldrey v Union Works Ltd* (1895) 72 LT 627; *Sadler v Worley* [1894] 2 Ch 170. See RSC Ord 5 r 4, Ord 88 r 1. As to the remedy of foreclosure generally see MORTGAGE vol 32 para 844 et seq.
2   *Sadler v Worley* [1894] 2 Ch 170.
3   *Re Continental Oxygen Co, Elias v Continental Oxygen Co* [1897] 1 Ch 511.
4   *Cumming v Metcalfe's London Hydro Ltd* (1895) 2 Mans 418.
5   This follows the practice under RSC 1883 Ord 51 r 1B (revoked and not replaced).
6   *Parkinson v Wainwright & Co and Wainwright* (1895) 64 LJ Ch 493.
7   *Re Day and Night Advertising Co, Upward v Day and Night Advertising Co* (1900) 48 WR 362.
8   *Re Crigglestone Coal Co, Stewart v Crigglestone Coal Co* [1906] 1 Ch 523.

1365. Sale. Where an order is made for the sale of the property charged by the debentures, the sale must generally be carried out under the directions of the court; and the purchase money will normally be ordered to be paid into court to the credit of the action. The court may, however, direct a sale to be carried out by laying proposals before the judge in chambers for his sanction, or by proceedings altogether out of court[1]. The judge will normally require to be satisfied by evidence that all the persons interested in the property to be sold are before the court or are bound by the order for sale[2]; every order authorising such proceedings altogether out of court will be prefaced by a declaration that the judge is so satisfied, and a statement of the evidence upon which the declaration is made[3]. Where an order for sale has been made, the court may authorise the trustees to sell where a majority of the holders of the debentures approve, if the trustees are acting in good faith and no injustice will be done to the minority[4].

A sale will not be ordered in the case of a company incorporated for purposes of a public nature and having statutory powers and duties[5].

1   See RSC Ord 31 r 2. An order for sale out of court generally requires the reserved bidding and the auctioneer's remuneration to be fixed by the master, and the purchase money to be paid directly into court. Where the master has by inadvertence inserted a lower figure than that fixed by the judge, there is nothing to compel the court to certify the highest bidder to be the purchaser when his bid is not as high as the reserve fixed by the judge: *Re Joseph Clayton Ltd* [1920] 1 Ch 257.
2   Where a contract for the sale of property is made subject to the approval of the court, that approval must be obtained before the date fixed for completion: *Re Sandwell Park Colliery Co* [1929] 1 Ch 277. The receiver should apply for leave to employ an agent for the sale; if he fails to do so, the agent is not entitled to any commission, though the court has a discretion to allow what seems equitable: *Re National Flying Services Ltd, Cousins v National Flying Services Ltd* [1936] Ch 271.
3   This follows the practice under RSC 1883 Ord 51 r 1A proviso (revoked and not replaced).
4   *Re Buenos Aires Port and City Tramways* (1920) 89 LJ Ch 597.
5   See the cases cited in para 1358 note 6 ante.

E.   PRACTICE IN DEBENTURE HOLDERS' ACTIONS

1366. Beginning debenture holders' action. The writ in a debenture holders' action must be entitled 'in the matter of' the particular company[1].

When a winding-up order has been made or a provisional liquidator has been appointed, no action or proceeding may be proceeded with or commenced against the company or its property except by leave of the court, and subject to such terms as the court may impose[2]. In either case, however, leave will be given almost invariably as a matter of course.

1 See the Supreme Court Practice 1995 vol 2 App, Form 1 note (a).
2 See the Insolvency Act 1986 s 130(2); para 2250 post (compulsory winding up); and para 2652 post (voluntary winding up).

1367. Parties. Usually the plaintiff is a debenture holder, suing on behalf of himself and all other debenture holders of the class to which he belongs[1]; and the defendants are the company, and any other incumbrancers on the same property, as in the case of proceedings to enforce ordinary mortgages[2].

If there is a trust deed securing the debentures, the trustees must also be made parties to the action[3]; and the relief claimed must include a claim that the trusts of the deed be carried into execution under the direction of the court.

In a foreclosure action by the holder of a mortgage of specific assets of a company which has subsequently given a floating charge by debentures on all its assets, the debenture holders should be made defendants, even when the principal money secured to them is not yet payable[4].

1 Holders or representatives of only one class of debentures cannot obtain judgments and orders for sale in the absence of holders of another class of debentures: *Parkinson v Wainwright & Co and Wainwright* (1895) 64 LJ Ch 493.
2 *Re Wilcox & Co (late W H Fox & Co) Ltd, Hilder v Wilcox & Co (late W H Fox & Co) Ltd* [1903] WN 64; and see *Re Crigglestone Coal Co, Stewart v Crigglestone Coal Co* [1906] 1 Ch 523. For a case where a debenture holder sued on behalf of himself only and no other holders and it was held that there was no estoppel as regards other debenture holders see *Cox v Dublin City Distillery (No 2)* [1915] 1 IR 345, CA.
3 *Mortgage Insurance Corpn Ltd v Canadian Agricultural Coal and Colonization Co Ltd* [1901] 2 Ch 377. The trustees may sue as plaintiffs, in which case they will represent the debenture holders, but they will normally be made defendants.
4 *Wallace v Evershed* [1899] 1 Ch 891; and see *Griffith v Pound* (1890) 45 ChD 553; *Fairfield Shipbuilding and Engineering Co Ltd v London and East Coast Express SS Co Ltd* [1895] WN 64.

1368. Representative action. A plaintiff suing on behalf of himself and other debenture holders cannot compromise or give up any of the rights of those he represents without the leave of the court[1]. If, after judgment, he has been paid off, and there is evidence that no other debentures have been issued, all further proceedings in the action will be stayed[2]. If the plaintiff becomes bankrupt and a trustee is appointed, his estate vests in his trustee in bankruptcy, and the action will be stayed unless his trustee continues it[3]. If any debenture holder objects to being represented by the plaintiff or any defendant appointed to represent his class, he may apply in the action to be added as a defendant, but at his own risk as to costs[4].

Where a debenture holder is sued in a representative capacity, an order may sometimes be obtained authorising him to defend in that capacity[5].

Trustees represent their beneficiaries[6]. Where foreclosure is sought and there are no trustees, the debenture holders who are subsequent incumbrancers must all be made parties[7]. It is not sufficient to make some of them parties as representing the whole[8]. The court may, however, direct a sale before all the persons interested are ascertained[9].

The court may give the conduct of the action to such person as it thinks fit[10]. The conduct of the action may be taken away from the plaintiff where he has an interest conflicting with the interests of the other debenture holders, as, for example, when he is or may be liable to the company; in such a case the court will give leave to add an independent debenture holder as defendant and transfer the conduct of the action to him[11].

1 *Re Calgary and Medicine Hat Land Co Ltd, Pigeon v Calgary and Medicine Hat Land Co Ltd* [1908] 2 Ch 652 at 659, 662, CA; *Collingham v Sloper, Foreign, American and General Investments Trust Co v Sloper* [1894] 3 Ch 716, CA.

2 *Re Alpha Co Ltd, Ward v Alpha Co Ltd* [1903] 1 Ch 203.

3 *Wolff v Van Boolen* (1906) 94 LT 502; and see RSC Ord 15 r 7; PRACTICE AND PROCEDURE vol 37 para 220; and BANKRUPTCY vol 3(2) (Reissue) para 423.

4 *Watson v Cave* (1881) 17 ChD 19, CA; *Fraser v Cooper, Hall & Co* (1882) 21 ChD 718; *Debenture Corpn v De Murrieta & Co Ltd* (1892) 8 TLR 496; and see *Re Services Club Estate Syndicate Ltd* [1930] 1 Ch 78.

5 *Fairfield Shipbuilding and Engineering Co Ltd v London and East Coast Express SS Co Ltd* [1895] WN 64; *Re Kent Coal Concessions Ltd* [1923] WN 328, CA. See, however, *Re Cadogan and Hans Place Estate (No 2) Ltd, Graham v Cadogan and Hans Place Estate (No 2) Ltd* (1906) 50 Sol Jo 499 (where it was said that such an order was unnecessary in the case of second debenture holders being defendants).

6 See RSC Ord 15 r 14 and PRACTICE AND PROCEDURE vol 37 para 243.

7 *Wallace v Evershed* [1899] 1 Ch 891.

8 *Griffith v Pound* (1890) 45 ChD 553; *Westminster Bank Ltd v Residential Properties Improvement Co Ltd* [1938] Ch 639, [1938] 2 All ER 374.

9 See paras 1364, 1365 ante.

10 See RSC Ord 15 r 17 and PRACTICE AND PROCEDURE vol 37 para 72.

11 *Re Services Club Estate Syndicate Ltd* [1930] 1 Ch 78; *Re Rhodesia Goldfields Ltd, Partridge v Rhodesia Goldfields Ltd* [1910] 1 Ch 239 at 240; *Watson v Cave* (1881) 17 ChD 19 at 21, CA.

1369. Procedure. Often, on the hearing of a motion for the appointment of a receiver, all the parties to the action attend and agree to treat the hearing of the motion as the trial of the action, and a judgment by consent is then taken; but, if this is not done, a statement of claim should be served, and, if no defence is served, or if the parties agree upon the form of the judgment, the action may then be disposed of as a short cause[1].

If a defendant fails to give notice of intention to defend within the time limited and has not acknowledged service, the plaintiff, upon filing an affidavit of service and serving a statement of claim, may proceed as if the party had given notice of intention to defend[2]. A master cannot dispense with a statement of claim against a defendant who does not acknowledge service, even when there are other defendants who do[3].

1 *Re Dupont Ltd, Dupont v Dupont Ltd* [1906] WN 14. As to setting down as a short cause and the papers required see the Supreme Court Practice 1995 paras 8/1-5/7, 8/1-5/8. Proposed minutes of judgment must always be left even if a common form judgment only is required: *Re Automatic Machines (Haydon and Urry's Patents) Ltd, Graafe v Automatic Machines (Haydon and Urry's Patents) Ltd* [1902] WN 236 per Swinfen Eady J.

2 See RSC Ord 13 r 6(1) and PRACTICE AND PROCEDURE vol 37 para 394.

3 *Re Norman, Norman v Norman* [1900] WN 159. As to acknowledging service, giving notice of intention to defend, service of defence, summons for directions, and motion for judgment in default of defence see PRACTICE AND PROCEDURE vol 37 paras 197 et seq, 267, 317 et seq, 406. On the summons for directions the order ought to direct the evidence to be taken on affidavit, and with the defendant's consent the action may then be tried on the earliest short cause day; the evidence filed on the application for a receiver and additional evidence may be allowed to be used: *Re Gutta Percha Corpn Ltd, Thornton v Gutta Percha Corpn Ltd* [1899] WN 251. As to setting down with affidavit evidence without consent cf *Re Pringle & Co Ltd* (1903) 89 LT 743; *Re Kitson Empire Lighting Co Ltd* [1910] WN 154.

1370. Receiver's register; proof of title. A receiver appointed by the court in a debenture holders' action to enforce registered debentures or registered debenture stock must, if so directed by the court, keep a register of transfers of, and other transmissions of title to, such debentures or stock ('the receiver's register')[1]. Where a receiver is so required to keep a receiver's register, then, on the application of any person entitled to debentures or debenture stock by virtue of any transfer or other transmission of title, and on production of such evidence of identity and title as the receiver may reasonably require, the receiver must register the transfer or other transmission of title in that register[2]. Any person aggrieved by any thing done or omission made by a receiver may apply to the court for rectification of the receiver's register, the application to be made by summons in the action in which the receiver was appointed[3]. The court hearing such an application may decide any question relating to the title of any person who is party to the application to have his name entered in or omitted from the receiver's register and generally may decide any question necessary or expedient to be decided for the rectification of that register[4].

Any entry made in the receiver's register, if verified by an affidavit made by the receiver or such other person as the court may direct, is evidence in all proceedings in the action in which the receiver was appointed of the transfer or transmission of title[5].

In an action to enforce bearer debentures or debenture stock in respect of which the company has issued debenture stock bearer certificates, the title of any person claiming to be the holder is sufficiently proved, in the absence of notice of any defect in the title, and notwithstanding that judgment has been given and that a certificate of holders has been made in the action, by the production of the debenture or debenture stock certificate, as the case may be, together with a certificate of identification signed by the person producing it identifying the debenture or certificate produced and certifying the person, giving his name and address, who is the holder of it[6]. Where such a debenture or certificate is produced in the chancery chambers, the solicitor of the plaintiff in the action must cause a notice to be indorsed on it stating that:

(1) the person whose name and address is specified in the notice, being the person named as the holder of the debenture or certificate in the certificate of identification so produced, has been recorded in chambers as the holder of the debenture or debenture stock certificate, as the case may be; and

(2) on producing the debenture or debenture stock certificate, that person will be entitled to receive payment of any dividend in respect of that debenture or stock unless before payment a new holder proves his title[7]; and

(3) if a new holder neglects so to prove his title, he may incur additional delay, trouble and expense in obtaining payment[8].

The solicitor of the plaintiff in the action must preserve any certificates of identification so produced and must keep a record of the debentures and debenture stock certificates so produced and of the names and addresses of the persons producing them and the holders thereof and, if the court requires it, must verify the record by affidavit[9].

Where in an action to enforce any debentures or debenture stock an order is made for payment in respect of the debentures or stock, the Accountant-General must not make a payment in respect of any such debenture or stock unless either there is produced to him the required certificate[10] or the court has in the case in question for special reason dispensed with the need for the certificate and directed payment to be made without it[11].

1 RSC Ord 87 r 1; and see the Supreme Court Practice 1995 para 87/1/1.
2 See RSC Ord 87 r 2(1); and see the Supreme Court Practice 1995 para 87/2/1. Before registering a transfer the receiver must, unless the due execution of the transfer is proved by affidavit, send by post to the registered holder of the debentures or debenture stock transferred at his registered office a notice stating that an application for the registration of the transfer has been made and that the transfer will be registered unless within the period specified in the notice the holder informs the receiver that he objects

to the registration; and no transfer may be registered until the period so specified has elapsed: RSC Ord 87 r 2(2). The period to be specified in the notice must in no case be less than seven days after a reply from the registered holder would in the ordinary course of post reach the receiver if the holder had replied to the notice on the day following the day when in the ordinary course of post the notice would have been delivered at the place to which it was addressed: RSC Ord 87 r 2(2). On so registering a transfer or other transmission of title, the receiver must indorse on the debenture or certificate of debenture stock, as the case may be, transferred or transmitted a memorandum of the registration, containing a reference to the action and to the order appointing him receiver: RSC Ord 87 r 2(3).

3 RSC Ord 87 r 3(1). The summons must in the first instance be served only on the plaintiff or other party having conduct of the action but the court may direct the summons or notice of the application to be served on any other person appearing to be interested: RSC Ord 87 r 3(2).

4 RSC Ord 87 r 3(3).

5 RSC Ord 87 r 4. In particular it is evidence for the purpose of any distribution of assets, notwithstanding that the transfer or transmission has taken place after the making of a certificate in the action certifying the holders of the debentures or debenture stock certificates: RSC Ord 87 r 4.

6 RSC Ord 87 r 5(1),(2). RSC Ord 87 r 5(2) applies notwithstanding that judgment has been given in the action and that a certificate has been made therein certifying the holders of such debentures or certificates as are referred to in RSC Ord 87 r 5(1): RSC Ord 87 r 5(2).

7 Ie in accordance with RSC Ord 87 r 5(2): see supra.

8 RSC Ord 87 r 5(3).

9 RSC Ord 87 r 5(4).

10 Ie the certificate for which RSC Ord 87 r 6(2) provides. For the purpose of obtaining any such payments, the debenture or debenture stock certificate must be produced to the solicitor of the plaintiff in the action or to such other person as the court may direct; and that solicitor or person must indorse thereon a memorandum of payment and must make and sign a certificate certifying that the statement set out in the certificate has been indorsed on the debenture or debenture stock certificate, as the case may be, and send the certificate to the Accountant-General: RSC Ord 87 r 6(2).

11 RSC Ord 87 r 6(1).

1371. Form of judgment. On the trial of a debenture holders' action, the court sometimes declares that the debenture holders are entitled to a charge[1]. A declaration of charge will be omitted from the judgment if there are debenture holders, other than those of the class which the plaintiff represents, who are not parties to the action[2], or if there is a question of priorities to be decided[3]. There is no power to make the declaration in chambers[4].

If, in a representative action by a debenture holder, a personal judgment against the company is asked for in order to reach property not charged, judgment cannot be given for the plaintiff for the whole amount secured by the debentures; but the court may declare that the debenture holders are entitled to stand in the position of judgment creditors and appoint a receiver of the uncharged property[5].

The usual form of judgment in a debenture holders' action directs an account of what is due to the debenture holders, an inquiry of what the property charged consists, an inquiry what other incumbrances affect the property and, if a receiver is appointed and there are preferential payments to be made, an inquiry whether there are any and what preferential debts[6].

Special inquiries are sometimes ordered, for example, as to determining priorities between claims of debenture holders. Under an inquiry directed by the judgment in a representative action as to the property charged by the debentures, the master may certify what uncalled capital, if uncalled capital is subject to the security, is due from the several shareholders, notwithstanding that no calls may actually be made in such an action; and, where the plaintiff is himself a shareholder and is found indebted in a sum of uncalled capital, he, being a party to the action, is bound by that finding, unless it is varied by the judge[7].

1 *Marwick v Lord Thurlow* [1895] 1 Ch 776; *Re Crigglestone Coal Co, Stewart v Crigglestone Coal Co* [1906] 1 Ch 523; *Brinsley v Lynton and Lynmouth Hotel and Property Co* (1895) 2 Mans 244; *Parkinson v Wainwright & Co and Wainwright* (1895) 64 LJ Ch 493; but, when he was the winding-up judge, Vaughan Williams J would not make such a declaration in a short cause on motion for judgment unless the company by its liquidator appeared and consented (see *Marwick v Lord Thurlow* supra). It is not the practice to insert a declaration in a judgment made by consent on a motion which is treated as the trial of the action; and the usual judgment in such a case does not estop the company or its liquidator from establishing the invalidity of any of the debentures: *Re Gregory Love & Co* [1916] 1 Ch 203 at 209. A company should not consent to a judgment including a charge, unless it is proved otherwise than by consent: *Re Gregory Love & Co* supra.

2 *Re Prince and Baugh Ltd, Bedell v Prince and Baugh Ltd* [1902] WN 96.

3 *Re Ehrmann Bros Ltd, Albert v Ehrmann Bros Ltd* (1904) 48 Sol Jo 298.

4 *Halifax and Huddersfield Union Banking Co v Radcliffe Ltd* [1895] WN 63.

5 *Hope v Croydon and Norwood Tramways Co* (1887) 34 ChD 730. Where a personal judgment for interest is not sought in a debenture holders' action, any debenture holder may begin a separate action for it: *Cleary v Brazil Rly Co* (1915) 85 LJKB 32.

6 See the form in *Re Burradon and Coxlodge Coal Co Ltd* [1929] WN 15, reverting to the form in *Re Wolverhampton District Brewery Ltd, Downes v Wolverhampton District Brewery Ltd* (1899) 44 Sol Jo 74, prior to the variation made by the Practice Note in *Debenture-Holders' Actions* (1900) 16 TLR 256. The same form had been adopted where no sum was presently due, but the security was in jeopardy: *Re Levison and Steiner Ltd* (1900) 44 Sol Jo 573; *Re Day and Night Advertising Co, Upward v Day and Night Advertising Co* (1900) 48 WR 362; cf *Re British Rly Carriage Metal Fittings etc Co Ltd* (1898) 43 Sol Jo 140 (judgment on admissions). As to the form of order for inquiries as to incumbrances where none is known to exist see *Re Addressograph Ltd, Backhouse v Addressograph Ltd* [1909] WN 260. A liquidator may in special circumstances appeal from the master's certificate as to the final accounts: *Re Gregory Love & Co* [1916] 1 Ch 203. Where, as is usually the case, interest on debentures is payable before principal, the fact that orders have been made for applying proceeds of sale in payment of principal will not be regarded as a final appropriation of the sums paid to principal, and the court will make the proper appropriation by a subsequent order: *Re Calgary and Medicine Hat Land Co Ltd, Pigeon v Calgary and Medicine Hat Land Co Ltd* [1908] 2 Ch 652, CA. As to the form of order and the inquiries directed where some of the debenture holders have not been registered in time see *Re Ehrmann Bros Ltd, Albert v Ehrmann Bros Ltd* (1904) 48 Sol Jo 298; and as to the effect on liability for income tax of appropriating money as principal or interest by orders in an action to administer the trusts of a debenture trust deed see *Smith v Law Guarantee and Trust Society Ltd* [1904] 2 Ch 569, CA.

7 *Madeley v Ross, Sleeman & Co* [1897] 1 Ch 505.

1372. Service of judgment. In ordinary cases the judgment in a debenture holders' action should not be served on the debenture holders, but notice should be given to them by circular or letter, or by advertisement if the case so requires[1]. Sums due to persons who do not put in their claims in answer to the advertisements are normally carried over to a fund[2]. Notice of judgment must be formally served if the court thinks it desirable and so directs[3].

1 Directions of Chancery Judges, May 1896. In the case of bearer debentures advertisements are invariably directed. As to the costs of serving notice of the judgment and of the meetings of debenture holders to sanction a scheme of arrangement see *Re Commonwealth Oil Corpn Ltd* [1917] 1 Ch 404. The costs of acknowledging and giving receipt for and returning debentures sent by a debenture holder in pursuance of the present form of notice of judgment are properly included in the plaintiff's costs of the action: *Re W Mate & Sons Ltd* [1920] 1 Ch 551; but distinguish *Re Ticehurst and District Water and Gas Co* (1915) 139 LT Jo 295. A debenture holder served with notice of judgment may not enter an appearance, but may with leave obtained on summons attend the proceedings: *Re W Mate & Sons Ltd* supra.

2 The court will exclude persons who have not sent in their claims after a long period of time and after the court has fixed a certain date before which the claims are to be brought or to be excluded: *Wilson v Church* (1911) 106 LT 31; *Wilson v Church* (1912) 133 LT Jo 282. See also *Elkins v Capital Guarantee Society* (1900) 16 TLR 423, CA; cf *Saragossa and Mediterranean Rly Co v Collingham* [1904] AC 159, HL (revsg *Collingham v Sloper* [1901] 1 Ch 769, CA).

3 See RSC Ord 44 r 3 and PRACTICE AND PROCEDURE vol 37 para 536.

1373. Costs. Even where the debentures do not rank pari passu and, in the event, nothing is payable in respect of his debentures, the plaintiff is entitled to the costs of the action except such, if any, as are incurred solely in supporting his own security[1].

As a general rule, the plaintiff in a representative action is entitled to costs only on the standard basis[2]; but, where the assets are insufficient for the payment of the debentures in full, he is entitled to costs on the indemnity basis[3]. If he is unable to pay the difference between indemnity and standard basis costs, and property has been recovered or preserved more than enough to pay the debenture holders, the solicitor is entitled to a charging order for the difference on so much of the property as belongs to the debenture holders[4].

Trustees of a debenture trust deed are entitled to be paid their costs before the funds are distributed among the debenture holders, even when they and the company appear by the same solicitor[5]. The defendant company is not entitled to costs unless the whole action fails, nor are second debenture holders who are made defendants; both must look to the surplus[6].

1 *Carrick v Wigan Tramways Co* [1893] WN 98. As to what these costs include see *Re W Mate & Sons Ltd* [1920] 1 Ch 551.
2 *Re Queen's Hotel Co, Cardiff Ltd, Re Vernon Tin Plate Co Ltd* [1900] 1 Ch 792.
3 *Re New Zealand Midland Rly Co, Smith v Lubbock* [1901] 2 Ch 357, CA (where the order was for costs as between solicitor and client, a basis no longer possible (see RSC Ord 62 r 12 and PRACTICE AND PROCEDURE); parties attending by leave were given party and party costs); and see *Re A Boynton Ltd, Hoffman v A Boynton Ltd* [1910] 1 Ch 519 (solicitor and client basis).
4 *Re W C Horne & Sons Ltd, Horne v W C Horne & Sons Ltd* [1906] 1 Ch 271 (where it was also held that the solicitor, who had acted as solicitor to the receiver in realising the assets, was entitled to a charging order for his costs in that capacity on the balance of the funds payable to the liquidator).
5 *Mortgage Insurance Corpn Ltd v Canadian Agricultural Coal and Colonization Co Ltd* [1901] 2 Ch 377; and see *Batten v Wedgwood Coal and Iron Co* (1884) 28 ChD 317.
6 *Re Clayton Engineering and Electrical Construction Co Ltd* (1904) 90 LT 283.

1374. Order of administration. Where there is a deficiency, the order for distribution of the amount realised in a debenture holders' action is:

(1) costs of realisation[1];
(2) costs including the receiver's remuneration;
(3) costs, charges, and expenses of the debenture trust deed, if any, including the trustees' remuneration where by the trust deed these are made a first charge on the amount realised;
(4) the plaintiff's costs of the action;
(5) the amount due to and available for preferential creditors to the extent to which they have priority[2]; and
(6) the amount due to and available for debenture holders[3].

1 This includes costs of an abortive sale: *Batten v Wedgwood Coal and Iron Co* (1884) 28 ChD 317.
2 See para 1334 ante.
3 *Re Glyncorrwg Colliery Co Ltd* [1926] Ch 951; *Batten v Wedgwood Coal and Iron Co* (1884) 28 ChD 317; *Re London United Breweries Ltd, Smith v London United Breweries Ltd* [1907] 2 Ch 511.

(iii) Interest on Securities

1375. Interest on securities. Where, as is usual in a debenture or debenture trust deed, the company agrees or covenants to pay the principal sum and interest at an agreed rate, and property of the company is charged with those payments, the charge is a security both for the principal and for interest at the agreed rate until payment, and on realisation of the security the debenture holder is entitled to interest at the agreed rate, notwithstanding that the company may be wound up or that he may have recovered judgment against the company[1].

Even if the debenture does not so provide, the principal money, if not paid on the appointed day, will continue to carry interest at the agreed rate[2]. Interest payable on debentures, although payable half-yearly, accrues from day to day[3].

A debenture holder who, in payment of interest, accepts cheques which by arrangement are not presented, is not thereby prevented from claiming to be a secured creditor in respect of that interest[4]. If in a debenture holders' action the amount of the principal only is certified, in the belief that the security is insufficient, and payment is made on this footing, this does not prevent the full interest being payable if the security proves sufficient[5].

1　*Economic Life Assurance Society v Usborne* [1902] AC 147, HL; *Re European Central Rly Co, ex p Oriental Financial Corpn* (1876) 4 ChD 33, CA. As to interest on judgment debts see PRACTICE AND PROCEDURE vol 37 para 551; and as to interest on debts proved in a winding up see para 2554 post.
2　*Price v Great Western Rly Co* (1847) 16 M & W 244.
3　*Re Rogers' Trusts* (1860) 1 Drew & Sm 338.
4　*Re J Defries & Sons Ltd, Eichholz v J Defries & Sons Ltd* [1909] 2 Ch 423.
5　*Re Calgary and Medicine Hat Land Co Ltd, Pigeon v Calgary and Medicine Hat Land Co Ltd* [1908] 2 Ch 652, CA.

(28)　INVESTIGATION OF COMPANIES AND THEIR AFFAIRS; REQUISITION OF DOCUMENTS

(i)　Investigations

A.　INVESTIGATION OF COMPANY'S AFFAIRS

1376. Appointment of inspectors on members' or company's own application. The Secretary of State may appoint one or more competent inspectors to investigate the affairs[1] of a company and to report on them in such manner as he may direct[2]. The appointment may be made:

(1)　in the case of a company having a share capital, on the application either of not less than 200 members or of members holding not less than one-tenth of the shares issued[3];

(2)　in the case of a company not having a share capital, on the application of not less than one-fifth in number of the persons on the company's register of members[4]; and

(3)　in any case, on application of the company[5].

The application must be supported by such evidence as the Secretary of State may require for the purpose of showing that the applicant or applicants has or have good reason for requiring the investigation[6]; and he may, before appointing inspectors, require the applicant or applicants to give security, to an amount not exceeding £5,000, or such other sum as he may by order specify, for payment of the costs of the investigation[7].

1　The company's goodwill, profits and losses, contracts and assets are included in its affairs: *R v Board of Trade, ex p St Martin Preserving Co Ltd* [1965] 1 QB 603, [1964] 2 All ER 561, DC (where assets were held to include the company's investment or other property interests, and its control of a subsidiary

company). As to whether the activities of a receiver and manager are affairs of the company for these purposes see *R v Board of Trade, ex p St Martin Preserving Co Ltd* supra.
2 Companies Act 1985 s 431(1). Section 431 does not apply to oversea companies: see s 453(1A)(a) (as substituted) and para 1385 post. As to the application of s 431 to unregistered companies see s 718(1), Sch 22 (as amended) and para 1767 post.

    Where an inspector appointed under s 431 obtains any information whilst acting in the course of any investigation, or discharging any functions, to which his appointment or authorisation relates, and is of the opinion that the information indicates that any person has or may have been engaged in money laundering, he must, as soon as is reasonably practicable, either disclose that information to a constable or disclose that information to the supervisory authority by whom he was appointed or authorised: Money Laundering Regulations 1993, SI 1993/1933, reg 16(3), (6)(c).
3 Companies Act 1985 s 431(2)(a). A writ of prohibition will not lie against the Secretary of State or an inspector appointed by him to prohibit an investigation: *Re Grosvenor and West End Railway Terminus Hotel Co Ltd* (1897) 76 LT 337, CA. See also *R v Board of Trade, ex p St Martin Preserving Co Ltd* [1965] 1 QB 603, [1964] 2 All ER 561, DC (an order of mandamus was obtained where the Secretary of State declined to appoint an inspector; the statutory provisions at that time required an appointment where the company had passed a special resolution declaring that its affairs ought to be investigated).
4 Companies Act 1985 s 431(2)(b). See also notes 2, 3 supra.
5 Ibid s 431(2)(c). See also notes 2, 3 supra.
6 Ibid s 431(3). See also note 2 supra.
7 Ibid s 431(4). See also note 2 supra. Such an order must be made by statutory instrument subject to annulment in pursuance of a resolution of either House of Parliament: s 431(4). At the date at which this volume states the law no such order had been made.

1377. Appointment of inspectors in other cases. Without prejudice to the above powers[1], the Secretary of State must appoint one or more competent inspectors to investigate the affairs[2] of a company and report on them in such manner as he directs, if the court[3] by order[4] declares that its affairs ought to be so investigated[5].

The Secretary of State may also make such an appointment if it appears to him that there are circumstances suggesting:

(1) that the company's affairs are being or have been conducted with intent to defraud its creditors or the creditors of any other person, or otherwise for a fraudulent or unlawful purpose, or in a manner which is unfairly prejudicial to some part of its members[6]; or

(2) that any actual or proposed act or omission of the company, including an act or omission on its behalf, is or would be so prejudicial, or that the company was formed for any fraudulent or unlawful purpose[7]; or

(3) that persons concerned with the company's formation or the management of its affairs have in connection therewith been guilty of fraud, misfeasance or other misconduct towards it or towards its members[8]; or

(4) that the company's members have not been given all the information with respect to its affairs which they might reasonably expect[9].

Inspectors may be so appointed[10] on terms that any report they may make is not for publication; and, in such a case, the provisions relating to the availability and publication of inspectors' reports[11] do not apply[12].

The Secretary of State must exercise the power to appoint inspectors in good faith but it is not incumbent upon him to disclose the material he has before him or the reasons for the inquiry[13]; nor is he required to desist from making an appointment because it may involve investigating fraudulent or criminal activity which should be investigated by the police or the Serious Fraud Office[14].

1 Ie the powers conferred by the Companies Act 1985 s 431: see para 1376 ante.
2 See para 1376 note 2 ante.
3 For the meaning of 'the court' see para 161 note 4 ante.

4 The application is by originating motion: RSC Ord 102 r 3(1)(b). The notice of motion need not be served on the Secretary of State but notice of the intended application should be sent to the solicitor of the Department of Trade and Industry with copies of any affidavits intended to be used at the hearing. Evidence should be filed proving that this has been done: *Practice Direction* [1954] 1 All ER 604, [1954] 1 WLR 563.

5 Companies Act 1985 s 432(1), (3). As to the application of s 432 (as amended) to oversea companies see para 1385 post; and as to the application of s 432 (as amended) to unregistered companies see s 718(1), Sch 22 (as amended) and para 1767 post.

Where an inspector appointed under s 432 (as amended) obtains any information whilst acting in the course of any investigation, or discharging any functions, to which his appointment or authorisation relates, and is of the opinion that the information indicates that any person has or may have been engaged in money laundering, he must, as soon as is reasonably practicable, either disclose that information to a constable or disclose that information to the supervisory authority by whom he was appointed or authorised: Money Laundering Regulations 1993, SI 1993/1933, reg 16(3), (6)(c).

6 Companies Act 1985 s 432(2)(a). See also note 5 supra. The power conferred by s 432(2) is exercisable with respect to a body corporate notwithstanding that it is in course of being voluntarily wound up: s 432(3). The reference in s 432(2)(a) to a company's members includes any person who is not a member but to whom shares in the company have been transferred or transmitted by operation of law: s 432(4). For the meaning of 'fraudulent purpose' and 'intent to defraud creditors' see the cases cited in para 2670 note 2 post.

While the provisions of s 432(1) are mandatory, those of s 432(2) merely empower the Secretary of State to appoint inspectors in the circumstances there specified.

7 Ibid s 432(2)(b). See also notes 5, 6 supra.
8 Ibid s 432(2)(c). See also notes 5, 6 supra.
9 Ibid s 432(2)(d). See also notes 5, 6 supra.
10 Ie under ibid s 432(2): see supra.
11 Ie ibid s 437(3): see para 1380 post.
12 Ibid s 432(2A) (added by the Companies Act 1989 s 55). See also note 5 supra.
13 *Norwest Holst Ltd v Secretary of State for Trade* [1978] Ch 201, [1978] 3 All ER 280, CA.
14 *Re London United Investments plc* [1992] Ch 578, [1992] 2 All ER 842, CA (the investigative powers in the companies legislation are separate from, even if they overlap, the investigative powers of other bodies).

1378. Inspectors' powers during investigation. If inspectors appointed under any of the above powers[1] to investigate the affairs of a company think it necessary for the purposes of their investigation to investigate also the affairs of another body corporate which is or at any relevant time has been the company's subsidiary[2] or holding company[3], or a subsidiary of its holding company or a holding company of its subsidiary, they have power to do so; and they must report on the affairs of the other body corporate so far as they think the results of their investigation of its affairs are relevant to the investigation of the affairs of the first-mentioned company[4].

1 Ie under the Companies Act 1985 s 431 (see para 1376 ante) or s 432 (as amended) (see para 1377 ante).
2 For the meaning of 'subsidiary' see para 827 ante.
3 For the meaning of 'holding company' see para 827 ante.
4 Companies Act 1985 s 433(1). As to the application of s 433(1) to oversea companies see para 1385 post; and as to the application of s 433(1) to unregistered companies see s 718(1), Sch 22 (as amended) and para 1767 post.

1379. Conduct of investigation. Where inspectors are appointed to investigate the affairs of a company[1], it is the duty of all officers and agents[2] of the company and of all officers and agents of any other body corporate whose affairs are investigated under the above powers[3]:

(1) to produce to the inspectors all documents[4] of or relating to the company or, as the case may be, the other body corporate which are in their custody or power;
(2) to attend before the inspectors when required to do so; and

(3) otherwise to give the inspectors all assistance in connection with the investigation which they are reasonably able to give[5].

If the inspectors consider that an officer or agent of the company or other body corporate, or any other person, is or may be in possession of information relating to a matter which they believe to be relevant to the investigation, they may require him:

(a) to produce to them any documents in his custody or power relating to that matter;

(b) to attend before them; and

(c) otherwise to give them all assistance in connection with the investigation which he is reasonably able to give;

and it is that person's duty to comply with the requirement[6].

An inspector may for the purposes of the investigation examine any person on oath, and may administer an oath accordingly[7].

The inspectors must act fairly in accordance with the rules of natural justice[8]. They must accordingly put to any witness any points of substance and give him a chance to explain or correct any statement prejudicial to him; but they are not required to put the substance of their conclusions to the witness for his comment, nor are they to be criticised for occasional omissions[9].

The common law privilege against self-incrimination having been impliedly excluded by the statutory provisions relating to investigations, those persons subject to investigation are not entitled to rely on the privilege as entitling them to refuse to answer the inspectors' questions[10].

An answer given by a person to a question put to him in exercise of these powers[11] may be used in evidence against him[12], although answers given as the result of informal questioning may not be included[13]. The public interest that all relevant evidence should be available to the court will normally override the public interest in maintaining the confidentiality of evidence given to inspectors[14].

If any person:

(i) fails to produce to the inspectors any documents which it is his statutory duty so to produce[15] or to give the inspectors all assistance in connection with the investigation which he is reasonably able to give[16]; or

(ii) refuses to attend before the inspectors when required to do so[17], or refuses to comply with the inspectors' requirement[18] where they consider that he may be in possession of information relating to a matter which they believe to be relevant to the investigation; or

(iii) refuses to answer any question put to him by the inspectors for the purposes of the investigation,

the inspectors may certify that fact in writing to the court[19]. The court may thereupon inquire into the case[20] and, after hearing any witnesses who may be produced against or on behalf of the alleged offender and after hearing any statement which may be offered in defence, may punish the offender in like manner as if he had been guilty of contempt of the court[21].

1 Ie under the Companies Act 1985 s 431 (see para 1376 ante) or s 432 (as amended) (see para 1377 ante).

2 For these purposes, a reference to officers or to agents includes past, as well as present, officers or agents, as the case may be; and 'agents', in relation to a company or other body corporate, includes its bankers and solicitors and persons employed by it as auditors, whether those persons are or are not officers of the company or other body corporate: ibid s 434(4). 'Agent' does not include a person's counsel acting as such: s 744. For the purposes of s 434(4), the reference to solicitors includes a body corporate recognised by the Law Society under the Administration of Justice Act 1985 s 9 (as amended) (see SOLICITORS vol 44(1) (Reissue) para 383 et seq): Solicitors' Incorporated Practices Order 1991, SI 1991/2684, arts 2(1),

3, 4(a), Sch 1. As to savings in respect of matters required to be disclosed by solicitors and bankers see para 1394 post.

3 Ie under the Companies Act 1985 s 433(1): see para 1378 ante.

4 For these purposes, 'documents' includes information recorded in any form; and, in relation to information recorded otherwise than in legible form, the power to require its production includes power to require the production of a copy of the information in legible form: ibid s 434(6) (added by the Companies Act 1989 s 56(1), (5)).

5 Companies Act 1985 s 434(1) (amended by the Companies Act 1989 s 56(1), (2)). As to the application of the Companies Act 1985 s 434 (as amended) to oversea companies see para 1385 post; and as to the application of s 434 (as amended) to unregistered companies see s 718(1), Sch 22 (as amended) and para 1767 post.

6 Ibid s 434(2) (substituted by the Companies Act 1989 s 56(1), (3)). See also note 5 supra.

7 Companies Act 1985 s 434(3) (substituted by the Companies Act 1989 s 56(1), (4)). See also note 5 supra. Cf *Karak Rubber Co Ltd v Burden* [1971] 3 All ER 1118, [1971] 1 WLR 1748 (answers given in the course of informal questioning inadmissible). The inspector is entitled to have present at the examination any person whom he may reasonably require to enable him properly to carry out his statutory duty: *Re Gaumont-British Picture Corpn Ltd* [1940] Ch 506, [1940] 2 All ER 415 (presence of a shorthand writer held to be reasonably necessary to enable the inspector to prepare his report).

8 *Re Pergamon Press Ltd* [1971] Ch 388, [1970] 3 All ER 535, CA (where it was observed that the inspectors' function under what is now the Companies Act 1985 s 432(2) (see para 1377 ante) is investigatory and not judicial). See also *R v Seelig* [1991] 4 All ER 429, [1992] 1 WLR 148, CA (where inspectors investigating the affairs of a company were held not to be persons charged with the duty of investigating offences or charging offenders for the purposes of the Police and Criminal Evidence Act 1984 s 67(9) (see CRIMINAL LAW vol 11(1) (Reissue) para 679) and therefore not bound by the Codes of Practice issued under that Act).

9 *Maxwell v Department of Trade and Industry* [1974] QB 523, [1974] 2 All ER 122, CA. The only relief which the court may give if these rules are not observed is a declaration that the rules of natural justice have not been followed, although the practical value of such a declaration is doubtful. The court cannot set aside the report, whether in whole or in part, or declare any part of it void: *Maxwell v Department of Trade and Industry* supra.

10 *R v Saunders* (1995) 140 Sol Jo LB 22, CA; *Re London United Investments plc* [1992] Ch 578, [1992] 2 All ER 842, CA; *R v Seelig* [1991] 4 All ER 429, [1992] 1 WLR 148, CA; *R v Harris* [1970] 3 All ER 746, [1970] 1 WLR 1252. The weight of authority now overrules any contrary position in so far as it was supported by *McClelland, Pope and Langley Ltd v Howard* [1968] 1 All ER 569n, HL; *Re Pergamon Press Ltd* [1971] Ch 388, [1970] 3 All ER 535, CA: see *Re London United Investments plc* supra at 600 and at 854. It may be that the court has power under the Companies Act 1985 s 436(1) (as substituted) (see infra), when a refusal to answer has been certified to it, to refuse to compel a person to answer, or to punish him for refusing to answer, if the court feels that continued questioning, in the circumstances and at the stage the case has reached, is oppressive and therefore unfair: *Re London United Investments plc* supra.

11 Ie the powers conferred by the Companies Act 1985 s 434 (as amended), whether as it has effect in relation to an investigation under any of ss 431-433 (as amended) (see paras 1376-1378 ante) or as applied by any other section in Pt XIV (ss 431-453) (as amended).

12 Ibid s 434(5). See also note 5 supra. Such answers may be used in evidence in either criminal or civil proceedings. For an example of their use in criminal proceedings see *R v Saunders* (1995) 140 Sol Jo LB 22, CA; and for an example of their use in civil proceedings see *London and County Securities Ltd v Nicholson* [1980] 3 All ER 861, [1980] 1 WLR 948. There is no unfairness per se in allowing the use in a criminal trial of evidence arising out of interviews conducted by inspectors in accordance with the statutory powers so as to require the exclusion of the evidence by the trial judge in the exercise of his discretion under the Police and Criminal Evidence Act 1984 s 78 (see CRIMINAL LAW vol 11(2) (Reissue) para 1060): *R v Saunders* supra; *R v Seelig* [1991] 4 All ER 429, [1992] 1 WLR 148, CA. Quaere whether the continued use of such interviews as evidence in criminal proceedings is likely to continue in the light of the decision in *Saunders v United Kingdom (Application 19187/91)* (1994) EHRR CD23 (where the use of such evidence, obtained in circumstances where there is no privilege against self-incrimination, was held by the European Commission on Human Rights to be unfair and a breach of the due process provisions of the European Convention on Human Rights).

A person who is subsequently charged with criminal offences as the result of an investigation has no right to require production of witness statements made by other parties to the inspector, or to call the inspector: *R v Cheltenham Justices, ex p Secretary of State for Trade* [1977] 1 All ER 460, [1977] 1 WLR 95.

13 *Karak Rubber Co Ltd v Burden* [1971] 3 All ER 1118, [1971] 1 WLR 1748.

14 *London and County Securities Ltd v Nicholson* [1980] 3 All ER 861, [1980] 1 WLR 948, distinguishing *Re Pergamon Press Ltd* [1971] Ch 388, [1970] 3 All ER 535, CA (where express but qualified assurances had been given to witnesses that their evidence would be treated as confidential).

15 Ie pursuant to the Companies Act 1985 s 434(1)(a) (as amended): see text head (1) supra.

16 Ie pursuant to ibid s 434(1)(c): see text head (3) supra.

17 Ie pursuant to ibid s 434(1)(b) (see text head (2) supra) or s 434(2)(b) (as substituted: see note 6 supra) (see text head (b) supra).

18 Ie to produce documents, to attend before them or to give all assistance pursuant to ibid s 434(2) (as substituted: see note 6 supra) (see text heads (a)–(c) supra).

19 Ibid s 436(1) (substituted by the Companies Act 1989 s 56(6)). As to the application of the Companies Act 1985 s 436 (as amended) to oversea companies see para 1385 post; and as to the application of s 436 (as amended) to unregistered companies see s 718(1), Sch 22 (as amended) and para 1767 post. For an example where inspectors did certify a refusal to the court under similar, but not identical, provisions relating to investigations into insider dealing under the Financial Services Act 1986 ss 177, 178(1) (as amended) see *Re an Inquiry under the Company Securities (Insider Dealing) Act 1985* [1988] AC 660, [1988] 1 All ER 203, HL and paras 1231, 1232 ante.

20 The application to the court for an order under this provision is by originating motion: RSC Ord 102 r 3(1)(c). For the meaning of 'the court' see para 161 note 4 ante. In the High Court the jurisdiction is assigned to the Chancery Division: RSC Ord 102 r 5(1). The notice of originating motion and all affidavits, notices and other documents in the proceedings must be entitled in the matter of the company and in the matter of the Companies Act 1985: RSC Ord 102 r 5(2).

21 Companies Act 1985 s 436(3). See also note 19 supra. As to punishment for contempt of court see CONTEMPT.

1380. Inspectors' reports. The inspectors may, and if so directed by the Secretary of State must, make interim reports to the Secretary of State; and on the conclusion of their investigation they must make a final report to him[1]. Any such report must be either written or printed as the Secretary of State directs[2]. Inspectors[3] may at any time and must, if the Secretary of State directs them to do so, inform him of any matters coming to their knowledge as a result of their investigations[4].

If it appears to the Secretary of State that matters have come to light in the course of the inspectors' investigation which suggest that a criminal offence has been committed, and those matters have been referred to the appropriate prosecuting authority, he may direct the inspectors to take no further steps in the investigation or to take only such further steps as are specified in the direction[5]. Where an investigation is the subject of such a direction, the inspectors must make a final report to the Secretary of State only where they were appointed in pursuance of an order of the court[6] or the Secretary of State directs them to do so[7].

If the inspectors were appointed in pursuance of an order of the court[8], the Secretary of State must furnish a copy of any report of theirs to the court[9].

In any case the Secretary of State may, if he thinks fit:

(1) forward a copy of any report made by the inspectors to the registered office[10] of the company[11];

(2) furnish a copy on request, and on payment of the prescribed fee[12], to any member of the company or other body corporate which is the subject of the report[13], any person whose conduct is referred to in the report, the auditors of that company or body corporate, the applicants for the investigation, and any other person whose financial interests appear to the Secretary of State to be affected by the matters dealt with in the report, whether as a creditor of the company or body corporate or otherwise[14]; and

(3) cause any such report to be printed and published[15].

1 Companies Act 1985 s 437(1). As to the application of s 437 (as amended) to oversea companies see para 1385 post; and as to the application of s 437 (as amended) to unregistered companies see s 718(1), Sch 22 (as amended) and para 1767 post.

2 Ibid s 437(1). See also note 1 supra. As to the admissibility of a copy of the inspectors' report as evidence in any legal proceedings see para 1392 post.

3 Ie any persons who have been appointed under ibid s 431 (see para 1376 ante) or s 432 (as amended) (see para 1377 ante).

4 Ibid s 437(1A) (added by the Financial Services Act 1986 s 182, Sch 13 para 7). See also note 1 supra.

5 Companies Act 1985 s 437(1B) (added by the Companies Act 1989 s 57). See also note 1 supra.

6 Ie under the Companies Act 1985 s 432(1): see para 1377 ante.

7 Ibid s 437(1C) (added by the Companies Act 1989 s 57). See also note 1 supra.

8 Ie under the Companies Act 1985 s 432 (as amended): see para 1377 ante.

9 Ibid s 437(2). See also note 1 supra.

10 As to the registered office of a company see para 150 ante.

11 Companies Act 1985 s 437(3)(a). See also note 1 supra.

12 For the meaning of 'prescribed' see para 24 note 3 ante. The fee so prescribed is ten pence for each page copied: Companies (Inspectors' Reports) (Fees) Regulations 1981, SI 1981/1686.

13 Ie by virtue of the Companies Act 1985 s 433(1): see para 1378 ante.

14 Ibid s 437(3)(b). See also note 1 supra.

15 Ibid s 437(3). See also note 1 supra. The provisions of s 437(3) do not apply where the inspectors are appointed under s 432(2A) (as added): see para 1377 ante. The discretion to publish or withhold publication is exercisable by the Secretary of State in the public interest: see *Lonrho plc v Secretary of State for Trade and Industry* [1989] 2 All ER 609, sub nom *R v Secretary of State for Trade and Industry, ex p Lonrho plc* [1989] 1 WLR 525, HL (the Secretary of State was held not to have acted unlawfully in withholding publication on the ground that publication might inhibit further inquiries and possible criminal proceedings). Publication of reports highly critical of named individuals without allowing the individuals concerned to vindicate their position in a court of law is not a breach of the due process provisions of the European Convention on Human Rights: *Fayed v United Kingdom (Application 17101/90)* (1994) 18 EHRR 393, ECtHR.

B. INVESTIGATION OF OWNERSHIP OF COMPANY

1381. Appointment and powers of inspectors. Where it appears to the Secretary of State that there is good reason to do so, he may appoint one or more competent inspectors to investigate and report on the membership of any company, and otherwise with respect to the company, for the purpose of determining the true persons who are or have been financially interested in its success or failure, real or apparent, or able to control or materially to influence its policy[1]. The appointment may define the scope of the inspectors' investigation, whether as respects the matter or the period to which it is to extend or otherwise, and in particular may limit the investigation to matters connected with particular shares or debentures[2].

If an application for such an investigation with respect to particular shares or debentures of a company is made to the Secretary of State by members of the company, and the number of applicants or the amount of shares held by them is not less than that required for an application by members for the appointment of inspectors to investigate a company's affairs[3], then, subject to the following provisions, the Secretary of State must appoint inspectors to conduct the investigation applied for[4]. The Secretary of State must not, however, appoint inspectors if he is satisfied that the application is vexatious; and, where inspectors are appointed, their terms of appointment must exclude any matter in so far as the Secretary of State is satisfied that it is unreasonable for it to be investigated[5]. Before appointing inspectors, the Secretary of State may require the applicant or applicants to give security, to an amount not exceeding £5,000 or such other sum as he may by order specify, for payment of the costs of the investigation[6].

If, on such an application for investigation by members of the company, it appears to the Secretary of State that the powers conferred by the statutory provisions relating to the obtaining of information as to those interested in shares[7] are sufficient for the purposes of investigating the matters which inspectors would be appointed to investigate, he may instead conduct the investigation under those statutory provisions[8].

Subject to the terms of their appointment, the inspectors' powers extend to the investigation of any circumstances suggesting the existence of an arrangement or understanding which, though not legally binding, is or was observed or likely to be observed in practice and which is relevant to the purposes of the investigation[9].

For the purposes of an investigation under the above provisions[10], the statutory provisions relating to the power of the inspectors to extend their investigations into the affairs of related companies[11], the production of documents and taking of evidence[12], the obstruction of inspectors[13] and inspectors' reports[14] apply as in the case of investigations into the affairs of a company[15], with the necessary modifications of references to the affairs of the company or to those of any other body corporate, but subject to the following provisions[16]. Those provisions apply to:

(1) all persons who are or have been, or whom the inspector has reasonable cause to believe to be or have been, financially interested in the success or failure or the apparent success or failure of the company or any other body corporate whose membership is investigated with that of the company, or able to control or materially influence its policy, including persons concerned only on behalf of others; and

(2) any other person whom the inspector has reasonable cause to believe possesses information relevant to the investigation,

as they apply in relation to officers and agents of the company or the other body corporate, as the case may be[17].

If the Secretary of State is of opinion that there is good reason for not divulging any part of a report made under these provisions[18], he may disclose the report[19] with the omission of that part; and he may cause to be kept by the registrar of companies a copy of the report with that part omitted, or in the case of any other such report, a copy of the whole report[20].

1 Companies Act 1985 s 442(1). Section 442 (as amended) does not apply to oversea companies: see s 453(1A)(c) (as substituted) and para 1385 post. As to the application of s 442 (as amended) to unregistered companies see s 718(1), Sch 22 (as amended) and para 1767 post.

Where an inspector appointed under s 442 (as amended) obtains any information whilst acting in the course of any investigation, or discharging any functions, to which his appointment or authorisation relates, and is of the opinion that the information indicates that any person has or may have been engaged in money laundering, he must, as soon as is reasonably practicable, either disclose that information to a constable or disclose that information to the supervisory authority by whom he was appointed or authorised: Money Laundering Regulations 1993, SI 1993/1933, reg 16(3), (6)(c).

2 Companies Act 1985 s 442(2). See also note 1 supra.

3 Ie under ibid s 431(2)(a) or (b): see para 1376 heads (1), (2) ante.

4 Ibid s 442(3) (substituted by the Companies Act 1989 s 62).

5 Companies Act 1985 s 442(3A) (substituted by the Companies Act 1989 s 62). See also note 1 supra.

6 Companies Act 1985 s 442(3B) (substituted by the Companies Act 1989 s 62). See also note 1 supra. Any such order must be made by statutory instrument which is subject to annulment in pursuance of a resolution of either House of Parliament: Companies Act 1985 s 442(3B) (as so substituted). At the date at which this volume states the law no such order had been made.

7 Ie ibid s 444: see para 1382 post.

8 Ibid s 442(3C) (substituted by the Companies Act 1989 s 62). See also note 1 supra.

9 Companies Act 1985 s 442(4). See also note 1 supra.

10 Ie ibid s 442 (as amended): see supra.

11 Ie ibid s 433(1): see para 1378 ante.

12 Ie ibid s 434 (as amended): see para 1379 ante.

13 Ie ibid s 436 (as amended): see para 1379 ante.

14 Ie ibid s 437 (as amended): see para 1380 ante.

15 See para 1376 et seq ante.

16 Companies Act 1985 s 443(1). Section 443 does not apply to oversea companies: see s 453(1A)(c) (as substituted) and para 1385 post. As to the application of s 443 to unregistered companies see s 718(1), Sch 22 (as amended) and para 1767 post.
17 Ibid s 443(2). See also note 16 supra.
18 Ie ibid ss 442, 443 (as amended).
19 Ie under ibid s 437 (as amended): see para 1380 ante.
20 Ibid s 443(3). See also note 16 supra.

1382. Power to obtain information as to persons interested in shares or debentures. If it appears to the Secretary of State that there is good reason to investigate the ownership of any shares in or debentures of a company, and that it is unnecessary to appoint inspectors for the purpose, he may require any person[1] whom he has reasonable cause to believe to have, or to be able to obtain, any information as to the present and past interests[2] in those shares or debentures and the names and addresses of the persons interested and of any persons who act or have acted on their behalf in relation to the shares or debentures, to give any such information to the Secretary of State[3].

A person who fails to give any information required of him under these provisions[4], or who in giving such information makes any statement which he knows to be false in a material particular[5], or recklessly makes any statement which is false in a material particular, is liable on conviction on indictment to imprisonment for a term not exceeding two years or a fine, or to both, or on summary conviction to a term of imprisonment not exceeding six months or a fine not exceeding the statutory maximum, or to both[6].

1 As to restrictions on the disclosure of privileged information by solicitors and bankers see para 1394 post.
2 For these purposes, a person is deemed to have an interest in shares or debentures if he has any right to acquire or dispose of them or of any interest in them, or to vote in respect of them, or if his consent is necessary for the exercise of any of the rights of other persons interested in them, or if other persons interested in them can be required, or are accustomed, to exercise their rights in accordance with his instructions: Companies Act 1985 s 444(2).
3 Ibid s 444(1). Section 444 does not apply to oversea companies: see s 453(1A)(c) (as substituted) and para 1385 post. As to the application of s 444 to unregistered companies see s 718(1), Sch 22 (as amended) and para 1767 post.
4 Ie under ibid s 444.
5 As to the materiality of misstatements see para 327 ante (where the matter is discussed in relation to offer documents).
6 Companies Act 1985 ss 444(3), 730, Sch 24. See also note 3 supra. For the meaning of 'the statutory maximum' see para 1161 ante.

1383. Power to impose restrictions on shares and debentures. If, in connection with an investigation of the ownership of a company[1] or of its shares or debentures[2], it appears to the Secretary of State that there is difficulty in finding out the relevant facts about any shares, whether issued or to be issued, he may by order direct that the shares shall until further order be subject to the restrictions[3] of Part XV of the Companies Act 1985[4]. If, however, the Secretary of State is satisfied that such an order may unfairly affect the rights of third parties in respect of shares, he may, for the purpose of protecting such rights and subject to such terms as he thinks fit, direct that such acts by such persons or descriptions of persons and for such purposes as may be set out in the order, shall not constitute a breach of the restrictions of Part XV of the Companies Act 1985[5].

1 Ie under the Companies Act 1985 s 442 (as amended): see para 1381 ante.
2 Ie under ibid s 444: see para 1382 ante. Section 445 (as amended), and Pt XV (ss 454-457 (as amended): see paras 1395-1397 post) in its application to orders under it, apply in relation to debentures as in relation to shares, save that s 445(1A) (as added: see note 5 infra) does not so apply: s 445(2) (amended by the Companies (Disclosure of Interests in Shares) (Orders imposing restrictions on shares) Regulations 1991, SI 1991/1646, regs 2, 5(b)).
3 Ie the restrictions of the Companies Act 1985 Pt XV (ss 454-457) (as amended).
4 Ibid s 445(1). Section 445 (as amended) does not apply to oversea companies: see s 453(1A)(c) (as substituted) and para 1385 post. As to the application of s 445 (as amended) to unregistered companies see s 718(1), Sch 22 (as amended) and para 1767 post.
    Where before 3 December 1981 shares in a company were directed by order of the Secretary of State to be subject to the restrictions imposed by the Companies Act 1948 s 174 (repealed), and the order remained in force on 1 July 1985, nothing in the Companies Consolidation (Consequential Provisions) Act 1985 prevents the continued application of the order with such effect as it had immediately before the repeal of the Companies Act 1948 s 174 took effect: Companies Consolidation (Consequential Provisions) Act 1985 s 23.
5 Companies Act 1985 s 445(1A) (added by the Companies (Disclosure of Interests in Shares) (Orders imposing restrictions on shares) Regulations 1991 regs 2, 5(a)). See also note 4 supra.

C. INVESTIGATION OF SHARE DEALINGS

1384. In general. If it appears to the Secretary of State that there are circumstances suggesting that contraventions may have occurred, in relation to a company's shares or debentures, of the provisions which restrict directors from dealing in options[1], or of the provisions which require a director to disclose shareholdings in his own company[2], including the provisions relating to spouses and children[3], he may appoint one or more competent inspectors to carry out such investigations as are requisite to establish whether or not such contraventions have occurred and to report the result of their investigations to him[4].

For the purposes of any such investigation, the provisions of the Companies Act 1985 which impose a duty to produce documents and assist inspectors[5] and those which relate to inspectors' reports[6] apply but with the substitution, for references to any other body corporate whose affairs are investigated as the result of any exercise of the inspectors' power to extend the investigation into the affairs of related companies[7], of a reference to any other body corporate which is, or has at any relevant time been, the company's subsidiary[8] or holding company[9] or a subsidiary of its holding company[10]; and the provisions which impose a duty to produce documents and assist inspectors[11] apply to the following persons as they apply to officers of the company or of the other body corporate:

(1) any individual who is an authorised person within the meaning of the Financial Services Act 1986[12];

(2) any individual who holds a permission to deal in the course of non-investment business granted by the Secretary of State[13];

(3) any officer, whether past or present, of a body corporate which is such an authorised person or holds such a permission;

(4) any partner, whether past or present, in a partnership which is such an authorised person or holds such a permission;

(5) any member of the governing body or officer, in either case whether past or present, of an unincorporated association which is such an authorised person or holds such a permission[14].

1 Ie the Companies Act 1985 s 323, Sch 13 (as amended): see para 614 ante.
2 Ie ibid s 324, Sch 13 (as amended): see paras 564, 565 ante.
3 Ie ibid s 328(3)-(5): see para 566 ante.

4 Ibid s 446(1). Such an appointment may limit the period to which the investigation is to extend or confine it to shares or debentures of a particular class, or both: s 446(2). Section 446 (as amended) does not apply to oversea companies (see s 453(1A)(c) (as substituted) and para 1385 post); nor does it apply to unregistered companies (see s 718(1), Sch 22 (as amended) and para 1767 post).

As to restrictions on the disclosure of privileged information by solicitors and bankers see para 1394 post.

Where an inspector appointed under s 446 (as amended) obtains any information whilst acting in the course of any investigation, or discharging any functions, to which his appointment or authorisation relates, and is of the opinion that the information indicates that any person has or may have been engaged in money laundering, he must, as soon as is reasonably practicable, either disclose that information to a constable or disclose that information to the supervisory authority by whom he was appointed or authorised: Money Laundering Regulations 1993, SI 1993/1933, reg 16(3), (6)(c).

5 Ie the Companies Act 1985 ss 434, 436 (as amended): see para 1379 ante.
6 Ie ibid s 437 (as amended): see para 1380 ante.
7 Ie under ibid s 433(1): see para 1378 ante.
8 For the meaning of 'subsidiary' see para 827 ante.
9 For the meaning of 'holding company' see para 827 ante.
10 Companies Act 1985 s 446(3)(a) (amended by the Financial Services Act 1986 s 182, Sch 13 para 8(a); the Companies Act 1989 s 212, Sch 24). See also note 4 supra.
11 See note 5 supra.
12 For these purposes, 'authorised person' means a person authorised under the Financial Services Act 1986 Pt I Ch III (ss 7-34 (as amended): see MONEY) to carry on investment business in the United Kingdom (ss 3, 207(1)) and includes a reference to a European institution carrying on home-regulated investment business in the United Kingdom (Banking Co-ordination (Second Council Directive) Regulations 1992, SI 1992/3218, reg 82(1), Sch 10 para 16). The Companies Act 1985 s 446 (as amended) has effect as if the references in s 446(4)(c)-(e) (see text heads (3)-(5) infra) to an authorised person within the meaning of the Financial Services Act 1986 included a reference to a European investment firm carrying on home-regulated investment business in the United Kingdom: Investment Services Regulations 1995, SI 1995/3275, reg 57, Sch 10 para 4.
13 Ie under the Financial Services Act 1986 ss 1, 2, Sch 1 para 23: see MONEY.
14 Companies Act 1985 s 446(4) (substituted by the Financial Services Act 1986 s 212(2), Sch 16 para 21). See also note 4 supra.

D. OVERSEA COMPANIES

1385. In general. The statutory provisions relating to the Secretary of State's powers of investigation[1] apply to bodies corporate[2] incorporated outside Great Britain which are carrying on business in Great Britain or which have at any time carried on business there as they apply to companies under the Companies Act 1985, but subject to the following exceptions, adaptations and modifications[3]. The statutory provisions relating to:

(1) the investigation of a company on the application of a company or its members[4];
(2) the power to bring civil proceedings on the company's behalf[5];
(3) the investigation of the ownership of a company and the power to obtain information as to those interested in shares or debentures[6];
(4) the investigation of share dealings[7],

do not apply to such bodies[8].

The other statutory provisions relating to the Secretary of State's powers of investigation apply to such bodies subject to such adaptations and modifications as may be specified by regulations made by the Secretary of State[9].

1 Ie the Companies 1985 Pt XIV (ss 431-453) (as amended): see para 1376 et seq ante and para 1386 et seq post.
2 For the meaning of 'body corporate' see para 89 note 8 ante.
3 Companies Act 1985 s 453(1) (substituted by the Companies Act 1989 s 70).
4 Ie the Companies Act 1985 s 431: see para 1376 ante.

5 Ie ibid s 438 (as amended): see para 1390 post.
6 Ie ibid ss 442-445 (as amended): see paras 1381-1383 ante.
7 Ie ibid s 446 (as amended): see para 1384 ante.
8 Ibid s 453(1A) (substituted by the Companies Act 1989 s 70).
9 Companies Act 1985 s 453(1B) (substituted by the Companies Act 1989 s 70). Such regulations must be made by statutory instrument subject to annulment in pursuance of a resolution of either House of Parliament: Companies Act 1985 s 453(2). At the date at which this volume states the law no such regulations had been made.

(ii) Requisition and Seizure of Books and Papers

1386. Secretary of State's power to require production of documents. The Secretary of State may at any time, if he thinks there is good reason to do so, give directions to a company requiring it, at such time and place as may be specified in the directions, to produce such documents[1] as may be so specified[2]. The Secretary of State may also at any time, if he thinks there is good reason to do so, authorise an officer of his or any other competent person, on producing, if so required, evidence of his authority, to require a company to produce to him, the officer or other person, forthwith any documents which he, the officer or other person, may specify[3].

Where, by virtue of the above provisions, the Secretary of State or an officer of his or other person has power to require the production of documents from a company, he or the officer or other person has the like power to require production of those documents from any person who appears to him or the officer or other person to be in possession of them; but, where any such person claims a lien on documents produced by him, the production is without prejudice to the lien[4].

The above power to require a company or other person to produce documents includes power:

(1) if the documents are produced, to take copies of them or extracts from them, and to require the person who produced them or any other person who is a present or past officer of, or is or was at any time employed by, the company in question, to provide an explanation of any of them[5];

(2) if the documents are not produced, to require the person who was required to produce them to state, to the best of his knowledge and belief, where they are[6].

If the requirement to produce documents or provide an explanation or make a statement is not complied with, the company or other person on whom the requirement was so imposed is guilty of an offence and is liable on conviction on indictment to a fine, or on summary conviction to a fine not exceeding the statutory maximum[7]. Where, however, a person is charged with such an offence in respect of a requirement to produce any documents, it is a defence to prove that they were not in his possession or under his control and that it was not reasonably practicable for him to comply with the requirement[8]. A statement made by a person in compliance with such a requirement may be used in evidence against him[9].

A person who, in purported compliance with any such requirement to provide an explanation or make a statement, provides or makes an explanation or statement which he knows to be false in a material particular or recklessly provides or makes an explanation or statement which is so false, is guilty of an offence and is liable on conviction on indictment to imprisonment for a term not exceeding two years or a fine, or to both, or on summary conviction to imprisonment for a term not exceeding six months or a fine not exceeding the statutory maximum, or to both[10].

Under the above provisions the Secretary of State may not require, or authorise an officer of his or other person to require, the production by a person carrying on the business of banking of a document relating to the affairs of a customer of his unless either it appears to the Secretary of State that it is necessary to do so for the purpose of investigating the affairs of the first-mentioned person, or the customer is a person on whom a statutory requirement[11] has been imposed[12].

1 For these purposes, 'documents' includes information recorded in any form; and, in relation to information recorded otherwise than in legible form, the power to require its production includes power to require the production of a copy of it in legible form: Companies Act 1985 s 447(9) (added by the Companies Act 1989 s 63(1), (7)).

2 Companies Act 1985 s 447(2) (amended by the Companies Act 1989 s 63(1), (2)(a), (3)). As to the application of the Companies Act 1985 s 447 (as amended) to oversea companies see para 1385 ante; and as to the application of s 447 (as amended) to unregistered companies see s 718(1), Sch 22 (as amended) and para 1767 post.

3 Ibid s 447(3) (amended by the Companies Act 1989 s 63(1), (2)(a), (3), (4)). An officer or other person must not abuse or misuse for any ulterior motive the discretions granted to him under the Companies Act 1985 s 447 (as amended): *R v Secretary of State for Trade, ex p Perestrello* [1981] QB 19, [1980] 3 All ER 28.

Where a person authorised to require the production of documents under the Companies Act 1985 s 447 (as amended) obtains any information whilst acting in the course of any investigation, or discharging any functions, to which his appointment or authorisation relates, and is of the opinion that the information indicates that any person has or may have been engaged in money laundering, he must, as soon as is reasonably practicable, either disclose that information to a constable or disclose that information to the supervisory authority by whom he was appointed or authorised: Money Laundering Regulations 1993, SI 1993/1933, reg 16(3), (6)(g).

4 Companies Act 1985 s 447(4) (amended by the Companies Act 1989 s 63(1), (2)(b), (3), (5)). See also note 2 supra.

5 Companies Act 1985 s 447(5)(a) (amended by the Companies Act 1989 s 63(1), (2)(b), (c), (3)). See also note 2 supra.

6 Companies Act 1985 s 447(5)(b) (amended by the Companies Act 1989 s 63(1), (2)(b), (3)). See also note 2 supra.

7 Companies Act 1985 s 447(6) (amended by the Companies Act 1989 s 63(1), (2)(c), (3), (6)); Companies Act 1985 s 730, Sch 24 (amended by the Companies Act 1989 s 63(1), (8)). See also note 2 supra. For the meaning of 'the statutory maximum' see para 1161 ante. The Companies Act 1985 s 732 (restriction on prosecutions: see para 1165 ante), s 733 (as amended) (liability of individuals for corporate default: see para 1162 ante) and s 734 (as amended) (criminal proceedings against unincorporated bodies: see para 1163 ante) apply to this offence: s 447(6) (as so amended).

8 Ibid s 447(7) (amended by the Companies Act 1989 s 63(1), (3)).

9 Companies Act 1985 s 447(8). See also note 2 supra.

10 Ibid s 451 (amended by the Companies Act 1989 s 67); Companies Act 1985 s 730, Sch 24. Section 732 (restriction on prosecutions: see para 1165 ante), s 733 (as amended) (liability of individuals for corporate default: see para 1162 ante) and s 734 (as amended) (criminal proceedings against unincorporated bodies: see para 1163 ante) apply to this offence: s 451 (as so amended). As to the application of s 451 (as amended) to oversea companies see para 1385 ante; and as to the application of s 451 (as amended) to unregistered companies see s 718(1), Sch 22 (as amended) and para 1767 post.

11 Ie a requirement under ibid s 447 (as amended) or the Insurance Companies Act 1982 s 43A (as added) or s 44(2)-(4) (as amended) (see INSURANCE vol 25 (Reissue) para 854).

12 Companies Act 1985 s 452(3) (amended by the Companies Act 1989 s 69(1), (4); the Insurance Companies (Third Insurance Directives) Regulations 1994, SI 1994/1696, reg 68(1), Sch 8 Pt I para 9(4)). See also note 10 supra. As to privileged information generally see para 1394 post.

1387. Security of information. No information or document relating to a company which has been obtained under the statutory power to require production of documents[1] may, without the previous consent in writing of that company, be published or disclosed, except to a competent authority[2]. This provision does not apply, however, where the publication or disclosure is required:

(1) with a view to the institution of, or otherwise for the purposes of, criminal proceedings[3];

(2) with a view to the institution of, or otherwise for the purposes of, any proceedings on an application under certain provisions[4] of the Company Directors Disqualification Act 1986[5];

(3) for the purposes of enabling or assisting any inspector appointed under Part XIV of the Companies Act 1985[6] or under certain provisions[7] of the Financial Services Act 1986 to discharge his functions[8];

(4) for the purpose of enabling or assisting any person authorised to exercise powers or appointed under certain provisions of the Insurance Companies Act 1982[9], the Companies Act 1985[10], the Financial Services Act 1986[11] or the Companies Act 1989[12] to discharge his functions[13];

(5) for the purpose of enabling or assisting the Secretary of State or the Treasury to exercise any of their functions under the Companies Act 1985, the insider dealing legislation[14], the Insurance Companies Act 1982, the Insolvency Act 1986, the Company Directors Disqualification Act 1986, the Financial Services Act 1986 or certain provisions[15] of the Companies Act 1989[16];

(6) for the purpose of enabling or assisting the Department of Economic Development for Northern Ireland to exercise any powers conferred on it by the enactments relating to companies or insolvency or for the purpose of enabling or assisting any inspector appointed by it under the enactments relating to companies to discharge his functions[17];

(7) for the purpose of enabling or assisting the Chief Registrar of friendly societies or the Assistant Registrar of friendly societies for Scotland to discharge his functions under the enactments relating to friendly societies[18];

(8) for the purpose of enabling or assisting the Friendly Societies Commission to discharge its functions under the Financial Services Act 1986[19];

(9) for the purpose of enabling or assisting the Occupational Pensions Regulatory Authority to discharge its functions under the Pension Schemes Act 1993 or the Pensions Act 1995 or any enactment in force in Northern Ireland corresponding to either of them[20];

(10) for the purpose of enabling or assisting the Bank of England to discharge its functions under the Banking Act 1987[21] or any other functions[22];

(11) for the purpose of enabling or assisting the Deposit Protection Board to discharge its functions under that Act[23];

(12) for any of certain purposes[24] mentioned in the Financial Services Act 1986[25];

(13) for the purpose of enabling or assisting a body established by order under the Companies Act 1989[26] to discharge its functions under Part II of that Act[27], or of enabling or assisting a recognised supervisory[28] or qualifying[29] body to discharge its functions as such[30];

(14) for the purpose of enabling or assisting the Industrial Assurance Commissioner or the Industrial Assurance Commissioner for Northern Ireland to discharge his functions under the enactments relating to industrial assurance[31];

(15) for the purpose of enabling or assisting the Insurance Brokers Registration Council to discharge its functions under the Insurance Brokers (Registration) Act 1977[32];

(16) for the purpose of enabling or assisting an official receiver to discharge his functions under the enactments relating to insolvency or for the purpose of enabling or assisting a body which is for the time being a recognised professional body for the purposes of the Insolvency Act 1986 in relation to insolvency practitioners[33], to discharge its functions as such[34];

(17) with a view to the institution of, or otherwise for the purposes of, any disciplinary proceedings relating to the exercise by a solicitor, auditor, accountant, valuer or actuary of his professional duties[35];

(18) with a view to the institution of, or otherwise for the purposes of, any disciplinary proceedings relating to the discharge by a public servant[36] of his duties[37];

(19) for the purpose of enabling or assisting an overseas regulatory authority[38] to exercise its regulatory functions[39].

The above provisions do not preclude publication or disclosure for the purpose of enabling or assisting any public or other authority for the time being designated for these purposes by the Secretary of State by an order in a statutory instrument to discharge any functions which are specified in the order[40].

A person who publishes or discloses any information or document in contravention of these provisions is guilty of an offence and is liable on conviction on indictment to imprisonment for a term not exceeding two years or a fine, or to both, or on summary conviction to imprisonment for a term not exceeding six months or a fine not exceeding the statutory maximum, or to both[41].

1 Ie under the Companies Act 1985 s 447 (as amended): see para 1386 ante.

2 Ibid s 449(1) (amended by the Companies Act 1989 ss 65(1), (2)(a), 212, Sch 24). For these purposes, each of the following is a competent authority: (1) the Secretary of State; (2) an inspector appointed under the Companies Act 1985 Pt XIV (ss 431-453 (as amended): see para 1376 et seq ante and para 1388 et seq post) or under the Financial Services Act 1986 s 94 (investigations: see MONEY) or s 177 (as amended) (investigations into insider dealing: see para 1231 ante); (3) any person authorised to exercise powers under the Insurance Companies Act 1982 s 44 (as amended) (power to obtain information and require production of documents: see INSURANCE vol 25 (Reissue) para 854), the Companies Act 1985 s 447 (as amended) (see para 1386 ante), the Financial Services Act 1986 s 106 (as amended) (exercise of investigative powers by officer etc: see MONEY) or the Companies Act 1989 s 84 (see para 1400 post); (4) the Department of Economic Development in Northern Ireland; (5) the Treasury; (6) the Bank of England (see BANKING vol 3(1) (Reissue) para 1 et seq); (7) the Lord Advocate; (8) the Director of Public Prosecutions (see CRIMINAL LAW vol 11(1) (Reissue) para 637) and the Director of Public Prosecutions for Northern Ireland; (9) any designated agency or transferee body within the meaning of the Financial Services Act 1986 (see MONEY) and any body administering a scheme under s 54 (as amended) or s 140, Sch 11 para 18 (schemes for compensation of investors: see MONEY); (10) the Chief Registrar of friendly societies (see FRIENDLY SOCIETIES vol 19(1) (Reissue) paras 131, 132); (11) the Friendly Societies Commission (see FRIENDLY SOCIETIES vol 19(1) (Reissue) paras 127-130); (12) the Industrial Assurance Commissioner (see INDUSTRIAL ASSURANCE vol 24 (Reissue) para 210); (13) any constable; (14) any procurator fiscal: Companies Act 1985 s 449(3) (substituted by the Companies Act 1989 s 65(1), (6); amended by the Friendly Societies Act 1992 s 120(1), (2), Sch 21 para 7(2), Sch 22).

    Any information which may be disclosed to a competent authority under these provisions may be disclosed to any officer or servant of the authority: Companies Act 1985 s 449(3A) (substituted by the Companies Act 1989 s 65(1), (6)).

3 Companies Act 1985 s 449(1)(a) (substituted by the Financial Services Act 1986 s 182, Sch 13 para 9(1)(a)).

4 Ie the Company Directors Disqualification Act 1986 s 6 (see para 1425 post), s 7 (see para 1427 post) or s 8 (as amended) (see para 1431 post).

5 Companies Act 1985 s 449(1)(ba) (added by the Insolvency Act 1985 s 109, Sch 6 para 4; amended by the Insolvency Act 1986 s 439(1), Sch 13 Pt I). See *Re Rex Williams Leisure plc (in administration)* [1994] Ch 350, [1994] 4 All ER 27, CA; *Re Samuel Sherman plc* [1991] 1 WLR 1070, [1991] BCC 699; and para 1390 text to notes 7-13 post.

6 Ie under the Companies Act 1985 Pt XIV (ss 431-453) (as amended).

7 Ie under the Financial Services Act 1986 s 94 or s 177 (as amended).

8 Companies Act 1985 s 449(1)(c) (substituted by the Companies Act 1989 s 65(1), (2)(b)).

9 Ie under the Insurance Companies Act 1982 s 43A (as added) or s 44 (as amended).

10 Ie under the Companies Act 1985 s 447 (as amended).

11 Ie under the Financial Services Act 1986 s 106 (as amended).

12 Ie under the Companies Act 1989 s 84.

13 Companies Act 1985 s 449(1)(cc) (added by the Companies Act 1989 s 65(1), (2)(c); amended by the Insurance Companies (Third Insurance Directives) Regulations 1994, SI 1994/1696, reg 68(1), Sch 8 Pt I para 9(2)).

14 Ie the Criminal Justice Act 1993 Pt V (ss 52-64): see para 1218 et seq ante.

15 Ie the Companies Act 1989 Pt II (ss 24-54) (eligibility for appointment as company auditor: see para 955 et seq ante), Pt III (ss 60-91 (as amended): investigations and powers to obtain information) or Pt VII (ss 154-191) (as amended) (financial markets and insolvency: see MONEY).

16 Companies Act 1985 s 449(1)(d) (substituted by the Financial Services Act 1986 s 212(3), Sch 13 para 9(1)(b), Sch 17 Pt I; amended by the Companies Act 1989 s 65(1), (2)(d); the Transfer of Functions (Financial Services) Order 1992, SI 1992/1315, art 10(1), Sch 4 para 1; the Criminal Justice Act 1993 s 79(13), Sch 5 Pt I para 4(2)).

17 Companies Act 1985 s 449(1)(dd) (added by the Financial Services Act 1986 Sch 13 para 9(1)(b)).

18 Companies Act 1985 s 449(1)(de) (added by the Friendly Societies Act 1992 Sch 21 Pt I para 7(1)).

19 Companies Act 1985 s 449(1)(df) (added by the Friendly Societies Act 1992 Sch 21 Pt I para 7(1)).

20 Companies Act 1985 s 449(1)(dg) (added by the Pensions Act 1995 s 122, Sch 3 para 12).

21 See BANKING.

22 Companies Act 1985 s 449(1)(f) (added by the Financial Services Act 1986 Sch 13 para 9(1)(c); amended by the Banking Act 1987 s 108(1), Sch 6 para 18(7)).

23 Companies Act 1985 s 449(1)(g) (added by the Financial Services Act 1986 Sch 13 para 9(1)(c)).

24 Ie the purposes mentioned in the Financial Services Act 1986 s 180(1)(b), (e), (h) or (n) (as amended) (exceptions from restrictions on disclosure): see MONEY.

25 Companies Act 1985 s 449(1)(h) (added by the Financial Services Act 1986 Sch 13 para 9(1)(c); amended by the Companies Act 1989 s 65(1), (2)(f)).

26 Ie the Companies Act 1989 s 46: see para 1005 ante. Section 46 comes into force on such day as the Secretary of State may appoint by order made by statutory instrument: s 215(2). At the date at which this volume states the law no such order had been made.

27 Ie under ibid Pt II (ss 24-54): see para 955 et seq ante.

28 Ie within the meaning of ibid Pt II (ss 24-54). For the meaning of 'supervisory body' see para 962 ante. As to the recognition of supervisory bodies see para 962 et seq ante.

29 Ie within the meaning of ibid Pt II (ss 24-54). For the meaning of 'qualifying body' see para 979 ante. As to the recognition of qualifying bodies see para 979 et seq ante.

30 Companies Act 1985 s 449(1)(hh) (added by the Companies Act 1989 s 65(1), (2)(g)).

31 Companies Act 1985 s 449(1)(i) (added by the Financial Services Act 1986 Sch 13 para 9(1)(c)).

32 Companies Act 1985 s 449(1)(j) (added by the Financial Services Act 1986 Sch 13 para 9(1)(c)). As to the Insurance Brokers Registration Council see INSURANCE vol 25 (Reissue) para 869 et seq.

33 Ie for the purposes of the Insolvency Act 1986 s 391: see para 2012 post. As to insolvency practitioners and their qualification see para 2007 et seq post; and as to official receivers see para 2263 et seq post.

34 Companies Act 1985 s 449(1)(k) (added by the Financial Services Act 1986 Sch 13 para 9(1)(c)).

35 Companies Act 1985 s 449(1)(l) (added by the Financial Services Act 1986 Sch 13 para 9(1)(c)).

36 For these purposes, 'public servant' means an officer or servant of the Crown or of any public or other authority for the time being designated for the purposes of the Companies Act 1985 s 449(1)(ll) (as added: see note 37 infra) by the Secretary of State by order made by statutory instrument: s 449(1A)(a) (added by the Financial Services Act 1986 Sch 13 para 9(2); substituted by the Companies Act 1989 s 65(1), (3)). A statutory instrument containing an order under the Companies Act 1985 s 449(1A)(a) (as so substituted) or s 449(1B) (as added and amended: see note 40 infra) is subject to annulment in pursuance of a resolution of either House of Parliament: s 449(4) (added by the Financial Services Act 1986 Sch 13 para 9(3); amended by the Companies Act 1989 s 65(1), (7)). At the date at which this volume states the law no such order had been made.

37 Companies Act 1985 s 449(1)(ll) (added by the Companies Act 1989 s 65(1), (2)(h)).

38 For these purposes, 'overseas regulatory authority' and 'regulatory functions' have the same meaning as in the Companies Act 1989 s 82 (see para 1398 notes 2, 5 post): Companies Act 1985 s 449(1A)(b) (added by the Financial Services Act 1986 Sch 13 para 9(2); substituted by the Companies Act 1989 s 65(1), (3)).

39 Companies Act 1985 s 449(1)(m) (added by the Financial Services Act 1986 Sch 13 para 9(1)(c); substituted by the Companies Act 1989 s 65(1), (2)(i)).

40 Companies Act 1985 s 449(1B) (added by the Financial Services Act 1986 Sch 13 para 9(2); amended by the Companies Act 1989 s 65(1), (4)). See also note 36 supra. Such an order may (1) impose conditions subject to which the publication or disclosure of any information or document is permitted; and (2) otherwise restrict the circumstances in which publication or disclosure is permitted: Companies Act 1985 s 449(1C) (added by the Financial Services Act 1986 Sch 13 para 9(2)).

The Companies Act 1985 s 449(1) (as amended) does not preclude the publication or disclosure of any such information as is mentioned in the Financial Services Act 1986 s 180(5) (see MONEY) by any person who by virtue of s 180 (as amended) is not precluded by s 179 (as amended) (see MONEY) from disclosing it: Companies Act 1985 s 449(1D) (added by the Financial Services Act 1986 Sch 13 para 9(2)).

For the purposes of the Companies Act 1985 s 449 (as amended):

(a) the Insolvency Practitioners Tribunal (see para 2036 post) is designated as an authority in relation to its functions under the Insolvency Act 1986 (Financial Services (Disclosure of Information) (Designated Authorities No 2) Order 1987, SI 1987/859, art 2(a));

(b) the body known as the Panel on Take-overs and Mergers (see para 1193 et seq ante) is designated as an authority in relation to all its functions (Financial Services (Disclosure of Information) (Designated Authorities No 2) Order 1987 art 2(c));

(c) the Occupational Pensions Board (to be dissolved and replaced by the Occupational Pensions Regulatory Authority from a day to be appointed: see the Pensions Act 1995 ss 1, 150 and SOCIAL SECURITY AND PENSIONS) is designated as an authority in relation to its functions under the Social Security Act 1973 and the Social Security Acts 1975 to 1986 (now substantially consolidated in the Pension Schemes Act 1993: see SOCIAL SECURITY AND PENSIONS) (Financial Services (Disclosure of Information) (Designated Authorities No 2) Order 1987 art 2(b));

(d) organs of the Society of Lloyd's, being organs constituted by or under the Lloyd's Act 1982, are designated as authorities in relation to their functions under the Lloyd's Acts 1871-1982 (see INSURANCE vol 25 (Reissue) para 21) and the byelaws made thereunder of the Society of Lloyd's (Financial Services (Disclosure of Information) (Designated Authorities) (No 3) Order 1987, SI 1987/1141, art 2(a));

(e) the Director General of Fair Trading is designated as an authority in relation to his functions under the Fair Trading Act 1973, other than Pt II (ss 13-33), the Restrictive Trade Practices Act 1976 and the Competition Act 1980 (Companies (Disclosure of Information) (Designated Authorities) Order 1988, SI 1988/1334, art 2(a); Financial Services (Disclosure of Information) (Designated Authorities) (No 6) Order 1989, SI 1989/2009, art 3(a)), and in relation to his functions under the Consumer Credit Act 1974, the Estate Agents Act 1979 and the Control of Misleading Advertisements Regulations 1988, SI 1988/915 (Financial Services (Disclosure of Information) (Designated Authorities) (No 6) Order 1989 art 3(b)-(d));

(f) the Monopolies and Mergers Commission is designated as an authority in relation to its functions under the Fair Trading Act 1973 and the Competition Act 1980 (Companies (Disclosure of Information) (Designated Authorities) Order 1988 art 2(b));

(g) the Charity Commissioners are designated as authorities in relation to their functions under the Charities Act 1960 (repealed: see now the Charities Act 1992 and the Charities Act 1993) and the Attorney General is designated as an authority in relation to his functions in connection with charities (Financial Services (Disclosure of Information) (Designated Authorities) (No 5) Order 1989, SI 1989/940, art 2);

(h) a person authorised by the Secretary of State under the Companies Act 1985 s 245C (as added) (rectification of defective accounts: see para 954 ante) is designated as an authority in relation to that person's functions relating to securing compliance by companies with the accounting requirements of the 1985 Act (Financial Services (Disclosure of Information) (Designated Authorities) (No 7) Order 1993, SI 1993/1826, art 2);

(i) the Director General of the National Lottery is designated as an authority in relation to his functions under the National Lottery etc Act 1993 ss 5-10, 15 (see BETTING) (Financial Services (Disclosure of Information) (Designated Authorities) (No 8) Order 1994, SI 1994/340, art 2).

41 Companies Act 1985 s 449(2) (amended by the Companies Act 1989 s 65(1), (5)); Companies Act 1985 s 730, Sch 24. For the meaning of 'the statutory maximum' see para 1161 ante. Section 732 (restriction on prosecutions: see para 1165 ante), s 733 (as amended) (liability of individuals for corporate default: see para 1162 ante) and s 734 (as amended) (criminal proceedings against unincorporated bodies: see para 1163 ante) apply to this offence: s 449(2) (as so amended).

1388. Punishment for destroying, mutilating etc company documents. An officer[1] of a company or of an insurance company to which Part II of the Insurance Companies Act 1982[2] applies, who:

(1) destroys, mutilates or falsifies, or is privy to the destruction, mutilation or falsification of a document[3] affecting or relating to the company's property or affairs; or

(2)　makes, or is privy to the making of, a false entry in such a document,

is guilty of an offence unless he proves that he had no intention to conceal the state of the company's affairs or to defeat the law[4]. Such a person is also guilty of an offence if he fraudulently either parts with, alters or makes an omission in any such document or is privy to any such act[5].

A person guilty of an offence under these provisions is liable on conviction on indictment to imprisonment for a term not exceeding seven years or a fine, or to both, or on summary conviction to imprisonment for a term not exceeding six months or a fine not exceeding the statutory maximum, or to both[6].

1　For the meaning of 'officer' see para 641 ante.
2　Ie the Insurance Companies Act 1982 Pt II (ss 15–71) (as amended): see INSURANCE vol 25 (Reissue) para 803 et seq. The Companies Act 1985 s 450(1) (as amended: see note 4 infra) has effect as if the reference to an insurance company to which the Insurance Companies Act 1982 Pt II (ss 15–71) (as amended) applies included a reference to an EC company lawfully carrying on insurance business in the United Kingdom: Insurance Companies (Third Insurance Directives) Regulations 1994, SI 1994/1696, reg 68(1), Sch 8 para 9(1)(c).
3　For these purposes, 'document' includes information recorded in any form: Companies Act 1985 s 450(5) (added by the Companies Act 1989 s 66(1), (4)). For the meaning of 'document' see para 151 ante.
4　Companies Act 1985 s 450(1) (amended by the Companies Act 1989 s 66(1), (2)). As to the application of the Companies Act 1985 s 450 (as amended) to oversea companies see para 1385 ante; and as to the application of s 450 (as amended) to unregistered companies see s 718(1), Sch 22 (as amended) and para 1767 post.
5　Ibid s 450(2). See also note 4 supra.
6　Ibid ss 450(3), 730, Sch 24. See also note 4 supra. For the meaning of 'the statutory maximum' see para 1161 ante. Section 732 (restriction on prosecutions: see para 1165 ante), s 733 (as amended) (liability of individuals for corporate default: see para 1162 ante) and s 734 (as amended) (criminal proceedings against unincorporated bodies: see para 1163 ante) apply to this offence: s 450(4) (substituted by the Companies Act 1989 s 66(1), (3)).

1389. Disclosure of information by Secretary of State or inspector. The Secretary of State may, if he thinks fit:

(1)　disclose any information obtained under the Companies Act 1985[1] to any person to whom, or for any purpose for which, disclosure is permitted[2]; or

(2)　authorise or require an inspector[3] to disclose such information to any such person or for any such purpose[4].

Such information may also be disclosed by an inspector[5] to another inspector appointed under the Companies Act 1985[5] or the Financial Services Act 1986[6] or a person authorised to exercise powers or appointed under the Insurance Companies Act 1982[7], the Companies Act 1985[8], the Financial Services Act 1986[9] or the provisions of the Companies Act 1989[10] permitting investigations to assist overseas regulatory authorities[11]. Any information which may be so disclosed[12] to any person may be disclosed to any officer or servant of that person[13].

If he thinks fit, the Secretary of State may disclose any information obtained in respect of interests in shares or debentures[14] to:

(a)　the company whose ownership was the subject of the investigation;

(b)　any member of the company;

(c)　any person whose conduct was investigated in the course of the investigation;

(d)　the auditors of the company; or

(e)　any person whose financial interests appear to the Secretary of State to be affected by matters covered by the investigation[15].

1 Ie information obtained under the Companies Act 1985 ss 434-446 (as amended): see para 1379 et seq ante.
2 Ie under ibid s 449 (as amended): see para 1387 ante.
3 Ie an inspector appointed under ibid Pt XIV (ss 431-453) (as amended): see para 1376 et seq ante.
4 Ibid s 451A(1), (2) (added by the Financial Services Act 1986 s 182, Sch 13 para 10; substituted by the Companies Act 1989 s 68). As to the application of the Companies Act 1985 s 451A (as added and amended) to oversea companies see para 1385 ante; and as to the application of s 451A (as added and amended) to unregistered companies see s 718(1), Sch 22 (as amended) and para 1767 post.
5 See note 3 supra.
6 Ie under the Financial Services Act 1986 s 94 (as amended) or s 177 (as amended): see MONEY.
7 Ie under the Insurance Companies Act 1982 s 43A (as added) or s 44 (as amended): see INSURANCE vol 25 (Reissue) para 854.
8 Ie under the Companies Act 1985 s 447 (as amended): see para 1386 ante.
9 Ie under the Financial Services Act 1986 s 106 (as amended): see MONEY.
10 Ie the Companies Act 1989 s 84: see para 1400 post.
11 Companies Act 1985 s 451A(3) (added by the Financial Services Act 1986 Sch 13 para 10; substituted by the Companies Act 1989 s 68; amended by the Insurance Companies (Third Insurance Directives) Regulations 1994, SI 1994/1696, reg 68(1), Sch 8 Pt I para 9(3)). See also note 4 supra.
12 Ie by virtue of the Companies Act 1985 s 451A(3) (as added and amended): see supra.
13 Ibid s 451A(4) (added by the Financial Services Act 1986 Sch 13 para 10; substituted by the Companies Act 1989 s 68). See also note 4 supra.
14 Ie information obtained under the Companies Act 1985 s 444: see para 1382 ante.
15 Ibid s 451A(5) (added by the Financial Services Act 1986 Sch 13 para 10; substituted by the Companies Act 1989 s 68). See also note 4 supra.

(iii) Power to bring Proceedings etc

1390. Proceedings arising from the exercise of investigative powers. Where it appears to the Secretary of State from any report made or information obtained during a company investigation[1] or any information obtained under the powers exercisable for the purpose of assisting overseas regulatory authorities[2] that it is expedient in the public interest that a company should be wound up, he may, unless the company is already being wound up by the court, present a petition for it to be wound up if the court thinks it just and equitable for it to be so[3].

The decision to present a petition may be made by the Secretary of State acting through one of his officers[4]. If the report makes detailed findings which are not directly challenged by evidence, the court is entitled to rely upon the report as prima facie evidence of the matters alleged and base its conclusions on it[5]. The same position applies if, the Secretary of State having decided that the public interest does not require the presentation of a petition, a contributory presents a petition based on the report[6].

If it appears to the Secretary of State from a report made by inspectors[7] or information or documents obtained during a company investigation[8] or any information obtained under the powers exercisable for the purpose of assisting overseas regulatory authorities[9] that it is expedient in the public interest that a disqualification order[10] should be made against any person who is or has been a director[11] or shadow director[11] of any company, he may apply to the court[12] for such an order to be made against that person[13].

If in the case of any company[14] the Secretary of State has received an inspectors' report[15] or exercised his power to require the production of documents or to obtain a warrant to enter and search any premises for such documents[16] and it appears to him that the company's affairs are being or have been conducted in a manner which is unfairly prejudicial to the interests of its members generally or of some part of its members, or that any actual or proposed act or omission of the company, including an act or omission on its behalf, is or would be so prejudicial, he may himself, in addition to presenting a petition for the winding up of the company, apply to the court by petition for an order under the statutory provisions[17] relating to the protection of members against unfair prejudice[18].

If from any report made or information obtained[19] it appears to the Secretary of State that any civil proceedings ought in the public interest to be brought by any body corporate, he may himself bring such proceedings in the name and on behalf of the body corporate[20]; but he must indemnify the body corporate against any costs or expenses incurred by it in or in connection with proceedings so brought[21].

1 Ie under the Companies Act 1985 Pt XIV (ss 431-453) (as amended): see para 1376 et seq ante.

2 Ie under the Companies Act 1989 s 83: see para 1399 post.

3 Insolvency Act 1986 s 124A(1)(a), (d), (2) (added by the Companies Act 1989 s 60(3)). See further para 2202 post. It is for the Secretary of State to form the opinion that the petition is expedient in the public interest, that is necessary to give him standing to present the petition: *Re Walter L Jacob & Co Ltd* [1989] BCLC 345, CA; *Re a Company (No 007816 of 1994)* [1995] 2 BCLC 539. It is for the court to determine if it is just and equitable to wind up the company balancing the conflicting interests of the opposing parties to the petition and giving such weight to the various factors as is appropriate in the particular case: *Re Walter L Jacob & Co Ltd* supra; *Re a Company (No 007816 of 1994)* supra. See also *Re a Company (No 007923 of 1994) (No 2)* [1995] 1 BCLC 594. While the court will take note that the source of the submission is a government department charged by parliament with wide-ranging responsibilities in relation to the affairs of companies, the submissions of the Secretary of State are not ipso facto endowed with such weight that those resisting a winding-up petition presented by him will find the scales loaded against them: *Re Walter L Jacob & Co Ltd* supra; *Re a Company (No 007816 of 1994)* supra. Cf *Re Lubin, Rosen and Associates Ltd* [1975] 1 All ER 577, [1975] 1 WLR 122 (winding-up order made against the wishes of the majority of creditors).

4 *Re Golden Chemical Products Ltd* [1976] Ch 300, [1976] 2 All ER 543. In such a case the affidavit verifying the petition should describe the officer's position in the department of the Secretary of State, depose that he was entrusted with the requisite power, and explain that he was the officer to whom it appeared expedient in the public interest that the company should be wound up. Neither the Secretary of State nor any of his departmental inspectors may be cross-examined as to his reason for this conclusion. The decision may be challenged only if made in bad faith or if immaterial matters have been taken into account or for misconduct: *Re Golden Chemical Products Ltd* (1976) Times, 9 December, DC; and see *Re Walter L Jacob & Co Ltd* [1989] BCLC 345 at 352.

    Having regard to the implications for a company if such a petition is presented, the Secretary of State might consider whether it would be right to defer advertising the petition until the last practical moment, at least where the company desires to continue trading and is not prima facie insolvent: *Re Golden Chemical Products Ltd* [1976] Ch 300 at 311, [1976] 2 All ER 543 at 551 per Brightman J. Where the company seeks to restrain the advertisement of the petition, the onus is on the company to show sufficient reason for departing from the normal practice of advertisement: *Re a Company (No 007946 of 1993)* [1994] 1 BCLC 565; *Re a Company (No 007923 of 1994)* [1995] 1 BCLC 440, CA. Advertisements there must be unless the company can show that advertisement may cause serious damage to its reputation and financial stability: *Re a Company (No 007923 of 1994)* supra. Cf *Applied Data Base Ltd v Secretary of State for Trade and Industry* [1995] 1 BCLC 272. As to advertisement of the petition see para 2222 post.

5 *Re Armvent Ltd* [1975] 3 All ER 441, [1975] 1 WLR 1679; *Re Allied Produce Co Ltd* [1967] 3 All ER 399n, [1967] 1 WLR 1469, following *Re Travel and Holiday Clubs Ltd* [1967] 2 All ER 606, [1967] 1 WLR 711; *Re SBA Properties Ltd* [1967] 2 All ER 615, [1967] 1 WLR 799; and distinguishing *Re ABC Coupler and Engineering Co Ltd (No 2)* [1962] 3 All ER 68, [1962] 1 WLR 1236 (where such allegations were contested). A report may be effectively challenged only by someone with knowledge of the facts testifying that the report is wrong; unsupported contravention is not sufficient: *Re Armvent Ltd* supra.

6 *Re St Piran Ltd* [1981] 3 All ER 270, [1981] 1 WLR 1300.

7 Ie under the Companies Act 1985 s 437 (as amended): see para 1380 ante.

8 Ie under ibid s 447 (as amended) (see para 1386 ante) or s 448 (as substituted) (see para 1393 post).

9 See note 2 supra.

10 For the meaning of 'disqualification order' see para 1417 post.

11 For the meaning of 'director' and 'shadow director' see para 1417 note 2 post.

12 Where the Secretary of State decides not to make such an application, the court can properly interfere only if the facts demonstrate that the only possible course open to the Secretary of State is to make an application to the court: *R v Secretary of State for Trade and Industry, ex p Lonrho plc* [1992] BCC 325, DC. For a case where a disqualification order was sought and obtained see *Re Samuel Sherman plc* [1991] 1 WLR 1070, [1991] BCC 699.

13 See the Company Directors Disqualification Act 1986 s 8(1) (as amended) and para 1431 post. Statements obtained under the Companies Act 1985 s 447 (as amended) are admissible even though hearsay; this affects weight but not admissibility: *Re Rex Williams Leisure plc (in administration)* [1994] Ch 350, [1994] 4 All ER 27, CA.

14 For the meaning of 'company' for these purposes see para 1406 note 2 post.

15 See note 7 supra.

16 See note 8 supra.

17 Ie the Companies Act 1985 Pt XVII (ss 459-461) (as amended): see para 1405 et seq post.

18 See ibid s 460(1) (as amended) and para 1406 post.

19 See note 1 supra.

20 Companies Act 1985 s 438(1) (amended by the Companies Act 1989 s 58). The Companies Act 1985 s 438 (as amended) does not apply to oversea companies: see s 453(1A)(b) (as substituted) and para 1385 ante. As to the application of s 438 (as amended) to unregistered companies see s 718(1), Sch 22 (as amended) and para 1767 post.

21 Ibid s 438(2). See also note 20 supra.

1391. Expenses of investigating a company's affairs. The expenses[1] of an investigation of a company's affairs[2] must be defrayed in the first instance by the Secretary of State; but he may recover those expenses from the persons liable in accordance with the following provisions[3]:

(1) a person who is convicted on a prosecution instituted as a result of the investigation, or is ordered to pay the whole or any part of the costs of civil proceedings brought by the Secretary of State[4], may in the same proceedings be ordered to pay those expenses to such extent as may be specified in the order[5];

(2) a body corporate in whose name such proceedings are brought[6] is liable to the amount or value of any sums or property recovered by it as a result of those proceedings; and any amount for which a body corporate is so liable is a first charge on the sums or property recovered[7];

(3) a body corporate dealt with by an inspectors' report, where the inspectors were appointed otherwise than of the Secretary of State's own motion[8], is liable, except where it was the applicant for the investigation, and except so far as the Secretary of State otherwise directs[9]; and

(4) where the inspectors were appointed on the company's application or that of its members[10], the applicant or applicants for the investigation is or are liable to such extent, if any, as the Secretary of State may direct[11].

The report of inspectors appointed otherwise than of the Secretary of State's own motion[12] may, if they think fit, and must, if the Secretary of State so directs, include a recommendation as to the directions, if any, which they think appropriate, in the light of their investigation, to be given under heads (3) or (4) above[13].

Subject to satisfaction of the Secretary of State's right to repayment, any liability to repay the Secretary of State imposed by heads (1) and (2) above is a liability also to indemnify all persons against liability under heads (3) and (4) above; and any such liability imposed by head (1) above is a liability also to indemnify all persons against liability under head (2) above[14]. A person liable under any of heads (1) to (4) above is entitled to contribution from any other person liable under the same head according to the amount of their respective liabilities under it[15].

The expenses to be defrayed by the Secretary of State under these provisions must, so far as not recovered under them, be paid out of money provided by Parliament[16];

and, for the purposes of these provisions, any costs or expenses incurred by the Secretary of State in or in connection with proceedings brought by him in the name of any body corporate[17], including any necessary indemnity[18], are to be treated as expenses of the investigation giving rise to the proceedings[19].

1 There is no limit to the amount of such expenses, provided that they are all of and incidental to the investigation: *Selangor United Rubber Estates Ltd v Cradock (No 4)* [1969] 3 All ER 965, [1969] 1 WLR 1773. In particular, such reasonable sums as the Secretary of State may determine in respect of general staff costs and overheads are to be treated as expenses of the investigation: Companies Act 1985 s 439(1) (substituted by the Companies Act 1989 s 59(1), (2)).

2 Ie under any of the powers conferred by the Companies Act 1985 Pt XIV (ss 431-453) (as amended): see para 1376 et seq ante.

3 Ibid s 439(1) (as substituted: see note 1 supra). As to the application of s 439 (as amended) to oversea companies see para 1385 ante; and as to the application of s 439 (as amended) to unregistered companies see s 718(1), Sch 22 (as amended) and para 1767 post.

4 Ie under ibid s 438 (as amended): see para 1390 ante.

5 Ibid s 439(2). See also note 3 supra.

6 See note 4 supra.

7 Companies Act 1985 s 439(3). See also note 3 supra.

8 See paras 1376, 1377 ante.

9 Companies Act 1985 s 439(4) (amended by the Companies Act 1989 s 59(1), (3)). See also note 3 supra.

10 Ie under the Companies Act 1985 s 431 (see para 1376 ante) or s 442(3) (as substituted) (see para 1381 ante).

11 Ibid s 439(5) (substituted by the Companies Act 1989 s 59(1), (4)). See also note 3 supra.

12 See note 8 supra.

13 Companies Act 1985 s 439(6). See also note 3 supra.

14 Ibid s 439(8). See also note 3 supra.

15 Ibid s 439(9). See also note 3 supra.

16 Ibid s 439(10). See also note 3 supra.

17 Ie under ibid s 438 (as amended): see para 1390 ante.

18 Ie any liability imposed by ibid s 438(2): see para 1390 ante.

19 Ibid s 439(7). See also note 3 supra.

1392. Inspectors' report to be evidence. A copy of any inspectors' report[1], certified by the Secretary of State to be a true copy, is admissible in any legal proceedings as evidence of the inspectors' opinion in relation to any matter contained in the report and, in proceedings under the Company Directors Disqualification Act 1986 for disqualification after investigation of a company[2], as evidence of any fact stated therein[3], but this is restricted to winding up or alternative relief and disqualification proceedings, and does not render the contents admissible in ordinary litigation[4]. A document purporting to be such a certificate as is mentioned above must be received in evidence and is deemed to be such a certificate, unless the contrary is proved[5].

1 Ie any report of inspectors appointed under the Companies Act 1985 Pt XIV (ss 431-453) (as amended): see para 1376 et seq ante.

2 Ie under the Company Directors Disqualification Act 1986 s 8 (as amended): see para 1431 post.

3 Companies Act 1985 s 441(1) (amended by the Insolvency Act 1985 s 109, Sch 6 para 3; the Insolvency Act 1986 s 439(1), Sch 13 Pt I; the Companies Act 1989 s 61). As to the application of the Companies Act 1985 s 441 (as amended) to oversea companies see para 1385 ante; and as to the application of s 441 (as amended) to unregistered companies see s 718(1), Sch 22 (as amended) and para 1767 post.

4 *Savings and Investment Bank Ltd v Gasco Investments (Netherlands) BV* [1984] 1 All ER 296, [1984] 1 WLR 271. Such a report is not a record for the purposes of the Civil Evidence Act 1968 s 4(1) and accordingly is not admissible under s 4(1) (see EVIDENCE vol 17 para 58) as evidence of any fact mentioned in it: *Savings and Investment Bank Ltd v Gasco Investments (Netherlands) BV* supra. Cf *Deutsche Rückversicherung AG v Walbrook Insurance Co Ltd, Group Josi Re (formerly known as Group Josi Reassurance SA) v Walbrook Insurance Co Ltd* [1994] 4 All ER 181, [1995] 1 WLR 1017, DC (where the plaintiff was entitled to rely on an inspectors' report in affidavits in support of a claim to interlocutory relief), not following *Savings*

and Investment Bank Ltd v Gasco Investments (Netherlands) BV supra. As to the proceedings which may be founded on the reports see para 1390 ante.
5 Companies Act 1985 s 441(2). See also note 3 supra.

1393. Entry and search of premises. A justice of the peace may issue a warrant under these provisions if satisfied on information on oath given by or on behalf of the Secretary of State, or by a person appointed or authorised to exercise powers under the Companies Act 1985[1]:

(1) that there are reasonable grounds for believing that there are on any premises documents[2] whose production has been required[3] and which have not been produced in compliance with the requirement[4]; or

(2) that there are reasonable grounds for believing that an offence has been committed for which the penalty on conviction on indictment is imprisonment for a term of not less than two years and that there are on any premises documents relating to whether the offence has been committed, that the Secretary of State, or the person so appointed or authorised, has power to require the production of the documents[5] and that there are reasonable grounds for believing that, if production was so required, the documents would not be produced but would be removed from the premises, hidden, tampered with or destroyed[6].

A warrant so issued continues in force until the end of the period of one month beginning with the day on which it is issued[7]; and the warrant authorises a constable, together with any other person named in it and any other constables:

(a) to enter the premises specified in the information, using such force as is reasonably necessary for the purpose;

(b) to search the premises and take possession of any documents appearing to be such documents as are mentioned in heads (1) or (2) above, as the case may be, or to take, in relation to any such documents, any other steps which may appear to be necessary for preserving them or preventing interference with them;

(c) to take copies of any such documents; and

(d) to require any person named in the warrant to provide an explanation of them or to state where they may be found[8].

If, in the case of a warrant under head (2) above, the justice of the peace is satisfied on information on oath that there are reasonable grounds for believing that there are also on the premises other documents relevant to the investigation, the warrant also authorises the actions mentioned in heads (a) to (d) above to be taken in relation to such documents[9].

Any person who intentionally obstructs the exercise of any rights conferred by a warrant so issued, or fails without reasonable excuse to comply with any requirement imposed in accordance with head (d) above, is guilty of an offence and liable on conviction on indictment to a fine or on summary conviction to a fine not exceeding the statutory maximum[10].

Any documents of which possession is taken under the above provisions may be retained for a period of three months or, if within that period proceedings to which the documents are relevant are commenced against any person for any criminal offence, until the conclusion of those proceedings[11].

1 Ie under the Companies Act 1985 Pt XIV (ss 431–453) (as amended): see para 1376 et seq ante.
2 For these purposes, 'document' includes information recorded in any form: ibid s 448(10) (substituted by the Companies Act 1989 s 64(1)). For the meaning of 'document' see para 151 ante.
3 See note 1 supra.

4 Companies Act 1985 s 448(1) (substituted by the Companies Act 1989 s 64(1)). As to the application of the Companies Act 1985 s 448 (as substituted) to oversea companies see para 1385 ante; and as to the application of s 448 (as substituted) to unregistered companies see s 718(1), Sch 22 (as amended) and para 1767 post.

For the purposes of s 449 (as amended) (see para 1387 ante) and s 451A (as added and substituted) (see para 1389 ante), documents obtained under s 448 (as substituted) are to be treated as if they had been obtained under the provision of Pt XIV (ss 431–453) (as amended) under which their production was or, as the case may be, could have been, required: s 448(8) (substituted by the Companies Act 1989 s 64(1)).

5 See note 1 supra.
6 Companies Act 1985 s 448(2) (substituted by the Companies Act 1989 s 64(1)). See also note 4 supra.
7 Companies Act 1985 s 448(5) (substituted by the Companies Act 1989 s 64(1)). See also note 4 supra.
8 Companies Act 1985 s 448(3) (substituted by the Companies Act 1989 s 64(1)). See also note 4 supra.
9 Companies Act 1985 s 448(4) (substituted by the Companies Act 1989 s 64(1)). See also note 4 supra.
10 Companies Act 1985 s 448(7) (substituted by the Companies Act 1989 s 64(1)); Companies Act 1985 s 730, Sch 24 (amended by the Companies Act 1989 s 64(2)(a), (b)). See also note 4 supra. For the meaning of 'the statutory maximum' see para 1161 ante. The Companies Act 1985 s 732 (restriction on prosecutions: see para 1165 ante), s 733 (as amended) (liability of individuals for corporate default: see para 1162 ante) and s 734 (as amended) (criminal proceedings against unincorporated bodies: see para 1163 ante) apply to this offence: s 448(7) (as so substituted).
11 Ibid s 448(6) (substituted by the Companies Act 1989 s 64(1)). See also note 4 supra.

1394. Privileged information. Nothing in the statutory provisions relating to company investigations[1] requires the disclosure to the Secretary of State or to an inspector appointed by him by any person of information which he would in an action in the High Court be entitled to refuse to disclose on grounds of legal professional privilege except, if he is a lawyer, the name and address of his client[2].

Nothing in the statutory provisions relating to the production of documents and evidence to inspectors[3], the investigation into the ownership of a company[4] or the investigation of share dealings[5] requires a person to disclose information or produce documents in respect of which he owes an obligation of confidence by virtue of carrying on the business of banking unless:

(1) the person to whom the obligation of confidence is owed is the company or other body corporate under investigation;

(2) the person to whom the obligation of confidence is owed consents to the disclosure or production; or

(3) the making of the requirement is authorised by the Secretary of State[6].

Nothing in the provisions relating to the requisition and seizure of documents[7] compels the production by any person of a document which he would in an action in the High Court be entitled to refuse to produce on grounds of legal professional privilege, or authorises the taking of possession of any such document which is in the person's possession[8].

1 Ie the Companies Act 1985 ss 431–446 (as amended): see para 1376 et seq ante.
2 Ibid s 452(1)(a). As to the application of s 452 (as amended) to oversea companies see para 1385 ante; and as to the application of s 452 (as amended) to unregistered companies see s 718(1), Sch 22 (as amended) and para 1767 post.
3 Ie ibid s 434 (as amended): see para 1379 ante.
4 Ie ibid s 443 (as amended): see para 1381 ante.
5 Ie ibid s 446 (as amended): see para 1384 ante.
6 Ibid s 452(1A) (added by the Companies Act 1989 s 69(1), (3)). See also note 2 supra. The Companies Act 1985 s 452(1A) (as so added) does not, however, apply where the person owing the obligation of confidence is the company or other body corporate under investigation under s 431 (see para 1376 ante), s 432 (as amended) (see para 1377 ante) or s 433 (see para 1378 ante): s 452(1B) (added by the Companies Act 1989 s 69(1), (3)).
7 Ie the Companies Act 1985 ss 447–451 (as amended): see para 1386 et seq ante.
8 Ibid s 452(2). See also note 2 supra.

(iv) Orders imposing Restrictions on Shares

1395. Consequences of order imposing restrictions on shares. So long as any shares are directed to be subject to the restrictions of Part XV of the Companies Act 1985[1], then, subject to any directions made in relation to an order[2] or subject in the case of an interim order[3] to the terms of that order[4]:

(1) any transfer of those shares or, in the case of unissued shares, any transfer of the right to be issued with them, and any issue of them, is void[5];

(2) no voting rights are exercisable in respect of the shares[6];

(3) no further shares may be issued in right of them or in pursuance of any offer made to their holder[7]; and

(4) except in a liquidation, no payment may be made of any sums due from the company on the shares[8], whether in respect of capital or otherwise[9].

Where shares are subject to the restrictions under head (1) above, any agreement to transfer the shares or, in the case of unissued shares, the right to be issued with them is void, except such agreement or right as may be made or exercised under the terms of directions made by the Secretary of State or the court[10] or of an interim order[11] or an agreement to transfer the shares on the making of an order[12] by the court or by the Secretary of State approving the transfer[13].

Where shares are subject to the restrictions under heads (3) or (4) above, an agreement to transfer any right to be issued with other shares in right of those shares, or to receive any payment on them, otherwise than in a liquidation, is void, except such agreement or right as may be made or exercised under the terms of directions made by the Secretary of State or the court[14] or of an interim order[15] or an agreement to transfer any such right on the transfer of the shares on the making of an order[16] by the court or by the Secretary of State approving the transfer[17].

1　Ie the Companies Act 1985 Pt XV (ss 454-457) (as amended): see infra and paras 1396, 1397 post. As to the provisions under which such restrictions may be imposed see s 210 (as amended) (imposition by the Secretary of State on failure to fulfil an obligation of disclosure: see para 745 ante), s 216 (as amended) (imposition by the court on failure by person required by public company to give information relating to interests in shares: see para 752 ante) and s 445 (as amended) (imposition by Secretary of State if, in connection with an investigation initiated by him, it appears to him that there is difficulty in finding out the relevant facts about any shares: see para 1383 ante).

2　Ie pursuant to ibid s 210(5A) (as added) (see para 745 ante), s 216(1B) (as added) (see para 752 ante), s 445(1A) (as added) (see para 1383 ante) or s 456(1A) (as added) (see para 1397 post).

3　Ie pursuant to ibid s 216(1A) (as added): see para 752 ante.

4　Ibid s 454(1) (amended by the Companies (Disclosure of Interests in Shares) (Orders imposing restrictions on shares) Regulations 1991, SI 1991/1646, regs 2, 6(a)). As to the application of the Companies Act 1985 s 454 (as amended) to unregistered companies see s 718(1), Sch 22 (as amended) and para 1767 post.

5　Ibid s 454(1)(a). See also note 4 supra.

6　Ibid s 454(1)(b). See also note 4 supra.

7　Ibid s 454(1)(c). See also note 4 supra.

8　This is not limited to payment of dividends or of capital on a reduction of capital or on redemption of shares but covers the proceeds of sale on a take-over: *Re Ashbourne Investments Ltd* [1978] 2 All ER 418, [1978] 1 WLR 1346.

9　Companies Act 1985 s 454(1)(d). See also note 4 supra.

10　See note 2 supra.

11　See note 3 supra.

12　Ie an order under the Companies Act 1985 s 456(3)(b) (as amended): see para 1397 post.

13 Ibid s 454(2) (amended by the Companies Act 1989 s 145, Sch 19 para 10(2); the Companies (Disclosure of Interests in Shares) (Orders imposing restrictions on shares) Regulations 1991 regs 2, 6(b)). See also note 4 supra.

14 See note 2 supra.

15 See note 3 supra.

16 See note 12 supra.

17 Companies Act 1985 s 454(3) (amended by the Companies Act 1989 Sch 19 para 10(2); the Companies (Disclosure of Interests in Shares) (Orders imposing restrictions on shares) Regulations 1991 regs 2, 6(c)). See also note 4 supra.

1396. Punishment for attempted evasion of restrictions. Subject to the terms of any directions made by the Secretary of State or the court[1] or of an interim order[2], a person who:

(1) exercises or purports to exercise any right to dispose of any shares which, to his knowledge, are for the time being subject to restrictions[3] or of any right to be issued with any such shares; or

(2) votes in respect of any such shares, whether as holder or proxy, or appoints a proxy to vote in respect of them; or

(3) being the holder of any such shares, fails to notify of their being subject to those restrictions any person whom he does not know to be aware of that fact but does know to be entitled, apart from the restrictions, to vote in respect of those shares whether as holder or as proxy; or

(4) being the holder of any such shares, or being entitled to any right to be issued with other shares in right of them, or to receive any payment on them, otherwise than in a liquidation, enters into any agreement which is void[4] as a consequence of an order imposing restrictions,

is liable on conviction on indictment to a fine or on summary conviction to a fine not exceeding the statutory maximum[5].

Subject to the terms of any directions made by the Secretary of State or the court[6] or of an interim order[7], if shares in a company are issued in contravention of the restrictions, the company, and every officer of it who is in default, is liable on conviction on indictment to a fine or on summary conviction to a fine not exceeding the statutory maximum[8].

A prosecution may not, however, be instituted under these provisions except by or with the consent of the Secretary of State[9].

1 Ie under the Companies Act 1985 s 210(5A) (as added) (see para 745 ante), s 216(1B) (as added) (see para 752 ante), s 445(1A) (as added) (see para 1383 ante) or s 456 (as amended) (see para 1397 post).

2 Ie under ibid s 216(1A) (as added): see para 752 ante.

3 Ie the restrictions in ibid Pt XV (ss 454-457) (as amended): see para 1395 ante.

4 Ie under ibid s 454(2) or (3): see para 1395 ante.

5 Ibid s 455(1) (amended by the Companies (Disclosure of Interests in Shares) (Orders imposing restrictions on shares) Regulations 1991, SI 1991/1646, regs 2, 7(a)); Companies Act 1985 s 730, Sch 24. For the meaning of 'the statutory maximum' see para 1161 ante. As to the application of s 455 (as amended) to unregistered companies see s 718(1), Sch 22 (as amended) and para 1767 post.

6 See note 1 supra.

7 See note 2 supra.

8 Companies Act 1985 s 455(2) (amended by the Companies (Disclosure of Interests in Shares) (Orders imposing restrictions on shares) Regulations 1991 regs 2, 7(b)); Companies Act 1985 s 730, Sch 24. See also note 5 supra. For the meaning of 'officer who is in default' see para 1161 ante.

9 Ibid ss 455(3), 732(1), (2)(c). See also note 5 supra.

1397. Relaxation and removal of restrictions. Where shares in a company are by order made subject to the restrictions of Part XV of the Companies Act 1985[1], application[2] may be made to the court for an order directing that the shares be no longer so subject[3].

Where the court is satisfied that an order subjecting the shares to such restrictions unfairly affects the rights of third parties in respect of shares, then the court, for the purpose of protecting such rights and subject to such terms as it thinks fit and in addition to any order it may make[4], may direct[5] on an application so made that such acts by such persons or descriptions of persons and for such purposes as may be set out in the order, shall not constitute a breach of the statutory restrictions[6].

If the order applying the restrictions was made by the Secretary of State[7], or he has refused to make an order disapplying them, the application may be made by any person aggrieved; and, if the order was made by the court in consequence of non-compliance by any person with a request by a public company to provide information relating to interests in shares in that company[8], it may be made by any such person or by the company[9].

Subject to the following provisions, an order of the court or the Secretary of State directing that shares are to cease to be subject to the restrictions may be made only if:

(1) the court or, as the case may be, the Secretary of State is satisfied that the relevant facts about the shares have been disclosed to the company and no unfair advantage has accrued to any person as a result of the earlier failure to make that disclosure[10]; or

(2) the shares are to be transferred for valuable consideration[11] and the court, in any case, or the Secretary of State, if the order was made by him[12], approves the transfer[13].

Where shares in a company are subject to the restrictions, the court may[14] on application[15] order the shares to be sold[16], subject to the court's approval as to the sale, and may also direct that the shares are to cease being subject to the restrictions; and an application to the court for this purpose may be made by the Secretary of State, unless the restrictions were imposed by court order for non-disclosure of a shareholding in a public company[17], or by the company[18]. Where an order for sale has been so made, then, on application[19] by the Secretary of State, unless the restrictions were imposed by court order for non-disclosure of a shareholding in a public company[20], or by the company, or by the person appointed by or in pursuance of the order to effect the sale, or by any person interested in the shares, the court may make such further order relating to the sale or to the transfer of the shares as it thinks fit[21].

Where shares are sold in pursuance of an order of the court, the proceeds of sale, less the costs of the sale, must be paid into court for the benefit of the persons who are beneficially interested in the shares; and any such person may apply[22] to the court for the whole or any part of those proceeds to be paid to him[23]. On any such application the court must order the payment to the applicant of the whole of the proceeds of sale together with any interest thereon or, if any other person had a beneficial interest in the shares at the time of their sale, such proportion of those proceeds and interest as is equal to the proportion which the value of the applicant's interest in the shares bears to the total value of the shares[24].

An order, whether of the Secretary of State or the court, directing that shares shall cease to be subject to the above restrictions[25], if it is expressed to be made with a view to permitting a transfer of the shares, or made under the power to approve a sale[26], may continue, either in whole or in part, so far as they relate to any right acquired or offer made before the transfer, the following restrictions[27]:

(a) that no further shares may be issued in right of those shares or in pursuance of any offer made to their holder; and

(b) except in a liquidation, no payment may be made of any sums due from the company on the shares, whether in respect of capital or otherwise[28].

1 Ie the Companies Act 1985 Pt XV (ss 454-457) (as amended): see infra and paras 1395, 1396 ante.

2 In the High Court the application is by originating motion: RSC Ord 102 r 3(1)(d).

3 Companies Act 1985 s 456(1). As to the application of s 456 (as amended) to unregistered companies see s 718(1), Sch 22 (as amended) and para 1767 post.

4 Ie under ibid s 456(1): see supra.

5 Ie on an application under ibid s 456(1): see supra.

6 Ibid s 456(1A) (added by the Companies (Disclosure of Interests in Shares) (Orders imposing restrictions on shares) Regulations 1991, SI 1991/1646, regs 2, 8(a)). See also note 3 supra. The Companies Act 1985 s 456(3) (as amended) (see infra) does not apply to an order made under s 456(1A) (as so added): s 456(1A) (as so added). The power of the court to give a direction under s 456(1A) (as so added) is exercisable in respect of any order made under s 210(5) (see para 745 ante), s 216(1) (see para 752 ante) or s 445(1) (see para 1383 ante), including such orders as may be in force on 18 July 1991: Companies (Disclosure of Interests in Shares) (Orders imposing restrictions on shares) Regulations 1991 reg 9. For earlier cases illustrating the adverse effect restrictions can have on third parties see *Re Geers Gross plc* [1988] 1 All ER 224, [1987] 1 WLR 1649, CA; *Re Lonrho plc (No 3)* [1989] BCLC 480; *Re Lonrho plc (No 4)* [1990] BCLC 151.

7 Ie under the Companies Act 1985 s 210(5) (see para 745 ante) or s 445(1) (see para 1383 ante).

8 Ie under ibid s 216 (as amended): see para 752 ante.

9 Ibid s 456(2). See also note 3 supra.

10 Ibid s 456(3)(a). See also note 3 supra. Once the information to which the company is entitled is supplied, the order imposing the restrictions should be discharged; a desire to produce evidence of new failures is no ground for adjournment of the hearing or continuation of the restrictions: *Re Ricardo Group plc* [1989] BCLC 566. Cf *Re Lonrho plc* [1988] BCLC 53 (the Companies Act 1985 s 456(3)(a) empowers the court to free shares subject to a restriction but does not require the court to do so particularly where it appears that the applicant to have the restriction lifted has not disclosed information reasonably required in relation to other shares of the company). See also *Re Ricardo Group plc (No 3)* [1989] BCLC 771 (restrictions released without disclosure of information where their continuation would prevent a take-over bid from going ahead to the prejudice of those shareholders who wanted to accept the bid). See also note 13 infra.

11 In the Companies Act 1985 s 456(3)(b) (as originally enacted) the word 'sold' was used instead of the words 'transferred for valuable consideration'. 'Sold' was held to denote an exchange of the shares for cash; a non-cash exchange was not then within the scope of the statutory provision: *Re Westminster Property Group plc* [1985] 2 All ER 426, [1985] 1 WLR 676, CA. As a result of the amendment of the Companies Act 1985 s 456(3)(b) (see note 13 infra) the decision in *Re Westminster Property Group plc* supra has been reversed.

12 Ie under the Companies Act 1985 s 210 (see para 745 ante) or s 445 (as amended) (see para 1383 ante).

13 Ibid s 456(3)(b) (amended by the Companies Act 1989 s 145, Sch 19 para 10(1)(a), (b)). See also note 3 supra. The Companies Act 1985 s 456(3) (as amended) only applies to a final order of the court and does not apply to an order made at an interlocutory stage, although the provision is nevertheless relevant as showing the type of circumstances requiring the maintenance of any restrictions: *Re TR Technology Investment Trust plc* [1988] BCLC 256. It is not sufficient to secure the release of shares from restrictions imposed under the Companies Act 1985 s 216 (see para 752 ante) for failure to comply with a notice under s 212 (see para 748 ante) to apply to the court to permit a sale on the open market; the company is entitled to the information requested under s 212: *Re Geers Gross plc* [1988] 1 All ER 224, [1987] 1 WLR 1649, CA; *Re TR Technology Investment Trust plc* supra. In exercising its discretion whether to approve a sale, the court is entitled to take into account the refusal to disclose relevant facts: *Re Geers Gross plc* supra.

14 Ie without prejudice to the power of the court to give directions under the Companies Act 1985 s 456(1A) (as added): see supra.

15 In the High Court the application is by originating motion: RSC Ord 102 r 3(1)(e).

16 Quaere whether the court would exercise this power where it interfered with the rights of parties to a pre-existing contract for sale: see *Re Westminster Property Group plc* [1985] 2 All ER 426, [1985] 1 WLR 676, CA (where the court thought that the proper procedure for removing the restrictions where shares are subject to a pre-existing contract would be to seek an order under the Companies Act 1985 s 456(3)(b) (as amended) (see supra)).

17 See note 8 supra.
18 Companies Act 1985 s 456(4) (amended by the Companies (Disclosure of Interests in Shares) (Orders imposing restrictions on shares) Regulations 1991 regs 2, 8(b)). See also note 3 supra. On granting an application for an order under the Companies Act 1985 s 456(4) (as so amended) or s 456(5) (see infra) the court may order that the applicant's costs be paid out of the proceeds of sale; and, if that order is made, the applicant is entitled to payment of his costs out of those proceeds before any person interested in the shares in question receives any part of those proceeds: s 457(3).
19 In the High Court the application, being an application in the already existing proceedings pursuant to ibid s 456(4) (as amended) (see supra), will be by ordinary summons in those proceedings.
20 See note 8 supra.
21 Companies Act 1985 s 456(5). See also notes 3, 18 supra.
22 In the High Court the application is by originating summons in the expedited form (RSC Ord 102 r 2(1), (2)); but, if there is no change of parties from the original order for payment under the Companies Act 1985 s 456(4) (see supra), an ordinary summons may suffice.
23 Ibid s 457(1). As to the application of s 457 to unregistered companies see s 718(1), Sch 22 (as amended) and para 1767 post.
24 Ibid s 457(2). See also note 23 supra.
25 Ie the restrictions of ibid Pt XV (ss 454–457) (as amended).
26 Ie under ibid s 456(4): see supra.
27 Ie the restrictions mentioned in ibid s 454(1)(c), (d): see para 1395 heads (3), (4) ante.
28 Ibid s 456(6). See also note 3 supra. Section 456(3) (as amended) (see supra) does not apply to an order directing that shares are to cease to be subject to any restrictions which have been continued in force in relation to those shares under s 456(6): s 456(7). See also *Re Ashbourne Investments Ltd* [1978] 2 All ER 418, [1978] 1 WLR 1346 (restrictions on transfer of shares lifted to enable take-over to proceed; restrictions on proceeds of sale continued).

(v) Powers exercisable to assist Overseas Regulatory Authorities

1398. Request for assistance by overseas regulatory authority. Certain investigative powers[1] are exercisable by the Secretary of State for the purpose of assisting an overseas regulatory authority[2] which has requested his assistance in connection with inquiries being carried out by it or on its behalf[3]. The Secretary of State[4] must not exercise these powers unless he is satisfied that the assistance requested by the overseas regulatory authority is for the purposes of its regulatory functions[5].

In deciding whether to exercise such powers the Secretary of State may take into account, in particular:

(1) whether corresponding assistance would be given in that country or territory to an authority exercising regulatory functions in the United Kingdom;

(2) whether the inquiries relate to the possible breach of a law, or other requirement, which has no close parallel in the United Kingdom or involves the assertion of a jurisdiction not recognised by the United Kingdom;

(3) the seriousness of the matter to which the inquiries relate, the importance to the inquiries of the information sought in the United Kingdom and whether the assistance could be obtained by other means;

(4) whether it is otherwise appropriate in the public interest to give the assistance sought[6].

Before deciding whether to exercise these powers in a case where the overseas regulatory authority is a banking supervisor[7], the Secretary of State must consult the Bank of England[8].

The Secretary of State may decline to exercise these powers unless the overseas regulatory authority undertakes to make such contribution towards the costs of their exercise as the Secretary of State considers appropriate[9].

1 Ie those conferred by the Companies Act 1989 s 83: see para 1399 post.
2 For these purposes, an 'overseas regulatory authority' means an authority which in a country or territory outside the United Kingdom exercises:
 (1) any function corresponding to:
  (a) a function under the Financial Services Act 1986 of a designated agency, transferee body or competent authority within the meaning of that Act (see MONEY);
  (b) a function of the Secretary of State under the Insurance Companies Act 1982 (see INSURANCE), the Companies Act 1985 or the Financial Services Act 1986; or
  (c) a function of the Bank of England under the Banking Act 1987 (see BANKING); or
 (2) any function in connection with the investigation of, or the enforcement of rules (whether or not having the force of law) relating to, conduct of the kind prohibited by the Criminal Justice Act 1993 Pt V (ss 52–64) (insider dealing: see para 1218 et seq ante); or
 (3) any function prescribed for these purposes by order of the Secretary of State, being a function which in his opinion relates to companies or financial services:
 Companies Act 1989 s 82(2) (amended by the Criminal Justice Act 1993 s 79(13), Sch 5 Pt I para 16). Any order made under head (3) supra must be made by statutory instrument which is subject to annulment in pursuance of a resolution of either House of Parliament: Companies Act 1989 s 82(2). References to financial services include, in particular, investment business, insurance and banking: s 82(7).
3 Ibid s 82(1).
4 The function of the Secretary of State under ibid s 82(3) (ie that of being satisfied as to whether assistance requested by an overseas regulatory authority is for the purpose of its regulatory functions) is exercisable by the Secretary of State and the Treasury concurrently: Transfer of Functions (Financial Services) Order 1992, SI 1992/1315, art 5, Sch 3 para 3.
5 Companies Act 1989 s 82(3). For these purposes, an authority's 'regulatory functions' means any functions falling within s 82(2) (as amended) (see note 2 supra) and any other functions relating to companies or financial services: s 82(3).
6 Ibid s 82(4).
7 For these purposes, a 'banking supervisor' means an overseas regulatory authority with respect to which the Bank of England has notified the Secretary of State, for the purposes of this provision, that it exercises functions corresponding to those of the Bank of England under the Banking Act 1987: Companies Act 1989 s 82(5).
8 Ibid s 82(5).
9 Ibid s 82(6).

1399. Power to require information, documents or other assistance. The following powers may be exercised for the purpose of assisting an overseas regulatory authority[1] if the Secretary of State considers there is good reason for their exercise[2].

The Secretary of State may require any person:

 (1) to attend before him at a specified time and place and answer questions or otherwise furnish information with respect to any matter relevant to the inquiries;
 (2) to produce at a specified time and place any specified documents[3] which appear to the Secretary of State to relate to any matter relevant to the inquiries; and
 (3) otherwise to give him such assistance in connection with the inquiries as he is reasonably able to give[4].

Where documents are so produced, the Secretary of State may take copies or extracts from them[5]; and, where a person claims a lien on a document, its production under these provisions is without prejudice to his lien[6].

The Secretary of State may examine a person on oath and may administer an oath accordingly[7]; but a person cannot be required under these provisions to disclose information or produce a document which he would be entitled to refuse to disclose or produce on grounds of legal professional privilege in proceedings in the High Court, except that a lawyer may be required to furnish the name and address of his client[8]. A statement by a person in compliance with a requirement imposed by these provisions may be used in evidence against him[9].

1　Ie in accordance with the Companies Act 1989 s 82 (as amended): see para 1398 ante. For the meaning of 'overseas regulatory authority' see para 1398 note 2 ante.

2　Ibid s 83(1).

3　For these purposes, 'documents' includes information recorded in any form; and, in relation to information recorded otherwise than in legible form, the power to require its production includes power to require the production of a copy of it in legible form: ibid s 83(8).

4　Ibid s 83(2). See also para 1379 ante.

5　Ibid s 83(4).

6　Ibid s 83(7).

7　Ibid s 83(3). See also para 1379 note 7 ante.

8　Ibid s 83(5).

9　Ibid s 83(6). See also para 1379 note 12 ante.

1400. Exercise of powers by officer etc. The Secretary of State may authorise an officer of his or any other competent person[1] to exercise on his behalf all or any of the powers[2] conferred by the above provisions[3]. No such authority must be granted except for the purpose of investigating:

(1)　the affairs, or any aspects of the affairs, of a person specified in the authority; or

(2)　a subject matter so specified,

being a person who, or subject matter which, is the subject of the inquiries being carried out by or on behalf of an overseas regulatory authority[4].

No person is bound to comply with a requirement imposed by a person exercising powers by virtue of an authority so granted unless he has, if required, produced evidence of his authority[5]; nor may a person by virtue of any such authority be required to disclose any information or produce any documents[6] in respect of which he owes an obligation of confidence by virtue of carrying on the business of banking unless:

(a)　the imposing on him of a requirement with respect to such information or documents has been specifically authorised by the Secretary of State; or

(b)　the person to whom the obligation of confidence is owed consents to the disclosure or production[7].

1　Where the Secretary of State authorises a person other than one of his officers to exercise any of these powers, that person must make a report to the Secretary of State in such manner as he may require on the exercise of those powers and the results of exercising them: Companies Act 1989 s 84(5).

2　Ie the powers conferred by ibid s 83: see para 1399 ante.

3　Ibid s 84(1). Where a person authorised to require the production of documents under s 84 obtains any information whilst acting in the course of any investigation, or discharging any functions, to which his appointment or authorisation relates, and is of the opinion that the information indicates that any person has or may have been engaged in money laundering, he must, as soon as is reasonably practicable, either disclose that information to a constable or disclose that information to the supervisory authority by whom he was appointed or authorised: Money Laundering Regulations 1993, SI 1993/1933, reg 16(3), (6)(g).

4　Companies Act 1989 s 84(2).

5　Ibid s 84(3).

6　For these purposes, 'documents' has the same meaning as in ibid s 83 (see para 1399 note 3 ante): s 84(4).

7　Ibid s 84(4).

1401. Penalty for failure to comply with the requirements. A person who without reasonable excuse fails to comply with a requirement to assist an investigation[1] commits an offence and is liable on summary conviction to imprisonment for a term not exceeding six months or a fine not exceeding level 5 on the standard scale, or to both[2].

A person who in purported compliance with any such requirement furnishes information which he knows to be false or misleading in a material particular, or recklessly furnishes information which is false or misleading in a material particular, commits an offence and is liable on conviction on indictment to imprisonment for a term not exceeding two years or a fine, or to both, or on summary conviction to imprisonment for a term not exceeding six months or a fine not exceeding the statutory maximum, or to both[3].

1 Ie a requirement imposed by the Companies Act 1989 s 83: see para 1399 ante.
2 Ibid s 85(1). For the meaning of 'the standard scale' see CRIMINAL LAW vol 11(2) (Reissue) para 808. For guidance on what constitutes 'reasonable excuse' see *Re an Inquiry under the Company Securities (Insider Dealing) Act 1985* [1988] AC 660, [1988] 1 All ER 203, HL.
3 Companies Act 1989 s 85(2). Summary proceedings for an offence under s 85 may, without prejudice to any jurisdiction otherwise exercisable, be taken against a body corporate or unincorporated association at any place at which it has a place of business and against an individual at any place where he is for the time being: s 91(1).

1402. Restrictions on disclosure of information. Information relating to the business or other affairs of a person which:

(1) is supplied by an overseas regulatory authority[1] in connection with a request for assistance; or

(2) is obtained by virtue of the powers to require information, documents or other assistance[2], whether or not any such requirement to supply it is made under such powers,

must not be disclosed, save as permitted below[3], for any purpose:

(a) by the primary recipient[4]; or

(b) by any person obtaining the information directly or indirectly from him,

without the consent of the person from whom the primary recipient obtained the information and, if different, the person to whom it relates[5].

Information is not, however, to be treated as information to which this restriction applies if the information has been made available to the public by virtue of being disclosed in any circumstances in which, or for any purpose for which, disclosure is not precluded[6] by this restriction[7].

A person who contravenes the restriction on disclosure of information commits an offence and is liable on conviction on indictment to imprisonment for a term not exceeding two years or a fine, or to both, or on summary conviction to imprisonment for a term not exceeding three months or a fine not exceeding the statutory maximum, or to both[8].

1 For the meaning of 'overseas regulatory authority' see para 1398 note 2 ante.
2 Ie the powers conferred by the Companies Act 1989 s 83: see para 1399 ante.
3 Ie under ibid s 87 (as amended): see para 1403 post.
4 For these purposes, 'primary recipient' means, as the case may be: (1) the Secretary of State; (2) any person authorised under ibid s 84 to exercise powers on his behalf (see para 1400 ante); and (3) any officer or servant of any such person: s 86(3).
5 Ibid s 86(1), (2).
6 Ie precluded by ibid s 86(1), (2): see supra.
7 Ibid s 86(4).
8 Ibid s 86(5).

1403. Exceptions from restrictions on disclosure. Information to which the restriction on disclosure applies[1] may be disclosed:

(1) to any person with a view to the institution of, or otherwise for the purposes of, relevant proceedings[2];

(2) for the purpose of enabling or assisting a relevant authority to discharge any relevant function, including functions in relation to proceedings[3];

(3) to the Treasury, if the disclosure is made in the interests of investors or in the public interest;

(4) if the information is or has been available to the public from other sources;

(5) in a summary or collection of information framed in such a way as not to enable the identity of any person to whom the information relates to be ascertained; or

(6) in pursuance of any Community obligation[4].

1 Ie information to which the Companies Act 1989 s 86 applies: see para 1402 ante.
2 For these purposes, 'relevant proceedings' are (1) any criminal proceedings; (2) civil proceedings arising under or by virtue of the Financial Services Act 1986 and proceedings before the Financial Services Tribunal; and (3) disciplinary proceedings relating to (a) the exercise by a solicitor, auditor, accountant, valuer or actuary of his professional duties; or (b) the discharge by a public servant of his duties: Companies Act 1989 s 87(2). 'Public servant' means an officer or servant of the Crown or of any public or other authority for the time being designated for the purposes of s 87(2) by order of the Secretary of State: s 87(3). Any order under s 87 (as amended) must be made by statutory instrument which is subject to annulment in pursuance of a resolution of either House of Parliament: s 87(6).
3 The relevant authorities and the relevant functions in relation to each such authority are set out in ibid s 87(4), Table (as amended). The Secretary of State may by order amend s 87(4), Table so as (1) to add any public or other authority to the Table and specify the relevant functions of that authority; (2) to remove any authority from s 87(4), Table; or (3) to add functions to, or remove functions from, those which are relevant functions in relation to an authority specified in s 87(4), Table; and the order may impose conditions subject to which, or otherwise restrict the circumstances in which, disclosure is permitted: s 87(5).
   The relevant authorities and the relevant functions in relation to each such authority are:

AUTHORITY	FUNCTIONS
the Secretary of State	functions under the enactments relating to companies, insurance companies or insolvency, or under the Financial Services Act 1986 or the Companies Act 1989 Pt II (ss 24-54), Pt III (ss 55-91) (as amended) or Pt VII (ss 154-191)
the Treasury	functions under the Financial Services Act 1986 or under the Companies Act 1989 Pt III (ss 55-91) (as amended) or Pt VII (ss 154-191)
an inspector appointed under the Companies Act 1985 Pt XIV (ss 431-453) (as amended) or the Financial Services Act 1986 s 94 (as amended) or s 177 (as amended)	functions under the Companies Act 1985 Pt XIV (ss 431-453) (as amended) or the Financial Services Act 1986 s 94 (as amended) or s 177 (as amended)
a person authorised to exercise powers or appointed under the Insurance Companies Act 1982 s 43A (as added) or s 44 (as amended), the Companies Act 1985 s 447 (as amended), the Financial Services Act 1986 s 106 (as amended) or the Companies Act 1989 s 84	functions under the Insurance Companies Act 1982 s 43A (as added) or s 44 (as amended), the Companies Act 1985 s 447 (as amended), the Financial Services Act 1986 s 106 (as amended) or the Companies Act 1989 s 84
an overseas regulatory authority	its regulatory functions within the meaning of the Companies Act 1989 s 82
the Department of Economic Development in Northern Ireland or a person appointed or authorised by that Department	functions conferred on it or him by the enactments relating to companies or insolvency
a designated agency within the meaning of the Financial Services Act 1986	functions under the Financial Services Act 1986 or the Companies Act 1989 Pt VII (ss 154-191)

AUTHORITY	FUNCTIONS
a transferee body or the competent authority within the meaning of the Financial Services Act 1986	functions under the Financial Services Act 1986
the body administering a scheme under the Financial Services Act 1986 s 54 (as amended)	functions under the scheme
a recognised self-regulating organisation, recognised professional body, recognised investment exchange, recognised clearing house or recognised self-regulating organisation for friendly societies (within the meaning of the Financial Services Act 1986)	functions in its capacity as an organisation, body, exchange or clearing house recognised under the Financial Services Act 1986
the Chief Registrar of friendly societies and the Assistant Registrar of Friendly Societies for Scotland	functions under the enactments relating to friendly societies or building societies
the Friendly Societies Commission	functions under the enactments relating to friendly societies or under the Financial Services Act 1986
the Bank of England	functions under the Banking Act 1987 and any other functions
the Deposit Protection Board	functions under the Banking Act 1987
a body established by order under the Companies Act 1989 s 46	functions under the Companies Act 1989 Pt II (ss 24–54)
a recognised supervisory or qualifying body within the meaning of the Companies Act 1989 Pt II (ss 24–54)	functions as such a body
the Industrial Assurance Commissioner and the Industrial Assurance Commissioner for Northern Ireland	functions under the enactments relating to industrial assurance
the Insurance Brokers Registration Council	functions under the Insurance Brokers (Registration) Act 1977
the Official Receiver or, in Northern Ireland, the Official Assignee for company liquidations or for bankruptcy	functions under the enactments relating to insolvency
a recognised professional body, within the meaning of the Insolvency Act 1986 s 391	functions in its capacity as such a body under the Insolvency Act 1986
the Building Societies Commission	functions under the Building Societies Act 1986
the Occupational Pensions Regulatory Authority	functions under the Pension Schemes Act 1993 or the Pensions Act 1995 or any enactment in force in Northern Ireland corresponding to either of them
the Director General of Fair Trading	functions under the Financial Services Act 1986
a person authorised by the Secretary of State under the Companies Act 1985 s 245C (as added)	functions relating to the securing of compliance by companies with the accounting requirements of the Companies Act 1985
the Director General of the National Lottery	functions under the National Lottery etc Act 1993 ss 5–10, 15

Companies Act 1989 s 87(4), Table (amended by the Friendly Societies Act 1992 s 120(1), (2), Sch 21 Pt I para 11, Sch 22 Pt I; the Transfer of Functions (Financial Services) Order 1992, SI 1992/1315, art 10(1), Sch 4 para 12; the Financial Services (Disclosure of Information) (Designated Authorities) (No 7) Order 1993, SI 1993/1826, art 3; the Financial Services (Disclosure of Information) (Designated Authorities) (No 8) Order 1994, SI 1994/340, art 3; the Insurance Companies (Third Insurance Directives) Regulations 1994, SI 1994/1696, reg 68(1), Sch 8 Pt I para 18; the Pensions Act 1995 s 122, Sch 3 para 19).

4 Companies Act 1989 s 87(1).

1404. Prosecution of offences. Proceedings for a failure to assist an investigation[1] or for a breach of the restrictions on disclosure of information[2] may not be instituted except by or with the consent of the Secretary of State or the Director of Public Prosecutions[3].

Where such an offence committed by a body corporate is proved to have been committed with the consent or connivance of, or to be attributable to any neglect on the part of, a director, manager, secretary or other similar officer of the body, or a person purporting to act in any such capacity, he as well as the body corporate is guilty of the offence and liable to be proceeded against and punished accordingly[4].

Where such an offence committed by a partnership is proved to have been committed with the consent or connivance of, or to be attributable to any neglect on the part of, a partner, he as well as the partnership is guilty of the offence and liable to be proceeded against and punished accordingly[5].

Where such an offence committed by an unincorporated association, other than a partnership, is proved to have been committed with the consent or connivance of, or to be attributable to any neglect on the part of, any officer of the association or any member of its governing body, he as well as the association is guilty of the offence and liable to be proceeded against and punished accordingly[6].

1 Ie under the Companies Act 1989 s 85: see para 1401 ante.
2 Ie under ibid s 86: see para 1402 ante.
3 Ibid s 89(a).
4 Ibid s 90(1). Where the affairs of a body corporate are managed by its members, s 90(1) applies in relation to the acts and defaults of a member in connection with his functions of management as to a director of a body corporate: s 90(2).
5 Ibid s 90(3).
6 Ibid s 90(4). Proceedings for an offence alleged to have been committed under s 85 or s 86 by an unincorporated association must be brought in the name of the association, and not in that of any of its members; and for the purpose of any such proceedings any rules of court relating to the service of documents apply as in relation to a body corporate: s 91(2). The Criminal Justice Act 1925 s 33 (as amended) and the Magistrates' Courts Act 1980 s 46, Sch 3 (as amended) (procedure on charge of offence against a corporation: see MAGISTRATES) apply in a case in which an unincorporated association is charged in England and Wales with an offence under the Companies Act 1989 s 85 or s 86 as they apply in the case of a corporation: s 91(3). A fine imposed on an unincorporated association on its conviction of such an offence must be paid out of the funds of the association: s 91(6).

(29) PROTECTION OF COMPANY'S MEMBERS AGAINST UNFAIR PREJUDICE

1405. Petition by members and others. A member[1] of a company[2] may apply to the court[3] by petition[4] for an order[5] on the ground that the company's affairs are being or have been conducted[6] in a manner which is unfairly prejudicial to the interests of its members generally or of some part of its members, including at least himself, or that any actual or proposed act[7] or omission of the company, including an act or omission on its behalf, is or would be so prejudicial[8].

The provisions[9] also apply to a person who is not a member of a company but to whom shares in the company have been transferred[10] or transmitted by operation of law[11] as they apply to a member of the company[12].

1　As to membership of a company see the Companies Act 1985 s 22 and para 369 ante. See also *Re Nuneaton Borough Association Football Club Ltd* [1989] BCLC 454, (1989) 5 BCC 377, CA (a person whose name is entered on the register of members with his consent is a member despite the absence of a binding contract between him and the company until the register is rectified by removal of his name). As to whether a majority shareholder can petition see *Re Baltic Real Estate Ltd (No 1)* [1993] BCLC 498 at 501, [1992] BCC 629 at 632; *Re Baltic Real Estate Ltd (No 2)* [1993] BCLC 503 at 506, 507, [1992] BCC 629 at 635, 636.

　　A member must show a tangible interest, ie that the company is not insolvent: *Re Commercial and Industrial Insulations Ltd* [1986] BCLC 191. Cf *Re Hailey Group Ltd* [1993] BCLC 459, sub nom *Re a Company (No 008126 of 1989)* [1992] BCC 542 (where the company became insolvent between the presentation and the hearing of the petition) (cited in para 1414 note 8 post).

2　For these purposes, and so far as applicable for the purposes of the Companies Act 1985 s 459 (as amended) in s 461(2) (see para 1414 post), 'company' means any company within the meaning of the Companies Act 1985 (see para 11 note 1 ante) or any company which is not such a company but is a statutory water company within the meaning of the Statutory Water Companies Act 1991 (see WATER): Companies Act 1985 s 459(3) (added by the Water Act 1989 s 190(1), Sch 25 para 71(3); amended by the Water Consolidation (Consequential Provisions) Act 1991 s 2(1), Sch 1 para 40(2)).

3　For the meaning of 'the court' see para 161 note 4 ante.

4　The power under the Insolvency Act 1986 s 411 (see para 2800 post) to make rules applies, so far as it relates to a winding-up petition, for the purposes of a petition under the Companies Act 1985 Pt XVII (ss 459-461 (as amended): see infra and para 1406 et seq post): s 461(6) (substituted by the Insolvency Act 1985 s 109, Sch 6 para 24; amended by the Insolvency Act 1986 s 439(1), Sch 13 Pt I). In exercise of the power so conferred the Lord Chancellor, with the concurrence of the Secretary of State, and after consulting the committee existing for that purpose under the Insolvency Act 1986 s 413 (as amended) (see para 2800 post), made the Companies (Unfair Prejudice Applications) Proceedings Rules 1986, SI 1986/2000 (see para 1411 post), which came into force on 29 December 1986: r 1(1).

5　Ie under the Companies Act 1985 Pt XVII (ss 459-461) (as amended).

6　Past conduct is clearly encompassed, even if remedied by the date of the petition or the date of the hearing (*Re Kenyon Swansea Ltd* [1987] BCLC 514, (1987) 3 BCC 259; and see *Re a Company (No 001761 of 1986)* [1987] BCLC 141 at 143; *Re a Company (No 00314 of 1989), ex p Estate Acquisition and Development Ltd* [1991] BCLC 154, [1990] BCC 221); but, if the conduct has been remedied, this may render useless a claim for relief (*Re Estate Acquisition & Development Ltd* [1995] BCC 338 at 352). Laches may bar relief under a petition under the Companies Act 1985 s 459 (as amended): *Re a Company (No 005134 of 1986), ex p Harries* [1989] BCLC 383, sub nom *Re DR Chemicals Ltd* (1989) 5 BCC 39; *Re a Company* [1986] BCLC 362 at 366, sub nom *Re a Company (No 007623 of 1984)* (1986) 2 BCC 99, 191 at 99, 195.

7　Threatened future conduct is included: *Re Whyte, Petitioner* (1984) 1 BCC 99, 044, Ct of Sess; *Re a Company* [1986] BCLC 362, sub nom *Re a Company (No 007623 of 1984)* (1986) 2 BCC 99, 191; *Re Kenyon Swansea Ltd* [1987] BCLC 514, (1987) 3 BCC 259; *Re Blue Arrow plc* [1987] BCLC 585, (1987) 3 BCC 618; *Re a Company (No 00314 of 1989), ex p Estate Acquisition and Development Ltd* [1991] BCLC 154, [1990] BCC 221. The petition must not, however, be premature: see *Re Gorwyn Holdings Ltd* (1985) 1 BCC 99, 479; *Re a Company (No 005685 of 1988), ex p Schwarcz (No 2)* [1989] BCLC 427 at 451, sub nom *Re Ringtower Holdings plc* (1989) 5 BCC 82 at 103.

8　Companies Act 1985 s 459(1) (amended by the Companies Act 1989 s 145, Sch 19 para 11(a)). The predecessor to the Companies Act 1985 s 459 was the Companies Act 1980 s 75 (repealed) which replaced a more restrictive provision, the Companies Act 1948 s 210 (repealed), which provided relief for members where the company's affairs were being conducted in an oppressive, ie burdensome, harsh and wrongful, manner: see *Elder v Elder and Watson Ltd* 1952 SC 49; *Scottish Co-operative Wholesale Society Ltd v Meyer* [1959] AC 324, [1958] 3 All ER 66, HL; *Re HR Harmer Ltd* [1958] 3 All ER 689, [1959] 1 WLR 62, CA; *Re Lundie Bros Ltd* [1965] 2 All ER 692, [1965] 1 WLR 1051; *Re Five Minute Car Wash Service Ltd* [1966] 1 All ER 242, [1966] 1 WLR 745; *Re Jermyn St Turkish Baths Ltd* [1971] 3 All ER 184, [1971] 1 WLR 1042, CA.

9　Ie the Companies Act 1985 Pt XVII (ss 459-461) (as amended).

10 See *Re a Company* [1986] BCLC 391, (1986) 2 BCC 99, 276 ('transferred' requires at least that a proper instrument of transfer should have been executed and delivered to the transferee or the company; an agreement to transfer is insufficient); and see *Re a Company (No 007828 of 1985)* (1986) 2 BCC 98, 951; *Re Quickdome Ltd* [1988] BCLC 370, (1988) 4 BCC 296.

11 Ie personal representatives or a trustee in bankruptcy: see para 518 ante. See *Re a Company (No 007828 of 1985)* (1986) 2 BCC 98, 951 (the existence of an alleged constructive trust over shares does not amount to a transmission by operation of law). See also *Murray's Judicial Factor v Thomas Murray & Sons (Ice Merchants) Ltd* [1993] BCLC 1437, Ct of Sess (a judicial factor appointed in place of the executor dative is entitled to be treated as a person to whom the shares of the deceased were transmitted).

12 Companies Act 1985 s 459(2). References to a member or members are to be construed accordingly: s 459(2).

1406. Petitions by the Secretary of State. In addition to or instead of presenting a petition[1] for the winding up of a company[2], the Secretary of State may apply to the court by petition for an order[3] if in the case of any company:

(1) he has received a report[4] from inspectors appointed to investigate the company[5], or he has exercised his powers to require production of a company's documents[6], or he has obtained a warrant to enter and search a company's premises[7], or, in the case of an insurance company, he has exercised his powers of investigation or his powers to obtain information and to require the production of a company's documents[8]; and

(2) it appears to him that the company's affairs are being or have been conducted in a manner which is unfairly prejudicial to the interests of its members generally or of some part of its members, or that any actual or proposed act or omission of the company, including an act or omission on its behalf, is or would be so prejudicial[9].

1 Ie under the Insolvency Act 1986 s 124A (as added): see para 1390 ante and para 2202 post.

2 For these purposes, 'company' means any body corporate which is liable to be wound up under the Companies Act 1985: s 460(2). For the meaning of 'body corporate' see para 89 note 8 ante. As to the companies which may be so wound up see para 2193 post. The reference to a company which is liable to be wound up includes a reference to a company which would be so liable but for the Water Industry Act 1991 s 25 (see WATER): see the Water Consolidation (Consequential Provisions) Act 1991 s 2(1), Sch 1 para 40(1). For the purpose of the Companies Act 1985 s 460(2), the Companies Act 1985 is to be read as including certain provisions of the Insolvency Act 1986, and also the Company Directors Disqualification Act 1986: see para 20 text to note 12 and note 12 ante.

3 Ie under the Companies Act 1985 Pt XVII (ss 459-461) (as amended): see para 1405 ante and para 1407 et seq post.

4 Ie pursuant to ibid s 437 (as amended): see para 1380 ante.

5 Ie appointed under ibid s 431 (see para 1376 ante) or s 432 (as amended) (see para 1377 ante).

6 Ie under ibid s 447 (as amended): see para 1386 ante.

7 Ie under ibid s 448 (as substituted): see para 1393 ante.

8 Ie under the Insurance Companies Act 1982 s 43A (as added) or s 44(2)-(6) (as amended): see INSURANCE vol 25 (Reissue) para 854 et seq.

9 Companies Act 1985 s 460(1) (amended by the Companies Act 1989 ss 145, 212, Sch 19 para 11(b), Sch 24; the Insurance Companies (Third Insurance Directives) Regulations 1994, SI 1994/1696, reg 68(1), Sch 8 Pt I para 9(5)).

1407. Conduct of the company's affairs in an unfairly prejudicial manner. The conduct complained of must relate to the conduct of the affairs of the company[1] of which the petitioner is a member, and a remedy is not available where the conduct complained of is merely that of an individual shareholder acting in a personal capacity[2].

The test of whether the company's affairs are being or have been conducted in a manner which is unfairly prejudicial to the petitioner is an objective, and not a subjective, test[3]. It is accordingly unnecessary for the petitioner to show that the persons controlling the company have acted deliberately in bad faith, or with a conscious intent to treat him unfairly[3].

There are two elements to the requirement of unfair prejudice: the conduct complained of must be prejudicial in the sense of causing prejudice or harm to the relevant interest of the members or some part of the members, and also unfairly so. Conduct may be unfair without being prejudicial, or prejudicial without being unfair, and it is not sufficient if the conduct satisfies only one of these tests[4].

In deciding what is fair or unfair for these purposes, it must be borne in mind that fairness is being used in the context of a commercial relationship, the contractual terms of which are set out in the articles of association[5]. The starting point is to ask whether the conduct of which the shareholder complains is in accordance with the articles and the powers which the shareholders have entrusted to the board. However, a finding that conduct was not in accordance with the articles does not necessarily render it unfair, as trivial or technical infringements of the articles will not give rise to relief[5]. Conduct may also be unfair without being unlawful where it does not accord with the understandings upon which the shareholders are associated[5].

1 *Re a Company (No 005685 of 1988), ex p Schwarcz (No 2)* [1989] BCLC 427 at 437, sub nom *Re Ringtower Holdings plc* (1989) 5 BCC 82 at 90. See also *Re Saul D Harrison & Sons plc* [1995] 1 BCLC 14, [1994] BCC 475 at 486, CA. As to the meaning of a company's affairs see *Re Stewarts (Brixton) Ltd* [1985] BCLC 4 (decided under the Companies Act 1948 s 210 (repealed): see para 1405 note 8 ante); *Re a Company (No 001761 of 1986)* [1987] BCLC 141; *Re Castleburn Ltd* [1991] BCLC 89, (1989) 5 BCC 652; *Nicholas v Soundcraft Electronics Ltd* [1993] BCLC 360, sub nom *Re a Company (No 002470 of 1988), ex p Nicholas* [1992] BCC 895 at 903, CA (withholding of sums due by parent company to subsidiary was an act in the conduct of the affairs of the subsidiary when the sums were withheld by the parent as part of the exercise of its general control of the affairs of the subsidiary); *Re Unisoft Group Ltd (No 3)* [1994] 1 BCLC 609 (the acts of the members themselves are not acts of the company nor are they part of the affairs of the company); *Re Estate Acquisition & Development Ltd* [1995] BCC 338.

2 See *Re a Company (No 001761 of 1986)* [1987] BCLC 141 (acquisition by shareholder of charge held by bank no cause of complaint); *Re Unisoft Group Ltd (No 3)* [1994] 1 BCLC 609 (allegations concerned activities of shareholders and alleged breach of shareholders' agreement); *Re Estate Acquisition & Development Ltd* [1995] BCC 338 (offer by one shareholder to another to purchase his shares cannot be treated as part of the conduct of the company's affairs).

3 *Re RA Noble & Sons (Clothing) Ltd* [1983] BCLC 273, applying *Re Bovey Hotel Ventures Ltd* (31 July 1981, unreported); and see *Re a Company (No 005134 of 1986), ex p Harries* [1989] BCLC 383, sub nom *Re DR Chemicals Ltd* (1989) 5 BCC 39; *Re Sam Weller & Sons Ltd* [1990] Ch 682, [1989] 3 WLR 923; *Re Elgindata Ltd* [1991] BCLC 959; *Re Macro (Ipswich) Ltd* [1994] 2 BCLC 354, [1994] BCC 781; *Re Saul D Harrison & Sons plc* [1995] 1 BCLC 14, [1994] BCC 475, CA; *Re Little Olympian Each-Ways Ltd (No 3)* [1995] 1 BCLC 636.

4 *Re Saul D Harrison & Sons plc* [1995] 1 BCLC 14, [1994] BCC 475, CA; *Re RA Noble & Sons (Clothing) Ltd* [1983] BCLC 273; *Re a Company (No 005685 of 1988), ex p Schwarcz (No 2)* [1989] BCLC 427 at 437, sub nom *Re Ringtower Holdings plc* (1989) 5 BCC 82 at 90; *Re Elgindata Ltd* [1991] BCLC 959; *Nicholas v Soundcraft Electronics Ltd* [1993] BCLC 360, sub nom *Re a Company (No 002470 of 1988), ex p Nicholas* [1992] BCC 895 at 903, CA; *Re Macro (Ipswich) Ltd* [1994] 2 BCLC 354, [1994] BCC 781.

5 *Re Saul D Harrison & Sons plc* [1995] 1 BCLC 14, [1994] BCC 475 at 486, CA; and see para 1408 post. See also *Re Macro (Ipswich) Ltd* [1994] 2 BCLC 354 at 404, [1994] BCC 781 at 832 (the concept of unfairness involves the balancing of many considerations); *Re BSB Holdings Ltd (No 2)* [1996] 1 BCLC 155.

1408. Conduct unfairly prejudicial to the interests of the members. Not only must it be unfairly prejudicial[1], but the conduct complained of must be unfairly prejudicial to the interests of the petitioner in his capacity as a member of the company[2] as opposed to any other interests which he might possess[3].

However, the court takes a broad view of what might properly be regarded as the petitioner's interests as a member of the company. The word 'unfairly', like the words 'just and equitable' in the context of winding up[4], enables the court to have regard to wider equitable considerations[5] and to recognise that behind a limited company, or amongst it, are individuals with rights, expectations and obligations inter se which are not necessarily submerged in the company structure[6]. In most cases, the basis of association will be adequately and exhaustively laid down in the articles, but cases in which further equitable considerations might arise will typically present one, or probably more, of the following features:

    (1) a personal relationship between the shareholders involving mutual confidence;

    (2) an agreement that some or all should participate in the management of the company; and

    (3) restrictions on the transfer of shares which would prevent a member from realising his investment[7].

A member's interests are not necessarily limited, therefore, to his strict legal rights under the articles and the Companies Acts but can extend also to legitimate expectations arising from the nature of the company and agreements and understandings between the parties[8].

A common case of such expectations being superimposed on a member's rights under the articles is the corporate quasi-partnership, in which members frequently have expectations of participating in the management and profits of the company, which arise from the understandings on which the company was formed and which it may be unfair for other members to ignore[9]. The member's interests as a member who ventures his capital in the company's business may include a legitimate expectation that he will continue to be employed as a director and his dismissal from that office and exclusion from management may therefore be unfairly prejudicial to his interests as a member[10].

This is not to say that the application of the statutory remedy[11] is confined to cases where the company is a quasi-partnership[12]; but, where the company is not a quasi-partnership, it will be more difficult to establish legitimate expectations beyond the member's strict legal rights[13]. If no such expectations exist, then a petitioner must show some abuse by directors of their powers or an infringement of the member's strict legal rights under the company's constitution or the companies legislation[14].

---

1 See para 1407 ante.

2 *Re a Company (No 004475 of 1982)* [1983] Ch 178 at 189, [1983] 2 All ER 36 at 44 per Lord Grantchester; *Re a Company* [1986] BCLC 376; *Re a Company (No 003843 of 1986)* [1987] BCLC 562, (1987) 3 BCC 624; *Re a Company (No 005685 of 1988), ex p Schwarcz (No 2)* [1989] BCLC 427, sub nom *Re Ringtower Holdings plc* (1989) 5 BCC 82; *Re a Company (No 00314 of 1989), ex p Estate Acquisition and Development Ltd* [1991] BCLC 154, [1990] BCC 221; *Jaber v Science and Information Technology Ltd* [1992] BCLC 764; *Re Unisoft Group Ltd (No 3)* [1994] 1 BCLC 609 at 626; *R & H Electric Ltd v Haden Bill Electrical Ltd, Re Haden Bill Electrical Ltd* [1995] 2 BCLC 280, sub nom *R & H Electrical Ltd v Haden Bill Electrical Ltd* [1995] BCC 958.

3 See *Re a Company (No 003843 of 1986)* [1987] BCLC 562, (1987) 3 BCC 624 (petitioner complained in capacity as a creditor or consultant pursuant to an agreement with the company); *Re JE Cade & Son Ltd* [1992] BCLC 213, [1991] BCC 360 (petitioner protecting his interests as a freeholder of a farm, not as a member of the company); *Re Unisoft Group Ltd (No 3)* [1994] 1 BCLC 609 at 626 (allegations concerned relationship as landlord and tenant); *Re Estate Acquisition & Development Ltd* [1995] BCC 338 (director seeking the disclosure of management information cannot show conduct which is unfairly prejudicial to his interests as a member).

4 Ie a winding up on the just and equitable ground under the Insolvency Act 1986 s 122(1)(g): see *Ebrahimi v Westbourne Galleries Ltd* [1973] AC 360, [1972] 2 All ER 492, HL. As to the scope of the just and equitable ground for winding up see paras 2208, 2209 post.

5 *Re Saul D Harrison & Sons plc* [1995] 1 BCLC 14, [1994] BCC 475 at 486, CA; and see *Re a Company* [1986] BCLC 376; *Re Posgate & Denby (Agencies) Ltd* [1987] BCLC 8, (1986) 2 BCC 99, 352; *Re Blue Arrow plc* [1987] BCLC 585, (1987) 3 BCC 618; *Re a Company (No 005685 of 1988), ex p Schwarcz (No 2)*

[1989] BCLC 427, sub nom *Re Ringtower Holdings plc* (1989) 5 BCC 82; *Re Tottenham Hotspur plc* [1994] 1 BCLC 655.

6 *Ebrahimi v Westbourne Galleries Ltd* [1973] AC 360 at 379, [1972] 2 All ER 492 at 500, HL.

7 *Ebrahimi v Westbourne Galleries Ltd* [1973] AC 360 at 379, [1972] 2 All ER 492 at 500, HL. Companies which reflect these features are often referred to as quasi-partnerships: see *Ebrahimi v Westbourne Galleries Ltd* supra. See para 2208 post.

8 *Re Saul D Harrison & Sons plc* [1995] 1 BCLC 14, [1994] BCC 475 at 486, CA; *Re a Company* [1986] BCLC 376; *Re Posgate & Denby (Agencies) Ltd* [1987] BCLC 8, (1986) 2 BCC 99, 352; *Re a Company (No 005685 of 1988), ex p Schwarcz (No 2)* [1989] BCLC 427, sub nom *Re Ringtower Holdings plc* (1989) 5 BCC 82; *R & H Electric Ltd v Haden Bill Electrical Ltd, Re Haden Bill Electrical Ltd* [1995] 2 BCLC 280, sub nom
R & H Electrical Ltd v Haden Bill Electrical Ltd [1995] BCC 958.

9 *Re Posgate & Denby (Agencies) Ltd* [1987] BCLC 8 at 14, (1986) 2 BCC 99, 352 at 99, 357. Cf *Re a Company (No 005134 of 1986), ex p Harries* [1989] BCLC 383, sub nom *Re DR Chemicals Ltd* (1989) 5 BCC 39 (company began as a quasi-partnership but relationship changed to a more commercial footing so ending any expectations as to participation in management).

10 *Re a Company* [1986] BCLC 376 at 379.

11 Ie the Companies Act 1985 s 459 (as amended): see para 1405 ante.

12 See *Re a Company (No 00314 of 1989), ex p Estate Acquisition and Development Ltd* [1991] BCLC 154 at 161, [1990] BCC 221 at 227. As to the meaning of quasi-partnership see text and note 7 supra.

13 See *Re Posgate & Denby (Agencies) Ltd* [1987] BCLC 8, (1986) 2 BCC 99, 352; *Re Blue Arrow plc* [1987] BCLC 585, (1987) 3 BCC 618 (listed public company; whole of parties' relationship in the articles and the companies legislation); *Re a Company (No 005685 of 1988), ex p Schwarcz (No 2)* [1989] BCLC 427, sub nom *Re Ringtower Holdings plc* (1989) 5 BCC 82 (public company; parties' relationship had been reduced to massively detailed agreements); *Re Elgindata Ltd* [1991] BCLC 959 (relationship negotiated at arm's length); *Re Tottenham Hotspur plc* [1994] 1 BCLC 655 (listed public company; no understandings beyond the company's constitution); *Re Estate Acquisition & Development Ltd* [1995] BCC 338 (no evidence of any expectations); *Re Saul D Harrison & Sons plc* [1995] 1 BCLC 14, [1994] BCC 475 at 486, CA (no evidence of any expectations).

14 *Re Saul D Harrison & Sons plc* [1995] 1 BCLC 14, [1994] BCC 475 at 486, CA.

1409. Types of unfairly prejudicial conduct. The categories of conduct which may amount to unfairly prejudicial conduct are not closed[1].

A member will be able to bring himself within the provisions of Part XVII of the Companies Act 1985[2] if he can show that the value of his shareholding has been seriously diminished or at least seriously jeopardised by a course of conduct on the part of those in control of the company; although the provisions are not limited to such cases[3].

Typical examples of what in most cases will constitute unfairly prejudicial conduct are:

(1) exclusion from management in circumstances where there is an expectation of participation[4];

(2) the diversion of business to another company in which the majority shareholder holds a greater interest[5];

(3) the awarding by the majority shareholder to himself of excessive financial benefits[6]; and

(4) abuses of power and breaches of the articles of association[7].

A rights issue of shares, even one made on a pro rata basis at an advantageous price[8], is nevertheless capable of amounting to unfairly prejudicial conduct if it is known that the objecting member did not have sufficient funds to take up the offer, and it was made for that reason, or where the objecting member was engaged in litigation with the majority, and the offer was designed to deplete the resources available to him to finance such litigation[9]. An allotment of shares secretly made in breach of the statutory provisions governing allotments[10] for the improper purpose of increasing the majority's holding and decreasing that of the minority is unfairly prejudicial conduct[11]; and so are calls made not in the interests of the company but for the purpose of putting pressure on a petitioner[12].

The passing of a special resolution to alter the company's articles of association may be unfairly prejudicial conduct; for example, where an alteration will affect the petitioner's legitimate expectation that he would control the management of the company; and even a proposal that such a resolution be passed may amount to unfairly prejudicial conduct[13]. However, in the absence of such special circumstances involving an abuse of the rights of the majority, a change in the articles is one of the ordinary incidents to which a member of a company cannot validly object[14].

Where an extraordinary general meeting of shareholders has been requisitioned by the members and there is unreasonable delay in convening the meeting, this will entitle the requisitioning members to present a petition on the grounds of unfairly prejudicial conduct[15].

Repeated failures to hold annual general meetings and to lay accounts before the members depriving members of their right to know and consider the state of the company's affairs is conduct unfairly prejudicial to their interests; as is holding an extraordinary general meeting on incorrect notice so invalidating an allotment of shares made at the meeting[16].

Although it is open to the court to find that serious mismanagement of a company's business constitutes conduct that is unfairly prejudicial to the interests of the shareholders[17], the court will normally be very reluctant to accept that managerial decisions can amount to unfairly prejudicial conduct[18].

A failure by the company to propound a scheme of arrangement which would enable the petitioner to dispose of his shares, or to purchase his shares under the statutory powers in that behalf, cannot be unfairly prejudicial, as a member has no recognisable interest in having any such scheme propounded; the provisions of the Companies Act 1985[19] have not been enacted with a view to enabling a locked-in shareholder to require the company to buy him out at a price which he considers adequately to reflect the value of the underlying assets of the company[20].

1 *Re BSB Holdings Ltd (No 2)* [1996] 1 BCLC 155.
2 Ie the Companies Act 1985 Pt XVII (ss 459–461) (as amended): see para 1405 et seq ante and para 1410 et seq post.
3 *Re RA Noble & Sons (Clothing) Ltd* [1983] BCLC 273; *Re Bovey Hotel Ventures Ltd* (31 July 1981, unreported); and see *McGuinness v Bremner plc* [1988] BCLC 673, Ct of Sess; *Re Elgindata Ltd* [1991] BCLC 959; *Re Little Olympian Each-Ways Ltd (No 3)* [1995] 1 BCLC 636.
4 See *R & H Electric Ltd v Haden Bill Electrical Ltd, Re Haden Bill Electrical Ltd* [1995] 2 BCLC 280, sub nom *R & H Electrical Ltd v Haden Bill Electrical Ltd* [1995] BCC 958; and see *Re a Company* [1986] BCLC 376; *Re Cumana Ltd* [1986] BCLC 430, CA; *Re Ghyll Beck Driving Range Ltd* [1993] BCLC 1126. See also *Ebrahimi v Westbourne Galleries Ltd* [1973] AC 360, [1972] 2 All ER 492, HL. In the absence of such an expectation, every director is subject to the possibility of removal and has no right to remain in office: *Re Estate Acquisition & Development Ltd* [1995] BCC 338; *Re a Company (No 005134 of 1986), ex p Harries* [1989] BCLC 383, sub nom *Re DR Chemicals Ltd* (1989) 5 BCC 39 (company changed from a quasi-partnership to commercial footing so ending expectation as to participation); *Re a Company (No 005685 of 1988), ex p Schwarcz (No 2)* [1989] BCLC 427, sub nom *Re Ringtower Holdings plc* (1989) 5 BCC 82. See also *Re Blue Arrow plc* [1987] BCLC 585, (1987) 3 BCC 618 (no expectation to remain as company president); *Re Tottenham Hotspur plc* [1994] 1 BCLC 655 (no expectation as to continued role as chief executive).
5 *Re Cumana Ltd* [1986] BCLC 430, CA; and see *Re Stewarts (Brixton) Ltd* [1985] BCLC 4 (decided under the Companies Act 1948 s 210 (repealed): see para 1405 note 8 ante); *Re London School of Electronics Ltd* [1986] Ch 211, [1985] 3 WLR 474; *Re Little Olympian Each-Ways Ltd (No 3)* [1995] 1 BCLC 636 (directors disposed of business at substantial undervalue to another company as part of transaction from which they benefited significantly); *Re Full Cup International Trading Ltd* [1995] BCC 682 at 690, 691.
6 *Re Cumana Ltd* [1986] BCLC 430, CA; *Re Elgindata Ltd* [1991] BCLC 959 (using company assets for personal benefit of majority shareholder). As to whether the failure to pay reasonable dividends while

maintaining significant benefits for the majority shareholders/directors could warrant a petition alleging unfairly prejudicial conduct see *Re a Company (No 00370 of 1987), ex p Glossop* [1988] BCLC 570, (1988) 4 BCC 506; *Re Sam Weller & Sons Ltd* [1990] Ch 682, [1989] 3 WLR 923.

7   *Re Saul D Harrison & Sons plc* [1995] 1 BCLC 14, [1994] BCC 475 at 486, CA; and see *Re Whyte, Petitioner* (1984) 1 BCC 99, 044, Ct of Sess (majority shareholders wanted to change composition of board with a probable view to compromising litigation which the company had commenced against a party associated with the majority); *Re a Company* [1986] BCLC 382 (board had an interest in one of two rival take-over bids for the company). However, the withholding of sums due by a parent company to a subsidiary as part of the exercise of the parent company's general control of the affairs of the subsidiary was not unfairly prejudicial when it was done in the interest of keeping the group afloat, something which was in the interests of the subsidiary: *Nicholas v Soundcraft Electronics Ltd* [1993] BCLC 360, sub nom *Re a Company (No 002470 of 1988), ex p Nicholas* [1992] BCC 895 at 903, CA.

8   As to the allotment of equity shares on a pre-emptive basis see para 457 et seq ante.

9   *Re a Company* [1985] BCLC 80; *Re Cumana Ltd* [1986] BCLC 430, CA (where there was no good financial reason for making a rights issue which the minority shareholder could not take up before capitalising profits). Cf *Re a Company* [1986] BCLC 362, sub nom *Re a Company (No 007623 of 1984)* (1986) 2 BCC 99, 191 (where the rights issue was motivated by a genuine desire to raise needed capital).

10   See the Companies Act 1985 s 89 et seq and para 457 ante.

11   *Re a Company (No 005134 of 1986), ex p Harries* [1989] BCLC 383, sub nom *Re DR Chemicals Ltd* (1989) 5 BCC 39.

12   *Re Hailey Group Ltd* [1993] BCLC 459, sub nom *Re a Company (No 008126 of 1989)* [1992] BCC 542.

13   *Re Kenyon Swansea Ltd* [1987] BCLC 514, (1987) 3 BCC 259; cf *Re Blue Arrow plc* [1987] BCLC 585, (1987) 3 BCC 618 (no such expectations existed). Quaere whether an alteration which involved the adoption of the provisions of Table A could ever be unfairly prejudicial to the members' interests for these purposes: *Re Estate Acquisition & Development Ltd* [1995] BCC 338. As to proposed acts see para 1405 note 7 ante.

14   *Re Estate Acquisition & Development Ltd* [1995] BCC 338; *Re a Company (No 005685 of 1988), ex p Schwarcz (No 2)* [1989] BCLC 427, sub nom *Re Ringtower Holdings plc* (1989) 5 BCC 82.

15   *McGuinness v Bremner plc* [1988] BCLC 673, Ct of Sess.

16   *Re a Company (No 00789 of 1987), ex p Shooter* [1990] BCLC 384.

17   See *Re Macro (Ipswich) Ltd* [1994] 2 BCLC 354, [1994] BCC 781 (specific acts of mismanagement repeated over many years causing financial loss to the company).

18   *Re Elgindata Ltd* [1991] BCLC 959 at 993, 994; *Re Macro (Ipswich) Ltd* [1994] 2 BCLC 354, [1994] BCC 781; *Re Saul D Harrison & Sons plc* [1995] 1 BCLC 14, [1994] BCC 475 at 486, CA. It is insufficient that the mere quality of management turns out to be poor: *Re Elgindata Ltd* supra at 993, 994.

19   See note 2 supra.

20   *Re a Company (No 004475 of 1982)* [1983] Ch 178, [1983] 2 All ER 36; *Re Estate Acquisition & Development Ltd* [1995] BCC 338 at 346.

1410. Conduct of the petitioner. While there is no overriding requirement that it should be just and equitable to grant relief or that the petitioner come with clean hands[1], the conduct of the petitioner may be relevant in a number of ways, as where the conduct complained of is found to be prejudicial but not unfair in the light of the petitioner's conduct[2]. The petitioner's conduct may also affect the relief granted by the court[3].

If the real object of the petition is to exert pressure to achieve a collateral purpose, this will be treated as an abuse of the process of the court and no order will be made[4].

1   *Re London School of Electronics Ltd* [1986] Ch 211, [1985] 3 WLR 474 (petitioner himself took wrongful action prompted by unfairly prejudicial conduct of majority). Cf *Nurcombe v Nurcombe* [1985] 1 All ER 65, [1985] 1 WLR 370, CA (a minority shareholders' action where the plaintiff had indirectly participated in the financial consequences of the act complained of, and could not therefore maintain the action); *Barrett v Duckett* [1995] 1 BCLC 243, CA.

2   *Re RA Noble & Sons (Clothing) Ltd* [1983] BCLC 273 (exclusion from participation not unfair in view of the petitioner's disinterest in the business).

3   Ie under the Companies Act 1985 s 461 (as amended): see para 1414 post. See also *Re London School of Electronics Ltd* [1986] Ch 211, [1985] 3 WLR 474; *Re Bird Precision Bellows Ltd* [1986] Ch 658, [1985] 3 All ER 523, CA (affg [1984] Ch 419, [1984] 3 All ER 444).

4   *Re Bellador Silk Ltd* [1965] 1 All ER 667.

1411. Procedure on petition. The following procedure applies in relation to petitions for relief against unfair prejudice presented to the court on or after 29 December 1986 by a member of a company[1], by a person treated as a member[2] or by the Secretary of State[3].

Except so far as inconsistent with the Companies Act 1985 and the following provisions, the Rules of the Supreme Court and the practice of the High Court apply to such proceedings[4] in the High Court, and the rules and practice of the county court apply to such proceedings[4] in a county court, with any necessary modifications[5].

The petition must be in the prescribed form[6] with such variations, if any, as the circumstances may require[7]. The petition must specify the grounds on which it is presented and the nature of the relief which is sought by the petitioner, and must be delivered to the court for filing with sufficient copies for service[8].

The court must fix a hearing for a day ('the return day') on which, unless the court otherwise directs, the petitioner and any respondent, including the company, must attend before the registrar in chambers for directions to be given in relation to the procedure on the petition[9]. On fixing the return day, the court must return to the petitioner sealed copies of the petition for service, each indorsed with the return day and the time of hearing[10].

The petitioner must, at least 14 days before the return day, serve a sealed copy of the petition on the company[11]. In the case of a petition by a company member[12], the petitioner must also, at least 14 days before the return day, serve a sealed copy of the petition on every respondent named in the petition[13].

On the return day, or at any time after it, the court must give such directions as it thinks appropriate with respect to the following matters:

(1) service of the petition on any person, whether in connection with the time, date and place of a further hearing, or for any other purpose;

(2) whether particulars of claim and defence are to be delivered, and generally as to the procedure on the petition;

(3) whether, and if so by what means, the petition is to be advertised[14];

(4) the manner in which any evidence is to be adduced at any hearing before the judge and in particular, but without prejudice to the generality of the above, as to:

(a) the taking of evidence wholly or in part by affidavit or orally;

(b) the cross-examination of any deponents to affidavits; and

(c) the matters to be dealt with in evidence;

(5) any other matter affecting the procedure on the petition or in connection with the hearing and disposal of the petition[15].

If complaint is made in respect of the conduct of the affairs of a number of companies which neither form a group nor have a common holding company, separate petitions should be presented in respect of each company[16].

Leave for service of the petition out of the jurisdiction is required[17].

When an order has been made by the court on the petition, the petitioner and every other person who has appeared on the hearing of the petition must, not later than the business day[18] following that on which the order is made, leave at the court all the documents required for enabling the order to be completed forthwith[19]. It is not necessary for the court to appoint a time, date and place for any person to attend to settle the order, unless in any particular case the special circumstances make an appointment necessary[20]. If the court considers that the order should be advertised, it must give directions as to the manner and time of advertisement[21].

To protect the company's position and that of the petitioner pending the hearing of the petition, interlocutory relief may be available[22].

1   Ie under the Companies Act 1985 s 459(1) (as amended): see para 1405 ante.
2   Ie a person treated as a member under ibid s 459(2): see para 1405 ante.
3   Companies (Unfair Prejudice Applications) Proceedings Rules 1986, SI 1986/2000, rr 1(1), (2), r 2(1). As to the Secretary of State's power to present a petition see the Companies Act 1985 s 460 (as amended) and para 1406 ante.
4   Ie proceedings under ibid Pt XVII (ss 459-461) (as amended): see para 1405 et seq ante and para 1412 et seq post.
5   Companies (Unfair Prejudice Applications) Proceedings Rules 1986 rr 1(2), 2(2).
6   For the prescribed form of petition see ibid r 3(1), Schedule.
7   Ibid r 3(1).
8   Ibid r 3(2).
9   Ibid r 3(3).
10 Ibid r 3(4).
11 Ibid r 4(1).
12 Ie a petition based upon the Companies Act 1985 s 459 (as amended): see para 1405 ante.
13 Companies (Unfair Prejudice Applications) Proceedings Rules 1986 rr 1(2), 4(2). As to the proper respondents see para 1412 post.
14 There is normally no advertisement of the petition: see *Re a Company (No 00687 of 1991)* [1992] BCLC 133, [1991] BCC 210.
15 Companies (Unfair Prejudice Applications) Proceedings Rules 1986 r 5.
16 *Re a Company* [1984] BCLC 307. If necessary, appropriate directions may be given for the separate petitions to be heard together or consecutively: *Re a Company* supra. In these proceedings, discovery pursuant to RSC Ord 24 r 3 (see DISCOVERY) is available; but, before it can be ordered in relation to documents belonging to a corporate entity which is not a respondent to the petition, it must be shown that the corporation is so under the control of the respondents as to be their alter ego: *Re Tecnion Investments Ltd* [1985] BCLC 434. For the meaning of 'holding company' see para 827 ante.
17 *Re Harrods (Buenos Aires) Ltd* [1992] Ch 72, [1991] 4 All ER 334, CA. See also *Re Baltic Real Estate Ltd (No 2)* [1993] BCLC 503, [1992] BCC 629 (leave for service out of the jurisdiction may be granted where the relief sought could result in respondents outside the jurisdiction having to deliver the relevant transfer and share certificates to the petitioner within the jurisdiction; on the facts, refused; petitioner did not have a good arguable case).
18 For the meaning of 'business day' see para 1320 note 4 ante.
19 Companies (Unfair Prejudice Applications) Proceedings Rules 1986 rr 1(2), 6(1).
20 Ibid r 6(2).
21 Ibid r 6(3).
22 See *Re a Company* [1985] BCLC 80; *Re Posgate & Denby (Agencies) Ltd* [1987] BCLC 8, (1986) 2 BCC 99, 352; *Re a Company (No 00596 of 1986)* [1987] BCLC 133, (1987) 2 BCC 99, 063; *Jaber v Science and Information Technology Ltd* [1992] BCLC 764 at 784; *Re Mountforest Ltd* [1993] BCC 565; *Re a Company (No 003061 of 1993), Safina v Comet Enterprises Ltd* [1994] BCC 883.

1412. Respondents to the petition. The statutory provisions relating to petitions for relief against unfair prejudice by a company member[1] do not indicate who may be, who has to be, or who cannot be, respondents; it is a matter for the court[2]. The company is made a respondent to the petition as a matter of course[3].

All members of the company whose interests would have been affected by the misconduct alleged or who would be affected by an order made by the court under its wide powers to give relief[4] should be made respondents to a petition or served with it[5]. This is so even if the members are not alleged to have been concerned in the alleged unfairly prejudicial conduct and are members against whom no relief is directly sought[6]. In circumstances where there are large numbers of inactive investors, it may, however, be sufficient to give them notice of the petition[7]. A former member may also properly be joined as a respondent where relief is sought against that person[8].

A third party, not a member of the company in respect of which the alleged unfairly prejudicial conduct occurred, should also be joined if it might be affected by the relief sought or was directly involved in the transactions which are said to be unfairly prejudicial[9].

If, however, the likelihood of the court's discretion being exercised so as to lead to relief against, or relief having any material effect upon, a given respondent can be seen to be so remote as to be perfectly hopeless, it would be abusive to require the respondent to remain as such or to be added as such[10].

1 Ie the Companies Act 1985 s 459 (as amended): see para 1405 ante.
2 *Re Little Olympian Each-Ways Ltd* [1994] 2 BCLC 420 at 425, sub nom *Supreme Travels Ltd v Little Olympian Each-Ways Ltd* [1994] BCC 947.
3 See the Companies (Unfair Prejudice Applications) Proceedings Rules 1986, SI 1986/2000, r 4(1) and para 1411 ante. The company may be affected by the petition in a number of ways: eg the composition of the corporators who are the embodiment of the company may change (see *Re BSB Holdings Ltd* [1993] BCLC 246 at 254, [1992] BCC 915 at 921, 922); it may have to give discovery of documents (see *Re Hydrosan Ltd* [1991] BCLC 418, [1991] BCC 19); and it may itself be affected by the relief sought such as an order to buy back the shares which are in issue (see *Re a Company (No 004502 of 1988), ex p Johnson* [1992] BCLC 701 at 703, [1991] BCC 234 at 235). As to costs incurred by the company see para 1413 post.
4 Ie under the Companies Act 1985 s 461: see para 1414 post.
5 *Re a Company (No 007281 of 1986)* [1987] BCLC 593, (1987) 3 BCC 375.
6 *Re a Company (No 007281 of 1986)* [1987] BCLC 593, (1987) 3 BCC 375. A member against whom no allegation is made and against whom no relief is sought need not take an active part in the proceedings: see *Re BSB Holdings Ltd* [1993] BCLC 246 at 253, [1992] BCC 915 at 921.
7 *Re a Company (No 007281 of 1986)* [1987] BCLC 593 at 599, (1987) 3 BCC 375 at 381. In cases of doubt, the court can give directions as to service of the petition on any person who has not been made a respondent: *Re a Company (No 007281 of 1986)* supra.
8 *Re a Company* [1986] 2 All ER 253, [1986] 1 WLR 281. Cf *Re Baltic Real Estate Ltd (No 1)* [1993] BCLC 498, [1992] BCC 629 (former shareholders not proper parties); but see *Re Little Olympian Each-Ways Ltd* [1994] 2 BCLC 420 at 429, sub nom *Supreme Travels Ltd v Little Olympian Each-Ways Ltd* [1994] BCC 947 at 954.
9 *Re BSB Holdings Ltd* [1993] BCLC 246, [1992] BCC 915; and see *Lowe v Fahey* [1996] 1 BCLC 262. It is not sufficient reason, in itself, for the joinder of a person as a further party that an existing respondent is owned or controlled by that person: *Re Baltic Real Estate Ltd (No 1)* [1993] BCLC 498, [1992] BCC 629; *Re Little Olympian Each-Ways Ltd* [1994] 2 BCLC 420 at 430, sub nom *Supreme Travels Ltd v Little Olympian Each-Ways Ltd* [1994] BCC 947 at 955.
10 *Re Little Olympian Each-Ways Ltd* [1994] 2 BCLC 420, sub nom *Supreme Travels Ltd v Little Olympian Each-Ways Ltd* [1994] BCC 947.

1413. Costs. The procedure whereby a shareholder who in good faith and on reasonable grounds brings a derivative action to remedy a wrong to the company is entitled to apply for an indemnity as to costs from the company[1] does not apply to petitions for relief on the grounds of unfairly prejudicial conduct where the substance of the complaint is a wrong done to the shareholder and not to the company[2].

It is a general principle of company law that the company's money should not be expended on disputes which are in substance between shareholders[3]. There is, however, no rule that in all cases active participation by a company in proceedings commenced by petition on the ground of unfair prejudice[4] is improper[5]. The test of whether such participation and expenditure is proper is whether it is necessary or expedient in the interests of the company as a whole; and only in cases of the most compelling circumstances proven by cogent evidence will advance approval of such participation and expenditure be given[6].

A respondent may seek security for costs where the petitioner is a limited company[7].

1 Ie the procedure devised in *Wallersteiner v Moir (No 2)* [1975] QB 373, [1975] 1 All ER 849, CA: see para 1171 note 11 ante.
2 *Re a Company (No 005136 of 1986)* [1987] BCLC 82. The question of the petitioner's costs is a matter for the discretion of the court: see *Re Elgindata Ltd (No 2)* [1993] 1 All ER 232, [1993] 1 WLR 1207, CA (petitioner deprived of part of his costs where he had caused a significant increase in the length of the proceedings).
3 *Re Crossmore Electrical & Civil Engineering Ltd* [1989] BCLC 137, (1989) 5 BCC 37, applying *Pickering v Stephenson* (1872) LR 14 Eq 322; and see *Re Kenyon Swansea Ltd* [1987] BCLC 514, (1987) 3 BCC 259; *Re Hydrosan Ltd* [1991] BCLC 418 at 420, [1991] BCC 19 at 20; *Re Elgindata Ltd* [1991] BCLC 959; *Re a Company (No 004502 of 1988), ex p Johnson* [1992] BCLC 701, [1991] BCC 234; *Re Milgate Developments Ltd, Re Kent and Provincial Investment plc* [1993] BCLC 291, [1991] BCC 24; *Re a Company (No 001126 of 1992)* [1994] 2 BCLC 146, [1993] BCC 325.
4 Ie a petition under the Companies Act 1985 s 459 (as amended): see para 1405 ante.
5 *Re a Company (No 001126 of 1992)* [1994] 2 BCLC 146, [1993] BCC 325. There may be cases (although unlikely nowadays) where active participation by the company would be ultra vires in the strict sense: *Re a Company (No 001126 of 1992)* supra. For the meaning of 'ultra vires' see para 1097 ante.
6 *Re a Company (No 001126 of 1992)* [1994] 2 BCLC 146, [1993] BCC 325. There is a heavy onus on a company, which has actively participated or has so incurred costs, to satisfy the court of the necessity or expedience of having done so: *Re a Company (No 001126 of 1992)* supra. The company can properly incur costs in preparing its list for discovery and on attendance by the company at the judgment so as to ensure that the company is able to contribute to framing an appropriate order: *Re a Company (No 001126 of 1992)* supra; *Re a Company (No 004502 of 1988), ex p Johnson* [1992] BCLC 701, [1991] BCC 234.
7 *Re Unisoft Group Ltd (No 1)* [1993] BCLC 1292, CA; affg [1993] BCLC 528 (a limited company which is a petitioner under the Companies Act 1985 s 459 (as amended) is 'a plaintiff' in 'other legal proceedings' for the purpose of s 726: see para 1183 ante). See also *Re Unisoft Group Ltd (No 2)* [1993] BCLC 532 (applicant for security must show that the company would be unable, and not may be unable, to meet its debts when an order for costs is made against it).

1414. Order for protection of members against unfair prejudice; in general.
If the court is satisfied that a petition under the statutory provisions relating to petitions for relief against unfair prejudice[1] is well founded[2], it may make such order as it thinks fit for giving relief in respect of the matters complained of[3].

Without prejudice to the generality of the above, the court's order may:

(1) regulate the conduct of the company's affairs in the future[4];
(2) require the company to refrain from doing or continuing an act complained of by the petitioner, or to do an act which the petitioner has complained it has omitted to do[5];
(3) authorise civil proceedings to be brought in the name and on behalf of the company by such person or persons and on such terms as the court may direct;
(4) provide for the purchase of the shares[6] of any members of the company by other members or by the company itself, and, in the case of a purchase by the company itself, the reduction of the company's capital accordingly[7].

The court's discretion as to the relief it may order extends to the refusal of specific relief where the court is unable to devise relief which would constitute an appropriate remedy or where some other course of action seems to be preferable[8].

If an order of the court requires the company not to make any, or any specified, alteration in the memorandum or articles, the company does not then have power without leave of the court to make any such alteration in breach of that requirement[9].

Any alteration in the company's memorandum or articles made by virtue of an order of the court is of the same effect as if duly made by resolution of the company, and the provisions of the Companies Act 1985 apply to the memorandum or articles as so altered accordingly[10].

An office copy of the order altering, or giving leave to alter, a company's memorandum or articles must, within 14 days from the making of the order, or such longer period as the court may allow, be delivered by the company to the registrar of companies for registration; and, if a company makes default in complying with this requirement, the company, and every officer of it who is in default, is liable on summary conviction to a fine not exceeding one-fifth of the statutory maximum and, on conviction after continued contravention, to a daily default fine not exceeding one-fiftieth of the statutory maximum[11].

If a petition is compromised, there is no reason why such compromise should not follow the usual *Tomlin* form[12]; but the petitioner should undertake to apply to dismiss the petition when the terms of the compromise have been fully implemented[13].

1 Ie the Companies Act 1985 s 459 (as amended) (see para 1405 ante) and s 460 (as amended) (see para 1406 ante).
2 There must be a finding of unfair prejudice before the court can make any order for relief: *Re Bird Precision Bellows Ltd* [1986] Ch 658, [1985] 3 All ER 523, CA; *Re a Company* [1986] BCLC 362, sub nom *Re a Company (No 007623 of 1984)* (1986) 2 BCC 99, 191; *Re a Company (No 004175 of 1986)* [1987] 1 WLR 585, [1987] BCLC 574; *Re a Company (No 004502 of 1988), ex p Johnson* [1992] BCLC 701, [1991] BCC 234. It follows that there is no jurisdiction to make interim orders in anticipation of the full hearing: *Re a Company (No 004175 of 1986)* supra.
3 Companies Act 1985 s 461(1). In all cases the petitioner should clearly state in his petition the relief to which he considers himself entitled: *Re Antigen Laboratories Ltd* [1951] 1 All ER 110n. The petition should include a prayer for such other order as the court thinks fit: *Re JE Cade & Son Ltd* [1992] BCLC 213 at 223, [1991] BCC 360 at 368. The court will consider such order as is appropriate at the time of the hearing and not at the time of the presentation of the petition: *Re Hailey Group Ltd* [1993] BCLC 459, sub nom *Re a Company (No 008126 of 1989)* [1992] BCC 542; *Re Little Olympian Each-Ways Ltd (No 3)* [1995] 1 BCLC 636. Relief need not be directed solely towards remedying the particular things that have happened: see *Re Hailey Group Ltd* supra; *Re a Company (No 00789 of 1987), ex p Shooter* [1990] BCLC 384 at 394. As to whether an order might be made where insolvency supervenes between the presentation of the petition and the hearing see *Re Hailey Group Ltd* supra and para 1415 post; and as to the respondents against whom relief might be ordered see para 1412 ante.
4 See *R & H Electric Ltd v Haden Bill Electrical Ltd, Re Haden Bill Electrical Ltd* [1995] 2 BCLC 280, sub nom *R & H Electrical Ltd v Haden Bill Electrical Ltd* [1995] BCC 958 (where the court ordered that the petitioner should cease to be chairman and a director, that his shares be purchased by the majority shareholders and that the company repay as soon as possible loans made to it by the petitioner).
5 See *McGuinness v Bremner plc* [1988] BCLC 673, Ct of Sess (directors delayed in convening meeting; court ordered extraordinary general meeting to be held on set date).
6 The most commonly sought relief is a purchase order, usually requiring the respondents to purchase the shares of the petitioners: see para 1415 post.
7 Companies Act 1985 s 461(2). For the meaning of 'company' where a petition is presented by a member of a company see para 1405 note 2 ante; and for the meaning of 'company' where a petition is presented by the Secretary of State see para 1406 note 2 ante. As to reduction of capital see para 215 ante.
8 See *Re Full Cup International Trading Ltd* [1995] BCC 682 (no relief which would meet the justice of the case and which would be more advantageous than a winding up was capable of being devised); *Re Hailey Group Ltd* [1993] BCLC 459, sub nom *Re a Company (No 008126 of 1989)* [1992] BCC 542 (purchase order refused where company had gone into administrative receivership between presentation and hearing of petition; in the circumstances no substantive relief granted). See also *Re Macro (Ipswich) Ltd* [1994] 2 BCLC 354, [1994] BCC 781 (purchase order made but appointment of additional directors refused as it might exacerbate not resolve the disputes between the parties); *Vujnovich v Vujnovich* [1990] BCLC 227, PC (winding up more appropriate remedy). As to purchase orders see para 1415 post.
9 Companies Act 1985 s 461(3). As to the ordinary power of a company to alter its memorandum or articles see paras 99, 538, 541 ante.
10 Ibid s 461(4).
11 Ibid ss 461(5), 730, Sch 24. For the meaning of 'officer who is in default', 'the statutory maximum' and 'daily default fine' see para 1161 ante.
12 As to such orders see PRACTICE AND PROCEDURE vol 37 para 388 note 5.

13 *Re a Company* [1981] 2 All ER 1007n, sub nom *Re a Company (No 003324 of 1979)* [1981] 1 WLR 1059n (decided under the Companies Act 1948 s 210 (repealed): see para 1405 note 8 ante).

1415. Orders for protection of members against unfair prejudice; purchase of shares. Where, as is often the case, the petition results in an order that the petitioner's shareholding should be bought out by the majority shareholders or by the company, there is no universal rule as to the appropriate method of [1], or date for [2], the calculation of the purchase price. Prima facie, the shares should be valued at the date of the order for purchase [3], but, depending on the circumstances of the case, the valuation may be directed to take place at the date of the presentation of the petition [4] or even at a date before such presentation [5]. The court is concerned that the valuation should be unaffected by any diminution to the company's value caused by the unfair conduct complained of [6]. In determining what is the proper price, there is a wide discretion in the court to do what is fair and equitable in the circumstances [7].

Where the sale is forced upon a blameless petitioner because of the unfairly prejudicial manner in which the affairs of the company have been conducted, the shares having been acquired on the incorporation of a quasi-partnership company, and it being expected that the holder of the shares would participate in the affairs of the company, the price fixed by the order will normally be pro rata to the value of the totality of the shares in question, without any discount to reflect the fact that the shares constitute a minority holding [8].

Where a minority shareholding is acquired as an investment, different considerations apply and the price fixed will normally be discounted to reflect the fact that it is a minority holding [9].

There may be cases in which the petitioner has acted in such a way as to merit, to some extent, the conduct of which he complains. In these cases it would be correct to treat him as if he had elected to sell his shares, and a suitable discount from the pro rata basis would be appropriate [10].

In some circumstances, it may be appropriate for the court to order that the majority shareholder transfer his shares to the petitioner [11]. Where the order is for the purchase by the petitioning shareholder of the shares of the offending majority, it is not normally proper to reflect the value of majority control by the award of a premium [12].

Conditions may be attached to a purchase order [13], but there is no basis for an award of interest upon the purchase price from a date earlier than the date of the order of the court [14]. Where the order is that the petitioner's shares should be bought by the majority shareholder, it is not correct, as a matter of principle, to include an escape clause [15] in the event of the majority shareholder being unable to complete the purchase, as the order represents compensation for wrongs inflicted which should not be affected by the impecuniosity of the majority shareholder [16].

A purchase order made when the company is insolvent is tantamount to a fine but there may be circumstances in which, despite the company's insolvency at the time of the hearing, the court would feel it necessary to impose an obligation to purchase the petitioner's shares [17].

A purchase order may be refused where such relief is inappropriate [18].

1 *Re Bird Precision Bellows Ltd* [1986] Ch 658 at 669, [1985] 3 All ER 523 at 529, CA per Oliver LJ (the merits of the case must determine the terms of the purchase).
2 *Re London School of Electronics Ltd* [1986] Ch 211, [1985] 3 WLR 474.
3 See *Re London School of Electronics Ltd* [1986] Ch 211, [1985] 3 WLR 474; *Re a Company (No 005134 of 1986), ex p Harries* [1989] BCLC 383, sub nom *Re DR Chemicals Ltd* (1989) 5 BCC 39; *Re Elgindata Ltd* [1991] BCLC 959; *Re Ghyll Beck Driving Range Ltd* [1993] BCLC 1126.

4 *Re London School of Electronics Ltd* [1986] Ch 211, [1985] 3 WLR 474 (unfair to value shares at date of judgment); *Re Cumana Ltd* [1986] BCLC 430, CA.

5 See *Re Cumana Ltd* [1986] BCLC 430 at 436, CA (date before petition might be permissible where wrongdoers took steps to depreciate shares in anticipation of presentation of petition); and see *Re a Company (No 002567 of 1982)* [1983] 1 WLR 927 at 937, [1983] BCLC 151 at 162; *Re OC (Transport) Services Ltd* [1984] BCLC 251; *Re London School of Electronics Ltd* [1986] Ch 211, [1985] 3 WLR 474; *R & H Electric Ltd v Haden Bill Electrical Ltd, Re Haden Bill Electrical Ltd* [1995] 2 BCLC 280, sub nom *R & H Electrical Ltd v Haden Bill Electrical Ltd* [1995] BCC 958.

6 *Re Little Olympian Each-Ways Ltd (No 3)* [1995] 1 BCLC 636 at 673. See notes 4, 5 supra. It may be difficult to place a value on the loss suffered by a company or the value the company would have had if the wrongdoing had not occurred: see *Re Macro (Ipswich) Ltd* [1994] 2 BCLC 354 at 409, [1994] BCC 781 at 837; and see *Re Full Cup International Trading Ltd* [1995] BCC 682 at 693. As to the particular difficulties regarding valuation where the company is a football club see *Re a Company (No 00789 of 1987), ex p Shooter* [1990] BCLC 384; *Re a Company (No 00789 of 1987), ex p Shooter (No 2)* [1991] BCLC 267, sub nom *Re Nuneaton Borough AFC Ltd (No 2)* [1991] BCC 44.

7 *Re Bird Precision Bellows Ltd* [1986] Ch 658, [1985] 3 All ER 523, CA (affg [1984] Ch 419, [1984] 3 All ER 444); *Re Elgindata Ltd* [1991] BCLC 959; *Re Little Olympian Each-Ways Ltd (No 3)* [1995] 1 BCLC 636.

8 *Re Bird Precision Bellows Ltd* [1986] Ch 658, [1985] 3 All ER 523, CA (affg [1984] Ch 419, [1984] 3 All ER 444); *Re London School of Electronics Ltd* [1986] Ch 211, [1985] 3 WLR 474; *Re Ghyll Beck Driving Range Ltd* [1993] BCLC 1126. Cf *Re a Company (No 005134 of 1986), ex p Harries* [1989] BCLC 383, sub nom *Re DR Chemicals Ltd* (1989) 5 BCC 39 (pro rata valuation not appropriate where relationship started as a quasi-partnership but subsequently changed to a more commercial footing; discounted basis of valuation appropriate).

9 *Re Elgindata Ltd* [1991] BCLC 959; *Re Bird Precision Bellows Ltd* [1984] Ch 419 at 430, [1984] 3 All ER 444 at 450 per Nourse J (cited in note 7 supra). See also *Re a Company (No 005134 of 1986), ex p Harries* [1989] BCLC 383, sub nom *Re DR Chemicals Ltd* (1989) 5 BCC 39 (cited in note 8 supra).

10 *Re Bird Precision Bellows Ltd* [1984] Ch 419 at 430, 431, [1984] 3 All ER 444 at 450 per Nourse J (cited in note 7 supra).

11 See *Re a Company (No 00789 of 1987), ex p Shooter* [1990] BCLC 384 (majority shareholder had shown himself to be unfit).

12 *Re Bird Precision Bellows Ltd* [1984] Ch 419 at 430, [1984] 3 All ER 444 at 450 per Nourse J (cited in note 7 supra).

13 See *Re a Company (No 00789 of 1987), ex p Shooter* [1990] BCLC 384 (purchaser to repay or procure the repayment to the vendor of sums paid by the vendor to the company).

14 *Re Bird Precision Bellows Ltd* [1986] Ch 658, [1985] 3 All ER 523, CA. See *Ferguson v Maclennan Salmon Co Ltd* [1990] BCC 702 (court can make interim order under the Companies Act 1985 s 461 (see para 1414 ante); where price fixed by share purchase order was to be appealed, payment on account at the lowest valuation likely to be made by the court was ordered and vendor was to transfer shares to nominee pending resolution of appeal).

15 Ie a provision which would enable the court to make some other order if the respondent is unable to raise the money.

16 *Re Cumana Ltd* [1986] BCLC 430, CA.

17 *Re Hailey Group Ltd* [1993] BCLC 459, sub nom *Re a Company (No 008126 of 1989)* [1992] BCC 542. For example, where the unfairly prejudicial conduct had prevented the petitioner from selling his shares at a proper price prior to the onset of insolvency; or where the purchase order was sought at a time when the company was solvent: see *Re Hailey Group Ltd* supra at 473 and at 555 (purchase order refused, having been sought only at eleventh hour).

18 *Re Full Cup International Trading Ltd* [1995] BCC 682 (purchase order unsuitable where on the facts valuation would be an extremely laborious and expensive process; a liquidator would be in a better position to determine value than the court directing accounts and inquiries); *Re Hailey Group Ltd* [1993] BCLC 459, sub nom *Re a Company (No 008126 of 1989)* [1992] BCC 542 (purchase order would not be granted where company had gone into administrative receivership between petition and hearing; no substantive relief granted) (cited in note 17 supra). See also para 1414 text to note 8 ante.

1416. Relationship between unfairly prejudicial provisions and other remedies. The existence of circumstances which would warrant a petition on the unfairly prejudicial ground does not by itself preclude a petitioner from seeking a winding up on the just and equitable ground[1]. It is, however, undesirable to include, as a matter of course, a petition for winding up as an alternative to a petition under the unfairly prejudicial provision[2]. It should be included only if that is the relief which the petitioner prefers or it is considered that it may be the only relief to which he is entitled[3].

It may be, in a particular case, that the facts are inadequate to support a petition on unfairly prejudicial grounds but indicate grounds which would warrant a winding up on the just and equitable ground[4]; alternatively, the facts may be inadequate to support a petition for winding up on the just and equitable ground but indicate arguable grounds for a petition alleging that the company's affairs are being carried on in an unfairly prejudicial manner[5].

The fact that the petitioner could have brought a derivative action with respect to the alleged conduct does not preclude his seeking relief under the unfairly prejudicial provision[6]. Where, however, a majority shareholder could remove from office the directors who are allegedly conducting the company's affairs in a manner unfairly prejudicial to that shareholder's interests, he should not seek the assistance of the court[7].

It is not the case that a petitioner is necessarily acting unreasonably in seeking to have his shares valued pursuant to a court order under the unfairly prejudicial provision rather than relying on a valuation under provisions in the company's articles of association[8].

The mere existence of a petition alleging unfairly prejudicial conduct, although it is a matter which bears upon the discretion of the court, is not an inevitable bar to the statutory power[9] of the court to call a meeting[10].

1   *Re a Company (No 001363 of 1988), ex p S-P* [1989] BCLC 579, (1989) 5 BCC 18. As to winding up on the just and equitable ground see paras 2208, 2209 post. See also para 1414 text to note 8 ante.
2   Ie the Companies Act 1985 s 459 (as amended): see para 1405 ante.
3   *Practice Direction* [1990] 1 All ER 1056, [1990] 1 WLR 490 para 1. If the petitioner fails to petition for winding up and the court ultimately considers that winding up is the only appropriate remedy, the court cannot so order under the Companies Act 1985 s 461 (see para 1414 ante) and it will be necessary to amend the petition to seek winding up: see *Re Full Cup International Trading Ltd* [1995] BCC 682 at 694.
4   *Re RA Noble & Sons (Clothing) Ltd* [1983] BCLC 273 (conduct prejudicial but not unfair therefore no relief possible under the Companies Act 1985 s 459 (as amended) but winding up would be granted since the personal relationship between the parties had been destroyed); *Jesner v Jarrad Properties Ltd* [1993] BCLC 1032, [1992] BCC 807.
5   See *Re a Company (No 00314 of 1989), ex p Estate Acquisition and Development Ltd* [1991] BCLC 154, [1990] BCC 221.
6   *Re a Company (No 005287 of 1985)* [1986] 1 WLR 281, [1986] BCLC 68; *Re Little Olympian Each-Ways Ltd (No 3)* [1995] 1 BCLC 636 at 665; *Lowe v Fahey* [1996] 1 BCLC 262.
7   *Re Baltic Real Estate Ltd (No 2)* [1993] BCLC 503, [1992] BCC 629.
8   *Re a Company (No 00330 of 1991), ex p Holden* [1991] BCLC 597, [1991] BCC 241 (not unreasonable because of the many difficulties in the expert's determination of valuation under the articles), applying *Virdi v Abbey Leisure Ltd* [1990] BCLC 342, sub nom *Re Abbey Leisure Ltd* [1990] BCC 60, CA. There must be questions of fact. In some cases a petitioner may be held to be unreasonable because it can be seen that it would be unreasonable to follow the contractual term; in other cases it will not: *Re a Company (No 00330 of 1991), ex p Holden* supra at 604 and at 247. This approach in effect overrules earlier authorities (see *Re a Company (No 00330 of 1991), ex p Holden* supra at 602, 603 and at 245, 246) which had decided that, when it was plain that the appropriate solution to a breakdown of relations was for the petitioner to sell his shares at a fair price and the articles contained provisions for an independent determination of a fair price, or a fair offer had been made for the shares, the presentation or maintenance of a petition under the Companies Act 1985 s 459 (as amended) would ordinarily be an abuse of process: *Re a Company* [1986] BCLC 362, sub nom *Re a Company (No 007623 of 1984)* (1986) 2 BCC 99, 191; *Re a Company (No 004377 of 1986)* [1987] BCLC 94, sub nom *Re XYZ Ltd* (1986) 2 BCC 99, 520; *Re a Company (No 003843 of 1986)* [1987] BCLC 562, (1987) 3 BCC 624; *Re a Company (No 003096 of 1987)* (1988) 4 BCC 80; *Re a Company (No 006834 of 1988), ex p Kremer* [1989] BCLC 365,

(1989) 5 BCC 218; *Re Boswell & Co (Steels) Ltd (Re a Company No 001567 of 1987)* (1989) 5 BCC 145; *Re Castleburn Ltd* [1991] BCLC 89, (1989) 5 BCC 652. See also *Virdi v Abbey Leisure Ltd* supra at 348, 349 and at 67.

9 Ie under the Companies Act 1985 s 371: see para 661 ante.

10 *Re Whitchurch Insurance Consultants Ltd* [1993] BCLC 1359, [1994] BCC 51; and see *Re Opera Photographic Ltd* [1989] 1 WLR 634, [1989] BCLC 763 (no subsisting petition under the Companies Act 1985 s 459 (as amended)); cf *Re Sticky Fingers Restaurant Ltd* [1992] BCLC 84, [1991] BCC 754 (subsisting petition; meeting ordered by the court but members restrained from removing petitioner from the board pending outcome of the petition).

(30) DISQUALIFICATION ORDERS

(i) Powers and Duty of Court to make Disqualification Order

1417. Disqualification order. A disqualification order against a person is an order that he may not, without leave of the court[1], be a director[2] of a company[3], or be a liquidator or administrator of a company, or be a receiver and manager of a company's property, or in any way, whether directly or indirectly, be concerned or take part in the promotion, formation or management of a company, for a specified period beginning with the date of the order[4].

Where a disqualification order is made against a person who is already subject to such an order, the periods specified in those orders run concurrently[5].

A disqualification order may be made on grounds which are or include matters other than criminal convictions notwithstanding that the person in respect of whom it is to be made may be criminally liable in respect of those matters[6].

The Company Directors Disqualification Act 1986 applies to building societies[7] and to incorporated friendly societies[8] as it applies to companies.

A person who is subject to a disqualification order is disqualified for being a charity trustee or trustee for a charity, except with the leave of the court[9].

Where an insolvent partnership is wound up as an unregistered company, certain of the provisions of the Company Directors Disqualification Act 1986 apply, subject to specified modifications[10].

1 See para 1440 post.

2 For these purposes, 'director' includes any person occupying the position of director, by whatever name called; and in the Company Directors Disqualification Act 1986 s 6 (see para 1425 post), s 7 (see paras 1427, 1428, 1430 post), s 8 (see para 1431 post) and s 9 (see para 1426 post) includes a shadow director: s 22(1),(4). See also *Re Lo-Line Electric Motors Ltd* [1988] Ch 477, [1988] 2 All ER 692 (decided under the Companies Act 1985 s 300 (repealed); person acting as de facto director, although not appointed as director was a 'director' for these purposes). 'Shadow director', in relation to a company, means a person in accordance with whose directions or instructions the directors of a company are accustomed to act, but so that a person is not deemed a shadow director by reason only that the directors act on advice given by him in a professional capacity: Company Directors Disqualification Act 1986 s 22(5). In other contexts it has been held that a company's bank might be a shadow director: *Re a Company (No 005009 of 1987)* (1988) 4 BCC 424. See also *Re Tasbian Ltd (No 3)* [1992] BCC 358, CA (outside investor). As to the distinction between de facto directors and shadow directors, which, it appears, are mutually exclusive classes, see *Re Hydrodan (Corby) Ltd* [1994] BCC 161; cf *Re Moorgate Metals Ltd* [1995] 1 BCLC 503; *Re Richborough Furniture Ltd* [1996] BCC 155.

3 For these purposes, 'company' includes any company which may be wound up under the Insolvency Act 1986 Pt V (ss 220-229 (as amended): see para 2899 et seq post): Company Directors Disqualification Act 1986 s 22(1),(2)(b).

4 Ibid s 1(1). The words 'be concerned in' should not be narrowly construed to mean 'take part in': *R v Campbell* [1984] BCLC 83, CA (decided under the Companies Act 1948 s 188(1) (repealed) where the meaning of 'be concerned or take part in' was considered). For the meaning of 'management' see *Re Clasper Group Services Ltd* (1988) 4 BCC 673 (decided under the Insolvency Act 1986 s 212(1)(c): see para 2448 post); *CCA v Brecht* (1989) 7 ACLC 40.

In each section of the Company Directors Disqualification Act 1986 which gives to a court power or, as the case may be, imposes on it the duty to make a disqualification order there is specified the maximum, and, in s 6 (see para 1425 post), the minimum, period of disqualification which may or, as the case may be, must be imposed by means of the order: s 1(2).

Any reference in the Company Directors Disqualification Act 1986 to provisions, or a particular provision, of the Companies Acts or the Insolvency Act 1986 includes the corresponding provisions or provision of the former Companies Acts including the Companies Act 1985, or, as the case may be, the Insolvency Act 1985; and any expression for whose interpretation provision is made by the Companies Act 1985 Pt XXVI (ss 735-744) (as amended) and not by the Company Directors Disqualification Act 1986 s 22(1)-(8) is to be construed in accordance with that provision: s 22(8),(9). For the meaning of 'the Companies Acts' see para 60 note 1 ante; and for the meaning of 'the former Companies Acts' see para 11 note 2 ante.

The Company Directors Disqualification Act 1986 ss 6-10 (see paras 1422, 1423, 1425-1428, 1430, 1431 post), s 15 (see para 1445 post), s 19(c) (see paras 1425, 1431 post), s 20 (see para 1446 post), Sch 1 (see para 1426 post) are deemed included in the Insolvency Act 1986 Pts I-VII (ss 1-251) (as amended) for the purposes of s 411 (power to make insolvency rules: see para 2800 post), s 414 (as amended) (fees orders: see para 2866 post), s 420 (orders extending provisions about insolvent companies to insolvent partnerships: see para 2916 post), s 422 (as amended) (modification of such provisions in their application to authorised institutions: see para 2312 post), and s 431 (summary proceedings: see para 2686 post): Company Directors Disqualification Act 1986 s 21(2).

5 Ibid s 1(3).

6 Ibid s 1(4). It is wrong in principle to make a compensation order against a person for fraudulent trading at the same time as to make a disqualification order: *R v Holmes* [1991] BCC 394.

7 Company Directors Disqualification Act 1986 s 22A(1) (added by the Companies Act 1989 s 211(3)). References in the Company Directors Disqualification Act 1986 to a company, or to a director or an officer of a company include, respectively, references to a building society within the meaning of the Building Societies Act 1986 (see BUILDING SOCIETIES vol 4(2) (Reissue) para 701) or to a director or officer, within the meaning of that Act (see BUILDING SOCIETIES vol 4(2) (Reissue) para 713 note 2), of a building society: Company Directors Disqualification Act 1986 s 22A(2) (added by the Companies Act 1989 s 211(3)). In relation to a building society the definition of 'shadow director' in the Company Directors Disqualification Act 1986 s 22(5) applies with the substitution of 'building society' for 'company': s 22A(3) (added by the Companies Act 1989 s 211(3)). In the application of the Company Directors Disqualification Act 1986 Sch 1 (as amended) (see para 1426 post) to the directors of a building society, references to provisions of the Insolvency Act 1986 or the Companies Act 1985 include references to the corresponding provisions of the Building Societies Act 1986: Company Directors Disqualification Act 1986 s 22A(4) (added by the Companies Act 1989 s 211(3)).

8 Company Directors Disqualification Act 1986 s 22B(1) (added by the Friendly Societies Act 1992 s 120(1), Sch 21 Pt I para 8). References in the Company Directors Disqualification Act 1986 to a company, or to a director or an officer of a company include, respectively, references to an incorporated friendly society within the meaning of the Friendly Societies Act 1992 (see FRIENDLY SOCIETIES vol 19(1) (Reissue) para 102) or to a member of the committee of management or officer, within the meaning of that Act (see FRIENDLY SOCIETIES vol 19(1) (Reissue) para 143 note 10), of an incorporated friendly society: Company Directors Disqualification Act 1986 s 22B(2) (added by the Friendly Societies Act 1992 Sch 21 Pt I para 8). In relation to an incorporated friendly society every reference to a shadow director must be omitted: Company Directors Disqualification Act 1986 s 22B(3) (added by the Friendly Societies Act 1992 Sch 21 Pt I para 8). In the application of the Company Directors Disqualification Act 1986 Sch 1 (as amended) (see para 1426 post) to the members of the committee of management of an incorporated friendly society, references to provisions of the Insolvency Act 1986 or the Companies Act 1985 include references to the corresponding provisions of the Friendly Societies Act 1992: Company Directors Disqualification Act 1986 s 22A(4) (added by the Friendly Societies Act 1992 Sch 21 Pt I para 8).

9 See the Charities Act 1993 s 72(1)(f),(3)(a) and CHARITIES vol 5(2) (Reissue) para 245.

10 See para 2929 post.

1418. Disqualification on conviction of indictable offence. The court[1] may make a disqualification order[2] against a person where he is convicted of an indictable offence, whether on indictment or summarily, in connection with the promotion, formation, management, liquidation or striking off of a company[3], or with the receivership or management of a company's property[4].

The maximum period of disqualification which may be imposed under these provisions is, where the disqualification order is made by a court of summary jurisdiction, five years, and in any other case, 15 years[5].

1 For these purposes, 'the court' means (1) any court having jurisdiction to wind up the company in relation to which the offence was committed; or (2) the court by or before which the person is convicted of the offence; or (3) in the case of a summary conviction in England and Wales, any other magistrates' court acting for the same petty sessions area: Company Directors Disqualification Act 1986 s 2(2).

2 See para 1417 ante.

3 For the meaning of 'company' see para 1417 note 3 ante.

4 Company Directors Disqualification Act 1986 s 2(1) (amended by the Deregulation and Contracting Out Act 1994 s 39, Sch 11 para 6). See *R v Georgiou* (1988) 4 BCC 322, CA; *R v Goodman* [1993] 2 All ER 789, [1994] 1 BCLC 349, CA (defendant convicted of insider dealing; the correct test to be applied was held to be whether the offence had some relevant factual connection with the management of the company).

5 Company Directors Disqualification Act 1986 s 2(3). Section 2 (as amended) does not apply in relation to anything done before 15 June 1982 by a person in his capacity as liquidator of a company or as receiver or manager of a company's property: s 19(a), Sch 2 para 1. Subject to this qualification, s 2 (as amended) applies in a case where a person is convicted on indictment of an offence which he committed (and, in the case of a continuing offence, had ceased to commit) before 15 June 1982; but in such a case a disqualification order under s 2 (as amended) cannot be made for a period in excess of five years: Sch 2 para 2(a). Section 2 (as amended) does not apply in a case where a person was convicted summarily in England and Wales if he had consented so to be tried before that date: Sch 2 para 2(b)(i). The significance of 15 June 1982 is that this was the date when the statutory predecessor of these provisions, the Companies Act 1981 s 93 (repealed), came into force: s 93(1),(1C) (repealed); Companies Act 1981 (Commencement No 4) Order 1982, SI 1982/672.

1419. Disqualification for persistent breaches of companies legislation. The court[1] may make a disqualification order[2] against a person where it appears to it that he has been persistently in default in relation to provisions of the companies legislation[3] requiring any return, account or other document to be filed with, delivered or sent, or notice of any matter to be given, to the registrar of companies[4].

On an application[5] to the court for such an order to be made, the fact that a person has been persistently in default in relation to such provisions as are mentioned above may, without prejudice to its proof in any other manner, be conclusively proved by showing that in the five years ending with the date of the application he has been adjudged guilty[6], whether or not on the same occasion, of three or more defaults in relation to those provisions[7].

The maximum period of disqualification which may be imposed under these provisions is five years[8].

1 For these purposes, 'the court' means any court having jurisdiction to wind up any of the companies in relation to which the offence or other default has been or is alleged to have been committed: Company Directors Disqualification Act 1986 s 3(4).

2 See para 1417 ante.

3 For these purposes, 'the companies legislation' means the Companies Act 1985, the Companies Consolidation (Consequential Provisions) Act 1985, the Insolvency Act 1986 Pts I–VII (ss 1–251) (as

amended) and, in Pt XV, ss 411, 413, 414 (as amended), 416, 417: Company Directors Disqualification Act 1986 s 22(1),(7); Companies Act 1985 s 744.

4 Company Directors Disqualification Act 1986 s 3(1). For these purposes, no account is to be taken of any offence which was committed, or any default order which was made, before 1 June 1977 (ie the date on which the Companies Act 1976 s 28 (repealed) came into force): Company Directors Disqualification Act 1986 s 19(b), Sch 2 para 5.

5 See further para 1432 et seq post.

6 A person is to be treated under the Company Directors Disqualification Act 1986 s 3(2) as being adjudged guilty of a default in relation to any provision of that legislation if (1) he is convicted, whether on indictment or summarily, of an offence consisting of a contravention of or failure to comply with that provision, whether on his own part or on the part of any company; or (2) a default order is made against him under certain provisions (see infra) in respect of any such contravention of or failure to comply with that provision, whether on his own part or on the part of any company: s 3(3) (amended by the Companies Act 1989 s 23, Sch 10 para 35(1),(2)(a),(b)). For these purposes a default order is an order under any of the following provisions: (a) the Companies Act 1985 s 242(4) (as substituted) (sic) (order requiring delivery of company accounts: see para 818 ante); (b) s 245B (as added) (order requiring preparation of revised accounts: see para 953 ante); (c) s 713 (as amended) (enforcement of company's duty to make returns: see para 69 ante); (d) the Insolvency Act 1986 s 41 (enforcement of receiver's or manager's duty to make returns: see para 1333 ante); (e) s 170 (enforcement of liquidator's duty to make returns: see para 2330 post): Company Directors Disqualification Act 1986 s 3(3) (as so amended).

7 Ibid s 3(2). An order made under the Companies Act 1976 s 28 (repealed) has effect as if made under the Company Directors Disqualification Act 1986 s 3 (as amended); and an application made before 15 June 1982 (see para 1418 note 5 ante) for such an order is to be treated as an application for an order under the Company Directors Disqualification Act 1986 s 3 (as amended): Sch 2 para 6. Under the Companies Act 1948 s 188 (repealed) it was not necessary to show that a person had been culpable, in the sense of evincing a deliberate disregard of the relevant provisions, in order to prove that he had been 'persistently in default'; but culpability could be taken into account in considering whether or not to disqualify and for how long: *Re Arctic Engineering Ltd (No 2)* [1986] 2 All ER 346, [1986] 1 WLR 686.

8 Company Directors Disqualification Act 1986 s 3(5).

1420. Disqualification for fraud etc in a winding up. The court[1] may make a disqualification order[2] against a person if, in the course of the winding up of a company, it appears that he:

(1) has been guilty of an offence for which he is liable, whether he has been convicted or not, under the fraudulent trading provisions[3]; or

(2) has otherwise been guilty, while an officer[4] or liquidator of the company or receiver or manager of its property, of any fraud in relation to the company or of any breach of his duty as such officer, liquidator, receiver or manager[5].

The maximum period of disqualification which may be imposed under these provisions is 15 years[6].

1 For these purposes, 'the court' means any court having jurisdiction to wind up the company in relation to which the offence or other default has been or is alleged to have been committed: Company Directors Disqualification Act 1986 s 4(2).

2 See para 1417 ante.

3 Company Directors Disqualification Act 1986 s 4(1)(a). The provisions referred to are the Companies Act 1985 s 458 (see para 1160 ante and para 2672 post) or the corresponding provisions of the former Companies Acts: Company Directors Disqualification Act 1986 s 22(8). For the meaning of 'the former Companies Acts' see para 11 note 2 ante.

4 For these purposes, 'officer' includes a shadow director: Company Directors Disqualification Act 1986 s 4(2). For the meaning of 'shadow director' see para 1417 note 2 ante. 'Officer' has the meaning given by the Companies Act 1985 s 744 (see para 641 ante): Company Directors Disqualification Act 1986 s 22(6).

5 Ibid s 4(1)(b). Section 4(1)(b) does not, however, apply in relation to anything done before 15 June 1982 (see para 1418 note 5 ante) by a person in his capacity as liquidator of a company or as receiver or manager of a company's property: s 19(a), Sch 2 para 1. Subject to this qualification, s 4 applies in

relation to an offence committed or other thing done before 15 June 1982; but a disqualification order made on the grounds of such an offence or other thing done must not be made for a period in excess of 5 years: Sch 2 para 3.

6 Ibid s 4(3). See also note 5 supra.

1421. Disqualification on summary conviction. Where a person is convicted of a summary offence[1], being for these purposes an offence of which a person is convicted, either on indictment or summarily, in consequence of a contravention of, or failure to comply with, any provision of the companies legislation[2] requiring a return, account or other document to be filed with, delivered or sent, or notice of any matter to be given, to the registrar of companies, whether the contravention or failure is on the person's own part or on the part of any company[3], the court by which he is convicted, or, in England or Wales, any other magistrates' court acting for the same petty sessions area, may make a disqualification order[4] against him if, during the five years ending with the date of the conviction, the person has had made against him, or has been convicted of, in total not less than three default orders[5] and offences counting for the purposes of these provisions[6].

The maximum period of disqualification which may be imposed under these provisions is five years[7].

1 For these purposes, the definition of 'summary offence' in the Interpretation Act 1978 s 5, Sch 1 (see STATUTES vol 44(1) (Reissue) para 1386) applies: Company Directors Disqualification Act 1986 s 5(4)(a).
2 For the meaning of 'the companies legislation' for these purposes see para 1419 note 3 ante.
3 Company Directors Disqualification Act 1986 s 5(1).
4 See para 1417 ante.
5 For these purposes, 'default order' means the same as in the Company Directors Disqualification Act 1986 s 3(3)(b) (see para 1419 note 6 head (2) ante): s 5(4)(b).
6 Ibid s 5(2),(3). The offences counting for the purposes of these provisions may include that of which he is convicted as mentioned in s 5(2) and any other offence of which he is convicted on the same occasion: s 5(3).
7 Ibid s 5(5). The powers of a court under s 5 are not exercisable in a case where a person is convicted of an offence which he committed, and, in the case of a continuing offence, had ceased to commit, before 15 June 1982 (see para 1418 note 5 ante): s 19(a), Sch 2 para 4. For the purposes of s 5, no account is to be taken of any offence which was committed, or any default order which was made, before 1 June 1977 (see para 1419 note 4 ante): s 19(b), Sch 2 para 5.

1422. Disqualification for participation in fraudulent or wrongful trading. Where the court makes a declaration under the fraudulent trading provisions[1] or the wrongful trading provisions[2] that a person is liable to make a contribution to a company's assets, then, whether or not an application for such an order is made by any person, the court may, if it thinks fit, also make a disqualification order against the person to whom the declaration relates[3].

The maximum period of disqualification which may be imposed under these provisions is 15 years[4].

1 Ie the Insolvency Act 1986 s 213: see para 2670 post.
2 Ie ibid s 214: see para 2673 post.
3 Company Directors Disqualification Act 1986 s 10(1).
4 Ibid s 10(2).

1423. Undischarged bankrupts. If a person, being an undischarged bankrupt[1], acts as director[2] of, or directly or indirectly takes part in or is concerned in the promotion, formation or management of, a company[3], except with the leave of the court[4], he is liable on conviction on indictment to imprisonment for a term not exceeding two years or a fine, or to both, or on summary conviction to imprisonment for a term not exceeding six months or a fine not exceeding the statutory maximum, or to both[5]. The offence is one of strict liability[6].

A person who acts in contravention of these provisions is also personally responsible for all the relevant debts of the company incurred whilst he was involved in its management[7].

In England and Wales, the leave of the court may not be given unless notice of intention to apply for it has been served on the official receiver[8]; and it is the latter's duty, if he is of opinion that it is contrary to the public interest that the application should be granted, to attend on the hearing of the application and oppose it[9].

1   See BANKRUPTCY.
2   For the meaning of 'director' see para 1417 note 2 ante.
3   For these purposes, 'company' includes an unregistered company or a company incorporated outside Great Britain which has an established place of business in Great Britain: Company Directors Disqualification Act 1986 s 22(1),(2)(a).
4   For these purposes, 'the court' is the court by which the person was adjudged bankrupt: ibid s 11(2).
5   Ibid ss 11(1), 13. For the meaning of 'the statutory maximum' see para 1161 ante.
6   *R v Brockley* [1994] 1 BCLC 606, CA.
7   See the Company Directors Disqualification Act 1986 s 15(1)(a) and para 1445 post.
8   References in the Company Directors Disqualification Act 1986 to the official receiver, in relation to the winding up of a company or the bankruptcy of an individual, are to any person who, by virtue of the Insolvency Act 1986 s 399 (see para 2263 post), is authorised to act as the official receiver in relation to that winding up or bankruptcy; and, in accordance with s 401(2) (see para 2267 post), references in the Company Directors Disqualification Act 1986 to an official receiver include a person appointed as his deputy: s 21(1).
9   Ibid s 11(3). As to the exercise of the discretion to grant leave to be a director under s 11 see *Re McQuillan* (1989) 5 BCC 137 (NI CA).

1424. Failure to pay under county court administration order. Where a court[1] revokes an administration order[2] against an individual, it may order that that person may not, except with the leave of the court which made the order, act as director or liquidator of, or directly or indirectly take part or be concerned in the promotion, formation or management of, a company[3], for such period not exceeding two years as may be specified in the order[4].

If a person acts in contravention of this provision, he is liable on conviction on indictment to imprisonment for a term not exceeding two years or a fine, or to both, or on summary conviction to imprisonment for a term not exceeding six months or a fine not exceeding the statutory maximum, or to both[5].

1   Ie under the Insolvency Act 1986 s 429: see BANKRUPTCY vol 3(2) (Reissue) para 877.
2   Ie under the County Courts Act 1984 Pt VI (ss 112–117): see BANKRUPTCY vol 3(2) (Reissue) 863 et seq.
3   For the meaning of 'company' see para 1417 note 3 ante.
4   Company Directors Disqualification Act 1986 s 12; Insolvency Act 1986 s 429(2).
5   Company Directors Disqualification Act 1986 s 13; Insolvency Act 1986 ss 429(5), 430, Sch 10. For the meaning of 'the statutory maximum' see para 1161 ante.

1425. Duty of court to disqualify unfit directors of insolvent companies. The court[1] must make a disqualification order[2] against a person in any case where, on an application for this purpose[3], the court is satisfied:

(1) that he is or has been a director[4] of a company which has at any time become insolvent[5], whether while he was a director or subsequently[6]; and

(2) that his conduct as a director[7] of that company, either taken alone or taken together with his conduct as a director of any other company or other companies[8], makes him unfit[9] to be concerned in the management of a company[10].

The minimum period of disqualification which may be imposed under these provisions is two years, and the maximum period which may be imposed is 15 years[11].

The above provisions apply both to foreigners outside the jurisdiction and to conduct which occurred outside the jurisdiction[12].

1 For these purposes, and for the purposes of the Company Directors Disqualification Act 1986 s 7 (see paras 1427, 1428, 1430 post), 'the court' means (1) in the case of a person who is or has been a director of a company which is being wound up by the court, the court by which the company is being wound up; (2) in the case of a person who is or has been a director of a company which is being wound up voluntarily, any court having jurisdiction to wind up the company; (3) in the case of a person who is or has been a director of a company in relation to which an administration order is in force, the court by which that order was made; and (4) in any other case, the High Court: s 6(3). For the meaning of 'director' see note 4 infra. The court continues to have jurisdiction to hear disqualification proceedings even after winding up is concluded: *Re The Working Project Ltd, Re Fosterdown Ltd, Re Davies Flooring (Southern) Ltd* [1995] 1 BCLC 226.

2 See para 1417 ante.

3 As to the mode of application and the procedure see para 1431 et seq post.

4 For these purposes, and for the purposes of the Company Directors Disqualification Act 1986 s 7 (see paras 1427, 1428, 1430 post), 'director' includes a shadow director: s 6(3). For the meaning of 'director' and 'shadow director' see para 1417 note 2 ante.

5 For these purposes, and for the purposes of ibid s 7 (see paras 1427, 1428, 1430 post), a company becomes insolvent if (1) the company goes into liquidation at a time when its assets are insufficient for the payment of its debts and other liabilities and the expenses of the winding up; (2) an administration order is made in relation to the company; or (3) an administrative receiver of the company is appointed: s 6(2).

Where an application is made for a disqualification order under s 6 by virtue of s 6(2)(a) (see text head (1) supra), and the company in question went into liquidation before 28 April 1986 (the coming into force of the provision replaced by s 6: see the Insolvency Act 1985 s 235, Sch 9 Pt II para 2; the Insolvency Act 1985 (Commencement No 3) Order 1986, SI 1986/463), the court may not make an order under the Company Directors Disqualification Act 1986 s 6 unless it could have made a disqualification order under the Companies Act 1985 s 300 (repealed) as it had effect immediately before 28 April 1986: Company Directors Disqualification Act 1986 s 19(c), Sch 2 para 7. The Insolvency Act 1986 s 247 applies as regards references to a company's insolvency and to its going into liquidation (see para 2008 note 3 post): Company Directors Disqualification Act 1986 s 22(3).

A company which has entered compulsory liquidation becomes insolvent for these purposes when the winding-up order is made and not when the winding-up petition is presented: *Re Walter L Jacob & Co Ltd, Official Receiver v Jacob* [1993] BCC 512. Where a petition for an administration order has been presented against a company, and an interim order has been made under the Insolvency Act 1986 s 9(4) (see para 2088 post), followed later by an administration order, the relevant date is the date of the latter order and not the interim order: *Secretary of State for Trade and Industry v Palmer* [1993] BCC 650, Ct of Sess. Where the company 'became insolvent' by reason of more than one of the triggering events, namely liquidation, administration, or administrative receivership, the time ran from the first of those events; but, where a company has returned to solvency after one of the triggering events, and then returns to insolvency and a further triggering event occurs, then the two-year period may start to run again from the second triggering event: *Re Tasbian Ltd* [1990] BCC 318, CA.

6 Company Directors Disqualification Act 1986 s 6(1)(a).

7 For these purposes, references to a person's conduct as a director of any company or companies include, where that company or any of those companies has become insolvent, that person's conduct in relation to any matter connected with or arising out of the insolvency of that company: ibid s 6(2).

8 See *Re Bath Glass Ltd* (1988) 4 BCC 130. The conduct of a director whilst director of a foreign company may be taken into account: *Re Eurostem Maritime Ltd* [1987] PCC 190. The word 'companies' is not limited to companies of limited liability: *Re Polly Peck International plc, Secretary of State for Trade and Industry v Ellis (No 2)* [1993] BCC 890 at 895.

9 As to the matters to be taken into account for determining unfitness of directors see para 1426 post.

10 Company Directors Disqualification Act 1986 s 6(1)(b). Despite the use of the word 'makes' in the present tense in s 6(1)(b), the question which the court must ask itself is not whether the director is presently unfit to be a director, but whether the relevant conduct specified in s 6(1)(b) alone has fallen below the standards of probity and competence appropriate for persons to be directors of companies; the court does not need to be satisfied that a disqualification order is necessary in the public interest; evidence tending to show that the director is unlikely to re-offend is relevant to mitigation and any application for leave under s 17 (see para 1440 post) only: *Secretary of State for Trade and Industry v Gray* [1995] 1 BCLC 276, CA.

11 Company Directors Disqualification Act 1986 s 6(4).

12 *Re Seagull Manufacturing Co Ltd (No 2)* [1994] 1 BCLC 273.

1426. Matters for determining unfitness of directors. Where it falls to a court to determine whether a person's conduct as a director[1] or shadow director[2] of any particular company or companies makes him unfit to be concerned in the management of a company, the court must, as respects his conduct as a director of that company or, as the case may be, each of those companies, have regard in particular to the following matters[3].

In all cases the court must have regard to:

(1) any misfeasance or breach of fiduciary or other duty by the director in relation to the company[4];

(2) any misapplication or retention by the director of, or any conduct by the director giving rise to an obligation to account for, any money or other property of the company[5];

(3) the extent of the director's responsibility for the company entering into any transaction liable to be set aside under the provisions against debt avoidance[6];

(4) the extent of the director's responsibility for any failure by the company to comply with any of the provisions relating to:

    (a) the company's duty to keep accounting records[7];

    (b) where and for how long records are to be kept[8];

    (c) the register of directors and secretaries[9];

    (d) the obligation to keep and enter up the register of members[10];

    (e) the location of the register of members[11];

    (f) the company's duty to make annual returns[12];

    (g) the company's duty to register charges it creates[13];

(5) the extent of the director's responsibility for any failure by the directors of the company to comply with the provisions relating to the preparation of annual accounts[14] or the approval and signature[15] of the accounts[16].

In addition, where the company has become insolvent[17], the court must also have regard to:

(i) the extent of the director's responsibility for the causes of the company becoming insolvent;

(ii) the extent of the director's responsibility for any failure by the company to supply any goods or services which have been paid for, in whole or in part;

(iii) the extent of the director's responsibility for the company entering into any transaction or giving any preference which is liable to be set aside[18];

(iv) the extent of the director's responsibility for any failure by the directors of the company to comply with the provisions relating to the duty to call creditors' meetings in a creditors' voluntary winding up[19];

(v) any failure by the director to comply with any obligation imposed on him by or under the provisions relating to:

(A) the company's statement of affairs where an administration order has been made[20];

(B) the statement of affairs where an administrative receiver has been appointed[21];

(C) the directors' duty to attend meetings and in respect of the statement of affairs in a creditors' voluntary winding up[22];

(D) the statement of affairs in a winding up by the court[23];

(E) the duty of anyone with company property to deliver it up[24]; and

(F) the duty[25] to co-operate with the office-holders[26].

1   For the meaning of 'director' see para 1417 note 2 ante.

2   For the meaning of 'shadow director' see para 1417 note 2 ante.

3   Company Directors Disqualification Act 1986 s 9(1)(a), Sch 1 Pt I. The Secretary of State may by order modify any of the provisions of Sch 1; and such an order may contain such transitional provisions as may appear to the Secretary of State necessary or expedient: s 9(4). The power to make such orders is exercisable by statutory instrument which is subject to annulment in pursuance of a resolution of either House of Parliament: s 9(5). Subject to such powers of modification, the references in Sch 1 to an enactment contained in the Companies Act 1985 or the Insolvency Act 1986 includes, in relation to any time before the coming into force of the enactment, the corresponding enactment in force at that time: Company Directors Disqualification Act 1986 s 9(3).

To reach a finding of unfitness the court must be satisfied that the director has been guilty of a serious failure or serious failures, whether deliberately or through incompetence, to perform those duties of a director which are attendant on the privilege of trading through companies with limited liability; any conduct of the director, whether as a director of the insolvent company or of that company or of other companies, may be relevant even if it does not fall within a specific section of company legislation: see *Re Bath Glass Ltd* (1988) 4 BCC 130 at 133 per Peter Gibson J. Ordinary commercial misjudgment is not in itself sufficient to justify disqualification, and in the normal case the evidence must show a lack of commercial probity; but disqualification will be appropriate where the evidence shows an extreme case of gross negligence or extreme incompetence: see *Re Lo-Line Electric Motors Ltd* [1988] Ch 477 at 486, [1988] 2 All ER 692 at 696.

In *Re Sevenoaks Stationers (Retail) Ltd* [1991] Ch 164 at 174, [1991] 3 All ER 578 at 581, CA Dillon LJ divided the possible periods of disqualification under the Company Directors Disqualification Act 1986 s 6 into three brackets: (1) the top bracket of disqualification for periods of 10-15 years, to be reserved for particularly serious cases, such as where a director had previously been disqualified; (2) the middle bracket of 6-10 years, to be reserved for serious cases which did not merit the top bracket; and (3) the bottom bracket of 2-5 years, where, although disqualification was mandatory, the conduct complained of was relatively not very serious. *Practice Note* [1996] 1 All ER 445; sub nom *Practice Direction* [1996] 1 WLR 170 para 15(b) appears to have adopted this bracketing: see para 2890 post.

Normally the application will include more than one complaint of misconduct. The types of misconduct, and cases where such misconduct has been discussed are numerous but include the following:

(a) failure to keep adequate accounting records or file returns (*Re Bath Glass Ltd* supra; *Re Rolus Properties Ltd* (1988) 4 BCC 446; *Re Chartmore Ltd* [1990] BCLC 673; *Re Pamstock Ltd* [1994] 1 BCLC 716; *Re Firedart Ltd, Official Receiver v Fairall* [1994] 2 BCLC 340; *Re Richborough Furniture Ltd* [1996] BCC 155);

(b) trading with 'phoenix' companies (*Re Swift 736 Ltd, Secretary of State for Trade and Industry v Ettinger* [1993] BCC 312, CA; *Re Douglas Construction Services Ltd* (1988) 4 BCC 553; *Re Lo-Line Electrical Motors Ltd* supra; *Re McNulty's Interchange Ltd* (1988) 4 BCC 533; *Re Ipcon Fashions Ltd* (1989) 5 BCC 773; *Re Keypak Homecare Ltd (No 2)* [1990] BCC 117; *Re Linvale Ltd* [1993] BCLC 654);

(c) continuing to draw remuneration whilst insolvent and drawing excessive remuneration (*Re Stanford Services Ltd* (1987) 3 BCC 326; *Re McNulty's Interchange Ltd* supra; *Re Ipcon Fashions Ltd* supra; *Re Cargo Agency Ltd* [1992] BCC 388; *Re Keypak Homecare Ltd (No 2)* supra; *Re ECM (Europe) Electronics Ltd* [1991] BCC 268; *Re Travel Mondial (UK) Ltd* [1991] BCC 224);

(d) inadequate capitalisation of a company (*Re Pamstock Ltd* supra; *Re Chartmore Ltd* supra; *Re Austinsuite Furniture Ltd* [1992] BCLC 1047);

(e) preferences and other breaches of duty (*Re Living Images Ltd* [1996] BCC 112 (diversion of corporate opportunities); *Secretary of State for Trade and Industry v Gray* [1995] 1 BCLC 276, CA; *Re Austinsuite Furniture Ltd* supra; *Re Godwin Warren Control Systems plc* [1992] BCC 557 (deception of company officers);

(f) trading with no reasonable prospect of paying creditors (*Re Living Images Ltd* supra; *Re Synthetic Technology Ltd, Secretary of State for Trade and Industry v Joiner* [1993] BCC 549; *Re Richborough Furniture Ltd* supra);

(g) trading at the expense of the Crown (*Re Dawson Print Group Ltd* (1987) 3 BCC 322; *Re Stanford Services Ltd* supra; *Re Lo-Line Electrical Motors Ltd* supra; *Re Sevenoaks Stationers (Retail) Ltd* supra; *Re Swift 736 Ltd, Secretary of State for Trade and Industry v Ettinger* supra);

(h) failure to co-operate with the official receiver (*Re Tansoft Ltd* [1991] BCLC 339).

4 See paras 582 ante and para 2448 et seq ante.
5 See para 582 et seq ante.
6 Ie the Insolvency Act 1986 Pt XVI (ss 423-425): see para 2612 et seq post.
7 Ie the Companies Act 1985 s 221 (as substituted): see para 801 ante.
8 Ie ibid s 222 (as substituted): see para 802 ante.
9 Ie ibid s 288 (as amended): see para 560 ante.
10 Ie ibid s 352: see para 379 ante.
11 Ie ibid s 353: see para 389 ante.
12 Ie ibid s 363 (as substituted): see para 1062 ante.
13 Ie ibid ss 399, 415: see para 1308 ante.
14 Ie ibid s 226 (as substituted) or s 227 (as substituted): see para 816 ante.
15 Ie ibid s 233 (as substituted): see para 937 ante.
16 Company Directors Disqualification Act 1986 Sch 1 Pt I (amended by the Companies Act 1989 ss 23, 139(4), Sch 10 para 35(1),(3)).
17 For these purposes, the Company Directors Disqualification Act 1986 s 6(2) (meaning of a company 'becoming insolvent': see para 1425 note 5 ante) applies as it applies for the purposes of s 6 and s 7: s 9(2).
18 Ie being a transaction or preference liable to be set aside under the Insolvency Act 1986 s 127 (see para 2460 post or ss 238-240 (see paras 2102, 2602 et seq post).
19 Ie ibid s 98: see para 2704 post.
20 Ie ibid s 22: see para 2103 post.
21 Ie ibid s 47: see para 2161 post.
22 Ie ibid s 99: see para 2706 post.
23 Ie ibid s 131: see para 2279 et seq post.
24 Ie ibid s 234: see para 2435 post.
25 Ie under ibid s 235: see para 2438 post.
26 Company Directors Disqualification Act 1986 s 9(1)(b), Sch 1 Pt II.

1427. Application by the Secretary of State. If it appears to the Secretary of State that it is expedient in the public interest that a disqualification order[1] should be made against any person, an application for the making of such an order against that person may be made by the Secretary of State or, if the Secretary of State so directs in the case of a person who is or has been a director[2] of a company which is being wound up by the court in England and Wales, by the official receiver[3].

Except with the leave of the court[4], such an application for the making of a disqualification order against any person may not be made after the end of the period of two years beginning with the day on which the company of which that person is or has been a director became insolvent[5].

If the proceedings are prosecuted in a dilatory manner, the proceedings may be struck out for want of prosecution[6].

1 Ie under the Company Directors Disqualification Act 1986 s 6: see para 1425 ante.
2 For the meaning of 'director' for these purposes see ibid s 6(3) and para 1425 note 4 ante.
3 Ibid s 7(1). For the meaning of 'the official receiver' see para 1423 note 8 ante. Where the company is not yet being wound up by the court, the Secretary of State may still direct the official receiver to bring proceedings pursuant to the powers in the Insolvency Act 1986 s 400 (see para 2264 post); but in such circumstances the proceedings must still be brought in the name of the Secretary of State, not the official receiver: *Re Probe Data Systems Ltd* (1989) 5 BCC 384; *Re NP Engineering and Security Products Ltd* [1995] 2 BCLC 585.
4 For the meaning of 'the court' for these purposes see the Company Directors Disqualification Act 1986 s 6(3) and para 1425 note 1 ante.

5 Ibid s 7(2). For the meaning of a company 'becoming insolvent' for these purposes see s 6(2) and para 1425 note 5 ante. Where an application is made under s 7(2) to bring proceedings out of time, the test is whether the Secretary of State or the official receiver has shown a good reason for the extension of time: *Re Crestjoy Products Ltd* [1990] BCC 23; *Secretary of State for Trade and Industry v McTighe, Re Copecrest Ltd* [1994] 2 BCLC 284, CA. The length of the delay, the reasons for the delay, the strength of the case against the director and the degree of prejudice caused by the delay are relevant factors to be taken into account by the court in determining whether to grant leave: *Re Probe Data Systems Ltd (No 3), Secretary of State for Trade and Industry v Desai* [1992] BCC 110 at 118; *Secretary of State for Trade and Industry v McTighe, Re Copecrest Ltd* supra. The list of factors is not exclusive of all other matters but in most cases it is likely to be so: *Re Polly Peck International plc, Secretary of State for Trade and Industry v Ellis (No 2)* [1993] BCC 890 at 894. Where it is sought to bring proceedings against a director of a company not originally joined as respondent, the correct procedure is to issue an originating summons separate from the existing proceedings seeking leave to issue proceedings out of time: *Re Westmid Packaging Services Ltd* [1995] BCC 203.

6 *Re Noble Trees Ltd* [1993] BCLC 1185; *Official Receiver v B Ltd* [1994] 2 BCLC 1; *Re Manlon Trading Ltd* [1995] 3 WLR 839, [1995] 1 BCLC 578, CA.

(ii) Procedure; Reports

1428. Reports to the Secretary of State. If it appears to the official receiver[1], the liquidator[2], the administrator[3], or the administrative receiver[4], that the conditions which impose a duty on the court to make a disqualification order[5] are satisfied as respects a person who is or has been a director[6] of the company in question, the official receiver, the liquidator, the administrator or, as the case may be, the administrative receiver, must forthwith report the matter to the Secretary of State[7].

1 Ie in the case of a company which is being wound up by the court in England and Wales. For the meaning of 'the official receiver' see para 1423 note 8 ante.

2 Ie in the case of a company which is being wound up otherwise than by the court.

3 Ie in the case of a company in relation to which an administration order is in force.

4 Ie in the case of a company of which there is an administrative receiver. For these purposes, 'administrative receiver' has the meaning given by the Insolvency Act 1986 s 251 (see para 1344 ante): Company Directors Disqualification Act 1986 s 22(3).

5 Ie the conditions mentioned in ibid s 6(1): see para 1425 ante.

6 For the meaning of 'director' for these purposes see ibid s 6(3) and para 1425 note 4 ante.

7 Ibid s 7(3). Where the liquidator of a company registered in England and Wales which passes a resolution for voluntary winding up on or after 29 December 1986, an administrative receiver of a company appointed, otherwise than under the Insolvency Act 1986 s 51, on or after 29 December 1986, or the administrator of a company registered in England and Wales in respect of which the court makes an administration order on or after 29 December 1986 makes such a report to the Secretary of State, it must be made in the form prescribed in the Insolvent Companies (Reports on Conduct of Directors) No 2 Rules 1986, SI 1986/2134, r 3(2), Schedule, Form D1, D2 or D6, as the case may be, and in the manner and to the extent required by the applicable form: r 3(1),(2).

Notwithstanding the revocation by r 2 of the Insolvent Companies (Reports on Conduct of Directors) Rules 1986, SI 1986/611, the provisions of rr 2, 3 of the latter continue to apply, and have effect in relation to any report to which the provisions of r 2 apply, and any interim return required to be made by r 3: Insolvent Companies (Reports on Conduct of Directors) No 2 Rules 1986 r 6. Under the Insolvent Companies (Reports on Conduct of Directors) Rules 1986 (revoked) any report made to the Secretary of State under the Insolvency Act 1985 s 12(5) (repealed and replaced by the Insolvency Act 1986 s 7(3)) by the liquidator of a company registered in England and Wales which passed a resolution for voluntary winding up on or after 28 April 1986, or by an administrative receiver of a company appointed, otherwise than under the Companies Act 1985 s 467 (repealed), on or after 28 April 1986, had to be made in the Insolvent Companies (Reports on Conduct of Directors) Rules 1986 r 2(2), Schedule, Form D1 or Form D2, as the case might be, and in the manner and to the extent provided in the applicable form: r 2(1),(2) (revoked).

The obligation on the liquidator to make a report as provided in r 2 under the Insolvency Act 1985 s 12(5) (repealed) applied only where it was a creditors' voluntary winding up (there having been no declaration of solvency by the directors under the Companies Act 1985 s 577 (repealed and replaced by the Insolvency Act 1986 s 89)) or the liquidation began as a members' voluntary winding up and at any time thereafter the liquidator formed the opinion that the company would not be able to pay its debts in full within the period stated in the directors' declaration under that provision, and also formed the opinion that, at the time when the company went into liquidation, its assets were insufficient for the payment of its debts and other liabilities and the expenses of the winding up: Insolvent Companies (Reports on Conduct of Directors) Rules 1986 r 2(3) (revoked).

When a report under the Insolvency Act 1985 s 12(5) (repealed) had to be made, then either (1) the liquidator, in the case of a company in creditors' voluntary winding up, there having been no declaration of solvency by the directors under the Companies Act 1985 s 577 (repealed); or (2) the liquidator, in the case of a company in voluntary winding up, if and when he formed the opinion that, at the time when the company went into liquidation, its assets were insufficient for the payment of its debts and other liabilities and the expenses of the winding up; or (3) the administrative receiver of a company, was under a duty not later than six months from the relevant date ('the relevant date' being, for cases falling within head (1) supra, the date of the liquidator's appointment; or for cases falling within head (2) supra, the date on which the liquidator formed the opinion there mentioned; or in the case of the administrative receiver, the date of his appointment), to furnish to the Secretary of State an interim return with respect to every person who was, on the date when the company went into liquidation or, as the case may be, the administrative receiver was appointed, a director or shadow director of the company, or had been a director or shadow director of the company at any time in the three years immediately preceding that date: Insolvent Companies (Reports on Conduct of Directors) Rules 1986 r 3(1),(2),(4) (revoked). The interim return had to be made in r 3(3), Schedule, Form D3, D4 or D5, as the case might be, and in the manner and to the extent provided in the applicable form: r 3(3) (revoked).

An interim return did not have to be provided under these provisions if the office-holder had, since the relevant date, made reports to the Secretary of State under the Insolvency Act 1985 s 12(5) (repealed) with respect to all the persons described in the Insolvent Companies (Reports on Conduct of Directors) Rules 1986 r 3(2) (revoked) (see supra) and, apart from this provision, required to be the subject of an interim return: r 3(5) (revoked).

If a liquidator or administrative receiver without reasonable excuse failed to comply with these provisions, he was liable to a fine not exceeding £400 and, on conviction after continued contravention, to a daily default fine not exceeding £40: r 3(6) (revoked).

1429. Returns by liquidators etc. Where it appears to the liquidator[1], to the administrative receiver[2], or to the administrator[3] (each of whom for the purpose of the following provisions is referred to as 'the office-holder'), that the company has at any time become insolvent[4], there may be furnished to the Secretary of State by the office-holder at any time during the period of six months from the relevant date[5], a return with respect to every person who was, on the relevant date, a director[6] or shadow director[7] of the company, or had been a director or shadow director of the company at any time in the three years immediately preceding that date[8].

It is, however, the duty of the responsible office-holder[9] to furnish a return complying with these provisions to the Secretary of State not later than the expiry of the period of six months from the relevant date where no return has been so furnished by a day one week before the expiry of that period[10].

If a responsible office-holder without reasonable excuse fails to comply with this duty, he is liable to a fine not exceeding £400 and, on conviction after continued contravention, to a daily default fine not exceeding £40[11].

1 Ie the liquidator of a company registered in England and Wales which passes a resolution for voluntary winding up on or after 29 December 1986: Insolvent Companies (Reports on Conduct of Directors) No 2 Rules 1986, SI 1986/2134, r 3(1)(a).
2 Ie an administrative receiver appointed on or after 29 December 1986: ibid r 3(1)(b). For the meaning of 'administrative receiver' see para 1428 note 4 ante.
3 Ie the administrator of a company registered in England and Wales in respect of which the court makes an administration order on or after 29 December 1986: ibid r 3(1)(c).
4 Ie within the meaning of the Company Directors Disqualification Act 1986 s 6(2): see para 1425 note 5 ante.

5 For these purposes, 'the relevant date' means: (1) in the case of a company in creditors' voluntary winding up, there having been no declaration of solvency by the directors under the Insolvency Act 1986 s 89 (see para 2700 post), the date of the passing of the resolution for voluntary winding up; (2) in the case of a company in members' voluntary winding up, the date on which the liquidator forms the opinion that, at the time when the company went into liquidation, its assets were insufficient for the payment of its debts and other liabilities and the expenses of winding up; (3) in the case of the administrative receiver, the date of his appointment; and (4) in the case of the administrator, the date of the administration order made in relation to the company; and for the purpose of head (3) supra, the only appointment of an administrative receiver to be taken into account in determining the relevant date is that appointment which is not that of a successor in office to an administrative receiver who has vacated office either by death or pursuant to s 45 (see para 2187 post): Insolvent Companies (Reports on Conduct of Directors) No 2 Rules 1986 r 4(4).

6 For the meaning of 'director' see para 1417 note 2 ante.

7 For the meaning of 'shadow director' see para 1417 note 2 ante.

8 Insolvent Companies (Reports on Conduct of Directors) No 2 Rules 1986 r 4(2). The return must be made in the form prescribed in r 4(3), Schedule, Form D3, D4, D5 or D7, as the case may be, and in the manner and to the extent required by the applicable form: r 4(3).

9 For these purposes, the responsible office-holder is the person in office in relation to the company on the day specified in ibid r 4(5) (see infra) or, where no person is in office on that day, the office-holder who vacated office nearest to that day: r 4(5).

10 Ibid r 4(5). A return need not be provided under these provisions if an office-holder has, since the relevant date, made reports to the Secretary of State under the Company Directors Disqualification Act 1986 s 7(3) (see para 1428 ante) with respect to all the persons falling within the Insolvent Companies (Reports on Conduct of Directors) No 2 Rules 1986 r 4(2) and, apart from r 4(6), required to be the subject of return: r 4(6).

11 Ibid r 4(7).

1430. Request for information from office-holders. The Secretary of State or the official receiver[1] may require the liquidator, administrator or administrative receiver[2] of a company or the former liquidator, administrator or administrative receiver of a company to furnish him with such information with respect to any person's conduct as a director[3] of the company, and to produce and permit inspection of such books, papers and other records relevant to that person's conduct as such a director, as the Secretary of State or the official receiver may reasonably require for the purpose of determining whether to exercise, or of exercising, any function[4] of his under the provisions of the Company Directors Disqualification Act 1986[5]. In such a case, the court, on the application of the Secretary of State or, as the case may be, the official receiver, may make an order directing compliance within such period as may be specified[6]; and the court's order may provide that all costs of and incidental to the application are to be borne by the person to whom the order is directed[7].

1 For the meaning of 'the official receiver' see para 1423 note 8 ante.

2 For the meaning of 'administrative receiver' see para 1428 note 4 ante.

3 See para 1427 note 2 ante.

4 Ie the functions of the Secretary of State and the official receiver under the Company Directors Disqualification Act 1986 s 7: see paras 1427, 1428 ante.

5 Ibid s 7(4). Documents and transcripts which have been obtained by an administrator under the Insolvency Act 1986 ss 235, 236 (see paras 2438, 2439 post) may be disclosed to the Secretary of State: *Re Polly Peck International plc, ex p Joint Administrators* [1994] BCC 15.

6 Insolvent Companies (Reports on Conduct of Directors) No 2 Rules 1986, SI 1986/2134, r 5(1),(2).

7 Ibid r 5(3). The right of the Secretary of State or the official receiver to apply for such an order does not establish that they have a present indefeasible legal right to production, such as to establish that the documents are in the power of the Secretary of State or the official receiver, and thus that those persons are liable to make discovery of them under RSC Ord 24: *Re Lombard Shipping and Forwarding Ltd* [1993] BCLC 238.

1431. Application for disqualification order after investigation of company. If it appears to the Secretary of State from a report made by inspectors appointed by him to investigate a company's affairs[1] or any alleged insider dealing[2] or from information or documents obtained under his power to require production of documents[3], or pursuant to an entry and search of premises on which such documents are believed to be[4], or as a result of the Director of the Serious Fraud Office's investigative powers[5], or the Secretary of State's powers to assist overseas regulatory authorities[6], that it is expedient in the public interest that a disqualification order[7] should be made against any person who is or has been a director[8] or shadow director[9] of any company, he may apply to the court[10] for such an order to be made against that person[11]. The court may make a disqualification order against a person where, on an application under this provision, it is satisfied that his conduct in relation to the company makes him unfit to be concerned in the management of a company[12].

The maximum period of disqualification which may be imposed under these provisions is 15 years[13].

1 Ie under the Companies Act 1985 s 437 (as amended): see para 1380 ante.
2 Ie under the Financial Services Act 1986 s 177 (as amended): see para 1231 ante. These provisions apply also in relation to the appointment of inspectors to investigate and report on the affairs etc of unit trust schemes: see s 94 (as amended) and MONEY.
3 Ie under the Companies Act 1985 s 447 (as amended) (see para 1386 ante) or the Financial Services Act 1986 s 105 (see MONEY).
4 Ie under the Companies Act 1985 s 448 (as substituted): see para 1393 ante.
5 Ie under the Criminal Justice Act 1987 s 2 (as amended): see CRIMINAL LAW vol 11(1) (Reissue) para 653.
6 Ie under the Companies Act 1989 s 83: see para 1399 ante.
7 See para 1417 ante.
8 For the meaning of 'director' see para 1417 note 2 ante.
9 For the meaning of 'shadow director' see para 1417 note 2 ante.
10 For these purposes, 'the court' means the High Court: Company Directors Disqualification Act 1986 s 8(3). As to the mode of application and the procedure see para 1434 et seq post. No application may be made in relation to a report made or information or documents obtained before 28 April 1986 (the date on which the provisions replaced by the Company Directors Disqualification Act 1986 s 8 came into force: see the Insolvency Act 1985 s 235, Sch 9 Pt II para 3; the Insolvency Act 1985 (Commencement No 3) Order 1986, SI 1986/463): Company Directors Disqualification Act 1986 s 19(c), Sch 2 para 8.
11 Ibid s 8(1) (amended by the Financial Services Act 1986 s 198(2); the Criminal Justice Act 1988 s 145(b); the Companies Act 1989 s 79).
12 Company Directors Disqualification Act 1986 s 8(2). As to determining such unfitness see para 1426 ante.
13 Ibid s 8(4).

1432. Application for disqualification order. A person intending to apply for the making of a disqualification order[1] by the court having jurisdiction to wind up a company must give not less than ten days' notice of his intention to the person against whom the order is sought; and on the hearing of the application the last-mentioned person may appear and himself give evidence or call witnesses[2]. On the hearing of any application[3] made by the Secretary of State or the official receiver or the liquidator, the applicant must appear and call the attention of the court to any matters which seem to him to be relevant, and may himself give evidence or call witnesses[4].

1 See para 1417 ante.
2 Company Directors Disqualification Act 1986 s 16(1). Failure to give proper notice is a procedural irregularity only which does not invalidate the application: *Secretary of State for Trade and Industry v Langridge* [1991] Ch 402, [1991] 3 All ER 591, CA. Where the court can of its own motion make a disqualification order, there is no statutory requirement of notice, though the rules of natural justice

require that a person should be given some notice that the court is contemplating making a disqualification order: *Secretary of State for Trade and Industry v Langridge* supra at 598 and at 414.
3 Ie under the Company Directors Disqualification Act 1986.
4 Ibid s 16(3). For the meaning of 'the official receiver' see para 1423 note 8 ante.

1433. Persons entitled to apply on grounds of general misconduct in connection with companies. An application to a court with jurisdiction to wind up companies for the making against any person of a disqualification order[1] on the grounds that that person has been convicted of an indictable offence[2], has been in persistent breach of companies legislation[3], has been guilty of fraud in the winding up[4], or has been convicted of summary offences[5], may be made by the Secretary of State or the official receiver[6], or by the liquidator or any past or present member or creditor of any company in relation to which that person has committed or is alleged to have committed an offence or other default[7].

1 See para 1417 ante.
2 Ie under the Company Directors Disqualification Act 1986 s 2 (as amended): see para 1418 ante.
3 Ie under ibid s 3: see para 1419 ante.
4 Ie under ibid s 4: see para 1420 ante.
5 Ie under ibid s 5: see para 1421 ante.
6 For the meaning of 'the official receiver' see para 1423 note 8 ante.
7 Company Directors Disqualification Act 1986 s 16(2). As to the mode of application and the procedure see para 1432 ante.

1434. Application on grounds of unfitness or following investigation into company's affairs. The following provisions[1] apply with respect to an application for a disqualification order[2] against any person ('the respondent') where made by the Secretary of State or the official receiver[3] on the grounds of the person's association with insolvent companies and unfitness to be concerned with the management of a company[4] or by the Secretary of State following an investigation[5] into the company's affairs[6]. Any such application must be made in the High Court by originating summons[7], and in a county court by originating application[8]; and the Rules of the Supreme Court 1965 or, as the case may be, the County Court Rules 1981, apply accordingly[9].

1 Ie para 1435 et seq post. Such provisions apply to applications made on or after 11 January 1988; and any applications made before that date are governed by the Insolvent Companies (Disqualification of Unfit Directors) Proceedings Rules 1986, SI 1986/612 (revoked): see the Insolvent Companies (Disqualification of Unfit Directors) Proceedings Rules 1987, SI 1987/2023, rr 1(1),(3), 11.
2 See para 1417 ante.
3 For the meaning of 'the official receiver' see para 1423 note 8 ante.
4 Ie under the Company Directors Disqualification Act 1986 s 7(1): see para 1427 ante.
5 Ie under ibid s 8: see para 1431 ante.
6 Insolvent Companies (Disqualification of Unfit Directors) Proceedings Rules 1987 r 1(3).
7 For the prescribed form of originating summons see RSC Appendix A, Form 10.
8 Such an application is nevertheless referred to in para 1435 et seq post as a summons: Insolvent Companies (Disqualification of Unfit Directors) Proceedings Rules 1987 r 2(b).
9 Ibid r 2. The Rules of the Supreme Court 1965 and the County Court Rules 1981, as the case may be, apply except where the Insolvent Companies (Disqualification of Unfit Directors) Proceedings Rules 1987 make provision to inconsistent effect: r 2.

1435. The case against the respondent. There must, at the time when the summons[1] is issued, be filed in court[2] evidence in support of the application for a

disqualification order[3]; and copies of the evidence must be served with the summons on the respondent[4].

The evidence must be by one or more affidavits, except where the applicant is the official receiver, in which case it may be in the form of a written report, with or without affidavits by other persons, which is treated as if it had been verified by affidavit by him and is prima facie evidence of any matter contained in it[5].

There must in the affidavit or affidavits or, as the case may be, the official receiver's report, be included a statement of the matters by reference to which the respondent is alleged to be unfit[6] to be concerned in the management of a company[7].

1 See para 1434 ante.
2 For these purposes, 'file in court' means deliver to the court for filing: Insolvent Companies (Disqualification of Unfit Directors) Proceedings Rules 1987, SI 1987/2023, r 1(2)(d).
3 See para 1417 ante.
4 Insolvent Companies (Disqualification of Unfit Directors) Proceedings Rules 1987 r 3(1). For the meaning of 'the respondent' see para 1434 ante. Non-compliance with r 3(1) is a mere irregularity; non-compliance does not nullify the proceedings and the court has power to waive any irregularity: *Re Copecrest Ltd* [1993] BCC 844 at 851, CA; *Re Jazzgold Ltd* [1994] 1 BCLC 38 at 42. A respondent may apply to strike out the summons and on the hearing of the application for striking out the court may consider further evidence filed by the applicant: *Re Jazzgold Ltd* supra.
5 Insolvent Companies (Disqualification of Unfit Directors) Proceedings Rules 1987 r 3(2). The report may be made by a deputy official receiver: *Re Homes Assured Corpn plc, Official Receiver v Dobson* [1994] 2 BCLC 71. Exhibits and annexures are also treated as prima facie evidence: *Re City Investment Centres Ltd* [1992] BCLC 956; *Re Moonbeam Cards Ltd* [1993] BCLC 1099. Statements obtained under the Companies Act 1985 s 447 (as amended) (see para 1386 ante) are admissible even though hearsay; this affects weight but not admissibility: *Re Rex Williams Leisure plc (in administration)* [1994] Ch 350, [1994] 4 All ER 27, CA.
6 See paras 1425, 1426, 1431 ante.
7 Insolvent Companies (Disqualification of Unfit Directors) Proceedings Rules 1987 r 3(3).

1436. Indorsement on summons. On the summons[1] the following information to the respondent[2] must be indorsed:

(1) that the application is made in accordance with the Insolvent Companies (Disqualification of Unfit Directors) Proceedings Rules 1987[3];

(2) the periods of disqualification which, in accordance with the relevant enactments, the court has power to impose[4];

(3) that the application for a disqualification order may[5] be heard and determined summarily, without further or other notice to the respondent, and that, if it is so heard and determined, the court may impose disqualification for a period of up to five years;

(4) that, if at the hearing of the application the court, on the evidence then before it, is minded to impose, in the respondent's case, disqualification for any period longer than five years, it will not make a disqualification order on that occasion but will adjourn the application to be heard, with further evidence, if any, at a later date to be notified; and

(5) that any evidence which the respondent wishes to be taken into consideration by the court must be filed in court[6] in accordance with provisions relating to time limits for the filing in court of evidence, which must be set out on the summons[7].

1 See para 1434 ante.
2 For the meaning of 'the respondent' see para 1434 ante.
3 Ie the Insolvent Companies (Disqualification of Unfit Directors) Proceedings Rules 1987, SI 1987/2023.

4 Ie where the application is made under the Company Directors Disqualification Act 1986 s 7, for a period of not less than two, and up to 15, years; and, where the application is under s 8, for a period of up to 15 years: Insolvent Companies (Disqualification of Unfit Directors) Proceedings Rules 1987 r 4(b).

5 Ie in accordance with the Insolvent Companies (Disqualification of Unfit Directors) Proceedings Rules 1987.

6 For the meaning of 'file in court' see para 1435 note 2 ante.

7 Insolvent Companies (Disqualification of Unfit Directors) Proceedings Rules 1987 r 4. As to the provisions relating to time limits for evidence see para 1438 post.

1437. Service and acknowledgment of summons. The summons[1] must be served on the respondent[2] by sending it by first class post to his last-known address; and the date of service is, unless the contrary is shown, deemed to be the seventh day next following that on which the summons was posted[3].

Where any process or order of the court or other document is required[4] to be served on any person who is not in England and Wales, the court may order service on him of that process or order or other document to be effected within such time and in such manner as it thinks fit, and may also require such proof of service as it thinks fit[5].

The summons served on the respondent must be accompanied by a form of acknowledgment of service, to be returned by him to the court within 14 days from the date of service, and for this purpose the practice and procedure of the High Court relating to acknowledgments of service apply to an application for an order[6] both in the High Court and, with such modifications as are required, in the county court[7].

The form of acknowledgment of service must state that the respondent should indicate:

(1) whether he contests the application on the grounds that, in the case of any particular company:
  (a) he was not a director[8] or shadow director[9] of the company at a time when conduct of his, or of other persons, in relation to that company is in question; or
  (b) his conduct as a director or shadow director of that company was not as alleged in support of the application for a disqualification order;

(2) whether, in the case of any conduct of his, he disputes the allegation that it makes him unfit to be concerned in the management of a company[10]; and

(3) whether he, while not resisting the application for a disqualification order, intends to adduce mitigating factors with a view to justifying only a short period of disqualification[11].

1 See para 1434 ante.

2 For the meaning of 'the respondent' see para 1434 ante.

3 Insolvent Companies (Disqualification of Unfit Directors) Proceedings Rules 1987, SI 1987/2023, r 5(1).

4 Ie under proceedings subject to the Insolvent Companies (Disqualification of Unfit Directors) Proceedings Rules 1987.

5 Ibid r 5(2).

6 Ie under the Insolvent Companies (Disqualification of Unfit Directors) Proceedings Rules 1987.

7 Ie save that any reference to RSC Appendix A, Form 15 relates to the form as modified by the Insolvent Companies (Disqualification of Unfit Directors) Proceedings Rules 1987.

8 For the meaning of 'director' see para 1417 note 2 ante.

9 For the meaning of 'shadow director' see para 1417 note 2 ante.

10 See paras 1419, 1426, 1431 ante.

11 Insolvent Companies (Disqualification of Unfit Directors) Proceedings Rules 1987 r 5.

1438. Evidence. The respondent[1] must, within 28 days from the date of service of the summons[2], file in court[3] any affidavit evidence in opposition to the application he wishes the court to take into consideration, and must forthwith serve upon the applicant a copy of such evidence[4]. The applicant must, within 14 days from receiving the copy of the respondent's evidence, file in court any further evidence in reply he wishes the court to take into consideration and must forthwith serve a copy of that evidence upon the respondent[5]. A respondent has no right to discovery from the applicant where the applicant is the Secretary of State or the official receiver where he is not also the liquidator, but he has such a right where the applicant is the official receiver who is also the liquidator[6].

1 For the meaning of 'the respondent' see para 1434 ante.
2 See para 1434 ante.
3 For the meaning of 'file in court' see para 1435 note 2 ante.
4 Insolvent Companies (Disqualification of Unfit Directors) Proceedings Rules 1987, SI 1987/2023, r 6(1). A respondent does not have the option of omitting to file affidavit evidence and giving evidence orally at the trial: *Re Rex Williams Leisure plc (in administration)* [1994] Ch 350, [1994] 4 All ER 27, CA.
5 Insolvent Companies (Disqualification of Unfit Directors) Proceedings Rules 1987 r 6(2).
6 *Re Lombard Shipping and Forwarding Ltd* [1993] BCLC 238. In practice a respondent will normally receive full discovery of relevant documents whoever has made the application.

1439. Hearing of application; commencement and setting aside of disqualification orders; summary procedure.   The date fixed for the hearing of the application must be not less than eight weeks from the date of issue of the summons[1]. The hearing must in the first instance be before the registrar[2] in open court[3]; and the registrar must either determine the case on the date fixed or adjourn it[4]. The registrar must adjourn the case for further consideration if:

(1) he forms the provisional opinion that a disqualification order ought to be made, and that a period of disqualification longer than five years is appropriate; or

(2) he is of opinion that questions of law or fact arise which are not suitable for summary determination[5].

If the registrar adjourns the case for further consideration, he must:

(a) direct whether the case is to be heard by a registrar, or, if he thinks it appropriate, by the judge, for determination by him;

(b) state the reasons for the adjournment; and

(c) give directions as to the following matters:

(i) the manner in which and the time within which notice of the adjournment and the reasons for it are to be given to the respondent[6];

(ii) the filing in court and the service of further evidence, if any, by the parties[7];

(iii) such other matters as the registrar thinks necessary or expedient with a view to an expeditious disposal of the application; and

(iv) the time and place of the adjourned hearing[7].

Where a case is adjourned other than to the judge, it may be heard by the registrar who originally dealt with the case or by another registrar[8].

In all cases where the trial is estimated to take ten days or more and in any other case where the court so directs, a pre-trial review will be held by a registrar or, if the matter is to be heard by a judge, by a judge in chambers[9].

The court may make a disqualification order against the respondent, whether or not the latter appears, and whether or not he has completed and returned the acknowledgment of service of the summons[10], or filed[11] evidence[12]; any disqualification order made in the absence of the respondent may be set aside or varied by the court on such terms as it thinks just[13].

Unless the court otherwise orders, a disqualification order takes effect at the beginning of the twenty-first day after the day on which the order is made[14].

Official receivers and deputy official receivers have right of audience in any proceedings to which the Insolvent Companies (Disqualification of Unfit Directors) Proceedings Rules 1987 apply, whether the application is made by the Secretary of State or by the official receiver at his direction, and whether made in the High Court or a county court[15].

No specific provision is made for appeals from disqualifications orders, but it has been held that the provisions relating to appeals in winding-up proceedings apply to proceedings under the Company Directors Disqualification Act 1986[16].

The costs of disqualification proceedings are in the discretion of the court, but the usual rules on costs will apply, so that the applicant will normally be liable to pay the costs of an unsuccessful application or if proceedings are discontinued, and the respondent will pay the costs on the standard basis if the application is successful[17].

Although on an application for a disqualification order it is not permissible for the parties merely to seek a consent order, the court has jurisdiction to deal with an application for a disqualification order by a summary procedure where the court is satisfied that the undisputed evidence is sufficient to establish unfitness, and that the potential impact of disputed evidence would not substantially affect the seriousness of that unfitness[18].

1 Insolvent Companies (Disqualification of Unfit Directors) Proceedings Rules 1987, SI 1987/2023, r 7(1). As to the summons referred to see para 1434 ante.

2 For these purposes, 'registrar' has the same meaning as in the Insolvency Rules 1986, SI 1986/1925, r 13.2(4),(5) (see para 2814 note 3 post): Insolvent Companies (Disqualification of Unfit Directors) Proceedings Rules 1987 r 1(2)(c).

3 Ibid r 7(2). All evidence should be filed before the first hearing of the summons: *Practice Note* [1996] 1 All ER 445; sub nom *Practice Direction* [1996] 1 WLR 170 para 2.

4 Insolvent Companies (Disqualification of Unfit Directors) Proceedings Rules 1987 r 7(3).

5 Ibid r 7(4).

6 For the meaning of 'the respondent' see para 1434 ante. The registrar's direction as to whether the matter should be heard by a judge or a registrar may at any time be varied by the court on application or of its own motion; if the direction is varied in the absence of all the parties, notice will be given to the parties: *Practice Note* [1996] 1 All ER 445; sub nom *Practice Direction* [1996] 1 WLR 170 para 4.

7 Insolvent Companies (Disqualification of Unfit Directors) Proceedings Rules 1987 r 7(5). The registrar will as far as possible give all the directions for trial at the first hearing: *Practice Note* [1996] 1 All ER 445; sub nom *Practice Direction* [1996] 1 WLR 170 para 4.

8 Insolvent Companies (Disqualification of Unfit Directors) Proceedings Rules 1987 r 7(6).

9 *Practice Note* [1996] 1 All ER 445; sub nom *Practice Direction* [1996] 1 WLR 170 para 8. *Practice Note* supra also provides for: the procedure for the setting down and fixing of the trial (paras 5, 6); time estimates (para 7); the documents to be prepared by the advocates (paras 10-12, 16); and the procedure in relation to hearings outside London (para 17).

10 See para 1437 ante.

11 Ie in accordance with the Insolvent Companies (Disqualification of Unfit Directors) Proceedings Rules 1987 r 6: see para 1438 ante.

12 Ibid r 8(1).

13 Ibid r 8(2).

14 Ibid r 9.

15 Ibid r 10.

16 *Re Tasbian Ltd (No 2)* [1990] BCC 322, CA; *Re Probe Data Systems Ltd (No 3), Secretary of State for Trade and Industry v Desai* [1992] BCLC 405, CA; *Secretary of State for Trade and Industry v Langley* [1993] BCLC 1340. As to the basis on which the appellate court will interefere with the decision of the trial court see *Secretary of State for Trade and Industry v Gray* [1995] 1 BCLC 276, CA.

17 *Re Southbourne Sheet Metal Co Ltd* [1993] 1 WLR 244, [1993] BCLC 135, CA; *Re Godwin Warren Control Systems plc* [1993] BCLC 80; *Secretary of State for Trade and Industry v Worth* [1994] 2 BCLC 113, CA. As to the costs of an application for leave under the Company Directors Disqualification Act 1986 s 17 (see para 1440 post) see *Secretary of State for Trade and Industry v Worth* supra.

18 See para 2890 post.

(iii) Effect of Disqualification Order; Consequences of Contravention

1440. Application for leave under a disqualification order. As regards the court to which application must be made for leave under a disqualification order[1]:

(1) where the application is for leave to promote or form a company, it is any court with jurisdiction to wind up companies; and

(2) where the application is for leave to be a liquidator, administrator or director of, or otherwise to take part in the management of, a company, or to be a receiver or manager of a company's property, it is any court having jurisdiction to wind up that company[2].

On the hearing of an application for leave made by a person against whom a disqualification order has been made on the application of the Secretary of State, the official receiver[3] or the liquidator, the Secretary of State, the official receiver or the liquidator must appear and call the attention of the court to any matters which seem to him to be relevant, and may himself give evidence or call witnesses[4].

It is desirable that, if proceedings to disqualify a director are outstanding, and the director wishes to apply for leave to continue as a director notwithstanding any disqualification order, that application should be heard at the same time as the disqualification proceedings[5]. Leave will be granted under a disqualification order only where the director shows that there is a need for such an order to be granted, and where the court can be satisfied that there is adequate protection for the public[6].

1 See para 1417 text to note 1 ante.
2 Company Directors Disqualification Act 1986 s 17(1).
3 For the meaning of 'the official receiver' see para 1423 note 8 ante.
4 Company Directors Disqualification Act 1986 s 17(2).
5 *Secretary of State for Trade and Industry v Worth* [1994] 2 BCLC 113, CA.
6 *Re Gibson Davies Ltd* [1995] BCC 11. Where leave is granted, it will often be subject to suitable safeguards designed to protect the public: see eg *Re Gibson Davies Ltd* supra at 17, 18; *Re Lo-Line Electric Motors Ltd* [1988] Ch 477, [1988] 2 All ER 692; *Re Chartmore Ltd* [1990] BCLC 673. Where a director appeals against a disqualification order and wishes to continue as a director pending the appeal, the correct method is normally to apply for leave under the Company Directors Disqualification Act 1986 s 17, although the Court of Appeal has jurisdiction to grant a stay on the order in exceptional cases: *Secretary of State for Trade and Industry v Bannister* [1995] BCC 1027, CA.

1441. Information to be provided to the Secretary of State in relation to disqualification orders. Where a disqualification order[1] is made on or after 29 December 1986 and where the court grants leave[2] under a disqualification order, or any action is taken by a court in consequence of which a disqualification order is varied or ceases to be in force, made or taken after that date, in relation to a disqualification order made before, on or after that date, specified officers of the court[3] must furnish to the Secretary of State certain specified particulars in the specified form and manner[4].

1 For these purposes, 'disqualification order' means an order of the court under any of the Company Directors Disqualification Act 1986 s 2 (as amended) and ss 3-6, 8, 10 (see para 1417 et seq ante): Companies (Disqualification Orders) Regulations 1986, SI 1986/2067, reg 1(2).
2 For these purposes, 'grant of leave' means a grant by the court of leave under the Company Directors Disqualification Act 1986 s 17 (see para 1440 ante) to any person in relation to a disqualification order: Companies (Disqualification Orders) Regulations 1986 reg 1(2).
3 The specified officers of the court are (1) where a disqualification order is made by the Crown Court, the chief clerk; (2) where a disqualification order or grant of leave is made by the High Court, the chief clerk; (3) where a disqualification order or grant of leave is made by a county court, the chief clerk; (4) where a disqualification order is made by a magistrates' court, the clerk to the justices; (5) where a disqualification order is made by the High Court of Justiciary, the Deputy Principal Clerk of Justiciary;

(6) where a disqualification order or grant of leave is made by a sheriff court, the sheriff clerk; and (7) where a disqualification order or grant of leave is made by the Court of Session, the Deputy Principal Clerk of Session: ibid reg 4(1).

Where a disqualification order is made by any of the courts mentioned in heads (1)-(7) supra and subsequently any action is taken by a court in consequence of which that order is varied or ceases to be in force, the officer of the first-mentioned court specified in heads (1)-(7) supra must furnish to the Secretary of State the particulars specified in reg 5(d) (see note 4 head (4) infra), in the form and manner there specified: reg 4(2).

4 Ibid regs 3, 4(2). The form in which the particulars are to be furnished is:

  (1) that set out in reg 5(a), Sch 1 (substituted by SI 1995/1509) with such variations as circumstances require when the person against whom the disqualification order is made is an individual, and the particulars contained therein are the particulars specified for that purpose;

  (2) that set out in reg 5(b), Sch 2 (substituted by SI 1995/1509) with such variations as circumstances require when the person against whom the disqualification order is made is a body corporate, and the particulars contained therein are the particulars specified for that purpose;

  (3) that set out in reg 5(c), Sch 3 (substituted by SI 1995/1509) with such variations as circumstances require when a grant of leave is made by the court, and the particulars contained therein are the particulars specified for that purpose;

  (4) that set out in reg 5(d), Sch 4 (substituted by SI 1995/1509) with such variations as circumstances require when any action is taken by a court in consequence of which a disqualification order is varied or ceases to be in force, and the particulars contained therein are the particulars specified for that purpose:

reg 5. The Companies (Disqualification Orders) (Amendment) Regulations 1995, SI 1995/1509, apply in relation to disqualification orders made on and after 1 July 1995 and to a grant of leave, or any action taken by a court in consequence of which a disqualification order is varied or ceases to be in force, made or taken after that date, in relation to a disqualification order made, before, on or after 1 July 1995: reg 2.

The time within which a prescribed officer is to furnish the Secretary of State with such particulars is a period of 14 days beginning with the day on which the disqualification order or grant of leave is made, or any action is taken by a court in consequence of which the disqualification order is varied or ceases to be in force, as the case may be: Companies (Disqualification Orders) Regulations 1986 reg 6.

The above regulations were made in pursuance of powers contained in the Company Directors Disqualification Act 1986 s 18(1), which provides that the Secretary of State may make regulations requiring officers of courts to furnish him with such particulars as the regulations may specify of cases in which a disqualification order is made, or any action is taken by a court in consequence of which such an order is varied or ceases to be in force, or leave is granted by a court for a person subject to such an order to do anything which otherwise the order prohibits him from doing; and the regulations may specify the time within which, and the form and manner in which, such particulars are to be furnished. Regulations under s 18 must be made by statutory instrument subject to annulment in pursuance of a resolution of either House of Parliament: s 18(5).

1442. Register of disqualification orders. The Secretary of State must, from the particulars furnished[1] in accordance with the statutory provisions[1], continue to maintain the register of orders[2] and of cases in which leave has been granted[3]. When an order of which entry is made in the register ceases to be in force, the Secretary of State must delete the entry from the register and all particulars relating to it which have been furnished to him under these provisions or any previous corresponding provision[4].

The register must be open to inspection on payment of such fee as may be specified by the Secretary of State[5].

1 Ie pursuant to the Company Directors Disqualification Act 1986 s 18(1) and the regulations made thereunder: see para 1441 ante.
2 Ie the register of orders set up by the Secretary of State under the Companies Act 1976 s 29 (repealed) and continued under the Companies Act 1985 s 301 (repealed).
3 Company Directors Disqualification Act 1986 s 18(2). As to the grant of leave under a disqualification order see para 1440 ante.
4 Ibid s 18(3).
5 Ibid s 18(4). No fee is payable for inspecting the register.

1443. Consequences of contravention of disqualification order; criminal penalties. If a person acts in contravention of a disqualification order[1], or of an order made following his failure to pay under a county court administration order[2] or is guilty of an offence under the provisions relating to undischarged bankrupts[3], he is liable on conviction on indictment to imprisonment for a term not exceeding two years or a fine, or both, or on summary conviction to imprisonment for a term not exceeding six months or a fine not exceeding the statutory maximum, or to both[4].

1 See para 1417 ante.
2 Ie under the Company Directors Disqualification Act 1986 s 12(2): see para 1424 ante.
3 Ie ibid s 11: see para 1423 ante.
4 Ibid s 13. For the meaning of 'the statutory maximum' see para 1161 ante.

1444. Offences by body corporate; disqualification orders. Where a body corporate[1] is guilty of an offence of acting in contravention of a disqualification order[2], and it is proved that the offence occurred with the consent or connivance of, or was attributable to any neglect on the part of any director, manager, secretary or other similar officer of the body corporate, or any person who was purporting to act in any such capacity he, as well as the body corporate, is guilty of the offence and liable to be proceeded against and punished accordingly[3].

Where the affairs of a body corporate are managed by its members, these provisions apply in relation to the acts and defaults of a member in connection with his functions of management as if he were a director of the body corporate[4].

1 A body corporate does not include a corporation sole, but includes a company incorporated elsewhere than in Great Britain: Companies Act 1985 s 740 (applied by the Company Directors Disqualification Act 1986 s 22(1),(6)).
2 See para 1443 ante.
3 Company Directors Disqualification Act 1986 s 14(1). As to the penalties see para 1443 ante.
4 Ibid s 14(2).

1445. Consequences of contravention; personal liability of persons acting while disqualified. A person is personally responsible for all the relevant debts[1] of a company[2] if at any time:

(1) in contravention of a disqualification order[3], or of the provisions relating to undischarged bankrupts[4], he is involved in the management of a company[5]; or

(2) as a person who is involved in the management of the company, he acts or is willing to act on instructions given without the leave of the court by a person whom he knows at that time to be the subject of a disqualification order or to be an undischarged bankrupt[6].

Where a person is personally responsible under these provisions for the relevant debts of a company, he is jointly and severally liable in respect of those debts with the company and any other person who, whether under these provisions or otherwise, is so liable[7].

1 For these purposes, the relevant debts of a company are (1) in relation to a person who is personally responsible under the Company Directors Disqualification Act 1986 s 15(1)(a) (see text head (1) infra), such debts and other liabilities of the company as are incurred at a time when that person was involved in the management of the company; and (2) in relation to a person who is personally responsible under

s 15(1)(b) (see text head (2) infra), such debts and other liabilities of the company as are incurred at a time when that person was acting or was willing to act on instructions given as mentioned in s 15(1)(b): s 15(3).

2 For the meaning of 'company' see para 1417 note 3 ante.

3 See para 1417 ante.

4 Ie the Company Directors Disqualification Act 1986 s 11: see para 1423 ante.

5 Ibid s 15(1)(a). For these purposes, a person is involved in the management of a company if he is a director of the company or if he is concerned, whether directly or indirectly, or takes part in the management of the company: s 15(4).

6 Ibid s 15(1)(b). For these purposes, a person who, as a person involved in the management of a company, has at any time acted on instructions given without the leave of the court by a person whom he knew at that time to be the subject of a disqualification order or to be an undischarged bankrupt is presumed, unless the contrary is shown, to have been willing at any time thereafter to act on any instructions given by that person: s 15(5).

7 Ibid s 15(2).

(iv) Admissibility in Evidence of Statements

1446. Admissibility in evidence of statements. In any proceedings, whether or not under the Company Directors Disqualification Act 1986, any statement made in pursuance of a requirement imposed by or under the provisions of that Act[1], or by or under rules made for the purposes of that Act under the Insolvency Act 1986[2], may be used in evidence against any person making or concurring in making that statement[3].

1 Ie the Company Directors Disqualification Act 1986 s 6 (see para 1425 ante), s 7 (see para 1427 et seq ante), s 8 (see para 1431 ante), s 9 (see para 1426 ante), s 10 (see para 1422 ante), s 15 (see para 1445 ante), s 19(c) (which relates to precluding any applications for a disqualification order under s 6 or s 8 where the relevant company went into liquidation before 28 April 1986: see paras 1425, 1431 ante), and Sch 1 (see para 1426 ante).

2 See the Insolvency Act 1986 s 411 and para 2800 post.

3 Company Directors Disqualification Act 1986 s 20.

(31) SCHEMES OF ARRANGEMENT, RECONSTRUCTION AND AMALGAMATION

(i) The Making of Schemes

1447. Sanctioning compromise or arrangement. Where a compromise or arrangement[1] is proposed between a company[2] and its creditors[3] or any class of them, or between the company and its members or any class of them[4], the court[5] may, on the application of the company or any creditor or member of the company or, in the case of a company being wound up, or an administration order[6] being in force in relation to a company, of the liquidator or administrator[6], order a meeting of the creditors or class of creditors, or of the members of the company or class of members, as the case may be, to be summoned in such a manner as the court directs[7].

If a majority in number representing three-fourths in value of the creditors or class of creditors or members or class of members[8], as the case may be, present and voting either in person or by proxy at the meeting agree to any compromise or arrangement, the compromise or arrangement, if sanctioned by the court, is binding on all the creditors or the class of creditors, or on the members or class of members, as the case may be, and also on the company or, in the case of a company in the course of being wound up, on the liquidator and contributories of the company[9].

The compromise proposed must be within the power of the company to effect, and, if not, its memorandum of association must be altered before the compromise will be approved[10].

The interests of creditors must always be safeguarded[11]; but in the case of a scheme which involves the application of the provisions of the Companies Act 1985 for facilitating such reconstructions or amalgamations[12], the protection of creditors is to be left to the procedure in relation to such provisions[13].

1 For the meaning of 'arrangement' see para 1455 post.
2 In the Companies Act 1985 s 425 (as amended) and s 426 (as amended) (see para 1450 post), 'company' means any company liable to be wound up under the Companies Act 1985: s 425(6)(a). The reference to a company which is liable to be wound up includes a reference to a company which would be so liable but for the Water Industry Act 1991 s 25 (see WATER): see the Water Consolidation (Consequential Provisions) Act 1991 s 2(1), Sch 1 para 40(1). As to companies so liable see paras 2193, 2899 et seq post. In the Companies Act 1985 s 425(6)(a), the reference to the Companies Act 1985 includes certain provisions of the Insolvency Act 1986, and also the Company Directors Disqualification Act 1986: see para 20 text to note 12 and note 12 ante. If the articles give the directors the necessary powers, they may present a petition on behalf of a company without first obtaining the company's approval in general meeting: see *Bruce, Peebles & Co Ltd v Bain & Co* 1918 SC 781, criticising *Dailuaine-Talisker Distilleries Ltd v Mackenzie* 1910 SC 913.
3 For the meaning of 'creditor' see para 1452 post.
4 As to classes see *Re Dominion of Canada Freehold Estate and Timber Co Ltd* (1886) 55 LT 347 at 352 and para 1451 post.
5 For the meaning of 'the court' see para 161 note 4 ante.
6 As to administration orders and administrators see para 2080 et seq post.
7 Companies Act 1985 s 425(1) (amended by the Insolvency Act 1985 s 109(1), Sch 6 para 11). See also *British and Commonwealth Holdings plc v Barclays Bank plc* [1996] 1 All ER 381, [1996] 1 WLR 1, CA.
    Where a statutory water company applies to the court under the Companies Act 1985 s 425(1) (as so amended) with a view to securing an order of the court in respect of a compromise or arrangement in anticipation of provision contained in a memorandum and articles having effect as mentioned in the Statutory Water Companies Act 1991 s 12(1)(b), the Companies Act 1985 Pt XIII (ss 425-427A) (as amended) applies (1) with the insertion after the words 'no effect until' in s 425(3) of the words 'the memorandum and articles come into force by virtue of an order made by the Secretary of State under section 12(1)(c) of the Statutory Water Companies Act 1991 and'; and (2) as if the Companies Act 1985 ss 427-430 (as amended) were omitted: Companies Act 1985 (Modifications for Statutory Water Companies) Regulations 1989, SI 1989/1461, reg 2; Interpretation Act 1978 s 17(2)(b).
8 A shareholding company which is a wholly-owned subsidiary of the purchasing company forms a separate class from the ordinary shareholders for the purpose of a meeting of the ordinary shareholders summoned by the court: *Re Hellenic and General Trust Ltd* [1975] 3 All ER 382, [1975] 1 WLR 123. For the meaning of 'wholly-owned subsidiary' see para 827 ante.
9 Companies Act 1985 s 425(2); and see para 1453 et seq post. The court will not deprive creditors of the protection afforded by these provisions by sanctioning on the liquidator's application a conditional agreement of compromise under the Insolvency Act 1986 s 167 (see para 2338 post): *Re Trix Ltd, Re Ewart Holdings Ltd* [1970] 3 All ER 397, [1970] 1 WLR 1421. Cf para 1453 post.
10 *Re Bramall & Ogden Ltd* [1981] LS Gaz R 813 (the company's memorandum of association only authorised a transaction under which the consideration was received by the company itself, not by its shareholders; sanction was withheld until appropriate amendments of the memorandum had been effected).
11 In *Re Sandwell Park Colliery Co Ltd* [1914] 1 Ch 589, this was effected by a provision that the company should not part with its assets to a new company until all its creditors had either been paid in full or assented to the scheme and accepted the new company as their debtor. As to the fairness of the arrangement and sufficiency of information see *Re Heron International NV* [1994] 1 BCLC 667.
12 Ie the Companies Act 1985 s 427: see para 1460 post.
13 *Clydesdale Bank Ltd, Petitioners* 1950 SC 30; *Re Bramall & Ogden Ltd* [1981] LS Gaz R 813.

1448. Procedure. The application for an order to summon meetings is made by originating summons in the expedited form[1]; and the proposed compromise or arrangement should be exhibited to the supporting affidavit. The order directing a meeting to be summoned usually appoints someone, for example, the liquidator, to act as chairman of the meeting, and directs him to report the result to the court. It also directs that advertisements are to be made and that notices convening the meeting, enclosing a copy of the proposed compromise or arrangement, and a form of proxy in the form settled in chambers, are to be sent. Where a class of creditors to be summoned consists of holders of bearer securities, the only practicable method of summoning them is to give public notice of the meeting by advertisement in selected newspapers. Where the company is not in winding up and a petition for winding up is not pending, the court cannot, after ordering meetings to be summoned and before approving the scheme, stay an execution on a judgment recovered before the order[2].

1　See RSC Ord 102 r 2(1),(2). In a proper case an order may be obtained that the hearing of the summons should be treated as vacation business: *Re Showerings, Vine Products and Whiteways Ltd* [1968] 3 All ER 276n, [1968] 1 WLR 1381.
2　*Booth v Walkden Spinning and Manufacturing Co Ltd* [1909] 2 KB 368, DC; cf *Bowkett v Fuller's United Electric Works Ltd* [1923] 1 KB 160, CA (where a winding-up petition had been presented and an execution was stayed under what is now the Insolvency Act 1986 s 126 (see para 2646 et seq post)). See also *Re Richards & Co* (1879) 11 ChD 676 (where the company was in winding up).

1449. Mergers and divisions of public companies; additional requirements. The statutory provisions relating to compromises and arrangements[1] are modified in cases involving the transfer of the undertaking, property and liabilities of public companies to other public companies, or, in some cases, companies, whether or not public companies, formed for the purpose of a merger or division in exchange for shares in the transferee companies receivable by shareholders of the transferor companies with or without an additional cash payment[2].

1　Ie the Companies Act 1985 ss 425–427 (as amended): see paras 1447, 1448 ante and paras 1450–1462 post.
2　See paras 1463–1478 post.

1450. Information to creditors or members. Where a meeting of creditors or members or any class of creditors or members is summoned[1], then, with every notice summoning the meeting sent to a creditor or member, there must be sent also a statement explaining the effect of the compromise or arrangement[2], and in particular stating any material interests of the directors of the company[3], whether as directors or as members or as creditors of the company or otherwise[4], and the effect of the compromise or arrangement on those interests[5] in so far as it is different from the effect on the like interests of other persons[6]. If, prior to the relevant class meetings, a director's material interests alter in such a way as possibly to affect the attitude of those receiving the statement, it is the duty of the directors to communicate the alteration to those to whom the original circular was sent[7]. Otherwise the company will have to satisfy the court that no reasonable shareholder would have changed his decision as to how to act on the scheme if the changes had been disclosed[8]. Every notice summoning the meeting, which is given by advertisement, must include either such a statement as mentioned above or a notification of the place at which, and the manner in which, creditors or members entitled to attend the meeting may obtain copies of the statement[9]; and in the latter case every such creditor or member, on making application in the manner indicated by the notice, must be furnished by the company free of charge with a copy of the statement[10]. Where the compromise or arrangement affects the rights of debenture holders of the company, the statement must give the like explanation as respects the trustees of any deed for securing the issue of the debentures as it is required to give as respects the company's directors[11].

If a company makes default in complying with any requirement of the provisions relating to information as to compromises[12], the company, and every officer[13] of it who is in default, is liable on conviction on indictment to a fine, or on summary conviction to a fine not exceeding the statutory maximum; and any liquidator or administrator[14] and any trustee of a deed for securing the issue of debentures of the company is deemed an officer of it for this purpose[15]. A person is not, however, so liable if he shows that the default was due to the refusal of any other person, being a director or trustee for debenture holders, to give the necessary particulars of his interests[16].

It is the duty of any director of the company, and of any trustee for its debenture holders, to give notice to the company of such matters relating to himself as may be necessary for the purposes of these provisions; and any person who makes default in complying with this provision is liable on summary conviction to a fine not exceeding one-fifth of the statutory maximum[17].

1 Ie under the Companies Act 1985 s 425 (as amended): see paras 1447, 1448 ante.
2 A copy of the heading to the scheme is not a sufficient statement (*Re Peter Scott & Co Ltd* 1950 SC 507) nor is a copy of the petition (*Re Rankin and Blackmore Ltd* 1950 SC 218).
3 For the meaning of 'company' see para 1447 note 2 ante.
4 The precise extent of the directors' interests must be disclosed (*Coltness Iron Co Ltd, Petitioners* 1951 SC 476), including interests held as trustees (*Second Scottish Investment Trust Co Ltd, Petitioners* 1962 SLT (Notes) 78).
5 A statement of the effect on the directors' interests is not required if the effect is the same as on the similar interests of other persons: *City Property Investment Trust Corpn Ltd, Petitioners* 1951 SC 570.
6 Companies Act 1985 s 426(1),(2). Failure to comply with this requirement in summoning a share-holders' meeting was held not sufficient to invalidate proceedings where all shares in the company were held by the bank which had originated the proposed scheme: *Re Clydesdale Bank Ltd* 1950 SC 30. The court did not refuse to sanction a scheme where there was a failure to disclose material but small interests of directors as trustees (*Second Scottish Investment Trust Co Ltd, Petitioners* 1962 SLT (Notes) 78), or a failure to disclose information which did not require to be disclosed in the statutory accounts (*Re National Bank Ltd* [1966] 1 All ER 1006, [1966] 1 WLR 819).
7 *Re Jessel Trust Ltd* [1985] BCLC 119.
8 *Re Minster Assets plc* [1985] BCLC 200. As to sufficiency of information see *Re Heron International NV* [1994] 1 BCLC 667.
9 Companies Act 1985 s 426(1),(3). Failure to comply with this requirement cannot be cured by sending the statement to all members entitled to attend the meeting (*City Property Investment Trust Corpn Ltd, Petitioners* 1951 SC 570), or by sending each shareholder a copy of the petition (*Re Rankin and Blackmore Ltd* 1950 SC 218). A scheme was sanctioned under the Companies (Consolidation) Act 1908 (repealed) (which contained no provision corresponding to the Companies Act 1985 s 426 (as amended)) in a case where advertisements were not inserted owing to an oversight, but notices were sent to and received by all except one of the shareholders: see *Re Anglo-Spanish Tartar Refineries Ltd* (1924) 68 Sol Jo 738.
10 Companies Act 1985 s 426(1),(5).
11 Ibid s 426(1),(4). As to the application of s 426 (as amended) to statutory water companies see para 1447 note 7 ante.
12 Ie the provisions of ibid s 426(1)-(5): see supra.
13 For the meaning of 'officer' see para 641 ante.
14 As to administrators see para 2092 et seq post.
15 Companies Act 1985 s 426(1),(6) (amended by the Insolvency Act 1985 s 109(1), Sch 6 para 12); Companies Act 1985 s 730, Sch 24. For the meaning of 'the statutory maximum' see para 1161 ante.
16 Ibid s 426(6).
17 Ibid ss 426(1),(7), 730, Sch 24.

1451. Advertisements, notices and proxies. The forms of any advertisements, notices and proxy papers that may be required are settled in the chambers of the winding-up court. The proxy papers used must be in the special form approved by the court where the company is in winding up[1]. In all cases the liquidator or chairman of the meeting, or, where the company is being wound up by the court, the official receiver, may be appointed as proxy[2]. Where, in the case of a company being wound up, the official receiver is acting as liquidator, foreign creditors may be authorised to give proxies to a person named by him, and to deposit them at a place named by him in the foreign country[3]. Proxies so given are valid, and may be used at the meeting, particulars of them being telegraphed to the chairman of the meeting[3].

Where there are several classes of creditors or contributories, and the scheme does not affect the rights of some particular class, it is not the practice, nor is it necessary, for notice of any meeting to be sent to the members of that class[4]. It is, however, necessary for different classes of those affected by the scheme to have separate meetings[5]. Thus, where there are matured and unmatured policy holders of an insurance company, a dissentient holder of a matured policy is not bound by a resolution passed at a meeting to which all the policy holders are summoned, as he is a member of the class of matured policy holders[6], and, for this purpose, holders of shares partly paid with the uncalled balance paid in advance of calls and carrying interest are a different class from holders of fully-paid shares[7]. Where a separate meeting of one class has not been held but is ordered to be convened on the application to sanction the scheme, the court, after the holding of that meeting, will sanction the scheme without requiring fresh meetings of the other classes[8].

1 *Practice Direction* (1896) 40 Sol Jo 545; *Re Magadi Soda Co Ltd* (1925) 94 LJ Ch 217. The order directing a meeting to be summoned should provide that proxies be in the form laid down in *Practice Direction* supra, or in such other form as may be settled in chambers: *Practice Direction* [1910] WN 154. There is no particular time for lodging proxies for a creditors' meeting: see *Lainière de Roubaix v Glen Glove and Hosiery Co Ltd* 1926 SC 91. Directors who, pursuant to the court's order, receive proxies are bound to use them: *Re Dorman, Long & Co Ltd, Re South Durham Steel and Iron Co Ltd* [1934] Ch 635. On the construction of a proxy see *Re Waxed Papers Ltd* [1937] 2 All ER 481, CA.

2 *Re General Mortgage Society (Great Britain) Ltd* [1942] Ch 274, [1942] 1 All ER 414; and see the Insolvency Rules 1986, SI 1986/1925, r 8.1(1),(3),(4) and paras 2417 et seq, 2708 note 2 post.

3 *Re English, Scottish and Australian Chartered Bank* [1893] 3 Ch 385, CA.

4 *Re Tea Corpn Ltd, Sorsbie v Tea Corpn Ltd* [1904] 1 Ch 12, CA; *Re Clydesdale Bank Ltd* 1950 SC 30. The dissent of a class which is not interested may be disregarded: *Re Tea Corpn Ltd, Sorsbie v Tea Corpn Ltd* supra; *Re Oceanic Steam Navigation Co Ltd* [1939] Ch 41 at 47, [1938] 3 All ER 740 at 742. As to the costs of notices of meetings to sanction a scheme of arrangement with debenture holders which should be allowed on taxation in a debenture holders' action see *Re Commonwealth Oil Corpn Ltd, Pearson v Commonwealth Oil Corpn Ltd* [1917] 1 Ch 404.

5 *Sovereign Life Assurance Co v Dodd* [1892] 2 QB 573, CA; *Re United Provident Assurance Co Ltd* [1910] 2 Ch 477 (where the scheme was subsequently sanctioned: see *Re United Provident Assurance Co Ltd* [1911] WN 40); and see *Lainière de Roubaix v Glen Glove and Hosiery Co Ltd* 1926 SC 91 (where a secured creditor was held to have voted wrongly at a meeting of unsecured creditors). The applicant for the sanction of the scheme has the responsibility for determining what creditors are to be summoned as constituting a class; objections must be taken on the hearing of the petition, and the applicant takes the risk of the petition being dismissed: *Practice Note* [1934] WN 142.

6 *Sovereign Life Assurance Co v Dodd* [1892] 2 QB 573, CA.

7 *Re United Provident Assurance Co Ltd* [1910] 2 Ch 477.

8 *Re United Provident Assurance Co Ltd* [1911] WN 40.

1452. Meaning of 'creditor'. Every person having a pecuniary claim against the company, whether actual or contingent, is a creditor. Thus debenture holders or other secured creditors can be bound by a scheme[1], and also foreign and Commonwealth creditors when their rights are in question in England[2]. The assignor of a lease to the company whom the company has indemnified against liability under the lease is barred by a scheme under which the assets and liabilities of the company giving the indemnity are to be transferred to another company, and cannot assert any claim to have the assets of the former company impounded to meet any claim arising under the indemnity[3].

A person who recovers judgment against the company in a claim for unliquidated damages subsequent to the scheme being approved is not bound thereby[4].

1 *Re Empire Mining Co* (1890) 44 ChD 402 at 409 (where dissentient debenture holders were deprived of their security).

2 *Re Alabama, New Orleans, Texas and Pacific Junction Rly Co* [1891] 1 Ch 213, CA; *New Zealand Loan and Mercantile Agency Co v Morrison* [1898] AC 349 at 357, PC; and see *Armani v Castrique* (1844) 13 M & W 443 at 447 per Pollock CB; *Dane v Mortgage Insurance Corpn Ltd* [1894] 1 QB 54 at 57, CA (where a scheme was sanctioned by the colonial as well as the English court in order to bind the company's assets in both jurisdictions).

3 *Craig's Claim* [1895] 1 Ch 267, CA; compromised on appeal sub nom *Craig v Midland Coal and Iron Co* (1896) 74 LT 744, HL.

4 *Trocko v Renlita Products Pty Ltd: Commonwealth Trading Bank (Claimant)* (1973) 5 SASR 207 (S Aust SC).

1453. Majorities required at meetings. The majority required is a majority in number representing three-fourths in value of those present and voting at the meeting in person or by proxy[1]. Where the debentures are registered, only the registered holder or his proxy may vote.

The court must be satisfied that the statutory provisions have been complied with, that the classes of creditors or members have been fairly represented by those who attended, and that the statutory majority approving the scheme is acting in good faith in the interest of the class it professes to represent[2]. The arrangement must also be such as a business person would reasonably approve, and fair and reasonable as regards the different classes, if any[2].

In the absence of any improper motive there is nothing to prevent a creditor who is also a shareholder from voting at a meeting of creditors or shareholders[3]; but the court will not sanction a scheme when the required majority is made up of persons not acting in good faith in the interest of the class to which they belong, as, for example, where their votes are given to rid themselves of their liability for amounts unpaid on their shares[4]. If, owing to insufficient notice or conflicting interests, there is a doubt whether the resolutions passed at any meeting really represent the views of the bulk of the members of the class, the court may direct another meeting to be called[5].

Where a person has two claims against a company and votes in respect of one only, he is not thereby estopped from ranking in a scheme of arrangement in respect of both claims[6].

Persons who enter into a secret bargain with a creditor by which, in return for a guarantee of payment of his claim, he agrees to support a scheme, are guilty of conspiracy[7].

1 See the Companies Act 1985 s 425(2) and para 1447 ante. Where, in the case of a company limited by guarantee, each member has precisely the same stake in the company, the position is the same as if each member owned a single share in it, and a three-fourths' majority of votes satisfies the requirements of s 425(2): *Re NFU Development Trust Ltd* [1973] 1 All ER 135, [1972] 1 WLR 1548. Even where the scheme involves the purchase by an outsider of all the issued shares of the company, it is not necessarily one which falls within the Companies Act 1985 ss 428–430F (as substituted) (see para 1202 et seq ante) and which thus requires approval by a 90% majority: *Re National Bank Ltd* [1966] 1 All ER 1006, [1966] 1 WLR 819. Cf para 1447 note 9 ante. The court will not sanction a scheme where in the case of creditors it is impossible to estimate the amount of debts: *Re Albert Life Assurance Co* (1871) 6 Ch App 381.

2 *Re Alabama, New Orleans, Texas and Pacific Junction Rly Co* [1891] 1 Ch 213, CA; *Re English, Scottish and Australian Chartered Bank* [1893] 3 Ch 385, CA; *Re Anglo-Continental Supply Co Ltd* [1922] 2 Ch 723 at 736; *Re Shandon Hydropathic Co Ltd* 1911 SC 1153; *Lainière de Roubaix v Glen Glove and Hosiery Co Ltd*

1926 SC 91; cf *Re Neath and Brecon Rly Co* [1892] 1 Ch 349, CA; *Re London Chartered Bank of Australia* [1893] 3 Ch 540 at 545. See also *Re Dorman, Long & Co Ltd, Re South Durham Steel and Iron Co Ltd* [1934] Ch 635 at 655-657.
3 *Re Madras Irrigation and Canal Co* [1881] WN 172.
4 *Re Wedgwood Coal and Iron Co* (1877) 6 ChD 627.
5 *Re Alabama, New Orleans, Texas and Pacific Junction Rly Co* [1891] 1 Ch 213 at 240, CA.
6 *Curtis v BURT Co Ltd* (1912) 28 TLR 585, CA.
7 *R v Potter* [1953] 1 All ER 296; and see CRIMINAL LAW vol 11(1) (Reissue) para 59 et seq.

1454. Concurrence of trustees. Where any securities of a company are subject to a trust, trustees may concur in any scheme or arrangement for the reconstruction of a company, for the sale of all or any part of its property and undertaking to another company, for its amalgamation with another company, for the release, modification or variation of any rights, privileges or liabilities attached to the securities subject to the trust or any of them[1], or for the acquisition of its securities, or of control of the company, by another company[2].

1 See the Trustee Act 1925 s 10(3)(a),(b),(c),(d) and TRUSTS vol 48 (Reissue) para 885. The scheme must not be construed as altering existing rights, unless the language used compels such an interpretation: *Re T H Downing & Co Ltd* [1940] 1 All ER 333, CA.
2 See the Trustee Act 1925 s 10(3)(bb) (as added) and TRUSTS vol 48 (Reissue) para 885. This provision in effect abrogates the decision in *Re Walker's Settlement, Royal Exchange Assurance Corpn v Walker* [1935] Ch 567, CA.

1455. Meaning of 'arrangement'. 'Arrangement' includes a reorganisation of the share capital of the company by the consolidation of shares of different classes or by the division of shares into shares of different classes or by both those methods[1]. The word 'arrangement' should not be limited to something analogous in some sense to 'compromise'[2].

1 Companies Act 1985 s 425(6)(b). By the Companies (Consolidation) Act 1908 s 45 (repealed), which was not re-enacted in later companies legislation, a separate procedure was provided for the reorganisation of share capital by the consolidation of shares of different classes or the division of shares into shares of different classes. Section 45 (repealed) was limited to the two kinds of reorganisation specified in it: *Re Schweppes Ltd* [1914] 1 Ch 322, CA, approving *Re Palace Hotel Ltd* [1912] 2 Ch 438, and overruling *Re Doecham Gloves Ltd* [1913] 1 Ch 226. A scheme for reorganisation of either of those kinds had to be effected under the Companies (Consolidation) Act 1908 s 45 (repealed), and could not be effected under s 120 (replaced in extended form by the Companies Act 1985 s 425 (as amended)): *Re Palace Hotel Ltd* supra; *Re J A Nordberg Ltd* [1915] 2 Ch 439.
    For other cases decided on the Companies (Consolidation) Act 1908 s 45 (repealed) see *Re Australian Estates and Mortgage Co Ltd* [1910] 1 Ch 414; *Re North Cheshire Brewery Co Ltd* (1920) 64 Sol Jo 463; *Re Vine and General Rubber Trust Ltd* (1913) 108 LT 709; *Re Garden Village (Hull) Ltd* [1923] 1 Ch 230.
2 *Re Guardianship Assurance Co Ltd* [1917] 1 Ch 431, CA, explaining the dictum of Buckley J in *Re General Motor Cab Co Ltd* [1913] 1 Ch 377 at 384, CA; and see *Re Odhams Press Ltd* [1925] WN 10; *Re Barclays Bank Ltd* (1918) 62 Sol Jo 752. It is not, however, appropriate to a scheme where membership rights are proposed to be confiscated or surrendered without compensation: *Re NFU Development Trust Ltd* [1973] 1 All ER 135, [1972] 1 WLR 1548.

1456. Compromises or arrangements sanctioned. Any kind of compromise or arrangement may be sanctioned[1].
The court may sanction schemes containing the following provisions: that first mortgage debenture holders are to be postponed to other debentures or charges about to be issued or created[2]; that, in place of debentures guaranteed by a third party, debentures without a guarantee are to be issued to the holders and the guarantor

released[3]; that debenture holders and other creditors of the company are to accept, in satisfaction of their debts, shares in a company to be formed[4]; that debentures, the interest on which is to be payable only out of the company's profits, are to be taken in satisfaction of debentures, the interest on which is payable whether profits are made or not[5]; that debentures repayable at periods of from three to five years shall be converted into debenture stock repayable only in a certain limited number of events[6]; or that shares in a company shall be sub-divided and that each shareholder shall surrender some of the shares resulting from the sub-division to another company whose undertaking is to be merged in that of the company whose shares they hold[7].

Arrangements may be entered into for the purpose of reconstructing the company, staying any pending winding-up proceedings, or distributing assets amongst creditors[8]. They may also involve reduction of the company's capital, but, if so, the proceedings must comply with the other requirements of the Companies Act 1985 applicable in such cases[9]. They may be concerned solely with the rights of classes of shareholders among themselves[10]. Where a company in winding up is to continue to carry on its business, the scheme should provide for the liquidation to be stayed, the liquidator discharged and the assets handed over by him to the company[11]. The court will not sanction a scheme which provides for payment of costs or remuneration unless it also provides for their taxation or allowance by the court[12].

A scheme of arrangement may be sanctioned under which the company's undertaking is to be transferred to a new company and members of the company are to receive fully-paid or partly-paid shares in the new company in the proportions specified in the scheme[13]. In such a case the court usually requires, as a condition of its sanction, provisions to be made for dissentient members to have the same rights as they would have had if the sale had been effected under the provision[14] permitting a liquidator to accept shares etc as consideration for the sale of the company's property[15]; and, where the scheme involves a sale of the company's undertaking to a new company in the manner contemplated by that provision, that provision must be complied with[16]. The court cannot sanction any scheme which involves the doing of an act which is ultra vires the company[17].

A scheme need not expressly reserve the rights of any creditors against sureties for the company's debts, as those rights are unaffected by a scheme[18]. It should provide that it may be modified with the court's approval; and the court has often acted on such a clause[19].

In case of ambiguity the provisions of a scheme should be construed in the sense in which an ordinary business person would understand them[20].

The court has no jurisdiction to sanction a scheme of which the company disapproves, and hence, unless it is proposed as part of the scheme that a general meeting of the company should be convened to obtain such approval, the court will not convene meetings to sanction a scheme of which the board of the company disapproves[21].

1 Ie sanctioned under the Companies Act 1985 s 425 (as amended): see para 1447 ante. The procedure under s 425 (as so amended) with its built-in safeguards should be adopted where what is proposed is in fact a compromise or arrangement rather than other procedures (eg under the Insolvency Act 1986 s 167: see para 2338 post): *Re Trix Ltd, Re Ewart Holdings Ltd* [1970] 3 All ER 397, [1970] 1 WLR 1421. Cf para 1453 note 1 ante. For the meaning of 'arrangement' see para 1455 ante.

2 *Re Western of Canada Oil, Lands and Works Co* [1874] WN 148.

3 *Shaw v Royce Ltd* [1911] 1 Ch 138.

4 *Slater v Darlaston Steel and Iron Co* [1877] WN 165; *Re Empire Mining Co* (1890) 44 ChD 402.

5 *Re Alabama, New Orleans, Texas and Pacific Junction Rly Co* [1891] 1 Ch 213, CA.

6 *Re Shandon Hydropathic Co Ltd* 1911 SC 1153.

7 *Re Guardian Assurance Co* [1917] 1 Ch 431, CA; *Re Barclays Bank Ltd* (1918) 62 Sol Jo 752. In Scotland a
   scheme has been sanctioned which involved an alteration in the memorandum of association in order to
   clarify the rights of the several classes of shareholders, these rights not being clearly stated in the
   memorandum: *Edinburgh Railway Access and Property Co v Scottish Metropolitan Assurance Co* 1932 SC 2.

8 *Re Dominion of Canada Freehold Estate and Timber Co Ltd* (1886) 55 LT 347; *Re Marine Investment Co, ex p
   Poole's Executors* (1873) 8 Ch App 702; and see *Re Stephen Walters & Sons Ltd* [1926] WN 236. As to
   provisions for ex gratia payments to officers and employees see now the Companies Act 1985 s 719 and
   para 1101 ante. As to the former law see *Hutton v West Cork Rly Co* (1883) 23 ChD 654, followed in
   Parke v Daily News Ltd [1962] Ch 927, [1962] 2 All ER 929.

9 *Re Cooper, Cooper and Johnson Ltd* [1902] WN 199; *Re White Pass and Yukon Rly Co Ltd* (1918) 63 Sol Jo
   55; and see *Re Stephen Walters & Sons Ltd* [1926] WN 236. As to a reduction of capital see para 215 et seq
   ante. A reduction and arrangement scheme has been sanctioned which involved the issue of participation certificates to shareholders, part of whose paid-up capital and whose arrears of dividend had been
   cancelled, with provision for the payment of dividend on the certificates, and their redemption at their
   nominal value, out of profits: see *Re Hoare & Co Ltd and Reduced* [1910] WN 87.

10 *Re Odhams Press Ltd* [1925] WN 10.

11 See para 2773 post.

12 *Re Mortgage Insurance Corpn* [1896] WN 4.

13 *Re Canning Jarrah Timber Co (Western Australia) Ltd* [1900] 1 Ch 708, CA; *Re Standard Exploration Co Ltd*
   (1902) Times, 21, 26 March; *Re Tea Corpn Ltd, Sorsbie v Tea Corpn Ltd* [1904] 1 Ch 12, CA; *Re Sandwell
   Park Colliery Co Ltd* [1914] 1 Ch 589. These cases were discussed in *Re Anglo-Continental Supply Co Ltd*
   [1922] 2 Ch 723. See also the Companies Act 1985 s 427 and paras 1460, 1462 post. Section 427(3)(e)
   specifically enables the court to make provisions for dissentients. For a scheme involving a transfer to
   another company and an application to the court under provisions now re-enacted in s 427 for
   facilitation of the scheme see *Re Star Tea Co Ltd* [1930] WN 4. For the position as to taxation of gains see
   CAPITAL GAINS TAXATION.

14 See the Insolvency Act 1986 s 110 and para 1480 et seq post.

15 See *Re Canning Jarrah Timber Co (Western Australia) Ltd* [1900] 1 Ch 708, CA; *Re Sandwell Park Colliery
   Co Ltd* [1914] 1 Ch 589 (where the scheme itself made provision for dissentient shareholders similar to
   those in the Companies Act 1985 s 427(3)). Cf *Re Standard Exploration Co Ltd* (1902) Times, 21, 26
   March; *Re Tea Corpn Ltd, Sorsbie v Tea Corpn Ltd* [1904] 1 Ch 12 (where no provisions for dissentients
   were included); *Re Anglo-Continental Supply Co Ltd* [1922] 2 Ch 723 (where provisions for dissentients
   were made which did not correspond with those in the Insolvency Act 1986 s 110); *Re Star Tea Co Ltd*
   [1930] WN 4.

16 *Re General Motor Cab Co Ltd* [1913] 1 Ch 377, CA (distinguished in *Re Sandwell Park Colliery Co Ltd*
   [1914] 1 Ch 589, and explained in *Re Anglo-Continental Supply Co Ltd* [1922] 2 Ch 723); *Re Guardian
   Assurance Co* [1917] 1 Ch 431 at 441, CA per Younger J and at 540 per Warrington LJ. See also *Re
   Needhams Ltd* [1923] WN 289.

17 *Re Oceanic Steam Navigation Co Ltd* [1939] Ch 41, [1938] 3 All ER 740. As to ultra vires acts generally see
   para 1097 et seq ante.

18 *Re London Chartered Bank of Australia* [1893] 3 Ch 540 at 546; *Dane v Mortgage Insurance Corpn Ltd* [1894]
   1 QB 54, CA; *Finlay v Mexican Investment Corpn* [1897] 1 QB 517. The scheme may vary the rights of
   creditors as to interest: *Re New English Bank of River Plate Ltd* (1898) 14 TLR 526, CA. When sanctioned
   by the court, a scheme has statutory operation and thus a discharge effected by the scheme of one of
   several joint debtors does not release the others: *Re Garner's Motors Ltd* [1937] Ch 594, [1937] 1 All ER
   671.

19 See *Re Canning Jarrah Timber Co (Western Australia) Ltd* [1900] 1 Ch 708, CA.

20 *Re Land Securities Co Ltd, ex p Farquhar* [1896] 2 Ch 320, CA (where it was held that 'under discount at
   the rate of 4% per annum' meant a rebate of interest at that rate).

21 *Re Savoy Hotel Ltd* [1981] Ch 351, [1981] 3 All ER 646.

1457. Petition for sanction of scheme. The application to the court to sanction
the scheme[1], after it has been approved at the meetings[2], is by petition[3]. If the
application is by the liquidator, he should be neutral[4]. If a winding up by the court is
pending, the court may hear a report by the official receiver[5].

1 See para 1447 ante.

2 The sanction of the meeting is generally obtained before the sanction of the court, but it is immaterial in
   what order the sanctions are obtained: *Re Dynevor, Dyffryn and Neath Abbey Collieries Co* (1879) 11 ChD
   605, CA.

3 RSC Ord 102 r 4(1)(f). As to proceedings on a petition under this rule see paras 252-254 ante. No summons for directions is required to be taken out unless there is included in the petition an application for an order under the Companies Act 1985 s 427 (see para 1460 post): RSC Ord 102 r 6(2)(a). As to the hearing of the petition in the vacation see *Re Showering, Vine Products and Whiteways Ltd* [1968] 3 All ER 276n, [1968] 1 WLR 1381.

4 *Re Alabama, New Orleans, Texas and Pacific Junction Rly Co* [1891] 1 Ch 213 at 233, CA.

5 See the Insolvency Rules 1986, SI 1986/1925, r 7.9(1)(a) and para 2839 post.

1458. Sanction of scheme. Sanction is by no means automatic[1], and the court may and often does impose conditions on its sanction to a scheme[2]. A scheme may be sanctioned even though one or more previous schemes have been sanctioned[3]. Once sanctioned, a scheme is binding on all contributories[4] and creditors, subject to the jurisdiction of the court, but cannot be pleaded as a defence to an action in a Commonwealth court by a non-assenting creditor suing for the whole of his debt[5]. An order sanctioning a scheme by virtue of which property is transferred may attract ad valorem stamp duty as a conveyance on sale[6].

Persons whose interests are affected by a scheme but who have not opposed it at a meeting or appeared at the hearing of the petition cannot appeal without leave from the order sanctioning the scheme[7].

1 Thus, in a case where, after the company's circular recommending a scheme of arrangement, there were dealings by certain directors in the company's shares, the court required to be satisfied, before it would sanction the scheme, that no reasonable shareholder would have come to a different conclusion in relation to the scheme if he had known of such dealings: *Re Minster Assets plc* [1985] BCLC 200 (the court was so satisfied).

2 Where the scheme proposes that a company in difficulties is to make over its assets to a new company, the sanction may be refused unless the scheme provides that the new company will undertake to obey the court's order as to any proceedings which the court may think it right to have taken against officers of the old company: *Practice Note* [1894] WN 166. In *Re Olympia Ltd* (1900) 16 TLR 564 the order on the assignment of the undertaking to a new company provided that the rights of the official receiver and liquidator to take misfeasance proceedings against officers of the transferor company should be preserved, and that the proceeds of any such proceedings should be held for the benefit of the shareholders of the transferor company. In *Re Canning Jarrah Timber Co (Western Australia) Ltd* [1900] 1 Ch 708, CA, the court gave its sanction to a scheme involving a sale to a new company (inter alia) on the liquidator's undertaking to pay the unsecured creditors in full out of the assets in his hands, not to act upon a resolution for the underwriting of the new company's shares, and to procure the cancellation of certain underwriting agreements. See also *Re Showerings, Vine Products and Whiteways Ltd* [1968] 3 All ER 276n, [1968] 1 WLR 1381 (conditions imposed as price of hearing in vacation). Shareholders opposing the scheme will be granted their costs only in the event of their being successful either in obtaining the court's refusal to sanction the scheme or in obtaining the alteration of the scheme: *Edinburgh Railway Access and Property Co v Scottish Metropolitan Assurance Co* 1932 SC 2, explaining *Re Thomas De la Rue & Co Ltd and Reduced* [1911] 2 Ch 361 at 367, 368 (where the costs of an unsuccessful dissentient shareholder were provided for). See also *Carruth v ICI Ltd* [1937] AC 707 at 757, 763, 771, HL; and para 265 text and note 9 ante. As to the protection of dissentient shareholders when the scheme involves a sale of the company's undertaking see para 1456 ante.

3 *Re Mortgage Insurance Corpn* [1896] WN 4.

4 *Nicholl v Eberhardt Co* (1889) 59 LJ Ch 103, CA.

5 *New Zealand Loan and Mercantile Agency Co v Morrison* [1898] AC 349, PC, approving *Gibbs & Sons v Société Industrielle et Commerciale des Metaux* (1890) 25 QBD 399, CA. Similarly, a Commonwealth scheme which has been sanctioned is no defence in England: see *Dane v Mortgage Insurance Corpn Ltd* [1894] 1 QB 54, CA.

6 *Sun Alliance Insurance Ltd v IRC* [1972] Ch 133, [1971] 1 All ER 135. As to conveyance on sale duty see STAMP DUTIES vol 44(1) (Reissue) para 1027 et seq; and as to reliefs from stamp duty see para 1491 et seq post.

7 *Re Securities Insurance Co* [1894] 2 Ch 410, CA.

1459. Registration of order sanctioning scheme. The court's order sanctioning a scheme has no effect until an office copy of it has been delivered to the registrar of companies for registration; and a copy of every such order must be annexed to every copy of the company's memorandum issued after the order has been made or, in the case of a company not having a memorandum, to every copy so issued of the instrument constituting or defining the company's constitution[1]. If a company makes default in complying with this provision, the company, and every officer of it who is in default, is liable on summary conviction to a fine not exceeding one-fifth of the statutory maximum[2].

1 Companies Act 1985 s 425(3). As to the application of s 425(3) to statutory water companies see para 1447 note 7 ante.
2 Ibid ss 425(4), 730, Sch 24. For the meaning of 'officer who is in default' and 'the statutory maximum' see para 1161 ante.

1460. Provisions for facilitating reconstruction and amalgamation. Where application is made to the court[1] for the sanctioning of a compromise or arrangement, and it is shown to the court that the compromise or arrangement has been proposed for the purposes of, or in connection with, a scheme for the reconstruction[2] of any company or companies[3], or the amalgamation[4] of any two or more companies, and that under the scheme the whole or any part of the undertaking or the property of any company concerned in the scheme ('a transferor company') is to be transferred to another company ('the transferee company'), the court may, either by the order sanctioning the compromise or arrangement or by any subsequent order, make provision for all or any of the following matters[5]:

(1) the transfer to the transferee company of the whole or any part of the undertaking and of the property[6] or liabilities[7] of any transferor company[8];

(2) the allotting or appropriation by the transferee company of any shares, debentures, policies or other like interests in that company which, under the compromise or arrangement, are to be allotted or appropriated by that company to or for any person[9];

(3) the continuation by or against the transferee company of any legal proceedings pending by or against any transferor company[10];

(4) the dissolution, without winding up, of any transferor company[11];

(5) the provision to be made for any persons who, within such time and in such manner as the court directs, dissent from the compromise or arrangement[12];

(6) such incidental, consequential and supplemental matters as are necessary to secure that the reconstruction or amalgamation is fully and effectively carried out[13].

If such an order provides for the transfer of property or liabilities, that property is, by virtue of the order, transferred to, and vests in, and those liabilities are, by virtue of the order, transferred to and become liabilities of, the transferee company; and property, if the order so directs, vests freed from any charge which, by virtue of the compromise or arrangement, is to cease to have effect[14].

1 Ie under the Companies Act 1985 s 425 (as amended): see para 1447 et seq ante. If the application under this provision is not included in the original petition (see para 1447 ante), the application is by originating summons: see para 1462 post.
2 For the meaning of 'reconstruction' see para 1461 post.

3 Notwithstanding the provisions of the Companies Act 1985 s 425(6)(a) (see para 1447 note 2 ante), 'company' for the purposes of this provision includes only a company as defined by s 735(1) (see para 11 ante): s 427(6).

4 For the meaning of 'amalgamation' see para 1461 post.

5 Companies Act 1985 s 427(1),(2). As to the disapplication of s 427 in the case of statutory water companies see para 1447 note 7 ante.

6 For these purposes, 'property' includes property, rights and powers of every description: ibid s 427(6). Non-transferable contracts are not included; thus contracts of personal services are not transferred: *Nokes v Doncaster Amalgamated Collieries Ltd* [1940] AC 1014, [1940] 3 All ER 549, HL. Nor are corporation tax allowances as to deductions for wear and tear and losses transferred: *United Steel Companies Ltd v Cullington (Inspector of Taxes)* [1940] AC 812, [1940] 2 All ER 170, HL; and see INCOME TAXATION vol 23 (Reissue) para 476.

7 For these purposes, 'liabilities' includes duties: Companies Act 1985 s 427(6). Duties as a personal representative are not transferred: *Re Skinner* [1958] 3 All ER 273, [1958] 1 WLR 1043.

8 Companies Act 1985 s 427(3)(a).

9 Ibid s 427(3)(b).

10 Ibid s 427(3)(c).

11 Ibid s 427(3)(d).

12 Ibid s 427(3)(e).

13 Ibid s 427(3)(f).

14 Ibid s 427(4).

1461. Meaning of 'reconstruction' and 'amalgamation'. Neither 'reconstruction' nor 'amalgamation'[1] has a precise legal meaning[2]. Where an undertaking is being carried on by a company and is in substance transferred, not to an outsider, but to another company consisting substantially of the same shareholders with a view to its being continued by the transferee company, there is a reconstruction[3]. It is none the less a reconstruction because all the assets do not pass to the new company, or all the shareholders of the transferor company are not shareholders in the transferee company, or the liabilities of the transferor company are not taken over by the transferee company[4].

Amalgamation is a blending of two or more existing undertakings into one undertaking, the shareholders of each blending company becoming substantially the shareholders in the company which is to carry on the blended undertakings[5]. There may be amalgamation either by the transfer of two or more undertakings to a new company, or by the transfer of one or more undertakings to an existing company[5]. Strictly 'amalgamation' does not, it seems, cover the mere acquisition by a company of the share capital of other companies which remain in existence and continue their undertakings[6], but the context in which the term is used may show that it is intended to include such an acquisition[7].

The question whether a winding up is for the purposes of reconstruction or amalgamation depends upon the whole of the circumstances of the winding up[8].

1 As to provisions for facilitating the reconstruction and amalgamation of companies see the Companies Act 1985 s 427 and para 1460 ante. The terms 'reconstruction' and 'amalgamation' are used, without being statutorily defined, in the Trustee Act 1925 s 10(3) (as amended): see para 1454 ante.

2 *Re South African Supply and Cold Storage Co, Wild v South African Supply and Cold Storage Co* [1904] 2 Ch 268 at 281.

3 *Hooper v Western Counties and South Wales Telephone Co Ltd* (1892) 68 LT 78 at 80; *Re South African Supply and Cold Storage Co, Wild v South African Supply and Cold Storage Co* [1904] 2 Ch 268 at 286; *Swithland Investments Ltd v IRC* [1990] STC 448.

4 *Re South African Supply and Cold Storage Co, Wild v South African Supply and Cold Storage Co* [1904] 2 Ch 268 at 286. The business and persons interested must, however, be substantially the same: *Re South African Supply and Cold Storage Co, Wild v South African Supply and Cold Storage Co* supra. For instances

where these requirements were not fulfilled see *Brooklands Selangor Holdings Ltd v IRC* [1970] 2 All ER 76, [1970] 1 WLR 429 (where, after the transfer of part of a company's undertaking, the stockholders in the new company comprised a majority in number, but less than half in value, of the stockholders in the original company); *Baytrust Holdings Ltd v IRC* [1971] 3 All ER 76, [1971] 1 WLR 1333 (where certain assets not required by a company in its business were passed on to its shareholders in the form of shares in a new company).

5 *Re South African Supply and Cold Storage Co, Wild v South African Supply and Cold Storage Co* [1904] 2 Ch 268 at 287; *Swithland Investments Ltd v IRC* [1990] STC 448.

6 See *Re Walker's Settlement, Royal Exchange Assurance Corpn v Walker* [1935] Ch 567, CA ('amalgamation' in the Trustee Act 1925 s 10(3)(c); but the actual decision in this case is nullified by the Trustee Investments Act 1961 s 9(1) (see para 1454 ante)).

7 See *Lever Bros Ltd v IRC* [1938] 2 KB 518 at 524, [1938] 2 All ER 808 at 809, CA (where it was said that the Finance Act 1927 s 55 (repealed) contemplated two methods of amalgamation 'or what is commonly called amalgamation': (1) where a company acquires the undertaking or part of the undertaking of another; and (2) where a company acquires the shares of another without acquiring the assets).

8 *Re South African Supply and Cold Storage Co, Wild v South African Supply and Cold Storage Co* [1904] 2 Ch 268 at 282; and see *Hooper v Western Counties and South Wales Telephone Co Ltd* (1892) 68 LT 78 (reconstruction); *Re Bank of Hindustan, China and Japan Ltd, Higg's Case* (1865) 2 Hem & M 657; *Re Empire Assurance Corpn, ex p Bagshaw* (1867) LR 4 Eq 341 at 349; *Imperial Bank of China, India and Japan v Bank of Hindustan, China and Japan* (1868) LR 6 Eq 91; *New Zealand Gold Extraction Co (Newbery-Vautin Process) v Peacock* [1894] 1 QB 622 at 627, 628, 632, CA; *Wall v London and Northern Assets Corpn* [1898] 2 Ch 469, CA; *Re Borax Co, Foster v Borax Co* [1899] 2 Ch 130 at 135; *Greenwich Pier Co v Thames River Conservators* (1905) 21 TLR 669 (amalgamation).

As to the amalgamation of insurance companies see INSURANCE; as to the fiscal problems involved in amalgamations see CAPITAL GAINS TAXATION and INCOME TAXATION; and as to relief from stamp duties see para 1491 et seq post.

1462. Application to facilitate reconstruction and amalgamation.

The necessary directions by the court to facilitate reconstruction and amalgamation[1] may be included in the order it makes on the hearing of the petition to sanction the scheme, but usually liberty is reserved in that order to apply for further directions[2]. Any such application must be made by originating summons in the general form[3].

Within seven days after the order[4] has been made, every company in relation to which it is made must cause an office copy of the order to be delivered to the registrar of companies for registration; and, if default is made in complying with this provision, the company, and every officer of it who is in default, is liable on summary conviction to a fine not exceeding one-fifth of the statutory maximum and, on conviction after continued contravention, to a daily default fine not exceeding one-fiftieth of the statutory maximum[5].

If a scheme by inadvertence orders or prohibits an act which otherwise the parties could not bind themselves to do or not do, it is to that extent a nullity[6].

1 Ie under the Companies Act 1985 s 427: see para 1460 ante.

2 Ie as to any of the matters set out in para 1460 ante: *Re Star Tea Co Ltd* [1930] WN 4. As to the practice of referring the matter to the registrar to make the necessary order see *Practice Note* [1939] WN 121.

3 RSC Ord 102 r 2(1),(2)(a). If the companies concerned in the application are the same as those concerned in the proceedings to sanction the scheme, so that no change is made in the title of the proceedings, an ordinary summons may in practice be employed.

4 It is unnecessary in the order to give details of the properties transferred or to except contracts which are not transferable (see para 1460 note 6 ante), such as those for personal services: *Re L Hotel Co Ltd and Langham Hotel Co Ltd* [1946] 1 All ER 319 (decided under the former RSC Ord 53B r 13, Appendix L Form 37 (revoked)). No form is now prescribed.

5 Companies Act 1985 ss 427(5), 730, Sch 24. For the meaning of 'officer who is in default', 'the statutory maximum' and 'daily default fine' see para 1161 ante.

6 *Re Skinner* [1958] 3 All ER 273, [1958] 1 WLR 1043, following *Nokes v Doncaster Amalgamated Collieries Ltd* [1940] AC 1014, [1940] 3 All ER 549, HL; and see *Re L Hotel Co Ltd and Langham Hotel Co Ltd* [1946] 1 All ER 319.

(ii) Mergers and Divisions of Public Companies

1463. Additional requirements. The statutory provisions relating to compromises and arrangements[1] are modified where:

(1) a compromise or arrangement[2] is proposed between a public company[3] and certain specified persons[4] for the purposes of, or in connection with, a scheme for the reconstruction of any company[5] or companies or the amalgamation of any two or more companies;

(2) the circumstances are those statutorily prescribed[6]; and

(3) the consideration for the transfer or each of the transfers envisaged[7] is to be shares in the transferee company[8] or any of the transferee companies receivable by members of the transferor company[9] or transferor companies, with or without any cash payment to members[10].

1 Ie the Companies Act 1985 ss 425-427 (as amended): see paras 1447-1462 ante.

2 For these purposes, 'compromise or arrangement' means a compromise or arrangement to which ibid s 427A(1) (added by the Companies (Mergers and Divisions) Regulations 1987, SI 1987/1991, reg 2(a), Schedule Pt I; amended by the Companies Act 1989 s 114(2)) applies: Companies Act 1985 s 427A(8) (added by the Companies (Mergers and Divisions) Regulations 1987 Schedule Pt I). As to compromises or arrangements in connection with the transfer of long-term business of an insurance company see the Insurance Companies Act 1982 s 49, Sch 2C para 1 (as added) and INSURANCE.

3 For the meaning of 'public company' see para 82 ante. In relation to a transferee company which is a Northern Ireland company, 'public company' means a public company within the meaning of the Companies (Northern Ireland) Order 1986, SI 1986/1032, art 12: Companies Act 1985 s 427A(8) (as added: see note 2 supra). For the meaning of 'transferee company' see note 8 infra; and for the meaning of 'Northern Ireland company' see note 5 infra.

4 Ie the persons specified in ibid s 425(1) (as amended): see para 1447 ante.

5 For these purposes, 'company' includes only a company as defined in ibid s 735(1) (see para 1447 note 2 ante) except that, in the case of a transferee company, it also includes a company as defined in the Companies (Northern Ireland) Order 1986 art 3 (a 'Northern Ireland company'): Companies Act 1985 s 427A(8) (as added: see note 2 supra).

6 Ie the circumstances specified in ibid s 427A(2), Cases 1-3 (as added): see para 1464 heads (1)-(3) post.

7 Ie in ibid s 427A(2), Cases 1-3 (as added), as appropriate.

8 For these purposes, 'transferee company' means a company to which a transfer envisaged in any of ibid s 427A(2), Cases 1-3 (as added) is to be made: s 427A(8) (as added: see note 2 supra).

9 For these purposes, 'transferor company' means a company whose undertaking, property and liabilities are to be transferred by means of a transfer envisaged in any of ibid s 427A(2), Cases 1-3 (as added): s 427A(8) (as added: see note 2 supra). 'Property' and 'liabilities' have the same meaning as in s 427 (see para 1460 notes 6, 7 respectively ante): s 427A(8) (as so added).

10 Ibid s 427A(1) (as added: see note 2 supra). Section 427A (as added) does not apply where the company in respect of which the compromise or arrangement is proposed is being wound up; nor does s 427A (as added) apply to compromises or arrangements in respect of which an application has been made to the court for an order under s 425(1) (as amended) (see para 1447 ante) before 1 January 1988: s 427A(4),(5) (added by the Companies (Mergers and Divisions) Regulations 1987 Schedule Pt I). Where the Companies Act 1985 s 427 (see para 1460 ante) would apply in the case of a scheme but for the fact that the transferee company or any of the transferee companies is a company within the meaning of the Companies (Northern Ireland) Order 1986 art 3 and thus not within the definition of 'company' in the Companies Act 1985 s 427(6) (see para 1460 note 3 ante), s 427 applies notwithstanding that fact: s 427A(6) (added by the Companies (Mergers and Divisions) Regulations 1987 Schedule Pt I). In the case of a scheme mentioned in the Companies Act 1985 s 427A(1) (as so added), for a company within the meaning of the Companies (Northern Ireland) Order 1986 art 3, the reference in the Companies Act 1985 s 427(5) (see para 1462 ante) to the registrar of companies has effect as a reference to the registrar as defined in the Companies (Northern Ireland) Order 1986 art 2: Companies Act 1985 s 427A(7) (added by the Companies (Mergers and Divisions) Regulations 1987 Schedule Pt I).

1464. Circumstances in which additional requirements apply. The circumstances specified[1] for the application of the statutory provisions[2] to mergers and divisions of public companies are:

(1) where, under the scheme[3], the undertaking, property[4] and liabilities[4] of the company[5] in respect of which the compromise or arrangement in question is proposed are to be transferred to another public company[6], other than one formed for the purpose of, or in connection with, the scheme ('Case 1 Scheme')[7];

(2) where, under the scheme, the undertaking, property and liabilities of each of two or more public companies concerned in the scheme, including the company in respect of which the compromise or arrangement in question is proposed, are to be transferred to a company, whether or not a public company, formed for the purpose of, or in connection with, the scheme ('Case 2 Scheme')[8];

(3) where, under the scheme, the undertaking, property and liabilities of the company in respect of which the compromise or arrangement in question is proposed are to be divided among and transferred to two or more companies each of which is either a public company, or a company, whether or not a public company, formed for the purpose of, or in connection with, the scheme ('Case 3 Scheme')[9].

Before sanctioning any compromise or arrangement[10], the court may, on the application of any pre-existing transferee company[11] or any member or creditor of it, or, an administration order[12] being in force in relation to the company, the administrator, order a meeting of the members of the company or any class of them or of the creditors of the company or any class of them to be summoned in such manner as the court directs[13].

1 Ie in the Companies Act 1985 s 427A(2) (added by the Companies (Mergers and Divisions) Regulations 1987, SI 1987/1991, reg 2(a), Schedule Pt I): see para 1463 ante.
2 Ie the Companies Act 1985 ss 425-427 (as amended): see paras 1447-1462 ante.
3 For these purposes, 'the scheme' means the scheme mentioned in ibid s 427A(1)(a) (as added) (see para 1463 head (1) ante): s 427A(8) (added by the Companies (Mergers and Divisions) Regulations 1987 Schedule Pt I).
4 For the meaning of 'property' and liabilities' see para 1463 note 9 ante.
5 For the meaning of 'company' see para 1463 note 5 ante.
6 For the meaning of 'public company' see para 1463 note 3 ante.
7 Companies Act 1985 s 427A(2), Case 1 (as added: see note 1 supra).
8 Ibid s 427A(2), Case 2 (as added: see note 1 supra).
9 Ibid s 427A(2), Case 3 (as added: see note 1 supra).
10 Ie under ibid s 425(2): see para 1447 ante.
11 For these purposes, 'pre-existing transferee company' means a transferee company other than one formed for the purposes of, or in connection with, the scheme: ibid s 427A(8) (as added: see note 3 supra).
12 As to administration orders see para 2080 et seq post.
13 Companies Act 1985 s 427A(3) (added by the Companies (Mergers and Divisions) Regulations 1987 Schedule Pt I).

1465. Meeting of transferee company. Subject to specified exceptions[1], the court must not sanction a compromise or arrangement[2] unless a majority in number representing three-fourths in value of each class of members of every pre-existing transferee company[3] concerned in the scheme[4], present and voting either in person or by proxy at a meeting, agree to the scheme[5].

1 Ie the Companies Act 1985 s 427A, Sch 15B para 10(1) (see para 1473 post), para 12(4) (see para 1475 post), para 14(2) (see para 1475 post) (all as added and renumbered).
2 Ie under ibid s 425(2): see para 1447 ante. For the meaning of 'compromise or arrangement' see para 1463 note 2 ante.
3 For the meaning of 'pre-existing transferee company' see para 1464 note 11 ante.
4 For the meaning of 'the scheme' see para 1464 note 3 ante.
5 Companies Act 1985 Sch 15B para 1 (added by the Companies (Mergers and Divisions) Regulations 1987, SI 1987/1991, reg 2(c), Schedule Pt II; renumbered by the Companies Act 1989 s 114(2)).

1466. Draft terms of merger. The court must not sanction the compromise or arrangement[1] under its statutory power[2] unless:

(1) a draft of the proposed terms of the scheme[3] ('the draft terms') has been drawn up and adopted by the directors of all the transferor[4] and pre-existing transferee[5] companies concerned in the scheme[6];

(2) in the case of each of those companies[7], the directors have delivered[8] a copy of the draft terms to the registrar of companies[9] and the registrar has published in the Gazette[10] notice of receipt by him of a copy of the draft terms from that company[11]; and

(3) that notice was so published at least one month before the date of any meeting of that company summoned[12] to approve the scheme[13].

The draft terms must give particulars of at least the following matters:

(a) in respect of each transferor company and transferee company[14] concerned in the scheme, its name, the address of its registered office and whether it is a company limited by shares or a company limited by guarantee and having a share capital[15];

(b) the number of shares in any transferee company to be allotted to members of any transferor company for a given number of their shares (the 'share exchange ratio') and the amount of any cash payment;

(c) the terms relating to the allotment of shares in any transferee company;

(d) the date from which the holding of shares in a transferee company will entitle the holders to participate in profits, and any special conditions affecting that entitlement;

(e) the date from which the transactions of any transferor company are to be treated for accounting purposes as being those of any transferee company;

(f) any rights or restrictions attaching to any shares or other securities in any transferee company to be allotted under the scheme to the holders of shares to which special rights or restrictions attach, or of other securities, in any transferor company, or the measures proposed concerning them;

(g) any amount or benefit paid or given or intended to be paid or given to any of the experts providing the statutory reports[16] or to any director of a transferor company or pre-existing transferee company, and the consideration for the payment of benefit[17].

Where the scheme is a Case 3 Scheme[18], the draft terms must also:

(i) give particulars of the property[19] and liabilities[19] to be transferred, to the extent these are known to the transferor company, and their allocation among the transferee companies;

(ii) make provision for the allocation among and transfer to the transferee companies of any other property and liabilities which the transferor company has or may subsequently acquire; and

(iii) specify the allocation to members of the transferor company of shares in the transferee companies and the criteria upon which that allocation is based[20].

1   For the meaning of 'compromise or arrangement' see para 1463 note 2 ante.

2   Ie under the Companies Act 1985 s 425(2): see para 1447 ante.

3   For the meaning of 'the scheme' see para 1464 note 3 ante.

4   For the meaning of 'transferor company' see para 1463 note 9 ante.

5   For the meaning of 'pre-existing transferee company' see para 1464 note 11 ante.

6   Companies Act 1985 s 427A(1), Sch 15B para 2(1)(a) (added by the Companies (Mergers and Divisions) Regulations 1987, SI 1987/1991, reg 2(c), Schedule Pt II; renumbered by the Companies Act 1989 s 114(2)).

7   For the meaning of 'company' see para 1463 note 5 ante.

8   Ie delivered pursuant to the Companies Act 1985 s 711(1)(s) (as added): see para 70 ante.

9   For the meaning of 'the registrar of companies' see para 1463 note 10 ante.

10   For the meaning of 'the Gazette' see para 70 note 1 ante. In relation to a company which is a Northern Ireland company, 'the Gazette' means the Belfast Gazette: Companies Act 1985 s 427A(8) (added by the Companies (Mergers and Divisions) Regulations 1987 reg 2(a), Schedule Pt I). For the meaning of 'Northern Ireland company' see para 1463 note 5 ante.

11   Companies Act 1985 Sch 15B para 2(1)(b) (added by the Companies (Mergers and Divisions) Regulations 1987 Schedule Pt II; renumbered by the Companies Act 1989 s 114(2)). The Companies Act 1985 Sch 15B para 2(1)(b) (as so added and renumbered) is subject to Sch 15B para 11(3) (as added and renumbered) (see para 1474 post): Sch 15B para 2(1)(b) (as so added and renumbered).

12   Ie under ibid s 425(1) (as amended) (see para 1447 ante) or for the purposes of Sch 15B para 1 (as added and renumbered) (see para 1465 ante).

13   Ibid Sch 15B para 2(1)(c) (added by the Companies (Mergers and Divisions) Regulations 1987 Schedule Pt II; renumbered by the Companies Act 1989 s 114(2)). The Companies Act 1985 Sch 15B para 2(1)(c) (as so added and renumbered) is subject to Sch 15B paras 10–14 (as added and renumbered) (see para 1473 et seq post): Sch 15B para 2(1)(c) (as so added and renumbered).

14   For the meaning of 'transferee company' see para 1463 note 8 ante.

15   With effect from 22 December 1980 a company cannot be formed as or become a company limited by guarantee with a share capital: Companies Act 1985 s 1(4).

16   Ie pursuant to ibid Sch 15B para 5 (as added and renumbered): see para 1469 post.

17   Ibid Sch 15B para 2(2) (added by the Companies (Mergers and Divisions) Regulations 1987 Schedule Pt II; renumbered by the Companies Act 1989 s 114(2)). The Companies Act 1985 Sch 15B para 2(2) (as so added and renumbered) is subject to Sch 15B para 12(2) (as added and renumbered) (see para 1475 post): Sch 15B para 2(2) (as so added and renumbered).

18   For the meaning of 'Case 3 Scheme' see para 1464 head (3) ante.

19   For the meaning of 'property' and 'liabilities' see para 1463 note 9 ante.

20   Companies Act 1985 Sch 15B para 2(3) (added by the Companies (Mergers and Divisions) Regulations 1987 Schedule Pt II; renumbered by the Companies Act 1989 s 114(2)).

1467. Documents and information to be made available. Subject to certain exceptions[1], the court must not sanction the compromise or arrangement[2] under its statutory power[3] unless:

    (1)   in the case of each transferor company[4] and each pre-existing transferee company[5] the directors have drawn up and adopted a report (a 'directors' report')[6];

    (2)   where the scheme is a Case 3 Scheme[7], the directors of the transferor company have reported to every meeting of the members or any class of members of that company duly summoned[8], and to the directors of each transferee company[9], any material changes in the property[10] and liabilities[10] of the transferor company between the date when the draft terms were adopted and the date of the meeting in question;

    (3)   where the directors of a transferor company have reported to the directors of a transferee company such a change as is mentioned in head (2) above, the latter have reported that change to every meeting of the members or any class of members of that transferee company duly summoned[11], or have sent a report of that change to every member who would have been entitled to receive a notice of such a meeting;

(4) a report by an expert (an 'expert's report')[12] has been drawn up on behalf of each transferor company and pre-existing transferee company;

(5) the members of any transferor company or transferee company were able to inspect at the registered office of that company copies of specified documents[13] in relation to every transferor company and pre-existing transferee company concerned in the scheme during a period beginning one month before, and ending on, the date of the first meeting of the members or any class of members of the first-mentioned transferor or transferee company duly summoned[14] and those members were able to obtain copies of those documents or any part of them on request during that period free of charge; and

(6) the memorandum and articles of association of any transferee company which is not a pre-existing transferee company, or a draft thereof, has been approved by ordinary resolution[15] of every transferor company concerned in the scheme[16].

1   Ie subject to the Companies Act 1985 s 427A(1), Sch 15B paras 10-14 (as added and renumbered): see para 1473 et seq post.
2   For the meaning of 'compromise or arrangement' see para 1463 note 2 ante.
3   Ie under the Companies Act 1985 s 425(2): see para 1447 ante.
4   For the meaning of 'transferor company' see para 1463 note 9 ante.
5   For the meaning of 'pre-existing transferee company' see para 1464 note 11 ante.
6   Ie a report complying with the Companies Act 1985 Sch 15B para 4 (as added and renumbered): see para 1468 post.
7   For the meaning of 'Case 3 Scheme' see para 1464 head (3) ante.
8   Ie summoned pursuant to the Companies Act 1985 s 425(1) (as amended): see para 1447 ante.
9   For the meaning of 'transferee company' see para 1463 note 8 ante.
10   For the meaning of 'property' and 'liabilities' see para 1463 note 9 ante.
11   Ie summoned pursuant to the Companies Act 1985 Sch 15B para 1 (as added and renumbered): see para 1465 ante.
12   Ie a report complying with ibid Sch 15B para 5 (as added and renumbered): see para 1469 post.
13   Ie the documents listed in ibid Sch 15B para 6(1) (as added and renumbered): see para 1470 post.
14   Ie summoned pursuant to ibid s 425(1) (as amended) (see para 1447 ante) or Sch 15B para 1 (as added and renumbered) (see para 1465 ante).
15   As to ordinary resolutions see para 681 ante.
16   Companies Act 1985 Sch 15B para 3 (added by the Companies (Mergers and Divisions) Regulations 1987, SI 1987/1991, reg 2(c), Schedule Pt II; renumbered by the Companies Act 1989 s 114(2)).

1468. Directors' report. The directors' report[1] must consist of:

(1) the statement explaining the effect of the compromise or arrangement[2]; and

(2) in so far as that statement does not contain the following matters, a statement setting out the legal and economic grounds for the draft terms[3], and in particular for the share exchange ratio[4], and, where the scheme is a Case 3 Scheme[5], for the criteria upon which the allocation to members of the transferor company[6] of shares in the transferee companies[7] was based, and specifying any special valuation difficulties[8].

Where the scheme is a Case 3 Scheme, the directors' report must also state whether a report has been made to the transferee company under the statutory provisions relating to the valuation of a non-cash consideration before allotment[9] and, if so, whether that report has been delivered[10] to the registrar of companies[11].

1   For the meaning of 'directors' report' see para 1467 head (1) ante.
2   Ie the statement required by the Companies Act 1985 s 426 (as amended): see para 1450 ante.
3   For the meaning of 'the draft terms' see para 1466 head (1) ante.
4   For the meaning of 'share exchange ratio' see para 1466 head (b) ante.
5   For the meaning of 'Case 3 scheme' see para 1464 head (3) ante.
6   For the meaning of 'transferor company' see para 1463 note 9 ante.

7 For the meaning of 'transferee company' see para 1463 note 8 ante.
8 Companies Act 1985 s 427A(1), Sch 15B para 4(1) (added by the Companies (Mergers and Divisions) Regulations 1987, SI 1987/1991, reg 2(c), Schedule Pt II; renumbered by the Companies Act 1989 s 114(2)).
9 Ie under the Companies Act 1985 s 103 (as amended): see para 468 ante.
10 Ie under ibid s 111: see para 474 ante.
11 Ibid Sch 15B para 4(2) (added by the Companies (Mergers and Divisions) Regulations 1987 Schedule Pt II; renumbered by the Companies Act 1989 s 114(2)). For the meaning of 'the registrar of companies' see para 1463 note 10 ante.

1469. Expert's report. Except where a joint expert is appointed[1], an expert's report[2] must consist of a separate written report on the draft terms[3] to the members of one transferor company[4] or pre-existing transferee company[5] concerned in the scheme[6] drawn up by a separate expert appointed on behalf of that company[7]. The court may, however, on the joint application of all the transferor companies and pre-existing transferee companies concerned in the scheme, approve the appointment of a joint expert to draw up a single report on behalf of all those companies[8]. An expert must be independent of any of the companies[9] concerned in the scheme, that is to say a person qualified at the time of the report to be appointed, or to continue to be, an auditor of those companies[10].

Where it appears to an expert that a valuation is reasonably necessary to enable him to draw up the report, and it appears to him to be reasonable for that valuation, or part of it, to be made, or for him to accept such a valuation, by another person who:

(1) appears to him to have the requisite knowledge and experience to make the valuation or that part of it; and

(2) is not an officer or servant[11] of any of the companies concerned in the scheme or any other body corporate[12] which is one of those companies' subsidiary[13] or holding company[14] or a subsidiary of one of those companies' holding company or a partner or employee of such an officer or servant,

he may arrange for or accept such a valuation, together with a report which will enable him to make his own report[15].

Where any valuation is made by a person other than the expert himself, the latter's report must state that fact and must also state the former's name and what knowledge and experience he has to carry out the valuation, and describe so much of the undertaking, property[16] and liabilities[16] as were valued by the other person, and the method used to value them, and specify the date of the valuation[17].

An expert's report must:

(a) indicate the method or methods used to arrive at the share exchange ratio[18] proposed;

(b) give an opinion as to whether the method or methods used are reasonable in all the circumstances of the case, indicate the values arrived at using each such method and, if there is more than one method, give an opinion on the relative importance attributed to such methods in arriving at the value decided on;

(c) describe any special valuation difficulties which have arisen;

(d) state whether, in the expert's opinion, the share exchange ratio is reasonable; and

(e) in the case of a valuation made by a person other than himself, state that it appeared to himself reasonable to arrange for it to be so made or to accept a valuation so made[19].

Each expert has the right of access to all such documents of all the transferor companies and pre-existing transferee companies concerned in the scheme, and the right to require from the companies' officers all such information, as he thinks necessary for the purpose of making his report[20].

1   Ie under the Companies Act 1985 s 427A(1), Sch 15B para 5(2) (added by the Companies (Mergers and Divisions) Regulations 1987, SI 1987/1991, reg 2(c), Schedule Pt II; renumbered by the Companies Act 1989 s 114(2)): see infra.
2   For the meaning of 'expert's report' see para 1467 head (4) ante.
3   For the meaning of 'the draft terms' see para 1466 head (1) ante.
4   For the meaning of 'transferor company' see para 1463 note 9 ante.
5   For the meaning of 'pre-existing transferee company' see para 1464 note 11 ante.
6   For the meaning of 'the scheme' see para 1464 note 3 ante.
7   Companies Act 1985 Sch 15B para 5(1) (added by the Companies (Mergers and Divisions) Regulations 1987 Schedule Pt II; renumbered by the Companies Act 1989 s 114(2)).
8   Companies Act 1985 Sch 15B para 5(2) (as added and renumbered: see note 1 supra).
9   For the meaning of 'company' see para 1463 note 5 ante.
10   Companies Act 1985 Sch 15B para 5(3) (added by the Companies (Mergers and Divisions) Regulations 1987 Schedule Pt II; renumbered by the Companies Act 1989 s 114(2)). As to auditors, their qualifications and disqualification for appointment, see para 955 et seq ante.
11   For these purposes, the reference to an officer or servant does not include an auditor: Companies Act 1985 Sch 15B para 5(5) (added by the Companies (Mergers and Divisions) Regulations 1987 Schedule Pt II; renumbered by the Companies Act 1989 s 114(2)).
12   For the meaning of 'body corporate' see para 89 note 8 ante.
13   For the meaning of 'subsidiary' see para 827 ante.
14   For the meaning of 'holding company' see para 827 ante.
15   Companies Act 1985 Sch 15B para 5(4) (added by the Companies (Mergers and Divisions) Regulations 1987 Schedule Pt II; renumbered by the Companies Act 1989 s 114(2)).
16   For the meaning of 'property' and 'liabilities' see para 1463 note 9 ante.
17   Companies Act 1985 Sch 15B para 5(6) (added by the Companies (Mergers and Divisions) Regulations 1987 Schedule Pt II; renumbered by the Companies Act 1989 s 114(2)).
18   For the meaning of 'share exchange ratio' see para 1466 head (b) ante.
19   Companies Act 1985 Sch 15B para 5(7) (added by the Companies (Mergers and Divisions) Regulations 1987 Schedule Pt II; renumbered by the Companies Act 1989 s 114(2)).
20   Companies Act 1985 Sch 15B para 5(8) (added by the Companies (Mergers and Divisions) Regulations 1987 Schedule Pt II; renumbered by the Companies Act 1989 s 114(2)).

1470. Inspection of documents. In relation to any company[1], the documents which must be made available for inspection[2] are:

(1)   the draft terms[3];

(2)   the directors' report[4];

(3)   the expert's report[5];

(4)   the company's annual accounts, together with the relevant directors' report and auditors' report, for the last three financial years[6] ending on or before the relevant date[7]; and

(5)   if the last of those financial years ended more than six months before the relevant date[7], an accounting statement consisting of:

     (a)   a balance sheet dealing with the state of affairs of the company as at a date not more than three months before the draft terms were adopted by the directors; and

     (b)   where the company would be required to prepare group accounts if that date were the last day of a financial year, a consolidated balance sheet dealing with the state of affairs of the company and its subsidiary undertakings[8] as at that date[9].

The statutory requirements[10] as to balance sheets forming part of a company's annual accounts, and the matters to be included in notes thereto, apply to any balance sheet required for the accounting statement, with such modifications as are necessary by reason of its being prepared otherwise than as at the last day of a financial year[11]. Any balance sheet required for the accounting statement must be approved by the board of directors and signed on behalf of the board by a director of the company[12].

1   For the meaning of 'company' see para 1463 note 5 ante.
2   Ie under the Companies Act 1985 s 427A(1), Sch 15B para 3(e) (as added and renumbered): see para 1467 ante.
3   See para 1466 ante.
4   Ie the report referred to in the Companies Act 1985 Sch 15B para 4 (as added and renumbered): see para 1467 ante.
5   See para 1469 ante.
6   For the meaning of 'financial year' see para 806 ante.
7   For these purposes, 'the relevant date' means one month before the first meeting of the company summoned under the Companies Act 1985 s 425(1) (as amended) (see para 1447 ante) or for the purposes of Sch 15B para 1 (as added and renumbered) (see para 1465 ante): Sch 15B para 6(1) (added by the Companies (Mergers and Divisions) Regulations 1987, SI 1987/1991, reg 2(c), Schedule Pt II; renumbered by the Companies Act 1989 s 114(2); amended by the Companies Act 1989 s 23, Sch 10 para 22(1),(4)).
8   For the meaning of 'subsidiary undertaking' see para 828 ante.
9   Companies Act 1985 Sch 15B para 6(1),(2) (added by the Companies (Mergers and Divisions) Regulations 1987 Schedule Pt II; renumbered by the Companies Act 1989 s 114(2); respectively amended and substituted by the Companies Act 1989 Sch 10 para 22(1)-(5)).
10   Ie the requirements of the Companies Act 1985: see paras 832, 833, 838 et seq ante. In relation to a company within the meaning of the Companies (Northern Ireland) Order 1986, SI 1986/1032, art 3 the reference to the requirements of the Companies Act 1985 is to be construed as reference to the corresponding requirements of the Companies (Northern Ireland) Order 1986: Companies Act 1985 Sch 15B para 6(5) (added by the Companies (Mergers and Divisions) Regulations 1987 Schedule Pt II; renumbered by the Companies Act 1989 s 114(2); substituted by the Companies Act 1989 Sch 10 para 22(1),(5)).
11   Companies Act 1985 Sch 15B para 6(3) (added by the Companies (Mergers and Divisions) Regulations 1987 Schedule Pt II; renumbered by the Companies Act 1989 s 114(2); substituted by the Companies Act 1989 Sch 10 para 22(1),(5)).
12   Companies Act 1985 Sch 15B para 6(4) (added by the Companies (Mergers and Divisions) Regulations 1987 Schedule Pt II; renumbered by the Companies Act 1989 s 114(2); substituted by the Companies Act 1989 Sch 10 para 22(1),(5)).

1471. Securities other than shares to which special rights attached. Where any security of a transferor company[1] to which special rights are attached is held by a person other than as a member or creditor of the company[2], the court must not sanction a compromise or arrangement[3] under its statutory power[4] unless, under the scheme[5], that person is to receive rights in a transferee company[6] of equivalent value[7]. The above provisions do not, however, apply in the case of any such security where the holder has agreed otherwise, or the holder is, or under the scheme is to be, entitled to have the security purchased by a transferee company involved in the scheme on terms which the court considers reasonable[8].

1   For the meaning of 'transferor company' see para 1463 note 9 ante.
2   For the meaning of 'company' see para 1463 note 5 ante.
3   For the meaning of 'compromise or arrangement' see para 1463 note 2 ante.
4   Ie under the Companies Act 1985 s 425(2): see para 1447 ante.
5   For the meaning of 'the scheme' see para 1464 note 3 ante.
6   For the meaning of 'transferee company' see para 1463 note 8 ante.
7   Companies Act 1985 s 427A(1), Sch 15B para 8(1) (added by the Companies (Mergers and Divisions) Regulations 1987, SI 1987/1991, reg 2(c), Schedule Pt II; renumbered by the Companies Act 1989 s 114(2)).

8 Companies Act 1985 Sch 15B para 8(2) (added by the Companies (Mergers and Divisions) Regulations 1987 Schedule Pt II; renumbered by the Companies Act 1989 s 114(2)).

1472. Date and consequences of compromise or arrangement. Where the court sanctions[1] a compromise or arrangement[2], it must in its order or in a subsequent order made under the provisions for facilitating company reconstructions or amalgamations[3] fix a date on which the transfer or transfers to the transferee company[4] or transferee companies of the undertaking, property[5] and liabilities[5] of the transferor company[6] are to take place; and any such order which provides for the dissolution of the transferor company must fix the same date for the dissolution[7].

If it is necessary for the transferor company to take any steps to ensure that the undertaking, property and liabilities are fully transferred, the court must fix a date, not later than six months after the date fixed for the transfer or transfers to take place, by which such steps must be taken, and for that purpose may postpone the dissolution of the transferor company until that date[8]. The court may postpone or further postpone the date so fixed if it is satisfied that the steps mentioned above[9] cannot be completed by the date, or latest date, so fixed[10].

1 Ie under the Companies Act 1985 s 425(2): see para 1447 ante.
2 For the meaning of 'compromise or arrangement' see para 1463 note 2 ante.
3 Ie the Companies Act 1985 s 427: see para 1460 ante.
4 For the meaning of 'transferee company' see para 1463 note 8 ante.
5 For the meaning of 'property' and 'liabilities' see para 1463 note 9 ante.
6 For the meaning of 'transferor company' see para 1463 note 9 ante.
7 Companies Act 1985 s 427A(1), Sch 15B para 9(1),(2) (added by the Companies (Mergers and Divisions) Regulations 1987, SI 1987/1991, reg 2(c), Schedule Pt II; renumbered by the Companies Act 1989 s 114(2)).
8 Companies Act 1985 Sch 15B para 9(3) (added by the Companies (Mergers and Divisions) Regulations 1987 Schedule Pt II; renumbered by the Companies Act 1989 s 114(2)).
9 Ie mentioned in the Companies Act 1985 Sch 15B para 9(3) (as added and renumbered): see supra.
10 Ibid Sch 15B para 9(4) (added by the Companies (Mergers and Divisions) Regulations 1987 Schedule Pt II; renumbered by the Companies Act 1989 s 114(2)).

1473. Additional requirements; general modifications. The court may sanction[1] a compromise or arrangement[2] notwithstanding that any meeting otherwise required[3] has not been summoned by a pre-existing transferee company[4] ('the relevant company') and no notice of receipt of a copy of the draft terms of the scheme[5] has been timeously published[6] and the members have not been able to exercise their statutory right to inspect the documents to be made available[7], if the court is satisfied that the following conditions have been complied with[8].

Subject to certain statutory provisions[9], the conditions mentioned above are:
(1) that the publication of notice of receipt of the draft terms[10] by the registrar of companies[11] took place in respect of the relevant company at least one month before the date of any meeting of members of any transferor company[12] concerned in the scheme[13] duly summoned[14] to approve the scheme;
(2) that the members of the relevant company were able to inspect at the registered office of that company the documents to be made available[15] in relation to every transferor company and transferee company[16] concerned in the scheme during a period ('the relevant period') beginning one month before, and ending on, the date of any such meeting, and that they were able to obtain copies of those documents or any part of them on request during that period free of charge; and
(3) that one or more members of the relevant company, who together held not less than 5% of the paid-up capital of that company which carried the right to vote at

general meetings of the company, would have been able during the relevant period to require that a meeting of each class of members be called for the purpose of deciding whether or not to agree to the scheme but that no such requisition had been made[17].

1 Ie pursuant to the Companies Act 1985 s 425(2): see para 1447 ante.
2 For the meaning of 'compromise or arrangement' see para 1463 note 2 ante.
3 Ie pursuant to the Companies Act 1985 s 427A(1), Sch 15B para 1 (as added and renumbered): see para 1465 ante.
4 For the meaning of 'pre-existing transferee company' see para 1464 note 11 ante.
5 For the meaning of 'the scheme' see para 1464 note 3 ante.
6 Ie in accordance with the Companies Act 1985 Sch 15B para 2(1)(c) (as added and renumbered): see para 1466 head (3) ante.
7 Ie pursuant to ibid Sch 15B para 3(e) (as added and renumbered): see para 1467 head (5) ante.
8 Ibid Sch 15B para 10(1) (added by the Companies (Mergers and Divisions) Regulations 1987, SI 1987/1991, reg 2(c), Schedule Pt II; renumbered by the Companies Act 1989 s 114(2)).
9 Ie subject to the Companies Act 1985 Sch 15B para 11(3) (as added and renumbered) (see para 1474 post) and Sch 15B para 12(3) (as added and renumbered) (see para 1475 post).
10 For the meaning of 'the draft terms' see para 1466 head (1) ante.
11 Ie pursuant to the Companies Act 1985 Sch 15B para 2(1)(b) (as added and renumbered): see para 1466 head (2) ante.
12 For the meaning of 'transferor company' see para 1463 note 9 ante.
13 For the meaning of 'the scheme' see para 1464 note 3 ante.
14 Ie summoned pursuant to the Companies Act 1985 s 425(1) (as amended): see para 1447 ante.
15 Ie the documents listed in ibid Sch 15B para 6(1) (as added, renumbered and amended): see para 1470 heads (1)-(5) ante.
16 For the meaning of 'transferee company' see para 1463 note 8 ante.
17 Companies Act 1985 Sch 15B para 10(2) (added by the Companies (Mergers and Divisions) Regulations 1987 Schedule Pt II; renumbered by the Companies Act 1989 s 114(2)).

1474. Additional requirements; modifications for Case 3 Schemes. Where the scheme is a Case 3 Scheme[1], the statutory provisions relating to the documents and information to be made available[2] are modified[3], if all members holding shares in, and all persons holding other securities of, any of the transferor companies[4] and pre-existing transferee companies[5] concerned in the scheme[6] on the date of the application to the court[7], being shares or securities which as at that date carry the right to vote in general meetings of the company, so agree[8].

The court may by order direct in respect of any transferor company or pre-existing transferee company that the requirements relating to delivering copies of the draft terms[9] and publication of notice of receipt of the draft terms[10] or inspection of the draft terms[11] shall not apply; and the court may by order direct that the general exception from the statutory requirements[12] shall not, with certain exceptions[13], apply to any pre-existing transferee company[14].

The court must not, however, make any such order[15] unless it is satisfied that the following conditions will be fulfilled:

(1) that the members of the company will have received or will have been able to obtain free of charge copies of the documents to be made available[16] in time to examine them before the date of the first meeting of the members or any class of members of the company[17] duly summoned[18];

(2) in the case of a pre-existing transferee company, where, in the circumstances postulated in the general exception from the statutory requirements[19], no meeting is held, that the members of that company will have received or will have been able to obtain free of charge copies of those documents in time to require a meeting[20];

(3) that the creditors of the company will have received or will have been able to obtain free of charge copies of the draft terms in time to examine them before the date of the meeting of the members or any class of members of the company, or, in the circumstances referred to in head (2) above, at the same time as the members of the company; and

(4) that no prejudice would be caused to the members or creditors of any transferor company concerned in the scheme by making the order in question[21].

1 For the meaning of 'Case 3 Scheme' see para 1464 head (3) ante.
2 Ie the Companies Act 1985 s 427A(1), Sch 15B para 6 (as added, renumbered and amended): see para 1467 ante.
3 Ie ibid Sch 15B para 3(a)-(d) (as added and renumbered) (see para 1467 heads (1)-(4) ante) do not apply and Sch 15B para 3(e) (as added and renumbered) (see para 1467 head (5) ante) does not apply as regards the documents listed in Sch 15B para 6(1)(b),(c),(e) (as added, renumbered and amended) (see para 1470 heads (2), (3), (5) ante).
4 For the meaning of 'transferor company' see para 1463 note 9 ante.
5 For the meaning of 'pre-existing transferee company' see para 1464 note 11 ante.
6 For the meaning of 'the scheme' see para 1464 note 3 ante.
7 Ie under the Companies Act 1985 s 425(1) (as amended): see para 1447 ante.
8 Ibid Sch 15B para 11(1),(2) (added by the Companies (Mergers and Divisions) Regulations 1987, SI 1987/1991, reg 2(c), Schedule Pt II; renumbered by the Companies Act 1989 s 114(2)).
9 Ie the Companies Act 1985 Sch 15B para 2(1)(b) (as added and renumbered): see para 1466 head (2) ante.
10 Ie ibid Sch 15B para 2(1)(c) (as added and renumbered): see para 1466 head (3) ante.
11 Ie ibid Sch 15B para 3(e) (as added and renumbered): see para 1467 head (5) ante.
12 Ie ibid Sch 15B para 10 (as added and renumbered): see para 1473 ante.
13 Ie with the omission of ibid Sch 15B para 10(2)(a),(b) (as added and renumbered): see para 1473 heads (1), (2) ante.
14 Ibid Sch 15B para 11(3) (added by the Companies (Mergers and Divisions) Regulations 1987 Schedule Pt II; renumbered by the Companies Act 1989 s 114(2)).
15 Ie an order under the Companies Act 1985 Sch 15B para 11(3) (as added and renumbered): see supra.
16 Ie the documents listed in ibid Sch 15B para 6(1) (as added, renumbered and amended): see para 1470 heads (1)-(5) ante.
17 For the meaning of 'the company' see para 1463 note 5 ante.
18 Ie summoned pursuant to the Companies Act 1985 s 425(1) (as amended) (see para 1447 ante) or for the purposes of Sch 15B para 1 (as added and renumbered) (see para 1465 ante).
19 Ie ibid Sch 15B para 10 (as added and renumbered): see para 1473 ante.
20 Ie a meeting pursuant to ibid Sch 15B para 10(2)(c) (as added and renumbered): see para 1473 head (3) ante.
21 Ibid Sch 15B para 11(4) (added by the Companies (Mergers and Divisions) Regulations 1987 Schedule Pt II; renumbered by the Companies Act 1989 s 114(2)).

1475. Transferee company or companies holding shares in transferor company; Case 1 Schemes. Where the scheme is a Case 1 Scheme[1], and in the case of every transferor company[2] concerned the shares in that company and such securities of that company, other than shares, as carry the right to vote at general meetings of that company, are all held by or on behalf of the transferee company[3], then the statutory provisions[4] apply subject to the following modifications[5]:

(1) the draft terms need not give particulars of:
   (a) the share exchange ratio[6] and the amount of any cash payment[7];
   (b) the terms relating to the allotment of shares in any transferee company[8]; or
   (c) the date from which the holding of shares in a transferee company will entitle the holders to participate in profits and any special conditions affecting that entitlement[9];

(2) neither the statutory provisions relating to the circulation of information[10] nor the necessity for drawing up[11] and making available[12] the directors' report[13] or the expert's report[14] apply[15];

(3) the court may sanction[16] the compromise or arrangement[17] notwithstanding that any meeting otherwise required[18] has not been summoned by any company[19] concerned in the scheme[20], that the notice of receipt by the registrar of companies of a copy of the draft terms[21] was not published at least one month before the date of any meeting of the company summoned to approve the scheme[22], and that members of any transferor or transferee company were not able timeously to inspect documents in accordance with their statutory right[23], if the court is satisfied that the following conditions have been complied with:

    (a) that the publication of notice of receipt of the draft terms by the registrar of companies[24] took place in respect of every transferor company and transferee company concerned in the scheme at least one month before the date of the order[25] ('the relevant date');

    (b) that the members of the transferee company were able to inspect at the registered office of that company copies of the documents to be made available[26] in relation to every transferor company or transferee company concerned in the scheme during a period ('the relevant period') beginning one month before, and ending on, the relevant date and that they were able to obtain copies of those documents or any part of them on request during that period free of charge; and

    (c) that one or more members of the transferee company who together held not less than 5% of the paid-up capital of the company which carried the right to vote at general meetings of the company would have been able during the relevant period to require that a meeting of each class of members be called for the purpose of deciding whether or not to agree to the scheme but that no such requisition has been made[27].

Alternatively, where the scheme is a Case 1 Scheme, and in the case of every transferor company concerned 90% or more, but not all, of the shares in that company and such securities of that company, other than shares, as carry the right to vote at general meetings of that company, are held by or on behalf of the transferee company, then the statutory provisions[28] apply subject to the following modifications[29].

The court may sanction[30] a compromise or arrangement notwithstanding that any meeting otherwise required[31] has not been summoned by the transferee company, that the notice of receipt by the registrar of companies of a copy of the draft terms was not published at least one month before the date of any meeting of the company summoned to approve the scheme[32], and that members of any transferor or transferee company were not able timeously to inspect documents in accordance with their statutory right[33], if the court is satisfied that the statutory conditions[34] have been complied with[35].

1 For the meaning of 'Case 1 Scheme' see para 1464 head (1) ante.
2 For the meaning of 'transferor company' see para 1463 note 9 ante.
3 For the meaning of 'transferee company' see para 1463 note 8 ante.
4 Ie the Companies Act 1985 s 427A, Sch 15B (as added, renumbered and amended).
5 Ibid Sch 15B para 12(1) (added by the Companies (Mergers and Divisions) Regulations 1987, SI 1987/1991, reg 2(c), Schedule Pt II; renumbered by the Companies Act 1989 s 114(2)).
6 For the meaning of 'share exchange ratio' see para 1466 head (b) ante.
7 Ie the matters mentioned in the Companies Act 1985 Sch 15B para 2(2)(b) (as added and renumbered): see para 1466 head (b) ante.

8 Ie the matters mentioned in ibid Sch 15B para 2(2)(c) (as added and renumbered): see para 1466 head (c) ante.

9 Ibid Sch 15B para 12(2) (added by the Companies (Mergers and Divisions) Regulations 1987 Schedule Pt II; renumbered by the Companies Act 1989 s 114(2)). The matters mentioned are those in the Companies Act 1985 Sch 15B para 2(2)(d) (as added and renumbered): see para 1466 head (d) ante.

10 Ie ibid s 426 (as amended): see para 1450 ante.

11 Ie ibid Sch 15B para 3(a),(d) (as added and renumbered): see para 1467 heads (1), (4) ante.

12 Ie ibid Sch 15B paras 3(e), 6(1)(b),(c) (as added and renumbered): see paras 1467 head (5), 1470 heads (2), (3) respectively ante.

13 See para 1468 ante.

14 See para 1469 ante.

15 Companies Act 1985 Sch 15B para 12(3) (added by the Companies (Mergers and Divisions) Regulations 1987 Schedule Pt II; renumbered by the Companies Act 1989 s 114(2)).

16 Ie pursuant to the Companies Act 1985 s 425(2): see para 1447 ante.

17 For the meaning of 'compromise or arrangement' see para 1463 note 2 ante.

18 Ie required by the Companies Act 1985 s 425 (as amended) (see para 1447 ante) or Sch 15B para 1 (as added and renumbered) (see para 1465 ante).

19 For the meaning of 'company' see para 1463 note 5 ante.

20 For the meaning of 'the scheme' see para 1464 note 3 ante.

21 Ie pursuant to the Companies Act 1985 Sch 15B para 2(1)(b) (as added and renumbered): see para 1466 head (2) ante.

22 Ie pursuant to ibid Sch 15B para 2(1)(c) (as added and renumbered): see para 1466 head (3) ante.

23 Ie pursuant to ibid Sch 15B para 3(e) (as added and renumbered): see para 1467 head (5) ante.

24 Ie pursuant to ibid Sch 15B para 2(1)(b) (as added and renumbered): see para 1466 head (2) ante.

25 Ie the order under ibid s 425(2): see para 1447 ante.

26 Ie the documents listed in ibid Sch 15B para 6(1)(a),(d),(e) (as added and renumbered): see para 1470 heads (1), (4), (5) ante.

27 Ibid Sch 15B para 12(4),(5) (added by the Companies (Mergers and Divisions) Regulations 1987 Schedule Pt II; renumbered by the Companies Act 1989 s 114(2)).

28 See note 4 supra.

29 Companies Act 1985 Sch 15B para 14(1) (added by the Companies (Mergers and Divisions) Regulations 1987 Schedule Pt II; renumbered by the Companies Act 1989 s 114(2)).

30 Ie under the Companies Act 1985 s 425(2): see para 1447 ante.

31 Ie required by ibid Sch 15B para 1 (as added and renumbered): see para 1465 ante.

32 Ie pursuant to ibid Sch 15B para 2(1)(c) (as added and renumbered): see para 1466 head (3) ante.

33 Ie pursuant to ibid Sch 15B para 3(e) (as added and renumbered): see para 1467 head (5) ante.

34 Ie the conditions specified in ibid Sch 15B para 10(2) (as added and renumbered) save that for this purpose the condition contained in Sch 15B para 10(2)(b) (as added and renumbered) is to be treated as referring only to the documents listed in Sch 15B para 6(1)(a),(d),(e) (as added and renumbered): see para 1470 ante.

35 Ibid Sch 15B para 14(2),(3) (added by the Companies (Mergers and Divisions) Regulations 1987 Schedule Pt II; renumbered by the Companies Act 1989 s 114(2)).

1476. Transferee company or companies holding shares in transferor company; Case 3 Schemes. Where the scheme is a Case 3 Scheme[1], and the shares in the transferor company[2] and such securities of that company, other than shares, as carry the right to vote at general meetings of that company, are all held by or on behalf of one or more transferee companies[3], the statutory provisions[4] apply subject to the following modifications[5].

The court may sanction[6] a compromise or arrangement[7] notwithstanding that any meeting otherwise required[8] has not been summoned by the transferor company, that the notice of receipt by the registrar of companies of a copy of the draft terms[9] was not published at least one month before the date of any meeting of the company summoned to approve the scheme[9], that there has been no report to every meeting of the changes in the property[10] and liabilities[10] of the transferor company[11], and that members of any transferor or transferee company were not able timeously to inspect documents to be made available in accordance with their statutory right[12], if the court is satisfied that the following conditions have been complied with[13]:

(1) that the publication of notice of receipt of the draft terms by the registrar of companies[14] took place in respect of every transferor company and transferee company concerned in the scheme at least one month before the date of the order[15];

(2) that one or more members of the transferee company who together held not less than 5% of the paid-up capital of the company which carried the right to vote at general meetings of the company would have been able during a period beginning one month before, and ending on, the date of the order[15] to require that a meeting of each class of members be called for the purpose of deciding whether or not to agree to the scheme but that no such requisition has been made;

(3) that the members of the transferor company and every transferee company concerned in the scheme were able to inspect at the registered office of the company of which they were members copies of the documents to be made available[16] in relation to every such company during a period beginning one month before, and ending on, the date of the order[17] ('the relevant date') and that they were able to obtain copies of those documents or any part of them on request during that period free of charge; and

(4) that the directors of the transferor company have sent to every member who would have been entitled to receive a notice of the meeting, had it been called, and to the directors of each transferee company, a report of any material changes in the property and liabilities of the transferor company between the date when the draft terms were adopted and a date one month before the relevant date[18].

1 For the meaning of 'Case 3 Scheme' see para 1464 head (3) ante.
2 For the meaning of 'transferor company' see para 1463 note 9 ante.
3 For the meaning of 'transferee company' see para 1463 note 8 ante.
4 Ie the Companies Act 1985 s 427A, Sch 15B (as added, renumbered and amended).
5 Ibid Sch 15B para 13(1) (added by the Companies (Mergers and Divisions) Regulations 1987, SI 1987/1991, reg 2(c), Schedule Pt II; renumbered by the Companies Act 1989 s 114(2)).
6 Ie pursuant to the Companies Act 1985 s 425(2): see para 1447 ante.
7 For the meaning of 'compromise or arrangement' see para 1463 note 2 ante.
8 Ie as required by the Companies Act 1985 s 425 (as amended): see para 1447 ante.
9 Ie pursuant to ibid Sch 15B para 2(1)(c) (as added and renumbered): see para 1466 head (3) ante.
10 For the meaning of 'property' and 'liabilities' see para 1463 note 9 ante.
11 Ie pursuant to the Companies Act 1985 Sch 15B para 3(b) (as added and renumbered): see para 1467 head (2) ante.
12 Ie pursuant to ibid Sch 15B para 3(e) (as added and renumbered): see para 1467 head (5) ante.
13 Ibid Sch 15B para 13(2) (added by the Companies (Mergers and Divisions) Regulations 1987 Schedule Pt II; renumbered by the Companies Act 1989 s 114(2)).
14 Ie pursuant to the Companies Act 1985 Sch 15B para 2(1)(b) (as added and renumbered): see para 1466 head (2) ante.
15 Ie the order under ibid s 425(2): see para 1447 ante.
16 Ie the documents listed in ibid Sch 15B para 6(1) (as added, renumbered and amended): see para 1470 heads (1)–(5) ante.
17 See note 15 supra.
18 Companies Act 1985 Sch 15B para 13(3) (added by the Companies (Mergers and Divisions) Regulations 1987 Schedule Pt II; renumbered by the Companies Act 1989 s 114(2)).

1477. Transferor company holding its own shares. The court must not sanction[1] a compromise or arrangement[2] under which any shares in a transferee company[3] are to be allotted to a transferor company[4] or its nominee in respect of shares in that transferor company held by it or its nominee[5].

1   Ie pursuant to the Companies Act 1985 s 425(2): see para 1447 ante.
2   For the meaning of 'compromise or arrangement' see para 1463 note 2 ante.
3   For the meaning of 'transferee company' see para 1463 note 8 ante.
4   For the meaning of 'transferor company' see para 1463 note 9 ante.
5   Companies Act 1985 s 427A(1), Sch 15B para 7 (added by the Companies (Mergers and Divisions) Regulations 1987, SI 1987/1991, reg 2(c), Schedule Pt II; renumbered by the Companies Act 1989 s 114(2)).

1478. Liability of transferee companies for default of another. Where the scheme is a Case 3 Scheme[1], each transferee company[2] is jointly and severally liable for any liability transferred to any other transferee company under the scheme[3] to the extent that that other has made default in satisfying that liability, but so that no transferee company is so liable for an amount greater than the amount arrived at by calculating the value at the time of the transfer of the property transferred to it under the scheme less the amount at that date of the liabilities[4] so transferred[5]. If a majority in numbers representing three-fourths in value of the creditors or any class of creditors of the transferor company[6] present and voting either in person or by proxy at a meeting duly summoned[7] so agree, the above provisions do not apply in respect of the liabilities of the creditors or that class of creditors[8].

1   For the meaning of 'Case 3 Scheme' see para 1464 head (3) ante.
2   For the meaning of 'transferee company' see para 1463 note 8 ante.
3   For the meaning of 'the scheme' see para 1464 note 3 ante.
4   For the meaning of 'liabilities' see para 1463 note 9 ante.
5   Companies Act 1985 s 427A(1), Sch 15B para 15(1) (added by the Companies (Mergers and Divisions) Regulations 1987, SI 1987/1991, reg 2(c), Schedule Pt II; renumbered by the Companies Act 1989 s 114(2)).
6   For the meaning of 'transferor company' see para 1463 note 9 ante.
7   Ie summoned pursuant to the Companies Act 1985 s 425(1) (as amended): see para 1447 ante.
8   Ibid Sch 15B para 15(2) (added by the Companies (Mergers and Divisions) Regulations 1987 Schedule Pt II; renumbered by the Companies Act 1989 s 114(2)).

(iii) Sale of Undertaking for Shares in Contemplation of Voluntary Winding Up

1479. Sale of undertaking. A sale of the company's undertaking with a view to winding up may be made and carried out by the company before liquidation under the powers conferred by its memorandum of association, or by the liquidator after the winding-up resolution[1]; or the agreement may be made by the company to be carried out by the liquidator. In any such case, if the agreement for sale contains provisions for the distribution of shares or other consideration among the members of the selling company, the sale must be carried out in accordance with the statutory provisions[2], and any clause in the memorandum or articles of the company is invalid in so far as it purports to authorise the distribution of such shares or consideration otherwise than in accordance with the statutory provisions or to deprive a dissenting shareholder of his rights under those provisions[3].

1   As to the powers of a liquidator in a voluntary winding up see paras 2718, 2719 post.
2   See para 1480 et seq post.
3   *Bisgood v Henderson's Transvaal Estates Ltd* [1908] 1 Ch 743, CA; *Etheridge v Central Uruguay Northern Extension Rly Co* [1913] 1 Ch 425; cf *Baring-Gould v Sharpinton Combined Pick and Shovel Syndicate* [1899]

2 Ch 80, CA; *Payne v Cork Co Ltd* [1900] 1 Ch 308; *Re Canning Jarrah Timber Co (Western Australia) Ltd* [1900] 1 Ch 708, CA.

The case may be different where the sale is of part of the assets only: see *Wall v London and Northern Assets Corpn* [1898] 2 Ch 469, CA. It has long been usual for companies to state in their memoranda that one of the objects is to sell the undertakings or any part of them for any consideration, and in particular for shares or other securities of any other company having similar objects, and to provide in their memoranda and articles for the distribution of such shares in specie among the members. Such a power was held to be valid, even when the whole of the company's assets were sold, and the winding up, which is required before the proceeds of the sale may be distributed amongst the shareholders, was not resolved upon at the same time: *Cotton v Imperial and Foreign Agency and Investment Corpn* [1892] 3 Ch 454. Hence dissentient members were deprived of the rights (see infra) which they would have possessed on a statutory reconstruction under the provisions now re-enacted in the Insolvency Act 1986 s 111 (see para 1480 post) to have their interests bought out. The fact that a resolution for voluntary winding up was passed at the time when the sale was sanctioned was held to be immaterial in *Doughty v Lomagunda Reefs Ltd* [1902] 2 Ch 837 (on appeal [1903] 1 Ch 673, CA); and see *Re Paterson, Laing and Bruce Ltd* (1902) 18 TLR 515. It was further held that, unless there was something in the memorandum or articles to qualify the meaning of 'shares', a company could, under the power of sale in its memorandum, accept partly-paid shares in another company: *Mason v Motor Traction Co Ltd* [1905] 1 Ch 419. Where the memorandum expressly gave power to sell for fully-paid or partly-paid shares, the Court of Appeal, without deciding that such a power was illegal, held that an agreement with another company which provided for the distribution of the partly-paid shares of the purchasing company among the shareholders of the selling company, and the proceeds of sale of the shares not taken up being applied in reduction of the purchase money, was not within the power: *Manners v St David's Gold and Copper Mines Ltd* [1904] 2 Ch 593, CA. An agreement under which the proceeds of the partly-paid shares unclaimed were to be distributed rateably amongst the members who might have claimed them was also held to be ultra vires in *Bisgood v Nile Valley Co Ltd* [1906] 1 Ch 747. In a somewhat similar case the agreement was held to be valid (*Fuller v White Feather Reward Ltd* [1906] 1 Ch 823), but the Court of Appeal in *Bisgood v Henderson's Transvaal Estates Ltd* supra subsequently approved *Bisgood v Nile Valley Co Ltd* supra and overruled *Cotton v Imperial and Foreign Agency and Investment Corpn* supra and *Fuller v White Feather Reward Ltd* supra, in so far as those cases decided that it was possible for a company to evade the provisions now embodied in the Insolvency Act 1986 ss 110, 111.

1480. Sale in voluntary winding up. Where a company ('the transferor company') is proposed to be or is being wound up voluntarily and the whole or part of its business or property is proposed to be transferred or sold to another company ('the transferee company'), whether or not a company within the meaning of the Companies Act 1985[1], the liquidator of the company being, or proposed to be, wound up ('the transferor company') may, with the requisite sanction[2], receive, in compensation or part compensation for the transfer or sale, shares, policies or other like interests in the transferee company for distribution[3] among the members of the transferor company[4]. Alternatively, the liquidator may, with that sanction, enter into any other arrangement[5] whereby the members of the transferor company may, in lieu of receiving cash, shares, policies or other like interests, or in addition thereto, participate in the profits of, or receive any other benefit from, the transferee company[6]. Any such sale or arrangement is binding on the members of the transferor company[7].

If a member of the transferor company who did not vote in favour of the special resolution sanctioning the arrangement expresses his dissent from it in writing, addressed to the liquidator and left at the company's registered office within seven days after the passing of the resolution, he may require the liquidator either to abstain from carrying the resolution into effect or to purchase his interest at a price to be determined by agreement or by arbitration in the manner specified[8].

1 See para 1481 post.
2 See para 1483 post. The sanction so required is (1) in the case of a members' voluntary winding up (see para 2698 et seq post), that of a special resolution of the company, conferring either a general authority on the liquidator or an authority in respect of any particular arrangement; and (2) in the case of a

creditors' voluntary winding up (see para 2698 et seq post), that of either the court or of the liquidation committee: Insolvency Act 1986 s 110(3). A special resolution is not invalid for these purposes by reason that it is passed before or concurrently with a resolution for voluntary winding up or for appointing liquidators; but, if an order is made within a year for winding up the company by the court, the special resolution is not valid unless sanctioned by the court: s 110(6).

3 As to the distribution of proceeds see para 1485 post: and as to relief from stamp duty see para 1491 et seq post.
4 Insolvency Act 1986 s 110(1),(2).
5 As to terms of the agreement see para 1482 post.
6 Insolvency Act 1986 s 110(4). By registering under the Companies Act 1985 an unregistered company can avail itself of this provision: *Southall v British Mutual Life Assurance Society* (1871) 6 Ch App 614.
7 Insolvency Act 1986 s 110(5).
8 Ibid s 111(1),(2). See further para 1488 post. Where the registered office of the company is abroad, notice given to the liquidator in England within the seven days' time limit is sufficient: *Brailey v Rhodesia Consolidated Ltd* [1910] 2 Ch 95. As to notice of dissent and the rights of a dissentient member and the manner specified for arbitration see further paras 1488–1490 post.

1481. When power of sale may be exercised. The statutory power of sale may be exercised even though the memorandum of association contains no power of sale[1]. The transferor company may sell to another company, whether or not a company within the meaning of the Companies Act 1985[2], but the transferor company cannot sell to an individual under the power[3], except perhaps to an agent or trustee for a company to be formed[4]. The sale binds both the shareholders and the creditors of the transferor company[5], although mortgagees may be entitled under the terms of their mortgage to prevent a sale of its assets[6].

1 *Clinch v Financial Corpn* (1868) LR 5 Eq 450 at 472 (affd (1868) 4 Ch App 117 at 121, 123); *Nicholl v Eberhardt Co* (1889) 59 LJ Ch 103, CA. The transferee company must have power under its memorandum to accept the transfer: *Pulbrook v New Civil Service Co-operation Ltd* (1877) 26 WR 11.
2 See the Insolvency Act 1986 s 110(1) and para 1480 ante. Under the Companies Act 1862 s 161 (repealed) a sale to a foreign company was permissible: *Re Irrigation Co of France, ex p Fox* (1871) 6 Ch App 176 at 192, CA. The Companies (Consolidation) Act 1908 (repealed), by introducing the definition of the word 'company' in s 285 (repealed: see now the Companies Act 1985 s 735(1) and para 11 note 1 ante), prevented a transfer to a foreign company *(Thomas v United Butter Co of France Ltd* [1909] 2 Ch 484), and such a transfer could only be effected under the Companies (Consolidation) Act 1908 s 120 (replaced by the Companies Act 1985 s 425 (as amended): see para 1447 et seq ante): *Re Anglo-Continental Supply Co Ltd* [1922] 2 Ch 723. The wording of the Insolvency Act 1986 s 110(1), however, permits a transfer to a foreign company. As to a company's change of residence see para 95 ante.
3 *Bird v Bird's Patent Deodorizing and Utilizing Sewage Co* (1874) 9 Ch App 358.
4 *Re Hester & Co Ltd* (1875) 44 LJ Ch 757 at 759; *Re Canning Jarrah Timber Co (Western Australia) Ltd* [1900] 1 Ch 708, CA.
5 *Re City and County Investment Co* (1879) 13 ChD 475, CA.
6 *Re Borax Co, Foster v Borax Co* [1899] 2 Ch 130; cf *Re H H Vivian & Co Ltd, Metropolitan Bank of England and Wales Ltd v H H Vivian & Co Ltd* [1900] 2 Ch 654.

1482. Agreement for sale. The agreement for sale[1] may validly provide that the transferor company shall call up its unpaid capital and transfer the amount so realised to the transferee company[2], or that shares in the transferee company shall be allotted either to the liquidator or directly to the members of the transferor company, and as either partly or fully paid up[3]. However, except with the consent of the members of the transferor company, a liability to pay cash cannot be imposed on those members by allotting them shares credited as partly paid up[4].

Even if he has not served notice of dissent, a member of the transferor company cannot be compelled to accept shares in the transferee company. If he has served no such notice, he is not entitled to receive compensation for his interest in the transferor company[5]; but, if the shares which he declines to accept are sold, he is entitled to the net proceeds of sale[6].

If members of the transferor company accept such shares, they become liable for the amount not credited as paid on them, the shareholder sometimes being required to make a payment of parts of the amount on application and on allotment[7].

The agreement for sale is not invalid because it provides that part of the purchase money shall be paid to the directors and secretary of the transferor company as compensation for loss of office, although proper disclosure of the proposed payment must be made to the shareholders[8].

The court has no power to authorise a sale to a transferee company in consideration of its agreeing to pay the creditors of the transferor company by instalments[9]; nor may it authorise an agreement or resolution compelling the members of that company to pay a premium upon the shares of the transferee company[10].

Subject to certain statutory relief, an agreement that the members of one company are, in exchange for their shares in it, to take shares in another company, is chargeable with ad valorem stamp duty[11].

1 See para 1480 ante.
2 *New Zealand Gold Extraction Co (Newbury-Vautin Process) v Peacock* [1894] 1 QB 622 at 630, CA; *Re Bank of South Australia (No 2)* [1895] 1 Ch 578, CA. The agreement cannot validly provide for a call to be made on the shares of the transferor company in case its assets do not realise a specified amount: *Clinch v Financial Corpn* (1868) 4 Ch App 117.
3 See eg *Re City and County Investment Co* (1879) 13 ChD 475 at 482, CA; *Postlethwaite v Port Phillip and Colonial Gold Mining Co* (1889) 43 ChD 452.
4 See *Re Imperial Mercantile Credit Association* (1871) LR 12 Eq 504; *Simpson v Palace Theatre Ltd* (1893) 69 LT 70, CA.
5 *Re Bank of Hindustan, China and Japan, ex p Los* (1865) 34 LJ Ch 609; *Re Bank of Hindustan, China and Japan, Higgs' Case* (1865) 2 Hem & M 657; *Re Bank of Hindustan, China and Japan, ex p Martin* (1865) 2 Hem & M 669; *Re Empire Assurance Corpn, ex p Bagshaw* (1867) LR 4 Eq 341; *Re London, Bombay and Mediterranean Bank Ltd, Drew's Case* (1867) 36 LJ Ch 785; and see para 1485 post.
6 *Re Lake View Extended Gold Mine (Western Australia) Ltd* [1900] WN 44.
7 *Weston v New Guston Co* (1889) 1 Meg 225, 352, CA; affd (1891) 64 LT 815, HL. Where the shares are to be taken as partly paid, the agreement should provide for the allotment being made directly to the members of the old company so as to free the liquidator from any liability: *Re City and County Investment Co* (1879) 13 ChD 475 at 482, CA; *Postlethwaite v Port Phillip and Colonial Gold Mining Co* (1889) 43 ChD 452 at 464, 465. A shareholder may be required to elect within a reasonable time whether he will accept such shares: *Zuccani v Nacupai Gold Mining Co* (1889) 61 LT 176, CA; *Burdett-Coutts v True Blue (Hannan's) Gold Mine* [1899] 2 Ch 616, CA.
8 See paras 594, 609 ante.
9 *Re General Exchange Bank* (1867) 15 WR 477.
10 *Imperial Bank of China, India and Japan v Bank of Hindustan, China and Japan* (1868) LR 6 Eq 91.
11 *Chesterfield Brewery Co v IRC* [1899] 2 QB 7. As to relief from stamp duty see para 1491 et seq post.

1483. Special resolution conferring authority. It is necessary to pass a special resolution conferring a general or special authority on the liquidator[1], authorising him to accept compensation for a transfer under the above provisions otherwise than in cash; it is not enough to pass special resolutions for voluntary winding up and for distributing the proceeds of any sale[2]. A special resolution sanctioning a transfer is not invalid because it is passed before or concurrently with a resolution to wind up the company or to appoint liquidators[3]. If, however, an order is made within a year to wind up the company by the court, the special resolution is not valid unless sanctioned by the court[3]. The court's sanction must be obtained at or after the making of the winding-up order and cannot be previously obtained in the voluntary winding up[4].

A special resolution is invalid unless the notice convening the meeting distinctly states that it is intended to proceed under the statutory provision[5]. It is invalid so far as it authorises the liquidator to pay for the underwriting of the transferee company's shares out of the transferor company's assets[6], unless the statutory requirements as to underwriting are complied with[7].

1 See para 1480 ante. As to special resolutions see para 683 ante.
2 *Etheridge v Central Uruguay Northern Extension Rly Co* [1913] 1 Ch 425.
3 See the Insolvency Act 1986 s 110(6) and para 1480 ante.
4 *Re Callao Bis Co* (1889) 42 ChD 169, CA.
5 *Imperial Bank of China, India and Japan v Bank of Hindustan, China and Japan* (1868) LR 6 Eq 91; *Re Irrigation Co of France, ex p Fox* (1871) 6 Ch App 176 at 193; *Etheridge v Central Uruguay Northern Extension Rly Co* [1913] 1 Ch 425; cf *Re Teede and Bishop Ltd* (1901) 70 LJ Ch 409.
6 *Re Canning Jarrah Timber Co (Western Australia) Ltd* [1900] 1 Ch 708, CA.
7 *Barrow v Paringa Mines (1909) Ltd* [1909] 2 Ch 658. As to underwriting shares see para 194 ante.

1484. Time limit for acceptance. A special resolution[1] directing shares in the transferee company to be offered to members of the transferor company and fixing a reasonable limit of time for acceptance is intra vires[2]. In the absence of such a stipulation, a reasonable time must be allowed, and, if the time is not reasonable, the members are not bound by it[3]. A contract for sale does not create a contractual relation between a member of the transferor company and the transferee company; and, if he applies for shares in the transferee company in pursuance of the scheme, he may withdraw his offer before it is accepted[4].

1 Ie a special resolution for the purpose of sanctioning a transfer: see para 1480 ante.
2 *Postlethwaite v Port Phillip and Colonial Gold Mining Co* (1889) 43 ChD 452; *Burdett-Coutts v True Blue (Hannan's) Gold Mine* [1899] 2 Ch 616, CA; cf *Nicholl v Eberhardt Co* (1889) 59 LJ Ch 103, CA.
3 *Zuccani v Nacupai Gold Mining Co* (1880) 61 LT 176, CA; *Re South Australian Petroleum Fields Ltd* [1894] WN 189.
4 *Re Metropolitan Fire Insurance Co, Wallace's Case* [1900] 2 Ch 671.

1485. Distribution of proceeds. The consideration for the sale must be distributed among the members of the transferor company in proportion to their rights and interests, under its regulations, in the company's assets remaining after payment of its liabilities, and any persons prejudicially affected by any other mode of distribution can only be bound by their individual consents[1]. Where the liquidator disposes of all the shares in the transferee company without reserving any for a member of the transferor company who is entitled to them, the court has no jurisdiction to award damages against the liquidator on a summons taken out in the winding up of the transferor company[2].

The question as to the validity of the sale cannot be decided in the winding-up proceedings; it can be decided only in an action instituted by a non-assenting shareholder suing on behalf of himself and all other shareholders[3].

A proper contract with regard to the fully or partly paid shares in the new company, and a return of the allotments, must be filed[4].

1 *Griffith v Paget* (1877) 6 ChD 511 at 517; *Postlethwaite v Port Phillip and Colonial Gold Mining Co* (1889) 43 ChD 452 at 469; *Simpson v Palace Theatre Ltd* (1893) 69 LT 70, CA; *Re North West Argentine Rly Co* [1900] 2 Ch 882 (where Wright J repudiated his former decision in *Re Beeston Pneumatic Tyre Co Ltd* (1898) 14 TLR 338).
2 *Re Hill's Waterfall Estate and Gold Mining Co* [1896] 1 Ch 947.

3 *Re Imperial Bank of China, India and Japan* (1866) 1 Ch App 339 at 347, 348; *Re International Life Assurance Society* (1868) 20 LT 433; *Clinch v Financial Corpn* (1868) LR 5 Eq 450 (affd 4 Ch App 117); cf *Re City and County Investment Co* (1879) 13 ChD 475, CA; *Re Hester & Co Ltd* (1875) 44 LJ Ch 757. An agreement for sale will not be set aside in the absence of the transferee company as a party: see *Doughty v Lomagunda Reefs Ltd* [1903] 1 Ch 673, CA.
4 As to filing contracts and returns see para 478 ante.

1486. Allotment to wrong person. Where, under a contract made before the reconstruction scheme is sanctioned, the purchaser is entitled to be registered as transferee of shares in the transferor company, and the vendor obtains the allotment of the shares in the transferee company to which the owner of the shares is entitled under the scheme, the allottee is a trustee of them for the purchaser, even though he has delayed registration of the transfer[1].

1 *Rooney v Stanton* (1900) 17 TLR 28, CA.

1487. Position of transferee company. The transferee company is in no sense the servant or agent of the transferor company, and is not bound by injunctions granted against it[1].

1 *Bosch v Simms Manufacturing Co Ltd* (1909) 25 TLR 419. Where a reconstruction has been carried out by forming a new company ('the transferee company') with the same name which takes over all the liabilities of the transferor company, payments made by the transferee company to a creditor of the transferor company who dealt with the transferee company under the belief that he was continuing to deal with the transferor company must be applied in discharge of debts of the transferor company, and not of those due to him by the transferee company: *Re Taurine Co Ltd, Anning and Cobb's Claim* (1877) 38 LT 53.

1488. Notice of dissent. A notice of dissent by a member[1] must contain a notice to the liquidator either to abstain from carrying the resolution into effect or to purchase the dissentient member's interest at a price to be determined by agreement or arbitration[2].

A deceased member's personal representatives, even though not registered as members, may exercise the right of dissent in respect of the shares registered in the deceased member's name, and a provision in the articles that they may not exercise any of the rights and privileges of a member in respect of those shares unless they are registered as members in respect of them does not prevent them from exercising the statutory right of dissent[3].

1 See para 1480 ante.
2 See the Insolvency Act 1986 s 111(2); para 1480 ante; and *Re Demerara Rubber Co Ltd* [1913] 1 Ch 331. As to the clauses to be inserted in the reconstruction or amalgamation agreement to provide funds to pay dissentients see *Re Hester & Co Ltd* (1875) 44 LJ Ch 757. As to provisions for dissentients where a scheme of arrangement under the Companies Act 1985 s 425 (as amended) involves a sale and a transfer of a company's undertakings to a new company see para 1447 ante. For the purposes of arbitration, the provisions of the Companies Clauses Consolidation Act 1845 with respect to the settlement of disputes by arbitration (see para 1747 post) are incorporated with the Insolvency Act 1986; and, in the construction of those provisions, the Insolvency Act 1986 is deemed the special Act, 'the company' means the transferor company, and any appointment directed by the incorporated provisions to be made under the hand of the secretary or any two of the directors may be made in writing by the liquidator or, if there is more than one liquidator, of any two or more of them (s 111(4)); but, if the articles provide for arbitration between the company and its members, either the provision in the

articles or the statutory mode of arbitration may be resorted to *(De Rosaz v Anglo-Italian Bank Ltd* (1869) LR 4 QB 462).

3 *Llewellyn v Kasintoe Rubber Estates Ltd* [1914] 2 Ch 670, CA.

1489. Arbitration as to amount payable. A provision in the articles purporting to exclude a reference to arbitration[1] and providing that the sum payable to a dissentient member shall be such sum as the liquidator can obtain by selling the shares to which the dissentient member, but for his dissent, would have been entitled is not binding on dissentient members[2]; nor is a provision which purports to authorise a sale for shares under the statutory power but which omits the provision[3] in favour of dissentient shareholders[4].

The amount payable to a dissentient shareholder is not determined by the price to be paid in shares by the transferee company. The value of a dissentient member's interest depends on the value of his proportionate share of the assets of the transferor company[5]. A commission to examine witnesses abroad may be granted in order to ascertain the value of those assets[6]. The court will not, however, allow a shareholder to examine officers of the company in order to obtain evidence for use on the arbitration[7]. Interest is not payable on the amount awarded until payment is demanded in writing, but it is payable from that time until the date of payment of the amount awarded[8].

1 For statutory provisions as to arbitration see para 1488 text and note 2 ante.
2 *Baring-Gould v Sharpington Combined Pick and Shovel Syndicate* [1899] 2 Ch 80, CA.
3 Ie the Insolvency Act 1986 s 111(2): see paras 1480, 1488 ante.
4 *Payne v Cork Co Ltd* [1900] 1 Ch 308; *Re Irrigation Co of France, ex p Fox* (1871) 6 Ch App 176. See also para 1479 note 3 ante.
5 *Re Mysore West Gold Mining Co Ltd* (1889) 42 ChD 535 at 538.
6 *Re Mysore West Gold Mining Co Ltd* (1889) 42 ChD 535.
7 *Re British Building Stone Co Ltd* [1908] 2 Ch 450. The company's books cannot be examined by the dissentient to see whether acceptance of the offer would be for his advantage: *Morgan's Case* (1884) 28 ChD 620.
8 *Re United States Direct Cable Co Ltd* (1879) 48 LJ Ch 665.

1490. Dissentient member's rights. If the liquidator elects to purchase a dissentient member's interest[1], the purchase money must be paid before the company is dissolved and must be raised by the liquidator in such manner as may be determined by special resolution[2]. Unless provision is made to satisfy money payable to a dissentient member, an injunction will be granted to restrain the liquidator from parting with the assets without providing for that member's claim[3].

A dissentient member is not entitled to have his name omitted from the list of contributories even if he transfers his shares to the liquidator[4], but the transfer relieves him from liability as to the costs of the liquidation[5].

Where a scheme is eminently unfair, a dissentient minority may stop it by obtaining a compulsory winding-up order[6].

1 As to a dissentient member's right to require the liquidator to elect see paras 1480, 1488 ante.
2 Insolvency Act 1986 s 111(3). As to special resolutions see para 683 ante.
3 *Re Hester & Co Ltd* (1875) 44 LJ Ch 757; *Baring-Gould v Sharpington Combined Pick and Shovel Syndicate* [1899] 2 Ch 80, CA; *Payne v Cork Co Ltd* [1900] 1 Ch 308.
4 *Re Imperial Land Co of Marseilles, ex p Jeaffreson* (1870) LR 11 Eq 109; *Vining's Case* (1870) 6 Ch App 96; *Part's Case* (1870) LR 10 Eq 622.
5 *Re Marine Investment Co, ex p Pool's Executors* (1873) 8 Ch App 702 at 710.
6 *Re Consolidated South Rand Mines Deep Ltd* [1909] 1 Ch 491.

(iv) Relief from Stamp Duty

1491. Exemption from ad valorem duty for the acquisition of a corporate undertaking on reconstruction. Where a company ('the acquiring company') acquires the whole or part of an undertaking of another company ('the target company') in pursuance of a scheme for the reconstruction[1] of the target company, then, if the first and second conditions set out below are fulfilled, stamp duty[2] is not chargeable on an instrument executed for the purposes of, or in connection with, the transfer of the undertaking or part[3].

The first condition is that the registered office of the acquiring company is in the United Kingdom and that the consideration for the acquisition:

(1) consists of or includes the issue of shares in the acquiring company to all the shareholders of the target company;

(2) includes nothing else (if anything) but the assumption or discharge by the acquiring company of liabilities of the target company[4].

The second condition is that:

(a) the acquisition is effected for bona fide commercial reasons and does not form part of a scheme or arrangement of which the main purpose, or one of the main purposes, is avoidance of liability to stamp duty, income tax, corporation tax or capital gains tax;

(b) after the acquisition has been made, each shareholder of each of the companies is a shareholder of the other; and

(c) after the acquisition has been made, the proportion of shares of one of the companies held by any shareholder is the same as the proportion of shares of the other company held by that shareholder[5].

This applies to any instrument executed after 24 March 1986 unless it is executed in pursuance of an unconditional contract made on or before 18 March 1986[6].

1　For this purpose, 'reconstruction' requires that the business and the persons interested must be substantially the same: *Re South African Supply and Cold Storage Co, Wild v South African Supply and Cold Storage Co* [1904] 2 Ch 268; *Brooklands Selangor Holdings Ltd v IRC* [1970] 2 All ER 76, [1970] 1 WLR 429; *Baytrust Holdings Ltd v IRC* [1971] 3 All ER 76, [1971] 1 WLR 1333; *Swithland Investments Ltd v IRC* [1990] STC 448; and see para 1461 ante.

2　Ie under the Stamp Act 1891 s 1, Sch 1, 'Conveyance or Transfer on Sale' (as amended): see STAMP DUTIES vol 44(1) (Reissue) para 1027.

3　Finance Act 1986 s 75(1),(2). An instrument on which stamp duty is not chargeable by virtue only of s 75(2) is not to be taken to be duly stamped unless it is stamped with the duty to which it would otherwise be liable, or it has, in accordance with the Stamp Act 1891 s 12 (as amended) (see STAMP DUTIES vol 44(1) (Reissue) para 1111) been stamped with a particular stamp denoting that it is not chargeable with any duty: Finance Act 1986 s 75(3).

4　Ibid s 75(4).

5　Ibid s 75(5).

6　Ibid s 75(6).

1492. Reduction in the rate of ad valorem duty for the acquisition of a corporate undertaking. Where a company ('the acquiring company') acquires the whole or part of an undertaking[1] of another company ('the target company'), then, if the condition set out below is fulfilled, and stamp duty[2] is chargeable on an instrument executed for the purposes of or in connection with:

(1) the transfer of the undertaking or part; or

(2) the assignment to the acquiring company by a creditor of the target company of any relevant debts[3] (secured or unsecured) owed by the target company,

the rate at which such duty is so charged must not exceed 50 pence for every £100 or part of £100 of the amount or value of the consideration for the sale to which the instrument gives effect[4].

The condition is that the registered office of the acquiring company is in the United Kingdom and that the consideration for the acquisition:

(a) consists of or includes the issue of shares in the acquiring company to the target company or to all or any or its shareholders;

(b) includes nothing else (if anything) but cash not exceeding 10% of the nominal value of those shares, or the assumption or discharge by the acquiring company of liabilities of the target company, or both[5].

This provision applies to any instrument executed on or after 27 October 1986[6].

1 'Undertaking' denotes the business or enterprise of the company, not its assets: *Baytrust Holdings Ltd v IRC* [1971] 3 All ER 76, [1971] 1 WLR 1333.
2 Ie under the Stamp Act 1891 s 1, Sch 1, 'Conveyance or Transfer on Sale' (as amended): see STAMP DUTIES vol 44(1) (Reissue) para 1027.
3 For these purposes, 'relevant debts' means (1) any debt in the case of which the assignor is a bank or trade creditor; and (2) any other debt incurred not less than two years before the date on which the instrument is executed: Finance Act 1986 s 76(6).
4 Ibid s 76(1),(2),(4). An instrument on which, by virtue only of s 76(2), the rate at which stamp duty is charged is not to exceed that mentioned in s 76(4) is not to be taken to be duly stamped unless it is stamped with the duty to which it would otherwise be liable or it has, in accordance with the Stamp Act 1891 s 12 (as amended) (see STAMP DUTIES vol 44(1) (Reissue) para 1111) been stamped with a particular stamp denoting that it is duly stamped: Finance Act 1986 s 76(5).
5 Ibid s 76(3).
6 Ibid s 76(7).

1493. Exemption from ad valorem duty for the acquisition of a company's share capital. Stamp duty is not chargeable[1] on an instrument transferring shares[2] in one company ('the target company') to another company ('the acquiring company') if the following conditions are fulfilled[3]. Those conditions are that:

(1) the registered office of the acquiring company is in the United Kingdom;

(2) the transfer forms part of an arrangement by which the acquiring company acquires the whole of the issued share capital of the target company;

(3) the acquisition is effected for bona fide commercial reasons and does not form part of a scheme or arrangement of which the main purpose, or one of the main purposes, is avoidance of liability to stamp duty, stamp duty reserve tax, income tax, corporation tax or capital gains tax;

(4) the consideration for the acquisition consists only of the issue of shares in the acquiring company to the shareholders of the target company;

(5) after the acquisition has been made, each person who immediately before it was made was a shareholder of the target company is a shareholder of the acquiring company;

(6) after the acquisition has been made, the shares in the acquiring company are of the same classes as were the shares in the target company immediately before the acquisition was made;

(7) after the acquisition has been made, the number of shares of any particular class in the acquiring company bears to all the shares in that company the same proportion as the number of shares of that class in the target company bore to all the shares in that company immediately before the acquisition was made; and

(8) after the acquisition has been made, the proportion of shares of any particular class in the acquiring company held by any particular shareholder is the same as

the proportion of shares of that class in the target company held by him immediately before the acquisition was made[4].

The above provisions apply to any instrument executed on or after 1 August 1986[5].

1   Ie under the Stamp Act 1891 s 1, Sch 1, 'Conveyance or Transfer on Sale' (as amended): see STAMP DUTIES vol 44(1) (Reissue) para 1027.
2   For these purposes, references to shares and share capital include references to stock: Finance Act 1986 s 77(4).
3   Ibid s 77(1). Section 77 is repealed from a day to be appointed by the Finance Act 1990 s 132, Sch 19 Pt VI.
4   Finance Act 1986 s 77(3). See also note 3 supra. An instrument on which stamp duty is not chargeable by virtue only of s 77(1) is not to be taken to be duly stamped unless it is stamped with the duty to which it would be liable but for s 77(1), or it has, in accordance with the Stamp Act 1891 s 12 (as amended) (see STAMP DUTIES vol 44(1) (Reissue) para 1111) been stamped with a particular stamp denoting that it is not chargeable with any duty: Finance Act 1986 s 77(2).
5   Ibid s 77(5). See also note 3 supra.

1494. Renounceable letters of allotment. Where there is an arrangement whereby:

(1)   rights under an instrument are renounced in favour of a person ('the benefici-ary');

(2)   the rights are rights to shares[1] in a company ('the company'); and

(3)   the beneficiary, or a person connected with[2] the beneficiary, or the beneficiary and such a person together, has or have control[3] of the company or will have such control in consequence of the arrangement,

the instrument is not exempt[4] from stamp duty[5].

These provisions apply to instruments if rights are renounced under them on or after 1 August 1985, except where the arrangement concerned includes an offer for the rights and on or before 27 June 1985 the offer became unconditional as to acceptances[6].

1   For these purposes, 'shares' includes stock: Finance Act 1985 s 81(4). References to shares in the company include references to its loan capital to which the Finance Act 1976 s 126(1) (repealed) does not apply by virtue of s 126(2) or (3) (repealed): Finance Act 1985 s 81(3). Section 81 (as amended) is repealed from a day to be appointed by the Finance Act 1990 s 132, Sch 19 Pt VI.
2   A person is connected with another if he would be so connected for the purposes of the Taxation of Chargeable Gains Act 1992 (see CAPITAL GAINS TAXATION vol 5(1) (Reissue) para 42): Finance Act 1985 s 81(6) (amended by the Taxation of Chargeable Gains Act 1992 s 290(1), Sch 10 para 9). See also note 1 supra.
3   A person has control of the company if he has power to control the company's affairs by virtue of holding shares in, or possessing voting power in relation to, the company or any other body corporate: Finance Act 1985 s 81(5). See also note 1 supra.
4   Ie not exempt by virtue of the Finance Act 1963 s 65(1) (renounceable letters of allotment etc) or the Finance Act (Northern Ireland) 1963 (corresponding provision for Northern Ireland) from stamp duty under the Stamp Act 1891 s 1, Sch 1, 'Conveyance or Transfer on Sale' (as amended) (see STAMP DUTIES vol 44(1) (Reissue) para 1027).
5   Finance Act 1985 s 81(1),(2). See also note 1 supra. See further STAMP DUTIES vol 44(1) (Reissue) para 1098.
6   Ibid s 81(7). See also note 1 supra.

1495. Exemption from ad valorem duty for conveyance or lease between associated bodies corporate. Relief from stamp duty[1] is also granted for convey-ances, leases and agreements for lease between associated bodies corporate[2].

Stamp duty[3] is not chargeable on any instrument where it is shown to the satisfaction of the Commissioners of Inland Revenue that its effect is to convey or transfer a beneficial interest in property from one body corporate to another, and that the bodies in question are associated[4] at the time the instrument is executed[5].

Stamp duty[6] is not chargeable on an instrument which is a lease, an agreement for a lease, or an agreement with respect to a letting where it is shown to the satisfaction of the Commissioners that:

(1) the lessor is a body corporate and the lessee is another body corporate;

(2) those bodies are associated at the time the instrument is executed;

(3) in the case of an agreement, the agreement is for the lease or letting to be granted to the lessee or to a body corporate which is associated with the lessee at the time the instrument is executed; and

(4) the instrument is not executed in pursuance of or in connection with an arrangement falling within heads (a) and (b) below[7].

The relief is not, however, available if the instrument is executed in pursuance of, or in connection with, an arrangement whereby:

(a) the consideration, or any part of the consideration, was to be provided or received, directly or indirectly, by a person other than a body corporate which at the relevant time[8] was associated with the transferor or the transferee[9] or with the lessor or lessee[10]; or

(b) the parties were to cease to be associated by reason of the transferor or a third body corporate ceasing to be the transferee's parent body[11] or the lessor or a third body corporate ceasing to be the lessee's parent body[12]; or

(c) in relation to a conveyance, the beneficial interest conveyed was previously conveyed or transferred by a person other than an associated body corporate[13].

In all such cases the instrument is not deemed to be duly stamped unless it is either stamped with the duty to which it would, but for the relief, be liable or has been stamped[14] with an adjudication stamp denoting that it is not chargeable with any duty or that it is duly stamped[15].

1 Ie under the Stamp Act 1891 s 1, Sch 1, 'Conveyance or Transfer on Sale' (as amended) and 'Lease or Tack' (as amended): see STAMP DUTIES vol 44(1) (Reissue) paras 1027 et seq, 1054 et seq.

2 See the Finance Act 1930 s 42 (as amended) (conveyances) and the Finance Act 1995 s 151 (leases).

3 Ie under the Stamp Act 1891 Sch 1, 'Conveyance or Transfer on Sale' (as amended).

4 For these purposes, and for the purposes of the Finance Act 1995 (see infra), bodies corporate are associated at a particular time if at that time one is the parent of the other or another body corporate is the parent of each: Finance Act 1930 s 42(2A) (added by the Finance Act 1995 s 149(1),(3)); Finance Act 1995 s 151(7). One body corporate is the parent of another at a particular time if at that time the first body is beneficial owner of not less than 75% of the ordinary share capital of the second body: Finance Act 1930 s 42(2B) (added by the Finance Act 1995 s 149(1),(3)); Finance Act 1995 s 151(8). Beneficial ownership is ownership either directly or through another body corporate or other bodies corporate, or partly directly and partly through another body corporate or other bodies corporate; and the Finance Act 1938 s 42(2), Sch 4 Pt I (determination of amount of capital held through other bodies corporate) applies for the purpose of the relief: Finance Act 1930 s 42(3) (substituted by the Finance Act 1967 s 27(2); amended by the Finance Act 1995 s 149(1),(4)); Finance Act 1995 s 151(10). 'Ordinary share capital', in relation to a body corporate, means all the issued share capital, by whatever name called, of the body corporate other than capital the holders of which have a right to a dividend at a fixed rate but have no other right to share in the profits of the body corporate: Finance Act 1930 s 42(4) (added by the Finance Act 1995 s 149(1),(5)); Finance Act 1995 s 151(9). Prior to the Finance Act 1995, the Finance Act 1930 s 42 (as amended) referred to 'issued share capital' and it was held that the amount of issued share capital is calculated by adding up the nominal value of the shares issued without regard either to market value or to different classes of share: *Canada Safeway Ltd v IRC* [1973] Ch 374, [1972] 1 All ER 666. Shares which have not yet been registered are not regarded as issued for this purpose: *National Westminster Bank plc v IRC* [1995] 1 AC 119, [1994] 3 All ER 1, HL.

5 Finance Act 1930 s 42(2) (substituted by the Finance Act 1967 s 27(2); amended by the Finance Act 1995 s 149(1),(2)).

6 Ie under the Stamp Act 1891 Sch 1, 'Lease or Tack' (as amended).

7 Finance Act 1995 s 151(1),(2). For these purposes, references to the lessor are to the person granting the lease or, in the case of an agreement, agreeing to grant the lease or letting; and references to the lessee are to the person being granted the lease or, in the case of an agreement, agreeing for the lease or letting to be granted to him or another: s 151(6).
8 For these purposes, the relevant time is the time of the execution of the instrument: Finance Act 1967 s 27(3)(a) (conveyances); Finance Act 1995 s 151(3) (leases).
9 Finance Act 1967 s 27(3)(a). Without prejudice to the generality of s 27(3)(a), an arrangement is treated as within s 27(3)(a) if it is one under which the transferor or the transferee, or a body corporate associated with either as there mentioned, was to be enabled to provide any of the consideration, or was to part with any of it, by or in consequence of the carrying out of a transaction or transactions involving, or any of them involving, a payment or other disposition by a person other than a body corporate so associated: s 27(3).
10 Finance Act 1995 s 151(3)(a). Without prejudice to the generality of s 151(3)(a), an arrangement is treated as within s 151(3)(a) if it is one under which the lessor or the lessee, or a body corporate associated with either at the relevant time, was to be enabled to provide any of the consideration, or was to part with any of it, by or in consequence of the carrying out of a transaction or transactions involving, or any of them involving, a payment or other disposition by a person other than the body corporate so associated: s 151(4).
11 Finance Act 1967 s 27(3)(c) (amended by the Finance Act 1995 s 149(6)).
12 Finance Act 1995 s 151(3)(b).
13 Finance Act 1967 s 27(3)(b).
14 Ie under the Stamp Act 1891 s 12 (as amended): see STAMP DUTIES vol 44(1) (Reissue) para 1111.
15 Finance Act 1930 s 42(1) (conveyances); Finance Act 1995 s 151(5) (leases).

(32) DEFUNCT COMPANIES; NON-TRADING PRIVATE COMPANIES

(i) Defunct Companies

1496. Registrar's power to strike defunct company off register. If the registrar of companies has reasonable cause to believe that a company is not carrying on business or in operation, he may send to the company by post a letter inquiring whether the company is carrying on business or in operation[1]. If the registrar does not, within one month of sending the letter, receive any answer to it, he must within 14 days after the expiration of that month send to the company by post a registered letter[2] referring to the first letter, and stating that no answer to it has been received, and that, if an answer is not received to the second letter within one month from its date, a notice will be published in the Gazette[3] with a view to striking the company's name off the register[4].

If the registrar either receives an answer to the effect that the company is not carrying on business or in operation, or does not within one month after sending the second letter receive any answer, he may publish in the Gazette, and send to the company by post, a notice that, at the expiration of three months from the date of that notice, the name of the company mentioned in it will, unless cause is shown to the contrary, be struck off the register and the company will be dissolved[5].

1 Companies Act 1985 s 652(1).
2 Any enactment which requires or authorises a document or other thing to be sent by registered post, whether or not it makes any other provision in relation thereto, has effect as if it required, or, as the case may be, authorised that thing to be sent by registered post or the recorded delivery service: Recorded Delivery Service Act 1962 s 1(1).
3 For the meaning of 'the Gazette' see para 70 note 1 ante.
4 Companies Act 1985 s 652(2). As to the address to which the notice is to be sent see para 1499 post.
5 Ibid s 652(3).

1497. Companies in liquidation. If, in a case where a company is being wound up, the registrar of companies has reasonable cause to believe either that no liquidator is acting, or that the affairs of the company are fully wound up, and the returns required to be made by the liquidator[1] have not been made for a period of six consecutive months, the registrar must publish in the Gazette[2] and send to the company or the liquidator, if any, a notice[3] that, at the expiration of three months from the date of that notice, the name of the company mentioned in it will, unless cause is shown to the contrary, be struck off the register and the company will be dissolved[4].

1 As to the returns required to be made by the liquidator see paras 2358, 2764-2767, 2780 post.
2 For the meaning of 'the Gazette' see para 70 note 1 ante.
3 Ie a like notice as is provided in the Companies Act 1985 s 652(3): see para 1496 ante. As to the address to which the notice is to be sent see para 1499 post.
4 Ibid s 652(4).

1498. Striking company off register; dissolution. At the expiration of the time mentioned in the notice sent by the registrar of companies[1], he may, unless cause to the contrary is previously shown by the company, strike its name off the register[2]. The registrar of companies must publish notice of this in the Gazette[3]; and, on the publication of that notice, the company is dissolved[4]. However, the liability, if any, of every director, managing officer and member of the company continues and may be enforced as if the company had not been dissolved[5]; and nothing in the above provision[6] affects the power of the court to wind up a company, the name of which has been struck off the register[7].

1 Ie the notice mentioned in the Companies Act 1985 s 652(4): see para 1497 ante.
2 Ibid s 652(5).
3 For the meaning of 'the Gazette' see para 70 note 1 ante.
4 Companies Act 1985 s 652(5).
5 Ibid s 652(6)(a). As to the effect of dissolution in ordinary cases see para 2691 post; and as to the power to declare a dissolution void see para 2696 post.
6 Ie ibid s 652(5): see supra.
7 Ibid s 652(6)(b). This proviso would appear to be intended to empower the court to wind up a company without first restoring it to the register; but as to the practical disadvantages of such an order see *Re Cambridge Coffee Room Association Ltd* [1952] 1 All ER 112n (cited in para 2692 note 5 post); cf *Re Beith Unionist Association Trustees* 1950 SC 1. As to restoration to the register see para 1504 post.

1499. Service of notices. A notice to be sent to a liquidator[1] may be addressed to him at his last known place of business; and a letter or notice to be sent to a company[1] may be addressed to the company at its registered office or, if no office has been registered, to the care of some officer of the company[2]. If there is no officer of the company whose name and address are known to the registrar of companies, the letter or notice may be sent to each of the persons who subscribed the memorandum, addressed to him at the address mentioned in the memorandum[2].

1 Ie under the Companies Act 1985 s 652: see paras 1496-1498 ante.
2 Ibid s 652(7).

(ii) Non-trading Private Companies

1500. Registrar's power to strike private company off register on application. On application by a private company[1], the registrar of companies may strike the company's name off the register[2]. Such an application must:

(1) be made on the company's behalf by its directors[3] or by a majority of them;

(2) be made in the prescribed form[4]; and

(3) contain the prescribed information[5].

Where a company makes such an application, any person who, in connection with the application, knowingly or recklessly furnishes any information to the registrar which is false or misleading in a material particular is guilty of an offence and liable on conviction on indictment to a fine or on summary conviction to a fine not exceeding the statutory maximum[6].

Any person who knowingly or recklessly makes an application to the registrar which purports to be an application to strike the company's name off the register[7], but which is not, is guilty of an offence and liable on conviction on indictment to a fine or on summary conviction to a fine not exceeding the statutory maximum[8].

The registrar must not, however, strike a company off the register until after the expiration of three months from the publication by him in the Gazette[9] of a notice stating that he may exercise his power under these provisions in relation to the company and inviting any person to show cause why he should not do so[10].

1 For the meaning of 'private company' see para 82 ante.

2 Companies Act 1985 s 652A(1) (added by the Deregulation and Contracting Out Act 1994 s 13(1), Sch 5 paras 1, 2).

3 For the meaning of 'director' see para 543 note 1 ante.

4 For the prescribed form of application see the Companies (Forms) (No 2) Regulations 1995, SI 1995/1479, reg 2, Form 652a. For the prescribed version of the form in Welsh see the Companies (Welsh Language Forms and Documents) (No 2) Regulations 1995, SI 1995/1480, reg 2, Form 652aCYM.

5 Companies Act 1985 s 652A(2) (added by the Deregulation and Contracting Out Act 1994 Sch 5 paras 1, 2). At the date at which this volume states the law no such information had been prescribed.

6 Companies Act 1985 s 652F(1) (added by the Deregulation and Contracting Out Act 1994 Sch 5 paras 1, 2); Companies Act 1985 s 730, Sch 24 (amended by the Deregulation and Contracting Out Act 1994 Sch 5 para 4). For the meaning of 'the statutory maximum' see para 1161 ante.

7 Ie purports to be an application under the Companies Act 1985 s 652A (as added).

8 Ibid s 652F(2) (added by the Deregulation and Contracting Out Act 1994 Sch 5 paras 1, 2); Companies Act 1985 s 730, Sch 24 (amended by the Deregulation and Contracting Out Act 1994 Sch 5 para 4).

9 For the meaning of 'the Gazette' see para 70 note 1 ante.

10 Companies Act 1985 s 652A(3) (added by the Deregulation and Contracting Out Act 1994 Sch 5 paras 1, 2).

1501. Duties in connection with making application. A person may not make an application on behalf of a company to strike its name off the register[1] if, at any time in the previous three months, the company has:

(1) changed its name;

(2) traded or otherwise carried on business[2];

(3) made a disposal[3] for value of property or rights which, immediately before ceasing to trade or otherwise carry on business, it held for the purpose of disposal for gain in the normal course of trading or otherwise carrying on business; or

(4) engaged in any other activity, except one which is:

(a) necessary or expedient for the purpose of making an application for the company to be struck off the register[4], or deciding whether to do so;

(b) necessary or expedient for the purpose of concluding the affairs of the company;

(c) necessary or expedient for the purpose of complying with any statutory requirement; or

(d) specified by the Secretary of State by order for these purposes[5].

A person may not make an application on behalf of a company to strike its name off the register[6] at a time when any of the following is the case:

(i) an application has been made to the court[7] on behalf of the company for the sanctioning of a compromise or arrangement and the matter has not been finally concluded[8];

(ii) a voluntary arrangement in relation to the company has been proposed[9] and the matter has not been finally concluded[10];

(iii) an administration order in relation to the company is in force[11] or a petition for such an order has been presented and not finally dealt with or withdrawn;

(iv) the company is being wound up[12], whether voluntarily or by the court, or a petition for the winding up of the company by the court has been presented and not finally dealt with or withdrawn;

(v) there is a receiver or manager of the company's property;

(vi) the company's estate is being administered by a judicial factor[13].

A person who makes an application on behalf of a company to strike its name off the register[14] must secure that a copy of the application is given[15], within seven days from the day on which the application is made, to every person who, at any time on that day, is a member of the company, an employee of the company, a creditor of the company, a director[16] of the company, a manager or trustee of any pension fund established for the benefit of employees of the company or a person of a description specified for these purposes by regulations made by the Secretary of State[17]; but this provision does not require a copy of the application to be given to a director who is a party to the application[18]. The duty so to give a copy of the application ceases to apply if the application is withdrawn[19] before the end of the period for giving the copy application[20].

A person who breaches or fails to comply with a duty imposed on him under the above provisions is guilty of an offence and liable on conviction on indictment to a fine or on summary conviction to a fine not exceeding the statutory maximum[21]; and a person who fails to perform a duty imposed on him to secure that a copy of the application is given to the specified persons[22] with the intention of concealing the making of the application in question from the person concerned is guilty of an offence and liable on conviction on indictment to imprisonment for a term not exceeding seven years or a fine, or to both, or on summary conviction to imprisonment for a term not exceeding six months or a fine not exceeding the statutory maximum, or to both[23].

In any proceedings for an offence under the above provisions consisting of a breach of a duty not to make an application in the specified circumstances[24] it is a defence for the accused to prove that he did not know, and could not reasonably have known, of the existence of the facts which led to the breach[25]; and in any proceedings for an offence consisting of failure to perform the duty to secure that a copy of the application is given to the specified persons[26], it is a defence for the accused to prove that he took all reasonable steps to perform the duty[27].

1 Ie under the Companies Act 1985 s 652A (as added): see para 1500 ante.

2 For these purposes, a company is not treated as trading or otherwise carrying on business by virtue only of the fact that it makes a payment in respect of a liability incurred in the course of trading or otherwise carrying on business: ibid s 652B(2) (added by the Deregulation and Contracting Out Act 1994 s 13(1), Sch 5 paras 1, 2).

3 For these purposes, 'disposal' includes part disposal: Companies Act 1985 s 652D(7) (added by the Deregulation and Contracting Out Act 1994 Sch 5 paras 1, 2).

4 See note 1 supra.

5 Companies Act 1985 s 652B(1) (added by the Deregulation and Contracting Out Act 1994 Sch 5 paras 1, 2). The Secretary of State may by order amend the Companies Act 1985 s 652B(1) (as so added) for

the purpose of altering the period in relation to which the doing of the things mentioned in s 652B(1)(a)-(d) (as so added) (see text heads (1)-(4) supra) is relevant: s 652B(9) (added by the Deregulation and Contracting Out Act 1994 Sch 5 paras 1, 2).

Any power to make an order or regulations under the Companies Act 1985 s 652B (as added) or s 652C (as added) (see para 1502 post): (1) includes power to make different provision for different cases or classes of case; (2) includes power to make such transitional provisions as the Secretary of State considers appropriate; and (3) is exercisable by statutory instrument subject to annulment in pursuance of a resolution of either House of Parliament: s 652D(5) (added by the Deregulation and Contracting Out Act 1994 Sch 5 paras 1, 2). At the date at which this volume states the law no such order had been made.

6   See note 1 supra.

7   Ie under the Companies Act 1985 s 425 (as amended): see para 1447 et seq ante.

8   For these purposes, the matter is finally concluded if (1) the application has been withdrawn; (2) the application has been finally dealt with without a compromise or arrangement being sanctioned by the court; (3) a compromise or arrangement has been sanctioned by the court and has, together with anything required to be done under any provision made in relation to the matter by order of the court, been fully carried out: ibid s 652B(4) (added by the Deregulation and Contracting Out Act 1994 Sch 5 paras 1, 2).

9   Ie under the Insolvency Act 1986 Pt I (ss 1-7): see para 2044 et seq post.

10   For these purposes, the matter is finally concluded if (1) no meetings are to be summoned under ibid s 3 (see paras 2052, 2054 post); (2) meetings summoned under s 3 fail to approve the arrangement with no, or the same, modifications; (3) an arrangement approved by meetings summoned under s 3, or in consequence of a direction under s 6(4)(b) (see para 2077 post), has been fully implemented; or (4) the court makes an order under s 6(5) (see para 2077 post) revoking approval given at previous meetings and, if the court gives any directions under s 6(6) (see para 2077 ante), the company has done whatever it is required to do under those directions: Companies Act 1985 s 652B(5) (added by the Deregulation and Contracting Out Act 1994 Sch 5 paras 1, 2).

11   Ie under the Insolvency Act 1986 Pt II (ss 8-27) (as amended): see para 2080 et seq post.

12   Ie under ibid Pt IV (ss 73-219) (as amended): see para 2190 et seq post.

13   Companies Act 1985 s 652B(3) (added by the Deregulation and Contracting Out Act 1994 Sch 5 paras 1, 2).

14   See note 1 supra.

15   For these purposes, and for the purposes of the Companies Act 1985 s 652C(2) (as added) (see para 1502 post), a document is treated as given to a person if it is delivered to him or left at his proper address or sent by post to him at that address: s 652D(1) (added by the Deregulation and Contracting Out Act 1994 Sch 5 paras 1, 2). For the purposes of the Companies Act 1985 s 652D(1) (as so added) and the Interpretation Act 1978 s 7 (service of documents by post: see STATUTES vol 44(1) (Reissue) para 1388) in its application to the Companies Act 1985 s 652D(1) (as so added), the proper address of any person is his last known address, except that (1) in the case of a body corporate, other than one to which s 652D(3) (as added) applies, it is the address of its registered or principal office; (2) in the case of a partnership, other than one to which s 652D(3) (as added) applies, it is the address of its principal office; and (3) in the case of a body corporate or partnership to which s 652D(3) (as added) applies, it is the address of its principal office in the United Kingdom: s 652D(2) (added by the Deregulation and Contracting Out Act 1994 Sch 5 paras 1, 2). The Companies Act 1985 s 652D(3) (as added) applies to a body corporate or partnership which (a) is incorporated or formed under the law of a country or territory outside the United Kingdom; and (b) has a place of business in the United Kingdom: s 652D(3) (added by the Deregulation and Contracting Out Act 1994 Sch 5 paras 1, 2). Where a creditor of the company has more than one place of business, the Companies Act 1985 s 652D(1) (as so added) has effect, so far as concerns the giving of a document to him, as if for the words from 'delivered' to the end there were substituted 'left, or sent by post to him, at each place of business of his with which the company has had dealings in relation to a matter by virtue of which he is a creditor of the company': s 652D(4) (added by the Deregulation and Contracting Out Act 1994 Sch 5 paras 1, 2). For these purposes, and for the purposes of the Companies Act 1985 s 652C (as added), 'creditor' includes a contingent or prospective creditor: s 652D(8) (added by the Deregulation and Contracting Out Act 1994 Sch 5 paras 1, 2).

16   For the meaning of 'director' see para 543 note 1 ante.

17   Companies Act 1985 s 652B(6) (added by the Deregulation and Contracting Out Act 1994 Sch 5 paras 1, 2).

18   Companies Act 1985 s 652B(7) (added by the Deregulation and Contracting Out Act 1994 Sch 5 paras 1, 2).

19   For these purposes, and for the purposes of the Companies Act 1985 s 652C (as added), an application under s 652A (as added) is withdrawn if notice of withdrawal in the prescribed form is given to the

registrar of companies: s 652D(6) (added by the Deregulation and Contracting Out Act 1994 Sch 5 paras 1, 2). For the prescribed form of withdrawal see the Companies (Forms) (No 2) Regulations 1995, SI 1995/1479, reg 2, Form 652c. For the prescribed version of the form in Welsh see the Companies (Welsh Language Forms and Documents) (No 2) Regulations 1995, SI 1995/1480, reg 2, Form 652cCYM.

20 Companies Act 1985 s 652B(8) (added by the Deregulation and Contracting Out Act 1994 Sch 5 paras 1, 2).
21 Companies Act 1985 s 652E(1) (added by the Deregulation and Contracting Out Act 1994 Sch 5 paras 1, 2); Companies Act 1985 s 730, Sch 24 (amended by the Deregulation and Contracting Out Act 1994 Sch 5 para 4). For the meaning of 'the statutory maximum' see para 1161 ante.
22 Ie a duty imposed on him by the Companies Act 1985 s 652B(6) (as added): see supra.
23 Ibid s 652E(2) (added by the Deregulation and Contracting Out Act 1994 Sch 5 paras 1, 2); Companies Act 1985 s 730, Sch 24 (as amended: see note 21 supra).
24 Ie a duty imposed by ibid s 652B(1) (as added) (see supra) or s 652B(3) (as added) (see supra).
25 Ibid s 652E(3) (added by the Deregulation and Contracting Out Act 1994 Sch 5 paras 1, 2).
26 See note 22 supra.
27 Companies Act 1985 s 652E(4) (added by the Deregulation and Contracting Out Act 1994 Sch 5 paras 1, 2).

1502. Directors' duties following application. In relation to any time after the day on which a company makes an application on behalf of a company to strike its name off the register[1] and before the day on which the application is finally dealt with or withdrawn[2], a person who is a director[3] of the company at the end of a day on which a person other than himself becomes a member of the company, an employee of the company, a creditor[4] of the company, a director of the company, a manager or trustee of any pension fund established for the benefit of employees of the company or a person of a description specified for these purposes by regulations made by the Secretary of State[5], must secure that a copy of the application is given[6] to that person within seven days from that day[7]. The duty so imposed ceases to apply if the application is finally dealt with or withdrawn before the end of the period for giving the copy application[8].

Where, at any time on or after the day on which a company makes an application to have its name struck off the register[9] and before the day on which the application is finally dealt with or withdrawn:

(1) the company changes its name, trades or otherwise carries on business[10], makes a disposal for value of any property or rights other than those which it was necessary or expedient for it to hold for the purpose of making, or proceeding with, an application to have its name struck off the register[11] or engages in any other activity, other than an excluded activity[12];

(2) an application is made to the court[13] on behalf of the company for the sanctioning of a compromise or arrangement;

(3) a voluntary arrangement in relation to the company is proposed[14];

(4) a petition is presented for the making of an administration order[15] in relation to the company;

(5) there arise any of the circumstances in which[16] the company may be voluntarily wound up;

(6) a petition is presented for the winding up of the company by the court[17];

(7) a receiver or manager of the company's property is appointed; or

(8) a judicial factor is appointed to administer the company's estate,

a person who, at the end of a day on which an event mentioned in any of heads (1) to (8) above occurs, is a director of the company must secure that the company's application is withdrawn forthwith[18].

A person who breaches or fails to comply with a duty imposed on him under the above provisions is guilty of an offence and liable on conviction on indictment to a fine or on summary conviction to a fine not exceeding the statutory maximum[19]; and a person who fails to perform a duty imposed on him to secure that a copy of the application is given to the specified persons[20] with the intention of concealing the making of the application in question from the person concerned is guilty of an offence and liable on conviction on indictment to imprisonment for a term not exceeding seven years or a fine, or to both, or on summary conviction to imprisonment for a term not exceeding six months or a fine not exceeding the statutory maximum, or to both[21].

In any proceedings for an offence consisting of failure to perform the duty to secure that a copy of the application is given to the specified persons[22], or to secure that the company's application is withdrawn in the specified circumstances[23], it is a defence for the accused to prove that at the time of the failure he was not aware of the fact that the company had made an application to be struck of the register[24] or that he took all reasonable steps to perform the duty[25].

1 Ie under the Companies Act 1985 s 652A (as added): see para 1500 ante.
2 As to when an application is withdrawn see para 1501 note 20 ante.
3 For the meaning of 'director' see para 543 note 1 ante.
4 For the meaning of 'creditor' see para 1501 note 15 ante.
5 As to the making of orders and regulations see para 1501 note 5 ante.
6 As to the giving of notice see para 1501 note 15 ante.
7 Companies Act 1985 s 652C(1),(2) (added by the Deregulation and Contracting Out Act 1994 s 13(1), Sch 5 paras 1, 2).
8 Companies Act 1985 s 652C(3) (added by the Deregulation and Contracting Out Act 1994 Sch 5 paras 1, 2).
9 See note 1 supra.
10 For these purposes, a company is not treated as trading or otherwise carrying on business by virtue only of the fact that it makes a payment in respect of a liability incurred in the course of trading or otherwise carrying on business: Companies Act 1985 s 652C(7) (added by the Deregulation and Contracting Out Act 1994 Sch 5 paras 1, 2).
11 See note 1 supra.
12 The activities so excepted are any activity which is (1) necessary or expedient for the purpose of making, or proceeding with, an application under the Companies Act 1985 s 652A (as added); (2) necessary or expedient for the purpose of concluding affairs of the company which are outstanding because of what has been necessary or expedient for the purpose of making, or proceeding with, such an application; (3) necessary or expedient for the purpose of complying with any statutory requirement; or (4) specified by the Secretary of State by order for these purposes: s 652C(6) (added by the Deregulation and Contracting Out Act 1994 Sch 5 paras 1, 2). At the date at which this volume states the law no such order had been made.
13 Ie under the Companies Act 1985 s 425 (as amended): see para 1447 et seq ante.
14 Ie under the Insolvency Act 1986 Pt I (ss 1-7): see para 2044 et seq ante.
15 Ie under ibid Pt II (ss 8-27) (as amended): see para 2080 et seq ante.
16 Ie under ibid s 84(1): see para 2698 post.
17 Ie under ibid Pt IV (ss 73-219) (as amended): see para 2190 et seq post.
18 Companies Act 1985 s 652C(4),(5) (added by the Deregulation and Contracting Out Act 1994 Sch 5 paras 1, 2).
19 Companies Act 1985 s 652E(1) (added by the Deregulation and Contracting Out Act 1994 Sch 5 paras 1, 2); Companies Act 1985 s 730, Sch 24 (amended by the Deregulation and Contracting Out Act 1994 Sch 5 para 4). For the meaning of 'the statutory maximum' see para 1161 ante.
20 Ie a duty imposed on him by the Companies Act 1985 s 652C(2) (as added): see supra.
21 Ibid s 652E(2) (added by the Deregulation and Contracting Out Act 1994 Sch 5 paras 1, 2); Companies Act 1985 s 730, Sch 24 (as amended: see note 19 supra).
22 See note 20 supra.
23 Ie the duty imposed by the Companies Act 1985 s 652C(5) (as added): see supra.
24 See note 1 supra.
25 Companies Act 1985 s 652E(5) (added by the Deregulation and Contracting Out Act 1994 Sch 5 paras 1, 2).

1503. Striking the company off the register. Where the registrar of companies strikes a company off the register[1], he must publish notice of that fact in the Gazette[2]; and, on publication of that notice, the company to which the notice relates is dissolved[3]. However, the liability, if any, of every director[4], managing officer and member of the company continues and may be enforced as if the company had not been dissolved[5].

Nothing in these provisions affects the power of the court to wind up a company the name of which has been struck off the register[6].

1 Ie under the Companies Act 1985 s 652A (as added): see para 1500 ante.
2 Ibid s 652A(4) (added by the Deregulation and Contracting Out Act 1994 s 13(1), Sch 5 paras 1, 2). For the meaning of 'the Gazette' see para 70 note 1 ante.
3 Companies Act 1985 s 652A(5) (added by the Deregulation and Contracting Out Act 1994 Sch 5 paras 1, 2).
4 For the meaning of 'director' see para 543 note 1 ante.
5 Companies Act 1985 s 652A(6) (added by the Deregulation and Contracting Out Act 1994 Sch 5 paras 1, 2).
6 Companies Act 1985 s 652A(7) (added by the Deregulation and Contracting Out Act 1994 Sch 5 paras 1, 2).

(iii) Restoration to the Register

1504. Defunct companies. If a company or any member[1] or creditor[2] of it feels aggrieved by the company having been struck off the register[3], the court may, on an application[4] by the company or the member or creditor made before the expiration of 20 years from publication in the Gazette[5] of the statutory notice[6], order the company's name to be restored to the register, if satisfied that the company was at the time of the striking off carrying on business or in operation, or otherwise that it is just that the company be restored to the register[7].

On an office copy of the order being delivered to the registrar of companies for registration, the company to which the order relates is deemed to have continued in existence as if its name had not been struck off[8]; and the court may by the order give such directions and make such provisions as seem just for placing the company and all other persons in the same position, as nearly as may be, as if the company had not been struck off[9].

The court will usually make the order if there is any business or property to be dealt with, but on the terms that all proper returns are to be made[10]. No application to set aside or modify an order for restoration to the register may, however, be made except on behalf of the company, and then only if there is some evidence that the board or the company in general meeting has considered the matter[11].

The power to restore applies where, when it was struck off the register, the company was in voluntary liquidation, and carrying on business only for the purposes of winding up[12].

1 For these purposes, 'member' includes personal representatives of a deceased member: *Re Bayswater Trading Co Ltd* [1970] 1 All ER 608, [1970] 1 WLR 343.
2 The person must be a member or creditor at the date of dissolution: *Re New Timbiqui Gold Mines Ltd* [1961] Ch 319, [1961] 1 All ER 865 (shares and debts acquired by transfers subsequent to dissolution); *Re Aga Estate Agencies Ltd* [1986] BCLC 346. 'Creditor' includes a person having an unquantified claim: *Re Harvest Lane Motor Bodies Ltd* [1969] 1 Ch 457, [1968] 2 All ER 1012. See *Re Test Holdings (Clifton) Ltd* [1970] Ch 285, [1969] 3 All ER 517 (where what is now the Companies Act 1985 s 653(1),(2) (as amended) is compared with s 651(1) (see para 2696 post)).
3 Ie under ibid s 652: see paras 1496-1499 ante.

4 As to applications for restoration see para 1506 post.

5 For the meaning of 'the Gazette' see para 70 note 1 ante.

6 Ie under the Companies Act 1985 s 652.

7 Ibid s 653(1),(2) (amended by the Deregulation and Contracting Out Act 1994 s 13(1), Sch 5 para 3(1),(2)(a),(b)). In considering whether it is 'just' to restore the company to the register, the personal circumstances of the shareholder may be relevant: *Re L Carroll Ltd* [1975] 1 NZLR 79 (NZ SC) (striking off due to illness). A company, even though not carrying on business, may be in operation: see *Re Financial Corpn Ltd* (1883) 27 Sol Jo 199 (voluntary winding up); *Re Estates Investment Co* (1883) 27 Sol Jo 585 (compulsory winding up). The court has no power to join a third party which has entered into a contract with the company after it has been struck off the register to proceedings to restore the company to the register: *Re Portrafram Ltd* [1986] BCLC 533.

8 Ie with retroactive effect: *Tyman's Ltd v Craven* [1952] 2 QB 100, [1952] 1 All ER 613 (proceedings in company's name before restoration rendered valid; applied in *Re Boxco Ltd* [1970] Ch 442, [1970] 2 All ER 183n). As to the effect of an order divesting the Crown of its title to bona vacantia see para 2692 note 5 post.

9 Companies Act 1985 s 653(3) (amended by the Deregulation and Contracting Out Act 1994 Sch 5 para 3(1),(4)). Thus in *Re Donald Kenyon Ltd* [1956] 3 All ER 596, [1956] 1 WLR 1397, the court directed that, in the case of creditors whose debts were not statute-barred at the date when the company was struck off, the period between the date of striking off and the date when its name was restored to the register should not be counted for the purposes of the Limitation Acts. In *Re Huntingdon Poultry Ltd* [1969] 1 All ER 328, [1969] 1 WLR 204, a petition for a similar direction was refused as being unnecessary. The above provisions do not apply where the company is already in liquidation: see *Re Vickers and Bott Ltd* [1968] 2 All ER 264n. This statutory fiction must not be negatived by terms in the order putting a creditor in the same position as if the company had been struck off, thus preserving any right against the directors on a warranty of authority: *Re Lindsay Bowman Ltd* [1969] 3 All ER 601, [1969] 1 WLR 1443; but cf *Re Brown Bayley's Steel Works Ltd* (1905) 21 TLR 374 and para 1506 text to note 15 post.

10 *Re Carpenter's Patent Davit Boat Lowering and Detaching Gear Co* (1888) 1 Meg 26; *Re Johannesburg Mining and General Syndicate Ltd* (1901) 45 Sol Jo 343; and see *Re Walter Wright Ltd* [1923] WN 128. In *Re New Timbiqui Gold Mines Ltd* [1961] Ch 319, [1961] 1 All ER 865, the court would not have made an order in any event as there was not sufficient evidence of likely benefit to members or creditors. See also *Re Lindsay Bowman Ltd* [1969] 3 All ER 601, [1969] 1 WLR 1443 (same point).

11 *Re Regent Insulation Co Ltd* (1981) Times, 4 November (application in name of company made ostensibly by a former managing director but actually in interests of insurance company).

12 *Re Outlay Assurance Society* (1887) 34 ChD 479.

1505. Non-trading private companies. On an application by a notifiable person[1] made before the expiration of 20 years from publication in the Gazette[2] of the relevant notice[3], the court, may, if satisfied:

(1) that any statutory duty[4] with respect to the giving to that person of a copy of the company's application to be struck off the register[5] was not performed;

(2) that the making of the company's application to be struck off the register involved a breach of duty[6]; or

(3) that it is for some other reason just to do so,

order the company's name to be restored to the register[7].

On an application by the Secretary of State made before the expiration of 20 years from publication in the Gazette of the relevant notice[8], the court may, if satisfied that it is in the public interest to do so, order the company's name to be restored[9].

On an office copy of the order being delivered to the registrar of companies for registration, the company to which the order relates is deemed to have continued in existence as if its name had not been struck off; and the court may by the order give such directions and make such provisions as seem just for placing the company and all other persons in the same position, as nearly as may be, as if the company had not been struck off[10].

1 For these purposes, 'notifiable person' means a person to whom a copy of the company's application under the Companies Act 1985 s 652A (as added) (see para 1500 ante) was required to be given under

s 652B (as added) (see para 1501 ante) or s 652C (see para 1502 ante): s 653(2C) (added by the Deregulation and Contracting Out Act 1994 s 13(1), Sch 5 para 3(1),(3)). As to applications for restoration see para 1506 post.

2 For the meaning of 'the Gazette' see para 70 note 1 ante.

3 Ie under the Companies Act 1985 s 652A(4) (as added): see para 1500 ante.

4 Ie under ibid s 652B (as added) or s 652C (as added).

5 Ie under ibid s 652A (as added): see para 1500 ante.

6 Ie under ibid s 652B(1) or (3) (as added): see para 1501 ante.

7 Ibid s 653(2A),(2B) (added by the Deregulation and Contracting Out Act 1994 Sch 5 para 3(1),(3)).

8 See note 3 supra.

9 Companies Act 1985 s 653(2A),(2D) (added by the Deregulation and Contracting Out Act 1994 Sch 5 para 3(1),(3)).

10 Companies Act 1985 s 653(3) (amended by the Deregulation and Contracting Out Act 1994 Sch 5 para 3(1),(4)).

1506. Procedure on application for restoration. The jurisdiction is exercised by the Chancery Division[1].

In the case of defunct companies[2], where the application is not made in conjunction with a winding-up petition, the application is made by originating summons[3]; but, where the application is made in conjunction with a winding-up petition, the application is by petition[4], which should be served on the registrar of companies[5]. Unless the company was already in course of liquidation when it was struck off the register[6], either the petition or notice of the petition should be served on the Treasury Solicitor[7]. If a member petitions, the company should be joined as a co-petitioner in order to give the usual undertaking to make the returns required by the Secretary of State[8]. If the company is in liquidation, the liquidator cannot petition in his own name, but must petition in the name of the company or join it as a petitioner[9]; and the company may itself petition even after dissolution, but an officer should be made co-petitioner so as to have somebody responsible for the registrar's costs[10]. The petitioner should ask that the order should direct, and it should direct, the registrar to advertise the order in his official name in the Gazette[11]. A third party suing the company for rescission of a contract is not entitled to be heard in opposition to the petition[12]. An affidavit must be filed proving that notice of the petition has been given to the Treasury Solicitor, and that he has stated that no objection is taken on behalf of the Crown to the making of the order prayed for; the order ought to be prefaced by a recital to that effect[13]. The court has no power to impose a penalty as a condition of making a restoration order[14]. The restoration of the name does not relieve directors or others from any liability; it does not relieve them from the personal liability incurred by carrying on business after the company has been dissolved, unless the court makes a special order[15].

Where a company is in winding up, it is not the practice for the Secretary of State to require or for the court to order the making of the returns which ought to have been sent to the registrar before the winding up[16].

In the case of non-trading private companies[17], the application is made by originating summons[18].

1 See eg *Re City Lands Investment Corpn Ltd* [1897] WN 162; *Re Chaco (Paraguay) Land Co Ltd* [1901] WN 124.

2 As to defunct companies see paras 1496-1499, 1504 ante.

3 RSC Ord 102 r 2(1),(2); and see the Supreme Court Practice 1995 paras 102/2/28-102/2/31.

4 RSC Ord 102 r 4(1)(g); and see the Supreme Court Practice 1995 paras 102/4/33-102/4/35. As to the practice on such a petition see para 252 ante.

5 *Re Conrad Hall & Co Ltd* (1916) 60 Sol Jo 666.

6 *Re Vickers and Bott Ltd* [1968] 2 All ER 264n.

7 *Re Home and Colonial Insurance Co Ltd* (1928) 44 TLR 718; and see note 11 infra.
8 *Re Walter Wright Ltd* [1923] WN 128.
9 *Re Johannesburg Mining and General Syndicate Ltd* (1901) 45 Sol Jo 343.
10 *Re Conrad Hall & Co Ltd* (1916) 60 Sol Jo 666.
11 *Re Johannesburg Mining and General Syndicate Ltd* (1901) 45 Sol Jo 343. For the meaning of 'the Gazette' see para 70 note 1 ante.
12 *Re Conrad Hall & Co Ltd* (1916) 60 Sol Jo 666. See further *Re Portrafram Ltd* [1986] BCLC 533.
13 *Practice Note* [1931] WN 99; and see *Practice Note* [1952] WN 170.
14 *Re Brown Bayley's Steel Works Ltd* (1905) 21 TLR 374; *Re Moses and Cohen Ltd* [1957] 3 All ER 232, [1957] 1 WLR 1007. As to costs on the making of the order see *Re Court Lodge Development Co Ltd* [1973] 3 All ER 425, [1973] 1 WLR 1097.
15 *Re Brown Bayley's Steel Works Ltd* (1905) 21 TLR 374. Cf para 1504 note 9 ante.
16 *Re Johannesburg Mining and General Syndicate Ltd* (1901) 45 Sol Jo 343.
17 As to non-trading private companies see paras 1500-1503, 1505 ante.
18 RSC Ord 102 r 2(1),(2). No application for striking off may be made if a non-trading private company is being wound up, whether voluntarily or by the court: see para 1501 ante.

(33) SECRETARY OF STATE FOR TRADE AND INDUSTRY

1507. Powers and duties in general. The numerous functions of the Secretary of State[1] in relation to the formation and supervision of companies have already been considered. For example, he may require the change of name of a company[2]; and his consent is required to a prosecution for the issue of shares in contravention of restrictions imposed by him[3].

The Secretary of State has power to open and staff registration offices at places in England and Wales[4]. As respects the companies themselves, his powers include power to specify words or expressions which may not, without his consent, be used as or as part of the name of any company applying for registration[5], or to require a company to abandon a misleading name[6]; to direct the holding of an annual general meeting if default has been made in the statutory requirements[7]; to appoint auditors if none is appointed by the company[8]; to extend the statutory period for delivery of accounts[9]; to modify the statutory provisions relating to the purchase by a company of its own shares[10]; and to investigate the ownership of a company and, in connection with that investigation, to impose restrictions on dealings in shares and debentures[11].

The Secretary of State also has power, on an order granted by the court, to inspect a company's books where it is suspected that an offence has been committed by an officer of the company[12]; power to investigate unit trust schemes[13]; and power to allow the formation of partnerships consisting of more than 20 members for the purpose of carrying on specified businesses[14].

1 As to the Secretary of State for Trade and Industry see TRADE AND INDUSTRY vol 47 (Reissue) para 2.
2 See para 114 ante.
3 See para 1396 ante.
4 See para 60 ante.
5 See para 156 ante.
6 See para 159 ante.
7 See para 658 ante.
8 See para 1031 ante.
9 See para 822 ante.
10 See para 240 ante.
11 See para 1383 et seq ante.
12 See para 1166 ante.
13 See the Financial Services Act 1986 s 94(1) and MONEY.
14 See para 21 ante.

1508. Power to contract out the Secretary of State's functions. If the Secretary of State by order so provides, any function of his which is conferred by or under any enactment and which, by virtue of any enactment or rule of law, may be exercised by an officer of his and which is not otherwise excluded[1] may be exercised by, or by employees of, such person (if any) as may be authorised in that behalf by the Secretary of State[2].

An order so made may provide that any such function may be exercised, and an authorisation given by virtue of such an order may, subject to the provisions of the order, authorise the exercise of such a function:

(1) either wholly or to such extent as may be specified in the order or authorisation;

(2) either generally or in such cases or areas as may be so specified; and

(3) either unconditionally or subject to the fulfilment of such conditions as may be so specified[3].

An authorisation given by virtue of such an order:

(a) must be for such period, not exceeding ten years, as is specified in the authorisation;

(b) may be revoked at any time by the Secretary of State; and

(c) must not prevent the Secretary of State or any other person from exercising the function to which the authorisation relates[4].

Where by virtue of such an order a person is authorised to exercise any function of the Secretary of State, anything done or omitted to be done by or in relation to the authorised person (or an employee of his) in, or in connection with, the exercise or purported exercise of the function is to be treated for all purposes as done or omitted to be done by or in relation to the Secretary of State in his capacity as such[5]; but this provision does not apply for the purposes of so much of any contract made between an authorised person and the Secretary of State as relates to the exercise of the function or for the purposes of any criminal proceedings brought in respect of anything done or omitted to be done by the authorised person (or any employee of his)[6].

Where by virtue of such an order a person is authorised to exercise any function of the Secretary of State and the order or authorisation is revoked at a time when a relevant contract[7] is subsisting, the authorised person is entitled to treat the relevant contract as repudiated by the Secretary of State (and not as frustrated by reason of the revocation)[8].

1   Ie by the Deregulation and Contracting Out Act 1994 s 71. A function is excluded from s 69 (see infra) if (1) its exercise would constitute the exercise of jurisdiction of any court or of any tribunal which exercises the judicial power of the State; or (2) its exercise, or a failure to exercise it, would necessarily interfere with or otherwise affect the liberty of any individual; or (3) it is a power or right of entry, search or seizure into or of any property; or (4) it is a power or duty to make subordinate legislation: s 71(1). Section 71(1)(b),(c) (see heads (2), (3) supra) does not exclude any function of the official receiver attached to any court: s 71(2). As to the official receiver see para 2263 et seq post.

2   Ibid ss 69(1), 79. In exercise of the powers so conferred the Secretary of State made the Contracting Out (Functions in relation to the Registration of Companies) Order 1995, SI 1995/1013, art 5, Sch 3: see para 1509 post. As to contracting out the functions of the registrar of companies see paras 61, 62 ante; and as to contracting out the functions of the official receiver see para 2265, 2266 post.

3   Deregulation and Contracting Out Act 1994 s 69(4).

4   Ibid s 69(5).

5   Ibid ss 72(1),(2), 79.

6   Ibid ss 72(3), 79.

7   For these purposes, 'relevant contract' means so much of any contract made between the authorised person and the Secretary of State as relates to the exercise of the functions: ibid ss 73(3), 79.

8   Ibid ss 73(2), 79.

1509. Contracted out functions of the Secretary of State. Any function of the Secretary of State which is listed below may be exercised by, or by employees of, such person (if any) as may be authorised in that behalf by the Secretary of State[1]:

(1) functions conferred by or under the following provisions of the Companies Act 1985:

    (a) those relating to the prohibition on registration of certain names except with the approval of the Secretary of State[2];

    (b) those relating to the extension by the Secretary of State of the period allowed for laying and delivering accounts and reports[3];

    (c) those relating to the extension of the period for delivering accounts and reports[4] of an oversea company[5];

(2) functions conferred by or under the Business Names Act 1985[6] relating to the prohibition of use of certain business names[7];

(3) functions conferred by or under the Business Names Act 1985[8] as applied[9] to European Economic Interest Groupings[10].

1 Contracting Out (Functions in relation to the Registration of Companies) Order 1995, SI 1995/1013, art 5.
2 Ie the Companies Act 1985 s 26(2): see para 156 ante.
3 Ie ibid s 244(5) (as substituted): see para 822 ante.
4 Ie ibid s 702(5) (as substituted): see para 1825 post.
5 Contracting Out (Functions in relation to the Registration of Companies) Order 1995 art 5, Sch 3 para 1.
6 Ie by or under the Business Names Act 1985 s 2: see para 167 ante.
7 Contracting Out (Functions in relation to the Registration of Companies) Order 1995 Sch 3 para 2.
8 See note 6 supra.
9 Ie by the European Economic Interest Groupings Regulations 1989, SI 1989/638, reg 17: see para 1831 post.
10 Contracting Out (Functions in relation to the Registration of Companies) Order 1995 Sch 3 para 3. For these purposes, 'European Economic Interest Grouping' means a European Economic Interest Grouping as defined in the the European Economic Interest Grouping Regulations 1989 reg 2(1) (see para 1831 post): Contracting Out (Functions in relation to the Registration of Companies) Order 1995 art 2(1).

1510. Powers in connection with winding up. The Secretary of State has power to present a petition for winding up[1], and has many other powers and duties in connection with the winding up of companies. In particular, he has power to appoint additional officers to carry out his functions in connection with winding up[2].

In a winding up by the court, the Secretary of State has a general power of surveillance over liquidators[3], and in particular may audit a liquidator's accounts[4], may carry out the functions of a committee of inspection where there is no committee[5], and may release the liquidator when the liquidator's duties have been completed[6]. In a voluntary winding up, the Secretary of State has a duty to investigate a report referred to him by the Director of Public Prosecutions in connection with suspected offences by directors in relation to the company[7].

The Secretary of State also has power to apply for the making of a disqualification order[8].

1 See para 1390 ante and para 2204 post.
2 See para 2311 post.
3 See para 2313 post.
4 See para 2359 post.
5 See para 2277 post.
6 See para 2383 post.

7 See para 2775 post.
8 See para 1427 ante.

1511. Annual report to Parliament. The Secretary of State must cause a general annual report of matters within the Companies Acts[1] to be prepared and laid before both Houses of Parliament[2]. A libel action does not lie against an officer of his department in respect of statements contained in a report prepared by him for and delivered to the Secretary of State in the performance of his duties, on winding-up matters, for the purpose of its being laid before Parliament as part of the Secretary of State's general annual report[3].

1 For the meaning of 'the Companies Acts' see para 60 note 1 ante. In the Companies Act 1985 s 729, references to the Companies Acts includes certain provisions of the Insolvency Act 1986, and also the Company Directors Disqualification Act 1986: see para 20 text to note 12 and note 12 ante.
2 Companies Act 1985 s 729.
3 *Burr v Smith* [1909] 2 KB 306, CA.

1512. Power to alter accounting requirements, tables, forms and monetary limits. The Secretary of State may by regulations made by statutory instrument modify the statutory provisions[1] relating to accounts[2].

Regulations which:

(1) add to the classes of documents required to be prepared, laid before the company in general meeting or delivered to the registrar;

(2) restrict the classes of company which have the benefit of any exemption, exception or special provision;

(3) require additional matter to be included in a document of any class; or

(4) otherwise render the requirements of the statutory provisions relating to accounts more onerous,

may not be made unless a draft of the instrument containing the regulations has been laid before Parliament and approved by a resolution of each House[3]. Otherwise a statutory instrument containing regulations under these provisions is subject to annulment in pursuance of a resolution of either House of Parliament[4].

Such regulations may:

(a) make different provision for different cases or classes of case;

(b) repeal and re-enact provisions with modifications of form or arrangement, whether or not they are modified in substance;

(c) make consequential amendments or repeals in other provisions of the Companies Act 1985 or in other enactments; and

(d) contain such transitional and other incidental and supplementary provisions as the Secretary of State thinks fit[5].

The Secretary of State also has power by regulations made in a statutory instrument:

(i) to alter Table A[6];

(ii) to alter the form of statement[7] to be published by insurance companies and deposit, provident or benefit societies[8]; and

(iii) to alter or add to Tables B, C, D, E and F[9].

The Secretary of State also has power by regulations in a statutory instrument to increase or decrease any of the money sums or prescribed percentages for the time being specified in various provisions in the Companies Act 1985[10] and the Insolvency Act 1986[11].

1 Ie the Companies Act 1985 Pt VII (ss 221–262A) (as amended): see para 801 et seq ante.
2 Ibid s 257(1) (substituted by the Companies Act 1989 s 20). In exercise of the power so conferred the Secretary of State made the Companies Act 1985 (Miscellaneous Accounting Amendments) Regulations 1996, SI 1996/189.
3 Companies Act 1985 s 257(2) (substituted by the Companies Act 1989 s 20).
4 Companies Act 1985 s 257(3) (substituted by the Companies Act 1989 s 20).
5 Companies Act 1985 s 257(4) (substituted by the Companies Act 1989 s 20). Any modification by regulations so made of the Companies Act 1985 s 258 (as substituted) or Sch 10A (as added) (parent and subsidiary undertakings: see paras 828, 829 ante) does not apply for the purposes of the enactments outside the Companies Acts unless the regulations so provide: Companies Act 1985 s 257(5) (substituted by the Companies Act 1989 s 20). For the meaning of 'the Companies Acts' see para 60 note 1 ante.
6 See the Companies Act 1985 s 8(1) and para 533 ante. If, in consequence of regulations under s 8, Table A is amended, the alteration does not affect a company registered before the alteration takes effect, or repeal as respects that company any portion of the Table: Companies Act 1985 s 8(3).
7 Ie ibid s 720, Sch 23: see para 939 ante.
8 Ibid s 720(7). At the date at which this volume states the law no such regulations had been made.
9 Ibid ss 3, 8(4). As to Table B see para 102 note 6 ante; as to Tables C and D see para 111 ante; as to Table E see para 116 ante; and as to Table F see para 85 note 5 ante. As to the Secretary of State's prospective power to prescribe a Table G see para 531 ante. At the date at which this volume states the law no such regulations subsequent to the Companies (Tables A to F) Regulations 1985, SI 1985/805, taking effect on 1 July 1985 had been made save for the Companies (Tables A to F) (Amendment) Regulations 1985, SI 1985/1052.
10 See the Companies Act 1985 s 118 (meaning of 'authorised minimum': see para 652 note 6 ante); and s 345 (enforcement of fair dealing by directors: see para 598 et seq ante).
11 Insolvency Act 1986 s 416(1). The provisions in question are s 117(2) (see para 2198 post), s 120(3) (sheriff court jurisdiction in Scotland), s 123(1)(a) (see para 2206 post), s 184(3) (see para 2643 post), s 206(1)(a),(b) (see para 2664 post): s 416(1). Any such order may contain such transitional provisions as may appear to the Secretary of State necessary or expedient: s 416(2). No such order increasing or reducing the money sums for the time being specified in s 117(2), s 120(3) or s 123(1)(a) can be made unless a draft of the order has been laid before, and approved by a resolution of, each House of Parliament: s 416(3). A statutory instrument containing an order other than one of the type mentioned supra is subject to annulment in pursuance of a resolution of either House of Parliament: s 416(4).

1513. Power to make regulations relating to inspection of registers etc. The Secretary of State may make provision by regulations as to the obligations of a company which is required by any provision of the Companies Act 1985 to make available for inspection any register, index or document or to provide copies of any such register, index or document, or part of it; and a company which fails to comply with the regulations is deemed to have refused inspection or, as the case may be, to have failed to provide a copy[1].

The regulations may make provision as to the time, duration and manner of inspection, including the circumstances in which and extent to which the copying of information is permitted in the course of inspection[2].

The regulations may define what may be required of the company as regards the nature, extent and manner of extracting or presenting any information for the purposes of inspection or the provision of copies[3].

Where there is power to charge a fee, the regulations may make provision as to the amount of the fee and the basis of its calculation[4].

Such regulations may make different provision for different classes of case[5].

Nothing in any provision of the Companies Act 1985 or in the regulations is to be construed as preventing a company from affording more extensive facilities than are required by the regulations or, where a fee may be charged, from charging a lesser fee than that prescribed or no fee at all[6].

Such regulations must be made by statutory instrument which is subject to annulment in pursuance of a resolution of either House of Parliament[7].

1 Companies Act 1985 s 723A(1) (added by the Companies Act 1989 s 143(1)). In exercise of the power so conferred the Secretary of State made the Companies (Inspection and Copying of Registers, Indices and Documents) Regulations 1991, SI 1991/1998 (see paras 229, 236, 390, 391, 560, 562, 574, 695, 755, 1294 ante) which came into force on 1 November 1991: reg 1.
2 Companies Act 1985 s 723A(2) (added by the Companies Act 1989 s 143(1)).
3 Companies Act 1985 s 723A(3) (added by the Companies Act 1989 s 143(1)).
4 Companies Act 1985 s 723A(4) (added by the Companies Act 1989 s 143(1)).
5 Companies Act 1985 s 723A(5) (added by the Companies Act 1989 s 143(1)).
6 Companies Act 1985 s 723A(6) (added by the Companies Act 1989 s 143(1)).
7 Companies Act 1985 s 723A(7) (added by the Companies Act 1989 s 143(1)).

1514. Power to make regulations relating to orders imposing restrictions on shares. The Secretary of State may by regulations made by statutory instrument make such amendments of the provisions of the Companies Act 1985 relating to orders imposing restrictions on shares[1] as appear to him necessary or expedient:

(1) for enabling orders to be made in a form protecting the rights of third parties;
(2) with respect to the circumstances in which restrictions may be relaxed or removed;
(3) with respect to the making of interim orders by a court[2].

The regulations may make different provision for different cases and may contain such transitional and other supplementary and incidental provisions as appear to the Secretary of State to be appropriate[3].

Such regulations must not be made unless a draft of the regulations has been laid before Parliament and approved by resolution of each House of Parliament[4].

1 Ie the Companies Act 1985 s 210(5) (see para 745 ante), s 216(1),(2) (see para 752 ante), s 445 (as amended) (see para 1383 ante) and Pt XV (ss 454–457 (as amended): see paras 1395–1397 ante).
2 Companies Act 1989 s 135(1),(2). In exercise of the power so conferred the Secretary of State made the Companies (Disclosure of Interests in Shares) (Orders imposing restrictions on shares) Regulations 1991, SI 1991/1646, which came into force on 18 July 1991: reg 1.
3 Companies Act 1989 s 135(3).
4 Ibid s 135(4).

1515. Power to make regulations relating to company insolvency. The Secretary of State may from time to time issue regulations with respect to so much of any matter that may be provided for in the rules as relates to the carrying out of the functions of the liquidator, administrator or administrative receiver of a company[1].

1 See the Insolvency Act 1986 s 411, Sch 8 para 27 and paras 2311, 2800 post.

1516. Insolvency Services Account. All money received by the Secretary of State in respect of proceedings under the Insolvency Act 1986 as it applies to England and Wales must be paid into the Insolvency Services Account kept by the Secretary of State with the Bank of England; and all payments out of money standing to the credit of the Secretary of State in that account must be made by the Bank of England in such manner as he may direct[1].

Whenever the cash balance standing to the credit of the Insolvency Services Account is in excess of the amount which, in the opinion of the Secretary of State, is required for the time being to answer demands in respect of companies' estates, he must notify the excess to the National Debt Commissioners[2], and pay into the Insolvency Services Investment Account[3] the whole or any part of the excess as the commissioners may require for investment in accordance with certain statutory provisions[4].

Whenever, in the Secretary of State's opinion, any part of the money so invested is required to answer any demand in respect of companies' estates, he must notify to the National Debt Commissioners the amount so required, and the commissioners must thereupon repay to the Secretary of State such sum as may be required to the credit of the Insolvency Services Account; and for that purpose may direct the sale of any such part of the securities in which the money has been invested as may be necessary[5].

The Secretary of State must for each year ending 31 March prepare a statement of the sums received or paid by him under the above provisions in such form and manner as the Treasury may direct and must transmit each statement to the Comptroller and Auditor General before the end of November next following the year[6].

1 Insolvency Act 1986 s 403(1). As to payments out of that account see para 2364 post; and as to the annual statement of sums relating to the account see para 2314 post.
2 As to the National Debt Commissioners see MONEY vol 32 para 225.
3 The Insolvency Services Investment Account is an account kept by the National Debt Commissioners with the Bank of England: Insolvency Act 1986 s 403(2)(b).
4 Ibid s 403(2). Any money standing to the credit of the Insolvency Services Investment Account, including any money received by the National Debt Commissioners by way of interest on or proceeds of any investment, may be invested by the commissioners in accordance with such directions as may be given by the Treasury, in any manner for the time being specified in the Trustee Investments Act 1961 s 1(1), Sch 1 Pt II (paras 1–24 (as amended): see TRUSTS vol 48 (Reissue) para 874): Insolvency Act 1986 s 404. The commissioners must for each year ending 31 March prepare a statement of the sums credited and debited to the account in such form and manner as the Treasury may direct and must transmit it to the Comptroller and Auditor General before the end of November next following the year (s 409(1)); and every such statement must include such additional information as the Treasury may direct (s 409(3)). The Comptroller and Auditor General must examine, certify and report on every such statement and must lay copies of it and of his report before Parliament: s 409(4).
    Where the annual account to be kept by the commissioners shows that, in the year for which it is made up, the gross amount of the interest accrued from the securities standing to the credit of the account exceeded the aggregate of (1) a sum, to be determined by the Treasury, to provide against the depreciation in the value of the securities; and (2) the sums paid into the account in pursuance of s 406 (see infra) together with the sums paid pursuant to s 406 to the Commissioners of Inland Revenue, then the National Debt Commissioners must, within three months after the account is laid before Parliament, cause the amount of the excess to be paid out of the account into the Consolidated Fund in such manner as may from time to time be agreed between the Treasury and the commissioners: s 405(1). Where such annual account shows that, in the year for which it is made up, the gross amount of interest accrued from the securities standing to the credit of the account was less than such aggregate, an amount equal to the deficiency must, at such times as the Treasury directs, be paid out of the Consolidated Fund into the account: s 405(2). If the account is insufficient to meet its liabilities, the Treasury may, on being informed of the insufficiency by the commissioners, issue the amount of the deficiency out of the Consolidated Fund and the Treasury must certify the deficiency to Parliament: s 405(3).
    Where under rules made by virtue of s 411, Sch 8 para 16 (see para 2800 note 2 post) a company has become entitled to any sum by way of interest, the Secretary of State must certify that sum and the amount of tax payable on it to the commissioners; and the commissioners must pay out of the Insolvency Services Investment Account (a) into the Insolvency Services Account, the sum so certified less the amount of tax so certified; and (b) to the Commissioners of Inland Revenue, the amount of tax so certified: s 406.
    In addition, the Secretary of State must from time to time pay into the Consolidated Fund out of the Insolvency Services Account so much of the sums standing to the credit of that account as represents: (i) dividends which were declared before such date as the Treasury may from time to time determine and have not been claimed; and (ii) balances ascertained before that date which are too small to be divided among the persons entitled to them: s 407(1). For these purposes, the sums standing to the credit of the Insolvency Services Account are deemed to include any sums paid out of that account and represented by any sums or securities standing to the credit of the Insolvency Services Investment Account: s 407(2). The Secretary of State may require the National Debt Commissioners to pay out of the Insolvency

Services Investment Account into the Insolvency Services Account the whole or part of any sum which the Secretary of State is required to pay out of that account under these provisions; and the commissioners may direct the sale of such securities standing to the credit of the Insolvency Services Investment Account as may be necessary for that purpose: s 407(3). If, after any such repayment, the Insolvency Services Account is insufficient to meet its liabilities, the Treasury may, on being so informed by the Secretary of State, issue the amount of the deficiency out of the Consolidated Fund; and the Treasury must certify such deficiency to Parliament: s 408.

5   Ibid s 403(3).
6   Ibid s 409(2).

(34) SHARE OPTION AND PROFIT SHARING SCHEMES; EMPLOYEE SHARE OWNERSHIP TRUSTS

(i) In general

1517. Introduction. An individual may obtain a right to acquire shares in a body corporate by reason of his office or employment as a director or employee of that or any other body corporate if that right is obtained in accordance with the provisions of an approved share option scheme and that right is obtained:

(1) in the case of a savings-related share option scheme, on or after 15 November 1980; or

(2) in the case of any other share option scheme, on or after 6 April 1984[1].

The trustees of an approved profit sharing scheme may appropriate shares which have been previously acquired by the trustees and as to which the statutory conditions are fulfilled to an individual who participates in the scheme[2].

A person may also acquire shares or an interest in shares in a company under an unapproved employee share scheme[3]; or he may acquire rights under an employee share ownership trust[4].

The statutory provisions relating to share incentive schemes[5] do not apply to an acquisition of shares, or of an interest in shares, made on or after 26 October 1987[6].

For the purposes of the Companies Act 1985, an employees' share scheme is a scheme for encouraging or facilitating the holding of shares or debentures in a company by or for the benefit of:

(a) the bona fide employees or former employees of the company, the company's subsidiary[7] or holding company[8] or a subsidiary of the company's holding company; or

(b) the wives, husbands, widows, widowers or children or stepchildren under the age of 18 of such employees or former employees[9].

1   See paras 1528, 1531 et seq post. As to whether there is a right to damages for loss of a share option where the contract of employment provides for the lapse of the option on cessation of employment see *Micklefield v SAC Technology Ltd* [1991] 1 All ER 275, [1990] 1 WLR 1002.
2   See paras 1529, 1531 et seq post.
3   See para 1518 et seq post.
4   See para 1576 et seq post.
5   Ie the Income and Corporation Taxes Act 1988 s 138 (repealed) and the Finance Act 1972 s 79 (repealed): see COMPANIES vol 7(1) (1988 Reissue) paras 507–515.
6   Finance Act 1988 s 88(1). Where (1) tax is chargeable by virtue of the Income and Corporation Taxes Act 1988 s 138(1)(a) (repealed) or the Finance Act 1972 s 79(4) (repealed) by reference to the market value, after 26 October 1987, of shares in a company which is not a dependent subsidiary on that date; and (2) that market value is greater than the market value of the shares on 26 October 1987, the amount on which tax is chargeable (and the question whether any tax is chargeable) is to be determined by reference to the market value on 26 October 1987 (and for this purpose 'market value' has the same

meaning as in the Income and Corporation Taxes Act 1988 s 138 (repealed)): Finance Act 1988 s 88(2). For the meaning of 'dependent subsidiary' see para 1520 post.

7 For the meaning of 'subsidiary' see para 827 ante.
8 For the meaning of 'holding company' see para 827 ante.
9 Companies Act 1985 s 743.

(ii) Unapproved Employee Share Schemes

1518. In general. The following provisions[1] apply where, on or after 26 October 1987, a person acquires shares[2] or an interest in shares[3] in a company in pursuance of a right conferred on him or an opportunity offered to him by reason of his office as a director[4] of, or his employment[5] by, that or any other company[6].

The following provisions do not, however, apply:

(1) in relation to an acquisition by a person who is not chargeable to tax under Case I of Schedule E[7] in respect of the office or employment in question[8];

(2) where the acquisition is made in pursuance of an offer to the public[9].

1 Ie the Finance Act 1988 Pt III Ch II (ss 77–89) (as amended): see infra and para 1519 et seq post. Part III Ch II (ss 77–89) (as amended), with the omission of s 79 (see para 1521 post) and s 80 (as amended) (see para 1522 post), has effect where shares, or an interest in shares, in a company which is not a dependent subsidiary on 26 October 1987 have been acquired before that date as it has effect, apart from s 88, where shares or an interest in shares are acquired on or after that date: s 88(3). In relation to shares which were, or an interest in shares which was, acquired before 26 October 1987 the removal or variation of a restriction to which the shares are subject is not a chargeable event for the purposes of s 78 (see para 1519 post) if, because of the Finance Act 1973 s 19, Sch 8 para 7 (repealed), the restriction would not have been regarded as one to which the shares were subject for the purposes of the Finance Act 1972 s 79(2)(c) (repealed): Finance Act 1988 s 88(4).

2 For these purposes, 'shares' includes stock and also includes securities as defined in the Income and Corporation Taxes Act 1988 s 254(1) (see INCOME TAXATION vol 23 (Reissue) para 881): Finance Act 1988 s 87(1).

3 For these purposes, references to an interest in any shares include references to an interest in the proceeds of sale of part of the shares: ibid s 87(1).

4 For these purposes, 'director' includes a person who is to be, or who has ceased to be, a director: ibid s 87(1).

5 Where a right to acquire shares or an interest in shares in a company is assigned to a person and the right was conferred on some other person by reason of the assignee's office as a director of, or his employment by, that or any other company, the assignee is treated for the purposes of ibid Pt III Ch II (ss 77–89) (as amended) as acquiring the shares or interest in pursuance of a right conferred on him by reason of that office or employment: s 87(4).

6 Ibid s 77(1) (amended by the Finance Act 1991 s 44(9),(10)). As to the duty to give information under s 77(1) (as so amended) see para 1526 post.

7 Ie the Income and Corporation Taxes Act 1988 s 19(1), Schedule E, Case I (as substituted): see INCOME TAXATION vol 23 (Reissue) para 668 et seq.

8 Finance Act 1988 s 77(2).

9 Ibid s 77(3). Where, in a case falling within s 68(1ZA) (as added), s 68(1) (as amended) applies or applied in relation to such a benefit as is there mentioned or would so apply or have applied, had there been any such benefit, any acquisition made on or after 16 January 1991 in pursuance of any of the offers which, in that case, fall to be regarded by virtue of s 68(1ZB) (as added) as together constituting a single offer of shares to the public for the purposes of s 68(1) (as amended) is to be regarded for the purposes of s 77(3) as an acquisition made in pursuance of an offer to the public: s 77(4) (added by the Finance Act 1991 s 44(9),(10)).

1519. Charge where restrictions removed etc. The person acquiring the shares[1] or interest in shares[2] is chargeable to tax if:

(1) a chargeable event occurs in relation to the shares at a time when he has not ceased to have a beneficial interest in them; and

(2) the shares are shares in a company which was not a dependent subsidiary[3] at the time of the acquisition and is not a dependent subsidiary at the time of the chargeable event[4].

Any of the following events is a chargeable event in relation to shares in a company for these purposes if it increases, or but for the occurrence of some other event would increase, the value[5] of the shares:

(a) the removal or variation of a restriction[6] to which the shares are subject;
(b) the creation or variation of a right relating to the shares;
(c) the imposition of a restriction on other shares in the company or the variation of a restriction to which such other shares are subject;
(d) the removal or variation of a right relating to other shares in the company[7].

A charge by virtue of these provisions is a charge under Schedule E[8], for the year of assessment in which the chargeable event occurs, on the amount by which the value of the shares is increased by the chargeable event or the amount by which it would be increased but for the occurrence of some other event (or, if the interest of the person chargeable is less than full beneficial ownership, on an appropriate part of that amount)[9].

An event is not a chargeable event in relation to shares in a company for these purposes unless the person who acquired the shares or interest has been a director[10] or employee[11] of that company, or, if it is different, the company as a director or employee of which he acquired the shares or interest, or an associated company[12] of such a company, at some time during the period of seven years ending with the date on which the event occurs[13].

Nor is an event a chargeable event for these purposes if it consists of:

(i) the removal of a restriction to which all shares of a class are subject from all those shares;
(ii) the variation of such a restriction in the case of all those shares;
(iii) the creation of a right relating to all shares of a class;
(iv) the variation of such a right in the case of all those shares;
(v) the imposition of a restriction on all shares of a class; or
(vi) the removal of a right relating to all shares of a class from all those shares,

and any of the following conditions is satisfied[14]:

(A) that at the time of the event the majority of the company's shares of the same class as those which, or an interest in which, the person acquired are held otherwise than by or for the benefit of directors or employees of the company, an associated company of the company or directors or employees of any such associated company;
(B) that at the time of the event the company is employee-controlled[15] by virtue of holdings of shares of that class;
(C) that at the time of the event the company is a subsidiary[16] which is not a dependent subsidiary and its shares are of a single class[17].

1 For the meaning of 'shares' see para 1518 note 2 ante.
2 For the meaning of references to an interest in any shares see para 1518 note 3 ante.
3 For the meaning of 'dependent subsidiary' see para 1520 post.
4 Finance Act 1988 s 78(1).
5 For these purposes, 'value', in relation to shares or a benefit, means the amount which the person holding the shares or receiving the benefit might reasonably expect to obtain from a sale in the open market: ibid s 87(1).
6 For these purposes, references to restrictions to which shares are subject, or to rights relating to shares, include references to restrictions imposed or rights conferred by any contract or arrangement or in any other way: ibid s 78(7).

7 Ibid s 78(2).
8 Ie under the Income and Corporation Taxes Act 1988 s 19(1), Schedule E (as amended): see INCOME TAXATION vol 23 (Reissue) para 654 et seq.
9 Finance Act 1988 s 78(3).
10 For the meaning of 'director' see para 1518 note 4 ante.
11 For these purposes, 'employee' includes a person who is to be, or who has ceased to be, an employee: Finance Act 1988 s 87(1).
12 For these purposes, 'associated company' has the same meaning as, by virtue of the Income and Corporation Taxes Act 1988 s 416 (as amended) (see INCOME TAXATION vol 23 (Reissue) para 1293 note 20), it has for the purposes of Pt XI (ss 414-422 (as amended): see INCOME TAXATION vol 23 (Reissue) para 1292 et seq): Finance Act 1988 s 87(1).
13 Ibid s 78(4).
14 Ibid s 78(5).
15 For these purposes, a company is 'employee-controlled' by virtue of shares of a class if (1) the majority of the company's shares of that class, other than any held by or for the benefit of an associated company, are held by or for the benefit of employees or directors of the company or a company controlled by the company; and (2) those directors and employees are together able as holders of the shares to control the company: ibid s 87(2). For these purposes, the Income and Corporation Taxes Act 1988 s 840 (meaning of 'control': see INCOME TAXATION vol 23 (Reissue) para 849) applies: Finance Act 1988 s 87(3).
16 For these purposes, 'subsidiary' means 51% subsidiary: ibid s 87(1).
17 Ibid s 78(6).

1520. Meaning of 'dependent subsidiary'. A company which is a subsidiary[1] is a dependent subsidiary throughout a period of account[2] of the company unless:

(1) the whole or substantially the whole of the company's business during the period of account (taken as a whole) is business carried on with persons who are not members of the same group[3] as the company[4];

(2) during the period of account either there is no increase in the value of the company as a result of intra-group transactions[5], or any such increase in value does not exceed 5% of the value of the company at the beginning of the period (or a proportionately greater or smaller percentage in the case of a period which is longer or shorter than a year)[6];

(3) the directors[7] of the principal company of the group give to the inspector of taxes, not later than two years after the end of the period of account, a certificate that in their opinion the conditions mentioned in heads (1) and (2) above are satisfied in relation to the period of account[8]; and

(4) there is attached to the certificate a report addressed to those directors by the auditors of the subsidiary that the auditors:

(a) have inquired into the state of affairs of the company with particular reference to the conditions mentioned in heads (1) and (2) above; and

(b) are not aware of anything to indicate that the opinion expressed by the directors in their certificate is unreasonable in all the circumstances[9].

1 For the meaning of 'subsidiary' see para 1519 note 16 ante.
2 For these purposes, 'period of account', in relation to a company, means the period for which it makes up its accounts: Finance Act 1988 s 86(3).
3 For these purposes, business carried on with any subsidiary of the company concerned is treated as carried on with a person who is not a member of the same group as the company unless the whole or substantially the whole of the business of that or any other subsidiary of the company during the company's period of account (taken as a whole) is carried on with members of the group other than the company and its subsidiaries (ibid s 86(2)); and 'group' means a principal company and all its subsidiaries (s 86(3)). 'Principal company' means a company of which another company is a subsidiary and which is not itself a subsidiary of another company: s 86(3).
4 Ibid s 86(1)(a).
5 For these purposes, 'intra-group transactions' means transactions between companies which are members of the same group on terms which are not such as might be expected to be agreed between

persons acting at arm's length (other than any payment for group relief, within the meaning given in the Income and Corporation Taxes Act 1988 s 402(6) (see INCOME TAXATION vol 23 (Reissue) para 940 note 10)): Finance Act 1988 s 86(3).

6 Ibid s 86(1)(b).
7 For the meaning of 'director' see para 1518 note 4 ante.
8 Finance Act 1988 s 86(1)(c).
9 Ibid s 86(1)(d).

1521. Charge for shares in dependent subsidiaries. The person acquiring the shares[1] or interest in shares[2] is chargeable to tax if the shares are shares in a company which:

(1) was a dependent subsidiary[3] at the time of the acquisition; or
(2) was not a dependent subsidiary at that time but becomes a dependent subsidiary before the person making the acquisition ceases to have any beneficial interest in the shares,

and there is a chargeable increase in the value[4] of the shares[5].

There is a chargeable increase in the value of shares in a case within head (1) above if the value of the shares at the earlier of:

(a) the expiration of seven years from the time of the acquisition; and
(b) the time when the person making the acquisition ceases to have any beneficial interest in the shares,

exceeds their value at the time of the acquisition[6].

There is a chargeable increase in the value of shares in a case within head (2) above if the value of the shares at the earlier or earliest of:

(i) the expiration of seven years from the time when the company becomes a dependent subsidiary; and
(ii) the time when the person making the acquisition ceases to have any beneficial interest in the shares; and
(iii) if the company ceases to be a dependent subsidiary, the time when it does so,

exceeds their value at the time when the company becomes a dependent subsidiary[7].

A charge by virtue of these provisions is a charge under Schedule E[8], for the year of assessment which includes the end of the period for which the chargeable increase is determined, on an amount equal to that increase (or, if the interest of the person chargeable is less than full beneficial ownership, on an appropriate part of that amount)[9].

Where, in accordance with the terms on which the acquisition was made, the consideration for the acquisition is subsequently increased, the amount chargeable to tax by virtue of these provisions is to be reduced by an amount equal to the increase in the consideration[10].

Where, in accordance with those terms, the person making the acquisition subsequently ceases to have a beneficial interest in the shares by a disposal made for a consideration which is less than the value of the shares or his interest in them at the time of the disposal, the amount on which tax is chargeable by virtue of these provisions is to be reduced so as to be equal to the excess of that consideration over the value of the shares or interest at the time of the acquisition[11].

In a case within head (2) above there is no chargeable increase in the value of shares in a company unless the person who acquired the shares or interest has been a director[12] or employee[13] of:

(A) that company; or
(B) if it is different, the company as a director or employee of which he acquired the shares or interest; or

(C) an associated company[14] of a company within heads (A) or (B) above,
at some time during the period of seven years ending with the time when the company
becomes a dependent subsidiary[15].

1 For the meaning of 'shares' see para 1518 note 2 ante.
2 For the meaning of references to an interest in any shares see para 1518 note 3 ante.
3 For the meaning of 'dependent subsidiary' see para 1520 ante.
4 For the meaning of 'value' see para 1519 note 5 ante.
5 Finance Act 1988 s 79(1).
6 Ibid s 79(2). Section 79(2) is subject to s 79(7) (see infra): s 79(2).
7 Ibid s 79(3).
8 Ie under the Income and Corporation Taxes Act 1988 s 19(1), Schedule E (as amended): see INCOME
   TAXATION vol 23 (Reissue) para 654 et seq.
9 Finance Act 1988 s 79(4).
10 Ibid s 79(5).
11 Ibid s 79(6).
12 For the meaning of 'director' see para 1518 note 4 ante.
13 For the meaning of 'employee' see para 1519 note 11 ante.
14 For the meaning of 'associated company' see para 1519 note 12 ante.
15 Finance Act 1988 s 79(7).

1522. Charge on special benefits. The person acquiring the shares[1] or interest in
shares[2] is chargeable to tax if he receives a special benefit by virtue of his ownership of
or interest in the shares[3].

If, when a benefit is received, the company is a dependent subsidiary[4] and its shares
are of a single class, the benefit is a special benefit[5]; but a benefit which does not fall
within the above provision[6] is a special benefit unless, when it becomes available, it is
available to at least 90% of the persons who then hold shares of the same class as those
which, or an interest in which, the person acquired and any of the following conditions
is satisfied[7]:

(1) that, when the benefit is received, the majority of the company's shares in
respect of which the benefit is received are held otherwise than by or for the
benefit of directors[8] or employees[9] of the company, an associated company[10] of
the company or directors or employees of any such associated company;

(2) that, when the benefit is received, the company is employee-controlled[11] by
virtue of holdings of shares of the class concerned;

(3) that, when the benefit is received, the company is a subsidiary[12] which is not a
dependent subsidiary and the majority of its shares in respect of which the
benefit is received are held otherwise than by or for the benefit of directors or
employees of the company, a company which is an associated company of the
company but is not its parent company[13] or directors or employees of a company
which is an associated company of the company[14].

A charge by virtue of the above provisions is a charge under Schedule E[15], for the
year of assessment in which the benefit is received, on an amount equal to the value[16] of
the benefit[17].

The above provisions[18] apply only if the person receiving the benefit has been a
director or employee of:

(a) the company[19]; or

(b) if it is different, the company or employee of which he acquired the shares or
interest; or

(c) an associated company of a company within heads (a) or (b) above,
at some time during the period of seven years ending with the date on which the
benefit is received[20].

A benefit is not chargeable by virtue of the above provisions[21] if it is chargeable to income tax apart from those provisions[22].

   1 For the meaning of 'shares' see para 1518 note 2 ante.
   2 For the meaning of references to an interest in any shares see para 1518 note 3 ante.
   3 Finance Act 1988 s 80(1).
   4 For the meaning of 'dependent subsidiary' see para 1520 ante.
   5 Finance Act 1988 s 80(1A) (substituted by the Finance (No 2) Act 1992 s 37).
   6 Ie within the Finance Act 1988 s 80(1A) (as substituted): see supra.
   7 Ibid s 80(2) (substituted by the Finance (No 2) Act 1992 s 37).
   8 For the meaning of 'director' see para 1518 note 4 ante.
   9 For the meaning of 'employee' see para 1519 note 11 ante.
  10 For the meaning of 'associated company' see para 1519 note 12 ante.
  11 For the meaning of 'employee-controlled' see para 1519 note 15 ante.
  12 For the meaning of 'subsidiary' see para 1519 note 16 ante.
  13 Finance Act 1988 s 80(3) (amended by the Finance (No 2) Act 1992 s 37).
  14 Ie under the Income and Corporation Taxes Act 1988 s 19(1), Schedule E (as amended): see INCOME
      TAXATION vol 23 (Reissue) para 654 et seq.
  15 For these purposes, a company is another company's parent company if the second company is a
      subsidiary of the first: Finance Act 1988 s 80(3A) (added by the Finance (No 2) Act 1992 s 37).
  16 For the meaning of 'value' see para 1519 note 5 ante.
  17 Finance Act 1988 s 80(4).
  18 Ie ibid s 80(1): see supra.
  19 Ie the company referred to in ibid s 80(1): see supra.
  20 Ibid s 80(5).
  21 Ie ibid s 80 (as amended).
  22 Ibid s 80(6).

1523. Changes in interest. Where a person's interest in shares[1] is increased or reduced, he is to be treated[2] as acquiring or disposing of a separate interest proportionate to the increase or reduction[3].

   1 For the meaning of 'shares' see para 1518 note 2 ante; and for the meaning of references to an interest in
      any shares see para 1518 note 3 ante.
   2 Ie for the purposes of the Finance Act 1988 Pt III Ch II (ss 77-89) (as amended): see para 1518 et seq ante
      and para 1524 et seq post.
   3 Ibid s 81.

1524. Company reorganisations etc. Where:
   (1) a person has acquired shares[1] or an interest in shares[2] ('the originally-acquired shares'); and
   (2) by virtue of his holding of those shares or the interest in them he acquires, whether or not for consideration, additional shares or an interest in additional shares ('the additional shares'),
the following provisions apply[3]:
   (a) the additional shares or the interest in them is treated[4] as having been acquired in accordance with the statutory provisions[5] and as having been acquired at the same time as the originally-acquired shares or the interest in them;
   (b) the additional shares and the originally-acquired shares are treated[6] as one holding of shares and the value[7] of the shares comprised in that holding at any time is to be determined accordingly, the value of the originally-acquired shares at the time of acquisition being attributed proportionately to all the shares in the holding; and
   (c) any consideration given for the acquisition of the additional shares or the interest in them is to be taken[8] to be an increase[9] in the consideration for the original acquisition[10].

If, on a person ceasing to have a beneficial interest in any shares, he acquires other shares or an interest in other shares and the circumstances are such that the shares in which he ceases to have a beneficial interest constitute[11] 'original shares' and the other shares constitute a 'new holding':

    (i)   the statutory provisions[12] which equate the original shares and the new holding apply[13]; and

    (ii) if any such consideration is given for the new holding[14], it is treated[15] as an increase[16] in the consideration for the shares; and

  (iii) if any such consideration is received for the disposal of the original shares[17], the consideration must be apportioned among the shares comprised in the new holding and the amount which would otherwise at any subsequent time be the value of any of those shares is to be taken to be increased by the amount of the consideration apportioned to them[18].

1 For the meaning of 'shares' see para 1518 note 2 ante.
2 For the meaning of references to an interest in any shares see para 1518 note 3 ante.
3 Finance Act 1988 s 82(1).
4 Ie for the purposes of ibid Pt III Ch II (ss 77–89) (as amended): see para 1518 et seq ante and paras 1525–1527 post.
5 Ie as mentioned in ibid s 77 (as amended): see para 1518 ante.
6 Ie for the purposes of ibid s 79: see para 1521 ante.
7 For the meaning of 'value' see para 1519 note 5 ante.
8 See note 6 supra.
9 Ie an increase falling within the Finance Act 1988 s 79(5): see para 1521 ante.
10 Ibid s 82(2).
11 Ie for the purposes of the Taxation of Chargeable Gains Act 1992 ss 127-130: see CAPITAL GAINS TAXATION vol 5(1) (Reissue) para 252.
12 Ie ibid s 127.
13 See note 4 supra.
14 Ie as is mentioned in the Taxation of Chargeable Gains Act 1992 s 128(1),(2).
15 See note 4 supra.
16 See note 7 supra.
17 Ie as is mentioned in the Taxation of Chargeable Gains Act 1992 s 128(3).
18 Finance Act 1988 s 82(3) (amended by the Taxation of Chargeable Gains Act 1992 s 290(1), Sch 10 para 16(1),(4)).

1525. Connected persons etc. Where a person acquires shares[1] or an interest in shares[2] in a company in pursuance of a right conferred on him or opportunity offered to him as a person connected[3] with a director[4] or employee[5] of that or any other company, the shares or interest are or is deemed to be acquired by the director or employee[6].

Where a person who acquires shares or an interest in shares disposes of the shares or interest otherwise than by a bargain at arm's length with a person who is not connected with him, he is deemed to continue to have a beneficial interest in the shares until there is a disposal of the shares or interest by such a bargain[7]; but this provision does not apply where shares, or an interest in shares, in a company are disposed of to the company in accordance with the terms on which the acquisition was made[8].

Where a person who has so made an acquisition[9] receives a benefit in the specified circumstances[10], the benefit is to be treated[11] as received by the person deemed[12] to have made the acquisition; and, where at a time when a person is deemed[13] to continue to have a beneficial interest in shares another person receives a benefit in such circumstances, the benefit is treated as received by him[14].

1 For the meaning of 'shares' see para 1518 note 2 ante.
2 For the meaning of references to an interest in any shares see para 1518 note 3 ante.
3 For these purposes, the Income and Corporation Taxes Act 1988 s 839 ('connected persons': see INCOME TAXATION vol 23 (Reissue) para 1250) applies: Finance Act 1988 s 87(3).
4 For the meaning of 'director' see para 1518 note 4 ante.
5 For the meaning of 'employee' see para 1519 note 11 ante.
6 Finance Act 1988 s 83(1).
7 Ibid s 83(2).
8 Ibid s 83(3).
9 Ie as mentioned in ibid s 83(1): see supra.
10 Ie the circumstances mentioned in ibid s 80 (as amended): see para 1522 ante.
11 Ie for the purposes of ibid s 80 (as amended).
12 Ie by ibid s 83(1).
13 Ie by ibid s 83(2): see supra.
14 Ibid s 83(4).

1526. Duty to give information. Where in any year of assessment a person acquires shares[1], or an interest in shares[2], in a company in the specified circumstances[3], that company and, if it is different, the company as a director[4] or employee[5] of which he acquires the shares or interest must give written particulars of the acquisition to the inspector of taxes within 30 days of the end of the year[6].

Where there occurs in relation to shares in a company an event which is a chargeable event[7] or a person receives a special benefit[8] in respect of shares, or an interest in shares, in a company, the company, and, if it is different, the company as a director or employee of which the person who acquired the shares or an interest in the shares made the acquisition, must within 60 days give to the inspector written particulars of the event or benefit and of the shares concerned[9].

1 For the meaning of 'shares' see para 1518 note 2 ante.
2 For the meaning of references to an interest in any shares see para 1518 note 3 ante.
3 Ie the circumstances described in the Finance Act 1988 s 77(1) (as amended): see para 1518 ante.
4 For the meaning of 'director' see para 1518 note 4 ante.
5 For the meaning of 'employee' see para 1519 note 11 ante.
6 Finance Act 1988 s 85(1). As to the penalty for non-compliance see INCOME TAXATION vol 23 (Reissue) para 1638.
7 Ie for the purposes of ibid s 78: see para 1519 ante.
8 Ie within the meaning given for the purposes of ibid s 80(1): see para 1522 ante.
9 Ibid s 85(2). As to the penalty for non-compliance see INCOME TAXATION vol 23 (Reissue) para 1638.

1527. Capital gains tax. Where an amount is chargeable to tax[1] on a person who acquires shares[2] or an interest in shares[3], then, on the first disposal of the shares, whether by him or another, after his acquisition, the statutory provisions relating to expenditure allowable in the computation of chargeable gains[4] apply as if a sum equal to the amount chargeable had formed part of the consideration given by the person making the disposal for his acquisition of the shares[5].

1 Ie under the Finance Act 1988 Pt III Ch II (ss 77–89) (as amended): see para 1518 et seq ante.
2 For the meaning of 'shares' see para 1518 note 2 ante.
3 For the meaning of references to an interest in any shares see para 1518 note 3 ante.
4 Ie the Taxation of Chargeable Gains Act 1992 s 38(1)(a): see CAPITAL GAINS TAXATION vol 5(1) (Reissue) para 32.
5 Finance Act 1988 s 84 (amended by the Taxation of Chargeable Gains Act 1992 s 290(1), Sch 10 para 16(1),(5)). The Finance Act 1988 s 84 (as so amended) applies with the appropriate modifications in a case to which s 83 (see para 1525 ante) applies: s 84 (as so amended). As to increase in expenditure by reference to tax charged in relation to shares etc see the Taxation of Chargeable Gains Act 1992 s 120 and CAPITAL GAINS TAXATION vol 5(1) (Reissue) para 201.

(iii) Share Option and Profit Sharing Schemes

A. IN GENERAL

1528. Approved share option schemes. The following provisions apply where, in accordance with the provisions of an approved[1] share option scheme, an individual obtains a right to acquire shares[2] in a body corporate by reason of his office or employment as a director or employee of that or any other body corporate and he obtains that right:

(1) in the case of a savings-related share option scheme[3], on or after 15 November 1980; or

(2) in the case of any other share option scheme, on or after 6 April 1984[4].

Tax is not chargeable[5] under any provision of the Tax Acts[6] in respect of the receipt of the right[7].

If he exercises the right in accordance with the provisions of the scheme at a time when it is approved:

(a) tax is not chargeable under any provision of the Tax Acts in respect of the exercise nor under the Finance Act 1988[8] in respect of the shares;

(b) the statutory provisions whereby assets are deemed to be acquired at market value[9] do not apply in calculating the consideration for the acquisition of the shares by him or for any corresponding disposal of them to him[10].

The above provisions[11] do not apply, however, in respect of a right obtained by a person under a scheme which is a savings-related share option scheme, which is exercised within three years of its being obtained by virtue of a provision included[12] in a scheme[13]; nor do the above provisions apply in relation to the exercise by a person of a right in accordance with the provisions of a scheme which is not a savings-related share option scheme if:

(i) the period beginning with his obtaining the right and ending with his exercising it is less than three, or greater than ten, years; or

(ii) the right is exercised within three years of the date on which he last exercised (in circumstances in which those provisions applied) any right obtained under the scheme or under any other approved share option scheme which is not a savings-related share option scheme (any such right exercised on the same day being disregarded)[14].

Where, in the case of a right obtained by a person under a scheme which is not a savings-related share option scheme, the aggregate of the amount or value of any consideration given by him for obtaining the right and the price at which he may acquire the shares by exercising the right is less than the market value, at the time he obtains the right, of the same quantity of issued shares of the same class, he is chargeable to tax under Schedule E[15] for the year of assessment in which he obtains the right on the amount of the difference; and the amount so chargeable is treated as earned income, whether or not it would otherwise fall to be so treated[16].

1 For these purposes, except where the context otherwise requires, 'approved', in relation to a scheme, means approved under the Income and Corporation Taxes Act 1988 ss 185-187, Sch 9 (as amended) (see para 1531 et seq post): s 187(2). For the meaning of 'scheme' see para 1531 note 3 post.

2 For these purposes, except where the context otherwise requires, 'shares' includes stock: ibid s 187(1).

3 For these purposes, 'savings-related share option scheme' has the meaning given by ibid Sch 9 (as amended) (see para 1531 note 3 post): s 185(10).

4 Ibid s 185(1). Where the provisions of a scheme which is not a savings-related share option scheme are approved in pursuance of an application made under the Finance Act 1984 s 38(1), Sch 10 para 1

(repealed) before 1 January 1985 (and the approval has not been withdrawn), the Income and Corporation Taxes Act 1988 s 185 (as amended) applies in relation to any right obtained before 1 July 1985 as if the scheme containing those provisions had been approved under the Finance Act 1984 Sch 10 (repealed) during the period beginning with the date on which that right was obtained and ending with the date on which those provisions were actually so approved: Income and Corporation Taxes Act 1988 s 185(9).

If, during the period beginning with 17 July 1995 and ending with 28 April 1996, any rights have been obtained by a person under an approved share option scheme in circumstances falling within the Finance Act 1996 s 115(2), the rights are to be treated for the purposes of the Income and Corporation Taxes Act 1988 ss 185, 187 (as amended) and Sch 9 (as amended) as being rights obtained otherwise than in accordance with the provisions of an approved share option scheme: Finance Act 1996 s 115(1). The circumstances so mentioned are circumstances such that, on the assumptions in s 115(3), there would, by virtue of the Income and Corporation Taxes Act 1988 Sch 9 para 28 (as amended) (see para 1552 post) or Sch 9 para 29 (as amended) (see para 1553 post), have been, with respect to the operation of the scheme, a contravention of any of the relevant requirements or of the scheme itself: Finance Act 1996 s 115(2). The assumptions so mentioned are (1) that the amendments made by s 114(2) had effect at all times on and after 17 July 1995; (2) that the amendments made by s 114(3)-(7) had effect in relation to rights obtained at any time on or after that date; and (3) that the provisions of Sch 16 paras 1(1) and 2-5 had effect at all times on and after 17 July 1995, but with the substitution for references to the day on which the Finance Act 1996 was passed of references to that date: s 115(3). For these purposes, rights obtained by a person on or after 17 July 1995 are to be treated as having been obtained by him before that date if (a) the scheme in question is one approved before that date; (b) an offer of the rights or an invitation to apply for them was made in writing to that person before that date; and (c) he obtained the rights within the period of 30 days beginning with the day on which the offer or invitation was made: s 115(4). 'Approved share option scheme' means an approved share option scheme within the meaning of the Income and Corporation Taxes Act 1988 s 185 (as amended) (see note 3 supra), other than a savings-related share option scheme; 'relevant requirements' has the meaning given in Sch 9 para 1(1) (see para 1531 note 3 post); and 'savings-related share option scheme' has the meaning given by Sch 9 (as amended) (see para 1531 note 3 post): Finance Act 1996 s 115(5).

An option which, when granted to an employee of a company, would have been understood by both the company and the employee as conferring rights to specified shares in the company, subject to the employee meeting key tasks set by the company and, if necessary, varied from time to time in a way which provided a fair measure of his performance, was a valid option under which the employee obtained a right to acquire shares within the Income and Corporation Taxes Act 1988 s 185(1): *IRC v Burton Group plc* [1990] STC 242.

5 Ie subject to the Income and Corporation Taxes Act 1988 s 185(6) (as substituted): see infra.
6 For these purposes, except so far as the context otherwise requires, 'the Tax Acts' means the Income and Corporation Taxes Act 1988 and all other provisions of the Income Tax Acts and the Corporation Tax Acts: Income and Corporation Taxes Act 1988 s 831(2). 'The Corporation Tax Acts' means the enactments relating to the taxation of the income and chargeable gains of companies and of company distributions (including provisions relating also to income tax); and 'the Income Tax Acts' means the enactments relating to income tax, including any provisions of the Corporation Tax Acts which relate to income tax: Income and Corporation Taxes Act 1988 s 831(1)(a),(b).
7 Ibid s 185(2) (amended by the Finance Act 1991 s 39(2),(3),(8); the Finance Act 1996 s 114(4),(5)). The Finance Act 1996 s 114(4),(5) has effect in relation to rights obtained on or after 29 April 1996: s 114(10).
8 Ie the Finance Act 1988 s 78 or s 79: see paras 1519, 1521 ante.
9 Ie the Taxation of Chargeable Gains Act 1992 s 17(1): see CAPITAL GAINS TAXATION vol 5(1) (Reissue) para 40. For these purposes, except where the context otherwise requires, 'market value' has the same meaning as in Pt VIII (ss 272-291 (as amended): see CAPITAL GAINS TAXATION vol 5(1) (Reissue) para 43): Income and Corporation Taxes Act 1988 s 187(1) (amended by the Taxation of Chargeable Gains Act 1992 s 290(1), Sch 10 para 14(1),(13)).
10 Income and Corporation Taxes Act 1988 s 185(3) (amended by the Taxation of Chargeable Gains Act 1992 Sch 10 para 14(1),(12)). The Income and Corporation Taxes Act 1992 s 185(3) (as so amended) is subject to s 185(4) (as amended) (see infra) and, except where Sch 9 para 27(3) (see para 1551 post) applies, s 185(5) (see infra): s 185(3) (as so amended).
11 Ie ibid s 185(3) (as amended): see supra.
12 Ie pursuant to ibid Sch 9 para 21: see para 1546 post.
13 Ibid s 185(4) (amended by the Finance Act 1991 s 39(2),(4),(8)).
14 Income and Corporation Taxes Act 1988 s 185(5).
15 Ie ibid s 19(1), Schedule E (as amended): see INCOME TAXATION vol 23 (Reissue) para 654 et seq.

16 Ibid s 185(6) (substituted by the Finance Act 1996 s 114(4),(6)). For the purposes of the Taxation of Chargeable Gains Act 1992 s 38(1)(a) (see CAPITAL GAINS TAXATION vol 5(1) (Reissue) para 32), the consideration given for shares acquired in the exercise of the right is not to be taken to have included that part of any amount on which income tax is payable in accordance with the Income and Corporation Taxes Act 1988 s 185(6) (as so substituted) which is attributable to the shares disposed of: s 185(7) (amended by the Taxation of Chargeable Gains Act 1992 Sch 10 para 14(1),(12); the Finance Act 1996 s 114(4),(7)).

Where a person is chargeable to tax under the Income and Corporation Taxes Act 1988 s 185(6) (as so substituted) on any amount (the 'amount of the discount') and subsequently, in circumstances in which s 185(3) (as amended) (see supra) does not apply (1) he is chargeable to tax under s 135 (see INCOME TAXATION vol 23 (Reissue) para 711), the amount of the gain on which he is chargeable to tax thereunder is reduced by that part of the amount of the discount which is attributable to the shares in question; or (2) he is treated by virtue of s 162 (as amended) (see INCOME TAXATION vol 23 (Reissue) para 746 et seq) as having had the benefit of a notional interest-free loan, the amount of the notional loan initially outstanding is reduced by that part of the amount of the discount which is attributable to the shares in question: s 185(8) (amended by the Finance Act 1996 s 114(4),(7)).

The Finance Act 1996 s 114(6),(7) has effect in relation to rights obtained on or after 29 April 1996: s 114(10).

1529. Approved profit sharing schemes. The following provisions apply where, after 5 April 1979, the trustees[1] of an approved[2] profit sharing scheme appropriate shares[3] which have previously been acquired by the trustees and as to which the specified conditions[4] are fulfilled to an individual who participates in the scheme[5] ('the participant')[6].

Notwithstanding that, by virtue of such an appropriation of shares as is mentioned above, the beneficial interest in the shares passes to the participant to whom they are appropriated:

(1) the value of the shares at the time of the appropriation is treated as not being income of his chargeable to tax under Schedule E[7]; and

(2) he is not chargeable[8] to income tax under Schedule E in respect of the shares[9] or in any case[9] where the shares are appropriated to him at an undervalue[10].

If, in respect of or by reference to any of a participant's shares[11], the trustees become or the participant becomes entitled, before the release date[12], to receive any money or money's worth ('a capital receipt'), the participant is chargeable to income tax under Schedule E for the year of assessment in which the entitlement arises on the appropriate percentage[13], determined as at the time the trustees become or the participant becomes so entitled, of so much of the amount or value of the receipt as exceeds the appropriate allowance[14] for that year[15].

If the trustees dispose of any of the participant's shares at any time before the release date or, if it is earlier, the date of the participant's death, the participant is chargeable[16] to income tax under Schedule E for the year of assessment in which the disposal takes place on the appropriate percentage of the locked-in value[17] of the shares at the time of the disposal[18].

If, at any time prior to the disposal of any of a participant's shares, a payment was made to the trustees to enable them to exercise rights arising under a rights issue, the above provisions[19] have effect as if the proceeds of the disposal were reduced by an amount equal to that proportion of that payment or, if there was more than one, the aggregate of those payments which, immediately before the disposal, the market value of the shares disposed of bore to the market value of all the participant's shares held by the trustees at that time[20].

If at any time the participant's beneficial interest in any of his shares is disposed of, the shares in question are treated for the purposes of the relevant provisions[21] as having been disposed of at that time by the trustees for the like consideration as was obtained for the disposal of the beneficial interest[22].

1 For these purposes, 'the trustees', in relation to an approved profit sharing scheme or the shares of a participant in such a scheme, means the body of persons for the establishment of which the scheme must provide as mentioned in the Income and Corporation Taxes Act 1988 ss 185-187 (as amended), Sch 9 para 30 (see para 1554 post): s 187(2). 'Participant', in relation to a profit sharing scheme, means an individual to whom the trustees of the scheme have appropriated shares: s 187(2).

2 For the meaning of 'approved' see para 1528 note 1 ante.

3 For the meaning of 'shares' see para 1528 note 2 ante.

4 Ie the conditions specified in the Income and Corporation Taxes Act 1988 Sch 9 Pt II (paras 7-15) (as amended): see paras 1537-1540 post.

5 For the meaning of 'scheme' see para 1531 note 3 post.

6 Income and Corporation Taxes Act 1988 s 186(1). Section 186(13), Sch 10 (as amended) (see para 1562 et seq post) has effect with respect to profit sharing schemes: s 186(13). Where the trustees of an approved scheme acquire any shares as to which the requirements of Sch 9 Pt II (paras 7-15) (as amended) are fulfilled and, within the period of 18 months beginning with the date of their acquisition, those shares are appropriated in accordance with the scheme, s 686 (as amended) (see INCOME TAXATION vol 23 (Reissue) para 1529) does not apply to income consisting of dividends on those shares received by the trustees; and, for the purpose of determining whether any shares are appropriated within that period, shares which were acquired at an earlier time are to be taken to be appropriated before shares of the same class which were acquired at a later time: s 186(11).

7 Ie ibid s 19(1), Schedule E (as amended): see INCOME TAXATION vol 23 (Reissue) para 654 et seq.

8 Ie by virtue of the Finance Act 1988 s 78 or s 79: see paras 1519, 1521 ante.

9 Ie by virtue of the Income and Corporation Taxes Act 1988 s 162 (as amended): see INCOME TAXATION vol 23 (Reissue) para 746 et seq.

10 Ibid s 186(2) (amended by the Finance Act 1988 s 89). For these purposes, 'undervalue' has the same meaning as in the Income and Corporation Taxes Act 1988 s 162 (as amended) (see INCOME TAXATION vol 23 (Reissue) para 746 note 11): s 186(2) (as so amended).

11 For these purposes, 'participant's shares', in relation to a participant in a profit sharing scheme, means, subject to ibid Sch 10 para 5(4) (see para 1566 post), shares which have been appropriated to the participant by the trustees: s 187(2).

12 For these purposes, 'release date', in relation to any of the shares of a participant in a profit sharing scheme, means the third anniversary of the date on which they were appropriated to him: ibid s 187(2) (amended by the Finance Act 1996 s 116(1)). The amendment made by the Finance Act 1996 s 116(1) has effect in relation to shares of a participant in a profit sharing scheme if the third anniversary of the appropriation of the shares to the participant occurs on or after 29 April 1996: s 116(2). If the third anniversary of the appropriation of any shares to a participant in a profit sharing scheme has occurred, but the fifth anniversary of their appropriation to him has not occurred, before 29 April 1996, then, in the application of the Income and Corporation Taxes Act 1988 ss 186, 187 (as amended) and Schs 9, 10 (as amended) in relation to those shares, the release date is 29 April 1996: Finance Act 1996 s 116(3).

13 For these purposes, except where the context otherwise requires, 'appropriate percentage' is to be construed in accordance with the Income and Corporation Taxes Act 1988 Sch 10 para 3 (as substituted) (see para 1564 post): s 187(2).

14 Ie as determined under ibid s 186(12) (as amended). 'The appropriate allowance', in relation to any year of assessment, means a sum which, subject to a maximum of £60, is the product of multiplying £20 by one plus the number of years which fall within the period of three years immediately preceding the year in question and in which shares were appropriated to the participant under the scheme; and, if in any year (and before the release date) the trustees become or the participant becomes entitled, in respect of or by reference to any of his shares, to more than one capital receipt, the receipts must be set against the appropriate allowance for that year in the order in which they are received: s 186(12) (amended by the Finance Act 1996 s 118(1)). The Finance Act 1996 s 118(1) has effect for the year 1997-98 and subsequent years of assessment: s 118(2).

15 Income and Corporation Taxes Act 1988 s 186(3), 187(2). Section 186(3) is subject to the provisions of s 186 (as amended) and Sch 10 para 4 (see para 1565 post): s 186(3).

16 Ie subject to ibid s 186(6),(7): see infra.

17 Subject to ibid Sch 10 paras 5, 6(6) (see paras 1566, 1567 respectively post), the locked-in value of a participant's shares at any time is (1) if prior to that time he has become chargeable to income tax by virtue of s 186(3) (see supra) on a percentage of the amount or value of any capital receipt which is referable to those shares, the amount by which their initial market value exceeds the amount or value of that capital receipt or, if there has been more than one such receipt, the aggregate of them; and (2) in any

other case, their initial market value: ss 186(5), 187(2). 'Initial market value', in relation to shares in a profit sharing scheme, has the meaning given by Sch 9 para 30(4) (see para 1554 note 11 post): s 187(2).

18 Ibid s 186(4). Subject to s 186(7) (see infra), if, on a disposal of shares falling within s 186(4), the proceeds of the disposal are less than the locked-in value of the shares at the time of the disposal, s 186(4) has effect as if that locked-in value were reduced to an amount equal to the proceeds of the disposal: s 186(6).

If (1) a disposal of shares falling within s 186(4) is a transfer to which Sch 9 para 2(2)(c) (see para 1532 post) applies; or (2) the Commissioners of Inland Revenue are of opinion that any other disposal falling with Sch 9 para 2(2)(c) is not at arm's length and accordingly direct that s 186(10) shall apply; or (3) a disposal of shares falling within Sch 9 para 2(2)(c) is one which is treated as taking place by virtue of s 186(9) (see infra) and takes place within the period of retention, then, for the purposes of the relevant provisions, the proceeds of the disposal are to be taken to be equal to the market value of the shares at the time of the disposal: s 186(10). 'Period of retention' has the meaning given by Sch 10 para 2 (see para 1532 post): s 187(2). For the meaning of 'the relevant provisions' see note 21 infra.

Where the disposal referred to in s 186(4) is made from a holding of shares which were appropriated to the participant at different times, then, in determining for the purposes of the relevant provisions the initial market value and the locked-in value of each of those shares, the disposal is treated as being of shares which were appropriated earlier before those which were appropriated later: s 187(8) (amended by the Finance Act 1996 ss 117(2), 205, Sch 41 Pt V). The Finance Act 1996 s 117(2) has effect in relation to the occurrence, on or after 29 April 1996, of events by reason of whose occurrence any provision of the Income and Corporation Taxes Act 1988 s 186 (as amended), s 187 (as amended) or Sch 9 (as amended) or Sch 10 (as amended) charges an individual to income tax under s 19(1), Schedule E (as amended): Finance Act 1996 s 117(3).

Any of the relevant provisions with respect to (i) the order in which any of a participant's shares are to be treated as disposed of for the purposes of those provisions; or (ii) the shares in relation to which an event is to be treated as occurring for any such purpose, has effect in relation to a profit sharing scheme notwithstanding any direction given to the trustees with respect to shares of a particular description or to shares appropriated to the participant at a particular time: Income and Corporation Taxes Act 1988 s 187(9).

19 Ie ibid s 186(4),(6): see supra.

20 Ibid s 186(7). For these purposes (1) no account is to be taken of any payment to the trustees if or to the extent that it consists of the proceeds of a disposal of rights arising under a rights issue; and (2) in relation to a particular disposal the amount of the payment or, as the case may be, of the aggregate of the payments referred to in s 186(7) is to be taken to be reduced by an amount equal to the total of the reduction, if any, previously made under s 186(7) in relation to earlier disposals; and any reference in s 186(7) or s 186(8)(a) (see head (1) supra) to the rights arising under a rights issue is a reference to rights conferred in respect of a participant's shares, being rights to be allotted, on payment, other shares or securities or rights of any description in the same company: s 186(8).

21 For these purposes, 'the relevant provisions' means ibid s 185 (as amended) (see para 1528 ante), s 186 (as amended) (see supra), Sch 9 (as amended) (see para 1531 et seq post) and Sch 10 (as amended) (see para 1562 et seq post): s 187(1).

22 Ibid s 186(9). For these purposes, there is no disposal of the participant's beneficial interest if and at the time when that interest becomes vested in any person on the insolvency of the participant or otherwise by operation of law: s 186(9)(a).

1530. Capital gains tax. Notwithstanding anything in a profit sharing scheme duly approved[1] or the statutory provisions relating to the participant's[2] being bound in contract with the grantor[3] or in the trust instrument[4] relating to that scheme, for the purposes of capital gains tax a person who is a participant in relation to that scheme is to be treated as absolutely entitled to his shares as against the trustees of the scheme[5].

The following provisions apply in any case where a right to acquire shares in a body corporate ('the old right') which was obtained by an individual by reason of his office or employment as a director or employee of that or any other body corporate is released in whole or in part for a consideration which consists of or includes the grant to that individual of another right ('the new right') to acquire shares in that or any other body corporate[6].

As respects the person to whom the new right is granted:

(1) without prejudice to the above provisions, the new right is not to be regarded for the purposes of capital gains tax as consideration for the release of the old right;

(2) the amount or value of the consideration given by him or on his behalf for the acquisition of the new right is to be taken[7] to be the amount or value of the consideration given by him or on his behalf for the old right; and

(3) any consideration paid for the acquisition of the new right is to be taken to be expenditure falling within the statutory provisions[8] relating to acquisition and disposal costs[9].

As respects the grantor of the new right, in determining[10] the amount or value of the consideration received for the new right, the release of the old right is to be disregarded[11].

The above provisions[12] have effect in relation to transactions effected on or after 28 November 1995[13].

1 Ie under the Income and Corporation Taxes Act 1988 ss 185–187, Sch 9 (as amended): see para 1531 et seq post.

2 For these purposes, 'participant' has the meaning given by ibid s 187 (as amended) (see para 1529 note 1 ante): Taxation of Chargeable Gains Act 1992 s 238(3).

3 Ie the Income and Corporation Taxes Act 1988 Sch 9 para 2(2): see para 1532 post.

4 For these purposes, 'the trust instrument' has the meaning given by ibid s 187 (as amended) (see para 1555 note 1 post): Taxation of Chargeable Gains Act 1992 s 238(3).

5 Ibid s 238(1). For the purposes of capital gains tax (1) no deduction may be made from the consideration for the disposal of any shares by reason only that an amount determined under the Income and Corporation Taxes Act 1988 s 186 (as amended) or s 187 (as amended) or Sch 9 (as amended) or Sch 10 (as amended) is chargeable to income tax under s 186(3) or (4); (2) any charge to income tax by virtue of s 186(3) is to be disregarded in determining whether a distribution is a capital distribution within the meaning of the Taxation of Chargeable Gains Act 1992 s 122(5)(b) (see CAPITAL GAINS TAXATION vol 5(1) (Reissue) para 243); (3) nothing in any provision of the Income and Corporation Taxes Act 1988 s 186 (as amended) or s 187 (as amended) or Sch 9 (as amended) or Sch 10 (as amended) with respect to (a) the order in which any of a participant's shares are to be treated as disposed of for the purposes of those provisions as they have effect in relation to profit sharing schemes; or (b) the shares in relation to which an event is to be treated as occurring for any such purpose, affects the rules applicable to the computation of a gain accruing on a part disposal of a holding of shares or other securities which were acquired at different times; and (4) a gain accruing on an appropriation of shares to which s 186(11) applies is not a chargeable gain: Taxation of Chargeable Gains Act 1992 s 238(2).

6 Ibid s 237A(1) (added by the Finance Act 1996 s 112(1)). The Taxation of Chargeable Gains Act 1992 s 238(4) (which provides that the release of an option under an approved share option scheme in exchange for another option, in connection with a company take-over, is not to involve a disposal, and which is superseded by s 237A(1) (as so added)) ceases to have effect: Finance Act 1996 ss 112(2), 205, Sch 41 Pt V.

7 Ie for the purposes of the Taxation of Chargeable Gains Act 1992 s 38(2): see CAPITAL GAINS TAXATION vol 5(1) (Reissue) para 32.

8 Ie ibid s 38(1)(b): see CAPITAL GAINS TAXATION vol 5(1) (Reissue) para 32.

9 Ibid s 237A(2) (added by the Finance Act 1996 s 112(1)).

10 Ie for the purposes of the Taxation of Chargeable Gains Act 1992.

11 Ibid s 237A(3) (added by the Finance Act 1996 s 112(1)).

12 Ie ibid s 237A (as added): see supra.

13 Finance Act 1996 s 112(3).

B. SUBMISSION OF SCHEME

1531. Approval of scheme. On the application of a body corporate ('the grantor') which has established a share option scheme[1] or a profit sharing scheme[2], the Commissioners of Inland Revenue must approve the scheme[3] if they are satisfied that it fulfils such of the statutory requirements[4] as apply in relation to the scheme in question[5]. Such an application must be made in writing and contain such particulars and be supported by such evidence as the commissioners may require[6].

Where the grantor has control[7] of another company or companies, the scheme may be expressed to extend to all or any of the companies of which it has control[8].

1 As to share option schemes see para 1528 ante.
2 As to profit sharing schemes see para 1529 ante.
3 For these purposes, 'scheme' means a savings-related share option scheme, a share option scheme which is not a savings-related share option scheme or a profit sharing scheme, as the context may require: Income and Corporation Taxes Act 1988 s 187(2). 'Savings-related share option scheme' means a scheme in relation to which the relevant requirements include the requirements of ss 185-187, Sch 9 Pt III (paras 16-26 (as amended): see para 1541 et seq post): Sch 9 para 1(1). 'The relevant requirements' means, in relation to any scheme, the requirements of Sch 9 (as amended) by reference to which the scheme is approved: Sch 9 para 1(1).
4 Ie such requirements of ibid s 187(2), Sch 9 Pt I (paras 1-6) (see infra and para 1532 et seq post), Sch 9 Pt II (paras 7-15 (as amended): see para 1537 et seq post) as apply in relation to the scheme in question and the requirements of Sch 9 Pt III (paras 16-26 (as amended): see para 1541 et seq post), Sch 9 Pt IV (paras 27-29 (as amended): see paras 1551-1553 post) or Sch 9 Pt V (paras 30-36 (as amended): see para 1554 et seq post).
5 Ibid Sch 9 para 1(1). For these purposes, 'grantor', in relation to any scheme, means the company which has established the scheme: s 187(2).
   By extra-statutory concession, if certain conditions are fulfilled, a jointly owned company and companies under the control of a jointly owned company are admitted as participating companies in an approved employee share scheme: see Inland Revenue booklet IR1 (1993) B27. As to the linkage between an approved discretionary share option scheme and a 'phantom' share scheme see Inland Revenue Decision RD5 (May 1992).
6 Income and Corporation Taxes Act 1988 Sch 9 para 1(2).
7 For these purposes, 'control' has the same meaning as in ibid s 840 (see INCOME TAXATION vol 23 (Reissue) para 849): s 187(2).
8 Ibid Sch 9 para 1(3). In Sch 9 (as amended) a scheme which is expressed so to extend is referred to as a 'group scheme': s 187(2), Sch 9 para 1(3). In relation to a group scheme the expression 'participating company' means the grantor or any other company to which for the time being the scheme is expressed to extend: s 187(2), Sch 9 para 1(4). See *IRC v Reed International plc, Reed International plc v IRC* [1995] STC 889, CA (Parliament could not have intended that a scheme extending to any company or companies of which the grantor did not have control should be capable of being a group scheme; moreover, the expression 'participating company' could only sensibly refer to companies of which the grantor had control; accordingly the amended SAYE scheme did not satisfy the requirements of the Income and Corporation Taxes Act 1988 Sch 9 para 26(3)).

1532. Non-approval of scheme. The Commissioners of Inland Revenue must not approve a scheme[1] if it appears to them that it contains features which are neither essential nor reasonably incidental to the purpose of providing for employees and directors benefits in the nature of rights to acquire shares[2] or, in the case of a profit sharing scheme[3], in the nature of interests in shares[4].

A profit sharing scheme must not be approved[5] unless the commissioners are satisfied that, whether under the terms of the scheme or otherwise, every participant[6] in the scheme is bound in contract with the grantor[7]:

(1) to permit his shares to remain in the hands of the trustees throughout the period of retention[8]; and

(2) not to assign, charge or otherwise dispose of his beneficial interest in his shares during that period; and

(3) if he directs the trustees[9] to transfer the ownership of his shares to him at any time before the release date[10], to pay to the trustees before the transfer takes place a sum equal to income tax at the basic rate on the appropriate percentage[11] of the locked-in value[12] of the shares at the time of the direction; and

(4) not to direct the trustees to dispose of his shares at any time before the release date in any other way except by sale for the best consideration in money that can reasonably be obtained at the time of the sale or, in the case of redeemable shares in a workers' co-operative[13], by redemption[14].

The commissioners must be satisfied in the case of a savings-related share option scheme[15] or a profit sharing scheme:

(a) that there are no features of the scheme, other than any which are included to satisfy the statutory requirements[16], which have or would have the effect of discouraging any description of employees or former employees who fulfil the specified conditions[17] from actually participating in the scheme; and

(b) where the grantor is a member of a group of companies[18], that the scheme does not and would not have the effect of conferring benefits wholly or mainly on directors of companies in the group or on those employees of companies in the group who are in receipt of the higher or highest levels of remuneration[19].

1   Ie under the Income and Corporation Taxes Act 1988 ss 185-187, Sch 9 (as amended): see para 1531 ante; infra; and para 1533 et seq post. For the meaning of 'scheme' see para 1531 note 3 ante.

2   For the meaning of 'shares' see para 1528 note 2 ante.

3   As to profit sharing schemes see para 1529 ante.

4   Income and Corporation Taxes Act 1988 Sch 9 para 2(1). See also *IRC v Burton Group plc* [1990] STC 242 (where there was held to be no substance in the Crown's claim that the power to impose new, or vary, existing key task conditions was a feature which was neither 'essential nor reasonably incidental to the purpose of providing for employees . . . benefits in the nature of rights to acquire shares' within the Income and Corporation Taxes Act 1988 Sch 9 para 2(1); the uncontradicted evidence was that the schemes were designed to ensure that they operated more effectively in the achievement of their purpose of providing share benefits for employees who contributed to the prosperity of the company).

5   Ie under the Income and Corporation Taxes Act 1988 Sch 9 para 1: see para 1531 ante.

6   For the meaning of 'participant' see para 1529 note 1 ante.

7   For the meaning of 'grantor' see para 1531 note 5 ante.

8   For the meaning of 'period of retention' see para 1529 note 18 ante.

9   For the meaning of 'the trustees' see para 1529 note 1 ante.

10   For the meaning of 'release date' see para 1529 note 12 ante.

11   For the meaning of 'appropriate percentage' see para 1529 note 13 ante.

12   For the meaning of 'locked-in value' see para 1529 note 17 ante.

13   For these purposes, 'workers' co-operative' means a registered industrial and provident society, within the meaning of the Income and Corporation Taxes Act 1988 s 486 (see INCOME TAXATION vol 23 (Reissue) para 164 note 4), which is a co-operative society and the rules of which include provisions which secure (1) that the only persons who may be members of it are those who are employed by, or by a subsidiary of, the society and those who are the trustees of its profit sharing scheme; and (2) that, subject to any provision about qualifications for membership which is from time to time made by the members of the society by reference to age, length of service or other factors of any description, all such persons may be members of the society; and, in this provision, 'co-operative society' has the same meaning as in the Industrial and Provident Societies Act 1965 s 1 (see INDUSTRIAL AND PROVIDENT SOCIETIES vol 24 (Reissue) para 8) or, as the case may be, the Industrial and Provident Societies (Northern Ireland) Act 1969: Income and Corporation Taxes Act 1988 s 187(10).

    Where, for the purpose of securing (and maintaining) approval of its profit sharing scheme in accordance with Sch 9 Pt I (paras 1-6) (as amended), the rules of a society which is a workers' co-operative or which is seeking to be registered under the Industrial and Provident Societies Act 1965 or the Industrial and Provident Societies Act (Northern Ireland) 1969 as a workers' co-operative contain (a) provision for membership of the society by the trustees of the scheme; (b) provision denying voting rights to those trustees; or (c) other provisions which appear to the registrar to be reasonably necessary for that purpose, those provisions must be disregarded in determining whether the society should be or continue to be registered under the Industrial and Provident Societies Act 1965 or the Industrial and Provident Societies Act (Northern Ireland) 1969 as a bona fide co-operative society: Finance Act 1986 s 24(4) (amended by the Income and Corporation Taxes Act 1988 Sch 29 para 32, Table); Finance Act 1986 s 24(5). 'The registrar' has the same meaning as in the Industrial and Provident Societies Act 1965 (see INDUSTRIAL AND PROVIDENT SOCIETIES vol 24 (Reissue) para 16 note 5) or the Industrial and Provident Societies Act (Northern Ireland) 1969 and 'co-operative society' has the same meaning as in the Industrial and Provident Societies Act 1965 (see INDUSTRIAL AND PROVIDENT SOCIETIES vol 24 para 8) or the Industrial and Provident Societies Act (Northern Ireland) 1969: Finance Act 1986 s 24(5).

14 Income and Corporation Taxes Act 1988 Sch 9 para 2(2).

15 For the meaning of 'savings-related share option scheme' see para 1531 note 3 ante.

16 Ie the requirements of the Income and Corporation Taxes Act 1988 Sch 9 (as amended).

17 Ie the conditions in ibid Sch 9 para 26(1) (as amended) (see para 1550 post) or, as the case may be, Sch 9 para 36(1) (as amended) (see para 1557 post).

18 For these purposes, 'a group of companies' means a company and any other companies of which it has control: ibid Sch 9 para 2(4). For the meaning of 'control' see para 1531 note 7 ante.

19 Ibid Sch 9 para 2(3).

1533. Withdrawal of approval. If, at any time after the Commisioners of Inland Revenue have approved a share option scheme[1], any of the relevant requirements[2] ceases to be satisfied or the grantor[3] fails to provide information requested by the commissioners[4], the commissioners may withdraw the approval with effect from that time or such later time as they may specify; but, where rights obtained under a savings-related share option scheme[5] before the withdrawal of approval from the scheme under these provisions are exercised after the withdrawal, certain statutory provisions[6] apply in respect of the exercise as if the scheme[7] were still approved[8].

If at any time after the commissioners have approved a profit sharing scheme[9]:

(1) a participant[10] is in breach of any of his statutory obligations[11]; or

(2) there is, with respect to the operation of the scheme, any contravention of any of the relevant requirements, the further requirements[12], the scheme itself or the terms of the trust[13]; or

(3) any shares[14] of a class of which shares have been appropriated to the participants receive different treatment in any respect from the other shares of that class, in particular, different treatment in respect of the dividend payable, repayment, the restrictions attaching to the shares or any offer of substituted or additional shares, securities or rights of any description in respect of the shares; or

(4) the commissioners cease to be satisfied that the scheme complies with certain of the statutory requirements[15]; or

(5) the trustees[16], the grantor or, in the case of a group scheme[17], a company which is or has been a participating company[18] fail or fails to furnish any information which they are or it is required to furnish to the commissioners[19],

the commissioners may withdraw the approval with effect from that time or from such later time as they may specify[20]. It is not, however, a ground for withdrawal of approval of a profit sharing scheme that shares which have been newly issued receive, in respect of dividends payable with respect to a period beginning before the date on which the shares were issued, treatment which is less favourable than that accorded to shares issued before that date[21].

1 As to share option schemes see para 1528 ante.

2 For the meaning of 'the relevant requirements' see para 1531 note 3 ante.

3 For the meaning of 'grantor' see para 1531 note 5 ante.

4 Ie under the Income and Corporation Taxes Act 1988 ss 185-187 (as amended), Sch 9 para 6: see para 1536 post.

5 For the meaning of 'savings-related share option scheme' see para 1531 note 3 ante.

6 Ie the Income and Corporation Taxes Act 1988 s 185(3) (as amended): see para 1528 ante.

7 For the meaning of 'scheme' see para 1531 note 3 ante.

8 Income and Corporation Taxes Act 1988 Sch 9 para 3(1).

9 As to profit sharing schemes see para 1529 ante.

10 For the meaning of 'participant' see para 1529 note 1 ante.
11 Ie his obligations under the Income and Corporation Taxes Act 1988 Sch 9 para 2(2)(a),(c),(d): see para
    1532 heads (1),(3),(4) ante.
12 Ie ibid s 186(13), Sch 10 (as amended): see para 1562 et seq post.
13 Ie the trust referred to in ibid Sch 9 para 30(1)(c): see para 1554 head (3) post.
14 For the meaning of 'shares' see para 1528 note 2 ante.
15 Ie the Income and Corporation Taxes Act 1988 Sch 9 para 2(3) (see para 1532 ante) or Sch 9 para 36 (as
    amended) (see para 1557 post).
16 For the meaning of 'the trustees' see para 1529 note 1 ante.
17 For the meaning of 'group scheme' see para 1531 note 8 ante.
18 For the meaning of 'participating company' see para 1531 note 8 ante.
19 See note 4 supra.
20 Income and Corporation Taxes Act 1988 Sch 9 para 3(2).
21 Ibid Sch 9 para 3(3).

1534. Alterations to scheme. If an alteration is made in the scheme[1] at any time
after the Commissioners of Inland Revenue have approved the scheme, the approval
does not have effect after the date of the alteration unless the commissioners have
approved the alteration[2].

1 For the meaning of 'scheme' see para 1531 note 3 ante.
2 Income and Corporation Taxes Act 1988 ss 185-187 (as amended), Sch 9 para 4.

1535. Aggrieved persons. If aggrieved:
  (1) in any case, by the failure of the Commissioners of Inland Revenue to approve
       the scheme[1] or to approve an alteration in the scheme or by the withdrawal of
       approval; or
  (2) in the case of a savings-related share option scheme[2], by the failure of the
       commissioners to decide that a condition subject to which the approval has been
       given is satisfied; or
  (3) in the case of a profit sharing scheme[3], by the failure of the commissioners to
       approve an alteration in the terms of the trust[4],
the grantor[5] may, by notice in writing given to the commissioners within 30 days from
the date on which it is notified of the commissioners' decision, require the matter to be
determined by the Special Commissioners[6]; and the Special Commissioners must hear
and determine the matter in like manner as an appeal[7].

1 For the meaning of 'scheme' see para 1531 note 3 ante.
2 For the meaning of 'savings-related share option scheme' see para 1531 note 3 ante.
3 Ie the trust referred to in the Income and Corporation Taxes Act 1988 ss 185-187 (as amended), Sch 9
   para 30(1)(c): see para 1554 head (3) post.
4 As to profit sharing schemes see para 1529 ante.
5 For the meaning of 'grantor' see para 1531 note 5 ante.
6 As to the Special Commissioners see INCOME TAXATION vol 23 (Reissue) paras 42-44.
7 Income and Corporation Taxes Act 1988 s 832(1), Sch 9 para 5.

1536. Commissioners' power to obtain information. The Commissioners of
Inland Revenue may by notice in writing require any person to furnish them, within
such time as they may direct, not being less than 30 days, with such information as they
think necessary for the performance of their functions under the relevant provisions[1]
and as the person to whom the notice is addressed has or can reasonably obtain,
including in particular information:

(1) to enable the commissioners to determine whether to approve a scheme[2] or withdraw an approval already given, or the liability to tax, including capital gains tax, of any person who has participated in a scheme; and

(2) in relation to the administration of a scheme and any alteration of the terms of a scheme[3].

1 For the meaning of 'the relevant provisions' see para 1529 note 21 ante.
2 For the meaning of 'scheme' see para 1531 note 3 ante.
3 Income and Corporation Taxes Act 1988 ss 185-187 (as amended), 832(1), Sch 9 para 6. As to the penalty for non-compliance see INCOME TAXATION vol 23 (Reissue) para 1638; and as to the cancellation of approval where information is not furnished see para 1533 ante.

C. REQUIREMENTS GENERALLY APPLICABLE

1537. Material interest in close company. The scheme[1] must not provide for any person to be eligible to participate in it, that is to say, to obtain and exercise rights under it, or in the case of a profit sharing scheme[2] to have shares[3] appropriated to him, at any time when he has, or has within the preceding 12 months had, a material interest[4] in a close company[5] which is:

(1) a company shares in which, in the case of a profit sharing scheme, are to be appropriated or, in the case of a share option scheme[6], may be acquired pursuant to the exercise of rights obtained under the scheme; or

(2) a company which has control[7] of such a company or is a member of a consortium which owns such a company[8].

1 For the meaning of 'scheme' see para 1531 note 3 ante.
2 As to profit sharing schemes see para 1529 ante.
3 For the meaning of 'shares' see para 1528 note 2 ante.
4 For the purposes of the application of the relevant provisions in relation to any share option scheme or profit sharing scheme, a person has a material interest in a company if he, either on his own or with one or more associates, or if any associate of his with or without such other associates (1) is the beneficial owner of, or able, directly or through the medium of other companies, or by any other indirect means to control, more than 25% or, in the case of a share option scheme which is not a savings-related share option scheme, more than 10%, of the ordinary share capital of the company; or (2) where the company is a close company, possesses, or is entitled to acquire, such rights as would, in the event of the winding up of the company or in any other circumstances, give an entitlement to receive more than 25%, or in the case of a share option scheme which is not a savings-related share option scheme more than 10%, of the assets which would then be available for distribution among the participators: Income and Corporation Taxes Act 1988 s 187(3) (amended by the Finance Act 1989 s 107, Sch 12 para 9). In the Income and Corporation Taxes Act 1988 s 187(3) (as so amended) 'associate' has the meaning given by s 417(3),(4) (as amended) (see INCOME TAXATION vol 23 (Reissue) para 1298); and 'participator' has the meaning given by s 417(1) (see INCOME TAXATION vol 23 (Reissue) para 1296): s 187(3) (as so amended). Section 187(3) (as so amended) has effect subject to the provisions of ss 185-187, Sch 9 Pt VI (paras 37-40 (as amended): see paras 1558-1561 post): s 187(4). For the meaning of 'ordinary share capital' see para 1211 note 4 ante; and for the meaning of 'the relevant provisions' see para 1529 note 21 ante.
5 For the meaning of 'close company' see INCOME TAXATION vol 23 (Reissue) para 1292. In determining whether a company is a close company for these purposes, ibid ss 414(1)(a), 415 (see INCOME TAXATION vol 23 (Reissue) paras 1292, 1294) are to be disregarded: Sch 9 para 8.
6 As to share option schemes see para 1528 ante.
7 For the meaning of 'control' see para 1531 note 7 ante.
8 Income and Corporation Taxes Act 1988 Sch 9 para 8. The provisions of Sch 9 Pt II (paras 7-15 (as amended): see supra and paras 1538-1540 post) apply in relation to all schemes unless otherwise stated: Sch 9 para 7. For the purposes of the relevant provisions, a company is a member of a consortium owning another company if it is one of a number of companies which between them beneficially own not less than three-quarters of the other company's ordinary share capital and each of which beneficially owns not less than one-twentieth of that capital: s 187(7).

1538. Specified age. In the case of a savings-related share option scheme[1] or a profit sharing scheme[2], the scheme must specify what age is to be the specified age for the purposes of the scheme[3].

The age specified must be the same for men and women and must be not less than 60 and not more than 75[4].

1 For the meaning of 'savings-related share option scheme' see para 1531 note 3 ante.
2 As to profit sharing schemes see para 1529 ante.
3 Income and Corporation Taxes Act 1988 ss 185-187 (as amended), Sch 9 para 8A(1) (added by the Finance Act 1991 s 38(1),(5),(6) in relation to a scheme not approved before 25 July 1991). 'Specified age', in relation to a scheme, means the age specified in pursuance of Sch 9 para 8A (as added) as the specified age for the purposes of the scheme: s 187(2) (amended by the Finance Act 1991 s 38(4)).
4 Income and Corporation Taxes Act 1988 Sch 9 para 8A(2) (added by the Finance Act 1991 s 38(1),(5), (6) in relation to a scheme not approved before 25 July 1991).

1539. Scheme shares. A share option scheme[1] must provide for directors and employees to obtain rights to acquire shares ('scheme shares') which satisfy the specified[2] requirements[3]. In the case of a profit sharing scheme[4], the shares to be acquired[5] by the trustees[6] ('scheme shares') must satisfy the specified[7] requirements[8].

Scheme shares must form part of the ordinary share capital[9] of the grantor[10] or a company which has control[11] of the grantor or a company which either is, or has control of, a company which is a member of a consortium owning either the grantor[12] or a company having control of the grantor[13].

Scheme shares must be shares[14] of a class quoted on a recognised stock exchange[15] or shares in a company which is not under the control of another company or shares in a company which is under the control of a company, other than a company which is, or would if resident in the United Kingdom be, a close company[16], whose shares are quoted on a recognised stock exchange[17].

Scheme shares must be:

(1) fully paid up;
(2) not redeemable; and
(3) not subject to any restrictions[18] other than restrictions which attach to all shares of the same class or a restriction authorised by the following provisions;

but head (2) above does not apply, in the case of a profit sharing scheme, in relation to shares in a workers' co-operative[19].

Except as provided below, the shares may be subject to a restriction imposed by the company's articles of association:

(a) requiring all shares held by directors or employees of the company or of any other company of which it has control to be disposed of on ceasing to be so held; and
(b) requiring all shares acquired, in pursuance of rights or interests obtained by such directors or employees, by persons who are not, or have ceased to be, such directors or employees to be disposed of when they are acquired[20].

A restriction is not so authorised, however, unless:

(i) any disposal required by the restriction will be by way of sale for a consideration in money on terms specified in the articles of association; and
(ii) the articles also contain general provisions by virtue of which any person disposing of shares of the same class[21] may be required to sell them on terms which are the same as those mentioned in head (i) above[22].

Except where scheme shares are shares in a company the ordinary share capital of which consists of shares of one class only, the majority of the issued shares of the same class either must be employee-control shares[23] or must be held by persons other than:

(A) persons who acquired their shares in pursuance of a right conferred on them or an opportunity afforded to them as a director or employee of the grantor or any other company and not in pursuance of an offer to the public;

(B) trustees holding shares on behalf of persons who acquired their beneficial interests in the shares as mentioned in head (A) above; and

(C) in a case where the shares fall within head (3) above, but not within head (1) above, companies which have control of the company whose shares are in question or of which that company is an associated company[24].

1 As to share option schemes see para 1528 ante.
2 Ie the requirements of the Income and Corporation Taxes Act 1988 ss 185–187, Sch 9 paras 10–14 (as amended): see infra.
3 Ibid Sch 9 para 9(1).
4 As to profit sharing schemes see para 1529 ante.
5 Ie as mentioned in the Income and Corporation Taxes Act 1988 Sch 9 para 30: see para 1554 post.
6 For the meaning of 'the trustees' see para 1529 note 1 ante.
7 Ie the requirements of the Income and Corporation Taxes Act 1988 Sch 9 paras 10–12, 14 (as amended): see infra.
8 Ibid Sch 9 para 9(2).
9 For the meaning of 'ordinary share capital' see para 1211 note 4 ante.
10 For the meaning of 'grantor' see para 1531 note 5 ante.
11 For the meaning of 'control' see para 1531 note 7 ante.
12 As to when a company is a member of a consortium owning another company see para 1537 note 8 ante.
13 Income and Corporation Taxes Act 1988 Sch 9 para 10 (amended by the Finance Act 1989 s 64, Sch 17 Pt IV).
14 For the meaning of 'shares' see para 1528 note 2 ante.
15 For the meaning of 'recognised stock exchange' see INCOME TAXATION vol 23 (Reissue) para 562 note 1.
16 For the meaning of 'close company' see INCOME TAXATION vol 23 (Reissue) para 1292.
17 Income and Corporation Taxes Act 1988 Sch 9 para 11.
18 In determining for these purposes, in the case of a share option scheme, whether scheme shares which are or are to be acquired by any person are subject to any restrictions, there must be disregarded as a restriction attaching to the shares any contract, agreement, arrangement or condition by which his freedom to dispose of the shares or of any interest in them or of the proceeds of their sale or to exercise any right conferred by them is restricted or by which such a disposal or exercise may result in any disadvantage to him or to a person connected with him: ibid Sch 9 para 13(1). Schedule 9 para 13(1) does not apply to so much of any contract, agreement, arrangement or condition as contains provisions similar in purpose and effect to any of the provisions of the Model Rules set out in the Model Code for Securities Transactions by Directors of Listed Companies issued by the Stock Exchange in November 1984: Income and Corporation Taxes Act 1988 Sch 9 para 13(2). In the case of schemes other than savings-related share option schemes, Sch 9 para 13(1) does not apply in relation to any terms of a loan making provision about how it is to be repaid or the security to be given for it: Sch 9 para 13(3) (added by the Finance Act 1989 s 69(1)). The Income and Corporation Taxes Act 1988 s 839 (meaning of 'connected persons': see INCOME TAXATION vol 23 (Reissue) para 1250) applies for the purposes of the relevant provisions: s 187(6). For the meaning of 'savings-related share option scheme' see para 1531 note 3 ante; and for the meaning of 'the relevant provisions' see para 1529 note 21 ante.
19 Ibid Sch 9 para 12(1). For the meaning of 'workers' co-operative' see para 1532 note 13 ante. As to the Inland Revenue's revised practice on certain share restrictions see Inland Revenue Statement of Practice dated 11 June 1985.
20 Income and Corporation Taxes Act 1988 Sch 9 para 12(2).
21 Ie whether or not held or acquired as mentioned in ibid Sch 9 para 12(2): see supra.
22 Ibid Sch 9 para 12(3).
23 For these purposes, shares in a company are employee-control shares if (1) the persons holding the shares are, by virtue of their holding, together able to control the company; and (2) those persons are or

have been employees or directors of the company or of another company which is under the control of
the company: ibid Sch 9 para 14(3).

24 Ibid Sch 9 para 14(1). In its application to a profit sharing scheme Sch 9 para 14(1) has effect with the
addition after the words 'ordinary share capital of which' of the words 'at the time of the acquisition of
the shares by the trustees': Sch 9 para 14(2). For these purposes, unless the context otherwise requires,
'associated company' has the same meaning as in s 416 (as amended) (see INCOME TAXATION vol 23
(Reissue) para 1293 note 20) except that in Sch 9 para 23 (see para 1544, 1546 post), s 416(1) has effect
with the omission of the words 'or at any time within one year previously': s 187(2).

1540. Release of rights. Except in the case of a profit sharing scheme[1], the scheme[2]
may provide that, if any company ('the acquiring company'):

(1) obtains control[3] of a company whose shares[4] are scheme shares[5] as a result of
making a general offer:

   (a) to acquire the whole of the issued ordinary share capital[6] of the company
   which is made on a condition such that, if it is satisfied, the person making
   the offer will have control of the company; or

   (b) to acquire all the shares in the company which are of the same class as the
   scheme shares;

(2) obtains control of a company whose shares are scheme shares in pursuance of a
compromise or arrangement sanctioned by the court[7]; or

(3) becomes bound or entitled to acquire shares in a company whose shares are
scheme shares[8],

any participant[9] in the scheme may at any time within the appropriate period[10], by
agreement with the acquiring company, release his rights under the scheme ('the old
rights') in consideration of the grant to him of rights ('the new rights') which are
equivalent to the old rights but relate to shares in a different company, whether the
acquiring company itself or some other[11] company[12].

The new rights are not to be regarded for these purposes as equivalent to the old
rights unless:

(i) the shares to which they relate satisfy the specified conditions[13] in relation to
scheme shares; and

(ii) the new rights will be exercisable in the same manner as the old rights and
subject to the provisions of the scheme as it had effect immediately before the
release of the old rights; and

(iii) the total market value[14], immediately before the release, of the shares which
were subject to the participant's old rights is equal to the total market value,
immediately after the grant, of the shares in respect of which the new rights are
granted to the participant; and

(iv) the total amount payable by the participant for the acquisition of shares in
pursuance of the new rights is equal to the total amount that would have been
payable for the acquisition of shares in pursuance of the old rights[15].

Where any new rights are granted pursuant to a provision included in a scheme by
virtue of these provisions, they are to be regarded[16] as having been granted at the time
when the corresponding old rights were granted[17].

Where a scheme which was approved before 1 August 1987 was altered before
1 August 1989 so as to include such a provision as is mentioned above ('an exchange
provision'), the scheme as altered may[18] apply that provision to rights obtained under
the scheme before the date on which the alteration takes effect[19]. If an exchange
provision is so applied in a case where, on or before 17 March 1987 but before the date
on which the alteration takes effect, an event has occurred by reason of which a person

holding rights under the scheme would be able to take advantage of the exchange provision:

    (A) the scheme may permit a person who held rights under the scheme immediately before that event to take advantage of the exchange provision; and

    (B) in a case where rights then held would otherwise, by reason of the event, have ceased to be exercisable, the scheme may provide that the exchange provision shall apply as if the rights were still exercisable[20].

The application of an exchange provision as mentioned above[21] is not itself to be regarded as the acquisition of a right[22].

1   As to profit sharing schemes see para 1529 ante.
2   For the meaning of 'scheme' see para 1531 note 3 ante.
3   For the meaning of 'control' see para 1531 note 7 ante.
4   For the meaning of 'shares' see para 1528 note 2 ante.
5   For the meaning of 'scheme shares' see para 1539 ante.
6   For the meaning of 'ordinary share capital' see para 1211 note 4 ante.
7   Ie under the Companies Act 1985 s 425 (as amended): see para 1447 ante.
8   Ie under ibid ss 428-430 (as substituted): see para 1202 et seq ante.
9   For the meaning of 'participant' see para 1529 note 1 ante.
10   For these purposes, 'the appropriate period' means (1) in a case falling within the Income and Corporation Taxes Act 1988 ss 185-187 (as amended), Sch 9 para 15(1)(a) (see text head (1) supra), the period of six months beginning with the time when the person making the offer has obtained control of the company and any condition subject to which the offer is made is satisfied; (2) in a case falling within Sch 9 para 15(1)(b) (see text head (2) supra), the period of six months beginning with the time when the court sanctions the compromise or arrangement; and (3) in a case falling within Sch 9 para 15(1)(c) (see text head (3) supra), the period during which the acquiring company remains bound or entitled as therein mentioned: Sch 9 para 15(2).
11   Ie some other company falling within ibid Sch 9 para 10(b) or (c): see para 1539 ante.
12   Ibid Sch 9 para 15(1).
13   Ie the conditions specified in ibid Sch 9 paras 10-14 (as amended): see para 1539 ante.
14   For the meaning of 'market value' see para 1528 note 10 ante.
15   Income and Corporation Taxes Act 1988 Sch 9 para 15(3).
16   Ie for the purpose of ibid s 185 (as amended) and Sch 9 (as amended) and for the purposes of the subsequent application, by virtue of a condition complying with Sch 9 para 15(3)(b) (see text head (ii) supra), of the provisions of the scheme.
17   Ibid Sch 9 para 15(4).
18   Ie by virtue of ibid Sch 9 para 15(5) and Sch 9 para 15(6)-(8): see infra.
19   Ibid Sch 9 para 15(5). Schedule 9 para 15(5) has effect subject to Sch 9 para 4 (see para 1534 ante): Sch 9 para 15(8).
20   Ibid Sch 9 para 15(6). Schedule 9 para 15(6) has effect subject to Sch 9 para 4 (see para 1534 ante): Sch 9 para 15(8).
21   Ie as mentioned in ibid Sch 9 para 15(5) or (6): see supra.
22   Ibid Sch 9 para 15(7).

D. REQUIREMENTS APPLICABLE TO SAVINGS-RELATED SHARE OPTION SCHEMES

1541. Consideration for shares. The scheme[1] must provide for the scheme shares[2] to be paid for with money not exceeding the amount of repayments made and any interest paid to them under a certified contractual savings scheme[3] which has been approved[4] by the Commisisoners of Inland Revenue[5].

Where the commissioners are satisfied that:

    (1) a person has entered into a certified contractual savings scheme before 15 November 1990; and

(2) he has obtained rights under a scheme established before that date to acquire shares in a company of which he is an employee or director, or a company of which such a company has control[6], using repayments made under the certified contractual savings scheme,

then repayments and interest paid under the certified contractual savings scheme are to be treated as repayments and interest paid under a scheme approved by the commissioners[7] and accordingly may be used for the purchase of shares under an approved[8] savings-related share option scheme[9].

The repayments and interest to which the above provisions[10] apply must not exceed the repayments and interest to which the participant[11] would have been entitled if the terms of the scheme had corresponded to those of a certified contractual savings scheme approved[12] by the commissioners[13].

1   For the meaning of 'scheme' see para 1531 note 3 ante.
2   For the meaning of 'scheme shares' see para 1539 ante.
3   For these purposes, 'certified contractual savings scheme' has the meaning given by the Income and Corporation Taxes Act 1988 s 326 (as amended) (see INCOME TAXATION vol 23 (Reissue) para 1220 note 1): s 187(2).
4   Ie for the purposes of ibid ss 185-187, Sch 9 (as amended): see para 1531 et seq ante and para 1542 et seq post.
5   Ibid Sch 9 para 16(1).
6   For the meaning of 'control' see para 1531 note 7 ante.
7   Ie for the purposes of the Income and Corporation Taxes Act 1988 Sch 9 (as amended) under Sch 9 para 16(1): see supra.
8   For the meaning of 'approved' see para 1528 note 1 ante.
9   Income and Corporation Taxes Act 1988 Sch 9 para 16(2). For the meaning of 'savings-related share option scheme' see para 1531 note 3 ante.
10 Ie ibid Sch 9 para 16(2): see supra.
11 For the meaning of 'participant' see para 1529 note 1 ante.
12 Ie under the Income and Corporation Taxes Act 1988 Sch 9 para 16(1): see supra.
13 Ibid Sch 9 para 16(3).

1542. Exercise of rights. The rights obtained under the scheme[1] must not be capable of being exercised[2] before the bonus date, that is to say, the date on which repayments under the certified contractual savings scheme[3] are due; and[4]:

(1) repayments under a certified contractual savings scheme may be taken as including or as not including a bonus;

(2) the time when repayments are due is, where repayments are taken as including the maximum bonus, the earliest date on which the maximum bonus is payable and in any other case the earliest date on which a bonus is payable under the scheme; and

(3) the question what is to be taken as so included must be required to be determined at the time when rights under the scheme are obtained[5].

1   For the meaning of 'scheme' see para 1531 note 3 ante.
2   Ie subject to the Income and Corporation Taxes Act 1988 ss 185-187, Sch 9 paras 18-21 (as amended): see paras 1543-1546 post.
3   For the meaning of 'certified contractual savings scheme' see para 1541 note 3 ante.
4   Ie for the purposes of the Income and Corporation Taxes Act 1988 Sch 9 para 17 and Sch 9 para 16 (see para 1541 ante).
5   Ibid s 187(2), Sch 9 para 17.

1543. Death before bonus date. The scheme[1] must provide that, if a person who has obtained rights under the scheme dies before the bonus date[2], the rights must be exercised, if at all, within 12 months after the date of his death and, if he dies within six months after the bonus date, the rights may be exercised within 12 months after the bonus date[3].

1 For the meaning of 'scheme' see para 1531 note 3 ante.
2 For the meaning of 'bonus date' see para 1542 ante.
3 Income and Corporation Taxes Act 1988 ss 185–187 (as amended), Sch 9 para 18.

1544. Ceasing to hold office or employment. The scheme[1] must provide that, if a person who has obtained rights under it ceases to hold the office or employment by virtue of which he is eligible to participate in the scheme[2] by reason of:

(1) injury or disability or redundancy[3]; or

(2) retirement on reaching the specified age[4] or any other age at which he is bound to retire in accordance with the terms of his contract of employment,

then the rights must be exercised, if at all, within six months of his so ceasing and, if he so ceases for any other reason within three years of obtaining the rights, they may not be exercised at all except pursuant to a specified provision[5] of the scheme; and, in relation to the case where he so ceases for any other reason more than three years after obtaining the rights, the scheme must either provide that the rights may not be exercised or that they must be exercised, if at all, within six months of his so ceasing[6].

1 For the meaning of 'scheme' see para 1531 note 3 ante.
2 For these purposes, no person is to be treated as ceasing to hold an office or employment by virtue of which he is eligible to participate in the scheme until he ceases to hold an office or employment in the grantor or in any associated company or company of which the grantor has control: Income and Corporation Taxes Act 1988 ss 185–187 (as amended), Sch 9 para 23. For the meaning of 'grantor' see para 1531 note 5 ante; for the meaning of 'associated company' see para 1539 note 24 ante; and for the meaning of 'control' see para 1531 note 7 ante.
3 Ie within the meaning of the Employment Protection (Consolidation) Act 1978: see EMPLOYMENT vol 16 (Reissue) para 412.
4 For the meaning of 'specified age' see para 1538 note 3 ante.
5 Ie such a provision as is mentioned in the Income and Corporation Taxes Act 1988 Sch 9 para 21(1)(e): see para 1546 head (5) post.
6 Ibid Sch 9 para 19 (amended by the Finance Act 1991 s 38(1),(2),(6)).

1545. Attainment of specified age. The scheme[1] must provide that, where a person who has obtained rights under it continues to hold the office or employment by virtue of which he is eligible to participate in the scheme after the date on which he reaches the specified age[2], he may exercise the rights within six months of that date[3].

1 For the meaning of 'scheme' see para 1531 note 3 ante.
2 For the meaning of 'specified age' see para 1538 note 3 ante.
3 Income and Corporation Taxes Act 1988 ss 185–187, Sch 9 para 20 (amended by the Finance Act 1991 s 38(1),(2),(6) in relation to a scheme not approved before 25 July 1991).

1546. Optional contents. The scheme[1] may provide that:

(1) if any person obtains control[2] of a company whose shares[3] are scheme shares[4] as a result of making a general offer[5], rights obtained under the scheme to acquire shares in the company may be exercised within six months of the time when the person making the offer has obtained control of the company and any condition subject to which the offer is made has been satisfied;

(2) if the court sanctions[6] a compromise or arrangement proposed for the purposes of or in connection with a scheme for the reconstruction of a company whose

shares are scheme shares or its amalgamation with any other company or companies, rights obtained under the share option scheme[7] to acquire shares in the company may be exercised within six months of the court sanctioning the compromise or arrangement;

(3) if any person becomes bound or entitled[8] to acquire shares in a company shares in which are scheme shares, rights obtained under the scheme to acquire shares in the company may be exercised at any time when that person remains so bound or entitled;

(4) if a company whose shares are scheme shares passes a resolution for voluntary winding up[9], rights obtained under a scheme to acquire shares in the company may be exercised within six months of the passing of the resolution;

(5) if a person ceases to hold an office or employment[10] by virtue of which he is eligible to participate in the scheme by reason only that:
   (a) that office or employment is in a company of which the grantor[11] ceases to have control; or
   (b) that office or employment relates to a business or part of a business which is transferred to a person who is neither an associated company[12] of the grantor nor a company of which the grantor has control,
   rights under the scheme held by that person may be exercised within six months of his so ceasing;

(6) if, at the bonus date[13], a person who has obtained rights under the scheme holds an office or employment in a company which is not a participating company[14], but which is an associated company of the grantor or a company of which the grantor has control, those rights may be exercised within six months of that date[15].

Where a scheme which has been approved before 1 August 1986 has been or is altered before 1 August 1988 so as to include such a provision as is specified in head (5) above, the scheme as altered may by virtue of these provisions apply that provision to rights obtained under the scheme before the date on which the alteration takes effect; and, where that provision is so applied in relation to such rights:

(i) the scheme may permit a person having such rights to take advantage of the provision notwithstanding that under the scheme he would otherwise be unable to exercise those rights after he has ceased to hold the office or employment in question; and

(ii) if, before the date on which the alteration takes effect, a person who held such rights on 18 March 1986 ceases, in either of the circumstances set out in head (5) above, to hold an office or employment by virtue of which he was eligible to participate in the scheme, then, so far as concerns the rights so held, the scheme may permit him to take advantage of the provision in question as if the alteration had been made immediately before he ceased to hold that office or employment; and

(iii) the application of the provision is not itself to be regarded[16] as the acquisition of a right[17].

1 For the meaning of 'scheme' see para 1531 note 3 ante.
2 For these purposes, a person is deemed to have obtained control of a company if he and others acting in concert with him have together obtained control of it: Income and Corporation Taxes Act 1988 ss 185–187 (as amended), Sch 9 para 21(2). For the meaning of 'control' see para 1531 note 7 ante.
3 For the meaning of 'shares' see para 1528 note 2 ante.
4 For the meaning of 'scheme shares' see para 1539 ante.
5 Ie an offer falling within the Income and Corporation Taxes Act 1988 Sch 9 para 15(1)(a)(i) or (ii): see para 1540 ante.

6 Ie under the Companies Act 1985 s 425 (as amended): see para 1447 ante.
7 As to share option schemes see para 1528 ante.
8 Ie under the Companies Act 1985 ss 428–430 (as substituted): see para 1202 ante.
9 As to voluntary winding up see para 2698 et seq post.
10 For these purposes, no person is to be treated as ceasing to hold an office or employment by virtue of which he is eligible to participate in the scheme until he ceases to hold an office or employment in the grantor or in any associated company or company of which the grantor has control: Income and Corporation Taxes Act 1988 Sch 9 para 23.
11 For the meaning of 'grantor' see para 1531 note 5 ante.
12 For the meaning of 'associated company' see para 1539 note 24 ante.
13 For the meaning of 'bonus date' see para 1542 ante.
14 For the meaning of 'participating company' see para 1531 note 8 ante.
15 Income and Corporation Taxes Act 1988 Sch 9 para 21(1) (amended by the Finance Act 1996 ss 113(1), 205, Sch 41 Pt V). Where a scheme approved before 29 April 1996 is altered before 5 May 1998 so as to include such a provision as is specified in the Income and Corporation Taxes Act 1988 Sch 9 para 21(1)(f) (as added) (see text head (6) supra), the scheme may apply the provision to rights obtained under the scheme before the alteration takes effect, whether the bonus date in relation to the rights occurred before or after 29 April 1996; and, where the provision is applied to such rights by virtue of this provision, its application to such rights is not of itself to be regarded as the acquisition of a right for the purposes of Sch 9 (as amended): Sch 9 para 21(4) (added by the Finance Act 1996 s 113(2)). The Income and Corporation Taxes Act 1988 Sch 9 para 21(4) (as so added) has effect subject to Sch 9 para 4 (see para 1534 ante): Sch 9 para 21(4) (as so added).
16 Ie for the purposes of ibid Sch 9 (as amended).
17 Ibid Sch 9 para 21(3). Schedule 9 para 21(3) has effect subject to Sch 9 para 4 (see para 1534 ante): Sch 9 para 21(3).

1547. Transfer etc of rights. Rights obtained by a person under the scheme[1] must not be capable[2] of being transferred by him or of being exercised later than six months after the bonus date[3].

1 For the meaning of 'scheme' see para 1531 note 3 ante.
2 Ie except as provided in the Income and Corporation Taxes Act 1988 ss 185–187 (as amended), Sch 9 para 18: see para 1543 ante.
3 Ibid Sch 9 para 22. For the meaning of 'bonus date' see para 1542 ante.

1548. Value of contributions. The scheme[1] must provide for a person's contributions under the certified contractual savings scheme[2] to be of such amount as to secure as nearly as may be repayment of an amount equal to that for which shares[3] may be acquired in pursuance of rights obtained under the scheme[4].

The scheme must not:

(1) permit the aggregate amount of a person's contributions under certified contractual savings schemes linked to approved[5] savings-related share option schemes[6] to exceed £250 monthly; nor

(2) impose a minimum on the amount of a person's contributions which exceeds £10 monthly[7].

1 For the meaning of 'scheme' see para 1531 note 3 ante.
2 For the meaning of 'certified contractual savings scheme' see para 1541 note 3 ante.
3 For the meaning of 'shares' see para 1528 note 2 ante.
4 Income and Corporation Taxes Act 1988 ss 185–187 (as amended), Sch 9 para 24(1). For this purpose, the amount of repayment under the certified contractual savings scheme is to be determined in accordance with Sch 9 para 17 (see para 1542 ante): Sch 9 para 24(1).
5 For the meaning of 'approved' see para 1528 note 1 ante.
6 For the meaning of 'savings-related share option scheme' see para 1531 note 3 ante.
7 Income and Corporation Taxes Act 1988 Sch 9 para 24(2) (amended by the Finance Act 1991 s 40). The Treasury may by order amend the Income and Corporation Taxes Act 1988 Sch 9 para 24(2) (as so

amended) by substituting for any amount for the time being there specified such amount as may be specified in the order: Sch 9 para 24(3).

1549. Price at which scheme shares may be acquired. The price at which scheme shares[1] may be acquired by the exercise of a right obtained under the scheme[2]:

(1) must be stated at the time the right is obtained; and

(2) must not be manifestly less than 80% of the market value[3] of shares[4] of the same class at that time or, if the Commissioners of Inland Revenue and the grantor[5] agree in writing, at such earlier time or times as may be provided in the agreement;

but the scheme may provide for such variation of the price as may be necessary to take account of any variation in the share capital of which the scheme shares form part[6].

1 For the meaning of 'scheme shares' see para 1539 ante.
2 For the meaning of 'scheme' see para 1531 note 3 ante.
3 For the meaning of 'market value' see para 1528 note 10 ante.
4 For the meaning of 'shares' see para 1528 note 2 ante.
5 For the meaning of 'grantor' see para 1531 note 5 ante.
6 Income and Corporation Taxes Act 1988 ss 185-187, Sch 9 para 25 (amended by the Finance Act 1989 s 62(1),(3)). See *IRC v Reed International plc, Reed International plc v IRC* [1995] STC 889, CA (existing option holders had not obtained a right), distinguishing *IRC v Eurocopy plc* [1991] STC 707.

1550. Eligibility. Every person who:

(1) is an employee or a full-time director of the grantor[1] or, in the case of a group scheme[2], a participating company[3]; and

(2) has been such an employee or director at all times during a qualifying period not exceeding five years; and

(3) is chargeable to tax in respect of his office or employment under Case I of Schedule E[4],

must be eligible to participate in the scheme, that is to say, to obtain and exercise rights under it, on similar terms, and those who do participate in the scheme must actually do so on similar terms[5].

For the above purposes, the fact that the rights to be obtained by the persons participating in a scheme vary according to the levels of their remuneration, the length of their service or similar factors are not to be regarded as meaning that they are not eligible to participate in the scheme on similar terms or do not actually do so[6].

A person must not be eligible[7] to participate in the scheme at any time unless he is at that time a director or employee of the grantor or, in the case of a group scheme, of a participating company[8].

1 For the meaning of 'grantor' see para 1531 note 5 ante.
2 For the meaning of 'group scheme' see para 1531 note 8 ante.
3 For the meaning of 'participating company' see para 1531 note 8 ante.
4 Ie under the Income and Corporation Taxes Act 1988 s 19(1), Schedule E, Case I (as substituted): see INCOME TAXATION vol 23 (Reissue) para 668 et seq.
5 Ibid ss 185–187, Sch 9 para 26(1) (amended by the Finance Act 1995 s 137(2) with effect for any scheme not approved before 1 May 1995).
6 Income and Corporation Taxes Act 1988 Sch 9 para 26(2).
7 Ie except as provided by ibid Sch 9 para 19 (as amended) (see para 1544 ante) or pursuant to such a provision as is referred to in Sch 9 para 21(1)(e) or (f) (as added) (see para 1546 heads (5), (6) ante).
8 Ibid Sch 9 para 26(3) (amended by the Finance Act 1996 s 113(3)). See *IRC v Reed International plc, Reed International plc v IRC* [1995] STC 889, CA (Parliament could not have intended that a scheme extending to any company or companies of which the grantor did not have control should be capable of

being a group scheme; moreover, the expression 'participating company' could only sensibly refer to companies of which the grantor had control; accordingly the amended SAYE scheme did not satisfy the requirements of the Income and Corporation Taxes Act 1988 Sch 9 para 26(3)).

E. REQUIREMENTS APPLICABLE TO OTHER SHARE OPTION SCHEMES

1551. Full-time directors or qualifying employees. A person must not be eligible to obtain rights under the scheme[1] at any time unless he is at that time a full-time director or qualifying employee[2] of the grantor[3] or, in the case of a group scheme, of a participating company, but the scheme may provide that a person may exercise rights under it after he has ceased to be a full-time director or qualifying employee[4].

The scheme must not permit any person obtaining rights under it to transfer any of them but may provide that, if a person who has obtained rights under it dies before exercising them, they may be exercised after, but not more than one year after, the date of his death[5].

1 For the meaning of 'scheme' see para 1531 note 3 ante.
2 For these purposes, 'qualifying employee', in relation to a company, means an employee of the company, other than one who is a director of the company or, in the case of a group scheme, of a participating company: Income and Corporation Taxes Act 1988 ss 185-187 (as amended), Sch 9 para 27(4) (amended by the Finance Act 1995 s 137(3), Sch 29 Pt VIII). For the meaning of 'group scheme' see para 1531 note 8 ante; and for the meaning of 'participating company' see para 1531 note 8 ante.
3 For the meaning of 'grantor' see para 1531 note 5 ante.
4 Income and Corporation Taxes Act 1988 Sch 9 para 27(1).
5 Ibid Sch 9 para 27(2). Where the scheme contains the provisions so permitted and any rights are exercised after the death of the person who obtained them but before the expiry of the period of ten years beginning with his obtaining them, s 185(3) (as amended) (see para 1528 ante) applies with the omission of the reference to s 185(5) (see para 1528 ante): Sch 9 para 27(3).

1552. Aggregate market value of shares not to exceed appropriate limit. The scheme[1] must provide that no person shall obtain rights under it which would, at the time they are obtained, cause the aggregate market value of the shares[2] which he may acquire in pursuance of rights obtained under the scheme or under any other share option scheme[3], not being a savings-related share option scheme[4], duly approved[5] and established by the grantor[6] or by any associated company[7] of the grantor (and not exercised) to exceed or further exceed £30,000[8].

1 For the meaning of 'scheme' see para 1531 note 3 ante.
2 For these purposes, the market value of shares is to be calculated as at the time when the rights in relation to those shares were obtained or, in a case where an agreement relating to them has been made under the Income and Corporation Taxes Act 1988 ss 185-187 (as amended), Sch 9 para 29 (as substituted) (see para 1553 post), such earlier time or times as may be provided in the agreement: Sch 9 para 28(3). For the meaning of 'market value' see para 1528 note 10 ante; and for the meaning of 'shares' see para 1528 note 2 ante.
3 As to share option schemes see para 1528 ante.
4 For the meaning of 'savings-related share option scheme' see para 1531 note 3 ante.
5 Ie under the Income and Corporation Taxes Act 1988 Sch 9 (as amended): see para 1537 et seq ante and para 1553 et seq post.
6 For the meaning of 'grantor' see para 1531 note 5 ante.
7 For the meaning of 'associated company' see para 1539 note 24 ante.
8 Income and Corporation Taxes Act 1988 Sch 9 para 28(1) (amended by the Finance Act 1996 s 114(1),(2)).

1553. Price for acquisition of shares. The price at which scheme shares[1] may be acquired by the exercise of a right obtained under the scheme[2]:

(1) must be stated at the time the right is obtained; and

(2) must not be manifestly less than the market value[3] of shares[4] of the same class at that time or, if the Commissioners of Inland Revenue and the grantor[5] agree in writing, at such earlier time or times as may be provided in the agreement[6].

The scheme may provide for such variation of the price at which share schemes may be acquired as may be necessary to take account of any variation in the share capital of which the scheme shares form part[7].

1 For the meaning of 'scheme shares' see para 1539 ante.
2 For the meaning of 'scheme' see para 1531 note 3 ante.
3 For the meaning of 'market value' see para 1528 note 10 ante.
4 For the meaning of 'shares' see para 1528 note 2 ante.
5 For the meaning of 'grantor' see para 1531 note 5 ante.
6 Income and Corporation Taxes Act 1988 ss 185-187 (as amended), Sch 9 para 29(1) (substituted by the Finance Act 1996 s 114(1),(3)). The Finance Act 1996 s 114(3) has effect in relation to rights obtained on or after 29 April 1996: s 114(10). See *IRC v Reed International plc, Reed International plc v IRC* [1995] STC 889, CA (existing option holders had not obtained a right), distinguishing *IRC v Eurocopy plc* [1991] STC 707.
7 Income and Corporation Taxes Act 1988 Sch 9 para 29(7) (substituted by the Finance Act 1991 s 39(1),(7)).

F. REQUIREMENTS APPLICABLE TO PROFIT SHARING SCHEMES

1554. Establishment of trustees. The scheme[1] must provide for the establishment of a body of persons resident in the United Kingdom ('the trustees'):

(1) who, out of moneys paid to them by the grantor[2] or, in the case of a group scheme[3], a participating company[4], are required by the scheme to acquire shares[5] in respect of which the specified conditions[6] are fulfilled; and

(2) who are under a duty to appropriate shares acquired by them to individuals who participate in the scheme, not being individuals who are ineligible[7]; and

(3) whose functions with respect to shares held by them are regulated by a trust which is constituted under the law of a part of the United Kingdom and the terms of which are embodied in an instrument which complies with the specified[8] provisions[9].

If at any time after the Commissioners of Inland Revenue have approved the scheme, an alteration is made in the terms of the trust referred to in head (3) above, the approval does not have any effect after the date of the alteration unless the commissioners have approved the alteration[10].

The scheme must provide that the total of the initial market values[11] of the shares appropriated to any one participant in a year of assessment will not exceed the relevant amount[12].

1 For the meaning of 'scheme' see para 1531 note 3 ante.
2 For the meaning of 'grantor' see para 1531 note 5 ante.
3 For the meaning of 'group scheme' see para 1531 note 8 ante.
4 For the meaning of 'participating company' see para 1531 note 8 ante.
5 For the meaning of 'shares' see para 1528 note 2 ante.
6 Ie the conditions specified in the Income and Corporation Taxes Act 1988 ss 185-187, Sch 9 paras 10-12, 14 (as amended): see para 1539 ante.
7 Ie by virtue of ibid Sch 9 para 8 (see para 1537 ante) or Sch 9 para 35 (see para 1556 post).
8 Ie the provisions specified in ibid Sch 9 paras 31-34 (as amended): see para 1555 post.

9　Ibid Sch 9 para 30(1).
10　Ibid Sch 9 para 30(2).
11　For these purposes, 'initial market value', in relation to a participant's shares, means the market value of those shares determined (1) except where head (2) infra applies, on the date on which the shares were appropriated to him; and (2) if the Commissioners of Inland Revenue and the trustees agree in writing, on or by reference to such earlier date or dates as may be provided for in the agreement: ibid Sch 9 para 30(4). For the meaning of 'market value' see para 1528 note 10 ante; and for the meaning of 'participant' see para 1529 note 1 ante.
12　Ibid Sch 9 para 30(3). For these purposes, 'relevant amount', in relation to a participant in a profit sharing scheme, means an amount which is not less than £3,000 and not more than £8,000 but which, subject to that, is 10% of his salary, determined under s 187(5), for the year of assessment in question or the preceding year of assessment, whichever is the greater: s 187(2) (amended by the Finance Act 1991 s 41). For the purposes of the Income and Corporation Taxes Act 1988 s 187(2) (as so amended), a participant's salary for a year of assessment means such of the emoluments of the office or employment by virtue of which he is entitled to participate in a profit sharing scheme as are liable to be paid in that year under deduction of tax pursuant to s 203 (as amended) after deducting therefrom amounts included by virtue of Pt V Ch II (ss 153-168G (as amended)): see INCOME TAXATION vol 23 (Reissue) para 727 et seq): s 187(5).

1555. Trust instrument. The trust instrument[1] must provide that, as soon as practicable after any shares[2] have been appropriated to a participant[3], the trustees[4] will give him notice in writing of the appropriation specifying the number and description of those shares and stating their initial market value[5].

The trust instrument must:

(1)　contain a provision prohibiting the trustees from disposing of any shares, except in the permitted manner[6], during the period of retention[7], whether by transfer to the participant or otherwise[8];

(2)　contain a provision prohibiting the trustees from disposing of any shares after the end of the period of retention and before the release date[9] except pursuant to a direction given by or on behalf of the participant or any person in whom the beneficial interest in his shares is for the time being vested and by a transaction which would not involve a breach of certain[10] of the participant's obligations[11];

(3)　contain a provision requiring the trustees to pay over[12] to the participant any money or money's worth received by them in respect of or by reference to any of his shares other than money's worth consisting of new shares[13] and to deal only pursuant to a direction given by or on behalf of the participant or any person in whom the beneficial interest in his shares is for the time being vested with any right conferred in respect of any of his shares to be allotted other shares, securities or rights of any description[14];

(4)　impose an obligation on the trustees to maintain such records as may be necessary to enable the trustees to carry out their statutory obligations[15] and, where the participant becomes liable to income tax under Schedule E[16] by reason of the occurrence of any event, to inform him of any facts relevant to determining that liability[17].

1　For these purposes, 'the trust instrument', in relation to an approved profit sharing scheme, means the instrument referred to in the Income and Corporation Taxes Act 1988 ss 185-187 (as amended), Sch 9 para 30(1)(c) (see para 1554 head (3) ante): s 187(2).
2　For the meaning of 'shares' see para 1528 note 2 ante.
3　For the meaning of 'participant' see para 1529 note 1 ante.
4　For the meaning of 'the trustees' see para 1529 note 1 ante.
5　Income and Corporation Taxes Act 1988 Sch 9 para 31.
6　Ie in the manner permitted by ibid Sch 10 para 1(1)(a),(b),(c) or (cc) (as amended): see para 1562 post.

7 For the meaning of 'period of retention' see para 1529 note 18 ante.
8 Income and Corporation Taxes Act 1988 Sch 9 para 32(1) (amended by the Finance Act 1994 s 101(5),(9),(10)).
9 For the meaning of 'release date' see para 1529 note 12 ante.
10 Ie obligations under the Income and Corporation Taxes Act 1988 Sch 9 para 2(2)(c) or (d): see para 1532 ante.
11 Ibid Sch 9 para 32(2).
12 Ie subject to their obligation under ibid Sch 10 para 7 (see para 1568 post) and to any such direction as is mentioned in Sch 10 para 4(2) (see para 1565 post).
13 Ie within the meaning of ibid Sch 10 para 5 (as amended): see para 1566 post.
14 Ibid Sch 9 para 33.
15 Ie under ibid Sch 10 para 7.
16 Ie under ibid s 19(1), Schedule E (as amended): see INCOME TAXATION vol 23 (Reissue) para 654 et seq.
17 Ibid Sch 9 para 34.

1556. Appropriation of shares. An individual is not eligible to have shares[1] appropriated to him under the scheme[2] at any time:

(1) unless he is at that time or was within the preceding 18 months a director or employee of the grantor[3] or, in the case of a group scheme[4], of a participating company[5];

(2) if in that year of assessment shares have been appropriated to him under another approved[6] scheme established by the grantor or by a company which controls[7] or is controlled by the grantor or which is controlled by a company which also controls the grantor or a company which is a member of a consortium owning the grantor[8] or which is owned in part by the grantor as a member of a consortium[9].

1 For the meaning of 'shares' see para 1528 note 2 ante.
2 For the meaning of 'scheme' see para 1531 note 3 ante.
3 For the meaning of 'grantor' see para 1531 note 5 ante.
4 For the meaning of 'group scheme' see para 1531 note 8 ante.
5 Income and Corporation Taxes Act 1988 ss 185-187 (as amended), Sch 9 para 35(1).
6 For the meaning of 'approved' see para 1528 note 1 ante.
7 For the meaning of 'control' see para 1531 note 7 ante.
8 As to when a company is a member of a consortium owning another company see para 1537 note 8 ante.
9 Income and Corporation Taxes Act 1988 Sch 9 para 35(2).

1557. Eligibility to participate. Every person who at any time:

(1) is an employee or a full-time director of the grantor[1] or, in the case of a group scheme[2], a participating company[3]; and

(2) has been such an employee or director at all times during a qualifying period, not exceeding five years, ending at that time; and

(3) is chargeable to tax in respect of his office or employment under Case I of Schedule E[4],

must then be eligible[5] to participate in the scheme[6] on similar terms and those who do participate must actually do so on similar terms[7].

For the above purposes, the fact that the number of shares to be appropriated to the participants[8] in a scheme varies by reference to the levels of their remuneration, the length of their service or similar factors is not to be regarded as meaning that they are not eligible to participate in the scheme on similar terms or do not actually do so[9].

1 For the meaning of 'grantor' see para 1531 note 5 ante.
2 For the meaning of 'group scheme' see para 1531 note 8 ante.

3 For the meaning of 'participating company' see para 1531 note 8 ante.

4 Ie the Income and Corporation Taxes Act 1988 s 19(1), Schedule E, Case I (as substituted): see INCOME TAXATION vol 23 (Reissue) para 668 et seq.

5 Ie subject to ibid ss 185-187 (as amended), Sch 9 para 8 (see para 1537 ante) and Sch 9 para 35 (see para 1556 ante).

6 For the meaning of 'scheme' see para 1531 note 3 ante.

7 Income and Corporation Taxes Act 1988 Sch 9 para 36(1) (amended by the Finance Act 1995 s 137(4) with effect for any scheme not approved before 1 May 1995).

8 For the meaning of 'participant' see para 1529 note 1 ante.

9 Income and Corporation Taxes Act 1988 Sch 9 para 36(2).

G. MATERIAL INTEREST TEST

1558. Interests under trusts. The following provisions apply in a case where the individual ('the beneficiary') was one of the objects of a discretionary trust and the property subject to the trust at any time consisted of or included any shares[1] or obligations of the company[2].

If neither the beneficiary nor any relevant associate[3] of his had received any benefit under the discretionary trust before 14 November 1986, then, as respects any time before that date, the trustees[4] of the settlement concerned are not to be regarded, by reason only of the matters referred to above[5], as having been associates[6] of the beneficiary[7].

If, on or after 14 November 1986:

(1) the beneficiary ceases to be eligible to benefit under the discretionary trust by reason of an irrevocable disclaimer or release executed by him under seal or the irrevocable exercise by the trustees of a power to exclude him from the objects of the trust; and

(2) immediately after he so ceases, no relevant associate of his is interested in the shares or obligations of the company which are subject to the trust; and

(3) during the period of 12 months ending with the date when the beneficiary so ceases, neither the beneficiary nor any relevant associate of his received any benefit under the trust,

the beneficiary is not regarded, by reason only of the matters referred to above[8], as having been interested in the shares or obligations of the company[9] at any time during the period of 12 months referred to in head (3) above[10].

1 For the meaning of 'shares' see para 1528 note 2 ante.

2 Income and Corporation Taxes Act 1988 ss 185-187 (as amended), Sch 9 para 37(1).

3 For these purposes, 'relevant associate' has the meaning given to 'associate' by ibid s 417(3) (as amended) (see INCOME TAXATION vol 23 (Reissue) para 1298) but with the omission of s 417(3)(c): Sch 9 para 37(4).

4 For the meaning of 'the trustees' see para 1529 note 1 ante.

5 Ie in the Income and Corporation Taxes Act 1988 Sch 9 para 37(1): see supra.

6 Ie as defined in ibid s 417(3),(4) (as amended): see INCOME TAXATION vol 23 (Reissue) para 1298.

7 Ibid Sch 9 para 37(2).

8 See note 5 supra.

9 Ie as mentioned in the Income and Corporation Taxes Act 1988 s 417(3)(c).

10 Ibid Sch 9 para 37(3).

1559. Options etc. A right to acquire shares[1], however arising, is to be taken[2] to be a right to control[3] them[4].

In any case where:

(1) the shares attributed to an individual[5] consist of or include shares which he or any other person has a right to acquire; and

(2) the circumstances are such that, if that right were to be exercised, the shares acquired would be shares which were previously unissued and which the company is contractually bound to issue in the event of the exercise of the right,

then, in determining at any time prior to the exercise of that right whether the number of shares attributed to the individual exceeds a particular percentage of the ordinary share capital of the company, that ordinary share capital is to be taken to be increased by the number of unissued shares referred to in head (2) above[6].

The above provisions have effect as respects any time after 5 April 1987[7].

1 For the meaning of 'shares' see para 1528 note 2 ante.
2 Ie for the purposes of the Income and Corporation Taxes Act 1988 s 187(3)(a) (as substituted): see para 1537 note 4 ante.
3 For the meaning of 'control' see para 1531 note 7 ante.
4 Income and Corporation Taxes Act 1988 ss 185-187 (as amended), Sch 9 para 38(1).
5 Any reference in ibid Sch 9 para 38(3) to the shares attributed to an individual is a reference to the shares which, in accordance with s 187(3)(a) (as substituted), fall to be brought into account in his case to determine whether their number exceeds a particular percentage of the company's ordinary share capital: Sch 9 para 38(2). For the meaning of 'ordinary share capital' see para 1211 note 4 ante.
6 Ibid Sch 9 para 38(3).
7 Ibid Sch 9 para 38(4).

1560. Shares held by trustees of approved profit sharing schemes. As respects any time before or after the passing of the Income and Corporation Taxes Act 1988, there must be disregarded[1]:

(1) the interest of the trustees[2] of an approved[3] profit sharing scheme[4] in any shares[5] which are held by them in accordance with the scheme and have not yet been appropriated to an individual; and

(2) any rights exercisable by those trustees by virtue of that interest[6].

1 Ie in applying the Income and Corporation Taxes Act 1988 s 187(3) (as amended): see para 1537 note 4 ante.
2 For the meaning of 'the trustees' see para 1529 note 1 ante.
3 For the meaning of 'approved' see para 1528 note 1 ante.
4 As to profit sharing schemes see para 1529 ante.
5 For the meaning of 'shares' see para 1528 note 2 ante.
6 Income and Corporation Taxes Act 1988 ss 185-187 (as amended), Sch 9 para 39.

1561. Shares subject to an employee benefit trust. Where an individual has an interest in shares[1] or obligations of the company as a beneficiary of an employee benefit trust[2], the trustees[3] are not to be regarded as associates[4] of his by reason only of that interest unless at any time on or after 14 March 1989:

(1) the individual, either on his own or with any one or more of his associates; or

(2) any associate of his, with or without other such associates,

has been the beneficial owner of, or able (directly or through the medium of other companies or by any other indirect means) to control[5], more than 25%, or in the case of a share option scheme[6] which is not a savings-related share option scheme[7] more than 10%, of the ordinary share capital[8] of the company[9].

1 For the meaning of 'shares' see para 1528 note 2 ante.
2 For these purposes, 'employee benefit trust' has the same meaning as in the Income and Corporation Taxes Act 1988 s 176(9), Sch 8 para 7 (see INCOME TAXATION vol 23 (Reissue) para 1193 note 7): ss 185-187 (as amended), Sch 9 para 40(2).

3 For the meaning of 'the trustees' see para 1529 note 1 ante.

4 For these purposes, the Income and Corporation Taxes Act 1988 Sch 8 para 7(9)-(12) (as amended) (see INCOME TAXATION vol 23 (Reissue) para 1193) applies to an individual as it applies for the purposes of Sch 8 para 7 (as amended) to an employee: Sch 9 para 40(4) (added by the Finance Act 1989 s 65).

5 For the meaning of 'control' see para 1531 note 7 ante.

6 As to share option schemes see para 1528 ante.

7 For the meaning of 'savings-related share option scheme' see para 1531 note 3 ante.

8 For the meaning of 'ordinary share capital' see para 1211 note 4 ante.

9 Income and Corporation Taxes Act 1988 Sch 9 para 40(1),(3) (added by the Finance Act 1989 s 65).

H. FURTHER PROVISIONS RELATING TO PROFIT SHARING SCHEMES

1562. Limitations on contractual obligations of participants. Any obligation placed[1] on the participant[2] does not prevent him from:

(1) directing the trustees[3] to accept an offer for any of his shares[4] ('the original shares') if the acceptance or agreement will result in a new holding being equated with the original shares for the purpose of capital gains tax; or

(2) directing the trustees to agree to a transaction affecting his shares or such of them as are of a particular class, if the transaction would be entered into pursuant to a compromise, arrangement or scheme applicable to or affecting:

    (a) all the ordinary share capital[5] of the company in question or, as the case may be, all the shares of the class in question; or

    (b) all the shares, or all the shares of the class in question, which are held by a class of shareholders identified otherwise than by reference to their employment or their participation in an approved[6] scheme; or

(3) directing the trustees to accept an offer of cash, with or without other assets, for his shares if the offer forms part of a general offer which is made to holders of shares of the same class as his or of shares in the same company and which is made in the first instance on a condition such that, if it is satisfied, the person making the offer will have control of that company[7]; or

(4) directing the trustees to accept an offer of a qualifying corporate bond[8], whether alone or with cash or other assets or both, for his shares if the offer forms part of a general offer which is made as mentioned in head (3) above; or

(5) agreeing after the expiry of the period of retention[9] to sell the beneficial interest in his shares to the trustees for the same consideration as would be required[10] to be obtained for the shares themselves[11].

No obligation placed on the participant[12] is to be construed as binding his personal representatives to pay any sum to the trustees[13].

If, in breach of his statutory obligation[14], a participant assigns, charges or otherwise disposes of the beneficial interest in any of his shares, then, as respects those shares, he is to be treated for the purposes of the relevant provisions[15] as if at the time they were appropriated to him he was ineligible to participate in the scheme[16].

1 Ie by virtue of the Income and Corporation Taxes Act 1988 ss 185-187 (as amended), Sch 9 para 2(2): see para 1532 ante.

2 For the meaning of 'participant' see para 1529 note 1 ante.

3 For the meaning of 'the trustees' see para 1529 note 1 ante.

4 For the meaning of 'shares' see para 1528 note 2 ante.

5 For the meaning of 'ordinary share capital' see para 1211 note 4 ante.

6 For the meaning of 'approved' see para 1528 note 1 ante.

7 Ie within the meaning of the Income and Corporation Taxes Act 1988 s 416 (as amended): see INCOME TAXATION vol 23 (Reissue) para 1295.

8 For these purposes, 'qualifying corporate bond' is to be construed in accordance with the Taxation of Chargeable Gains Act 1992 s 117 (as amended) (see CAPITAL GAINS TAXATION vol 5(1) (Reissue) para 248): Income and Corporation Taxes Act 1988 s 186(13), Sch 10 para 1(4) (added by the Finance Act 1994 s 101(1)-(3),(7)).
9 For the meaning of 'period of retention' see para 1529 note 18 ante.
10 Ie in accordance with the Income and Corporation Taxes Act 1988 Sch 9 para 2(2)(d).
11 Ibid Sch 10 para 1(1) (amended by the Finance Act 1994 s 101(1)-(3),(7)).
12 Ie by virtue of the Income and Corporation Taxes Act 1988 Sch 9 para 2(2)(c).
13 Ibid Sch 10 para 1(2).
14 Ie under ibid Sch 9 para 2(2)(b).
15 For the meaning of 'the relevant provisions' see para 1529 note 21 ante.
16 Income and Corporation Taxes Act 1988 Sch 10 para 1(3). Schedule 10 para 6 (see para 1567 post) applies accordingly: Sch 10 para 1(3).

1563. Period of retention. For the purposes of any of the relevant provisions[1], 'the period of retention', in relation to any of a participant's shares[2], means the period beginning on the date on which they are appropriated to him and ending on the second anniversary of that date or, if it is earlier:

(1) the date on which the participant[3] ceases to be a director or employee of the grantor[4] or, in the case of a group scheme[5], a participating company[6] by reason of injury or disability or on account of his being dismissed by reason of redundancy[7]; or

(2) the date on which the participant reaches the relevant age[8]; or

(3) the date of the participant's death; or

(4) in a case where the participant's shares are redeemable shares in a workers' co-operative[9], the date on which the participant ceases to be employed by, or by a subsidiary of, the co-operative[10].

1 For the meaning of 'the relevant provisions' see para 1529 note 21 ante.
2 For the meaning of 'participant's shares' see para 1529 note 11 ante.
3 For the meaning of 'participant' see para 1529 note 1 ante.
4 For the meaning of 'grantor' see para 1531 note 5 ante.
5 For these purposes, in the case of a group scheme, the participant is not to be treated as ceasing to be a director or employee of a participating company until such times as he is no longer a director or employee of any of the participating companies: Income and Corporation Taxes Act 1988 s 186(13), Sch 10 para 2. For the meaning of 'group scheme' see para 1531 note 8 ante.
6 For the meaning of 'participating company' see para 1531 note 8 ante.
7 Ie within the meaning of the Employment Protection (Consolidation) Act 1978: see EMPLOYMENT vol 16 (Reissue) para 412.
8 For these purposes, the reference to the relevant age is a reference, in the case of a scheme approved before 25 July 1991 (ie the day on which the Finance Act 1991 was passed), in the case of a man, to the age of 65 and, in the case of a woman, to the age of 60 and, in the case of a scheme approved on or after that day, to the specified age: Income and Corporation Taxes Act 1988 Sch 10 para 2 (amended by the Finance Act 1988 Sch 13 para 9; the Finance Act 1991 s 38(3); the Pensions Act 1995 s 126, Sch 4 para 12(b)). For the meaning of 'specified age' see para 1538 note 3 ante.
9 For the meaning of 'workers' co-operative' see para 1532 note 13 ante.
10 Income and Corporation Taxes Act 1988 Sch 10 para 2 (as amended: see note 8 supra).

1564. The appropriate percentage. For the purposes of any of the relevant provisions[1] charging an individual to income tax under Schedule E[2] by reason of the occurrence of an event relating to any of his shares[3], 'the appropriate percentage', in relation to those shares, is 100%, save that, where the individual ceases to be a director or employee of the grantor[4] or, in the case of a group scheme[5], a participating company[6] as mentioned in the above provisions[7] or reaches the relevant age before the event occurs, the appropriate percentage is[8] 50%[9].

For these purposes, the reference to the relevant age is to be construed as follows[10].

Where the scheme is approved before 25 July 1991 and the event occurs before 30 November 1993, the relevant age is, in the case of a man, 65 and, in the case of a woman, 60[11].

Where:

(1) the scheme is approved before 25 July 1991;

(2) the event occurs on or after 30 November 1993;

(3) the scheme defines the period of retention[12] by reference to the age of 60 for both men and women; and

(4) the reference to that age is incorporated in the definition by virtue of an alteration approved[13] by the Commissioners of Inland Revenue before the event occurs,

the relevant age is 60[14].

Where:

(a) the scheme is approved before 25 July 1991;

(b) the event occurs on or after 30 November 1993; and

(c) the above provisions[15] do not apply,

the relevant age is, in the case of a man, 65 and, in the case of a woman, 60[16].

Where the scheme is approved on or after 25 July 1991, the relevant age is the specified age[17].

1 For the meaning of 'the relevant provisions' see para 1529 note 21 ante.

2 Ie under the Income and Corporation Taxes Act 1988 s 19(1), Schedule E (as amended): see INCOME TAXATION vol 23 (Reissue) para 654 et seq.

3 For the meaning of 'shares' see para 1528 note 2 ante.

4 For the meaning of 'grantor' see para 1531 note 5 ante.

5 For the meaning of 'group scheme' see para 1531 note 8 ante.

6 For the meaning of 'participating company' see para 1531 note 8 ante.

7 Ie as mentioned in the Income and Corporation Taxes Act 1988 s 186(13), Sch 10 para 2(a): see para 1563 head (1) ante.

8 Ie unless ibid Sch 10 para 6(4) applies: see para 1567 post.

9 Ibid Sch 10 para 3(1),(2) (substituted by the Finance Act 1996 s 117(1)). The Finance Act 1996 s 117(1) has effect in relation to the occurrence, on or after 29 April 1996, of events by reason of whose occurrence any provision of the Income and Corporation Taxes Act 1988 s 186 (as amended), s 187 (as amended) or Sch 9 (as amended) or Sch 10 (as amended) charges an individual to income tax under s 19(1), Schedule E (as amended): Finance Act 1996 s 117(3).

10 Income and Corporation Taxes Act 1988 Sch 10 para 3A(1) (added by the Finance Act 1994 s 100(1),(3)).

11 Income and Corporation Taxes Act 1988 Sch 10 para 3A(2) (added by the Finance Act 1994 s 100(1),(3); amended by the Pensions Act 1995 s 126, Sch 4 para 12(c)).

12 For the meaning of 'period of retention' see para 1529 note 18 ante.

13 Ie under the Income and Corporation Taxes Act 1988 ss 185, 187, Sch 9 para 4: see para 1534 ante.

14 Ibid Sch 10 para 3A(3) (added by the Finance Act 1994 s 100(1),(3)).

15 Ie the Income and Corporation Taxes Act 1988 Sch 10 para 3A(3) (as added): see supra.

16 Ibid Sch 10 para 3A(4) (added by the Finance Act 1994 s 100(1),(3); amended by the Pensions Act 1995 Sch 4 para 12(d)).

17 Income and Corporation Taxes Act 1988 Sch 10 para 3A(5) (added by the Finance Act 1994 s 100(1),(3)). For the meaning of 'specified age' see para 1538 note 3 ante.

1565. Capital receipts. Money or money's worth is not a capital receipt[1] if or, as the case may be, to the extent that:

(1) it constitutes income in the hands of the recipient for the purposes of income tax; or

(2) it consists of the proceeds of a disposal[2]; or

(3) it consists of new shares[3].

If, pursuant to a direction given by or on behalf of the participant[4] or any person in whom the beneficial interest in the participant's shares[5] is for the time being vested, the trustees dispose of some of the rights arising under a rights issue[6] and use the proceeds of that disposal to exercise other such rights, the money or money's worth which constitutes the proceeds of that disposal is not[7] a capital receipt[8].

If the amount or value of a capital receipt would otherwise exceed the sum which, immediately before the entitlement to the receipt arose, was the locked-in value[9] of the shares to which the receipt is referable, the receipt is treated[10] as if the amount or value of the receipt were equal to that locked-in value[11].

1 Ie for the purposes of the Income and Corporation Taxes Act 1988 s 186(3): see para 1529 ante.
2 Ie a disposal falling within ibid s 186(4): see para 1529 ante.
3 Ibid s 186(13), Sch 10 para 4(1). For these purposes, 'new shares' has the meaning given in Sch 10 para 5 (as amended) (see para 1566 note 10 post): Sch 10 para 4(1).
4 For the meaning of 'participant' see para 1529 note 1 ante.
5 For the meaning of 'participant's shares' see para 1529 note 11 ante.
6 Ie as defined in the Income and Corporation Taxes Act 1988 s 186(8): see para 1529 ante.
7 See note 1 supra.
8 Income and Corporation Taxes Act 1988 Sch 10 para 4(2).
9 For the meaning of 'locked-in value' see para 1529 note 17 ante.
10 Ie the Income and Corporation Taxes Act 1988 s 186(3) does not apply in relation to a capital receipt if the entitlement to it arises after the death of the participant to whose shares it is referable: Sch 10 para 4(4).
11 Ibid Sch 10 para 4(3).

1566. Company reconstructions. The following provisions apply where there occurs in relation to any of a participant's shares[1] ('the original holding') a transaction which results in a new holding[2] being equated with the original holding for the purposes of capital gains tax; and any such transaction is referred to below as a 'company reconstruction'[3].

Where an issue of shares of any of the following descriptions (in respect of which a charge to income tax arises) is made as part of a company reconstruction, those shares are treated for these purposes as not forming part of the new holding, that is to say:

(1) certain redeemable shares or securities[4];
(2) share capital issued in specified circumstances[5]; and
(3) certain other[6] share capital[7].

In relation to a profit sharing scheme[8], references in the relevant provisions[9] to a participant's shares are to be construed, after the time of the company reconstruction, as being or, as the case may be, as including references to any new shares[10]; and, for the purposes of the relevant provisions:

(a) a company reconstruction is treated as not involving a disposal of shares comprised in the original holding;
(b) the date on which any new shares are to be treated as having been appropriated to the participant is that on which the corresponding shares[11] were appropriated; and
(c) the specified conditions[12] are treated as fulfilled with respect to any new shares if they were, or were treated as, fulfilled with respect to the corresponding shares[13].

For the purposes of the relevant provisions, if, as part of a company reconstruction, trustees[14] become entitled to a capital receipt[15], their entitlement to the capital receipt is to be taken to arise before the new holding comes into being and, in certain circumstances[16] before the date on which the locked-in value of any shares comprised in the original holding falls to be ascertained[17].

The above provisions[18] apply where there occurs in relation to any of a participant's shares ('the original holding') a relevant transaction[19] which would result in a new holding being equated with the original holding for the purposes of capital gains tax, were it not for the fact that what would be the new holding consists of or includes a qualifying corporate bond[20].

1 For the meaning of 'participant's shares' see para 1529 note 11 ante.
2 In the context of a new holding, any reference to shares includes securities and rights of any description which form part of the new holding for the purposes of the Taxation of Chargeable Gains Act 1992 Pt IV Ch II (ss 126–140D (as amended): see CAPITAL GAINS TAXATION vol 5(1) (Reissue) para 252 et seq): Income and Corporation Taxes Act 1988 Sch 10 para 5(7) (amended by the Taxation of Chargeable Gains Act 1992 s 290(1), Sch 10 para 14(1),(58)). In relation to shares comprised in the new holding, the Income and Corporation Taxes Act 1988 s 186(5) (see para 1529 ante) applies as if the references therein to the initial market value of the shares were references to their locked-in value immediately after the company reconstruction, which is to be determined as follows: (1) ascertain the aggregate amount of locked-in value immediately before the reconstruction of those shares comprised in the original holding which had at that time the same locked-in value; and (2) distribute that amount pro rata among (a) such of those shares as remains in the new holding; and (b) any new shares in relation to which those shares are the corresponding shares, according to their market value immediately after the date of their reconstruction; and s 186(5)(a) applies only to capital receipts after the date of the reconstruction: Sch 10 para 5(5).
3 Ibid Sch 10 para 5(1),(3).
4 Ie redeemable shares or securities issued as mentioned in ibid s 209(2)(c): see INCOME TAXATION vol 23 (Reissue) para 881.
5 Ie in circumstances such that ibid s 210(1) applies: see INCOME TAXATION vol 23 (Reissue) para 884.
6 Ie share capital to which ibid s 249 (as amended) applies: see INCOME TAXATION vol 23 (Reissue) para 934 et seq.
7 Ibid Sch 10 para 5(2).
8 As to profit sharing schemes see para 1529 ante.
9 For the meaning of 'the relevant provisions' see para 1529 note 21 ante.
10 For these purposes, 'new shares' means shares comprised in the new holding which were issued in respect of, or otherwise represent, shares comprised in the original holding: Income and Corporation Taxes Act 1988 Sch 10 para 5(3).
11 For these purposes, 'corresponding shares', in relation to any new shares, means those shares in respect of which the new shares are issued or which the new shares otherwise represent: ibid Sch 10 para 5(3).
12 Ie the conditions in ibid Sch 9 paras 10–12, 14 (as amended): see para 1539 ante.
13 Ibid Sch 10 para 5(4). Schedule 10 para 5(4) is subject to Sch 10 para 5(5)–(7) (as amended) (see infra): Sch 10 para 5(4).
14 For the meaning of 'the trustees' see para 1529 note 1 ante.
15 For the meaning of 'capital receipt' see para 1529 ante.
16 Ie for the purposes of the Income and Corporation Taxes Act 1988 Sch 10 para 5(5): see supra.
17 Ibid Sch 10 para 5(6).
18 Ie ibid Sch 10 para 5(2)–(6): see supra.
19 For these purposes, 'relevant transaction' means a transaction mentioned in the Taxation of Chargeable Gains Act 1992 Pt IV Ch II (ss 126–140D) (as amended) (see CAPITAL GAINS TAXATION vol 5(1) para 252 et seq): Income and Corporation Taxes Act 1988 Sch 10 para 5A(1) (added by the Finance Act 1994 s 101(1),(4),(8)).
20 Income and Corporation Taxes Act 1988 Sch 10 para 5A(1) (as added: see note 19 supra). For these purposes, 'qualifying corporate bond' is to be construed in accordance with the Taxation of Chargeable Gains Act 1992 s 117 (as amended) (see CAPITAL GAINS TAXATION vol 5(1) (Reissue) para 248): Income and Corporation Taxes Act 1988 Sch 10 para 5A(3) (added by the Finance Act 1994 s 101(1),(4),(8)).
   In the Income and Corporation Taxes Act 1988 Sch 10 para 5(2)–(6) (see supra) as applied by Sch 10 para 5A (as added): (1) references to a company reconstruction are to the transaction referred to in Sch 10 para 5A(1) (as added); (2) references to the new holding are to what would be the new holding were it not for the fact mentioned in Sch 10 para 5A(1) (as added); (3) references to the original holding are to be construed in accordance with Sch 10 para 5A(1) (as added), and not Sch 10 para 5(1); (4) references to shares, in the context of the new holding, include securities and rights of any description which form part of the new holding: Sch 10 para 5A(2) (added by the Finance Act 1994 s 101(1),(4),(8)).

1567. Excess or unauthorised shares. The following provisions apply in any case where:

(1) the total amount of the initial market value[1] of all the shares[2] which are appropriated to an individual in any one year of assessment, whether under a single approved[3] profit sharing scheme[4] or under two or more such schemes, exceeds the relevant amount[5]; or

(2) the trustees[6] of an approved profit sharing scheme appropriate shares to an individual at a time when he is ineligible[7] to participate in the scheme[8].

For the purposes of any of the relevant provisions[9] charging an individual to income tax under Schedule E[10] by reason of the occurrence of an event relating to any of his shares:

(a) the appropriate percentage[11] in relation to excess[12] or unauthorised[13] shares is in every case 100%; and

(b) the event is treated[14] as relating to shares which are not excess or unauthorised shares before shares which are[15].

Excess or unauthorised shares which have not been disposed of before the release date[16] or, if it is earlier, the date of the death of the participant[17] whose shares they are, are treated for the purposes of the relevant provisions as having been disposed of by the trustees immediately before the release date or, as the case may require, the date of the participant's death, for a consideration equal to their market value[18] at that time[19].

The locked-in value[20] at any time of any excess or unauthorised shares is their market value at that time[21].

Where there has been a company reconstruction[22], a new share[23] is treated as an excess or unauthorised share if the corresponding share[24] or, if there was more than one corresponding share, each of them was an excess or unauthorised share[25].

1 For the meaning of 'initial market value' see para 1529 note 17 ante.
2 For the meaning of 'shares' see para 1528 note 2 ante.
3 For the meaning of 'approved' see para 1528 note 1 ante.
4 As to profit sharing schemes see para 1529 ante.
5 For these purposes, if a number of shares is appropriated to an individual at the same time under two or more approved profit sharing schemes, the same proportion of the shares appropriated at that time under each scheme is regarded as being appropriated before the relevant amount is exceeded: Income and Corporation Taxes Act 1988 s 186(13), Sch 10 para 6(3). For the meaning of 'relevant amount' see para 1554 note 12 ante.
6 For the meaning of 'the trustees' see para 1529 note 1 ante.
7 Ie by virtue of the Income and Corporation Taxes Act 1988 ss 185–187 (as amended), Sch 9 para 8 (see para 1537 ante) or Sch 9 para 35 (see para 1556 ante).
8 Ibid Sch 10 para 6(1).
9 For the meaning of 'the relevant provisions' see para 1529 note 21 ante.
10 Ie under the Income and Corporation Taxes Act 1988 s 19(1), Schedule E (as amended): see INCOME TAXATION vol 23 (Reissue) para 654 et seq.
11 For the meaning of 'appropriate percentage' see para 1529 note 13 ante.
12 For these purposes, 'excess shares' means any share which caused the relevant amount to be exceeded and any share appropriated after that amount was exceeded: Income and Corporation Taxes Act 1988 Sch 10 para 6(2).
13 For these purposes, 'unauthorised shares' means any share appropriated as mentioned in ibid Sch 10 para 6(1)(b) (see supra): Sch 10 para 6(2).
14 Ie without prejudice to ibid s 187(8): see para 1529 note 18 ante.
15 Ibid Sch 10 para 6(4).
16 For the meaning of 'release date' see para 1529 note 12 ante.
17 For the meaning of 'participant' see para 1529 note 1 ante.
18 For the meaning of 'market value' see para 1528 note 10 ante.
19 Income and Corporation Taxes Act 1988 Sch 10 para 6(5).

20 For the meaning of 'locked-in value' see para 1529 note 17 ante.
21 Income and Corporation Taxes Act 1988 Sch 10 para 6(6).
22 Ie to which ibid Sch 10 para 5 (as amended) applies: see para 1566 ante.
23 Ie within the meaning of ibid Sch 10 para 5: see para 1566 note 10 ante.
24 Ie within the meaning of ibid Sch 10 para 5: see para 1566 note 11 ante.
25 Ibid Sch 10 para 6(7).

1568. PAYE deduction of tax. Where the trustees[1] of an approved[2] profit sharing scheme[3] receive a sum of money which constitutes, or forms part of, the proceeds of a disposal of shares[4] or a capital receipt[5] in respect of which a participant[6] in the scheme[7] is chargeable to income tax[8], the trustees must pay out of that sum of money to the company[9] an amount equal to that on which income tax is so payable; and the company must then pay over that amount to the participant but, in so doing, must make a PAYE deduction[10].

Where a participant disposes of his beneficial interest in any of his shares to the trustees of the scheme and the trustees are deemed[11] to have disposed of the shares in question, these provisions apply as if the consideration payable by the trustees to the participant on the disposal had been received by the trustees as the proceeds of disposal[12] of shares[13].

The company to which the payment mentioned above[14] is to be made is the company:

(1) of which the participant is an employee or director at the time the trustees receive the sum of money referred to above[15]; and

(2) whose employees are at that time eligible, subject to the terms of the scheme and the statutory provisions[16], to be participants in the approved profit sharing scheme concerned;

and, if there is more than one company which falls within heads (1) and (2) above, such one of those companies as the Commissioners of Inland Revenue may direct[17].

Where the trustees of an approved profit sharing scheme receive a sum of money to which the above provisions[18] apply but:

(a) there is no company which falls within heads (1) and (2) above; or

(b) the commissioners are of opinion that it is impracticable for the company which falls within heads (1) and (2) above (or, as the case may be, any of them) to make a PAYE deduction and accordingly direct that this provision shall apply,

then, in paying over to the participant the proceeds of the disposal or the capital receipt, the trustees must make a PAYE deduction in respect of an amount equal to that on which income tax is payable as mentioned above[19] as if the participant were a former employee of the trustees[20].

Where the trustees of an approved profit sharing scheme receive a sum of money to which the above provisions[21] apply and the commissioners direct that this provision shall apply:

(i) the trustees must make the payment mentioned above[22] to the company specified in the commisioners' direction; and

(ii) that company must pay over that amount to the participant but, in so doing, must make a PAYE deduction, and for that purpose, if the participant is not an employee of that company, he is to be treated as a former employee;

but no such direction must be given except with the consent of the trustees, the company or companies (if any) specified above[23] and the company specified in the direction[24].

Where any person is so required to make a PAYE deduction in respect of any amount, that amount is to be treated[25] as an amount of income payable to the recipient and assessable to income tax under Schedule E[26] and accordingly such deduction must be made as is[27] required[28].

Where, in connection with a transfer of a participant's shares[29], the trustees receive a sum[30], that sum is to be treated for the purpose of the Income Tax Acts[31] as a sum deducted by the trustees pursuant to a requirement to make a PAYE deduction[32] and as referable to the income tax to which, as a result of the transfer, the participant is[33] chargeable[34].

Unless the commisioners otherwise direct, in the application of these provisions to a sum of money which constitutes or forms part of the proceeds of a disposal of, or a capital receipt referable to, excess or unauthorised shares[35], the trustees must determine the amount of the payment mentioned above[36] or, as the case may be, the amount of PAYE deduction to be made[37] as if the shares were not excess or unauthorised shares[38].

1 For the meaning of 'the trustees' see para 1529 note 1 ante.
2 For the meaning of 'approved' see para 1528 note 1 ante.
3 As to profit sharing schemes see para 1529 ante.
4 Ie falling within the Income and Corporation Taxes Act 1988 s 186(4): see para 1529 ante.
5 For the meaning of 'capital receipt' see para 1529 ante.
6 For the meaning of 'participant' see para 1529 note 1 ante.
7 For the meaning of 'scheme' see para 1531 note 3 ante.
8 Ie under the Income and Corporation Taxes Act 1988 s 19(1), Schedule E (as amended) (see INCOME TAXATION vol 23 (Reissue) para 654 et seq) in accordance with s 186 (as amended) (see para 1529 ante).
9 Ie the company specified in ibid s 186(13), Sch 10 para 7(3): see infra.
10 Ibid Sch 10 para 7(1).
11 Ie by virtue of ibid s 186(9): see para 1529 ante.
12 Ie disposal of shares falling within ibid s 186(4): see para 1529 ante.
13 Ibid Sch 10 para 7(2).
14 Ie mentioned in ibid Sch 10 para 7(1): see supra.
15 Ie referred to in ibid Sch 10 para 7(1).
16 Ie the provisions of ibid ss 185-187, Sch 9 (as amended): see para 1531 et seq ante.
17 Ibid Sch 10 para 7(3).
18 Ie ibid Sch 10 para 7(1).
19 Ie as mentioned in ibid Sch 10 para 7(1).
20 Ibid Sch 10 para 7(4).
21 See note 18 supra.
22 See note 14 supra.
23 See note 9 supra.
24 Income and Corporation Taxes Act 1988 Sch 10 para 7(5).
25 Ie for the purposes of ibid s 203 (as amended) and any regulations made thereunder: see INCOME TAXATION vol 23 (Reissue) para 765.
26 Ie ibid s 19(1), Schedule E (as amended).
27 Ie as is required by any regulations made under ibid s 203 (as amended).
28 Ibid Sch 10 para 7(6).
29 Ie to which ibid Sch 9 para 2(2)(c) applies: see para 1532 ante. For the meaning of 'participant's shares' see para 1529 note 11 ante.
30 Ie such a sum as is referred to in ibid Sch 9 para 2(2)(c).
31 For the meaning of 'the Income Tax Acts' see para 1528 note 6 ante.
32 Ie under the Income and Corporation Taxes Act 1988 Sch 10 para 7(4): see supra.
33 Ie by virtue of ibid s 186(4).
34 Ibid Sch 10 para 7(7).
35 Ie within the meaning of ibid Sch 10 para 6: see para 1567 notes 12, 13 ante.
36 See note 14 supra.
37 See note 32 supra.
38 Income and Corporation Taxes Act 1988 Sch 10 para 7(8).

I. OLD STYLE SHARE OPTION SCHEMES

1569. Application of provisions. The following provisions[1] apply to any share option scheme[2] approved[3] by the Commissioners of Inland Revenue before 29 April 1996 in consequence of their being satisfied that the scheme[4] fulfils the statutory requirements[5]. The following provisions do not, however, apply to a share option scheme if, before the end of 1996, the grantor[6] gives notice to the commissioners that those provisions are not to apply[7]. Where a notice is so given to the commissioners, the scheme ceases to be approved with effect from the day on which the notice is given[8].

1   Ie the Finance Act 1996 s 114(9), Sch 16: see infra and paras 1570-1572 post.
2   As to share option schemes see para 1528 ante.
3   For these purposes, 'approved' has the same meaning as in the Income and Corporation Taxes Act 1988 s 187 (as amended) (see para 1528 note 1 ante): Finance Act 1996 Sch 16 para 5(1).
4   For these purposes, 'scheme' has the same meaning as in the Income and Corporation Taxes Act 1988 s 187 (as amended) (see para 1531 note 3 ante): Finance Act 1996 Sch 16 para 5(1).
5   Ibid Sch 16 para 1(1). The statutory requirements are the Income and Corporation Taxes Act 1988 ss 185-187, Sch 9 Pt IV (paras 27-29 (as amended): see paras 1551-1553 ante), as well as such requirements of Sch 9 Pt I (paras 1-6) (see paras 1531-1536 ante) and Sch 9 Pt II (paras 7-15 (as amended): see paras 1537-1540 ante) as apply in relation to the scheme: Finance Act 1996 Sch 16 para 1(1).
6   For these purposes, 'grantor' has the same meaning as in the Income and Corporation Taxes Act 1988 s 187 (as amended) (see para 1531 note 5 ante): Finance Act 1996 Sch 16 para 5(1).
7   Ibid Sch 16 para 1(2).
8   Ibid Sch 16 para 1(3).

1570. Limit on aggregate value of options. A share option scheme approved before 29 April 1996[1] has effect, notwithstanding anything included in it to the contrary, as if it provided that no person shall, on or after 29 April 1996, obtain rights under it which would, at the time they are obtained, cause the aggregate market value[2] of the shares[3] which that person may acquire in pursuance of rights obtained under the scheme or under any other share option scheme, not being a savings–related share option scheme[4], duly approved[5] and established by the grantor[6] or an associated company[7] of the grantor (and not exercised) to exceed or further exceed £30,000[8].

1   Ie a share option scheme to which the Finance Act 1996 s 114(9), Sch 16 applies: see para 1569 ante.
2   For these purposes, 'market value' has the same meaning as in the Income and Corporation Taxes Act 1988 s 187 (as amended) (see para 1528 note 9 ante): Finance Act 1996 Sch 16 para 5(1).
3   For these purposes, 'shares' has the same meaning as in the Income and Corporation Taxes Act 1988 s 187 (as amended) (see para 1528 note 2 ante): Finance Act 1996 Sch 16 para 5(1).
4   For these purposes, 'savings-related share option scheme' has the same meaning as in the Income and Corporation Taxes Act 1988 s 187 (as amended) (see para 1531 note 3 ante): Finance Act 1996 Sch 16 para 5(1).
5   Ie under the Income and Corporation Taxes Act 1988 ss 185-187, Sch 9 (as amended): see para 1531 et seq ante.
6   For the meaning of 'grantor' see para 1569 note 6 ante.
7   For these purposes, 'associated company' has the same meaning as in the Income and Corporation Taxes Act 1988 s 187 (as amended) (see para 1539 note 24 ante): Finance Act 1996 Sch 16 para 5(1).
8   Ibid Sch 16 para 2(1). The Income and Corporation Taxes Act 1988 Sch 9 para 28(3) (market value of shares to be calculated as at time when rights obtained etc: see para 1552 ante) has effect for the purposes of the Finance Act 1996 Sch 16 para 2(1) as it has effect for the purposes of the Income and Corporation Taxes Act 1988 Sch 9 para 28: Finance Act 1996 Sch 16 para 2(2).

1571. Price at which shares may be obtained. A share option scheme approved before 29 April 1996[1] has effect, notwithstanding anything in it to the contrary, as if it provided that the price at which scheme shares[2] may be acquired by the exercise of a right obtained, on or after 29 April 1996, under the scheme[3] must not be manifestly less than the market value[4] of shares[5] of the same class at that time or, if the Commissioners of Inland Revenue and the grantor[6] agree in writing, at such earlier time or times as may be provided in the agreement[7].

1   Ie a share option scheme to which the Finance Act 1996 s 114(9), Sch 16 applies: see para 1569 ante.
2   For these purposes, 'scheme shares' has the same meaning as in the Income and Corporation Taxes Act 1988 Sch 9 Pt IV (paras 27-29 (as amended): see paras 1551-1553 ante): Finance Act 1996 Sch 16 para 5(1).
3   For the meaning of 'scheme' see para 1569 note 4 ante.
4   For the meaning of 'market value' see para 1570 note 2 ante.
5   For the meaning of 'shares' see para 1570 note 3 ante.
6   For the meaning of 'grantor' see para 1569 note 6 ante.
7   Finance Act 1996 Sch 16 para 3.

1572. Commissioners' approval to alterations.   For the purposes of the statutory provisions under which the approval of the Commissioners of Inland Revenue is not to have effect from the date of any alteration in the scheme[1], the alterations made by the above provisions[2] in any scheme approved before 29 April 1996[3] are to be taken to have been approved by the commissioners before 29 April 1996[4].

1   Ie the Income and Corporation Taxes Act 1988 ss 185-187 (as amended), Sch 9 para 4: see para 1534 ante.
2   Ie the Finance Act 1996 s 114(9), Sch 16 paras 2, 3: see paras 1570, 1571 ante.
3   Ie a share option scheme to which ibid Sch 16 applies: see para 1569 ante.
4   Ibid Sch 16 para 4.

J. TAX CONSEQUENCES FOR COMPANY

1573. Costs of establishing share option or profit sharing schemes; relief. Where a company incurs expenditure on or after 1 April 1991 on establishing a share option scheme[1] which the Commissioners of Inland Revenue approve[2] and under which no employee or director obtains rights before such approval is given or a company incurs expenditure on establishing a profit sharing scheme[3] which the commissioners approve and under which the trustees acquire no shares before such approval is given, the expenditure may be deducted in computing for the purposes of Schedule D[4] the profits or gains[5] of a trade[6] carried on by the company[7].

In a case where:

(1)   the above provisions apply; and
(2)   the approval is given after the end of the period of nine months beginning with the day following the end of the period of account in which the expenditure is incurred,

then, for the purpose of applying the above provisions, the expenditure is to be treated as incurred in the period of account in which the approval is given, and not the period of account mentioned in head (2) above[8].

1   As to share option schemes see para 1528 ante.
2   For these purposes, references to approving are to approving under the Income and Corporation Taxes Act 1988 ss 185-187, Sch 9 (as amended) (see para 1531 et seq ante): s 84A(4) (added by the Finance Act 1988 s 42).
3   As to profit sharing schemes see para 1529 ante.

4 Ie the Income and Corporation Taxes Act 1988 s 18(1), Schedule D (as amended): see INCOME TAXATION vol 23 (Reissue) para 135.
5 For the meaning of 'profits or gains' see INCOME TAXATION vol 23 (Reissue) para 1 note 3.
6 For the meaning of 'trade' see INCOME TAXATION vol 23 (Reissue) para 152.
7 Income and Corporation Taxes Act 1988 s 84A(1),(2)(a),(5) (added by the Finance Act 1991 s 42). If the company is an investment company or a company in the case of which the Income and Corporation Taxes Act 1988 s 75 (as amended) (see INCOME TAXATION vol 23 (Reissue) para 1338) applies by virtue of s 76 (as amended) (see INCOME TAXATION vol 23 (Reissue) para 1361), any such sum is treated as expenses of management: s 84A(2)(b) (added by the Finance Act 1991 s 42).
8 Income and Corporation Taxes Act 1988 s 84A(3) (added by the Finance Act 1991 s 42).

1574. Share option schemes. Where:

(1) an option is granted on or after 16 March 1993;
(2) the option consists of a right to acquire shares in a body corporate and is obtained by an individual by reason of his office or employment as a director or employee of that or any other body corporate; and
(3) the statutory provisions relating to disposals and acquisitions being treated as made at market value[1] would otherwise apply for the purposes of calculating the consideration for the grant of the option,

both the grantor of the option and the person to whom the option is granted are treated for the purposes of the Taxation of Chargeable Gains Act 1992 as if those statutory provisions did not apply for the purposes of calculating the consideration and accordingly as if the amount or value of the consideration was its actual amount or value[2].

Where the option is granted wholly or partly in recognition of services or past services in any office or employment, the value of those services must not be taken into account in calculating the actual amount or value of the consideration[3].

1 Ie the Taxation of Chargeable Gains Act 1992 s 17(1): see CAPITAL GAINS TAXATION vol 5(1) (Reissue) para 40.
2 Ibid s 149A(1),(2) (added by the Finance Act 1993 s 104; amended by the Finance Act 1996 s 111(1)-(3)). The Finance Act 1996 s 111 has effect in relation to any right to acquire shares in a body corporate obtained on or after 28 November 1995 by an individual by reason of his office or employment as a director or employee of a body corporate: s 111(6).
3 Taxation of Chargeable Gains Act 1992 s 149A(3) (added by the Finance Act 1993 s 104).

1575. Payments to trustees of approved profit sharing schemes. Any sum expended in making a payment to the trustees of an approved profit sharing scheme[1] by a company which is in relation to that scheme the grantor[2] or a participating company[3] may be deducted in computing for the purposes of Schedule D[4] the profits or gains[5] of a trade[6] carried on by that company if, and only if, one of the following conditions is fulfilled[7]:

(1) that before the expiry of the relevant period[8] the sum in question is applied by the trustees[9] in the acquisition of shares for appropriation to individuals who are eligible to participate in the scheme by virtue of their being or having been employees or directors of the company making the payment; and
(2) that the sum is necessary to meet the reasonable expenses of the trustees in administering the scheme[10].

1 For these purposes, 'approved profit sharing scheme' means a profit sharing scheme approved under the Income and Corporation Taxes Act 1988 ss 185-187, Sch 9 (as amended) (see para 1531 et seq ante): s 85(5).
2 For these purposes, 'the grantor' has the meaning given by ibid Sch 9 para 1(3) (see para 1531 ante): s 85(5).

3 For these purposes, 'participating company' has the meaning given by ibid Sch 9 para 1(4) (see para 1531 note 8 ante): s 85(5).
4 Ie ibid s 18(1), Schedule D (as amended): see INCOME TAXATION vol 23 (Reissue) para 135.
5 For the meaning of 'profits or gains' see INCOME TAXATION vol 23 (Reissue) para 1 note 3.
6 For the meaning of 'trade' see INCOME TAXATION vol 23 (Reissue) para 152.
7 Income and Corporation Taxes Act 1988 s 85(1)(a). If the company is an investment company or a company in the case of which s 75 (as amended) (see INCOME TAXATION vol 23 (Reissue) para 1338) applies by virtue of s 76 (as amended) (see INCOME TAXATION vol 23 (Reissue) para 1361), any such sum is treated as expenses of management: s 85(1)(b).
8 For these purposes, 'the relevant period' means the period of nine months beginning on the day following the end of the period of account in which the sum in question is charged as an expense of the company incurring the expenditure or such longer period as the Commissioners of Inland Revenue may allow by notice in writing given to that company: ibid s 85(3).
9 For these purposes, the trustees of an approved profit sharing scheme are to be taken to apply sums paid to them in the order in which the sums are received by them: ibid s 85(4).
10 Ibid s 85(2).

(iv) Employee Share Ownership Trusts

A. IN GENERAL

1576. Tax relief. Where:

(1) a company expends a sum in making a payment by way of contribution to the trustees of a trust which is a qualifying employee share ownership trust[1] at the time the sum is expended;

(2) at that time the company or a company which it then controls[2] has employees who are eligible to benefit under the terms of the trust deed;

(3) at that time the company is resident in the United Kingdom;

(4) before the expiry of the expenditure period[3] the sum is expended by the trustees for one or more of the qualifying purposes[4]; and

(5) before the end of the claim period[5] a claim for relief under these provisions is made,

the sum may be deducted in computing for the purposes of Schedule D[6] the profits or gains of a trade carried on by the company[7].

For these purposes, the trustees of an employee share ownership trust are to be taken to expend sums paid to them in the order in which the sums are received by them, irrespective of the number of companies making payments[8].

1 For the meaning of 'qualifying employee share ownership trust' see para 1583 post.
2 For these purposes, the question whether one company is controlled by another is to be construed in accordance with the Income and Corporation Taxes Act 1988 s 840 (see INCOME TAXATION vol 23 (Reissue) para 849): Finance Act 1989 s 67(3).
3 For these purposes, the expenditure period is the period of nine months beginning with the day following the end of the period of account in which the sum is charged as an expense of the company, or such longer period as the Commissioners of Inland Revenue may allow by notice given to the company: ibid s 67(5).
4 For these purposes, each of the following is a qualifying purpose: (1) the acquisition of shares in the company which established the trust; (2) the repayment of sums borrowed; (3) the payment of interest on sums borrowed; (4) the payment of any sum to a person who is a beneficiary under the terms of the trust deed; (5) the meeting of expenses: ibid s 67(4).
5 For these purposes, the claim period is the period of two years beginning with the day following the end of the period of account in which the sum is charged as an expense of the company: ibid s 67(6).
6 Ie the Income and Corporation Taxes Act 1988 s 18(1), Schedule D (as amended): see INCOME TAXATION vol 23 (Reissue) para 135 et seq.
7 Finance Act 1989 s 67(1),(2)(a). If the company is an investment company or a company in the case of which the Income and Corporation Taxes Act 1988 s 75 (as amended) (see INCOME TAXATION vol 23

(Reissue) para 1338) applies by virtue of s 76 (as amended) (see INCOME TAXATION vol 23 (Reissue) para 1361), any such sum is treated as expenses of management: Finance Act 1989 s 67(2)(b).
8 Ibid s 67(7).

1577. Principal charges to tax. The following provisions apply where a chargeable event[1] occurs in relation to the trustees of an employee share ownership trust[2].

In such a case:

(1) the trustees are treated as receiving, when the event occurs, annual profits or gains whose amount is equal to the chargeable amount[3];

(2) the profits or gains are chargeable to tax under Case VI of Schedule D[4] for the year of assessment in which the event occurs; and

(3) the rate at which the tax is chargeable is the rate applicable to trusts for the year of assessment in which the event occurs[5].

If the whole or any part of the tax assessed on the trustees is not paid before the expiry of the period of six months beginning with the day on which the assessment becomes final and conclusive, a notice of liability to tax may be served on a qualifying company[6] and the tax or the part unpaid, as the case may be, is payable by the company on service of the notice[7]. Where a notice of liability is so served, any interest which is due on the tax or the part, as the case may be, and has not been paid by the trustees, and any interest accruing due on the tax or the part, as the case may be, after the date of service are payable by the company[8]. Where a notice of liability is so served and any amount payable by the company, whether on account of tax or interest, is not paid by the company before the expiry of the period of three months beginning with the date of service, the amount unpaid may be recovered from the trustees, without prejudice to the right to recover it instead from the company[9].

1 Ie within the meaning of the Finance Act 1989 s 69 (as amended): see para 1578 post.
2 Ibid s 68(1). As to employee share ownership trusts see para 1583 et seq post.
3 Ie within the meaning of ibid s 70 (as amended): see para 1579 post.
4 Ie the Income and Corporation Taxes Act 1988 s 18(2),(3), Schedule D, Case VI (as amended): see INCOME TAXATION vol 23 (Reissue) para 610 et seq.
5 Finance Act 1989 s 68(2) (amended by the Finance Act 1993 s 79, Sch 6 paras 20, 25(1)).
6 For these purposes, each of the following is a qualifying company: (1) the company which established the employee share ownership trust; (2) any company which, before it is sought to serve a notice of liability on it under the Finance Act 1989 s 68(3), has paid a sum to the trustees and the sum has been deducted as mentioned in s 67(2)(a) (see para 1576 ante) or treated as mentioned in s 67(2)(b) (see para 1576 ante): s 68(6),(7).
7 Ibid s 68(3).
8 Ibid s 68(4).
9 Ibid s 68(5).

1578. Chargeable events. Each of the following is a chargeable event[1] in relation to the trustees of an employee share ownership trust[2]:

(1) the transfer[3] of securities[4] by the trustees, if the transfer is not a qualifying transfer[5];

(2) the transfer of securities by the trustees to persons who are at the time of the transfer beneficiaries under the terms of the trust deed, if the terms on which the transfer is made are not qualifying terms[6];

(3) the retention[7] of securities by the trustees at the expiry of the qualifying period[8] beginning with the date on which they acquired[9] them;

(4) the expenditure of a sum by the trustees for a purpose other than a qualifying purpose[10].

If trustees agree to take a transfer of securities, they are treated[11] as becoming entitled to them when the agreement is made and not on a later transfer made pursuant to the agreement[12]. If trustees agree to transfer securities to another person, the other person is treated[13] as becoming entitled to them when the agreement is made and not on a later transfer made pursuant to the agreement[14].

1   Ie for the purposes of the Finance Act 1989 s 68 (as amended): see para 1577 ante.
2   As to employee share ownership trusts see para 1583 et seq post.
3   For these purposes, trustees transfer securities to another person when that other becomes entitled to them: Finance Act 1989 s 69(8)(b).
4   For these purposes, the following are securities: (1) shares; (2) debentures: ibid s 69(12).
5   For these purposes, a transfer is a qualifying transfer if it is made to a person who at the time of the transfer is a beneficiary under the terms of the trust deed: ibid s 69(2). A transfer is also a qualifying transfer if (1) it is made to the trustees of a scheme which at the time of the transfer is a profit sharing scheme approved under the Income and Corporation Taxes Act 1988 ss 185-187, Sch 9 (as amended) (see para 1531 et seq ante); and (2) it is made for a consideration which is not less than the price the securities might reasonably be expected to fetch on a sale in the open market: Finance Act 1989 s 69(3). A transfer is also a qualifying transfer if it is made by way of exchange in circumstances mentioned in the Capital Gains Tax Act 1979 s 85(1) (repealed) or the Taxation of Chargeable Gains Act 1992 s 135(1) (see CAPITAL GAINS TAXATION vol 5(1) (Reissue) para 258): Finance Act 1989 s 69(3A) (added by the Finance (No 2) Act 1992 s 36).
6   For these purposes, a transfer of securities is made on qualifying terms if (1) all the securities transferred at the same time, other than those transferred on a transfer such as is mentioned in the Finance Act 1989 s 69(4ZA) (as added) (see infra), are transferred on similar terms; (2) securities have been offered to all the persons who are beneficiaries under the terms of the trust deed by virtue of a rule which conforms with s 74, Sch 5 para 4(2),(3) or (4) (as amended) (see para 1589 post) when the transfer is made; and (3) securities are transferred to all such persons who have accepted: s 69(4) (amended by the Finance Act 1996 s 120(2),(3)). The fact that terms vary according to the levels of remuneration of beneficiaries, the length of their service, or similar factors, is not regarded as meaning that the terms are not similar: Finance Act 1989 s 69(6). A transfer of securities is also made on qualifying terms if (a) it is made to a person exercising a right to acquire shares; and (b) that right was obtained in accordance with the provisions of a savings-related share option scheme within the meaning of the Income and Corporation Taxes Act 1988 Sch 9 (as amended) (see para 1531 note 3 ante) which was established by, or by a company controlled by, the company which established the trust and which is approved under Sch 9 (as amended); and (c) that right is being exercised in accordance with the provisions of that scheme; and (d) the consideration for the transfer is payable to the trustees: Finance Act 1989 s 69(4ZA) (added by the Finance Act 1996 s 120(2),(4)). The Finance Act 1996 s 120 has effect in relation to trusts established on or after 29 April 1996: s 120(12).
7   For these purposes, trustees retain securities if they remain entitled to them: Finance Act 1989 s 69(8)(c). In ascertaining for these purposes whether particular securities are retained, securities acquired earlier by the trustees are treated as transferred by them before securities acquired by them later: s 69(7).
8   For these purposes, the qualifying period is (1) seven years, in the case of trusts established on or before 3 May 1994 (ie the day on which the Finance Act 1994 was passed); (2) 20 years, in the case of other trusts; and, for this purpose, a trust is established when the deed under which it is established is executed: Finance Act 1989 s 69(4A) (added by the Finance Act 1994 s 102, Sch 13 para 6).
9   For these purposes, trustees acquire securities when they become entitled to them, subject to the exceptions in the Finance Act 1989 s 69(9) (as amended): s 69(8)(a). The exceptions are these: (1) if securities are issued to trustees in exchange in circumstances mentioned in the Taxation of Chargeable Gains Act 1992 s 135(1), they are treated as having acquired them when they became entitled to the securities for which they are exchanged; (2) if trustees become entitled to securities as a result of a reorganisation, they are treated as having acquired them when they became entitled to the original shares which those securities represent, construing 'reorganisation' and 'original shares' in accordance with s 126 (see CAPITAL GAINS TAXATION vol 5(1) (Reissue) paras 255, 252 note 3 respectively): Finance Act 1989 s 69(9) (amended by the Taxation of Chargeable Gains Act 1992 s 290(1), Sch 10 para 19(1)).
10 Finance Act 1989 s 69(1) (amended by the Finance Act 1994 Sch 13 para 6). For these purposes, each of the following is a qualifying purpose: (1) the acquisition of shares in the company which established the trust; (2) the repayment of sums borrowed; (3) the payment of interest on sums borrowed; (4) the payment of any sum to a person who is a beneficiary under the terms of the trust deed; (5) the meeting of expenses: Finance Act 1989 s 69(5).

11 Ie for the purposes of ibid s 69 (as amended).
12 Ibid s 69(10).
13 Ie for the purposes of ibid s 69 (as amended).
14 Ibid s 69(11).

1579. Chargeable amounts. The following provisions have effect to determine[1] the chargeable amount[2]. If the chargeable event is[3]:

(1) the transfer of securities by the trustees, where the transfer is not a qualifying transfer;

(2) the transfer of securities by the trustees to persons who are at the time of the transfer beneficiaries under the terms of the trust deed, where the terms on which the transfer is made are not qualifying terms;

(3) the retention of securities by the trustees at the expiry of the qualifying period beginning with the date on which they acquired them,

the following rules apply:

(a) if the event constitutes a disposal of those securities by the trustees for the purposes of the Taxation of Chargeable Gains Act 1992, the chargeable amount is an amount equal to the sums allowable[4] under that Act;

(b) if the event does not constitute such a disposal, the chargeable amount is an amount equal to the sums which would be so allowable had the trustees made a disposal of the securities for the purposes of the 1992 Act at the time the chargeable event occurs[5].

If the chargeable event is the expenditure of a sum by the trustees for a purpose other than a qualifying purpose[6], the chargeable amount is an amount equal to the sum concerned[7].

1 Ie for the purposes of the Finance Act 1989 s 68 (as amended): see para 1577 ante.
2 Ibid s 70(1).
3 Ie if the chargeable event falls within ibid s 69(1)(a),(b) or (c): see para 1578 heads (1)-(3) ante.
4 Ie under the Taxation of Chargeable Gains Act 1992 s 38(1)(a): see CAPITAL GAINS TAXATION vol 5(1) (Reissue) para 32.
5 Finance Act 1989 s 70(2) (amended by the Taxation of Chargeable Gains Act 1992 s 290(1), Sch 10 para 19(2)).
6 Ie if the chargeable event falls within the Finance Act 1989 s 69(1)(d): see para 1578 head (4) ante.
7 Ibid s 70(3).

1580. Further charge to tax; borrowing. The following provisions apply where:

(1) a chargeable event[1] occurs in relation to the trustees of an employee share ownership trust[2];

(2) at the time the event occurs, anything is outstanding in respect of the principal of an amount or amounts borrowed at any time by the trustees; and

(3) the chargeable event is a specified[3] event[4].

If any of the total outstanding amount[5] is repaid[6] after the initial chargeable event[7] occurs, a further chargeable event occurs in relation to the trustees at the end of the year of assessment in which the repayment is made[8].

In such a case:

(a) the trustees are treated as receiving, when the further event occurs, annual profits or gains whose amount is equal to the chargeable amount[9];

(b) the profits or gains are chargeable to tax under Case VI of Schedule D[10] for the year of assessment at the end of which the further event occurs; and

(c) the rate at which the tax is chargeable is the rate applicable to trusts for the year of assessment at the end of which the further event occurs[11].

1 Ie within the meaning of the Finance Act 1989 s 69 (as amended): see para 1578 ante.

2 As to employee share ownership trusts see para 1583 et seq post.

3 Ie an event as regards which the Finance Act 1989 s 72(2)(b) applies: see para 1581 head (2) post.

4 Ibid s 71(1). Section 68(3)-(7) (see para 1577 ante) applies where tax is assessed by virtue of s 71 (as amended) as it applies where tax is assessed by virtue of s 68 (as amended): s 71(11).
In a case where (1) a chargeable event (within the meaning of s 69 (as amended)) occurs in relation to the trustees in circumstances mentioned in s 71(1); (2) a sum falls to be included in the total outstanding amount found for the time the event occurs; (3) another chargeable event (within the meaning of s 69 (as amended)) occurs in relation to the trustees in circumstances mentioned in s 71(1); and (4) the same sum or a part of it would otherwise fall to be included in the total outstanding amount found for the time the event occurs, the sum or part, as the case may be, must not be included in the total outstanding amount found for the time the other chargeable event occurs: s 71(9). For the meaning of 'the total outstanding amount' see note 5 infra.

5 For these purposes, 'the total outstanding amount' means the total amount outstanding, at the time the initial chargeable event occurs, in respect of the principal of an amount or amounts borrowed at any time by the trustees: ibid s 71(2)(b).

6 In ascertaining for these purposes whether a repayment is in respect of a particular amount, amounts borrowed earlier are taken to be repaid before amounts borrowed later: ibid s 71(10).

7 For these purposes, 'the initial chargeable event' means the event referred to in ibid s 71(1)(a) (see text head (1) supra): s 71(2)(a).

8 Ibid s 71(3).

9 For these purposes, the chargeable amount is an amount equal to the aggregate of the total outstanding amount repaid in the year of assessment: ibid s 71(5). However, in a case where s 72(2)(b) (see para 1581 post) had effect in the case of the initial chargeable event, for the purposes of s 71(4), the chargeable amount is an amount equal to the smaller of (1) the aggregate of the total outstanding amount repaid in the year of assessment; and (2) an amount found by applying the formula A-B-C, where A is the amount which would be the chargeable amount for thr initial chargeable event apart from s 72(2) (see para 1581 post), B is the chargeable amount for the initial chargeable event and C is the amount, if any, found under s 71(8): s 71(6),(7). If, before the further chargeable event occurs, one or more prior chargeable events have occurred in relation to the trustees by virtue of the prior repayment of any of the total outstanding amount found for the time the initial chargeable event occurs, the amount found under this provision is an amount equal to the chargeable amount for the prior chargeable event or to the aggregate of the chargeable amounts for the prior chargeable events, as the case may be: s 71(8).

10 Ie the Income and Corporation Taxes Act 1988 s 18(2),(3), Schedule D, Case VI (as amended): see INCOME TAXATION vol 23 (Reissue) para 610 et seq.

11 Finance Act 1989 s 71(4) (amended by the Finance Act 1993 s 79, Sch 6 paras 20, 25(1)).

1581. Limit on chargeable amount. If a chargeable event[1] ('the event in question') occurs in relation to the trustees of an employee share ownership trust[2], the following rules apply:

(1) the amount which would otherwise be the chargeable amount for the event in question must be aggregated, for the purposes of head (2) below, with the chargeable amounts for other chargeable events, if any, occurring in relation to the trustees before the event in question;

(2) if the amount which would otherwise be the chargeable amount for the event in question, or the aggregate found under head (1) above, if there is one, exceeds the deductible amount[3], the chargeable amount for the event in question is the amount it would otherwise be less an amount equal to the excess;

(3) the statutory provisions relating to chargeable amounts and the further charge to tax[4] have effect subject to head (2) above[5].

1 For these purposes, each of the following is a chargeable event in relation to the trustees of an employee share ownership trust: (1) an event which is a chargeable event by virtue of the Finance Act 1989 s 69 (as amended) (see para 1578 ante); (2) an event which is a chargeable event by virtue of s 71 (as amended) (see para 1580 ante): s 72(1).

2 As to employee share ownership trusts see para 1583 et seq post.
3 For these purposes, the deductible amount, as regards the event in question, is an amount equal to the total of the sums falling within the Finance Act 1989 s 72(4): s 72(3). A sum falls within this provision if it has been received by the trustees before the occurrence of the event in question and (1) it has been deducted as mentioned in s 67(2)(a) (see para 1576 ante), or treated as mentioned in s 67(2)(b) (see para 1576 ante), before the occurrence of that event; or (2) it would fall to be so deducted or treated if a claim for relief under s 67 (see para 1576 ante) had been made immediately before the occurrence of that event: s 72(4).
4 Ie ibid s 70(2),(3) (see para 1579 ante) and s 71(5) (see para 1580 ante).
5 Ibid s 72(2).

1582. Power to obtain information. An inspector of taxes may by notice in writing require a return to be made by the trustees of an employee share ownership trust[1] if they have at any time received a sum which has been deducted[2] in computing the profits or gains of a trade carried on by the company or treated[3] as expenses of management[4]. Where he requires such a return to be made, the inspector must specify the information to be contained in it[5]. The information which may be specified is information the inspector needs for the purposes of the statutory provisions relating to employee share ownership trusts[6] and may include information about:

(1) sums received, including sums borrowed, by the trustees;
(2) expenditure incurred by them;
(3) assets acquired by them;
(4) transfers of assets made by them[7].

The information which may be:

(a) required under head (1) above may include the persons from whom the sums were received[8];
(b) required under head (2) above may include the purpose of the expenditure and the persons receiving any sums[9];
(c) specified under head (3) above may include the persons from whom the assets were acquired and the consideration furnished by the trustees[10];
(d) included under head (4) above may include the persons to whom assets were transferred and the consideration furnished by them[11].

In a case where a sum has been deducted[12] in computing the profits or gains of a trade carried on by the company or treated[13] as expenses of management, the inspector must send to the trustees to whom the payment was made a certificate stating that a sum has been so deducted or so treated and what sum has been so deducted or so treated[14].

1 As to employee share ownership trusts see para 1583 et seq post.
2 Ie as mentioned in the Finance Act 1989 s 67(2)(a): see para 1576 ante.
3 Ie as mentioned in ibid s 67(2)(b): see para 1576 ante.
4 Ibid s 73(1). As to the penalty for non-compliance see INCOME TAXATION vol 23 (Reissue) para 1638.
5 Ibid s 73(2).
6 Ie ibid ss 68–72 (as amended): see para 1576 et seq ante.
7 Ibid s 73(3).
8 Ibid s 73(4).
9 Ibid s 73(5).
10 Ibid s 73(6).
11 Ibid s 73(7).
12 See note 1 supra.
13 See note 2 supra.
14 Finance Act 1989 s 73(8).

B. NATURE OF TRUST

1583. Qualifying trusts. A trust is a qualifying employee share ownership trust at the time it is established if the specified conditions[1] are satisfied in relation to the trust at that time[2].

1 Ie the conditions set out in the Finance Act 1989 s 74, Sch 5 paras 2-11 (as amended): see para 1584 et seq post.
2 Ibid Sch 5 para 1. As to the establishment of the trust see para 1584 post.

1584. Establishment of trust. The trust must be established under a deed ('the trust deed')[1]; and it must be established by a company ('the founding company') which, at the time the trust is established, is resident in the United Kingdom and not controlled[2] by another company[3]. A trust is established when the deed under which it is established is executed[4].

1 Finance Act 1989 s 74, Sch 5 para 2(1).
2 For these purposes, the question whether one company is controlled by another is to be construed in accordance with the Income and Corporation Taxes Act 1988 s 840 (see INCOME TAXATION vol 23 (Reissue) para 849): Finance Act 1989 Sch 5 para 15.
3 Ibid Sch 5 para 2(2).
4 Ibid Sch 5 para 17 (added by the Finance Act 1994 s 102, Sch 13 paras 1, 8).

1585. Trustees of a trust established on or before 3 May 1994. The trust deed[1] must:
(1) provide for the establishment of a body of trustees[2];
(2) appoint the initial trustees, contain rules for the retirement and removal of trustees and contain rules for the appointment of replacement and additional trustees[3];
(3) provide that at any time while the trust subsists ('the relevant time'):
   (a) the number of trustees must not be less than three;
   (b) all the trustees must be resident in the United Kingdom;
   (c) the trustees must include one person who is a trust corporation, a solicitor[4], or a member of such other professional body as the Commissioners of Inland Revenue may from time to time allow for these purposes;
   (d) most of the trustees must be persons who are not and have never been directors of any company which falls within the founding company's group[5] at the relevant time;
   (e) most of the trustees must be persons who are employees of companies which fall within the founding company's group at the relevant time, and who do not have and have never had a material interest[6] in any such company;
   (f) the trustees falling within head (e) above must, before being appointed as trustees, have been selected by a majority of the employees of the companies falling within the founding company's group at the time of the selection or by persons elected to represent those employees[7].
The above provisions apply in relation to trusts established on or before 3 May 1994[8].

1 For the meaning of 'the trust deed' see para 1584 ante.
2 Finance Act 1989 s 74, Sch 5 para 3(1).

3 Ibid Sch 5 para 3(2).
4 For these purposes, the reference to a solicitor includes a body corporate recognised by the Law Society under the Administration of Justice Act 1985 s 9 (as amended) (see SOLICITORS vol 44(1) (Reissue) para 383 et seq): Solicitors' Incorporated Practices Order 1991, SI 1991/2684, arts 2(1), 3, 4(a), Sch 1.
5 For these purposes, a company falls within the founding company's group at a particular time if (1) it is the founding company; or (2) it is at that time resident in the United Kingdom and controlled by the founding company: Finance Act 1989 Sch 5 para 3(4). For the meaning of 'the founding company' see para 1584 ante; and for the meaning of 'control' see para 1584 note 2 ante.
6 For these purposes, a person is treated as having a material interest in a company if he, either on his own or with one or more of his associates, or if any associate of his with or without other such associates (1) is the beneficial owner of, or able (directly or through the medium of other companies or by any other indirect means) to control, more than 5% of the ordinary share capital of the company; or (2) possesses, or is entitled to acquire, such rights as would, in the event of the winding up of the company or in any other circumstances, give an entitlement to receive more than 5% of the assets which would then be available for distribution among the participators: ibid Sch 5 para 16(1). 'Associate' has the same meaning as in the Income and Corporation Taxes Act 1988 s 417(3),(4) (as amended) (see INCOME TAXATION vol 23 (Reissue) para 1298) but subject to the Finance Act 1989 Sch 5 para 16(3); 'control' has the meaning given by the Income and Corporation Taxes Act 1988 s 840 (see INCOME TAXATION vol 23 (Reissue) para 849); and 'participator' has the same meaning as in Pt XI (ss 414–422 (as amended): see INCOME TAXATION vol 23 (Reissue) para 1296): Finance Act 1989 Sch 5 para 16(2). Where a person has an interest in shares or obligations of the company as a beneficiary of an employee benefit trust, the trustees are not regarded as associates of his by reason only of that interest unless Sch 5 para 16(5) applies in relation to him: Sch 5 para 16(3). In Sch 5 para 16(3) 'employee benefit trust' has the same meaning as in the Income and Corporation Taxes Act 1988 s 176(9), Sch 8 para 7 (as amended) (see INCOME TAXATION vol 23 (Reissue) para 1193 note 7), except that in its application for this purpose Sch 8 para 7(5)(b) has effect as if it referred to 27 July 1989 (ie the day on which the Finance Act 1989 was passed) instead of to 14 March 1989: Sch 5 para 16(4). This provision applies in relation to a person if at any time on or after 27 July 1989 (a) he, either on his own or with any one or more of his associates; or (b) any associate of his, with or without other such associates, has been the beneficial owner of, or able (directly or through the medium of other companies or by any other indirect means) to control, more than 5% of the ordinary share capital of the company: Sch 5 para 16(5). The Income and Corporation Taxes Act 1988 Sch 8 para 7(9)–(12) (as added) (see INCOME TAXATION vol 23 (Reissue) para 1193) applies for the purposes of the Finance Act 1989 Sch 5 para 16(5) as it applies for the purposes of the Income and Corporation Taxes Act 1988 Sch 8 para 7: Finance Act 1989 Sch 5 para 16(6).
7 Ibid Sch 5 para 3(3).
8 Ibid Sch 5 para 3(5) (added by the Finance Act 1994 s 102, Sch 13 paras 1, 2).

1586. Trusts established after 3 May 1994. Where a trust is established after 3 May 1994, the trust deed[1] must make provision as mentioned in one of heads (1) to (3) below:

(1) provision for the establishment of a body of trustees and complying with the statutory provisions[2];

(2) provision for the establishment of a body of trustees and complying with the statutory provisions[3];

(3) provision that at any time while the trust subsists there must be a single trustee[4].

1 For the meaning of 'the trust deed' see para 1584 ante.
2 Ie the Finance Act 1989 s 74, Sch 5 para 3(2)–(4): see para 1585 ante.
3 Ie ibid Sch 5 para 3B(2)–(9) (as added): see para 1587 post.
4 Ibid Sch 5 para 3A (added by the Finance Act 1994 s 102, Sch 13 paras 1, 3).

1587. Establishment of a body of trustees. The following are the provisions which must be complied with[1] in relation to the establishment of a body of trustees of a trust established after 3 May 1994[2].

The trust deed[3] must:

(1) appoint the initial trustees, contain rules for the retirement and removal of trustees and contain rules for the appointment of replacement and additional trustees[4];

(2) be so framed that at any time while the trust subsists the following conditions are fulfilled as regards the persons who are then trustees[5]:

(a) the number of trustees must not be less than three[6];

(b) all the trustees must be resident in the United Kingdom[7];

(c) the trustees must include at least one person who is a professional trustee[8] and at least two persons who are non-professional trustees[9];

(d) at least half of the non-professional trustees must have been, before being appointed as trustees, selected in accordance with the specified[10] procedure[11];

(e) all the trustees so selected must be persons who are employees of companies which fall within the founding company's group[12] at the relevant time, and who do not have and have never had a material interest[13] in any such company[14].

1 Ie under the Finance Act 1989 s 74, Sch 5 para 3A(b) (as added): see para 1586 head (2) ante.

2 Ibid Sch 5 para 3B(1) (added by the Finance Act 1994 s 102, Sch 13 paras 1, 3).

3 For the meaning of 'the trust deed' see para 1584 ante.

4 Finance Act 1989 Sch 5 para 3B(2) (added by the Finance Act 1994 Sch 13 paras 1, 3).

5 Finance Act 1989 Sch 5 para 3B(3) (added by the Finance Act 1994 Sch 13 paras 1, 3). In the Finance Act 1989 Sch 5 para 3B(4) (as added) (see infra) 'the relevant time' means that time: Sch 5 para 3B(3) (added by the Finance Act 1994 Sch 13 paras 1, 3).

6 Finance Act 1989 Sch 5 para 3B(4)(a) (added by the Finance Act 1994 Sch 13 paras 1, 3).

7 Finance Act 1989 Sch 5 para 3B(4)(b) (added by the Finance Act 1994 Sch 13 paras 1, 3).

8 For these purposes, a trustee is a professional trustee at a particular time if (1) the trustee is then a trust corporation, a solicitor, or a member of such other professional body as the Commissioners of Inland Revenue may at that time allow for these purposes; (2) the trustee is not then an employee or director of any company then falling within the founding company's group; and (3) the trustee meets the requirements of the Finance Act 1989 Sch 5 para 3B(6) (as added); and a trustee is a non-professional trustee at a particular time if the trustee is not then a professional trustee: Sch 5 para 3B(5) (added by the Finance Act 1994 Sch 13 paras 1, 3). A trustee meets the requirements of this provision if (a) he was appointed as an initial trustee and, before being appointed as trustee, was selected by, and only by, the persons who later became the non-professional initial trustees; or (b) he was appointed as replacement or additional trustee and, before being appointed as trustee, was selected by, and only by, the persons who were the non-professional trustees at the time of the selection: Finance Act 1989 Sch 5 para 3B(6) (added by the Finance Act 1994 Sch 13 paras 1, 3). As to when a company falls within the founding company's group see note 12 infra.

9 Finance Act 1989 Sch 5 para 3B(4)(c) (added by the Finance Act 1994 Sch 13 paras 1, 3).

10 Trustees are selected in accordance with this provision if the process of selection is one under which (1) all the persons who are employees of the companies which fall within the founding company's group at the time of the selection, and who do not have and have never had a material interest in any such company, are, so far as is reasonably practicable, given the opportunity to stand for selection; (2) all the employees of the companies falling within the founding company's group at the time of the selection are, so far as is reasonably practicable, given the opportunity to vote; and (3) persons gaining more votes are preferred to those gaining less: Finance Act 1989 Sch 5 para 3B(7) (added by the Finance Act 1994 Sch 13 paras 1, 3). Trustees are selected in accordance with this provision if they are selected by persons elected to represent the employees of the companies falling within the founding company's group at the time of the selection: Finance Act 1989 Sch 5 para 3B(8) (added by the Finance Act 1994 Sch 13 paras 1, 3). As to when a company falls within the founding company's group see note 12 infra.

11 Finance Act 1989 Sch 5 para 3B(4)(d) (added by the Finance Act 1994 Sch 13 paras 1, 3).

12 For these purposes, a company falls within the founding company's group at a particular time if (1) it is at that time resident in the United Kingdom; and (2) it is the founding company or it is at that time controlled by the founding company: Finance Act 1989 Sch 5 para 3B(9) (added by the Finance Act 1994 Sch 13 paras 1, 3). For the meaning of 'the founding company' see para 1584 ante.

13 For the meaning of 'material interest' see para 1585 note 6 ante.
14 Finance Act 1989 Sch 5 para 3B(4)(e) (added by the Finance Act 1994 Sch 13 paras 1, 3).

1588. Single trustee. The following provisions apply where the trust deed[1] provides that, at any time while the trust subsists, there must be a single trustee[2].

The trust deed must:

(1) be so framed that at any time while the trust subsists the trustee is a company which at that time is resident in the United Kingdom and controlled[3] by the founding company[4], appoint the initial trustee and contain rules for the removal of any trustee and for the appointment of a replacement trustee[5];

(2) be so framed that, at any time while the trust subsists, the company which is then the trustee is a company so constituted that the following conditions are then fulfilled as regards the persons who are then directors of the company[6]:

(a) the number of trustees must be not less than three[7];

(b) all the directors must be resident in the United Kingdom[8];

(c) the directors must include at least one person who is a professional director[9] and at least two persons who are non-professional directors[10];

(d) at least half of the non-professional directors must have been, before being appointed as directors, selected in accordance with the specified[11] procedure[12];

(e) all the directors so selected must be persons who are employees of companies which fall within the founding company's group[13] at the relevant time, and who do not have and have never had a material interest[14] in any such company[15].

1 For the meaning of 'the trust deed' see para 1584 ante.
2 Finance Act 1989 s 74, Sch 5 para 3C(1) (added by the Finance Act 1994 s 102, Sch 13 paras 1, 3).
3 For the meaning of 'control' see para 1584 note 2 ante.
4 For the meaning of 'the founding company' see para 1584 ante.
5 Finance Act 1989 Sch 5 para 3C(2) (added by the Finance Act 1994 Sch 13 paras 1, 3).
6 Finance Act 1989 Sch 5 para 3C(3) (added by the Finance Act 1994 Sch 13 paras 1, 3). In the Finance Act 1989 Sch 5 para 3C(4) (as added) (see infra) 'the relevant time' is that time and 'the trust company' is that company (sic): Sch 5 para 3C(3) (as so added).
7 Ibid Sch 5 para 3C(4)(a) (added by the Finance Act 1994 Sch 13 paras 1, 3).
8 Finance Act 1989 Sch 5 para 3C(4)(b) (added by the Finance Act 1994 Sch 13 paras 1, 3).
9 For these purposes, a director is a professional director at a particular time if (1) the director is then a solicitor or a member of such other professional body as the Commissioners of Inland Revenue may at that time allow for these purposes; (2) the director is not then an employee of any company then falling within the founding company's group; (3) the director is not then a director of any such company, other than the trust company; and (4) the director meets the requirements of the Finance Act 1989 Sch 5 para 3C(6) (as added); and a director is a non-professional director at a particular time if the director is not then a professional director: Sch 5 para 3C(5) (added by the Finance Act 1994 Sch 13 paras 1, 3). A director meets the requirements of this provision if (a) he was appointed as an initial director and, before being appointed as director, was selected by, and only by, the persons who later became the non-professional initial directors; or (b) he was appointed as a replacement or additional director and, before being appointed as director, was selected by, and only by, the persons who were the non-professional directors at the time of the selection: Finance Act 1989 Sch 5 para 3C(6) (added by the Finance Act 1994 Sch 13 paras 1, 3).
10 Finance Act 1989 Sch 5 para 3C(4)(c) (added by the Finance Act 1994 Sch 13 paras 1, 3).
11 Directors are selected in accordance with this provision if the process of selection is one under which (1) all the persons who are employees of the companies which fall within the founding company's group at the time of the selection, and who do not have and have never had a material interest in any such company, are, so far as is reasonably practicable, given the opportunity to stand for election; (2) all the employees of the companies falling within the founding company's group at the time of the selection are, so far as is reasonably practicable, given the opportunity to vote; and (3) persons gaining more votes are preferred to those gaining less: Finance Act 1989 Sch 5 para 3C(7) (added by the Finance Act 1994

Sch 13 paras 1, 3). Directors are selected in accordance with this provision if they are selected by persons elected to represent the employees of the companies falling within the founding company's group at the time of the selection: Finance Act 1989 Sch 5 para 3C(8) (added by the Finance Act 1994 Sch 13 paras 1, 3). As to when a company falls within the founding company's group see note 13 infra.

12 Finance Act 1989 Sch 5 para 3C(4)(d) (added by the Finance Act 1994 Sch 13 paras 1, 3).

13 For these purposes, a company falls within the founding company's group at a particular time if it is at that time resident in the United Kingdom and it is the founding company or it is at that time controlled by the founding company: Finance Act 1989 Sch 5 para 3C(9) (added by the Finance Act 1994 Sch 13 paras 1, 3).

14 For the meaning of 'material interest' see para 1585 note 6 ante.

15 Finance Act 1989 Sch 5 para 3C(4)(e) (added by the Finance Act 1994 Sch 13 paras 1, 3).

1589. Beneficiaries. The trust deed[1] must contain provision as to the beneficiaries under the trust, in accordance with the following rules[2].

The trust deed:

(1) must provide that a person is a beneficiary at a particular time ('the relevant time') if:

    (a) he is at the relevant time an employee or director of a company which at that time falls within the founding company's group[3];

    (b) at each given time in a qualifying period[4] he was an employee or director of a company falling within the founding company's group at that given time; and

    (c) in the case of a director, at that given time he worked as a director of the company concerned at the rate of at least 20 hours a week, ignoring such matters as holidays and sickness[5];

(2) may provide that a person is a beneficiary at a given time if at that time he is eligible to participate in a savings–related share option scheme[6] which was established by a company within the founding group and which is approved[7];

(3) may provide that a person is a beneficiary at a particular time ('the relevant time') if:

    (a) he has at each given time in a qualifying period[8] been an employee or director of a company falling within the founding company's group at that given time;

    (b) he has ceased to be an employee or director of the company or the company has ceased to fall within that group; and

    (c) at the relevant time a period of not more than 18 months has elapsed since he so ceased or the company so ceased, as the case may be[9];

(4) may provide for a person to be a beneficiary if the person is a charity[10] and the circumstances are such that:

    (a) there is no person who is a beneficiary within any rule which is included in the deed and conforms with heads (1), (2) or (3) above; and

    (b) the trust is in consequence being wound up[11];

(5) must not provide for a person to be a beneficiary unless he falls within any rule which is included in the deed and conforms with heads (1), (2), (3) or (4) above[12];

(6) must provide that, notwithstanding any other rule which is included in it, a person cannot be a beneficiary at a particular time ('the relevant time') by virtue of a rule which conforms with heads (2), (3) or (4) above if:

    (a) at that time he has a material interest[13] in the founding company; or

    (b) at any time in the period of one year preceding the relevant time he has had a material interest in that company[14].

1 For the meaning of 'the trust deed' see para 1584 ante.
2 Finance Act 1989 s 74, Sch 5 para 4(1).
3 For these purposes, a company falls within the founding company's group at a particular time if (1) it is at that time resident in the United Kingdom; and (2) it is the founding company or it is at that time controlled by the founding company: ibid Sch 5 para 4(9). For the meaning of 'the founding company' see para 1584 ante; and for the meaning of 'control' see para 1584 note 2 ante.
4 For these purposes, a qualifying period is a period (1) whose length is not more than five years; (2) whose length is specified in the trust deed; and (3) which ends with the relevant time (within the meaning of ibid Sch 5 para 4(2)): Sch 5 para 4(5) (amended by the Finance Act 1996 ss 119(1), 205, Sch 41 Pt V). The Finance Act 1996 s 119 applies to trusts established on or after 29 April 1996: s 119(2).
5 Finance Act 1989 Sch 5 para 4(2).
6 Ie within the meaning of the Income and Corporation Taxes Act 1988 ss 185-187, Sch 9 (as amended): see para 1531 note 3 ante.
7 Finance Act 1989 Sch 5 para 4(2A) (added by the Finance Act 1996 s 120(1)). For these purposes, 'approved' means approved under the Income and Corporation Taxes Act 1988 Sch 9 (as amended) (see para 1531 et seq ante): Finance Act 1989 Sch 5 para 4(2A) (as so added). Where a trust deed contains a rule conforming with Sch 5 para 4(2A) (as so added), it must provide that the only powers and duties which the trustees may exercise in relation to persons who are beneficiaries by virtue only of that rule are those which may be exercised in accordance with the provisions of a scheme such as is mentioned in Sch 5 para 4(2A) (as so added): Sch 5 para 4(2B) (added by the Finance Act 1996 s 120(1)). The Finance Act 1996 s 120 applies to trusts established on or after 29 April 1996: s 120(12).
8 For these purposes, a qualifying period is a period (1) whose length is equal to that of the period specified in the trust deed for the purposes of a rule which conforms with the Finance Act 1989 Sch 5 para 4(2) (see supra); and (2) which ends when the person or company, as the case may be, ceased as mentioned in Sch 5 para 4(3)(b): Sch 5 para 4(6).
9 Ibid Sch 5 para 4(3).
10 For these purposes, a charity is a body established for charitable purposes only: ibid Sch 5 para 4(10).
11 Ibid Sch 5 para 4(4) (amended by the Finance Act 1996 s 120(2),(5)). See also note 7 supra.
12 Finance Act 1989 Sch 5 para 4(7) (amended by the Finance Act 1996 s 120(2),(6)). See also note 7 supra.
13 For the meaning of 'material interest' see para 1585 note 6 ante.
14 Finance Act 1989 Sch 5 para 4(8) (amended by the Finance Act 1996 s 120(2), (7)). See also note 7 supra.

1590. Trustees' functions. The trust deed[1] must contain provision as to the functions of the trustees[2]; and those functions must be so expressed that it is apparent that their general functions are:

(1) to receive sums from the founding company and other sums, by way of loan or otherwise;

(2) to acquire securities[3];

(3) to transfer securities or sums, or both, to persons who are beneficiaries under the terms of the trust deed;

(4) to grant rights to acquire shares to persons who are beneficiaries under the terms of the trust deed;

(5) to transfer securities to the trustees of approved profit sharing schemes[4] for a price not less than the price the securities might reasonably be expected to fetch on a sale in the open market;

(6) pending transfer, to retain the securities and to manage them, whether by exercising voting rights or otherwise[5].

1 For the meaning of 'the trust deed' see para 1584 ante.
2 Finance Act 1989 s 74, Sch 5 para 5(1).
3 For these purposes, the following are securities: (1) shares; and (2) debentures: ibid Sch 5 para 14.
4 Ie profit sharing schemes approved under the Income and Corporation Taxes Act 1988 ss 185-187, Sch 9 (as amended): see para 1531 et seq ante.
5 Finance Act 1989 Sch 5 para 5(2) (amended by the Finance Act 1996 s 120(2),(8)). The Finance Act 1996 s 120 applies to trusts established on or after 29 April 1996: s 120(12).

1591. Sums received by trustees. The trust deed[1] must:

(1) require that any sum received by the trustees:
    (a) must be expended within the relevant period[2];
    (b) may be expended only for one or more of the qualifying purposes[3]; and
    (c) must, while it is retained by them, be kept as cash or be kept in an account with a bank or building society[4];

(2) provide that, in ascertaining for the purposes of a relevant rule[5] whether a particular sum has been expended, sums received earlier by the trustees shall be treated as expended before the sums received by them later[6];

(3) provide that, where the trustees pay sums to different beneficiaries at the same time, all the sums must be paid on similar terms[7].

1 For the meaning of 'the trust deed' see para 1584 ante.
2 For these purposes, the relevant period is the period of nine months beginning with the day found as follows: (1) in a case where the sum is received from the founding company, or a company which is controlled by that company at the time the sum is received, the day following the end of the period of account in which the sum is charged as an expense of the company from which it is received; (2) in any other case, the day the sum is received: Finance Act 1989 s 74, Sch 5 para 6(2). For the meaning of 'the founding company' see para 1584 ante; and for the meaning of 'control' see para 1584 note 2 ante.
3 For these purposes, each of the following is a qualifying purpose: (1) the acquisition of shares in the founding company; (2) the repayment of sums borrowed; (3) the payment of interest on sums borrowed; (4) the payment of any sum to a person who is a beneficiary under the terms of the trust deed; (5) the meeting of expenses: ibid Sch 5 para 6(3).
4 Ibid Sch 5 para 6(1).
5 For these purposes, a relevant rule is one which is included in the trust deed and conforms with ibid Sch 5 para 6(1) (see supra): Sch 5 para 6(4).
6 Ibid Sch 5 para 6(4).
7 Ibid Sch 5 para 6(5). For these purposes, the fact that terms vary according to the levels of remuneration of beneficiaries, the length of their service, or similar factors, is not to be regarded as meaning that the terms are not similar: Sch 5 para 6(6).

1592. Securities. The trust deed[1] must provide[2] that securities[3] acquired by the trustees must be shares in the founding company[4] which:

(1) form part of the ordinary share capital of the company;
(2) are fully paid up;
(3) are not redeemable; and
(4) are not subject to any restrictions other than restrictions which attach to all shares of the same class or any authorised restriction[5].

A restriction is so authorised if:

(a) it is imposed by the founding company's articles of association;
(b) it requires all shares held by directors or employees of the founding company, or of any other company which it controls[6] for the time being, to be disposed of on ceasing to be so held; and
(c) it requires all shares acquired, in pursuance of rights or interests obtained by such directors or employees, by persons who are not, or have ceased to be, such directors or employees to be disposed of when they are acquired[7].

A restriction is not so authorised unless:

(i) any disposal required by the restriction will be by way of sale for a consideration in money on terms specified in the articles of association; and
(ii) the articles also contain general provisions by virtue of which any person disposing of shares of the same class, whether or not held or acquired as mentioned above[8], may be required to sell them on terms which are the same as those mentioned in head (i) above[9].

The trust deed must provide:

(A) that shares in the founding company may not be acquired by the trustees at a price exceeding the price they might reasonably be expected to fetch on a sale in the open market[10];

(B) that shares in the founding company may not be acquired by the trustees at a time when that company is controlled by another company[11].

1 For the meaning of 'the trust deed' see para 1584 ante.
2 Ie subject to the Finance Act 1989 s 74, Sch 5 para 8 (as amended): see para 1593 post.
3 For the meaning of 'securities' see para 1590 note 3 ante.
4 For the meaning of 'the founding company' see para 1584 ante.
5 Finance Act 1989 Sch 5 para 7(1).
6 For the meaning of 'control' see para 1584 note 2 ante.
7 Finance Act 1989 Sch 5 para 7(2).
8 Ie as mentioned in ibid Sch 5 para 7(2): see supra.
9 Ibid Sch 5 para 7(3).
10 Ibid Sch 5 para 7(4).
11 Ibid Sch 5 para 7(5).

1593. Acquisition and transfer of securities. The trust deed[1]:

(1) may provide that the trustees may acquire securities[2] other than shares in the founding company[3]:

(a) if they are securities issued to the trustees in exchange in the specified circumstances[4]; or

(b) if they are securities acquired by the trustees as a result of a reorganisation[5] and the original shares[6] the securities represent are shares in the founding company[7];

(2) must provide that:

(a) where the trustees transfer securities to a beneficiary, they must do so on qualifying terms[8];

(b) the trustees must transfer securities before the expiry of the qualifying period[9] beginning with the date on which they acquired them[10];

(3) must provide that, in ascertaining for the purposes of a relevant rule[11] whether particular securities are transferred, securities acquired earlier by the trustees shall be treated as transferred by them before securities acquired by them later[12].

1 For the meaning of 'the trust deed' see para 1584 ante.
2 For the meaning of 'securities' see para 1590 note 3 ante.
3 For the meaning of 'the founding company' see para 1584 ante.
4 Ie the circumstances mentioned in the Taxation of Chargeable Gains Act 1992 s 135(1): see CAPITAL GAINS TAXATION vol 5(1) (Reissue) para 258.
5 For these purposes, 'reorganisation' is to be construed in accordance with ibid s 126 (see CAPITAL GAINS TAXATION vol 5(1) (Reissue) para 255): Finance Act 1989 s 74, Sch 5 para 8(b) (amended by the Taxation of Chargeable Gains Act 1992 s 290(1), Sch 10 para 19(5)).
6 For these purposes, 'original shares' is to be construed in accordance with ibid s 126 (see CAPITAL GAINS TAXATION vol 5(1) (Reissue) para 252 note 3): Finance Act 1989 Sch 5 para 8(b) (as amended: see note 5 supra).
7 Ibid Sch 5 para 8 (amended by the Taxation of Chargeable Gains Act 1992 Sch 10 para 19(5)).
8 For these purposes, a transfer of securities is made on qualifying terms if (1) all the securities transferred at the same time, other than those transferred on a transfer such as is mentioned in the Finance Act 1989 Sch 5 para 9(2ZA) (as added) (see infra), are transferred on similar terms; (2) securities have been offered to all the persons who are beneficiaries under the terms of the trust deed by virtue of a rule which conforms with Sch 5 para 4(2),(3) or (4) (as amended) (see para 1589 ante) when the transfer is made; and (3) securities are transferred to all such persons who have accepted: Sch 5 para 9(2) (amended by the Finance Act 1996 s 120(2),(9)). For these purposes, the fact that terms vary according to the levels of remuneration of beneficiaries, the length of their service, or similar factors, is not to be regarded as meaning that the terms are not similar: Finance Act 1989 Sch 5 para 9(3). A transfer of securities is also

made on qualifying terms if (a) it is made to a person exercising a right to acquire shares; and (b) that right was obtained in accordance with the provisions of a savings-related share option scheme within the meaning of the Income and Corporation Taxes Act 1988 ss 185-187, Sch 9 (as amended) (see para 1531 note 3 ante) which was established by, or by a company controlled by, the founding company and which is approved under Sch 9 (as amended); and (c) that right is being exercised in accordance with the provisions of that scheme; and (d) the consideration for the transfer is payable to the trustees: Finance Act 1989 Sch 5 para 9(2ZA) (added by the Finance Act 1996 s 120(2),(10)). The Finance Act 1996 s 120 applies to trusts established on or after 29 April 1996: s 120(12).

 9 For these purposes, the qualifying period is (1) seven years, in the case of trusts established on or before 3 May 1994 (ie the date on which the Finance Act 1994 was passed); (2) 20 years, in the case of other trusts: Finance Act 1989 Sch 5 para 9(2A) (added by the Finance Act 1994 s 102, Sch 13 paras 1, 7).
10 Finance Act 1989 Sch 5 para 9(1).
11 For these purposes, a relevant rule is one which is included in the trust deed and conforms with ibid Sch 5 para 9(1) (see supra): Sch 5 para 9(5).
12 Ibid Sch 5 para 9(4).

1594. Other features. The trust deed[1] must not contain features which are not essential or reasonably incidental to the purpose of acquiring sums and securities[2], granting rights to acquire shares to persons who are eligible to participate in savings-related share option schemes duly approved[3], transferring shares to such persons, transferring sums and securities to employees and directors and transferring securities to the trustees of approved[3] profit sharing schemes[4].

 1 For the meaning of 'the trust deed' see para 1584 ante.
 2 For the meaning of 'securities' see para 1590 note 3 ante.
 3 Ie approved under the Income and Corporation Taxes Act 1988 ss 185-187, Sch 9 (as amended): see para 1531 et seq ante.
 4 Finance Act 1989 s 74, Sch 5 para 10 (amended by the Finance Act 1996 s 120(2),(11)). The Finance Act 1996 s 120 applies to trusts established on or after 29 April 1996: s 120(12).

1595. Rules about acquisition etc. The trust deed[1] must provide that, for the purpose of the deed, the trustees:

(1) acquire securities[2] when they become entitled to them;
(2) transfer securities to another person when that other becomes entitled to them;
(3) retain securities if they remain entitled to them[3].

If, however, the deed provides that the trustees may acquire specified securities other than shares in the founding company[4], it must provide for the following exceptions to any rule which is included in it and conforms with head (1) above, namely that:

(a) if securities are issued to the trustees in exchange in the specified circumstances[5], they are to be treated as having acquired them when they became entitled to the securities for which they are exchanged;
(b) if the trustees become entitled to securities as a result of a reorganisation[6], they are to be treated as having acquired them when they became entitled to the original shares[7] which those securities represent[8].

The trust deed must also provide that:

(i) if the trustees agree to take a transfer of securities, for the purposes of the deed they become entitled to them when the agreement is made and not on a later transfer made pursuant to the agreement;
(ii) if the trustees agree to transfer securities to another person, for the purposes of the deed the other person becomes entitled to them when the agreement is made and not on a later transfer made pursuant to the agreement[9].

1 For the meaning of 'the trust deed' see para 1584 ante.
2 For the meaning of 'securities' see para 1590 note 3 ante.
3 Finance Act 1989 s 74, Sch 5 para 11(1).
4 Ie if the deed provides as mentioned in ibid Sch 5 para 8 (as amended): see para 1593 ante. For the meaning of 'the founding company' see para 1584 ante.
5 Ie in the circumstances mentioned in the Taxation of Chargeable Gains Act 1992 s 135(1): see CAPITAL GAINS TAXATION vol 5(1) (Reissue) para 258.
6 For these purposes, 'reorganisation' is to be construed in accordance with ibid s 126 (see CAPITAL GAINS TAXATION vol 5(1) (Reissue) para 255): Finance Act 1989 Sch 5 para 11(2)(b) (amended by the Taxation of Chargeable Gains Act 1992 s 290(1), Sch 10 para 19(5)).
7 For these purposes, 'original shares' is to be construed in accordance with ibid s 126 (see CAPITAL GAINS TAXATION vol 5(1) (Reissue) para 252 note 3): Finance Act 1989 Sch 5 para 11(2)(b) (as amended: see note 6 supra).
8 Ibid Sch 5 para 11(2) (amended by the Taxation of Chargeable Gains Act 1992 Sch 10 para 19(5)).
9 Finance Act 1989 Sch 5 para 11(3).

1596. Position after trusts' establishment. A trust established on or before 3 May 1994 which was at the time it was established a qualifying employee share ownership trust[1] continues to be one, except that it is not such a trust at any time when the specified requirements[2] are not satisfied[3].

A trust established after 3 May 1994 which was at the time it was established a qualifying employee share ownership trust continues[4] to be one[5].

A trust is an employee share ownership trust at a particular time ('the relevant time') if it was a qualifying employee share ownership trust at the time it was established; and it is immaterial whether or not it is a qualifying employee share ownership trust at the relevant time[6].

1 As to qualifying employee share ownership trusts see para 1583 ante.
2 Ie the requirements mentioned in the Finance Act 1989 s 74, Sch 5 para 3(3)(a)-(f): see para 1585 ante.
3 Ibid Sch 5 para 12 (amended by the Finance Act 1994 s 102, Sch 13 paras 1, 4).
4 Ie subject to the Finance Act 1989 Sch 5 para 12A(2),(3) (as added). If the trust deed makes provision under Sch 5 para 3A(a) (as added) (see para 1586 ante), the trust is not a qualifying employee share ownership trust at any time when the requirements mentioned in Sch 5 para 3(3)(a)-(f) (see para 1585 heads (3)(a)-(f) ante) are not satisfied: Sch 5 para 12A(2) (added by the Finance Act 1994 Sch 13 paras 1, 5). If the trust deed makes provision under the Finance Act 1989 Sch 5 para 3A(b) (as added) (see para 1586 ante), the trust is not a qualifying employee share ownership trust at any time when the conditions mentioned in Sch 5 para 3B(4)(a)-(e) (as added) (see para 1587 heads (2)(a)-(e) ante) are not satisfied: Sch 5 para 12A(3) (added by the Finance Act 1994 Sch 13 paras 1, 5). If the trust deed makes provision under the Finance Act 1989 Sch 5 para 3A(c) (as added) (see para 1586 head (3) ante), the trust is not a qualifying employee share ownership trust at any time when (1) there is not a single trustee; (2) the trustee is not a company which is resident in the United Kingdom and controlled by the founding company; or (3) the conditions mentioned in Sch 5 para 3C(4)(a)-(e) (as added) (see para 1588 heads (2)(a)-(e) ante) are not satisfied as regards the directors of the trustee: Sch 5 para 12A(3) (added by the Finance Act 1994 Sch 13 paras 1, 5). For the meaning of 'the founding company' see para 1584 ante; and for the meaning of 'control' see para 1584 note 2 ante.
5 Finance Act 1989 Sch 5 para 12A(1) (added by the Finance Act 1994 Sch 13 paras 1, 5).
6 Finance Act 1989 Sch 5 para 13.

(iii) Tax Consequences for Company

1597. Costs of establishing employee share ownership trusts. Where a company incurs expenditure on or after 1 April 1991 on establishing a qualifying employee share ownership trust[1], the expenditure may be deducted in computing for the purposes of Schedule D[2] the profits or gains[3] of a trade[4] carried on by the company[5].

In a case where:

(1) the above provisions apply; and

(2) the trust is established after the end of the period of nine months beginning with the day following the end of the period of account in which the expenditure is incurred,

for the purpose of applying the above provisions the expenditure is treated as incurred in the period of account in which the trust is established, and not the period of account mentioned in head (2) above[6].

1 For these purposes, 'qualifying employee share ownership trust' is to be construed in accordance with the Finance Act 1989 s 74, Sch 5 (as amended) (see para 1583 ante): Income and Corporation Taxes Act 1988 s 85A(4) (added by the Finance Act 1991 s 41).

2 Ie the Income and Corporation Taxes Act 1988 s 18(1), Schedule D (as amended): see INCOME TAXATION vol 23 (Reissue) para 135 et seq.

3 For the meaning of 'profits or gains' see INCOME TAXATION vol 23 (Reissue) para 1 note 3.

4 For the meaning of 'trade' see INCOME TAXATION vol 23 (Reissue) para 152.

5 Income and Corporation Taxes Act 1988 s 85A(1),(2)(a),(6) (added by the Finance Act 1991 s 41). If the company is an investment company or a company in the case of which the Income and Corporation Taxes Act 1988 s 75 (as amended) (see INCOME TAXATION vol 23 (Reissue) para 1338) applies by virtue of s 76 (as amended) (see INCOME TAXATION vol 23 (Reissue) para 1361), any such sum is treated as expenses of management: s 85A(1),(2)(b),(6) (added by the Finance Act 1991 s 41). For these purposes, the trust is established when the deed under which it is established is executed: Income and Corporation Taxes Act 1988 s 85A(5) (added by the Finance Act 1991 s 41).

6 Income and Corporation Taxes Act 1988 s 85A(3) (added by the Finance Act 1991 s 41).

1598. Roll-over relief. A form of roll-over relief applies on the disposal of shares to employee share ownership trusts[1].

1 See the Taxation of Chargeable Gains Act 1992 ss 227–236 (as amended) and CAPITAL GAINS TAXATION vol 5(1) (Reissue) para 204 et seq.

3. COMPANIES REGULATED BY THE COMPANIES CLAUSES ACTS

(1) IN GENERAL

1599. Object of the Companies Clauses Acts. The Companies Clauses Acts 1845 to 1889[1] are:

(1) the Companies Clauses Consolidation Act 1845 as amended by the Companies Clauses Consolidation Act 1888 and the Companies Clauses Consolidation Act 1889[2]; and

(2) the Companies Clauses Act 1863 as amended by the Companies Clauses Act 1869.

The Companies Clauses Consolidation Act 1845 was passed in order to comprise in one general Act the provisions relating to the constitution and management of companies which were at that time usually introduced into special Acts of Parliament incorporating a company; and the Companies Clauses Act 1863 was passed with the same object. By passing these general Acts the legislature has to a great extent avoided the necessity for repeating in each special Act incorporating a company provisions with regard to its constitution and management which are common to all such companies[3].

Many companies have been and are from time to time incorporated by special Act of Parliament for the purpose of carrying on undertakings of a public nature. In some cases the special Act incorporating the company provides for the dissolution of a company previously incorporated, either by a special Act or pursuant to the Companies Act 1985 or the Acts which it replaces, and also for the transfer to the new company of the undertaking and assets of the dissolved company[4].

The Companies Clauses Acts are of declining importance as more and more companies are incorporated under the Companies Acts[5] and the class of companies incorporated by special Act is thereby diminished[6].

1 This collective title was given by the Short Titles Act 1896 s 2, Sch 2.
2 This Act was repealed by the Statute Law Revision Act 1908.
3 Companies Clauses Consolidation Act 1845 preamble (repealed by the Statute Law Revision Act 1891). The Companies Act 1985, following the precedent set out in the Joint Stock Companies Act 1856, the Companies Act 1862, the Companies (Consolidation) Act 1908, the Companies Act 1929 and the Companies Act 1948, allows the tables referred to in those Acts to be adopted as standard forms of the regulations governing companies registered under that Act. As to the continuance of the former Tables A etc so far as they applied to any company existing on 1 July 1985 see para 9 ante. For a comparison between the Acts mentioned and the Companies Clauses Consolidation Act 1845 see *Barton v London and North Western Rly Co* (1889) 24 QBD 77 at 87, CA.
4 Stamp duty is chargeable on the special Act as a conveyance on sale (see the Finance Act 1895 s 12; the Finance Act 1949 s 36(4); STAMP DUTIES vol 44(1) (Reissue) para 1050; and *A-G v Felixstowe Gas Light Co* [1907] 2 KB 984), subject to exemptions from duty on certain transactions by way of reconstruction and amalgamation (see the Finance Act 1986 ss 75-77 and para 1491 et seq ante). As to stamp duty generally see STAMP DUTIES vol 44(1) (Reissue) para 1001 et seq.
5 See para 7 ante.
6 On the registration of the memorandum of a new company under the Companies Act 1985, the registrar must certify under his hand or authenticate by his official seal that the company is incorporated and, in the case of a limited company, that the company is limited: see s 13(1),(2) and para 91 ante. From the date of incorporation mentioned in the certificate the subscribers of the memorandum of association, together with such other persons as may from time to time become members of the company, become ipso facto a body corporate by the name contained in the memorandum, capable forthwith of exercising all the functions of an incorporated company: see s 13(3),(4) (as amended) and para 92 ante.

1600. Application of the Companies Clauses Acts. All the clauses and provisions of the Companies Clauses Consolidation Act 1845 apply to every joint stock company incorporated by any special Act of Parliament passed after 8 May 1845 for the purpose of carrying on any undertaking whatsoever, unless they are expressly varied or excepted by the special Act[1]; and the special Act and the Companies Clauses Consolidation Act 1845, and any other Act incorporated with the special Act are, save as mentioned above, to be construed together as forming one Act[2].

Part III of the Companies Clauses Act 1863, which provides for the creation and issue of debenture stock[3], applies to every company having power to raise money on mortgage or bond by virtue of any Act of Parliament[4]; but none of the other provisions of that Act applies to a company unless made expressly applicable by its special Act[5].

1 As to the application of the Companies Act 1985 to a company incorporated by special Act as being an unregistered company see s 718, Sch 22 (as amended) and para 1765 et seq post.
2 Companies Clauses Consolidation Act 1845 s 1.
3 See the Companies Clauses Act 1863 Pt III (ss 22-35) (amended by the Companies Clauses Act 1869).
4 Companies Clauses Act 1869 s 3.
5 See the Companies Clauses Act 1863 ss 3, 12, 22, 36.

1601. Differences between companies incorporated under special Acts and under the Companies Act 1985. The process of incorporating a company by special Act[1] is to be distinguished from the quite different method, lately from time to time adopted by Parliament, of conferring by statute special powers for special purposes on a company, incorporated or to be incorporated, in the ordinary way by registration under the Companies Act 1985[2].

Except where the provisions of the Companies Act 1985 have been specifically applied to companies incorporated by special Acts as unregistered companies[3], such companies differ in many important respects of constitution, powers and management from companies regulated by the Companies Act 1985[4].

1 See paras 1599, 1600 ante.
2 See para 1599 text and notes 5, 6 ante.
3 See para 1600 note 1 ante.
4 See para 1602 et seq post.

1602. Application of general companies legislation. The provisions of the Companies Act 1985 which apply to companies regulated by the Companies Clauses Acts have already been mentioned[1]. The provisions of the Business Names Act 1985[2], the Company Directors Disqualification Act 1986[3] and Part V of the Criminal Justice Act 1993[4] also apply.

1 See para 1600 note 1 ante.
2 See the Business Names Act 1985 s 1(1)(c) and paras 166–172 ante.
3 See the Company Directors Disqualification Act 1986 s 22(2) and para 1417 et seq ante.
4 See the Criminal Justice Act 1993 s 60(3)(a) and para 1218 text and note 15 ante.

1603. Statutory definitions. In the Companies Clauses Consolidation Act 1845[1] and in the special Act certain words[2] and expressions have special meanings unless there is something in the subject or the context repugnant to such a construction[3]. Thus 'lands' extends to messuages, lands, tenements and hereditaments of any tenure; and 'lease' includes an agreement for a lease[4].

'The company' is the company constituted by the special Act; and the 'directors' are the directors of the company and include all persons having the direction of the undertaking, whether under the name of directors, managers, committee of management or under any other name. 'The secretary' means the secretary of the company and includes a clerk[4].

'Shareholder' means a shareholder, proprietor or member of the company; and in referring to any such shareholder, expressions properly applicable to a person are to apply to a corporation[4].

A 'justice' is a justice of the peace acting for the place where the matter requiring his cognisance arises, and who is not interested[5] in the matter[6].

1 The Companies Clauses Consolidation Act 1845 and the Companies Clauses Consolidation Act 1888 are to be construed together as one Act: s 1. These statutory definitions are, therefore, also relevant to the construction of the 1888 Act: see eg *Phillips v Parnaby* [1934] 2 KB 299, DC.
2 The singular includes the plural, the masculine gender includes the feminine, and 'month' is a calendar month: Companies Clauses Consolidation Act 1845 s 3.
3 Ibid s 3. 'Superior courts' was defined as 'Her Majesty's Superior Courts of Record at Westminster or Dublin as the case may require'. The former is now the High Court of Justice: see the Supreme Court Act 1981 s 19.
    'Prescribed' as used in the Companies Clauses Consolidation Act 1845 is to be construed to refer to such matter as the same is prescribed or provided for in the special Act; and the sentence in which that word occurs is construed as if, instead of the expression 'prescribed', the expression 'prescribed for that purpose in the special Act' had been used: Companies Clauses Consolidation Act 1845 s 2.

4 Ibid s 3.
5 'Interest' in the matter in dispute disqualifies a person from acting as judge in the matter on the maxim that no man shall be judge in his own cause: see eg *R v Manchester, Sheffield and Lincolnshire Rly Co* (1867) LR 2 QB 336; and for cases on the meaning of 'interest' for the purposes of disqualification see further MAGISTRATES vol 29 para 250 et seq.
6 Companies Clauses Consolidation Act 1845 s 3.

1604. Inspection of special Acts. The company must at all times after the expiration of six months after the passing of its special Act keep in its principal office of business a copy of the special Act, printed by the Queen's printers[1]. If it fails to do so, it is liable to a penalty not exceeding level 2 on the standard scale for every such offence and also, in the case of a continuing offence, to a penalty of £5 a day[2]. It must permit persons interested to inspect its Act and make extracts and copies from it at all reasonable hours on payment[3].

1 Companies Clauses Consolidation Act 1845 s 161.
2 Ibid s 162 (amended by the Criminal Law Act 1977 s 31(6); the Criminal Justice Act 1982 s 46). For the meaning of 'the standard scale' see CRIMINAL LAW vol 11(2) (Reissue) para 808.
3 Companies Clauses Consolidation Act 1845 s 161. The payments (eg ten pence for inspection) are provided for by the Local Government Act 1972 ss 228(5),(7), 270(1). The Companies Clauses Consolidation Act 1845 s 161 also requires the deposit in the offices of local authorities of copies of special Acts by railway, canal and similar undertakings operating in more than one place, and the same provisions as to inspection apply.

(2) POWERS AND LIABILITIES OF COMPANIES REGULATED BY THE COMPANIES CLAUSES ACTS

1605. Powers conferred by statute. The powers of a company to which the Companies Clauses Acts apply are limited and circumscribed by the special Act creating it and any Act altering its powers. They extend no further than is therein expressly stated or is necessarily required for carrying into effect the purposes of its incorporation. It does not have power to deal with its property and incur liabilities in the same way as an ordinary individual, as is the case with a corporation created by charter[1]. Such a company, therefore, has only the powers expressly or by inference given to it by its special Act or Acts, with the superadded powers given to it by the Companies Clauses Acts or such of those Acts as are applicable.

Even with the consent of all its shareholders, the company cannot do or contract to do anything outside the scope of its powers, however advantageous it may appear to be, and any act purported to be done by the company which exceeds these powers is ultra vires[2]. Such companies, being bodies corporate, may acquire and hold real or personal property in joint tenancy in the same manner as if they were individuals; but this acquisition and holding is subject to the same restrictions as attach to the acquisition and holding of property by a body corporate in severalty[3].

1 *Baroness Wenlock v River Dee Co* (1883) 36 ChD 675n at 685n, CA; *Eastern Counties Rly Co v Hawkes* (1855) 5 HL Cas 331; *A-G v Great Eastern Rly Co* (1880) 5 App Cas 473 at 486, HL; and see CORPORATIONS.
2 *Ashbury Railway Carriage and Iron Co v Riche* (1875) LR 7 HL 653, the principle of which applies to companies incorporated by Act of Parliament: see *A-G v Great Eastern Rly Co* (1880) 5 App Cas 473 at 486, HL per Lord Watson; and see para 97 et seq ante. As to the extension of the provisions of the Companies Act 1985 ss 35-35B (see paras 1093, 1107-1109 ante) to such companies see para 1767 post.
3 Bodies Corporate (Joint Tenancy) Act 1899 s 1. The former restrictions which existed on the assurance or holding of land in mortmain have been abolished: see the Charities Act 1960 ss 38, 48(2), Sch 7 Pt II; the Education Act 1973 s 1(4), Sch 2 Pt I.

1606. Form of contracts. The former general rule that contracts entered into by a corporation aggregate had, with certain exceptions, to be made under seal[1] never applied to companies governed by the Companies Clauses Consolidation Act 1845, which have always been subject to the special provision in that Act with respect to the making of contracts[2], not radically different from those contained in the Corporate Bodies' Contracts Act 1960[3].

1 See eg *Ludlow Corpn v Charlton* (1840) 6 M & W 815 and CORPORATIONS.
2 See the Companies Clauses Consolidation Act 1845 s 97 and para 1709 post.
3 The Corporate Bodies' Contracts Act 1960 does not apply to any company formed and registered under the Companies Act 1985 or an existing company as defined in that Act (see para 11 ante): Corporate Bodies' Contracts Act 1960 s 2 (amended by the Companies Consolidation (Consequential Provisions) Act 1985 s 30, Sch 2). See further CORPORATIONS.

1607. Liability for torts and crimes. The rule that a corporation aggregate is liable to be sued for its torts[1] applies to companies governed by the Companies Clauses Acts[2], as also does the rule that in certain cases corporations may be indicted or fined in respect of criminal or quasi-criminal offences[3].

1 As to the liability of a corporation aggregate to be sued for torts see CORPORATIONS vol 9 para 1374 et seq.
2 *Poulton v London and South Western Rly Co* (1867) LR 2 QB 534; *Maund v Monmouthshire Canal Co* (1842) Car & M 606; *Cooke v Midland Great Western Rly of Ireland* [1909] AC 229, HL; *Goff v Great Northern Rly Co* (1861) 3 E & E 672; *Moore v Metropolitan Rly Co* (1872) LR 8 QB 36.
3 *R v Birmingham and Gloucester Rly Co* (1842) 3 QB 223; *Whitfield v South Eastern Rly Co* (1858) EB & E 115; and see CRIMINAL LAW vol 11(1) (Reissue) para 35.

(3) NAME, OFFICE AND SERVICE

1608. Manner and effect of change of name. The name given to the company by its special Act cannot be changed except by another Act. If the special Act incorporates the statutory provisions relating to change of name[1], the following provisions apply. The change of name does not affect the powers vested in the company by its original name, and any reference in any statute to the company by its original name is interpreted as if a reference to the company by its new name was substituted[2].

No proceeding, whether civil or criminal, which is pending at the passing of the special Act either at the instance of or against the company, by its original name, is affected in any way by its change of name[3]. Nor is any document or instrument whatever discharged or affected by reason of the company or its undertaking being called in it by the original name of the company or undertaking[3]. It is not necessary in any such proceeding, document or instrument to aver that the company or its undertaking had been known by its original name, and that by the special Act the name of the company and its undertaking were changed, and that the company had since been known by its new name, and its undertaking by its new name: but it is sufficient to describe the company by its new name and its undertaking by its new name[3].

The change of name does not invalidate anything done before the passing of the special Act effecting the change under or by virtue of any other Act[4]; nor does it affect any deeds, instruments, purchases, sales, securities and contracts made before the passing of the special Act under any other Act or with reference to its purposes[5].

1 Ie the Companies Clauses Act 1863 Pt IV (ss 36–39). The company may have been incorporated either before or after 28 July 1863, the date of the passing of the Act: s 36. As to the prohibition of the use of certain business names see the Business Names Act 1985 s 2 and para 166 et seq ante.

2 Companies Clauses Act 1863 s 36.
3 Ibid s 37.
4 Ibid s 38.
5 Ibid s 39.

1609. Service on company. Any summons, notice, writ or other proceeding requiring to be served upon the company may be served by being left at or transmitted through the post[1] directed to its principal office, or one of its principal offices where there are more than one, or by being given personally to the secretary or, in case there is no secretary, then by being given to any one director of the company[2]. Where there is a secretary, service on a director is not sufficient[3]. The principal office of the company is the office where the general superintendence and management of its business are carried on[4].

1 This includes registered post *(TO Supplies (London) Ltd v Jerry Creighton Ltd* [1952] 1 KB 42, [1951] 2 All ER 992), and recorded delivery under the Recorded Delivery Service Act 1962 (s 1(1)).
2 Companies Clauses Consolidation Act 1845 s 135. See also the Companies Act 1985 s 725 and para 151 ante. The provisions of the Companies Clauses Consolidation Act 1845 s 135 are not affected by RSC Ord 65 r 3 (which provides for the service of writs of summons on corporations in the absence of statutory provision providing therefor). As to the service of process generally see PRACTICE AND PROCEDURE vol 37 para 145 et seq. Notice to a secretary received in another capacity has been held to be a good notice: *Re Sketchley, ex p Boulton* (1857) 1 De G & J 163. As to the effect of non-receipt on a default judgment see para 1146 note 4 ante.
3 *Lawrenson v Dublin Metropolitan Junction Rly Co* (1877) 37 LT 32, CA (where the plaintiff was secretary).
4 *Garton v Great Western Rly Co* (1858) EB & E 837; revsd (1859) EB & E 846; *Palmer v Caledonian Rly Co* [1892] 1 QB 823, CA; cf *Wilson v Caledonian Rly Co* (1850) 5 Exch 822.

1610. Service on members. A notice requiring to be served by the company upon a person holding its shares or stock may, unless expressly required to be served personally, be served by being sent by post to his registered or other known address within such period as to admit of its being delivered in the due course of delivery within the period, if any, prescribed for the giving of the notice[1]. In proving such service it is sufficient to prove that the notice was properly directed and put into the post office[1].

With respect to any share or stock to which two or more persons are jointly entitled, notice must be given to the person named first in the appropriate register, and notice so given is sufficient notice to all the proprietors of the share or stock[2].

1 Companies Clauses Consolidation Act 1845 s 136. Cf the Companies (Tables A to F) Regulations 1985, SI 1985/805, Schedule, Table A arts 111–116. As to Table A generally see para 529 et seq ante.
2 Companies Clauses Consolidation Act 1845 s 137. Cf the Companies (Tables A to F) Regulations 1985 Schedule, Table A art 112.

1611. Advertisement of notices. All notices required to be given by advertisement must be advertised in the prescribed newspaper or, if no newspaper is prescribed, or if the prescribed newspaper has ceased to be published, in a newspaper circulating in the district within which the company's principal place of business is situated[1]. In the absence of evidence that the newspaper in which notice of a meeting is advertised circulates in the district, the proceedings at the meeting are a nullity[2].

1 Companies Clauses Consolidation Act 1845 s 138.
2 *Swansea Dock Co v Levien* (1851) 20 LJ Ex 447.

1612. Authentication of documents. Every summons, notice or other document requiring authentication by the company may be signed by two directors, or by the treasurer or secretary of the company, and need not be under the common seal[1]. It may be in writing or in print, or partly in writing and partly in print[1].

1 Companies Clauses Consolidation Act 1845 s 139.

(4) CAPITAL

(i) Amount and Description of Capital

1613. Authorised capital. The amount of the capital which the company is authorised to raise is prescribed by the special Act, and the company is precluded from raising capital in excess of that amount.

The special Act also prescribes how the authorised capital is to be raised, whether by way of subscriptions for shares or stock[1], or whether partly by way of such subscriptions and partly by way of loan[2].

1 See para 1614 post.
2 See para 1615 post.

1614. Subscribed capital. The special Act may provide for the division of the subscribed capital[1] into shares of prescribed number and amount, or it may provide that the subscribed capital is to be in the form of a general capital stock, each subscriber being entitled to an aliquot part of the stock proportionate to the amount subscribed by him. It may also confer upon the company power to issue different classes of shares and different classes of stock with preferential or other rights attached to them.

The Companies Clauses Consolidation Act 1845 contains elaborate provisions with regard to shares and shareholders[2], and provides for the conversion of fully paid shares into stock[3]; but it does not contain any provisions with regard to preference shares, nor does it provide for the issue of stock. The Companies Clauses Act 1863, however, supplies this deficiency[4].

1 Ie the capital to be raised by way of subscription.
2 See para 1626 et seq post.
3 See para 1666 post.
4 See para 1620 et seq post.

1615. Loan capital. In the case of a company authorised by a special Act to raise capital by way of loan, the special Act may prescribe how the capital may be obtained, whether by the creation of mortgages or the issue of bonds[1] or debentures or debenture stock[2] or in any other form. In certain cases a company may issue redeemable debenture stock[3]. Mortgages or bonds must be carefully distinguished from debenture stock. The principal distinction is that the holder of debenture stock, instead of being a lender entitled to repayment of his capital at the time fixed by the instrument, obtains a charge on the company's undertaking for the interest on the money paid by him, which is in the nature of a perpetual annuity[4].

1 See para 1670 et seq post.
2 See para 1687 et seq post.

3 See the Statutory Companies (Redeemable Stock) Act 1915 and para 1617 post.
4 *Re Burry Port and Gwendreath Valley Rly Co* (1885) 54 LJ Ch 710 at 713. As to the misdescription of bonds as 'debentures' and mortgages as 'mortgage debentures' see also para 1670 note 2 post.

1616. Excess borrowing. A limit on the amount of the capital which may be raised by way of loan is usually prescribed by the special Act, and borrowing in excess of the amount so prescribed is ultra vires and creates no debt[1]. Directors are in the position of special agents, having authority to affix the company's seal to mortgage and other deeds which are intra vires the company, but having no power to affix the seal so as to bind the company in any case where the deed is one the execution of which the legislature has expressly or impliedly forbidden[2].

Prohibition against borrowing more than a specified sum is, in substance, disobeyed only when and so far as an obligation to pay more than that sum is contracted. So far as money borrowed has been applied in discharging debts or liabilities which could be enforced against the company, the lender is entitled to have the loan treated as valid[3].

Money borrowed to pay off bonds or mortgages given or made under the statutory powers and so applied is deemed to be borrowed within the statutory powers[4].

1 *Fountaine v Carmarthen Rly Co* (1868) LR 5 Eq 316 at 325. The issue of debenture stock extinguishes the powers of borrowing or reborrowing to the extent of the money so raised: see para 1691 post.
2 *Chambers v Manchester and Milford Rly Co* (1864) 5 B & S 588 at 605–608; *Landowners West of England and South Wales Land Drainage and Inclosure Co v Ashford* (1880) 16 ChD 411; *Re Cork and Youghal Rly Co* (1869) 4 Ch App 748 at 757, 758.
3 Cf *Re Wrexham, Mold and Connah's Quay Rly Co* [1899] 1 Ch 440 at 446, 447, CA; *Fountaine v Carmarthen Rly Co* (1868) LR 5 Eq 316 at 325; *Re Cork and Youghal Rly Co* (1869) 4 Ch App 748 at 759; *Yorkshire Railway Wagon Co v Maclure* (1882) 21 ChD 309, CA; and see para 1237 ante.
4 Companies Clauses Act 1869 s 4.

1617. Redeemable capital. Certain statutory companies[1] are empowered by statute[2], where preference or debenture stock[3] was authorised to be created or issued before 19 May 1915[4], to create and issue that stock so as to be redeemable on terms and conditions specified in a resolution[5] passed at a special company meeting[6]. If the resolution so provides, the company may call in and pay off the stock or any part of it at any time before the fixed redemption date and redeem it either by paying it off or by issuing to any consenting stockholder any other stock in substitution. Further, such companies may, for the purpose of providing money for paying off the stock or providing substituted stock, create and issue new stock, either redeemable or irredeemable, or reissue stock originally created and issued in pursuance of these provisions. The creation and issue for the purpose of any particular class of stock must not make the total nominal amount of that stock issued exceed the amount of that class of stock which the company is for the time being authorised to create[7].

1 For these purposes, 'statutory company' means any railway, canal, dock, water or other company incorporated by special Act which is for the time being authorised under an Act to construct, work, own or carry on any railway, canal, dock, water or other public undertaking, and includes any person or body of persons so authorised: Statutory Companies (Redeemable Stock) Act 1915 s 2(1). As to the power of statutory water companies to issue redeemable stock see the Statutory Water Companies Act 1991 ss 2, 3 and WATER.
2 Ie by the Statutory Companies (Redeemable Stock) Act 1915.
3 The provisions apply equally to preference shares and debentures: ibid s 2(2).
4 Ie the date of the commencement of the Act: ibid s 1(5). Except with Treasury consent redeemable stock was not to be created or issued during the 1914–18 war and a period of 12 months thereafter: s 1(5).
5 For the purposes of the Act, a resolution passed before the commencement of the Act and after the outbreak of the 1914–18 war for the creation or issue of redeemable stock has the same effect as if the Act had been in operation when the resolution was passed: ibid s 1(4).

6 Ibid s 1(1).
7 Ibid s 1(2). Companies coming under these provisions may set aside out of revenue, after provision has been made for the various payments mentioned in the Act, a fund for the purpose of redeeming the stock at maturity, and may invest that fund and apply it either in redeeming the stock or in purchasing any of the stock, in which case the stock purchased is to be cancelled: s 1(3).

(ii) Increase of Subscribed Capital under the Companies Clauses Consolidation Act 1845

1618. Creation of new shares. Unless the special Act otherwise provides, the whole or part of the additional sum authorised to be borrowed by the special Act[1] may be raised, with the previous authority of a general meeting, by creating new shares; and new shares may be issued to pay off part of an existing loan[2]. The capital so raised must be considered as part of the general share capital and is subject to the same provisions as if it had been part of the original share capital, except as to the times of making and the amount of calls, which the company may fix as it thinks fit[3].

1 See the Companies Clauses Consolidation Act 1845 ss 38-55.
2 Ibid s 56. As to capital duty see para 1628 post.
3 Ibid s 57.

1619. Issue of new shares. If, when any increase of the subscribed capital takes place by the creation of new shares, the existing shares are at a premium, the sum to be raised must, unless it is otherwise provided by the special Act, be divided into shares of such an amount as will conveniently allow them to be apportioned among the shareholders in proportion to their holding. The new shares must be offered by letter under the hand of the secretary to the shareholders, in proportion to their holding[1].

The new shares vest in and belong to the shareholders who accept them and pay for them at the time and by the instalments fixed by the company. If any shareholder fails for one month after the offer of new shares to accept them and pay the required instalments, the company may dispose of them in such manner as it deems most for its advantage[2].

If the existing shares are not at a premium, the new shares may be of such amount and may be issued in such manner and on such terms as the company thinks fit[3]. They may be issued at a discount[4].

1 Companies Clauses Consolidation Act 1845 s 58. The letter may be given to the shareholder or sent by post to his registered address, or left at his usual or last place of abode: s 58.
2 Ibid s 59. The time prescribed is of the essence of this transaction and the shareholder will lose his right to the new shares if he fails to accept within the prescribed time: cf *Pearson v London and Croydon Rly Co* (1845) 14 Sim 541; *Campbell v London and Brighton Rly Co* (1846) 5 Hare 519. Cf also the Companies Clauses Act 1863 s 20 proviso, which permits the time for acceptances to be extended: see para 1623 post.
3 Companies Clauses Consolidation Act 1845 s 60.
4 *Statham v Brighton Marine Palace and Pier Co* [1899] 1 Ch 199; and see para 1629 et seq post.

(iii) Increase of Subscribed Capital under the Companies Clauses Act 1863

1620. Increase of share capital. Where a company is authorised by a special Act[1] to raise any additional sum or sums by the issue of new ordinary shares or new ordinary stock, the company, with the sanction of the proportion prescribed by that Act[2] of the votes of the shareholders and stockholders entitled to vote in that behalf at meetings of the company, present (personally or by proxy) at a specially convened meeting, may from time to time create and issue, according to the authority given by that Act, such new ordinary shares of such nominal amount and subject to the payment of calls of such amounts and at such times as the company thinks fit, or such new ordinary stock as the company thinks fit[3].

1 The Companies Clauses Act 1863 Pt II (ss 12–21) will apply only if incorporated by the special Act: s 12. See para 1600 ante. The company may have been incorporated either before or after 28 July 1863, the date of the passing of the Act: s 12.

2 If no proportion is prescribed, the proportion is three-fifths: ibid s 12.

3 Ibid s 12. As to capital duty see para 1628 post.

1621. Preference shares. There was no general provision in the Companies Clauses Consolidation Act 1845 authorising the creation of preference shares or regulating, as to companies empowered by special Act to create such shares, the exercise of that power. Before the passing of the Companies Clauses Act 1863, however, certain companies had been empowered by special Acts to issue preference shares and, in effect, to attach to them the right to a dividend, not only of a preferential but also of a cumulative character[1].

The 1863 Act provides that a company authorised by a special Act[2] to raise any additional sum or sums by the issue of new preference shares or new preference stock or, at the company's option, by either of these modes, may from time to time with the same sanction as for the issue of new ordinary shares, create and issue, according to the authority given by the special Act, such new shares or new stock, either ordinary or preference, and either of one class and with the same privileges, or of several classes and with different privileges, and of the same or different amounts, and respectively with any fixed, fluctuating, contingent, preferential, perpetual, terminable, deferred or other dividend or interest, not exceeding the rate prescribed by the special Act, or, if no rate is so prescribed, 5%[3], and subject to the payment of calls of such amounts and at such times as the company thinks fit[4]. Any preference assigned to any shares or stock so issued does not affect any guarantee, preference or priority in the payment of dividend or interest on any shares or stock that may have been granted by the company under or confirmed by any previous Act, or that may be otherwise lawfully subsisting[4].

The preference shares or stock so issued are entitled to the preferential dividend or interest assigned to them out of the annual profits in priority to the company's ordinary shares and stock, but they are non-cumulative[5].

In the absence of special provision the preference shareholders have no priority over ordinary shareholders as to repayment of capital, but the assets must be distributed rateably among all the shareholders in proportion to their capital[6].

The terms and conditions to which any preference share or preference stock is subject must be clearly stated on the certificate of that preference share or portion of preference stock[7].

1 In such special Acts, the so-called preference 'dividend' was in the nature of interest chargeable upon profits generally, and therefore in effect cumulative: see *Henry v Great Northern Rly Co* (1857) 1 De G & J 606 at 636, 648; *Matthews v Great Northern Rly Co* (1859) 28 LJ Ch 375 at 378; *Corry v Londonderry and Enniskillen Rly Co* (1860) 29 Beav 263; *Staples v Eastman Photographic Materials Co* [1896] 2 Ch 303 at 309, 310, CA per Kay LJ; and see *Lamplough v Kent Waterworks (Company of Proprietors)* [1903] 1 Ch 575, CA (affd sub nom *Kent Waterworks (Company of Proprietors) v Lamplough* [1904] AC 27, HL).

2 See para 1620 note 1 ante.

3 Companies Clauses Act 1863 s 13.

4   Ibid s 13. Section 13 and s 14 (see infra) limit a company to which this part of the Act applies in respect of its power to attach rights of dividend to its preference shares, but not in respect of its power to attach other privileges: *Windermere District Gas and Water Co v Whitehead* [1931] 1 Ch 558. As to capital duty see para 1628 post.
5   Companies Clauses Act 1863 s 14; cf *Staples v Eastman Photographic Materials Co* [1896] 2 Ch 303, CA.
6   *Re Accrington Corpn Steam Tramways Co* [1909] 2 Ch 40.
7   Companies Clauses Act 1863 s 15.

1622. Cancellation of unissued shares. If, after having created new shares or new stock, the company determines not to issue the whole, it may cancel the unissued shares or stock[1].

1   Companies Clauses Act 1863 s 16.

1623. Disposal of new shares. If, at the time of the issue of new shares or new stock, the ordinary shares or ordinary stock are or is at a premium, then, unless before the issue of the new shares or stock the company otherwise determines, the new shares or stock must be of such amount as will conveniently allow the same to be apportioned among the holders of the ordinary stock and ordinary shares in proportion, as nearly as conveniently may be, to their holding, and must be offered to them at par in that proportion[1]. It is not obligatory on the company so to apportion or offer any new shares or stock unless the amount of every new share or portion of new stock to be so offered would, if so apportioned, be at least the sum prescribed in the special Act, and, if no such sum is prescribed, then at least £10[1].

The offer must be made by letter under the hand of the company treasurer or secretary, given to every holder of ordinary shares or stock or sent by post addressed to him according to his address in the shareholders' or stockholders' address book, or left for him at his usual or then last known place of abode in England, Scotland or Northern Ireland[2], as the case may require; and every such offer made by letter sent by post is considered as made on the day on which the letter in due course of delivery ought to be delivered at the place to which it is addressed[3].

The new shares or portions of new stock so offered vest in and belong to the shareholders or stockholders who accept them or their nominees[4].

Any shareholder or stockholder failing to signify his acceptance of the whole or part of the new shares or stock offered him within the time prescribed by the special Act or, if no time is so prescribed, within one month[5] is deemed to have declined the offer either wholly or in part[6]; but, where, from absence abroad or other cause satisfactory to the directors, he omits to signify his acceptance within the time prescribed, the directors may permit him to accept them[7].

Subject to the above right of pre-emption, the company may from time to time dispose of new shares and new stock at such times, to such persons, on such terms and conditions, and in such manner as the directors think advantageous to the company[8].

1   Companies Clauses Act 1863 s 17; cf the Companies Clauses Consolidation Act 1845 s 58. See further para 1619 ante.
2   See the Irish Free State (Consequential Adaptation of Enactments) Order 1923, SR & O 1923/405.
3   Companies Clauses Act 1863 s 18.
4   Ibid s 19; cf the Companies Clauses Consolidation Act 1845 s 59. See further para 1619 ante.
5   Companies Clauses Act 1863 s 20.
6   Ibid s 20. The corresponding section of the Companies Clauses Consolidation Act 1845 does not contain any such provision in favour of shareholders not signifying acceptance within the prescribed time: see s 59 and para 1619 ante.

7 Companies Clauses Act 1863 s 20 proviso.
8 Ibid s 21 (amended by the Companies Clauses Act 1869 s 5), whereby it was made clear that the legislature contemplated and authorised new shares or stock of companies governed by these Acts being thereafter issued at a discount: see *Statham v Brighton Marine Palace and Pier Co* [1899] 1 Ch 199; *Webb v Shropshire Rlys Co* [1893] 3 Ch 307 at 329, CA.

(iv) Application of Capital

1624. Application of share and loan capital. All the money raised by the company, whether by subscriptions of the shareholders or by loan or otherwise, must be applied:
(1) in paying the costs and expenses incurred in obtaining the special Act and all expenses incident thereto; and
(2) in carrying the purposes of the company into execution[1].

1 Companies Clauses Consolidation Act 1845 s 65. As to the limits on companies' powers generally, and as to ultra vires acts, see paras 1605-1607 ante.

1625. Promotion expenses. The only persons entitled to require and, if necessary, sue for, payment out of the proposed company's funds of the costs they have incurred are those who have acted directly for the company contemplated by the Bill, without being employed to do the work by any other person for hire or reward; those who have been employed by some other person for hire or reward to do the work must look for payment to the person who employed them[1].

These costs and expenses include money advanced for the purpose of paying parliamentary fees[2]. A promise by promoters of a railway company to pay a sum of money to an influential landowner for his countenance and support does not constitute an expense incident to obtaining the special Act which the company is liable to or lawfully can pay[3]. The period of limitation[4] does not begin to run against a person who is entitled to sue a company for the costs and expenses mentioned until the company has assets with which to pay him[5].

1 *Re Skegness and St Leonard's Tramways Co, ex p Hanly* (1888) 41 ChD 215 at 233, 239, CA; *Re Kent Tramways Co* (1879) 12 ChD 312, CA; *Wyatt v Metropolitan Board of Works* (1862) 11 CBNS 744. Where the company's Act sanctioned two only out of six lines of railway originally projected by the Bill, the company's solicitor was held entitled to be paid out of the company's funds the costs incurred in relation to the four unsanctioned lines, but the special Act expressly provided that the costs incidental and preparatory to obtaining the Act should be paid by the company: *Re Tilleard* (1863) 3 De GJ & Sm 519. As to the rights of a solicitor employed in promoting a company see further para 1724 post.
2 *Scott v Lord Ebury* (1867) LR 2 CP 255 at 263; and see PARLIAMENT.
3 *Earl of Shrewsbury v North Staffordshire Rly Co* (1865) LR 1 Eq 593 at 619; and see *Cutbill v Shropshire Rly Co* (1891) 7 TLR 381 (where promoters had advanced the parliamentary deposit). Funds of a company may probably be lawfully applied in opposing in Parliament the passing of an Act calculated to prejudice the company's undertaking: *A-G v Andrews* (1850) 2 Mac & G 225 at 230.
4 Ie under the Limitation Act 1980 s 5: see LIMITATION OF ACTIONS.
5 *Re Kensington Station Act* (1875) LR 20 Eq 197 at 206, 207.

1626. Division of capital into shares. The Companies Clauses Consolidation Act 1845 makes provision for the division of the capital of the company into shares of a prescribed number and amount, numbered in arithmetical progression beginning with the number one, each share being distinguished by its appropriate number[1].

1 Companies Clauses Consolidation Act 1845 s 6 which, together with ss 7-13 (as amended), comprises the part of the Act described as relating to distribution of capital. A person may become a member even

though the particular shares in respect of which he is a member may not be capable of identification by numbers: *Portal v Emmens* (1876) 1 CPD 201 at 210, 211 (affd 1 CPD 664, CA); *Irish Peat Co v Philips* (1861) 1 B & S 598 at 626, 627, 638; *East Gloucestershire Rly Co v Bartholomew* (1867) LR 3 Exch 15. 'Share' indicates simply a right to participate in the profits of a particular joint stock undertaking (*Morrice v Aylmer* (1874) 10 Ch App 148 at 155 per James LJ; affd (1875) LR 7 HL 717), and to attend and vote at the general meetings of the company (*Nanney v Morgan* (1887) 37 ChD 346 at 352, CA per Cotton LJ).

(5) SUBSCRIBED CAPITAL

(i) Shares

1627. Nature of shares. All shares in the company's undertaking are personal estate, and transmissible as such[1]. They are not of the nature of real estate[1]; and, even if the undertaking comprises land, they are not an interest in land within the statutory provisions[2] requiring a contract for the sale or other disposition to be in writing, incorporating all the expressly agreed terms of the contract in one document or, where contracts are exchanged, in each and signed by or on behalf of each party to the contract[3]. They are choses in action[4] and not goods[5]. Certificates for shares or for the stock into which they have been converted are not goods or documents of title to goods[6].

1 Companies Clauses Consolidation Act 1845 s 7.
2 Ie the Law of Property (Miscellaneous Provisions) Act 1989 s 2: see SALE OF LAND.
3 *Bradley v Holdsworth* (1838) 3 M & W 422; and see *Bligh v Brent* (1837) 2 Y & C Ex 268 at 294.
4 *Colonial Bank v Whinney* (1886) 11 App Cas 426, HL; and see CHOSES IN ACTION vol 6 (Reissue) para 8. As to charging orders on shares or stock see EXECUTION vol 17 para 555 et seq; and as to vesting orders of shares or stock see MENTAL HEALTH vol 30 (Reissue) paras 1482-1484; TRUSTS vol 48 (Reissue) para 769 et seq.
5 See *Humble v Mitchell* (1839) 11 Ad & El 205 at 208. See also the definition of 'goods' in the Sale of Goods Act 1979 s 61(1) (see SALE OF GOODS vol 41 para 639).
6 *Freeman v Appleyard* (1862) 32 LJ Ex 175; *Williams v Colonial Bank* (1888) 38 ChD 388 at 408, CA (affd sub nom *Colonial Bank v Cady and Williams* (1890) 15 App Cas 267, HL).

1628. Capital duty. On and after 31 July 1973 no stamp duty is chargeable on any statement of the amount of the share capital of a company unless the obligation to deliver the statement arose before that date or the period within which it was required to be delivered or sent began on or before that date[1]. Nor is stamp duty chargeable on documents relating to chargeable transactions of capital companies[1] in relation to any transaction occuring on or after 22 March 1988[2].

1 Finance Act 1973 s 49(1).
2 See para 280 ante.

1629. Issue of shares at a discount. New shares issued under the Companies Clauses Consolidation Act 1845[1] and new shares or stock to which the Companies Clauses Act 1863[2] applies[3] may be issued at a discount[4].

The Companies Clauses Act 1863[5] regulates the issue of any shares forming part of the capital, whether original or additional, authorised to be raised by any special Act of a company passed before the parliamentary session of 1869[6]. Any shares the creation of which has been authorised by a company, but which have not been issued before the passing of the Companies Clauses Act 1869, must not be issued on any terms other than those on which they might have been issued if that Act had not been passed, except where the company has authorised the issue on other terms in the proper manner[7]. That Act does not alter or extend the provisions of any Act relating to share capital in respect of which the amount of profits to be divided is limited to a fixed rate per cent upon the company's paid-up capital[8].

1 See the Companies Clauses Consolidation Act 1845 ss 56-60 and paras 1618, 1619 ante.
2 See the Companies Clauses Act 1863 Pt II (ss 12-21) (as amended) and paras 1620-1623 ante.
3 *Statham v Brighton Marine Palace and Pier Co* [1899] 1 Ch 199; *Webb v Shropshire Rlys Co* [1893] 3 Ch 307, CA.
4 *Statham v Brighton Marine Palace and Pier Co* [1899] 1 Ch 199.
5 Companies Clauses Act 1863 ss 12-21; Companies Clauses Act 1869 ss 5, 6. It is clear that, in the particular cases to which those statutory provisions refer, companies may issue their unissued original shares, as well as new shares, at a discount. The question whether, in other cases and in the absence of power in the special Act, original as opposed to new shares or stock may be issued at a discount was left open in *Webb v Shropshire Rlys Co* [1893] 3 Ch 307, CA (decided upon the terms of the special Act). In *Statham v Brighton Marine Palace and Pier Co* [1899] 1 Ch 199, Romer J held that original shares not subscribed for may be issued at a discount. See these two cases discussed in *Newburgh and North Fife Rly Co v North British Rly Co* 1913 SC 1166.
6 Companies Clauses Act 1869 s 6.
7 Ibid s 7. The authorisation referred to probably means that, in the case postulated by s 7, there must, before the issue of shares, be a resolution passed by the company in the manner prescribed by the Companies Clauses Act 1863 s 12 (see para 1620 ante), expressly authorising the particular terms of issue intended; cf the Companies Clauses Act 1869 s 2 and para 1687 note 4 post.
8 Ibid s 8.

1630. Allotment of shares. There are no special provisions in the Companies Clauses Acts with reference to the allotment of shares in companies regulated by those Acts[1], but in general[2] certain provisions[3] of the Companies Act 1985 respecting allotment apply[4].

1 As to the companies so regulated see para 1599 et seq ante.
2 As to the exceptions, ie the bodies corporate to which the unregistered companies' legislation does not apply, see the Companies Act 1985 s 718(2); the Companies (Unregistered Companies) Regulations 1985, SI 1985/680 (amended by SI 1990/438; SI 1990/1394; SI 1990/2571); and para 1767 post.
3 Ie the Companies Act 1985 ss 82, 86, 87. As to the extent of the repeal of ss 82, 86, 87 see para 450 note 5 ante. See also para 1694 post.
4 See ibid s 718(3); the Companies (Unregistered Companies) Regulations 1985 reg 4, Schedule; and para 1767 post.

(ii) Shareholders

A. DESCRIPTION OF SHAREHOLDER

1631. How shareholders are constituted. Every person who has subscribed[1] the prescribed sum or more to the capital of the company or has otherwise become entitled to a share in the company and whose name has been entered on the register of shareholders is deemed to be a shareholder of the company[2].

A scripholder may be entitled, in certain events and on certain terms, to come in and take shares without being liable to be registered against his will as a shareholder[3]. Generally a person becomes entitled to shares by sending the company a signed application form and receiving notice of an allotment pursuant to the application, and consequently a binding contract, by offer and acceptance, is constituted, as in the cases of companies under the Companies Act 1985[4]. Although there cannot be a register in the strict sense of the term until the book containing it is sealed at the first ordinary meeting of a company[5], there are shareholders before that time, inasmuch as the first ordinary meeting is a meeting of shareholders[6]. A transferee whose name is on the register of transfers may be a shareholder without his name being on the register of shareholders[7].

Where the special Act contains the usual provision that the company must not issue any share and that no share will vest in the person accepting it unless and until a sum not being less than one-fifth part of the amount of the share has been paid up in respect of it, anyone who has subscribed for shares and whose name is entered on the register is deemed to be a shareholder, and accordingly is liable for calls, notwithstanding that, when the call is made, the prescribed one-fifth has not been paid up on the shares[8]. Where, however, there is such a provision as to the issue and vesting of shares, and a person who has agreed to take shares but has paid nothing on them executes a transfer which is registered by the company, the transfer operates as a new contract between the transferor, the transferee and the company, whereby the transferee becomes the taker of the shares and the transferor is discharged from his agreement to take them[9].

1 'Subscribed' primarily referred to the signing of the subscription or parliamentary contracts (formerly in vogue when application was made for a special Act to incorporate a company for the execution of some public undertaking), whereby a number of signatories bound themselves to contribute specified sums for the purpose of the undertaking: *Portal v Emmens* (1876) 1 CPD 664 at 669, CA. For forms of subscription contracts and of the subscribers' agreements which usually accompanied them see *Cork and Youghal Rly Co v Paterson* (1856) 18 CB 414 at 415, 422, 433; *Burke v Lechmere* (1871) LR 6 QB 297 at 303. A subscription contract is now neither necessary nor usual, and signing such a contract is not the only way of subscribing; anyone who has agreed in writing to take shares is for this purpose a subscriber: *Portal v Emmens* (1876) 1 CPD 664 at 669, CA; *Re Littlehampton SS Co Ltd, Gregg's Case* (1866) 15 WR 82.

2 Companies Clauses Consolidation Act 1845 s 8. Taking s 8 in conjunction with the definition of shareholder in s 3 (see para 1603 ante), a person who has become entitled to a share, even though he has paid no subscription and no register has been formed, may be a shareholder: *Portal v Emmens* (1876) 1 CPD 664, CA.

3 *McIlwraith v Dublin Trunk Connecting Rly Co* (1871) 7 Ch App 134 at 140; cf *Ormerod's Case* (1867) LR 5 Eq 110. Where the conditions of the issue of scrip certificates merely entitle the scripholder at some future time to an allotment of shares, a scripholder who sells his scrip before registration or whose scrip is forfeited for non-payment of instalments is not liable for shares: *Eustace v Dublin Trunk Connecting Rly Co* (1868) LR 6 Eq 182; *Re Asiatic Banking Corpn, ex p Collum* (1869) LR 9 Eq 236.

4 See *Nicol's Case, Tufnell and Ponsonby's Case* (1885) 29 ChD 421 at 426, CA and para 442 ante. See also paras 369 et seq, 440 ante.

5 See para 1633 post.

6 Se the Companies Clauses Consolidation Act 1845 s 66 and para 1727 post.

7 *Portal v Emmens* (1876) 1 CPD 664, CA; cf *Kipling v Todd* (1878) 3 CPD 350, CA.

8 *East Gloucestershire Rly Co v Bartholomew* (1867) LR 3 Exch 15 at 18, 24; *McEuen v West London Wharves and Warehouses Co* (1871) 6 Ch App 655.

9 *Morton's Case* (1873) LR 16 Eq 104.

1632. Non-recognition of trust affecting shares. The company is not bound to see to the execution of any trust, whether express, implied or constructive, to which any shares are subject[1]. The receipt of the party in whose name any share stands in the company's books or, if it stands in the names of more persons than one, the receipt of one of the persons named in the register of shareholders, is a sufficient discharge to the company for any dividend or other sum payable in respect of the share, notwithstanding any trusts to which the share may then be subject, and whether or not the company has had notice of them; and the company is not bound to see to the application of the money paid upon such receipt[1]. Therefore, as between themselves and the company, executors or trustees registered as the holders of shares have and are subject to precisely the same rights and liabilities as other joint holders; they are joint holders in their individual capacity, and any transfer of the shares must be executed by all of them; the company has nothing to do with the character in which they hold the shares[2].

Where, however, directors make an illegal application of the company's funds by investing them in the purchase, in the name of the chairman of the board, of shares in another company, notwithstanding the illegality of the transaction, the chairman is a trustee of the shares for his company and is compellable to transfer them as it directs[3].

1 Companies Clauses Consolidation Act 1845 s 20.
2 *Barton v North Staffordshire Rly Co* (1888) 38 ChD 458 at 464, 465; *Barton v London and North Western Rly Co* (1889) 24 QBD 77 at 89, CA; and see *Muir v City of Glasgow Bank* (1879) 4 App Cas 337, HL; *Re City of Glasgow Bank, Bell's Case* (1879) 4 App Cas 547, HL; *Cuninghame v City of Glasgow Bank* (1879) 4 App Cas 607, HL; cf *Re Shelley, ex p Stewart* (1864) 4 De GJ & Sm 543 at 547, 548; and cf the Companies Act 1985 s 360; and see para 385 ante.
3 *Great Eastern Rly Co v Turner* (1872) 8 Ch App 149; cf *Murray v Pinkett* (1846) 12 Cl & Fin 764, HL.

1633. Register of shareholders. The company must keep a book, called the 'Register of Shareholders', in which must be entered in alphabetical order the names of the corporations, and the names and additions of the persons entitled to shares in the company, with the number of shares to which each shareholder is entitled, distinguishing each share by its number and the amount of the subscriptions paid on the shares. This book must be authenticated by the company's common seal being affixed to it at the first ordinary meeting, or at the next subsequent meeting, and so from time to time at each ordinary meeting of the company[1]. The provision as to distinguishing each share by its number is directory, and the insertion of the distinguishing numbers in the register is not essential[2]. Nor is the direction as to the time at which the register is to be made up an essential condition to its validity, and a register made up later may be valid[3]. The register need not necessarily consist of a single volume; where it is contained in several volumes, and only the last one of the series is sealed, the whole of the register is admissible in evidence[4].

1 Companies Clauses Consolidation Act 1845 s 9. An unsatisfied judgment creditor is entitled to inspect the register without fee: see s 36 and para 1646 post. The register is prima facie evidence against a shareholder sued for calls: see s 28 and para 1643 post. 'Additions' means the persons' occupations, residences etc.
2 *East Gloucestershire Rly Co v Bartholomew* (1867) LR 3 Exch 15. Cf the position where the register is being relied upon as sole evidence in an action: see para 1643 post.
3 *Burke v Lechmere* (1871) LR 6 QB 297 at 304; *Wolverhampton New Waterworks Co v Hawksford* (1861) 11 CBNS 456, Ex Ch.
4 *Inglis v Great Northern Rly Co* (1852) 19 LTOS 149, HL; and see *Bain v Whitehaven and Furness Junction Rly Co* (1850) 3 HL Cas 1; cf *London Grand Junction Rly Co v Freeman* (1841) 2 Man & G 606 at 637 (a case before the Act).

1634. Shareholders' address book. In addition to the register of shareholders[1], the company must provide a book called the 'Shareholders' Address Book', in which the secretary must from time to time enter in alphabetical order the corporate names and places of business of the shareholders who are corporations, and the surnames of the other shareholders with their respective christian names, places of abode and descriptions, so far as these are known to the company[2].

Every shareholder or, if a corporation, its clerk or agent may at all convenient times examine this book without charge, and may require a copy of the whole or of any part of it[3]. This right to have a copy is a private right conferred on a person as a member of the company and not as a member of the public[4]. The remedy to enforce the right is by an injunction to restrain the company from continuing to refuse to supply him, or a mandatory injunction directing the company to supply him; and the court cannot inquire into the applicant's motives[4].

1 See para 1633 ante.
2 Companies Clauses Consolidation Act 1845 s 10.
3 Ibid s 10. For every 100 words so required to be copied the company may demand a sum not exceeding two pence: s 10 (amended by the Decimal Currency Act 1969 s 10(1)). The figure has been rounded down in consequence of the withdrawal of the halfpenny from 31 December 1984.
4 *Davies v Gas Light and Coke Co* [1909] 1 Ch 708, CA.

B. SHARE CERTIFICATES

1635. Delivery and effect of certificates. On the demand of the holder of any share, a company must cause to be delivered to him a certificate of the proprietorship of the share under its common seal, specifying the share in the undertaking to which he is entitled[1]. The certificate may be according to the statutory form or to the like effect[2]; and for the certificate the company may demand any sum not exceeding the amount prescribed in the special Act or, if no amount is prescribed, a sum not exceeding 12 pence[3]. The certificate is a solemn affirmation under the company's seal that a certain amount of shares or stock stands in the name of the holder named in the certificate[4], and is a representation, binding on the company by way of estoppel, that the amount stated in the certificate to have been paid on the shares has been paid[5].

The certificate is admissible in all courts as prima facie evidence of the title of the shareholder, his executors, administrators, successors or assigns to the share specified in it[6], but it is not conclusive evidence of title[7]; and the want of it does not prevent the holder of any share from disposing of it[8].

1 Companies Clauses Consolidation Act 1845 s 11.
2 Ibid s 11. For the form of certificate see s 11, Sch (A).
3 Ibid ss 2, 11 (amended by the Decimal Currency Act 1969 ss 9, 10(1), Sch 1). The figure has been rounded down in consequence of the withdrawal of the halfpenny from 31 December 1984.
4 *Shropshire Union Railways and Canal Co v R* (1875) LR 7 HL 496 at 509.
5 Cf *Bloomenthal v Ford* [1897] AC 156, HL. As to the estoppel created by the issue of a share certificate see para 488 ante.
6 Companies Clauses Consolidation Act 1845 s 12.
7 *Powell v London and Provincial Bank* [1893] 1 Ch 610 at 617 (affd [1893] 2 Ch 555, CA); cf *Burkinshaw v Nicholls* (1878) 3 App Cas 1004, HL; *Shropshire Union Railways and Canal Co v R* (1875) LR 7 HL 496; *Société Générale de Paris v Walker* (1885) 11 App Cas 20 at 35, HL; and see para 487 ante.
8 Companies Clauses Consolidation Act 1845 s 12.

1636. New certificates. If the certificate is worn out or damaged, it may be produced at some meeting of the directors and they may order it to be cancelled, and thereupon another similar certificate must be given to the person in whom the property of the certificate, and of the share mentioned in it, is at the time vested[1]. If the certificate is lost or destroyed and the loss is proved to the satisfaction of the directors, a similar certificate must be given to the person entitled to it[1]. In either case the secretary must make a due entry of the substituted certificate in the register of shareholders[1]. For every certificate so given or exchanged the company may demand any sum not exceeding the amount prescribed by the special Act or, if no amount is prescribed, a sum not exceeding 12 pence[2].

1　Companies Clauses Consolidation Act 1845 s 13.
2　Ibid ss 2, 13 (amended by the Decimal Currency Act 1969 s 10(1)). The figure has been rounded down in consequence of the withdrawal of the halfpenny from 31 December 1984. The note at the foot of a share certificate, requiring its production prior to the registration of a transfer, is not a representation that a transfer will not be registered without its production: *Rainford v James Keith and Blackman Co Ltd* [1905] 1 Ch 296 (revsd on another ground [1905] 2 Ch 147, CA); and see para 489 ante.

C. SHAREHOLDERS' LIABILITY FOR CALLS OR CAPITAL NOT PAID UP

1637. Shareholders' liability in general. The persons who have subscribed[1] any money towards an undertaking, or their legal representatives[2], must pay the sums subscribed or those portions as are from time to time called for by the company at the times and places it appoints[3]. The company's remedy by action for recovery of calls is enforceable only against persons who were shareholders when the calls were made[4].

1　'Subscribed' is used with reference primarily to subscription of the parliamentary contract and subscribers' agreement which, in 1845, were required by the standing orders of both Houses of Parliament in the case of companies to which the Companies Clauses Consolidation Act 1845 applies: see para 1631 note 1 ante. See also *Cromford Rly Co v Lacey* (1829) 3 Y & J 80 at 86, 90. The provision also applies to the modern method of subscription by application for shares in a company after its incorporation. Liability to pay calls is incurred by so subscribing as to become entitled to shares: *Waterford, Wexford, Wicklow and Dublin Rly Co v Pidcock* (1853) 8 Exch 279 at 283, 285; *Edwards v Kilkenny and Great Southern and Western Rly Co* (1863) 14 CBNS 526.
2　'Legal representatives' applies to executors who are in the possession of shares and renders them liable for calls upon those shares; but an executor cannot be sued personally in the form indicated by the Companies Clauses Consolidation Act 1845 s 26 for a call made in his testator's lifetime: *Birkenhead, Lancashire and Cheshire Junction Rly Co v Cotesworth* (1850) 5 Exch 226 at 228. See also para 1642 post.
3　Companies Clauses Consolidation Act 1845 s 21.
4　*Wolverhampton New Waterworks Co v Hawksford* (1859) 6 CBNS 336 at 353, 357. In an action for calls under the Companies Clauses Consolidation Act 1845 the form of remedy given by s 25 (see para 1642 post) must be followed: *Wolverhampton New Waterworks Co v Hawksford* supra at 356, 357.

1638. Power to make calls. A company may from time to time make calls upon the shareholders in respect of the amount of capital subscribed or owing by them, as it thinks fit, provided that at least 21 days' notice is given of each call, that no call exceeds the amount, if any, prescribed by the special Act, that successive calls are not made at less than the interval, if any, prescribed, and that the aggregate amount of calls made in any one year does not exceed the prescribed amount, if any[1]. Every shareholder is liable to pay the amount of the calls so made in respect of the shares held by him to the persons and at the times and places from time to time appointed by the company[2].

1　Companies Clauses Consolidation Act 1845 ss 2, 22.
2　Ibid s 22. The particulars as to the persons to whom and the times and places at which payment is to be made must be specified in the notice of the call, but may be decided by the directors subsequent to the board's actual resolution to make the call: *Great North of England Rly Co v Biddulph* (1840) 7 M & W 243 at 262; *London and Brighton Rly Co v Fairclough* (1841) 2 Man & G 674 at 703; *Sheffield, Ashton-under-Lyne and Manchester Rly Co v Woodcock* (1841) 7 M & W 574.

1639. How calls are made. The power to make calls may be, and usually is, exercised by the directors[1]. A call is generally deemed to have been made when the resolution to call for the money is passed; the resolution need not specify either the time or the place for payment, it being only a determination that an application is to be made to each shareholder for a portion of the amount of his shares[2]. The resolution is not invalid merely because it is prospective. Thus, a resolution may be passed on 13 March that a call be made on 30 March, payable on 1 May following[3]. A call may validly be made payable by instalments[4]; but probably, in that case, the company cannot maintain an action for any part of the call until the last instalment is due, the day appointed for payment of the last instalment being, in that case, the day appointed for the payment of the call within the meaning of the statute[5].

If the directors make a call which is for any reason invalid, they must before proceeding to make a valid call rescind the resolution for the invalid call[6].

1 *Ambergate, Nottingham and Boston and Eastern Junction Rly Co v Mitchell* (1849) 4 Exch 540.
2 *R v Londonderry and Coleraine Rly Co* (1849) 13 QB 998 at 1005; *Newry and Enniskillen Rly Co v Edmunds* (1848) 2 Exch 118 at 122.
3 *Sheffield, Ashton-under-Lyne and Manchester Rly Co v Woodcock* (1841) 7 M & W 574 at 589.
4 *Ambergate, Nottingham, Boston and Eastern Junction Rly Co v Norcliffe* (1851) 6 Exch 629.
5 *Ambergate, Nottingham and Boston and Eastern Junction Rly Co v Coulthard* (1850) 5 Exch 459; *Birkenhead, Lancashire and Cheshire Junction Rly Co v Webster* (1851) 6 Exch 277 at 278; *Re Jennings, ex p Belfast and County Down Rly Co* (1851) 1 I Ch R 654 at 656.
6 *Welland Rly Co v Berrie* (1861) 6 H & N 416 at 422.

1640. Liability for calls. The making of the call and notice of its having been made are two distinct things[1]. Consequently a shareholder who transfers his shares after a call has been made on them continues liable to pay the call, as between himself and the company, even if at the time of the transfer he has not received the notice[2]. This right of the company against a transferor does not, however, affect any right of his against the transferee under the contract of transfer[3].

The person whose name appears on the register is alone personally liable to the company for calls. The company cannot, therefore, compel an equitable mortgagee or other owner of shares to pay calls on them[4]; nor can it sue a transferee for calls until his name has been entered on a duly sealed register[5].

1 *R v Londonderry and Coleraine Rly Co* (1849) 13 QB 998.
2 See the Companies Clauses Consolidation Act 1845 s 16 and para 1652 post.
3 *R v Londonderry and Coleraine Rly Co* (1849) 13 QB 998. The purchaser of a share with an uncalled liability is bound to indemnify his vendor against calls made after the date of the contract of sale: *Spencer v Ashworth, Partington & Co* [1925] 1 KB 589, CA; and see para 491 ante.
4 *Newry and Enniskillen Rly Co v Moss* (1851) 14 Beav 64.
5 *Newry and Enniskillen Rly Co v Edmunds* (1848) 2 Exch 118 at 127; cf *McEuen v West London Wharves and Warehouses Co* (1871) 6 Ch App 655; and see para 1631 ante.

1641. Minor's liability. A minor[1] is capable of becoming a shareholder in a company governed by the Companies Clauses Consolidation Act 1845, and it seems that an action for calls may be maintained against him even during his minority[2]. If, having been registered while a minor, he attains his majority and then permits his name to continue registered, he is liable to be sued for calls, whether made during or since his minority[3]. Where, however, he has become a shareholder by contract, he may repudiate the contract either during his minority or when he comes of age, and after that repudiation cannot be sued for calls[4].

1 As to the attainment of majority at the age of 18 see the Family Law Reform Act 1969 s 1 and CHILDREN vol 5(2) (Reissue) para 601.
2 *Leeds and Thirsk Rly Co v Fearnley* (1849) 4 Exch 26; cf *Re Royal Naval School, Seymour v Royal Naval School* [1910] 1 Ch 806.

3 *Cork and Bandon Rly Co v Cazenove* (1847) 10 QB 935 at 939.
4 *Newry and Enniskillen Rly Co v Coombe* (1849) 3 Exch 565 at 574, 575. A minor may repudiate a contract
   to take shares but cannot recover sums paid on allotment and on call unless there has been a total failure
   of consideration: *Steinberg v Scala (Leeds) Ltd* [1923] 2 Ch 452, CA. See further para 374 ante.

1642. Recovery of payment and interest. If, before or on the day appointed for
payment, a shareholder does not pay the amount of any call to which he is liable, he is
liable to pay interest at the rate allowed by law from the day appointed for payment to
the time of the actual payment[1]. The company may sue him in any court having
competent jurisdiction and recover the amount, with lawful interest, from the day on
which the call was payable[2].

In an action for calls it is sufficient for the company to allege that the defendant is the
holder of one share or more in the company, stating the number of shares, and is
indebted to it in the sum to which the calls in arrear amount in respect of one call or
more upon one share or more (stating the number and amount of each of those calls),
by which an action has accrued to the company by virtue of the Companies Clauses
Consolidation Act 1845 and the special Act[3]. An allegation in the pleading that the
defendant is a holder may be supported by proof that he was so when the call was
made[4]. An action in this statutory form cannot be maintained against the executors of a
deceased shareholder personally, where the call was made in his lifetime[5]. The
limitation period in an action in the statutory form is six years[6].

1 Companies Clauses Consolidation Act 1845 s 23. Interest on a judgment debt is at 8% per annum:
  Judgments Act 1838 s 17 (amended by the Judgments Debts (Rate of Interest) Order 1993, SI 1993/564,
  art 2) and probably the current rate of interest for the time being is the rate demandable by a company
  under the Companies Clauses Consolidation Act 1845 s 23: see *London, Chatham and Dover Rly Co v
  South Eastern Rly Co* [1892] 1 Ch 120 at 133, 136, 137, CA; affd [1893] AC 429, HL. See also *Maine and
  New Brunswick Electrical Power Co v Hart* [1929] AC 631, PC and MONEY.
2 Companies Clauses Consolidation Act 1845 s 25. As to forfeiture in case of non-payment see para 1655
  et seq post.
3 Ibid s 26. Where the statement of claim is framed in strict accordance with s 26, interest may be
  recovered, even though not expressly claimed: cf *Southampton Dock Co v Richards* (1840) 1 Man & G 448
  at 464. As to the court's general power to award interest see the Supreme Court Act 1981 s 35A (added
  by the Administration of Justice Act 1982 s 15(1), Sch 1 Pt I) and PRACTICE AND PROCEDURE.
4 *Belfast and County Down Rly Co v Strange* (1848) 1 Exch 739 at 742; *Wilson v Birkenhead, Lancashire and
  Cheshire Junction Rly Co* (1851) 6 Exch 626 at 628; *Inglis v Great Northern Rly Co* (1852) 19 LTOS 149,
  HL.
5 *Birkenhead, Lancashire and Cheshire Junction Rly Co v Cotesworth* (1850) 5 Exch 226 at 228.
6 Limitation Act 1980 s 9(1).

1643. Evidence. At the trial of the action it is sufficient to prove that, at the time of
making the call, the defendant was a holder of one share or more in the undertaking
and that the call was in fact made, and notice of the making of the call given as directed
by the Companies Clauses Consolidation Act 1845 or the special Act[1]. It is not
necessary to prove the appointment of the directors who made the call, or any other
matter[2]. The company is thereupon entitled to recover what is due upon the call, with
interest, unless it appears either that the call exceeds the prescribed amount, that due
notice was not given, that the prescribed interval between two successive calls had not
elapsed, or that calls amounting to more than the sum prescribed for the total amount
of calls in one year had been made within that period[3].

The production of the register of shareholders is prima facie evidence of the
defendant being a shareholder, and of the number and amount of his shares[4], without
proof that the company's seal has been duly affixed at a meeting[5]. If the company relies

on this provision, the register must contain within itself all the particulars necessary to charge the defendant with liability in the action[6], and all the provisions of the enactment as to how the register is to be kept must be scrupulously observed[7]. In addition, if it is proved that such person has become, by subscribing the prescribed sum or otherwise, entitled to a share in the company, the evidence that he is a shareholder is conclusive.

If there is no register or if the register is so defective as to be inadmissible in evidence, other evidence must be adduced to prove that a person is a shareholder[8].

The defendant may disprove the prima facie liability arising from his name being on the register by showing that the company had no authority to put, and ought not to have put, his name there[9]. He may, however, be precluded by his own conduct from denying, as against the company, that he is a shareholder; and, if he has so acted as, in effect, to claim the position of a shareholder, he may be estopped from raising some objection which he might otherwise have raised to his liability for calls[10].

  1   Companies Clauses Consolidation Act 1845 s 27.
  2   Ibid s 27.
  3   Ibid s 27; *R v Londonderry and Coleraine Rly Co* (1849) 13 QB 998 at 1006.
  4   Companies Clauses Consolidation Act 1845 s 28. However, where B, acting professedly on behalf of himself and his co-trustees, T and another, accepted an allotment of shares which in the sealed register were entered as held by 'B and others', the entry was held to be no evidence against T: *Birkenhead, Lancashire and Cheshire Junction Rly Co v Brownrigg* (1849) 4 Exch 426. Cf the Civil Evidence Act 1968 s 4 (admissibility of records as to facts stated): see EVIDENCE vol 17 para 58.
  5   See the Companies Clauses Consolidation Act 1845 s 9 (cited in para 1633 ante); *Derbyshire Rly Co v Tomlinson* (1848) 12 LTOS 124; *London and North Western Rly Co v M'Michael* (1850) 5 Exch 855.
  6   *East Gloucestershire Rly Co v Bartholomew* (1867) LR 3 Exch 15 at 22.
  7   *Bain v Whitehaven and Furness Junction Rly Co* (1850) 3 HL Cas 1 at 22 per Lord Brougham; *East Gloucestershire Rly Co v Bartholomew* (1867) LR 3 Exch 15 at 20, 27; and see *Waterford, Wexford, Wicklow and Dublin Rly Co v Pidcock* (1853) 8 Exch 279 at 283.
  8   *Portal v Emmens* (1876) 1 CPD 201 at 212 (affd 1 CPD 664, CA); *Wolverhampton New Waterworks Co v Hawksford* (1861) 11 CBNS 456 at 470, 471, Ex Ch.
  9   *Waterford, Wexford, Wicklow and Dublin Rly Co v Pidcock* (1853) 8 Exch 279; *Newry and Enniskillen Rly Co v Edmunds* (1848) 2 Exch 118 at 126; cf *Guest v Worcester, Bromyard and Leominster Rly Co* (1868) LR 4 CP 9.
10   See eg *Cromford Rly Co v Lacey* (1829) 3 Y & J 80; *Cheltenham and Great Western Union Rly Co v Daniel* (1841) 2 QB 281 at 292; *Sheffield, Ashton-under-Lyne and Manchester Rly Co v Woodcock* (1841) 7 M & W 574 at 580, 582.

1644. Proceedings in Scotland to recover calls. Although in general the Companies Clauses Consolidation Act 1845 does not extend to Scotland[1], if any shareholder residing in Scotland fails to pay the amount of any call made upon him by the company, the company may proceed against him in Scotland and sue for and recover the amount of the call, or declare his share forfeited, in the manner provided by the Companies Clauses Consolidation (Scotland) Act 1845 in regard to shareholders of any company in Scotland[2].

  1   Companies Clauses Consolidation Act 1845 s 163.
  2   Ibid s 164. For an instance of the exercise of this power see *Inglis v Great Northern Rly Co* (1852) 19 LTOS 149, HL.

1645. Execution against shareholders for company's debts. If any execution has been issued against the property or effects of a company, and there cannot be found sufficient on which to levy that execution, then execution may be issued against any of the shareholders to the extent of their shares respectively in the company's capital not then paid up, upon an order of the court in which the action or other proceeding has been brought or instituted made upon motion in open court after notice to the persons sought to be charged or by summons in chambers[1].

Execution against shareholders will be granted only after proof of total[2] or partial[3] failure of execution against the company, and only against persons who were shareholders at the time of the failure of that execution, whether they were so at the date of the judgment or not[4].

The court may order execution to issue, or may order that any issue or question necessary to determine the rights of the parties be tried in any of the ways in which any question in an action may be tried, and in either case such terms as to costs or otherwise as are just may be imposed[5].

1 Companies Clauses Consolidation Act 1845 s 36; RSC Ord 46 rr 2, 4. The court may order execution so to issue against a shareholder who has not in fact taken up any shares if he is liable to do so: *Portal v Emmens* (1876) 1 CPD 664, CA. A director who by a resignation in good faith has surrendered his inchoate right to take shares is treated as being thereby divested of any liability in respect of the holding of shares, and execution will not be ordered against him: *Kipling v Todd* (1878) 3 CPD 350, CA; *Mammatt v Brett* (1886) 54 LT 165.

2 A mere statement by a solicitor's clerk that abortive writs of fieri facias have issued against the company is insufficient: *Re Emery, Hitchins v Kilkenny and Great Southern and Western Rly Co* (1850) 10 CB 160. Returns of nulla bona to writs of fieri facias coupled with an unanswered affidavit of no effects have been held sufficient evidence: *Rastrick v Derbyshire, Staffordshire and Worcestershire Junction Rly Co* (1853) 9 Exch 149; *Ridgway v Security Mutual Life Assurance Society* (1856) 18 CB 686. The return of nulla bona need not have been filed before the application is made: *Ilfracombe Rly Co v Devon and Somerset Rly Co* (1866) LR 2 CP 15.

3 *Rigby v Dublin Trunk Rly Co* (1867) LR 2 CP 586 at 588; *Ilfracombe Rly Co v Poltimore* (1868) LR 3 CP 288.

4 *Nixon v Brownlow, Nixon v Green* (1858) 3 H & N 686.

5 RSC Ord 46 r 4(3). This supersedes, but does not abolish, the old remedy by scire facias: see further Chitty's Archbold's Practice (14th Edn) 1072-1077. As to the circumstances in which writs of scire facias might be issued see eg *Re Emery, Hitchins v Kilkenny and Great Southern and Western Rly Co* (1850) 10 CB 160; *Hitchins v Kilkenny and Great Southern and Western Rly Co* (1854) 15 CB 459. Cf *Healey v Chichester and Midhurst Rly Co* (1870) LR 9 Eq 148. RSC Ord 46 r 2(1)(d) refers generally to relief being subject to the fulfilment of a condition.

1646. Inspection of and evidence by register. For the purpose of ascertaining the names of the shareholders and the amount of capital remaining to be paid upon their respective shares, any person entitled to execution may at all reasonable times inspect the register of shareholders without fee[1]. The right to inspect is enforceable by application to the court in the action in which the judgment against the company was recovered[2], and includes a right to take a copy of the material part or parts of the register[3].

The register is prima facie evidence that any particular person is or is not a shareholder, but is not conclusive[4]. A shareholder who is registered in respect of partly paid shares may show that, as between himself and the company, he is not liable for calls[5].

1 Companies Clauses Consolidation Act 1845 s 36.

2 *Meader v Isle of Wight Ferry Co* (1861) 9 WR 750.

3 *Mutter v Eastern and Midlands Rly Co* (1888) 38 ChD 92 at 106, CA, approved in *Re Balaghât Gold Mining Co* [1901] 2 KB 665 at 667, CA; *Ormerod, Grierson & Co v St George's Ironworks Ltd* [1905] 1 Ch 505, CA; *Davies v Gas Light and Coke Co* [1909] 1 Ch 708, CA.

4 *Rastrick v Derbyshire, Staffordshire and Worcestershire Junction Rly Co* (1853) 9 Exch 149 at 151; *Edwards v Kilkenny and Great Southern and Western Rly Co* (1863) 14 CBNS 526 at 531; *Portal v Emmens* (1876) 1 CPD 664 at 668, CA; *Kipling v Todd* (1878) 3 CPD 350 at 357, CA. As to evidence by register see further para 1643 ante.

5 *Guest v Worcester, Bromyard and Leominster Rly Co* (1868) LR 4 CP 9.

1647. Reimbursement of shareholder. If by means of the execution any shareholder has paid any sum of money beyond the amount then due from him in respect of calls, he must forthwith be reimbursed that additional sum by the directors out of the company's funds[1].

If proceedings to enforce the creditor's judgment have been commenced against a shareholder, a payment by him in good faith under those proceedings, at whatever stage they may be, is a good answer against another creditor[2].

1 Companies Clauses Consolidation Act 1845 s 37. The right to reimbursement under the 1845 Act does not arise unless the shareholder submits to execution, but payment under threat of execution would by the general law confer a right of reimbursement under an implied contract of indemnity: see eg *North v Walthamstow UC* (1898) 67 LJQB 972.
2 *Kernaghan v Dublin Trunk Connecting Rly Co, James' Case* (1867) LR 3 QB 47 at 49.

1648. Payment of subscriptions in advance of calls. If it thinks fit, a company may receive from any of its shareholders payment in advance of all or any part of the money due upon their shares, beyond the sums actually called for[1]. Upon the principal money so paid in advance, or so much of it as from time to time exceeds the amount of the calls then made upon the shares in respect of which the advance is made, the company may pay interest at such rate as the shareholder paying that sum in advance and the company agree upon, but not exceeding the legal rate of interest for the time being[2].

1 Companies Clauses Consolidation Act 1845 s 24.
2 Ibid s 24. As to the legal rate of interest see para 1642 note 1 ante.

D. TRANSFER AND TRANSMISSION OF SHARES

1649. Obligations of seller and buyer of shares. In ordinary cases the mutual obligations of the seller and the buyer of shares are briefly as follows. The seller must at the time fixed by the contract or, if no time is fixed, within a reasonable time[1], deliver to the buyer, against payment of the agreed price, a duly executed transfer of, and the certificate for, the shares agreed to be sold, and must do nothing to prevent the registration of the buyer as transferee. Where the contract is subject to the Rules and Regulations of the Stock Exchange, there is no implied term that, if the company refuses to register the transfer, the price is to be refunded[2]. The buyer must:

(1) prepare a proper instrument of transfer and send it to the seller for execution, although in practice the seller's broker prepares and procures the seller's execution of the transfer and then sends it to the buyer[3];
(2) on receipt of a transfer duly executed by the seller and of the relative certificates, pay the agreed price;
(3) procure the registration of the transfer[4]; and
(4) pay and indemnify the seller against all liability for calls made subsequently to the contract of sale[5].

In the absence of any stipulation in the contract to the contrary, a purchaser of shares is entitled to all dividends on them declared after the date of the contract[6] but not to dividends declared before the date of the contract the payment of which is postponed[7].

A contract for the sale of shares may be enforced by an action for specific performance[8].

Where a company acting on a forged transfer alters its register of shareholders by striking out the name of the true owner and inserting that of the transferee, the true owner is in general entitled to obtain rectification of the register[9]. Statutory provision is made by which a company may form a compensation fund in respect of losses arising from forged transfers[10].

1   *De Waal v Adler* (1886) 12 App Cas 141, PC.
2   *London Founders Association v Clarke Ltd and Palmer* (1888) 20 QBD 576 at 579, 585, CA; *Maxted v Paine* (1871) LR 6 Exch 132 at 150, Ex Ch. As to the law governing contracts made subject to the Rules and Regulations of the Stock Exchange see STOCK EXCHANGE.
3   *Stephens v De Medina* (1843) 4 QB 422 at 429; *Bowlby v Bell* (1846) 3 CB 248 at 294.
4   *Sayles v Blane* (1849) 14 QB 205; *Wynne v Price* (1849) 3 De G & Sm 310. The seller is not entitled to rescind the contract if registration of the purchaser is refused by the company, but he must rely on his right to be indemnified against calls: *Casey v Bentley* [1902] 1 IR 376, CA.
5   *Wynne v Price* (1849) 3 De G & Sm 310; *Maxted v Paine* (1871) LR 6 Exch 132, Ex Ch. As to this liability to indemnify the seller against calls see further para 492 ante.
6   *Black v Homersham* (1878) 4 Ex D 24. As to the need for registration of the transfer to entitle the purchaser to receive dividends see para 1651 post.
7   *Re Kidner, Kidner v Kidner* [1929] 2 Ch 121.
8   *Duncuft v Albrecht* (1841) 12 Sim 189, LC; *Cheale v Kenward* (1858) 3 De G & J 27. Such an action is within the scope of RSC Ord 86 r 1: *Woodlands v Hind* [1955] 2 All ER 604, [1955] 1 WLR 688; and see para 490 ante.
9   See para 515 ante.
10   See para 516 ante.

1650. How shares are transferred. The statutory provisions[1] grouped as relating to the transfer and transmission of shares govern all cases in which the property in shares or stock passes from the proprietor to another person[2]. They are not restricted to transfers by actual sale and purchase for money, and apply to a transfer for a nominal consideration by way of voluntary settlement[3].

Subject to the regulations in the Companies Clauses Consolidation Act 1845[4] or in the special Act, every shareholder may sell and transfer all or any of his shares or stock[5]. Every transfer must be by duly stamped deed in which the consideration must be truly stated; the deed may be according to the statutory form or to the like effect[6]. A deed executed by the transferor and duly registered is essential to pass the legal title[7]. The company is not bound to register a deed differing materially from the statutory form[8], which requires execution by the transferee as well as by the transferor[9].

When duly executed, the transfer deed must be delivered to the secretary, and must be kept by him[10]. This delivery is essential to the legal efficacy of a transfer[11].

1   Ie the Companies Clauses Consolidation Act 1845 ss 14–19.
2   *Copeland v North Eastern Rly Co* (1856) 6 E & B 277 at 283.
3   *Copeland v North Eastern Rly Co* (1856) 6 E & B 277.
4   See the Companies Clauses Consolidation Act 1845 ss 15–17; para 1651 et seq post; and *Nanney v Morgan* (1887) 37 ChD 346 at 353, CA.
5   Companies Clauses Consolidation Act 1845 s 14. As to the amounts in which stock may be transferred see the Decimal Currency Act 1969 s 8 and para 210 ante.
6   Companies Clauses Consolidation Act 1845 s 14. For a form of transfer see s 14, Sch (B).
7   *McEuen v West London Wharves and Warehouses Co* (1871) 6 Ch App 655; *Powell v London and Provincial Bank* [1893] 2 Ch 555 at 560, CA.
8   *R v General Cemetry Co* (1856) 6 E & B 415 at 419, 420; *Roots v Williamson* (1888) 38 ChD 485.
9   See the Companies Clauses Consolidation Act 1845 s 14, Sch (B).
10   Ibid s 15.
11   *Nanney v Morgan* (1887) 37 ChD 346, CA.

1651. Registration of transfers. The secretary must enter a memorial of the transfer in a book called the 'Register of Transfers', indorsing the entry on the transfer deed and, on demand, delivering a new certificate to the purchaser[1]. For every entry, indorsement and certificate the company may demand any sum not exceeding the prescribed amount or, if no amount is prescribed, a sum not exceeding 12 pence[2]. On the request of the purchaser of any share, an indorsement of the transfer must be made on the certificate instead of a new certificate being granted, and this indorsement, signed by the secretary, is considered in every respect the same as a new certificate[3]. Until the transfer has been delivered to the secretary, the seller of the share continues liable to the company for any calls that may be made upon the share, and the purchaser is not entitled to receive any share of the profits of the undertaking or to vote in respect of the share[3].

Where a valid and duly executed deed of transfer of shares has been left with the secretary for registration, mere neglect on the company's part to register the transfer does not affect the transferee's right to be treated as the legal owner of the shares[4]. Registration, unless preceded by a valid transfer, does not, however, give the transferee a good title[5]. A company cannot refuse to register a real and absolute transfer merely because it is made to a pauper with the object of escaping from liability to calls[6].

Registration of a transfer may be enforced by mandamus[7].

1 Companies Clauses Consolidation Act 1845 s 15.
2 Ibid s 15 (amended by the Decimal Currency Act 1969 s 10(1)). The figure has been rounded down in consequence of the withdrawal of the halfpenny from 31 December 1984.
3 Companies Clauses Consolidation Act 1845 s 15.
4 *Nanney v Morgan* (1887) 37 ChD 246 at 354, CA.
5 *Powell v London and Provincial Bank* [1893] 2 Ch 555 at 560, CA.
6 *R v Lambourn Valley Rly Co* (1888) 22 QBD 463 at 465; and see *Re Discoverers' Finance Corpn Ltd, Lindlar's Case* [1910] 1 Ch 312, CA.
7 *R v Carnatic Rly Co* (1873) LR 8 QB 299; *R v Lambourn Valley Rly Co* (1888) 22 QBD 463; *R v London and North Western Rly Co* [1894] 2 QB 512. As to mandamus see ADMINISTRATIVE LAW vol 1(1) (Reissue) para 128 et seq.

1652. Transfer when calls unpaid. A shareholder is not entitled to transfer any share after a call has been made until he has paid the call or until he has paid all calls for the time being due on every share held by him[1]. Neglect to do so, if waived, as it may be, by the company, does not make the transfer void; and, if directors consent to and register a transfer of shares on which there is a call in arrear, the property in the shares passes, and the transferor ceases to be a shareholder in respect of them, though he may remain liable to the company for the amount of the call[2]. Where a shareholder executes a transfer after the directors have passed a resolution to make a call but before he has received notice of it, the company is not bound to register the transfer and a mandamus to compel registration will be refused[3]. The company's right in such a case to compel the transferor to pay a call does not, however, affect any right which he in his turn may have against the transferee under the contract between them[4].

The company cannot refuse to register a transfer of fully paid shares or stock on the ground that the transferor holds other shares on which a call is in arrear[5].

1 Companies Clauses Consolidation Act 1845 s 16; *R v Wing* (1851) 17 QB 645 at 650, 651.
2 *Re Hoylake Rly Co, ex p Littledale* (1874) 9 Ch App 257 at 259, 262.
3 *R v Londonderry and Coleraine Rly Co* (1849) 13 QB 998 at 1005.
4 *R v Londonderry and Coleraine Rly Co* (1849) 13 QB 998; and see paras 509, 1640 ante.
5 *Hubbersty v Manchester, Sheffield and Lincolnshire Rly Co* (1867) LR 2 QB 471, Ex Ch.

1653. Closing register of transfers. The directors may close the register of transfers for the prescribed period or, if no period be prescribed, then for a period not exceeding 14 days previous to each ordinary meeting[1], and may fix a day for the closing, of which seven days' notice must be given by advertisement[2]. As between the company and the party claiming under it, but not otherwise, any transfer made during the time when the transfer books are so closed is to be considered as made subsequently to the ordinary meeting[3].

1　For the meaning of 'ordinary meeting' see para 1727 post.
2　As to notice by advertisement see para 1611 ante.
3　Companies Clauses Consolidation Act 1845 s 17. Section 17 does not imply that a transfer immediately on execution is effectual as between transferor and transferee though not as between them and the company: *Nanney v Morgan* (1887) 35 ChD 598 at 604, 605; affd 37 ChD 346, CA.

1654. Transmission of shares. If the interest in any share becomes transmitted in consequence of the death, bankruptcy[1] or insolvency of any holder, or by any other lawful means[2] than by a transfer under the Companies Clauses Consolidation Act 1845 or the special Act, the transmission must be authenticated by a declaration in writing or in such other manner as the directors require[3]. The declaration must state the manner in which and the person to whom the share has been so transmitted, and must be made and signed by some credible person before a justice[4], before a master of the High Court, or before a commissioner for oaths[5]. It must be left with the secretary, who must thereupon enter the name of the person entitled under the transmission in the register of shareholders. For every entry the company may demand a sum not exceeding the prescribed amount and, where no amount is prescribed, a sum not exceeding 25 pence; until the transmission has been so authenticated, no person claiming by virtue of it is entitled to receive any share of the profits of the undertaking, or to vote as a shareholder in respect of any such share[6].

If the transmission has taken place by virtue of any testamentary instrument or by intestacy[7], the probate or letters of administration, or an official extract, together with the declaration, must be produced to the secretary, who must then enter the declaration in the register of transfers[8].

The personal representative of a deceased shareholder may, however, leave the shares standing in the deceased's name, in which case he cannot transfer or vote in respect of them, or receive dividends on them and, though he may be liable for calls, will be so only in his representative capacity. If he wishes to deal with the shares or to vote or receive dividends in respect of them, he may procure himself to be registered as a shareholder in the manner described above, in which case he will become a shareholder in the company, with and subject to the ordinary rights and liabilities of a shareholder[9]. If two or more personal representatives are so registered as joint holders, a transfer by one only is invalid[10].

1　See BANKRUPTCY.
2　These words do not cover a transfer by conveyance: *Copeland v North Eastern Rly Co* (1856) 6 E & B 277 at 284.
3　Companies Clauses Consolidation Act 1845 s 18.
4　For the meaning of 'justice' see para 1603 ante.
5　Companies Clauses Consolidation Act 1845 s 18; Commissioners for Oaths Act 1889 s 1(2) (amended by the Courts Act 1971 s 56(4), Sch 11 Pt IV; the Courts and Legal Services Act 1990 ss 113(2), 125(7),

Sch 20). Every solicitor holding a practising certificate which is in force has the powers conferred by a commissioner for oaths by the Commissioners for Oaths Act 1889; and accordingly, unless the context otherwise requires, every reference to such a commissioner in an enactment or instrument includes a reference to such a solicitor: see the Solicitors Act 1974 s 81(1) and SOLICITORS vol 44(1) (Reissue) para 94.

6 Companies Clauses Consolidation Act 1845 s 18 (amended by the Decimal Currency Act 1969 s 10(1)). When the transmission is to persons as executors, it must be stated in the declaration that that is so, and their names must be given: *Barton v London and North Western Rly Co* (1889) 24 QBD 77 at 88, CA. The provision as to leaving the declaration is not obligatory in the sense that the person entitled must leave the declaration with the secretary, but it is obligatory in the sense that such declaration can only be effective against the company if it is so left. The company cannot compel a person entitled by transmission to have his name put on the register, but, if he wishes to make his claim to the transmitted shares effective against the company, he must follow the course prescribed by the Companies Clauses Consolidation Act 1845 ss 18, 19 (as amended): *Barton v London and North Western Rly Co* supra.

7 The transmission here referred to is the transmission in consequence of death mentioned in the Companies Clauses Consolidation Act 1845 s 18 (as amended): *Copeland v North Eastern Rly Co* (1856) 6 E & B 277 at 284.

8 Companies Clauses Consolidation Act 1845 s 19.

9 *Barton v London and North Western Rly Co* (1889) 24 QBD 77 at 88, 89, CA.

10 *Barton v London and North Western Rly Co* (1889) 24 QBD 77, CA; *Barton v North Staffordshire Rly Co* (1888) 38 ChD 458 at 464.

E. FORFEITURE, CANCELLATION AND SURRENDER OF SHARES

1655. When shares may be forfeited. If a shareholder fails to pay any call payable by him, together with interest, if any, then, at any time after the expiration of two months from the day appointed for payment, the directors may declare forfeited the share in respect of which the call was payable, whether the company has sued for the amount of the call or not[1].

The remedy of forfeiture is additional to that by action, and is a further security for unpaid calls, in the nature of a mortgage or pledge. Hence, until the company has finally disposed of the shares and the debts and the costs have been satisfied, it may go on with its action for calls in arrear[2]. When it has sold the forfeited shares and converted them into money, the defendant is entitled to credit to the extent of the net proceeds of the sale. If the forfeited shares are cancelled and converted into other shares, he is entitled to the benefit of the value of the new shares, in satisfaction wholly or pro tanto of his liability[3].

1 Companies Clauses Consolidation Act 1845 s 29. As to forfeiture of shares generally see para 522 et seq ante.

2 *Great Northern Rly Co v Kennedy* (1849) 4 Exch 417 at 425; *Inglis v Great Northern Rly Co* (1852) 19 LTOS 149, HL; cf *Birmingham, Bristol and Thames Junction Rly Co v Locke* (1841) 1 QB 256. As to the position where the shares are sold for more than sufficient to pay the debt and the costs see para 1658 post.

3 *Great Northern Rly Co v Kennedy* (1849) 4 Exch 417 at 425; *Inglis v Great Northern Rly Co* (1852) 19 LTOS 149, HL.

1656. Notice of intention to forfeit shares. Before declaring any share forfeited, the directors must cause notice of their intention to be left at or transmitted by post to the usual or last place of abode of the person appearing by the register of shareholders to be the proprietor of the share[1]. If the shareholder is abroad, or if his usual or last place of abode is not known to the directors, by reason of its being imperfectly described in the shareholders' address book or otherwise, or if the interest in the share is known by the directors to have become transmitted otherwise than by transfer, as previously mentioned[2], but a declaration of the transmission has not been registered, and so the address of the parties to whom the share may have been transmitted, or may for the time being belong, is not known to the directors, they must give public notice of their intention in the London Gazette, if the company's principal place of business is situated in England, and also in some newspapers[3]. These notices must be given 21 days at least before the directors make a declaration of forfeiture[4].

1 Companies Clauses Consolidation Act 1845 s 30.
2 See ibid s 18 and para 1654 ante.
3 Ibid s 30. As to the giving of notice by advertisement in newspapers see para 1611 ante.
4 Ibid s 30. A notice does not, however, excuse a shareholder from payment of calls in arrear: see *Birmingham, Bristol and Thames Junction Rly Co v Locke* (1841) 1 QB 256.

1657. Confirmation of declaration of forfeiture. The declaration of forfeiture does not take effect so as to authorise the sale or other disposition of any share until it has been confirmed at a general meeting of the company to be held after the expiration of two months at least from the day on which the notice of intention to make the declaration has been given[1]. At that meeting the company may confirm the forfeiture, and by an order at that meeting or at any subsequent general meeting may direct the forfeited share to be sold or otherwise disposed of[2].

1 Companies Clauses Consolidation Act 1845 s 31. As to the notice of intention to forfeit shares see para 1656 ante.
2 Ibid s 31.

1658. Sale of forfeited shares. After confirmation[1] the directors may sell the forfeited share either by public auction or by private contract and, if there is more than one forfeited share, then either separately or together[2]. Any shareholder may purchase any share so sold[2].

The company must not sell or transfer more of a defaulter's shares than will be sufficient, as nearly as can be ascertained at the time of the sale, to pay the arrears then due from him on account of any calls, together with interest and the expenses attending the sale and declaration of forfeiture[3]. If the money produced by the sale of any forfeited shares is more than sufficient, the surplus must, on demand, be paid to the defaulter[3]. A company which has wrongfully forfeited and sold shares is liable in damages to the person wronged[4].

1 See para 1657 ante.
2 Companies Clauses Consolidation Act 1845 s 32.
3 Ibid s 34.
4 *Catchpole v Ambergate, Nottingham and Boston and Eastern Junction Rly Co* (1852) 1 E & B 111.

1659. Evidence of forfeiture; protection of purchaser. A declaration in writing by some credible person not interested in the matter, made before any justice[1] or master of the Supreme Court, that the call in respect of a share was made, that due notice was given, that default was made in payment of the call, and that the forfeiture of the share was declared and confirmed in the proper manner[2], is sufficient evidence of the facts stated in it[3].

This declaration, and the receipt of the treasurer of the company for the price of the share, constitute a good title to the share, and a certificate of proprietorship must be delivered to the purchaser[4]. He is then deemed the holder of the share and discharged from all calls due prior to the purchase[4]. He is not bound to see to the application of the purchase money, nor is his title to the share affected by any irregularity in the proceeding in reference to the sale[4].

1 For the meaning of 'justice' see para 1603 ante.
2 See paras 1655-1657 ante.
3 Companies Clauses Consolidation Act 1845 s 33; Supreme Court Act 1981 s 19(2); and see COURTS.
4 Companies Clauses Consolidation Act 1845 s 33.

1660. Effect of paying arrears before sale. If the arrears of calls, interest and expenses are paid before any share forfeited and vested in the company has been sold, the share reverts to the person to whom it belonged before the forfeiture, as if the calls had been duly paid[1]. Where a forfeiture has been regularly effected, the defaulter may recover the ownership of his share on this ground only; the court will not relieve against the forfeiture on the ground that by accident he never received the notice of forfeiture[2].

1 Companies Clauses Consolidation Act 1845 s 35. The fact that the defaulter has a right to redeem until and at the last moment before sale shows that the forfeited shares are, during the period between forfeiture and sale, a security only: *Great Northern Rly Co v Kennedy* (1849) 4 Exch 417 at 426.
2 Cf *Sparks v Liverpool Waterworks Co* (1807) 13 Ves 428.

1661. Cancellation of forfeited shares. Where any share of the capital of a company whose special Act incorporates the statutory provisions as to cancellation[1] is declared forfeited[2], and the forfeiture is confirmed by a meeting, and notice of the forfeiture has been given, then, if the directors are unable to sell the share for a sum equal to the arrears of calls, interest and expenses, the company may, at any general meeting held not less than two months after the notice is given, in case payment of the arrears of calls, interest and expenses is not made by the registered holder of the share before the meeting is held, resolve that the share be cancelled instead of being sold, and the share is then cancelled accordingly[3]. If payment is made before the meeting is held, the share reverts to the shareholder and must be re-entered in the company's register[4].

A declaration in writing made by some credible person before a justice[5] stating that a sum of money sufficient to pay the arrears of calls, interest and expenses due in respect of the share could not, at the time of the cancellation of the share, be obtained for the same upon the stock exchange prescribed in the special Act, or if no stock exchange is prescribed, the Stock Exchange, is sufficient evidence of the fact so declared[6].

1 Ie the Companies Clauses Act 1863 Pt I (ss 3-11), which applies only where incorporated: see s 3.
2 Ie under the provisions contained in the Companies Clauses Consolidation Act 1845 ss 29-35: see para 1655 et seq ante.
3 Companies Clauses Act 1863 s 4.
4 Ibid s 7.
5 For the meaning of 'justice' see para 1603 ante.
6 Companies Clauses Act 1863 s 5.

1662. Effect of cancelling shares. Where it is resolved that any share must be cancelled, then from and after the passing of the resolution the holder is precluded from all right and interest in and in respect of the share[1]. The cancellation does not, however, affect the liability of the last registered holder to pay the company all arrears of calls, interest and expenses due in respect of the share at the time of the cancellation, or the company's power to enforce payment by action or otherwise[1]. If the company enforces payment of arrears, the value of the share at the time of the cancellation must be deducted from the amount due[2].

1 Companies Clauses Act 1863 s 6.
2 Ibid s 7.

1663. Cancellation with shareholder's consent. Where any share is declared forfeited, or where any sum payable on any share remains unpaid, the company may, with the registered holder's written consent and with the sanction of a general meeting, resolve that the share be cancelled[1]. The share is then immediately cancelled and all liabilities and rights with respect to it absolutely extinguished[1]. A company must not pay or refund to the shareholder any sum of money for or in respect of the cancellation of any share[2].

1 Companies Clauses Act 1863 s 8.
2 Ibid s 10.

1664. Surrender of shares. A company whose special Act incorporates the statutory provisions as to surrender[1] may, on such terms as it thinks fit, from time to time accept surrenders of any shares which have not been fully paid up[2].

A company must not pay or refund to any shareholder any sum of money for or in respect of the surrender of any share[3].

1 Ie the Companies Clauses Act 1863 ss 9–11: see s 3.
2 Ibid s 9.
3 Ibid s 10.

1665. Issue of new shares. In lieu of any shares that have been cancelled or surrendered, a company may from time to time issue new shares of amounts which will allow them to be conveniently apportioned or disposed of according to the resolution of any ordinary or extraordinary meeting of the company, fixing the amounts and times of payment of the calls on them, and disposing of them on such terms and conditions as may be so resolved upon[1]. The aggregate nominal amount of the new shares must not exceed the aggregate nominal amount of the shares in lieu of which they are issued, after deducting the amount actually paid up in respect of the shares cancelled or surrendered[1].

1 Companies Clauses Act 1863 s 11.

(iii) Stock and Stockholders

1666. Issue of stock and conversion of shares. The special Act may authorise the company to issue stock instead of shares, and the Companies Clauses Consolidation Act 1845 provides for the conversion of fully paid shares into stock. Under that Act, with the consent of three-fifths of the votes of the shareholders present in person or by proxy at any general meeting, when due notice for that purpose has been given, the company may from time to time convert or consolidate all or any part of the shares then existing in the capital and in respect of which the whole money subscribed has been paid up, into a general capital stock to be divided amongst the shareholders according to their respective interests in it[1].

After the conversion, all the provisions of the 1845 Act or the special Act which require or imply that the capital must be divided into shares of any fixed amount and distinguished by numbers cease to have effect as to so much of the capital as is converted into stock[2]. The stock is transferable in the same manner and subject to the same regulations and provisions as the original shares[3].

The company must keep a register of transfers, and for every entry may demand any sum not exceeding the amount prescribed in the special Act or, if no amount is prescribed, a sum not exceeding 12 pence[4].

1 Companies Clauses Consolidation Act 1845 s 61; and see the provisions as to new stock contained in the Companies Clauses Act 1863 Pt II (ss 12-21) (see paras 1620-1623 ante).
2 Companies Clauses Consolidation Act 1845 s 62.
3 For the provisions as to the transfer of shares see para 1649 et seq ante.
4 Companies Clauses Consolidation Act 1845 ss 2, 62 (amended by the Decimal Currency Act 1969 s 10(1)). The figure has been rounded down in consequence of the withdrawal of the halfpenny from 31 December 1984. There is no distinction between stock and shares as regards the requisites of a valid and effectual transfer: *Nanney v Morgan* (1887) 37 ChD 346 at 353, CA.

1667. Register of stockholders. The company must from time to time cause the names of the stockholders with the amounts of their interests to be entered in a book to be kept for the purpose called 'The Register of Holders of Consolidated Stock'[1]. This book must be accessible at all reasonable times to the holders of shares or stock in the undertaking[2].

1 Companies Clauses Consolidation Act 1845 s 63.
2 Ibid s 63. The right of inspection given under s 63 may be exercised without assigning any reason for it, and may be enforced by an injunction restraining interference or by a mandatory injunction: *Holland v Dickson* (1888) 37 ChD 669. The right includes a right to take copies: *Mutter v Eastern and Midlands Rly Co* (1888) 38 ChD 92 at 105, CA. Cf the Companies Clauses Act 1863 s 28 and para 1689 post.

1668. Participation in dividends. A stockholder is entitled to participate in the dividends and profits of the company according to the amount of his holding[1]. For the purpose of voting at meetings, qualification for the office of director and other purposes, he has the same rights in proportion to his holding as would have been conferred by shares of equal amount in the capital but, except for the right to the participation in dividends and profits, no rights are conferred by any aliquot part of that amount of consolidated stock which would have been conferred by a corresponding holding in shares[1].

1 Companies Clauses Consolidation Act 1845 s 64.

1669. Preference stock. The statutory provisions relating to the issue of preference shares, the cancellation of unissued shares and the apportionment of new shares[1], and as to the issue of redeemable preference shares[2], apply to stock as well as to shares.

1 See the Companies Clauses Act 1863 ss 13-21 and para 1621 et seq ante.
2 See the Statutory Companies (Redeemable Stock) Act 1915 and para 1617 ante.

(6) LOAN CAPITAL

(i) Borrowing on Mortgage or Bond

1670. Power to borrow on mortgage or bond. If so authorised by its special Act, the company may, subject to the restrictions contained in that Act, borrow on mortgage or bond such sums of money as are from time to time authorised by a general meeting[1], not exceeding in the whole the sum prescribed, and, for securing the repayment of the money so borrowed, with interest, may mortgage the undertaking and the future calls on the shareholders or give bonds[2]. The giving of a power to borrow on mortgage or bond, without more, impliedly prohibits any other mode of borrowing, for example on Lloyd's bonds[3] or by overdrawing a bank account[4].

Mortgages and bonds under the Companies Clauses Consolidation Act 1845 may validly be issued at a discount[5]. They are not bills of sale[6] within the meaning of the Bills of Sale Acts 1878 and 1882[7].

1 The provision as to a general meeting is directory, and as against the company a lender need not show that it has been observed: *Landowners West of England and South Wales Land Drainage and Inclosure Co v Ashford* (1880) 16 ChD 411 at 438 (decided on an analogous clause in a special Act).
2 Companies Clauses Consolidation Act 1845 s 38. The bonds given by a statutory company pursuant to the Companies Clauses Acts are not infrequently described as 'debentures' and the mortgages as 'mortgage debentures': *Edmonds v Blaina Furnaces Co* (1887) 36 ChD 215 at 219 per Chitty J.
3 *Chambers v Manchester and Milford Rly Co* (1864) 5 B & S 588. As to Lloyd's bonds see further DEEDS vol 12 para 1394.
4 *Landowners West of England and South Wales Land Drainage and Inclosure Co v Ashford* (1880) 16 ChD 411 at 437.
5 *Webb v Shropshire Rlys Co* [1893] 3 Ch 307 at 320, 330, CA.
6 *Re Standard Manufacturing Co* [1891] 1 Ch 627 at 644, 648, CA; and see BILLS OF SALE vol 4(1) (Reissue) para 665.
7 As to the nature and meaning of a bill of sale see BILLS OF SALE vol 4(1) (Reissue) paras 601, 619.

1671. Borrowing again. If, after having borrowed any part of the money authorised by its special Act to be borrowed on mortgage or bond, the company pays it off, it may again borrow the amount paid off, and so from time to time. This power of reborrowing may not be exercised without the authority of a general meeting of the company unless the money is reborrowed in order to pay off any existing mortgage or bond[1]. A mortgage or bond issued for cash by way of reborrowing to a lender who has no notice of any irregularity may, however, be valid even though the reborrowing was not authorised by a general meeting[2].

If a company's goods are sold under a judgment obtained by a mortgagee or a bondholder who obtains payment of his debt out of the proceeds of sale, the transaction is equivalent to payment off by the company[3].

1 Companies Clauses Consolidation Act 1845 s 39.
2 *Fountaine v Carmarthen Rly Co* (1868) LR 5 Eq 316 at 323-325; *Landowners West of England and South Wales Land Drainage and Inclosure Co v Ashford* (1880) 16 ChD 411 at 438; *Re Romford Canal Co, Pocock's Claim, Trickett's Claim, Carew's Claim* (1883) 24 ChD 85 at 92.
3 *Fountaine v Carmarthen Rly Co* (1868) LR 5 Eq 316.

1672. Meaning of 'undertaking'. In the Companies Clauses Consolidation Act 1845, 'the undertaking' means the undertaking or works of whatever nature which by the special Act is or are authorised to be executed[1].

Although various ingredients go to make up an undertaking, the term describes not the ingredients but the complete work[2] from which the earnings arise. So far as mortgage contracts are concerned, the undertaking is made over as a thing complete or to be completed, as a going concern, with internal and parliamentary powers of management not to be interfered with; and under a contract pledging it as security the undertaking cannot be destroyed, broken up or annihilated[3]. The undertaking's tolls and other earnings are available to satisfy the mortgage, but the mortgagees cannot, by seizing the company's assets or calling on the court to seize them, either prevent its completion or reduce it into its original elements when it has been completed[4].

1 Companies Clauses Consolidation Act 1845 s 2. In the case of a railway company, the undertaking included the land actually used for the railway, with the stations and other buildings and the rails, and, under a mortgage in the statutory form, the mortgagee had a title to them paramount to that of a judgment creditor of the company who had issued an elegit. The court would interfere by injunction, at the instance of a mortgagee, to restrain a subsequent judgment creditor from impairing the subject matter of the mortgage by elegit proceedings: *Legg v Mathieson* (1860) 2 Giff 71 at 78, 79; *Gardiner v London, Chatham and Dover Rly Co, Drawbridge v Same, ex p Grissell* (1866) 15 LT 494; *Wildy v Mid-Hants Rly Co* (1868) 18 LT 73 (where the money secured by the mortgage had not become due at the date when the proceedings were commenced but the security was in jeopardy).

2 A company with powers to mortgage its undertaking may mortgage surplus land not required for the purposes of the undertaking (*Stagg v Upper Medway Navigation Co* [1903] 1 Ch 169, CA), or chattels, such as barges, which it has a statutory power to own and use *(Reeve v Upper Medway Navigation Co* (1905) 21 TLR 400).

3 *Gardner v London, Chatham and Dover Rly Co, Drawbridge v Same, Gardner v Same (No 2), Imperial Mercantile Credit Association v Same* (1867) 2 Ch App 201; *Legg v Mathieson* (1860) 2 Giff 71; *Re Salisbury Railway and Market House Co Ltd* [1969] 1 Ch 349, [1967] 1 All ER 813.

4 *Hart v Eastern Union Rly Co* (1852) 7 Exch 246 at 265, 266 (affd sub nom *Eastern Union Rly Co v Hart* (1852), 8 Exch 116); *Wickham v New Brunswick and Canada Rly Co* (1865) LR 1 PC 64 at 78; *Re Portsmouth Borough (Kingston, Fratton and Southsea) Tramways Co* [1892] 2 Ch 362 at 366.

1673. Evidence of authority to borrow. Where the special Act restricts the company from borrowing any money on mortgage or bond until a definite portion of its capital has been subscribed or paid up, or where by the Companies Clauses Consolidation Act 1845 or the special Act the authority of a general meeting is required for such borrowing, the certificate of a justice[1] that that definite portion of the capital has been subscribed or paid up, and a copy of the order of a general meeting authorising the borrowing, certified by a director or by the secretary, are sufficient evidence of the fact of the capital having been subscribed or paid up, and of the order having been made[2]. Upon production to a justice of the company's books and of such other evidence as he thinks sufficient, he must grant the certificate[2]. A copy of an order of a general meeting is not conclusive evidence as between the directors and the company, if no such order has in fact been made, but it is evidence on which a lender may reasonably act[3].

1 For the meaning of 'justice' see para 1603 ante.
2 Companies Clauses Consolidation Act 1845 s 40.
3 *Fountaine v Carmarthen Rly Co* (1868) LR 5 Eq 316 at 322, 323.

1674. Form of mortgage. Every mortgage or bond securing money borrowed by the company must be by deed under its common seal, duly stamped and truly stating the consideration, and it may be either according to the statutory form or to the like effect[1]. Where the seal has been affixed without due authority, the company is not bound by the instrument[2], except as against a lender who takes the security without notice, actual or imputed, of the irregularity[3]. The mortgage or bond is not invalid if the true consideration is not disclosed in express terms in it. The consideration is required to be stated for the purpose of enabling the document to be properly stamped[4].

1　Companies Clauses Consolidation Act 1845 s 41, Schs (C), (D).
2　*D' Arcy v Tamar, Kit Hill and Callington Rly Co* (1867) LR 2 Exch 158.
3　*County of Gloucester Bank v Rudry Merthyr Steam and House Coal Colliery Co* [1895] 1 Ch 629 at 632, CA. As to how far a person dealing with a company is entitled to assume that the company's rules of internal management have been complied with see para 1137 et seq ante; as to the lender's duty to acquaint himself with the company's 'external position' by reason of having constructive notice of its powers see para 1236 et seq ante; as to extension of the provisions of the Companies Act 1985 ss 35-35B (as substituted) (see paras 1093, 1107-1109 ante) to such companies see para 1767 post; and as to the effect of such extension on borrowing powers see para 1236 text and note 3 ante.
4　*Landowners West of England and South Wales Land Drainage and Inclosure Co v Ashford* (1880) 16 ChD 411 at 438.

1675. Effect of mortgages in statutory form. Although the statutory form of mortgage purports to assign the whole undertaking to each mortgagee as if he were the sole and first incumbrancer, the respective mortgagees are entitled only to the property comprised in the mortgages in proportion to the sums advanced by them[1]. The sums advanced must be repaid with interest, without any preference by reason of priority of the date of any mortgage or of the meeting at which it was authorised[2]. Whatever the property charged by the mortgage may be, every mortgagee must bring that property into hotchpot with all the other mortgagees. All the mortgage claims and all the subject matters of the mortgages are consolidated, the whole charge being made upon the whole subject matter, and the whole proceeds being distributed pari passu[3]. The mortgagees are entitled rateably to the tolls, sums and premises comprised in their mortgages, and, further, to be repaid their advances, with interest generally, and not merely out of tolls and the like[4]; but they are not entitled to any specific lien on any of the company's property or effects[5].

A mortgage in the statutory form does not entitle the mortgagee to bring an action to recover the company's land[6], or for sale or foreclosure of it[7]. Where, however, a railway has been sold under a special Act and the proceeds paid into court, a holder of a mortgage in the statutory form is entitled to payment out of the fund in court in priority to a subsequent judgment creditor[8].

1　Companies Clauses Consolidation Act 1845 s 42; and see s 41, Sch (C).
2　Ibid s 42.
3　*Landowners West of England and South Wales Land Drainage and Inclosure Co v Ashford* (1880) 16 ChD 411 at 439.
4　*Bowen v Brecon Rly Co, ex p Howell* (1867) LR 3 Eq 541.
5　*Russell v East Anglian Rly Co* (1850) 3 Mac & G 125. See also note 8 infra.
6　*Doe d Myatt v St Helen's and Runcorn Gap Rly Co* (1841) 2 QB 364 (a decision on a mortgage in form similar to that set out in the Companies Clauses Consolidation Act 1845 Sch (C)).

7 *Furness v Caterham Rly Co* (1858) 25 Beav 614.
8 *Furness v Caterham Rly Co* (1859) 27 Beav 358 at 361, 362. The lien of the mortgagees of a railway company on its undertaking under the Railway Companies Act 1867 s 23 (repealed) was not a specific charge upon or claim against the sale proceeds of its surplus land: *Re Hull, Barnsley and West Riding Junction Rly Co* (1888) 40 ChD 119 at 127, CA. See RAILWAYS.

1676. Effect of mortgage on uncalled capital. Even though it comprises future calls on shareholders, no mortgage, unless it expressly so provides, precludes the company from receiving any calls to be made by it and applying them to the purposes of the company[1]. A mortgagee of unpaid capital, it seems, prevails against a judgment creditor of the company, who is entitled to proceed by way, in effect, of execution against a shareholder whose shares are not fully paid up, and against a liquidator making calls in the winding up of the company[2].

1 Companies Clauses Consolidation Act 1845 s 43. Section 43 has no application where the undertaking has been in effect abandoned: *Re Glyn Valley Tramway Co Ltd* [1937] Ch 465 at 472, [1937] 3 All ER 15 at 19. As to mortgages of uncalled capital by companies governed by the Companies Act 1985 see para 1245 ante.
2 *Re Pyle Works* (1890) 44 ChD 534 at 587, CA per Lindley LJ, the decision in which (but not specifically the dictum of Lindley LJ) was approved in *Newton v Anglo-Australian Investment Co's Debenture Holders* [1895] AC 244, PC. The remedy by scire facias referred to in the former of these cases has been superseded: see para 1645 note 5 ante.

1677. Bondholders' rights. According to the amount of the money secured, the obligees in bonds given by the company are proportionally entitled to be paid, out of its tolls or other property, the sums secured, without any preference one above another by reason of priority of date of any bond or of the meeting at which it was authorised[1].

Bondholders are not assignees of the undertaking or tolls[2]; nor are they entitled to any specific equitable lien on any of the company's property or effects[3]. Their only remedy appears to be the obtaining of a judgment[4] and, as against them, any judgment creditor of the company may seize its goods and chattels under a writ of fieri facias[5].

1 Companies Clauses Consolidation Act 1845 s 44.
2 *Bowen v Brecon Rly Co, ex p Howell* (1867) LR 3 Eq 541 at 548.
3 *Russell v East Anglian Rly Co* (1850) 3 Mac & G 125 at 141, 143. As to bondholder's liens in the case of railway companies see para 1675 note 8 ante.
4 *Bowen v Brecon Rly Co, ex p Howell* (1867) LR 3 Eq 541.
5 *Russell v East Anglian Rly Co* (1850) 3 Mac & G 125.

1678. Register of mortgages and bonds. A register of mortgages and bonds must be kept by the secretary, and, within 14 days after the date of the mortgage or bond, an entry or memorial, specifying its number and date, the sums secured and the names of the parties, with their proper additions[1], must be made in the register[2]. The register may be perused, without payment, at all reasonable times by any of the shareholders, by any mortgagee or bond creditor or by any person interested in any mortgage or bond[2]. The right to inspect includes the right to take copies or extracts[3]. An applicant for inspection is not bound to state the grounds of his application, and his right, if disputed, may be enforced by injunction[4].

1 For the meaning of 'additions' see para 1633 note 1 ante.
2 Companies Clauses Consolidation Act 1845 s 45. Cf the Companies Act 1985 s 407 and para 1296 ante.
3 *Mutter v Eastern and Midlands Rly Co* (1888) 38 ChD 92, CA; and see para 1634 ante. As to the employment of agents to make inspections see para 1298 note 3 ante.
4 *Holland v Dickson* (1888) 37 ChD 669; cf *Davies v Gas Light and Coke Co* [1909] 1 Ch 708, CA.

1679. Fixing time for repayment of principal. The company may, if it thinks proper, fix a period for the repayment of the principal money borrowed, with interest, in which case it must cause the period to be inserted in the mortgage or bond[1]. Upon its expiration, the principal sum, together with arrears of interest, must, on demand, be paid to the party entitled to the mortgage or bond[1]. If no other place of payment is inserted in the instrument, the principal and interest are payable at the company's principal office or place of business[1].

  1 Companies Clauses Consolidation Act 1845 s 50.

1680. Repayment of principal where no time fixed. If no time is fixed in the mortgage or bond for the repayment of the money borrowed, the person entitled to the mortgage or bond may, at the expiration or at any time after the expiration of 12 months from the date of the instrument, demand payment of the principal money secured, with all arrears of interest, upon giving six months' previous notice for that purpose[1]. Similarly, the company may at any time, on giving like notice, pay off the money borrowed[1]. If given by a mortgagee or bond creditor, the notice must be delivered to the secretary or left at the company's principal office[2]. If given by the company, it must be given either personally to the mortgagee or bond creditor or left at his residence or, if he is unknown to the directors or cannot after inquiry be found, must be given by advertisement in the London Gazette, and in some newspaper[3].

  1 Companies Clauses Consolidation Act 1845 s 51. Every notice must be in writing, or print, or both: s 51.
  2 Ibid s 51.
  3 Ibid s 51. As to newspaper advertisements see para 1611 ante.

1681. Mortgagees' and bondholders' remedies. In default of payment, a right of action arises on the mortgage or bond[1]. A mortgagee or a bondholder, as the case may be, may sue on behalf of himself and all other holders of the same issue of mortgages or bonds and, after obtaining on interlocutory motion the appointment of a receiver of the undertaking, may obtain a judgment declaring that he and those on whose behalf he sues are entitled to stand in the position of judgment creditors of the company for the principal and interest due upon their securities, and appointing the existing receiver to be receiver of all property of the company not included in the interlocutory order[2]. With the leave of the court the plaintiff may then issue execution[3], and, if he fails to obtain satisfaction of his debt, he may obtain an order on petition for the company to be wound up[4] as an unregistered company[5]. If, by means of an execution, an individual holder has obtained satisfaction of his debt, he cannot afterwards be made to refund, for the benefit of other holders, any part of what he has received[6].

  1 *Hart v Eastern Union Rly Co* (1852) 7 Exch 246 at 265, 266, 268 (affd sub nom *Eastern Union Rly Co v Hart* (1852) 8 Exch 116); *Bowen v Brecon Rly Co, ex p Howell* (1867) LR 3 Eq 541.
  2 *Russell v East Anglian Rly Co* (1850) 3 Mac & G 104; *Bowen v Brecon Rly Co, ex p Howell* (1867) LR 3 Eq 541; *Hope v Croydon and Norwood Tramways Co* (1877) 34 ChD 730.
  3 *Bowen v Brecon Rly Co, ex p Howell* (1867) LR 3 Eq 541; *Re Potteries, Shrewsbury and North Wales Rly Co* (1869) 5 Ch App 67 (decided under the Railway Companies Act 1867 s 9 (repealed)).
  4 *Re Portsmouth Borough (Kingston, Fratton and Southsea) Tramways Co* [1892] 2 Ch 362, not following *Re Herne Bay Waterworks Co* (1878) 10 ChD 42 (where a judgment had not been first obtained), and disapproving *Re Exmouth Docks Co* (1873) LR 17 Eq 181 on this point.

5 Ie under the Insolvency Act 1986 s 221 (as amended): see para 2900 post.
6 *Fountaine v Carmarthen Rly Co* (1868) LR 5 Eq 316 at 324.

1682. Interest on mortgages and bonds. The interest on money borrowed upon a mortgage or bond must be paid at the periods appointed in it or, if no period is appointed, half-yearly, and in preference to any dividends payable to the company's shareholders[1]. Where a company gives a bond for a principal sum to be paid on a specified day with interest in the meantime, and does not pay or offer to pay the principal at the date fixed, the bondholder is entitled to interest from the date fixed for payment until actual payment of the principal sum[2]. If a bondholder sues the company on its covenant to pay and recovers judgment, the original debt merges in the judgment debt, which carried interest at the appropriate statutory rate[3] unless the parties have agreed that any judgment should carry a different rate of interest[4].

Where the company has given notice of its intention to pay off a mortgage or bond at a time when it may lawfully be paid off, all further interest ceases to be payable on the mortgage or bond at the expiration of the notice unless, on demand of payment made pursuant to the notice or at any time afterwards, the company fails to pay the principal and interest due at the expiration of the notice[5].

1 Companies Clauses Consolidation Act 1845 s 48.
2 *Price v Great Western Rly Co* (1847) 16 M & W 244. The rate of interest allowed as from the date specified to that of actual payment is not necessarily the same as that payable up to the time specified for payment: see *Cook v Fowler* (1874) LR 7 HL 27 and MONEY.
3 Interest on a judgment debt is at 8% per annum: Judgments Act 1838 s 17 (amended by the Judgments Debts (Rate of Interest) Order 1993, SI 1993/564, art 2); and see *Re European Central Rly Co, ex p Oriental Financial Corpn* (1876) 4 ChD 33, CA.
4 *Economic Life Assurance Society v Usborne* [1902] AC 147, HL.
5 Companies Clauses Consolidation Act 1845 s 52.

1683. Appointment of receiver by justices. Where the mortgagees of a company are empowered by the special Act to enforce the payment of arrears of interest, or arrears of principal and interest, due on the mortgages by the appointment of a receiver, a mortgagee may, without prejudice to his right to sue for the sum in the High Court, require the appointment of a receiver by application to justices[1]:

(1) if the interest accruing upon any mortgage is not paid within 30 days after it has become payable, and after a demand in writing; or

(2) if the principal money owing upon any mortgage is not paid within six months after it has become payable, and after a demand in writing, provided his debt amounts to the sum prescribed by the special Act; if it does not, he may combine with other mortgagees entitled to make the application whose debts, together with his debt, amount to the prescribed sum[2].

The application must be made to two justices who may, on the application, after hearing the parties, by order in writing appoint some person to receive the whole or part of the tolls or sums liable to the payment of the amount due until that amount and all costs, including the charges of receiving the tolls or sums, are fully paid[3]. On the appointment being made, all such tolls and sums must be paid to the person appointed[3]. The money received is so much money received by or to the use of the party to whom the interest, or principal and interest, as the case may be, is then due, and on whose behalf the receiver has been appointed; and, after the interest and costs, or principal, interest and costs, have been so received, the power of the receiver ceases[3].

1 For the meaning of 'justice' see para 1603 ante.
2 Companies Clauses Consolidation Act 1845 s 53.
3 Ibid s 54.

1684. Appointment of receiver by High Court. The statutory provisions for the appointment of a receiver[1] do not oust or exclude the ordinary jurisdiction of the High Court to appoint a receiver[2]; and a mortgagee may either bring an action to recover his interest and principal or apply for the appointment of a receiver of tolls or sums liable to the payment of such principal and interest[3]. Where the security is in jeopardy, a receiver may be appointed before the money secured has become payable[4]. As a general rule, mortgagees or bondholders cannot have a manager of the undertaking appointed by the court, nor can they have it sold[5], though, if such a company is ordered to be wound up, its undertaking may be sold by the liquidator[6].

1 See para 1683 ante.
2 *Fripp v Chard Rly Co, Fripp v Bridgewater and Taunton Canal and Stolford Rly and Harbour Co* (1853) 11 Hare 241 at 259; *Russell v East Anglian Rly Co* (1850) 3 Mac & G 125 at 144; and see the Supreme Court Act 1981 s 37(1) and RECEIVERS.
3 *Gardner v London, Chatham and Dover Rly Co, Drawbridge v Same, Gardner v Same (No 2), Imperial Mercantile Credit Association v Same* (1867) 2 Ch App 201 at 213; *Hart v Eastern Union Rly Co* (1852) 7 Exch 246 at 265, 266, 268 (affd 8 Exch 116); and see the cases cited in para 1358 note 7 ante.
4 *Wildy v Mid-Hants Rly Co* (1868) 18 LT 73; and see paras 1348, 1358 ante.
5 This rule applies to all companies incorporated for carrying on a public undertaking: *Gardner v London, Chatham and Dover Rly Co* (1867) 2 Ch App 201 at 212; *Blaker v Herts and Essex Waterworks Co* (1889) 41 ChD 399; *Marshall v South Staffordshire Tramways Co* [1895] 2 Ch 36, CA, disapproving *Bartlett v West Metropolitan Tramways Co* [1893] 3 Ch 437, [1894] 2 Ch 286; cf *Re Crystal Palace Co, Fox v Crystal Palace Co* (1911) 104 LT 898, CA; affd sub nom *Saunders v Bevan* (1912) 107 LT 70, HL. A judgment creditor could obtain the appointment of a manager in the case of a railway company: see the Railway Companies Act 1867 and RAILWAYS vol 38 para 812. When the company has ceased to exist as a going concern, debenture holders are entitled to a charge on the assets in priority to unsecured creditors: *Re Glyn Valley Tramway Co Ltd* [1937] Ch 465, [1937] 3 All ER 15. As to the law relating to the appointment of a receiver or manager of companies governed by the Companies Act 1985 see para 1320 et seq ante.
6 *Marshall v South Staffordshire Tramways Co* [1895] 2 Ch 36 at 53, CA; *Pegge v Neath District Tramways Co Ltd* [1895] 2 Ch 508 at 511.

1685. Transfer of mortgage or bond and interest. A person entitled to a mortgage or bond may from time to time transfer his interest to any other person; the transfer must be by deed[1] duly stamped, truly stating the consideration, and it may be in the statutory form[2] or to the like effect[3]. If a mortgage or bond has been transferred in accordance with these provisions, an action on the mortgage or bond must be brought in the transferee's name[4].

Interest on a mortgage or bond is transferable only by deed duly stamped[5].

1 *Powell v London and Provincial Bank* [1893] 2 Ch 555 at 560, CA.
2 For the statutory form of transfer see the Companies Clauses Consolidation Act 1845 s 46, Sch (E).
3 Ibid s 46.
4 *Vertue v East Anglian Rlys Co* (1850) 5 Exch 280 at 285, 286. As to the rights of a transferee when there have been irregularities in the issue of a mortgage or bond see para 1244 ante; and see *Dickson v Swansea Vale Rly Co* (1868) LR 4 QB 44; *Re South Essex Estuary Co, ex p Chorley* (1870) LR 11 Eq 157; *Re Romford Canal Co, Pocock's Claim, Trickett's Claim, Carew's Claim* (1883) 24 ChD 85.
5 Companies Clauses Consolidation Act 1845 s 49.

1686. Registration of transfer. A transfer must be produced to the secretary within 30 days after its date if it is executed within the United Kingdom, or otherwise within

30 days after its arrival in the United Kingdom, and he must thereupon enter it in the register of mortgages and bonds[1]. For such entry the company may demand a sum not exceeding the prescribed sum or, where no sum is prescribed, the sum of 12 pence[2].

Until registration of the transfer the company is not in any manner responsible to the transferee in respect of a mortgage, but after such entry the transfer entitles him to the full benefit of the original mortgage or bond, and no party, having made a transfer, can release or discharge the mortgage or bond transferred or any money secured by it[3].

1 See para 1678 ante.
2 Companies Clauses Consolidation Act 1845 s 47 (amended by the Decimal Currency Act 1969 s 10(1)). The figure has been rounded down in consequence of the withdrawal of the halfpenny from 31 December 1984.
3 Companies Clauses Consolidation Act 1845 s 47.

(ii) Debenture Stock

1687. Power to issue debenture stock. A company having power to raise money on mortgage or bond by virtue of an Act of Parliament, or authorised by any special Act to create and issue debenture stock[1], may create and issue debenture stock subject to the provisions of the Companies Clauses Act 1863[2].

In either case, with the sanction of such proportion of the votes of the shareholders and stockholders, entitled to vote in that behalf present personally or by proxy at a meeting of the company specially convened for the purpose, as is prescribed in its special Act and, if no proportion is prescribed, then of three-fifths of such votes, a company may from time to time raise all or any part of the money which for the time being it has raised or is authorised to raise on mortgage or bond, by the creation and issue, at such times, in such amounts and manner, on such terms, subject to such conditions and with such rights and privileges, as it thinks fit, of debenture stock[3], instead of and to the same amount as the whole or any part of the money which may for the time being be owing by the company on mortgage or bond, or which it may from time to time have power to raise on mortgage or bond. To the stock so created it may attach such fixed and perpetual preferential interest, payable half-yearly or otherwise, and commencing at once or at any future time or times, when and as the debenture stock is issued, or otherwise, as it thinks fit[4].

The creation of the stock, as distinguished from its issue, is effected by the resolution authorising the issue, fixing the rate of interest and prescribing the other conditions on which the stock is to be held[5]. In certain cases debenture stock may be created or issued so as to be redeemable[6].

1 Wherever 'debenture stock' is mentioned in the Companies Clauses Act 1863 Pt III (ss 22–35), the provisions of Pt III (ss 22–35) (amended by the Companies Clauses Act 1869) are deemed to apply to mortgage preference stock, and to funded debt, as the case may require, in all respects as if mortgage preference stock or funded debt were debenture stock: Companies Clauses Act 1863 s 35.
2 The provisions of ibid Pt III (ss 22–35) (as amended: see note 1 supra) are deemed to be incorporated with the company's special Act: Companies Clauses Act 1869 s 3. As to the application of the Companies Clauses Act 1863 Pt III (ss 22–35) (as so amended) to every company having power to raise money on mortgage or bond by virtue of any Act of Parliament see para 1600 ante.
   The provisions of Pt III (ss 22–35) (as so amended) were also applied with modifications to the power of railway companies to create and issue debenture stock by the Railway Companies Act 1867 s 24 (repealed): see *Re Mersey Rly Co* [1895] 2 Ch 287.
   No such corresponding limitations on the creation and issue of debentures and debenture stock are contained in the Companies Act 1985.
3 See note 1 supra.

4 Companies Clauses Act 1863 s 22 (amended by the Companies Clauses Act 1869 s 1). Since the passing of the 1869 Act a company entitled to issue debenture stock may attach to it any rate of interest which the exigencies of its financial position at the time of the creation of the stock may require; and any special Act of a company passed before the passing of the 1869 Act prescribing any rate, is to be read as if no rate had been prescribed therein: s 1. Debenture stock, authorised but not issued before that Act, could not be issued on any terms other than those on which it might have been issued before that Act without further authority of the company: s 2.
5 *Re Burry Port and Gwendreath Valley Rly Co* (1885) 54 LJ Ch 710 at 713.
6 See para 1617 ante.

1688. Priority of charge created by debenture stock. The debenture stock, with the interest on it, is a charge[1] on the company's undertaking, prior to all its shares or stock, and is transmissible and transferable in the same manner and according to the same regulations and provisions as its other stock, and in all other respects has the incidents of personal estate[2].

The issue of debenture stock does not in any way affect any mortgage or bond at any time legally granted by the company before the creation of such stock, or any power of the company to raise money on mortgage or bond, except in so far as its borrowing powers are extinguished by such issue[3], the holders of all such mortgages and bonds being entitled to the same priorities, rights and privileges in all respects as they would have been entitled to if the special Act authorising the issue of debenture stock had not been passed[4], the result being that the priority of mortgages and bonds granted before the creation of the debenture stock is saved, as also are the company's existing borrowing powers[5].

The interest on debenture stock has priority of payment over all dividends or interest on any shares or stock of the company, whether ordinary, preference or guaranteed, and ranks next to the interest payable on its mortgages or bonds for the time being legally granted before the creation of the debenture stock, but the holders of debenture stock created and issued under the same special Act are not, as among themselves, entitled to any preference or priority[6].

1 Debenture stock is not a charge in the ordinary sense of the word; owing to its nature it confers only a limited right to enforce the interest payable on it: see para 1690 post.
2 Companies Clauses Act 1863 s 23; and see paras 1627, 1650 ante.
3 See ibid s 34 and para 1691 post.
4 Ibid s 30.
5 *Re Burry Port and Gwendreath Valley Rly Co* (1885) 54 LJ Ch 710 at 713; and see *Harrison v Cornwall Minerals Rly Co* (1881) 18 ChD 334, CA; affd sub nom *Fenton v Harrison* (1883) 8 App Cas 780, HL.
6 Companies Clauses Act 1863 s 24; *Re Mersey Rly Co* [1895] 2 Ch 287 at 296, 297, CA.

1689. Certificates and register of holders. The company must deliver to every holder of debenture stock a certificate stating the amount of stock held by him, and all regulations or provisions for the time being applicable to certificates of shares in the company apply, mutatis mutandis, to certificates of debenture stock[1].

The company must enter in a register to be kept for the purpose the names and addresses of the persons and corporations entitled to the debenture stock, and the amounts of the stock to which they are entitled. The register must be accessible for inspection at all reasonable times to every mortgagee, bondholder, debenture stock-holder, shareholder and stockholder of the company, without payment[2], and every such person is entitled to see the whole register and make such copies as he thinks fit, for this provision is aimed (inter alia) at enabling any such person to communicate with the whole body of people interested on some matter which concerns them all[3].

1   Companies Clauses Act 1863 s 29: see paras 1635, 1636 ante.
2   Ibid s 28.
3   *Mutter v Eastern and Midlands Rly Co* (1888) 38 ChD 92 at 107, CA; *Holland v Dickson* (1888) 37 ChD 669; and see para 1667 ante. As to the remedies for enforcing the right see *Davies v Gas Light and Coke Co* [1909] 1 Ch 708, CA (decided under the Companies Clauses Consolidation Act 1845 s 10: see para 1634 ante).

1690. Nature of security. The holder of debenture stock is not a creditor of a company except as to the annual interest; he has only a right to a perpetual annuity, payable out of the concern. Unless expressly issued as redeemable in the cases where that is permissible[1], the capital cannot be called in or paid off. There is a charge[2], but no conveyance or assignment to the stockholder, or to any trustee for him; but there is an entry in the books of the concern that there is so much debenture stock on which there is so much to be paid half-yearly to each holder.

The shareholder has a security of a special and limited kind on the company's assets and, if the interest on the stock is in arrear, with a right to obtain or join with other holders in obtaining the appointment of a receiver, but with no right to take possession of a single item of the company's property in specie[3]. He is not a member of the company, and is not entitled to vote or be present at any of its meetings[4], although he has the rights and powers of a mortgagee of the undertaking, other than the right to require repayment of the principal money paid up on the stock[5].

1   See para 1617 ante.
2   See para 1688 ante.
3   *Attree v Hawe* (1878) 9 ChD 337 at 349, CA; *Lawrence v West Somerset Mineral Rly Co* [1918] 2 Ch 250; *Cross v Imperial Continental Gas Association* [1923] 2 Ch 553. A debenture stockholder having no enforceable charge is not entitled, if his annuity is not in arrear, to interfere with the ownership, possession or dominion of the company as the statutory owners and managers: *Lawrence v West Somerset Mineral Rly Co* supra; *Cross v Imperial Continental Gas Association* supra.
4   Companies Clauses Act 1863 s 31; *Re Bodman, Bodman v Bodman* [1891] 3 Ch 135 at 137, 138.
5   Companies Clauses Act 1863 s 31; and see para 1679 et seq ante.

1691. Effect of issue of debenture stock at a discount. The powers of borrowing and reborrowing by a company are extinguished to the extent of the money raised by the issue of debenture stock[1].

A company empowered to create debenture stock and governed by the Companies Clauses Acts may issue such stock at a discount or, within the limits of its borrowing powers, by way of collateral security for a loan, and, in the last-mentioned case, with reservation of a right of redemption[2].

1   Companies Clauses Act 1863 s 34.
2   *Webb v Shropshire Railways Co* [1893] 3 Ch 307 at 330, CA; *Whitehaven Joint Stock Banking Co v Reed* (1886) 54 LT 360, CA; cf *Re Anglo-Danubian Steam Navigation and Colliery Co* (1875) LR 20 Eq 339.

1692. Application of proceeds; accounts. The money raised by debenture stock must be applied exclusively either in paying off money due by the company on mortgage or bond, or for the purposes to which the money would be applicable if it were raised on mortgage or bond instead of on debenture stock[1].

Separate and distinct accounts must be kept by the company showing how much money has been received on account of debenture stock, and how much money, borrowed or owing on mortgage or bond or which it has power so to borrow, has been paid off by debenture stock, or raised by it instead of being so borrowed[2].

1 Companies Clauses Act 1863 s 32; and see para 1624 ante.
2 Ibid s 33.

1693. Recovery of interest in arrears. If the interest on debenture stock is not paid within 30 days after it is payable, any one or more of the stockholders holding, individually or collectively, the nominal amount prescribed in the special Act and, if no sum is prescribed, a sum equal to one-tenth of the aggregate amount which the company is for the time being authorised to raise by mortgage, by bond and by debenture stock, or the sum of £10,000, whichever of the two last-mentioned sums is the smaller sum, may, without prejudice to the right to sue in any court of competent jurisdiction for the interest in arrear, require the appointment of a receiver[1].

The application for a receiver must be made to two justices of the peace, who may by order in writing appoint some person to receive the whole or part of the tolls or sums liable to the payment of the interest until all the arrears of interest then due on the debenture stock, with all costs, including the charges of receiving the tolls or sums, are fully paid[2]. On the appointment being made, all such tolls or sums must be paid to and received by the person appointed[2]. All money so received is deemed so much money received to the use of the several persons interested in the same, according to their several priorities; and the receiver must distribute it rateably, and without priority, among all the proprietors of debenture stock to whom interest is in arrear, after satisfying the interest on the company's mortgages and bonds[2]. When the full amount of interest and costs has been so received, the receiver's power ceases, and he is bound to account to the company, and to pay it any balance in his hands[2].

If the interest on debenture stock is in arrear for 30 days after any of the days on which the same is payable, the stockholder for the time being may, without prejudice to his power to apply for the appointment of a receiver, recover the arrears, with costs, by action against the company in any court of competent jurisdiction[3].

1 Companies Clauses Act 1863 s 25. The High Court has jurisdiction to appoint a receiver in a proper case: see the cases regarding mortgagees and bondholders.
2 Ibid s 26.
3 Ibid s 27. At a time when periods of limitation in respect of specialties and statutory causes of action were the same, it was held that the cause of action was statutory: see *Re Cornwall Minerals Rly Co* [1897] 2 Ch 74. If this is correct, the period of limitation is now six years (see the Limitation Act 1980 s 9(1)); sed quaere, as the statute merely authorises the issue. If the cause of action is in respect of a specialty, the period will be 12 years: s 8(1).

(7) PROSPECTUS AND OFFER FOR SALE

1694. Statutory provisions. There are no special provisions in the Companies Clauses Acts concerning prospectuses and offer documents of companies regulated by those Acts[1]. However, the provisions of the Financial Services Act 1986 and the Public Offers of Securities Regulations 1995 relating to offers of listed[2] and unlisted[3] securities respectively apply[4].

1 As to the companies so regulated see para 1599 et seq ante.
2 Ie the Financial Services Act 1986 Pt IV (ss 142–156B) (as amended): see paras 281–299 and 339–348 ante.
3 Ie the Public Offers of Securities Regulations 1995, SI 1995/1537: see paras 300–320, 339–344 and 349–353 ante.
4 See the Financial Services Act 1986 ss 1, 2, Sch 1 para 1 (as amended); the Public Offers of Securities Regulations 1995 reg 3(b).

1695. Misrepresentation. The common law remedy by an action of deceit for damages[1], the equitable remedy by an action for rescission[2] of a contract to take shares or debentures on the ground of misrepresentation and the statutory provision for damages for innocent misrepresentation[3] apply to companies regulated by the Companies Clauses Acts[4] equally with companies subject to the provisions of the Companies Act 1985.

1 See paras 321, 332 et seq ante.
2 See paras 321, 324 et seq ante.
3 See the Misrepresentation Act 1967 and MISREPRESENTATION.
4 As to the companies so regulated see para 1599 et seq ante.

(8) REGULATION AND MANAGEMENT

(i) In general

1696. How company's powers are exercised. The directors are invested with the management and superintendence of the company's affairs, and they may lawfully exercise all its powers, except as to such matters as are directed by the Companies Clauses Consolidation Act 1845 or the special Act to be transacted by a general meeting[1]. The exercise of these powers is subject to the provisions of the 1845 Act and the special Act, and also to the control and regulation of any general meeting specially convened for the purpose, but not so as to render invalid any act done by the directors prior to any resolution passed by such a general meeting[2].

The principles applicable to litigation in the company's name or by shareholders suing on behalf of their class, and those relating to interference of the court in the company's internal management, are in substance the same as those which apply to companies subject to the Companies Act 1985[3].

1 The Companies Clauses Consolidation Act 1845 s 91 specifies the powers to be exercised at a general meeting: see para 1726 post. Other powers which may be exercised only at a general meeting include the power to issue new ordinary or preference shares or stock (see para 1620 ante), to cancel forfeited shares (see para 1663 ante), and to borrow on mortgage or bond (see paras 1670, 1671 ante) or by issuing debenture stock (see para 1687 ante).
2 Ibid s 90. For miscellaneous examples of directors' powers see *Hutton v West Cork Rly Co* (1883) 23 ChD 654, CA (gratuity out of company's funds to its employees); *Exeter and Crediton Rly Co v Buller* (1847) 5 Ry & Can Cas 211 at 217 (power to use the company's name in proceedings); *Peel v London and North Western Rly Co* [1907] 1 Ch 5, CA (paying for the postage and stamping of proxy papers), followed in *Wilson v London, Midland and Scottish Rly Co* [1940] Ch 393, [1940] 2 All ER 92, CA; *Ambergate, Nottingham and Boston and Eastern Junction Rly Co v Mitchell* (1849) 4 Exch 540 (making calls without the special authority of a general meeting); *Thairlwall v Great Northern Rly Co* [1910] 2 KB 509 (deciding within reasonable limits when and how dividends declared by a general meeting shall be paid); *Re Galway and Salthill Tramway Co* [1918] 1 IR 62 (no power to present petition to wind up); cf the Companies (Tables A to F) Regulations 1985, SI 1985/805, Schedule, Table A art 70 (cited in para 589 note 1 ante). As to Table A generally see para 529 et seq ante. See also para 582 et seq ante.
3 See *Hoole v Great Western Rly Co* (1867) 3 Ch App 262; *Wilson v London, Midland and Scottish Rly Co* [1940] Ch 393, [1940] 2 All ER 92, CA; and paras 1110 et seq, 1169 et seq ante.

1697. Annual returns. There are no provisions in the Companies Clauses Acts with reference to annual returns in respect of companies regulated by those Acts[1] but, in general[2], with one modification[3], the provisions of the Companies Act 1985 relating to them[4] apply[5].

1   As to the companies so regulated see para 1599 et seq ante.
2   For the exceptions, namely the bodies corporate to which the unregistered companies legislation does not apply, see the Companies Act 1985 s 718(2); the Companies (Unregistered Companies) Regulations 1985, SI 1985/680 (amended by SI 1990/438; SI 1990/1394; SI 1990/2571); and para 1766 post.
3   References in the relevant provisions to the company's registered office are to be taken as references to its principal office: ibid reg 5(b).
4   Ie the Companies Act 1985 Pt XI Ch III (ss 363-365 (as amended): see paras 1063-1065 ante). As to the application of administrative provisions in relation to provisions so applied see para 1699 post.
5   See ibid s 718(3); the Companies (Unregistered Companies) Regulations 1985 reg 4, Schedule and para 1767 post.

1698. Investigations. There are no special provisions in the Companies Clauses Acts with reference to the investigation of the affairs of companies regulated by those Acts[1] but, in general[2], the relevant provisions[3] of the Companies Act 1985 apply[4].

1   As to the companies so regulated see para 1599 et seq ante.
2   As to the exceptions, namely the bodies corporate to which the unregistered companies legislation does not apply, see the Companies Act 1985 s 718(2) and para 1766 post.
3   Ie ibid Pt XIV (431-453 (as amended): see para 1376 et seq ante), except s 446 (as amended) (see para 1384 ante).
4   Ibid s 718(1), Sch 22 (amended by the Companies Act 1989 s 71).

1699. Administrative provisions of the Companies Act 1985. In relation to the provisions of the Companies Act 1985, which apply to companies regulated by the Companies Clauses Acts[1], certain miscellaneous administrative provisions[2] of the 1985 Act in general[3] apply[4].

1   See paras 1630, 1694, 1697, 1698 ante and paras 1719, 1736 post.
2   Those which apply in any event are miscellaneous provisions about registration, namely the Companies Act 1985 s 706 (as substituted) (size and durability of documents delivered to the registrar: see para 64 ante), s 707 (as substituted) (delivery to the registrar of documents otherwise than in legible form: see para 65 ante), s 707A (as added) (keeping of company records by the registrar (see para 68 ante), s 708 (as amended) (fees payable to the registrar: see para 66 ante), s 709 (as substituted) (inspection of documents kept by the registrar: see para 67 ante), s 710 (as substituted) (public notice by the registrar of receipt and issue of certain documents: see para 67 ante), s 710A (as added) (provision and authentication by registrar of documents in non-legible form: see para 67 ante), s 713 (as amended) (enforcement of company's duty to make returns: see para 69 ante) and s 715A (as added) (interpretation): s 718(1), Sch 22 (amended by the Companies Act 1989 s 127(7)). Those which apply by virtue of an exercise by the Secretary of State of his powers under the Companies Act 1985 s 718(3) contained in the Companies (Unregistered Companies) Regulations 1985, SI 1985/680 (amended by SI 1990/438; SI 1990/1394; SI 1990/2571), are the Companies Act 1985 s 18 (statutory and other amendments of memorandum and articles to be registered: see para 100 ante), ss 35-35B (as substituted) (company's capacity, powers of directors to bind it: see paras 1107-1109 ante), ss 36-36C (as substituted and added) (company contracts and execution of documents by companies: see paras 54, 1129, 1130 ante), s 40 (as amended) (official seal for security documents: see para 1118 ante), s 42 (events affecting a company's status to be officially notified: see para 71 ante), ss 82, 86, 87 (allotments: see paras 450, 456 ante), s 185(4) (as amended) (exemption from duty to prepare certificates where shares etc issued to stock exchange nominee: see para 482 ante), s 186 (as amended) (certificates as evidence of title: see paras 487 ante), s 287 (as substituted) (registered office: see para 150 ante), ss 343-347 (as amended) (register to be kept of certain transactions not disclosed in accounts and related matters: see paras 606, 607 ante), s 351(1),(2),(5)(a) (as amended) (particulars of company to be given in correspondence: see para 1135 ante), s 711 (as amended) (public notice by registrar with respect to certain documents: see para 70 ante) and s 720 (certain companies to publish periodical statement: see para 939 ante): Companies (Unregistered Companies) Regulations 1985 reg 4, Schedule (amended by SI 1990/438; SI 1990/1394; SI 1990/2571).
3   For the exceptions, namely the bodies corporate to which the unregistered companies legislation does not apply, see the Companies Act 1985 s 718(2); the Companies (Unregistered Companies) Regulations 1985 reg 2; and para 1766 post.
4   See the Companies Act 1985 s 718(1), Sch 22 (as amended) and para 1767 et seq post.

(ii) Directors

1700. Appointment and number of directors. The number of directors[1] is the number prescribed in the special Act, which usually also appoints the first directors[2]. If that Act does not contain negative words, such as 'not less than' a specified number, a provision as to the number of directors may be directory only, as when it is provided elsewhere in that Act that directors are not bound to fill a vacancy on the board[3].

Where the company is authorised by its special Act to increase or reduce the number of directors, it may from time to time, in general meeting, after due notice for that purpose, increase or reduce their number within the prescribed limits, if any, and determine the order of rotation in which they are to go out of office, and what number is to be a quorum at their meetings[4].

1 For the meaning of 'director' see para 1603 ante.
2 Companies Clauses Consolidation Act 1845 ss 2, 81. The special Act usually also appoints the first directors. The special Act appointing the first directors may oblige them to continue in office until the first ordinary meeting held after the passing of the Act: *Re South London Fish Market Co* (1888) 39 ChD 324, CA. Generally it should be noted that guidance may be obtained from decisions with regard to directors of companies registered under the Companies Act 1985 or the Acts which it replaces: see further para 557 et seq ante.
3 See *Thames Haven Dock and Rly Co v Rose* (1842) 4 Man & G 552 at 559. Cf the cases cited in para 632 note 9 ante, which go to show that a provision in the articles of a company that the directors shall not be less than a given number is imperative.
4 Companies Clauses Consolidation Act 1845 s 82.

1701. Tenure of office. Unless the special Act provides otherwise, the directors appointed by it hold office until the first ordinary meeting[1] to be held in the year next after that in which the special Act was passed[2]. At this meeting the shareholders present, personally or by proxy, may either re-elect the directors appointed by the special Act, or any number of them, or may elect a new body of directors, or directors to supply the places of those not re-elected[2]. At the first ordinary meeting to be held every year afterwards directors to replace those then retiring from office in accordance with the statutory provisions[3] must be elected by the shareholders present, personally or by proxy[4]. Unless they are removed or disqualified or resign, the persons elected at any such meeting continue to be directors until others are elected in their stead[4]. The directors cannot legally agree to an arrangement with contractors or others which would have the effect of depriving the shareholders of their power of appointing their own directors[5].

1 For the meaning of 'ordinary meeting' see para 1727 post.
2 Companies Clauses Consolidation Act 1845 s 83.
3 Ie ibid s 88 (retirement of directors in rotation): see para 1717 post.
4 Ibid s 83.
5 *James v Eve* (1873) LR 6 HL 335 at 342.

1702. Quorum to elect directors. If at any meeting at which an election of directors ought to take place[1] the prescribed quorum[2] is not present within one hour from the time appointed for the meeting, no election of directors can be made, but the meeting stands adjourned to the following day at the same time and place[3]. If at the adjourned meeting the prescribed quorum is not present within one hour from the time appointed for the meeting, the existing directors continue to act, and retain their powers until new directors are appointed at the first ordinary meeting of the following year[3].

1　These words are merely another way of saying 'if at the first ordinary meeting to be held in the year': see *Grundt v Great Boulder Proprietary Gold Mines Ltd* [1948] Ch 145, [1948] 1 All ER 21, CA. See also the Companies Clauses Consolidation Act 1845 s 83 and para 1701 ante.
2　As to what constitutes a quorum see ibid s 72 and para 1730 post.
3　Ibid s 84.

1703. Casual vacancy in office of director. If a director dies or resigns or becomes disqualified or incompetent to act as such, or ceases to be a director by any other cause than that of going out of office by rotation[1], the remaining directors[2], if they think proper to do so, may elect in his place some other shareholder, duly qualified, to be a director[3]. The director so elected continues in office so long only as the person in whose place he has been elected would have been entitled to continue if he had remained in office[3].

1　See the Companies Clauses Consolidation Act 1845 s 88 (retirement in rotation of directors) and para 1717 post.
2　'Remaining directors' includes a sole continuing director: *Channel Collieries Trust Ltd v Dover, St Margaret's and Martin Mill Light Rly Co* [1914] 2 Ch 506, CA.
3　Companies Clauses Consolidation Act 1845 s 89.

1704. Qualification to be director. No person is capable of being a director unless he is a shareholder and possesses the prescribed number, if any, of shares; and a person holding an office or place of trust or profit under the company, or interested in any contract with the company, cannot be a director[1]. A director must not accept any other office or place of trust or profit under the company, or be interested in any contract with it, during the time he is a director[1]. If the special Act prescribes a certain share qualification for the directors and names a person as one of the first directors, he is in effect constituted by the Act a shareholder to the extent of the prescribed share qualification; and, if, in neglect of his duty, he fails to take up that number of shares and to procure himself to be registered in respect of them, he is liable in respect of that number of shares[2].

1　Companies Clauses Consolidation Act 1845 s 85. Section 85 does not apply to directors named in the special Act: *Portal v Emmens* (1876) 1 CPD 664 at 667, CA. Notwithstanding anything in the Companies Clauses Consolidation Act 1845, as applied to any company, but subject to any provision of a memorandum and articles having effect by virtue of an order under the Statutory Water Companies Act 1991 s 12 (adoption of memorandum and articles: see WATER) and to any modification of any such memorandum and articles, the following provisions have effect in relation to any statutory water company: s 10(1). Any person employed as chief engineer, general manager or secretary of the company may, whether or not he is a shareholder of the company, be appointed a director of the company either by the directors or in the manner provided by the Companies Clauses Consolidation Act 1845: Statutory Water Companies Act 1991 s 10(2). No appointment may, however, be so made if the appointment would increase the number of the directors of the company in question beyond the maximum prescribed by any provision of any enactment or statutory order relating to the company; and not more than one director of the company may hold office by virtue of these provisions at the same time: s 10(3). A person so appointed (1) does not cease to be a director by reason that he is employed as mentioned in s 10(2); but (2) if he was appointed by the directors, ceases to be a director as from the date of the next ordinary general meeting of the company unless his appointment is approved at that meeting by a majority of the votes of the proprietors of the company entitled to vote or voting, whether personally or by proxy, at the meeting: s 10(4). The provisions of the Companies Clauses Consolidation Act 1845 requiring directors to retire by rotation have effect as if a person appointed by virtue of these provisions were not a director: Statutory Water Companies Act 1991 s 10(5).

2 *Portal v Emmens* (1876) 1 CPD 664, CA; and see *Kincaid's Case* (1870) LR 11 Eq 192; *Forbes' Case* (1875) LR 19 Eq 353. The holding of the prescribed number of shares is a condition precedent to qualify for election as a director: *Channel Collieries Trust Ltd v Dover, St Margaret's and Martin Mill Light Rly Co* [1914] 2 Ch 506, CA.

1705. Consequences of director's interest in company's contract. If a director at any time after his election accepts or continues to hold any other office or place of trust or profit under the company, or is either directly or indirectly concerned in any contract with it or participates in any manner in the profits of any work to be done for it, his office of director becomes vacant, and thenceforth he must cease from voting or acting as such[1]. A member of any incorporated joint stock company is not, however, disqualified or prevented from acting as a director of a company subject to the Companies Clauses Consolidation Act 1845 by reason of any contract entered into between the two companies, although he must not vote on any question as to any contract with the joint stock company[2]. A director cannot validly deal, on behalf of the company, with himself or with a firm in which he is a partner; as a fiduciary agent of the company he cannot enter into engagements in which his personal interest may possibly conflict with his duty to the company[3]. The disqualification applies only to contracts with the company in the execution of its enterprise; hence a director may be a partner in a banking company which is the company's bank[4].

The consequences of a director being interested in a contract with his company are:

(1) the statutory consequence that he ceases to hold office[5]; and

(2) the legal consequence that the contract is voidable at the instance of the company[6].

A contract between two companies sanctioned by both in general meeting is not, however, to be treated as invalid and ultra vires one of the companies merely because the directors of that company are so interested in the contract[7].

1 Companies Clauses Consolidation Act 1845 s 86; *Portal v Emmens* (1876) 1 CPD 664, CA.

2 Companies Clauses Consolidation Act 1845 s 87. It is, however, immaterial that the director is also a director of other joint stock companies: *Wilson v London, Midland and Scottish Rly Co* [1940] Ch 393, [1940] 2 All ER 92, CA.

3 *Aberdeen Rly Co v Blaikie Bros* (1854) 1 Macq 461 at 471, HL; *Great Luxembourg Rly Co v Magnay (No 2)* (1858) 25 Beav 586; and see para 595 ante.

4 *Sheffield, Ashton-under-Lyne and Manchester Rly Co v Woodcock* (1841) 7 M & W 574.

5 Companies Clauses Consolidation Act 1845 s 86.

6 *Hely-Hutchinson v Brayhead Ltd* [1968] 1 QB 549 at 573, [1967] 3 All ER 98, CA, not following *Kaye v Croydon Tramways Co* [1898] 1 Ch 358 at 368, CA, where Lindley MR said that the director could not enforce the contract; *Flanagan v Great Western Rly Co* (1868) LR 7 Eq 116 at 123 (same point).

7 *Kaye v Croydon Tramways Co* [1898] 1 Ch 358, CA; *Foster v Oxford, Worcester and Wolverhampton Rly Co* (1853) 13 CB 200.

1706. Director ceasing to hold shares. The office of a director becomes vacant if at any time he ceases to be a holder of the prescribed number of shares in the company[1]. If he executes an equitable mortgage of his qualifying shares and the mortgagee gives notice of the mortgage to the company, the mortgagor's position as a director is at once determined[2]. Where he creates, in favour of his creditor, a mere equitable lien on his qualifying shares, his ownership of the shares is probably not so affected by notice to the company's secretary not to register any transfer of them without the creditor's consent as to deprive him of his office[3].

1 Companies Clauses Consolidation Act 1845 s 86.
2 *Re Pearse, ex p Littledale* (1855) 6 De GM & G 714 at 724, 733.
3 *Cumming v Prescott* (1837) 2 Y & C Ex 488 at 496.

1707. Directors' remuneration. Except as otherwise provided by the special Act, the powers of the company to determine what remuneration is to be paid to the directors must be exercised at a general meeting of the company[1]. A general meeting, if duly called, may vote the remuneration of directors, even for past services[2].

1 Companies Clauses Consolidation Act 1845 s 91.
2 *Hutton v West Cork Rly Co* (1883) 23 ChD 654 at 658, 672, CA; cf *Kaye v Croydon Tramways Co* [1898] 1 Ch 358, CA.

1708. Appointment of committees. The directors may appoint one or more committees, consisting of such number of directors as they think fit, within the limits, if any, prescribed in the special Act, and they may grant to such committees power to do any acts relating to the company's affairs which the directors could lawfully do, and which they from time to time think proper to entrust to them[1].

A committee may meet from time to time and adjourn from place to place, as it thinks proper, for carrying into effect the purposes of its appointment. No committee can exercise the powers entrusted to it except at a meeting at which there is present the prescribed quorum or, if no quorum is prescribed, a quorum to be fixed for that purpose by the general body of directors[2]. At all committee meetings one of the members present must be appointed chairman[2]. All questions at any committee meeting must be determined by a majority of votes of the members present and in case of an equal division of votes the chairman has a casting vote in addition to his vote as a committee member[2].

1 Companies Clauses Consolidation Act 1845 ss 2, 95; and see *D'Arcy v Tamar, Kit Hill and Callington Rly Co* (1867) LR 2 Exch 158, explained in *Re Bonelli's Telegraph Co, Collie's Claim* (1867) LR 12 Eq 246 at 259.
2 Companies Clauses Consolidation Act 1845 s 96.

1709. How contracts may be made. The power which may be granted to a committee to make contracts, as well as the directors' power to make contracts[1], on behalf of the company, is exercisable as follows:

(1) any contract which, if made between private persons, would by law be required to be in writing and under seal may be made by the committee or the directors on behalf of the company in writing, and under the company's common seal, and may be varied or discharged in the same manner[2];

(2) any contract which, if made between private persons, would by law be required to be in writing and signed by the parties to be charged may be made by the committee or the directors or any person acting under the company's express or implied authority on behalf of the company in writing, signed by the committee or any two of them, or any two of the directors or by such authorised person and may be varied or discharged in the same manner[3];

(3) any contract which, if made between private persons, would by law be valid even though made by parol only, and not reduced into writing, may be made by the committee or the directors or any person acting under the company's express or implied authority on behalf of the company by parol only, without writing, and may be varied or discharged in the same manner[4].

Any contract so made is effectual in law[5] and binds the company and its successors, and all other parties to it and their personal representatives[6]; and on any default in the execution of any such contract, either by the company or by any other party to it, such actions may be brought, either by or against the company, as might be brought had the same contract been made between private persons only[7].

Contracts binding on the company may be made in other ways if there is power so to make them[8]. Thus a company established for the purpose of trading may, independently of the statutory provision, validly make all contracts which are of ordinary occurrence in its trade and all contracts, not expressly regulated by any statute, which relate to objects or purposes for which it was incorporated, without the formality of a seal[9].

A company's rights and obligations under its contracts, when once validly made, are in all respects the same as those of individuals[10].

1 As to minutes and copies of contracts see para 1715 post.
2 Companies Clauses Consolidation Act 1845 s 97.
3 Ibid s 97; Corporate Bodies' Contracts Act 1960 s 1(1)(a),(3).
4 Companies Clauses Consolidation Act 1845 s 97; Corporate Bodies' Contracts Act 1960 s 1(1)(b),(3).
5 This does not of course apply where there is a valid defence, eg on the ground that the contract was ultra vires the company. As to ultra vires acts see para 1605 ante.
6 Companies Clauses Consolidation Act 1845 s 97; Corporate Bodies' Contracts Act 1960 s 1(2).
7 Companies Clauses Consolidation Act 1845 s 97.
8 *Wilson v West Hartlepool Rly Co* (1865) 2 De GJ & Sm 475 at 496.
9 *South of Ireland Colliery Co v Waddle* (1869) LR 4 CP 617 at 618, Ex Ch; cf *Cope v Thames Haven Dock and Rly Co* (1849) 3 Exch 841. As to the making of contracts not under seal see further CORPORATIONS.
10 *Greene v West Cheshire Rly Co* (1871) LR 13 Eq 44 at 49; *London and Birmingham Rly Co v Winter* (1840) Cr & Ph 57 at 63.

1710. Contracts under seal. In order to bind a company by a bond, the seal must be affixed by or by the authority of the directors or a committee of the directors, acting together at a properly constituted meeting[1].

Where directors have only the power of affixing the company's seal under certain prescribed rules, a person dealing with them is taken to have notice of those rules; and, if there is something which may only be done by them under limited powers, the person so dealing must at his peril see that those powers are not being exceeded. If, however, they have power to bind the company, but certain preliminaries are required to be gone through on the part of the company before their power may be duly exercised, the person so dealing is not bound to see that all those preliminaries have been observed, but is entitled to presume that the directors are acting regularly[2].

1 *D'Arcy v Tamar, Kit Hill and Callington Rly Co* (1867) LR 2 Exch 158. Cf *Clarke v Imperial Gas Light and Coke Co* (1832) 4 B & Ad 315 (company incorporated under a private Act which made specific provision as to affixing the seal).
2 *Royal British Bank v Turquand* (1856) 6 E & B 327, Ex Ch; *Fountaine v Carmarthen Rly Co* (1868) LR 5 Eq 316 at 322; *Re Romford Canal Co, Pocock's Claim, Trickett's Claim, Carew's Claim* (1883) 24 ChD 85; cf *Duck v Tower Galvanizing Co* [1901] 2 KB 314 at 318; *County of Gloucester Bank v Rudry Merthyr Steam and House Coal Colliery Co* [1895] 1 Ch 629, CA; and see *Williams v Chester and Holyhead Rly Co* (1851) 15 Jur 828 at 830; *Webb v Herne Bay Comrs* (1870) LR 5 QB 642; para 1137 et seq ante and CORPORATIONS.

1711. Other circumstances in which contracts bind the company. A company may make a parol contract for the temporary occupation of land required for carrying out its undertaking and may be sued on such a contract in respect of the occupation; and, even though no evidence other than the occupation of the land by the company is adduced, the court will, in the absence of evidence to negative a parol contract, assume that it had been made[1]. The directors may ratify a written contract made by the company's manager without authority, and, if they do so, it becomes in effect the company's contract[2]. It has, however, been held that, in the absence of an order of the directors or of a duly authorised committee or of something from which authority in the engineer to make a parol contract may be inferred, the mere fact of work having been done, as for example by a contractor on the order of the company's engineer, is not enough to render the company liable[3].

1 *Lowe v North Western Rly Co* (1852) 18 QB 632 at 638. Where a company has had the use of goods ordered by its clerk, sufficient evidence exists for the court to find that the company, by its directors, entered into a binding contract to buy: *Pauling v London and North Western Rly Co* (1853) 8 Exch 867. In some cases a corporation has not been allowed to take the benefit of a misapprehension on the faith of which some person has expended money on the corporation's land, but a contract in favour of such persons has been implied: *Crampton v Varna Rly Co* (1872) 7 Ch App 562 at 568; *Laird v Birkenhead Rly Co* (1859) John 500 at 510.

2 *Wilson v West Hartlepool Rly Co* (1865) 2 De GJ & Sm 475. See also *Leominster Canal Navigation Co v Shrewsbury and Hereford Rly Co* (1857) 3 K & J 654 (purchase of undertaking authorised to be purchased); *Serrell v Derbyshire, Staffordshire and Worcestershire Junction Rly Co* (1850) 9 CB 811 at 828 (cheque dishonestly drawn). Since the passing of the Corporate Bodies' Contracts Act 1960 the ostensible authority of the person purporting to make the contract on behalf of the company would be sufficient: see s 1(1) and para 1709 ante.

3 *Homersham v Wolverhampton Waterworks Co* (1851) 6 Exch 137 at 141. As to the effect of the Corporate Bodies' Contracts Act 1960 s 1(1) see note 2 supra.

1712. Directors' liability. No director, by being party to or executing as director any contract or instrument on behalf of the company, or lawfully executing any of the powers given to the directors, incurs any personal liability[1]. The directors are entitled to be indemnified out of the company's capital for all payments made or liability, losses, costs and damages incurred in the due execution of their powers, and for the purposes of such indemnity may apply the company's funds and, if necessary, make calls on unpaid capital[2].

A director indorsing a certificate for debenture stock[3] with a warranty, contrary to the fact, that the amount of stock represented by the certificate is within the amount which the company has power to issue, is personally liable for breach of warranty, if money is lent to the company on the faith of the warranty[4]. Promoters of a company who afterwards become its first directors and who obtain an advance of money on their personal credit will not escape from their personal liability to the lender merely by showing that the money was applied in payment of expenses incidental to the passing of the special Act, and that the company has purported to ratify their act in obtaining the advances[5].

1 Companies Clauses Consolidation Act 1845 s 100. Where acts have been honestly done by directors within their authority, they cannot generally be made personally liable 'even though bad consequences may ensue': *Charitable Corpn v Sutton* (1742) 2 Atk 400 at 405. However, if, being agents of the company, they exercise its functions for the purpose of improperly alienating its property or otherwise injuring its interests, the company is entitled to sue them, and to obtain redress from them: *A-G v Wilson* (1840) Cr & Ph 1 at 24, 25. As to actions of deceit against directors see para 332 et seq ante.

2 Companies Clauses Consolidation Act 1845 s 100.

3 As to debenture stock see para 1687 et seq ante.

4 *Whitehaven Joint Stock Banking Co v Reed* (1886) 54 LT 360, CA; and see AGENCY.

5 *Scott v Lord Ebury* (1867) LR 2 CP 255 at 264, 270.

1713. Meetings of directors. The directors hold meetings at such times as they appoint for the purpose, and may meet and adjourn from time to time and from place to place as they think proper[1]. Any two of them may at any time require the secretary to call a meeting of the directors[1]. In order to constitute a meeting of directors there must be present at least the quorum prescribed in the special Act or, where no quorum is prescribed, one-third of the directors[2].

All questions at any such meeting must be determined by the majority of votes of the directors present, and in case of an equal division of votes the chairman has a casting vote in addition to his vote as a director[3]. In order to do effectually such an act as authorising the affixing of the company's seal to a bond the directors, or at least a quorum of them, must act jointly and as a board at a meeting[4].

1 Companies Clauses Consolidation Act 1845 s 92.
2 A quorum of directors means a quorum competent to transact the business before the meeting: cf *Re Greymount-Point Elizabeth Rly and Coal Co Ltd, Yuill v Greymouth-Point Elizabeth Rly and Coal Co Ltd* [1904] 1 Ch 32. See further para 632 ante.
3 Companies Clauses Consolidation Act 1845 s 92. In general, although the majority can bind the minority, the minority have a right to be heard: *Great Western Rly Co v Rushout* (1852) 5 De G & Sm 290.
4 *D'Arcy v Tamar, Kit Hill and Callington Rly Co* (1867) LR 2 Exch 158, explained in *Re Bonelli's Telegraph Co, Collie's Claim* (1871) LR 12 Eq 246 at 259, 260; *County of Gloucester Bank v Rudry Merthyr Steam and House Coal Colliery Co* [1895] 1 Ch 629 at 632, 635, CA; followed in *Re Haycraft Gold Reduction and Mining Co* [1900] 2 Ch 230 at 235.

1714. Chairman of directors. At the first meeting of directors held after the passing of the special Act, and at the first meeting of the directors held after each annual appointment of directors, the directors must choose one of themselves to act as chairman for the following year, and may also, if they think fit, choose another director to act as deputy chairman for the same period[1]. If the chairman or deputy chairman dies or resigns, or ceases to be a director or otherwise becomes disqualified to act, the directors must fill the vacancy at the next meeting; every chairman or deputy chairman elected to fill a vacancy continues in office so long only as the person in whose place he may be so elected would have been entitled to continue if the vacancy had not occurred[1].

If at any meeting neither the chairman nor deputy chairman is present, the directors present must choose one of their number to be chairman of the meeting[2].

1 Companies Clauses Consolidation Act 1845 s 93.
2 Ibid s 94.

1715. Minutes of meetings etc. The directors must cause notes, minutes or copies of all appointments made or contracts entered into by the directors, and of the orders and proceedings of all meetings of the company and of the directors and committees of directors[1] to be entered in books which must be kept under the directors' superintendence[2]. Every entry must be signed by the chairman of the meeting, and, if so signed, is to be received as evidence in all courts without proof of the meeting having been duly convened or held, of the persons making or entering the orders or proceedings being shareholders or directors or members of committee, of the signature of the chairman, or of the fact of his having been chairman, all of which matters are presumed until the contrary is proved³. The signature required to authenticate the minutes is that of the director who has presided at the particular meeting, but the signature need not be attached at the time of that meeting; it may be given at a subsequent meeting⁴.

1   As to the committees of directors see the Companies Clauses Consolidation Act 1845 s 95 and para 1708 ante.
2   Ibid s 98.
3   Ibid s 98; cf *Sheffield, Ashton-under-Lyne and Manchester Rly Co v Woodcock* (1841) 7 M & W 574; *Miles v Bough* (1842) 3 QB 845 at 866.
4   *Southampton Dock Co v Richards* (1840) 1 Man & G 448 at 463, 467; *West London Rly Co v Bernard* (1843) 3 QB 873 at 877. Where a meeting was held on one day and adjourned until the next, and the director who was in the chair on both occasions signed the minutes of the adjourned meeting only, the minutes of both meetings were admitted in evidence: *Inglis v Great Northern Rly Co* (1852) 19 LTOS 149 at 150, HL. A fact stated in minutes may, if necessary, be proved by other evidence: *Inglis v Great Northern Rly Co* supra. Minutes, though duly signed, are not admissible in evidence for the purpose of establishing, in favour of the company, the facts stated in the minutes, eg against a bondholder suing the company: *Hill v Manchester and Salford Waterworks Co* (1833) 5 B & Ad 866 at 875, 876.

1716.   Effect of informalities in appointment of directors.   All acts done by any meeting of the directors, or of a committee of directors¹, or by any person acting as a director, are as valid as if every such person had been duly appointed and qualified, notwithstanding that it is afterwards discovered that there was some defect in the appointment of any of them or that any of them was disqualified².

1   As to committees of directors see para 1708 ante.
2   Companies Clauses Consolidation Act 1845 s 99; and see *Channel Collieries Trust Ltd v Dover, St Margaret's and Martin Mill Light Rly Co* [1914] 2 Ch 506, at 514, 515, CA. Cf para 545 ante.

1717.   Retirement of directors by rotation.   Subject to the provision under which a company may determine the order of rotation in which directors go out of office¹, directors must retire at the times and in the proportions laid down in the Companies Clauses Consolidation Act 1845². In the case of the first elected directors³, the number prescribed in the special Act and, if no number is prescribed, one-third of the directors, to be determined by ballot among themselves unless they otherwise agree, must go out of office at the end of the first year; at the end of the second year the prescribed number and, if no number is prescribed, one-half of the remaining number of the directors to be determined in like manner, must go out of office; and at the end of the third year the prescribed number and, if no number is prescribed, the remainder of the directors, must go out of office⁴.

At the first ordinary meeting in every subsequent year the prescribed number and, if no number is prescribed, one-third of the directors, being those who have been longest in office, must go out of office⁴.

If the prescribed number of directors is some number not divisible by three, and the number of directors to retire is not prescribed, the directors must in each case determine what number of directors, as nearly one-third as may be, are to go out of office, so that the whole number must go out of office in three years⁵.

In each instance the places of the retiring directors must be filled by an equal number of qualified shareholders⁶. A retiring director may be re-elected immediately or at any future time⁶.

1 See the Companies Clauses Consolidation Act 1845 s 82 and para 1700 ante.
2 Ibid s 88.
3 Ie those elected at the first ordinary meeting held in the year next after that in which the special Act was
   passed: see ibid s 83 and para 1701 ante. As to the qualification of directors see para 1704 ante.
4 Ibid s 88.
5 Ibid s 88 proviso.
6 Ibid s 88.

1718. Power to choose and remove directors. Except as otherwise provided by
the special Act and subject to the directors' power to fill casual vacancies in the office of
director[1], the company's powers to choose and remove directors can be exercised only
at a general meeting[2]. A general meeting has power to remove directors provided
proper notice as to the object of the meeting is given, and may fill vacancies if all the
directors are removed or if the directors decline to exercise the power of filling casual
vacancies[3].

1 See the Companies Clauses Consolidation Act 1845 s 89 and para 1703 ante.
2 Ibid s 91.
3 *Isle of Wight Rly Co v Tahourdin* (1883) 25 ChD 320, CA; *West Somerset Mineral Rly Co v Robinson* (1917)
   34 TLR 132.

1719. Register of directors and secretaries. There are no special requirements in
the Companies Clauses Acts with reference to the keeping of a register of directors and
secretaries of companies regulated by those Acts[1]; but, in general[2], the provisions of the
Companies Act 1985 relating to that register[3] apply[4].

1 As to the companies so regulated see para 1599 et seq ante.
2 As to the exceptions, ie the bodies corporate to which the unregistered companies legislation does not
   apply, see the Companies Act 1985 s 718(2); the Companies (Unregistered Companies) Regulations
   1985, SI 1985/680 (amended by SI 1990/438; SI 1990/1394; SI 1990/2571); and para 1766 post.
3 Ie the Companies Act 1985 ss 288-290 (as amended): see paras 560, 649 ante. As to the application of
   certain administrative provisions of that Act see para 1699 ante.
4 Ibid s 718(1), Sch 22; and see para 1767 et seq post.

(iii) Other Officers

1720. Statutory requirements. Besides the directors, the company is required by
statute to appoint a secretary[1], auditors[2], and a book-keeper[3], and it may have other
officers such as treasurer and collector[4].

Except as otherwise provided by the special Act, the company's powers as to the
choice of auditors, and the remuneration of the auditors, treasurer and secretary, can be
exercised only at a general meeting of the company[5]. A person employed by the
directors as secretary may, however, maintain an action against the company to
recover remuneration for his services even though there has been no determination of
a general meeting on the subject, but directors agreeing, without authority, to pay a
salary to a secretary may, as between themselves and the general body of shareholders,
have been guilty of a breach of trust[6].

1 See the Companies Clauses Consolidation Act 1845 ss 3, 10, 15, 18, 40, 45. For the meaning of
   'secretary' see para 1603 ante. As to his position and duties see para 646 et seq ante. There are no special
   requirements as to keeping a register of securities: see para 1719 ante.
2 See ibid s 101 and para 1740 post.
3 See ibid s 119.

4 See para 1721 post.
5 Companies Clauses Consolidation Act 1845 s 91.
6 *Bill v Darenth Valley Rly Co* (1856) 1 H & N 305 at 306.

1721. Security by officers. Before any person entrusted with the custody or control of money, whether as treasurer, collector or other officer of the company, enters upon his office, the directors must take sufficient security from him for the faithful execution of his office[1].

1 Companies Clauses Consolidation Act 1845 s 109. Where the security of a surety is taken, any variation of the agreement to which he has subscribed, which is made without his consent or knowledge, or may prejudice him *(North Western Rly Co v Whinray* (1854) 10 Exch 77 at 82), or may amount to the substitution of a new agreement for the original agreement, will discharge the surety, even though the original agreement might, notwithstanding that variation, be substantially performed *(Bonar v Macdonald* (1850) 3 HL Cas 226 at 238, 239; *Phillips v Foxall* (1872) LR 7 QB 666 at 672, 680). Where by statute the nature of a principal's office is so changed that its duties are materially altered so as to affect the surety's risk, the surety is discharged: *Pybus v Gibb* (1856) 6 E & B 902 at 911. The amalgamation of two companies by statute impliedly or expressly preserving rights against a surety does not so alter the position of an officer of one of the companies who continues to hold that office under the amalgamated companies as to discharge his surety: *London, Brighton and South Coast Rly Co v Goodwin* (1849) 3 Exch 320 at 332; *Eastern Union Rly Co v Cochrane* (1853) 9 Exch 197. As to fidelity guarantees see further GUARANTEE vol 20 (Reissue) para 201.

1722. Officers' duty to account. When required by the directors, every officer must make out and deliver to them or to any person appointed by them a true and perfect written account under his hand of all money received by him on behalf of the company, stating how, to whom and for what purpose that money has been disposed of, together with vouchers and receipts[1]. He must also pay to the directors or to any person appointed by them all money which appears to be owing from him upon the balance of those accounts[1].

Any officer failing to render that account, to produce and deliver up all the vouchers and receipts in his possession or power, to pay the balance when required, or, for three days after being required, failing to deliver up to the directors or to any person appointed by them all papers and writings, property, effects, matters and things in his possession or power relating to the execution of the Companies Clauses Consolidation Act 1845, or the special Act, or any Act incorporated with it, or belonging to the company, may be summoned before two or more justices[2] who may determine the matter in a summary way and may adjust and declare the balance owing by him[3]. If it appears, either upon his confession, or upon evidence, or upon inspection of the account, that any of the company's money is in his hands or owing by him to the company, the justices may order him to pay the amount[3].

1 Companies Clauses Consolidation Act 1845 s 110.
2 For the meaning of 'justice' see para 1603 ante.
3 Companies Clauses Consolidation Act 1845 s 111.

1723. Officers' refusal to account. If an officer refuses to make out his written account, or to produce and deliver to the justices his vouchers and receipts, or to deliver up any property in his possession or power belonging to the company[1], they may commit him to prison until he has delivered up all the vouchers and receipts, if any, in his possession or power, and all property, if any, in his possession or power, belonging to the company[2]. Further, if any director or other person acting on behalf of the company makes oath that he has good reason to believe, upon stated grounds, and does believe, that the officer intends to abscond, the justice before whom the complaint is made, instead of issuing his summons, may issue his warrant to bring the officer before two justices[3]. However, no person executing the warrant may keep the officer in custody longer than 24 hours without bringing him before some justice[3]. The justice before whom the officer may be brought may either discharge him, if he thinks there is no sufficient ground for his detention, or order him to be detained in custody so as to be brought before two justices unless the officer gives satisfactory bail for his appearance before them[3].

No such proceeding against an officer will deprive the company of any remedy which it might otherwise have against him or his surety[4].

1 See para 1722 ante. For the meaning of 'justice' see para 1603 ante.
2 Companies Clauses Consolidation Act 1845 s 112.
3 Ibid s 113.
4 Ibid s 114.

1724. Solicitor. A solicitor is not ordinarily, but may be, an officer of a company[1]. The mere fact that a solicitor has been employed in bringing out a new company does not entitle him to claim payment from it[2], but in the case of companies formed under private Acts provision is usually made by the Act incorporating the company for the costs, charges and expenses incident to obtaining the Act and forming the company to be paid out of the company's assets when formed. Such a provision, being intended to benefit the promoters, does not entitle a solicitor employed under a retainer from the promoters to obtain payment of his costs directly from the company[3]. To enable him to do so he must establish either that the company has, after its formation, entered into a new contract with himself to pay him[4] or, perhaps, that he has no claim against the promoters, being in fact a promoter himself and having only the company to look to for payment[5].

1 See para 651 notes 1, 2 ante.
2 *Re English and Colonial Produce Co Ltd* [1906] 2 Ch 435, CA.
3 *Wyatt v Metropolitan Board of Works* (1862) 11 CBNS 744 (distinguishing *Tilson v Warwick Gas Light Co* (1825) 4 B & C 962, and *Carden v General Cemetery Co* (1839) 5 Bing NC 253, which had been followed in *Hitchins v Kilkenny Rly Co* (1850) 9 CB 536); *Re Kent Tramways Co* (1879) 12 ChD 312, CA; *Re Skegness and St Leonard's Tramways Co, ex p Hanly* (1888) 41 ChD 215, CA; and see *Re Manchester, Middleton and District Tramways Co* [1893] 2 Ch 638 at 644–652. It has been suggested that, to prevent circuity of action, the solicitor might claim directly against the company: *Re Manchester, Middleton and District Tramways Co* supra at 651 per Kekewich J; cf *Terrell v Hutton* (1854) 4 HL Cas 1091. See also para 1625 ante.
4 *Nichols v Regent's Canal Co* (1894) 63 LJQB 641 (revsd on the facts, without affecting the proposition in the text, sub nom *Nichols v North Metropolitan Rly and Canal Co* 71 LT 836, CA; affd (1896) 74 LT 744, HL); *Terrell v Hutton* (1854) 4 HL Cas 1091.
5 *Re Brampton and Longtown Rly Co, Shaw's Claim* (1875) 10 Ch App 177; *Re Skegness and St Leonard's Tramways Co, ex p Hanly* (1888) 41 ChD 215 at 241, CA per Bowen LJ; cf *Savin v Hoylake Rly Co* (1865) LR 1 Exch 9; *Muir v Forman's Trustee* (1903) 5 F 546. It is difficult to see how this can happen in the case of a solicitor acting as such, who necessarily acts on instructions and who, therefore, looks to the person instructing him for his costs: see *Re Skegness and St Leonard's Tramways Co, ex p Hanly* supra at 241 per Lindley LJ, followed in *Re Manchester, Middleton and District Tramways Co* [1893] 2 Ch 638 at 650 per Kekewich J. Prior to its repeal by the Administration of Justice Act 1965 s 34(1), Sch 2, where the undertaking was abandoned, under the Parliamentary Deposits and Bonds Act 1892 s 1(2) the solicitor was entitled to claim against the parliamentary depositors as a creditor.

(iv) Byelaws

1725. Power to make byelaws. The company may from time to time make such byelaws as it thinks fit for the purpose of regulating the conduct of its officers and employees and for providing for the due management of its affairs[1], and may alter or repeal them and make others[2]. The byelaws must not be repugnant to the general law, or to the provisions of the Companies Clauses Consolidation Act 1845, or the special Act[3]. They must be in writing, sealed with the company's common seal, and a copy must be given to each of its officers and employees affected by them[4].

By its byelaws the company may impose reasonable penalties upon all its officers or employees offending against them as it thinks fit, not exceeding level 1 on the standard scale or not exceeding a lesser amount for any one offence[5].

The production of a written or printed copy of the byelaws, with the company's common seal affixed, is sufficient evidence of them in all prosecutions under them[6].

1 A byelaw to the effect that a company's canal must not be used on Sundays is void, as an attempt to deal with a matter outside the cognisance of the company: *Calder and Hebble Navigation Co v Pilling* (1845) 14 M & W 76.
2 Companies Clauses Consolidation Act 1845 s 124.
3 Ibid s 124. As to the making of byelaws by companies and the validity of those byelaws see CORPORATIONS.
4 Ibid s 124.
5 Ibid s 125 (amended by the Criminal Law Act 1977 s 31(6); the Criminal Justice Act 1982 s 46). For the meaning of 'the standard scale' see CRIMINAL LAW vol 11(2) (Reissue) para 808.
6 Companies Clauses Consolidation Act 1845 s 127.

(v) General Meetings

1726. Powers exercisable only in general meeting. Except as otherwise provided by the special Act, the following powers of the company may be exercised only at a general meeting of the company[1]:

(1) the choice and removal of the directors, except as already mentioned[2], and the increasing or reducing of their number where authorised by the special Act[3];
(2) the choice of auditors[4];
(3) the determination as to the remuneration of the directors, auditors, treasurer and secretary;
(4) the determination as to the amount of money to be borrowed on mortgage[5];
(5) the determination as to the augmentation of capital[6]; and
(6) the declaration of dividends[7].

1 Companies Clauses Consolidation Act 1845 s 91.
2 See ibid ss 83, 89 and paras 1700, 1701, 1703, 1718 ante.
3 See ibid s 82 and para 1700 ante.
4 See ibid ss 101, 104 and paras 1740, 1742 post.
5 See ibid ss 38, 39 and paras 1670, 1671 ante.
6 See ibid s 56 and paras 1618, 1619 ante. See also the Companies Clauses Act 1863 Pt II (ss 12–21) and para 1620 et seq ante.
7 See the Companies Clauses Consolidation Act 1845 s 120 and para 1744 post.

1727. Ordinary and extraordinary meetings. The first general meeting of the shareholders of the company must be held within the time prescribed by the special Act or, if no time is so prescribed, within one month of the passing of that Act[1]. Subsequent general meetings must be held at the periods prescribed by that Act or, if no periods are prescribed, in February and August each year or at such other stated periods as are appointed for that purpose by an order of a general meeting[2]. These meetings are called 'ordinary meetings'[3].

Every general meeting of the shareholders other than an ordinary meeting is called an 'extraordinary meeting'[3].

1 Companies Clauses Consolidation Act 1845 ss 2, 66.
2 Ibid ss 2, 66.
3 Ibid s 68.

1728. Notice and place of meeting. At least 14 clear days' public notice of all meetings, whether ordinary or extraordinary, must be given by advertisement[1], specifying the place, day and hour of the meeting[2]. No business except that which may be appointed by the Companies Clauses Consolidation Act 1845 or the special Act to be done at an ordinary meeting[3] can be transacted at any ordinary meeting unless special notice of that business has been given in the advertisement convening the meeting[4]. Thus, the voting of remuneration to directors is a matter requiring special notice[5]. In the case of an extraordinary meeting the notice must always specify the purpose for which the meeting is called, and the meeting cannot enter upon any business not set forth in the notice upon which it has been convened[6].

The whole purpose, as distinguished from the details, must be fairly stated in the notice, which must not be so framed as to mislead those to whom it is addressed; if there are several purposes, the notice will not be sufficient in respect of any purpose not indicated in it[7].

All meetings, whether ordinary or extraordinary, must be held in the place prescribed by the special Act and, if no place is so prescribed, at some place appointed by the directors[8].

1 For the method of giving notice by advertisement and the effect of non-compliance with the statutory requirements see para 1611 ante.
2 Companies Clauses Consolidation Act 1845 s 71.
3 Eg the election of directors (see ibid s 83 and para 1700 ante) or of auditors (see s 101 and para 1740 post).
4 Ibid s 67.
5 *Hutton v West Cork Rly Co* (1883) 23 ChD 654 at 659, CA.
6 Companies Clauses Consolidation Act 1845 s 69.
7 *Kaye v Croydon Tramways Co* [1898] 1 Ch 358 at 369, 370, 373, CA; *Tiessen v Henderson* [1899] 1 Ch 861.
8 Companies Clauses Consolidation Act 1845 ss 2, 66.

1729. Convening extraordinary meetings. Extraordinary meetings may be convened by the directors at such times as they think fit[1].

The number of shareholders prescribed by the special Act, holding in the aggregate shares to the amount prescribed by that Act or, where the number of shareholders or the amount of shares is not prescribed, 20 or more shareholders, holding in the aggregate not less than one-tenth of the company's capital, may by writing under their hands at any time require the directors to call an extraordinary meeting[2]. The requisition must fully express the object of the meeting required to be called, and must be left at the company's office or given to at least three directors or left at their last or usual places of abode[3]. Upon the receipt of the requisition the directors must forthwith convene a meeting of the shareholders, and, if they fail to do so within 21 days, the shareholders signing the requisition may call it by giving 14 days' public notice[3].

If the object of the requisition is such that in no manner and by no machinery can it be legally carried into effect, the directors are justified in refusing to act upon it; but, if the object stated can be carried into effect, it is the directors' duty to call the meeting[4]. If, upon receiving a requisition, the directors issue a notice convening a meeting so worded as not to be a proper compliance with the requisition, the requisitionists are justified in calling the meeting, as upon a failure by the directors to do so[5].

1 Companies Clauses Consolidation Act 1845 s 68.
2 Ibid ss 2, 70.
3 Ibid s 70.
4 *Isle of Wight Rly Co v Tahourdin* (1883) 25 ChD 320 at 334, CA.
5 *Isle of Wight Rly Co v Tahourdin* (1883) 25 ChD 320 at 333, CA.

1730. Quorum at general meeting. In order to constitute a meeting, whether ordinary or extraordinary, there must be present, either personally or by proxy, the quorum prescribed by the special Act, and, if no quorum is prescribed, then shareholders holding in the aggregate not less than one-twentieth of the company's capital, and being in number not less than one for every £500 of that required proportion of capital, unless that number would be more than 20, in which case 20 shareholders, holding not less than one-twentieth of the capital, form a quorum[1].

If within one hour from the time appointed for the meeting a quorum is not present, no business can be transacted at the meeting other than the declaring of a dividend, in case that is one of the objects of the meeting, and, except in the case of a meeting for the election of directors, the meeting must be adjourned indefinitely[2]. If and so long as the total number of shares issued represents less than the amount of capital required to be represented at a general meeting, no valid meeting can be held[3].

1 Companies Clauses Consolidation Act 1845 ss 2, 72.
2 Ibid s 72.
3 *Re Skegness and St Leonard's Tramways Co, ex p Hanly* (1888) 41 ChD 215 at 225, 231, 237, CA. Cf *Channel Collieries Trust Ltd v Dover, St Margaret's and Martin Mill Light Rly Co* [1914] 1 Ch 568 at 576 (where Sargant J interpreted the phrase 'one-twentieth of the share capital of the company' as used in the order incorporating the railway company as meaning one-twentieth of its issued share capital); affd on other grounds [1914] 2 Ch 506, CA.

1731. Chairman. At every meeting of the company one or other of the following persons is to preside as chairman, namely the chairman of the directors, or in his absence the deputy chairman, if any, or in their absence some one of the directors chosen for that purpose by the meeting, or in the absence of the chairman, deputy chairman and all the directors, any shareholder chosen for that purpose by a majority of the shareholders present at the meeting[1].

1 Companies Clauses Consolidation Act 1845 s 73.

1732. Business at meetings; adjournment. The shareholders present at any meeting must proceed in the execution of the company's powers with respect to the matters for which the meeting has been convened, and those only[1]. Any meeting may be adjourned from time to time and from place to place[1]. No business can, however, be transacted at any adjourned meeting other than the business left unfinished at the meeting from which the adjournment took place[1].

1 Companies Clauses Consolidation Act 1845 s 74.

1733. Voting rights. At all general meetings every shareholder is entitled to vote according to the scale of voting prescribed by the special Act and, where no scale is prescribed, every shareholder has one vote for every share up to ten, and an additional vote for every five shares beyond the first ten shares up to 100, and an additional vote for every ten shares beyond the first 100 shares, but a shareholder is not entitled to vote at any meeting unless he has paid all calls then due upon his shares[1].

Where several persons are jointly entitled to a share, the person whose name stands first in the register of shareholders is, for the purpose of voting[2], deemed the sole proprietor, and on all occasions his vote, either in person or by proxy, must be allowed as the vote in respect of the share without proof of the concurrence of the other holders[3].

A shareholder who by reason of mental disorder is incapable of managing his affairs may vote by his receiver[4]; and a shareholder who is a minor[5] may vote by his guardian or any one of his guardians[6]; and every such vote may be given either in person or by proxy[6].

1 Companies Clauses Consolidation Act 1845 ss 2, 75.
2 But presumably not for the purpose of calculating voting rights in accordance with this provision.
3 Companies Clauses Consolidation Act 1845 s 78.
4 See the Mental Health Act 1983 ss 95, 96, 99 and MENTAL HEALTH vol 30 (Reissue) para 1441 et seq. The Companies Clauses Consolidation Act 1845 s 79 has ceased to have effect in relation to persons within the jurisdiction under the Mental Health Act 1983 Pt VIII (ss 93–113) (as amended): see s 113, Sch 3 and MENTAL HEALTH vol 30 (Reissue) para 1443.
5 As to the attainment of majority at the age of 18 see the Family Law Reform Act 1969 s 1 and CHILDREN vol 5(2) (Reissue) para 601.
6 Companies Clauses Consolidation Act 1845 s 79.

1734. Manner of voting; proxies. The votes may be given either personally or by proxies who are shareholders, by written authorisation according to the statutory form or in a form to the like effect under the hand of the shareholder nominating the proxy or, if the shareholder is a corporation, then under its common seal[1]. Every proposition at a meeting must be determined by the majority of votes of the parties present, including proxies, the chairman of the meeting being entitled not only to vote as a principal and proxy but to have a casting vote if there is an equality of votes[2].

Where the shareholder is a body corporate, the proxy may be any member of that body, even though not personally a shareholder in the company[3]. During the continuance of his appointment, the proxy is to be taken to be a shareholder in the company to which his appointment relates, holding the number of shares held by the corporation by whom he is appointed, for all purposes except the transfer of any share or the giving of receipts for any dividend[4]. His appointment may be made and revoked by the corporation in the statutory forms[5].

No person is entitled to vote as a proxy unless the instrument appointing him has been transmitted to the secretary of the company within the period prescribed by the special Act or, if no period is prescribed, not less than 48 hours before the time appointed for holding the meeting at which the proxy is to be used[6].

1 Companies Clauses Consolidation Act 1845 s 76, Sch (F). As to stamps on and the insertion of the date of the meeting in proxies see paras 674, 679 ante. As to payment by directors for the stamps (if any) and postage on proxies see paras 676, 1696 note 2 ante. Proxy forms in the directors' names may be sent to some only of the shareholders at the expense of the company without contravening the Act, and the court will not interfere if the motive in so acting is honest, eg to ensure the presence of a quorum at the meeting, and not improper, eg to ensure a favourable vote: see *Wilson v London, Midland and Scottish Rly Co* [1940] Ch 393, [1940] 2 All ER 92, CA. However, as to the sending out of invitations to appoint

named persons as proxies to some only of the shareholders in the case of companies regulated by the Companies Act 1985 see s 372(6) and para 676 ante.

2 Companies Clauses Consolidation Act 1845 s 76.

3 Ibid s 76 proviso (amended by the Companies Clauses Consolidation Act 1888 s 2; the Companies Clauses Consolidation Act 1889 s 2).

4 Companies Clauses Consolidation Act 1888 s 3.

5 Ibid s 4.

6 Companies Clauses Consolidation Act 1845 ss 2, 77.

1735. Evidence of resolutions. Whenever in the Companies Clauses Consolidation Act 1845 or the special Act the consent of any particular majority of votes at any meeting of the company is required in order to authorise any proceeding of the company, that particular majority is required to be proved only in the event of a poll being demanded at the meeting[1]. If a poll is not demanded, a declaration by the chairman that the resolution authorising that proceeding has been carried and an entry to that effect in the book of the company's proceedings is sufficient authority for the proceeding, without proof of the number or proportion of votes recorded in favour of or against it[2].

1 Companies Clauses Consolidation Act 1845 s 80.

2 Ibid s 80. As to the functions of the chairman with respect to a poll see further para 672 ante.

(vi) Accounts and Audit

1736. Application of certain provisions of the Companies Act 1985. In general[1] the accounts of the company and their audit, and the qualifications, appointment and removal of its auditors are governed with one modification[2] by certain provisions of the Companies Act 1985[3] which are applied[4], and the operation of the relevant provisions of the Companies Clauses Acts is suspended in so far as they are inconsistent with those provisions[5]. To the extent to which and in any case where the provisions of the Act of 1985 do not apply, the following provisions[6] still apply.

1 For the exceptions ie the bodies corporate to which the unregistered companies legislation does not apply see the Companies Act 1985 s 718(2); the Companies (Unregistered Companies) Regulations 1985, SI 1985/680 (amended by SI 1990/438; SI 1990/1394; SI 1990/2571); and para 1767 post.

2 References in the provisions of the Companies Act 1985 to the company's registered office are to be taken as references to its principal office: Companies (Unregistered Companies) Regulations 1985 reg 5(b).

3 Ie (1) the Companies Act 1985 Pt VII (ss 221-262A (as amended): see para 801 et seq ante), except ss 252, s 253 (as substituted) (see paras 923, 924 ante); (2) Schs 4-6 (as amended) (see para 831 et seq ante); (3) Sch 7 (as amended) (see para 1066 et seq ante), except paras 2-2B (as substituted) (see para 1071 ante) and paras 7, 8 (see para 1074 ante); (4) Sch 8 (as substituted and amended) (see para 904 et seq ante); (5) Sch 9, except paras 2(a)-(d), 3(c)-(e), 10(1)(c) (sic); (6) Sch 10 (sic); and (7) Sch 10A (as added) (see paras 828, 829 ante): see the Companies (Unregistered Companies) Regulations 1985 reg 4, Schedule (amended by SI 1990/438) and para 1767 post. As to the Companies Act 1985 s 720, Sch 23 (which apply to insurance companies) see para 939 ante. As to the application of certain administrative provisions in relation to the provisions so applied see para 1699 ante.

4 Ie by ibid s 718, Sch 22 (as amended); the Companies (Unregistered Companies) Regulations 1985 reg 4, Schedule (amended by SI 1990/438). See further para 1765 et seq post.

5 Companies Act 1985 s 718(5).

6 See paras 1737-1742 post.

1737. Accounts to be kept. The directors must cause full and true accounts to be kept of all sums of money received or expended on account of the company by the directors and all persons employed by or under them, and of the matters and things for which those sums of money have been received or disbursed and paid[1], and must appoint a book-keeper to enter those accounts in books to be provided for the purpose[2].

1 Companies Clauses Consolidation Act 1845 s 115. Separate and distinct accounts must also be kept by the company as regards money raised by issuing debenture stock: Companies Clauses Act 1863 s 33; and see para 1692 ante. Cf the duty to keep accounting records imposed by the Companies Act 1985 s 221 (as substituted): see para 801 ante. For the application of s 221 (as substituted) in lieu of the provision here stated see para 1736 text and note 3 ante.
2 Companies Clauses Consolidation Act 1845 s 119.

1738. Balance sheets. The company's books must be balanced at the periods prescribed by the special Act and, if no periods are prescribed, 14 days at least before each ordinary meeting[1]. On the books being balanced, an exact balance sheet must forthwith be made up, exhibiting a true statement of the capital stock, credits and property of every description belonging to the company, and the debts due by it at the date of making the balance sheet, and a distinct view of the profit or loss which has arisen on the company's transactions[2] in the course of the preceding half-year[3]. Before each ordinary meeting the balance sheet must be examined by the directors, or any three of them, and be signed by the chairman or deputy chairman[4].

At the ordinary meeting the directors must produce to the shareholders the balance sheet, applicable to the period immediately preceding the meeting, together with the auditors' report[5].

1 Companies Clauses Consolidation Act 1845 ss 2, 116.
2 A transaction resulting in a realised profit from a capital asset must be brought within the scope of the distinct view: *Cross v Imperial Continental Gas Association* [1923] 2 Ch 553.
3 Companies Clauses Consolidation Act 1845 s 116.
4 Ibid s 116. As to the application of the provisions of the Companies Act 1985 relating to balance sheets in lieu of the provisions here stated see para 1736 text and note 3 ante.
5 Companies Clauses Consolidation Act 1845 s 118.

1739. Inspection of books and balance sheets. The books duly balanced[1], together with the balance sheet, must for the periods prescribed by the special Act and, if no periods are prescribed, for 14 days previous to each ordinary meeting, and for one month afterwards, be open for the inspection of the shareholders at the company's principal office or place of business[2]. Shareholders are not, however, entitled at any time, except during these periods, to demand the inspection of the books, unless in virtue of a written order signed by three directors[3].

Every book-keeper must permit any shareholder to inspect the books and to take copies or extracts at any reasonable time during the periods when the books are so open for inspection[4]. Failure to comply with these requirements involves forfeiture to the shareholder, for every offence, of a sum not exceeding £5[4].

The account books must also be open at all reasonable times to the inspection of the company's respective mortgagees and bond creditors with liberty to take extracts without fee or reward[5].

1 See para 1738 ante.
2 Companies Clauses Consolidation Act 1845 ss 2, 117.

3 Ibid s 117. A shareholder is not entitled to an order of mandamus calling on the directors to permit him
   to inspect the books which are to be kept under ss 115, 119 (see para 1737 ante) unless he can prove
   some genuine motive for the inspection, and not merely idle curiosity: *R v Directors of London and St
   Katharine Docks Co* (1874) 44 LJQB 4. Cf the provisions as to balance sheets in the Companies Act 1985
   ss 227-251 (as substituted): see para 816 et seq ante. As to the application of those provisions in lieu of the
   provisions here stated see para 1736 text and note 3 ante.
4 Companies Clauses Consolidation Act 1845 s 119.
5 Ibid s 55. Entries in these books are not, however, admissible in evidence in favour of the company, for
   the purpose of establishing the matters there mentioned, as against a creditor suing it: *Hill v Manchester
   and Salford Waterworks Co* (1833) 5 B & Ad 866 at 876.

1740. Appointment and qualification of auditors. Except as otherwise provided
by the special Act, the company's powers as regards the choice of auditors and their
remuneration can be exercised only at a general meeting of the company[1]. Except
where the special Act directs them to be appointed otherwise than by the company, the
company must at the first ordinary meeting after the passing of the special Act elect the
number of auditors prescribed by that Act or, if no number is prescribed, two auditors,
in the manner provided for the election of directors[2]. At the first ordinary meeting in
each year afterwards the company must in the same manner elect an auditor to supply
the place of the retiring auditor[3]. Every auditor so elected, if he has not been removed
or become disqualified, and has not resigned, continues to be an auditor until another is
elected in his stead[4].

Where no other qualification is prescribed by the special Act, every auditor must
have at least one share in the undertaking[5]. He must not hold any office in the company
or be in any other manner interested in its concerns except as a shareholder[6].

1 Companies Clauses Consolidation Act 1845 s 91. As regards unnationalised railway companies,
   including light railway companies, and tramways, the provisions of that Act respecting auditors were
   formerly modified by the Regulation of Railways Act 1868 ss 11, 12 (repealed as obsolete by the
   Transport Act 1962 s 95(1), Sch 12, Pt I). As to the accounts of the various transport boards see the
   Transport Act 1962 s 24 (as amended) and RAILWAYS vol 38 para 787.
2 Companies Clauses Consolidation Act 1845 ss 2, 101.
3 Ibid s 101. As to the retirement of auditors see para 1742 post; and as to the application of the provisions
   of the Companies Act 1985 ss 221-262 (as substituted) relating to auditors in lieu of the provisions here
   stated see para 1736 text and note 3 ante.
4 Companies Clauses Consolidation Act 1845 s 101.
5 Ibid s 102. As regards unnationalised railway companies, including light railway companies, and
   tramways, it was formerly unnecessary for the auditor to hold any share: see the Regulation of Railways
   Act 1868 s 11 (repealed: see note 1 supra).
6 Companies Clauses Consolidation Act 1845 s 102.

1741. Auditors' duties. The directors must deliver to the auditors the half-yearly or
other periodical accounts and balance sheet at least 14 days before the ensuing ordinary
meeting at which they are required to be produced to the shareholders[1]. It is the
auditors' duty to receive from the directors the accounts and balance sheet and to
examine them[2], but they may employ accountants and other persons as they think
proper at the company's expense[3]. They must either make a special report on the
accounts or simply confirm them[3]. Their report or confirmation must be read,
together with the directors' report, at the ordinary meeting[3]. If the auditors differ, they
may make separate reports, and each of them may separately employ an accountant[4].

1　Companies Clauses Consolidation Act 1845 s 106.
2　Ibid s 107.
3　Ibid s 108.
4　*Steele v Sutton Gas Co* (1883) 12 QBD 68 at 69.

1742. Retirement of auditors. One of the auditors, to be determined in the first instance by ballot between themselves, unless they otherwise agree, and afterwards by seniority, must go out of office at the first ordinary meeting in each year, but the auditor going out is immediately eligible for re-election[1]. Any vacancy which takes place among the auditors in the course of the current year may be supplied at any general meeting, if the company thinks fit, by election of the shareholders[2].

The statutory provision[3] respecting the failure of an ordinary meeting at which directors ought to be chosen applies, with any necessary changes in points of detail, to any ordinary meeting at which an auditor ought to be appointed[4].

1　Companies Clauses Consolidation Act 1845 s 103.
2　Ibid s 104.
3　Ie ibid s 84: see para 1702 ante.
4　Ibid s 105.

(vii) Dividends

1743. Power to pay dividends. Subject as mentioned below, a company incorporated by special Act may, like a company regulated by the Companies Act 1985, pay dividends[1] on its shares[2]. Certain provisions relating to the dividends on preference shares are imposed by statute[3]. The rate of dividend on ordinary shares is in nearly every case limited either by the special Act itself or by the provisions of a general Act; and, where a limit is imposed, it is usual to provide that arrears of dividend may only be paid out of profits earned in subsequent years. Where there are two cases of ordinary shares entitled to a dividend at different rates, and the dividend on both classes is in arrear, the ratio existing between the respective rates of dividend must be preserved in paying off arrears of dividend in subsequent years[4].

No dividend can be paid in respect of any share until all calls then due in respect of that and every other share held by the person to whom the dividend may be payable have been paid[5].

1　As to the taxation of company distributions see paras 733, 734 ante.
2　See para 717 et seq ante.
3　See the Companies Clauses Act 1863 ss 13, 14 and para 1621 ante.
4　*Weymouth Waterworks Co v Coode and Hasell* [1911] 2 Ch 520.
5　Companies Clauses Consolidation Act 1845 s 123.

1744. Declaration of dividend. Before every ordinary meeting at which a dividend is intended to be declared, the directors must cause a scheme to be prepared showing the profits, if any, of the company for the period current since the preceding ordinary meeting at which a dividend was declared, and apportioning them, or as much as they may consider applicable to the purposes of dividend, among the shareholders according to the shares held by them, the amount paid on them and the periods during which those amounts have been paid[1]. The scheme must be exhibited at the meeting, at which a dividend may be declared according to the scheme[2]. Except as otherwise provided by the special Act, the company's powers as to the declaration of dividends can be exercised only at a general meeting[3].

1 Companies Clauses Consolidation Act 1845 s 120. It is the directors' duty to act strictly in accordance with s 120: *Henry v Great Northern Rly Co* (1857) 1 De G & J 606.
2 Companies Clauses Consolidation Act 1845 s 120.
3 Ibid s 91.

1745. Reserve fund. Before apportioning the profits to be divided among the shareholders, the directors may, if they think fit, set aside such sum as they think proper to meet contingencies, or for enlarging, repairing or improving the works connected with the undertaking or any part of it, and may divide the balance only among the shareholders[1].

1 Companies Clauses Consolidation Act 1845 s 122 (repealed in relation to water companies by the Water Act 1945 s 62, Sch 5).

1746. No dividend out of capital. The company must not pay any dividend by which its capital stock will be in any way reduced[1]. However, a return of any portion of the capital stock, with the consent of all the mortgagees and bond creditors of the company, after due notice being given for that purpose at an extraordinary meeting to be convened for that object, is not a payment of dividend[2].

1 Companies Clauses Consolidation Act 1845 s 121. This provision relates to the company's paid-up capital and not to its capital assets generally, and so a company may pay a dividend out of a realised profit on its capital assets: *Cross v Imperial Continental Gas Association* [1923] 2 Ch 553. A payment by a company of dividends on shares out of surplus revenue arising from an annuity from another company is not a payment of dividends out of capital: *Lawrence v West Somerset Mineral Rly Co* [1918] 2 Ch 250.
2 Companies Clauses Consolidation Act 1845 s 121. See generally para 717 et seq ante.
  As the claim for dividends is equivalent to an action on a simple contract, the period of limitation is six years: Limitation Act 1980 s 5; and see *Re Compania de Electricidad de la Provincia de Buenos Aires Ltd* [1980] Ch 146, [1978] 3 All ER 668 (not following *Re Artisans' Land and Mortgage Corpn* [1904] 1 Ch 796). Time begins to run in favour of a company from the date when a dividend becomes payable: *Re Severn and Wye and Severn Bridge Rly Co* [1896] 1 Ch 559 at 565.

(9) SETTLEMENT OF DISPUTES

1747. Application of the Arbitration Act 1950. With some exceptions[1], certain provisions of the Arbitration Act 1950[2] apply to the settlement of disputes authorised or directed to be settled by arbitration by the Companies Clauses Consolidation Act 1845, or the special Act, or any Act incorporated with it, as if the arbitration were pursuant to an arbitration agreement, except in so far as the Arbitration Act 1950 is inconsistent with that other Act or with any rules or procedure authorised or recognised by that Act[3]. The fact that any particular provision contained in the 1950 Act is additional to the provisions of the 1845 Act does not of itself show that there is any inconsistency in the Acts, the test being whether the provisions of the 1950 Act can be read into the 1845 Act without any conflict between the two[4].

1 The provisions of the Arbitration Act 1950 Pt I (ss 1-34) (as amended) which do not apply to statutory arbitrations are those specified in s 31(2) (as amended): see ARBITRATION vol 2 (Reissue) para 601 note 2.
2 Ie ibid Pt I (ss 1-34) (as amended). For these provisions see generally ARBITRATION vol 2 (Reissue) para 608 et seq.
3 See ibid s 31(1) and ARBITRATION vol 2 (Reissue) para 601. The effect of s 31 (as amended) is to apply the provisions of Pt I (ss 1-34) (as amended), not expressly excluded, to arbitrations (inter alia) under the

Companies Clauses Consolidation Act 1845 except in so far as the arbitrations under that Act are conducted pursuant to provisions inconsistent with the provisions of the 1950 Act. Its effect is in no way to introduce into arbitrations under the 1950 Act any of the provisions for arbitration contained in the Companies Clauses Consolidation Act 1845 ss 128-134. Those provisions do not, therefore, apply to a reference for trial before an arbitrator ordered by the court under RSC Ord 36 (made under powers conferred by the Supreme Court Act 1981 s 68, repealing the Administration of Justice Act 1956 s 15, which itself repealed (inter alia) the Supreme Court of Judicature (Consolidation) Act 1925 s 89, which itself replaced the Arbitration Act 1889 s 14 (repealed)): see *Zelma Gold Mining Co v Hoskins* [1895] AC 100 at 103, PC. Under the Companies Clauses Consolidation Act 1845 s 134 the submission to arbitration could be made a rule of court on the application of either of the parties. As to enforcing arbitration awards see the Arbitration Act 1950 s 26 (as amended) and ARBITRATION vol 2 (Reissue) para 713.

4   *Tabernacle Permanent Building Society v Knight* [1892] AC 298 at 306, HL.

1748. Appointment of arbitrators. When any dispute has arisen, authorised or directed by the Companies Clauses Consolidation Act 1845, or the special Act, or any Act incorporated with it[1], to be settled by arbitration, then, unless both parties concur in the appointment of a single arbitrator, each party, on the request of the other by written nomination under his hand, must appoint an arbitrator to whom the dispute is to be referred[2]. After the appointment has been made, neither party can revoke it without the other's consent, nor does the death of either operate as a revocation[2].

If for the space of 14 days after a dispute has arisen, and after a written request has been served by one party on the other to appoint an arbitrator, the latter fails to appoint an arbitrator, the party making the request, and having himself appointed an arbitrator, may appoint that arbitrator to act on behalf of both parties, and that arbitrator may proceed to hear and determine the matters in dispute, in which case the award or determination of the single arbitrator is final[2].

If before the matters referred are determined an arbitrator appointed by either party dies, or becomes incapable or refuses or for seven days neglects to act as arbitrator, the party by whom he was appointed may by written nomination appoint some other person to act in his place, and if, for seven days after written notice from the other party, he fails to do so, the remaining or other arbitrator may proceed ex parte[3]. Every arbitrator so substituted has the same powers and authorities as were vested in the former arbitrator at the time of his death, refusal or disability[3].

1   See para 1747 note 1 ante. The provisions of the Companies Clauses Consolidation Act 1845 with respect to the settlement of disputes by arbitration are incorporated into the Insolvency Act 1986 for the purposes of arbitrations under s 111: see s 111(4) and para 1488 ante.
2   Companies Clauses Consolidation Act 1845 s 128.
3   Ibid s 129.

1749. Appointment of umpire. Where more than one arbitrator has been appointed, they must, before entering on the matters referred to them, by written appointment under their hands appoint an umpire to decide any matters on which they differ[1]. If the umpire dies, or refuses or for seven days neglects to act, they must forthwith appoint another umpire in his place[1]. The decision of the umpire on the matters so referred to him is final[1].

If in either case the arbitrators refuse or for seven days after request of either party to the arbitration neglect to appoint an umpire, the Secretary of State[2] may, in any case in which a railway company is one party to the arbitration, on the application of either party to that arbitration, appoint an umpire whose decision on the matter on which the arbitrators differ is to be final[3].

1 Companies Clauses Consolidation Act 1845 s 130.
2 Ibid s 131 refers to the Board of Trade. As to the Board of Trade see CONSTITUTIONAL LAW vol 8 para 1266; TRADE AND INDUSTRY vol 47 (Reissue) para 2 note 2.
3 Ibid s 131.

1750. Conduct of arbitration; costs. The arbitrators or their umpire may call for the production of any documents in the possession or power of either party which they or he may think necessary for determining the question in dispute, and may examine the parties or their witnesses on oath, and administer the oaths necessary for that purpose[1].

Except where it is otherwise provided by the Companies Clauses Consolidation Act 1845 or the special Act or any Act incorporated with it, the costs of and attending an arbitration are in the discretion of the arbitrators or their umpires, as the case may be[2].

1 Companies Clauses Consolidation Act 1845 s 132.
2 Ibid s 133.

(10) RECOVERY OF CLAIMS, DAMAGES AND PENALTIES

1751. Bankruptcy claims. If any person against whom the company has any claim becomes bankrupt or insolvent, then in all proceedings against his estate the company's secretary or treasurer may represent the company, and act in its behalf, as if that claim had been his own claim[1].

1 Companies Clauses Consolidation Act 1845 s 140.

1752. Recovery of amounts ascertained by justices. Where any damages, costs or expenses are directed to be paid by the Companies Clauses Consolidation Act 1845 or the special Act or any Act incorporated with it, and the method of ascertaining the amount or enforcing payment is not provided for, that amount, in case of dispute, must be ascertained by two justices[1].

1 Companies Clauses Consolidation Act 1845 s 142. Cf with ss 142, 144-147, 156 (see infra and para 1753 et seq post) the Lands Clauses Consolidation Act 1845 s 136 (as amended); and see COMPULSORY ACQUISITION. For the meaning of 'justice' see para 1603 ante.

1753. Procedure before justices. Where any question of compensation, expenses, charges or damages is referred to the determination of any one justice or more, any justice may on the application of either party summon the other party to appear before one justice or before two justices as the case may require, at a time and place named in the summons[1]. Upon the appearance of the parties, or in the absence of any of them, upon proof of due service of the summons, the question may be determined and the parties and their witnesses may be examined on oath, the costs being in the discretion of the justices[1].

1 Companies Clauses Consolidation Act 1845 s 144. For the meaning of 'justice' see para 1603 ante.

1754. Publication of particulars of offences. The company must publish short particulars of the several offences for which any penalty is imposed by the Companies

Clauses Consolidation Act 1845 or the special Act or any Act incorporated with it, or by any byelaw of the company[1], affecting other persons than its shareholders, officers or employees, and of the amount of every such penalty, and must cause such particulars to be painted or printed upon paper and pasted on a board to be hung up on some conspicuous part of its principal place of business[2]. Where the penalties are of local application, it must cause the boards to be affixed in some conspicuous place in the immediate neighbourhood to which the penalties are applicable, and no such penalty is recoverable unless it has been so published and kept published[2].

If any person pulls down any board put up or affixed for the purpose of publishing any byelaw or penalty, or obliterates any of the letters or figures thereon, he must forfeit for every such offence a sum not exceeding level 1 on the standard scale and must defray the expenses attending the restoration of such board[3].

1   As to byelaws see para 1725 ante.
2   Companies Clauses Consolidation Act 1845 s 145.
3   Ibid s 146 (amended by the Criminal Damage Act 1971 s 11(8), Schedule Pt I; the Criminal Law Act 1977 s 31(6); the Criminal Justice Act 1982 s 46). For the meaning of 'the standard scale' see CRIMINAL LAW vol 11(2) (Reissue) para 808.

1755. Recovery of penalties. Every penalty or forfeiture imposed by the Companies Clauses Consolidation Act 1845 or the special Act or any Act incorporated with it, or by any byelaw of the company made in pursuance thereof, the recovery of which is not otherwise provided for, may be recovered by summary proceeding before two justices[1].

1   Companies Clauses Consolidation Act 1845 s 147 (amended by the Summary Jurisdiction Act 1884 s 4, Schedule; the Statute Law Revision Act 1892). For the meaning of 'justice' see para 1603 ante.

1756. Arrest of offenders. Any officer or agent of the company, and all persons called by him to his assistance, may seize and detain any person who has committed any offence against the provisions of the Companies Clauses Consolidation Act 1845 or the special Act or any Act incorporated with it[1], and whose name and residence are unknown to him, and convey him before some justice[2] without warrant[3]. The justice must proceed with all convenient despatch to the hearing and determining of the complaint[3].

1   Infringement of byelaws is an offence against the Companies Clauses Consolidation Act 1845: see s 125 and para 1725 ante.
2   For the meaning of 'justice' see para 1603 ante.
3   Companies Clauses Consolidation Act 1845 s 156.

1757. Appeals. Any party aggrieved by any determination or adjudication of any justice with respect to any penalty or forfeiture may appeal to the Crown Court[1].

1   Companies Clauses Consolidation Act 1845 s 159 (amended by the Summary Jurisdiction Act 1884 s 4, Schedule; the Courts Act 1971 s 56(2), Sch 9 Pt I). As to appeals to the Crown Court see the Supreme Court Act 1981 ss 45, 48 (as amended) and CRIMINAL LAW vol 11(2) (Reissue) para 1470.

4. UNREGISTERED AND UNINCORPORATED COMPANIES

(1) LEGAL AND ILLEGAL COMPANIES

(i) In general

1758. Lawful company associations. Companies formed in pursuance of letters patent or of some Act of Parliament other than the Companies Act 1985[1], unincorporated companies, associations and partnerships which were in existence before 2 November 1862[2], and any body of persons approved by the Secretary of State[3] for the purposes of certain war risks reinsurance[4], are associations which are not rendered illegal by the Companies Act 1985[5] or any former enactment relating to companies[6], even though those associations consist of more than 20[7] persons associated for carrying on business which has for its object the acquisition of gain[8], and are not registered under present or former company legislation.

A company which is a lawful association within one or other of the above categories may be an unregistered company within one or both of the two meanings of that term which are discussed subsequently[9].

Few, if any, unincorporated companies[10] which were in existence before 2 November 1862 now remain, and the legislation relating to stannaries and cost book companies has been repealed as being obsolete[11].

Notwithstanding the repeal of the Chartered Companies Act 1837 and the Chartered Companies Act 1884[12], the power of Her Majesty to grant a charter of incorporation of limited duration or to extend or renew such a charter or privileges of such a charter is not affected[13].

1 Ie including one of the former Companies Acts referred to in note 6 infra.
2 Ie the date when the Companies Act 1862 came into full operation: s 2 (repealed). Cf para 21 text and notes 12, 13 ante.
3 The functions of the Minister of Transport under the Marine and Aviation Insurance (War Risks) Act 1952 (see note 4 infra) were transferred to the Board of Trade by the Transfer of Functions (Sea Transport, etc) Order 1968, SI 1968/2038. As to the exercise of the Board of Trade's functions concurrently with the Secretary of State for Trade and Industry see TRADE AND INDUSTRY vol 47 (Reissue) para 2.
4 See the Marine and Aviation Insurance (War Risks) Act 1952 s 1(1)(b) and INSURANCE vol 25 (Reissue) para 794 et seq. The Companies Act 1985 s 716 (as amended) (prohibition of partnerships with more than 20 members: see para 21 ante) or any corresponding enactment previously in force is deemed not to have invalidated the formation of any insurance company which immediately before 3 November 1966 was carrying on in Great Britain insurance business of any class relevant for the purposes of the Insurance Companies Act 1974 Pt I (ss 10-11) (repealed), and was carrying on business of that class on 25 July 1973: see the Insurance Companies Act 1982 s 89 (as amended) and INSURANCE vol 25 (Reissue) para 24.
5 Ie by the Companies Act 1985 s 716 (as amended): see para 21 ante.
6 Ie the Companies Act 1948 s 434; the Companies Act 1929 s 357; the Companies (Consolidation) Act 1908 s 1; and the Companies Act 1862 s 4 (all repealed).
7 In the case of banking partnerships, the limit was formerly ten: see the Companies Act 1948 s 429 (repealed). The Companies Act 1967 raised the limit to 20, provided that, if there were more than ten, each partner had been authorised by the Department of Trade and Industry: see s 119. Both provisions were repealed by the Banking Act 1979 s 51(2), Sch 7 (repealed).
8 The prohibition enacted by the Companies Act 1985 s 716 (as amended) does not extend to companies which do not carry on business or do not carry it on for acquisition of gain. Neither 'business' nor 'gain' is susceptible of precise definition: see *Armour v Liverpool Corpn* [1939] Ch 422 at 437, [1939] 1 All ER 363 at 371 per Simonds J; and see generally paras 21, 22 ante. Nothing in the Companies Act 1985 s 716 (as amended) is to be taken to prevent the formation of an employers' association which is neither registered as a company under the Companies Act 1985 nor otherwise incorporated: see the Trade

Union and Labour Relations (Consolidation) Act 1992 s 127(3) and TRADE AND INDUSTRY vol 47 (Reissue) para 1202. For the meaning of 'employers' association' see TRADE AND INDUSTRY vol 47 (Reissue) para 1201.
9 See para 1765 et seq post.
10 These unincorporated companies were usually formed under deeds of settlement which set out the company's objects and constitution. The question sometimes arose as to whether such companies had power to transfer the whole of their undertaking to new companies. See *Re Era Assurance Co, Williams' Case, Anchor Case* (1860) 30 LJ Ch 137; *Kearns v Leaf* (1864) 1 Hem & M 681; *Doman's Case* (1876) 3 ChD 21; *Re Argus Life Assurance Co* (1888) 39 ChD 571.
11 Companies Consolidation (Consequential Provisions) Act 1985 s 28.
12 The Chartered Companies Act 1837 and the Chartered Companies Act 1884 were repealed by the Statute Law (Repeals) Act 1993 s 1(1), Sch 1 Pt V. As to the Chartered Companies Act 1837 and the Chartered Companies Act 1884 see COMPANIES vol 7(2) (1988 Reissue) para 2379 et seq.
13 Statute Law (Repeals) Act 1993 s 1(2), Sch 2 para 11.

1759. Companies illegal under the Companies Acts. No company, association or partnership consisting of more than 20 persons may be formed for the purpose of carrying on any business that has for its object the acquisition of gain by the company, association or partnership, or by its individual members, unless it is registered as a company under the Companies Act 1985, or is formed in pursuance of some other Act of Parliament, or of letters patent[1]. Companies formed in contravention of the above prohibitions and restrictions are illegal[2]; and, where such a company is formed, the law can take no cognisance of its existence except perhaps from a penal point of view[3].

1 Companies Act 1985 s 716(1). As to s 716 (as amended) see further paras 21, 1758 ante and PARTNERSHIP vol 35 (Reissue) para 26. The words 'company', 'association' and 'partnership' are used interchangeably in this provision. For the meaning of 'company' see paras 1, 11 note 1 ante.
2 *Re Thomas, ex p Poppleton* (1884) 14 QBD 379.
3 *Re Padstow Total Loss and Collision Assurance Association* (1882) 20 ChD 137 at 145, 146, 149, CA. See, however, paras 1761-1764 post.

1760. Companies formed for an illegal purpose. A company of a dangerous and mischievous character or formed for a fraudulent purpose is probably illegal at common law[1] and a company the proposed constitution of which involves an offence against the general law cannot properly be registered[2]. In the event of such a company being registered, the certificate of incorporation would not be conclusive as to the legality of its objects as set out in its memorandum[3], and the company would be an illegal company[4]. Thus a company formed to set up a lottery in England[5] (other than a company authorised by the Director General of the National Lottery by licence to run the National Lottery or to promote lotteries as part of the National Lottery[6]) or to sell tickets in England in a lottery in a foreign state where lotteries are legal, would, if registered under the Companies Act 1985, be an illegal company[7]; but a company formed to set up a lottery in a foreign state where such lotteries are legal would not be illegal[8].

The fact that some only of the regulations of a company are illegal does not necessarily make the company an illegal one, or prevent the court from giving effect to such of the rules as are legal[9]; but, where the objects of a company include an illegal object, and other objects of the company, although in themselves legal, are mere applications of the governing principle stated in the illegal object, the company is an illegal company[10]. If a company is formed for legal purposes, the commission by it of illegal acts does not make it an illegal company[11].

1 Lindley's Law of Companies (6th Edn) 183. An Act of 1719 (6 Geo 1 c 18) ss 18, 19 (repealed; popularly known as 'the Bubble Act') declared to be illegal and void dangerous and mischievous undertakings and

attempts tending to the common grievance, prejudice and inconvenience of the King's subjects, or great numbers of them, and more particularly by unincorporated companies presuming to act as if they were corporate bodies, and pretending to make their shares or stocks transferable, without any legal authority by Act of Parliament or charter; but, even before that Act was repealed, there were conflicting decisions as to whether acting, by an unincorporated company, as a corporation, without the authority of a statute or charter, and pretending to be possessed of transferable stock, was illegal: *Duvergier v Fellows* (1828) 5 Bing 248 at 267; *Blundell v Winsor* (1837) 8 Sim 601; *Walburn v Ingilby* (1883) 1 My & K 61 at 76. After that Act had been partly repealed in 1825 (by 6 Geo 4 c 91), notwithstanding the recital in the repealing Act that the several undertakings, attempts, practices, acts, matters and things referred to in the repealed Act should be adjudged and dealt with in like manner as they might have been adjudged and dealt with 'according to the common law, notwithstanding the Act', the mere raising and transfer of stock in an unincorporated company was not an offence at common law: *Garrard v Hardey* (1843) 5 Man & G 471; *Harrison v Heathorn* (1843) 6 Man & G 81.

2 *R v Registrar of Joint Stock Companies, ex p More* [1931] 2 KB 197 at 201, CA; *R v Registrar of Companies, ex p Bowen* [1914] 3 KB 1161; *Bowman v Secular Society Ltd* [1917] AC 406, HL.

3 See para 91 ante.

4 The Companies Act 1985 s 13(7) (conclusiveness of the certificate of incorporation: see para 91 ante) does not bind the Crown: *Bowman v Secular Society Ltd* [1917] AC 406 at 439, 440, HL; and see the cases cited in note 1 supra. In practice the registrar will refuse to register such a company, and consequently the question of what is the status of such a company has never been decided. In the event of such a company being registered, it would appear that the Attorney General could institute proceedings by way of certiorari to cancel the registration: see para 91 ante.

5 As to lotteries see BETTING vol 4(1) (Reissue) para 148 et seq.

6 See the National Lottery etc Act 1993 ss 5(1), 6(1) and BETTING.

7 *R v Registrar of Joint Stock Companies, ex p More* [1931] 2 KB 197, CA.

8 *Macnee v Persian Investment Corpn* (1890) 44 ChD 306. See further BETTING vol 4(1) (Reissue) para 41. In *Macnee v Persian Investment Corpn* supra the company was held not to be an illegal company in the proper sense of the term, as no illegality was shown in the memorandum of association of the company. See supra and note 11 infra.

9 *Strick v Swansea Tin-Plate Co* (1887) 36 ChD 558; *Swaine v Wilson* (1889) 24 QBD 252, CA. See also *Re General Co for the Promotion of Land Credit* (1870) 5 Ch App 363; affd sub nom *Princess Reuss v Bos* (1871) LR 5 HL 176; and see *McGlade v Royal London Mutual Insurance Society Ltd* [1910] 2 Ch 169, CA.

10 *Bowman v Secular Society Ltd* [1917] AC 406 at 421, HL.

11 *Macnee v Persian Investment Corpn* (1890) 44 ChD 306 at 311. Thus it would appear that a money-lending company which failed to comply with the then statutory requirements as to moneylenders was not an illegal company but was merely liable to the penalties imposed by those requirements: see further *Lodge v National Union Investment Co Ltd* [1907] 1 Ch 300. The same would appear to apply to a company which carries on the business of dentistry without complying with the requirements of the Dentists Act 1984 ss 42, 43 (see MEDICINE vol 30 (Reissue) para 310), or which carries on business under the style or title of 'architect' without complying with the requirements of the Architects (Registration) Acts 1931 to 1969 (see BUILDING CONTRACTS vol 4(2) (Reissue) para 508). See also Lindley's Law of Companies (6th Edn) 186, where it is questioned whether the failure of bankers to make the return required under penalties by the Bank Charter Act 1844 s 21 (repealed) made a banking partnership or company composed in part of members whose names had not been returned in accordance with that Act illegal.

(ii) Effect of Company being Illegal

1761. Proceedings by or against illegal companies. An illegal company cannot sustain an action to recover a debt incurred for money lent, either to members or outsiders[1], or on any contract made directly for the purpose of carrying on its business[2]. A trustee for the illegal company is in no better position[3]. The fact that it began with less than 20[4] members does not prevent it from becoming illegal by an increase beyond that number[5]. If, however, while it is illegal by reason of its having more than 20[6] members, it lends money to a member, and then registers under the Companies Act 1985, instalments of the debt being paid before and after the date of registration, it is inferred that all members have agreed that transactions prior to registration shall be binding, and the society may recover the balance of the loan[7].

Money lent to an illegal company for the purpose of carrying out its objects cannot be recovered[8], and persons making other contracts with an illegal company may not be able to enforce them against it[9]. Persons subscribing to the formation of a company, the agreement to form which is illegal, may, however, recover the money before it is actually applied to the illegal purpose[10], and the court will order any persons who have received the money subscribed to render an account[11]; but the question, even now, seems open whether the courts will assist members of illegal companies to recover their subscriptions from the persons who have been the recipients of them, and, if so, by what means[12].

The members of an illegal company may be beneficial owners of property, and, if an officer of the company embezzles funds entrusted to him, he may be indicted for theft[13].

1 *Jennings v Hammond* (1882) 9 QBD 225.
2 *Jennings v Hammond* (1882) 9 QBD 225. As to void and illegal contracts see generally CONTRACT vol 9 para 386 et seq.
3 *Shaw v Benson* (1883) 11 QBD 563, CA.
4 See para 21 ante.
5 *Re Thomas, ex p Poppleton* (1884) 14 QBD 379.
6 See para 21 ante.
7 *Re Thomas, ex p Poppleton* (1884) 14 QBD 379.
8 *Phillips v Davies* (1888) 5 TLR 98.
9 *Re Padstow Total Loss and Collision Assurance Association* (1882) 20 ChD 137, CA.
10 *Strachan v Universal Stock Exchange (No 2)* [1895] 2 QB 697, CA; *Burge v Ashley and Smith Ltd* [1900] 1 QB 744, CA.
11 *Greenberg v Cooperstein* [1926] Ch 657.
12 See *Greenberg v Cooperstein* [1926] Ch 657 at 666; *Hume v Record Reign Jubilee Syndicate* (1899) 80 LT 404; *Sheppard v Oxenford* (1855) 1 K & J 491; *Marrs v Thompson* (1902) 86 LT 759, DC; *Re One and All Sickness and Accident Assurance Association* (1909) 25 TLR 674.
13 *R v Tankard* [1894] 1 QB 548; *R v Stainer* (1870) LR 1 CCR 230. The offence of embezzlement as such has been abolished and the Larceny Act 1916 repealed (see the Theft Act 1968 ss 32(1), 33, Sch 3), and the offence has been replaced by the offence of theft (see the Theft Act 1968 and CRIMINAL LAW vol 11(1) (Reissue) para 541 et seq).

1762. Winding up. An illegal company cannot be wound up by the court under the Insolvency Act 1986 on its own petition or that of a member[1], or on the petition of a creditor, at any rate if the petitioner had notice of the illegality[2]. If a winding-up order is made, it is effective unless and until discharged on appeal and, while it exists, the illegality of the company is not a bar to proceedings in the winding up[3].

1 *Re Mexican and South American Mining Co, Barclay's Case* (1858) 26 Beav 177 at 179, 180; *Re London and Eastern Banking Corpn, Longworth's Case* (1859) 1 De G F & J 17 at 30, 31, CA.
2 *Re Padstow Total Loss and Collision Assurance Association* (1882) 20 ChD 137, CA; *Re South Wales Atlantic SS Co* (1876) 2 ChD 763, CA; *Re Arthur Average Association for British, Foreign and Colonial Ships, ex p Hargrove & Co* (1875) 10 Ch App 542 at 545n; *Re Ilfracombe Permanent Mutual Benefit Building Society* [1901] 1 Ch 102. The court may, however, administer a trust where the beneficiaries exceed 20, even though the trust involves the carrying on of some business, provided the business is carried on by trustees who are less than 20 in number: *Smith v Anderson* (1880) 15 ChD 247, CA.
3 *Re Padstow Total Loss and Collision Assurance Association* (1882) 20 ChD 137, CA; *Re Arthur Average Association for British, Foreign and Colonial Ships, ex p Hargrove & Co* (1875) 10 Ch App 542; *Re Arthur Average Association* (1876) 3 ChD 522; *Re Queen's Average Association, ex p Lynes* (1878) 38 LT 90; *Re London Marine Insurance Association, Andrews and Alexander's Case, Chatt's Case, Cook's Case, Crew's Case* (1869) LR 8 Eq 176.

1763. Company's right to set up illegality. An illegal company may set up its own illegality in answer to proceedings against it[1]; but, where effect is given to the defence, the company may not be allowed costs[2].

  1 *Phillips v Davies* (1888) 5 TLR 98; *Re Ilfracombe Permanent Mutual Benefit Society* [1901] 1 Ch 102; cf *Re Padstow Total Loss and Collision Assurance Association* (1882) 20 ChD 137, CA; *Doolan v Midland Rly Co* (1877) 2 App Cas 792 at 806, HL.
  2 *Phillips v Davies* (1888) 5 TLR 98; *Re Ilfracombe Permanent Mutual Benefit Building Society* [1901] 1Ch 102.

1764. Sale of shares. The sale of shares or scrip in an illegal company or intended company is illegal[1]; and a broker who is employed to sell or purchase them cannot recover from his principal any commission or any sums expended on his behalf[2]. The buyer cannot recover any purchase money paid to the broker[3].

  1 *Josephs v Pebrer* (1825) 3 B & C 639; *Buck v Buck* (1808) 1 Camp 547.
  2 *Josephs v Pebrer* (1825) 3 B & C 639; cf *Re Edmond, ex p Neilson* (1863) 3 De GM & G 556.
  3 *Buck v Buck* (1808) 1 Camp 547.

(2) UNREGISTERED COMPANIES

1765. Meaning of 'unregistered company'. Certain provisions of the Companies Act 1985 relating to the formation and management of companies registered under the 1985 Act apply also to unregistered companies[1]; and in this context 'unregistered company' refers to certain bodies incorporated in, and having a principal place of business in, Great Britain[2]. For convenience, these provisions are described subsequently as 'the business provisions'. In this sense 'unregistered company' is to be distinguished from 'oversea company'[3].

Those provisions similarly apply to any unincorporated body of persons entitled by virtue of letters patent to any of the privileges conferred by the (now repealed) Chartered Companies Act 1837[4] and not registered under any other public general Act of Parliament[5]. Notwithstanding the repeal of the Chartered Companies Act 1837[6] and the Chartered Companies Act 1884, the power of Her Majesty to grant a charter of incorporation of limited duration or to extend or renew such a charter or privileges of such a charter is not affected[7].

In Part V of the Insolvency Act 1986[8], however, 'unregistered company' has a different meaning[9].

  1 See the Companies Act 1985 s 718 and paras 1766-1770 post.
  2 See ibid s 718(1) and para 1766 post.
  3 For the meaning of 'oversea company' see para 1790 post. As to the provisions relating to oversea companies see para 1790 et seq post.
  4 As to the repeal of the Chartered Companies Act 1837 and the Chartered Companies Act 1884 see para 1758 note 12 ante.
  5 See the Companies Act 1985 s 718(4).
  6 See note 4 supra.
  7 Statute Law (Repeals) Act 1993 s 1(2), Sch 2 para 11.
  8 Ie the Insolvency Act 1986 Pt V (ss 220-229) (as amended): see para 2899 et seq post.
  9 See para 2899 post.

1766. Application of the business provisions. Certain specified[1] provisions[2] of the Companies Act 1985 apply or may be made by regulations to apply, with certain qualifications, to all bodies corporate[3] incorporated in, and having a principal place of business in, Great Britain, except:

(1) any body incorporated by or registered under any public general Act of Parliament[4];

(2) any body not formed for the purpose of carrying on a business which has for its object the acquisition of gain[5] by the body or its individual members; and

(3) any body for the time being exempted by direction of the Secretary of State, or before him by the Board of Trade[6].

1 As to the provisions specified see the Companies Act 1985 s 718, Sch 22 (as amended) and para 1767 post.

2 For the meaning of 'the business provisions' see para 1765 ante.

3 For the meaning of 'body corporate' see para 89 note 8 ante.

4 The exception of 'any body incorporated by or registered under any public general Act of Parliament' will not except a company incorporated under a special Act, even though that Act incorporates the provisions of the Companies Clauses Acts. As to the distinction between public and general Acts and local and personal Acts see *R v LCC* [1893] 2 QB 454 at 462, CA and STATUTES vol 44(1) (Reissue) para 1206 et seq; and as to the companies to which the Companies Clauses Acts apply see para 1599 et seq ante.

5 For the meaning of 'gain' cf para 22 ante.

6 Companies Act 1985 s 718(1),(2). As to the scope of the business provisions see para 1767 post; and as to the winding up of unregistered companies see para 2899 et seq post.

1767. Scope of the business provisions. Some of the business provisions[1] apply without further action being required; others apply so far only as may be specified by regulations made by the Secretary of State and to such bodies corporate as may be so specified, and subject to such adaptations and modifications, if any, as may be specified in such regulations[2].

The provisions which apply automatically[3] are:

(1) provisions relating to the register of directors and secretaries[4];

(2) provisions relating to the investigation of companies and their affairs[5];

(3) provisions relating to the effect of an order imposing restrictions on shares made by the Secretary of State[6];

(4) provisions relating to fraudulent trading[7];

(5) miscellaneous provisions about registration[8];

(6) provisions supplemental to provisions which themselves apply automatically or are made to apply by regulations made by the Secretary of State[9]; and

(7) provisions relating to interpretation which apply so far as requisite for the interpretation of other provisions which themselves apply automatically or are made to apply by regulations made by the Secretary of State[10].

The provisions which may be made to apply by regulations made by the Secretary of State[11] are:

(a) provisions requiring statutory and other amendments of the memorandum and articles to be registered[12];

(b) provisions relating to the company's capacity and the power of its directors to bind it[13];

(c) provisions relating to company contracts and the execution of documents by companies[14];

(d) provisions relating to an official seal for share certificates etc[15];

(e) provisions requiring events affecting a company's status to be officially notified[16];

(f) provisions relating to allotments[17];

(g) provisions relating to exemption from the duty to prepare certificates where shares etc are issued to a stock exchange nominee[18];

(h) provisions relating to certificates as evidence of title[19];

(i) provisions relating to accounts and audit[20];

(j) provisions relating to the registered office[21];

(k) provisions relating to the invalidity of certain transactions involving directors etc[22];

(l) provisions relating to the register to be kept of certain transactions not disclosed in the accounts, and related matters[23];

(m) provisions relating to the giving of particulars of the company in correspondence[24];

(n) provisions relating to the annual return[25];

(o) provisions relating to the appointment etc of auditors[26];

(p) provisions relating to the giving of public notice by the registrar of receipt and issue of certain documents[27]; and

(q) provisions relating to the obligation of certain companies to publish periodical statements[28].

1　For the meaning of 'the business provisions' see para 1765 ante.

2　Companies Act 1985 s 718(1),(3), Sch 22 (amended by the Financial Services Act 1986 s 212(2),(3), Sch 16 para 26, Sch 17 Pt I; the Companies Act 1989 ss 23, 71, 106, 108(3), 109(2), 123(5), 127(7), 130(5), 143(11), 145, 212, Sch 10 para 23, Sch 19 para 21, Sch 24; the Companies Act 1985 (Bank Accounts) Regulations 1991, SI 1991/2705, reg 7, Sch 3 para 2; the Companies Act 1985 (Insurance Companies Accounts) Regulations 1993, SI 1993/3246, reg 5(1), Sch 2 para 9).

3　Ie those listed in the Companies Act 1985 Sch 22 (as amended: see note 2 supra) against which the words 'subject to s 718(3)' do not appear in the third column.

4　Ie ibid ss 288-290 (as amended): see paras 560, 649 ante.

5　Ie ibid Pt XIV (ss 431-453 (as amended): see paras 1376 et seq ante), except s 446 (as amended) (investigation of share dealing: see para 1384 ante).

6　Ie ibid Pt XV (ss 454-457 (as amended): see paras 1395-1397 ante), so far only as relates to orders under s 445 (as amended) (see para 1383 ante).

7　Ie ibid Pt XVI (s 458): see para 1160 ante.

8　Ie ibid ss 706-710A (as amended), s 713 (as amended), s 715A (as added): see paras 64-67, 69 ante.

9　Ie ibid ss 721-723, 723A (as added), 725, 730 (as amended), 731, 732, Sch 24 (as amended): see paras 378, 655, 1146, 1161, 1164, 1165, 1513 ante and para 1778 post.

10　Ie ibid Pt XXVI (ss 735-744) (as amended).

11　Where, against any provision of the Companies Act 1985 specified in the first column of Sch 22 (as amended: see note 2 supra), there appears in the third column the entry 'subject to section 718(3)', it means that the provision is to apply by virtue of s 718 so far only as may be specified by regulations made by the Secretary of State and to such bodies corporate as may be so specified: s 718(3). In the exercise of the powers so conferred the Secretary of State made the Companies (Unregistered Companies) Regulations 1985, SI 1985/680 (amended by SI 1990/438; SI 1990/1394; SI 1990/2571). The provisions of the Companies Act 1985 specified in the Companies (Unregistered Companies) Regulations 1985 reg 4, Schedule (amended by SI 1990/438; SI 1990/1394; SI 1990/2571) apply to any unregistered company, subject to the modifications and extensions set out in reg 6 (as amended) (see paras 70 note 1, 100 note 1, 482 note 8, 487 note 3, 853 note 1, 1107 note 1, 1109 note 1, 1118 note 2, 1129 note 2, 1130 note 1, 1135 note 1 ante): regs 4, 5(e). For the purposes of the application to any unregistered company of the provisions which apply by virtue of reg 4, that company is deemed to be a company registered in England and Wales or Scotland, as the case may be, if its principal office on 5 January 1976, or in the case of a company incorporated after that date, immediately after its incorporation, was situated in England and Wales or Scotland, as the case may be; and 'registrar of companies' is to be construed accordingly: reg 5(a). References to the registered office are to be construed as references to its principal office in England, Wales or Scotland, as the case may be (reg 5(b)); and references to a public company are to be construed as references to an unregistered company which has power under the instrument constituting or regulating it to offer its shares or debentures to the public, and references to a private company are to be construed as references to an unregistered company which does not have such power (reg 5(c)). As to expenses and commission incurred before 1 January 1985 see reg 5(d).

12 Ie the Companies Act 1985 s 18: see para 100 note 1 ante. Section 18 has been so applied: Companies (Unregistered Companies) Regulations 1985 Schedule.

13 Ie the Companies Act 1985 ss 35–35B (as substituted): see paras 1107–1109 ante. Sections 35–35B (as substituted) have been so applied: Companies (Unregistered Companies) Regulations 1985 Schedule (amended by SI 1990/2571).

14 Ie the Companies Act 1985 ss 36–36C (as substituted and added): see paras 54, 1129, 1130 ante. Sections 36–36C (as substituted and added) have been so applied: Companies (Unregistered Companies) Regulations 1985 Schedule (amended by SI 1990/1934).

15 Ie the Companies Act 1985 s 40 (as amended): see para 1118 note 1 ante. Section 40 (as amended) has been so applied: Companies (Unregistered Companies) Regulations 1985 Schedule.

16 Ie the Companies Act 1985 s 42: see para 71 ante. Section 42 has been so applied: Companies (Unregistered Companies) Regulations 1985 Schedule.

17 Ie the Companies Act 1985 s 82 (see para 450 ante), s 86 (see para 456 ante) and s 87 (see para 456 ante). Sections 82, 86, 87 have been so applied: Companies (Unregistered Companies) Regulations 1985 Schedule. As to the extent of the repeal of the Companies Act 1985 ss 82, 86, 87 see para 450 note 5 ante.

18 Ie ibid s 185(4) (as amended): see para 482 note 8 ante. Section 185(4) (as amended) has been so applied: Companies (Unregistered Companies) Regulations 1985 Schedule.

19 Ie the Companies Act 1985 s 186 (as amended): see para 487 note 3 ante. Section 186 (as amended) has been so applied: Companies (Unregistered Companies) Regulations 1985 Schedule.

20 Ie the Companies Act 1985 Pt VII (ss 221–262A) (as amended), with Schs 4–10A (as amended): see paras 809 note 1, 853 note 1 ante. The following provisions have been so applied: (1) Pt VII (ss 221–262A) (as amended), except ss 252, s 253 (as substituted) (see paras 923, 924 ante); (2) Schs 4–6 (as amended) (see para 831 et seq ante); (3) Sch 7 (as amended) (see para 1066 et seq ante), except paras 2–2B (as substituted) (see para 1071 ante) and paras 7, 8 (see para 1074 ante); (4) Sch 8 (as substituted and amended) (see para 904 et seq ante); (5) Sch 9, except paras 2(a)–(d), 3(c)–(e), 10(1)(c) (sic); (6) Sch 10 (sic); and (7) Sch 10A (as added) (see paras 828, 829 ante): Companies (Unregistered Companies) Regulations 1985 Schedule (amended by SI 1990/438).

21 Ie the Companies Act 1985 s 287 (as substituted): see para 150 ante. Section 287 (as substituted) has been so applied: Companies (Unregistered Companies) Regulations 1985 Schedule.

22 Ie the Companies Act 1985 s 322A (as added): see para 613 ante. Section 322A (as added) has been so applied: Companies (Unregistered Companies) Regulations 1985 Schedule (amended by SI 1990/2571).

23 Ie the Companies Act 1985 ss 343–347 (as amended): see paras 606, 607 ante. Sections 343–347 (as amended) have been so applied: Companies (Unregistered Companies) Regulations 1985 Schedule.

24 Ie the Companies Act 1985 s 351(1),(2),(5)(a) (as amended): see para 1135 note 1 ante. Section 351(1),(2),(5)(a) (as amended) has been so applied: Companies (Unregistered Companies) Regulations 1985 Schedule.

25 Ie the Companies Act 1985 ss 363–365 (as substituted): see paras 1062–1065 ante. Sections 363–365 (as substituted) have been so applied: Companies (Unregistered Companies) Regulations 1985 Schedule (amended by SI 1990/2571).

26 Ie the Companies Act 1985 ss 384–394A (as amended): see para 1027 et seq ante. Sections 384–394A (as amended), except s 385A (as added) (see para 1029 ante), s 386 (as substituted) (see para 1030 ante) and s 393 (as substituted) (see para 1051 ante), have been so applied: Companies (Unregistered Companies) Regulations 1985 Schedule (amended by SI 1990/438).

27 Ie the Companies Act 1985 s 711 (as amended): see para 70 note 1 ante. Section 711 (as amended) has been so applied: Companies (Unregistered Companies) Regulations 1985 Schedule.

28 Ie the Companies Act 1985 s 720: see para 939 ante. Section 720 has been so applied: Companies (Unregistered Companies) Regulations 1985 Schedule.

1768. Consequences of application of the business provisions. The application of the business provisions[1] does not repeal or revoke in whole or in part any enactment, royal charter or other instrument constituting or regulating any body in relation to which those provisions apply, or restrict Her Majesty's power to grant a charter in lieu of or supplementary to any such charter; but, in relation to any such body, the operation of any such enactment, charter or instrument is suspended in so far as it is inconsistent with any of the business provisions as they apply for the time being to that body[2].

1 For the meaning of 'the business provisions' see para 1765 ante.
2 Companies Act 1985 s 718(5).

1769. Application of other relevant legislation. The Business Names Act 1985 applies to any person who has a place of business in Great Britain[1]; the Company Directors Disqualification Act 1986 applies to all companies which may be wound up[2] under the provisions of the Insolvency Act 1986[3]; the provisions of the Financial Services Act 1986 and the Public Offers of Securities Regulations 1995 relating to offers of listed[4] and unlisted[5] securities respectively apply generally[6]; and the insider dealing legislation[7] also applies[8].

1 See the Business Names Act 1985 s 1(1) and para 166 et seq ante.
2 Ie under the Insolvency Act 1986 Pt V (ss 220–229) (as amended): see para 2899 et seq post.
3 See the Company Directors Disqualification Act 1986 s 22(2)(b) and para 1417 et seq ante.
4 Ie the Financial Services Act 1986 Pt IV (ss 142–156B) (as amended): see paras 281–299 and 339–348 ante.
5 Ie the Public Offers of Securities Regulations 1995, SI 1995/1537: see paras 300–320, 339–344 and 349–353 ante.
6 See the Financial Services Act 1986 ss 1, 2, Sch 1 para 1 (as amended); the Public Offers of Securities Regulations 1995 reg 3(b).
7 Ie the Criminal Justice Act 1993 Pt V (ss 52–64): see para 1218 et seq ante.
8 See ibid s 60(3) and para 1218 text and note 15 ante.

1770. Power to make regulations. The power to make regulations conferred on the Secretary of State for any of the above purposes[1] is exercisable by statutory instrument subject to annulment in pursuance of a resolution of either House of Parliament[2].

1 Ie under the Companies Act 1985 s 718(1),(3): see paras 1766, 1767 ante.
2 Ibid s 718(6).

5. COMPANIES FORMED OUTSIDE ENGLAND AND WALES

(1) IN GENERAL

1771. Scope. This Part deals with companies formed outside England and Wales, namely in Scotland[1], in Northern Ireland[2], in other parts of the Commonwealth[3], in the Republic of Ireland[4], and in foreign countries[5]; and with European Economic Interest Groupings[6].

1 See para 1777 et seq post.
2 See para 1779 et seq post.
3 See para 1781 et seq post.
4 See para 1785 post.
5 See para 1786 et seq post.
6 See para 1831 et seq post.

1772. Domicile and residence. The nationality and domicile of a company are determined by its place of registration, and its residence by the place where its central management and control are actually to be found[1].

1 See para 94 ante. As to change of residence by a company see para 95 ante.

1773. Service out of the jurisdiction. With certain exceptions in the case of Scottish and Irish companies, companies, like individuals, may in certain cases be served out of the jurisdiction by leave of the court where service cannot be effected within the jurisdiction[1].

1 RSC Ord 11 r 1. Cf Ord 10 r 2, Ord 65 r 3 and the Companies Act 1985 s 695 (as amended) (cited in para 1814 post). See further PRACTICE AND PROCEDURE vol 37 para 171 et seq.

1774. Registration of charges. The provisions of the Companies Act 1985 relating to the registration of charges[1] extend to charges on property in England and Wales which are created, and to charges on property in England and Wales which is acquired, by a company, whether a company within the meaning of that Act or not, incorporated outside Great Britain which has an established place of business in England and Wales[2].

These provisions apply whether or not the company has registered the required statutory particulars[3]. They apply even if the company ceases to have a place of business in England and Wales before its liquidation[4]; and in the application of these provisions, at any rate if the winding up of the company is similar to an English liquidation, the term 'liquidator' includes the foreign liquidator[4].

1 Ie the Companies Act 1985 ss 395–408 (as amended): see para 1296 et seq ante. These provisions apply to floating charges so created: see *Slavenburg's Bank NV v Intercontinental Natural Resources Ltd* [1980] 1 All ER 955, [1980] 1 WLR 1076.
2 Companies Act 1985 s 409(1). For the meaning of 'established place of business' see para 1790 post. In relation to such a company, s 406 (copies of instruments creating charges to be kept by companies at their registered office: see para 1296 ante) and s 407 (register of charges to be kept by companies at their registered office: see para 1297 ante) apply with the substitution of a reference to the company's principal place of business in England and Wales for the reference to the company's registered office: s 409(2).
     Section 409 is repealed from a day to be appointed by the Companies Act 1989 s 92(b) and replaced from a day to be appointed by the Companies Act 1985 Pt XXIII Ch III (ss 703A–703N) (added by the Companies Act 1989 ss 92(b), 105, Sch 15). At the date at which this volume states the law no such days had been appointed. As to the proposed new registration system in respect of oversea companies generally see para 1827 post.
3 Ie those required under the Companies Act 1985 s 691 (as amended): see paras 1804, 1805 post. See also *Slavenburg's Bank NV v Intercontinental Natural Resources Ltd* [1980] 1 All ER 955, [1980] 1 WLR 1076; *Re Alton Corpn* [1985] BCLC 27.
4 *Slavenburg's Bank NV v Intercontinental Natural Resources Ltd* [1980] 1 All ER 955, [1980] 1 WLR 1076.

1775. Investigation of company's affairs. The statutory provisions relating to the Secretary of State's powers of investigation[1] apply to bodies corporate incorporated outside Great Britain which are carrying on business in Great Britain or which have at any time carried on business there as they apply to companies under the Companies Act 1985, but subject to the following adaptations and modifications[2]. The statutory provisions relating to:
     (1)   an investigation on the application of a company or its members[3];
     (2)   the power to bring civil proceedings on the company's behalf[4];
     (3)   an investigation of the ownership of a company and the power to obtain information as to those interested in shares[5];
     (4)   the investigation of share dealings[6],
do not apply to such bodies[7].

The other statutory provisions relating to the Secretary of State's powers of investigation apply to such bodies subject to such adaptations and modifications as may be specified by regulations made by the Secretary of State[8].

1　Ie the Companies Act 1985 Pt XIV (ss 431-453) (as amended): see para 1376 et seq ante.
2　Ibid s 453(1) (substituted by the Companies Act 1989 s 70).
3　Ie the Companies Act 1985 s 431: see para 1376 ante.
4　Ie ibid s 438 (as amended): see para 1390 ante.
5　Ie ibid ss 442-445 (as amended): see paras 1381-1383 ante.
6　Ie ibid s 446 (as amended): see para 1384 ante.
7　Ibid s 453(1A) (substituted by the Companies Act 1989 s 70).
8　Companies Act 1985 s 453(1B) (substituted by the Companies Act 1989 s 70). Such regulations must be made by statutory instrument subject to annulment in pursuance of a resolution of either House of Parliament: Companies Act 1985 s 453(2). At the date at which this volume states the law no such regulations had been made.

1776. Application of other relevant legislation. The Business Names Act 1985 applies to any person who has a place of business in Great Britain[1]; the Company Directors Disqualification Act 1986 applies to all companies which may be wound up[2] under the provisions of the Insolvency Act 1986[3]; the provisions of the Financial Services Act 1986 and the Public Offers of Securities Regulations 1995 relating to offers of listed[4] and unlisted[5] securities respectively apply generally[6]; and the insider dealing legislation[7] also applies[8].

1　See the Business Names Act 1985 s 1(1) and para 166 et seq ante.
2　Ie under the Insolvency Act 1986 Pt V (ss 220-229) (as amended): see para 2899 et seq post.
3　See the Company Directors Disqualification Act 1986 s 22(2)(b) and para 1417 et seq ante.
4　Ie the Financial Services Act 1986 Pt IV (ss 142-156B) (as amended): see paras 281-299 and 339-348 ante.
5　Ie the Public Offers of Securities Regulations 1995, SI 1995/1537: see paras 300-320, 339-344 and 349-353 ante.
6　See the Financial Services Act 1986 ss 1, 2, Sch 1 para 1 (as amended); the Public Offers of Securities Regulations 1995 reg 3(b).
7　Ie the Criminal Justice Act 1993 Pt V (ss 52-64): see para 1218 et seq ante.
8　See ibid s 60(3) and para 1218 note 15 ante.

(2) COMPANIES FORMED IN SCOTLAND

1777. The legislation. The Companies Act 1985 applies in Scotland as in England and Wales with the additions and subject to the modifications specified in it. The concept of a floating charge was first introduced to the law of Scotland in 1961[1], and, whilst originally such a charge could be enforced only in a liquidation and not by the appointment of a receiver, it may now be enforced by such an appointment[2]. Any receiver so appointed in respect of the whole or any part of the property or undertaking of a company and in consequence of the company having created a charge which, as created, was a floating charge, may exercise his powers in England and Wales so far as their exercise is not inconsistent with English law[3]. Companies incorporated in Scotland by special Act after 8 May 1845 for the purpose of carrying on any undertaking are governed by the Companies Clauses Acts[4].

1 See the Companies (Floating Charges) (Scotland) Act 1961 ss 1, 4 (repealed).
2 See the Insolvency Act 1986 Pt III Ch II (ss 50–71) (as amended).
3 See ibid s 72(1) and para 1339 ante.
4 Ie the Companies Clauses Consolidation (Scotland) Act 1845, the Companies Clauses Act 1863 and the Companies Clauses Act 1869: see para 1599 et seq ante.

1778. Service within the jurisdiction. A document may be served on a company regulated by the Companies Act 1985 whose registered office is situated in Scotland by leaving it at, or sending it by post[1] to, the company's registered office[2]. Where a company registered in Scotland carries on business in England and Wales, however, the process of any court in England and Wales may be served on the company by leaving it at, or sending it by post to, the company's principal place of business in England and Wales, addressed to the manager or other head officer in England and Wales of the company[3]; and, where process is so served, the person issuing out the process must send a copy of it by post to the company's registered office[4].

A statutory corporation incorporated in Scotland under Acts which contain no special provisions as to service may be sued and served in England and Wales in the same way as any other corporation aggregate, even though the cause of action did not arise in England and Wales, provided the corporation carries on business in England and Wales[5].

1 This includes registered post (*TO Supplies (London) Ltd v Jerry Creighton Ltd* [1952] 1 KB 42, [1951] 2 All ER 992) and consequentially recorded delivery under the Recorded Delivery Service Act 1962. Service is deemed to be effected by properly addressing, prepaying and posting a letter containing the process and, unless the contrary is proved, to have been effected at the time at which the letter would be delivered in the ordinary course of post: Interpretation Act 1978 s 7. See also PRACTICE AND PROCEDURE vol 37 para 169.
2 Companies Act 1985 s 725(1). See also para 1146 ante.
3 Ibid s 725(2). In *Re Burland's Trade Mark, Burland v Broxburn Oil Co* (1889) 41 ChD 542, leave to serve the writ out of the jurisdiction was given in an action for an injunction to restrain infringements in England of a trade mark where the defendant company had its registered office in Scotland and branches in England.
4 Companies Act 1985 s 725(3). As to the service of process on foreign corporations see CONFLICT OF LAWS vol 8(1) (Reissue) para 990.
5 *Logan v Bank of Scotland* [1904] 2 KB 495 at 498, 499, CA; and see RSC Ord 65 r 3 and PRACTICE AND PROCEDURE vol 37 para 159.

(3) COMPANIES FORMED IN NORTHERN IRELAND

1779. Historical outline. Before 1 January 1922 the Companies Acts 1908 to 1917[1] applied in Ireland as in England, subject to certain modifications specified in them. The Government of Ireland Act 1920, which provided for the establishment of Parliaments for Southern Ireland and Northern Ireland, enacted that all existing laws, institutions and authorities in Ireland should continue with necessary modifications as if that Act had not been passed, subject to repeal, abolition, alteration and adaptation as respects matters within the powers of the Parliaments of Southern and Northern Ireland[2], and further provided for the adaptation by Order in Council of any enactments so far as necessary or proper to give effect to the provisions of the Act[3]. The Parliament of Northern Ireland was duly established in accordance with the Act, and as a result of an Order in Council[4] having effect as from 1 January 1922 the jurisdiction over companies registered in Northern Ireland was transferred to the Parliament of Northern Ireland as from that date, and those companies became governed by the Companies Acts 1908 to 1917 from then onwards[5], as adapted by that Order in Council, subject to those Acts being repealed or amended by the Parliament of Northern Ireland.

The Companies Act (Northern Ireland) 1930, an Act to amend the law governing companies registered in Northern Ireland, with the exception of certain provisions which took effect on 17 June 1930, was to take effect only as a result of an Order in Council[6]. This Act was replaced by the Companies Act (Northern Ireland) 1932, which came into force on 1 January 1933[7]. This was replaced by the Companies Act (Northern Ireland) 1960, which came into force on 1 April 1961[8], and the Companies (Amendment) Act (Northern Ireland) 1963.

By the Northern Ireland Constitution Act 1973 the Parliament of Northern Ireland ceased to exist[9], being replaced by a new constitution[10], and certain of the above provisions of the Government of Ireland Act 1920 were repealed[11], but neither the abolition of the Parliament of Northern Ireland nor the repeal of any provision relating to that Parliament affected the validity or otherwise of any Act of that Parliament[12].

By the Northern Ireland Act 1974 it was provided that, during the interim period (expressed to be for a period of one year from 17 July 1974 but subsequently extended[13]), Her Majesty might, by Order in Council[14], make laws for Northern Ireland[15]. Pursuant to this provision, there were made the Companies (Northern Ireland) Orders 1978[16], 1981[17] and 1982[18], and the Companies (Beneficial Interests) (Northern Ireland) Order 1983[19].

Parallel with the consolidation effected by the Companies Act 1985 and its associated Acts, the present company law of Northern Ireland is now contained in the following orders, namely the Companies (Northern Ireland) Order 1986[20], the Business Names (Northern Ireland) Order 1986[21] and the Companies Consolidation (Consequential Provisions) Order 1986[22].

1 Ie the Companies (Consolidation) Act 1908; the Companies Act 1913; the Companies (Foreign Interest) Act 1917; the Companies (Particulars as to Directors) Act 1917.
2 Government of Ireland Act 1920 s 61; Statute Law Revision Act 1927 s 1, Schedule Pt I.
3 Government of Ireland Act 1920 s 69(a).
4 Government of Ireland (Companies, Societies &c) Order 1922, SR & O 1922/184.
5 See note 1 supra.
6 Companies Act (Northern Ireland) 1930 s 108(3) (repealed).
7 See the Companies Act (Northern Ireland) 1932 s 339(2) (repealed) by which that Act was to come into force on the day on which the Companies Act (Northern Ireland) 1930 was brought into general force: Order in Council dated 15 November 1932, SR & O (NI) 1932/140 (bringing the 1930 Act into force on 1 January 1933).
8 Companies Act (Northern Ireland) 1960 s 405(2) (repealed); Order dated 16 February 1961, SR & O (NI) 1961/34.
9 Northern Ireland Constitution Act 1973 s 31(1).
10 The provisions relating to the composition and election of the Northern Ireland Assembly were separately enacted in the Northern Ireland Assembly Act 1973 whilst the Northern Ireland Constitution Act 1973 Pt II (ss 4–16) contains the principal provisions as to the new legislative and executive authorities. Section 10(4) was repealed by the Statutue Law (Repeals) Act 1981 s 1(1), Sch 1 Pt IV.
11 Northern Ireland Constitution Act 1973 s 41(1)(a), Sch 6 Pt I.
12 Ibid s 42(2).
13 As to the current extension see the Northern Ireland Act 1974 (Interim Period Extension) Order 1995, SI 1995/1895, art 2 extending the interim period until 16 July 1996.
14 Ie exercisable by statutory instrument: see the Statutory Instruments Act 1946 s 1(1) and STATUTES vol 44(1) (Reissue) para 1503. As to the procedure required see the Northern Ireland Act 1974 s 1(3), Sch 1 para 1(4)–(6).
15 Ibid Sch 1 para 1(1)(b).
16 Ie the Companies (Northern Ireland) Order 1978, SI 1978/1042 (revoked).
17 Ie the Companies (Northern Ireland) Order 1981, SI 1981/838 (revoked).

18 Ie the Companies (Northern Ireland) Order 1982, SI 1982/1534 (revoked).
19 Ie the Companies (Beneficial Interests) (Northern Ireland) Order 1983, SI 1983/1119 (revoked).
20 Ie the Companies (Northern Ireland) Order 1986, SI 1986/1032. See also the Companies (Northern Ireland) Order 1989, SI 1989/2404; the Insolvency (Northern Ireland) Order 1989, SI 1989/2405; the Companies (Northern Ireland) Order 1990, SI 1990/593; and the Companies (No 2) (Northern Ireland) Order 1990, SI 1990/1504.
21 Ie the Business Names (Northern Ireland) Order 1986, SI 1986/1033.
22 Ie the Companies Consolidation (Consequential Provisions) (Northern Ireland) Order 1986, SI 1986/1035. The repeal of the previous legislation was effected by art 22, Sch 2.

1780. Application of the Companies Act 1985. Unless the contrary intention appears, 'existing company' as used in the Companies Act 1985 does not include a company formed and registered in Northern Ireland under the Joint Stock Companies Acts[1], the Companies Act 1862, or the Companies (Consolidation) Act 1908[2]. Except where otherwise expressly provided, nothing in the Companies Act 1985, other than provisions which relate expressly to companies registered or incorporated in Northern Ireland or outside Great Britain[3], applies to or in relation to companies registered or incorporated in Northern Ireland[4]; and, subject to any such provision, and to any express provision as to extent, the Companies Act 1985 does not extend to Northern Ireland[5]. It is expressly provided that nothing in the provisions of the Companies Act 1985 which govern the application of that Act to companies formed or registered under former Acts[6] is to apply to companies registered in Northern Ireland[7]; nor may a company registered in Northern Ireland under the Companies Act 1862 or the Companies (Consolidation) Act 1908 register under the provisions of the Companies Act 1985[8] which authorise companies not formed under companies legislation to register[9]. Further, a company registered in Northern Ireland under the Joint Stock Companies Acts, or under the legislation (past or present) relating to companies in Great Britain, may not be wound up as an unregistered company[10] under the Insolvency Act 1986[11].

1 See para 11 note 2 ante.
2 See the Companies Act 1985 s 735(1)(b),(c),(4) and para 11 ante.
3 The provisions of the Companies Act 1985 relating to companies incorporated outside Great Britain are s 305 (as amended) (particulars of directors on company correspondence: see para 561 ante), ss 691–699 (as amended) (registration under Pt XXIII (ss 690A–703R) (as amended): see para 1790 et seq post). As to sale or transfer in a voluntary winding up see the Insolvency Act 1986 ss 110, 111 and para 1480 et seq ante. As to winding up under Pt V (ss 220–229) (as amended) see para 2899 et seq post (where the winding up of foreign companies is discussed).
    As a result of the Government of Ireland (Companies, Societies, etc) Order 1922, SR & O 1922/184, art 7(e), companies incorporated in Northern Ireland after 1 January 1922 which established a place of business in England, like companies incorporated outside the United Kingdom, had to comply with the registration obligations imposed by the Companies (Consolidation) Act 1908 s 274 and the Companies (Particulars as to Directors) Act 1917 which were similar to those imposed by the Companies Act 1929 s 344. The Companies Act 1985 s 691 (as amended) continues that obligation with certain additions which do not apply to companies already established in England: see para 1804 et seq post.
4 Ibid s 745(1).
5 Ibid s 745(2). Equally, except in so far as the Companies Consolidation (Consequential Provisions) Act 1985 has effect for maintaining the continuity of the law (see para 10 ante) or (1) repeals any enactment which extends to Northern Ireland; or (2) amends any enactment which extends to Northern Ireland otherwise than by the insertion of provisions expressed not so to extend, nothing in that Act extends to Northern Ireland: s 33.
6 Ie the Companies Act 1985 Pt XXII Ch I (ss 675–679).
7 Ibid s 679.

8 Ie ibid Pt XXII Ch II (ss 680–690) (as amended).
9 Ibid s 680(2).
10 Ie under the Insolvency Act 1986 Pt V (ss 220–229) (as amended): see para 2899 et seq post.
11 See ibid s 220(1)(b) and para 2899 post. As to when an unregistered company having a principal place of business in Northern Ireland may be wound up in England see para 2902 post.

(4) COMPANIES FORMED IN OTHER PARTS OF THE COMMONWEALTH AND IN THE REPUBLIC OF IRELAND

1781. Companies incorporated outside Great Britain. Companies incorporated[1] in parts of the Commonwealth outside Great Britain are governed by the companies legislation in force in the part of the Commonwealth in which they were incorporated. Companies incorporated outside Great Britain, whether or not in the Commonwealth, which establish a place of business[2] in Great Britain on or after 1 July 1985, or which had established a place of business before that date and continued at that date to have a place of business in Great Britain, namely oversea companies[3], are governed by certain provisions of Part XXIII of the Companies Act 1985[4].

Oversea companies must comply with the provisions of the Companies Act 1985 relating to registration[5].

1 A company formed in a British possession, which was empowered to sue and be sued in the name of one of its officers, was held not to be a corporation: *Aldridge v Cato* (1872) LR 4 PC 313. A judgment recovered in the British possession against the officer may, however, be enforced in England against a member resident here although he was not a party to the proceedings abroad: *Bank of Australasia v Harding* (1850) 9 CB 661; *Bank of Australasia v Nias* (1851) 16 QB 717; *Kelsall v Marshall* (1856) 1 CBNS 241.
2 For the meaning of 'place of business' see para 63 note 1 ante.
3 For the meaning of 'oversea company' see para 1790 post.
4 Ie the Companies Act 1985 Pt XXIII (ss 690A–703R) (as amended): see paras 1790 et seq, 2913, 2914 post.
5 See para 1790 et seq post.

1782. Branch registers of certain oversea companies kept in Great Britain. If, by virtue of the law in force in certain specified countries or territories[1], companies incorporated under that law have power to keep in Great Britain branch registers of their members resident in Great Britain, Her Majesty may, by Order in Council[2], direct that the provisions of the Companies Act 1985 relating to the location of the register at the company's registered office[3] and inspection of the register of members[4] and to the court's power to rectify that register[5] shall apply, subject to any modifications and adaptations specified in the Order, to and in relation to any such branch registers kept in Great Britain, as they apply to and in relation to the registers of companies within the meaning of that Act[6].

1 The countries and territories so specified are all those specified in the Companies Act 1985 s 362(1), Sch 14 Pt I (see para 398 note 2 ante) plus (1) the Channel Islands and the Isle of Man; (2) Botswana, Zambia and Tonga; and (3) any territory for the time being under Her Majesty's protection or administered by the government of the United Kingdom under the Trusteeship System of the United Nations: s 362(3), Sch 14 para 9(2).
2 At the date at which this volume states the law no such order had been made.
3 Ie so much of the Companies Act 1985 s 353 as requires a company's register of members to be kept at its registered office: see para 389 ante.
4 Ie ibid s 356 (as amended): see paras 390, 391 ante.

5 Ie ibid s 359: see para 393 ante.
6 Ibid Sch 14 para 9(1). The provisions relating to overseas branch registers (see para 398 et seq ante) may be applied to companies registered in any territories under Her Majesty's protection: see s 362(5) and para 402 ante.

1783. Miscellaneous provisions applicable. The provisions of the Company Directors Disqualification Act 1986 relating to undischarged bankrupts acting as directors of companies[1], and those of the Companies Act 1985 relating to the statement of particulars with respect to directors' names on company correspondence etc[2], apply to a company incorporated outside Great Britain which has an established place of business in Great Britain[3], but in the case of the last-mentioned provision, only where it had established such a place of business on or after 23 November 1916[4].

Provided that the provisions of the Insolvency Act 1986 relating to such sale or transfer are complied with[5], the whole or part of a company in voluntary liquidation may be sold or transferred to a company incorporated outside the United Kingdom[6].

1 Ie the Company Directors Disqualification Act 1986 s 11: see para 1423 ante.
2 Ie the Companies Act 1985 s 305 (as amended): see para 561 ante.
3 Company Directors Disqualification Act 1986 s 22(2)(a); Companies Act 1985 s 305(2)(b).
4 See ibid s 305(2)(b) and para 561 ante.
5 Ie the Insolvency Act 1986 ss 110, 111: see para 1480 et seq ante.
6 See ibid s 110(1)-(3) and para 1481 ante.

1784. Channel Islands and Isle of Man companies. With the exceptions specified below, the provisions of the Companies Act 1985[1] requiring documents to be forwarded or delivered to or filed with the registrar of companies and applying to companies formed and registered under Part I of that Act[2] apply also, if they would not otherwise, to an oversea company[3] incorporated in the Channel Islands or the Isle of Man[4].

Those provisions apply to such a company:

(1) if it has established a place of business[5] in England and Wales, as if it were registered in England and Wales;

(2) if it has established a place of business in Scotland, as if it were registered in Scotland; and

(3) if it has established a place of business both in England and Wales and in Scotland, as if it were registered in both England and Wales and Scotland;

with such modifications as may be necessary and, in particular, apply in a similar way to documents relating to things done outside Great Britain as if they had been done in Great Britain[6].

The above obligation does not, however, apply:

(a) to resolutions altering the company's objects[7];

(b) to alterations of the memorandum or articles by statute or statutory instrument[8];

(c) to the directors' duty to file accounts[9];

(d) to notices to the registrar of companies of change of directors or secretary[10]; and

(e) to copies of resolutions[11] altering a company's memorandum or articles[12].

Her Majesty may, by Order in Council, direct that such of the provisions of the Insolvency Act 1986 as are specified in the Order, being provisions formerly contained in the Insolvency Act 1985, shall extend to any of the Channel Islands[13] with such modifications as may be so specified[14]. In other respects companies incorporated in the Channel Islands or the Isle of Man rank as oversea companies for the purposes of English company legislation[15].

1 For the purposes of the Companies Act 1985 s 699(1), references to the Companies Act 1985 include references to certain provisions of the Insolvency Act 1986, and also the Company Directors Disqualification Act 1986: see para 20 note 12 ante.

2 As to such requirements see paras 88, 100, 691 ante.

3 Ie an oversea company to which the Companies Act 1985 s 691 (as amended) applies: see paras 1804, 1805 post. For the meaning of 'oversea company' see para 1790 post.

4 Ibid s 699(1) (amended by the Oversea Companies and Credit and Financial Institutions (Branch Disclosure) Regulations 1992, SI 1992/3179, reg 3(1), Sch 2 paras 1, 14).

5 For the meaning of 'place of business' see para 63 note 1 ante.

6 Companies Act 1985 s 699(2).

7 Ie under ibid s 6(1): see para 1186 ante.

8 Ie under ibid s 18: see para 100 ante.

9 Ie under ibid s 242(1) (as substituted): see para 817 ante.

10 Ie under ibid s 288(2): see para 560 ante.

11 Ie copies of certain resolutions and agreements to be sent to the registrar of companies within 15 days under ibid s 380 (as amended) (see para 691 ante), so far as applicable to a resolution altering the company's memorandum or articles.

12 Ibid s 699(3).

13 This provision also extends to 'any colony': Insolvency Act 1986 s 442.

14 Ibid s 442.

15 Companies Act 1985 s 699(1). As to the provisions governing such companies see para 1781 et seq ante and para 1790 et seq post.

1785. Republic of Ireland. 'Existing company' as defined in the Companies Act 1985[1] does not include a company registered in the Republic of Ireland[2] under the Joint Stock Companies Acts[3], the Companies Act 1862 or the Companies (Consolidation) Act 1908[4]. The provisions of the Companies Act 1985 which govern the application of that Act to companies formed or registered under former Acts[5] do not apply to companies registered in the Republic of Ireland[6]. In other respects companies there registered rank as 'oversea companies' for the purposes of English company legislation[7].

1 For the meaning of 'existing company' see para 11 ante.

2 The Republic of Ireland is the territory formerly known as Eire and, before that, the Irish Free State: see the Irish Free State (Agreement) Act 1922 s 1, Schedule para 1; the Eire (Confirmation of Agreements) Act 1938 s 1 (repealed); and the Ireland Act 1949 s 1(3). Under the 1949 Act the Republic ceased to be a member of the British Commonwealth. Laws existing in the territory in 1922 were continued in force after the establishment of the Irish Free State until repealed by the Irish Parliament: see the Irish Free State Constitution art 73 and the Irish Free State Constitution Act 1922. The existing company law included the Companies Acts 1908 to 1917: see para 1779 note 1 ante.

3 For the meaning of 'the Joint Stock Companies Acts' see para 11 note 2 ante.

4 Companies Act 1985 s 735(1)(b). It has been held in the Republic of Ireland that an English company could not be wound up there as an unregistered company under provisions now enacted in the Insolvency Act 1986 Pt V (ss 220–229 (as amended): see para 2899 et seq post): *Re Portarlington Electric Light and Power Co Ltd* [1922] 1 IR 100.

5 Ie the Companies Act 1985 Pt XXII Ch 1 (ss 675–679).

6 Ibid s 679. As a result of the Irish Free State (Consequential Adaptation of Enactments) Order 1923, SR & O 1923/405, companies incorporated in what is now the Republic of Ireland and establishing a place of business in Great Britain after 27 March 1923 (the date on which that Order in Council came into force), had to comply with the obligation with regard to registration imposed on companies incorporated outside the United Kingdom so establishing a place of business by the Companies (Consolidation) Act 1908 and the Companies (Particulars as to Directors) Act 1917; and that obligation, which was similar to that imposed by the Companies Act 1929 s 344(1) (repealed), was continued by s 344(3) (repealed) in the case of those of such companies which continued to have an established place of business in Great Britain on 1 November 1929. The arrangement is again continued by the Companies Act 1985 s 691 (as amended): see paras 1804, 1805 post.

7 For the meaning of 'oversea company' see para 1790 post. As to the provisions governing such companies see para 1781 et seq ante and para 1790 et seq post.

(5) COMPANIES FORMED IN FOREIGN COUNTRIES

(i) Recognition of Foreign Companies

1786. Recognition of foreign company. A company which purports to have been incorporated in a foreign country may be recognised as a corporation in England[1] and, as such, capable of suing and being sued. The universal succession of one foreign corporate body to another will also be recognised[2].

1 As to the principles on which recognition is accorded or withheld see CONFLICT OF LAWS vol 8(1) (Reissue) para 983 et seq; and as to EC requirements relating to recognition see para 6 ante.
2 *National Bank of Greece and Athens SA v Metliss* [1958] AC 509, [1957] 3 All ER 608, HL (creditor's action against successor to foreign guarantor company).

1787. Recognition under the Foreign Corporations Act 1991. If at any time:
(1) any question arises whether a body which purports to have, or as the case may be appears to have, lost corporate status under the laws of a territory which is not at that time a recognised state[1] should or should not be regarded as having legal personality as a body corporate under the law of any part of the United Kingdom; and
(2) it appears that the laws of that territory are at that time applied by a settled court system in that territory,
that question and any other material question[2] relating to that body must be determined (and account taken of those laws) as if that territory were a recognised state[3]. Any registration or other thing done before 25 September 1991[4] is valid if it would have been valid before that date had the provisions described above then been in force[5].

1 For these purposes, a 'recognised state' is a territory which is recognised by Her Majesty's government in the United Kingdom as a state: Foreign Corporations Act 1991 s 1(2)(a). The laws of a territory which is so recognised are taken to include the laws of any part of the territory which are acknowledged by the federal or other central government of the territory as a whole: s 1(2)(b). As to the recognition of foreign states see Dicey and Morris *The Conflict of Laws* (12th Edn, 1993) 1109 and FOREIGN RELATIONS.
2 Foreign Corporations Act 1991 s 1(1).
3 For these purposes, a material question is a question, whether as to capacity, construction or otherwise, which in the case of a body corporate falls to be determined by reference to the laws of the territory under which the body is incorporated: ibid s 1(2)(c).
4 Ie the day on which the Foreign Corporations Act 1991 came into force: see s 2(3).
5 Ibid s 1(3).

1788. Application of the Companies Act 1985. A company incorporated in a foreign country is not included within the meaning of 'existing company' as defined in the Companies Act 1985[1], but is included in the words 'body corporate' as defined in that Act[2]. Some of the provisions of the Companies Act 1985 deal with foreign companies[3], and, if they carry on insurance business, they are subject to the provisions of the Insurance Companies Act 1982[4].

1 For the meaning of 'existing company' see para 11 ante; and see *Bulkeley v Schutz* (1871) LR 3 PC 764 at 769; *Bateman v Service* (1881) 6 App Cas 386 at 392, PC.
2 For the meaning of 'body corporate' see para 89 note 8 ante.
3 The Companies Act 1985 s 305 (as amended) (disclosure of names of directors of a company on company correspondence etc: see para 561 ante) applies to such a company which established a place of business within Great Britain after 23 November 1916 (s 305(2)(b)). As to registration under Pt XXIII

Chs I, II (ss 691-703) (as amended) see para 1790 et seq post; and as to winding up an unregistered company under the Insolvency Act 1986 Pt V (ss 220-229) (as amended) see para 2909 post. A sale or transfer of the undertaking of a company in voluntary liquidation may be made to a foreign company: see para 1481 note 2 ante.

4 See the Insurance Companies Act 1982 ss 15, 87 (as amended) and INSURANCE vol 25 (Reissue) para 803.

1789. Application of other relevant legislation. The Business Names Act 1985 applies to any person who has a place of business in Great Britain[1]; the Company Directors Disqualification Act 1986 applies to all companies which may be wound up[2] under the provisions of the Insolvency Act 1986[3]; the provisions of the Financial Services Act 1986 and the Public Offers of Securities Regulations 1995 relating to offers of listed[4] and unlisted[5] securities respectively apply generally[6]; and the insider dealing legislation[7] also applies[8].

1 See the Business Names Act 1985 s 1(1) and para 166 et seq ante.
2 Ie under the Insolvency Act 1986 Pt V (ss 220-229) (as amended): see para 2899 et seq post.
3 See the Company Directors Disqualification Act 1986 s 22(2)(b) and para 1417 et seq ante.
4 Ie the Financial Services Act 1986 Pt IV (ss 142-156B) (as amended): see paras 281-299 and 339-348 ante.
5 Ie the Public Offers of Securities Regulations 1995, SI 1995/1537: see paras 300-320, 339-344 and 349-353 ante.
6 See the Financial Services Act 1986 ss 1, 2, Sch 1 para 1 (as amended); the Public Offers of Securities Regulations 1995 reg 3(b).
7 Ie the Criminal Justice Act 1993 Pt V (ss 52-64): see para 1218 et seq ante.
8 See ibid s 60(3) and para 1218 note 15 ante.

(ii) Oversea Companies

A. REGISTRATION

(A) *In general*

1790. General registration requirements. Certain special requirements relating to registration[1] are imposed on oversea companies, that is to say companies incorporated elsewhere than in Great Britain which on or after 1 July 1985 establish a place of business[2] in Great Britain and companies incorporated elsewhere than in Great Britain which had before that date established a place of business and continued to have an established place of business in Great Britain at that date[3].

Some of the special requirements so imposed are of general application[4]; but others depend upon whether:

(1) the company is incorporated outside the United Kingdom and Gibraltar with a branch in Great Britain[5]; or

(2) the company is incorporated outside the United Kingdom and Gibraltar and has no branch in the United Kingdom[6].

A company establishes a place of business in Great Britain if it carries on part of its business activities there. Such activity need not be either a substantial part of, or more than incidental to, its main objects[7]; but there must be a more or less permanent location, not necessarily owned or leased but associated with the company and from which its business is conducted habitually or with some degree of regularity[8].

1 See para 1791 et seq post.
2 'Place of business' includes a share transfer or share registration office: Companies Act 1985 s 744. See also *Lord Advocate v Huron and Erie Loan and Savings Co* 1911 SC 612; *Act Dampskib 'Hercules' v Grand Trunk Pacific Rly Co* [1912] 1 KB 222, CA.
3 Companies Act 1985 ss 744, 746 (amended by the Companies Act 1989 s 212, Sch 24). As to the requirements with which any such company would have had to comply see the Companies (Consolidation) Act 1908 s 274; the Companies (Particulars as to Directors) Act 1917; the Companies Act 1929 s 344; the Companies Act 1948 s 407 (all repealed).
4 See paras 1810-1812 post.
5 See paras 1791 et seq, 1813 post.
6 See paras 1803 et seq, 1814 post.
7 *South India Shipping Corpn Ltd v Export-Import Bank of Korea* [1985] 2 All ER 219, [1985] 1 WLR 585, CA.
8 *Re Oriel Ltd* [1985] 3 All ER 216, [1986] 1 WLR 180, CA (mere presence of director at his residence followed by the company's entry into business dealings not sufficient).

(B) *Companies incorporated outside the United Kingdom and Gibraltar and having a Branch in Great Britain*

1791. Application of the statutory provisions. The following provisions[1] apply to any limited company which is incorporated outside the United Kingdom and Gibraltar and has a branch[2] in Great Britain[3].

1 Ie the Companies Act 1985 s 690A(2), Sch 21A (as added): see para 1792 et seq post.
2 For these purposes, except in ibid s 699A (as added) (see para 1816 post) and s 699A(2), Sch 21C (as added) (see paras 1817, 1818 post), 'branch' means a branch within the meaning of EC Council Directive 89/666 (OJ L395, 30.12.89, p 36): Companies Act 1985 s 698(2)(b) (added by the Oversea Companies and Credit and Financial Institutions (Branch Disclosure) Regulations 1992, SI 1992/3179, reg 3(1), Sch 2 para 13(1),(3)). Where a branch comprises places of business in more than one part of the United Kingdom, the branch is treated as being situated in that part of the United Kingdom where its principal place of business is situated: Companies Act 1985 s 698(2)(a) (added by the Oversea Companies and Credit and Financial Institutions (Branch Disclosure) Regulations 1992 Sch 2 para 13(1),(3)). For the meaning of 'place of business' see para 1790 note 2 ante.
3 Companies Act 1985 s 690A(1) (added by the Oversea Companies and Credit and Financial Institutions (Branch Disclosure) Regulations 1992 Sch 2 paras 1, 2).

1792. Duty to register. Within one month of having opened a branch in a part of Great Britain[1], a company[2] must deliver to the registrar of companies[3] for registration a return in the prescribed form[4] containing the specified particulars about the company[5] and the specified particulars about the branch[6] and, if the company is incorporated outside the United Kingdom and Gibraltar, has a branch in Great Britain and is not a credit or financial institution[7], the specified particulars[8] in relation to the registration of documents[9].

The return must be accompanied by the specified[10] documents[11], except where:

(1) at the time the return is delivered, the company has another branch in the United Kingdom;

(2) the return contains a statement to the effect that the specified documents[12] are included in the material registered in respect of the other branch; and

(3) the return states where the other branch is registered and what is its registered number[13].

If, at the date on which the company opens the branch in Great Britain, the company is subject to any winding-up proceedings[14] or insolvency proceedings[15], the company must deliver the appropriate return[16] within one month of that date[17]. If, on or before that date, a person has been appointed to be liquidator of the company and continues in that office at that date, the liquidator's statutory duty to make a return within 14 days of his appointment[18] has effect as if it required a return to be made within one month of the date of the branch being opened[19].

1 For these purposes, the reference to having opened a branch in a part of Great Britain includes a reference to a branch having become situated there on ceasing to be situated elsewhere: Companies Act 1985 s 690A(2), Sch 21A para 1(4) (added by the Oversea Companies and Credit and Financial Institutions (Branch Disclosure) Regulations 1992, SI 1992/3179, reg 3(1), Sch 2 paras 1, 3). For the meaning of 'branch' see para 1791 note 2 ante.

2 As to the companies to which these provisions apply see para 1791 ante.

3 For the meaning of 'the registrar of companies' see para 1798 post.

4 For the prescribed form of return see the Companies (Forms) (Amendment) Regulations 1992, SI 1992/3006, reg 4(1), Sch 2, Form BR1.

5 Ie such particulars as are specified in the Companies Act 1985 Sch 21A para 2 (as added): see para 1793 post.

6 Ie such particulars as are specified in ibid Sch 21A para 3 (as added): see para 1794 post.

7 Ie if the company is one to which ibid s 699AA (as added) applies: see para 1819 post.

8 Ie such particulars in relation to the registration of documents under ibid s 699AA(2), Sch 21D (as added) (see paras 1820, 1821 post) as are specified in Sch 21A para 4 (as added): see para 1795 post.

9 Ibid Sch 21A para 1(1) (added by the Oversea Companies and Credit and Financial Institutions (Branch Disclosure) Regulations 1992 Sch 2 paras 1, 3).
    Any limited company incorporated outside the United Kingdom and Gibraltar which, immediately after 31 December 1992, had a branch in England and Wales which it had there immediately before 1 January 1993, is treated for the purposes of the Companies Act 1985 Sch 21A para 1(1) (as so added) as having opened on 1 January 1993 any branch which it had in England and Wales immediately after 31 December 1992 and had there immediately before 1 January 1993: Oversea Companies and Credit and Financial Institutions (Branch Disclosure) Regulations 1992 reg 5, Sch 4 para 1(1),(2). Where any such company was a registered oversea company in relation to England and Wales immediately before 1 January 1993, the Companies Act 1985 Sch 21A para 1(1) (as so added) has effect, in its application by virtue of the Oversea Companies and Credit and Financial Institutions (Branch Disclosure) Regulations 1992 Sch 4 para 1(2), with the substitution for 'one month' of 'six months': Sch 4 para 1(1),(3). For the purposes of Sch 4 para 1(3), a company is a registered oversea company in relation to England and Wales if it has duly delivered documents to the registrar for England and Wales under the Companies Act 1985 s 691 (as amended) (see para 1804 post) and has not subsequently given notice to him under s 696(4) (as amended) (see para 1808 post) that it has ceased to have an established place of business there: Oversea Companies and Credit and Financial Institutions (Branch Disclosure) Regulations 1992 Sch 4 para 1(4). For the meaning of 'place of business' see para 1790 note 2 ante.

10 Ie the documents specified in the Companies Act 1985 Sch 21A para 5 (as added) (see para 1796 post) and, if the company is one to which Sch 21D Pt I (paras 1–6 (as added): see para 1820 post) applies, the documents specified in Sch 21A para 6 (as added) (see para 1796 post).

11 Ibid Sch 21A para 1(2) (added by the Oversea Companies and Credit and Financial Institutions (Branch Disclosure) Regulations 1992 Sch 2 paras 1, 3).

12 See note 10 supra.

13 Companies Act 1985 Sch 21A para 1(3) (added by the Oversea Companies and Credit and Financial Institutions (Branch Disclosure) Regulations 1992 Sch 2 paras 1, 3).

14 Ie any proceedings referred to in the Companies Act 1985 s 703P(1) (as added): see para 2913 post.

15 Ie any proceedings referred to in ibid s 703Q(1) (as added): see para 2914 post.

16 Ie under ibid s 703P(1) (as added) or s 703Q(1) (as added), as the case may be.

17 Ibid Sch 21A para 1(5) (added by the Oversea Companies and Credit and Financial Institutions (Branch Disclosure) Regulations 1992 Sch 2 paras 1, 3).

18 Ie the Companies Act 1985 s 703P(3),(4) (as added): see para 2913 post.

19 Ibid Sch 21A para 1(5) (as added: see note 17 supra).

1793. Particulars about the company. The particulars about the company to be contained in the return to the registrar of companies[1] are:

(1) the corporate name of the company[2];

(2) its legal form[3];

(3) if it is registered in the country of its incorporation, the identity of the register in which it is registered and the number with which it is so registered[4];

(4) a list of its directors[5] and secretary[6], containing:
  (a) with respect to each director, the specified particulars, that is to say, in the case of an individual, his name[7], any former name[8], his usual residential address, his nationality, his business occupation (if any), particulars of any other directorships held by him and his date of birth and, in the case of a corporation or Scottish firm, its corporate or firm name and registered or principal office[9];
  (b) with respect to the secretary (or, where there are joint secretaries, with respect to each of them), the specified particulars, that is to say, in the case of an individual, his name, any former name and his usual residential address and, in the case of a corporation or Scottish firm, its corporate or firm name and registered or principal office, except that, where all the partners in a firm are joint secretaries of the company, the name and principal office of the firm may be stated instead of each individual's name, former name and usual residential address[10];
(5) the extent of the powers of the directors to represent the company in dealings with third parties and in legal proceedings, together with a statement as to whether they may act alone or must act jointly and, if jointly, the name of any other person concerned[11]; and
(6) whether the company is[12] a credit or financial institution[13].

In the case of a company which is not incorporated in a member State, those particulars also include:
  (i) the law under which the company is incorporated[14];
  (ii) in specified cases[15] the period for which the company is required by the law under which it is incorporated to prepare accounts, together with the period allowed for the preparation and public disclosure of accounts for such a period[16]; and
  (iii) unless disclosed by the specified documents[17], the address of its principal place of business in its country of incorporation, its objects and the amount of its issued share capital[18].

Where:
(A) at the time a return is delivered[19] by the company to the registrar of companies the company has another branch[20] in the same part of Great Britain as the branch covered by the return; and
(B) the company has delivered the required particulars[21] to the registrar with respect to that branch or, to the extent it is required to do so[22], and has no outstanding obligation to make a return to the registrar in respect of that branch[23] in relation to any alteration to those particulars,

the company may adopt the particulars so delivered as particulars which the registrar is to treat as having been filed by the return by referring in the return to the fact that the particulars have been filed in respect of that other branch and giving the number with which the other branch is registered[24].

1 Ie the particulars referred to in the Companies Act 1985 s 690A(2), Sch 21A para 1(1)(a) (as added): see para 1792 ante.
2 Ibid Sch 21A para 2(1)(a) (added by the Oversea Companies and Credit and Financial Institutions (Branch Disclosure) Regulations 1992, SI 1992/3179, reg 3(1), Sch 2 paras 1, 3).
3 Companies Act 1985 Sch 21A para 2(1)(b) (added by the Oversea Companies and Credit and Financial Institutions (Branch Disclosure) Regulations 1992 Sch 2 paras 1, 3).
4 Companies Act 1985 Sch 21A para 2(1)(c) (added by the Oversea Companies and Credit and Financial Institutions (Branch Disclosure) Regulations 1992 Sch 2 paras 1, 3).

5 For these purposes, 'director', in relation to an oversea company, includes a shadow director: Companies Act 1985 s 698(1) (renumbered by the Oversea Companies and Credit and Financial Institutions (Branch Disclosure) Regulations 1992 Sch 2 para 13(1),(2)). For the meaning of 'shadow director' and 'director' see para 543 note 1 ante.

6 For these purposes, 'secretary' includes any person occupying the position of secretary by whatever name called: Companies Act 1985 s 698(1) (as renumbered: see note 5 supra).

7 For these purposes, 'name' means a person's forename and surname, except that, in the case of a peer, or an individual usually known by a title, the title may be stated instead of his forename and surname, or in addition to either or both of them: ibid Sch 21A para 2(5)(a) (added by the Oversea Companies and Credit and Financial Institutions (Branch Disclosure) Regulations 1992 Sch 2 paras 1, 3).

8 For these purposes, the reference to a former name does not include: (1) in the case of a peer, or an individual normally known by a title, the name by which he was known previous to the adoption of or succession to the title; (2) in the case of any person, a former name which was changed or disused before he attained the age of 18 years or which has been changed or disused for 20 years or more; (3) in the case of a married woman, the name by which she was known previous to the marriage: Companies Act 1985 Sch 21A para 2(5)(b) (added by the Oversea Companies and Credit and Financial Institutions (Branch Disclosure) Regulations 1992 Sch 2 paras 1, 3).

9 Companies Act 1985 Sch 21A para 2(1)(d)(i),(3) (added by the Oversea Companies and Credit and Financial Institutions (Branch Disclosure) Regulations 1992 Sch 2 paras 1, 3).

10 Companies Act 1985 Sch 21A para 2(1)(d)(ii),(4) (added by the Oversea Companies and Credit and Financial Institutions (Branch Disclosure) Regulations 1992 Sch 2 paras 1, 3).

11 Companies Act 1985 Sch 21A para 2(1)(e) (added by the Oversea Companies and Credit and Financial Institutions (Branch Disclosure) Regulations 1992 Sch 2 paras 1, 3).

12 Ie whether the company is an institution to which the Companies Act 1985 s 699A (as added) (see para 1816 post) or the equivalent provision in Northern Ireland applies.

13 Ibid Sch 21A para 2(1)(f) (added by the Oversea Companies and Credit and Financial Institutions (Branch Disclosure) Regulations 1992 Sch 2 paras 1, 3).

14 Companies Act 1985 Sch 21A para 2(2)(a) (added by the Oversea Companies and Credit and Financial Institutions (Branch Disclosure) Regulations 1992 Sch 2 paras 1, 3).

15 Ie in the case of a company to which the Companies Act 1985 s 699A(2), Sch 21C Pt I paras 2, 3 (as added) (see para 1817 post) or s 699AA(2), Sch 21D Pt I paras 2, 3 (as added) (see para 1820 post) applies.

16 Ibid Sch 21A para 2(2)(b) (added by the Oversea Companies and Credit and Financial Institutions (Branch Disclosure) Regulations 1992 Sch 2 paras 1, 3).

17 Ie the documents specified in the Companies Act 1985 Sch 21A para 5 (as added): see para 1796 post.

18 Ibid Sch 21A para 2(2)(c) (added by the Oversea Companies and Credit and Financial Institutions (Branch Disclosure) Regulations 1992 Sch 2 paras 1, 3).

19 Ie under the Companies Act 1985 Sch 21A para 1(1) (as added): see para 1792 ante.

20 For the meaning of 'branch' see para 1791 note 2 ante.

21 Ie the particulars required by the Companies Act 1985 Sch 21A para 2(1)(b)-(f) (as added) (see text heads (2)-(6) supra) and Sch 21A para 2(2)-(5) (as added) (see supra).

22 Ie by virtue of ibid s 692A(4), Sch 21B (as added): see para 1801 post.

23 Ie under ibid Sch 21A para 7 (as added): see para 1797 post.

24 Ibid Sch 21A para 2(6) (added by the Oversea Companies and Credit and Financial Institutions (Branch Disclosure) Regulations 1992 Sch 2 paras 1, 3).

1794. Particulars about the branch. The particulars about the branch to be contained in the return to the registrar of companies[1] are:

(1) the address of the branch[2];

(2) the date on which it was opened;

(3) the business carried on at it;

(4) if different from the name of the company, the name in which that business is carried on;

(5) a list of the names and addresses of all persons resident in Great Britain authorised to accept on the company's behalf service of process in respect of the business of the branch and of any notices required to be served on the company in respect of the business of the branch;

(6) a list of the names and usual residential addresses of all persons authorised to represent the company as permanent representatives of the company for the business of the branch;

(7) the extent of the authority of any person falling within head (6) above, including whether that person is authorised to act alone or jointly; and

(8) if a person falling within head (6) above is not authorised to act alone, the name of any person with whom he is authorised to act[3].

1 Ie the particulars referred to in the Companies Act 1985 s 690A(2), Sch 21A para 1(1)(b) (as added): see para 1792 ante.
2 For the meaning of 'branch' see para 1791 note 2 ante.
3 Companies Act 1985 Sch 21A para 3 (added by the Oversea Companies and Credit and Financial Institutions (Branch Disclosure) Regulations 1992, SI 1992/3179, reg 3(1), Sch 2 paras 1, 3).

1795. Particulars relating to credit and financial institutions. The particulars to be contained in the return to the registrar of companies[1] are:

(1) whether it is intended to register documents[2] in respect of the branch[3] or in respect of some other branch in the United Kingdom; and

(2) if it is, where that other branch is registered and what is its registered number[4].

1 Ie the particulars referred to in the Companies Act 1985 s 690A(2), Sch 21A para 1(1)(c) (as added): see para 1792 ante.
2 Ie under ibid Sch 21A para 2(2) (as added) (see para 1793 ante) or, as the case may be, Sch 21D para 10(1) (as added) (see para 1821 post).
3 For the meaning of 'branch' see para 1791 note 2 ante.
4 Companies Act 1985 Sch 21A para 4 (added by the Oversea Companies and Credit and Financial Institutions (Branch Disclosure) Regulations 1992, SI 1992/3179, reg 3(1), Sch 2 paras 1, 3).

1796. Documents required. The documents to be contained in the return to the registrar of companies[1] are:

(1) a certified copy of the charter, statutes or memorandum and articles of the company, or other instrument constituting or defining the company's constitution; and

(2) if any of the documents mentioned in head (1) above is not written in the English language, a translation of it into English certified in the prescribed manner[2] to be a correct translation[3].

If, however, the company is one required to make disclosure under parent law, the documents to be contained in the return to the registrar of companies[4] are:

(a) copies of the latest accounting documents[5] prepared in relation to a financial period[6] of the company to have been publicly disclosed in accordance with the law of the country in which it is incorporated before the end of the period allowed for compliance in respect of the branch[7] or, if earlier, the date on which the company complies in respect of the branch; and

(b) if any of the documents mentioned in head (a) above is not written in the English language, a translation of it into English certified in the prescribed manner[8] to be a correct translation[9].

1 Ie the first documents mentioned in the Companies Act 1985 s 690A(2), Sch 21A para 1(2) (as added): see para 1792 ante.
2 For these purposes, and for the purposes of ibid Sch 21A para 6(1)(b) (as added) (see infra), Sch 21A para 7 (as added) (see para 1797 post), s 699A(2), Sch 21C para 2(b) (as added) (see para 1817 post), Sch 21C para 3(b) (as added) (see para 1817 post), Sch 21C para 12(2) (as added) (see para 1818 post), s 699AA(2),

Sch 21D para 2(4) (as added) (see para 1820 post) and Sch 21D para 10(2) (as added) (see para 1821 post), a translation of a document into English is certified to be a correct translation:

(1) if the translation was made in the United Kingdom, by:
    (a) a notary public in any part of the United Kingdom;
    (b) a solicitor (if the translation was made in Scotland), a solicitor of the Supreme Court of Judicature of England and Wales (if it was made in England or Wales), or a solicitor of the Supreme Court of Judicature of Northern Ireland (if it was made in Northern Ireland);
    (c) a person certified by a person mentioned in heads (1)(a) and (1)(b) supra to be known to him to be competent to translate the document into English; or

(2) if the translation was made outside the United Kingdom, by:
    (a) a notary public;
    (b) a person authorised in the place where the translation was made to administer an oath;
    (c) any of the British officials mentioned in the Commissioners for Oaths Act 1889 s 6 (as amended) (see para 818 note 7 ante); or
    (d) a person certified by a person mentioned in heads (2)(a), (2)(b) or (2)(c) supra, to be known to him to be competent to translate the document into English:

Companies (Forms) (Amendment) Regulations 1992, SI 1992/3006, regs 2, 3.

3 Companies Act 1985 Sch 21A para 5 (added by the Oversea Companies and Credit and Financial Institutions (Branch Disclosure) Regulations 1992, SI 1992/3179, reg 3(1), Sch 2 paras 1, 3).

4 Ie the second documents mentioned in the Companies Act 1985 Sch 21A para 1(2) (as added): see para 1792 ante.

5 For these purposes, 'accounting documents' is to be construed in accordance with ibid Sch 21D para 6 (as added) (see para 1820 note 6 post): Sch 21A para 6(2) (added by the Oversea Companies and Credit and Financial Institutions (Branch Disclosure) Regulations 1992 Sch 2 paras 1, 3).

6 For these purposes, 'financial period' is to be construed in accordance with the Companies Act 1985 Sch 21D para 6 (as added) (see para 1820 note 7 post): Sch 21A para 6(2) (as added: see note 5 supra).

7 For the meaning of 'branch' see para 1791 note 2 ante.

8 See note 2 supra.

9 Companies Act 1985 Sch 21A para 6(1) (added by the Oversea Companies and Credit and Financial Institutions (Branch Disclosure) Regulations 1992 Sch 2 paras 1, 3).

1797. Alterations. If, after a company[1] has delivered a return[2] to the registrar of companies, any alteration is made in:

(1) its charter, statutes or memorandum and articles, or other instrument constituting or defining its constitution; or

(2) any of the specified particulars to be contained in the return,

the company must, within the specified time, deliver to the registrar for registration a return in the prescribed form[3] containing the prescribed particulars of the alteration[4]. In the case of an alteration in any of the documents referred to in head (1) above, the return must be accompanied by a certified copy of the document as altered, together with, if the document is not written in the English language, a translation of it into English certified in the prescribed manner[5] to be a correct translation[6].

The time so specified for the delivery of the return is:

(a) in the case of an alteration in any of the particulars about the branch[7], 21 days after the alteration is made; or

(b) in the case of any other alteration, 21 days after the date on which notice of the alteration in question could have been received in Great Britain in due course of post, if dispatched with due diligence[8].

Where a company's return to the registrar[9] includes a statement to the effect that the specified documents are included in the material registered in respect of another branch[10], and the statement ceases to be true so far as concerns the documents to be contained in the return[11], the company must, within 21 days after the date on which notice of the fact that the statement in the earlier return has ceased to be true could have been received in Great Britain in due course of post, if dispatched with due diligence, deliver to the registrar for registration in respect of the branch to which the return relates:

(i) the specified documents[11]; or

(ii) a return in the prescribed form[12] containing a statement to the effect that those documents are included in the material which is registered in respect of another branch of the company in the United Kingdom and stating where the other branch is registered and what is its registered number[13].

1 As to the companies to which these provisions apply see para 1791 ante.
2 Ie a return under the Companies Act 1985 s 690A(2), Sch 21A para 1(1) (as added): see para 1792 ante.
3 For the prescribed form of return see the Companies (Forms) (Amendment) Regulations 1992, SI 1992/3006, reg 4(1), Sch 2, Form BR2 (alteration to constitution documents), Form BR3 (alteration of company particulars), Form BR4 (change of directors or secretary or of their particulars), Form BR5 (change of address or other branch particulars), Form BR6 (change of person authorised to accept service or to represent the branch of an oversea company or of any change in their particulars).
4 Companies Act 1985 Sch 21A para 7(1) (added by the Oversea Companies and Credit and Financial Institutions (Branch Disclosure) Regulations 1992, SI 1992/3179, reg 3(1), Sch 2 paras 1, 3).
    Where a company has more than one branch in Great Britain and an alteration relates to more than one of those branches, the Companies Act 1985 Sch 21A para 7(1) (as so added) has effect to require the company to deliver a return in respect of each of the branches to which the alteration relates: Sch 21A para 7(3) (added by the Oversea Companies and Credit and Financial Institutions (Branch Disclosure) Regulations 1992 Sch 2 paras 1, 3). For these purposes: (1) an alteration in any of the particulars specified in the Companies Act 1985 Sch 21A para 2 (as added) (see para 1793 ante) is treated as relating to every branch of the company, though, where the company has more than one branch in a part of Great Britain, a return in respect of an alteration in any of those particulars which gives the branch numbers of two or more such branches is treated as a return in respect of each branch whose number is given; but (2) an alteration in the company's charter, statutes or memorandum and articles, or other instrument constituting or defining its constitution, is only treated as relating to a branch if the document altered is included in the material registered in respect of it: Sch 21A para 7(4) (added by the Oversea Companies and Credit and Financial Institutions (Branch Disclosure) Regulations 1992 Sch 2 paras 1, 3).
5 For the prescribed manner of certification see para 1796 note 2 ante.
6 Companies Act 1985 Sch 21A para 7(1) (as added: see note 4 supra).
7 Ie in the case of an alteration in any of the particulars specified in ibid Sch 21A para 3 (as added): see para 1793 ante. For the meaning of 'branch' see para 1791 note 2 ante.
8 Ibid Sch 21A para 7(2) (added by the Oversea Companies and Credit and Financial Institutions (Branch Disclosure) Regulations 1992 Sch 2 paras 1, 3).
9 See note 2 supra.
10 Ie where a company's return contains a statement to the effect mentioned in the Companies Act 1985 Sch 21A para 1(3)(b) (as added): see para 1792 ante.
11 Ie the documents specified in ibid Sch 21A para 5 (as added): see para 1796 ante.
12 For the prescribed form of return see the Companies (Forms) (Amendment) Regulations 1992 Sch 2, Form BR7.
13 Companies Act 1985 Sch 21A para 8(1)–(3) (added by the Oversea Companies and Credit and Financial Institutions (Branch Disclosure) Regulations 1992 Sch 2 paras 1, 3). The Companies Act 1985 Sch 21A para 8(2) (as so added) also applies where, after a company has made a return under Sch 21A para 8(2)(b) (as so added) (see text head (ii) supra), the statement to the effect that those documents are included in the material which is registered in respect of another branch of the company in the United Kingdom ceases to be true: Sch 21A para 8(4) (added by the Oversea Companies and Credit and Financial Institutions (Branch Disclosure) Regulations 1992 Sch 2 paras 1, 3). For the purposes of the Companies Act 1985 Sch 21A para 8(2)(b) (as so added), where the company has more than one branch in a part of Great Britain, a return which gives the branch numbers of two or more such branches is treated as a return in respect of each branch whose number is given: Sch 21A para 8(5) (added by the Oversea Companies and Credit and Financial Institutions (Branch Disclosure) Regulations 1992 Sch 2 paras 1, 3).

1798. Registrar to whom documents to be delivered. References to the registrar, in relation to a limited company which is incorporated outside the United

Kingdom and Gibraltar and has a branch in Great Britain[1], are to be construed in accordance with the following provisions[2].

The documents which a company is required to deliver to the registrar must be delivered:

(1) to the registrar for England and Wales, if required to be delivered in respect of a branch in England and Wales; and

(2) to the registrar for Scotland, if required to be delivered in respect of a branch in Scotland[3].

If a company closes a branch in a part of Great Britain[4], it must forthwith give notice of that fact to the registrar for that part; and from the date on which notice is so given it is no longer obliged to deliver documents to that registrar in respect of that branch[5].

1 Ie a company to which the Companies Act 1985 s 690A (as added) applies (see para 1791 ante), except references in s 699A(2), Sch 21C (as added) (see paras 1817, 1818 post). For the meaning of 'branch' see para 1791 note 2 ante.

2 Ibid s 695A(1) (added by the Oversea Companies and Credit and Financial Institutions (Branch Disclosure) Regulations 1992, SI 1992/3179, reg 3(1), Sch 2 paras 1, 10).

3 Companies Act 1985 s 695A(2) (added by the Oversea Companies and Credit and Financial Institutions (Branch Disclosure) Regulations 1992 Sch 2 paras 1, 10).

4 For these purposes, the reference to closing a branch in either part of Great Britain includes a reference to a branch ceasing to be situated in that part on becoming situated elsewhere: Companies Act 1985 s 695A(4) (added by the Oversea Companies and Credit and Financial Institutions (Branch Disclosure) Regulations 1992 Sch 2 paras 1, 10).

5 Companies Act 1985 s 695A(3) (added by the Oversea Companies and Credit and Financial Institutions (Branch Disclosure) Regulations 1992 Sch 2 paras 1, 10).

1799. Registration of branches. For each limited company which is incorporated outside the United Kingdom and Gibraltar and has a branch in Great Britain[1], the registrar of companies[2] must keep, in such form as he thinks fit, a register of the branches registered[3] by the company[4]. The registrar must allocate to every branch so registered by him a number, which is known as the branch's registered number[5]. Branches' registered numbers must be in such form, consisting of one or more sequences of figures or letters, as the registrar may from time to time determine[6]. Upon adopting a new form of registered number, the registrar may make such changes of existing registered numbers as appear to him necessary[7].

A change of a branch's registered number has effect from the date on which the company is notified by the registrar of the change; but for a period of three years beginning with the date on which that notification is sent by the registrar, the statutory requirement[8] as to the use of the branch's registered number on business letters and order forms is satisfied by the use of either the old number or the new[9].

Where an oversea company, being a limited company which is incorporated outside the United Kingdom and Gibraltar and has a branch in Great Britain[10], files particulars, in any circumstances permitted by the Companies Act 1985, by adopting particulars already filed in respect of another branch or including in one document particulars which are to relate to two or more branches, the registrar must ensure that the particulars concerned become part of the registered particulars of each branch concerned[11].

1 Ie a company to which the Companies Act 1985 s 690A (as added) applies: see para 1791 ante. For the meaning of 'branch' see para 1791 note 2 ante.

2 For the meaning of 'the registrar of companies' see para 1798 ante.

3 Ie under the Companies Act 1985 s 690A(2), Sch 21A para 1 (as added): see para 1792 ante.

4 Ibid s 705A(1) (added by the Oversea Companies and Credit and Financial Institutions (Branch Disclosure) Regulations 1992, SI 1992/3179, reg 3(2)).

5 Companies Act 1985 s 705A(2) (added by the Oversea Companies and Credit and Financial Institutions (Branch Disclosure) Regulations 1992 reg 3(2)).
6 Companies Act 1985 s 705A(3) (added by the Oversea Companies and Credit and Financial Institutions (Branch Disclosure) Regulations 1992 reg 3(2)).
7 Companies Act 1985 s 705A(4) (added by the Oversea Companies and Credit and Financial Institutions (Branch Disclosure) Regulations 1992 reg 3(2)).
8 Ie the requirement of the Companies Act 1985 s 693(2) (as added): see para 1800 post.
9 Ibid s 705A(5) (added by the Oversea Companies and Credit and Financial Institutions (Branch Disclosure) Regulations 1992 reg 3(2)).
10 See note 1 supra.
11 Companies Act 1985 s 705A(6) (added by the Oversea Companies and Credit and Financial Institutions (Branch Disclosure) Regulations 1992 reg 3(2)).

1800. Obligation to state company's name etc. Every limited company which is incorporated outside the United Kingdom and Gibraltar and has a branch in Great Britain[1] must, in the case of each branch of the company registered by it[2], cause the following particulars to be stated in legible characters in all letter paper and order forms used in carrying on the business of the branch:

(1) the place of registration of the branch; and
(2) the registered number of the branch[3].

Every such company, which is not incorporated in a member State and which is required by the law of the country in which it is incorporated to be registered, must, in the case of each branch of the company registered by it, cause the following particulars to be stated in legible characters in all letter paper and order forms used in carrying on the business of the branch:

(a) the identity of the registry in which the company is registered in its country of incorporation; and
(b) the number with which it is registered[4].

Every such company which is not incorporated in a member State must, in the case of each branch of the company registered by it, cause the following particulars to be stated in legible characters in all letter paper and order forms used in carrying on the business of the branch:

(i) the legal form of the company;
(ii) the location of its head office; and
(iii) if applicable, the fact that it is being wound up[5].

1 Ie a company to which the Companies Act 1985 s 690A (as added) applies: see para 1791 ante. For the meaning of 'branch' see para 1791 note 2 ante.
2 Ie under ibid s 690A(2), Sch 21A para 1 (as added): see para 1792 ante.
3 Ibid s 693(2) (added by the Oversea Companies and Credit and Financial Institutions (Branch Disclosure) Regulations 1992, SI 1992/3179, reg 3(1), Sch 2 paras 1, 6).
4 Companies Act 1985 s 693(3) (added by the Oversea Companies and Credit and Financial Institutions (Branch Disclosure) Regulations 1992 Sch 2 paras 1, 6).
5 Companies Act 1985 s 693(4) (added by the Oversea Companies and Credit and Financial Institutions (Branch Disclosure) Regulations 1992 Sch 2 paras 1, 6).

1801. Change in registration regime. Where a company ceases to be a limited company which is incorporated outside the United Kingdom and Gibraltar and has a branch in Great Britain[1] and, immediately after ceasing to be such a company:

(1) continues to have in Great Britain a place of business[2] which it had immediately before ceasing to be such a company; and

(2) does not have a branch in Northern Ireland,

it is treated[3] as having established the place of business on the date when it ceased to be such a company[4].

Where a limited company incorporated outside the United Kingdom and Gibraltar:

(a) ceases to have a branch in Northern Ireland; and

(b) both immediately before and immediately after ceasing to do so, has a place of business, but not a branch, in Great Britain,

it is treated[5] as having established the place of business on the date when it ceased to have a branch in Northern Ireland[6].

Where a company:

(i) becomes a limited company which is incorporated outside the United Kingdom and Gibraltar and has a branch in Great Britain;

(ii) immediately after becoming such a company, has in a part of Great Britain an established place of business but no branch; and

(iii) immediately before becoming such a company, had an established place of business in that part,

the statutory provisions relating to registration[7] continue to apply[8] to the company, in relation to that part, until such time as it gives notice to the registrar for that part that it is a limited company which is incorporated outside the United Kingdom and Gibraltar and has a branch in Great Britain[9].

1 Ie a company to which the Companies Act 1985 s 690A (as added) applies: see para 1791 ante.

2 For the meaning of 'place of business' see para 1790 note 2 ante.

3 Ie for the purposes of the Companies Act 1985 s 691 (as amended): see paras 1804, 1805 post.

4 Ibid s 692A(1) (added by the Oversea Companies and Credit and Financial Institutions (Branch Disclosure) Regulations 1992, SI 1992/3179, reg 3(1), Sch 2 paras 1, 4). Where a company which becomes a company to which the Companies Act 1985 s 690A (as added) applies was, immediately before becoming such a company ('the relevant time'), a company to which s 691 (as amended) applies, the company need not include the particulars specified in s 690A(2), Sch 21A para 2(1)(d) (as added) (see para 1793 ante) in the first return to be delivered under Sch 21A para 1(1) (as added) (see para 1792 ante) to the registrar of companies for a part of Great Britain if at the relevant time (1) it had an established place of business in that part; (2) it had complied with its obligations under s 691(1)(b)(i) (see para 1804 post); and (3) it had no outstanding obligation to make a return to the registrar for that part under s 692(1), so far as concerns any alteration of the kind mentioned in s 692(1)(b) (as substituted) (see para 1805 post), and if it states in the return that the particulars have been previously filed in respect of a place of business of the company in that part, giving the company's registered number: s 692A(4), Sch 21B para 1(1),(2) (added by the Oversea Companies and Credit and Financial Institutions (Branch Disclosure) Regulations 1992 Sch 2 paras 1, 5).

   The company is not required to deliver the documents mentioned in the Companies Act 1985 Sch 21A para 5 (as added) (see para 1796 ante) with the first return to be delivered under Sch 21A para 1(1) (as added) for a part of Great Britain if at the relevant time (a) it had an established place of business in that part; (b) it had delivered the documents mentioned in s 691(1)(a) to the registrar for that part; and (c) it had no outstanding obligation to make a return to that registrar under s 692(1), so far as concerns any alteration in any of the documents mentioned in s 692(1)(a), and, if it states in the return that the documents have been previously filed in respect of a place of business of the company in that part, giving the company's registered number: Sch 21B para 1(3) (added by the Oversea Companies and Credit and Financial Institutions (Branch Disclosure) Regulations 1992 Sch 2 paras 1, 5).

   Where a company which becomes a company to which the Companies Act 1985 s 691 (as amended) applies was, immediately before becoming such a company ('the relevant time'), a company to which s 690A (as added) applies, the company is not required to deliver the documents mentioned in s 691(1)(a) to the registrar for a part of Great Britain if at the relevant time (i) it had a branch in that part; (ii) the documents mentioned in Sch 21A para 5 (as added) were included in the material registered in respect of the branch; and (iii) it had no outstanding obligation to make a return to the registrar for that part under Sch 21A para 7 (as added), so far as concerns any alteration in any of the documents mentioned in Sch 21A para 7(1)(a) (as added), and, if it states in the return that the documents have been previously filed in respect of a branch of the company, giving the branch's registered number: Sch 21B para 2(1),(2) (added by the Oversea Companies and Credit and Financial Institutions (Branch

Disclosure) Regulations 1992 Sch 2 paras 1, 5). The company need not include the particulars mentioned in the Companies Act 1985 s 691(1)(b)(i) in the return to be delivered under s 691(1)(b) to the registrar for a part of Great Britain if at the relevant time (A) it had a branch in that part; (B) it had complied with its obligations under Sch 21A para 1(1)(a) (as added) in respect of the branch, so far as the particulars required by Sch 21A para 2(1)(d) (as added) are concerned; and (C) it had no outstanding obligation to make a return to the registrar for that part under Sch 21A para 7 (as added), so far as concerns any alteration in any of the particulars required by Sch 21A para 2(1)(d) (as added), and, if it states in the return that the particulars have been previously filed in respect of a branch of the company, giving the branch's registered number: Sch 21B para 2(3) (added by the Oversea Companies and Credit and Financial Institutions (Branch Disclosure) Regulations 1992 Sch 2 paras 1, 5). Where the Companies Act 1985 Sch 21B para 2(3) (as so added) applies, the reference in s 692(1)(b) to the list of the directors and secretary is to be construed as a reference to the list contained in the return under Sch 21A para 1(1) (as added) with any alteration in respect of which a return under Sch 21A para 7(1) (as added) has been made: Sch 21B para 3(4) (added by the Oversea Companies and Credit and Financial Institutions (Branch Disclosure) Regulations 1992 Sch 2 paras 1, 5).

5 See note 3 supra.

6 Companies Act 1985 s 692A(2) (added by the Oversea Companies and Credit and Financial Institutions (Branch Disclosure) Regulations 1992 Sch 2 paras 1, 4).

7 Ie the Companies Act 1985 s 691 (as amended) and s 692 (see para 1806 ante).

8 Ie notwithstanding ibid s 690B (as added): see para 1803 post.

9 Ibid s 692A(3) (added by the Oversea Companies and Credit and Financial Institutions (Branch Disclosure) Regulations 1992 Sch 2 paras 1, 4).

1802. Penalties. If an oversea company fails to comply with its obligation to deliver documents to the registrar of companies or to register a branch[1], the company, and every officer or agent of the company who knowingly and wilfully authorises or permits the default, is liable on summary conviction to a fine not exceeding one-fifth of level 5 on the standard scale and, on conviction after continued contravention, to a daily default fine not exceeding £100[2].

If an oversea company fails to comply with its obligation to state its name and other particulars in company documents[3], the company, and every officer or agent of the company who knowingly and wilfully authorises or permits the default, is liable on summary conviction to a fine not exceeding one-fifth of the statutory maximum and, on conviction after continued contravention in the case of a continuing offence, to a daily default fine not exceeding one-fiftieth of the statutory maximum[4].

1 Ie the Companies Act 1985 s 695A (as added) (see para 1798 ante) or s 690A(2), Sch 21A (as added) (see para 1792 et seq ante).

2 Ibid s 697(3) (added by the Oversea Companies and Credit and Financial Institutions (Branch Disclosure) Regulations 1992, SI 1992/3179, reg 3(1), Sch 2 paras 1, 12); Companies Act 1985 s 730, Sch 24 (amended by the Oversea Companies and Credit and Financial Institutions (Branch Disclosure) Regulations 1992 reg 4, Sch 3 paras 3, 9(1),(2)). For the meaning of 'daily default fine' see para 1161 ante; and for the meaning of 'the standard scale' see CRIMINAL LAW vol 11(2) (Reissue) para 808.

3 Ie fails to comply with the Companies Act 1985 s 693(2)-(4) (as added): see para 1800 ante.

4 Ibid ss 697(1), 730, Sch 24. For the meaning of 'the statutory maximum' see para 1161 ante.

(c) *Companies other than those incorporated outside the United Kingdom and Gibraltar and having a Branch in the United Kingdom*

1803. Application of the statutory provisions. The following provisions[1] do not apply to a limited company which is incorporated outside the United Kingdom and Gibraltar and has a branch[2] in the United Kingdom[3].

1 Ie the Companies Act 1985 s 691 (as amended) (see paras 1804, 1805 post) and s 692 (see para 1806 post).

2 For the meaning of 'branch' see para 1791 note 2 ante.

3 Companies Act 1985 s 690B (added by the Oversea Companies and Credit and Financial Institutions (Branch Disclosure) Regulations 1992, SI 1992/3179, reg 3(1), Sch 2 paras 1, 2).

1804. Registration of particulars. When a company incorporated outside Great Britain[1] establishes a place of business[2] in Great Britain, it must, within one month of doing so, deliver to the registrar of companies[3] for registration:

(1) a certified[4] copy of its charter, statutes or memorandum and articles or other instrument constituting or defining its constitution, and, if the instrument is not written in the English language, a certified translation of it[5]; and

(2) a return in the prescribed form[6] containing:

    (a) a list of its directors[7] and secretary[8], containing certain specified particulars[9];

    (b) a list of the names and addresses of some one or more persons resident in Great Britain authorised to accept on its behalf service of process and any notices required to be served on the company[10];

    (c) a list of the documents delivered in compliance with head (1) above[11]; and

    (d) a statutory declaration (made by a director or secretary of the company, or by any person whose name and address are given in the list required by head (2)(b) above), stating the date on which the company's place of business in Great Britain was established[12].

Failure to register such particulars does not render a contract made by the company ipso facto illegal[13].

1 As to the companies to which these provisions apply see para 1803 ante.
2 For the meaning of 'place of business' see para 1790 note 2 ante.
3 For the meaning of 'registrar of companies' see para 1807 note 2 post.
4 For these purposes, 'certified' means certified in the prescribed manner to be a true copy or a correct translation: Companies Act 1985 s 698(1) (renumbered by the Oversea Companies and Credit and Financial Institutions (Branch Disclosure) Regulations 1992, SI 1992/3179, reg 3(1), Sch 2 para 13(1),(2)). For the prescribed manner of certification see para 90 note 3 ante. For the purposes of the Companies Act 1985 s 691(1)(a), a copy of an instrument constituting or defining a company's constitution must be certified, in the place of incorporation of the company, to be a true copy by (1) an official of the Government to whose custody the original is committed; or (2) a notary public; or (3) an officer of the company on oath taken before (a) a person having authority in that place to administer an oath; or (b) any of the British officials mentioned in the Commissioners for Oaths Act 1889 s 6 (as amended) (see para 818 note 7 ante): Companies (Forms) Regulations 1985, SI 1985/854, reg 7(4).
5 Companies Act 1985 s 691(1)(a). As to the penalty for contravention see para 1809 post.
6 For the prescribed form of return see the Companies (Forms) (Amendement) Regulations 1992, SI 1992/3006, reg 4(1), Sch 2, Form 691.
7 For the meaning of 'director' see para 1793 note 5 ante.
8 For the meaning of 'secretary' see para 1793 note 6 ante.
9 Companies Act 1985 s 691(1)(b)(i). As to the particulars see para 1805 post.
10 Ibid s 691(1)(b)(ii). As to service of process see para 1814 post. No fee is now prescribed.
11 Ibid s 691(1)(b)(iii).
12 Ibid s 691(1)(b)(iv).
13 *Curragh Investments Ltd v Cook* [1974] 3 All ER 658, [1974] 1 WLR 1559.

1805. Particulars about the company. The particulars about the company to be contained in the return to the registrar of companies[1] are with respect to each director[2]:

(1) in the case of an individual:

    (a) his name[3];

    (b) any former name[4];

    (c) his usual residential address;

    (d) his nationality;

(e) his business occupation, if any;

(f) if he has no business occupation but holds other directorships, particulars of them; and

(g) his date of birth;

(2) in the case of a corporation or Scottish firm, its corporate or firm name and registered or principal office[5].

The particulars about the company to be contained in the return to the registrar of companies are with respect to the secretary[6] (or, where there are joint secretaries, with respect to each of them):

(i) in the case of an individual, his name, any former name and his usual residential address;

(ii) in the case of a corporation or Scottish firm, its corporate or firm name and registered or principal office[7].

Where all the partners in a firm are joint secretaries of the company, the name and principal office of the firm may be stated instead of the particulars required by head (i) above[7].

1 Ie under the Companies Act 1985 s 691(1): see para 1804 ante.
2 For the meaning of 'director' see para 1793 note 5 ante.
3 For these purposes, 'name' means a person's Christian name (or other forename) and surname, except that, in the case of a peer, or an individual usually known by a title, the title may be stated instead of his Christian name (or other forename) and surname, or in addition to either or both of them: Companies Act 1985 s 691(4)(a) (substituted by the Companies Act 1989 s 145, Sch 19 para 6).
4 For these purposes, the reference to a former name does not include: (1) in the case of a peer, or an individual normally known by a British title, the name by which he was known previous to the adoption of or succession to the title; or (2) in the case of any person, a former name which was changed or disused before he attained the age of 18 years or which has been changed or disused for 20 years or more; (3) in the case of a married woman, the name by which she was known previous to the marriage: Companies Act 1985 s 691(4)(b) (substituted by the Companies Act 1989 Sch 19 para 6).
5 Companies Act 1985 s 691(2) (substituted by the Companies Act 1989 Sch 19 para 6).
6 For the meaning of 'secretary' see para 1793 note 6 ante.
7 Companies Act 1985 s 691(3) (substituted by the Companies Act 1989 Sch 19 para 6).

1806. Registration of altered particulars. If any alteration is made in:

(1) the charter, statutes or memorandum and articles of an oversea company[1] or other instrument constituting or defining its constitution; or

(2) the directors[2] or secretary[3] of an oversea company or the particulars contained in the list of directors and secretary; or

(3) the names or addresses of the persons authorised to accept service on behalf of an oversea company[4],

the company must, within the time specified below, deliver to the registrar of companies[5] for registration a return containing the prescribed particulars[6] of the alteration[7]. If any change is made in the corporate name of an oversea company, the company must, within the time specified below, deliver to the registrar of companies for registration a return containing the prescribed particulars[8] of the change[9].

The time for delivery of the above returns is, in the case of an alteration in the names or addresses of the persons authorised to accept service on behalf of the company, 21 days after the making of the alteration, and in all other cases, 21 days after the date on which notice of the alteration or change in question could have been received in Great Britain in due course of post, if dispatched with due diligence[10].

1 For the meaning of 'oversea company' see para 1790 ante. As to the companies to which these provisions apply see para 1803 ante.

2 For the meaning of 'director' see para 1793 note 5 ante.

3 For the meaning of 'secretary' see para 1793 note 6 ante.

4 As to the registration of such documents or documents containing such information see paras 1804, 1805 ante.

5 For the meaning of 'registrar of companies' see para 1807 note 2 post.

6 For the prescribed forms of particulars see the Companies (Forms) Regulations 1985, SI 1985/854, reg 4(1), Sch 3, Form 692(1)(a) (in respect of text head (1) supra), Form 692(1)(b) (in respect of text head (2) supra), and Form 692(1)(c) (in respect of text head (3) supra).

7 Companies Act 1985 s 692(1). No fee is now payable on registration.

8 For the prescribed form of return see the Companies (Forms) Regulations 1985 Sch 3, Form 692(2).

9 Companies Act 1985 s 692(2).

10 Ibid s 692(3). As to the penalty for contravention see para 1809 post.

1807. Documents to be filed at registration office. Any document which an oversea company[1] is required to deliver to the registrar of companies[2] must be delivered to the registrar at the registration office in England and Wales or Scotland, according to where the company has established a place of business[3]. If the company has established a place of business both in England and Wales and in Scotland, the document must be delivered at the registration office both in England and Wales and in Scotland[4].

1 Ie an oversea company to which the Companies Act 1985 s 691 (as amended) applies: see paras 1804, 1805 ante.

2 References in ibid Pt XXIII (ss 690A–703R) (as amended) (see para 1791 et seq ante and para 1808 et seq post), except references in s 699A(2), Sch 21C (as added) (see paras 1817, 1818 post) to the registrar of companies, in relation to a company to which s 691 (as amended) applies, are to be construed in accordance with s 696(1),(2) (as amended): s 696(3) (amended by the Oversea Companies and Credit and Financial Institutions (Branch Disclosure) Regulations 1992, SI 1992/3179, reg 3(1), Sch 2 para 11(b), Sch 3 paras 3, 4).

3 Companies Act 1985 s 696(1) (amended by the Oversea Companies and Credit and Financial Institutions (Branch Disclosure) Regulations 1992 Sch 2 para 11(a)). The Companies Act 1985 s 696 (as amended) is substituted from a day to be appointed by the Companies Act 1989 s 145, Sch 19 para 13 (amended by the Oversea Companies and Credit and Financial Institutions (Branch Disclosure) Regulations 1992 reg 4, Sch 3 para 17). At the date at which this volume states the law no such day had been appointed. For the meaning of 'place of business' see para 1790 note 2 ante.

4 Companies Act 1985 s 696(2). As to the penalty for contravention see para 1809 post.

1808. Notice that company no longer has place of business. If an oversea company[1] ceases to have a place of business[2] in either part of Great Britain, it must forthwith give notice of that fact to the registrar of companies[3] for that part; and, as from the date on which notice is so given, the company's obligation to deliver any document to the registrar ceases[4].

1 Ie an oversea company to which the Companies Act 1985 s 691 (as amended) applies: see paras 1804, 1805 ante.

2 For the meaning of 'place of business' see para 1790 note 2 ante.

3 For the meaning of 'the registrar of companies' see para 1807 note 2 ante.

4 Companies Act 1985 s 696(4) (amended by the Oversea Companies and Credit and Financial Institutions (Branch Disclosure) Regulations 1992, SI 1992/3179, reg 3(1), Sch 2 para 11(c)). As to the penalty for non-compliance see para 1809 post.

1809. Penalties. If an oversea company[1] fails to comply with any of the above statutory requirements[2], the company, and every officer or agent of the company who knowingly and wilfully authorises or permits the default, is liable on summary conviction to a fine not exceeding one-fifth of the statutory maximum and, on conviction after continued contravention in the case of a continuing offence, to a daily default fine not exceeding one-fiftieth of the statutory maximum[3].

1 For the meaning of 'oversea company' see para 1790 ante.
2 Ie the Companies Act 1985 s 691 (as amended) (see paras 1804, 1805 ante), s 692 (see para 1806 ante) and s 696 (as amended) (see paras 1807, 1808 ante).
3 Ibid ss 697(1), 730, Sch 24. For the meaning of 'the statutory maximum' and 'daily default fine' see para 1161 ante.

B. GENERAL OBLIGATIONS

1810. Regulation of names. If it appears to the Secretary of State that the corporate name of an oversea company[1] is a name by which the company, had it been formed under the Companies Act 1985, would on the relevant date[2] have been precluded from being registered by virtue of the statutory prohibitions[3], the Secretary of State may serve a notice on the company, stating why the name would not have been registered[4].

If the corporate name of an oversea company is in the Secretary of State's opinion too like a name appearing on the relevant date in the registrar of companies'[5] index of company and corporate names[6] or which should have appeared in that index on that date, or is the same as a name which should have so appeared, the Secretary of State may serve a notice on the company specifying the name in the index which the company's name is too like or which is the same as the company's name[7].

No notice may, however, be served on a company under the above provisions later than 12 months after the relevant date[8].

An oversea company on which a notice is so served[9]:

(1) may deliver to the registrar of companies for registration a statement in the prescribed form[10] specifying a name approved by the Secretary of State other than its corporate name under which it proposes to carry on business in Great Britain; and

(2) may, after that name has been registered, at any time deliver to the registrar for registration a statement in the prescribed form[10] specifying a name approved by the Secretary of State (other than its corporate name) in substitution for the name previously registered[11].

The name by which an oversea company is for the time being so registered is, for all purposes of the law applying in Great Britain (including the Companies Act 1985 and the Business Names Act 1985) deemed to be the company's corporate name[12]. This does not, however, affect references to the corporate name in these provisions, or any rights or obligations of the company, or render defective any legal proceedings by or against the company; and any legal proceedings that might have been continued or commenced against the company by its corporate name or its name previously registered under these provisions may be continued or commenced against it by its name for the time being so registered[13].

An oversea company on which a notice is so served[14] must not at any time after the expiration of two months from the service of that notice (or such longer period as may be specified in that notice) carry on business in Great Britain under its corporate name; but nothing in this provision, or in that imposing penalties for its contravention, invalidates any transaction entered into by the company[15].

The Secretary of State may withdraw a notice so served at any time before the end of the period for compliance[16]; and the prohibition on carrying on business under its corporate name[17] does not apply to a company served with a notice which has been withdrawn[18].

1 For the meaning of 'oversea company' see para 1790 ante.
2 For these purposes, the relevant date, in relation to a company, is the date on which it has complied with the Companies Act 1985 s 690A(2), Sch 21A para 1 (as added) (see para 1792 ante) or s 691(1) (see para 1804 ante) or, if there is more than one such date, the first date on which it has complied with Sch 21A para 1 (as added) or s 691(1), as the case may be, since becoming an oversea company: s 694(3A) (added by the Oversea Companies and Credit and Financial Institutions (Branch Disclosure) Regulations 1992, SI 1992/3179, reg 3(1), Sch 2 para 7(1),(4)). Where, however, the company's corporate name has changed since the date so ascertained, the relevant date is the date on which the company has, in respect of the change or, if more than one, the latest change, complied with the Companies Act 1985 Sch 21A para 7(1) (as added) (see para 1797 ante) or s 692(2) (see para 1806 ante), as the case may be: s 694(3B) (added by the Oversea Companies and Credit and Financial Institutions (Branch Disclosure) Regulations 1992 Sch 2 para 7(1),(4)).
3 Ie those contained in the Companies Act 1985 s 26: see para 156 ante. Such registration might have been precluded either because the name fell within s 26(1), or, if it fell within s 26(2), because the Secretary of State would not approve the company being registered with that name: see para 156 ante.
4 Ibid s 694(1) (amended by the Oversea Companies and Credit and Financial Institutions (Branch Disclosure) Regulations 1992 Sch 2 para 7(1),(2)).
5 For the meaning of 'the registrar of companies' see paras 1798, 1807 note 2 ante.
6 Ie under the Companies Act 1985 s 714 (as amended): see para 72 ante.
7 Ibid s 694(2).
8 Ibid s 694(3) (amended by the Oversea Companies and Credit and Financial Institutions (Branch Disclosure) Regulations 1992 Sch 2 para 7(1),(3)).
9 Ie under the Companies Act 1985 s 694(1) (as amended) or s 694(2): see supra.
10 For the prescribed forms of statement see the Companies (Forms) (Amendment) Regulations 1992, SI 1992/3006, reg 4(1), Sch 2, Form 694(4)(a) (name, other than corporate name, under which business is proposed to be carried on), Form 694(4)(b) (name, other than corporate name, under which business is proposed to be carried on in substitution for a name previously registered).
11 Companies Act 1985 s 694(4).
12 Ibid s 694(5). As to business names see para 166 et seq ante.
13 Ibid s 694(5)(a),(b).
14 See note 9 supra.
15 Companies Act 1985 s 694(6). As to the penalty for non-compliance see para 1812 post.
16 Ie the period mentioned in ibid s 694(6): see supra.
17 Ie that contained in ibid s 694(6): see supra.
18 Ibid s 694(7).

1811. Obligation to state company's name and other particulars. Every oversea company[1] must:

(1) in every prospectus[2] inviting subscriptions for its shares or debentures in Great Britain, state the country in which the company is incorporated[3];

(2) conspicuously exhibit on every place where it carries on business in Great Britain the name of the company and the country in which it is incorporated[4];

(3) cause the company's name and the country in which it is incorporated to be stated in legible characters in all its bill-heads and letter paper, and in all notices and other official publications of the company[5]; and

(4) if the liability of the members of the company is limited, cause notice of that fact to be stated in legible characters in every such prospectus as above mentioned and in all bill-heads, letter paper, notices and other official publications of the company in Great Britain, and to be affixed on every place where it carries on its business[6].

1 For the meaning of 'oversea company' see para 1790 ante.
2 For the meaning of 'prospectus' see para 105 note 2 ante.
3 Companies Act 1985 s 693(1)(a) (renumbered by the Oversea Companies and Credit and Financial Institutions (Branch Disclosure) Regulations 1992, SI 1992/3179, reg 3(1), Sch 2 para 6). The

Companies Act 1985 s 693(1)(a) (as so renumbered) and the words 'in every such prospectus as above mentioned and' in s 693(1)(d) (as renumbered: see note 6 infra) are repealed by the Financial Services Act 1986 s 212(3), Sch 17 Pt I to the following extent:
  (1) in so far as they apply in relation to any investment which is listed or the subject of an application for listing under Pt IV (ss 142-156B (as amended): see para 281 et seq ante) (Financial Services Act 1986 (Commencement No 3) Order 1986, SI 1986/2246, art 5, Sch 4);
  (2) in so far as they apply to a prospectus offering for subscription, or to any form of application for, units in a body corporate which is a recognised scheme (Financial Services Act 1986 (Commencement) (No 8) Order 1988, SI 1988/740, art 2, Schedule).
4 Companies Act 1985 s 693(1)(b) (renumbered by the Oversea Companies and Credit and Financial Institutions (Branch Disclosure) Regulations 1992 Sch 2 para 6). See also note 3 supra. As to the penalty for contravention see para 1812 post.
5 Companies Act 1985 s 693(1)(c) (renumbered by the Oversea Companies and Credit and Financial Institutions (Branch Disclosure) Regulations 1992 Sch 2 para 6). As to the penalty for contravention see para 1812 post.
6 Companies Act 1985 s 693(1)(d) (renumbered by the Oversea Companies and Credit and Financial Institutions (Branch Disclosure) Regulations 1992 Sch 2 para 6). As to the penalty for contravention see para 1812 post.

1812. Penalties. If an oversea company[1] carries on business in breach of the statutory requirements relating to its name[2], the company, and every officer or agent of the company who knowingly and wilfully authorises or permits the default, is liable on indictment to a fine, or on summary conviction to a fine not exceeding the statutory maximum and, on conviction after continued contravention in the case of a continuing offence, to a daily default fine not exceeding one-tenth of the statutory maximum[3].

If an oversea company fails to comply with its obligation to state its name and other particulars in company documents[4], the company, and every officer or agent of the company who knowingly and wilfully authorises or permits the default, is liable on summary conviction to a fine not exceeding one-fifth of the statutory maximum and, on conviction after continued contravention in the case of a continuing offence, to a daily default fine not exceeding one-fiftieth of the statutory maximum[5].

1 For the meaning of 'oversea company' see para 1790 ante.
2 Ie contravenes the Companies Act 1985 s 694(6) (as amended): see para 1810 ante.
3 Ibid ss 697(2), 730, Sch 24. For the meaning of 'the statutory maximum' and 'daily default fine' see para 1161 ante.
4 Ie fails to comply with ibid s 693(1) (as renumbered): see para 1811 ante.
5 Ibid ss 697(1), 730, Sch 24.

C. SERVICE OF DOCUMENTS

1813. Companies incorporated outside the United Kingdom and Gibraltar and having a branch in Great Britain. Any process or notice required to be served on a limited company which is incorporated outside the United Kingdom and Gibraltar and has a branch in Great Britain[1] in respect of the carrying on of the business of a branch registered by it[2] is sufficiently served if:
  (1) addressed to any person whose name has, in respect of the branch, been delivered to the registrar of companies[3] as a person authorised to accept service of process and of any notices to be served on the company in respect of the business of the branch[4]; and
  (2) left at or sent by post to the address for that person which has been so delivered[5].
Where:
  (a) such a company makes default, in respect of a branch, in delivering to the registrar the required particulars[6]; or

(b) all the persons whose names have, in respect of a branch, been delivered to the registrar as persons authorised to accept service of process and of any notices to be served on the company in respect of the business of the branch are dead or have ceased to reside in Great Britain, or refuse to accept service on the company's behalf, or for any reason cannot be served,

a document may be served on the company in respect of the carrying on of the business of the branch by leaving it at, or sending it by post to, any place of business[7] established by the company in Great Britain[8].

Where such a company has more than one branch in Great Britain, any notice or process required to be served on the company which is not required to be served in respect of the carrying on of the business of one branch rather than another is treated for these purposes as required to be served in respect of the carrying on of the business of each of its branches[9].

1 Ie a company to which the Companies Act 1985 s 690A (as added) applies: see para 1791 ante. For the meaning of 'branch' see para 1791 note 2 ante.
2 Ie under ibid s 690A(2), Sch 21A para 1 (as added): see para 1792 ante.
3 For the meaning of 'the registrar of companies' see para 1798 ante.
4 Ie a person falling within the Companies Act 1985 Sch 21A para 3(e) (as added): see para 1794 head (5) ante.
5 Ibid s 694A(1),(2) (added by the Oversea Companies and Credit and Financial Institutions (Branch Disclosure) Regulations 1992, SI 1992/3179, reg 3(1), Sch 2 paras 1, 8).
6 Ie the particulars mentioned in the Companies Act 1985 Sch 21A para 3(e) (as added).
7 For the meaning of 'place of business' see para 1790 note 2 ante.
8 Companies Act 1985 s 694A(1),(3) (added by the Oversea Companies and Credit and Financial Institutions (Branch Disclosure) Regulations 1992 Sch 2 paras 1, 8).
9 Companies Act 1985 s 694A(1),(4) (added by the Oversea Companies and Credit and Financial Institutions (Branch Disclosure) Regulations 1992 Sch 2 paras 1, 8).

1814. Other oversea companies. Any process or notice required to be served on an oversea company[1] is sufficiently served if addressed to any person whose name has been delivered to the registrar of companies[2] as authorised to accept service[3] and left at or sent by post[4] to the address which has been so delivered[5]. Where, however, such a company has made default in delivering to the registrar the name and address of a person resident in Great Britain who is authorised to accept on behalf of the company service of process or notices[6], or if at any time all the persons whose names and addresses have been so delivered are dead or have ceased so to reside or refuse to accept service on the company's behalf[7], or for any reason cannot be served, a document may be served on the company by leaving it at, or sending it by post to, any place of business[8] established by the company in Great Britain[9].

Where the company itself is the plaintiff, the writ should state that the company is a foreign corporation registered in England and Wales under the Companies Act 1985, and the registered name and address of the person to be served should be given[10].

1 Ie an oversea company to which the Companies Act 1985 s 691 (as amended) applies: see paras 1804, 1805 ante.
2 For the meaning of 'the registrar of companies' see para 1807 note 2 ante.
3 See para 1804 ante.
4 See para 1778 note 1 ante.
5 Companies Act 1985 s 695(1) (amended by the Oversea Companies and Credit and Financial Institutions (Branch Disclosure) Regulations 1992, SI 1992/3179, reg 3(1), Sch 2 Pt I paras 1, 9). See also *Boocock v Hilton International Co* [1993] 4 All ER 19, [1993] 1 WLR 1065, CA (the Companies Act 1985 s 695 (as amended) was held to be a complete code for the service of documents on an oversea company; but in this instance the court exercised its discretion under RSC Ord 2 r 1 and treated the non-compliance with the Companies Act 1985 s 695 as an irregularity).

6 See para 1804 ante.

7 Under the Companies (Consolidation) Act 1908 (repealed) it was held that service on a person whose name and address had been given was good service, even where he refused to accept it on the ground that his authority to do so had ceased: *Employers' Liability Assurance Corpn v Sedgwick, Collins & Co* [1927] AC 95, HL. In view of the wording of the Companies Act 1985 s 695(2), it is doubtful how far this case is now good law.

8 For the meaning of 'place of business' see para 1790 note 2 ante.

9 Companies Act 1985 s 695(2); *Deverall v Grant Advertising Inc* [1955] Ch 111, [1954] 3 All ER 389, CA. Service of a writ may be effected on a foreign company within the jurisdiction only if the company is carrying on business here, in which case service should be effected under the above provisions and not those of the Rules of the Supreme Court: *The Theodohos* [1977] 2 Lloyds Rep 428.

10 See the Supreme Court Practice 1995 vol 2 App A, Form 1 note (f).

D. DELIVERY OF ACCOUNTS AND REPORTS

(A) *In general*

1815. In general. The obligation to deliver accounts and reports depends upon whether:

(1) the company is a credit or financial institution incorporated or otherwise formed outside the United Kingdom and Gibraltar, having its head office outside the United Kingdom and Gibraltar and a branch in Great Britain[1];

(2) the company is incorporated outside the United Kingdom and Gibraltar with a branch in Great Britain, but not being an institution to which head (1) above applies[2]; or

(3) the company is a company other than an institution to which head (1) above applies or a limited company incorporated outside the United Kingdom and Gibraltar with a branch in the United Kingdom[3].

1 See paras 1816–1818 post.
2 See paras 1819–1821 post.
3 See paras 1822–1826 post.

(B) *Credit and Financial Institutions*

1816. Credit and financial institutions. The following provisions[1] apply to any credit[2] or financial[3] institution which is incorporated or otherwise formed outside the United Kingdom and Gibraltar, whose head office is outside the United Kingdom and Gibraltar and which has a branch[4] in Great Britain[5].

1 Ie the Companies Act 1985 s 699A(2), Sch 21C (as added): see paras 1817, 1818 post.

2 For these purposes, 'credit institution' means a credit institution as defined in EC Council Directive 77/780 (OJ L322, 17.12.77, p 30) art 1 (see BANKING), that is to say an undertaking whose business is to receive deposits or other repayable funds from the public and to grant credits for its own account: Companies Act 1985 s 699A(3) (added by the Oversea Companies and Credit and Financial Institutions (Branch Disclosure) Regulations 1992, SI 1992/3179, reg 2(3)). 'Undertaking' has the same meaning as in the Companies Act 1985 Pt VII (ss 221–262A (as amended): see para 806 note 5 ante): s 699A(3) (as so added).

3 For these purposes, 'financial institution' means a financial institution within the meaning of EC Council Directive 89/117 (OJ L44, 16.2.89, p 40) art 1 (see BANKING): Companies Act 1985 s 699A(3) (as added: see note 2 supra).

4 For these purposes, 'branch', in relation to a credit or financial institution, means a place of business which forms a legally dependent part of the institution and which conducts directly all or some of the operations inherent in its business: ibid s 699A(3) (as added: see note 2 supra).

5 Ibid s 699A(1) (added by the Oversea Companies and Credit and Financial Institutions (Branch Disclosure) Regulations 1992 reg 2(1)).

1817. Institutions required to prepare accounts under parent law. The following provisions apply to any institution[1] which is required by its parent law[2] to prepare and have audited accounts for its financial periods[3] and whose only or principal branch[4] within the United Kingdom is in Great Britain[5].

Such an institution must, within one month of becoming such an institution, deliver to the registrar of companies for registration:

(1) copies of the latest accounting documents[6] of the institution prepared in accordance with its parent law to have been disclosed[7] before the end of the period allowed for compliance with this provision or, if earlier, the date of compliance with it; and

(2) if any of the documents mentioned in head (1) above is not written in the English language, a translation of it into English, certified in the prescribed manner[8] to be a correct translation[9].

Such an institution must deliver to the registrar for registration:

(a) copies of all the accounting documents of the institution prepared in accordance with its parent law which are disclosed on or after the end of the period allowed for compliance or, if earlier, the date on which it complies with the above provision[10]; and

(b) if any of the documents mentioned in head (a) above is not written in the English language, a translation of it into English, certified in the prescribed manner[11] to be a correct translation[12].

The period allowed for delivery, in relation to a document required to be so delivered[13], is three months from the date on which the document is first disclosed[14].

Where an institution's parent law permits it to discharge its obligation with respect to the disclosure of accounting documents by disclosing documents in a modified form, it may discharge its obligation under the above provisions[15] by delivering copies of documents modified as permitted by that law[16].

Neither of the above provisions[17] requires an institution to deliver documents to the registrar if at the end of the period allowed for compliance:

(i) it is not required by its parent law to register them;

(ii) they are made available for inspection at each branch of the institution in Great Britain; and

(iii) copies of them are available on request at a cost not exceeding the cost of supplying them[18].

Where, however, an institution is not so required to deliver documents and any of the conditions specified in heads (i) to (iii) above ceases to be met, the institution must deliver the documents to the registrar for registration within seven days of the condition ceasing to be met[19].

The documents which an institution is required to deliver to the registrar under these provisions must be delivered:

(A) to the registrar for England and Wales if the institution's only branch, or, if it has more than one, its principal branch within the United Kingdom, is in England and Wales; or

(B) to the registrar for Scotland if the institution's only branch, or, if it has more than one, its principal branch within the United Kingdom is in Scotland[20].

If an institution fails to comply with the above provisions[21] before the end of the period allowed for compliance, it, and every person who immediately before the end of that period was a director of it, or, in the case of an institution which does not have directors, a person occupying an equivalent office, is guilty of an offence and liable on conviction on indictment to a fine or on summary conviction to a fine not exceeding the statutory maximum and, on conviction after continued contravention, to a daily default fine not exceeding £100[22]. It is, however, a defence for the person charged with such an offence to prove that he took all reasonable steps for securing compliance with the above provisions[23].

1 Ie any institution to which the Companies Act 1985 s 699A (as added) applies: see para 1816 ante.
2 For these purposes, 'parent law', in relation to an institution, means the law of the country in which the institution has its head office: ibid s 699A(2), Sch 21C para 8(1) (added by the Oversea Companies and Credit and Financial Institutions (Branch Disclosure) Regulations 1992, SI 1992/3179, reg 2(2)).
3 For these purposes, 'financial period', in relation to an institution, means a period for which the institution is required or permitted by its parent law to prepare accounts: Companies Act 1985 Sch 21C para 8(1) (as added: see note 2 supra).
4 For these purposes, 'branch' has the meaning given by ibid s 699A (as added) (see para 1816 note 4 ante): Sch 21C para 1(2) (added by the Oversea Companies and Credit and Financial Institutions (Branch Disclosure) Regulations 1992 reg 2(2)).
5 Companies Act 1985 Sch 21C para 1(1) (added by the Oversea Companies and Credit and Financial Institutions (Branch Disclosure) Regulations 1992 reg 2(2)).
6 For these purposes, the following are accounting documents in relation to a financial period of an institution: (1) the accounts of the institution for the period, including, if it has one or more subsidiaries, any consolidated accounts of the group; (2) any annual report of the directors, or, in the case of an institution which does not have directors, the persons occupying equivalent offices, for the period; (3) the report of the auditors on the accounts mentioned in head (1) supra; and (4) any report of the auditors on the report mentioned in head (2) supra: Companies Act 1985 Sch 21C para 8(2) (added by the Oversea Companies and Credit and Financial Institutions (Branch Disclosure) Regulations 1992 reg 2(2)).
7 For these purposes, references to disclosure are to public disclosure, except where an institution is not required under its parent law, any enactment (including any subordinate legislation within the meaning of the Interpretation Act 1978 s 21: see STATUTES vol 44(1) (Reissue) para 1381) having effect for Great Britain or its constitution publicly to disclose its accounts, in which case such references are to the disclosure of the accounts to the persons for whose information they have been prepared: Companies Act 1985 Sch 21C para 8(1) (as added: see note 2 supra).
8 For the prescribed manner of certification see para 1796 note 2 ante.
9 Companies Act 1985 Sch 21C para 2(1) (added by the Oversea Companies and Credit and Financial Institutions (Branch Disclosure) Regulations 1992 reg 2(2)). Where such an institution had, immediately prior to becoming such an institution, a branch in Northern Ireland which was its only or principal branch within the United Kingdom, it may, instead of delivering the documents mentioned in the Companies Act 1985 Sch 21C para 2(1)(a) (as so added) (see text head (1) supra), deliver thereunder a notice that it has become an institution required to prepare acccounts under parent law, provided that those documents have been delivered to the registrar for Northern Ireland pursuant to the Companies (Northern Ireland) Order 1986, SI 1986/1032: Companies Act 1985 Sch 21C para 2(1) (as so added).
10 Ie ibid Sch 21C para 2(1) (as added): see supra.
11 See note 8 supra.
12 Companies Act 1985 Sch 21C para 3(1) (added by the Oversea Companies and Credit and Financial Institutions (Branch Disclosure) Regulations 1992 reg 2(2)).
13 Ie under the Companies Act 1985 Sch 21C para 3(1) (as added): see supra.
14 Ibid Sch 21C para 3(2) (added by the Oversea Companies and Credit and Financial Institutions (Branch Disclosure) Regulations 1992 reg 2(2)).
15 Ie under the Companies Act 1985 Sch 21C para 2 (as added) or Sch 21C para 3 (as added): see supra.
16 Ibid Sch 21C para 4 (added by the Oversea Companies and Credit and Financial Institutions (Branch Disclosure) Regulations 1992 reg 2(2)).
17 Ie neither the Companies Act 1985 Sch 21C para 2 (as added) nor Sch 21C para 3 (as added): see supra.
18 Ibid Sch 21C para 5(1) (added by the Oversea Companies and Credit and Financial Institutions (Branch Disclosure) Regulations 1992 reg 2(2)).
19 Companies Act 1985 Sch 21C para 5(2) (added by the Oversea Companies and Credit and Financial Institutions (Branch Disclosure) Regulations 1992 reg 2(2)).
20 Companies Act 1985 Sch 21C para 6 (added by the Oversea Companies and Credit and Financial Institutions (Branch Disclosure) Regulations 1992 reg 2(2)).

21 Ie the Companies Act 1985 Sch 21C paras 2, 3 or 5(2) (as added): see supra.
22 Ibid Sch 21C para 7(1) (added by the Oversea Companies and Credit and Financial Institutions (Branch Disclosure) Regulations 1992 reg 2(2)); Companies Act 1985 s 730, Sch 24 (amended by the Oversea Companies and Credit and Financial Institutions (Branch Disclosure) Regulations 1992 reg 4, Sch 3 para 9(1),(2)). For the meaning of 'the statutory maximum' and 'daily default fine' see para 1161 ante.
23 Companies Act 1985 Sch 21C para 7(2) (added by the Oversea Companies and Credit and Financial Institutions (Branch Disclosure) Regulations 1992 reg 2(2)).

1818. Companies not required to prepare accounts under parent law. The following provisions apply to any institution[1] which is incorporated and is not required by the law of the country in which it has its head office to prepare and have audited accounts[2].

Such an institution must in respect of each financial year of the institution prepare the like accounts and directors' report, and cause to be prepared such an auditors' report, as would be required if the institution were[3] an oversea company[4].

Such an institution must, in respect of each financial year of the institution, deliver to the registrar of companies copies of the accounts and reports prepared in accordance with the above provisions[5]. If any document comprised in those accounts or reports is in a language other than English, the company must annex to the copy delivered a translation into English, certified in the prescribed manner[6] to be a correct translation[7].

The period allowed for so delivering accounts and reports is 13 months after the end of the relevant accounting reference period[8]. If, however, the relevant accounting reference period is the institution's first and is a period of more than 12 months, the period allowed is 13 months from the first anniversary of the institution's becoming an institution not required to prepare accounts under parent law[9]. If the relevant accounting reference period is treated as shortened by virtue of a notice given by the institution[10], the period allowed is that applicable in accordance with the above provisions or three months from the date of the notice, whichever last expires[11]. If for any special reason the Secretary of State thinks fit, he may, on an application made before the expiry of the period otherwise allowed, by notice in writing to an institution not required to prepare accounts under parent law extend that period as may be specified in the notice[12].

The documents which an institution is required to deliver to the registrar under these provisions must be delivered:

  (1) to the registrar for England and Wales if the institution's only branch[13], or, if it has more than one, its principal branch within Great Britain, is in England and Wales; or

  (2) to the registrar for Scotland if the institution's only branch, or, if it has more than one, its principal branch within Great Britain is in Scotland[14].

If the above requirements[15] are not complied with before the end of the period allowed for delivering accounts and reports, or if the accounts and reports delivered do not comply with the requirements of the Companies Act 1985, the institution and every person who immediately before the end of that period was a director of the institution is liable on conviction on indictment to a fine or on summary conviction to a fine not exceeding the statutory maximum and, on conviction after continued contravention, to a daily default fine not exceeding £100[16]. It is, however, a defence for a person charged with such an offence to prove that he took all reasonable steps for securing that the requirements in question would be complied with[17]; but it is not a defence in relation to a failure to deliver copies to the registrar to prove that the documents in question were not in fact prepared as required[18] by the Companies Act 1985[19].

1 Ie any institution to which the Companies Act 1985 s 699A (as added) applies: see para 1816 ante.
2 Ibid s 699A(2), Sch 21C para 9(1) (added by the Oversea Companies and Credit and Financial Institutions (Branch Disclosure) Regulations 1992, SI 1992/3179, reg 2(2)).
3 Ie as would be required if the company were a company to which the Companies Act 1985 s 700 (as substituted) applied: see para 1823 post.
4 Ibid Sch 21C para 10 (added by the Oversea Companies and Credit and Financial Institutions (Branch Disclosure) Regulations 1992 reg 2(2)). The Companies Act 1985 ss 223-225 (as substituted and amended) (see paras 806-808 ante) apply to such an institution subject to the following modifications: (1) for the references to the incorporation of the company there must be substituted references to the institution becoming an institution not required to prepare accounts under parent law; and (2) s 225(4) (as substituted) (see para 808 ante) must be omitted: Sch 21C para 11 (added by the Oversea Companies and Credit and Financial Institutions (Branch Disclosure) Regulations 1992 reg 2(2)).
5 Companies Act 1985 Sch 21C para 12(1) (added by the Oversea Companies and Credit and Financial Institutions (Branch Disclosure) Regulations 1992 Sch 2 reg 2(2)).
6 For the prescribed manner of certification see para 1796 note 2 ante.
7 Companies Act 1985 Sch 21C para 12(2) (added by the Oversea Companies and Credit and Financial Institutions (Branch Disclosure) Regulations 1992 reg 2(2)).
8 Companies Act 1985 Sch 21C para 13(1) (added by the Oversea Companies and Credit and Financial Institutions (Branch Disclosure) Regulations 1992 reg 2(2)). For these purposes, 'the relevant accounting reference period' means the accounting reference period by reference to which the financial year for the accounts in question was determined: Companies Act 1985 Sch 21C para 13(5) (added by the Oversea Companies and Credit and Financial Institutions (Branch Disclosure) Regulations 1992 reg 2(2)).
9 Companies Act 1985 Sch 21C para 13(2) (added by the Oversea Companies and Credit and Financial Institutions (Branch Disclosure) Regulations 1992 reg 2(2)).
10 Ie under the Companies Act 1985 s 225 (as substituted and amended): see para 808 ante.
11 Ibid Sch 21C para 12(3) (added by the Oversea Companies and Credit and Financial Institutions (Branch Disclosure) Regulations 1992 reg 3(1), Sch 2 paras 15, 18).
12 Companies Act 1985 Sch 21C para 13(4) (added by the Oversea Companies and Credit and Financial Institutions (Branch Disclosure) Regulations 1992 reg 2(2)).
13 For these purposes, 'branch' has the meaning given by the Companies Act 1985 s 699A (as added) (see para 1816 note 4 ante): Sch 21C para 9(2) (added by the Oversea Companies and Credit and Financial Institutions (Branch Disclosure) Regulations 1992 reg 2(2)).
14 Companies Act 1985 Sch 21C para 14 (added by the Oversea Companies and Credit and Financial Institutions (Branch Disclosure) Regulations 1992 reg 2(2)).
15 Ie the Companies Act 1985 Sch 21C para 12 (as added): see supra.
16 Ibid Sch 21C para 15(1) (added by the Oversea Companies and Credit and Financial Institutions (Branch Disclosure) Regulations 1992 reg 2(2)); Companies Act 1985 s 730, Sch 24 (amended by the Oversea Companies and Credit and Financial Institutions (Branch Disclosure) Regulations 1992 reg 4, Sch 3 para 9(1),(2)). For the meaning of 'the statutory maximum' and 'daily default fine' see para 1161 ante.
17 Companies Act 1985 Sch 21C para 15(2) (added by the Oversea Companies and Credit and Financial Institutions (Branch Disclosure) Regulations 1992 reg 2(2)).
18 Ie as required by the Companies Act 1985 Sch 21C (as added).
19 Ibid Sch 21C para 15(3) (added by the Oversea Companies and Credit and Financial Institutions (Branch Disclosure) Regulations 1992 reg 2(2)).

(C) *Companies (other than Credit and Financial Institutions) incorporated outside the United Kingdom and Gibraltar having a Branch in Great Britain*

1819. Application of the statutory provisions. The following provisions[1] apply to any limited company which is incorporated outside the United Kingdom and Gibraltar, has a branch[2] in Great Britain and is not[3] a credit or financial institution which is incorporated or otherwise formed outside the United Kingdom and Gibraltar, whose head office is outside the United Kingdom and Gibraltar and which has a branch in Great Britain[4].

1 Ie the Companies Act 1985 s 699AA(2), Sch 21D (as added): see paras 1820, 1821 post.
2 For the meaning of 'branch' see para 1791 note 2 ante.
3 Ie which is not an institution to which the Companies Act 1985 s 699A (as added) applies: see para 1816 ante.
4 Ibid s 699AA(1) (added by the Oversea Companies and Credit and Financial Institutions (Branch Disclosure) Regulations 1992, SI 1992/3179, reg 3(1), Sch 2 paras 15, 16).

1820. Companies required to make disclosure under parent law. The following provisions apply to any company[1] which is required by its parent law[2] to prepare, have audited and disclose[3] accounts[4].

In respect of each branch[5] which such a company has in Great Britain, the company must deliver to the registrar of companies for registration in respect of the branch copies of all the accounting documents[6] prepared in relation to a financial period[7] of the company which are disclosed in accordance with its parent law on or after the end of the period allowed for compliance in respect of registration of the branch[8] or, if earlier, the date on which the company complies with that obligation to register in respect of the branch[9].

Where the company's parent law permits it to discharge its obligation with respect to the disclosure of accounting documents by disclosing documents in a modified form, it may discharge the above obligation[10] by delivering copies of documents modified as permitted by that law[11]. If any document which is so delivered is in a language other than English, the company must annex to the copy delivered a translation of it into English, certified in the prescribed manner[12] to be a correct translation[13].

The above provisions do not, however, require documents to be delivered in respect of a branch if:

(1) before the end of the period allowed for compliance, they are delivered in respect of another branch in the United Kingdom; and

(2) the particulars registered[14] in respect of the branch indicate an intention that they are to be registered in respect of that other branch and include the details[15] of that other branch[16].

The period allowed for delivery, in relation to a document required to be so delivered[17], is three months from the date on which the document is first disclosed in accordance with the company's parent law[18].

If a company fails to comply with the above provisions[19] before the end of the period allowed for compliance, it, and every person who immediately before the end of that period was a director of it, is guilty of an offence and liable on conviction on indictment to a fine or on summary conviction to a fine not exceeding the statutory maximum and, on conviction after continued contravention, to a daily default fine not exceeding £100[20]. It is, however, a defence for the person charged with such an offence to prove that he took all reasonable steps for securing compliance with the above provisions[21].

1 Ie any company to which the Companies Act 1985 s 699AA (as added) applies: see para 1819 ante.
2 For these purposes, 'parent law', in relation to a company, means the law of the country in which the company is incorporated: ibid s 699AA(2), Sch 21D para 6(1) (added by the Oversea Companies and Credit and Financial Institutions (Branch Disclosure) Regulations 1992, SI 1992/3179, reg 3(1), Sch 2 paras 15, 18).
3 For these purposes, references to disclosure are to public disclosure: Companies Act 1985 Sch 21D para 6(1) (as added: see note 2 supra).
4 Ibid Sch 21D para 1 (added by the Oversea Companies and Credit and Financial Institutions (Branch Disclosure) Regulations 1992 Sch 2 paras 15, 18).
5 For the meaning of 'branch' see para 1791 note 2 ante.

6 For these purposes, the following are accounting documents in relation to a financial period of the company: (1) the accounts of the company for the period, including, if it has one or more subsidiaries, any consolidated accounts of the group; (2) any annual report of the directors for the period; (3) the report of the auditors on the accounts mentioned in head (1) supra; and (4) any report of the auditors on the report mentioned in head (2) supra: Companies Act 1985 Sch 21D para 6(2) (added by the Oversea Companies and Credit and Financial Institutions (Branch Disclosure) Regulations 1992 Sch 2 paras 15, 18).

7 For these purposes, 'financial period', in relation to a company, means a period for which the company is required or permitted by its parent law to prepare accounts: Companies Act 1985 Sch 21D para 6(1) (as added: see note 2 supra).

8 Ie under ibid s 690A(2), Sch 21A para 1 (as added): see para 1792 ante.

9 Ibid Sch 21D para 2(1),(2) (added by the Oversea Companies and Credit and Financial Institutions (Branch Disclosure) Regulations 1992 Sch 2 paras 15, 18).

10 Ie under the Companies Act 1985 Sch 21D para 2(2) (as added): see supra.

11 Ibid Sch 21D para 2(3) (added by the Oversea Companies and Credit and Financial Institutions (Branch Disclosure) Regulations 1992 Sch 2 paras 15, 18).

12 For the prescribed manner of certification see para 1796 note 2 ante.

13 Companies Act 1985 Sch 21D para 2(4) (added by the Oversea Companies and Credit and Financial Institutions (Branch Disclosure) Regulations 1992 Sch 2 paras 15, 18).

14 Ie under the Companies Act 1985 Sch 21A (as added): see para 1792 et seq ante.

15 Ie the details of that other branch mentioned in ibid Sch 21A para 4(b) (as added): see para 1795 ante.

16 Ibid Sch 21D para 3 (added by the Oversea Companies and Credit and Financial Institutions (Branch Disclosure) Regulations 1992 Sch 2 paras 15, 18).

17 Ie under the Companies Act 1985 Sch 21D para 2 (as added): see supra.

18 Ibid Sch 21D para 4 (added by the Oversea Companies and Credit and Financial Institutions (Branch Disclosure) Regulations 1992 Sch 2 paras 15, 18).

19 Ie the Companies Act 1985 Sch 21D para 2 (as added): see supra.

20 Ibid Sch 21D para 5(1) (added by the Oversea Companies and Credit and Financial Institutions (Branch Disclosure) Regulations 1992 Sch 2 paras 15, 18); Companies Act 1985 s 730, Sch 24 (amended by the Oversea Companies and Credit and Financial Institutions (Branch Disclosure) Regulations 1992 reg 4, Sch 3 para 9(1),(2)). For the meaning of 'the statutory maximum' and 'daily default fine' see para 1161 ante.

21 Companies Act 1985 Sch 21D para 5(2) (added by the Oversea Companies and Credit and Financial Institutions (Branch Disclosure) Regulations 1992 Sch 2 paras 15, 18).

1821. Companies not required to make disclosure under parent law. The following provisions apply to any company[1] which is not required by the law of the country in which it is incorporated to prepare, have audited and publicly disclose accounts[2].

Such a company must in respect of each financial year of the company prepare the like accounts and directors' report, and cause to be prepared such an auditors' report, as would be required if the company were[3] an oversea company[4].

Such a company must, in respect of each financial year of the company, deliver to the registrar of companies copies of the accounts and reports prepared in accordance with the above provisions[5]. If any document comprised in those accounts or reports is in a language other than English, the company must annex to the copy delivered a translation into English, certified in the prescribed manner[6] to be a correct translation[7]. A company required so to deliver accounts in respect of a financial year must deliver them in respect of each branch[8] which it has in Great Britain at the end of that year[9].

The above provisions do not, however, require documents to be delivered in respect of a branch if:

(1) before the end of the period allowed for compliance, they are delivered in respect of another branch in the United Kingdom; and

(2) the particulars registered[10] in respect of the branch indicate an intention that they are to be registered in respect of that other branch and include the details[11] of that other branch[12].

The period allowed for so delivering accounts and reports is 13 months after the end of the relevant accounting reference period[13]. If, however, the relevant accounting reference period is the company's first and is a period of more than 12 months, the period allowed is 13 months from the first anniversary of the company's becoming a company not required to make disclosure under parent law[14]. If the relevant accounting reference period is treated as shortened by virtue of a notice given by the company[15], the period allowed is that applicable in accordance with the above provisions or three months from the date of the notice, whichever last expires[16]. If for any special reason the Secretary of State thinks fit, he may, on an application made before the expiry of the period otherwise allowed, by notice in writing to a company not required to make disclosure under parent law extend that period as may be specified in the notice[17].

If the above requirements[18] are not complied with before the end of the period allowed for delivering accounts and reports, or if the accounts and reports delivered do not comply with the requirements of the Companies Act 1985, the company, and every person who immediately before the end of that period was a director of the company, is liable on conviction on indictment to a fine or on summary conviction to a fine not exceeding the statutory maximum and, on conviction after continued contravention, to a daily default fine not exceeding £100[19]. It is, however, a defence for a person charged with such an offence to prove that he took all reasonable steps for securing that the requirements in question would be complied with[20]; but it is not a defence in relation to a failure to deliver copies to the registrar to prove that the documents in question were not in fact prepared as required by the Companies Act 1985[21].

1 Ie any company to which the Companies Act 1985 s 699AA (as added) applies: see para 1819 ante.
2 Ibid s 699AA(2), Sch 21D para 7 (added by the Oversea Companies and Credit and Financial Institutions (Branch Disclosure) Regulations 1992, SI 1992/3179, reg 3(1), Sch 2 paras 15, 18).
3 Ie as would be required if the company were a company to which the Companies Act 1985 s 700 (as substituted) applied: see para 1823 post.
4 Ibid Sch 21D para 8 (added by the Oversea Companies and Credit and Financial Institutions (Branch Disclosure) Regulations 1992 Sch 2 paras 15, 18). The Companies Act 1985 ss 223-225 (as substituted and amended) (see paras 806-808 ante) apply to such a company subject to the following modifications: (1) for the references to the incorporation of the company there must be substituted references to the company becoming a company not required to make disclosure under parent law; and (2) s 225(4) (as substituted) (see para 808 ante) must be omitted: Sch 21D para 9 (added by the Oversea Companies and Credit and Financial Institutions (Branch Disclosure) Regulations 1992 Sch 2 paras 15, 18).
5 Companies Act 1985 Sch 21D para 10(1) (added by the Oversea Companies and Credit and Financial Institutions (Branch Disclosure) Regulations 1992 Sch 2 paras 15, 18).
6 For the prescribed manner of certification see para 1796 note 2 ante.
7 Companies Act 1985 Sch 21D para 10(2) (added by the Oversea Companies and Credit and Financial Institutions (Branch Disclosure) Regulations 1992 Sch 2 paras 15, 18).
8 For the meaning of 'branch' see para 1791 note 2 ante.
9 Companies Act 1985 Sch 21D para 10(3) (added by the Oversea Companies and Credit and Financial Institutions (Branch Disclosure) Regulations 1992 Sch 2 paras 15, 18). The Companies Act 1985 Sch 21D para 10(3) (as so added) is without prejudice to s 695A(3) (as added) (see para 1798 ante): Sch 21D para 10(4) (added by the Oversea Companies and Credit and Financial Institutions (Branch Disclosure) Regulations 1992 Sch 2 paras 15, 18).
10 Ie under the Companies Act 1985 s 690A(2), Sch 21A para 1 (as added): see para 1792 ante.
11 Ie the details of that other branch mentioned in ibid Sch 21A para 4(b) (as added): see para 1795 ante.
12 Ibid Sch 21D para 11 (added by the Oversea Companies and Credit and Financial Institutions (Branch Disclosure) Regulations 1992 Sch 2 paras 15, 18).

13 Companies Act 1985 Sch 21D para 12(1) (added by the Oversea Companies and Credit and Financial Institutions (Branch Disclosure) Regulations 1992 Sch 2 paras 15, 18). For these purposes, 'the relevant accounting reference period' means the accounting reference period by reference to which the financial year for the accounts in question was determined: Companies Act 1985 Sch 21D para 12(5) (added by the Oversea Companies and Credit and Financial Institutions (Branch Disclosure) Regulations 1992 Sch 2 paras 15, 18).

14 Companies Act 1985 Sch 21D para 12(2) (added by the Oversea Companies and Credit and Financial Institutions (Branch Disclosure) Regulations 1992 Sch 2 paras 15, 18).

15 Ie under the Companies Act 1985 s 225 (as substituted and amended): see para 808 ante.

16 Ibid Sch 21D para 12(3) (added by the Oversea Companies and Credit and Financial Institutions (Branch Disclosure) Regulations 1992 Sch 2 paras 15, 18).

17 Companies Act 1985 Sch 21D para 12(4) (added by the Oversea Companies and Credit and Financial Institutions (Branch Disclosure) Regulations 1992 Sch 2 paras 15, 18).

18 Ie the Companies Act 1985 Sch 21D para 10 (as added): see supra.

19 Ibid Sch 21D para 13(1) (added by the Oversea Companies and Credit and Financial Institutions (Branch Disclosure) Regulations 1992 Sch 2 paras 15, 18); Companies Act 1985 s 730, Sch 24 (amended by the Oversea Companies and Credit and Financial Institutions (Branch Disclosure) Regulations 1992 reg 4, Sch 3 para 9(1),(2)). For the meaning of 'the statutory maximum' and 'daily default fine' see para 1161 ante.

20 Companies Act 1985 Sch 21D para 13(2) (added by the Oversea Companies and Credit and Financial Institutions (Branch Disclosure) Regulations 1992 Sch 2 paras 15, 18).

21 Companies Act 1985 Sch 21D para 13(3) (added by the Oversea Companies and Credit and Financial Institutions (Branch Disclosure) Regulations 1992 Sch 2 paras 15, 18).

(D) *Companies (other than Credit and Financial Institutions and Companies incorporated outside the United Kingdom and Gibraltar and having a Branch in the United Kingdom)*

1822. Application of the statutory provisions. The following provisions[1] do not apply to any credit or financial institution[2] which is incorporated or otherwise formed outside the United Kingdom and Gibraltar, whose head office is outside the United Kingdom and Gibraltar, and which has a branch[3] in Great Britain or to any limited company which is incorporated outside the United Kingdom and Gibraltar and has a branch in the United Kingdom[4].

1 Ie the Companies Act 1985 ss 700-703 (as substituted): see paras 1823-1826 post.

2 Ie any institution to which ibid s 699A (as added) applies: see para 1816 ante.

3 For the meaning of 'branch' see para 1791 note 2 ante.

4 Companies Act 1985 s 699B (added by the Oversea Companies and Credit and Financial Institutions (Branch Disclosure) Regulations 1992, SI 1992/3179, reg 2(3); amended by reg 3(1), Sch 2 paras 15, 17). It is apprehended that this provision should be read as '[the Companies Act 1985] s 699B', although the Oversea Companies and Credit and Financial Institutions (Branch Disclosure) Regulations 1992 reg 2(3) in fact refers to '[the Companies Act 1985] s 669B'.

1823. Preparation of accounts and reports. Every oversea company[1] must, in respect of each financial year[2] of the company, prepare the like accounts and directors' report, and cause to be prepared such an auditors' report[3], as would be required if the company were formed and registered under the Companies Act 1985[4].

The Secretary of State may by order:

(1) modify the above requirements for the purpose of their application to oversea companies;

(2) exempt an oversea company from those requirements or from such of them as may be specified in the order[5].

Such an order may make different provision for different cases or classes of case and may contain such incidental and supplementary provisions as the Secretary of State thinks fit[6].

1 For the meaning of 'oversea company' see para 1790 ante. As to the companies to which these provisions do not apply see para 1822 ante.
2 As to the company's financial year see para 1824 post.
3 As to the preparation etc of accounts and reports by or for companies registered under the Companies Act 1985 see para 801 et seq ante.
4 Ibid s 700(1) (substituted by the Companies Act 1989 s 23, Sch 10 para 13).
5 Companies Act 1985 s 700(2) (substituted by the Companies Act 1989 Sch 10 para 13). In exercise of the power so conferred the Secretary of State made the Oversea Companies (Accounts) (Modifications and Exemptions) Order 1990, SI 1990/440.
6 Companies Act 1985 s 700(3) (substituted by the Companies Act 1989 Sch 10 para 13). Any such order must be made by statutory instrument which is subject to annulment in pursuance of a resolution of either House of Parliament: Companies Act 1985 s 700(4) (substituted by the Companies Act 1989 Sch 10 para 13).

1824. Financial year and accounting reference periods. The statutory provisions relating to a company's financial year and accounting reference periods[1] apply to an oversea company[2], subject to the following modifications[3]. For the references to the incorporation of the company references to the company establishing a place of business in Great Britain are to be substituted[4]; and the statutory restriction on the frequency with which the current accounting reference period may be extended[5] is to be omitted[6].

1 Ie the the Companies Act 1985 ss 223-225 (as substituted and amended): see paras 806-808 ante.
2 For the meaning of 'oversea company' see para 1790 ante. As to the companies to which these provisions do not apply see para 1822 ante.
3 Companies Act 1985 s 701(1) (substituted by the Companies Act 1989 s 23, Sch 10 para 13).
4 Companies Act 1985 s 701(2) (substituted by the Companies Act 1989 Sch 10 para 13).
5 Ie the Companies Act 1985 s 225(4) (as substituted and amended): see para 808 ante.
6 Ibid s 701(2) (substituted by the Companies Act 1989 Sch 10 para 13).

1825. Delivery of accounts and reports. An oversea company[1] must in respect of each financial year[2] of the company deliver to the registrar of companies copies of the accounts and reports prepared[3] in accordance with the statutory requirements[4]. If any document comprised in those accounts or reports is in a language other than English, the directors must annex to the copy delivered a translation of it into English, certified in the prescribed manner[5] to be a correct translation[6].

In relation to such an oversea company the period allowed for delivering accounts and reports is 13 months after the end of the relevant accounting reference period[7]. If, however, the relevant accounting reference period is the company's first and is a period of more than 12 months, the period allowed is 13 months from the first anniversary of the company's establishing a place of business[8] in Great Britain[9]. If the relevant accounting period is treated as shortened by virtue of a notice given[10] by the company, the period allowed is that applicable in accordance with the above provisions or three months from the date of the notice, whichever last expires[11]. If for any special reason the Secretary of State thinks fit, he may, on an application made before the expiry of the period otherwise allowed, by notice in writing to an oversea company, extend that period by such further period as may be specified in the notice[12].

1 For the meaning of 'oversea company' see para 1790 ante. As to the companies to which these provisions do not apply see para 1822 ante.
2 For the meaning of 'financial year' see para 1824 ante.
3 Ie prepared in accordance with the Companies Act 1985 s 700 (as substituted): see para 1823 ante.
4 Ibid s 702(1) (substituted by the Companies Act 1989 s 23, Sch 10 para 13). As to the penalty for non-compliance see para 1826 post.

5 For the prescribed manner of certification see para 818 note 7 ante.
6 Companies Act 1985 s 702(1) (as substituted: see note 4 supra).
7 Ibid s 702(2) (substituted by the Companies Act 1989 Sch 10 para 13). For these purposes, 'the relevant accounting reference period' means the accounting reference period by reference to which the financial year for the accounts in question was determined: Companies Act 1985 s 702(6) (substituted by the Companies Act 1989 Sch 10 para 13).
8 For the meaning of 'place of business' see para 1790 note 2 ante.
9 Companies Act 1985 s 702(3) (substituted by the Companies Act 1989 Sch 10 para 13).
10 Ie under the Companies Act 1985 s 225 (as substituted and amended): see para 808 ante.
11 Ibid s 702(4) (substituted by the Companies Act 1989 Sch 10 para 13).
12 Companies Act 1985 s 702(5) (substituted by the Companies Act 1989 Sch 10 para 13). The functions conferred on the Secretary of State by the Companies Act 1985 s 702(5) (as so substituted) may be exercised by, or by employees of, such person (if any) as may be authorised in that behalf by the Secretary of State: Contracting Out (Functions in relation to the Registration of Companies) Order 1995, SI 1995/1013, art 5, Sch 3 para 1(c). As to the contracting out of functions of the Secretary of State generally see paras 1508, 1509 ante.

1826. Penalty for non-compliance. If the statutory requirements to deliver to the registrar of companies copies of the accounts and reports[1] are not complied with before the end of the period allowed for delivery[2] or, if the accounts and reports delivered do not comply with the requirements of the Companies Act 1985, the company, and every person who immediately before the end of that period was a director of the company, is guilty of an offence and liable on conviction on indictment to a fine or on summary conviction to a fine not exceeding the statutory maximum and, on conviction after continued contravention, to a daily default fine not exceeding one-tenth of the statutory maximum[3].

It is a defence for a person charged with such an offence to prove that he took all reasonable steps for securing that the requirements in question would be complied with[4]; but it is not a defence to a failure to deliver copies to the registrar to prove that the documents in question were not in fact prepared as required by the Companies Act 1985[5].

1 Ie the Companies Act 1985 s 702(1) (as substituted): see para 1825 ante.
2 As to the period allowed for the delivery of accounts see para 1825 ante.
3 Companies Act 1985 s 703(1) (substituted by the Companies Act 1989 s 23, Sch 10 para 13); Companies Act 1985 s 730, Sch 24 (amended by the Companies Act 1989 Sch 10 para 24(1),(4)). As to the companies to which these provisions do not apply see para 1822 ante. For the meaning of 'the statutory maximum' and 'daily default fine' see para 1161 ante.
4 Companies Act 1985 s 703(2) (substituted by the Companies Act 1989 Sch 10 para 13).
5 Companies Act 1985 s 703(3) (substituted by the Companies Act 1989 Sch 10 para 13).

E. REGISTRATION OF CHARGES

1827. Proposed new registration system. The Companies Act 1989[1] adds new provisions[2] for securing the registration in Great Britain of charges on the property of a registered oversea company[3]. The provisions come into force on such day as the Secretary of State may by order made by statutory instrument appoint[4], such day not having yet been appointed.

The proposed new system of registration relates to:

(1) introductory provisions[5];
(2) charges requiring registration[6];
(3) the charges register to be maintained by the registrar of companies[7];
(4) a company's duty to deliver particulars of a charge for registration[8];

(5) the registrar to whom particulars etc are to be delivered[9];

(6) the effect of failure to deliver particulars for registration, late delivery and the effect of errors and omissions[10];

(7) delivery of further particulars or a memorandum of a charge ceasing to affect a company's property[11];

(8) provisions with respect to voidness of charges[12];

(9) additional information to be registered[13];

(11) copies of instruments and the register to be kept by the company[14];

(12) the power to make further provision by regulations[15];

(13) provisions as to the situation of property[16];

(14) other supplementary provisions[17];

(15) an index of defined expressions[18].

A similar proposed new system is to be introduced with respect to charges created by companies registered in England and Wales[19].

1 Ie the Companies Act 1989 ss 92(b), 105, Sch 15.
2 Ie the Companies Act 1985 Pt XXIII Ch III (ss 703A-703N).
3 Companies Act 1989 ss 92(b), 105.
4 See ibid s 215(2).
5 Ie the Companies Act 1985 s 703A (added by the Companies Act 1989 Sch 15; amended by the Oversea Companies and Credit and Financial Institutions (Branch Disclosure) Regulations 1992, SI 1992/3179, reg 4, Sch 3 paras 11, 12).
6 Ie the Companies Act 1985 s 703B (added by the Companies Act 1989 Sch 15; amended by the Oversea Companies and Credit and Financial Institutions (Branch Disclosure) Regulations 1992 Sch 3 paras 11, 13).
7 Ie the Companies Act 1985 s 703C (added by the Companies Act 1989 Sch 15).
8 Ie the Companies Act 1985 s 703D (added by the Companies Act 1989 Sch 15; amended by the Oversea Companies and Credit and Financial Institutions (Branch Disclosure) Regulations 1992 Sch 3 paras 11, 14).
9 Ie the Companies Act 1985 s 703E (added by the Companies Act 1989 Sch 15; amended by the Oversea Companies and Credit and Financial Institutions (Branch Disclosure) Regulations 1992 Sch 3 paras 11, 15).
10 Ie the Companies Act 1985 s 703F (added by the Companies Act 1989 Sch 15).
11 Ie the Companies Act 1985 s 703G (added by the Companies Act 1989 Sch 15).
12 Ie the Companies Act 1985 s 703H (added by the Companies Act 1989 Sch 15).
13 Ie the Companies Act 1985 s 703I (added by the Companies Act 1989 Sch 15).
14 Ie the Companies Act 1985 s 703J (added by the Companies Act 1989 Sch 15).
15 Ie the Companies Act 1985 s 703K (added by the Companies Act 1989 Sch 15).
16 Ie the Companies Act 1985 s 703L (added by the Companies Act 1989 Sch 15).
17 Ie the Companies Act 1985 s 703M (added by the Companies Act 1989 Sch 15).
18 Ie the Companies Act 1985 s 703N (added by the Companies Act 1989 Sch 15).
19 See the Companies Act 1989 ss 92(b), 93-104 and para 1316 ante.

(iii) Actions and Proceedings

1828. Actions by and against foreign companies. A foreign company may sue or be sued in an English court[1]. The lex fori regulates the procedure and the parties to be joined[2]. When a foreign company is plaintiff, it must indorse on its writ of summons its address, which must be that of its domicile or residence, and not merely that of its place of business[3].

It is not open to the English court to control the exercise of a fiduciary power arising in the internal management of a foreign company[4].

1 As to the effect of misnomer see para 1169 note 2 ante.
2 See CONFLICT OF LAWS vol 8(1) (Reissue) para 1066.

3 RSC Ord 6 r 5(1)(a); *Stoy v Rees* (1890) 24 QBD 748, CA (plaintiff could not be found at address given; security for costs ordered). It must also indorse on the writ its solicitor's name or firm and a business address of his within the jurisdiction and, if the solicitor is the agent of another, the name or firm and business address of his principal: RSC Ord 6 r 5(1)(a). It must act by a solicitor: RSC Ord 5 r 6(2).

4 *Pergamon Press Ltd v Maxwell* [1970] 2 All ER 809, [1970] 1 WLR 1167.

1829. Action by minority of shareholders. A minority of the shareholders of a foreign company may sue the directors or managing body in England and the foreign company to restrain the foreign company from acting ultra vires its constitution[1].

1 *Pickering v Stephenson* (1872) LR 14 Eq 322. The possibility of the applicable foreign law having provisions comparable to the Companies Act 1985 ss 35-35B (as substituted) (see para 1093, 1107-1109 ante) must be borne in mind.

1830. Security for costs. When suing or applying to the court, a foreign company[1] may be ordered to give security for costs[2] unless it has sufficient available assets within the jurisdiction[3] or unless the defendant admits his liability, or admits it subject to a counterclaim[4], or the liability has been proved in English proceedings[5].

1 The principle that security for costs should not be ordered, on the ground of residence outside the jurisdiction of the courts of England and Wales against a plaintiff resident in another part of the United Kingdom, only applies to individual plaintiffs and does not apply to insolvent companies: *DSQ Property Co Ltd v Lotus Cars Ltd* [1987] 1 WLR 127 (although the plaintiff was resident in Northern Ireland, the court had jurisdiction under RSC Ord 23 r 1(1)(a) to order that it should give security for costs), not following *Wilson Vehicle Distributions Ltd v Colt Car Co Ltd* [1984] BCLC 93.

2 RSC Ord 23 r 1; *Re Alabama Portland Cement Co Ltd* (1909) 25 TLR 691; *Re Norman* (1849) 11 Beav 401; *Cochrane v Fearon* (1845) 2 Eq Rep 813; *Naamlooze Vennootschap Beleggings Compagnie 'Uranus' v Bank of England* [1948] 1 All ER 465, CA.

3 *Redondo v Chaytor* (1879) 4 QBD 453 at 457, CA; *Hamburger v Poetting* (1882) 30 WR 769; *Ebrard v Gassier* (1884) 28 ChD 232, CA; *Re Apollinaris Co's Trade Marks* [1891] 1 Ch 1, CA; *Clarke v Barber* (1890) 6 TLR 256; *Redfern v Redfern and Herbert* (1890) 63 LT 780. The onus of proving that it has sufficient assets so available lies on the company: *Sacker v Bessler & Co* (1887) 4 TLR 17.

4 *Winterfield v Bradnum* (1878) 3 QBD 324, CA; *De St Martin v Davis & Co* [1884] WN 86.

5 *Re Contract and Agency Corpn Ltd* (1887) 57 LJ Ch 5. As to security for costs by a defendant foreign company, counterclaiming or otherwise, see PRACTICE AND PROCEDURE vol 37 para 298 et seq.

(6) EUROPEAN ECONOMIC INTEREST GROUPINGS

(i) In general

1831. Application of the statutory provisions. The Business Names Act 1985[1] applies in relation to a European Economic Interest Grouping[2] which carries on business in Great Britain as if it were a company formed and registered under the Companies Act 1985[3].

Specified provisions[4] of the Companies Act 1985 apply to European Economic Interest Groupings, and their establishments, registered or in the process of being registered[5], as if they were companies formed and registered or in the process of being registered under the 1985 Act and as if in those provisions any reference to the 1985 Act included a reference to the European Economic Interest Grouping Regulations 1989 and any reference to a registered office included a reference to an official address, but subject to any limitations mentioned in relation to those provisions[6] and to the omission of any reference to a daily default fine[7].

Part III of the Insolvency Act 1986[8] applies to European Economic Interest Groupings and their establishments as if they were companies registered under the Companies Act 1985[9].

Where a European Economic Interest Grouping is wound up as an unregistered company[10], specified provisions[11] of the Company Directors Disqualification Act 1986 apply in relation to it as if any reference to a director or past director of a company included a reference to a manager of the European Economic Interest Grouping and any other person who has or has had control or management of its business and the European Economic Interest Grouping were a company as defined[12] by the Company Directors Disqualification Act 1986[13].

1 As to the Business Names Act 1985 see para 166 et seq ante.
2 For these purposes, 'European Economic Interest Grouping' means a grouping being formed in pursuance of EC Council Regulation 2137/85 (OJ L199, 31.7.1985, p 1) (see EUROPEAN COMMUNI-TIES vol 51 para 11·66 et seq): European Economic Interest Grouping Regulations 1989, SI 1989/638, reg 2(1). EC Council Regulation 2137/85 is set out in the European Economic Interest Grouping Regulations 1989 reg 2(1), Sch 1.
3 Ibid reg 17.
4 Ie the provisions of the Companies Act 1985 specified in the European Economic Interest Grouping Regulations 1989 reg 18, Sch 4. The provisions of the Companies Act 1985 which so apply are:
    (1) s 26(1)(c)-(e),(2),(3) (see para 156 ante);
    (2) s 28(2)-(5),(7), so far as it relates to a direction given under s 28(2) (see paras 159, 160 ante);
    (3) s 29(1)(a) (see para 157 ante);
    (4) Pt XII (ss 395-424) for the purposes of the creation and registration of charges to which it applies (see para 1296 et seq ante);
    (5) s 432(1),(2) (see para 1377 ante);
    (6) s 434 (as amended) (see para 1379 ante), so far as it refers to inspectors appointed under s 432 (as amended) as applied by the European Economic Interest Grouping Regulations 1989 reg 18 and Sch 4;
    (7) the Companies Act 1985 s 436 (as amended) (see para 1379 ante), so far as it refers to inspectors appointed under s 432 (as amended), and to s 434 (as amended), as applied by the European Economic Interest Grouping Regulations 1989 reg 18 and Sch 4;
    (8) the Companies Act 1985 ss 437-439 (as amended) (see paras 1380, 1390, 1391 ante);
    (9) s 441 (as amended) (see para 1380 ante), so far as it applies to inspectors appointed under s 432 (as amended) as applied by the European Economic Interest Grouping Regulations 1989 reg 18 and Sch 4;
    (10) the Companies Act 1985 s 447 (as amended) (see para 1386 ante), as if s 447(1)(d) (repealed) referred to any European Economic Interest Grouping which is carrying on business in Great Britain or has at any time carried on business there, whether or not any such European Economic Interest Grouping is a body corporate;
    (11) ss 448-452 (as amended) (see paras 1386-1389, 1393, 1394 ante);
    (12) s 458 (see para 1160 ante and para 2672 post);
    (13) Pt XVIII (ss 462-487) (as amended) relating to floating charges and receivers (Scotland);
    (14) s 694 (as amended) (see para 1810 ante) as if it referred to:
        (a) the registered name of a European Economic Interest Grouping whose establishment is registered or is in the process of being registered under the European Economic Interest Grouping Regulations 1989 reg 12 (see para 1840 post) with the necessary modifications;
        (b) reg 10 (see para 1838 post) as applied by reg 12(7) (see para 1840 post) in addition to the Companies Act 1985 s 26 (see para 156 ante);
        (c) in s 694(4)(a), a statement in the European Economic Interest Grouping Regulations reg 2(2), Sch 2, Form EEIG6; and
        (d) in the Companies Act 1985 s 694(4)(b), a statement in the European Economic Interest Grouping Regulations Sch 2, Form EEIG7;
    (15) the Companies Act 1985 s 697(2) (see para 1810 ante), as if it referred to a European Economic Interest Grouping whose establishment is registered or is in the process of being registered under the European Economic Interest Grouping Regulations 1989 reg 12;
    (16) the Companies Act 1985 s 704(5) (see para 60 ante);
    (17) s 705(2) (as substituted) (see para 63 ante);

(18) s 706 (as substituted) (see para 64 ante), s 707 (as substituted) (see para 65 ante) and s 710(1)-(3),(5) (repealed), as if they referred to documents and particulars delivered to or furnished by the registrar under the European Economic Interest Grouping Regulations 1989;

(19) the Companies Act 1985 s 714(1) (see para 72 ante), as if it referred to European Economic Interest Groupings or their establishments registered under the European Economic Interest Grouping Regulations 1989 or in Northern Ireland;

(20) the Companies Act 1985 s 718(2) (see para 1766 ante), as if it included a reference to a European Economic Interest Grouping registered in Great Britain under the European Economic Interest Grouping Regulations 1989;

(21) the Companies Act 1985 s 725 (see paras 151, 1146, 1778 ante);

(22) s 730 and Sch 24 (as amended) (punishment of offences), so far as they refer to offences under sections applied by the European Economic Interest Grouping Regulations 1989 reg 18 and Sch 4;

(23) the Companies Act 1985 s 731 (see para 1164 ante);

(24) s 732 (see para 1165 ante) and s 733 (as amended) (see para 1162 ante), so far as they refer to ss 447-451 (as amended) as applied by the European Economic Interest Grouping Regulations 1989 reg 18 and Sch 4.

Nothing in the European Economic Interest Grouping Regulations 1989 creates any new criminal offence punishable to a greater extent than is permitted under the European Communities Act 1972 s 2(2), Sch 2 para 1(1)(d) (see EUROPEAN COMMUNITIES vol 51 para 3·39): European Economic Interest Grouping Regulations reg 21.

Any function of the registrar of companies for England and Wales conferred by or under any provision of the Companies Act 1985 listed in the Contracting Out (Functions in relation to the Registration of Companies) Order 1995, SI 1995/1013, art 3, Sch 1 paras 2, 3 (see para 62 heads (2), (3) ante) to the extent specified therein where any such provision is applied to European Economic Interest Groupings by the European Economic Interest Grouping Regulations 1989 reg 18 and Sch 4 may be exercised by, or by employees of, such person (if any) as may be authorised in that behalf by the registrar of companies for England and Wales: Contracting Out (Functions in relation to the Registration of Companies) Order 1995 Sch 1 para 8. As to the contracting out of the registrar of companies' functions generally see paras 61, 62 ante.

 5 Ie under the European Economic Interest Grouping Regulations 1989.
 6 Ie mentioned in ibid Sch 4: see note 4 supra.
 7 Ibid reg 18. For the meaning of 'daily default fine' see para 1161 ante.
 8 Ie the Insolvency Act 1986 Pt III (ss 28-72) (as amended): see para 1318 et seq ante and para 2147 et seq post.
 9 European Economic Interest Grouping Regulations 1989 reg 19(1).
 10 Ie under the Insolvency Act 1986 Pt V (ss 220-229) (as amended): see para 2899 et seq post.
 11 Ie the Company Directors Disqualification Act 1986 ss 1, 2 (as amended), 4-11 (as amended), 12(2), 15-17, 20, 22, Sch 1 (as amended): see para 1417 et seq ante.
 12 Ie as defined by ibid s 22(2)(b): see para 1417 note 3 ante.
 13 European Economic Interest Grouping Regulations 1989 reg 20.

1832. Legal personality. From the date of registration of a European Economic Interest Grouping[1] in Great Britain mentioned in a certificate of registration given by the registrar of companies[2], the European Economic Interest Grouping is[3] a body corporate by the name contained in the contract[4].

 1 For the meaning of 'European Economic Interest Grouping' see para 1831 note 2 ante.
 2 Ie under the European Economic Interest Grouping Regulations 1989, SI 1989/638, reg 9(5): see para 1837 post.
 3 Ie subject to ibid reg 11: see para 1839 post.
 4 Ibid reg 3. For these purposes, 'the contract' means the contract for the formation of a European Economic Interest Grouping: reg 2(1).

1833. Transfer of official address. Notice of any proposal to transfer the official address of a European Economic Interest Grouping[1] registered in Great Britain to any other place must, where such transfer would result in a change in the law applicable to the contract[2], be filed at the registry where the European Economic Interest Grouping was registered by delivery of a notice[3] in the prescribed form[4].

Where the registrar[5], being the competent authority[6], receives such a notice within the period of two months beginning with its publication in the Gazette[7] and opposes that transfer on the grounds of public interest, that transfer does not take effect[8].

1 For the meaning of 'European Economic Interest Grouping' see para 1831 note 2 ante.
2 Ie under EC Council Regulation 2137/85 (OJ L199, 31.7.1985, p 1) art 2: see EUROPEAN COMMUNITIES vol 51 para 11·66. For the meaning of 'the contract' see para 1832 note 4 ante.
3 Ie in pursuance of the European Economic Interest Grouping Regulations 1989, SI 1989/638, reg 13(1): see para 1841 post.
4 Ibid reg 4(1). For the prescribed form of notice see regs 2(2), 4(1), Sch 2, Form EEIG4.
5 For these purposes, 'the registrar' has the meaning given by ibid reg 9(1) (see para 1837 post) and reg 12(1) (see para 1840 post): reg 2(1).
6 Ie within the meaning of EC Council Regulation 2137/85 art 14(4): see EUROPEAN COMMUNITIES vol 51 para 11·67.
7 For the meaning of 'the Gazette' see para 70 note 1 ante. As to the publication of documents see para 1843 post.
8 European Economic Interest Grouping Regulations 1989 reg 4(2).

1834. Managers. A manager of a European Economic Interest Grouping[1] registered in Great Britain may be a legal person other than a natural person, on condition that it designates one or more natural persons to represent it and notice of particulars of each such person is sent to the registrar in the prescribed form[2] as though he were a manager[3]. Any natural person so designated is subject to the same liabilities as if he himself were a manager[4].

There must be delivered to the registrar[5] notice of appointment of any manager and the following particulars with respect to each manager:

(1) his present Christian name[6] and surname[7];
(2) any former Christian name or surname[8];
(3) his usual residential address;
(4) his nationality;
(5) his business occupation, if any;
(6) the date of his birth;

and, in the case of a legal person other than a natural person, its name and registered or principal office[9].

1 For the meaning of 'European Economic Interest Grouping' see para 1831 note 2 ante.
2 For the prescribed form of notice see the European Economic Interest Grouping Regulations 1989, SI 1989/638, regs 2(2), 5(1), Sch 2, Form EEIG3.
3 Ibid reg 5(1).
4 Ibid reg 5(2).
5 Ie in accordance with ibid reg 13(1): see para 1841 post. For the meaning of 'the registrar' see para 1833 note 5 ante.
6 For these purposes, the Companies Act 1985 s 289(2) (as substituted) (see para 560 ante) applies as regards the meaning of 'Christian name': European Economic Interest Grouping Regulations 1989 regs 2(1), 5(4).
7 For these purposes, the Companies Act 1985 s 289(2) (as substituted) (see para 560 ante) applies as regards the meaning of 'surname': European Economic Interest Grouping Regulations 1989 regs 2(1), 5(4).

8 For these purposes, the Companies Act 1985 s 289(2) (as substituted) (see para 560 ante) applies as regards the meaning of 'former Christian or surname': European Economic Interest Grouping Regulations 1989 regs 2(1), 5(4).
9 Ibid reg 5(3).

1835. Cessation of membership. For the purpose of the national law on liquidation, winding up, insolvency or cessation of payments, a member of a European Economic Interest Grouping[1] ceases to be a member if:

(1) in the case of an individual:
    (a) a bankruptcy order has been made against him in England and Wales; or
    (b) sequestration of his estate has been awarded[2] by the court in Scotland;

(2) in the case of a partnership:
    (a) a winding-up order has been made against the partnership in England and Wales;
    (b) a bankruptcy order has been made against its members in England and Wales on a bankruptcy petition presented under the Insolvent Partnerships Order 1994[3]; or
    (c) sequestration of the estate of the partnership has been awarded[4] by the court in Scotland;

(3) in the case of a company, the company goes into liquidation in Great Britain; or

(4) in the case of any legal person or partnership, it is otherwise wound up or otherwise ceases to exist after the conclusion of winding up or insolvency[5].

1 For the meaning of 'European Economic Interest Grouping' see para 1831 note 2 ante.
2 Ie under the Bankruptcy (Scotland) Act 1985.
3 Ie under the Insolvent Partnerships Order 1994, SI 1994/2421: see para 2916 et seq post.
4 See note 2 supra.
5 European Economic Interest Grouping Regulations 1989, SI 1989/638, reg 6; Interpretation Act 1978 s 17(2)(a).

1836. Competent authority. The Secretary of State is the competent authority for the purposes of making an application to the court[1] for the winding up of a European Economic Interest Grouping[2] in certain circumstances[3].

The court may, on an application by the Secretary of State, order the winding up of a European Economic Interest Grouping which has an official address in Great Britain, if the European Economic Interest Grouping acts contrary to the public interest and it is expedient in the public interest that the European Economic Interest Grouping should be wound up and the court is of the opinion that it is just and equitable for it to do so[4].

The court is, on an application by the Secretary of State, the competent authority for the purpose of prohibiting[5] any activity carried on in Great Britain by a European Economic Interest Grouping where such activity is in contravention of the public interest there[6].

1 Ie under EC Council Regulation 2137/85 (OJ L199, 31.7.1985, p 1) art 32(1): see EUROPEAN COMMUNITIES vol 51 para 11·73.
2 For the meaning of 'European Economic Interest Grouping' see para 1831 note 2 ante.
3 European Economic Interest Grouping Regulations 1989, SI 1989/638, reg 7(1).
4 Ibid reg 7(2).
5 Ie under EC Council Regulation 2137/85 art 38: see EUROPEAN COMMUNITIES.
6 European Economic Interest Grouping Regulations 1989 reg 7(3).

(ii) Registration etc

1837. Registration of European Economic Interest Grouping whose official address is in Great Britain. The registrar for the purposes of registration of a European Economic Interest Grouping[1] in Great Britain where its official address is in Great Britain is the registrar within the meaning of the Companies Act 1985[2] and the contract[3] must be delivered:

(1) to the registrar or other officer performing under the 1985 Act the duty of registration of companies in England and Wales, if the contract states that the official address of the European Economic Interest Grouping is to be situated in England and Wales, or that it is to be situated in Wales; and

(2) to the registrar or other officer performing under the 1985 Act the duty of registration of companies in Scotland, if the contract states that the official address of the European Economic Interest Grouping is to be situated in Scotland[4].

With the contract there must be delivered a registration form in the prescribed form[5] containing a statement of the names and the specified[6] particulars[7].

The registrar must not register a European Economic Interest Grouping under these provisions unless he is satisfied that all the specified requirements[8] in respect of registration and of matters precedent and incidental to it have been complied with but he may accept a declaration in the prescribed form[9] as sufficient evidence of compliance[10]. Subject thereto, the registrar must retain the contract, and any certified translation[11], so delivered to him and register the European Economic Interest Grouping[12].

On the registration of a European Economic Interest Grouping, the registrar must give a certificate that the European Economic Interest Grouping has been registered stating the date of registration[13]. The certificate must be signed by the registrar, or authenticated by his official seal[14]. A certificate of registration so given in respect of a European Economic Interest Grouping is conclusive evidence that the specified requirements[15] in respect of registration and of matters precedent and incidental to it have been complied with and that the European Economic Interest Grouping is an organisation authorised to be registered, and is duly registered[16].

Where a European Economic Interest Grouping is to be registered with the contract written in any language other than English, the contract to be delivered to the registrar may be in the other language provided that it is accompanied by a certified translation into English[17].

Where a European Economic Interest Grouping has published a proposal to transfer its official address to a place in Great Britain[18], the registrar responsible for the registration of the European Economic Interest Grouping with the new official address must, where the transfer of the official address has not been opposed[19], register the European Economic Interest Grouping with its new official address on receipt of a registration form in the prescribed form[20] containing evidence of the publication of the transfer proposal and a statement that no competent authority has opposed[21] the transfer[22].

Any communication or notice may be addressed to a European Economic Interest Grouping where its official address is in Great Britain at its official address stated on the prescribed form[23] or in the case of any change in the situation of that address at any new official address stated on[24] the prescribed form[25].

1 For the meaning of 'European Economic Interest Grouping' see para 1831 note 2 ante.

2 See para 60 note 3 ante.

3 For the meaning of 'the contract' see para 1832 note 4 ante.
4 European Economic Interest Grouping Regulations 1989, SI 1989/638, regs 2(1), 9(1). For the fee payable to the registrar of companies for registration of a European Economic Interest Grouping whose official address is in Great Britain see the European Economic Interest Grouping (Fees) Regulations 1989, SI 1989/950, reg 3, Schedule, Fee 1.
5 For the prescribed form of registration see the European Economic Interest Grouping Regulations 1989 regs 2(2), 9(2), Sch 2, Form EEIG1.
6 Ie the particulars set out in EC Council Regulation 2137/85 (OJ L199, 31.7.1985, p 1) art 5: see EUROPEAN COMMUNITIES vol 51 para 11·67.
7 European Economic Interest Grouping Regulations 1989 reg 9(2).
8 Ie all the requirements of the European Economic Interest Grouping Regulations 1989 and EC Council Regulation 2137/85.
9 For the prescribed form of declaration see the European Economic Interest Grouping Regulations 1989 regs 2(2), 9(3), Sch 2, Form EEIG1.
10 Ibid reg 9(3).
11 For these purposes, 'certified translation' means a translation certified to be a correct translation:
    (1) if the translation was made in the United Kingdom, by:
        (a) a notary public in any part of the United Kingdom;
        (b) a solicitor (if the translation was made in Scotland), a solicitor of the Supreme Court of Judicature of England and Wales (if it was made in England or Wales) or a solicitor of the Supreme Court of Judicature of Northern Ireland (if it was made in Northern Ireland); or
        (c) a person certified by a person mentioned supra to be known to him to be competent to translate the document into English; or
    (2) if the translation was made outside the United Kingdom, by:
        (a) a notary public;
        (b) a person authorised in the place where the translation was made to administer an oath;
        (c) any of the British officials mentioned in the Commissioners for Oaths Act 1889 s 6 (as amended) (see para 818 note 7 ante);
        (d) a person certified by a person mentioned in heads (2)(a),(b) or (c) supra to be known to him to be competent to translate the document into English:
    European Economic Interest Grouping Regulations 1989 reg 2(3).
12 Ibid reg 9(4).
13 Ibid reg 9(5).
14 Ibid reg 9(6).
15 See note 8 supra.
16 European Economic Interest Grouping Regulations 1989 reg 9(7).
17 Ibid reg 9(8).
18 Ie under EC Council Regulation 2137/85 art 14(1): see EUROPEAN COMMUNITIES vol 51 para 11·67.
19 Ie under ibid art 14(4): see EUROPEAN COMMUNITIES vol 51 para 11·67.
20 See note 5 supra.
21 See note 19 supra.
22 European Economic Interest Grouping Regulations 1989 reg 9(9).
23 Ie on ibid Sch 2, Form EEIG1.
24 Ie on ibid Sch 2, Form EEIG4.
25 Ibid reg 9(10).

1838. Prohibition on registration of certain names. A European Economic Interest Grouping[1] may not be registered in Great Britain[2] by a name which includes any of the following words or expressions, or abbreviations thereof, that is to say, 'limited', 'unlimited' or 'public limited company' or their Welsh equivalents[3].

1 For the meaning of 'European Economic Interest Grouping' see para 1831 note 2 ante.
2 Ie under the European Economic Interest Grouping Regulations 1989, SI 1989/638, reg 9: see para 1837 ante.
3 Ibid reg 10(1). As to the Welsh equivalents see para 154 ante. In determining for the purposes of the Companies Act 1985 s 26(1)(c) (see para 156 ante) (as applied by the European Economic Interest Grouping Regulations 1989 reg 18, Sch 4: see para 1831 note 4 ante) whether one name is the same as another, there are to be disregarded the words 'European Economic Interest Grouping' or the initials

'EEIG' or their authorised equivalents in official languages of the European Community, other than English, the authorised equivalents being set out in reg 10(2), Sch 3: regs 2(1), 10(2).

1839. Change of name. Where a European Economic Interest Grouping[1] changes its name, the registrar[2] must[3] enter the new name on the register in place of the former name and must issue a certificate of registration altered to meet the circumstances of the case[4]. A change of name has effect from the date on which the altered certificate is issued[5].

1 For the meaning of 'European Economic Interest Grouping' see para 1831 note 2 ante.
2 For the meaning of 'the registrar' see para 1833 note 5 ante.
3 Ie subject to the provisions of the Companies Act 1985 s 26 (see para 156 ante) which apply by virtue of the European Economic Interest Grouping Regulations 1989, SI 1989/638, regs 10, 18, Sch 4: see paras 1838, 1831 note 4 respectively ante.
4 Ibid regs 2(1), 11(2). Regulation 10(2) applies in determining under the Companies Act 1985 s 28(2) (see para 159 ante) (as applied by the European Economic Interest Grouping Regulations 1989 reg 18, Sch 4) whether a name is the same as or too like another: regs 2(1), 11(1).
5 Ibid reg 11(3).

1840. Registration of establishment of European Economic Interest Grouping whose official address is outside the United Kingdom. The registrar for the purposes of registration under these provisions of a European Economic Interest Grouping[1] establishment situated in Great Britain where the European Economic Interest Grouping's official address is outside the United Kingdom is the registrar[2] within the meaning of the Companies Act 1985[3].

For the purpose of such registration, save where an establishment is already so registered in Great Britain, there must be delivered, within one month of the establishment becoming so situated at any place in Great Britain, to the registrar at the registration office in England and Wales or Scotland, according to where the establishment is situated, a certified copy of the contract[4] together with:

(1) a certified translation[5] into English of the contract and other documents and particulars to be filed with it[6] if the contract and other documents and particulars, or any part thereof, are not in English; and

(2) a registration form in the prescribed form[7] containing a statement of the specified[8] names and particulars[9].

The registrar must not register a European Economic Interest Grouping estalishment under these provisions unless he is satisfied that all the specified requirements[10] in respect of registration and of matters precedent and incidental to it have been complied with but he may accept a declaration in the prescribed form[11] as sufficient evidence of compliance[12]. Subject thereto, the registrar must retain the copy of the contract, and any certified translation, delivered to him and register the European Economic Interest Grouping establishment[13].

Any communication or notice may be addressed to a European Economic Interest Grouping where its official address is outside the United Kingdom at any of its establishments in Great Britain[14].

If a European Economic Interest Grouping fails to comply with any of the above provisions[15], the European Economic Interest Grouping, and any officer[16] of it who intentionally authorises or permits the default, is guilty of an offence and liable on summary conviction to a fine not exceeding level 3 on the standard scale and, if failure to comply with any such provision continues after conviction, the European Economic Interest Grouping, and any such officer, is guilty of a further offence of failure to comply with that provision and is liable to be proceeded against and punished accordingly[17].

1 For the meaning of 'European Economic Interest Grouping' see para 1831 note 2 ante.
2 See para 60 note 3 ante.
3 European Economic Interest Grouping Regulations 1989, SI 1989/638, regs 2(1), 12(1). Regulation 10 (see para 1838 ante) applies to a European Economic Interest Grouping establishment to be registered under reg 12 as it applies to a European Economic Interest Grouping to be registered under reg 9 (see para 1837 ante): reg 12(7).
4 For the meaning of 'the contract' see para 1832 note 4 ante.
5 For the meaning of 'certified translation' see para 1837 note 11 ante.
6 Ie under EC Council Regulation 2137/85 (OJ L199, 31.7.1985, p 1) art 10: see EUROPEAN COMMUNI- TIES vol 51 para 11–67.
7 For the prescribed form of registration see the European Economic Interest Grouping Regulations 1989 regs 2(2), 12(2), Sch 2, Form EEIG2.
8 Ie the particulars set out in EC Council Regulation 2137/85 arts 5, 10: see EUROPEAN COMMUNITIES vol 51 para 11·67.
9 European Economic Interest Grouping Regulations 1989 reg 12(2),(3).
10 Ier all the requirements of the European Economic Interest Grouping Regulations 1989 and EC Council Regulation 2137/85.
11 For the prescribed form of declaration see the European Economic Interest Grouping Regulations 1989 regs 2(2), 12(4), Sch 2, Form EEIG2.
12 Ibid reg 12(4).
13 Ibid reg 12(5).
14 Ibid reg 12(6).
15 Ie any provision of ibid reg 12(2): see supra.
16 For these purposes, 'officer', in relation to a European Economic Interest Grouping, includes a manager, or any other person provided for in the contract as an organ of the European Economic Interest Grouping: ibid reg 2(1).
17 Ibid reg 12(8). For the meaning of 'the standard scale' see CRIMINAL LAW vol 11(2) (Reissue) para 808.

1841. Filing of documents. The documents and particulars required to be filed in Great Britain[1] must be filed within 15 days (or, in the case of a European Economic Interest Grouping[2] whose official address is outside the United Kingdom, 30 days) of the event to which the document in question relates by delivery to the registrar[3] for registration of a notice, together with a certified translation[4] into English of any documents and particulars, or any part thereof, which are not in English, of specified information[5].

The registrar must retain the documents and particulars and any certified translation so delivered to him[6].

If a European Economic Interest Grouping fails to comply with any of the above provisions, the European Economic Interest Grouping, and any officer[7] of it who intentionally authorises or permits the default, is guilty of an offence and liable on summary conviction to a fine not exceeding level 3 on the standard scale and, if the failure to comply with any such provision continues after conviction, the European Economic Interest Grouping, and any such officer, is guilty of a further offence of failure to comply with that provision and is liable to be proceeded against and punished accordingly[8].

1 Ie the documents and particulars referred to in EC Council Regulation 2137/85 (OJ L199, 31.7.1985, p 1) art 7(a)–(j) and required to be filed under art 7 in Great Britain: see EUROPEAN COMMUNITIES vol 51 para 11·67.
2 For the meaning of 'European Economic Interest Grouping' see para 1831 note 2 ante.
3 For the meaning of 'the registrar' see para 1833 note 5 ante.
4 For the meaning of 'certified translation' see para 1837 note 11 ante.
5 European Economic Interest Grouping Regulations 1989, SI 1989/638, reg 13(1). The notice must be so given (1) in the case of EC Council Regulation 2137/85 art 7(d) where the official address of the

European Economic Interest Grouping is in Great Britain, in the European Economic Interest Grouping Regulations 1989 regs 2(2), 13(1)(a), Sch 2, Form EEIG3 of the names of the managers and the particulars referred to in reg 5(3) (see para 1834 ante), of particulars of whether they may act alone or must act jointly and of the termination of any manager's appointment; (2) in the cases of EC Council Regulation 2137/85 art 7(a),(c),(e)-(j), and in the case of art 7(d) where the official address of the European Economic Interest Grouping is outside the United Kingdom, in the European Economic Interest Grouping Regulations 1989 regs 2(2), 13(1)(b), Sch 2, Form EEIG4 of the documents and particulars referred to in Form EEIG4; and (3) in the cases of EC Council Regulation 2137/85 art 7(b), in the European Economic Interest Grouping Regulations 1989 regs 2(2), 13(1)(c), Sch 2, Form EEIG5 of the setting up or closure of an establishment of a European Economic Interest Grouping in Great Britain, except where reg 12(1) (see para 1840 ante) applies: reg 13(1)(a)-(c).

6 Ibid reg 13(2).

7 For the meaning of 'officer' see para 1840 note 16 ante.

8 European Economic Interest Grouping Regulations 1989 reg 13(3). For the meaning of 'the standard scale' see CRIMINAL LAW vol 11(2) (Reissue) para 808.

1842. Inspection of documents. Any person may:
   (1) inspect any document or particulars kept[1] by the registrar[2] or a copy thereof; and
   (2) require the registrar to deliver or send by post to him a copy or extract of any such document or particulars or any part thereof[3].

1 Ie under the European Economic Interest Grouping Regulations 1989, SI 1989/638: see para 1831 et seq ante and paras 1843, 1844 post.

2 For the meaning of 'the registrar' see para 1833 note 5 ante.

3 European Economic Interest Grouping Regulations 1989 reg 14. Any function of the registrar of companies for England and Wales conferred by or under reg 14 may be exercised by, or by employees of, such person (if any) as may be authorised in that behalf by the registrar of companies for England and Wales: Contracting Out (Functions in relation to the Registration of Companies) Order 1995, SI 1995/1013, art 3, Sch 1 para 7. As to the contracting out of the registrar of companies' functions generally see paras 61, 62 ante.

   For the fee payable to the registrar of companies for inspection of documents and particulars under the European Economic Interest Grouping Regulations 1989 reg 14 except the index kept by the registrar of companies under the Companies Act 1985 s 714(1) (see para 72 ante) as applied by the European Economic Interest Grouping Regulations 1989 reg 18 and Sch 4 (see para 1831 note 4 ante) see the European Economic Interest Grouping (Fees) Regulations 1989, SI 1989/950, reg 3, Schedule, Fee 2 (substituted by SI 1991/1228); and for the fee payable to the registrar for delivering or sending by post by him of a copy or extract of any document or particulars, or any part thereof, delivered to him and kept by him by virtue of the European Economic Interest Grouping Regulations 1989 reg 14 see the European Economic Interest Grouping (Fees) Regulations 1989 Schedule, Fee 3 (substituted by SI 1991/1228).

1843. Publication of documents in the Gazette and the Official Journal. The registrar[1] must cause to be published in the Gazette[2]:
   (1) the documents and particulars issued or received by him[3]; and
   (2) in the case of certain of those documents and particulars[4] a notice, stating in the notice the name of the European Economic Interest Grouping[5], the description of the documents or particulars and the date of receipt[6].
The registrar must forward to the Office for Official Publications of the European Communities specified information[7] within one month of the publication of the relevant documents and particulars in the Gazette[8].

1 For the meaning of 'the registrar' see para 1833 note 5 ante.

2 For the meaning of 'the Gazette' see para 70 note 1 ante.

3 Ie under the European Economic Interest Grouping Regulations 1989, SI 1989/638, and referred to in EC Council Regulation 2137/85 (OJ L199, 31.7.1985, p 1) art 8(a),(b): see EUROPEAN COMMUNITIES vol 51 para 11·67.

4 Ie in the case of those documents and particulars referred to in ibid art 7(b)–(j): see EUROPEAN COMMUNITIES vol 51 para 11·67.
5 For the meaning of 'European Economic Interest Grouping' see para 1831 note 2 ante.
6 European Economic Interest Grouping Regulations 1989 reg 15(1).
7 Ie the information referred to in EC Council Regulation 2137/85 art 11: see EUROPEAN COMMUNITIES vol 51 para 11·67.
8 European Economic Interest Grouping Regulations 1989 reg 15(2).

1844-2000. Identification. If a European Economic Interest Grouping[1] fails to comply with its obligations in relation to the information to be indicated on letters, order forms and similar documents[2], it is guilty of an offence and liable on summary conviction to a fine not exceeding level 3 on the standard scale[3].

If an officer[4] of a European Economic Interest Grouping or a person on its behalf issues or authorises the issue of any letter, order form or similar document not complying with the above obligations[5], he is guilty of an offence and liable on summary conviction to a fine not exceeding level 3 on the standard scale[6].

1 For the meaning of 'European Economic Interest Grouping' see para 1831 note 2 ante.
2 Ie fails to comply with EC Council Regulation 2137/85 (OJ L199, 31.7.1985, p 1) art 25: see EUROPEAN COMMUNITIES vol 51 para 11·69.
3 European Economic Interest Grouping Regulations 1989, SI 1989/638, reg 16(1). For the meaning of 'the standard scale' see CRIMINAL LAW vol 11(2) (Reissue) para 808.
4 For the meaning of 'officer' see para 1840 note 16 ante.
5 Ie not complying with the requirements of EC Council Regulation 2137/85 art 25.
6 European Economic Interest Grouping Regulations 1989 reg 16(2).

INDEX

Companies

This Index relates only to entries appearing in Volumes 7(1) and 7(2). A consolidated Index for Volumes 7(1), 7(2) and 7(3) appears in Volume 7(3).

References are to paragraph numbers; superior figures refer to notes

References are to paragraph numbers; superior figures refer to notes

AUDITOR—*continued*
  delegation order—*continued*
    annual report and accounts of body established, 1012
    contents, 1005, 1009
    effect, 1005
    fees, 1010
    financial provisions, 1008
    functions within scope, 1005n[1]
    legislative functions under, 1011
    liability in damages, exemption under, 1023
    name, members and chairman of body established, 1007
    proceedings of body established, 1009
    regulations, powers of Secretary of State, 1014
    status of body established, 1006
    supplementary provisions, 1013
  duties—
    articles, provisions in, 1036
    contract, regulated by, 1037
    generally, 1037
    report, as to, 1059–1061
    statutory, 1037
    third parties, towards, 1038
    trade union, towards, 1040
  false and misleading statements, 1001
  firm controlled by qualified persons: meaning, 964
  fit and proper person, 965
  improper dividend, liability, 722
  improper payments by directors, liability for, 1037
  indemnity clauses in articles, 1036
  independence, 958, 966
  information, right to, 1034
  information about firms available to public, 973, 995, 996
  jurisdiction and procedure as to offences, 1004
  lack of independence, ineligibility on ground of, 958
  misfeasance, liability, 1039
  monopoly situation, 1021
  non-audit work—
    associates of auditor, 1044
    disclosure of remuneration, 1046
    persons not regarded as associates, 1045
    regulations as to remuneration, power to make, 1043
    remuneration, 1043
  offences on ceasing to hold office, 1053
  officer of company, 1039
  overseas qualifications, approval of, 989
  partnership appointed as, effect, 957
  persons eligible for appointment, 956
  persons not regarded as associates of, 1045
  position of, 1039
  professional indemnity insurance, 972
  professional integrity, 966
  qualification—
    appropriate: meaning, 978
    authorisation under Companies Act 1967 . . 990

AUDITOR—*continued*
  qualification—*continued*
    examination subjects, 984n[1]
    notice as to retention of, 978
    overseas, approval of, 989
    qualifying bodies, 979
    recognition—
      application for, 980
      competition grounds, refusal on, 1015
      compliance order, 999
      entry requirements, 981
      examination, 984
      grant or refusal, 987
      practical training, 985
      professional experience, 983
      revocation, 988, 1020
      rules etc of qualifying body, 986
      theoretical instruction, 982
    rules as to holding of, 964
  qualifying body—
    meaning, 979
    amendment of enactments on change of name, merger or transfer, 1026
    changes of rules or guidance, notice of, 1016
    competition. *See* competition *above*
    compliance order, 999
    fees payable by, 1022
    international obligations, compliance with, 1000
    matters to be notified to Secretary of State, 997, 998
    recognition of qualification. *See under* qualification *above*
    restrictive trade practices exemption, 1021
  register—
    contents, 991
    copies of entries, 994
    false indication of entry on, 1001
    injunction, enforcement of provisions by, 991
    inspection, 993
    keeping and maintenance, 992
    location, 993
    regulations, power to make, 991
  removal—
    auditors not appointed annually, 1051
    compensation etc, right to, 1047
    notice of intended resolution, 1048
    notice to registrar, 1047
    powers, 1047
    representations, 1048
    resolution, by, 1047
    statement on, 1052, 1053
    statutory rights on, 1047, 1048
  remuneration—
    benefits in kind, 1042
    disclosure, 1046
    fixing of, 1042
    non-audit work, 1043
    note to company's accounts, 1042
    report. *See* AUDITORS' REPORT
    representations on removal, 1048

AUDITOR—*continued*
resignation—
extraordinary general meeting, 1050
notice of, 1049
statement, circulation of, 1050
statement to be lodged with registrar, 1052, 1053
resolutions of private company, rights as to, 1035
rights—
attendance at company meetings etc, 1035
compensation on termination of appointment, 1047
information, to, 1034
resolutions of private company, as to, 1035
trade union's auditor, of, 1040
working papers, to, 1041
service of notices, 1024
statement by—
ceasing to hold office, on, 1052, 1053
circulation to members, 1050
summary proceedings, 1004
supervisory body—
meaning, 962
admission and expulsion of members, 970
amendment of enactments on change of name, merger or transfer, 1026
changes of rules or guidance, notice of, 1016
competition. *See* competition *above*
compliance order, 999
costs of compliance with rules, 974
discipline, 970
fees payable by, 1022
firms information available to public—
inspection and copies, 996
requirements, 973, 995
fit and proper persons, auditors to be, 965
international obligations, compliance with, 1000
investigation of complaints, 971
liability in damages, exemption, 1023
matters to be notified to Secretary of State, 997, 998
members, 962
monitoring and enforcement, 969
power of Secretary of State to require information, 998
procedures for maintaining competence, 968
professional indemnity insurance etc, 972
professional integrity and independence, 966
promotion and maintenance of standards, 975
qualifications of auditors, 964
recognition—
application for, 963
competition grounds, refusal on, 1015
false indication of, 1001
grant or refusal, 976
revocation, 977, 1020
register of auditors, 973, 991–994
restrictive trade practices exemption, 1021
service of notices, 1024
technical standards, 967
technical standards, 967

AUDITOR—*continued*
third parties, duties towards, 1038
time limit for prosecution of offences, 1003
trade union, of, 1040
trading stamp schemes, 990
transfer of functions of Secretary of State. *See* delegation order *above*
unquoted companies, 990
vacation of office on becoming ineligible, 960
working papers, rights as to, 1041
written resolutions, rights as to, 698
AUDITORS' REPORT
meaning, 938n^{12}
AGM, laying before, 817
Companies Clauses Acts, under, 1741
companies registrar, delivery to, 818
compromise or arrangement by public company, inspection provisions, 1470
contents, 1059
disclosure of information to auditor, 1061
distribution of copies, 823
duty to report, 1059
failure to sign, 1060
group accounts, 1059
initial accounts, 710
investigation for purposes of, 1061
last annual accounts, 708
prospectus, in, 312
qualified: meaning, 913n^{10}
redemption or purchase of own shares by private company, 236
relevant: meaning, 938n^{3}
revised accounts, 943
revised directors' report, on, 1081
signature, 1060
translation into English, 88
BALANCE SHEET
company's. *See under* COMPANY
BANKING COMPANY
meaning, 117n^{8}, 920n^{2}
annual accounts, special provisions, 926, 927
disclosure requirements, modification, 928
exemption from audit, restriction, 1055
loans to directors, 601
record of loans to directors, 606
summary financial statement, form and content, 921
BANKING PARTNERSHIP
meaning, 929n^{1}
accounts regulations, powers of Secretary of State, 929
BANKRUPT
disqualification order, 1423
receiver and manager, ineligible for appointment as, 1326
BANKRUPTCY
calls on shares, effect on, 428
director of company, restriction, 553
membership of company, cessation of, 435
qualification shares, 558
transmission of shares on, 518

CHARGE (COMPANY)—*continued*
  delivery of particulars to registrar, validity
    dependent on, 1299
  existing charges on property acquired, 1309
  extension of time for registration, 1314, 1315
  floating. *See* FLOATING CHARGE
  foreign property, on, registration, 1304
  future property, on, 1247
  inspection of company's register and instru-
    ments, 1298
  instruments, inspection of, 1298
  memorandum of satisfaction, entry on register,
    1313
  new system of registration, 1316
  Northern Ireland, property in, registration, 1305
  public company's own shares, on, 214
  rectification of register, 1314, 1315
  register. *See* company's register *above*; regis-
    tration *below*
  registers, on, 1248
  registration—
    certificate of, 1311
    charges required to be registered, 1299
    commission and discount, statements as to,
      1302
    companies formed outside England and
      Wales, 1774
    company, by. *See* company's register *above*
    current practice, 1300
    debentures, series of, 1303
    default, 1308
    duty to register, 1308
    existing charges on property acquired, 1309
    extension of time, 1314, 1315
    foreign property, 1304
    indorsement on debentures, 1312
    oversea company, 1827
    proposed new system, 1316
    rectification, 1314, 1315
    retention of title clauses, 1301
    sale of property subject to charge, 1307
    satisfaction or release, of, 1313
    Scotland or Northern Ireland, property in,
      1305
    series of debentures, 1303
    time of creation of charge, 1306
  release, registration of, 1313
  retention of title clauses, 1301
  sale of property subject to, 1307
  satisfaction, registration of, 1313
  Scotland, property in, registration, 1305
  time of creation, 1306
  uncalled capital, on, 1245, 1246
CHARGE ON PROPERTY
  company's. *See* CHARGE (COMPANY); DEBEN-
    TURE; FLOATING CHARGE
CHARGING ORDER
  debentures, 1258
  shares, as to, 386

CHARITABLE COMPANY
  alteration of objects, 1184
CHARITABLE PURPOSE
  directors' report as to gifts for, 1072
CHARITY TRUSTEES
  disqualification order, 1417
CHARTERED COMPANY
  powers as to, 1758n[12, 13]
CHILD
  director, of—
    disclosure of interests, 566
    loans to, 607
    share options, prohibition on dealing in, 614
CLERGYMAN
  director of company, restriction, 554
CLOSE COMPANY
  material interest in: meaning, 1537n[4]
  profit sharing scheme restriction, 1537
  share option scheme restriction, 1537
COMMAND PAPERS
  Cmd—
    1749 (Jenkins Report), 18n[1]
    6659 (Cohen Report), 17n[1]
  Cmnd 5179 (Treaty of Rome), 4n[1], 5n[1]
COMMONWEALTH
  companies incorporated in, application of legis-
    lation, 1781
COMPANIES CLAUSES ACTS
  meaning, 1599
  accounts—
    audit. *See* auditors *below*
    balance sheet, 1738, 1739
    Companies Act 1985, application of, 1736
    debenture stock, 1692
    duty to keep, 1737
    inspection of books and balance sheet, 1739
    officers' duty to account, 1722
  administrative provisions of Companies Act
    1985 . . 1699
  advertisement of notices, 1611
  allotment of shares, 1630
  annual returns, 1697
  appeals, 1757
  application of, 1600
  arbitration—
    application of Arbitration Act 1950 . . 1747
    appointment of arbitrators, 1748
    conduct of, 1750
    costs, 1750
    umpire's appointment, 1749
  arrest of offenders, 1756
  auditors—
    appointment, 1740
    casual vacancies, 1742
    confirmation of accounts, 1741
    duties, 1741
    duty to appoint, 1720
    number of, 1740
    qualification, 1740

References are to paragraph numbers; superior figures refer to notes

COMPANIES CLAUSES ACTS—*continued*
  ultra vires—*continued*
    excess borrowing, 1616
  undertaking: meaning, 1672
  unregistered company. *See* UNREGISTERED
    COMPANY
COMPANY
  meaning. *See under* WORDS AND PHRASES *post*
  accounting principles—
    alternative accounting rules—
      additional information required, 815
      application of depreciation rules, 814
      current cost basis, 813
      depreciation rules, 813, 814
      intangible fixed assets, 813
      market value, determination of, 813
      revaluation reserve, 815
      stocks, 813
      tangible fixed assets, 813
    depreciation rules, 813, 814
    general principles, 809
    historical cost accounting rules—
      meaning, 810
      current assets, 811
      debts, 812
      depreciation rules, 813, 814
      determination of particular fixed asset
        items, 811
      development costs, 811
      diminution of asset value, 810
      fixed asset value, 810
      fungible assets, 812
      LIFO and FIFO, 812
      production cost, determination of, 812
      purchase price, determination of, 812
      raw materials and consumables, 812
      stocks, 812
      supplementary provisions, 812
      tangible assets, 812
      use of, 810
  accounting records—
    accounting standards, 803
    alteration of requirements by Secretary of
      State, 805
    articles of association as to, 804
    contents, 801
    duty to keep, 801
    financial year, 806
    inspection by directors and shareholders, 804
    lien over, restriction, 801n[4]
    location, 802
    non-compliance, penalties, 801
    non-eligible form, inspection provisions, 656
    outside Great Britain, 802
    preservation of, duration, 802
    subsidiaries, 801
    Table A provisions, 804n[3]
  accounting reference date—
    alteration, 808
    determination of, 807
    extension, limit of, 808
    notice of, 807, 808

COMPANY—*continued*
  accounting reference period, 807
  accounting requirements, power to change,
    1512
  accounting standards, 803
  accounts—
    accounting reference date, 807, 808
    accounting reference period, 807
    annual. *See* annual accounts *below*
    auditors' report. *See* AUDITORS' REPORT
    Companies Clauses Acts. *See under* COM-
      PANIES CLAUSES ACTS
    contents, 825
    directors' emoluments and benefits—
      meaning, 865n[1]
      aggregate amount, 866
      chairman's, 867
      compensation for loss of office, 869
      details required, 867
      emoluments: meaning, 866n[2]
      pensions, 868
      provisions generally, 865
      sums paid to third parties, 870
    directors' report. *See under* DIRECTOR OF
      COMPANY
    distributions, as to. *See* COMPANY DISTRI-
      BUTION (relevant accounts)
    exemption from audit. *See under* AUDIT
    financial year, 806
    form of, 825
    general rules, 831
    group accounts. *See* GROUP ACCOUNTS
    individual. *See* annual accounts *below*
    information supplementary to—
      balance sheet, as to. *See* balance sheet *below*
      directors' etc emoluments. *See* directors'
        emoluments and benefits *supra*
      general provisions, 839
      loans etc to company officers, 874
      loans etc to directors. *See* loans etc to direc-
        tors *infra*
      profit and loss account, as to. *See* profit and
        loss account *below*
      related undertakings. *See* related undertak-
        ings *infra*
    investment companies, 936
    loans etc to company officers, 874
    loans etc to directors—
      disclosure requirements, 871
      excluded transactions, 873
      record of transactions not shown in
        accounts, 606
      required particulars, 872
    negligence of secretary in preparation of, 650
    non-statutory—
      meaning, 938n[5]
      publication, 938
    notes to—
      auditors' remuneration, 1042
      general provisions, 838

References are to paragraph numbers; superior figures refer to notes

COMPANY—*continued*
  debenture. *See* DEBENTURE; DEBENTURE
    HOLDER
  debts, balance sheet information, 845
  deed of settlement—
    meaning, 34n³
    memorandum and articles, substitution by, 34
    power to register under 1985 Act, 24
  defunct. *See* DEFUNCT COMPANY
  demerger. *See* DEMERGER
  development costs, treatment for distribution
    purposes, 706
  directing mind of, 1157
  director. *See* COMPANIES CLAUSES ACTS (direc-
    tors); DIRECTOR OF COMPANY
  disabled persons, directors' report as to employ-
    ment of, 1075
  discovery of documents, 1180
  distribution. *See* COMPANY DISTRIBUTION;
    DIVIDEND
  domicile, 94, 150, 1772
  dormant—
    exemption from audit, 1058
    revision of defective accounts, 951
  duties, statutory, 1088
  EC Council Directives, 5
  EC legislation—
    companies: meaning, 4n¹
    freedom of establishment, 5
    mutual recognition of companies, 6
    Treaty requirements in general, 4
  employees—
    involvement, directors' report, 1076
    profit and loss account particulars, 851
  enforcement of judgments and orders against,
    1181
  execution of documents, 1130
  exercise of powers—
    agent, through. *See* agent *above*
    articles, authorised by, 1090
    capacity, 1093
    court interference—
      acts outside scope of, 1110
      jurisdiction, 1111
    delegated powers, 1138
    general statutory powers, 1089
    intra vires, binding on company, 1098
    limit on, 1087
    liquidation, effect of, 1112
    parties not bound to inquire as to capacity or
      authority, 1109
    special resolution, by, 1091
    ultra vires, 1102
  financial year—
    determination of, 806
    subsidiary undertaking, 857
  fixed assets—
    balance sheet information, 842
    directors' report, 1070
  floating charge and floating security. *See* FLOAT-
    ING CHARGE
  foreign. *See* FOREIGN COMPANY; OVERSEA
    COMPANY

COMPANY—*continued*
  formation—
    articles. *See* ARTICLES OF ASSOCIATION
    certificate of incorporation, 91
    effect of incorporation, 92
    memorandum. *See* MEMORANDUM OF
      ASSOCIATION
    outside England and Wales, 1771
    particulars of directors and secretaries, 89
    persons: meaning, 83
    private company: meaning, 82
    public company: meaning, 82
    registration of documents, 88
    single member companies, 81
    statement as to directors, 88, 89
    statutory declaration, 88
    statutory provisions generally, 80
    types of company, 80
    Welsh company's documents, 90
  fraudulent trading. *See* FRAUDULENT TRADING
  freedom of establishment, 5
  funding of director's expenditure on duty to
    company, 600
  general commercial company, objects clause, 86
  good faith, person dealing in, 1093
  group accounts. *See* GROUP ACCOUNTS
  guarantee of ultra vires acts, 1105
  head office: meaning, 94
  illegal—
    'Bubble Act', 1760n¹
    Companies Acts, under, 1759
    illegal purpose, formed for, 1760
    pleading illegality, 1763
    proceedings by or against, 1761
    sale of shares or scrip, 1764
    winding up, 1762
  incorporation—
    certificate. *See under* COMPANY REGIS-
      TRATION
    effect, 92
    status on, 1
    See also COMPANY REGISTRATION
  increase of capital. *See under* SHARE CAPITAL
  indemnification of directors, 625
  index of members' names, 381
  insider dealing. *See* INSIDER DEALING
  insolvent—
    meaning, 1425n⁵
    directors' powers, exercise of, 586
    disqualification of unfit directors, 1425
    matters for determining unfitness of directors,
      1426
    returns by liquidators etc, 1429
    share transfer where, 503
  inspection of registers etc—
    duties, 230
    non-legible form, kept in, 656
  interrogatories, 1180
  investigation—
    affairs, of. *See under* COMPANY INVESTI-
      GATION

COMPANY REGISTRATION—*continued*
non-1985 Act companies—*continued*
classes entitled to register, 24
contributories' liability, 35
creditors, 30
documents to be delivered, 78
existing constitution, continuance of, 32
fees, 73
joint stock company. *See under* JOINT STOCK
COMPANY
name requirements, 79
pending actions and execution, 31
provisions not applying, 27
restrictions, 25
substitution of deed of settlement, 34
vesting of property, 29
winding up and stay of actions, 36
oversea company. *See under* EUROPEAN ECON-
OMIC INTEREST GROUPING; OVERSEA
COMPANY
prohibited companies, 23
promoter's expenses, payment by company, 52
prospectus as to unlisted securities, 302
public company's capital reduced below authorised minimum, 269
purchase of own shares, 229
redemption of shares, 220
refusal for non-compliance with requirements,
88
registered number—
allocation, 63
change of, 63
requirement for—
carrying on business: meaning, 22
gain: meaning, 22
partnerships of more than 20 persons, 21
re-registration. *See* REREGISTRATION
resolutions and agreements, 691
restoration to register—
defunct company, 1504
private company, 1505
procedure, 1506
return of allotments, 478, 480, 481
revised directors' report, 1085
single member company, 24n⁹
special class rights, 185
special register body, 23
status of company after, 97
striking off register—
defunct companies, 1496–1499
non-trading private companies, 1500–1503
sub-division of capital, 208
Table A, adoption of, 529
trade unions, 23n¹
Welsh companies, 90
winding-up, with view to, 24
COMPENSATION
allotment contravening restrictions, for, 455
Companies Clauses Acts provisions, 1752, 1753
forged transfer, as to, 516
loss of office of director. *See* DIRECTOR OF
COMPANY (compensation for loss of office)

COMPENSATION—*continued*
misstatements in offer documents. *See* MISREP-
RESENTATION IN OFFER DOCUMENT
(statutory compensation)
COMPETITION
company audit work. *See under* AUDITOR
CONDITION PRECEDENT
call on shares, to, 419
company borrowing, to, 1243
forfeiture of shares, to, observance of, 525
qualification shares as, 559
re-registration of old public company, 134
CONNECTED PERSON
employee share schemes, 1525
CONSENT ORDER
unfair prejudice, relief from, 1414
CONSPIRACY
company officers' criminal liability, 1159
secret bargain with creditor, 1453
CONSTRUCTION (INTERPRETATION)
company objects clause, 1095
memorandum and articles, 1096
underwriting letters, 198
CONTRACT
articles of association as. *See under* ARTICLES OF
ASSOCIATION
company and a director or his firm, between, 596
company's powers. *See* COMPANY (contracts)
declaration of director's interest in, 594
sale of shares, for, 490
sole members who are directors, with, 597
shares, to take. *See under* MEMBER OF COMPANY
CONTRACT OF EMPLOYMENT
director's. *See* DIRECTOR OF COMPANY (service
contract)
receiver and manager, effect of employment of,
644
winding up, effect of, 644
CONTRIBUTION
director's right to, 626
misstatement in offer document, as to, 341
CONTRIBUTORY
calls. *See* CALL ON SHARES
non-1985 Act companies registered under the
Act, liability, 35
reduction of capital, effect on liability, 270
CORPORATION TAX
demerger relief. *See* DEMERGER
distributions, exemption, 733
receiver's liability, 1323
COSTS
debenture holders' action, 1373
disqualification order proceedings, 1439
misstatement in offer document, as to, 342
unfair prejudice, proceedings for relief from,
1413
CREDIT INSTITUTION
oversea. *See under* OVERSEA COMPANY
CREDITOR
balance sheet information, 845
compromise or arrangement, schemes of. *See*
SCHEMES OF ARRANGEMENT, RECON-
STRUCTION AND AMALGAMATION

References are to paragraph numbers; superior figures refer to notes

DEBENTURE HOLDER—*continued*
  action—*continued*
    hearing of motion treated as trial of action,
      1369
    judgment, form of, 1371
    leave for, 1366
    order of administration, 1374
    parties, 1367
    pleadings, 1369
    procedure, 1369
    proof of title, 1370
    receiver's register, 1370
    representative action, 1368
    service of judgment, 1372
    writ of summons, 1366
  administrative receiver. *See* ADMINISTRATIVE
    RECEIVER
  annual accounts and reports, entitlement to
    receive, 823, 824
  assignee's position, 1244
  cancellation of alteration of objects, 1185
  compromise, rights modified by, 1288
  court's power to enforce security, 1346
  directors, appointment of, 546
  foreclosure or sale, 1363–1365
  guarantee, enforcement of, 1346
  investigation as to, 1382
  liability for acts of receiver, 1329
  meetings—
    advertisement, notice by, 1151
    provisions as to, 1287
  modification of rights of, 1286–1288
  notice by company to, 1151
  priority, 1274
  promoter, remedies against, 47
  receiver and manager. *See* RECEIVER AND MAN-
    AGER
  register—
    Companies Clauses Acts, under, 1689
    duly closed, 1294n[1]
    inspection and copies, 1294
    location, 153, 1293
    non-legible form, in, 1295
    application to court, by, 1346
    security, under, 1317
  representative action, 1368
  sale, remedy of, 1363, 1365
  scheme of arrangement, effect, 1288
  voting, 1287
  winding up petition, presentation of, 1346
DECEIT
  misrepresentation in offer document. *See under*
    MISREPRESENTATION IN OFFER DOCU-
    MENT
DEED
  company, execution by, 1130
DEFAMATION
  auditor's statement on ceasing to hold office,
    1052
  company meeting, at, 1154

DEFAMATION—*continued*
  newspaper reports of company meetings, privi-
    lege, 693, 1155
DEFENCE (PLEADING)
  insider dealing, as to, 1225–1228
  misrepresentation in offer document as, 323
  misstatement in offer document, as to, 340
DEFUNCT COMPANY
  companies in liquidation, 1497
  preliminary inquiry, 1496
  restoration to register, 1504, 1506
  service of notices, 1499
  striking off register—
    companies in liquidation, 1497
    liability of directors etc, 1498
    notice of, 1498
    notice of intention, 1496
    registrar's powers, 1496
DELEGATION
  auditors, as to. *See* AUDITOR (delegation order)
  directors' powers, 587
DEMERGER
  advance clearance of distributions and payments,
    1215
  anti-avoidance provisions, 1212
  capital gains tax relief, 1213
  chargeable payments connected with exempt
    distributions, 1214
  conditions for relief, 1212
  distributing company: meaning, 1212n[4]
  exempt distributions, 1211
  extra-statutory concession as to retention of
    share capital, 1212n[15]
  group: meaning, 1211n[1]
  holding company: meaning, 1212n[8]
  information, power to obtain, 1217
  interest in trade, 1212n[17]
  notice requiring information, 1217
  public companies, additional requirements. *See*
    SCHEMES OF ARRANGEMENT, RECON-
    STRUCTION AND AMALGAMATION (pub-
    lic company)
  returns, 1216
  trading activities, 1211n[7]
  75% subsidiary: meaning, 1211n[6]
DIRECTIONS
  receiver and manager, application by, 1331
DIRECTOR OF COMPANY
  meaning, 543n[1]
  accountability, 592
  additional, power to appointment, 548
  administrator, removal by, 639
  age limit, 552, 637
  agent of company, as, 582, 1115
  alternate directors, 640
  appearance in court in person, 1182
  appointment—
    additional directors, 548
    alternate directors, 640
    automatic restrictions, 551–554
    casual vacancies, 547
    debenture holders, by, 546
    defective, 545

DIRECTOR OF COMPANY—*continued*
qualification shares. *See* QUALIFICATION
   SHARES
quantum meruit for services rendered, 575
quorum, 632
ratification of acts beyond powers of, 590
reappointment, 634
rectification of register of members, 392
refusal to register share transfer, 498
register of. *See* REGISTER OF DIRECTORS AND
   SECRETARIES
relief from liability, court's powers, 624
removal, 639
remuneration—
   accounts, particulars to shown in, 581
   apportionment, 577
   articles, according to, 575, 576
   fixing of, 576
   managing director, 588
   payment of, 577
   proof in winding up, 579
   qualification, and, 576
   quantum meruit, 575
   receiver's appointment, restriction, 579n[6]
   recovery of sums improperly received, 575
   right to, 575
   special, 576, 580
   special resolution altering, effect, 577
   tax-free payments, 578
   waiver of, 575
report—
   AGM, laying before, 817
   approval and signing, 1068
   compromise or arrangement by public com-
     pany, 1467, 1468
   contents—
     asset values, 1070
     charitable gifts, 1072
     directors' interests, 1071
     generally, 1066
     miscellaneous items, 1073
     political gifts, 1072
     revised report, 1079
   default, 818
   defective, revision of. *See* revised *infra*
   delivery to registrar, 818
   distribution of copies, 823
   duty to prepare, 1066
   employee involvement, 1076
   employment etc of disabled persons, 1075
   failure to sign, 1068
   false statements, 1069
   payment practice, 1077
   penalties for failure to comply, 1066
   purchase of own shares, disclosure require-
     ments, 1074
   revised—
     meaning, 1079n[2]
     approval and signature, 1080
     auditors' report on, 1081
     content, 1079
     copies, supply of, 1083

DIRECTOR OF COMPANY—*continued*
report—*continued*
   revised—*continued*
     date of, 1080n[12]
     delivery to registrar, 1085
     effect, 1082
     laying before meeting, 1084
     publication, 1083
     regulations, power to make, 1078
     voluntary revision, 1078
   signature, 1068
   small companies, 1067
   translation into English, 818
reports on conduct of, 1428
representations as to removal from office, 639
requirement of, 543
reserve fund, discretion as to, 728
resignation, 636
resolution—
   date of, 630
   quorum, 629n[5], 632
   registration, 691
   validity, 628n[5]
retirement—
   age limit, 637
   articles, under, 634
   casual vacancies, 638
   failure to declare interest, on, 635
   reappointment, 634
   resignation, 636
   Table A, 634n[2, 3, 5, 6]
returns by liquidator etc where company
   becomes insolvent, 1429
revised report. *See under* report *above*
revision of accounts. *See under* COMPANY
   (annual accounts)
sales to company by, disclosure of interests, 595
secretary as, restriction, 551
security given on borrowing, 1239
sequestration of property, 1181
serious loss of capital, duty on, 213
service contract—
   appropriate locations, 562n[1]
   custody of, 562
   default as to, 562
   exceptions, 562
   inspection, 562
   more than 5 years, for, 563
   subsidiaries, 562
   written memorandum of terms, 562
service on, 151
share option scheme. *See* SHARE OPTION
   SCHEME
share options, prohibition on dealing in, 614
sole members, contracts with company, 597
statement on company formation, 88, 89
stationery requirements, 561
statutory declaration on company formation, 88
sums paid to third parties as to services of, 870
tax-free payments, prohibition, 578
termination of liability, 619

DIRECTOR OF COMPANY—*continued*
  tortious liability, 621
  travelling etc expenses, 580
  trustee company of employee share ownership
    trust, conditions as to, 1588
  trustees of company property, as, 591
  ultra vires—
    court's power to give relief, 624
    dividends, 721
    doctrine of, 590
    notice of meeting to ratify acts, 666
    person dealing in good faith, 583
    ratification of acts, 590, 1098
    See also liability *above*
  unauthorised acts of agent, ratification of, 629
  undischarged bankrupt, 553
  unlimited liability, 627
  unqualified person, penalty, 556
  vacation of office, 634
DIRECTOR GENERAL OF FAIR TRADING
  competition in company audit work, functions
    as to, 1017–1019
DIRECTOR OF PUBLIC PROSECUTIONS
  consent to prosecution—
    company, of, 1165
    insider dealing, 1223
    investigation assisting overseas regulatory
      authority, as to, 1404
DISABLED PERSON
  directors' report as to employment of, 1075
DISCOUNT
  allotment of shares at, 187, 465
DISCOVERY OF DOCUMENTS
  company, order against, 1180
  disqualification order application, as to, 1438
  receiver, order against, 1329
DISCIPLINARY PROCEEDINGS
  Take-Over Code, as to, 1198, 199
DISQUALIFICATION ORDER
  meaning, 555, 1417
  acknowledgment of summons, 1437
  adjournment of hearing, 1439
  admissibility of evidence, 1446
  affidavit evidence, 1435, 1438
  appeals, 1439n[16]
  application for—
    company investigation, after, 1431, 1434
    hearing, 1439
    leave application heard with, 1440
    persons entitled, 1433
    procedure and time limit, 1432
    unfitness, as to, 1434
  building societies, application to, 1417n[7]
  case against respondent, 1435
  charity trustees, 1417
  companies regulated by Companies Clauses
    Acts, 1602
  company: meaning, 1417n[3]
  company formed outside England and Wales,
    1776
  company investigation, after, 1431, 1434

DISQUALIFICATION ORDER—*continued*
  contravention—
    body corporate, by, 1444
    criminal penalties, 1443
    personal liability, 1445
  conviction of indictable offence, on, 1418
  corporate offences, 1444
  costs, 1439
  county court administration order, default
    under, 1424
  criminal penalties, 1443
  default of appearance etc, 1439
  determination of unfitness of directors, matters
    to consider, 1426
  director: meaning, 1417n[2]
  discovery, 1438
  discretionary grounds, 555
  duration, 1417n[4], 1426n[3]
  effective date, 1439
  evidence, 1435, 1438, 1446
  European Economic Interest Grouping, appli-
    cation of provisions, 1831
  foreign companies, 1789
  fraud etc in winding up, 1420
  fraudulent trading, 1422
  friendly societies, application of provisions,
    1417n[8]
  hearing, 1439
  indorsement on summons, 1436
  information as to conduct of directors, request
    for, 1430
  insider dealing, 1223
  insolvent partnerships, 1417
  leave under—
    application for, 1440
    cases requiring, 1440
    information requirements, 1441
  mandatory grounds, 555
  matters for determining unfitness, 1426
  office-holder—
    meaning, 1429
    reports on conduct of directors, 1428
    request for information from, 1430
    returns by, 1429
  oversea company, 1783
  particulars to be furnished to Secretary of State,
    1441n[4]
  persistent breaches of companies legislation,
    1419
  personal liability where acting while disqualified,
    1445
  persons able to apply, 1433
  pre-trial review, 1439
  promoter of company, 59
  register of, 1442
  reports as to need to impose, 1428
  respondent—
    meaning, 1434
    case against, 1435
    evidence in reply, 1438
  returns by liquidators etc, 1429
  right of audience, 1439

DISQUALIFICATION ORDER—*continued*
  Secretary of State, application by, 1427
  service of summons, 1437
  shadow director: meaning, 1417n[2]
  specified officers of court, 1441n[3]
  subsequent order to run concurrently, 1417
  summary conviction, on, 1421
  summary procedure, 1439
  time limit for application for, 1432
  types of misconduct, 1426n[3]
  undischarged bankrupt, 1423
  unfit directors of insolvent companies, 1425
  unregistered companies, 1769
  wrongful trading, 1422
DISTRESS FOR RATES
  floating charge, effect on, 1265
DISTRESS FOR RENT
  floating charge, effect on, 1265
DISTRIBUTION
  company assets and profits. *See* COMPANY DIS-
    TRIBUTION; DIVIDEND
DIVIDEND
  meaning, 717
  amount, provision in articles, 723
  arrears on preference shares, priority, 725
  capitalisation of profits, 732
  court interference, 721
  'cum dividend' and 'ex dividend' sales, 730
  declaration of, 723
  forfeiture where unclaimed, 727
  future, sale of right to, 730
  guarantee by vendor of business, 720
  improper, liability, 722
  in specie, 732
  income tax, 726, 734
  injunction by preference shareholders restrain-
    ing, 725
  interim—
    meaning, 722n[2]
    injunction by preference shareholders, 725
    power to declare, 722
    rescission of declaration, 723
    Table A, 722n[3]
  method of payment, 724n[10]
  paid-up shares, in, 732
  participation in, 730
  preference shares, on, 725
  recoverability, 724
  reserve fund, discretion as to, 728
  right to, 718
  secret reserve, 729
  settled shares, on, 731
  shares not fully paid-up, on, 719
  Table A, 718n[2]
  tax-free, calculation of, 726
  trustee, payment to, 731
  ultra vires, 721
  unclaimed, forfeiture of, 727
  warrant: meaning, 717
DOMICILE
  company, of, 94, 150

DOMICILE—*continued*
  company formed outside England and Wales,
    1772
EC COMPANY LAW
  directives, 5
EEA UNDERTAKING
  meaning, 808n[11]
  alteration of accounting reference date, 808
EEC TREATY
  companies requirements generally, 4
ELECTION (CHOICE)
  annual general meeting, to dispense with, 659
  authority for allotment by private company, as
    to, 448
EMPLOYEE
  company's power to provide for on cessation or
    transfer of business, 1101
  involvement in company, directors' report, 1076
  profit sharing scheme. *See* PROFIT SHARING
    SCHEME
  share option scheme. *See* SHARE OPTION
    SCHEME
  share ownership trust. *See* EMPLOYEE SHARE
    OWNERSHIP TRUST
  share scheme. *See* EMPLOYEE SHARE SCHEME
  solicitor as, 651
EMPLOYEE BENEFIT TRUST
  meaning, 1561n[2]
  shares subject to, material interest test, 1561
EMPLOYEE SHARE OWNERSHIP TRUST
  meaning, 1596
  acquisition and transfer of securities, 1593, 1595
  beneficiaries, 1589
  borrowing, further charge to tax, 1580
  charge to tax—
    borrowing, 1580
    chargeable amounts, 1579, 1580n[9]
    chargeable events, 1578
    limit on chargeable amount, 1581
    principal charges, 1577
  chargeable amount—
    borrowing, as to, 1580n[9]
    generally, 1579
    limit on, 1581
  chargeable events, 1578
  conditions as to directors of single trustee com-
    pany, 1588
  conditions for tax relief, 1576
  costs of establishment, tax treatment, 1597
  establishment, 1584
  founding company—
    meaning, 1584
    group, within, 1585n[5]
  information, power to obtain, 1582
  material interest: meaning, 1585n[6]
  position after establishment, 1596
  post-3 May 1994 . . 1586
  pre-4 May 1994 . . 1585
  principal charges to tax, 1577
  professional trustees, 1587n[8]
  qualifying companies, 1577n[6]
  qualifying period, 1578n[8], 1589n[4]

References are to paragraph numbers; superior figures refer to notes

References are to paragraph numbers; superior figures refer to notes

References are to paragraph numbers; superior figures refer to notes

INVESTMENT AGREEMENT
  meaning, 356n[1]
  misleading statements and practices, 356
INVESTMENT BUSINESS
  authorisation, cancellation etc on obstruction of
    insider dealing investigation, 1232
  investigation of share dealings, 1384
INVESTMENT COMPANY
  meaning, 703, 936n[2]
  accounts, special provisions, 936
  distributions, special provisions, 703
IRELAND, REPUBLIC OF
  companies legislation, application of, 1785
ISLE OF MAN
  companies legislation, application of, 1784
  Take-over Code, application of, 1195
JOINT STOCK COMPANY
  meaning (registration), 25n[2]
  alteration of articles, extent of power, 538
  alteration of objects, powers, 34
  certificate of incorporation, 28
  Northern Ireland, application of Companies Act
    1985 . . 1780
  promoter: meaning, 37n[1]
  registration—
    documents required, 76
    power to register, 24
    public company , as, 77
    restriction on power, 25
  share transfer methods, 496n[2]
JOINT TENANCY
  company's powers, 1190
JOINT VENTURE
  group accounts, 885, 893
JUDGMENT
  debenture holders' action, 1371, 1372
JURISDICTION
  compliance orders as to auditors' regulatory
    bodies, 999
  register of members, to rectify, 394
LAND
  company's power to hold, 1188
LEGAL MORTGAGEE
  company member, liability as, 385
LEGAL PROCEEDINGS
  company, by or against. *See under* COMPANY
  company investigation, following, 1390
  oversea company. *See under* OVERSEA COMPANY
  receiver, by or against, leave for, 1357
  receiver and manager, powers of, 1322
LEGAL PROFESSIONAL PRIVILEGE
  company investigations, 1394
  criminal proceedings against body corporate,
    1168
LETTER
  underwriting of shares, 198
LIABILITY INSURANCE
  director's liability, against, 623
LIEN
  shares, on. *See under* MEMBER OF COMPANY

LIMITATION PERIOD
  deceit by misrepresentation in offer document,
    337
  misstatement in offer document, as to, 343
LIMITED COMPANY
  guarantee, limited by. *See* LIMITED COMPANY
    (GUARANTEE)
  reregistration. *See* REREGISTRATION
  shares, limited by. *See* LIMITED COMPANY
    (SHARES)
  word 'limited', without—
    alteration of memorandum or articles, 114
    designated agencies, 113
    exemption from requirement, 112
LIMITED COMPANY (GUARANTEE)
  articles of association, 111, 530
  capital, statement in memorandum, 178
  division of undertaking into shares, effect, 109
  'limited', exemption as to, 112
  members' liability 412
  memorandum—
    division of undertaking into shares, effect, 109
    form and content, 84, 108
    void provisions, 110
  old public company, re-registration. *See under*
    REREGISTRATION
  registration of single member companies, 24n[9]
  single member company, power to form, 81
  Table A, adoption of, 111
  Table C, application of, 85n[5]
  Table D, application of, 85n[5]
LIMITED COMPANY (SHARES)
  acquisition of own shares, 362
  articles, contents, 103
  capital, statement in memorandum, 178
  'limited', exemption as to, 112
  members' liability, 413
  memorandum, contents of, 84, 102
  old public company, re-registration. *See under*
    REREGISTRATION
  partnership company. *See* PARTNERSHIP COM-
    PANY
  private company, 105–107
  public company, nature and powers, 104
  registration of single member companies, 24n[9]
  share warrant. *See* SHARE WARRANT
  single member company, power to form, 81
  surrender of shares, 520
  Table A. *See* TABLE A
  Table B, application of, 85n[5]
  Table F, application of, 85n[5]
LIMITED PARTNERSHIP
  private company, advantages of, 107
LIQUIDATOR
  continuance of employees' employment by, 644
  disqualification order. *See* DISQUALIFICATION
    ORDER
  floating charges, 1266
  receiver, appointment as, 1351
  regulations as to, power to make, 1515

LIQUIDATOR—*continued*
report as to conditions for imposition of disqualification order, 1428
LISTED SECURITIES
capitalisation issue, 732n[1]
disclosure of directors' interests to investment
exchange, 567
offer to subscribe or purchase. *See* OFFER
(LISTED SECURITIES)
LOAN
company, to. *See* COMPANY (borrowing)
director, to. *See under* DIRECTOR OF COMPANY
LOSS OF OFFICE
director, of. *See* DIRECTOR OF COMPANY (compensation for loss of office)
MANAGER
company, of. *See* COMPANY (manager); DIREC-
TOR OF COMPANY (managing)
receiver and. *See* RECEIVER AND MANAGER
MARKET MAKER
defence as to insider dealing, 1226
MARRIED WOMAN
membership of company, contractual liability,
375
transfer of shares by, 504
MEDIUM-SIZED COMPANY
meaning (accounts), 901
annual accounts. *See under* COMPANY (annual
accounts)
delivery of accounts, 912, 913
revised accounts, 948
MEETING
companies. *See* COMPANIES CLAUSES ACTS
(meetings); DIRECTOR OF COMPANY
(meetings); MEMBERS' MEETING
debenture holders, 1287
directors, of. *See under* DIRECTOR OF COMPANY
members of company, of. *See* COMPANIES
CLAUSES ACTS (general meeting); MEM-
BERS' MEETING
shareholders'. *See* COMPANIES CLAUSES ACTS
(general meeting); MEMBERS' MEETING
MEMBER
company, of. *See* COMPANIES CLAUSES ACTS
(shareholders); MEMBER OF COMPANY;
MEMORANDUM OF ASSOCIATION (subscriber)
MEMBER OF COMPANY
meaning, 358
acquisition of shares by company's nominee, 365
action against company for individual wrong,
1173
agent's contract to take shares, 372
agreement to become. *See* contract *below*
alteration of rights on reduction of capital, 250
annual accounts and reports entitlement to
receive, 823, 824
articles as contract, 141–143
assent or sanction of intra vires acts, 696
bankrupt, 435
beneficial interest: meaning, 364
bearer of share warrant, 384, 494
calls. *See* CALL ON SHARES
cessation—
bankruptcy, 435

MEMBER OF COMPANY—*continued*
cessation—*continued*
methods, 434
winding up corporate member, 435
circulation of resolutions of, 688
Companies Clauses Acts. *See* COMPANIES
CLAUSES ACTS (shareholders)
company acquiring own shares, general rule
against, 362
company limited by shares, 439
compromise or arrangement, information as to,
1450
consent to entry on register of, effect, 369
contract—
agent, by, 372
agreement: meaning, 369
application for allotment, 442
company, by, 373
completion of, 442
conditional offer, 443
enforcement, 376
express, 370
implied, 371
issue of shares, 446
married woman, 375
minors, 374
mistake and misrepresentation, 442
nature of, 369
option to take shares, 377
oral, 442
principles generally, 440
registration, 478, 480
control over directors, 589
copies of memorandum and articles, 101
copies of resolutions to be supplied to, 692
decisions reached without meetings, 696
dividend. *See* DIVIDEND
enforcement of agreement to take shares, 376
express contract to take shares, 370
forfeiture of shares. *See under* SHARE IN COM-
PANY
forged transfer, remedies, 515, 516
holding company, of, restrictions, 363
implied contract to take shares, 371
indebted to company, transfer of shares by, 502
index of names, 381
injunction against company, 1173
insider dealing. *See* INSIDER DEALING
interrogatories, 1180
joint holders—
calls on shares, 427
entry in register, 383
liability—
allotment contravening restrictions, 475
alteration of memorandum or articles as to,
415
calls. *See* CALL ON SHARES
company limited by guarantee, 412
company limited by shares, 413
extent generally, 409
legal mortgagee, 385
less than 2 members, 410
redemption or purchase of shares by company, where, 414
reduction of capital, after, 270

MEMBER OF COMPANY—*continued*
 liability—*continued*
  subscribers', 360
  trustees, 385
  unlimited company, 411
  articles, by, 430n[1]
 lien on shares—
  company's lien, 430
  extent, 431
  loss or discharge, 433
  priority, 432
 married women, 375
 minors, 374
 notice by company to, 1149, 1150
 notice of memorandum and articles, 145
 option to take shares, 377
 payment for shares. *See under* ALLOTMENT
 persons held to be, 358
 pre-emption rights. *See under* SHAREHOLDER
 register. *See* REGISTER OF MEMBERS
 representative actions, 1174–1176
 representative capacity, suing in, 1175
 requisition for meeting, 662
 rights—
  articles, under, 407
  general law, under, 408
  memorandum, under, 406
  source of, 403
  statutory—
   collectively, 405
   individual member, 404
 service on, 1149, 1150
 shares held by or for public company, 366
 sole member. *See* SINGLE MEMBER COMPANY
 specific performance of agreement to take shares, 376
 statements of, circulation by company, 688
 subscriber of memorandum. *See under* MEMOR-
  ANDUM OF ASSOCIATION
 summary financial statement. *See under* PUBLIC
  COMPANY
 supplementary provisions as to private companies, 367
 surrender of shares, 520, 521
 transfer of shares. *See* SHARE TRANSFER
 transmission of shares on death etc, 518
 undertaking as to work or services for payment
  for shares, 464, 474
 unfair prejudice. *See* UNFAIR PREJUDICE
 winding up of, 435
MEMBERS' MEETING
 adjournment, 669
 annual general meeting—
  accounts and reports to be laid before, 817
  default as to, 658
  dividend, sanction of, 723
  election to dispense with, 659
  period of notice, 657n[3]
  register of directors' interests, production of,
   574
  requirement to hold, 658
  statutory provisions generally, 658

MEMBERS' MEETING—*continued*
 annual general meeting—*continued*
  time between, 658
 articles, provisions in, 657
 auditors' rights as to, 1035
 authority of board for, 663
 chairman, 668
 Companies Clauses Acts. *See* COMPANIES
  CLAUSES ACTS (general meeting)
 compromise or arrangement, as to, 1447
 convening—
  authorisation, 663
  court, by, 661
  notice, 660
  pecuniary advantage of director, notice provisions, 665
  period of notice, 660
  requisition for, 662
  Secretary of State, by, 658
 copies of minutes, supply to members, 695
 corporation representatives, 678
 court, convened by, 661
 decisions reached without, 696
 defamation, liability, 1154, 1155
 evidence as to—
  inspection of minute books, 695
  minutes, 694
  Table A, 694n[5]
 extraordinary general meeting—
  meaning, 657
  period of notice, 657n[3]
  resigning auditor, requisitioned by, 1050
  serious loss of capital, on, 213
 general meeting—
  agent's acts, ratification, 1125
  appointment of auditor—
   laying of accounts, 1028
   private company not laying accounts, 1029,
    1030
  auditors' rights, 1035
  chairman, 668
  Companies Clauses Acts. *See under* COM-
   PANIES CLAUSES ACTS
  directors' report, laying of, 1084
  dispensing with laying of accounts of private
   company before, 923, 924
  fixing of auditor's remuneration, 1042
  increase of capital, 201n[5]
  market purchase of own shares, authorising,
   226
  minutes, 694
  ratification of directors' ultra vires acts, 1098
  revised accounts, laying of, 946
  Secretary of State, called by, 658
  termination of auditors' appointment, 1051
 inspection of minute books, 695
 insufficient notice, 664
 minutes, 694
 newspaper reports of, defamation in, 1155
 notice of meetings, 660
 ordinary—
  meaning, 657
  See also annual general meeting *above*
 poll, 672

PRIVATE COMPANY—*continued*
  authority for allotment, election as to duration of, 448
  elective resolutions, 686
  election to dispense with laying of accounts before general meeting, 923, 924
  failure to deliver accounts, civil penalty, 819
  financial assistance for acquisition of shares, 276–278
  limited partnership, advantages over, 107
  offer for sale to the public, $105n^2$
  pre-emption rights, 459
  purchase of own shares. *See under* PURCHASE OF OWN SHARES
  redeemable shares. *See under* REDEEMABLE SHARES
  re-registration. *See* RE-REGISTRATION
  removal of auditors not appointed annually, 1051
  restoration to register, 1505, 1506
  restrictions on powers, 105
  special resolution, required majority, 683
  striking off register—
    directors' duties after application, 1502
    duties as to application for, 1501
    liability of directors etc after, 1503
    notice of, 1503
    registrar's power, 1500
  supplementary provisions on re-registration as public company, 367
  written resolutions, 697–699
PRIVILEGE
  newspaper reports of company meetings, 693, 1155
PRODUCTION OF DOCUMENTS FOR INSPECTION
  company documents—
    offence suspected, where, 1166
    powers, 1386
PROFESSIONAL INDEMNITY INSURANCE
  auditors, 972
PROFIT AND LOSS ACCOUNT
  company's. *See under* COMPANY
PROFIT SHARING SCHEME
  meaning, 1517
  aggrieved persons, 1535
  alterations to, effect, 1534
  appropriate allowance, $1529n^{14}$
  appropriate percentage, $1529n^{13}$, 1564
  appropriation of shares, eligibility for, 1556
  approved—
    meaning, $1528n^1$
    aggrieved persons, 1535
    alterations to scheme, 1534
    application of provisions, 1529
    capital gains tax, 1530
    conditions for approval, 1531
    release date, $1529n^{12}$
    trustees: meaning, $1529n^1$
    withdrawal of approval, 1533
  capital receipts, 1565
  commissioners' power to obtain information, 1536

PROFIT SHARING SCHEME—*continued*
  company reconstructions, 1566
  contractual obligations of participants, limitations on, 1562
  costs of establishing, tax treatment, 1573
  eligibility to participate, 1557
  establishment of trustees, 1554
  excess or unauthorised shares, 1567
  group scheme: meaning, $1531n^8$
  initial market value of shares, $1554n^{11}$
  limitations on contractual obligations of participants, 1562
  locked-in value of participant's shares, $1529n^{17}$
  material interest—
    close company, in, 1537
    employee benefit trust, shares subject to, 1561
    options etc, 1559
    relevant associate: meaning, $1558n^3$
    shares held by trustees, 1560
    trusts, interests under, 1558
  new holding on company reconstruction, 1566
  non-approval, 1532
  participating company: meaning, $1531n^8$
  PAYE, 1568
  period of retention, 1563
  release of rights, 1540
  relevant amount of participation, $1554n^{12}$
  scheme shares, 1539
  specified age, 1538
  statutory provisions generally, 1517
  tax consequences—
    costs of establishing scheme, 1573
    payments to trustees, 1575
  trust instrument, contents, 1555
  trustees—
    deduction of tax under PAYE, 1568
    duties, 1555
    establishment of, 1554
    payments to, tax treatment, 1575
    shares held by, material interest test, 1560
  unauthorised shares, 1567
  withdrawal of approval, 1533
PROFITS
  company distributions. *See* COMPANY DISTRIBUTION; DIVIDEND
PROMISSORY NOTE
  company's powers. *See* COMPANY (bills and notes)
PROMOTER OF COMPANY
  meaning, 37
  actions constituting promotion, 38
  agent, exclusion as, 41
  borrowing by company from, 1241
  commencement and cessation, 40
  company's remedies other than rescission, 46
  criminal liability, 58
  debenture holders' remedies, 47
  disclosure—
    acts amounting to, 49
    duty of, 48
    independent executive, 50

References are to paragraph numbers; superior figures refer to notes

REGISTER OF DIRECTORS' INTERESTS—
continued
refusal of inspection, 574
requirement to keep, 571
time for making entries, 572n[4]
REGISTER OF MEMBERS
branch—
    oversea companies, 1782
    overseas branches. *See* overseas branch register
      below
charge on, 1248
charging order, 386
closure, 390
consent to entry on, effect, 369
contents, 379
copies of, 391
custody of, 389
entry necessary for membership, 382
equitable interests, 385
evidence, as, 388
exchange control, 387
executors, entry of, 518
firms, 383
form of, 378
former members, removal of entries, 379
index of names, 381
inspection, 390
joint holders, 383
liability for entries or deletions, limitation, 379
maintenance of, 378
non-legible form, inspection requirements, 656
overseas branch register—
    meaning, 398
    ceasing to keep, 400
    companies required to keep, 398
    extension to foreign countries by Order in
      Council, 402
    inspection, 399
    non-legible form, inspection requirements,
      656
    notice requirements, 398
    provisions as to keeping of, 399
    rectification, 399
    requirement to keep, 398
    specified countries, 398n[2]
    transfers of shares, 401
particulars to be entered in, 379
principal register: meaning, 398
Public Trustee, 385
rectification—
    application to court, 395
    court, by, 393
    directors, by, 392
    jurisdiction, 394
    misrepresentation in offer document, 322
    order for, 397
    overseas branch register, 399
    procedure, 395
    respondents, 395
    uncertificated units, 392
    winding up, after, 396
register of directors' interests to be kept with, 573

REGISTER OF MEMBERS—*continued*
registered office, to be kept at, 153
share warrants, 384
stop notice, 386
subscribers of memorandum, 379
trustee in bankruptcy, 435
trusts, notice of, 385
uncertificated securities, 379
REGISTRAR OF COMPANIES
meaning, 60n[3]
appointment, 60
charges register. *See* CHARGE (COMPANY)
    (registration)
companies' registered numbers, 63
contracting out functions—
    excluded functions, 61n[1]
    functions within scope, 62
    powers, 61
delegation of functions, 60
delivery of documents—
    generally, 60
    legible form, in, 64
    non-legible form, in, 65
    public notice of, 70, 71
enforcement of company's duty to make returns,
    69
fees—
    non-1985 Act companies, 73
    power to regulate, 66
    re-registration, 73
index of company names, 72
inspection of records of, 67
keeping of company records, 68
lack of notice by, effect, 71
officers, 60
offices, 60
official seal: meaning, 28n[3]
powers of Secretary of State, 60
public notice of receipt and issue of documents,
    70, 71
registration by. *See* COMPANY REGISTRATION
REGISTRATION
companies. *See* COMPANY REGISTRATION
company charges. *See under* CHARGE (COM-
    PANY)
EEIGs. *See under* EUROPEAN ECONOMIC
    INTEREST GROUPING
memorandum and articles, 87, 88
order sanctioning scheme of arrangement etc,
    1459
share transfer. *See under* SHARE TRANSFER
REGULATIONS
business names, as to, 171
inspection of company registers etc, as to, 230
power to make—
    accounting body changes, on, 1026
    accounting requirements, as to, 805, 1512
    accounts of banking partnerships, as to, 929
    annual returns, as to, 1065
    auditors register, as to, 991
    business provisions, as to, 1767

SHARE IN COMPANY—*continued*
  disclosure of interests—*continued*
    interest notification date, 741n[12]
    interests to be disclosed, 736
    investigation—
      company, by, 748
      company's report to members, 751
      failure to provide information, 752
      inspection of report, 755
      requisition, on, 750
    joint interests, 743
    material interests, 736n[4]
    notifiable interests, 736, 743
    particulars required, 737
    percentage level, 736n[11]
    persons acting together, 741
    register. *See* register of acquisitions and disposals *below*; REGISTER OF DIRECTORS' INTERESTS
    regulations, power to make, 746
    relevant share capital, 735n[1]
    restrictions on shares, power to impose, 745
    time for, 737
    unidentifiable interests, 743
    wide obligation of disclosure: meaning, 741n[10]
  discount, allotment at, 187
  employee share ownership trust. *See* EMPLOYEE SHARE OWNERSHIP TRUST
  equity share—
    meaning, 189n[5]
    merger relief, 189
  forfeiture—
    articles, under, 522
    calls, liability for, 425, 526
    conditions precedent, compliance with, 525
    exercise of power, 524
    extent of power, 523
    irregular, 525
    notice, 525
    observance of conditions, 525
    powers, 522
    reallotment of forfeited shares, 528
    reinstatement, 527
    Table A, under, 522
  founders' shares, 180n[1]
  illegal company, in, 1764
  insider dealing. *See* INSIDER DEALING
  issue of. *See* SHARE ISSUE
  lien on. *See under* MEMBER OF COMPANY
  locality of, 94
  mortgage of, 519
  nature of, 437
  nominal capital divided into, 436
  nominee, acquisition by, 365
  non-cash consideration. *See under* ALLOTMENT
  numbering, 438
  offer for sale, evidence of, 105n[2]
  offer for subscription or purchase. *See* OFFER (LISTED SECURITIES); OFFER (UNLISTED SECURITIES)
  old public company, held by or charged to, 137
  option scheme. *See* SHARE OPTION SCHEME

SHARE IN COMPANY—*continued*
  option to take shares at par, 195
  ownership, investigation of, 1382
  paid up—
    meaning, 445
    one-quarter, minimum for allotment, 466
  payment for. *See under* ALLOTMENT
  personal estate, as, 437
  pre-emption rights. *See under* SHAREHOLDER
  preference. *See* PREFERENCE SHARE
  private company, supplementary provisions, 367
  public company—
    charges on own shares, 214
    disclosure of interests. *See* disclosure of interests *above*
    held by or for, 366
  purchase of own shares by company. *See* PURCHASE OF OWN SHARES
  purchase order where unfair prejudice, 1415
  qualification shares. *See* QUALIFICATION SHARES
  redeemable. *See* REDEEMABLE SHARES
  register of acquisitions and disposals—
    company's investigations, interests found on, 749
    contents and form, 747
    deletions, restrictions, 754
    inspection, 747, 755
    removal of entries, 753
    statutory provisions, 747
  repudiation of, 442
  restrictions on—
    attempted evasion, 1396
    consequences of order, 1395
    person aggrieved, application by, 1397
    power to impose, 745, 1383
    regulations, power to make, 1514
    relaxation and removal, 1397
    sale under court direction, 1397
    third parties' rights, affecting, 1397
  sale of undertaking for, with view to winding up. *See under* SCHEMES OF ARRANGEMENT, RECONSTRUCTION AND AMALGAMATION
  settled, payment of dividend, 731
  share premium account, 188
  stop notice, 386
  sub-division—
    notice to registrar, 208
    powers, 207
  subscription or purchase, offers for. *See* OFFER (LISTED SECURITIES); OFFER (UNLISTED SECURITIES)
  subsidiary undertaking, held by—
    disclosure requirements, 858
    notes to group accounts, 892
  sub-underwriting, 199, 325
  surrender—
    company limited by shares, 520
    transfer to nominee distinguished, 520
    unlimited company, 521

References are to paragraph numbers; superior figures refer to notes

References are to paragraph numbers; superior figures refer to notes

References are to paragraph numbers; superior figures refer to notes

UNLIMITED COMPANY—*continued*
member of partnership, accounting provisions. *See under* PARTNERSHIP (accounts)
members' liability, 411
memorandum of association, 115
reduction of capital, 217
registered as limited, application of legislation, 13
re-registration. *See* RE-REGISTRATION
share capital to be stated in articles, 178, 534
surrender of shares, 521
Table A, adoption of, 116
Table E, 85n⁵, 116n³, 530

UNLISTED SECURITIES
offer for subscription or purchase. *See* OFFER (UNLISTED SECURITIES)
statutory compensation. *See under* MISREPRESENTATION IN OFFER DOCUMENT

UNREGISTERED COMPANY
meaning, 1765
alteration of instrument constituting, 100n¹
application of legislation, 14
business name, 1769
business provisions—
  meaning, 1765
  application of, 1766
  consequences of application of, 1768
  regulations applying, power to make, 1767
  scope of, 1767
construction of references to memorandum or articles, 1109n¹
disqualification of directors etc, 1769
European Economic Interest Grouping wound up as, 1831
insider dealing, 1769
lawful company associations, 1758
Northern Ireland company, 1780
offer documents, 1769
oversea company distinguished, 1765
regulations, power to make, 1770

VALUATION
non-cash assets, 469, 472
non-cash consideration, 468, 471

VALUE ADDED TAX
receiver and manager, liability of, 1323

VOTING RIGHTS
Companies Clauses Acts, under, 1733

WAIVER
directors' remuneration, of, 575

WINDING UP
contract of employment, effect on, 644
crystallisation of floating charge, 1263
debentures redeemable on, 1290
fraud in, disqualification order, 1420
illegal company, 1762
member of company, of, 435
minority shareholders' or derivative actions, restriction, 1112
powers of Secretary of State, 1510
rectification of register of members after, 396
reduction of capital, 242
sale with view to, scheme for. *See under* SCHEMES OF ARRANGEMENT, RECONSTRUCTION AND AMALGAMATION
stay of actions as to non-1985 Act companies registered under the Act, 36
stay of proceedings on, 1182

WINDING-UP ORDER
status of receiver, receiver and manager or administrative receiver, 1336

WINDING-UP PETITION
debenture holder's remedy, 1346
investigation of company, following, 1390
unfair prejudice, alternative remedies, 1416

WRIT OF FIERI FACIAS
company, against, 1181
floating charge, effect on, 1265

WRIT OF SEQUESTRATION
company's, director's or officer's property, 1181

WRIT OF SUMMONS IN ACTION
debenture holders' action, 1366

WRONGFUL TRADING
disqualification order, 1422

Words and Phrases

These Words and Phrases relate only to entries appearing in Volumes 7(1) and 7(2).
A consolidated Words and Phrases for Volumes 7(1), 7(2) and 7(3) appears in Volume 7(3).

Words in parentheses indicate the context in which the word or phrase is used

accountant with the appropriate qualifications, 77n¹⁰
accounting documents (oversea company), 1796n⁵
accounting reference date, 807
accounting reference period—
  (company), 807
  relevant, 822n³
accounting standards, 803
accounts—
  (qualifying partnership), 932n⁵

accounts—*continued*
annual, 826
individual, 816
initial, 707
interim, 707
non-statutory, 938n⁵
original, 941n³
relevant (distributions), 707
revised, 941n²

References are to paragraph numbers; superior figures refer to notes

References are to paragraph numbers; superior figures refer to notes

References are to paragraph numbers; superior figures refer to notes

References are to paragraph numbers; superior figures refer to notes